ADOLESCENCE AND EMERGING ADULTHOOD

PEARSON

At Pearson, we take learning personally. Our courses and resources are available as books, online and via multi-lingual packages, helping people learn whatever, wherever and however they choose.

We work with leading authors to develop the strongest learning experiences, bringing cutting-edge thinking and best learning practice to a global market. We craft our print and digital resources to do more to help learners not only understand their content, but to see it in action and apply what they learn, whether studying or at work.

Pearson is the world's leading learning company. Our portfolio includes Penguin, Dorling Kindersley, the Financial Times and our educational business, Pearson International. We are also a leading provider of electronic learning programmes and of test development, processing and scoring services to educational institutions, corporations and professional bodies around the world.

Every day our work helps learning flourish, and wherever learning flourishes, so do people.

To learn more please visit us at: www.pearson.com/uk

ADOLESCENCE AND EMERGING ADULTHOOD

A CULTURAL APPROACH

Jeffrey J. Arnett and Malcolm Hughes

Harlow, England • London • New York • Boston • San Francisco • Toronto • Sydney • Auckland • Singapore • Hong Kong
Tokyo • Seoul • Taipei • New Delhi • Cape Town • São Paulo • Mexico City • Madrid • Amsterdam • Munich • Paris • Milan

Pearson Education Limited

Edinburgh Gate
Harlow
Essex CM20 2JE
England

and Associated Companies throughout the world

Visit us on the World Wide Web at:
www.pearson.com/uk

First published 2012

© Pearson Education Limited 2012

ISBN 978-1-4082-5390-8

British Library Cataloguing-in-Publication Data
A catalogue record for this book is available from the British Library

Library of Congress Cataloging-in-Publication Data
Arnett, Jeffrey Jensen.
 Adolescence and emerging adulthood : a cultural approach / Jeff Arnett and Malcolm Hughes.
    p. cm.
  Includes bibliographical references and index.
  ISBN 978-1-4082-5390-8
  1. Adolescence—Cross-cultural studies. 2. Teenagers—Cross-cultural studies.
  3. Young adults—Cross-cultural studies. 4. Adolescent psychology—Cross-cultural
studies. I. Hughes, Malcolm. II. Title.
  HQ796.A7255 2012
  305.235—dc23

                                    2012003952

10 9 8 7 6 5 4 3 2 1
16 15 14 13 12

Typeset in 10/12 pt BasicCommercial by 73
Printed and bound in Malaysia (CTP-PJB)

BRIEF CONTENTS

CONTENTS

Part 2 Contexts   233

Part 3 Problems and resilience   447

PREFACE

Why read this book; why write it?

The proposal for this text book was written four months after my son Tom Hughes was killed in a road traffic accident. He was 19 years of age. In his short life he learned an enormous amount, achieved a great deal, and knew what it was to love and be loved. He was bright, funny, outgoing, generous and popular. But Tom was also frustrated, disaffected and disengaged, and his academic achievement in no way reflected his potential. He revelled in the peer-social dimensions of school, but found relationships with teachers, the curriculum and the methods of delivery did not match ways in which he learned best; which would capture his imagination and provoke him to make the necessary investment of effort and time in order to achieve. Many other dimensions of Tom's family and social life did compensate in part for this, but the style and nature of English schooling in the first decade of the 21st century failed to address his learning needs and potential. The adaptation is made in response to my perception that much of services for young people in the UK fails to account for the developmental needs of our young people.

This book is not just about schools and schooling; far from it. Of course, schools and families are the two main 'institutions', which support young people on a safe journey from childhood to young adulthood. Are dysfunctional families and failing schools responsible for the creation of an underclass of alienated and angry young people, or is there another explanation? What is going on during adolescence and early adulthood? What are the issues that our young people have to face? Is there a 'crisis of childhood' where young people are not the focus of our care, protection and attention, but 'perceived as a source of disruption, if not actual threat' (Foley et al, 2001)[1].

In an article *British Childhood* (New Statesman, 2008) Suzanne Moore asks 'Why are our young people so unhappy?' and argues that it is because "we have become a society that fears, demonises and silences them. The fault is ours, not theirs." She quotes the Children's Society's claim that in 2006, 20% of our children have mental health problems and one in twelve is self harming. She further argues that 'over-testing our children has not made them cleverer; criminalising them has not made them behave better……….countries that are doing better than us do so because therapeutic and family interventions are not only more effective than punishment, but also cheaper.'

Consider the tragic case of Victoria Climbié, killed by her great aunt and the man with whom they lived. You may remember that in response to these terrible events, the UK Government published *Every Child Matters: Change for Children* (DfES, 2004) and passed the Children Act 2004. Also published as part of the Every Child Matters agenda was *The Common Core of Skills and Knowledge for the Children's Workforce* (DfES, 2005) which sets out the basic skills and knowledge needed by people (including volunteers) whose work brings them into regular contact with children, young people and families.

The skills and knowledge of the Common Core are described under six *main headings*:

1 Effective communication and engagement
2 Child and young person development
3 Safeguarding and promoting the welfare of the child
4 Supporting transitions
5 Multi-agency working
6 Sharing information

Over time, the UK government expects everyone working with children, young people and families to be able to demonstrate a basic level of competence in these six areas of the Common Core. The Core forms part of qualifications for working with children, young people and families and acts as a foundation for training and development programmes. Four of the six *main headings* are what we might term 'transferable skills' that might and probably should apply in any number of professional settings, but numbers 2 and 3 are very different. Number 3 speaks specifically of safeguarding and promoting the welfare of the child and addresses Section 11 of the Children Act 2004 which places a statutory duty on key people to make arrangements to safeguard and promote the welfare of children.

Number 2 of the *main headings* (Child and young person development) places a clear responsibility on all those who aspire to working with children to be expert in child and young person development. It is also as a response to this requirement and responsibility, that this adaptation is written.

A European Adaptation of an American Text

The 4th edition of the original text *Adolescence and Emerging Adulthood* begins with Jeff Arnett writing 'I am delighted that with this edition of *Adolescence and Emerging Adulthood*', which begs the question why wouldn't he be? The consistent characteristics of the first four editions include the very high quality of the writing, the rigour of the scholarship and the acclaim of reviewers, course tutors and students. When asked by Pearson to consider adapting such a highly successful and influential text as *Adolescence and Emerging Adulthood* for the European market, we began by testing out how viable and desirable an adapted text would be.

The approach taken in the original editions did provide a rich and diverse global exploration of cultural practices, customs, and beliefs about adolescence. In taking a cultural approach to development Jeff infused discussion of every aspect of development with a cultural perspective. However, the emphasis on American cultures particularly in some of the key features of each chapter meant that European students, particularly those in the United Kingdom would be looking for a more familiar national contexts for exploring the development of adolescents and those in emergent adulthood. Early reviews of adapted material supported the view that there was a need for a text focused on the European and particularly the UK market.

Readers of the original editions also noted the strong personal voice of Jeff Arnett throughout the book, particularly in relation to the cultural emphasis and in deepening the reader's knowledge and understanding the nature of emergent adulthood. My task was to preserve much of Jeff's authority and style, complementing his work by providing themes and examples in personal and professional contexts that would be familiar and pertinent to new readers. The most important reviewer of this text has been Jeff himself, who has consistently provided guidance and affirmation that his original work has been respected and appropriately adapted, and that new material has matching rigour and usefulness.

Emerging Adulthood

The title *Adolescence and Emerging Adulthood* uses a relatively new term to the UK, that of Emerging Adulthood. Jeff in the Preface to the 4th Edition of *Adolescence and Emerging Adulthood* explains how he came to identify, define and apply the term.

'Adolescence in our time begins far earlier than it did a century ago, because puberty begins for most people in industrialised countries at a much earlier age, due to advances in nutrition and health care. Yet, if we measure the end of adolescence in terms of taking on adult roles such as marriage, parenthood, and stable full-time work, adolescence also ends much later than it has in the past, because these transitions are now postponed for many people into at least the mid-20s.

My research over the past decade has focused on development among young people from their late teens through their mid-20s in the United States and Europe. I concluded, on the basis of this research, that this period is not really adolescence, but it is not really adulthood either, not even "young adulthood." In my view, the transition to adulthood has become so prolonged that it constitutes a separate period of the life course in industrialised societies, lasting about as long as adolescence. This view is now widely held by other scholars as well.'

This textbook includes not only adolescence (ages 10–18) but also 'emerging adulthood,' extending from (roughly) ages 19 to 25. The theory of emerging adulthood, is conceptualised by Jeff is as the age of identity explorations, of instability, self-focus, of feeling in-between, and the age of possibilities. We describe this theory in some detail in the first chapter, and use it as the framework for discussing emerging adulthood in the chapters that follow.

The Historical Context

Students will have a richer understanding of adolescent development if they are able to contrast the lives of young people in the present with the lives of young people in other times. Toward this end, we provide historical material in each chapter. Furthermore, each chapter contains a *Historical Focus* feature that describes some aspect of young people's development during a specific historical period - for example, the rise of youth culture, and work among British adolescents in the 19th century.

An emphasis on the historical context of development is perhaps especially important now, with the accelerating pace of cultural change that has taken place around the world in recent decades due to the influence of globalization. Especially in economically developing countries, the pace of change in recent decades has been dramatic, and young people often find themselves growing up in a culture that is much different than the one their parents grew up in. Globalisation is a pervasive influence on the lives of young people today, in ways both promising and potentially troubling, and for this reason we have made it one of the unifying themes of the book.

An Interdisciplinary Approach

We offer interdisciplinary approach to theories and research. Psychology is of course represented abundantly, because this is the discipline in which most research on adolescent development takes place. However, we also integrate materials from a wide range of other fields. Much of the theory and research that is the basis for a cultural understanding of adolescence comes from anthropology, so anthropological studies are strongly represented. Students often find this material fascinating, because it challenges effectively their assumptions about what they expect adolescence to be like. Interesting and important cultural material on adolescence also comes from sociology, especially with respect to European and Asian societies, and these studies find a place here. The field of history is notably represented, for providing the historical perspective discussed above. Other disciplines used for material include education, psychiatry, medicine, and family studies.

The integration of materials across disciplines means drawing on a variety of research methods. The reader will find many different research methods represented here, from questionnaires and interviews, ethnographic research to biological measurements. Each chapter contains a *Focus on Research* feature, in which the methods used in a specific study are described.

Professional Contexts

A new feature of this text are the *Professional Focus* features in each chapter. Although adolescence and youth studies are fascinating as subjects of academic study, many students are also considering future careers providing services to children, young people and their families. Even those who have no intention of furthering a career in children's services will find the discussion of professional contexts provided useful to exemplify the application of theory and research in challenging circumstances such as teenage pregnancy, traveller children dropping out of school, child carers and supporting transgender young people.

Thinking Critically

Each chapter contains a number of *Thinking Critically* questions. Critical thinking has become a popular term in academic circles particularly to define in part the academic level at which students are expected to reflect on their learning. The purpose of the critical thinking questions is to inspire students to attain a higher level of analysis and reflection about the ideas and information in the chapters than they would be likely to reach simply by reading the chapter. With the critical thinking questions we seek to encourage students to connect ideas across chapters, to consider hypothetical questions, and to apply the chapter materials to their own lives. Often, the questions have no 'right answer.' Although they are mainly intended to assist students in attaining a high level of thinking as they read, the questions also serve as lively material for group discussions or writing assignments.

Connect and Extend

Students often ask 'What is the difference between just passing the course and gaining a distinction or first class grade?' The answer in part is the extent to which students can call upon a width and depth of reading particularly in relation to current and groundbreaking classic research. Despite many colleges and universities housing extensive collections of books and journals, access to these collections at times when students are ready and primed to take on extending their thinking is not always possible. A new feature of this text is *Connect and Extend*, regularly inserted into the text, and containing a short description of an important piece of work and full referencing. What is different is that all the texts are available in full on-line via an electronic database accessible through college and university library web pages. In this case we have used EBSCO host Electronic Journals Service at http://ejournals.ebsco.com/Home.asp

A Companion Web Site

A website complements the text (visit www.pearsoned.co.uk/arnett). This website contains case study material to illustrate topics such as ethnic identity and eating disorders. In addition, the website contains:

- **responses to the *Thinking Critically* features** which provide fresh ideas and approaches and contributions from readers and course leaders

- **additional *Connect and Extend* features** with the most up-to-date research and contributions from readers and course leaders

- **online quizzes** that include instant scoring and responses.

- **web links** specific to each chapter that provide a valuable source of supplementary materials for learning and research.

- **an extensive teaching section** that includes PowerPoint slides, presentation graphics, lecture ideas and seminar activities.

One of the ways in which the website can work for students and course leaders is to keep the information in the text fresh and up to date. An example of why this is important is *Teachers* TV. In the text, particularly in Chapter 10 *School*, examples are used drawing on excellent video material from Teachers TV a website and free-to-air television channel which provided video and support materials for those who work in children's services. Government funding was withdrawn April 2011 and Teachers TV ceased to exist, but all the content 3,500 15 minute programmes in the archive will still be available to watch on-line at any of these web sites:

Distributer	Website
Phoenix TTV Limited	www.teachersmedia.co.uk/
viewmy.tv Limited	www.viewmy.tv
TSL Education Ltd	www.tes.co.uk/video
Axis 12 Limited	www.teachfind.com/
Promethean Planet	www.prometheanplanet.com/PDTV
Teach Pro Limited	www.schoolsworld.tv
Laser Learning Ltd	www.laserlearning.tv

Source: http://www.education.gov.uk/schools/toolsandinitiatives/teacherstv/ accessed 15th September 2011

ABOUT THE AUTHORS

Jeffrey Jensen Arnett is a Research Professor in the Department of Psychology at Clark University in Worcester, Massachusetts. During 2005 he was a Fulbright Scholar at the University of Copenhagen, Denmark. He has also taught at Oglethorpe University and the University of Missouri. He was educated at Michigan State University (undergraduate), the University of Virginia (graduate school), and the University of Chicago (postdoctoral studies). His research interests are in risk behavior (especially cigarette smoking), media use in adolescence (especially music), and a wide range of topics in emerging adulthood. He is editor of the *Journal of Adolescent Research* and of two encyclopedias, the *International Encyclopedia of Adolescence* (2007) and the *Encyclopedia of Children, Adolescents, and the Media* (2006). His book *Emerging Adulthood: The Winding Road from the Late Teens through the Twenties,* was

The author with his wife Lene Jensen and soon-to-be adolescents Miles and Paris, age 9. © Jeffrey J. Arnett

published in 2004 by Oxford University Press. His edited book (with Jennifer Tanner), *Emerging Adults in America: Coming of Age in the 21st Century,* was published by APA Books in 2006. He lives in Worcester, Massachusetts with his wife Lene Jensen and their nine-year-old twins, Miles and Paris. For more information on Dr. Arnett and his research, see **www.jeffreyarnett.com.**

Malcolm Hughes is Senior Research Fellow in Developmental Psychology at the University of the West of England, Bristol, UK. For over two decades he was a school leader and taught physical education, music and mathematics before moving to lead postgraduate initial teacher training and continuing professional development at UWE. He has co-authored a number of influential and widely read higher education texts including *Psychology of Education* and *Child Development, Theory and Practice 0-11,* both for Pearson Education. He has also co-authored a wide range of classroom teaching and assessment resources for secondary and primary schools, mainly in mathematics and information technology.

Mal has held many posts as organist, conductor and director of music in parish churches, choral societies and community choirs in Oxfordshire, Buckinghamshire, and Herefordshire. He is a Licentiate of the Royal Academy of Music in voice and an Associate of the Royal College of Organists. He enjoys stage direction, singing, golf and (these days watching) rugby, walking, home improvement projects, and arranging many

The author with his wife in Rhodes © Malcolm Hughes

styles of choral music. Mal lives in Ledbury, Herefordshire with his wife Sue. They have five grown-up children and two grandchildren.

AUTHOR'S ACKNOWLEDGEMENTS

Preparing a textbook is an enormous enterprise that involves a wide network of people, none more so than Jeff Arnett himself who has been most generous to allow an adaptation to be made of his outstanding original text. I also thank Catherine Yates, Editor in Chief - Humanities & Social Sciences, Pearson UK whose continued confidence and support helped persuade me to take on the project. My thanks also to Katy Robinson the then Associate Editor of the book, Lauren Hayward, Desk Editor Pearson UK and Ros Woodward who have taken the book from rough manuscript to finished textbook.

The reviewers of the proposal and draft chapters were indispensable for the many comments and suggestions for improvement they provided. I am grateful for the time and care expended by these reviewers to give such detailed, expert and well-informed reviews.

Finally, I wish to thank my wife Sue for her support, scholarship and encouragement that has made this book possible. The adaptation is dedicated to my son Tom Hughes (1990–2009).

Malcolm W H Hughes
University of the West of England

PUBLISHER'S ACKNOWLEDGEMENTS

We are grateful to the following for permission to reproduce copyright material:

Figures

Figure 1.2 from Emerging adulthood: A theory of development from the late teens through the twenties, *American Psychologist*, Vol. 55, pp. 469–480 (Arnett, J.J. 2000), American Psychological Association, reprinted with permission; Figure 2.2 from E.D. Nottelmann, E.J. Susman, J.H. Blue, G. Inoff-Germain, L.D. Dorn, D.L. Loriaux, G.B. Cutler and G.P. Chrousos, Gonadal and adrenal hormone correlates of adjustment in early adolescence, in, *Biological-Psychological Interactions in Early Adolescence*, pp. 246–260 (Learner, R.M. and Foch, T.T. (Eds.) 1987), Hillsdale, NJ: Erlbaum. Copyright 1987, reproduced with permission of Taylor & Francis Group LLC - Books in the format Textbook and Other book via Copyright Clearance Center; Figures 2.3 and 2.5 adapted from M. Grumbach, J. Roth, S. Kaplan and R. Kelch, Hypothalamic-pituitary regulation of puberty in man: Evidence and concepts derived from clinical research, in, *Control of the Onset of Puberty* (Grumbach, M., Grave, G. and Mayer, F. (Eds.) 1990), Lippincott, Williams & Wilkins, used with permission of Lippincott, Williams & Wilkins and the authors; Figure 2.4 adapted from W.A. Marshall, Puberty, in, *Human Growth. Volume 2: Postnatal Growth* (Falkner, F. and Tanner, J.M. (Eds.) 1978), with kind permission from Springer Science + Business Media B.V.; Figure 2.6 from Eurostat (hlth_is_bmia), © European Communities, 1995–2010; Figure 2.8 from *Growth at Adolescence*, 2nd ed., Blackwell, Oxford (Tanner, J.M. 1962), reproduced with permission of Blackwell Publishing Ltd.; Figure 2.9 adapted from *Worldwide variation in human growth*, Cambridge, MA: Cambridge University Press (Eveleth, P.B. and Tanner, J.M. 1990); Figure 2.10 adapted from Variations in the pattern of pubertal changes in boys, *Archives of Disease in Childhood*, Vol. 45 (239), p. 22 (Marshall, W.A. and Tanner, J.M. 1970), Copyright © 1970, BMJ Publishing Group Ltd. and the Royal College of Paediatrics and Child Health, with permission from BMJ Publishing Group Ltd.; Figure 2.11 from A naturalistic study of the involvement of children and adolescents with their mothers and friends: Developmental differences in expressive behavior, *Journal of Adolescent Research*, Vol. 4 (1), pp. 3–14 (Montemayor, R. and Flannery, D.J. 1989), Copyright © 1989, Sage Publications, reprinted by permission of Sage Publications; Figure 3.3 from Optimistic bias in adolescent and adult smokers and nonsmokers, *Addictive Behaviors*, Vol. 25 (4), pp. 625–632 (Arnett, J.J. 2000), with permission from Elsevier; Figure 3.4 from Behavioral correlates of mental growth: Birth to thirty-six years, *American Psychologist*, Vol. 23, pp. 1–17 (Bayley, N. 1968), American Psychological Association, reprinted with permission; Figures 3.5 and 3.6 from *Adolescence*, 10th ed. (Santrock, J.W. 2005) Copyright © 2005 The McGraw-Hill Companies, Inc., reproduced with permission of McGraw-Hill Companies, Inc. - Books in the format Textbook and Other book via Copyright Clearance Center; Figure 5.1 from *General Social Survey (GSS) 1977–2006*, National Opinion Research Center; Figure 5.2 from Content analysis of contemporary teen magazines for adolescent females, *Youth and Society*, Vol. 23 (1), pp. 99-120 (Evans, E.D., Rutberg, J., Sather, C. and Turner, C. 1991), Copyright © 1991, Sage Publications, reprinted by permission of Sage Publications; Figure 5.3 from Sex differences in mathematical ability: Fact or artifact?, *Science*, Vol. 210 (4475), pp. 1262–1264 (Benbow, C.P. and Stanley, J.C. 1980), The American Association for the Advancement of Science (AAAS), reprinted with permission from AAAS and the authors; Figure 6.1 from A longitudinal study of self esteem: Implications of adolescent development, *Journal of Youth and Adolescence*, Vol. 26, No. 2, pp. 117–141 (Zimmerman, M.A., Copeland, L.A., Shope, J.T. and Dielman, T.E. 1997), Copyright © 1997 Springer Netherlands, with kind permission from Springer Science + Business Media and the authors; Figure 6.2 from *How Social Role Transitions From Adolescence to Adulthood Relate to Trajectories of Well-Being and Substance Use*, Institute of Social Research (Schulenberg, J.E., O'Malley, P.M., Bachman, J.G., Johnston, L.D. and Laetz, V..B. 2003) The Monitoring the Future Study, Occasional Paper 56, the University of Michigan, Figure 1 'Average Well-Being During the Transition to Adulthood'; Figure 6.3 from Identity formation revisited: A rejoinder to Waterman on developmental and cross-cultural issues, *Developmental Review*, Vol. 19 (4), pp. 480–496 (Meeus, W., Iedema, J. and Vollebergh, W. 1999), Academic Press, with permission from Elsevier;

Figure 7.1 from Changes in adolescents' daily interactions with their families from ages 10 to 18: disengagement and transformation, *Development Psychology*, Vol. 32 (4), pp. 744–754 (Larson, R. W., Richards, M. H., Moneta, G., Holmbeck, G. and Duckett, E. 1996), American Psychological Association, reprinted with permission; Figure 7.2 from I. Granic, T.J. Dishion and T. Hollenstein, The family ecology of adolescence: A dynamic systems perspective on normative development, in, *Blackwell Handbook of Adolescence*, pp. 60–91 (Adams, G.R. and Berzonsky, M.D. (Eds.) 2008), © 2006 Blackwell Publishing Ltd., Figure 4.4, p. 73, with permission of John Wiley and Sons; Figure 7.3 from Regional differences in the transition to adulthood, *Annals of the American Academy of Political and Social Science*, Vol. 580 (1), pp. 40–69 (Iacovou, M. 2002), Copyright © 2002, American Academy of Political and Social Science, reprinted by permission of Sage Publications; Figure 7.4 from *Marriage, Divorce and Children's Adjustment*, 2nd ed., Newbury Park, CA: Sage (Emery, R.E. 1999), reproduced with permission of Sage Publications, Inc. Books in the format Textbook and Other book via Copyright Clearance Center; Figure 7.5 from http://www.statistics.gov.uk/cci/nugget.asp?id=1655, Source: Office for National Statistics licensed under the Open Government Licence v.1.0.; Figure 8.2 from R. Larson and M. Richards, Waiting for the weekend: Friday and Saturday nights as the emotional climax of the week, in, *Temporal Rhythms in Adolescence: Clocks, Calendars, and the Coordination of Daily Life*, pp. 37–52 (Crouter, A.C. and Larson, R.W. (Eds.) 1998), New Directions for Child and Adolescent Development, Vol. 82. Copyright © 1998 by Jossey-Bass Inc. Publishers, all rights reserved, reproduced with permission of John Wiley & Sons, Inc.; Figure 8.3 from *Being Adolescent: Conflict and Growth in the Teenage Years*, New York: Basic Books (Csikszentmihalyi, M. and Larson, R.W. 1986) Copyright © 1986 Mihaly Csikszentmihalyi, Reed Larson, reprinted by permission of Basic Books, a member of the Perseus Books Group; Figure 9.1 from R.J. Sternberg, Triangulating love, in, *The Psychology of Love*, pp. 119–138 (Sternberg, R.J. and Barnes, M.L. (Eds.) 1988), New Haven, CT: Yale University Press, p. 122, Copyright © by Yale University; Figure 9.2 from The culture of harassment in secondary schools, *American Educational Research Journal*, Vol. 33 (2), pp. 383–417 (Lee, V., Croninger, R., Linn, E. and Chen, X. 1996), Copyright © 1996, American Educational Research Association, reprinted by permission of Sage Publications; Figure 9.5 from *Risk and Protection: Youth and HIV/AIDS in Sub-Saharan Africa*, New York: The Alan Guttmacher Institute (Bankole, A., Singh, S., Woog, V. and Wulf, D. 2004) p. 5; Figure 10.1 from M.E. Fussell and M.E. Greene, Demographic trends affecting youth around the world, in, *The World's Youth: Adolescence in Eight Regions of the Globe*, p. 32 (Mortimer, J. and Larson, R. (Eds.) 2002), Cambridge, England: Cambridge University Press; Figure 10.2 from *PISA 2009 at a Glance*, OECD Publishing (2011) http://dx.doi.org/10.1787/9789264095298-en; Figure 10.3 from *Ethnicity and Education: the Evidence on Minority Ethnic Pupils Aged 5–16*, Department for Education and Skills. Research topic paper 0208-2006DOM-EN (2006), Source: Office for National Statistics licensed under the Open Government Licence v.1.0.; Figure 11.1 adapted from *Labour Force Survey*, Office for National Statistics, Source: Office for National Statistics licensed under the Open Government Licence v.1.0.; Figure 11.2 adapted from *NEET Statistics Quarterly Brief*, DCSF (2007), Source: Office for National Statistics licensed under the Open Government Licence v.1.0.; Figure 11.3 adapted from Client Caseload Information System (CCIS) data, Source: Office for National Statistics licensed under the Open Government Licence v.1.0.; Figure 11.4 adapted from Welsh Assembly statistical article (2009): Young people not in education, employment or training (NEET) (Year to 30 June 2009), http://wales.gov.uk/docs/statistics/2010/100120neet0609en.pdf, Source: Office for National Statistics licensed under the Open Government Licence v.1.0.; Figure 12.4 from *Monitoring the Future: National survey results on drug use, 1975–2007: Volume II, College students and adults ages 19–45*, Bethesda, MD: National Institute on Drug Abuse (Johnston, L.D., O'Malley, P.M., Bachman, J.G. and Schulenberg, J.E. 2008) (NIH Publication No. 08–6418B); Figure 12.5 from *A General Theory of Crime*, Stanford, CA: Stanford University Press (Gottfredson, M. and Hirschi, T. 1990) p. 125, Copyright © 1990 by the Board of Trustees of the Leland Stanford Jr. University, all rights reserved. Used with the permission of Stanford University Press, www.sup.org; Figures 12.7 and 12.8 from *Deliberate Self-Harm in Oxford 2008*, Centre for Suicide Research (Hawton, K., Casey, D., Bale, E., Shepherd, A., Bergen, H. and Simkin, S. 2009)

Tables

Table 2.3 from Hospital Episode Statistics, HES, Copyright © 2011, re-used with the permission of The Health and Social Care Information Centre. All rights reserved; Table 4.2 from From obedience to autonomy: Changes in traits desired in children, 1924–1978, *Public Opinion Quarterly*, Vol. 52 (1), pp. 33–52

(Alwin, D.F. 1988), by permission of Oxford University Press; Table 4.3 from A congregation of one: Individualized religious beliefs among emerging adults, *Journal of Adolescent Research*, Vol. 17, pp. 451–467 (Arnett, J.J. and Jensen, L.A. 2002), Copyright © 2002, Sage Publications; Table 5.1 from The measurement of psychological androgyny, *Journal of Consulting and Clinical Psychology*, Vol. 42, pp. 155–162 (Bem, S.L. 1974), American Psychological Association, reprinted with permission; Table 5.2 from Creating gender equality: Cross-national gender stratification and mathematical performance, *Sociology of Education*, Vol. 66, pp. 91–103 (Baker, D.P. and Perkins-Jones, D. 1993), Copyright © 1993, American Sociological Association, reproduced with permission of Sage Publications Inc. Journals in the format Textbook and Other book via Copyright Clearance Center; Table 7.4 from Eurostat, 2007 pp. 3–4, © European Communities, 1995–2010; Table 9.2 from Interpersonal context as an influence on the sexual timetables of youths: Gender and ethnic effects, *Journal of Research on Adolescence*, Vol. 9, pp. 25–52 (Feldman, S.S., Turner, R.A. and Araujo, K. 1999), Society for Research on Adolescence, Copyright 1999, reproduced with permission of Taylor & Francis Informa UK Ltd - Journals in the format Textbook and Other book via Copyright Clearance Center; Table 9.3 from *Love and Sex: Cross-Cultural Perspectives*, New York: University Press of America (Hatfield, E. and Rapson, R.L. 2005) Copyright 2005, reproduced with permission of University Press of America in the format Textbook and Other book via Copyright Clearance Center; Table 9.4 from Perceptions of sexual harassment in Swedish high schoools: Experiences and school-environment problems, *The European Journal of Public Health*, Vol. 15 (1), pp. 78–85 (Witkowska, E. and Menckel, E. 2005), by permission of Oxford University Press; Table 9.5 from http://rds.homeoffice.gov.uk/rds/pdfs10/recorded-crime-2002–2010.xls, accessed 19 November 2010, Source: Office for National Statistics licensed under the Open Government Licence v.1.0.; Table 9.6 from Prevalence and stability of sexual orientation components during adolescence and young adulthood, *Archives of Sexual Behavior*, Vol. 36 (3), pp. 385–394 (Savin-Williams, R.C. and Ream, G.L. 2007), Copyright © 2006, Springer Science + Business Media, Inc., with kind permission from Springer Science + Business Media and the authors; Table 10.2 from National Center for Education Statistics (2006), U.S. Department of Education, Institute of Education Sciences; Table 10.3 from *Annual Population Survey*, Office for National Statistics, Source: Office for National Statistics licensed under the Open Government Licence v.1.0.; Table 11.1 from Occupations of the people of the United Kingdom, 1801–81, *Journal of the Statistical Society of London*, Vol. 49, pp. 314–436 (Booth, C. 1886); Table 11.2 adapted from P.J. Aronson, J.T. Mortimer, C. Zierman and M. Hacker, Generational differences in early work experiences and evaluations, in, *Adolescents, Work and Family: An Intergenerational Developmental Analysis* (Mortimer, J.T. and Finch, M.D. (Eds.) 1996), Thousand Oaks, CA: Sage, Copyright 1996, reproduced with permission of Sage Publications, Inc. Books in the format Textbook and Other book via Copyright Clearance Center; Table 11.3 from Office for National Statistics (2001) Omnibus Survey, Source: Office for National Statistics licensed under the Open Government Licence v.1.0.

Text

Poetry on page 87 from A Dedication to My Wife by T.S. Eliot, *Collected Poems 1909–1962*, Faber and Faber Ltd.; General Displayed Text on pages 117–8 from NHS Choices, Attention Deficit Hyperactivity Disorder (ADHD), 'jwest' comment 23 February 2011, http://www.nhs.uk/conditions/attention-deficit-hyperactivity-disorder/Pages/Introduction.aspx, content supplied by NHS Choices; General Displayed Text on page 138 from Scout promise and law, http://scouts.org.uk/supportresources/2943/scout-promise-law-and-motto?cat=7,132, reproduced by permission of The Scout Association, Registered Charity no. 306101 (England and Wales) and SC038437 (Scotland); Poetry on page 183 from *Mirrors*, Mermaids UK: Young Voices, Copyright Mermaids support group - www.mermaids.org.uk; Poetry on page 184 from *Day by Day*, Mermaids UK: Young Voices, Copyright Mermaids support group - www.mermaids.org.uk; Poetry on page 243 from My experience of being an only (an extract). Guest writing, http://www.onlychild.org.uk; Extracts on pages 246, 276 and 277 from *Childline Casenotes: Calls to ChildLine About Running Away and Homelessness*, NSPCC (2007); General Displayed Text on page 384 from My smart school still failed me, *The Guardian*, 12 September 2004; General Displayed Text on pages 484–5 from National Probation Service 2011, http://www.nationalprobationservice.co.uk/page1.html, contains public sector information licensed under the Open Government Licence v1.0.

Picture Credits

The publisher would like to thank the following for their kind permission to reproduce their photographs:
(Key: b-bottom; c-centre; l-left; r-right; t-top)

4 Mary Evans Picture Library: Edwin Mullan Collection. **5 Corbis:** Bettmann. **6 Corbis:** Bettmann (t, b). **9 Getty Images:** Imagno. **10 Pearson Education Ltd. 14 Photofusion Picture Library:** Bob Watkins (bl, bc), Liz Somerville (br) **16 Panos Pictures:** Dean Chapman. **19 Corbis:** Kazuyoshi Nomachi. **23 Library of Congress. 25 Pearson Education Ltd. 30 Rex Features:** Mark Campbell. **31 Alamy Images:** © Stock Connection Distribution. **32 Alamy Images:** Imagebroker. **33 Getty Images:** Eco Images (tr). **Alamy Images:** amana images inc. (tl). **37 Pearson Education Ltd. 39 TopFoto:** Dinodia / M.L.Corvetto. **51 Pearson Education Ltd. 56 Alamy Images:** © Trinity Mirror / Mirrorpix / Alamy. **57 Getty Images:** Erza Shaw. **65 TopFoto:** The Image Works / Sasa Kralj / Trace Images (b). **Wiley-Blackwell, Oxford.:** Blackwell Science Ltd (t). **67 Himalayan Academy.** . **73 Mary Evans Picture Library. 76 Pearson Education Ltd. 83 Science Photo Library Ltd:** BILL ANDERSON / SCIENCE PHOTO LIBRARY. **89 Getty Images:** Eco Images. **92 B&C Alexander/Arcticphoto.com.** **93 Alamy Images:** Jon Parker Lee. **96 Alamy Images:** © Robin Beckham / BEEPstock / Alamy. **98 Pearson Education Ltd. 100 Mary Evans Picture Library:** Peter Higginbotham Collection. **103 Science Photo Library Ltd:** CC Studio. **105 Science Photo Library Ltd:** Damien Lovegrove. **109 Alamy Images:** samc. **115 Alamy Images:** Darren Baker. **116 Getty Images:** Franck Fife / AFP. **118 Imagemore Co., Ltd: 122 TopFoto:** The Image Works / Richard Lord. **128 Alamy Images:** Miriam Reik. **130 Alamy Images:** vario images GmbH & Co.KG (tc); Peter Phipp / Travelshots.com (tl). **Panos Pictures:** J. Holmes (tr). **131 Alamy Images:** Graham Oliver. **135 Panos Pictures:** Pennie Tweedie. **137 Pearson Education Ltd. 140 Alamy Images:** Tim Graham (t); Robert Fried (b). **145 Corbis:** Ashley Cooper. **147 Corbis:** Reuters Photographer / Reuters. **152 Alamy Images:** John Powell / Bubbles. **156 Getty Images:** Jo Metson Scott. **158 Corbis:** Sion Touhig. **159 Darren Stein. 163 Alamy Images:** Tina Manley. **168 Corbis:** Peter Johnson. **169 Mary Evans Picture Library. 171 Getty Images:** Topical Press Agency / Hulton Archive. **174 Alamy Images:** Blend Images (c); Ace Stock Limited (t). **177 Alamy Images:** Bubbles photolibrary. **179 Press Association Images:** AP. **184 http://www.mermaidsuk.org.uk/.** **186 Getty Images:** Blend Images. **191 Panos Pictures:** Morris Carpenter. **199 Pearson Education Ltd. 207 Pearson Education Ltd. 212 Bridgeman Art Library Ltd:** Germanisches Nationalmuseum, Nuremberg, Germany. **217 Mary Evans Picture Library:** SIGMU.

219 Pearson Education Ltd. 221 Pearson Education Ltd. 223 Corbis: AMIT DAVE / Reuters. **224 Pearson Education Ltd:** Pearson Education Ltd. Jules Selmes. **226 Pearson Education Ltd. 228 Press Association Images:** Martin Rickett. **236 Pearson Education Ltd. 241 Pearson Education Ltd. 243 Getty Images:** Asger Carlsen. **245 Panos Pictures:** Giacomo Pirozzi. **246 Shutterstock.com:** Carme Balcells. **249 Alamy Images:** Catchlight Visual Services. **250 Getty Images:** Harry Hook. **251 Pearson Education Ltd. 254 Alamy Images:** Rubberball. **255 Inmagine Limited. 259 Alamy Images:** Ace Stock Limited. **261 Corbis:** Moodboard. **264 Getty Images:** Archive Holdings Inc.. **265 Getty Images:** Topical Press. **266 Getty Images:** Michael Krasowitz. **268 Shutterstock.com:** ejwhite. **281 Pearson Education Ltd. 285 Alamy Images:** Megapress. **287 Pearson Education Ltd. 288 Pearson Education Ltd. 290 Alamy Images:** Janine Wiedel Photolibrary. **292 The Kobal Collection:** Columbia Pictures. **294 Pearson Education Ltd. 296 Adam Lawrence:** (b). **The Kobal Collection:** Warner Bros TV / Bright / Kauffman / Crane Pro (t). **297 Company Pictures/Stormdog:** Peter Wolfes. **302 Pearson Education Ltd. 306 Getty Images:** Pennie Tweedie. **310 Corbis:** Martin Ruetschi / Keystone. **313 Alamy Images:** Images.com. **314 Getty Images:** Hulton Archvie (tl); Hulton Archive (tr); Bert Hardy / Hulton Archive (cl). **Alamy Images:** Blend Images (cr). **316 Alamy Images:** MBI. **321 Getty Images:** Fuse. **325 The Kobal Collection:** Universal. **326 Alamy Images:** Gaertner. **328 Alamy Images:** Profimedia International s.r.o. **330 Alamy Images:** Design Pics Inc.. **336 TopFoto:** The Image Works / Hari Mahidhar / DPA. **339 Alamy/Juice Images: 343 Woodfin Camp & Associates / Francios Perri / Cosmos 347 Shutterstock.com:** Aaron Amat. **352 Alamy Images:** Julio Etchart. **358 Getty Images:** David Hanson. **359 Corbis:** Atlantide Phototravel. **360 Shutterstock.com:** Angela Farley. **368 Education Photos:** John Walmsley. **373 Pearson Education Ltd. 376 iAfrika Photos/Shaun Harris. 387 Amana Images. 391 Education Photos:** John Walmsley. **397 Alamy Images:** MIXA. **399 Shutterstock.com:** Patricia Marks **400 Getty Images/Yellow Dog Productions 406 Alamy Images:** Aurora Photos. **411 Woodfin Camp & Associates/M&E Bernheim 412 Alamy Images:** Wolfgang Kaehler. **414 Panos Pictures:** Sean Sprague. **416 Library of Congress. 418 Mary Evans Picture Library:** Country Life / IPC Media Ltd. **419 Pearson Education Ltd. 423 Alamy Images:** Picture Partners. **425 Pearson Education Ltd. 431 Pearson Education Ltd. 426 Alamy/Juice Images 433 Tony Mottram. 451 Getty Images:**

Jupiterimages. **452 Science Photo Library Ltd:** Richard Hutchings. **458 Alamy Images:** Andrew Lever. **459 TopFoto**. **465 Getty Images:** Flickr Unreleased. **471 Pearson Education Ltd. 473 Science Photo Library Ltd:** AJ Photo. **476 Corbis:** Les Stone / Sygma. **478 Getty Images:** Tony Latham. **482 Reuters:** David Gray. **485 Alamy Images:** Mark Harvey

Cover images: *Front:* **Getty Images**

In some instances we have been unable to trace the owners of copyright material, and we would appreciate any information that would enable us to do so.

CHAPTER 1
INTRODUCTION

OUTLINE

In her bedroom at the top of the Victorian terrace in Redland, Bristol, UK, 14-year-old Emily is standing in front of a full-length mirror with a dismayed look, trying to decide whether to wear her hair down for school or to tie it back in a ponytail. Her self-absorbed gaze takes in the shapeless maroon jumper and skirt and the knee-high socks. 'I look awful,' she says to herself. 'I'm getting so fat!' For the past three years her body has been changing rapidly, and now she is alarmed to find it becoming rounder and larger seemingly with each day. Vaguely she hears her mum calling her from downstairs, probably urging her to hurry up and leave for school, but the music channel on her new flat-screen TV is so loud it drowns out what her mother is saying. 'Good weed, white wine,' Rihanna sings. 'I come alive in the night time.'

In the dim dawn light of a simple reed house in Tehuantepec, Mexico, 16-year-old Conchita leans over an open, barrel-shaped oven. Although it is just dawn, she has already been working for two hours making tortillas. It is difficult work, kneeling beside the hot oven, and hazardous, too; she has several scars on her arm from the times she has inadvertently touched the hot steel. She thinks with some resentment of her younger brother, who is still sleeping and who will soon be rising and going off to school. Like most girls in her village, Conchita can neither read nor write because it is only the boys who go to school.

But she finds consolation in looking ahead to the afternoon, when she will be allowed to go to the centre of town to sell the tortillas she has made beyond those that her family will need that day. There she will see her girlfriends, who will also be selling tortillas and other things for their families. And there she hopes to see the boy who spoke to her, just a few words, in the town square two Sunday evenings ago. The following Sunday evening she saw him waiting in the street across from her home, a sure sign that he is courting her. But her parents would not allow her out, so she hopes to get a glimpse of him in town (based on Chinas, 1992).

In Amakiri, Nigeria, 18-year-old Omiebi is walking to school. He is walking quickly, because the time for school to begin is near, and he does not want to be one of the students who arrive after morning assembly has started and are grouped together and made to kneel throughout the assembly. Up ahead he sees several of his fellow students, easily identifiable by the grey uniforms they are all required to wear, and he breaks into a trot to join them. They greet him, and together they continue walking. They joke nervously about the exam coming up for the West African School Certificate. Performance on that exam will determine who is allowed to go on to university.

Omiebi is feeling a great deal of pressure to do well in the exam. He is the oldest child of his family, and his parents have high expectations that he will go to university and become a lawyer, then help his three younger brothers go to university or find good jobs in Lagos, the nearest big city. Omiebi is not really sure he wants to be a lawyer, and he would find it difficult to leave the girl he has recently begun seeing. However, he likes the idea of moving away from tiny Amakiri to the university in Lagos, where, he has heard, all the homes have electricity and all the latest movies are showing in the cinemas. He and his friends break into a run over the last stretch, barely making it to school and joining their classes before the assembly starts (based on Hollos and Leis, 1989).

THREE ADOLESCENTS, IN THREE DIFFERENT CULTURES, with three very different lives. Yet all are adolescents: All have left childhood but have not yet reached adulthood; all are developing into physical and sexual maturity and learning the skills that will enable them to take part in the adult world.

'The adolescent stage has long seemed to me one of the most fascinating of all themes. These years are the best decade of life . . . It is a state from which some of the bad, but far more of the good qualities of life and mind arise.'
– G. Stanley Hall, *Adolescence* (1904), pp. XVIII, 351, Volume 1

Although all of them are adolescents, what makes these three adolescents so different is that they are growing up in three distinct cultures. Throughout this book we will take a cultural approach to understanding development in **adolescence** by examining the ways that cultures differ in what they allow adolescents to do and what they require them to do, the different things that cultures teach adolescents to believe, and the different patterns that cultures provide for adolescents' daily lives. Adolescence is in part a cultural construction, not simply a biological phenomenon. Puberty – the set of biological changes involved in reaching physical and sexual maturity – is universal, and the same biological changes take place in puberty for young people everywhere, although with differences in timing and in cultural meanings. Adolescence, however, is more than the events and processes of puberty. Adolescence is a period of the life course between the time puberty begins and the time adult status is approached, when young people are developing and preparing to take on the roles and responsibilities of adulthood in their culture. Developmental psychology is the study of how individuals develop and change during particular periods of their lives – we will draw much on what developmental and behavioural psychologists have learned in the last hundred years or so about how adolescents think and behave. We will also draw on important ideas of social psychology, the study of how people interrelate with others and the effects on behaviour of the relationships people experience. Adolescents are often referred to as young people or 'the youth', and those interested in what happens during adolescence – parents, young people themselves, and professional practitioners including teachers, counsellors and youth workers – are described as students or researchers of youth studies.

CONNECT AND EXTEND

To establish the European and cultural focus of this text our first *Connect and Extend* feature is about the impact of musical culture on Polish adolescents. The clue is in the title. Read 'Education and the music culture of Polish adolescents' by Elzbieta Szubertowska in the *Psychology of Music*, Volume 33, Number 3 (July 2005), pp. 317–330

The approach taken in this book is to weave together the most significant approaches and ideas of developmental, social and behavioural psychology and of youth studies, to present a picture of what it means to be a young person – an adolescent. To say that adolescence is culturally and socially constructed means that cultures vary in how they define adult status and in the content of the adult roles and responsibilities adolescents are learning to fulfil. Almost all cultures and societies have some kind of adolescence, but the length and content and daily experiences of adolescence vary greatly among cultures (Larson et al., 2010).

In this chapter, we will lay a foundation for understanding the social and cultural basis of adolescence by beginning with a look at how adolescence has changed throughout the history of 'Western' cultures and societies. Historical change is also cultural change; for example, Europe of the early twenty-first century is different culturally from Europe of 1900 or 1800. Seeing how adolescence changes as cultures and societies change will emphasise the cultural and social basis of adolescence.

Another way this chapter will lay the foundation for the rest of the book is by introducing the concept of **emerging adulthood**. This textbook focuses on adolescence (roughly ages 10 to 18) but also 'looks ahead' to young adulthood (roughly ages 18 to 25). This period is also sometimes referred to as emerging adulthood – a new idea, a new way of thinking about this age period. Each chapter contains information about emerging adulthood as well as maintaining the focus on adolescence and youth studies.

This chapter also sets the stage for what follows by discussing the scientific study of adolescence and emerging adulthood. We will present some of the basic features of the scientific method as it is applied in psychological and sociological research on these age periods. It is important to understand adolescence and emerging adulthood not just as periods of the life course but as areas of scientific inquiry, with certain standard methods and certain conventions for determining what is valid and what is not.

Finally, this chapter will provide the foundation for the chapters to come by previewing the major themes and the framework of the book. This will introduce you to themes that will be repeated often in subsequent chapters, and will let you know where we are headed through the course of the book. Special attention will be given to the cultural approach that is central to this book, by presenting an overview of adolescence in various regions of the world.

ADOLESCENCE IN WESTERN CULTURES: A BRIEF HISTORY

Seeing how people in other times have viewed adolescence provides a useful perspective for understanding how adolescence is understood in our own time. In this brief historical survey, we begin with ancient times 2500 years ago and proceed through the early twentieth century.

Adolescence in Ancient Times

Ideas about adolescence as a stage of the life course go back a long way in the history of Western cultures. In ancient Greece (4th and 5th centuries BC), the source of so many ideas that influenced Western history, both Plato and Aristotle viewed adolescence as the third distinct stage of life, after infancy (birth to age 7) and childhood (ages 7 to 14). In their framework, adolescence extended from age 14 to 21. Both of them viewed adolescence as the stage of life in which the capacity for reason first developed. Writing (in 4 BC) in *The Republic*, Plato argued that serious education should begin only at adolescence. Before age 7, according to Plato, there is no point in beginning education because the infant's mind is too undeveloped to learn much, and during childhood (ages 7 to 14) education should focus on sports and music, which children can grasp. Education in science and mathematics should be delayed until adolescence, when the mind is finally ready to apply reason in learning these subjects.

Aristotle, who was a student of Plato's during his own adolescence, had a view of adolescence that was in some ways similar to Plato's. Aristotle viewed children as similar to animals, in that both are ruled by the impulsive pursuit of pleasure. It is only in adolescence that we become capable of exercising reason and making rational choices. However, Aristotle argued that it takes the entire course of adolescence for reason to become fully established. At the beginning of adolescence, in his view, the impulses remain in charge and even become more problematic now that sexual desires have developed. It is only toward the end of adolescence – about age 21, according to Aristotle – that reason establishes firm control over the impulses.

THINKING CRITICALLY

Plato and Aristotle argued that young people are not capable of reason until at least age 14. Consider some examples of how the question of when young people are capable of reason is still an issue in our time. Afterwards you might like to compare your thinking with ours as we present our ideas at **www.pearsoned.co.uk/arnett**.

Adolescence From Early Christian Times Through the Middle Ages

A similar focus on the struggle between reason and passion in adolescence can be found in early Christianity. One of the most famous and influential books of early Christianity was Saint Augustine's autobiographical *Confessions*, which he wrote *circa* AD 400. In his *Confessions*, Augustine described his life from early childhood until his conversion to Christianity at age 33. A considerable portion of the autobiography focused on his teens and early 20s, when he was a reckless young man living an impulsive, pleasure-seeking life. He drank large quantities of alcohol, spent money extravagantly, had sex with many young women, and fathered a child outside of marriage. In the autobiography, he repents his reckless youth and argues that conversion to Christianity is the key not only to eternal salvation but to the establishment of the rule of reason over passion here on earth, within the individual.

'The young are in character prone to desire and ready to carry any desire they may have formed into action. Of bodily desires it is the sexual to which they are most disposed to give way, and in regard to sexual desire they exercise no self-restraint.'
– Aristotle, *Rhetoric, circa* 330 BC

Over the following millennium, from Augustine's time through the Middle Ages, the historical record on adolescence is sparse, as it is on most topics. However, one well-documented event that sheds some light on the history of adolescence is the 'Children's Crusade', which took place in 1212. Despite its name, it was composed mostly of young people in their teens, including many university students (Gray, 2006). In those days, university students were younger than today, usually entering between ages 13 and 15.

The Children crossing the Alps

During the Children's Crusade, European adolescents attempted to travel to Jerusalem, with disastrous results.

'For this space then (from my nineteenth year, to my eight and twentieth), we lived seduced and seducing, deceived and deceiving, in diverse lusts.'
– Augustine, *Confessions*, A.D. 400

The young crusaders set out from Germany for the Mediterranean coast, believing that when they arrived there the waters would part for them as the Red Sea had for Moses. They would then walk over to the Holy Land (Jerusalem and the areas where Jesus Christ had lived), where they would appeal to the Muslims to allow Christian pilgrims to visit the holy sites. Adults, attempting to take the Holy Land by military force, had already conducted several Crusades. The Children's Crusade was an attempt to appeal to the Muslims in peace, inspired by the belief that Jesus had decreed that the Holy Land could be gained only through the innocence of youth.

'The very children put us to shame. While we sleep they go forth joyfully to conquer the Holy Land.'
– Pope Innocent III (1212), referring to the Children's Crusade

Unfortunately, the 'innocence' of the young people – their lack of knowledge and experience – made them a ripe target for the unscrupulous. Many were robbed, raped or kidnapped along the way. When the remainder arrived at the Mediterranean Sea, the sea did not open after all, and the ship owners who promised to take them across instead sold them to the Muslims as slaves. The Children's Crusade was a total disaster, but the fact that it was undertaken at all suggests that many people of that era viewed adolescence as a time of innocence and saw that innocence as possessing a special value and power.

Adolescence From 1500 to 1890

Beginning in about 1500, young people in some European societies typically took part in what historians term **life-cycle service**, a period in their late teens and 20s in which they would engage in domestic service, farm service or apprenticeships in various trades and crafts (Ben-Amos, 1994). Life-cycle service involved moving out of the family household and into the household of a 'master' to whom the young person was in service for a period lasting (typically) seven years. Young women were somewhat less likely than young men to engage in life-cycle service, but even among women a majority left home during adolescence, most often to take part in life-cycle service as a servant in a family.

Life-cycle service was common in Western countries from about 1500 to about 1800. This woodcut shows a printer's apprentice.

Life-cycle service faded during the eighteenth and nineteenth centuries. As the population grew and the national economy became less based in farming and more industrialised, young people increasingly left their small towns in their late teens for the growing cities. In the cities, without ties to a family or community, young people soon became regarded as a social problem in many respects. Rates of crime, premarital sex and alcohol use among young people all increased in the late eighteenth and early nineteenth centuries (Wilson and Herrnstein, 1985). In response, new institutions of social control developed – religious associations, literary societies, YMCAs and YWCAs (first opened in 1844 and focused on education and the development of 'body, mind and spirit') – where young people were monitored by adults (Kett, 1977). This approach worked remarkably well: in the second half of the nineteenth century rates of crime, premarital pregnancies, alcohol use and other problems among young people all dropped sharply (Wilson and Herrnstein, 1985).

The Age of Adolescence, 1890–1920

Although we have been using the term *adolescence* in this brief history for the sake of clarity and consistency, it was only towards the end of the nineteenth century and the beginning of the twentieth that *adolescence*

CONNECT AND EXTEND

For a paper which argues that any focus on a youth culture of music, dance and style negates an accurate exploration of the cultural identities and experiences of the majority of young people, read 'In defence of subculture: young people, leisure and social divisions' by Tracy Shildrick and Robert MacDonald in the *Journal of Youth Studies*, Volume 9, Number 2 (2006), pp. 125–140

became a widely used term (Locke and Bogin, 2006). Before this time, young people in their teens and early twenties were more often referred to as **youth** or simply as young men and young women (Modell and Goodman, 1990). However, towards the end of the nineteenth century important changes took place in this age period in Western countries that made a change of terms appropriate.

The years 1890–1920 were crucial in establishing the characteristics of modern adolescence. Key changes during these years included the enactment of laws restricting child labour, new requirements for children to attend secondary school, and the development of the field of adolescence as an area of research and study. For these reasons, historians call the years 1890–1920 the 'Age of Adolescence' (Tyack, 1990).

Towards the end of the nineteenth century, the Industrial Revolution was proceeding at full throttle in Western countries. There was a tremendous demand for labour to work the mines, shops and factories. Adolescents and even pre-adolescent children were especially in demand, because they could be hired cheaply. Few countries had laws restricting the ages of children in the workplace, even for work such as coal mining (Tyack, 1990). Nor did many restrict the number of hours children or adults could work, so children often worked 12-hour days for just a few pence a day.

As more and more young people entered the workplace, however, concern for them also increased among urban reformers, youth workers and educators. In the view of these adults the young people were being exploited and harmed (physically and morally) by their involvement in adult work. These activists successfully fought for legislation that prohibited companies from hiring pre-teen children and severely limited the number of hours that could be worked by young people in their early teens (Hendrick, 2007).

Along with laws restricting child labour came laws requiring a longer period of schooling. Up until the late nineteenth century, many countries did not have any

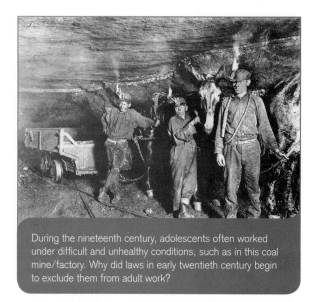

During the nineteenth century, adolescents often worked under difficult and unhealthy conditions, such as in this coal mine/factory. Why did laws in early twentieth century begin to exclude them from adult work?

G. Stanley Hall, the founder of the researcherly study of adolescence.

laws requiring children to attend school, and those that did required attendance only through primary school (Tyack, *ibid.*). However, between 1890 and 1920

Table 1.1 Key terms

Here are some terms used throughout the book that you should be sure to know

Culture	*Culture* is the total pattern of a group's customs, beliefs, art and technology. Thus, a culture is a group's common way of life, passed on from one generation to the next.
The West	Europe, the United States, Canada, Australia and New Zealand make up the West. They are all industrialised countries, all representative democracies with similar kinds of governments, and they share to some extent a common cultural history. In the present, they are all characterised to different degrees by secularism, consumerism and capitalism. *The West* usually refers to the majority culture in each of the countries, but each country also has cultural and ethnic groups that do not or only partly share the characteristics of the majority culture.
Industrialised countries	The term *industrialised countries* includes the countries of the West along with Eastern countries such as Japan and South Korea. All have highly developed economies that have passed through a period of industrialisation and are now based mainly on services (such as law, banking, sales and accounting) and information (such as computer-related companies). China, Brazil and India are examples of countries sometimes referred to as newly industrialised countries – more industrialised than developing countries but with a significant proportion of the population not engaged in industrial activity.
Majority culture	The majority culture in any given society is the culture that sets most of the norms and standards and holds most of the positions of political, economic, intellectual and media power. The term *majority culture* will be used often in this book to refer to the mostly white middle-class majority in European societies.
Society	A *society* is a group of people who interact in the course of sharing a common geographical area. A single society may include a variety of cultures with different customs, religions, family traditions and economic practices. Thus, a society is different from a culture: Members of a culture share a common way of life, whereas members of a society may not. For example, European society includes a variety of different cultures, such as the white majority culture, Mediterranean culture, black European culture and Asian European culture. They share certain characteristics by virtue of being Europeans – for example, within a European society, all are subject to the same laws, and they go to similar schools – but there are differences within European societies that make different groups culturally distinct.
Traditional cultures	The term *traditional culture* refers to a culture that has maintained a way of life based on stable traditions passed from one generation to the next. These cultures do not generally value change but rather place a higher value on remaining true to cultural traditions. Often traditional cultures are 'preindustrial', which means that the technology and economic practices typical in industrialised countries are not widely used. However, this is not always true; Japan, for example, is still in many ways traditional, even though it is also one of the most highly industrialised countries in the world. When we use the term traditional cultures, naturally this does not imply that all such cultures are alike. They differ in a variety of ways, but they have in common that they are firmly grounded in a relatively stable cultural tradition, and for that reason they provide a distinct contrast to the cultures of the West.

continued

Table 1.1 *continued*

Developing countries	Most previously traditional, preindustrial cultures are becoming industrialised today as a consequence of globalisation. The term ***developing countries*** is used to refer to countries where this process is taking place. Examples include most of the countries of Africa and some of South America, as well as Asian countries such as Thailand and Vietnam.
Socioeconomic status	The term ***socio-economic status (SES)*** is often used to refer to social class, which includes educational level, income level and occupational status. For adolescents and emerging adults, because they have not yet reached the social class level they will have as adults, *SES* is usually used in reference to their parents' levels of education income and occupation.
Young people	In this book the term ***young people*** is used as shorthand to refer to adolescents and emerging adults together.

many European countries began to pass laws requiring attendance not only at primary school but secondary school as well. As a consequence, the proportion of adolescents in school increased dramatically. This change contributed to making this time the Age of Adolescence, because it marked a more distinct separation between adolescence as a period of continued schooling and adulthood as a period that begins after schooling is finished.

The third major contributor to making the years 1890–1920 the Age of Adolescence was the work of G. Stanley Hall and the beginning of the study of adolescence as a distinct field of interest (Kohlstedt, 2005). Hall was a remarkable person whose achievements included obtaining the first PhD in psychology in the United States and becoming the founder of the American Psychological Association. In addition, Hall was one of the initiators of the **child study movement** in the United States, which advocated scientific research on child and adolescent development and the improvement of conditions for children and adolescents in the family, school and workplace.

'At no time of life is the love of excitement so strong as during the season of accelerated development of adolescence, which craves strong feelings and new sensations.'
– G. Stanley Hall, *Adolescence* (1904), Volume 1, p. 368

Among his accomplishments, Hall wrote the first textbook on adolescence, published in 1904 as a two-volume set ambitiously titled *Adolescence: Its Psychology and Its Relations to Physiology, Anthropology, Sociology, Sex, Crime, Religion, and Education.* Hall's textbook covered a wide range of topics, such as physical health and development, adolescence cross-culturally and historically, and adolescent love. A surprising number of Hall's observations have been verified by more recent research, such as his description of biological development during puberty, his assertion that depressed mood tend to peak in the mid-teens, and

CONNECT AND EXTEND

To read an account of how educational psychologists and philosophers of the 1890s, including G. Stanley Hall, related curriculum methods to perceived developmental stages in children, read 'Nature, not books: scientists and the origins of the nature-study movement in the 1890s' by Sally Gregory Kohlstedt in *Isis*, Volume 96, Number 3 (2005), pp. 324–352. You may want to refer back to this paper when reading Chapter 3, Cognitive foundations.

Laws requiring children to attend school were passed in the early twentieth century.

re-enacts the evolutionary development of the human species as a whole. He believed the stage of adolescence reflected a stage in the human evolutionary past when there was a great deal of upheaval and disorder, with the result that adolescents experience a great deal of **storm and stress** as a standard part of their development. (For more on the 'storm and stress' debate, see the upcoming Historical Focus feature). No reputable researcher today adheres to the theory of recapitulation. Nevertheless, Hall did a great deal to focus attention and concern on adolescents, not only among academics across the globe but among the public at large. Thus, he was perhaps the most important figure in making the years 1890–1920 the Age of Adolescence.

This brief history of adolescence provides only a taste of what adolescence has been like in various eras of history. However, because the history of adolescence is one of the themes of this book, historical information will appear in every chapter in the form of a Historical Focus feature, and here is the first one.

his claim that adolescence is a time of heightened responsiveness to peer (Arnett, 2006a). However, much of what he wrote is dated and obsolete (Youniss, 2006). To a large extent, he based his ideas on the now-discredited theory of **recapitulation**, which held that the development of each individual recapitulates or

HISTORICAL FOCUS

The 'Storm and Stress' Debate

One of G. Stanley Hall's ideas that is still debated today among researchers is his claim that adolescence is inherently a time of storm and stress. According to Hall, it is normal for adolescence to be a time of considerable upheaval and disruption. As Hall described it, adolescent storm and stress is reflected in especially high rates of three types of difficulties during the adolescent period: conflict with parents, mood disruptions and risk behaviour (such as substance use and crime).

Hall (1904) favoured the **Lamarckian** evolutionary ideas that many prominent thinkers in the early twentieth century considered to be a better explanation of evolution than Darwin's theory of natural selection. In Jean-Baptiste Lamarck's now-discredited theory, evolution takes place as a result of accumulated experience. Organisms pass on their characteristics from one generation to the next not in the form of genes (which were unknown at the time Lamarck and Darwin devised their theories) but in the form of memories and acquired characteristics. These memories and acquired characteristics would then be re-enacted or *recapitulated* in the development of each individual in future generations. Thus Hall, considering development during adolescence, judged it to be 'suggestive of some ancient period of storm and stress' (1904, Volume 1, p. xiii). In his view, there must have been a period of human evolution that was extremely difficult and tumultuous; ever since, the memory of that period had been passed from one generation to the next and was recapitulated in the development of each individual as the storm and stress of adolescent development.

In the century since Hall's work established adolescence as an area of scientific study, the debate over adolescent storm and stress has simmered steadily and boiled to the surface periodically. Anthropologists, led by Margaret Mead (1928), countered Hall's claim that a tendency toward storm and stress in adolescence is universal and biological by describing non-Western cultures in which adolescence was neither

➤

stormy nor stressful. In contrast, psychoanalytic theorists, particularly Anna Freud (1969; 1968; 1958; 1946), have been the most outspoken proponents of the storm and stress view.

Anna Freud viewed adolescents who did not experience storm and stress with great suspicion, claiming that their outward calm concealed the inward reality that they must have 'built up excessive defences against their drive activities and are now crippled by the results' (1968, p. 15). She viewed storm and stress as universal and inevitable, to the extent that its absence signified a serious psychological problem: 'To be normal during the adolescent period is by itself abnormal' (1958, p. 267).

What do more recent studies indicate about the validity of the storm and stress view? A clear consensus exists among current researchers that the storm and stress view proposed by Hall and made more extreme by Anna Freud and other psychoanalysts is not valid for most adolescents (Steinberg, 2001; Susman et al., 2003). The claim that storm and stress is characteristic of all adolescents, and that the source of it is purely biological, is clearly false. Researchers today tend to emphasise that most adolescents like and respect their parents, that for most adolescents their mood disruptions are not so extreme that they need psychological treatment, and that most of them do not engage in risky behaviour on a regular basis.

On the other hand, studies in recent decades have also indicated some support for what might be called a 'modified' storm and stress view. Research evidence (e.g. Whalen et al., 2002; Ayman-Nolley and Taira, 2000) supports the existence of some degree of storm and stress with respect to conflict with parents, mood disruptions and risk behaviour. Not all adolescents experience storm and stress in these areas, but adolescence is the period when storm and stress is more likely to occur than at other ages.

Conflict with parents tends to be higher in adolescence than before or after adolescence (Smetana, 2005). Adolescents report greater extremes of mood and more frequent changes of mood, compared with pre-adolescents or adults (Reid et al., 2009), and depressed mood is more common in adolescence than it is in childhood or adulthood (Bond et al., 2005). Rates of most types of risk behaviour rise sharply during adolescence and peak during late adolescence or emerging adulthood. The different aspects of storm and stress have different peak ages: conflict with parents in early to mid-adolescence (De Goede et al., 2009) mood disruptions in mid-adolescence (Holsen et al., 2000), and risk behaviour in late adolescence and emerging adulthood (Fergusson et al., 2005).

We will explore each aspect of storm and stress in more detail in later chapters. For now, however, it should be emphasised that even though evidence supports a modified storm and stress view, this does not mean that storm and stress is typical of all adolescents in all places and times. Cultures vary in the degree of storm and stress experienced by their adolescents, with storm and stress relatively low in traditional cultures and relatively high in Western cultures (Gkoltsiou et al., 2008; Blacher and McIntyre, 2006; Attree, 2005). Also, within every culture individuals vary in the amount of adolescent storm and stress they experience.

Risk behaviour peaks in late adolescence and emerging adulthood.

THINKING CRITICALLY

Do you agree or disagree with the view that adolescence is inevitably a time of storm and stress? Specify what you mean by storm and stress, and explain the basis for your view.

ADOLESCENCE AND EMERGING ADULTHOOD

'When our mothers were our age, they were engaged . . . They at least had some idea what they were going to do with their lives . . . I, on the other hand, will have a degree in [subjects] that are ambiguous at best and impractical at worst (English and political science), no ring on my finger and no idea who I am, much less what I want to do . . . Under duress, I will admit that this is a pretty exciting time. Sometimes, when I look out across the wide expanse that is my future, I can see beyond the void. I realise that having nothing ahead to count on means I now have to count on myself; that having no direction means forging one of my own.'

– Kristen, age 22 (Page, 1999, pp. 18, 20)

In the various eras of history described in the previous section, when people referred to adolescents (or youth or whatever term a particular era or society used), they usually indicated that they meant not just the early teen years but the late teens and into the 20s as well. When G. Stanley Hall initiated the scientific study of adolescence early in the twentieth century, he defined the age range of adolescence as beginning at 14 and ending at 24 (Hall, 1904, Volume 1, p. xix). In contrast, today's academics generally consider adolescence to begin at about age 10 and end by about age 18. Studies published in the major journals on adolescence rarely include samples with ages higher than 18 (Arnett, 2000a). What happened between Hall's time and our own to move researchers' conceptions of adolescence forwards chronologically in the life course?

Two changes stand out as explanations. One is the decline that took place during the twentieth century in the typical age of the initiation of puberty. At the beginning of the twentieth century, the median age of **menarche** (a girl's first menstruation) in Western countries was about 15 (Lakshman et al., 2008). Because menarche takes place relatively late in the typical sequence of pubertal changes, this means that the initial changes of puberty would have begun at ages 13 to 15 for most boys and girls (usually earlier for girls than for boys), which is just where Hall designated the beginning of adolescence. However, the median age of menarche (and, by implication, other pubertal changes) declined steadily between 1900 and 1970 before levelling out, so that by now the typical age of menarche in the West is around $12\frac{1}{2}$ (Vigil et al., 2005). The initial changes of puberty begin about two years earlier, thus the designation of adolescence as beginning at about age 10.

As for when adolescence ends, the change in this age may have been inspired not by a biological change but by a social change: the growth of secondary school attendance as a normal experience for adolescents in Western countries. Because attending secondary school is now nearly universal among British and other European adolescents and because secondary schooling and further education is increasingly extended to age 18 or 19, it makes sense for researchers studying adolescents to place the end of adolescence at age 18 or 19. Hall did not choose 18 as the end of adolescence because for most adolescents of his time no significant transition took place at that age. Education ended earlier, work began earlier, and leaving home took place later. Marriage and parenthood did not take place for most people until their mid-20s (van Poppel et al., 2008), which may have been why Hall designated age 24 as the end of adolescence.

Hall viewed the late teens and early 20s as an especially interesting time of life. We agree, and we think it would be a mistake to cut off our study of adolescence in this book at age 18. A great deal happens in the late teens and early 20s that is related to development earlier in adolescence and that has important implications for the path that development takes in adulthood. Jeff Arnett has termed this period *emerging adulthood*, and considers it to include roughly the ages 18 to 25 (Arnett, 2010; 2007a; 2006b; 2004a; 2000a; 1998a).

CONNECT AND EXTEND

For a Finnish study of the association between health-related lifestyle and different probabilities of ending up in low or high social positions in emerging adulthood read 'Health-related lifestyle in adolescence – origin of social class differences in health?' by A. H. Rimpelä, M. K. Rimpelä, L. K. Koivusilta in *Health Education Research*, Volume 14, Number 3 (June 1999), pp. 339–355

Five characteristics distinguish emerging adulthood from other age periods (Reifman et al., 2007; Arnett, *ibid*.). Emerging adulthood is:

1 the age of identity explorations;

2 the age of instability;

3 the self-focused age;

4 the age of feeling in-between; and

5 the age of possibilities.

Perhaps the most distinctive characteristic of emerging adulthood is that it is the *age of identity explorations*. That is, it is an age when people explore various possibilities in love and work as they move towards making enduring choices. Through trying out these different possibilities they develop a more definite identity, including an understanding of who they are, what their capabilities and limitations are, what their beliefs and values are, and how they fit into the society around them. Developmental and social psychologist Erik Erikson (1950), who was the first to develop the idea of identity, asserted that it is mainly an issue in adolescence. That was over 60 years ago, and today some scholars consider that the exploration of identity, though beginning in adolescence, is more particularly pursued in emerging adulthood (Côté, 2006; Schwartz et al., 2005).

The explorations of emerging adulthood also make it the *age of instability*. As emerging adults explore different possibilities in love and work, their lives are often unstable. A good illustration of this instability is their frequent moves from one residence to another. As Figure 1.1 shows, rates of residential change are much higher at ages 18–29 than at any other period of life. This reflects the explorations going on in emerging adults' lives. Some move out of their parents' household for the first time in their late teens to attend a university, whereas others move out simply to be independent (Moogan and Baron, 2003). They may move again when they drop out of university or when they graduate. They may move to cohabit with a romantic partner and then move out when the relationship ends. Some move to another part of the country or of the world to study or work. For nearly half of emerging adults, residential change includes moving back in with their parents at least once (Bell and Lee, 2008). In

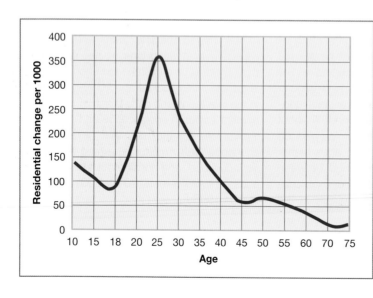

Figure 1.1 Rate of residential change by age. Why does the rate peak in emerging adulthood?

Source: Goldscheider and Goldscheider (1994).

some countries in southern Europe, emerging adults remain at home rather than moving out; nevertheless, they may still experience instability in education, work and love relationships (Douglass, 2007; 2005).

'But when, by what test, by what indication does manhood commence? Physically, by one criterion, legally by another. Morally by a third, intellectually by a fourth – and all indefinite.'
– Thomas De Quincey, *Autobiography* (1821), p. 14

Emerging adulthood is also a *self-focused age*. Most emerging adults move out of their parents' home at age 18 or 19 and do not marry and have their first child until at least their late 20s and increasingly into their 30s (Nabukera et al., 2009). Even in countries where emerging adults remain home through their early 20s, such as in southern Europe and Asian countries, including Japan, they establish a more independent lifestyle than they had as adolescents (Douglass, 2005). Emerging adulthood is a time in-between adolescents' reliance on parents and adults' long-term commitments in love and work, and during these years emerging adults focus on themselves as they develop the knowledge, skills and self-understanding they will need for adult life. In the course of emerging adulthood, they learn to make independent decisions about everything from what to have for dinner to whether or not to go on to postgraduate study.

To say that emerging adulthood is a self-focused time is not meant pejoratively. There is nothing wrong with being self-focused during emerging adulthood. It

is normal, healthy and temporary. The goal of their self-focusing is learning to stand alone as self-sufficient persons, but emerging adults do not see self-sufficiency as a permanent state. Rather, they view it as a necessary step before committing themselves to lasting relationships with others, in love and work.

Another distinctive feature of emerging adulthood is that it is an *age of feeling in-between*, not adolescent but not fully adult either. When asked, "Do you feel that you have reached adulthood?" the majority of emerging adults respond neither yes nor no but with the ambiguous "in some ways yes, in some ways no" (Arnett, *ibid.*). As Figure 1.2 shows, it is only when people reach their late 20s and early 30s that a clear majority feel they have reached adulthood. Most emerging adults have the subjective feeling of being in a transitional period of life, on the way to adulthood but not there yet. This 'in-between' feeling in emerging adulthood has been found in a wide range of countries, including Argentina (Facio and Micocci, 2003), Israel (Mayseless and Scharf, 2003), China (Nelson et al., 2004), the Czech Republic (Macek et al., 2007), and Denmark (Arnett et al., 2009).

Finally, emerging adulthood is the *age of possibilities*, when many different futures remain possible, when little about a person's direction in life has been decided for certain. It tends to be an age of high hopes and great expectations, in part because few of their dreams have been tested in the fires of real life. The dreary, dead-end jobs, the bitter divorces, the disappointing and disrespectful children that some of them will find themselves experiencing in the years to come – few of them imagine in emerging adulthood that this is

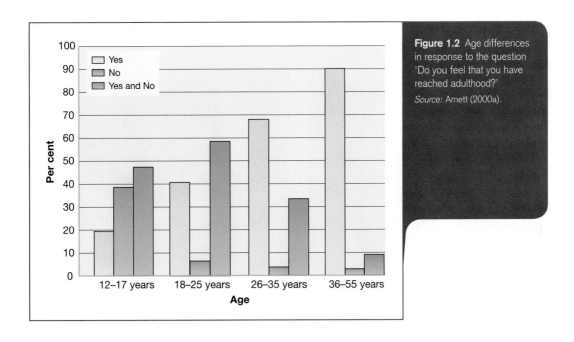

Figure 1.2 Age differences in response to the question 'Do you feel that you have reached adulthood?'
Source: Arnett (2000a).

what the future holds. This optimism in emerging adulthood has been found in other countries as well (e.g. Nelson and Chen, 2007).

One feature of emerging adulthood that makes it the age of possibilities is that emerging adults typically have left their family of origin but are not yet committed to a new network of relationships and obligations. For those who have come from a troubled family, this is their chance to try to straighten the parts of themselves that have become twisted. No longer dependent on their parents, and no longer subject to their parents' problems on a daily basis, they may be able to make independent decisions – perhaps to move to a different area or go to college or university – that turn their lives in a dramatically different direction (Masten et al., 2006). Even for those who have come from families that are relatively happy and healthy, emerging adulthood is an opportunity to transform themselves so that they are not merely made in their parents' images but have made independent decisions about what kind of person they wish to be and how they wish to live. For this limited window of time – seven, perhaps ten years – the fulfilment of all their hopes seems possible, because for most people the range of their choices for how to live is greater than it has ever been before and greater than it will ever be again.

Emerging adulthood does not exist in all cultures. Cultures vary widely in the ages that young people are expected to enter full adulthood and take on adult responsibilities (see Chapter 4). Emerging adulthood exists only in cultures in which young people are allowed to postpone entering adult roles such as marriage and parenthood until at least their mid-20s. In many industrialised countries, the median age of marriage is at a record high; about 28 for women (see Table 1.2) and has risen steeply over the past 40 years (Arnett,

2006b). This postponement of adult responsibilities into the mid- to late 20s makes possible the explorations of emerging adulthood. Thus, emerging adulthood exists mainly in industrialised societies such as most of Europe, Australia, New Zealand, the United States, Canada and Japan (Bynner, 2005; Douglass, *ibid.*).

However, in many other areas of the world, emerging adulthood is becoming more prevalent as cultures become more industrialised and more integrated into a global economy (Galambos and Martinez, 2007; Macek et al., 2007; Nelson and Chen, 2007). With growing industrialisation and economic integration worldwide, emerging adulthood is even more likely to become increasingly common around the world in the twenty-first century.

Table 1.2 Median Marriage Age (Females) in Selected Countries

Industrialised countries	Age	Developing countries	Age
United States	26	Egypt	19
Canada	28	Morocco	20
Germany	30	Ghana	19
France	29	Nigeria	17
Italy	29	India	20
Japan	29	Indonesia	19
Australia	28	Brazil	21

Sources: Population Reference Bureau (2000); United Nations Economic Commission for Europe, 2005; Douglass (2007)

A young person in three periods: early adolescence (ages 10–14), late adolescence (ages 15–18) and emerging adulthood (ages 18–25).

In this book, then, we will cover three periods: **early adolescence**, from age 10 to 14; **late adolescence**, from age 15 to 18; and emerging adulthood, from age 19 to about 25. Including all three of these periods will provide a broad age range for our examination of the various aspects of young people's development – the biological, psychological and social changes they experience over time. Because studies on early and late adolescence are more abundant than studies on emerging adulthood, most of the information in the book will refer to adolescence, but each chapter will contain some information on emerging adulthood.

THINKING CRITICALLY

Is 25 a good upper age boundary for the end of emerging adulthood? Where would you put an upper age boundary, and why? In your view, what marks the attainment of adulthood for yourself and for others more generally?

THE TRANSITION TO ADULTHOOD

So far, we have argued that adolescence is generally viewed as beginning with the first noticeable changes of puberty. The end of adolescence, as we have defined it here, is also quite clear: at age 18, when most people in industrialised societies have reached the end of their secondary school education. Age 18 also marks the beginning of emerging adulthood, as that is when most young people begin the exploratory activities that characterise emerging adulthood. But what marks the end of emerging adulthood? If emerging adulthood is in many ways a period of transition from adolescence to full adulthood, how does a person know when the transition to adulthood is complete? The answer to this question is complex and varies notably among cultures. First, we examine cultural similarities in views of adulthood, then cultural variations.

The Transition to Adulthood: Cross-cultural Themes

'Sometimes I feel like I've reached adulthood, and then I'll sit down and eat ice cream . . . But I guess in some ways I feel like I'm an adult. I'm a pretty responsible person. I mean, if I say I'm going to do something, I do it. Financially, I'm fairly responsible with my money. But there are still times where I think, "I can't believe I'm 25." A lot of times I don't really feel like an adult.'
– Lisa, age 25 (Arnett, 2004, p. 14)

In industrialised societies, there are a variety of possible ways one could define the transition to adulthood. Legally, the transition to adulthood takes place in most respects at age 18. This is the age at which a person becomes an adult for various legal purposes, such as signing legally binding documents and being eligible to vote. One could also define the transition to adulthood as entering the roles that are typically considered to be part of adulthood: full-time work, marriage and parenthood (Rankin & Kenyon, 2012).

But what about young people themselves? How do young people today conceptualise the transition to adulthood? In the past decade, many studies have examined what young people in industrialised societies view as the key markers of the transition to adulthood. The results of the studies have been remarkably similar, in countries including South Korea (Arnett, 2001), Argentina (Facio and Micocci, 2003), Israel (Mayseless and Scharf, 2003), the United States (Nelson, 2003), China (Nelson et al., 2004), the United Kingdom (Horowitz and Bromnick, 2007), the Czech Republic (Macek, 2007) and Romania (Nelson, 2009). In these

CONNECT AND EXTEND

The timing of when people come to define themselves as adults is based on cultural influences and established cultural norms. Read 'Demarcating role transitions as indicators of adulthood in the 21st century: who are they?' by Lela Rankin and DenYelle Kenyon in the *Journal of Adult Development*, Preprint (January 2012), pp. 1–6

studies young people from their early teens to their late 20s agreed that the most important markers of the transition from adolescence to adulthood are *accepting responsibility for oneself, making independent decisions* and *becoming financially independent*, in that order. These three criteria rank highest not just across cultures and nations but across ethnic groups and social classes.

Note the similarity among these three highest ranking criteria: all three are characterised by **individualism**; that is, all three emphasise the importance of learning to stand alone as a self-sufficient person without relying on anyone else. The values of individualism, such as independence and self-expression, are often contrasted with the values of **collectivism**, such as duties and obligations to others. The criteria for adulthood favoured by emerging adults in industrialised societies reflect the individualistic values of those societies (Douglass, 2005; Harkness et al., 2000).

The Transition to Adulthood: Cultural Variations

In addition to the top three criteria for adulthood that have been found across cultures – accepting responsibility for oneself, making independent decisions and becoming financially independent – studies have found distinctive cultural criteria as well. Young Israelis viewed completing military service as important for becoming an adult, reflecting Israel's requirement of mandatory military service (Mayseless and Scharf, *ibid.*). Young Argentines especially valued being able to support a family financially, perhaps reflecting the economic upheavals Argentina has experienced for many years (Facio and Miccoci, *ibid.*). Emerging adults in Korea and China viewed *being able to support their parents financially* as necessary for adulthood, reflecting the collectivistic value of obligation to parents found in Asian societies (Naito and Gielen, 2003; Nelson et al., 2004).

What about traditional cultures? Do they have different ideas about what marks the beginning of adulthood, compared to industrialised societies? The answer appears to be yes. Anthropologists have found that in virtually all traditional, non-Western cultures, the transition to adulthood is clearly and explicitly marked by *marriage* (Grant and Furstenberg, 2007). It is only after marriage that a person is considered to have attained adult status and is given adult privileges and responsibilities. In contrast, very few of the young people in the studies mentioned above indicated that they considered marriage to be an important marker of the transition to adulthood. In fact, in industrialised societies marriage ranks near the bottom in surveys of possible criteria for adult status.

What should we make of that contrast? One possible interpretation would be that traditional cultures elevate marriage as the key transition to adulthood because they prize the collectivistic value of **interdependence** more highly than the individualistic value of independence, and marriage signifies that a person is taking on new interdependent relationships outside the family of origin (Shweder et al., 2006). Marriage is a social event rather than an individual, psychological process, and it represents the establishment of a new network of relationships with all the kin of one's marriage partner. This is especially true in traditional cultures, where family members are more likely than in the West to be close knit and to have extensive daily contact with one another. Thus, cultures that value interdependence view marriage as the most important marker of entering adulthood because of the ways marriage confirms and strengthens interdependence.

Still, these conclusions about traditional cultures are based mainly on the observations of the anthropologists who have studied them. If you asked young people in these cultures directly about their own conceptions of what marks the beginning of adulthood, perhaps you would get a variety of answers other than marriage. For example in an early study, anthropologists Susan and Douglas Davis (1989) asked young

Marriage is of great significance as a marker of adulthood in traditional cultures. Here, a Burmese bride and groom (centre) and their attendants.

Moroccans (aged 9 to 20), 'How do you know you're grown up?' They found that the two most common types of responses were (1) those that emphasised chronological age or physical development, such as the beginning of facial hair among boys; and (2) those that emphasised character qualities, such as developing self-control (see the *Cultural Focus* feature). Few of the young people mentioned marriage, even though Davis and Davis stated that in Moroccan culture generally, 'after marriage, one is considered an adult' (p. 59). This suggests that further and more up-to-date investigation of young people's conceptions of the transition to adulthood in traditional cultures may prove enlightening and that their views may not match the conceptions of adulthood held by adults.

THE SCIENTIFIC STUDY OF ADOLESCENCE AND EMERGING ADULTHOOD

Insights into development during adolescence and emerging adulthood can be gained in many ways. For example, there are some excellent autobiographies of these periods such as *This Boy's Life* by Tobias Wolff (1987) and the autobiography of Anne Frank (1942/1997). Journalists have written accounts of various aspects of these periods, often focusing on a particular young person or a small group (for one example see Bamberger, 2004). Some terrific novels have been written that focus on adolescence and emerging adulthood, such as J. D. Salinger's *Catcher in the Rye* (1951/1964), Anchee Min's *Katherine* (1995) and Russell Banks's *The Rule of the Bone* (1995). More examples of accounts of adolescence and emerging adulthood are given in the upcoming Youth in the media feature and in many other chapters of this text.

We draw on sources in all these areas for illustrations and examples. However, the main focus in this book will be on the scientific study of adolescence and emerging adulthood. You will be learning about development during adolescence and emerging adulthood as an area of the social sciences. You will read about the most important and influential studies that have contributed to this field. In every chapter of the book you will find a *Research Focus* feature that explores a specific study in depth and discusses in detail the methods used in the study.

What does it mean for researchers to engage in the scientific study of adolescence and emerging adulthood? It means to apply the standards of the **scientific method** to the questions we investigate (Salkind, 2003). The scientific method includes standards of **hypotheses**, **sampling**, **procedure**, method, analysis and interpretation.

Every scientific study begins with an idea: a researcher wants to find an answer to a question, and on the basis of a theory or previous research, the researcher proposes one or more hypotheses. A hypothesis is the researcher's idea about one possible answer to the question of interest. For example, a researcher may be interested in the question 'Why are girls more likely than boys to become depressed in adolescence?' and propose the hypothesis 'Girls are more likely to become depressed because they tend to blame themselves when they experience conflict with others.' The researcher would then design a study to test that hypothesis. The hypotheses of a study are crucial, because they influence the sampling, measures, analysis and interpretation that follow.

With respect to sampling, researchers who study adolescents and emerging adults seek to obtain a **sample** that represents the **population** they are interested in. Suppose, for example, a researcher wants to study adolescents' attitudes towards contraception. The waiting room of a clinic offering contraceptive services would probably not be a good place to look for

CONNECT AND EXTEND

For a longitudinal study of whether certain types of stressful events explain gender differences in depressive symptoms among adolescents, read 'Stress and emotional reactivity as explanations for gender differences in adolescents' depressive symptoms' by Anna Charbonneau, Amy Mezulis and Janet Hyde in the *Journal of Youth and Adolescence*, Volume 38, Number 8 (September 2009), pp. 1050–1058

a sample, because the adolescents coming to such a clinic are quite likely to have more favourable attitudes towards contraception than adolescents in general; otherwise, why would they be coming to a place that offers contraceptive services? Instead, if the population of interest is adolescents in general, it might be better to sample them through schools or through a telephone survey that selected households randomly from the community.

On the other hand, if a researcher is particularly interested in attitudes towards contraception among the population of adolescents who are already using or planning to use contraception, then a clinic offering contraceptive services would be a good place to find a sample. It all depends on the population the researcher wishes to study and on the questions the researcher wishes to address. The goal is to seek out a sample that will be **representative** of the population of interest (e.g. Spencer, 2006). If the sample is representative of the population, then the findings from the sample will be **generalisable** to the population. In other words, the findings from the sample will make it possible to draw conclusions about not just the sample itself but also the larger population of adolescents that the sample is intended to represent.

The third consideration of the scientific method, *procedure*, refers to the way the study is conducted and the data are collected. One standard aspect of the procedure in scientific studies of human beings is **informed consent** (Iqbal, 2002). Human subjects in any scientific study are supposed to be presented with a well-constructed **consent form** before they participate (Bhattacharya, 2007). Consent forms typically include information about who is conducting the study, what the purposes of the study are, what participation in the study involves (e.g. filling out a questionnaire on contraceptive use), what risks (if any) are involved in participating, and what the person can expect to receive in return for participation. Consent forms also

usually include a statement indicating that participation in the study is voluntary and that persons may withdraw from participation in the study at any time.

The use of consent forms is not always possible (for example, in telephone surveys), but whenever possible they are included in the procedure for researchers studying adolescents and emerging adults. For adolescents under age 18, the consent of one of their parents is also usually required as part of a study's procedures.

Another aspect of the procedure is the circumstances of the data collection. Researchers try to collect data in a way that will not be biased. For example, researchers must be careful not to phrase questions in an interview or a questionnaire in a way that seems to lead people toward a desired response. They must also assure participants that their responses will be confidential, especially if the study concerns a sensitive topic such as sexual behaviour or drug use.

The scientific method also includes a variety of specific methods for data collection. A method is a strategy for collecting data. In the next section, we will consider a variety of methods used in research on adolescence and emerging adulthood. This will also be a way of introducing some of the classic and historic studies on adolescence and emerging adulthood that we will be referring to often in the course of the book.

THINKING CRITICALLY

You have probably read about topics concerning adolescence and emerging adulthood in newspapers and magazines. Find a recent article and analyse to what extent it meets the criteria for scientific research.

CULTURAL FOCUS

Moroccan Conceptions of Adolescence

The anthropologists Susan Davis and Douglas Davis (e.g. 2007) have been studying adolescents in Morocco for nearly three decades, originally as part of the Harvard Adolescence Project described in this chapter. One of the questions that has interested them in their research concerns the qualities Moroccans associate with adolescence.

The most important concept in Moroccan views of adolescence is *'aql*, an Arabic word that has connotations of reasonableness, understanding and rationality. Self-control and self-restraint are also part of *'aql*: to possess 'aql means to have control over your needs and passions and to be able and willing to restrain them out of respect for those around you. Moroccans see 'aql as a quality expected of adults and often lacking in adolescents.

'Aql is expected to develop in both males and females during adolescence, but males are believed to take a decade longer to develop it fully! This appears to be due to sharp differences in gender roles and expectations. Unlike males, females are given a variety of responsibilities from an early age, such as household work and taking care of

Moroccan adolescents.

younger siblings, so it is more important for them to develop 'aql earlier to meet the demands of these responsibilities. It is quite common, not just in Morocco but worldwide in traditional cultures, that much more work is required of females in adolescence than of males.

Another term Moroccans use in reference to adolescence is *taysh*, which means reckless, rash and frivolous. This quality is especially associated with awakening sexuality and the possible violations of social norms this awakening may inspire (female virginity before marriage is very important to Moroccans). Taysh is a quality associated with adolescence in the views of many Moroccans, as illustrated in this exchange between Susan Davis and Naima, a mother of two adolescents:

Susan: What does this word taysh mean?

Naima: It starts at the age of 15, 16, 17, 18, 19 until 20. [It lasts] until she develops her 'aql. She is frivolous [taysha] for about four years.

Susan: How do you know they have reached that age? How would you know when Najet [her daughter, age 13] gets there?

Naima: You can recognise it. The girl becomes frivolous. She starts caring about her appearance, dressing well, wearing fancy clothes and showy things, you understand. . . . She also messes up her school schedule. She either leaves too early or comes too late [i.e. she may be changing her schedule to meet boys]. You have to be watchful with her at that juncture. If you see she is on the right path, you leave her alone. If you notice that she is too late or far off the timing, then you have to set the record straight with her until the age of adolescence is over. When she is 20 years of age, she recovers her ability to reason and be rational.

Susan: When your son Saleh [age 14] reaches the age of adolescence, how would you know it?

Naima: I will notice that he doesn't come home on time, he will start skipping school . . . He will start following girls. . . . Girls will start complaining, 'Your son is following me.' This is the first consequence.

Susan: So it's similar to the girl – the girl will dress in a fancy way, while the boy will start getting interested in her.

Naima: That's it.

Moroccans explicitly state that marriage marks the end of adolescence and the entry into adulthood. However, from their use of the terms 'aql and taysh, we can see that the transition to adulthood also involves intangible qualities similar to the ones important in other cultures. Can you see the similarities between 'aql and taysh and the qualities important in conceptions of the transition to adulthood discussed in this chapter?

THINKING CRITICALLY

How is the Moroccan conception of adolescence similar to and different from the view of Plato and Aristotle described earlier in this chapter?

Methods Used in Research

Researchers conduct research on adolescence and emerging adulthood in a variety of academic disciplines, including developmental and behavioural psychology, sociology, anthropology, education and medicine. They use a variety of different methods in their investigations.

Two key issues with many methods are **reliability** and **validity**. There are a variety of types of reliability, but in general, a method has high reliability if it obtains similar results on different occasions (e.g. Dadds et al., 2008). For example, if a questionnaire asked girls in their last year of secondary school to recall when their first menstrual period occurred, the questionnaire would be considered reliable if most of the girls answered the same on one occasion as they did when asked the question again six months later. Or, if adolescents were interviewed about the quality of their relationships with their parents, the measure would be reliable if the adolescents' answers were the same for two different interviewers (e.g. Daving et al., 2001).

Validity refers to the truthfulness of a method (González-Tejera et al., 2005). A method is valid if it measures what it claims to measure. For example, IQ tests are purported to measure intellectual abilities, but as we shall see in Chapter 3, this claim is controversial. Critics claim that IQ tests are not valid (i.e. that they do not measure what they are supposed to measure). Notice that a measure is not necessarily valid even if it is reliable. It is widely agreed that IQ tests are

reliable – people generally score about the same on one occasion as they do on another – but the validity of the tests is disputed. In general, it is more difficult to establish validity than reliability.

We will examine questions of reliability and validity throughout the book. For now, we turn to the methods.

Questionnaires

The most commonly used method in social science research is the questionnaire (Salkind, 2003). Usually, questionnaires have a **closed-question** format, which means that participants are provided with specific responses to choose from (e.g. Margolese et al., 2005). Sometimes the questions have an **open-ended question** format, which means that participants are allowed to state their response following the question. One advantage of closed questions is that they make it possible to collect and analyse responses from a large number of people in a relatively short time. Everyone responds to the same questions from the same response options. For this reason, closed questions have often been used in large-scale surveys conducted on adolescents and emerging adults. One of the most famous of these surveys is the Monitoring the Future survey conducted annually (see the *Research Focus* feature for more information about this survey).

Interviews

Although questionnaires are the dominant type of method used in the study of adolescence and emerging adulthood, the use of questionnaires has certain limitations. For example, when a closed-question format questionnaire is used, the range of possible responses is already specified, and the participant must choose from the responses provided. The researcher tries to cover the responses that seem most plausible and most likely, but it is impossible in a few

CONNECT AND EXTEND

Attention-deficit/hyperactivity disorder (ADHD) is a highly prevalent neurobehavioural disorder, with genetic and environmental origins, which persists into adolescence. For an overview of the reliability and validity of research in this area read 'Attention-deficit/hyperactivity disorder: diagnosis, lifespan, comorbidities, and neurobiology' by Thomas J. Spencer, Joseph Biederman and Eric Mick in the *Journal of Pediatric Psychology*, Volume 32, Number 6 (July 2007), pp. 631–631

brief response options to do justice to the depth and diversity of human experience. For example, if a questionnaire contains an item such as 'How close are you to your mother? A. very close; B. somewhat close; C. not very close; D. not at all close,' it is probably true that an adolescent who chooses 'very close' really is closer to his or her mother than the adolescent who chooses 'not at all close'. But this alone does not begin to capture the complexity of the relationship between an adolescent and a parent.

RESEARCH FOCUS   R

Data Collection with Adolescents

Adolescence and emerging adulthood spans a 15-year period. During this time young people's developmental change and their cultural and sociological contexts influence their behaviour when responding to researchers and research instruments. Nursing professor Carol Dashiff discusses the problems that can be anticipated in data collection with adolescents in her 2001 article 'Data collection with adolescents' in the *Journal of Advanced Nursing*.

Dashiff groups some of the potential problems into those associated with adolescent developmental capacities, adolescent developmental change and stability, gender and ethnicity. Some of the potential problems discussed are quite specific to certain settings or to certain data collection methods. For example, in education settings, research instruments are used to collect data in a group context where peer pressure can affect responses. More private methods of data collection, perhaps computer-based questionnaires, may not suffer the same potential detriment from peer pressure as focus groups and more qualitative methods (see *Research Focus* features in Chapters 9 and 11). In home settings, rehearsed response patterns and family expectations can also affect the validity of the views obtained from adolescents.

Dashiff argues that it's not just understanding the setting that matters; by applying what we know about adolescent development – the biological, cognitive and emotional development of adolescents – researchers can make research instruments and procedures, such as questionnaires and interviews, more robust in terms of validity and reliability. Carol Dashiff's discussion of the part that ethnicity may well may play when designing and implementing data collection with adolescents is particularly important to us as authors when reviewing and critiquing adolescent research. Let's take an important and historic example.

The 'Monitoring the Future' Study

One of the best-known and most enduring studies of American adolescents is the Monitoring the Future (MTF) study. Beginning in 1975, every year the MTF study has surveyed thousands of adolescents on a wide range of topics, including substance use, political and social attitudes, and gender roles. The survey involves about 50,000 adolescents annually of ages 13, 15 and 17 in 420 schools. (For detailed information on the study, see **www.monitoringthefuture.org**.)

A European example of a large-scale survey is the British Social Attitudes survey. Every year since 1983 the British Social Attitudes report has interviewed 3000 people to 'lift the lid' on what people of all ages in Britain think about today's issues and debates. You can get the most recent reports (currently 2010) by going to the website: **http://www.natcen.ac.uk/**.

These kinds of studies, not surprisingly, are called **national surveys**. A **survey** is a study that involves asking people questions about their opinions, beliefs or behaviour (Salkind, 2003). Usually, closed questions are used, meaning that participants are asked to select from a predetermined set of responses, so that their responses can be easily added and compared. Studies can be cross-sectional (a large-scale snapshot at one point in time) or longitudinal studies which collect survey data from a group (which can be sizeable) over a period of time. These ideas are explored in Chapter 11.

➤

If it is a national survey that does not mean, of course, that every person in the country is asked the survey questions! Instead, as this chapter describes, researchers seek a sample – that is, a relatively small number of people whose responses are taken to represent the larger population from which they are drawn. Usually, national surveys such as the one described here use a procedure called **stratified sampling**, in which they select participants so that various categories of people are represented in proportions equal to their presence in the population (e.g. Rivlin and Faragher, 2007). For example, if we know that 52 per cent of the 13- to 17-year-olds in a nation are female, we want the sample to be 52 per cent female; if we know that 13 per cent of 13- to 17-year-olds in a local authority are British Asian, the sample should be 13 per cent British Asian; and so on. The categories used to select a stratified sample often include age, gender, ethnic group, education and socio-economic status (SES).

The other characteristic of a large-scale or national survey is usually that the stratified sample is also a **random sample**, meaning that the people selected for participation in the study are chosen randomly – no one in the population has a better or worse chance of being selected than anyone else (Salkind, *ibid.*). You could do this by putting all possible participants' names in a hat and pulling out as many participants as you needed or by going through a phone book and putting your finger down in random places, but these days the selection of a random sample for national and large-scale surveys is usually done by a computer program. Selecting a random sample enhances the likelihood that the sample will be genuinely representative of the larger population. The MTF study selects a random sample of 350 pupils within each school. In addition, a random sample of MTF participants is followed every two years after school, extending (so far) into their 30s.

Although the MTF study includes many topics, it is best known for its findings regarding substance use. We will examine these findings in detail in Chapter 12.

Interviews are intended to provide the kind of individuality and complexity that questionnaires usually lack (Arnett, 2007b; Briggs, 1989). Therefore interviews are part of what scholars call qualitative – as opposed to quantitative – research (see below). An interview allows a researcher to hear adolescents and emerging adults describe their lives in their own words, with all the uniqueness and richness that such descriptions make possible. An interview also allows a researcher to know the whole person and see how the various parts of the person's life are intertwined. For example, an interview on an adolescent's family relationships might reveal how the adolescent's relationship with her mother is affected by her relationship with her father, and how the whole family has been affected by certain events – perhaps a family member's loss of a job, psychological problems, medical problems or substance abuse.

Interviews provide **qualitative** data, as contrasted with the **quantitative** data of questionnaires, and qualitative data can be interesting and informative. However, like questionnaires, interviews have limitations (Salkind, *ibid.*). Because interviews do not typically provide preclassified responses the way questionnaires do, interview responses have to be coded according to some plan of classification. For example, if you asked the interview question 'What occupation do you plan to

have by age 30?' you might get a fascinating range of responses from a sample of adolescents or emerging adults. Those responses would help to inform you about the entire range of occupations young people imagine themselves having as adults. However, to make sense of the data and present them in a scientific format, at some point you would have to code the responses into categories – business, arts, professional/technical, trades and so on. Only in this way would you be able to say something about the pattern of responses among your sample.

Coding interview data takes time, effort and money. This is one of the reasons far more studies are conducted using questionnaires than using interviews. However, some excellent studies have been conducted using interview data. For example, sociologists Marata Tienda and William Wilson conducted studies of hundreds of ethnic minority young adults in poor neighbourhoods (Tienda and Wilson, 2002). Their research focuses on the difficulties many young urban blacks face in pursuing educational and occupational opportunities. They analyse the connections between high unemployment among young blacks and the schools they attend, the neighbourhoods they live in, their beliefs about work and education, their family circumstances, and employers' views of them as potential employees. Tienda and Wilson's writing combines quantitative and qualitative data to portray the lives of young blacks in a way that is extremely lively, insightful and enlightening. The quantitative data provide the reader with a clear understanding of the overall pattern of young people's lives in urban areas, but at the same time their qualitative examples bring to life the individual perspectives and circumstances of the people they studied. We will learn more about this and other interview studies, especially in Chapter 11 on work.

Ethnographic Research

Another way researchers have learned about adolescence and emerging adulthood is through **ethnographic research** (Caldas, 2008; Griffin, 2001). In ethnographic research, researchers spend a considerable amount of time among the people they wish to study, often by actually living among them. Information gained in ethnographic research typically comes from researchers' observations, experiences and conversations with the people they are studying. Ethnographic research is commonly used by anthropologists, usually in studying non-Western cultures. Anthropologists usually report the results of their research in an **ethnography**, a book that presents an anthropologist's observations of what life is like in a particular culture.

The first ethnography on adolescence was written by Margaret Mead (1928). Mead studied the people of Samoa, a group of islands in the South Pacific. One of the inspirations of her study was to see whether the "storm and stress" said by G. Stanley Hall to be typical of American adolescents would also be present in a non-Western culture where life was much different than in American society. She reported that, contrary to Hall's claim that adolescent storm and stress is biologically based and therefore universal, most adolescents in Samoa passed through adolescence smoothly, with little sign of turmoil or upheaval.

After Mead's ethnography of Samoan adolescence, several decades passed before anthropologists gave much attention to adolescence. However, in the 1980s two eminent anthropologists, Beatrice and John Whiting,

Margaret Mead and a Samoan adolescent.

set out to remedy this neglect. They initiated the **Harvard Adolescence Project**, in which they sent young researchers to do ethnographic research in seven different cultures in various parts of the world: the Inuit (Eskimos) of the Canadian Arctic; Aborigines in northern Australia; Muslims in Thailand; the Kikuyu of Kenya; the Ijo of Nigeria; rural Romania; and Morocco.

The project produced a series of extremely interesting and enlightening classic ethnographies (Davis and Davis, 1989; Hollos and Leis, 1989; Burbank, 1988; Condon, 1987). These ethnographies show the enormous variation that exists in the nature of adolescence in cultures around the world. We draw from these ethnographies often in the course of this book.

CONNECT AND EXTEND

For an example of ethnographic research in relation to a number of key themes in this book read 'Feminist media ethnography in India: Exploring power, gender, and culture in the field' by R. Parameswaran in *Qualitative Inquiry*, Volume 7, Number 1 (February 1, 2001), pp. 69–103

Biological Measurement

The biological changes of puberty are a central part of adolescent development, so research on adolescence includes measurement of biological functioning. One area of this research has focused on the timing and pace of different aspects of physical development during puberty, such as genital changes and the growth of pubic hair. Several decades ago a British physician, J. M. Tanner, conducted a series of studies that carefully monitored adolescents' physical changes and established valid information about the timing and sequence of these changes (Eveleth and Tanner, 1990; Tanner, 1962). More recently, researchers have conducted research measuring hormonal levels at various points during adolescence and looked at the ways hormonal levels are related to adolescents' moods and behaviour (e.g. McBurnett et al., 2005; Susman et al., 2003). There has also been a recent surge of interest in research on adolescent brain functioning (e.g. Forbes et al., 2009; Halari et al., 2009; Musso et al., 2007). We will examine biological research on adolescence in various chapters of the book, especially Chapter 2 (Biological Foundations).

Experimental Research

An approach used in many kinds of scientific research is the **experimental research method** (Salkind, *ibid*.). In the simplest form of this design, two groups of participants are randomly selected from a population, with one group (the **experimental group**) receiving a treatment of some kind and the other group (the **control group**) receiving no treatment. Because participants were randomly assigned to either the experimental group or the control group, it can be reasonably assumed that the two groups did not differ prior to the experiment. Following the treatment of the experimental group, the two groups are given a post-treatment (or non-treatment) test, and any differences between the two groups are attributed to the treatment.

The experimental research method is frequently used in media research. For example, in one study black adolescents aged 11–16 were randomly assigned to an experimental group that viewed rap videos or a control group that did not (Johnson et al., 1995). Following the experimental group's treatment – their exposure to the rap videos – both groups responded to a story about teen dating violence. It was found that in the post-test, girls (but not boys) in the experimental group showed greater acceptance of dating violence than girls in the control group.

Another area of adolescent research for which the experimental research method is commonly used is **interventions**. Interventions are programmes or schemes intended to change the attitudes or behaviour of the participants. For example, a variety of programmes have been developed to prevent adolescents from starting to smoke cigarettes, by promoting critical thinking about cigarette advertising or by attempting to change attitudes associating smoking with peer acceptance (e.g. Horn et al., 2005). The adolescents participating in such studies are usually randomly assigned to either the experimental group receiving the intervention or the control group that does not receive the intervention. After the intervention, the two groups are assessed for their attitudes and behaviour regarding smoking. If the intervention worked, the attitudes or behaviour of the experimental group should be less favourable towards smoking than those of the control group.

Natural Experiments

Experiments are in many ways the scientific ideal, because they allow scientists to identify cause and effect with some precision. In the experiment just described, by assigning adolescents randomly to the experimental group or the control group and then exposing only the experimental group to the antismoking intervention, the results provide definite evidence of whether or not the intervention caused changes to occur in attitudes and behaviour related to smoking. However, many of the most important questions researchers seek to answer regarding adolescence and emerging adulthood cannot be answered through these kinds of experiments. For example, although many researchers are interested in how teaching quality influences adolescents' learning, they cannot assign adolescents randomly to high-quality or low-quality teaching, for obvious ethical reasons.

Because researchers usually cannot control the environments adolescents and emerging adults experience, they sometimes take advantage of **natural experiments**. A natural experiment is a situation that exists naturally – in other words, the researcher does not control the situation – but which provides interesting scientific information to the perceptive observer. For example, although researchers cannot assign adolescents randomly to high- or low-quality teaching, they can assess adolescents' learning before and after they experience higher or lower ability teachers, thus taking advantage of a natural experiment to learn more about the influence of school quality (e.g. Brand et al., 2003).

One important natural experiment used in the study of adolescents and emerging adults is adoption. The question of how genes and environment interact in development is of great interest to researchers who study adolescents and emerging adults, and adoption provides important insights into this question. Unlike in most families, children in adoptive families are raised by adults with whom they have no biological relationship. Because one set of parents provides the child's genes and a different set of parents provides the environment, it is possible to examine the relative contributions of genes and environment to the child's development. Similarities between adoptive parents and adopted children are likely to be due to the environment provided by the parents, because the parents and children are biologically unrelated. Similarities between adopted children and their biological parents are likely to be due to genetics, because the environment the children grew up in was not provided by the biological parents. One surprising result of adoption studies on intelligence is that adoptees are actually *less* similar to their adoptive parents in adolescence than they were in childhood, even though they have lived with them longer (Malouff et al., 2012; Stams et al., 2000). Chapter 3, on cognitive development, presents more on this intriguing research.

Twin studies are another type of natural experiment. Identical or **monozygotic (MZ) twins** have exactly the same genotype, whereas fraternal or **dizygotic (DZ) twins** have about half their genotype in common, the same as other siblings. By comparing the degree of similarity in MZ compared to DZ twins, we gain information about the extent to which a characteristic is genetically based. If MZ twins are more similar on a characteristic than DZ twins are, this may be due to genetics, since MZ twins are more genetically similar.

Throughout the book, we present studies using a wide variety of methods. For now, the methods just

described provide you with an introduction to the approaches used most often – their strengths and weaknesses, the challenges and opportunities of research.

Analysis and Interpretation

Once the data for a study have been collected using methods of one kind or another, statistical analyses are usually conducted to examine relationships between different parts of the data. Often, the analyses are determined by the hypotheses that generated the study. For example, a researcher studying adolescents' relationships with parents may hypothesise, based on a theory or on past research, that adolescents are closer to their mothers than to their fathers, then test that hypothesis with a statistical analysis comparing the quality of adolescents' relationships with mothers and with fathers.

Once the data are analysed, they must be interpreted. When scientists write up the results of their study for publication in a scientific journal, they interpret the results of the study in light of relevant theories and previous research. One of the key issues in interpreting research is the issue of **correlation versus causation**. A correlation is a predictable relationship between two variables: knowing one of the variables allows you to predict the other with some degree of accuracy. However, just because two variables are correlated does not mean that one causes the other.

Consider an example. In studies of adolescent work, a negative correlation is typically found between hours worked and commitment to school (e.g. Barling and Kelloway, 1999). That is, the more adolescents work, the less committed to school they tend to be. But whether this correlation also means causation requires interpretation. One possible interpretation is that working many hours causes adolescents to be less committed to school. Another possible interpretation is that being less committed to school causes adolescents to work more hours. It is also possible that both high work hours and low commitment to school are caused by a third variable: a relatively low IQ, or a personality high in sensation seeking, or growing up in a low-income family. Although the issue of correlation versus causation can be unravelled to some extent by using a **longitudinal study** design – mentioned earlier – that follows adolescents over time, and by considering the results of other studies that have asked similar questions in different ways, the conclusions drawn also depend on the judgement of the researchers who are interpreting the data. Misinterpreting correlation as causation is a mistake made frequently, even by scientists, as we will see in the course of this book.

Monozygotic (MZ) twins can be used in research as participants in a natural experiment, because they have exactly the same genotype.

CONNECT AND EXTEND

What sense can you make of this: 'There was a significant correlation between the genetic influences on [major depressive disorder] MDD and [conduct disorder] CD' (from the abstract)? Your challenge is to establish for yourself the meaning of 'correlation' by reading: 'Common genetic and environmental influences on major depressive disorder and conduct disorder' by Anjali Subbarao, Soo Rhee, Susan Young, Marissa Ehringer, Robin Corley and John Hewit in the *Journal of Abnormal Child Psychology*, Volume 36, Number 3 (April 2008), pp. 433–444

THINKING CRITICALLY

From your daily life, think of an example of how you or people you know may have mistaken correlation for causation. Then think of how you would design a study to show whether or not causation is truly involved.

THINKING CRITICALLY

Choose a topic on adolescence and emerging adulthood that you would be interested in studying. Which methodological approach would you use, and why?

Once a researcher writes a paper about a study they have undertaken – describing the methods used, the results of the statistical analyses and the interpretation of the results – the researcher typically submits the manuscript to a professional journal. The editor of the journal then sends the manuscript out for review by other researchers. In other words, the manuscript is **peer reviewed** for its scientific accuracy and credibility and for the importance of its contribution to the field. The editor relies on the reviews by the researchers' peers in deciding whether or not to accept the manuscript for publication. If the editor determines that the paper has passed the peer-review process successfully, the article is published in the journal. Some of the journals that publish peer-reviewed articles on adolescence and emerging adulthood are *Journal of Adolescent Research, Youth & Society, Journal of Adolescence, Journal of Youth Studies, Journal of Youth & Adolescence* and *Journal of Research on Adolescence*. In addition to research articles, most journals publish occasional theoretical articles and review articles that integrate findings from numerous other studies. Researchers studying adolescence and emerging adulthood also publish the results of their research in books, and often these books go through the peer-review process, as has this current text.

Theories and Research

A crucial part of the scientific process in any field is the development of theories. A good theory presents a set of interconnected ideas in an original and insightful way and points the way to further research. Theories and research are intrinsically connected: a theory generates hypotheses that can be tested in research, and research leads to modifications of the theory, which generate further hypotheses and further research. A good example of this is G. Stanley Hall's storm and stress theory – you may begin to appreciate the contribution that this scholar had on the work of all of us across the world who research and write about adolescence and emerging adulthood! His theory has generated a great deal of research in the past century; in turn, this research has resulted in modifications of his theory because it showed that storm and stress was not as extreme and was not universal in adolescence as he had proposed. Research still continues on the questions his theory provoked and the last decade has been as important as the century before in testing out Hall's theories of adolescence (Stroud et al., 2009; Huan et al., 2008; Alriksson-Schmidt et al., 2007; Caldwell et al., 2004; Raby, 2002; Griffin, 2001; Ayman-Nolley and Taira, 2000). It's really worth tracing the citations that we have used here using your online access to academic databases.

Of course we will also direct your attention to exciting and sometimes challenging alternative viewpoints and research using our features.

This book includes no separate chapter on theories, not because we do not think theories are important but because we think theories and research are intrinsically connected and should be presented together. Theories are presented in every chapter in relation to the research they have generated and the questions they have raised for future research. However, in the next section we present an outline of a cultural theory of development that applies to a wide range of topics.

Bronfenbrenner's Ecological Theory

One important and defining cultural theory is Urie Bronfenbrenner's **ecological theory** of human development (Bronfenbrenner, 2005; 2000; Bronfenbrenner and Morris, 1998). Bronfenbrenner presented his theory as a reaction to what he viewed as an overemphasis in developmental psychology on the immediate environment, especially the mother–child relationship. The immediate environment is important, Bronfenbrenner argued, but much more than this is involved in children's development. Bronfenbrenner's theory was intended to draw attention to the broader cultural environment that people experience as they develop, and to the ways the different levels of a person's environment interact. Bronfenbrenner also added a biological dimension to his framework and termed it a 'bioecological theory', but the distinctive contribution of the theory remains in its portrayal of the cultural environment.

According to Bronfenbrenner, five key levels or *systems* play a part in human development (see Figure 1.3):

- The **microsystem** is Bronfenbrenner's term for the immediate environment, the settings where people experience their daily lives. This is where the person's direct interactions and relationships take place. Microsystems in most cultures include relationships with each parent, with siblings, and perhaps with extended family (if any live in close

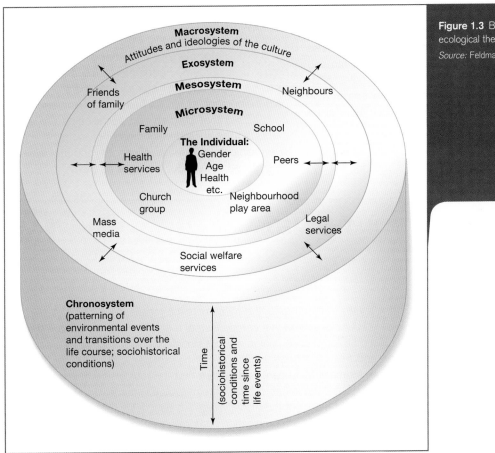

Figure 1.3 Bronfenbrenner's ecological theory.
Source: Feldman (2003).

proximity and are seen on a regular basis); with peers/friends; with teachers; and with other adults (such as coaches, religious leaders and employers). Bronfenbrenner emphasises that the child is an *active* agent in the microsystems; for example, children are affected by their parents but children's behaviour affects their parents as well; children are affected by their friends but they also make choices about whom to have as friends. The microsystem is where most research in developmental psychology has focused; today, however, most developmental psychologists use the term **context** rather than microsystem to refer to immediate environmental settings.

- The **mesosystem** is the network of interconnections between the various microsystems. For example, a child who is experiencing abusive treatment from parents may become difficult to handle in relationships with teachers; or, if a parent's employer demands longer hours in the workplace, the parent's relationship with the child may be affected.

- The **exosystem** refers to the societal institutions that have indirect but potentially important influences on development. In Bronfenbrenner's theory, these institutions include schools, religious institutions and media. For example, in Asian countries such as South Korea, competition to get into college is intense and depends chiefly on adolescents' performance in a national exam at the end of high school; consequently, the high school years are a period of extreme academic stress.

- The **macrosystem** is the broad system of **cultural beliefs** and values, and the economic and governmental systems that are built on those beliefs and values. For example, in countries such as Iran and Saudi Arabia, cultural beliefs and values are based in the religion of Islam, and the economic and governmental systems of those countries are also based on the teachings of Islam. In contrast, in the West, beliefs in the value of individual freedom are reflected in a free market economic system and in governmental systems of representative democracy.

- Finally, the **chronosystem** refers to changes that occur in developmental circumstances over time, both with respect to individual development and to historical changes. For example, with respect to individual development, losing your job is a much different experience at 15 than it would be at 45; with respect to historical changes, the occupational opportunities open to young women in many countries are much broader than they were half a century ago.

'So what', did we hear you ask? Well, there are many characteristics of Bronfenbrenner's ecological theory that make it important and useful for the cultural approach that will be taken in this book. Many developmental theories make no mention of culture, but culture is an important component of Bronfenbrenner's theory. He recognises that cultural beliefs and values are the basis for many of the other conditions of children's development. Furthermore, his theory recognises the importance of historical changes as influences on development, as we will here. Also, Bronfenbrenner emphasised that children and adolescents are active participants in their development, not merely the passive recipients of external influences, and that view will be stressed throughout this book as well.

FOCUS ON YOUTH IN THE MEDIA

Yob or Ladette?

I (MH) was 15 or 16 when I became aware of the phrase 'the medium is the message'. An enlightened teacher of English (Mr Elwyn Jones) led our class through a comparison of a then current news story: the IRA (Irish Republican Army) had launched a terrorist campaign against British troops in Ireland. Mr Jones presented audio recordings of radio and television news and copies of newspaper leading articles. He explained that a Canadian philosopher, Marshall McLuhan, had written that the part of the media – the medium – in which a message or story is presented influences how the message is perceived. (I can also remember Mr Jones talking about McLuhan's theory of the global village – a description of how the world would contract into a village as electrical and digital communication technologies allow the instantaneous transfer of information from any point to every quarter. Was this a premonition of the World Wide Web?)

What I learned from Mr Jones was that the media were incredibly powerful in forming our perceptions of the world and moulding our views about right and wrong, goodness, and matters of conscience. Our defining views of adolescence and adolescents are formed by what we see, read or hear from the many forms of the media that impact on our daily experience of the world. Therefore, each chapter of this book contains a *Focus on Youth in the Media* feature that will provide a glimpse of one aspect of adolescence or emerging adulthood. What, for example, is the view taken in one part of the media, the press, about youth cultures variously described, but here called yobs and ladettes. Let's take a couple of examples.

Dated 19 April 2005, a journalist at the *Daily Mail* newspaper reported under the headline of 'Tories' five-point plan to tackle yob culture' that the British Conservative Party (the Tories), the then opposition party to the UK government, had made plans to address what was then seen as the growing problem of yob culture. Interestingly, nowhere in this article is yob culture described or defined. It seems to be taken for granted that readers will already have formed a perception of yob culture as a slang term for loutish or thuggish behaviour by individuals or groups of young males and the idioms, clothes, language and associated attitudes. The word derives from a backwards reading of the word 'boy' (yob). Much of the article refers to a general societal fear of yobs and the main cause of loutish or thuggish behaviour – alcohol; 'Britain's binge-drinking yob culture'.

Under the plans, announced by the then Conservative party leader Michael Howard, a Conservative government would: put a stop to 'all you can drink' promotions; give local councils new powers to block new and late-night licence applications; and recruit more police.

The news media quoted Howard at a press conference saying that it was time to frighten the yobs in the same way as the yobs were frightening the rest of the law-abiding community. He highlighted the differences between the yob culture and family culture repeatedly using terms of 'law-abiding', 'right' and 'decent' when talking about families and 'fear' and 'nightmare' when talking about yobs. Howard also emphasised the division in society between those who do the right thing and those who do wrong, and that anti-social, yobbish behaviour was usually fuelled by cheap alcohol. Much of this alcohol is bought illegally by and for the youngsters, leading Mr Howard and others of similar views to believe that the policing of licensing arrangements and the closing down of late night shops selling cheap alcohol will go some way to cut down yobbish behaviour.

It is the so called culture of binge drinking - drinking large quantities of strong alcohol in a short period of time - linked to fighting, vandalism and street crimes that Howard associates with a climate of fear amongst the general public. It is not clear in the newspaper reports of the time how the 'five-point plan to tackle yob culture' will frighten the yobs, which is Mr Howard's confessed intention but the connection between some boys behaviour and the availability of large amounts of cheap booze on our streets, late at night is more explicit. Read more at: **http://www.dailymail.co.uk/news/article-345463/**.

Of course it isn't just boys who are part of the 'yob culture'. Girls and young women who behave in similar ways to 'the yobs' are called ladettes. In May 2008 James Slack, also writing in the *Daily Mail*, uses this term in the headline 'Ladettes' crimewave as girls aged 10 to 17 carry out 15,700 assaults and 1000 muggings a year'. Slack quotes more statistics to support an argument that ladette crime is fuelled by alcohol crime and is part of a growing problem of youth crime. For example, Slack reports that:

1 Girls were also responsible for 5748 incidents of criminal damage and almost 1000 drugs offences, according to the Youth Justice Board (YJB).

2 There has now been a 25 per cent leap in offending by girls aged 10 to 17 over a period of only three years. The YJB's Annual Workload Data report shows that girls committed 59,236 crimes in 2006/07, up from 47,358 in 2003/04.

3 Cases of violence by young people, ranging from common assault to murder, are up by 39 per cent over three years. There is a reoffending rate among these of more than 37 per cent.

Elaine Arnull of London's South Bank University is reported as commenting:

'The bigger picture is that behaviour is changing and there is a link between girls using alcohol and violence.'

Arnull then goes on to argue and is quoted as saying:

'It is fights between girls, principally – things like fights at school that the police weren't called to in the past. Most offending by girls, especially violent offending, is of a very low level. It doesn't mean it's insignificant, but it is hair-pulling fights between girls.'

Nevertheless, despite this caricaturing of ladette violence by Arnull as 'hair-pulling fights between girls', James Slack does report alarm among the police and government ministers at the rise of ladette behaviour and the overall substantial rise in teenage crime over a three-year period.

Read more at: **http://www.dailymail. co.uk/news/article-1019810/**. What do you make of the ways in which these two 'stories' are written: the language used; the quotations selected; the statistics presented?

There is alarm amongst the police and government at the rise of ladette behaviour.

The purpose of this feature is to activate your interest in the ways in which youth cultures are perceived and communicated. Our main text is largely based upon empirical research and meta-analysis of academic research in a number of different psychological and sociological disciplines. Our *Focus on Youth in the Media* feature is aimed at grounding your understanding of that research in the prevalent popular media and so to be able to judge the consequences of how adolescence and emerging adulthood is portrayed. Each *Focus on Youth in the Media* feature is, quite obviously, our selection and you will appreciate that some parts of the media, particularly newspapers, often skew their news reports and social comment according to political leanings either to the right or left (in part the meaning of 'the medium is the message'). To provide a balanced view further case studies and web links to new examples of youth in the media can be found on the companion website at **www.pearsoned.co.uk/arnett.**

Some parts of the theory will be addressed differently in this book. We think media play a more central and direct role in development than they do in Bronfenbrenner's theory – see the *Focus on Youth in the Media* feature in each chapter. We also emphasise the macrosystem of cultural beliefs and values as the basis of the rest of the socialisation environment to a greater extent than Bronfenbrenner does. Nevertheless, Bronfenbrenner's theory is a useful way of thinking about development, and we will refer back to it at various points in the book.

CONNECT AND EXTEND

For a study that simultaneously examines the effect of factors related to school, leisure, family and the individual on adolescent smoking (these determining factors occupy the micro- and mesosystems of Bronfenbrenner's ecological theory) read 'An ecological system approach to adolescent smoking behaviour' by Nora Wiium and Bente Wold in the *Journal of Youth and Adolescence*, Volume 38, Number 10 (November 2009), pp. 1351–1363

ADOLESCENCE AROUND THE WORLD: A BRIEF REGIONAL OVERVIEW

The heart of this textbook is its cultural approach. Throughout the book it is emphasised that adolescents and emerging adults around the world have very different lives, depending on their culture. What it is like to be an adolescent or an emerging adult in the British middle class is different in many ways from being a young person in Egypt, or Thailand, or Brazil – and also different from being a young person in some British minority cultures, such as the urban African British culture or the culture of recent British Asian immigrants. Although the physical changes of puberty are similar everywhere, cultures differ greatly in how they respond to these changes and in what they allow and expect from their adolescents. Cultural context underlies every aspect of young people's lives, from their family relations to their school participation to their sexuality to their media use. As background for understanding the cultural material presented in the chapters to come, here is a brief overview of the cultural context of adolescence in the major regions of the world.

Sub-Saharan Africa

Africa has been described as 'a rich continent whose people are poor' (Nsamenang, 1998). The countries of Africa are extremely rich in natural resources such as oil, gold and diamonds. Unfortunately, due to exploitation by the West in the nineteenth century followed by corruption, waste and war in the twentieth, this natural wealth has not yet translated into economic prosperity for the people of Africa. On the contrary, sub-Saharan Africa has the worst performance of any region of the world on virtually every measure of living standards, including income per person, access to clean water, life expectancy and prevalence of disease (United Nations Development Programme, 2009). Consequently, adolescents in Africa face challenges to their physical health and survival that are more formidable than in any other region of the world.

Although the problems facing young people in Africa are daunting, there are some bright spots, too. In the past decade, the civil wars that flared in many countries in the 1990s died down. Several African governments, most notably South Africa, moved towards more open, stable and democratic governments. Recent economic

African adolescents often care for younger siblings.

growth in Africa has been among the strongest of any world region (Zakaria, 2008). There is hope that these positive changes will endure and provide Africa's adolescents with a more promising future.

African cultures also have strengths in their tradition of large families and strong, supportive family relationships (Nsamenang, 2010). In nearly all other regions of the world, birth rates have fallen steadily in recent decades and most women have only one or two children. However, in Africa the current birth rate is five children per woman (Population Reference Bureau, 2009). Consequently, African adolescents typically have many siblings, and they often have responsibilities for caring for their younger siblings. In adolescence and beyond, African siblings have close ties of mutual obligation and support (Nsamenang et al., 2007).

North Africa and the Middle East

In North Africa and the Middle East, the Muslim religion is the predominant influence on all aspects of cultural life. The strength of Islam varies from countries in which all government policies are based on Islamic principles and texts (e.g. Kuwait and Saudi Arabia) to countries in which the influence of Islam is strong but a semblance of democracy and diversity of opinion also exist (e.g. Jordan and Morocco). At the time of writing many of the countries of the Middle East are in political and social revolution and so the relevance of commentary here is dependent upon the outcomes at your time of reading of a fast moving and ever-changing political and social context.

Patriarchal authority – in which the father's authority in the family is to be obeyed unquestioningly – has a long tradition in the cultures of North Africa and

Adolescents in North Africa and the Middle East blend Islamic traditions with modern ways.

the Middle East and is supported by Islam (Booth, 2002). Discussion of family rules in Muslim families is uncommon. Even to suggest such a thing would be considered an unacceptable affront to the authority of the parents, especially the father.

Part of the tradition of patriarchal authority is the dominance of men over women. Islamic societies have a long tradition of keeping tight control over women's appearance and behaviour. In many Islamic societies girls and women are required and/or choose to wear a **chador** or **burka**, which are garments that cover the hair and part or all of the face and body. Muslim girls and women are often expected to wear these garments in public as a way of being modest, beginning at puberty. In some Islamic societies women are not allowed to go out of the house unless accompanied by a male (Booth, 2002). Virginity before marriage is highly prized, and violation of this taboo can result in the most severe punishments, even death (Constable, 2000). Although in many Muslim countries young women exceed young men in educational attainment (UNDP, 2009), in adulthood women are generally discouraged from working outside the home. Consequently, adolescent girls in many countries in North Africa and the Middle East face sharply limited opportunities in adulthood.

Although the cultures of North Africa and the Middle East are deeply rooted in Islamic traditions, they are changing in response to globalisation. Many young people in this region today are highly attracted to the popular culture and information technologies of the West (e.g. Davis and Davis, 2007; Booth, 2002). Nevertheless, Islam currently remains strong, even among the young, and the strength of fundamentalist Islam is growing.

Asia

Asia comprises a vast and diverse area, ranging from countries that are highly industrialised (e.g. Japan) to countries that have recently industrialised (e.g. South Korea) to countries that are rapidly industrialising (e.g. China). In the case of China and some other Asian (and South American) countries it is difficult to characterise them as developing countries, or partly or wholly industrialised. We have tentatively used the term 'newly industrialised' and await the responses of our peers to this description. Nevertheless, many Asian countries share certain common characteristics and challenges.

The cultures of Asia have been profoundly influenced by Confucianism, a set of beliefs and precepts

Asian cultures such as Japan strongly emphasise education.

Many Indian adolescents work in manufacturing jobs such as carpet weaving.

attributed to the philosopher Confucius, who lived around 550 to 480 BC. One of the tenets of Confucianism is **filial piety**, which holds that children should respect, obey and revere their parents, especially the father. Part of filial piety is the expectation that the children, in particular the oldest son, have the responsibility of caring for their parents when the parents become elderly (Nelson et al., 2004). Consequently, Asian adolescents are more likely than adolescents in other parts of the world to have a grandparent living in their household (Stevenson and Zusho, 2002).

The Confucian tradition places a strong emphasis on education, which is one of the reasons for the intense focus on education in the lives of young people in Asian cultures today. As we will see in Chapter 10, secondary school tends to present strong pressures for young people in Asian societies, because performance in college entrance exams largely determines their path through adult life. This system is facing increasing criticism within Asian societies by those who argue that young people should not be subjected to such pressure at a young age and should be allowed more time for fun (Nelson and Chen, 2007; Lee and Larson, 2000).

India

Geographically, India is part of Asia, but it has such a large population (over a billion people) and a distinctive cultural tradition that it merits separate attention here. Unlike the rest of Asia, India's cultural tradition is based not in Confucianism but in the Hindu religion. However, India also has the second largest Muslim population in the world (after Indonesia), nearly 300 million.

India is one of the few countries in the world that does not have compulsory education for children or adolescents (Chaudhary and Sharma, 2007; Verma and Saraswathi, 2002). Consequently, many young people are illiterate, especially girls in rural areas. Many parents do not believe girls should be educated beyond a minimal ability to write letters and keep household accounts. Rural areas in India have relatively few schools, and those that exist tend to be poorly funded and staffed by teachers who are poorly trained. Access to education is much higher in urban areas, for girls as well as boys. In its urban areas India also has a large number of highly educated emerging adults, especially in fields such as medicine and information technologies, and they have made India a world economic leader in these areas (Chaudhary and Sharma, 2007).

Also contributing to high illiteracy in India is widespread child and adolescent labour, with jobs ranging from carpet weaving to mines, cigarette manufacturing and gem polishing, often in extremely unsafe and unhealthy conditions (Sanghera, 2008; ILO, 2002). Parents often prefer to have their children and adolescents working, and thus contributing to the family income, rather than attending school. Consequently, the government has taken few steps to restrict child and adolescent labour.

A distinctive feature of Indian culture is the **caste system**. According to this tradition, people are believed to be born into a particular caste based on their moral and spiritual conduct in their previous life (reincarnation is central to the Hindu beliefs held by most Indians). A person's caste then determines his or her status in Indian society. Only persons of elite castes are considered to be eligible for positions of wealth and power. Persons of lower castes are considered worthy only of the lowest paying, dirtiest, lowest status jobs. Also, marrying outside one's caste is strongly discouraged.

CONNECT AND EXTEND

Multiple deprivations are widespread in rural India. Literacy levels remain stubbornly low, albeit gradually improving. Caste, class, religion, gender, age and disability all impact on access to education, participation and successful completion (from the abstract). Read 'Widening access, widening participation, widening success: an Indian case study' by Mary Thornton in *Research in Post-Compulsory Education*, Volume 11, Number 1 (2006), pp. 19–30

Adolescents from lower castes are less likely to attend school than adolescents from higher castes, which restricts the jobs available to them as adults (Verma and Saraswathi, 2000).

Family relations are notably strong and warm in Indian families. Adolescents in India spend most of their leisure time with their families rather than with their friends, and they are happiest when with their families (Larson et al., 2000). Even highly educated emerging adults in India often prefer to have their parents arrange their marriage, which shows how deeply they trust and rely on their parents (Reddy and Gibbons, 1999). Indian families are discussed in further detail in Chapter 5.

Latin America

Latin America comprises a vast land area of diverse cultures but they share a common history of colonisation by southern European powers, particularly Spain, and a common allegiance to the Roman Catholic religion. For young people in Latin America, two of the key issues for the twenty-first century are political stability and economic growth (Galambos and Martinez, 2007). For many decades the countries of Latin America have experienced repeated episodes of political and economic instability, but today prospects look somewhat brighter. Although political instability continues in some countries, for the most part Latin American countries have now established stable democracies. Economically, too, the situation has improved in recent years in most of Latin America. However unemployment among adults is high throughout Latin America, and unemployment among young people is even higher, often exceeding 25 per cent (Galambos and Martinez, 2007; Welti, 2002).

If the recent trend of political stability can be sustained, economic growth in Latin America is likely to improve. Young people in Latin America are obtaining increased education, which should help prepare them for the increasingly information-based global economy. Also, the birth rate in this region has declined sharply in the past two decades, and consequently the children who are now growing up should face less competition in the job market as they enter adolescence and emerging adulthood (Galambos and Martinez, 2007).

The West

'The West' is less a regional grouping than a cultural grouping that refers to the countries of Europe, the United States, Canada, Australia and New Zealand. Western countries are notably stable, democratic and affluent. Young people in the West generally have access to opportunities for secondary, further and higher education, and they can choose from a wide range of occupations (Arnett, 2002b). Most young people in the West have a wide range of leisure opportunities. In contrast to adolescents in other regions of the world, adolescents in the West spend most of their time (outside school) in leisure with their friends, rather than studying or working for their families. A substantial proportion of their leisure is media based, including television, computer games, text messaging, listening to portable music and using social networking websites such as MySpace and Facebook.

Although young people in Western countries are obtaining increased education, with many of them remaining in school through their early 20s, educational opportunities are not evenly distributed in most Western countries (Arnett, 2002b). Emerging adults in minority groups often obtain higher education at rates considerably lower than emerging adults in the majority cultures (see evidence cited in Chapter 10). Unemployment is also high among emerging adults in Western countries, especially among minorities (Sneeding and Phillips, 2002). Throughout Western countries, young minorities are disadvantaged in the workplace in part because of lower levels of education

CONNECT AND EXTEND

For a paper that explores the relationship between culture and ethnicity and the development of paranoia in both mental health settings and in the wider world, read 'Culture, ethnicity, and paranoia' by P. Sen and A. Chowdhury in *Current Psychiatry Reports*, Volume 8, Number 3 (May 2006), pp. 174–178

and training and in part because of prejudice and discrimination from the majority (Boromisza-Habashi and Rappoport, 2007; Gounev and Bezlov, 2006; van der Slik and Konig, 2006; Stephenson, 2006; Gary, 2005; Shelton et al., 2005). You might note that when we stray into areas of philosophical or scientific controversy we cite far more evidence for the argument we are trying to make than just one or two academic papers. It is worth looking out for this in the chapters ahead.

Implications of Cultural Context

The overview we have just presented gives a brief look at the cultural contexts of adolescence and emerging adulthood, and you will be learning a lot more about young people's lives in different parts of the world in the course of the book. However, even this general overview shows you how different it is to be an adolescent or emerging adult depending on where in the world you live. Adolescents in some cultures are likely to be in school for most of a typical day through their teens and even into emerging adulthood; adolescents in other cultures begin working early in life and have little chance of obtaining education beyond primary school. Adolescents in some cultures grow up as part of a large extended family; adolescents in other cultures grow up in a small nuclear family and may not even have a sibling. Emerging adults in some cultures have a wide range of occupational possibilities; for emerging adults in other cultures the range is narrow or nonexistent, as lack of education leaves them unprepared for any but the most unskilled labour, or, for young women, as cultural beliefs about women's roles exclude them from the workplace.

This is why cultural context is essential to a full understanding of the adolescent and emerging adult experience. Throughout the book, we present examples from many different cultures for each topic we address. In each chapter we also present a feature called *Cultural Focus*, which looks in more detail at one particular culture with respect to the topic of the

chapter. In addition, we often critique research from a cultural perspective. By the time you finish this book we would like you to be able to *think culturally*, so that you can analyse and critique research for whether it does or does not take culture and ethnicity into account– and how those two constructs differ.

OTHER THEMES OF THE BOOK

In addition to the cultural approach, a number of other themes will be part of every chapter: historical contrasts, the interdisciplinary approach, professional applications and implications, gender issues and globalisation.

Historical Contrasts

In the same way that we can learn a lot about adolescence and emerging adulthood from comparing different cultures, we can also learn a great deal by comparing the lives of adolescents and emerging adults today to the lives of their counterparts in other times. Throughout the book, we provide historical information on each of the topics we discuss. Also, each chapter has a feature entitled *Historical Focus* that provides more detailed information on a specific issue in a specific historical period.

Interdisciplinary Approach

Many researchers studying adolescence and emerging adulthood are psychologists. They have been trained in psychology, and they work in the psychology departments of colleges and universities. However, many researchers in other disciplines also study adolescence and emerging adulthood. Anthropology's recent studies we have already discussed. Sociology has a long tradition of research on adolescence and emerging adulthood, including some of the most important studies in such areas as peer relations, delinquency, and the transition to adulthood. Medical doctors, especially psychiatrists and paediatricians, have also made important contributions, most notably concerning the biology of adolescence and emerging adulthood and the treatment of psychological disorders that may occur during these age periods, such as depression. Researchers in education have contributed insightful work on adolescents' and emerging adults' development in relation to school, as well as other topics. In recent decades historians have published a number of excellent studies on adolescence and emerging adulthood.

The boundaries we set up between different disciplines are useful in some ways, but they are essentially artificial. If you want to understand development in adolescence and emerging adulthood, you should seek insights wherever you can find them. We want you to have as full an understanding of adolescence and emerging adulthood as possible by the time you finish this book, and toward that goal we will use material from developmental, behavioural and cognitive psychology, anthropology, sociology, education, history and other disciplines.

Professional Applications and Implications

There will be many reasons why you are reading this text. Perhaps it might be that you are engaged in a programme of study which includes or leads to professional qualification and status as a member of the young people's workforce. All members of the children's and young people's workforce need to understand the ways in which young people grow and develop, and be able apply that knowledge in whatever professional context or role to which they aspire. Teachers, psychologists, youth workers, social workers, carers, paediatric nurses, family welfare officers, counsellors – yes the list goes on and on – are professional practitioners who can make a huge difference to the way in which our young people achieve a successful transition from childhood to adulthood. To explore some of the challenges and opportunities that confront professional practitioners we include in each chapter a *Focus on Professional Practice* feature and there are many more case studies and links on our companion website at **www.pearsoned.co.uk/arnett.**

Gender Issues

In every culture, gender is a key issue in development throughout the life span (Hatfield and Rapson, 2006; Carroll and Wolpe, 2005). The expectations cultures have for males and females are different from the time they are born. Children become aware of their own gender by the time they are about 2 or 3 years old, and with this awareness they grow sensitive to the differences in what is considered appropriate behaviour for each gender. Differences in cultural expectations related to gender typically become more pronounced at puberty. Adolescence and emerging adulthood are, among other things, periods of preparation for taking on adult roles in the family and in work. In most cultures, these roles differ considerably depending on whether you are male or female, so the expectations for male and female adolescents and emerging adults differ accordingly. Expected behaviours in the courtship and sexual behaviour that are typically part of adolescence and emerging adulthood also differ considerably between males and females in most cultures.

Although all cultures have different expectations for males and females, the degree of the differences varies greatly among cultures. In the majority cultures of the West these days, the differences are relatively blurred; men and women hold many of the same jobs, wear many of the same clothes (e.g. jeans, T-shirts), and enjoy many of the same entertainments. If you have grown up in the West, you may be surprised to learn how deep gender differences go in many other cultures. For example, in Morocco, boys are more or less expected to become sexually experienced before marriage (Davis and Davis, 2007). Girls, on the other hand, are expected to be virgins on their wedding night. Thus, the boys' first sexual experience is typically with a prostitute. The morning after a wedding, bride and groom are obliged to hang the sheet from their bed out of the window, complete with a bloody stain on it to prove that the girl's hymen was broken on the wedding night, confirming that she had been a virgin until that time.

Although nothing comparable to this exists in the West, there are gender-specific expectations in the West, too. Even now, there are fewer male nurses or personal assistants or full-time fathers, and there are few female truck drivers or engineers or MPs. The differences in expectations for males and females may be more subtle in the West than in some other cultures, but they remain powerful, and they are a key part of adolescence and emerging adulthood. Throughout the book, we pay attention to gender differences for each

FOCUS ON PROFESSIONAL PRACTICE

Paediatric Psychology

Adolescent development can be so absorbing that many scholars want to apply what they have learned in their professional lives. One set of fascinating career pathways in which you can apply what you currently studying (in part by reading *Adolescence and Emerging Adulthood*) is in the area of paediatric psychology. The term *paediatric psychology* was first coined by Logan Wright as 'dealing primarily with children in a medical setting which is non-psychiatric in nature' (1967, p. 323). A couple of definitions might help to describe what paediatric psychology is and what it isn't! Paediatrics is the branch of medicine dealing with children and young people and psychology is the scientific study of the human mind and its functions that affect behaviour in a given context. Wright specifically excludes psychiatry as psychiatry is the highly specialist study and treatment of mental disease whereas psychology concentrates on the relationship between behaviour, mental functioning, health and relationships. So, paediatric psychologists study and advise on abnormal and normal personal construct theory (Green, 2005) and behaviour in young people.

Educational Psychologist

Educational psychologists work with and advise teachers, parents and pupils to improve learning outcomes for pupils. They apply research and theories to the school setting and so promote effective schools (Hymer et al., 2002). Ed psychs, as they are sometimes called, conduct assessments on individual pupils to determine interventions and so promote increased gains in attainment. They also make assessments that verify eligibility for special education provision including gifted and talented programmes and advise teachers and parents on strategies to improve pupils' learning, behaviour and motivation (Swinson and Cording, 2002; Tierney and Dowd, 2000).

Educational psychologists conduct assessments on individual pupils to determine interventions and so promote increased gains in attainment.

Clinical Psychologist

Within the field of clinical psychology, some psychologists specialise in child and adolescent psychology. Young people face challenges that are not exclusive but can be distinctive to their age group, and clinical psychologists specialising in the treatment of young people assess the needs of and develop interventions to prevent common psychological problems. For example, some abnormal behaviours – referred to as psychopathologies – common in children, such as attention deficit disorder (Tervo et al., 2002) and conduct disorder (Cukrowicz et al., 2006) can cause major problems at home or at school, and eating disorders can remain a serious and long-term threat to health and welfare of young people (Boyd et al., 2007). Other adolescents need help coping with major life changes, such as hospitalisation for long periods (Ametller et al., 2005), or their parents divorcing (Dunlop et al., 2001) or the disablement or death of a parent, sibling or friend (Dillen et al., 2009). Clinicians specialising in youngsters assess and help meet those needs by supporting young people to explore, understand and moderate their potentially damaging behaviours. Much of this treatment is on a one-to-one basis but can include group therapy techniques.

Researcher

Child psychologists have to earn a higher research degree in order to become a child psychologist, which requires original research and the successful completion and defence of a thesis. Therefore, they are deemed qualified to conduct and publish psychological research – although publication requires peers to agree that the findings are valid, and the methods used are reliable. This is research into the normal and abnormal development of children, considering questions such as: the learning and behaviour of children with chronic illness or disability (e.g. Gilbert, 2004); the role of play and imagination (e.g. Jago, 2006); the nature of family relationships and childhood friendships (e.g. Cross and Fletcher, 2009); runaways and the homeless (e.g. Kurtz et al., 2000); and the normal and abnormal development of cognition (e.g. Petrina et al., 2012). Researchers are typically employed by or affiliated to universities (Lin and Bozeman, 2006), where they conduct their research and perhaps teach undergraduate and postgraduate students.

Source: format adapted from 'Careers in paediatric psychology' by Dawn Walls-Thumma at **http://www.ehow.co.uk/list_6695563_careers-pediatric-psychology.html** accessed 02.04.2011

---

of the topics we address, and Chapter 5 is devoted specifically to gender issues. By the end of the book, we want you to have a broader sense of how males and females are treated differently in cultures around the world, and of how your own culture has shaped your development in gender-specific ways you may not have realised before now.

Globalisation

Researchers on adolescence have recently begun giving more attention to cultural influences on development in adolescence and emerging adulthood. However, this attention to culture comes at a time in world history when the boundaries that give cultures their distinctiveness are becoming steadily fainter (Zakaria, 2008), and the world is becoming increasingly integrated into a global culture – a 'global village', as the social philosopher Marshall McLuhan put it some years ago. No traditional culture has remained exempt from these changes. You can go to the remotest rainforest culture in Venezuela, the northernmost Arctic village in Canada, or the smallest mountain village of New Guinea, and you will find that every one of them is being drawn inexorably into a common world culture. Our exploration of development in adolescence and emerging adulthood would not be complete without an account of these changes, which reflect the **globalisation** of adolescence and emerging adulthood (Larson et al., 2010).

Globalisation means that increasing worldwide technological and economic integration is making the world 'smaller', more homogeneous. As a consequence of the globalisation of adolescence and emerging adulthood, young people around the world experience increasingly similar environments. Adolescents and emerging adults in many parts of the world are growing up listening to much of the same music, watching many of the same films, going to school for an increasing number of years, learning how to use personal computers, drinking the same soft drinks, and wearing the same brands of jeans. The appeal of being connected to a global culture appears to be especially high among adolescents and emerging adults (Straker, 2007; Schlegel, 2001). Perhaps this is because they are more capable than children of seeking out information beyond the borders of their own culture – through travel and the Internet, for example – and are less committed to established roles and a set way of life than adults are.

THINKING CRITICALLY

Have you travelled to another country in recent years? If so, can you think of examples you have witnessed that reflect the globalisation of adolescence? Perhaps you can think of examples you have read about or heard about? What positive and negative consequences do you anticipate from the globalisation of adolescence?

Globalisation does not mean that young people everywhere are growing up in exactly the same way or becoming exactly alike in their cultural identity. The more typical pattern worldwide is that young people are becoming increasingly **bicultural** in their identities, with one identity for participation in their local culture and one identity for participation in the global culture (Papastergiadis, 2005), for example through e-mail or in interactions with foreign visitors. It should also be noted that although many young people participate eagerly in the global culture, other adolescents and emerging adults are at the forefront of growing resistance to globalisation, for example in protests against the actions of the World Bank and the International Monetary Fund (Ignatow, 2008; Osland, 2003; Van Aelst and Walgrave, 2002; Welti, 2002).

The globalization of adolescence: A Venezuelan adolescent's T-shirt depicts characters from the American TV show *The Simpsons*.

CONNECT AND EXTEND

'The events of 11 September 2001 and their aftermath have prompted several obituaries of the so-called "Anti-globalization movement". Even before that date, the movement was struggling to cope with the problem of violence at its set piece summit protests in Genoa and elsewhere' (from the abstract). Read 'Globalization and its discontents' by Duncan Green and Matthew Griffith in *International Affairs*, Volume 78, Number 1 (January 2002), pp. 49–68

Throughout this book we present examples of how globalisation is affecting the lives of adolescents and emerging adults. We will consider how this trend is likely to affect their futures in both positive and negative ways.

FRAMEWORK OF THE BOOK

Following this introductory chapter, the book is divided into three sections. The first section, Foundations, includes chapters on five different areas of development: Biological foundations, Cognitive foundations, Cultural beliefs, Gender, and The self. These chapters describe the areas that form the foundation for young people's development across a variety of aspects of their lives. Together, these chapters form the basis for understanding development as it takes place in various contexts.

Thus, the first section sets the stage for the second section, called Contexts. Context is the term researchers use to refer to the environmental settings in which development takes place. This section has chapters on six different contexts: Family relationships; Friends and peers; Love and sexuality; School; and Work.

The third section is entitled Problems and Resilience. The sole chapter in this section addresses problems ranging from risky car driving to drug use to depression. It also examines **resilience**, which is the ability of children and adolescents who are at risk for problems to avoid falling prey to those risks.

SUMMING UP

This chapter has introduced you to the central ideas and concepts that we will be considering throughout the rest of the book. The following summarises the key points we have discussed:

- The cultural approach taken in this book means that adolescence and emerging adulthood will be portrayed as being culturally constructed; cultures determine what the experience of these age periods is like. It is emphasised that what it is like to be an adolescent or an emerging adult varies widely among cultures.
- Adolescence has a long history in Western societies as a specific period of life between childhood and adulthood. However, it was only during the years 1890–1920 that adolescence developed into its modern form, as a period of life when young people are largely excluded from adult work and spend their time mostly among their peers.
- *Emerging adulthood* is the term for the period from ages 18 to 25. The distinctive characteristics of this age period are that it is the age of identity explorations; the age of instability; the self-focused age; the age of feeling in-between; and the age of possibilities.

- The scientific method includes standards of hypotheses, sampling, procedure, method, analysis and interpretation. A variety of specific methods for data collection are used in the study of adolescence and emerging adulthood, ranging from questionnaires and interviews, ethnographic research and experimental research.
- Bronfenbrenner's ecological theory emphasises the cultural environment that people experience as they develop and the ways the different levels of a person's environment interact. There are five levels or *systems* in the theory: microsystem, mesosystem, exosystem, macrosystem and chronosystem.
- The cultural context of adolescence and emerging adulthood varies widely by world regions. These cultural differences influence a variety of aspects of development in adolescence and emerging adulthood, from physical health to education and work, to family relationships.
- The book is divided into three major sections: Foundations, Contexts, and Problems and Resilience.

In each chapter, this *Summing Up* section briefly restates the main points of the chapter and then offers some reflections on what we know at this point and what we have yet to learn.

The study of adolescence and emerging adulthood is relatively new. Adolescence has been established as a distinct field only since G. Stanley Hall's work was published a century ago; emerging adulthood is only just now becoming a distinct area of study. As you will see in the chapters to come, a remarkable amount has already been learned about these age periods. However, so far most research has focused on young people in the majority cultures of the West. That focus is now broadening to include other groups in our European societies as well as young people in other cultures around the world. One goal of this book is to make you familiar with research on adolescence and emerging adulthood in many different cultures, so that you will be able to take a cultural approach in your own understanding of how young people develop during these years.

INTERNET RESOURCES

http://www.earaonline.org

The website for the European Association for Research on Adolescence. Information on membership and conferences, and recent news pertaining to the organisation.

http://www.s-r-a.org

The official website of the Society for Research on Adolescence (SRA), which is the main organisation for researchers on adolescence. Contains information about conferences and publications related to adolescence.

http://www.ssea.org

The website of the Society for the Study of Emerging Adulthood. Contains information about conferences on emerging adulthood, resources for teaching courses on emerging adulthood, and a bibliography of useful articles and books on the topic.

FURTHER READING

G. S. Hall *Adolescence: Its Psychology and its Relation to Physiology, Anthropology, Sociology, Sex, Crime, Religion, and Education* **(Vols I & II). Englewood Cliffs, NJ: Prentice Hall (1904)**

These are two thick volumes, each over 500 pages, but you may find it enjoyable to browse through them to get a sense of Hall's ideas. This will also give you a sense of how the scientific approach to the study of adolescence has changed since Hall's time.

Roger Harrison and Christine Wise, *Working with Young People*. **Sage Publications Ltd; published in Association with the Open University (24 August 2005)**

An excellent introductory text grounded in professional practice that is relevant for students interested in a career in youth work.

Ann Wheal, *Adolescence: Positive Approaches to Working with Young People*. **Russell House Publishing Ltd; 2nd rev edn (1 July 2006)**

This book is for all those interested in working with adolescents and emerging adults. It is well grounded in the practicalities of various career routes and the kinds of qualities required and the challenges that need to be met.

Kerry Young, *The Art of Youth Work*. **Russell House Publishing Ltd; 2nd edn (15 May 2006)**

This edition argues that youth work is centrally concerned with making relationships with young people, which support them in creating themselves and the values and meanings that shape their lives and guide their actions in the world.

For more web links and further reading, plus practice tests, case studies, PowerPoint presentations and discussion of the *Critical Thinking* features, log on to **www.pearsoned.co.uk/arnett**.

PART 1

FOUNDATIONS

CHAPTER 2
BIOLOGICAL FOUNDATIONS

OUTLINE

'I had my first period at 11 which was a lot earlier than any of my friends and earlier than I ever expected to get it. I was quite upset when it first happened – I thought I had hurt myself as I was too young (I thought) for my period. I went straight to my older sister in tears and she explained everything to me. It was quite scary at such a young age to be dealing with it and it took a while for me to fully understand.'

Emily, age 17 (Hughes, unpublished data)

'I knew a bit about [menstruation] but not a lot. I wasn't really prepared and didn't tell my mum for two days. She asked why I hadn't told her but I'd been too embarrassed.'

Bev – pseudonym – age 16 (Hughes, unpublished data)

'When my body started to change, I noticed more people's reactions to me, rather than changes in the mirror. I guess I was a late starter, maybe 15/16? I used to walk half way to school by myself before meeting friends to go the remainder of the way. Lorry drivers started beeping at me and yelling "phwoar" out of their windows. Of course my outer reaction was either to completely ignore them or "Oh for goodness sake", while my inner reaction was "woo hoo!"'

Steph, age 20 (Hughes, unpublished data)

'I vividly remember being one of the first boys in my class to get spots. It was the start of Year 8 (aged 12–13 years). That meant being the butt of jokes for a while. I tried every cream available but they just didn't seem to do anything. They were concentrated on my forehead and nose. I soon lost faith in the creams and just stuck to washing normally. By the time I was 16 things had improved.'

Edd, age 21 (Hughes, unpublished data)

'Growing [pubic] hair, I didn't think much of it, hair started off a light colour and then as I got older I got more of it and it was darker. Mates started growing hair before me and some after so nothing struck me as wrong, so I just, I didn't really notice it.'

Chris, age 24 (Hughes, unpublished data)

'Wet dreams were often the talk of the playground and I must have been slow in them happening to me. Of course I knew what to expect from the conversations us boys had had for months. It was messy and seemed to get everywhere. My mum never said anything but the next evening I had clean bed linen! I was 14 years old at the time'.

Jon – pseudonym – age 19 (Hughes, unpublished data)

THESE EXAMPLES ILLUSTRATE THE WIDE RANGE of reactions that adolescents have to some of the events that indicate the early development of physical and sexual maturity. They also suggest the ways that different families influence young people's interpretations of the biological events of puberty, in part by informing them – or neglecting to inform them – about the changes that will be taking place in their bodies. The foregoing quotes also suggest the intensely personal nature of those events. Notice Emily's use above of 'my' in: 'I thought I had hurt myself as I was too young (I thought) for *my* period'; not *a* period, but 'my period'. In this chapter we deal, and necessarily so, with these personal 'biological' events in a straightforward way, but not forgetting the social impact on adolescents that the events of puberty can have.

Although adolescence is a socially constructed period of life, the biological changes of puberty are a central part of development during adolescence in all cultures. Many changes take place, and they are often dramatic. There you are, growing at a more or less steady rate through childhood, and then suddenly an out-and-out metamorphosis begins – growth spurt, pubic hair, underarm hair, acne, changes in body shape, breast development and menarche in girls, first ejaculation and facial hair in boys, and much more. The changes are often exciting and joyful, but adolescents experience them with other emotions as well – fear, shock, annoyance and anxiety. Reaching the key changes earlier or later than most peers is especially a source of anxiety.

The biological changes of puberty are similar across cultures, but in this chapter we will see that biological events interact with social influences. Culture influences the timing of biological events, and societies respond in a variety of ways to the biological changes that signify adolescents' attainment of physical – and sexual – maturity. Adolescents, in turn, rely on information provided by their families and friends for interpreting the changes taking place within their bodies and in their physical appearance.

In this chapter we will begin with a description of the hormonal changes that lead to the biological changes of puberty. This will be followed by a description of the physical changes of puberty, including changes in height, weight, muscle-to-fat ratio and strength. Next will be a description of primary sex characteristics (sperm and egg production) and secondary sex characteristics (such as the growth of pubic hair and the development of breasts). Then we will examine cultural, social and psychological responses to puberty, including the different experiences of adolescents who mature relatively early or relatively late. The chapter closes with an examination of the interactions between genetic and environmental influences.

THE BIOLOGICAL REVOLUTION OF PUBERTY

'Puberty is the attainment of fertility, a process encompassing morphological, physiological and behavioural development'.
(Ebling, 2005: p 675)

In the foregoing quote, scientist Professor Fran Ebling manages to encapsulate in one sentence one of the most complex and important aspects of adolescent development, the process, the happening, the inescapable human experience of **puberty**. Puberty happens to us all; all living organisms; all humans since time began, since homo-sapiens started to become the most powerful species on earth. Puberty 'happened' to me, it happened to you (or will do if you are academically precocious and reading this text at an early age). What is puberty?

THINKING CRITICALLY

Take a few moments to think about Fran Ebling's definition of puberty. Is there anything missing from the definition? The meanings of 'morphological' and 'physiological' are important to understand the implications of the remainder of this chapter to your current study of adolescence and emerging adulthood.

The word puberty is derived from the Latin word *pubescere*, which means 'to grow hairy'. Of course, adolescents do a lot more in puberty than just grow hairy – just check back to Fran Ebling's definition of puberty above. After developing gradually and steadily during childhood, the body at puberty undergoes a biological revolution that dramatically changes the adolescent's anatomy, physiology and physical appearance. By the time adolescents enter emerging adulthood, they look very different from how they looked before puberty; their bodies function much differently and they are biologically prepared for sexual reproduction. These changes result from events that occur in the endocrine system. Although what comes next may feel like a technical explanation of what happens in the body during puberty, it is important to understand and to be able to discuss the biology of

change in the terms used by experts in developmental sciences, and by practitioners working in children's services.

The Endocrine System

The **endocrine system** consists of glands in various parts of the body. These glands release chemicals called **hormones** into the bloodstream, and the hormones affect the development and functioning of the body. Let us take a look at each of the glands that are part of the endocrine system and at the hormones they secrete during puberty (see Figure 2.1).

The Initiation of Puberty in the Hypothalamus

The hormonal changes of puberty begin in the **hypothalamus**, a bean-sized structure located in the lower part of the brain, beneath the cortex. The hypothalamus has profound and diverse effects on physiological and psychological motivation and functioning in areas such as eating, drinking and sexuality. In addition to these functions, the hypothalamus stimulates and regulates the production of hormones by other glands. To initiate puberty, the hypothalamus begins gradually to

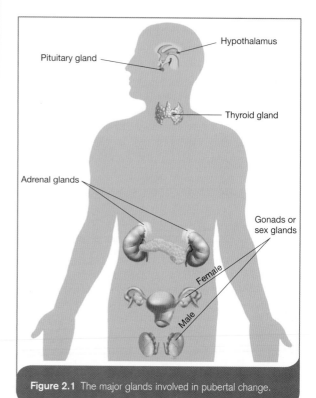

Figure 2.1 The major glands involved in pubertal change.

CONNECT AND EXTEND

Aesthetic sport athletes are subject to pressures to be thin. To find out the effects on competitive female gymnasts, aged 10–15 years read 'Disturbed eating in young, competitive gymnasts: differences between three gymnastics disciplines' by Sanna Nordin, Gillian Harris and Jennifer Cumming in the *European Journal of Sport Science*, Volume 3, Number 5 (2003), pp. 1–14

increase its production of **gonadotropin-releasing hormone (GnRH)**, releasing GnRH in pulses at intervals of about two hours (DeRose and Brooks-Gunn, 2006). The increase in GnRH begins in middle childhood, at least a year or two before even the earliest bodily changes of puberty.

But what causes the hypothalamus to increase GnRH production? Recent evidence indicates that this increase occurs once a threshold level of body fat is reached (Alsaker and Flammer, 2006). During middle childhood the proportion of fat in the body gradually increases, and once the threshold level is reached the increase in GnRH is triggered in the hypothalamus. Fat cells produce a protein, **leptin**, which provides the signal to the hypothalamus (Shalatin and Philip, 2003; Mantzoros, 2000; Spear, 2000). Consequently, for adolescents who are excessively thin due to illness, extreme exercise such as intense gymnastic training, or malnutrition, puberty is delayed. Other factors known to influence the timing of puberty include genetics, stress, socioeconomic status (SES) and environmental toxins (Ge and Natsuaki, 2009; Belsky et al., 2007; DeRose & Brooks-Gunn, 2006; Finkelstein, 2001a; Kipke, 1999).

The Pituitary Gland and the Gonadotropins

The increase in GnRH affects the **pituitary gland**, a gland about 1 cm located at the base of the brain. GnRH is appropriately named gonadotropin-releasing hormone because that is what it does when it reaches the pituitary gland – it causes hormones called **gonadotropins** to be released from the pituitary. The two gonadotropins are **follicle-stimulating hormone (FSH)** and **luteinising hormone (LH)**. FSH and LH stimulate the development of **gametes** – egg cells in the ovaries of the female and sperm in the testes of the male. FSH and LH also influence the production of sex hormones by the ovaries and testes, which will be described in more detail below.

The Gonads and the Sex Hormones

The ovaries and testes are also known as the **gonads**, or sex glands. In response to stimulation from the FSH and LH released by the pituitary gland, the gonads increase their production of the **sex hormones**. There are two classes of sex hormones, the **oestrogens** and the **androgens**. With respect to pubertal development, the most important oestrogen is **estradiol** and the most important androgen is **testosterone**. Increases in these hormones are responsible for most of the observable bodily changes of puberty, such as breast growth in females and facial hair in males.

Estradiol and testosterone are produced in both males and females, and throughout childhood the levels of these hormones are about the same in boys and girls (DeRose and Brooks-Gunn, *ibid.*). However, once puberty begins the balance changes dramatically, with females producing more estradiol than males and males producing more testosterone than females (Shirtcliff et al., 2009) – see Figure 2.2. By the mid-teens, estradiol production is about eight times as high in females as it was before puberty, but only about twice as high for males (Dorn et al., 2009). Similarly, in males testosterone production is about 20 times as high by the mid-teens as it was before puberty, but in females it is only about four times as high (Dorn et al., *ibid.*).

Androgens are produced not only by the sex glands but also by the adrenal glands. At puberty, the pituitary gland increases production of a hormone known as **adrenocorticotropic hormone (ACTH)**, which causes the adrenal glands to increase androgen production (Archibald et al., 2003). The androgens released by the adrenal gland have the same effects as the androgens released by the testes, contributing to changes such as the development of increased body hair.

The Feedback Loop in the Endocrine System

From infancy onward, a **feedback loop** runs between the hypothalamus, the pituitary gland, the gonads and the adrenal glands. The feedback loop monitors and

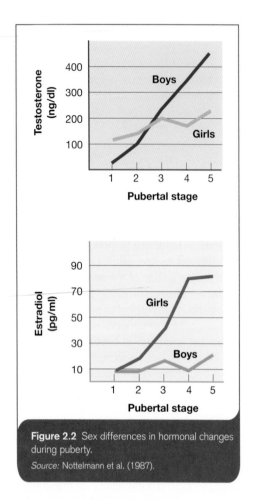

Figure 2.2 Sex differences in hormonal changes during puberty.

Source: Nottelmann et al. (1987).

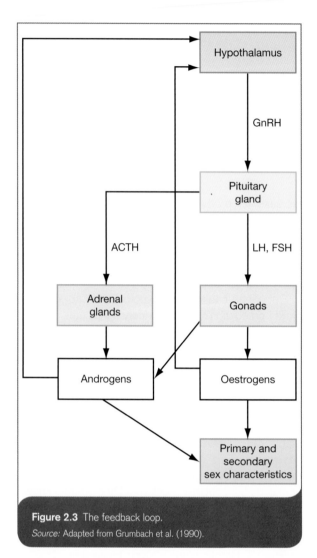

Figure 2.3 The feedback loop.

Source: Adapted from Grumbach et al. (1990).

adjusts the levels of the sex hormones (see Figure 2.3). The hypothalamus monitors the levels of androgens and oestrogens in the bloodstream, and when the sex hormones reach an optimal level, called the **set point**, the hypothalamus reduces its production of GnRH. The pituitary responds to the reduction in GnRH by reducing its production of FSH, LH and ACTH; the gonads and adrenal glands, in turn, respond to lower levels of FSH and LH by reducing the amount of sex hormones they produce.

Think of this like the heating thermostat that is commonly found in many homes which have central heating. If you set a domestic heating thermostat at 20 °C, when the temperature falls below that level the heating boiler comes on. As the boiler heats the rooms, the temperature rises, and when it reaches 20 °C again the boiler turns off. In your body, when the levels of the sex hormones fall below set points, production by the gonads increases. Once the levels rise again to a set point, the production of sex hormones decreases.

When puberty begins, the set points rise for androgens and oestrogens in the hypothalamus. The set point for androgens rises higher in males than in females and the set point for oestrogens rises higher in females than in males. In other words, during childhood the gonads produce only a relatively small amount of sex hormones before the set point of the hypothalamus is reached and the hypothalamus signals the gonads to decrease production of the sex hormones. As puberty begins, however, and the set points for the sex hormones rise in the hypothalamus, the gonads can produce an increasing amount of the sex hormones before the hypothalamus instructs them to decrease production. To return to the heating thermostat metaphor, it is as if the thermostat were set at 5 °C during childhood, so that the 'heat' of sex hormone production is triggered only occasionally. In the course of puberty, it is as if the thermostat is set to 25 °C, and the 'heat' of sex hormone production rises accordingly.

What do you think are some of the social and psychological consequences of the fact that girls mature about two years earlier than boys during puberty? Jot down some ideas and compare your ideas with those in the upcoming sections.

Stages of Development

Before considering the effects of these changes in hormone levels on growth it is worth noting that very many recent studies (e.g. Calcaterra et al., 2009; Zunquin et al., 2009; Badouraki et al., 2008; Du Pasquier-Fediaevsky et al., 2005; Žukauskaite et al., 2005; Battaglia et al., 2002) into changes including growth during puberty – those 'set off' by changes to hormone production – use a common five-stage model of pubertal changes. The five-stage model most commonly used was first developed during the 1960s by the British biologist and paediatrician James Tanner (1962; 1970; 1971). Later this chapter, in the *Research Focus* feature on Tanner's longitudinal research on

pubertal development, will explore how his five-stage model was developed. For now, it is worth noting the principal features of the five stages that will contextualise the upcoming discussion of individual changes and patterns of growth during puberty, post-pubertal adolescence and emerging adulthood.

Some versions of these five-stage tables include average ages and later on we will consider the usefulness of averaging out the ages at which researchers have observed these changes. At this point in the chapter it is useful to understand that all stage models (even Tanner's much-quoted and often-used model (see Tables 2.1 and 2.2)) are not able to demonstrate the continuous aspect of growth and development, and that individuals and individual aspects of growth can and do vary. It is also worth noting that much of the seminal, definitive and much-quoted work on physical development during puberty and adolescence was conducted during the 1960s and 1970s. We might conjecture that research interest in adolescence grew from the development of teenage culture in Britain, other parts of Europe and in North America during the late 1950s and 1960s – as we discussed in Chapter 1. You should note that research interest has continued in refining our understanding of 'normal' and particularly abnormal development during puberty and adolescence, but in general

Table 2.1 Tanner's Five Stages of Puberty – Boys

Stage	Genitals	Testicle length	Pubic hair	Annual height velocity	Other
1	infrequent erections	less than 1.6 cm	only villus hair (short, fine, light-coloured)	5.0 to 6.0 cm	adrenarche – increase in activity of the adrenal glands just before puberty
2	skin of scrotum thins and reddens; frequent erections	2.5 to 3.2 cm	sparse, straight, slightly pigmented	7.0 to 8.0 cm	leaner body
3	lengthening of penis	3.3 to 4.0 cm	coarser, darker, curled	8.0 cm	some temporary swelling of breasts, voice 'breaks', deepens
4	thickening of penis, darkening of scrotum skin	4.1 to 4.5 cm	adult type, but not beyond pubic area	10.0 cm	acne, underarm hair, voice deepens
5	adult genitals	up to 5 cm	spreading on to inner thigh	full height usually reached at age 18 or 19	beard growth, continuing muscle development

Table 2.2 Tanner's Five Stages of Puberty – Girls

Stage	Breasts	Pubic hair	Annual height velocity	Other
1	elevation of nipple	villus hair only	5.0 to 6.0 cm	adrenarche
2	breast buds palpable, enlarged areola	sparse, slightly pigmented	7.0 to 8.0 cm	clitoral enlargement; labia pigmentation
3	mammary extends beyond edge of areola	coarser, darker, curled	8.0 cm	acne, underarm hair
4	nipple mound stacked on areola mound	adult type, but not beyond pubic area	less than 7.0 cm	first menstruation
5	integral nipple mound	spreading on to inner thigh	final height reached at about age 16	adult genitals

more recent studies have confirmed or built on the original research. Therefore, in the remainder of the chapter we have cited the original seminal research alongside more recent complementary or follow-up studies.

Physical Growth During Puberty

The increases in the levels of the sex hormones discussed in a previous section result in a variety of dramatic changes in the bodies of adolescents. One of these changes is the rate of physical growth. After proceeding at an even pace since early childhood, growth suddenly surges when puberty arrives. In fact, one of the earliest signs of puberty for both girls and boys is the **adolescent growth spurt**. Figure 2.4 shows the typical rate of growth in height from birth to age 19, including the adolescent growth spurt. At **peak height velocity**, when the adolescent growth spurt is at its maximum, girls grow at about 9 cm per year, and boys grow at about 10.5 cm per year

(Tanner, 1971). The peak of bone growth velocity is 14 years (± 1.0 y) in boys and 12.5 (± 0.9 y) in girls and bone growth is maximal approximately six months after peak height velocity (Whiting et al., 2004). However, this varies between ethnic groups (Burrows et al., 2009). For all children, the rate of growth at peak height velocity is the highest it has been since they were 2 years old. It is worth noting again the similarities of some changes during puberty and those at 2 years of age and this idea will be referred to in this and other chapters.

As Figure 2.4 shows, girls typically reach the beginning of their growth spurt (and their peak height velocity) about two years earlier than boys. This is true of other aspects of physical development in puberty as well: girls mature about two years ahead of boys. Throughout childhood – until the growth spurt begins – boys are slightly taller on average than girls of the same age (DeRose and Brooks-Gunn, *ibid*.). Girls become taller on average for about two years in early adolescence, from age 11 to 13, the two years when they have hit their growth spurt but boys have

CONNECT AND EXTEND

To find out about ethnic differences in growth patterns between countries, read 'Secular trends in growth: the narrowing of ethnic differences in stature' by Stanley J. Ulijaszek in *Nutrition Bulletin*, Volume 26, Number 1 (March 2001), pp. 43–51

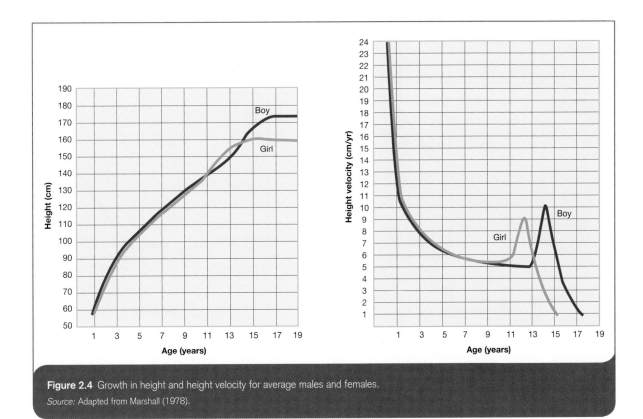

Figure 2.4 Growth in height and height velocity for average males and females.
Source: Adapted from Marshall (1978).

not. However, the earlier maturation of girls contributes to their smaller adult height, because the adolescent growth spurt also marks the beginning of the end of growth in height. Because girls begin their growth spurt earlier, they also reach their final height earlier – about age 16, on average, compared with about age 18 for boys (Archibald et al., 2003). Higher levels of testosterone also contribute to a higher average final height in boys (Donfield et al., 2007; Underwood & Van Wyk, 1981 – here's an example of earlier research with more recent follow-up or complementary research).

Girls typically reach their growth spurt two years earlier than boys.

During the adolescent growth spurt, not all parts of the body grow at the same pace. A certain amount of **asynchronicity** in growth during this time explains why some adolescents have a 'gangly' look early in puberty, as some parts of the body grow faster than others. The **extremities** – feet, hands and head – are the first to hit the growth spurt, followed by the arms and legs (Archibald et al., 2003). Some parts of the head grow more than others. The forehead becomes higher and wider, the mouth widens, the lips become fuller, and the chin, ears and nose become more prominent (Lopez, 2003; Mussen et al., 1990). The torso, chest and shoulders are the last parts of the body to reach the growth spurt and therefore the last to reach the end of their growth.

In addition to the growth spurt, a spurt in muscle growth occurs during puberty, primarily because of the increase in growth hormones (Naughton et al., 2000; Tanner, 1971) and as boys experience greater increases in testosterone than girls do, they also experience greater increases in muscle growth. As Figure 2.5 shows, girls and boys before puberty are very similar in their muscle mass.

Levels of body fat also surge during puberty, but body fat increases more for girls than for boys, as Figure 2.5 shows. As a consequence of these sex differences in muscle and fat growth, by the end of puberty boys have about 1.5 times as much muscle as

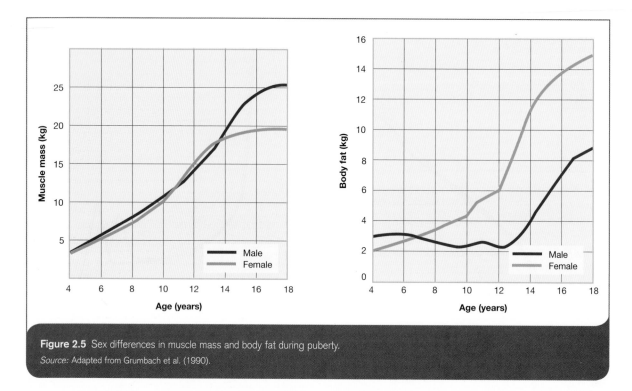

Figure 2.5 Sex differences in muscle mass and body fat during puberty.
Source: Adapted from Grumbach et al. (1990).

girls. Boys have a muscle-to-fat ratio of about 3:1, whereas the muscle-to-fat ratio for girls is 5:4 (de Guzman, 2006; Steinberg, 2006; Archibald et al., 2003; Grumbach et al., 1974). Other sex differences in body shape also develop during puberty. Hips and shoulders widen among both girls and boys, but hips widen more than shoulders in girls and shoulders widen more than hips in boys.

THINKING CRITICALLY

Given that girls naturally gain substantially more body fat than boys during puberty, why do some cultures create physical ideals that demand thinness in females once they reach puberty?

In both boys and girls, the heart becomes larger during puberty – on average, its weight almost doubles – and the heart rate falls, but boys' hearts grow more than girls' hearts do and their heart rates fall to a lower level (Irwin et al., 2003). By age 17, the average girl's heart rate is about five beats per minute faster than the average boy's (Joffe, 2000). A similar change takes place in the growth of the lungs. A measure of lung size called **vital capacity**, which means the amount of air that can be exhaled after a deep breath, increases rapidly for both boys and girls during puberty, but increases more for boys than for girls (Ford and Coleman, 1999). These sex differences in physical growth and functioning result in sex differences in strength and athletic ability during adolescence and beyond. Before puberty, boys and girls are about equal in strength and athletic performance, but during puberty boys overtake girls, and the difference remains throughout adulthood (DeRose and Brooks-Gunn, 2006).

Gender differences also exist in cultural expectations for physical activity in many cultures, with adolescent girls sometimes being discouraged from participating in sports in order to conform to cultural ideas of what it means to be 'feminine'. Boys are more likely to exercise in adolescence, and this gender difference contributes to the difference in athletic performance between adolescent boys and girls (Eiðsdóttir et al., 2008). A World Health Organisation (WHO) survey of 15-year-olds in 26 Western countries found that in every country, boys were more likely than girls to say they exercised vigorously at least twice a week outside of school (Smith, 2000). Across countries, about three-quarters of boys exercised at least twice a week, compared with about half of girls. In studies that take amount of exercise into account, the muscle-to-fat ratio is still higher for boys than for girls, but the difference is not as large as in studies that do not take exercise into account (DeRose and Brooks-Gunn, *ibid.*).

CONNECT AND EXTEND

For a fascinating account of the association of exercise in adolescence with exercise in adulthood (and with a cultural focus), read 'Who is physically active? Cultural capital and sports participation from adolescence to middle age – a 38-year follow-up study' by Lars-Magnus Engstrom in *Physical Education and Sport Pedagogy*, Volume 13, Number 4 (October 2008), pp. 319–343

Obesity

Although it is normal and healthy for young people to gain some weight during puberty, for many young people their weight gain goes well beyond what is healthy. Obesity has become a major health problem in industrialised countries and is becoming a problem in some developing countries as well (Hong et al., 2007; Werner and Bodin, 2007). The obesity pandemic originated in the US (see Figure 2.6 for statistics relating to 2004) before crossing to Europe and the world's other rich nations. It has, remarkably, penetrated even the world's poorest countries, especially in their urban areas. Obesity is defined by medical authorities as weighing 20 per cent or more above the maximum healthy weight for height, for males, and 25 per cent or more for females (Davies and Fitzgerald, 2008). WHO projects that by 2015, across the globe approximately 2.3 billion adults will be overweight; more than 700 million will be obese (WHO, 2010).

Across the developed world, obesity in adolescents has been increasing rapidly (Kosti and Panagiotakos, 2006; Lobstein et al., 2004). The rate of increase in obesity is increasing in Europe (Jackson-Leach and Lobstein, 2006) and there seems to be no sign of any improvement, although some countries face greater challenges than others. – see Figure 2.7.

The 'epidemic of obesity' is now very common in the UK. Almost a decade ago a national survey – the Health Survey for England 2004 – found the prevalence of obesity was a staggering 25 per cent in 11 to 15-year-olds (Reilly, 2006). Look at the trends in the figures for England issued by the UK's National Health

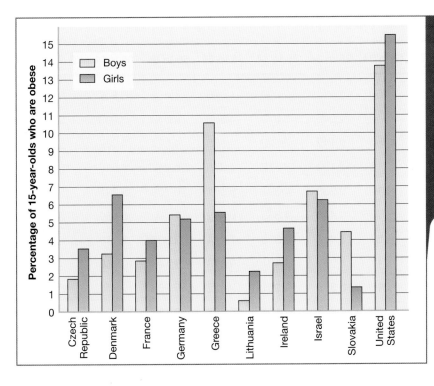

Figure 2.6 Rates of obesity among adolescents in selected countries. Why are rates of obesity so high among adolescents in the United States?

Source: Bowman (2004).

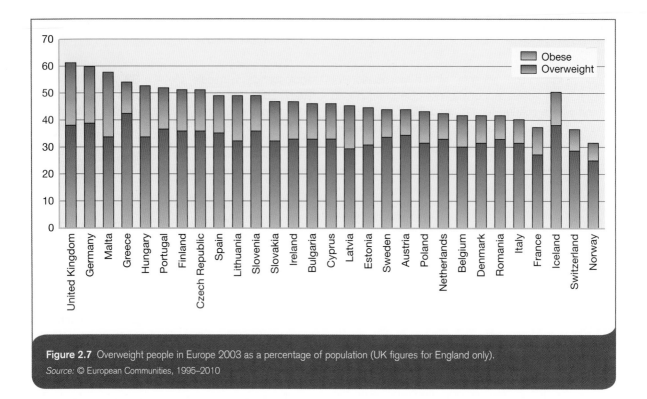

Figure 2.7 Overweight people in Europe 2003 as a percentage of population (UK figures for England only).
Source: © European Communities, 1995–2010

Service (presented here in Table 2.3) of hospital admissions in England with a primary or secondary diagnosis of obesity. What are the percentage increases for the different age groups compared with the total admissions for obesity?

Table 2.3 shows (as you might already have calculated) a five-fold increase in the diagnosis of obesity across all age groups and a shocking eight-fold increase in the 16 to 24 age group – the largest increase of any age group. Obese adolescents have higher leptin levels

Table 2.3 Hospital Admissions in England with a Diagnosis of Obesity, by Age Group, 1998/99 to 2008/09

	Total	Under 16	16 to 24	25 to 34	35 to 44	45 to 54	55 to 64	65 to74	75 and over
1998/99	21,344	654	560	1,972	2,990	4,286	4,683	3,847	2,340
1999/00	21,900	726	612	2,046	3,278	4,538	4,540	3,903	2,249
2000/01	22,878	781	654	2,142	3,522	4,656	4,877	4,009	2,190
2001/02	23,777	856	715	2,129	3,512	4,878	5,217	4,226	2,222
2002/03	29,237	1,117	912	2,288	4,371	5,661	6,721	5,391	2,738
2003/04	33,546	1,355	1,026	2,449	4,845	6,452	7,790	6,432	3,175
2004/05	40,741	1,506	1,457	3,449	5,953	7,424	9,086	7,813	4,036
2005/06	52,019	1,727	1,717	4,252	7,401	9,858	12,146	10,056	4,840
2006/07	67,211	1,896	2,316	5,319	9,961	12,922	15,882	12,571	6,296
2007/08	80,914	2,104	3,169	7,218	12,101	15,683	18,489	14,496	7,512
2008/09	102,987	2,229	4,326	9,899	15,508	19,971	23,136	18,234	9,531

Source: Hospital Epsiode Statistics, HES. The NHS Information Centre for Health and Social Care

CONNECT AND EXTEND

For a comprehensive overview of trends in child-hood and adolescent obesity read 'Childhood obesity: an overview' by John J. Reilly in *Children & Society*, Volume 21, Number 5 (September 2007), pp. 390–396

(Shalatin and Phillip, 2003) so it may be that increased obesity has contributed to the earlier onset of puberty (Cesario and Hughes, 2007; Žukauskaite et al., 2005) and that earlier onset of puberty has led to increased risks of endometrial (of the uterus) cancer among women in later life (Xu et al., 2006).

What is responsible for the disturbing trends in obesity among adolescents? Not surprisingly, diet and exercise are implicated. A more street-oriented lifestyle and a more commercialised leisure time for adolescents are associated with a higher intake of fast food (Roos et al., 2004) and fast-food meals, for example McDonald's, Burger King and KFC, tend to be extremely high in calories, and loaded with fat and sugar (Bowman, 2004). Furthermore, fast-food portions have increased dramatically (Fleming and Towey, 2003), as the burgers, drinks and French fry portions have become 'supersized'. Alongside the higher intake of fast foods has grown a culture of car use, fed by a fear of walking or cycling through school neighbour-hoods and parental responses that emphasised children's safety at the expense, it is argued by some, of developing their independence (Lorenc et al., 2008). European adolescents exercise less than medical experts recommend (Rabin et al., 2007), and young females have especially low rates of exercise (Mackey and La Greca, 2007). Where adolescent girls do take up exercise to improve fitness, weight-related sport participation is significantly associated with body dissatisfaction, and lower self-esteem (de Bruin et al., 2009).

One comparatively recent study found a steep decline in physical activity from age 9 to 15 (Nader et al., 2008). Rather than using reports of physical activity from the participants or their parents, the researchers had the participants wear an 'accelerometer', a device that measures movement, for one week. At age 9, children engaged in about three hours of physical activity a day on both weekdays and weekends. However, from age 9 to 15 the rate of physical activity declined steadily, and at age 15 physical activity was down to less than an hour on weekdays and just a half-hour on weekends. The study did not investigate the reasons for the decline.

Time watching television has been found to be related to obesity (Dowda et al., 2001), but people in many parts of Europe watch about the same amount of television (van den Broek, 2002) and this hasn't changed in the UK much in the last ten years (BARB, 2010). Small differences in television viewing times cannot explain the cross-national differences in obesity. Of course, television has also been found to be the prime promotional medium for unhealthy foods such as savoury snacks and confectionary consumed by children across many European countries (Matthews, 2008) so there may be a less obvious 'television effect' than just a sedentary lifestyle.

Computer games have also been blamed (Davies and Fitzgerald, 2008), but again, computer games are popular in countries with widely different rates of adolescent obesity. Similarly, obesity has been found to run in families – when parents are obese, adolescents are at higher risk of obesity (Davies and Fitzgerald, 2008; Corrado et al., 2004; Dowda et al., 2001) – which suggests that heredity may be involved, but this cannot explain the steep increase in obesity in recent decades.

Obesity in adolescence is a source of concern not just because it is unhealthy in adolescence but because it predicts long-term health problems (Davies and Fitzgerald, 2008; Fleming and Towey, 2003). About 80 per cent of obese adolescents remain obese in adulthood (Engeland et al., 2004). A variety of health risks result from obesity in adulthood, including diabetes, stroke and heart disease (Boyle, 2004; Corrado et al., 2004). To address the problem, medical professionals have developed interventions intended to reduce obesity during childhood and adolescence, usually through schools and community groups (Gao et al., 2008). Successful programmes have a variety of components, including nutrition education, dietary assessment, modifications of meals offered in the school and efforts to increase physical activity (Stice et al., 2006; Graf et al., 2008). Such programmes can face barriers, especially resistance from adolescents who see no need to change and parents who are disinclined to become more involved. Yet even comparatively short-term changes as part of school and community interventions can lead to longer-term improvement (Macias-Cervantes et al., 2009).

FOCUS ON YOUTH IN THE MEDIA

'Fat Kids' on YouTube

The year 2005 saw the launch of an Internet media phenomenon – YouTube – that some would argue has had as much global and social impact as the development of the original World Wide Web (Harley and Fitzpatrick, 2009; Søraker, 2008). YouTube is a video-sharing website on which users can upload and view videos. The website was created in 2005 by three former PayPal employees and uses video technology to display film clips, TV clips, music videos, video blogs and home-made movies. Some of the picture quality is very poor but that adds to the sense of authenticity and the cutting-edge nature of some of what is available (Gehl, 2009). In November 2006, about a year after its launch, YouTube was bought for $1.65 billion, and now operates as a subsidiary of Google. It is one of the main ways in which adolescents and young adults access and view music videos (Webb, 2007).

The YouTube site contains enormous numbers of clips of accidents, 'funny' falls, some set up or choreographed by the youngsters involved, and others 'captured' as a result of many youngsters using their iPhones or smart phones to video themselves and their friends in the typical pursuits of adolescence. If you enter search terms into the site, the main page almost instantly gives access and choice of many thousands of video clips. Log on now and try 'obese adolescents' – you'll see a few interesting short documentary films on gastric banding, summer camps and a suggested association between obesity and bullying. When we tried it, one of the 120 results (April 2011) or so included the pejorative but widely used term 'fat kid'. Entering 'fat kid' into the search box garnered 42,500 results and we narrowed that down by following the suggested: 'fat kid falls'; 'fat kid falls in water'; and 'fat kid gets shot with paint balls'. For 'fat kid falls', there were 7100 results which included 'fat kid falls off rollercoaster'.

We watched 'fat kid falls off rollercoaster'. We're not sure if that is mum sitting beside her youngster but she seems to find his extreme discomfort and terror highly amusing and the more we watched the clip, the funnier it seemed to get. Why is this? Is it because of the young man's reaction alone or because of his size and his reaction? The more clips you watch, the more you wonder to what extent unfortunate and potentially painful things happening to youngsters who look obese are funnier to many of us than the same thing happening to adolescents who don't appear to be obese. **http://www.youtube.com/watch?v=dXsoa6rd-n8**

Billy Bunter

Was Billy Bunter in the Greyfriars stories of the 1940s and 1950s funny because of the silly situations he got himself into at boarding school or because it was a fat boy who got himself into silly situations at boarding school? Billy Bunter became a television character and was played in 40 half-hour episodes by Gerald Campion in a BBC television series between 1952 and 1961. The television show was totally centred on Bunter, his attempts to steal food or 'tuck' and his depiction as almost constantly eating. What a figure of fun he is! The programmes were filmed in black and white, and 12 still exist in the BBC's Film and Videotape Archive. You can watch some of this wonderful historic material on YouTube. For

Billy Bunter

another example of 'fat and funny' search on YouTube for Chunky in the 1980s teenage adventure movie, *The Goonies.*

More recently, in the animation series *Family Guy* the young character Stewie is seen following fat people around playing a tuba. 'Cut it out!' they say, 'I have a glandular problem', before falling forward like a felled tree. Again, you can check out these clips on YouTube and look for more examples.

What is happening here? Is fat funny? The association between compulsive eating, fatness, misfortune and funny situations is made throughout the popular media (Dorey and McCool, 2009; Evans et al., 2006; Giles, 2003) and appears to be across time – as we have seen – and different cultures (F. Johnson et al., 2008; Greenhalgh et al., 2005). We are drawn into enjoying the humour of poking fun at the obese, even those of us who 'carry a little extra' ourselves.

THINKING CRITICALLY

What do you think are some of the social and psychological consequences of adolescents becoming obese? Who is to blame and what makes you think that? How can adolescent obesity be best tackled by families, schools, and health and social services?

Physical Functioning in Emerging Adulthood

For most people, the peak of their physical functioning comes during emerging adulthood.

Although most people reach their maximum height by the end of adolescence, in other ways emerging adulthood rather than adolescence is the period of peak physical functioning. Even after maximum height is attained, the bones continue to grow in density, and peak bone mass is reached in the 20s (Zumwalt, 2008). A measure of physical stamina called **maximum oxygen uptake (VO$_2$ max)** – which reflects the ability of the body to take in oxygen and transport it to various organs – improves significantly during adolescence (Wong et al., 2008), during emerging adulthood (Bangsbo et al., 2008) and peaks in the early 20s (Neder et al., 1999; Plowman et al., 1979). Similarly, **cardiac output**, the quantity of blood flow from the heart, peaks at around age 25 (Bromley et al., 2006; Lakatta, 1990). Reaction time is also faster in the early 20s than at any other time of life (Der and Deary, 2006). Studies of grip strength among men show the same pattern, with a peak in the 20s followed by a steady decline (Massy-Westropp et al., 2004) All together, for most people emerging adulthood is the time of life when they are at the zenith of their fitness and strength.

Emerging adulthood is also the period of the lifespan with the least susceptibility to physical illnesses (Case and Deaton, 2005). This is especially true in modern times, when vaccines and medical treatments have dramatically lowered the risk of diseases such as polio that used to strike mainly during these years (Dobson, 2008). Emerging adults are no longer vulnerable to the illnesses and diseases of childhood, and with rare exceptions they are not yet vulnerable to diseases such as cancer and heart disease that rise in prevalence later in adulthood. The immune system is at its most effective during the emerging adult years. Consequently, the late teens and early 20s are the years of fewest hospital stays and fewest days spent sick at home (Anderson et al., 2007). In many ways, then, your youth is an exceptionally healthy time of life.

This is not the whole story, however. The lifestyles of many emerging adults often include a variety of factors that can undermine physical and mental health, such as poor nutrition, lack of sleep, and the high stress of trying to juggle university and work or multiple jobs (Ma et al., 2002; Steptoe and Wardle, 2001). Furthermore, in the industrialised countries the late teens and early 20s are the years of highest incidence of a variety of types of disease, injury, and death due to risky behaviour (see Chapter 12).

CONNECT AND EXTEND

How do practitioners in an outpatient clinic identify adolescents prone to risk-taking behaviours? Researchers in Barcelona identified five variables (e.g. relationship with parents and teachers) to create a screening tool to detect at least one of ten risky behaviours (e.g. driving while intoxicated, riding with an intoxicated driver, not always using a seat belt, and not always using a helmet). This is a really interesting paper rooted in professional practice. Read 'Behaviour evaluation for risk-taking adolescents (BERTA): an easy to use and assess instrument to detect adolescent risky behaviours in a clinical setting' by Joan-Carles Suris, Manel Nebot and Núria Parera in the *European Journal of Pediatrics*, Volume 164, Number 6 (June 2005), pp. 371–376

Although driving or being a passenger in a car should not be considered a risky behaviour, there is a higher than average risk of death and injury to young drivers and their passengers. In England during 2007, 32 per cent of car driver deaths and 40 per cent of car passenger deaths were people aged between 17 and 24. Young male drivers were much more likely to be killed or seriously injured in a car accident than young female drivers; 1,815 male drivers aged between 17 and 24 were killed or seriously injured in 2007, compared with 665 female drivers in the same age group (Office for National Statistics, 2010a).

In 2006, just over one-quarter (26 per cent) of 10 to 25 year olds in England and Wales were victims of personal crime including robbery, assault and wounding (Office for National Statistics, 2010b). Rates of contracting sexually transmitted diseases, including HIV, are highest in the early 20s (Weinstock et al., 2004; Teitler, 2002). Most kinds of substance use and abuse also peak in the early 20s (Eisner, 2002). We will discuss the causes of these problems in Chapter 12 but for now we need to return to our description of the changes that take place during puberty. In addition to the changes in physical growth and functioning described so far, two other kinds of changes take place in the adolescent's body in response to increased sex hormones during puberty.

Primary Sex Characteristics

Primary sex characteristics involve the production of eggs and sperm and the development of the sex organs. **Secondary sex characteristics** are other bodily changes of puberty, not including the ones related directly to reproduction.

Egg and Sperm Production

As previously explained, increases in the sex hormones at puberty cause eggs to develop in the ovaries of females and sperm to be produced in the testes of males. The development of the gametes is quite different for the two sexes. Females are born with about 400,000 immature eggs in each ovary. By puberty, this number has declined to about 80,000 in each ovary. Once a girl reaches menarche (her first menstrual period) and begins having menstrual cycles, one egg develops into a mature egg, or **ovum** (plural: ova), every 28 days or so. Females release about 400 eggs over the course of their reproductive lives.

In contrast, males have no sperm in their testes when they are born, and they do not produce any until they reach puberty. The first production of sperm in boys is called **spermarche** and it takes place on average at age 12 (Finkelstein, 2001b). Once spermarche arrives, boys produce sperm in astonishing quantities. There are between 30 and 500 million sperm in the typical male ejaculation, which means that the average male produces millions of sperm every day. If you are a man, you will probably produce over a million sperm during the time you read this chapter – even if you are a fast reader!

Why so many? One reason is that the environment of the female body is not very hospitable to sperm. The female's immune system registers sperm as foreign bodies and begins attacking them immediately. A second reason is that sperm have, in relation to their size, a long way to go to reach the ovum. They have to make their way along and through the various structures of the female reproductive anatomy. So it helps to have a lot of sperm wiggling their way toward the ovum, because this increases the likelihood that some of them may make it to the ovum at the right time for fertilisation to take place.

The Male and Female Reproductive Anatomy

The changes of puberty prepare the body for sexual reproduction, and during puberty the sex organs undergo a number of important changes as part of that preparation. In males, both the penis and the testes grow substantially in puberty (King, 2005). The penis doubles in length and diameter. In its mature form, the flaccid (limp) penis averages 6 to 8 cm in length and about 3 cm in diameter. The tumescent (erect) penis averages 14 to 16 cm in length and 3½ cm in diameter. The growth of the testes during puberty is even more pronounced – they increase 2½ times in length and 8½ times in weight, on average. The dramatic growth of the testes reflects the production of the many millions of sperm.

In females, the external sex organs are known as the **vulva**, which includes the **labia majora** (Latin for 'large lips'), the **labia minora** (Latin for 'small lips') and the **clitoris**. The vulva grows substantially in puberty (King, 2005). The ovaries also increase greatly in size and weight. Just as the testes grow as a consequence of sperm production, the growth of the ovaries reflects the growth of maturing ova. Furthermore, the uterus doubles in length during puberty, growing to a mature length of about 7½ cm, about the size of a closed fist. The vagina also increases in length, and its colour deepens.

As noted earlier, an ovum is released in each monthly cycle. The two ovaries typically alternate months, with one releasing an ovum and then the other. The ovum moves along the fallopian tube and travels to the uterus. During this time, a lining of blood builds up in the uterus in preparation for the possibility of receiving and providing nutrients for the fertilised egg. If the ovum becomes fertilised by a sperm during its journey to the uterus, the fertilised egg begins dividing immediately. When it reaches the uterus it implants in the wall of the uterus and continues developing. If the ovum is not fertilised, it is evacuated during menstruation along with the blood lining of the uterus.

Although menarche is a girl's first menstruation, it is not the same as the first ovulation. On the contrary, the *majority* of a girl's menstrual cycles in the first two years after menarche do not include ovulation, and in the third and fourth years only about a third to a half of cycles include ovulation (Finkelstein, 2001c). It is only after four years of menstruation that girls consistently ovulate with each menstrual cycle. This early inconsistency leads some sexually active adolescent girls to believe they are infertile, but this is an unfortunate misunderstanding. Fertility may be inconsistent and unpredictable during the first four years after menarche, but it is certainly possible for most girls. Whether boys experience a similar lag between spermarche and the production of sperm capable of fertilising an egg is not known.

Secondary Sex Characteristics

All the primary sex characteristics are directly related to reproduction. In addition to these changes, numerous other bodily changes take place as part of puberty but are not directly related to reproduction. These changes are known as secondary sex characteristics.

Some secondary sex characteristics develop for only males or only females, but for the most part the changes that happen to one sex also happen to the other, to some degree. Both males and females grow hair in their pubic areas and underneath their arms. Both also grow facial hair – you knew that males do, but you may not have realised that females also grow hair, just a slight amount, on their faces during puberty. Similarly, increased hairiness on the arms and legs is more pronounced in males, but females also grow more hair on their limbs at puberty. Boys also begin to grow hair on their chests and sometimes on their shoulders and backs as well, whereas girls typically do not.

Both males and females experience various changes in their skin and bones (Yingling, 2009). The skin becomes rougher, especially around the thighs and upper arms. The sweat glands in the skin increase production, making the skin oilier and more prone to acne, and resulting in a stronger body odour. Also, bones become harder and thicker throughout the body (Zumwalt, 2008). Males and females both experience a deepening of the voice as the vocal cords lengthen, with males experiencing a deeper drop in pitch. Although testosterone concentrations were not predictive of the rate or amount of pitch change, there is a correlation with testis volume (Harries et al., 1997).

CONNECT AND EXTEND

When adolescents perceive their skin to be poorly evaluated by others, this has implications for self-perception and acts as a barrier to exercise participation. For the evidence read 'Not just "skin deep": psychosocial effects of dermatological-related social anxiety in a sample of acne patients' by Tom Loney, Martyn Standage and Stephen Lewis in the *Journal of Health Psychology,* Volume 13, Number 1 (January 2008), pp. 47–54

'I was about six months younger than everyone else in my class, and so for about six months after my friends had begun to develop (that was the word we used, develop), I was not particularly worried. I would sit in the bath and look down at my breasts and know that any day now, they would start growing like everyone else's. They didn't ... "Don't worry about it", said my friend Libby some months later, when things had not improved. "You'll get them after you're married." "What are you talking about?" I said. "When you get married," Libby explained, "your husband will touch your breasts and rub them and kiss them and they'll grow."'

(Nora Ephron, 2000, pp. 2–4)

Breast development, a secondary sex characteristic that occurs in females, also occurs in a substantial proportion of males. About a quarter of boys experience enlargement of the breasts by about midway through puberty. This can be a source of alarm, embarrassment and anxiety for adolescent boys, but for the majority of them the enlargement recedes within a year (Bembo and Carlson, 2004; Tanner, 1970).

For girls, the breasts go through a series of predictable stages of development (Figure 2.8). The earliest indication of breast development, a slight enlargement of the breasts known as **breast buds**, is also one of the first outward signs of puberty in most girls (Žukauskaite et al., 2005; Tanner, 1971, *ibid*.). During this early stage, there is also an enlargement of the area surrounding the nipple, called the **areola**. In the later stages of breast development, the breasts continue to enlarge, and the areola first rises with the nipple to form a mound above the breast, then recedes to the level of the breast while the nipple remains projected (Archibald et al., 2003).

Table 2.4 provides a useful summary and reminder of the physical changes in males and females during puberty.

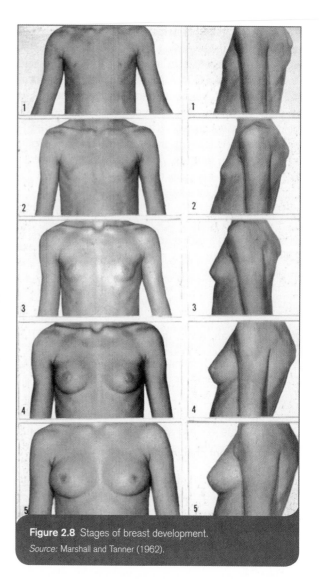

Figure 2.8 Stages of breast development.
Source: Marshall and Tanner (1962).

THINKING CRITICALLY

Puberty involves the development of sexual maturation. Among the secondary sex characteristics described here, which are viewed in your culture as enhancing sexual interest and attractiveness between males and females? Which are not?

The Order of Pubertal Events

In our earlier discussion of James Tanner's five-stage model of the order of pubertal changes we showed that puberty is composed of many events and processes, typically stretching out over several years. A great deal of variability exists among individuals in the timing of pubertal events. Among young people in industrialised countries the first pubertal events may occur as early as age 8 in girls and age 9 or 10 in boys, or as late as age 13 (Ge et al., 2007; Sun et al., 2005). The duration between the initiation of the first pubertal event and full pubertal maturation can be as short as a year and a half or as long as six years (Tanner, 1962) or even nine years if you accept much of the available wisdom

Table 2.4 Summary of Physical Changes During Adolescence

Both sexes	Males only	Females only
Pubic hair	Sperm production	Ovulation/menstruation
Underarm hair	Wider shoulders and chest	Breast development
Facial hair	Increased proportion of muscle to fat	Broader hips/pelvis
Arm and leg hair	Chest hair	Increased proportion of fat to muscle
Rougher skin (especially thighs, upper arms)	Shoulder and back hair	
Oilier skin, stronger body odour		
Harder bones		
Lower voice		
Growth spurt		
Larger forehead		
Wider mouth		
Fuller lips		
More prominent chin, ears, nose		

that puberty can start as early as 8 for girls, 9/10 for boys and finish as late as 17 for girls and 19 for boys. Even James Tanner's (1962) findings about the timing of puberty are open to criticism that his time frames are a result of the particular group he researched, and that human variation is part of what makes each of us unique and special. One thing is clear though, what happens during puberty is really important to what else happens during adolescence and emerging adulthood.

In the early teens (consequent to the time frames suggested by Tanner) some adolescents may have nearly finished their pubertal development while others have barely begun. Because adolescents experience the first events of puberty at different ages and proceed through puberty at different rates, age alone is a very poor predictor of an adolescent's pubertal development (Archibald et al., 2003). This is an important idea.

CONNECT AND EXTEND

Pupils shift their time of day preferences from 'morningness' to 'eveningness' during the age of puberty. Therefore, early school start times may have a negative influence on school functioning, adolescent health and academic attainment. For the evidence from a German study read 'Correlation between morningness–eveningness and final school leaving exams' by Christoph Randler and Daniela Frech in *Biological Rhythm Research*, Volume 37, Number 3 (2006), pp. 233 – 239

More consistency can be seen in the order of pubertal events than in the ages they begin or the amount of time it takes to complete them (Finkelstein, 2001b; Archibald et al., *ibid.*). For girls, downy pubic hair is often the first sign of the beginning of puberty, followed closely by the appearance of breast buds (for about 20 per cent of girls, breast buds precede the first sign of pubic hair). The next event for girls is usually the growth spurt, along with the growth of the sexual and reproductive organs (vulva, uterus and vagina). Menarche, the development of underarm hair and the secretion of increased skin oil and sweat occur relatively late in puberty for most girls.

For boys, the first outward sign of puberty is usually the growth of the testes, along with or closely followed by the beginning of pubic hair (Archibald et al., *ibid.*). These events are followed (usually about a year later) by the initiation of the growth spurt and the increased growth of the penis, along with the beginning of the deepening of the voice. Spermarche takes place at age 12 to 14 for most boys. In boys as in girls, the growth of underarm hair and the secretion of increased skin oil and sweat take place relatively late in puberty. For boys, facial hair is also one of the later developments of puberty, usually beginning about four or five years after the first outward events of puberty.

Virtually all the studies we have been considering in this section have been conducted with white adolescents in the West. In fact, the main source of our information about physical growth and functioning in adolescence remains the studies by Tanner and his colleagues (see the later *Research Focus* feature), which were mostly conducted 40 to 50 years ago on British adolescents who were in foster homes. Tanner's findings have been verified in numerous studies of white adolescents in the United States (e.g. Archibald et al., *ibid.*; Susman et al., 2003), but we do not have similarly detailed information on other ethnic and cultural groups around the world.

However, three historical studies demonstrate the variations that may exist in other groups. Among the Kikuyu, a culture in Kenya, boys show the first physical changes of puberty *before* their female peers (Worthman, 1987), a reversal of the Western pattern. In a study of Chinese girls, Lee et al. (1963) found that pubic hair began to develop in most girls about two years after the development of breast buds, and only a few months before menarche. This is a sharp contrast to the pattern for the girls in Tanner's studies, who typically began to develop pubic hair at about the same time they developed breast buds, usually two years before menarche (Tanner, 1971).

Given a similar environment, variation in the order and timing of pubertal events among adolescents appears to be due to genetics. The more similar two people are genetically, the more similar they tend to be in the timing of their pubertal events, with identical twins – hardly surprisingly – the most similar of all (Ge et al., 2007; van den Berg and Boomsma, 2007). However, the key phrase here is 'given a similar environment'. In reality, the environments adolescents experience differ greatly, both within and between countries. These differences have an effect on the timing of puberty, as we will see in detail in the following section.

CULTURAL, SOCIAL AND PSYCHOLOGICAL RESPONSES TO PUBERTY

Whatever their culture, all humans go through the physical and biological changes of puberty. However, even here culture's effects are profound. Cultural diets and levels of health and nutrition influence the timing of the initiation of puberty. Perhaps more importantly, cultures define the meaning and significance of pubertal change in different ways. These cultural definitions in turn influence the ways that adolescents interpret and experience their passage through puberty. First we will look at culture and pubertal timing and the meaning of puberty. Then we will examine social and personal responses to puberty, with a focus on differences between adolescents who mature relatively early and adolescents who mature relatively late.

Culture and the Timing of Puberty

How do cultures influence the timing of the initiation of puberty? The definition of culture includes a group's 'technologies' such as food production and medical care. The age at which puberty begins is strongly influenced by the extent to which food production provides for adequate nutrition and medical care provides for good health throughout childhood. In general, puberty begins earlier in cultures where good nutrition and medical care are widely available (Ebling, 2005).

Persuasive historical evidence for the influence of technologies on pubertal timing comes from records showing a steady decrease in the average age of menarche in industrialised countries over the past 150 years. This kind of change in a population over time is called a **secular trend** (Moreno et al., 2005). As you can see from Figure 2.9, a secular trend downward in

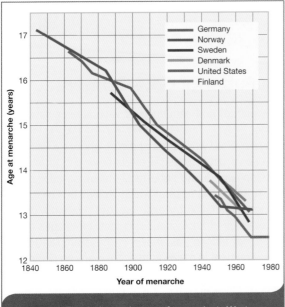

Figure 2.9 The decline in the age of menarche in Western countries.
Source: Adapted from Eveleth and Tanner (1990).

et al., 2002). In countries that have undergone rapid economic development in recent decades, such as China and South Korea, a corresponding decline in the average age of menarche has been recorded (Cho et al., 2010; Graham et al., 1999; Park et al., 1999).

With respect to nutrition in particular, substantial evidence shows that girls who are involved in activities in which there is a great deal of pressure to keep their weight down, such as ballet, skating and gymnastics, experience later menarche and have inconsistent periods once they begin to menstruate (Vadocz et al., 2002; Picard, 1999). The body appears to respond to lower than expected weight gain as a nutritional deficiency and so it delays menarche.

THINKING CRITICALLY

In your view, what potential social and psychological problems may develop as a consequence of girls showing signs of reaching puberty (such as initial breast development) as early as 8 or 9 years old?

the age of menarche has occurred in many European countries and the USA. Menarche is not a perfect indicator of the initiation of puberty – as we have discussed, the first outward signs of puberty appear much earlier for most girls, and of course menarche does not apply to boys. However, menarche is a reasonably good indicator of when other events have begun, and it is a reasonable assumption that if the downward secular trend in the age of puberty has occurred for females, it has occurred for males as well. Menarche is also the only aspect of pubertal development for which we have records going back so many decades. Scholars believe that the secular trend in the age of menarche is due to improvements in nutrition and medical care that have taken place during the past 150 years (Archibald et al., 2003). As medical advances have reduced illnesses and advances in food production have enhanced nutrition, puberty has come sooner. As promised earlier, now seems a good time to look in some detail at the historic research of James Tanner and his colleagues into the various aspects of puberty as this relates closely to the earlier timing of puberty that is shown clearly in Figure 2.10.

Further evidence of the role of nutrition and medical care in pubertal timing comes from cultural comparisons in the present. When we look around the world, we find that the average age of menarche is lowest in industrialised countries, where adequacy of nutrition and medical care contributes to higher birth weights and childhood growth trajectories (dos Santos Silva

Given that the secular trend in the age of menarche was steadily downward for over a century in industrialised countries, will girls someday begin menstruating in middle childhood or even earlier? Apparently not. In most industrialised countries the median age of menarche has been more or less stable since about 1970 (McDowell et al., 2007; Susman et al., 2003). Although there is some evidence that a downward secular trend for breast development and pubic hair may have continued since that time (Herman-Giddens et al., 2001), human females appear to have a genetically established **reaction range** for the age of menarche. This means that genes establish a range of possible times when menarche may begin and environment determines the actual timing of menarche within that range.

To summarise, the healthier the environment, the lower the timing of menarche. However, the reaction range has boundaries. Even under relatively unhealthy conditions, most girls will eventually reach menarche, and even in conditions of optimal health there is a lower boundary age below which menarche is unlikely to fall. Because the timing of menarche in industrialised countries has changed little in recent decades, it appears that girls in these countries have reached the lower boundary age of their reaction range for menarche.

RESEARCH FOCUS

R

Tanner's Longitudinal Research on Pubertal Development

James M. Tanner was a British biologist who studied the pattern and sequence of various aspects of physical development during puberty (Marshall and Tanner, 1970; Tanner, 1991; 1971; 1962). His research took place mainly during the 1960s and 1970s and involved white boys and girls who were living in state-run foster homes in Great Britain. Through the use of direct physical evaluations and photographs, he made careful assessments of growth and development during puberty. By following adolescents over a period of many years, he was able to establish the typical ages at which various processes of pubertal development begin and end, as well as the range of variation for each process. His work on adolescents' physical development is widely accepted by scholars of adolescence; in fact, the stages of various aspects of pubertal development are known as 'Tanner stages', as shown in the examples for breast development in females (see Figure 2.8), genital development in males (see accompanying photo) and in Tables 2.1 and 2.2 of this chapter.

Tanner and his colleagues focused on specific aspects of physical development during puberty: the growth spurt; the development of pubic hair; genital maturity in boys; the development of breasts in girls; and menarche in girls (Figure 2.10). For breast development (girls), genital maturity (boys) and pubic hair, Tanner defined a sequence of five stages as described earlier in this chapter. Remember that stage 1 is the prepubertal stage, when no physical changes have appeared; stage 5 is the stage when maturity has been reached and growth is completed; and stages 2, 3 and 4 describe levels of development in between. In addition to the stages, Tanner described other bodily changes such as muscle growth and the composition of the blood (Tanner, 1971).

The adolescents Tanner studied were mainly from low SES families, and many of them probably did not receive optimal physical care during childhood (Marshall and Tanner, 1970). They were living in foster homes, which can indicate that there may have been problems of some kind in their original families. Thus, the adolescents in Tanner's studies were not selected randomly and were in many ways not truly representative of the larger population of adolescents, even the larger population of white British adolescents. Nevertheless, Tanner's description of development in puberty has held up very well. Since his original studies, Tanner and his colleagues have also researched development during puberty in other

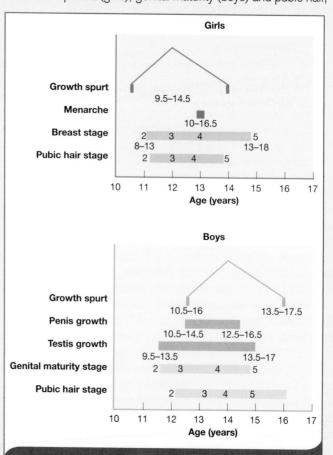

Figure 2.10 Typical age ranges for pubertal development.
Source: Adapted from Marshall and Tanner (1970), p. 22.

countries in various parts of the world and have found – as reported earlier – that the timing and pace of development during puberty vary widely depending on the levels of nutrition and medical care available to adolescents (Eveleth and Tanner, 1990).

Tanner's research was longitudinal. A longitudinal study is a study in which the same individuals are followed across time and data on them are collected on more than one occasion. The range of time involved can vary from a few weeks to an entire lifetime. This kind of study is different from a **cross-sectional study**, which examines many individuals at one point in time. Both kinds of studies are valuable, but there are certain kinds of information that can be gained only with a longitudinal study. For example, in Tanner's research, the only way to find out how long it typically takes for females to develop from stage 1 to stage 5 of breast development is through a longitudinal study. If breast development were assessed with a cross-sectional study, it would be difficult to tell for each girl how long it had taken for her to develop to that stage and how long it would take for her to develop to the next stage. With a longitudinal study, this can be assessed quite precisely.

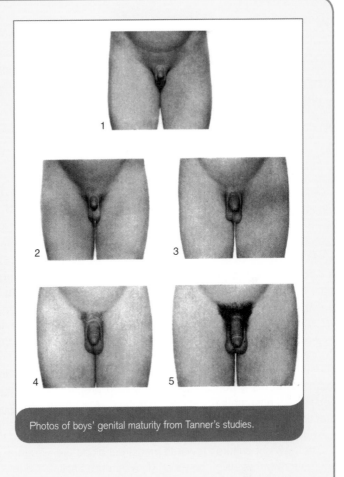

Photos of boys' genital maturity from Tanner's studies.

Cultural Responses to Puberty: Puberty Rituals

Puberty has been marked with rituals in many cultures through history as the departure from childhood and the entrance into adolescence, particularly in traditional cultures. Not all traditional cultures have such rituals, but they are quite common, especially for girls. In a landmark study, anthropologists Alice Schlegel and Herbert Barry (1991) analysed information on adolescent development across 186 traditional cultures and reported that the majority had some kind of ritual initiation into adolescence at the beginning of puberty: 68 per cent had a puberty ritual for boys, 79 per cent for girls.

Schlegel and Barry found that menarche is the pubertal event that is most often marked by ritual. In many cultures, menarche initiates a monthly ritual related to menstruation that lasts throughout a

Menarche is often marked by a ritual in traditional cultures. Here, girls of the N'Jembe tribe of West Africa prepare for their initiation.

CONNECT AND EXTEND

For a disturbing account from the north of Ireland of how women used menstrual blood as a means of resisting the state – an extraordinary cultural phenomenon – read 'Menstrual blood as a weapon of resistance' by Theresa O'Keefe in the *International Feminist Journal of Politics,* Volume 8, Number 4 (2006), pp. 535–556

woman's reproductive life. It is remarkably common for cultures to have strong beliefs concerning the power of menstrual blood. Such beliefs are not universal, but they have been common in all parts of the world, in a wide variety of cultures. Menstrual blood is often believed to present a danger to the growth and life of crops, to the health of livestock, to the success of hunters and to the health and well-being of other people, particularly the menstruating woman's husband (Howie and Shail, 2005). Consequently, the behaviour and movement of menstruating women in the developing world are often restricted in many domains, including food preparation and consumption, social activities, religious practices, bathing, school attendance and sexual activities (Mensch et al., 1998).

The views of cultures towards menstrual blood are not uniformly negative, however (Howie and Shail, 2005). For example, it is sometimes seen as promoting fertility and is used in fertility rituals. Some cultures use menstrual blood in the treatment of medical conditions, and some use it to make love potions (Hatfield, 2005). Sometimes both positive and negative beliefs about menstruation exist within the same culture.

A historical example of cultural ambivalence towards menstruation was found among the Asante, a culture in the African nation of Ghana (Buckley and Gottlieb, 1988). Among the Asante, menstruating women were subject to numerous stringent regulations concerning where they may go and what they may do, and the penalty for violating these taboos could be death. However, the Asante also celebrated girls' menarche with an elaborate ritual celebration. The menarcheal girl sat in public view under a canopy (a symbol of honour usually reserved for royalty), while others came before her to congratulate her, present her with gifts and perform songs and dances in her honour. Thus, on this occasion menstruation was celebrated, even though the

rest of the time it was viewed with a great deal of dread and fear.

There are few examples in industrial countries of 'coming of age' rituals similar to that of the many colourful and challenging rituals to be found amongst the hunter–gatherer cultures of Africa and South America. One interesting example of a puberty ritual for both males and females comes from the islands known as Samoa, in the Pacific Ocean near New Zealand. The traditional rite of passage – a ceremony marking the coming of age – involved an elaborate process of tattooing between the ages of 14 and 16 of much of the body and lower limbs. Samoa became known to many early in the twentieth century when the anthropologist Margaret Mead wrote a book about Samoan adolescence, *Coming of Age in Samoa* (1928), which was widely read in Europe (and, in fact, all over the world). Many people were fascinated by the stark contrast between adolescence in Samoa and adolescence in the West.

Of course, it is unlikely that here in Europe we will come into much contact with Samoan young people but we do have 'sub-cultures' within our broadly comparable pan-European culture that might also have outward signs of coming of age. (Some European adolescents do indeed submit to tattooing and body piercing – perhaps as a sign of increasing independence from their parents, who may not be too pleased about a pierced tongue or a beautiful butterfly adorning a young ankle.)

Countries of Europe are increasingly multi cultural – an observation explicitly explored in Chapter 4, but throughout this book – and many of the cultural differences that are found in our nation states are to an increasing extent based upon religious–ethnic differences rather than regional–tribal differences; an idea that we explored in Chapter 1. In the *Cultural Focus* feature that follows rituals of 'coming of age' based upon religious–ethnic differences are explored.

CULTURAL FOCUS

Coming of Age

In the Hindi tradition, two forms of Upanayana – initiation – can be found. For boys the ceremony of Kesanta Kala marks the first shaving of facial hair and the Ritu Kala marks a girl's first menstruation. Both ceremonies are an initiation into society and mark spiritual adulthood and responsibility. The ceremonies are informal, often taking place at home without a priest, where older members of the family give their blessings, sing spiritual songs and offer gifts, including a first sari for the girl.

Muslims celebrate the full public reading or reciting of the Qur'an Khatam Qur'an at around the time of puberty. In some parts of the world celebrations include the circumcision of boys to mark their progress to adulthood but in Europe circumcision is more usually performed at the age of 7 or seven days after birth. The nearest the Sikh tradition has to an initiation into adulthood is the Amrit where the initiate joins Khalsa, the community of Sikhs who belong to God, by observing the disciplines of the religion. The private ceremony includes drinking from a bowl shared by all those who are Khalsa.

Christian young people will traditionally have prepared for and attend a service of confirmation. At confirmation the teenager will confirm the declarations of faith made by their godparents and parents at their infant baptism into the Church. The youngsters have reached the age of reason when they can declare their faith for themselves and so receive

At Ritu Kala the gift of a first sari is an outward sign that the young Hindi girl has become a woman.

the Holy Spirit and the bread and wine of communion and become full members of the Church. In some parts of the Church that do not practise infant baptism, this initiation includes baptism by full immersion in a special large bath at the front of the church. The initiate 'dies' to their old life as a child by being 'buried' under the water and then is pulled upwards to the surface: reborn into a new life as an adult.

In the Orthodox Jewish tradition, the granting of the status of bar mitzvah (boys) and bat mitzvah (girls) when aged 13 is a sign that each is a son or daughter of the Commandments, which marks the transfer from childhood to adulthood. A full explanation of the ceremonies and traditions associated with bar and bat mitzvah is given in the *Cultural Focus* feature in Chapter 4.

Traditionally, when girls told their mothers they had reached menarche, it is believed that an Orthodox Jewish mother responded with a sudden sharp slap to her daughter's face. This gesture was intended to inform the daughter to 'wake up' to all the responsibilities awaiting her in a new life as her woman. Following menarche, and each time they afterwards menstruated, Orthodox Jewish women were obliged to have a ritual bath called **mikveh** a week after their period was finished, as a way of cleansing themselves of the impurity believed to be associated with menstruation. Today, the slap has largely 'been retired' or replaced with a ceremonial tap on the cheek (Houseman, 2007), though the ritual bath remains.

Source: Ridgeon, L. (ed.) (2003) *Major World Religions from their Origins to the Present.* London: Routledge

THINKING CRITICALLY

Are there any rituals in Western cultures that are comparable to the puberty rituals in traditional cultures? Should people in Western cultures recognise and mark the attainment of puberty more than they do now? If so, why, and how? If not, why not?

Social and Personal Responses to Puberty

'I think I was about 13 when I had my first period. I remember finding blood in my knickers, just a little bit. I knew what it was and wasn't frightened but I was embarrassed. My mum had got me "starter" packs of Tampax ages before – and we had obviously done all that stuff in school. I just didn't want to hear things like "Oh, you're growing up" or "You're turning into a woman"! I put the knickers under my bed, gross I know but it served the purpose of me not having to tell anyone. Then I forgot them. Mum found them when she was cleaning. Needless to say, I shouldn't have worried. She was quite cool about it. She just said, "Oh, have you started your periods?" to which I huffily (at the time, I thought nonchalantly) replied "Yeah, so?" and she left it at "OK," and started adding tampons to her shopping list.'

— Stephanie, age 20 (Hughes, unpublished data)

Although puberty is not marked in European cultures in quite the same way as other world cultures, European parents, family members and friends of the family do respond to the changes in adolescents' bodies that signify puberty and the development of sexual maturity. Adolescents in turn form their personal responses to puberty based in part on the information provided by their parents and older siblings. First, let's look at the adjustments that take place in parent–adolescent relations when puberty begins, then at adolescents' personal responses to puberty.

Parent–Adolescent Relations and Puberty

When young people reach puberty, the metamorphosis that takes place affects not only them personally but their relations with those closest to them, especially their parents. Just as adolescents have to adjust to the changes taking place in their bodies, parents have to adjust to the new person their child is becoming.

How do parent–adolescent relations change at puberty? For the most part, studies of adolescents and their parents find that relations tend to become cooler when pubertal changes become evident (De Goede et al., 2009; Järvinen and Østergaard, 2009; Branje et al., 2004; Hay and Ashman, 2003). Conflict increases and closeness decreases. Parents and adolescents seem to be less comfortable in each other's presence when puberty is reached, especially in their physical closeness. In one especially creative early study demonstrating this change, researchers went to a shopping centre and an amusement park and observed 122 pairs of mothers and children aged 6 to 18 (Montemayor and Flannery, 1989). For each pair, the researchers observed them for 30 seconds and recorded whether they were talking, smiling, looking at or touching each other. The most notable result of the study is shown in Figure 2.11. Early adolescents (ages 11–14) and their mothers were much less likely than younger children and their mothers to touch each other, and late adolescents (ages 15–18) and their mothers touched even less. Mothers and early adolescents talked more than mothers and younger children, suggesting that parent–child communication styles shift towards talking and away from touching as puberty is reached.

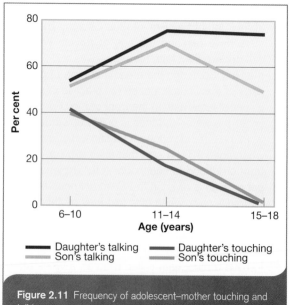

Figure 2.11 Frequency of adolescent–mother touching and talking.
Source: Montemayor and Flannery (1989).

CONNECT AND EXTEND

12-year-old Dutch adolescent girls and their mothers were observed during a conflict interaction task. To find out what happened read 'Conflict management in mother–daughter interactions in early adolescence'

by Susan Branje in *Behaviour*, Volume 145, Number 11 (November 2008), pp. 1627–1651

Other studies have found that the physical changes of puberty, not age alone, lead to the change in parent–adolescent relations. If a child reaches puberty relatively early, relations with parents change relatively early; if a child reaches puberty relatively late, relations with parents change relatively late (Miller et al., 2009). Studies have also found that conflict with parents tends to be especially high for adolescents who mature early (Pagani et al., 2009; Sagestrano et al., 1999).

What is it about reaching puberty that causes parent–child relations to change? Various explanations have been proposed, focusing mostly on how the biologically based **incest taboo** between parents and children becomes activated once children reach sexual maturity, resulting in more distant relations (Belsky et al., 2007). If this explanation were true, however, one would expect to find distancing between pubertal youngsters and their parents in nearly all cultures, but this is not the case. In fact, the studies that have found distancing to take place at puberty have been mainly studies of white families (Lewis et al., 2000; Sagestrano et al., 1999). Distancing from parents is not as common in young people who have close and supportive peer friendships (Lieberman et al., 1999), have strong parental attachments during infancy (Hamilton, 2000) or in divorced mother-headed families (Molina and Chassin, 1996). Family researcher Yvette Soloman argues that some distancing is inevitable and healthy in pursuit of young teenagers' 'project of the self' and that distancing in cutting off the flow of information to parents begins to define adolescents' 'privacy, power and identity' (Soloman, 2002, p. 965).

Excessive distancing is also not typical in traditional cultures. An interesting counter-example is provided by anthropologists Alice Schlegel and Herbert Barry's (1991) earlier and comprehensive survey of traditional cultures, which found that girls in traditional cultures often grow closer to their mothers during adolescence because they frequently spend much of their days side by side in shared labour. However, Desiree Qin's much more recent study of Chinese immigrant families (2009a) found that Chinese immigrant fathers' and mothers' adaptation after migration (the effect of the majority culture) influenced their relations with their children. Furthemore, the cultural norm of high academic expectations created tensions with the majority culture, and led to parent–child alienation.

THINKING CRITICALLY

Alice Schlegel and Herbert Barry's survey of traditional cultures found that girls in such cultures often grow closer to their mothers during adolescence because girls often spend much of their days side by side with their mothers in shared labour. That might be one reason but can you think of any others?

In traditional cultures and the majority cultures of Europe and North America, adolescents of both sexes tend to be closer to their mothers than to their fathers (Crockett et al., 2009; Laham et al., 2005; Dalheim-Englund et al., 2004; Claes, 1998). If increased distance in adolescence were due to the incest taboo, one would expect adolescent sons to be closer to fathers, not mothers. Thus, for the time being an unanswered question appears to be, what is it about European majority cultures that leads to greater distancing between parents and children when children reach puberty?

Another finding with regard to parents and puberty is that puberty tends to begin earlier for girls in families with a stepfather or other adult male not biologically related to the girl (Belsky et al., 2007; Ellis and Garber, 2000). This has been found to occur in other mammals as well. Exposure to unrelated adult males causes females to reach puberty earlier, evidently because of exposure to the males' **pheromones**, which are

CONNECT AND EXTEND

Do girls exposed to a stressful environment (due to father abandoning their family) show an early onset of puberty or is it that a gene, predisposing the father to family abandonment, is passed to their daughters causing early puberty, precocious sexuality and behaviour problems? Read some 'joined-up thinking' in 'Parent–daughter transmission of the androgen receptor gene as an explanation of the effect of father absence on age of menarche' by David E. Comings, Donn Muhleman, James P. Johnson and James P. MacMurray in *Child Development*, Volume 73, Number 4 (July 2002), pp. 1046–1051

airborne chemicals produced by the sweat glands (Miracle et al., 2003). Why the pheromones of unrelated males would stimulate puberty in girls is not well understood. It has also been found that family stress and conflict are related to early puberty in girls (Ellis and Garber, 2000). Again, the reason for this is not known.

Personal Responses to Menarche and Semenarche

Although menarche occurs relatively late in pubertal development for most girls, their responses to it have received a great deal of attention from researchers. This may be because menarche is a more momentous event than other female pubertal changes. The growth of pubic hair, the development of breasts, and most other pubertal changes occur gradually, almost imperceptibly from one day to the next, whereas menarche is suddenly there one day, when there was nothing to herald it the day before. Similarly, menarche is easier for scientists to measure – it is easier to identify when menarche begins than to pinpoint the beginning of other more gradual changes. Menarche also holds a special significance in that it signifies that ovulation is beginning and reproductive maturity is arriving. Of course, boys' first ejaculation holds a similar significance, but it has received far less research, perhaps because of its relation to masturbation, a taboo topic in most cultures (Laqueur, 2004).

What follows is an in-depth look at the reaction of girls to menarche and to subsequent cycles of menstruation, and boys are pretty much left out of the account. Why is this? Parents and professionals working with this age group will tell you that there is no more defining moment of transfer from childhood to adolescence than menarche. There are important social, educational and developmental effects of a well-handled menarche and accommodation to a regular menstruation cycle. Boys reactions to first and subsequent ejaculations are rarely shared with parents, do not result in changes of mood or attitude and are not subject to commercial advertising and social commentary. Therefore, for the time being, we will concentrate on girls.

How do girls respond to menarche? Research carried out in the last decade or so (Lee, 2009; Bramwell and Zeb, 2006; Rembeck and Gunnarsson, 2004; Lu, 2001; Beausang and Razor, 2000) provides some inconsistent conclusions but the short answer would be: positively for the most part but with shades of ambivalence. This recent research has confirmed an early study of over 600 girls by family researchers Jeanne Brooks-Gunn and Diane Ruble (1982) which found that girls often reported that menarche made them feel more 'grown up'. Many girls also indicated that they welcomed menarche because it allowed them to catch up with peers who had already begun menstruating and signified their capacity to bear children. Recent studies that follow girls over time confirm that menarche is followed by increases in social maturity, prestige with peers, and self-esteem (e.g. Archibald et al., 2003).

'Each time I have a period …. I have the feeling that in spite of all the pain, unpleasantness, and nastiness, I have a sweet secret and that is why, although it is nothing but a nuisance to me in a way, I always long for the time that I shall feel the secret within me again.'
— Anne Frank (1942/1997) *Diary of a Young Girl*, p.117

Not all reactions to menarche are positive, however. Some girls do not live with their mothers and have to wait for an available female to answer questions, do not have a female available to ask, or feel embarrassed discussing menstruation with their fathers (Kalman, 2003). During the nineteenth century many girls received no information about menarche before it occurred, and they often responded with shock and fear when they were one day surprised by it (see the *Historical Focus* feature). Across cultures, evidence from anthropological studies in cultures as diverse as rural Turkey, Malaysia and Wales suggests that even today girls often are provided with no information at all to prepare them for menarche, with the result that it is experienced with fear and dismay (Howie and Shail, 2005). The following is an example from an Egyptian woman's memoir:

'It would be difficult for anyone to imagine the panic that seized hold of me one morning when I woke to find blood trickling down beneath my thighs . . . I was obliged to overcome the fear and shame which possessed me and speak to my mother. I asked her to take me to a doctor for treatment. To my utter surprise she was calm and cool and did not seem to be affected by her daughter's serious condition. She explained that this was something that happened to all girls and that it recurs every month for a few days. On the last day when the flow ceased, I was to cleanse myself of this "impure blood" by having a hot bath . . . . I was therefore to understand that in me there was something degrading which appeared regularly in the form of this impure blood, and that it was something to be ashamed of, to hide from others.'
(Saadawi, 1980, p. 45)

Even when girls receive information in advance of menarche, in some cultures it may be information that shapes their views of menstruation in negative ways. For example, in a recent Chinese study, a majority of pre-menarcheal girls expected menstruation to be annoying, embarrassing and confusing, whereas only 10 per cent expected to feel happy or excited (Yeung, 2005). Negative expectations of menarche were especially high among girls who accepted traditional Chinese beliefs about menstruation, such as beliefs that menstruation brings bad luck, that women should not wash their hair or eat cold food while menstruating, and that it is easier to get sick during or after menstruation. A study of Mexican premenarcheal girls found similarly negative expectations for menarche, based in similarly negative cultural views of menstruation (Marván et al., 2007).

Research also indicates that girls whose mothers, peers or other sources have led them to expect menstruation to be unpleasant report greater discomfort once menarche occurs (Tang et al., 2004; Teitelman, 2004).

The results of studies of girls' responses to menarche indicate vividly that the degree to which cultures provide knowledge and shape expectations for menarche can have important effects on how girls experience it. However, studies also indicate that most girls and women experience a certain amount of discomfort associated with menstruation. Among adolescent girls, most report some degree of **premenstrual syndrome (PMS)**, the combination of behavioural, emotional and physical symptoms that occur in the week before menstruation (Dean et al., 2006). Various studies have found that from half to three-quarters of adolescent girls experience discomfort related to their menstrual cycles, with symptoms including cramps, backaches, headaches, fatigue and depression, as well as general discomfort (Yonkers et al., 2006; Meaden et al., 2005). The most common source of discomfort is cramps, experienced by up to 50 per cent of girls and women (Finkelstein, 2001c). Even among girls whose experience of menarche is mostly positive, many dislike the messiness of dealing with menstrual blood and the obligation of carrying around supplies to deal with it every month (Tang et al., 2003). Also, some girls report disliking the limits menstruation places on their activities.

'A girl could claim to have her period for months and nobody would ever know the difference. Which is exactly what I did. All you had to do was make a big fuss … and walk around clutching your stomach and moaning three to five days a month about the Curse and you could convince anybody … "I can't go. I have cramps." "I can't do that. I have cramps." And most of all, gigglingly, blushingly: "I can't swim, I have cramps." Nobody ever used the hard-core word. Menstruation. God, what an awful word. Never that. "I have cramps".'
– Nora Ephron (2000, pp. 2–3).

CONNECT AND EXTEND

For a disturbing but important study on PMS and the abuse of adolescent girls read 'Sexual abuse and perimenstrual symptoms in adolescent girls' by C. S. Al-Mateen, P. D. Hall, R. R. Brookman, A. M. Best and N. N. Singh in the *Journal of Interpersonal Violence*, Volume 14, Number 11 (November 1, 1999), pp. 1211–1224

Seen in this light, it is easier to understand the ambivalence girls often experience when they begin menstruating. They like the confirmation that they are developing normally towards reproductive maturity, but they may not like the discomfort and practical requirements that accompany menstruation each month. However, adolescent girls and adult women experience a great range of physical responses to menstruation. At the extreme, a very small proportion of girls and women experience premenstrual symptoms that are severe enough to interfere with their daily functioning; on the other hand, some experience no symptoms at all, and there is a great deal of variability in between these two extremes (Yonkers et al., 2008; Dean et al., 2006). Poor diet, high stress, alcohol use, insufficient sleep and lack of exercise all make PMS symptoms more severe (Daley, 2008). Ibuprofen and other medications can provide effective treatment for cramps (Finkelstein, 2001c).

As already noted, for boys the closest analogy to menarche is first ejaculation, sometimes known as **semenarche** (not to be confused with spermarche, which was described earlier in this chapter). Very little research has taken place on this topic. Two small earlier studies (Stein and Reiser, 1993; Gaddis and Brooks-Gunn, 1985) found that boys' reactions to semenarche were mostly positive. They enjoyed the pleasurable sensations of it, and, like girls' experience of menarche, it made them feel more grown up. However, ambivalence existed for boys as well. Many reported that surprise or fear was part of the experience. Most girls in Western countries now receive some information about menarche before it happens, but parents rarely talk to their boys about semenarche (Frankel, 2002).

Culture certainly influences boys' interpretation of semenarche. It may occur through 'wet dreams' or masturbation, and there is a long history of shame and censure associated with masturbation (Laqueur, 2004; Frankel, 2002). Perhaps for this reason, boys tend to tell no one after they experience semenarche (Gaddis and Brooks-Gunn, 1985). In contrast, a study of boys in Nigeria found that boys tended to tell their friends about semenarche soon after it took place (Adegoke, 1993), perhaps reflecting less of a stigma associated with masturbation in Nigerian culture.

THINKING CRITICALLY

What kind of preparation for menarche/semenarche would you recommend be provided for today's adolescents? At what age? If schools or youth organisations provide information on menarche/semenarche, should that information include a discussion of the relationship between these events and sexuality?

Early and Late Pubertal Timing

'Everybody thought there was something wrong with me because I still looked like a ten-year-old until I was fifteen or sixteen. That has been really a bad experience for me, because everybody was changing around me and I was standing still. I was changing in my head but not my body. My parents were even going to take me to the doctor to see if I was deformed or something like that, but they didn't, and finally last year I started to grow. My voice started changing and everything, so I guess I'm normal after all, but I think it's going to be awhile before I stop feeling like I'm different from everybody else.'
– Steven, age 17 (quoted in Bell, 1998, p. 14)

In some respects, social and personal responses to puberty are intertwined. That is, one factor which determines how adolescents respond to reaching puberty is how others respond. In industrialised societies, one aspect of others' responses that adolescents seem to be acutely aware of concerns perceptions of whether they have reached puberty relatively early or relatively late compared with their peers.

CONNECT AND EXTEND

To examine the relations among timing of puberty, timing of first experience of sexual arousal, strength of sex drive, and sexual attitudes and behaviours in young men and women read 'Timing of puberty and sexuality in men and women' by Jennifer Ostovich and John Sabini in *Archives of Sexual Behavior*, Volume 34, Number 2 (April 2005), pp. 197–206

HISTORICAL FOCUS

Menarche as a Taboo Topic

Some traditional cultures have harboured false beliefs about menstruation, such as the belief that menstrual blood has magical power that can cause crops to fail. However, false beliefs about menstruation are not exclusive to traditional cultures. Erroneous and even bizarre beliefs about menstruation were widespread until relatively recent times. Furthermore, menarche has been shrouded in shame and secrecy, leaving many girls entirely ignorant of it until they suddenly found themselves bleeding incomprehensibly.

Throughout the nineteenth century, menstruation and menarche were regarded as taboo topics in most middle-class families. An 1895 study of secondary school girls indicated that 60 per cent had no knowledge of menarche before it occurred. A popular 1882 advice book for mothers railed against the 'criminal reserve' and 'pseudo-delicacy' that led mothers to fail to prepare their girls for menarche. Another nineteenth-century advice writer reported that 'numbers of women' had written to tell her that they were totally unprepared for menarche, including one who wrote, 'It has taken me nearly a lifetime to forgive my mother for sending me away to boarding school without telling me about it.'

Why such secrecy? Probably because the middle class of that era believed they had a duty to protect girls' 'innocence' for as long as they could. Children who grew up on farms learned a lot about the facts of life by observing and caring for farm animals, but parents in more urban middle-class households sought to protect their children from such raw realities. They associated menarche with budding sexuality, and they were zealous about protecting girls' virginity until marriage. As part of this effort, they often attempted to delay menarche by having girls avoid sexually 'stimulating' foods such as pickles! Menarche came anyway, pickles or not, but they believed it was best to keep girls in ignorance of menarche – and sexuality – for as long as possible.

In the course of the twentieth century, as the sexual restrictiveness of the nineteenth century faded, menarche and menstruation gradually became more openly discussed and a substantial amount of information was communicated through the media. In the 1920s, as mass-produced 'sanitary napkins' became popular (previously, cotton rags or cheesecloth had been typically used to staunch menstrual blood), advertisements for sanitary napkins helped to open up discussion of menstruation. Companies making sanitary napkins distributed pamphlets on menstruation to girls through mothers, teachers and uniformed youth organisations during the 1930s and 1940s. In the 1940s a cartoon produced by the Disney Company, 'The Story of Menstruation', was seen by many millions of school girls, and magazines for girls provided advice on how to handle menstruation while remaining active.

Today, it is rare for a girl to experience menarche in total ignorance of what is happening to her body. Perhaps because menarche now takes place at around age 12, cultural beliefs in European society no longer associate menarche with sexuality but rather with health and hygiene. It may be that dissociating menarche from sex has been important in allowing it to be discussed more openly. As we will see in later chapters, however, open discussions of adolescent sexuality remain rare in our society.

Nineteenth century mothers rarely discussed menarche with their daughters.

Within cultures, the timing of puberty appears to be based mainly on genetic factors (Anderson et al., 2007). Mothers' age of menarche strongly predicts their daughters' (Belsky et al., 2007). Sisters' ages of menarche are highly correlated, and correlations are especially high between identical twin sisters (Ge et al., 2007; van den Berg & Boomsma, 2007). However, as noted earlier in the chapter, there is some evidence that environmental factors such as stress may trigger earlier puberty (DeRose & Brooks-Gunn, 2006).

The timing of puberty is especially important in industrialised countries. One interesting feature of puberty rites in traditional cultures is that eligibility for the rites is not typically based on age but on pubertal maturation. This is obvious with regard to rites related to menarche; a girl participates the first time she menstruates. However, boys' participation in puberty rites is also based on maturation rather than age. Typically, the adults of the community decide when a boy is ready, based on his level of physical maturation and on their perceptions of his psychological and social readiness (Ball, 2010). Consequently, the precise age of reaching puberty matters little in traditional cultures; everyone gets there eventually.

In contrast, chronological age has much more significance in industrialised countries. The school systems in industrialised countries group children on the basis of age rather than developmental maturity. As a result, Year 8 in British schools, for example, includes children who are all 12 or 13 years old, but their pubertal development is likely to vary widely, from those who have not experienced any pubertal changes to those who are well on the way to full maturity. Grouping them together in the same classrooms for many hours each day adds to the intensity of comparisons between them and makes them highly aware of whether they are early, late or 'on time', compared with others.

A great deal of research has been conducted on early versus late maturation among adolescents in the West, extending back over a half century. The results are complex. They differ depending on gender, and the short-term effects of maturing early or late appear to differ from the long-term effects. The effects also differ depending on the area of development considered: body image, popularity, school performance or behaviour problems. To help clarify these differences, we will look at the results of these studies separately for girls and boys.

Early and Late Maturation Among Girls

The effects of early maturation are especially negative for girls. Findings over the last decade and from a variety of industrialised countries concur that early-maturing girls are at risk of many different but often related problems:

depressed mood; negative body image; eating disorders; substance use; delinquency; aggressive behaviour; school problems; and conflict with parents (Westling et al., 2008; Lynne et al., 2007; Mendle et al., 2007; Obeidallah et al., 2004; Weichold et al., 2003; Lanza and Collins, 2002; Wichstrom, 2001; Sagestrano et al., 1999).

Why is early maturation such a problem for girls? One likely reason involves cultural values about physical appearance. Because early maturation typically leads to a shorter and heavier appearance, it is a disadvantage in Western cultures that value thinness in females' appearance. This may help to explain why early-maturing girls have higher rates of depressed mood, negative body image and eating disorders (Mendle et al., 2007; Lien et al., 2006).

A second reason for the problems of early-maturing girls is that their early physical development draws the attention of older boys, who then introduce them to an older group of friends and to substance use, delinquency and early sexual activity (Westling et al., 2008; Lynne et al., 2007; Weichold et al., 2003). So when early-maturing girls have higher rates of these behaviours than other girls their age, it may be because they are behaving more like their friends who are older than they are.

THINKING CRITICALLY

In the light of the difficulties often experienced by early-maturing girls, can you think of anything families, communities or schools could do to assist them?

Late-maturing girls share few of early-maturing girls' problems, although they suffer from teasing and negative body image during the years when other girls have begun to develop and they have not (Weichold et al., 2003). By their late teens, however, they tend to have a more favourable body image than other girls (Simmons and Blyth, 1987), probably because they are more likely to end up with the lean body build that tends to be regarded as attractive in Western majority cultures.

Studies on the long-term effects of early maturation for girls are mixed. Some studies find that most of the negative effects diminish by the late teens (Weichold et al., 2003; Posner, 2006). However, in women, earlier menarche is associated with more parental marital conflict throughout childhood (birth to age 11); more independence from parents in late childhood (age 8–11); earlier age at dating men; more boyfriends; younger age at first sexual intercourse; older age of first intercourse partner relative to own age at first intercourse; and more intercourse partners (Kim and Smith, 1999). Also, a

FOCUS ON PROFESSIONAL PRACTICE

Giving Advice on Contraception

At the beginning of this chapter we quoted UK scientist Fran Ebling's definition of puberty which included 'Puberty is the attainment of fertility'. The attainment of fertility by girls creates new possible outcomes for engaging in sexual activity, most obviously becoming pregnant. Teenage pregnancy is generally considered, in most majority European cultures, to be a problem for the young person, for her family and for society at large, and in Chapter 9 we will look at contraceptive use and non-use. As previously noted, menarche, particularly early menarche, often draws the attention of older boys, who then introduce young girls to an older group of friends and to early sexual activity (Westling et al., 2008; Lynne et al., 2007; Weichold et al., 2003). This is often at a time for 12 to 15-year-olds when support for contraceptive use is not well established.

Research in 2009 by paediatricians Jeanelle Sheeder, Kristina Tocce and Catherine Stevens-Simon explored the reasons for ineffective contraceptive use before adolescent pregnancy among an ethnically diverse group of 1,568 pregnant 13–18-year-olds. The researchers intended to identify new ways to increase the impact of pregnancy prevention interventions by professional services on the number of children born to adolescents.

Surprisingly, the most commonly endorsed category for ineffective use of contraception among these adolescents was that they were 'not ready to prevent pregnancy' – not that they didn't know how to prevent pregnancy or were unready when sex occurred. Indeed, logistical barriers and misperceptions about the need for contraception were the least frequently endorsed categories. This means that many of the young mothers-to-be considered that being pregnant was compatible with their other life goals for this stage in their lives. These life goals included gaining recognition as an adult, winning independence from parents and establishing a full partnership including marriage with the father. The adolescents who were not ready to prevent conception consistently differed from those who were; they were more apt to already live in non-chaotic environments with an adult father of the child rather than their parents. They had already established goals compatible with adolescent childbearing.

What should those professionals working with this age group do in the light of this kind of research? What interventions are possible or advisable? The researchers conclude that:

'The most expedient way to strengthen the impact of pregnancy prevention programs on adolescent childbearing is to shift the focus of intervention from overcoming logistical barriers and misperceptions about the need for contraception, to helping young women develop goals that make adolescent childbearing a threat to what they want in life. This means intervening actively enough to ensure that goal setting translates into an internal desire to postpone childbearing beyond adolescence.'

(Sheeder et al., 2009, p. 295)

Jeanelle Sheeder and her colleagues neatly state the problem and a logical overall aim for interventions but what kind of interventions would 'translate into an internal desire to postpone childbearing'? In what ways can professionals support goal setting for this age group and have the desired impact? Perhaps there are different opportunities for different professional groups and it is a shared understanding that is important; that the task goes well beyond providing advice about contraception, and providing the contraceptives to prevent teenage pregnancy. It is to provide the support and advice to prevent the aspiration to adolescent pregnancy as a life choice.

later study reported that at age 24, women who had been early maturers had more psychological and social problems than women who had reached puberty 'on time' (Graber et al., 2004). Given the current research findings, particularly that of British psychologists Kenneth Kim and Peter Smith (1999), more up-to-the-minute research into the long-term consequences of early maturation seems warranted.

CONNECT AND EXTEND

Read more about the likely effects of girls and boys maturing late in 'Pubertal timing and substance use: the effects of gender, parental monitoring and deviant peers' by E. Westling, J. A. Andrews, S. E. Hampson and M. Peterson in the *Journal of* *Adolescent Health,* volume 42 (2008), pp. 555–563. What are the signs that professionals might need to intervene?

Early and Late Maturation Among Boys

In contrast to girls, for whom early maturation has overwhelmingly negative effects, the effects of early maturation for boys are positive in some ways and negative in others. Early-maturing boys tend to have more favourable body images and to be more popular than other boys (Weichold et al., 2003). This may be because early-maturing boys get their burst of growth and muscular development before other boys do, which gives them a distinct advantage in the sports activities that are so important to male prestige in secondary schooling. Also, the earlier development of facial hair, lowered voice and other secondary sex characteristics may make early-maturing boys more attractive to girls. Early-maturing boys may also have a long-term advantage. One study that followed early-maturing adolescent boys 40 years later found that they had achieved greater success in their careers and had higher marital satisfaction than later-maturing boys (Taga et al., 2006).

However, not everything about being an early-maturing boy is favourable. Like their female counterparts, early-maturing boys tend to become involved

Adolescents of the same age have many different levels of physical maturity. How does age-grouping of schools accentuate these differences?

earlier in delinquency, sex and substance use (Westling et al., 2008; Wichstrom, 2001; Williams and Dunlop, 1999). Some studies report that early-maturing boys have higher rates of emotional distress (Ge et al., 2001), despite their more positive body images. Specifically, earlier spermarche is associated with less emotional closeness to mother throughout childhood (birth to age 11); less internalising symptoms (anxiousness/depression) in late childhood (age 8–11); earlier age at dating women; more girlfriends; more likelihood of having had intercourse; and earlier age at first intercourse (Kim and Smith, 1999).

Late-maturing boys can also show evidence of problems. Compared to boys who mature 'on time', late-maturing boys have higher rates of alcohol use and delinquency (Williams and Dunlop, 1999). They also have lower attainment in school (Weichold et al., 2003). There is some evidence that late-maturing boys have elevated levels of substance use and deviant behaviour well into emerging adulthood (Biehl et al., 2007; Graber et al., 2004).

So, the effects of early and late maturation differ considerably between girls and boys. For girls, early maturation puts them at risk for a host of problems, but late maturation does not. For boys, both early and late maturation make them at risk for problems, but early maturation also includes some benefits. The problems of early-maturing girls appear to be due in part to their associations with older boys, but the sources of the problems of early- and late-maturing boys are not clear.

As you read about these studies of early- and late-maturing boys and girls, keep in mind that each of these groups displays a great deal of variance. Although early and late maturation are related to certain kinds of general outcomes on a group level, the effects for individuals will naturally depend on their particular experiences and relationships – the upcoming **nature–nurture debate** will help to explain this.

Also remember that, so far, nearly all the studies conducted on pubertal timing have involved adolescents in the majority ethnic societies of industrialised countries – white youngsters (e.g. Güre et al., 2006; Lien et al., 2006). We suggested earlier that the effects of maturing early or late may be due to schooling by age that exists in these countries, but right now we do not know how adolescents respond to pubertal timing in cultures where schooling by age does not exist. Nor do we know much about the effect of maturing early or late in minority cultures. Is there anything professionals should know about physical developmental issues when working with young people and families from minority groups?

BIOLOGICAL DEVELOPMENT AND THE ENVIRONMENT: THE THEORY OF GENOTYPE-ENVIRONMENT INTERACTIONS

For many decades in the social sciences, scholars have debated the relative importance of biology and the environment in human development. Some scholars have claimed that human behaviour can be explained by biological factors (nature) and that environment matters little, whereas others have claimed that biology is largely irrelevant and that differences in human behaviour can be better explained by environmental factors (nurture). In recent years, most scholars have reached a consensus that both biology and environment play key roles in human development, although they continue to debate the relative strength of nature and nurture (Lerner, 2006).

Given the profound biological changes that take place in adolescence and emerging adulthood, nature–nurture issues are perhaps especially relevant to these periods of life. One influential theory on this topic that we will be relying on occasionally in this book is the **theory of genotype–environment interactions** (Eaves et al., 2003; Jang et al., 2001). According to this theory, both genotype (a person's inherited genes) and environment make essential contributions to human development. However, the relative strengths of genetics and the environment are difficult to unravel because our genes can influence the kind of environment we experience. To some extent our genotypes help us to create our own environments by giving us a propensity to seek out and accommodate to some experiences, rather than

others. These genotype–environment interactions take three forms: passive, evocative and active.

Passive genotype–environment interactions occur in biological families because parents provide both genes and environment for their children. This may seem obvious, but it has profound implications for how we think about development. Take this father–daughter example. Dad has been good at drawing things ever since he was a boy, and now he makes a living as a commercial illustrator. One of the first birthday presents he gives to his little girl is a set of crayons and coloured pencils for drawing. She seems to like it, and he provides her with increasingly sophisticated materials as she grows up. He also teaches her a number of drawing skills as she seems ready to learn them. By the time she reaches adolescence, she's quite a proficient artist herself and draws a lot of the art for school clubs and social events. She goes to college and majors in architecture, and then goes on to become an architect. It is easy to see how she became so good at drawing, given an environment that stimulated her drawing abilities so much – that makes perfect sense!

Not so fast. It is true that Dad provided her with a stimulating environment, but he also provided her with half her genes. If there are any genes that contribute to drawing ability – such as genes that promote spatial reasoning and fine motor coordination – she may well have received those from Dad, too. The point is that in a biological family, it is very difficult to separate genetic influences from environmental influences because *parents provide both*, and they are likely to provide an environment that reinforces the tendencies they have provided to their children through their genes.

So you should be sceptical when you read studies about parents and adolescents in biological families claiming that the behaviour of parents is the cause of the characteristics of adolescents. Remember from Chapter 1: correlation is not necessarily causation! Just because a *correlation* exists between the behaviour of parents and the characteristics of adolescents does not mean the parents *caused* the adolescents to have those characteristics. Maybe causation was involved, but in biological families it is difficult to tell. The correlation could be due to the similarity in genes between the biological parents and their adolescents, rather than to the environment the biological parents provided.

One good way to unravel this tangle is through adoption studies (e.g. Wynne et al., 2006) These studies avoid the problem of passive genotype–environment interactions because one set of parents provided the adolescents' genes but a different set of parents provided the environment. So when adolescents are more similar to their adoptive parents than to their biological parents, it is possible to make a strong case that this similarity is due to the environment provided by the adoptive parents, and when adolescents are more similar to their biological parents than to their adoptive parents it is likely that genes played a strong role. We will examine specific adoption studies in future chapters but hold the principle in until then.

Evocative genotype–environment interactions occur when a person's inherited characteristics evoke responses from others in their environment. If you had a son who started reading at age 3 and seemed to love it, you and others in the family might buy him more books; if you had a daughter who could sink 20-foot putts at age 12, you might arrange to send her to a golf academy. Did you ever babysit or work in a setting where there were many children or families? Perhaps you still do. If so, you probably found that children differ in how sociable, cooperative and obedient they are. In turn, you may have found that you reacted differently to them, depending on their characteristics. That is what is meant by evocative genotype–environment interactions – with the crucial addition of the assumption that characteristics such as reading ability, athletic ability and sociability are at least partly based on genetics.

Active genotype–environment interactions occur when people seek out environments that correspond to their genotypic characteristics. The child who reads easily may ask for books as birthday gifts; the adolescent with an ear for music may ask for piano lessons; the emerging adult for whom reading has always been slow and difficult may choose to begin working full time after secondary school rather than going to university or college. The idea here is that people are drawn to environments that match their inherited abilities.

Genotype–Environment Interactions Over Time

The three types of genotype–environment interactions operate throughout childhood, adolescence and emerging adulthood, but their relative balance changes over time (Eaves et al., 2003). In childhood, passive genotype–environment interactions are especially pronounced, and active genotype–environment interactions are relatively weak. This is because the younger a child is, the more parents control the daily environment the child experiences and the less autonomy the child has to seek out environmental influences outside the family. However, with age, especially as children move through adolescence and emerging adulthood, the balance changes. Parental control diminishes, so passive genotype–environment interactions also diminish. Autonomy increases, so active genotype–environment interactions also increase. Evocative genotype–environment interactions remain relatively stable from childhood through adolescence and into emerging adulthood.

The theory of genotype–environment interactions is by no means universally accepted by scholars of human development. In fact, it has been the source of vigorous debate in the field (Loehlin et al., 2009; O'Connor et al., 2003). Some scholars question the theory's claim that characteristics such as sociability, reading ability and athletic ability are substantially inherited. However, it is currently one of the most important new theories of human development, and you should be familiar with it as part of your understanding of development during adolescence and emerging adulthood. We find the theory provocative and illuminating, and we will be referring to it in the chapters to come.

THINKING CRITICALLY

Are you a good case study of genotype–environment interaction? Think of one of your abilities in relation to the genes and environment your parents have provided for you, and describe how the various types of genotype–environment interactions may have been involved in your development of that ability. Of course, if you were adopted or a twin, that could add an additional intriguing aspect to your personal case study.

CONNECT AND EXTEND

'Parental engagement in children's learning in the home makes the greatest difference to student achievement.' Find out more by reading 'Do parents know they matter? Engaging all parents in learning' by Alma Harris and Janet Goodall in *Educational Research*, Volume 50, Number 3 (2008), pp. 277–289

SUMMING UP

This chapter has presented the biological changes that take place during puberty as well as the cultural, social and personal responses that result from these changes. Here are the main points we have covered in this chapter:

- During puberty, a set of remarkable transformations takes place in young people's bodies. Hormonal changes lead to changes in physical functioning and to the development of primary and secondary sex characteristics.

- The hormonal changes of puberty begin in the hypothalamus, initiated when a threshold level of leptin is reached. The chain of events in the endocrine system runs from the hypothalamus to the pituitary gland to the gonads and adrenal glands to the hypothalamus again, in a feedback loop that monitors the levels of the sex hormones (androgens and oestrogens). The set points for the sex hormones rise in the course of puberty.

- Physical growth during puberty includes the growth spurt as well as increases in muscle mass (especially in boys) and body fat (especially in girls). The heart and lungs also grow dramatically, especially for boys.

- Obesity has become a serious public health problem in industrialised countries and the prevalence of this problem increases sharply during adolescence. The increase in obesity in recent years is due mainly to increases in consumption of foods high in fat and sugar (especially fast food) and a decrease in rates of exercise.

- In many respects, emerging adulthood is a time of optimum physical functioning for most people, when athletic performance peaks and susceptibility to illness and disease is at its nadir. However, emerging adults are at higher risk than people of other ages for certain problems due to lifestyle and behaviour, including automobile fatalities, murder and sexually transmitted diseases.

- Primary sex characteristics are related directly to reproduction. Females are born with all their eggs already in their ovaries, but males produce sperm only once they reach puberty.

- Secondary sex characteristics develop at puberty but are not directly related to reproduction. Girls show the first development of secondary sex characteristics about two years earlier than boys. The order of pubertal events is quite predictable, but adolescents vary greatly in the ages the events begin and how long it takes to complete them.

- Cultures influence the timing of puberty through cultural technologies in nutrition and medical care. The initiation of puberty is earlier when nutrition and medical care are good, and consequently the age of beginning puberty decreased steadily in industrialised countries during the twentieth century and is now decreasing in newly developed and developing countries.

- Many traditional cultures have rituals that give meaning to pubertal changes, usually focused on menarche for girls and on tests of courage, strength and endurance for boys.

- Cultures influence adolescents' experiences of puberty by providing or failing to provide young people with information about what is happening to their bodies. Menarche can be traumatic when girls are unprepared for it, but girls today typically know about it long before it arrives.

- In industrialised countries, the cultural practice of organising schooling by age group means that the timing of puberty has important consequences for adolescents who begin puberty relatively early or relatively late. Early maturation is especially problematic for girls.

- According to the theory of genotype–environment interactions, the influences of genetics and the environment are difficult to separate because in some ways genes shape the kind of environment we experience. During adolescence and emerging adulthood, passive genotype–environment interactions decrease and active genotype–environment interactions increase.

Perhaps the most notable single fact in this chapter is that the typical age of reaching puberty has declined steeply in industrialised countries over the past 150 years, so that now the first evident changes of puberty take place between ages 10 and 12 for most adolescents in these countries, sometimes even earlier. Reaching puberty means reaching sexual maturity, and in many ways the cultural beliefs and practices of industrialised countries still have not adjusted to the fact that young people now reach the threshold of sexual maturity at such an early age. Parents are often unsure of when or how to talk to children about their changing bodies and their sexual feelings. Teachers and counsellors are often equally unsure about what to communicate to children. Adolescent peers exchange information among themselves, but what they tell each other is not always accurate or healthy. Consequently, adolescents often experience their biological changes with limited information about the psychological and social implications of what is happening to their bodies.

In this area even more than in most of the areas we will discuss in this book, we know little about the experiences of young people outside of the middle-class majority cultures of Europe, Australasia and North America. How do young people in traditional cultures respond to the biological changes of puberty? What about adolescents in minority cultures in Western societies? In the decades to come, research on these questions may provide us with better information about the different ways that cultures may enhance young people's passage through the dramatic transformations of puberty.

INTERNET RESOURCES

http://www.e-lfh.org.uk/projects/ah/index.html

An extraordinary UK government project providing e-learning to help improve the health outcomes and experiences of all young people The information is intended to be understandable to the general public, not just physicians and other health care providers. Many sessions incorporate video clips and case studies to help you understand the views of both young people and professionals on a host of subjects, from confidentiality and self-harm to puberty and acne.

http://www.childrenfirst.nhs.uk/kids/news/features/my_health/understanding_puberty.html

There is a huge amount of information available to young people via the Internet. Here is a good example of what can be done.

FURTHER READING

S. Attwood, *Making Sense of Sex: A Forthright Guide to Puberty, Sex and Relationships for People with Asperger's Syndrome.* **Jessica Kingsley Publishers (2008)**

Just what the title suggests. Here is important information for all professionals working with a wide range of young people who may display a range of challenging behaviours.

J. Bancroft, *Adolescence and Puberty.* **Oxford University Press (1990)**

This wide-ranging relevant volume presents an in-depth picture of adolescent sexuality and behaviour. Here, 19 scientists representing ten disciplines explore the biological, psychological and cultural factors involved in the onset of puberty and its associated emotional changes.

C. Haywood (ed.). *Puberty and Psychopathology.* **Cambridge University Press (2003)**

A collection of chapters on the physical, social and psychological changes of puberty, with a focus on how those changes place some adolescents at risk of psychological problems.

M. Ross, *Coming of Age.* **Heinemann (2004)**

This book investigates the ways in which children become adults in various religions and cultures around the world. Coming of age is usually celebrated between the ages of 12 and 21. Religious ceremonies, such as confirmation and bat mitzvah, and initiation rites, such as the Latin-American celebration for girls called quinceaera, are explored.

For more reviews, responses to the *Thinking Critically* features, case studies, web links and practice tests, log on to **www.pearsoned.co.uk/arnett.**

CHAPTER 3
COGNITIVE FOUNDATIONS

OUTLINE

Mario has a problem. It is early morning, and he is standing with some friends on the beach just north of Galéria, Corsica, in the Mediterranean. The friends (all in their late teens) have planned a fishing trip for today, but as Mario looks out over the ocean he notices signs that disturb him. The movement and colour of the clouds, the height and activity of the waves, all suggest a storm on the way. He calculates the strength and direction of the wind and how they are likely to change in the next few hours. He looks over their equipment – nets, a small outboard motorboat with a single motor (no oars or sails), some bottled water. If they were planning with safety in mind they would at least take oars, but he knows that a large part of the appeal of the trip is the risk involved, with the opportunity it presents to demonstrate their courage. The small boat, the threatening weather and jagged underwater rocks will present them with ample opportunity today to test their bravery. These are the challenges that have faced his father, all their fathers and generations of proud Corsicans. As he matches the anticipated challenges with their capacities, he is confident they will measure up to them. Quelling his doubts, he helps push the boat out into the surf, jumps in the boat and they set off (based on Marshall, 1979).

Elke has a problem. She is sitting in the staff room of a hospital in Bremen, Germany, analysing the medical charts of a patient being treated for ovarian cysts. Something is not quite right – the diagnosis is ovarian cysts but the levels of some of the patient's hormones are much higher than normal, and suggest that something else besides the cysts is problematic. At age 22, Elke has been studying medicine for three years and has learned a great deal, but she is well aware that she has not yet accumulated the knowledge and experience the doctors have. She wonders whether she should she tell them what she thinks?

Mike has a problem. He is sitting in his Year 8 classroom in Leighton Buzzard, UK and puzzling over the maths quiz in front of him. 'Amy received 70 per cent of the votes in the election for school netball captain,' reads the first question. 'If her opponent received the remaining 21 votes, how many people voted in the election?' Mike stares at the question and tries to remember how to solve such a problem. He was working on one last night that was just like this; how did it go? He has difficulty recalling it, and his attention begins to drift off to other topics – the hockey game coming up this Thursday, the 60 pence song he was listening to on his iPod on the way to school, the legs of the girl in the pleated skirt two rows in front of him – wow! 'Ten minutes,' intones the teacher from the front of the room. 'You have ten more minutes.' Seized with panic, he focuses again on the problem in front of him.

ADOLESCENTS AND EMERGING ADULTS ALL over the world confront intellectual challenges as part of their daily lives. Often, as in the cases of Mario and Elke, their challenges are similar in type and magnitude to the challenges faced by adults, although usually they have less authority and responsibility than adults have. In industrialised countries, many of the intellectual challenges adolescents face take place in a school setting, as in Mike's case. As we shall see, however, the changes that occur in cognitive development during adolescence and emerging adulthood affect all aspects of their lives, not just their school performance.

In this chapter we will look at changes in how adolescents and emerging adults think, how they solve problems, and changes in their capacities for memory and attention; changes that scholars call **cognitive development**. We begin by talking about Jean Piaget's theory of cognitive development and some of the research based on it. Piaget's theory (referred to as Piagetian) describes general changes in mental structures and problem-solving abilities that take place during childhood and adolescence. Next we will discuss some of the cognitive changes that occur during emerging adulthood and consider theory and research on information processing. In contrast to the Piagetian approach, which describes general changes in cognitive development, the information-processing approach focuses on a detailed examination of specific cognitive abilities such as attention and memory.

Later in the chapter we will look at the practical use of cognitive abilities in critical thinking and decision making, and the ways that ideas about cognitive development can be applied to social topics. Following this discussion, we will examine the major intelligence tests and studies that have used these tests to investigate the cognitive development of adolescents and emerging adults, and present exciting and relatively 'new' findings on brain development in adolescence and emerging adulthood. Finally, we will discuss the role of culture in cognitive development.

PIAGET'S THEORY OF COGNITIVE DEVELOPMENT

In our view, the most influential theory of cognitive development from infancy through adolescence is the one developed by the Swiss psychologist **Jean Piaget** who lived from 1896 to 1980. Piaget was quite the adolescent prodigy. He developed an early fascination with the workings of the natural world and published articles on molluscs while still in his early teens.

After receiving his PhD at age 21 for his studies of molluscs, Piaget shifted his attention to human development. He took a job testing children's intelligence and became intrigued by the kinds of wrong answers children gave. It seemed to him that children of the same age not only answered the questions in similar ways when they gave the correct answer, but also gave similar kinds of wrong answers. Piaget deduced that age differences in patterns

Jean Piaget.

of wrong answers reflected differences in how children of various ages *thought* about the questions. Furthermore, he concluded that older children not only know more than younger children, they also think differently.

This early insight became the basis of much of Piaget's work over the next 60 years, during which his observations convinced him that not only do children of different ages think differently but that changes in cognitive development proceed in distinct stages (Piaget, 1972). Each stage involves a different way of thinking about the world. An important part of identifying **stages** means that at any point during each person's growth and development, their cognitive abilities are organised into a coherent **mental structure** that persists across all aspects of thinking. For example, take rearranging things; what some psychologists call problems of **conservation**. Somebody who knows that 15 objects remain 15 objects even if they are rearranged is also likely to know that there could be the same amount of water in a short wide glass as a tall thin one. So all thinking within a stage is part of the same mental structure (Keating, 2004; Hansen and Monk, 2002). As Piaget focused on how cognition changes with age, his approach (and the approach of those who have explored and extended his work) is known as the **cognitive-developmental approach**.

According to Piaget, the driving force behind development from one stage to the next is **maturation** (Inhelder and Piaget, 1958). All of us have within our genotypes (see 'Biological development and the environment: the theory of genotype–environment interactions' in Chapter 2) a prescription for cognitive development that prepares us for certain changes at certain ages. A reasonably 'normal' environment is necessary for cognitive development to occur but, according to Piaget, the effect of the environment on maturation is limited. According to the theory, you cannot teach an 8-year-old something that only a 13-year-old can learn, no matter how sophisticated your teaching techniques. In the same way, by the time the 8-year-old reaches age 13, the biological processes of maturation will make it easy for him or her to understand the world as a typical child of 13 understands it, and no special teaching will be required.

Piaget's emphasis on the importance of maturation contrasts with the views of other theorists such as the psychologist Howard Gardner, who believe in few inherent limits to development, that environmental stimulation can override them (Flavell et al., 2002), that newborns posses considerable innate or easily developed cognitive capacities and that Piaget underestimated the power of the 'inborn cognitive architecture' (Gardner, 2006). Piaget portrayed maturation as an active process in which children seek out information and stimulation in the environment that matches the maturity of their thinking. This idea contrasts with the view of other theorists such as the behaviourists (more about them later) who saw the environment as acting on the child through rewards and punishments rather than seeing children as proactive agents of their own development.

Piaget proposed that the active construction of reality takes place through the use of **schemes**, which are structures for organising and interpreting information. For infants, schemes are based on sensory and motor information such as that received through sucking and grasping, but after infancy schemes become symbolic and representational, as words, ideas and concepts.

The two processes involved in the use of schemes are **assimilation** and **accommodation**. Assimilation occurs when new information is altered to fit (to be

CONNECT AND EXTEND

To find out what might characterise cognitive maturation through adolescence read 'Maturation of cognitive processes from late childhood to adulthood' by Beatriz Luna, Krista E. Graver, Trinity A. Urban, Nicole A. Lazar and John A. Sweeney in *Child Development*, Volume 75, Number 5 (September 2004), pp. 1357–1372

assimilated into) an existing scheme, whereas accommodation entails changing the scheme to adapt to the new information. Assimilation and accommodation usually take place together in varying degrees; they are 'two sides of the same cognitive coin' (Flavell et al., 2002, p. 5). For example, an infant who has been breast feeding may use mostly assimilation and a slight degree of accommodation when learning to suck from the nipple on a bottle, but if sucking on a ball or the dog's bone the infant would be able to use assimilation less and need to use accommodation more.

People of other ages, too, use both assimilation and accommodation whenever they are processing cognitive information. One example is right in front of you. In the course of reading this textbook, you will read things that seem familiar to you from your own experience or previous reading, so that you can easily assimilate them to what you already know. Other information, perhaps the information about cultures other than your own, will be contrary to the schemes you have developed and will require you to use accommodation in order to expand your knowledge and understanding of development in adolescence and emerging adulthood.

Stages of Cognitive Development in Childhood and Adolescence

Based on his own research and his collaborations with his colleague Barbel Inhelder, Piaget devised a theory of cognitive development to describe the stages that children's thinking passes through as they grow up (Inhelder and Piaget, 1958; Piaget, 1972; see Table 3.1). Piaget termed the first two years of life the **sensorimotor stage**. Cognitive development in this stage involves learning how to coordinate the activities of the senses (such as watching an object as it moves across your field of vision) with motor activities (such as reaching out to grab the object). Next, from about age 2 to about age 7, is the **preoperational stage**. Here the child becomes capable of representing the world symbolically, such as through the use of language and in play such as using a broom to represent a horse. However, children in this stage are still very limited in their ability to use mental operations – that is, in their ability to manipulate objects mentally and reason about them in a way that accurately represents how the world works. For example, children of this age are easily enchanted by stories about how a pumpkin changes into a stagecoach or a frog into a prince, because with their limited understanding of the world these are not just fanciful tales but real possibilities.

Concrete operations is the next stage, lasting from about age 7 to about age 11. During this stage, children become more adept at using **mental operations**, and this skill leads to a more advanced understanding of the world. For example, they understand that if you take water from a short wide glass and pour it into a taller, thinner glass, the amount of water remains the same (a problem of conservation that we talked about earlier). Mentally, they can reverse this action and conclude that the amount of water could not have changed just because it was poured into a different container. However, despite these new understandings, children in this stage focus on what can be experienced and manipulated in the physical environment (Doherty and Hughes, 2009; Woolfolk et al., 2008). They have difficulty transferring their reasoning to situations and problems that require them to think systematically about possibilities and hypotheses. That is where the next stage, formal operations, comes in.

Table 3.1 Piaget's Stages of Cognitive Development

Ages	Stage	Characteristics
0–2	Sensorimotor	Learns to coordinate the activities of the senses with motor activities.
2–7	Preoperational	Capable of symbolic representation, such as in language, but has limited ability to use mental operations.
7–11	Concrete operations	Capable of using mental operations, but only in 'concrete', immediate experience; experiences difficulty thinking hypothetically.
11–15/20	Formal operations	Capable of thinking logically and abstractly, capable of formulating hypotheses and testing them systematically; thinking is more complex, for example thinking in contemporaneous and sometimes interacting trains of thought, and thinking about thinking (metacognition).

Formal Operations in Adolescence

The stage of **formal operations** begins at about age 11 and reaches completion somewhere between ages 15 and 20, according to Piaget (1972), so this is the stage most relevant to cognitive development in adolescence. Children in concrete operations can perform simple tasks that require logical and systematic thinking, but formal operations allows adolescents to reason about complex tasks and problems involving multiple variables. Essentially, formal operations involves the development of an ability to think scientifically and apply the rigour of the scientific method to cognitive tasks.

To demonstrate how this works, let us look at one of the tasks Piaget used to test whether a child has progressed from concrete to formal operations. This task is known as the **pendulum problem** (Inhelder and Piaget, 1958). Children and adolescents are shown a pendulum (consisting of a weight hanging from a string and then set in motion) and asked to try to figure out what determines the speed at which the pendulum sways from side to side. Is it the heaviness of the weight, the length of the string, the height from which the weight is dropped or the force with which it is dropped? They are given various weights and various lengths of string to use in their deliberations.

Children in concrete operations tend to approach the problem with random attempts, often changing more than one variable at a time. They may try the heaviest weight on the longest string dropped from medium height with medium force, then a medium weight on the smallest string dropped from medium height with lesser force. When the speed of the pendulum changes, it remains difficult for them to say what caused the change because they altered more than one variable. If they happen to arrive at the right answer – it's the length of the string (but you knew that already!) – they find it difficult to explain why. This is crucial to understand how Piagetian theory is constructed and applied; cognitive advances at each stage are reflected not just in the solutions children devise for problems but in their explanations for how they arrived at the solution.

It is only with formal operations that we can find the right answer to a problem like this and explain why it is the right answer. The formal operational thinker approaches the pendulum problem by utilising the kind of hypothetical thinking involved in a scientific experiment. The thought process spoken out loud could be something like this.

'Let's see, it could be weight; let me try changing the weight while keeping everything else the same. No, that's not it; same speed. Maybe it's length; if I change the length while keeping everything else the same, that seems to make a difference; it goes faster with a shorter string. But let me try height, too; no change; then force; no change there, either. So it's length, and only length, that makes the difference.' Thus, the formal operational thinker changes one variable while holding the others constant and tests the different possibilities systematically. Through this process, the formal operational thinker arrives at an answer that is not only correct but can be explained and defended. The capacity for this kind of thinking, which Piaget (1972) termed **hypothetical-deductive reasoning**, is at the heart of Piaget's concept of formal operations.

The pendulum problem.

THINKING CRITICALLY

Think of a real-life example of how you have used hypothetical-deductive reasoning. A stern test of your critical thinking ability is to think here of an example outside of normal scientific activity; perhaps something more to do with personal issues. The key is to find a problem with a number of variables, one of which is the key to solving the problem.

CONNECT AND EXTEND

Theory of mind is a *theory* based upon our presumption that others have a mind like our own, because we can only really 'observe' our own minds. Would Piaget agree? Read 'Where is the "theory" in theory of mind?' by Alan Costall and Ivan Leudar in *Theory & Psychology*, Volume 14, Number 5 (October 2004), pp. 623–646

In Piaget's research, as well as the research of many others (e.g. Lee and Freire, 2003; Elkind, 2001), adolescents perform the pendulum problem and similar tasks significantly better than pre-adolescent children. The transitional period from concrete operations to formal operations on these tasks usually takes place between the ages 11 and 14 (Keating, 2004). However, there may be something about the pendulum test itself that makes it difficult for even older teenagers. For example, it has been noted in one European study that secondary schools pupils and even university undergraduates have difficulty answering question about the simple pendulum (Czudková and Musilová, 2000) and a later study in Spain found an association between formal operations thinking of middle teenagers as measured using a Spanish version of the Tobin and Capie (1981) Test of Logical Thinking (TOLT) and their ability to deal with mechanics problems such as the pendulum test (Oliva, 2003). This study would seem to show that transition from concrete to formal thinking has usually taken place by the age of 15 and that the mechanical problems of a pendulum are not so straightforward as Piaget's experiments appeared to assume.

The problems Piaget used to assess the attainment of formal operations were essentially scientific problems, involving the capacity to formulate hypotheses, test them systematically and then make deductions (that is, draw conclusions) on the basis of the results (Piaget and Inhelder, 1969; Inhelder and Piaget, 1958). However, a number of other aspects of formal operations focus less on scientific thinking and more on logical or applied reasoning (Gaines, 2009; Keating, 2004). These include the development of capacities for **abstract thinking, complex thinking** and thinking about thinking (called **metacognition**). Piaget discussed all of these capacities, but since then, and as we shall see, other scholars have also conducted considerable research on them.

Abstract Thinking

Something that is abstract is something that is strictly a mental concept or process; it cannot be experienced directly, through the senses. Examples of abstract concepts include time, friendship and faith. You were introduced to several abstract concepts in Chapters 1 and 2, including culture, the West and adolescence itself. You cannot actually see, hear, taste or touch these things; they exist only as ideas. *Abstract* is often contrasted with *concrete*, which refers to things you can experience through the senses. The contrast is especially appropriate here because the stage preceding formal operations was termed by Piaget 'concrete operations'. Children in concrete operations can apply logic only to things they can experience directly, concretely, whereas the capacity for formal operations includes the ability to think abstractly and apply logic to mental operations as well (Schmidt and Thompson, 2008; Fischer and Pruyne, 2003; Piaget, 1972).

Suppose I tell you that $A = B$ and $B = C$, and then ask you, does $A = C$? It is easy for you, as a university student, to see that the answer is yes, even though you have no idea what A, B and C represent. However, children thinking in terms of concrete operations tend to be mystified by this problem. They need to know what A, B and C represent. In contrast, you realise that it does not matter what they are. The same logic applies to A, B and C no matter what they represent.

But abstract thinking involves more than just the capacity to solve this kind of logical puzzle. It also involves the capacity to think about abstract concepts such as justice, freedom, goodness, evil and time. Adolescents become capable of engaging in discussions about politics, morality and religion in ways they could not when they were younger because with adolescence they gain the capacity to understand and use the abstract ideas involved in such discussions (McIntosh et al., 2007; Granqvist, 2002; Gillies, 2000). It may useful at this point to 'bear in mind' that recent research on brain development suggests that the capacity for abstract thinking is based on a growth spurt in the brain in late adolescence and emerging adulthood which strengthens the connections between the frontal cortex and the other parts of the brain (Fischer and Pruyne, 2003; Thompson et al., 2000). As already promised, we will discuss brain development and important recent research later in the chapter.

Complex Thinking

Formal operational thinking is more complex than the kind of thinking that occurs in concrete operations. Concrete operational thinkers tend to focus on one aspect of things, usually the most obvious, but formal operational thinkers are more likely to see things in greater complexity and perceive multiple aspects of a situation or an idea. This greater complexity can be seen in, for example, the use of metaphor and sarcasm.

Metaphor

With formal operations, adolescents become capable of understanding metaphors that are more subtle than metaphors they may have understood earlier (Levorato and Cacciari, 2002). Metaphors are complex because they have more than one meaning, the literal, 'concrete' meaning as well as less obvious, more subtle meanings. Poems and novels are full of metaphors. Consider, for example, this passage in a poem by T. S. Eliot entitled 'A Dedication to My Wife':

> No peevish winter wind shall chill
> No sullen tropic sun shall wither
> The roses in the rose-garden which is ours and
> ours only.

On one level, the meaning of the passage is about the hardiness of the roses in a garden, but there is a second meaning as well. The roses are a metaphor of the author's optimism for the enduring vitality of the love between him and his wife. Adolescents can grasp multiple meanings such as this to a degree that children usually cannot (Genereux and McKeough, 2007; Gibbs et al., 2002).

One recent study examined understandings of metaphors in adolescents and emerging adults ages 11–29 (Duthie et al., 2008). For the metaphors the study used sayings such as 'One bad apple spoils the whole barrel.' Early adolescents tended to describe the meanings of the metaphors in concrete terms (e.g. age 11, 'There's a big barrel of apples and a woman picks up one that is rotten and there are worms in it and the worms go to all the other apples'). In later adolescence and emerging adulthood, understanding of the metaphors became more abstract and more focused on their social meanings (e.g. age 21, 'One bad comment can spoil the entire conversation').

Sarcasm

Sarcasm is another example of complex communication. As with metaphors, more than one interpretation is possible. 'Nice shirt' someone says to you as they greet you. That has a literal meaning, as a compliment for your fine taste in fashion. But depending on who says it, and how they say it, it could have another and quite different meaning: 'What a stupid looking shirt! You look like an idiot.' Adolescents become capable of understanding (and using) sarcasm in a way children cannot, and as a result sarcasm is more often part of adolescents' conversations (Pexman and Glenright, 2007). Media that employ sarcasm, such as *Mad* magazine and *The Simpsons* television show, are more popular among adolescents than other age groups, perhaps because adolescents enjoy using their newly developed abilities for understanding sarcasm (Katz et al., 2004).

One early but important study examined how understanding of sarcasm changes from middle childhood through adolescence (Demorest et al., 1984). Participants of various ages were presented with stories in which they were asked to judge whether a particular remark was sincere, deceptive or sarcastic (for example, 'That new haircut looks terrific'). Children aged 9 or younger had difficulty identifying sarcastic remarks, but 13-year-olds were better at it than 9-year-olds, and university students were better than 13-year-olds.

CONNECT AND EXTEND

A commonly used test of social perception including the ability to recognise sarcasm is *The Awareness of Social Inference Test (TASIT)* written by Skye McDonald, Sharon Flanagan and Jennifer Rollins. First published in 2002 by Pearson, it has itself been subject to tests of reliability and clinical trials. Do some surfing to find out the scope and applicability of the test.

Metacognition: Thinking About Thinking

One of the abstractions adolescents develop is the capacity to think about their own thoughts. They become aware of their thinking processes in a way that children are not, and this ability enables them to monitor and reason about those processes. This capacity for 'thinking about thinking', known as metacognition, enables adolescents to learn and solve problems more efficiently (Klaczynski, 2006; 2005; Roeschl-Heils et al., 2003; Rozencwajg, 2003; Kuhn, 1999). In fact, one study indicates that instructing adolescents in metacognitive strategies improves their overall academic performance (Kramarski, 2004).

Metacognition first develops in adolescence, but it continues to develop in emerging adulthood and beyond. One study compared adolescents and adults of various ages (Vukman, 2005). They were given various problems and asked to 'think out loud' so that the researchers could record their metacognitive processes. Self-awareness of thinking processes rose from adolescence to emerging adulthood and again from emerging adulthood to mid-life, then declined in later adulthood.

I (MH) can give a personal example. My first degree is in mathematics. When solving a new kind of problem, my tutor taught me to divide my page into two columns. Down the left-hand side I wrote the workings of the solution and down the right a running record of what I was thinking. My long-suffering tutor (I really wanted to do psychology rather than mathematics) wanted to understand my thinking and, more importantly, wanted me to understand my own thinking. When I 'hit a brick wall' during my search for a solution to a problem I traced back my thinking to decisions I had taken, alternatives I had ignored or gaps in the logic. By this method my tutor, and more importantly I, could generally find any error in the process of thinking through the problem and finding the solution.

You probably use metacognition to some degree as you read; almost certainly you use it when studying for an exam. As you move along from sentence to sentence, you may monitor your comprehension and ask yourself, 'What did that sentence mean? How is it connected to the sentence that preceded it? How can I make sure I remember what that means?' As you study for an examination, you look over the material you are required to know, asking yourself if you know what the concepts mean, finding the gaps in your understanding and determining which are the most important ideas for you to know.

Metacognition applies not only to learning and problem solving but also to social topics – thinking about what you think of others and what they think of you. We will explore these topics in the section on social cognition later in the chapter.

Limitations of Piaget's Theory

Piaget's theory of cognitive development has endured remarkably well. Decades after he first presented it, Piagetian theory remains the dominant theory of cognitive development from birth to the end of adolescence (Doherty & Hughes, *ibid.*). However, that does not mean that the theory has been verified in every respect. On the contrary, Piaget's theory of formal operations is the part of Piagetian theory that has been critiqued the most and which requires more modification than his ideas about development at younger ages (Keating, 2004; Lee and Freire, 2003). The limitations of Piaget's theory of formal operations fall into two related categories: individual differences in the attainment of formal operations and the cultural basis of adolescent cognitive development.

Individual Differences in Formal Operations

You may recall from earlier in the chapter that Piaget's theory of cognitive development puts a strong emphasis on maturation. Although he acknowledged some degree of **individual differences**, especially in the timing of transitions from one stage to the next, Piaget asserted that most people proceed through the same stages at about the same ages because they experience the same maturational processes (Inhelder and Piaget, 1958). Every 8-year-old is in the stage of concrete operations; every 15-year-old should be a formal operational thinker. Furthermore, Piaget's idea of stages means that 15-year-olds should reason in formal operations in all aspects of their lives because the same mental structure should be applied no matter what the nature of the problem (Keating, 2004).

Abundant research over time indicates decisively that these claims were inaccurate, especially for formal operations (e.g. Lee and Freire, 2003; Overton and Byrnes, 1991). In adolescence and even in adulthood, a great range of individual differences exists in the extent to which people use formal operations. Some adolescents and adults use formal operations over a wide range of situations; others use it selectively; still others appear to use it rarely or not at all. One early review indicated that by the age of 13/14 years, only about one-third of adolescents can be said to have reached formal operations (Strahan, 1983). These results were shown to be reliable over time by a number of quasi-longitudinal studies (e.g. Shayer and Ginsburg, 2009). Other reviews find that, on any particular Piagetian task of formal operations, the success rate among late adolescents and adults is only 40 per cent to 60 per cent, depending on the task and on individual factors such as educational background (Keating, 2004; Lawson and Wollman, 2003). Thus even in emerging adulthood and beyond, a large proportion of people use formal operations either inconsistently or not at all.

Even people who demonstrate the capacity for formal operations tend to use it selectively, for problems and situations in which they have the most experience and knowledge (Flavell et al., 2002; Klaczynski et al., 1998). For example, adolescents who are experienced chess players may apply formal operational thinking to chess strategies, even though they may not have performed well on standard Piagetian tasks such as the pendulum problem or the Tower of London task (Unterrainer et al., 2006). An adolescent with experience working on cars ('scientifically' working out what the problem is) may find it easy to apply principles of formal operations in that area but have difficulty performing classroom tasks in mathematical or historical thinking that require formal operations.

Having said that, it is interesting to note that specific kinds of experience, in the form of science and maths education, is also important for the development of formal operations. Adolescents who have successfully completed courses in maths and science are more likely than other adolescents to exhibit formal operational thought (Keating, 2004; Lawson and Wollman, 2003), especially when the courses involve hands-on experience. This makes sense, if you think about the kinds of reasoning required for formal operations. The hypothetical-deductive reasoning that is so important to formal operations is taught as part of maths and science classes; it is the kind of thinking that is the basis of the scientific method. Not surprisingly, it is easier for adolescents to develop this kind of thinking if they have systematic instruction in it, and the more they have applied hypothetical-deductive thinking to problems in classes, the more likely they are to perform well on tasks (such as the pendulum problem) used to assess formal operations.

Professor of Educational Psychology, William Gray (1990) and more recently psychologist and science educator Peter Sutherland (2005, 1999) suggest that Piaget underestimated how much effort, energy and knowledge it takes to use formal operations. According to Gray concrete operations are sufficient for most daily tasks and problems, and because formal operations are so much more difficult and taxing, people often will not use formal operations even if they have the capacity to do so. Formal operations might be useful for scientific thinking, but most people will not go to the time and trouble to apply it to every aspect of their daily lives. When people have a problem, they generally do not feel the need to understand the true nature of the problem, they just want it resolved. Thus, it could be argued that the concept of formal operations is inadequate for describing how most people – adolescents as well as adults – solve practical problems and draw causal inferences in their everyday lives (Keating, 2004). Perhaps that is why you might have found it difficult in an earlier Thinking critically feature to identify your use of hypothetical-deductive reasoning outside of a maths or science context.

Culture and Formal Operations

Do cultures differ in whether their members reach formal operations at all? It is now widely accepted that cultures vary greatly in the prevalence with which their members display an understanding of formal

In traditional cultures, practical activities sometimes require formal operations. Here, adolescents in Indonesia help build a subsistence farm.

CONNECT AND EXTEND

Many educators face the problem of how to handle the different ways in which young people from different cultures approach learning. For a very readable example try 'Cognitive style and socialisation: an exploration of learned sources of style in Finland, Poland and the UK' by Jeanne Hill, Arja Puurula, Agnieszka Sitko-Lutek and Anna Rakowska in *Educational Psychology*, Volume 20, Number 3 (2000), pp. 285–305

operations on the kinds of tasks that Piaget and others have used to measure it (Downing et al., 2007; Suizzo, 2000). A consensus has formed among scholars that in many cultures formal operational thought (as measured with Piagetian tasks) does not develop and that this is particularly true in cultures that do not have formal schooling (Cole, 1996).

Piaget responded to these criticisms (1972) by suggesting that even though all persons reach the potential for formal operational thinking, they apply it first (and perhaps only) to areas in which their culture has provided them with the most experience and expertise. In other words, it may not make sense to give such tasks as the pendulum problem to people in all cultures because the materials and the task may be unfamiliar to them. However, if you use materials and tasks familiar to them and relevant to their daily lives, you may find that they display formal operational thinking under those conditions.

Studies like the ones described in the upcoming *Cultural Focus* feature and the example of Mario at the start of this chapter indicate that Piaget's ideas about cognitive development in adolescence can be applied to different cultures as long as they are adapted to the ways of life of each culture. However, in every culture there is likely to be considerable variation in the extent to which adolescents and adults display formal operational thought, from persons who display it in a wide variety of circumstances to persons who display it little or not at all. Finally some theorists (e.g. Susanne Prediger, 2001) view mathematics as a 'culture of formal thinking' and thus it follows that the learning of mathematics (and other forms of training in formal thinking) can be understood as intercultural learning.

COGNITIVE DEVELOPMENT IN EMERGING ADULTHOOD: POSTFORMAL THINKING

In Piaget's theory, formal operations lie at the end point of cognitive development. Once the ability to use formal operations is fully attained, by age 20 at the latest, cognitive maturation is complete. However, like many aspects of Piaget's theory of formal operations, this view has been altered by research, which indicates that cognitive development often continues in important ways during emerging adulthood. This research has inspired theories of cognitive development beyond formal operations, known as **postformal thinking** (Sinnott, 2003; 1998) and two of the most notable aspects of postformal thinking in emerging adulthood concern advances in pragmatism and reflective judgement.

Pragmatism

Pragmatism involves adapting logical thinking to the practical constraints of real-life situations. Theories of postformal thought emphasising pragmatism have been developed over three decades by several scholars (e.g. Sinnott, 2003; Labouvie-Vief, 2006; 1998; Labouvie-Vief and Diehl, 2002; Basseches, 1989; 1984) all of whom propose that the problems faced in normal adult life often contain complexities and inconsistencies that cannot be addressed with the logic of formal operations.

According to psychologist Gisela Labouvie-Vief (2006; 1998; 1990; 1982), cognitive development in emerging adulthood is distinguished from adolescent

THINKING CRITICALLY

If abstract thinking is required for the formation of ideas about wealth, power and disadvantage, right and wrong, and good and evil, how can you explain why such ideas exist even in cultures in which maths and science education is rare?

CONNECT AND EXTEND

How pragmatic are students about attending lectures? Read 'Should we still lecture or just post examination questions on the Web?: the nature of the shift towards pragmatism in undergraduate lecture attendance' by Sara Dolnicar in *Quality in Higher Education*, Volume 11, Number 2 (2005), pp. 103–115

thinking by a greater recognition and incorporation of practical limitations to logical thinking. Labouvie-Vief proposes that adolescents exaggerate the extent to which logical thinking will be effective in real life. In contrast, emerging adulthood brings a growing awareness of how social factors, and other factors specific to a given situation, must be taken into account in approaching most of life's problems.

For example, in one study (1990) Labouvie-Vief presented adolescents and emerging adults with stories and asked them to predict what they thought would happen. One story described a man who was a heavy drinker, especially at parties. His wife had warned him that if he came home drunk one more time, she would leave him and take the children. Some time later he went to an office party and came home drunk. What would she do?

Labouvie-Vief found that adolescents tended to respond strictly in terms of the logic of formal operations:

the wife said she would leave if her husband came home drunk once more, he came home drunk, therefore she will leave. In contrast, emerging adults considered many possible dimensions of the situation. Did he apologise and beg her not to leave? Did she really mean it when she said she would leave him? Does she have a place to go? Has she considered the possible effects on the children?

Rather than relying strictly on logic, with a belief in definite wrong and right answers, the emerging adults tended to be postformal thinkers in the sense that they realised that the problems of real life often involve a great deal of complexity and ambiguity. However, Labouvie-Vief (2006) emphasises that with postformal thinking, as with formal thinking, not everyone continues to move to higher levels of cognitive complexity, and many people continue to apply earlier, more concrete thinking in emerging adulthood and beyond.

CULTURAL FOCUS

Formal Operations Among the Sami

Until recent decades, children and adolescents of the Laplanders (now referred to as Sami) of Northern Europe had never attended school (Stern, 2003). If Sami adolescents had tried to perform the tasks of formal operations, they would probably have done poorly (Miettinen and Peisa, 2002).

But did they, nevertheless, possess and use formal operational thinking? Consider the kind of work adolescent boys and girls performed by the age of 12 or 13 (Meinander, 2011).

Boys
Harnessing dog team for sledge
Pushing and pulling sledge when stuck in snow
Preparing bows and arrows, harpoons and spears for hunting
Helping to build snowhouses
Helping to erect skin tents
Hunting polar bears, seals, etc.
Fishing

Girls
Cutting fresh ice
Fetching water
Gathering moss for fire
Caring for infants and small children
Sewing
Tanning animal skins
Cooking

Not all these tasks would require formal operations. Assigning them to adolescents (rather than children) may have been appropriate simply because adolescents' larger physical size meant they could perform many tasks better than children, such as fetching water and helping to move a sledge that was stuck in the snow. Other tasks, however, would be likely to demand the kind of thinking involved in formal operations.

Take the hunting trips that adolescent boys would participate in with their fathers, or sometimes undertake by themselves. To become successful, a boy would have to think through the components involved in a hunt and test his knowledge of hunting through experience. If he were unsuccessful on a particular outing, he would have to ask himself why. Was it because of the location he chose, the equipment he took along or the tracking method he used? Or were there other (at this point unknown or unappreciated) causes? On the next hunt he might alter one or more of these factors to see if his success improved. This would be hypothetical-deductive reasoning, altering and testing different variables to arrive at the solution to a problem.

Or take the example of an adolescent girl learning to tan animal hides. Tanning is an elaborate process, involving several complicated steps. Girls were given responsibility for this task on their own beginning at about age 14. If a girl failed to do it properly, as would sometimes happen, the hide would be ruined, and her family would be disappointed and angry with her. She would have to ask herself, where did the process go wrong? Mentally, she would work her way back through the various steps in the process, trying to identify her error. This, too, is formal operational thinking, mentally considering various hypotheses in order to identify a promising idea to test.

In recent decades, globalisation has come to the Laplanders of Northern Europe, and adolescents spend most of their day in school rather than working alongside their parents (Stern, 2003; Kral et al., 2002). As a result, they have a greater range of opportunities than they had before. Some of them go to larger nearby cities after secondary school to receive professional training of various kinds. By now, they face many of the same cognitive demands as adolescents in the Scandinavian and Russian majority cultures.

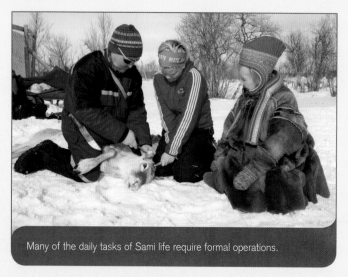
Many of the daily tasks of Sami life require formal operations.

As has so often happened in the course of globalisation, however, there have been negative repercussions as well (Higgins et al., 2008; Kassam, 2006; Leineweber and Arensman, 2003; Kral et al., 2002). Many adolescents find school boring and irrelevant to their lives, and some of them turn to smoking, alcohol, glue sniffing and shoplifting to add excitement. Sami young people are not only in transition between childhood and adulthood but it could be argued are still in transition between two (seemingly) incompatible ways of life, and the transition is not easy to make.

CONNECT AND EXTEND

A useful European perspective on using dialectic thinking (reconciling contradictory arguments) in lifelong learning contexts is provided by teacher-trainer Ted Bailey in 'Analogy, dialectics and lifelong learning', *International Journal of Lifelong Education*, Volume 22, Number 2 (2003), pp. 132–146

A similar theory of cognitive development in emerging adulthood has been presented by psychologist Professor Michael Basseches (e.g. 1989). Like Labouvie-Vief, Basseches views cognitive development in emerging adulthood as involving a recognition that formal logic can rarely be applied to the problems most people face in their daily lives. **Dialectical thought** is Basseches's term for the kind of thinking that develops in emerging adulthood, involving a growing awareness that problems often have no clear solution and that two opposing strategies or points of view may each have some merit. Problems also have to be addressed without all the relevant information. For example, people may have to decide whether to leave a job they dislike without knowing whether their next job will be more satisfying.

Some cultures may promote dialectical thinking more than others. Kaiping Peng and Richard Nisbett (1999) have proposed that Chinese culture traditionally promotes dialectical thought; the approach to learning strives to reconcile contradictions and combine opposing perspectives by seeking a middle ground. In contrast, they argue, the Western hemisphere approach tends to apply logic in a way that polarises contradictory perspectives in an effort to determine which is correct.

THINKING CRITICALLY

Think of a problem you have had lately. Can you apply the insights of Labouvie-Vief and Basseches to the problem?

Reflective Judgement

Reflective judgement is another cognitive quality that has been found to develop in emerging adulthood. It is the capacity to evaluate the accuracy and logical coherence of evidence and arguments. An influential theory of the development of reflective judgement in emerging

adulthood has been proposed by educational psychologist William Perry (1999), who based his theory on his studies of university students in their late teens and early 20s. According to Perry adolescents tend to engage in **dualistic thinking**, which means they often see situations and issues in polarised terms – an act is either right or wrong, with no in-between; a statement is either true or false, regardless of the nuances or the situation to which it is being applied. In this sense, adolescents lack reflective judgement. However, reflective judgement begins to develop for most people in their late teens. First a stage of **multiple thinking** takes

Reflective judgement tends to improve during university.

CONNECT AND EXTEND

Contrast emerging relativism in childhood with the ability of young adults to compare the merits of competing views by reading 'Children's thinking about diversity of belief in the early school years: judgments of relativism, tolerance and disagreeing persons' by Cecilia Wainryb, Leigh A. Shaw, Marcie Langley, Kim Cottam and Renee Lewis in *Child Development*, Volume 75, Number 3 (May, 2004), pp. 687–703

place, in which emerging adults believe there are two or more sides to every story, two or more legitimate views of every issue, and that it can be difficult to justify one position as the only true or accurate one. In this stage, people tend to value all points of view equally, even to the extent of asserting that it is impossible to make any judgements about whether one point of view is more valid than another.

By the early 20s, according to William Perry, multiple thinking develops into **relativism**. Like people in the stage of multiple thinking, relativists are able to recognise the legitimacy of competing points of view. However, rather than denying that one view could be more persuasive than another, relativists attempt to compare the merits of competing views. Finally, by the end of their university years, many emerging adults reach a stage of **commitment** in which they commit themselves to certain points of view they believe to be the most valid, while being open to re-evaluating their views if new evidence is presented to them.

Research on reflective judgement indicates that significant gains may take place in emerging adulthood (Kitchener et al., 2006; King and Kitchener, 2004; 2002). However, the gains that take place in emerging adulthood appear to be due more to education than to maturation (Labouvie-Vief, 2006; Pirttilae-Backman and Kajanne, 2001) – that is, people who pursue a university education during emerging adulthood show greater advances in reflective judgement than people who do not. Also, Perry and his colleagues acknowledged that the development of reflective judgement is likely to be more common in a culture that values pluralism and whose educational system promotes tolerance of diverse points of view. However, thus far, little cross-cultural research has taken place on reflective judgement.

THE INFORMATION-PROCESSING APPROACH

The approach of Piaget and the Piagetians – scholars who continued his line of theory and research – describes how adolescents and emerging adults develop capacities such as hypothetical-deductive reasoning, abstract thinking and reflective judgement. The focus is on how the development of these general cognitive capacities is reflected in young people's performance on specific tasks such as the pendulum problem. Piaget also emphasised the way cognitive abilities change with age, from pre-adolescence to adolescence, from concrete operations to formal operations.

However, the **information-processing (IP) approach** to understanding cognitive development in adolescence is quite different. Rather than viewing cognitive development as **discontinuous**, that is, as separated into distinct stages, the way Piaget did, the information-processing approach views cognitive change as **continuous**; gradual and steady. The

THINKING CRITICALLY

Citizens of the United Kingdom can vote in European, national and local elections from the age of 18. In fact it would be perfectly possible for an 18-year-old to be elected leader of a political party and, if winners of a general election, to be prime minister. It is feasible but perhaps not desirable for such a young person to elected prime minister. What cognitive qualities might be insufficiently developed at 18 for a person to be capable of exercising the duties of the office? (William Pitt, the Younger (28 May 1759–23 January 1806) was a politician who, in 1783, became the youngest British prime minister of the United Kingdom at the age of 24. He was ridiculed for his youthfulness.)

information-processing approach does not have a developmental focus – how mental structures and ways of thinking change with age – but focuses on the thinking processes that exist at all ages (Daurignac et al., 2006; Bishop, 2000). Nevertheless, some studies of information processing do compare adolescents or emerging adults to people of other ages.

The original model for the information-processing approach was the computer (Green, 2001; Mooney et al., 1999). Information-processing researchers and theorists have tried to break down human thinking into separate parts in the same way that the functions of a computer are separated into capacities for *attention*, *processing* and *memory*. In the pendulum problem, someone taking the information-processing approach would examine how adolescents draw their attention to the most relevant aspects of the problem, process the results of each trial, remember the results, and retrieve the results from previous trials to compare to the most recent trial. In this way the IP approach is a **componential approach** (Shiotsu and Weir, 2007) because it involves breaking down the thinking process into its various components.

More recent models of information processing have moved away from a simple computer analogy and recognised that the brain is more complex than any computer (Ashcraft, 2002). Rather than occurring in a step-by-step fashion as in a computer, in human thinking the different components operate simultaneously, as Figure 3.1 illustrates. Nevertheless, the focus of IP theory remains on the components of the thinking process, especially attention and memory.

Let us look at each of the components of information processing and how they change during adolescence and emerging adulthood. For all of the components, adolescents perform better than younger children, and for some, emerging adults perform better than adolescents.

Attention

Information processing begins with stimulus information that enters the senses (see Figure 3.1), but much of what you see, hear and touch is processed no further. For example, as you are reading this chapter, there may be sounds in the environment, other sights in your visual field, and the feeling of your body in the seat where you are reading, but if you are focusing on what you are reading most of this information goes no further than sensory memory. The only information you process is the information on which you focus your attention. Are you able to read a textbook while someone else in the same room is watching television? Are you able to have a conversation at a party where music and other conversations are blaring loudly all around you? These are tasks that require **selective attention** – the ability to focus on relevant information while screening out information that is irrelevant (Sreenivasan and Jha, 2007; Weerd et al., 2006; Yeh et al., 2005; Mason et al., 2003). Adolescents tend to be better than pre-adolescent children at tasks that require selective attention, and emerging adults are generally better than adolescents (Huang-Pollock et al., 2002). Adolescents are also more adept than pre-adolescents at tasks that require **divided attention** – reading a book and listening to music at the same time, for example – but even for adolescents divided attention may result in less efficient learning than if attention were focused entirely on one thing. One interesting and relevant study (I'm – MH – listening to music while writing this!) found that watching TV interfered with adolescents' homework performance but listening to music did not (Pool et al., 2003).

One aspect of selective attention is the ability to analyse a set of information and select the most important parts of it for further attention. When you listen to a lecture, for example, your attention may fluctuate. You may monitor the information being presented and increase or decrease your level of attention according to your judgement of the information's importance. This aspect of selective attention is also a key part of problem solving; one of the initial steps of solving any problem is to decide where to direct your attention. For example, I'm (MH) trying to concentrate on writing this part of the chapter as my wife is giving me instructions on where and when to

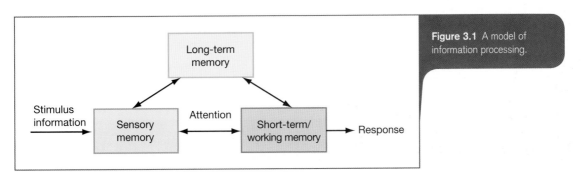

Figure 3.1 A model of information processing.

Capacities for selective attention and divided attention improve during adolescence.

meet for lunch. She is also trying to give me a lot of other information about which friends we are meeting that may or may not be relevant to me turning up at the right time and the right place. Adolescents are better than children at focusing on the most relevant aspects of a problem

THINKING CRITICALLY

Design a simple study to assess the abilities of adolescents or emerging adults for selective attention, and a separate study on their learning abilities under conditions of divided attention – perhaps performing a range of tasks while watching television. What would you expect to find?

(Slater, 2007; Sweeney, 2007; Brown and Wright, 2001). I wonder if husbands get better or worse at selective attention during lifespan development?

Storing and Retrieving Information: Short-term and Long-term Memory

Memory is a key part of information processing, perhaps even the most important part. IP theories liken memory to a store model; a model that suggests information is held in three parts – the **sensory register**, two types of **short-term memory** and **long-term memory**. Drawing your attention to something and processing information about it would not do you much good if you could not store the results in your memory and call them back into your mind when you needed them. The sensory register allows us to briefly store data. Try this – look at a picture, then close your eyes and you should see a visual image trace for a brief time. Some of the data received and held briefly in the sensory register is then selected for transfer to the **central executive** for action. Short-term memory is for information that is currently the focus of your attention. It has a limited capacity and retains information for only a short time, usually 15 to 30 seconds. Auditory information goes into a **phonological loop** (Baddeley and Larsen, 2007) and visual information on to a visuo-spatial sketchpad (see Figure 3.2 and nearby *Connect and Extend*). Information is either transferred into long-term memory through rehearsal or use (resending it around the loop) or it is lost.

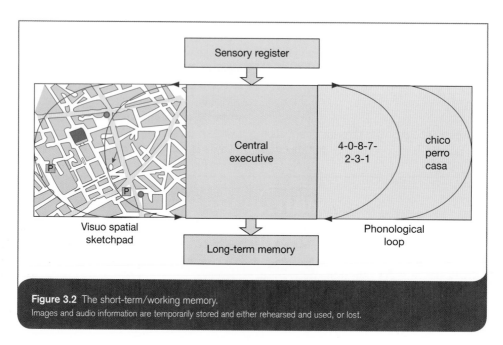

Figure 3.2 The short-term/working memory.
Images and audio information are temporarily stored and either rehearsed and used, or lost.

CONNECT AND EXTEND

Read an examination of working memory in teenagers (13–17 years) in 'Verbal working memory in children with mild intellectual disabilities' by M. VanderMolen, J. VanLuit, M. Jongmans and M. VanderMolen in *Journal of Intellectual Disability Research*, Volume 51, Number 2 (February 2007), pp. 162–169.

There are two types of short-term memory (Ashcraft, 2002). One type is involved in the input and storage of new information. This type of short-term memory has a limited capacity. The most common test of short-term memory capacity is to recite lists of numbers or words, gradually increasing the length, and see how many a person can remember without making a mistake. So if I give you the list: 1, 6, 2, 9, you can probably remember that pretty easily. Now try this: 8, 7, 1, 5, 3, 9, 2, 4, 1. Not so easy, is it? But you are certainly better at this kind of test now than when you were 8 or 10. Short-term memory capacity increases throughout childhood and early adolescence until the mid-teens, and remains stable after about age 16 (Crone et al., 2006; Luciana et al., 2005).

The other type of short-term memory is known as **working memory** (Cowan et al., 2002; Kail and Hall, 2001; Baddeley, 2000). Working memory is a 'mental workbench' where you keep information as you are working on it (Ashcraft, 2002). It is where you analyse and reason about information in the course of making decisions, solving problems and comprehending written and spoken language. The information may be new (in the short-term memory 'loops', or it may be called up from long-term memory, or some combination of the two. The size of a person's working memory is highly correlated with overall intelligence (Colom et al., 2003). Like short-term memory capacity for new information, the capacity of working memory increases from childhood through the mid-teens and then stabilises (Keage et al., 2008; Conklin et al., 2007; Luciana et al., 2005).

Long-term memory is memory for information that is committed to longer-term storage, so that you can draw on it again after a period when your attention has not been focused on it. The capacity of long-term memory is unlimited, and information is retained indefinitely. You can probably think of things you experienced ten or more years ago that you can still call up from your long-term memory. Long-term memory improves substantially between childhood and adolescence (Scherf et al., 2006; Luna et al., 2004; Fry and Hole, 1996).

THINKING CRITICALLY

Why do we have very few memories of the first few years of life, particularly the first two years? They should be locked away somewhere in our long-term memories having been transferred from our short-term and working memories. What are your first memories and why do you think you *can* 'find' them in your long-term memory when so much else seems to have been lost?

An early and important experiment by Robert Sternberg and his colleagues demonstrates how increases in working memory take place between childhood and adolescence (Sternberg and Nigro, 1980). They presented analogies to 8-year-olds, 11-year-olds, 14-year-olds and university students. For example, 'Sun is to moon as asleep is to . . . ?'

1 Star
2 Bed
3 Awake
4 Night

There was improvement with age, especially marked improvement between the younger pupils (7–11 years) and older students (13–22 years). Sternberg attributed the differences to short-term working memory capacities. Why use a test about analogies? Analogies take a considerable amount of short-term memory space. You have to keep the first set of words ('sun is to moon') and the nature of their relationship in your working memory continuously as you consider the other possible pairings ('asleep is to star . . . asleep is to bed . . .') and analyse their relationships as well. Before adolescence, children do not have enough working memory capacity to perform tasks like this very effectively. (The best answer is 'awake', in case you are wondering.)

Long-term memory also improves in adolescence. Adolescents are more likely than pre-adolescent children to use **mnemonic devices** (memory strategies), such as organising information into coherent patterns (Kwon et al., 2002). Think of what you do, for example, when you sit down to read a textbook chapter. You probably have various organisational strategies you have developed over the years (if you do not, you would be wise to develop some), such as writing a chapter outline, making notes in the margins, organising information into categories, underlining key passages, and so on. By planning your reading in these ways, you remember (and learn) more effectively.

Another way long-term memory improves in adolescence is that adolescents have more experience and more knowledge than children do, and these advantages enhance the effectiveness of long-term memory (Keating, 2004). Having more knowledge helps you learn new information and store it in long-term memory. This is a key difference between short-term and long-term memory. Because the capacity of short-term memory is limited, the more information you have in there already, the less effectively you can add new information to it. With long-term memory, however, the capacity is essentially unlimited, and the more you know the easier it is to learn new information.

What makes it easier is that you already have information in your memory that you can use to form associations with the new information, which makes it more likely that the new information will be remembered (Pressley and Schneider, 1997). For example, if you have already had a course in child development or human development, some of the concepts (such as concrete operations) and 'big names' (such as Piaget) already presented here may be familiar to you. If so, the new information you come across here will be easier for you to remember than for someone who has never had a related course before, because you can make associations between the new information and the knowledge you already have. Notice the relation to Piaget's concepts of assimilation and accommodation: The more information you have in your long-term memory, the more you can assimilate new information and the less accommodation is required.

Processing Information: Speed and Automaticity

Two other aspects of information processing also advance in adolescence. Adolescents generally process information with greater speed and **automaticity** than children (de Ridder et al., 2007). With regard to speed, think of the example of a computer or video game. Adolescents are generally better at such games than children because the games typically require the player to respond to changing circumstances, and adolescents are faster at processing information as those changes occur. In experimental situations involving tasks such as matching letters, there is an increase in speed of processing from age 10 through the late teens (Luna et al., 2004), with the largest gains coming in the early part of this age period.

Video games require speed of information processing.

THINKING CRITICALLY

Among the subjects you have studied in your secondary school or university education, in which have you found information easiest to remember, and which hardest? In what ways do the memory concepts presented here help explain why some subjects and some topics are easier than others for retaining information?

CONNECT AND EXTEND

A common mistake is to think that automaticity is gained only through rote learning. Isabelle De Ridder, Lieve Vangehuchten and Marta Seseña Gómez give another perspective in 'Enhancing automaticity through task-based language learning', *Applied Linguistics*, Volume 28, Number 2 (June 2007), pp. 309–315

HISTORICAL FOCUS

Gender and Cognitive Development in Emerging Adulthood

In most cultures throughout history, opportunities for enhancing cognitive development through education have been much more limited for females than for males. In Europe and other developed countries, this issue pertains particularly to emerging adulthood. Historically, there has been much more debate over and resistance to the idea that females should receive higher education. Many men in the eighteenth and nineteenth centuries were vehemently opposed to the idea that females should be allowed to attend colleges and universities.

Arguments against allowing young women the opportunity for higher education had two main features. One was the claim that 'too much' education for young women would be hazardous to them, because it would spoil their feminine qualities and because it might exhaust them and even make them ill. A second was the claim that women were inherently inferior to men intellectually, and therefore higher education would be wasted on them.

The first claim, that intellectual stimulation was hazardous to young women, was especially prevalent in the eighteenth century. A popular verse during that century read:

Why should girls be learn'd and wise?
Books only serve to spoil their eyes.
The studious eye but faintly twinkles
And reading paves the way to wrinkles.

This argument continued to be stated during the nineteenth century, but as women began to break through the barriers to higher education, some men claimed that women were 'scientifically' shown to be cognitively inferior. Even though a lot of scientific activity took place in the nineteenth century, a lot of pseudoscience did too. Some of the worst pseudoscience attempted to establish biologically based group differences in intelligence (Sowerwine, 2003). Even scientists who were otherwise respectable were infected by pseudoscientific reasoning when it came to issues of intelligence. Paul Broca, perhaps the most important figure in neurology in the nineteenth century, claimed that the smaller brains of women demonstrated their intellectual inferiority. He knew very well that brain size is related to body size and that women's smaller brain size simply reflected their smaller body size rather than inferior intelligence, but his prejudice against the cognitive capacities of women allowed him to talk himself out of it:

'We might ask if the small size of the female brain depends exclusively on the small size of her body . . . . But we must not forget that women are, on average, a little less intelligent than men . . . . We are therefore permitted to suppose that the relatively small size of the female brain depends in part upon her physical inferiority and in part upon her intellectual inferiority.' (1861, quoted in Gould, 1981, p. 104)

➤

Even worse were the pseudoscientific claims of Gustave Le Bon, the French scholar who was one of the founders of social psychology. He commented:

'In the most intelligent races, as among the Parisians, there are a large number of women whose brains are closer in size to those of gorillas than to the most developed male brains. This inferiority is so obvious that no one can contest it even for a moment; only its degree is worth discussion. All psychologists who have studied the intelligence of women . . . recognise today that they represent the most inferior forms of human evolution and that they are closer to children and savages than to an adult, civilised man. They excel in fickleness, inconstancy, absence of thought and logic, and incapacity to reason. Without doubt there exist some distinguished women, very superior to the average man, but they are as exceptional as the birth of any monstrosity, as, for example, of a gorilla with two heads; consequently we may neglect them entirely.' (1879, quoted in Gould, 1981, p. 48)

Keep in mind that Broca and Le Bon were not regarded as cranks or fools, but were two of the most important scholars of their time. They both reflected and affected attitudes towards the cognitive capacities of females that many people held in those days.

It wasn't until 1878 that the University of London became the first university in the UK to admit women to its degrees. In 1880, four women passed the BA examination and in 1881 two women obtained a BSc. By 1895, over 10 per cent of the graduates were women and by 1900 the proportion had increased to 30 per cent. In just over two decades this huge increase in numbers was nothing short of revolutionary and the revolution continued throughout the twentieth century and across the developed world. Now a decade into the twenty-first century females in Western countries exceed males' performance on nearly every measure of educational achievement (UNDP, 2009). However, it remains true in most of the developing world that females receive less education than males (UNICEF, 2005). It is also true that certain prejudices against females' cognitive abilities continue to exist, as we will discuss in the chapters on gender and school.

In the nineteenth century there were strong prejudices against women with regard to their intellectual abilities.

Automaticity is closely related to speed and to working memory capacity (Barsalou, 1992). The more automatic a cognitive task is, the faster you are able to do it. Also, the more automatic a task is, the less working memory capacity it takes, leaving more room for other tasks. For example, if you have automatic accurate recall of multiplication tables and associated numbers facts, then you are likely to be more able to solve mathematical problems involving more than one calculation. This author (MH) has spent many hours tutoring 16- and 17-year-olds in preparation for public examinations in mathematics. These youngsters understood the principles of basic trigonometry but were so frustratingly slow because they struggled with recalling nine times eight!

THINKING CRITICALLY

Think of an example of a task you performed today in which you demonstrated automaticity.

Limitations of the Information-processing Approach

Like Piaget's theory of cognitive development, the information-processing approach has not been without its critics. According to the critics, information-processing theorists and researchers are guilty of **reductionism**, which means breaking up a complex phenomenon into separate parts to such an extent that the meaning and coherence of the phenomenon as a whole become lost. From this perspective, what information-processing scholars see as a strength – the focus on the separate components of cognitive processes – is actually a weakness. In the words of Professor Deanna Kuhn, an influential developmental psychologist, this approach leads scholars to the false conclusion that 'the performance is *nothing but* the serial execution of a specified set of individual processes' (Kuhn, 1992, p. 236, emphasis in original).

According to the critics, by taking a reductionist approach, information-processing scholars have lost the holistic perspective that characterised Piaget's work. That is, they fail to consider how human cognition works as a whole rather than as a set of isolated parts. The analogy of a computer once favoured by information-processing scholars is misguided because human beings are not computers. Computers have no capacity (currently!) for self-reflection, and no awareness of how their cognitive processes are integrated, organised and monitored. Because self-reflection and self-awareness are central to human cognition, critics argue, overlooking them leaves the information-processing approach insufficient and inadequate.

Computers also lack emotions, and according to some scholars emotions must be taken into account when considering cognitive functioning. Evidence suggests that adolescents' emotions tend to be more intense and more variable than either pre-adolescent children's or adults' emotions (e.g. Larson et al., 2002), so this would seem to be an especially important consideration with regard to adolescent cognition. In one early study, researchers presented three dilemmas to secondary school pupils, university students and adults (Blanchard-Fields, 1986). The dilemmas were intended to vary in the degree of emotional involvement they elicited from the participants. The low-involvement dilemma concerned conflicting accounts of a war between two fictitious nations, whereas the high-involvement dilemmas concerned a conflict between parents and their adolescent son over whether he should join them on a visit to his grandparents, and a man and a woman disagreeing over whether her unintended pregnancy should end in abortion. The researchers found that the secondary school pupils and university students showed less advanced reasoning about the high-involvement dilemmas than about the low-involvement dilemmas, whereas the adults showed similar reasoning levels for all three dilemmas. This study indicates both that emotions can affect cognition and that the effect may be greater for adolescents and emerging adults than for adults. Recent brain research, as we shall later discuss, seems to support this conclusion (Sercombe and Paus, 2009).

CONNECT AND EXTEND

What is the daily emotional experience of adolescence? Read 'Continuity, stability and change in daily emotional experience across adolescence' by Reed W. Larson, Giovanni Moneta, Maryse H. Richards and Suzanne Wilson in *Child Development*, Volume 73, Number 4 (July 2002), pp. 1151–1165

PRACTICAL COGNITION: CRITICAL THINKING AND DECISION MAKING

Some research on cognitive development in adolescence and emerging adulthood has been especially concerned with how cognition operates in real life, applied to practical situations. Two areas of research on practical cognition in adolescence and emerging adulthood are critical thinking and decision making.

The Development of Critical Thinking

In combination, the changes in cognitive development during adolescence described thus far have the potential to provide adolescents with a greater capacity for **critical thinking**, which is thinking that involves not merely memorising information but analysing it, making judgements about what it means, relating it to other information, and considering how it might be valid or invalid.

According to the cognitive psychologist Daniel Keating (Keating, 2004; Keating and Sasse, 1996), cognitive development in adolescence provides the potential for critical thinking in several ways. First, a wider range of knowledge is available in long-term memory, across a variety of domains; thus, the ability to analyse and make judgements about new information is enhanced because more previous knowledge is available for comparison. Second, the ability to consider different kinds of knowledge simultaneously is increased, which makes it possible to think of new combinations of knowledge. Third, more metacognitive strategies are available for applying or gaining knowledge, such as planning and monitoring one's own comprehension; these strategies make it possible to think more critically about what is being learned.

However, Keating and others stress that critical-thinking skills do not develop automatically or inevitably in adolescence. On the contrary, critical thinking in adolescence requires a foundation of skills and knowledge obtained in childhood, along with an educational environment in adolescence that promotes and values critical thinking. According to Keating, gaining specific knowledge and learning critical-thinking skills are complementary goals. Critical thinking promotes gaining knowledge of a topic because it leads to a desire for underlying explanations, and gaining knowledge of a topic makes critical thinking possible because it makes relevant knowledge available for analysis and critique.

Given the potential usefulness of critical thinking in the learning process, one might expect that critical-thinking skills would be a primary goal of teaching in schools. However, observers of educational systems generally agree that schools do a mixed and sometimes poor job of promoting critical thinking (Weinstock et al., 2009; Ernst and Monroe, 2004; Keating, 2004; Gruber and Boreen, 2003). Assessments of adolescents' critical-thinking skills generally find that few adolescents develop such skills and use them capably, in part because such skills are so rarely promoted in the classroom. Instead of promoting the complementary development of knowledge and critical thinking, a great deal of secondary school teaching is limited to promoting the rote memorisation of facts, with the limited goal that students will be able to remember those facts until such time as an examination is taken (Barzilai and Zohar, 2008; Gruber and Boreen, 2003).

Asian secondary schools have been observed to have an especially strong emphasis on rote learning and to discourage critical thinking (Stevenson and Zusho, 2002). In contrast, some scholars argue that European secondary schools are better at providing a classroom environment that promotes critical thinking (Hamilton and Hamilton, 2006). In this textbook, the *Thinking Critically* questions in each chapter are intended to promote critical thinking on adolescence and emerging adulthood. They also provide you with examples of what critical thinking means.

THINKING CRITICALLY

Did your secondary school successfully promote critical thinking? If not, why do you think it did not? What barriers exist to the promotion of critical thinking in schools?

Can Adolescents Make Competent Decisions?

We saw in Chapter 1 that making independent decisions is one of the qualities that most adolescents and emerging adults in a variety of cultures consider to be a crucial part of becoming an adult (Arnett, 2004). What do studies tell us about whether adolescents possess the cognitive abilities to make decisions competently? The answer to this question has important implications, given that adolescents in many societies are confronted with decisions about whether to use drugs (including alcohol and cigarettes), when to become sexually active, and which educational path to pursue.

CONNECT AND EXTEND

To address the issue of autonomy as it relates to adolescent lifestyles or 'ways of living', read 'Autonomy and adolescence: a concept analysis' by Hila J. Spear and Pamela Kulbok in *Public Health* *Nursing*, Volume 21, Number 2 (1 March 2004), pp. 144–152

This area also has political and legal implications in debates over whether adolescents should have the right to make independent decisions about using contraception, obtaining an abortion or pursuing various medical treatments. In the United Kingdom, teenagers who are 16 and 17 years of age are entitled to consent to their own treatment, and this consent cannot be overruled by their parents.

Children who are under 16 years of age can also consent to their own treatment if it is thought that they have sufficient intelligence, competence and understanding to fully appreciate what is involved in their treatment. No one except the courts can override the consent of a child who is under 16 years of age. However, a person who has parental responsibility for a child, or a teenager aged 16 or 17, can override that consent if the child refuses treatment.

As far as UK law is concerned, 10 years old is the legal age of 'criminal responsibility'. Therefore, children under the age of 10 are not considered to have reached an age where they can be held responsible for their crimes, so they cannot be charged with any criminal offence. Children over 10 can be convicted for breaking the law. Furthermore, crimes committed by adolescents are treated under a different legal system than crimes committed by adults, and usually more leniently, which reflects a perception that adolescents should not be held responsible for bad decisions in the same way adults are.

One prominent current perspective on adolescent decision making is **behavioural decision theory** (Fischoff, 2005; Jacobs and Klaczynski, 2005). According to this perspective, the decision-making process includes: (1) identifying the range of possible choices; (2) identifying the consequences that would result from each choice; (3) evaluating the desirability of each consequence; (4) assessing the likelihood of each consequence; and (5) integrating this information into a decision.

Studies indicate that competence in this process varies substantially with age. Compared with pre-adolescent children, early adolescents generally identify a wider range of possible choices, are better at anticipating the consequences of the possible choices and are better at evaluating and integrating information (Keating, 2004). In each of these respects, however, early adolescents are less skilled than late adolescents or emerging adults (Byrnes et al., 1999).

For example, in an early and often-cited study Lewis (1981) presented adolescents aged 12, 15 and 18 with hypothetical situations regarding decisions about medical procedures. The 18-year-olds were more likely than the younger groups to mention risks to be considered (83 per cent, 50 per cent and 40 per cent, from oldest to youngest), to recommend consultation with an outside specialist (62 per cent, 46 per cent and 21 per cent) and to anticipate possible consequences (42 per cent, 25 per cent and 11 per cent).

Most studies comparing late adolescents and adults have found few differences between them in the decision-making processes they use (e.g. Fischoff, 2005). Why is it, then, that adolescents are so much more likely than adults to take risks such as driving while intoxicated or trying illegal drugs? One possible explanation is that adolescents and adults make different evaluations about the desirability of the possible consequences (Maggs, 1999). For example, in deciding whether to try an illegal drug that is being handed

Are adolescents competent to make major decisions, such as about legal or medical issues?

CONNECT AND EXTEND

Decision making for those with attention deficit-hyperactivity disorder (ADHD) is particularly challenging. Contrary to earlier beliefs, ADHD frequently persists into adolescence and adulthood and is associated with poor health choices and risk-taking behaviour. Read 'STOP, LOOK AND LISTEN: the challenge for children with ADHD' by Julie B. Meaux in *Issues in Comprehensive Pediatric Nursing*, Volume 23, Number 1 (2000), pp. 1–13

around at a party, both adolescents and adults may identify the same range of choices and the same possible consequences from these choices such as the possible pleasurable feelings from the drug and the possibility of being considered daring or timid by others for trying or not trying it. However, adolescents and adults may evaluate these consequences differently. Adolescents may be more attracted to the possible sensation-seeking pleasure of the drug, more eager to be considered daring and more worried about being considered timid by others (Reyna and Farley, 2006). They may also evaluate the potential consequences of taking the drug as less negative than adults would. As a consequence, adolescents would be more likely than adults to try illegal drugs even though both adolescents and adults would be going through the same decision-making process (Gibbons et al., 2003).

A recent 'dual-processing' theory by Paul Klaczynski (2005; 2001; 2000) has proposed that adolescent decision making is based on two different cognitive systems, one that is *analytic* and uses the reasoning of formal operations, and another that is *heuristic*, that is, based on intuitive factors such as past experience, emotions and unconscious motivations. Klaczynski finds that even as analytic reasoning advances in the course of adolescence, heuristic factors continue to affect decision making and do not necessarily lessen in impact. His research indicates that adolescents tend to accept an argument based on questionable analytic reasoning if they have intuitive reasons for accepting the argument. This distorting effect of heuristic factors in decision making declines during adolescence, but decision making by emerging adults remains affected by an overreliance on intuitive feelings.

A similar view of adolescents' decision making has been proposed by psychologists Laurence Steinberg and Elizabeth Cauffman (2001; Steinberg, 2008; Cauffman and Woolard, 2005; Grisso et al., 2003). They argue that differences in decision-making abilities between adolescents and adults should be divided into two broad categories: those attributed to cognitive factors and those attributed to psychosocial factors (i.e.

social and emotional maturity). According to Steinberg and Cauffman, most studies of decision-making abilities among adolescents and adults have explored only cognitive factors. However, they view this approach as too narrow and as being likely to underestimate the differences between adolescents and adults. Instead, they propose that mature decision making should be viewed as the product of the interaction between cognitive and psychosocial factors, with competent decision making potentially undermined by a deficiency in either area.

The implication of their theory is that even though adolescents may be able to show the same level of cognitive ability as adults in making a decision, adolescents may make different decisions because they are more likely than adults to be affected by psychosocial factors, such as the emotions of the moment and the desire to be accepted by peers. Research using this model indicates that it is especially adolescents aged 15 and younger whose decision-making competence is impaired by psychosocial immaturity (Grisso et al., 2003).

Your reading around this subject (perhaps in the nearby *Connect and Extend* feature on youngsters with ADHD) may lead you to agree with researchers who consider that, even in adulthood, the process of making decisions is rarely based purely on reason and is often inaccurate because of reasoning errors or the influence of social and emotional factors (Jacobs and Klaczynski, 2005; 2002; Klaczynski, 2001; Byrnes et al., 1999). Decision-making abilities may improve from childhood through adolescence, into emerging adulthood and beyond, but at all ages the process of decision making is often subject to errors and distortions.

THINKING CRITICALLY

By what age, if at all, should adolescents be allowed to decide whether to get a tattoo, whether to use birth control, and whether to live on their own? Justify your answer in terms of the decision-making theories presented here.

Adolescents' decision making is strongly influenced by psychosocial factors.

SOCIAL COGNITION

Cognitive development is discussed in this 'early' chapter of *Adolescence and Emerging Adulthood* because it is an area of development that provides a foundation for a wide range of other aspects of development, from family relations and friendships to school performance and risk behaviour.

This means that the cognitive concepts we have discussed in relation to the physical world can be applied to social topics as well. **Social cognition** is the term for the way we think about other people, social relationships and social institutions (Evans, 2008). As social cognition (like cognitive development generally) is reflected in so many other areas of adolescent development, we will be discussing social cognition throughout the book. Here, as an introduction, we examine two aspects of social cognition: perspective taking and adolescent egocentrism.

Perspective Taking

Have you had a conversation lately with a young child? If you have, you may have found that such conversations tend to go most smoothly when the focus of the conversation is on them rather than you. Young children tend to assume that topics which focus on themselves are of

great interest not only to themselves but to others, and it rarely occurs to them to ask themselves how your interests might differ from theirs. As children grow into adolescence, they become better at **perspective taking**, the ability to understand the thoughts and feelings of others. Of course, understanding the thoughts and feelings of others remains a challenge even for most adults, but most people improve at this as they grow up. Therefore adolescence – arguably the most conspicuous period of 'growing up' – is an especially important period in the development of perspective taking.

Robert Selman (Selman, 1980; 1976; Selman and Byrne, 1974) was one of the earliest and most influential scholars on the development of perspective taking (De Lisi, 2005). On the basis of his research, he proposed a theory describing how perspective taking develops through a series of stages, from early childhood through adolescence. In the course of these stages, according to Selman, the egocentrism of childhood gradually develops into the mature perspective-taking ability of adolescence.

Selman used mainly interviews as the method of his research. In the interviews, children and adolescents were provided with hypothetical situations and asked to comment on them. For example:

'Dr. Miller has just finished his training to be a doctor. He was setting up an office in a new town and wanted to get a lot of patients. He didn't have much money to start out with. He found an office and was trying to decide if he should spend a lot of money to make it fancy, by putting down a fancy rug, buying fancy furniture, and expensive lighting, or if he should keep it plain, with no rug, plain furniture, and a plain lamp.' (Selman, 1980, p. 42)

Responses indicating perspective-taking abilities are then elicited by asking questions concerning the doctor's thinking about attracting new patients, and asking about the point of view of patients and of society in general on the doctor's behaviour (e.g. 'What do you think society thinks about doctors spending money to make their offices fancy to attract people?').

Selman's research indicates that until adolescence, children's capacity for perspective taking is limited in various ways. Young children have difficulty separating their own perspective from those of others. When they reach ages 6 to 8, children begin to develop perspective-taking skills but have difficulty comparing perspectives. By pre-adolescence (ages 8 to 10), most children can understand that others may have a point of view that is different from their own. They also realise that taking another's perspective can assist them in understanding others' motives, intentions and actions.

According to Selman, in early adolescence, about ages 10 to 12, children become capable for the first time of **mutual perspective taking**. That is, early adolescents understand that their perspective-taking interactions with others are mutual – just as you understand that another person has a perspective that is different from your own, you also realise that other people understand that you have a perspective that is different from theirs. Also, unlike pre-adolescents, early adolescents have begun to be able to imagine how their view and the view of another person might appear to a third person. In the Dr Miller example just presented, this stage would be reflected in the ability to explain the doctor's perceptions of how others might view both him and his patients.

According to Selman's theory, social cognition develops further in late adolescence. After mutual perspective taking comes **social and conventional system perspective taking**, meaning that adolescents come to realise that their social perspectives and those of others are influenced not just by their interactions with each other but also by their roles in the larger society. In the Dr Miller example, this stage would be reflected in an understanding of how the role of doctor is perceived by society and how that would influence the perspective of the doctor and his patients.

In general, Selman's research has demonstrated that perspective-taking abilities improve from childhood through adolescence. However, his research also shows that there is only a loose connection between age and perspective-taking abilities. Adolescents may reach the stage of mutual perspective taking as early as age 11 or as late as age 20. Notice that this is similar to the findings we discussed earlier on Piagetian formal operations. In both theories there is a wide range of individual differences, and people of any given age vary a great deal in their cognitive skills.

Other studies of perspective taking have found it plays an important role in adolescents' peer relationships. For example, studies over three decades and building on Selman's theories have found that adolescents' perspective-taking abilities are related to their popularity among peers and skills of social adaptation (Allen et al., 2005; Kurdek and Krile, 1982), to their success at making new friends, and avoiding antisocial behaviour and depressive symptoms (Sund

et al., 2003; Vernberg et al., 1994). Being able to take the perspective of others helps adolescents to be aware of how the things they say and do might please or displease others. Perspective taking is also related to how adolescents treat others. In a study of Brazilian adolescents (Eisenberg et al., 2001), perspective-taking abilities were found to predict sympathy and **prosocial behaviour**, meaning behaviour that is kind and considerate. Since perspective taking promotes these qualities, it makes sense that adolescents who are good at perspective taking would also be good at making friends.

A more recently developed concept related to perspective taking is the concept of **theory of mind**. Theory of mind is the ability to attribute mental states to one's self and others, including beliefs, thoughts, and feelings (Kuhn, 2002). So far, most research using the theory of mind idea has been on young children, looking at how they first develop an understanding that others have a mental life independent from their own (Lillard, 2007). Happily for us, some of this theory of mind research is turning towards adolescence. For example, a recent study using techniques for measuring brain activity found that increased understanding of theory of mind from childhood to adolescence was related to increased activation of the frontal cortex when performing theory of mind tasks (Moriguchi et al., 2007). Again, another recent study looked at adolescents' theory of mind in relation to their family lives and found that adolescents were quite advanced in describing their parents' thoughts and feelings concerning the marital relationship (Artar, 2007). This is an area of theoretical development to watch in the years to come and you can begin by referring to the nearby *Connect and Extend* feature.

Adolescent Egocentrism

'I remember a time in secondary school when everybody in the posse (the name for our gang of girls) wore FCUK T-shirts. They were pricey – much more than I could afford from the clothing allowance my mum gave me. I always suspected that others in the gang were laughing at me for

CONNECT AND EXTEND

Make a start at exploring theory of mind by reading 'Adolescent egocentrism and theory of mind: in the context of family relations' by M. Artar in *Behavior* *and Personality: an international journal,* Volume 35, Number 9 (2007), pp. 1211–1220

not having some of these "tees" and that I stuck out from the others. Now I wouldn't wear one if you paid me.'

– Emma, aged 24 (Hughes, unpublished data)

'During early adolescence I believed/pretended that a movie crew was following me around and taping everything I did. They personally picked me because I was the most popular girl in school and had the most interesting life. Or so I thought!'

– Denise, age 21 (Arnett, unpublished data)

We have seen that adolescents become less egocentric than younger children as they learn to take the perspectives of others. However, cognitive development in adolescence also leads to new kinds of egocentrism that are distinctly adolescent.

It was noted earlier in the chapter that cognitive development in adolescence includes the development of metacognition, which is the capacity to think about thinking. This development includes the ability to think about not only your own thoughts but also the thoughts of others. When these abilities first develop, adolescents may have difficulty distinguishing their thinking about their own thoughts from their thinking about the thoughts of others, resulting in a distinctive kind of **adolescent egocentrism**. Ideas about adolescent egocentrism were first put forward by Piaget (1967) and were developed further by psychologist David Elkind (1985; 1967; Alberts et al., 2007). According to Elkind, adolescent egocentrism has two aspects, the imaginary audience and the personal fable.

The Imaginary Audience

The **imaginary audience** results from adolescents' limited capacity to distinguish between their thinking about themselves and their thinking about the thoughts of others. Because they think about themselves so much and are so acutely aware of how they might appear to others, they conclude that others must also be thinking about them a great deal. Because they exaggerate the extent to which others think about them, they imagine a rapt audience for their appearance and behaviour.

The imaginary audience makes adolescents much more self-conscious than they were before formal operations. Do you remember waking up at 13 or 14 with a pimple on your forehead, or discovering a stain on the back of your sports kit and wondering how long it had been there, or saying something in class that made everybody laugh (even though you didn't intend it to be funny)? Of course, experiences such as these are not much fun as an adult either, but are worse in adolescence because the imaginary audience makes it seem as though 'everybody' knows about your humiliation and will remember it for a long, long time.

The imaginary audience is not something that simply disappears when adolescence ends. Adults are also egocentric to some extent; they imagine (and sometimes exaggerate) an audience for their behaviour. It is just that this tendency is stronger in adolescence, when formal operations are first developing and the capacity for distinguishing between our own perspective and the perspective of others is less developed.

The Personal Fable

The **personal fable** is built on the imaginary audience, according to Elkind (1985; 1967; Alberts et al., 2007). The belief in an imaginary audience that is highly conscious of how you look and act leads to the belief that there must be something special, something unique, about you – otherwise, why would others be so preoccupied with you? Adolescents' belief in the uniqueness of their personal experiences and their personal destiny is the 'personal fable'.

The personal fable can be the source of adolescent anguish, when it makes them feel that 'no one understands me' because no one can share their unique experience (Scott and Strading, 2006). It can be the source of high hopes, too, as adolescents imagine their unique personal destiny leading to the fulfilment of their dreams to be a rock musician, or a Premiership footballer, or a Hollywood star, or simply successful in the field of their choice. It can also contribute to risky behaviour by adolescents whose sense of uniqueness leads them to believe that adverse consequences from behaviour such as unprotected sex and drunk driving 'won't happen to me' (Alberts et al., 2007).

CONNECT AND EXTEND

To develop a fuller understanding of the diverse social processes that influence young people's behaviour in risk taking, read 'Towards a sociological understanding of youth and their risk-taking' by Alan France, *Journal of Youth Studies*, Volume 3, Number 3 (2000), pp. 317–331

FOCUS ON YOUTH IN THE MEDIA

The Real and the Imaginary Audience: Part of a Personal Myth?

In the last section we explained that adolescents in particular imagine their unique personal destiny leading to the fulfilment of their dreams to be a rock musician, or a Premiership footballer or a celebrity. TV reality shows such as *Britain's got Talent*, *Pop Idol*, *The X Factor* and *Big Brother* are of enormous interest to teenagers as they can share the experience of the lucky few living the dream of being discovered. For the vast majority of adolescents, these dreams or fantasies remain private – a kind of secret life, sometimes constructed to protect the self from inadequacy or loneliness (Adamo, 2004). Perhaps that is why the author James Thurber chose 'The Secret Life of Walter Mitty' as the title for one of his short stories in 1939. The central character, Walter Mitty is a timid, gentle young man with a vivid fantasy life: in short order he imagines himself a wartime pilot, an emergency-room surgeon, and a devil-may-care killer. The character's name has come into more general use to describe a fantasist – a Walter Mitty character – to refer to an ineffectual dreamer – played and sung brilliantly by Danny Kaye in a later film.

One of these 'Walter Mitty characters' is the eponymous Billy Liar in the 1959 novel by Keith Waterhouse, adapted into a TV series, a play, a film and a musical starring Michael Crawford and Elaine Page in her 'West End' debut. Billy Liar is William Fisher, a working-class 19-year-old living with his parents in a fictional Yorkshire town. Bored by his lowly job as a clerk for an undertaker, Billy spends his time indulging in fantasies and dreams of life in the big city as a comedy writer. He lies compulsively to everyone he comes across. For example, Billy claims that his father is a retired naval captain. His fantasy life spills over into his love life; he is engaged to two girlfriends, and in love with a third. Billy Liar inspired a number of pop and rock tracks. Morrissey was heavily influenced by the novel, borrowing many lines from it, in particular for The Smiths' 1984 song 'William, It Was Really Nothing'. The title for the fourth and final studio Smiths' album *Strangeways Here We Come* (1987) is based on a line from the film adaption, where one of the Billy's friends shouts 'Borstal, here we come'.

Look for the lyrics of *William, It really was nothing* using a web search. Find the section that speaks of not staying with a 'fat girl'.

Of course for the most part, there is no problem with developing a personal fable in which the youngster can live out their dreams of being famous, brave, popular or the best at something. Most fantasies are played to an imagined audience. It's no good being famous, brave, popular or the best at something if nobody is looking. The reaction of the audience – perhaps a particular girl or boy that needs to be impressed – is also fantasised, and this is a kind of private playing up to an audience that is harmless. However, real-life playing to an audience of peers in risky situations can be a problem.

For example, one craze widely reported in the British press in the summer of 2007 was 'tombstoning'. Participants of tombstoning jump from a structure such as a pier or harbour wall into the sea. The title was adopted because of the way a person falls and plunges into deep water, in a similar way a stone would. Tombstoning is an adrenaline-fuelled activity which has occurred around the British coast for generations and is particularly popular with groups of teenage boys who often challenge each other to take on something dangerous in relatively high profile public settings. However in 2007 it gained public attention for the wrong reasons, with a number of young people killed or seriously injured.

One tragic case was the death of 16-year-old Sam Boyd who died after jumping from the harbour wall at Minehead, Somerset. It was about 8 pm and the harbourside was busy with visitors and locals enjoying the evening sunshine. Sam was with a group of friends when he jumped into the sea dressed in ordinary clothes and disappeared beneath the surface. When he reappeared, he swam for a short distance, started crying for help and then sank into the deep water. His body was found by HM Coastguard 6 hours later and he was pronounced dead on arrival at hospital.

It's not absolutely clear in Sam's shocking case that his friends at Minehead Harbour encouraged him to 'tombstone' off the harbour wall but their presence as an audience is likely to contribute to Sam wanting to be the brave 'devil-couldn't-care-less' character that perhaps was part of his personal fable, and tragically became a reality. Search the Internet to find out more about Sam and other cases.

The very dangerous and potentially disastrous activity of 'tombstoning' – jumping into water from harbour walls and sea cliffs.

Like the imaginary audience, the personal fable diminishes with age, but it never disappears entirely for most of us. Even most adults like to think there is something special, if not unique, about their personal experiences and their personal destiny. But the personal fable tends to be stronger in adolescence than at later ages because with age our experiences and conversations with others lead us to awareness that our thoughts and feelings are not as exceptional as we thought. As predicted by the theory, personal fable scores increased from early to mid-adolescence and were correlated with participation in risk behaviours such as substance use. Boys score higher than girls on both personal fable scores and reports of risk behaviour (Alberts et al., 2007).

A concept related to the personal fable, known as the **optimistic bias**, has been researched more extensively than the personal fable itself. The idea of the optimistic bias comes out of health psychology, and it concerns a specific aspect of the personal fable: the tendency to assume that accidents, diseases and other misfortunes are more likely to happen to others than to ourselves (Fife-Schaw and Barnett, 2004). Research in this area has found that both adolescents and adults have an optimistic bias with regard to health risk behaviours such as driving while intoxicated or smoking cigarettes, but adolescents tend to have a stronger optimistic bias than adults (Klein and Helweg-Larsen, 2002; Weinstein, 1998).

For example, in one study adolescent and adult smokers and non-smokers were asked about the risks of smoking for others and for themselves (Arnett, 2000b). As you can see from Figure 3.3, strong

THINKING CRITICALLY

Do you think most emerging adults have outgrown adolescent egocentrism? Give examples of the imaginary audience and the personal fable that you have witnessed among your peers or, perhaps, experienced yourself.

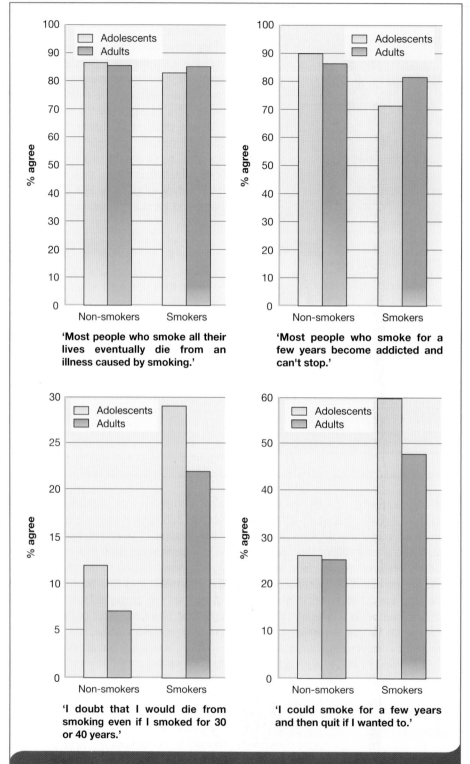

Figure 3.3 Adolescent and adult smokers' perceptions of the risks of smoking. Does this study show evidence of the optimistic bias in adolescence?

majorities of both adolescents and adults, both smokers and non-smokers, believed that smoking is addictive and deadly for 'most people'. However, when they applied the risk to themselves, there was evidence of an optimistic bias. Smokers were more likely than non-smokers to believe that they would not die as a consequence of smoking for 30 to 40 years.

Still, even most of the smokers believed that smoking would eventually be fatal for them personally, if they smoked long enough. The real heart of the optimistic bias for smoking seems to be in relation to addiction. Although the great majority of both adolescents and adults believed that 'Most people who smoke for a few years become addicted and can't stop', 48 per cent of the adult smokers and 60 per cent of the adolescent smokers believed that 'I could smoke for a few years and then quit if I wanted to'. These findings indicate that one of the reasons adolescents take up smoking in spite of the well-known health risks is that they hold an optimistic bias with regard to addiction. They do not believe they will ultimately die from smoking, not because they do not believe smoking is deadly but because they believe they will quit smoking long before it kills them. The findings also show that many adults, too, have an optimistic bias about their smoking behaviour, but it may not be as strong among adults as it is among adolescents.

THE PSYCHOMETRIC APPROACH: INTELLIGENCE TESTING

Thus far, we have looked mostly at group patterns in cognitive functioning, describing the cognitive functioning of adolescents and emerging adults in general. Another way to look at cognitive development is to focus on individual differences, that is, on how various individuals within a group (all 16-year-olds, for example) might differ in their cognitive abilities. This is the goal of intelligence tests. Attempting to understand human cognition by evaluating cognitive abilities with intelligence tests is known as the **psychometric approach**.

Let us begin by looking at the characteristics of the most widely used intelligence tests and then examine some of the research on intelligence tests that pertains most directly to adolescence. Following that we will consider an alternative way of conceptualising and measuring intelligence.

The Stanford-Binet and Wechsler Intelligence Tests

The first intelligence test was developed in 1905 by a French psychologist named **Alfred Binet**. Binet's test was brief, consisting of just 30 items, and assessed performance in areas such as memory and abstract thinking. In the years since its original development it has been revised and expanded several times. Some of the most important revisions were conducted by Louis Terman of Stanford University, USA in the 1920s, and the test is now known as the **Stanford-Binet**. The most recent revision of the test includes four content areas: verbal reasoning, quantitative reasoning, abstract/visual reasoning, and short-term memory (Bain and Allin, 2005). It can be given to people from age 2 through to adulthood. The test results in an overall score called the IQ (for **intelligence quotient**). It can be used to assess abilities within the normal range of intelligence as well as problems such as cognitive delays, mental retardation and learning disabilities.

The other widely used IQ tests are the Wechsler scales, including the **Wechsler Intelligence Scale for Children (WISC-IV)** for children aged 6 to 16 and the **Wechsler Adult Intelligence Scale (WAIS-IV)** for persons aged 16 and over. The Wechsler tests contain two kinds of subtests, **verbal subtests** and **performance subtests**. The results of the Wechsler tests provide a verbal IQ and a performance IQ as well as an overall IQ. More detail on the WISC-IV and the WAIS-IV are provided in the *Research Focus* feature.

As the *Research Focus* feature indicates, **relative performance** on IQ tests is very stable – people who score higher than average in childhood tend to score higher than average as adolescents and adults, and people who score lower than average in childhood tend to score lower than average as adolescents and adults. However, some interesting patterns of change occur in **absolute performance** from mid-adolescence through to young adulthood (Moffitt et al., 1993). Figure 3.4 shows how scores on the WAIS subtests changed from age 16 to age 38 in one longitudinal study (Bayley, 1968). Notice how absolute scores on the verbal subtests generally improved from age 16 to 38, whereas absolute scores on the performance subtests tended to peak in the mid-20s and then decline.

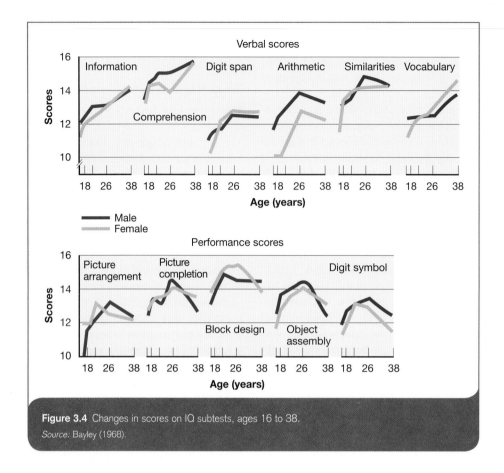

Figure 3.4 Changes in scores on IQ subtests, ages 16 to 38.
Source: Bayley (1968).

RESEARCH FOCUS   R

The Wechsler IQ Tests

Among the most widely used IQ tests are the Wechsler scales. Children and early adolescents (ages 6 to 16) are typically tested using the Wechsler Intelligence Scale for Children (WISC-IV), and older adolescents and adults (ages 16 and over) with the Wechsler Adult Intelligence Scale (WAIS-IV). The 'IV' in the names indicates that this is the fourth version of the tests that has been developed. Early versions of the tests were criticised for being biased against some minority cultures (Miller-Jones, 1989). Therefore special efforts were made in more recent versions of the tests to eliminate any items that might require a particular cultural background (Psychological Corporation, 2000).

The Wechsler scales consist of 11 subtests, of which 6 are verbal subtests and 5 are performance subtests. The results provide an overall IQ score, a verbal IQ score, a performance IQ score, and scores for each of the 11 subtests. More detail on each of the subscales of the WAIS-IV is provided in Table 3.2, so you can get an idea of what IQ tests really measure.

A great deal of research has gone into the development of the Wechsler scales (Kaufman and Lichtenberger, 2006; Ryan and Lopez, 2001). One goal of this research was to establish **age norms**. Age norming means that a typical score for each age is established by testing a large random sample of people from a variety of geographical areas and social class backgrounds. An individual's IQ score is determined by comparing the individual's performance on the test to the 'norm', or typical score,

Table 3.2 The WAIS-IV: Sample Items

Verbal Subtests

Arithmetic: Word problems. 'How long does it take to drive 140 miles at a constant speed of 30 miles an hour?'

Comprehension: Practical knowledge. 'Why is it important to use postal codes when you address envelopes?'

Digit Span: Short-term memory. Sequences of numbers of increasing length are recited. The subject repeats each sequence.

Information: General knowledge questions. 'Who wrote Treasure Island?'

Similarities: Describe relationship between two things. 'In what ways are an apple and a potato alike?'

Vocabulary: Give definitions. 'What does 'didactic' mean?'

Performance subtests

(Scores in these tests are based on speed as well as accuracy of responses).

Block Design: Blocks are provided having two faces all white, two faces all red, and two faces half red and half white. A card is shown with a geometrical pattern, and the subject arranges the blocks to match the pattern.

Digit Symbol: Numbers are presented with matching symbols. Sequences of symbols are presented with an empty box below each symbol. The subject writes the matching number in the box below each symbol.

Matrix Reasoning: Patterns are shown with one area of the pattern missing. The subject chooses from five options one that will 'fill in' the missing area.

Picture Arrangement: Cards are presented depicting a sequence of activities. The subject is asked to place the cards in an order that tells a logical and coherent story.

Picture Completion: Cards are presented depicting an object or scene with something missing. The subject is required to identify what is missing. (For example, a chair is shown with only three legs).

for people his or her age. The **median** – the point at which half of the sample scores above and half below – is assigned the score of 100, and other scores are determined according to how high or low they are in relation to the median.

Two other important considerations in the research to develop the Wechsler tests were reliability and validity. As discussed in Chapter 1, reliability is a measurement of the extent to which responses on a measure are consistent. There are a number of kinds of reliability, but one of the most important is **test-retest reliability**, which examines whether persons' scores on one occasion are similar to their scores on another occasion. The Wechsler IQ tests have high test-retest reliability, which improves as people get older (Psychological Corporation, 2000). For most people, little change in IQ scores takes place after about age 10 (Carr, 2005; Bird et al., 2004; Kittler et al., 2004).

Of course, that does not mean that your mental abilities never advance after age 10! Keep in mind that IQ is a relative score. It indicates how you compare with other people your age. So, people who score higher than their peers at age 10 are also likely to score above the median average at age 20, 30, 40, and so on; people whose IQs are below median average at age 10 are also likely to score below the median average as they become older, relative to other people of the same age. Some earlier research suggested that there are exceptions to this general pattern in that some people change dramatically in IQ during childhood or adolescence, for better or worse (Moffitt et al., 1993), but the more typical pattern, and the pattern generally accepted today, is one of great stability in IQ scores over the lifespan.

We have talked about the reliability of the tests, but what about validity? Remember that the validity of a research instrument is the extent to which it measures what it claims to measure. For IQ tests, the validity question would be 'Do IQ tests really measure intelligence?' Some evidence regarding this question is presented in this chapter. However, questions about validity are much harder to answer than questions about reliability, and the validity of IQ tests remains hotly debated among scholars and in the general public. In general, it can be concluded at this point that IQ tests have reasonably good **predictive validity**; that is, high IQ scores in adolescence predict relatively high educational attainment in emerging adulthood and occupational success in young adulthood and beyond (Dandy and Nettlebeck, 2002). High IQs in adolescence are also predictive of positive outcomes in adulthood unrelated to education and occupation, for example lower likelihood of divorce, alcoholism or suicide (Voracek, 2006).

CONNECT AND EXTEND

Does low IQ predict reading disability? A sample of 443 Spanish children ranging in age from 7 to 13 years were classified into four groups according to IQ scores and reading disabled and normally achieving readers were compared. Read 'The relative roles of IQ and cognitive processes in reading disability' by Juan Jimenez, Linda Siegel, Isabel O'Shanahan and Laurie Ford in *Educational Psychology*, Volume 29, Number 1 (January 2009), pp. 27–43

These patterns reflect a distinction that some scholars have made between what has been termed fluid and crystallised intelligence (Sligh et al., 2005). **Fluid intelligence** refers to mental abilities that involve speed of analysing, processing and reacting to information, which is the kind of ability tapped by the performance subtests (performance tests reward speed of response, whereas verbal tests do not). IQ tests indicate that this kind of intelligence peaks in emerging adulthood. **Crystallised intelligence**, in contrast, refers to accumulated knowledge and enhanced judgement based on experience. Subtests such as Information, Comprehension and Vocabulary assess this kind of intelligence, and absolute scores on these subtests tend to improve through the 20s and 30s.

THINKING CRITICALLY

What aspects of 'intelligence' does the WAIS-IV *not* include, in your view?

Intelligence Tests and Adolescent Development

An enormous amount of research using IQ tests has been conducted since they were first developed. With respect to adolescence, the most notable results concern adoption studies.

As described in Chapter 1, adoption studies take advantage of a natural experiment – a situation that exists naturally, beyond the control of a researcher but which still provides interesting scientific information to the perceptive observer. Adoption is a natural experiment in the sense that, unlike in most families, children in adoptive families are raised by adults with whom they have no biological relationship. This eliminates the problem of passive genotype–environment interactions we discussed in Chapter 2, in which it is difficult to know the extent to which similarities between parents and children in biological families are due to genes or environment because the parents provide both. Similarities between adoptive parents and adopted children are likely to be due to the environment provided by the parents because the parents and children are biologically unrelated. Similarities between adopted children and their biological parents are likely to be due to genetics because the environment the children grew up in was not provided by the biological parents.

An interesting pattern occurs in adoption studies that follow children from birth through adolescence. In early and middle childhood, a substantial correlation in IQ exists between adopted children and their adoptive parents. However, by the time adopted children reach adolescence, the correlation between their IQs and the IQs of their adoptive parents has declined, even though the number of years they have all been in the same family has increased (Beckett et al., 2007; McGue et al., 2007; Duyme et al., 1999). How could this be?

What may explain it is a gradual decline with age in the influence of the immediate family environment on intellectual development, and a gradual increase in active genotype–environment interactions – that is, in the degree to which children choose their own environmental influences (Wong et al., 2006) in early and middle childhood, parents have a great deal of control over the kind of environment their children experience. Parents control decisions about how much time their children spend on homework, how much television they watch, what they do for fun on the weekends, who they play with, and so on. However, adolescents make many of these decisions for themselves (Gucray, 2005). Parents are still important influences on adolescents, but adolescents have much more autonomy than younger children. Adolescents have a greater say in how much time they spend on homework, how much of their free time they spend reading or watching television, and who their friends will be. All these decisions contribute to intellectual development, and as a consequence adopted adolescents bear less resemblance in IQ to their adoptive parents than younger adopted children do. This is a story of how during adolescence neighbourhood often takes over from parents in influencing adolescents' behaviour, educational attainment and future employment (Schneiders et al., 2003). This is an important idea and one that we will explore further throughout this text and particularly in Chapter 8, Friends and peers.

A particularly interesting line of adoption research concerns **transracial adoption**, specifically involving

Black children raised by white parents tend to have higher than average IQs.

black children who have been adopted by white parents (Burrow and Finley, 2004). It should not be a surprise to you that one of the most bitter controversies surrounding intelligence tests concerns racial differences in IQ. Sub-Saharan Africans score lower than European whites on the most widely used IQ tests and Oriental peoples of East Asia have higher median average intelligence by about 5 IQs points than European whites (Lynn, 2003). However, scholars disagree vehemently over the source of these group differences. Some assert that the differences are due to genetic ethnic/racial differences in intelligence (e.g. Lynn, 2006; Herrnstein and Murry, 1995). Others assert that the differences simply reflect the fact that IQ tests concern knowledge obtained in the majority culture, which whites are more likely than minorities to have grown up in (e.g. Fraser, 1995; Brody, 1992). Transracial adoption represents an extraordinary natural experiment, in that it involves raising black children in the white-dominated majority culture.

What do these studies find? In general, they indicate that when black children are raised in adoptive white families their IQs are as high (or higher) than the average IQ for whites (Weinberg et al., 1992). Their IQ scores decline somewhat in adolescence but nevertheless remain relatively high (Burrow and Finley, 2004).

CONNECT AND EXTEND

For a comprehensive summary of issues around the validity of IQ tests particularly in relation to race, read Professor John Oller's influential and widely referenced paper, 'Monoglottosis: what's wrong with the idea of the IQ meritocracy and its racy cousins?', *Applied Linguistics*, Volume 18, Number 4 (December 1997), pp. 467–507

This indicates that overall differences in IQ between white and black teenagers are due to cultural and social class differences rather than to genetics.

Does IQ Predict Educational Attainment?

As early as in 1991, James Flynn proposed that students from Asian cultural backgrounds typically achieve at higher levels than non-Asian students with the same IQs. Can this be demonstrated, and how important is IQ in determining educational attainment? In an important study a decade or so ago two researchers Justin Dandy and Ted Nettelbeck found that mathematics grades for Chinese and Vietnamese Australian children were higher. They spent more time studying and were more likely to desire an occupation requiring tertiary qualifications than Anglo-Celtic Australian peers. Consistent with Flynn's hypothesis, students from Asian backgrounds obtained higher mathematics grades than their Anglo-Celtic Australian peers with the same IQ. However, study and occupational aspirations formed only part of a more complex interaction with these factors to produce high achievement. So straightforward IQ may not be the whole story. Are there other kinds of cognition that can be conceived of and measured as intelligences?

Other Conceptions of Intelligence: The Theory of Multiple Intelligences

For many centuries there have been three main themes to how intelligence is viewed: (1) a person's capacity to learn; (2) the total knowledge a person has acquired; and (3) the ability to adapt successfully to new situations and to the environment in general (Woolfolk et al., 2008). The 'total knowledge' conception of intelligence underlies the construction of intelligence tests, and it is the one that most people hold. In one historic study, scholars and non-scholars indicated the abilities they believed to be characteristic of an intelligent person (Sternberg et al., 1981). The scholars (psychologists studying intelligence) and non-scholars (from a variety of backgrounds) provided similar responses. Both groups viewed intelligence as being comprised mainly of verbal abilities (e.g. 'good vocabulary', 'high reading comprehension') and problem-solving skills (e.g. 'reasons logically', 'can apply knowledge to the situation at hand').

In recent years, however, alternative theories of intelligence have been proposed. These theories have sought to present a conception of intelligence that is much broader than the traditional one. One of the most influential alternative theories of intelligence has been presented by Howard Gardner. Gardner's (1999; 1989; 1983) **theory of multiple intelligences** includes eight types of intelligence. In Gardner's view only two of them, linguistic and logical–mathematical intelligences, are evaluated by intelligence tests. The other intelligences are spatial (the ability to think three dimensionally); musical; bodily kinaesthetic (the kind that athletes and dancers excel in); naturalist (ability for understanding natural phenomena); interpersonal (ability for understanding and interacting with others); and intrapersonal (self-understanding). As evidence for the existence of these different types of intelligence, Gardner argues that each involves different cognitive skills, that each can be destroyed by damage to a particular part of the brain, and that each appears in extremes in geniuses as well as in *idiots savants* (the French term for people who are low in general intelligence but possess an extraordinary ability in one specialised area).

Gardner argues that schools should give more attention to the development of all eight kinds of intelligence and develop programmes tailored to each

According to Howard Gardner, there are eight different kinds of intelligence. This gymnast is demonstrating bodily-kinaesthetic intelligence.

child's individual profile of intelligences. He has proposed methods for assessing different intelligences, such as measuring musical intelligence by having people attempt to sing a song, play an instrument, or orchestrate a melody (Gardner, 1999). However, thus far neither Gardner nor others have developed reliable and valid methods for analysing the intelligences he proposes (Kornhaber, 2004). Gardner has also been criticised for extending the boundaries of intelligence too widely. When an adolescent learns to play piano more quickly than her peers, is this an indication of musical 'intelligence' or simply of musical talent? Gardner himself has been critical of the concept of 'emotional intelligence' proposed by Daniel Goleman and others (Goleman, 1997), arguing persuasively that the capacity to empathise and cooperate with others is better viewed as 'emotional sensitivity' rather than intelligence (Gardner, 1999). However, Gardner is vulnerable to a similar criticism for proposing 'interpersonal' and 'intrapersonal' intelligences.

THINKING CRITICALLY

Do you agree that all the mental abilities described by Gardner are different types of intelligence? If not, which types would you remove? Are there other types you would add?

The underlying issue in alternative theories of intelligence is the question of how intelligence should be defined. If intelligence is defined simply as the mental abilities required to succeed in school, the traditional approach to conceptualising and measuring intelligence is generally successful. However, if one wishes to define intelligence more broadly, as the entire range of human mental abilities, the traditional approach may be seen as too narrow, and an approach such as Gardner's may be preferred.

PROFESSIONAL FOCUS

The Effects of ADHD on Cognition and Intelligence

As a comment added to a UK National Health Service website on attention deficit-hyperactivity disorder (ADHD) 'jwest' wrote on 23 February 2011:

'I am 17 and not very hyper but I was as a child. I used to sing loudly in public, much to the annoyance of my mum and could be quite bossy and controlling in the playground. However other symptoms such as inattentiveness and impulsiveness I do seem to posses (*sic*).'

'I have a very short attention span and in class I often find it very difficult to concentrate on what the teacher is saying. I am forgetful and when long tasks or instructions are explained to me my mind often just switches off. I would find it almost impossible to listen to complicated directions. If I find something difficult I quite often just give up if I find it uninteresting. For example when I used to do maths, I would completely ignore the teacher speaking for the beginning of the lesson and then find that I didn't no (*sic*) what she had asked us to do. I am very fidgety. I am constantly tapping a foot or a finger and I often get very anxious in certain situations and react physically (like begin sweating or shaking). I have very bad attendance at school and this is partly because I find it boring despite my interest in the subjects I do.'

'When I was younger I used to steal from shops and I read somewhere this can be a result of ADHD. Sometimes, particularly with my family, I have a very short fuse and can explode. I was wondering if anyone could tell me if this sounds like a case of ADHD. Sorry for the essay.'

We can't vouch for the provenance of these comments – like so much that you discover when 'surfing the net' – but we think this an authentic voice of someone in late adolescence, trying to understand their own behaviour. The behaviour described by 'jwest' does tick all the boxes for a diagnosis of ADHD to be made as the symptoms of attention deficit-hyperactivity disorder is organised in two sets of behavioural problems: symptoms of inattentiveness; and symptoms of hyperactivity and impulsiveness. You can find those symptoms listed on a number of websites and there is a good deal of agreement between professionals about the behaviour problems presented. What is noticeable is that many writers take great pains to suggest that although ADHD can often lead to underachievement at school – as well as poor social interaction with other children and adults and problems with discipline – the condition has no affect on intelligence (e.g. Rayner et al., 2005; Indredavik et al., 2004). How can this be?

Attention, as we have previously noted, is vital to cognition as information garnered from 'paying attention' is temporarily stored in the short-term memories and used in the working memory (Webster et al., 2009). Remember also that there are three main themes to how intelligence is viewed: (1) a person's capacity to learn; (2) the total knowledge a person has acquired; and (3) the ability to adapt successfully to new situations and to the environment in general (Woolfolk et al., 2008). What sense can we make then that ADHD has no effect upon a person's capacity to learn and the development of the fluid intelligences of analysing, processing and reacting to information? Is it – as suggested by a number of writers (e.g. Roebroeck et al., 2006; Crawford et al., 2005; Potter and Newhouse, 2004) – that mild to moderate ADHD allows quick-fire learning and other cognitive processes which may not be so considered but are equally powerful; just shorter and more intense? Is it an issue of time?

We may be unsure of the causes of ADHD but we do have a common experience of the symptoms.

Those at the more severe end of the ADHD spectrum are increasingly prescribed with mephylphenidate – Ritalin is the brand name (Monastra et al., 2002). The effect of these drugs is – in the words of one user – smartbenne123 on the same website as jwest – 'to allow the neuro transmitters in the frontal cortex to fire up and pass full messages through to the synaptic membrane … enabling things like impulsivity to reduce, self-control to be supported and allowing that space and time to develop learning techniques to cope'. Although the science of this is arguable, the view does usefully concentrate on the time issue. It is becoming more widely accepted that ADHD is largely caused by genetic factors affecting cognition at the level of DNA (e.g. Langley et al., 2010). Is part of the treatment for ADHD also a matter of chemistry? Should Ritalin be prescribed more widely to provide the 'time and space' for youngsters with ADHD to learn other coping strategies? Some writers even characterise these questions as 'The right to Ritalin or the right to childhood' (e.g. Frazzetto et al., 2007). These are important decisions and questions for the professional community working with our adolescents and young people.

BRAIN DEVELOPMENT IN ADOLESCENCE

In recent years, there has been a surge of research on neurological development in adolescence and emerging adulthood that casts new light on cognitive development during these years (Casey et al., 2008; Giedd, 2008; Keating, 2004). Research technologies, especially **PET scans** (Positron Emission Tomography) and **fMRI** (functional Magnetic Resonance Imaging), have made possible a more advanced understanding of how the brain develops, because these technologies show how different parts of the brain function when performing a cognitive task (e.g. solving a maths problem). This research unveils the underlying neurological basis for the kinds of changes we have discussed in this chapter in areas such as decision making and reflective judgement.

It has long been known that by age 6 the brain is already 95 per cent of its adult size. However, when it comes to brain development, size is not everything. Of more importance are the connections or **synapses** between the **neurons** (brain cells) (see Figure 3.5).

Now scientists have learned that a considerable thickening of synaptic connections occurs around the time puberty begins, ages 10–12, a process neuroscientists call **overproduction** or **exuberance**. It had been known for decades that overproduction occurs during prenatal development and through the first 18 months of life, but now it turns out that a new period of overproduction occurs in early adolescence as well (Giedd, 2008; Giedd et al., 1999). Overproduction of synaptic connections occurs in many parts of the brain's **grey matter**, its outer layer, but is especially concentrated in the **frontal lobes**, the part of the brain that is right behind your forehead (Keating, 2004). The frontal lobes are involved in most of the higher functions of the brain, such as planning ahead, solving problems and making moral judgements.

The findings about overproduction in early adolescence are surprising and fascinating, but equally fascinating is what follows it. Overproduction peaks at about age 11 or 12, but obviously that is not when our cognitive abilities peak. In the years that follow a massive amount of **synaptic pruning** takes place, in which the overproduction of synapses is whittled down considerably. In fact, between the ages of 12 and 20 the average brain loses 7 per cent to 10 per cent of its grey matter through synaptic pruning (Sowell et al., 1999). 'Use it or lose it' seems to be the operating principle; synapses that are used remain, whereas those that are not used whither away. Recent research using fMRI methods shows that synaptic pruning is especially rapid among adolescents with high intelligence (Shaw et al., 2006).

Synaptic pruning allows the brain to work more efficiently, as brain pathways become more specialised. Imagine if you had to drive somewhere, and there were either many different back roads to get to your destination or one direct smooth main road. You would get there a lot faster if you took the main road. Synaptic pruning is like scrapping the many back roads in favour of one smooth main road. However, the down-side is that as the brain specialises in this way, it also becomes less flexible and less amenable to change.

Myelination is another important process of neurological growth in adolescence. Myelin is a blanket of fat wrapped around the main part of the neuron (Figure 3.5). It serves the function of keeping the brain's electrical signals on one path and increasing their speed. Like overproduction, myelination was previously thought to be over prior to puberty but has now been found to continue through the teens (Giedd, 2008; Sowell et al., 2002; Paus et al., 1999). This is another indication of how brain functioning is becoming faster and more efficient during adolescence. However, like synaptic pruning, myelination also makes brain functioning less flexible and changeable.

CONNECT AND EXTEND

There are many excellent summaries of early brain development on the shelves of your library. Start with Chapter 6 (Neonatral behaviour and learning) in John Doherty and Malcolm Hughes' *Child* *Development Theory and Practice 0–11*. Try to draw out the similarities with and differences to brain development during adolescence

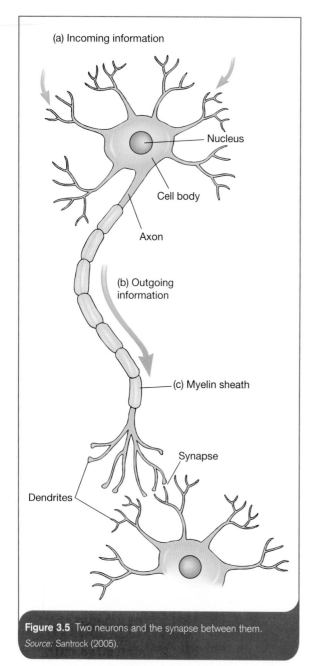

(a) Incoming information

Nucleus

Cell body

Axon

(b) Outgoing information

(c) Myelin sheath

Synapse

Dendrites

Figure 3.5 Two neurons and the synapse between them.
Source: Santrock (2005).

humour, and that it continues to grow through adolescence and well into emerging adulthood (Strauch, 2003). In fact, the cerebellum is the last structure of the brain to stop growing, not completing its phase of overproduction and pruning until the mid-20s, even after the frontal lobes.

So what can we conclude about brain development in adolescence and emerging adulthood on the basis of this new research? First, it is clear that the brain grows a lot more, and a lot differently, than we had known in the past. Second, the new findings confirm in many ways what we had known from studies using other methods, that adolescents are different and more advanced in their thinking than children are, but their cognitive development is not yet mature. Their abilities in areas such as making decisions, anticipating the consequences of their actions, and solving complex problems are not as advanced as they will be once they have reached adulthood and their basic brain development is more or less complete. Third, there are both gains and losses in the course of brain development in adolescence and emerging adulthood. The same neurological changes that make thinking faster and more efficient also make it more rigid and less flexible. After adolescence it is easier for people to make mature judgements about complicated issues, but not as many neurological options remain open for learning new things. However, for the most part the neurological changes of adolescence and emerging adulthood increase cognitive abilities substantially.

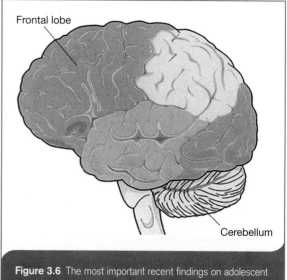

Frontal lobe

Cerebellum

Figure 3.6 The most important recent findings on adolescent brain development involve the frontal lobes and the cerebellum.
Source: Santrock (2005)

Finally, one last recent surprise for researchers studying brain development in adolescence has been in the growth of the **cerebellum** (see Figure 3.6). This is perhaps the biggest surprise of all because the cerebellum is part of the lower brain, well beneath the cortex, and has long been thought to be involved only in basic functions such as movement. Now, however, it turns out that the cerebellum is important for many higher functions as well, such as mathematics, music, decision making, and even social skills and understanding

CONNECT AND EXTEND

An excellent short book on brain-based explanations for teenagers' behaviour is *Why are They so Weird? What's really going on in a teenager's brain* by Barbara Strauch (Bloomsbury, London, 2004). This is not an academic reader but draws on recent academic work by respected researchers including Jay Giedd and Paul Grasby. Watch out for some unsupported explanations and a bias towards genetic factors. Nevertheless, a rattling good read!

CULTURE AND COGNITIVE DEVELOPMENT

Although they differ in many ways, the three major perspectives on cognitive development discussed in this chapter – cognitive-developmental, information processing and psychometric – all underemphasise the role of culture in cognitive development. The goal of theories and research from these perspectives has been to discover principles of cognitive development that apply to all people in all times and all cultures – in other words, to strip away the effect of culture on cognition in an effort to identify universal human cognitive characteristics (e.g. Rogoff, 2003). The recent research on brain development that we have just been discussing also de-emphasises the role of culture.

However, in recent years a cultural approach to cognition has gained increased attention from scholars on childhood and adolescence. This approach is founded on the ideas of the Russian psychologist Lev **Vygotsky** (1896–1934). Vygotsky died of tuberculosis when he was just 37, and it took decades before his ideas about cognitive development were translated and recognised by scholars outside Russia. It is only in the past two decades that his work has been widely influential among Western scholars, but his influence is increasing as interest in understanding the cultural basis of development continues to grow (Daniels et al., 2007; Maynard and Martini, 2005; Gardiner, 2001).

Vygotsky's theory is often referred to as a *sociocultural* theory because in his view cognitive development is inherently both a social and a cultural process (Mahn, 2003; Tudge and Scrimsher, 2002). It is social because children learn through interactions with others and require assistance from others in order to learn what they need to know. It is cultural because what children need to know is determined by the culture they live in. As we have seen in this chapter, there are distinct cultural differences in the knowledge adolescents must acquire: fishing skills in the unpredictable Mediterranean; a range of understandings and skills needed for surviving in the harsh Arctic environment of the Sami; the verbal and the scientific reasoning skills taught in schools.

Two of Vygotsky's most influential ideas are the **zone of proximal development** and **scaffolding**. The zone of proximal development is the gap between what adolescents can accomplish alone and what they are capable of doing if guided by an adult or a more competent peer. According to Vygotsky, children and adolescents learn best if the instruction they are provided with is near the top of the zone of proximal development, so that they need assistance at first but gradually become capable of performing on their own.

Scaffolding refers to the degree of assistance provided to the adolescent in the zone of proximal development. According to Vygotsky, scaffolding should gradually decrease as children become more competent. When adolescents begin learning a task, they require substantial instruction and involvement from the teacher, but as they gain knowledge and skill the teacher should gradually scale back the amount of direct instruction provided. These ideas underscore the social nature of learning in Vygotsky's theory. In his view learning always takes place via a social process, through the interactions between someone who possesses knowledge and someone who is in the process of obtaining it.

A much referenced example of scaffolding and the zone of proximal development can be found in earlier research by Fabienne Tanon (1994), who studied weaving skills among male adolescents in the Dioula culture in Ivory Coast, on the Western coast of Africa. An important part of the Dioula economy is making and selling large handmade cloths with elaborate designs. The training of weavers begins when they are aged 10–12 and continues for several years. Boys grow up watching their fathers weave, but it is in early adolescence that they begin learning weaving skills themselves. Teaching takes place through scaffolding: The boy attempts a simple weaving pattern, the father corrects his mistakes, and the boy tries again. When the boy gets it right, the father gives him a more complex pattern, thus raising the upper boundary of the zone of proximal development so that the boy continues to be challenged and his skills continue to improve. As the boy becomes more competent at weaving, the scaffolding provided by the father diminishes. Eventually the boy gets his own loom, but he continues to consult with his father for several years before he can weave entirely by himself.

According to Vygotsky, cognitive development is always a social and cultural process. Here, a father in Haiti teaches his daughter how to weave baskets.

THINKING CRITICALLY

Think of an example of learning in your own culture that involves scaffolding and the zone of proximal development.

One scholar who has been important in extending Vygotsky's theory is Professor of Psychology Barbara Rogoff. Her idea of **guided participation** refers to the teaching interaction between two people (often an adult and a child or adolescent) as they participate in a culturally valued activity. The guidance is 'the direction offered by cultural and social values, as well as social partners' (Rogoff, 1995, p. 142) as learning takes place. This is like Vygotsky's idea of scaffolding, except that Rogoff is even more explicit than Vygotsky in emphasising the importance of cultural values in determining what children and adolescents learn and how they learn it.

For example, in one study Rogoff and her colleagues observed a troop of early adolescent Scouts as they sold and delivered Scout biscuits as a fundraising project (Rogoff et al., 1995). The girls' involvement in the project reflected scaffolding and guided participation, as they began by taking a small observational role but gradually moved towards active participation and finally towards taking greater responsibilities in managing the sales (e.g. making calculations of how much money was due from each customer and keeping track of which customers had or had not paid). The project demonstrated the sociocultural basis of cognitive development. The girls' learning was social, because they were taught through participation in biscuit selling with older girls, mothers, troop leaders and even customers (who sometimes helped with the calculations). Their learning was also cultural, because it involved participation in a culturally valued activity and the implicit expression of cultural values such as efficiency, competition, cooperation and responsibility.

The growing interest in a cultural approach to cognitive development is part of a broader perspective that has come to be known as **cultural psychology**. In this perspective, cognition is inseparable from culture. Rather than trying to strip away the effect of culture on cognition, cultural psychologists seek to examine the ways that culture and cognition are interrelated and the profound effects that culture has on cognitive development (Shweder et al., 2006). Instead of seeking to

CONNECT AND EXTEND

Read some Rogoff for yourself. Try 'Cognition as a collaborative process' in W. Damon (ed.), *Handbook of Child Psychology* (5th edn, Vol. 2, 1998) or her own book published in 2003 *The Cultural Nature of Human Development*.

develop tests of cognitive abilities to examine underlying structures that apply to all aspects of thinking, cultural psychologists seek to analyse how people use cognitive skills in the activities of their daily lives (Segall et al., 1999). Cultural psychology is being applied to an increasing range of developmental topics, but thus far the main focus has been on culture and cognition.

Despite the rise of cultural psychology, far more research is still being conducted using the cognitive-developmental, information-processing and psychometric approaches than is conducted using a cultural approach (Segall et al., *ibid.*). Nevertheless, the cultural approach to adolescent cognition promises to grow in importance in the years to come and so we will be taking a good long look at the effect of culture on the development of adolescents and young adults in many chapters of this book, but particularly in the next chapter, Cultural beliefs.

SUMMING UP

In this chapter we have examined a variety of aspects of cognitive development in adolescence and emerging adulthood. The following summarises the key points we have discussed:

- Piaget's theory of formal operations explains many of the changes that take place cognitively between pre-adolescence and adolescence, in areas including abstract thinking complex thinking and metacognition. However, research has shown that not all persons in all cultures reach formal operations, and most people do not use formal operations in all aspects of their lives.
- Cognitive development in emerging adulthood is distinguished by the development of certain aspects of postformal thinking, especially pragmatism and reflective judgement.
- The information-processing approach focuses on separating cognitive functioning into different components, including attention, various aspects of processing information and various aspects of memory. However, the information-processing approach has been criticised for losing a sense of the overall thinking process in the course of breaking it down into components.
- Two aspects of practical cognition are critical thinking and decision making. Adolescents reach the potential for critical thinking, but teaching techniques in many secondary schools rarely bring this potential out; colleges and universities have more success with emerging adults. Adolescents appear to be capable of

making some decisions using the same processes as adults, although psychosocial factors such as the emotions of the moment may be more likely to influence their decisions.
- Social cognition also changes during adolescence, in areas including perspective taking and adolescent egocentrism.
- Absolute scores on intelligence tests improve from the teens through the 30s for verbal tests, but scores on performance tests peak in the mid-20s. Howard Gardner has proposed a theory of multiple intelligences as an alternative to traditional conceptions of intelligence.
- Recent research on brain development shows that a process of overproduction and synaptic pruning takes place in the course of adolescence, which leads to more efficient but less flexible cognitive functioning. Furthermore, the cerebellum shows a surprising amount of growth in adolescence and emerging adulthood, leading to enhanced cognitive abilities in areas such as mathematics and social skills.
- Most research on cognitive development in adolescence and emerging adulthood has ignored culture in favour of seeking universal principles of cognition. However, in recent years there has been growing attention to the ideas of Vygotsky that emphasise the sociocultural basis of cognitive development, especially scaffolding and the zone of proximal development. The new field of cultural psychology emphasises the cultural context of cognition.

The three major approaches discussed in this chapter – cognitive-developmental, information processing and psychometric – should be thought of as complementary rather than competing. The cognitive-developmental approach provides an overall view of cognitive changes in adolescence and emerging adulthood. From this approach we gain insights into how mental structures change with age and how changes in mental structures result in a wide range of other cognitive changes, from hypothetical-deductive reasoning to the use of sarcasm to reflective judgement. The information-processing approach focuses on the components of cognitive functioning, in areas such as attention and memory. From this approach we learn how the components of cognition work at their most basic level. We also learn how abilities for performing these functions change with age from childhood through adolescence and emerging adulthood. The psychometric approach focuses on measuring individuals' cognitive abilities. From this approach we learn about the range of individual differences in various cognitive abilities at any given age and also how the typical level of these cognitive abilities changes with age.

Together, these three approaches provide a broad understanding of cognitive changes in adolescence and emerging adulthood, especially when combined with other areas of study that are derived from these approaches, such as practical cognition and social cognition. However, the glaring omission in our understanding is the cultural basis of cognitive development. As all three of the major approaches have neglected cultural factors in the course of seeking universal principles of cognitive development, at this point we know relatively little about the role of culture in cognitive development during adolescence and emerging adulthood. This neglect is now being rectified in the new field of cultural psychology, which has already begun to change our understanding of cognitive development in childhood and which is likely to do the same for adolescence and emerging adulthood in the years to come.

INTERNET RESOURCES

www.piaget.org

This is the official website for the Jean Piaget Society. The Society is not solely about Piaget; instead, it is a society of scholars interested in cognitive development. It was named after Piaget to honour his contributions in this area. This website contains information about conferences and publications (books, articles, a newsletter) on topics related to cognitive development.

http://www.iqtest.com

If you have never taken an IQ test try this website. The website owners promise that

'Our original IQ test is the most scientifically valid IQ test available on the web today. Previously offered only to corporations, schools, and in certified professional applications, it is now available to you. In addition to measuring your general IQ, our exclusive test assesses your performance in 13 different areas of intelligence, revealing your key cognisant strengths and weaknesses.'

You could compare their claims with other sites offering free IQ tests online.

FURTHER READING

S. J. Gould, *The Mismeasure of Man*. New York: Norton (1981).

In this book Gould describes the history of intelligence testing and how the tests have often been used to discriminate against women and minority groups in society. Gould is a superb writer, highly readable, insightful and relevant.

J. E. Jacobs and P. A. Klaczynsky, *The Development of Judgment and Decision Making in Children and Adolescents*. Mahwah, NJ: Erlbaum (2005).

An excellent summary of research on decision making, along with new theoretical ideas, by two of the top scholars in this area.

J. Piaget, 'Intellectual evolution from adolescence to adulthood', *Human Development,* 15, 1–12 (1972).

I recommend that you read something Piaget has written, instead of simply reading how others describe his ideas. He has an insightful and original style of expression. This article would be a good choice because it focuses on issues related to adolescence and emerging adulthood.

R. A. Shweder, J. Goodnow, G. Hatano, R. A. Levine, H. Markus and P. Miller, 'The cultural psychology of development: one mind, many mentalities', in W. Damon (ed.), *Handbook of Child Development* (6th ed, Vol. 1, pp. 865–937) New York: Wiley (2006).

An excellent overview of cultural psychology. This chapter defines cultural psychology and applies it to moral development, language development, cognitive development and the development of the self.

For more reviews, responses to the *Thinking Critically* features, case studies, web links and practice tests, log on to **www.pearsoned.co.uk/arnett**.

CHAPTER 4
CULTURAL BELIEFS

OUTLINE

'Should young people accept their parents' authority without question? Or do parents have an obligation to treat their children as equals or near-equals by the time the children reach adolescence and emerging adulthood?'

'When making decisions about the future, which should come first – young people's individual desires and ambitions or the well-being of their families?'

'Should young people spend their leisure time – Friday and Saturday evenings, for example – with their parents at home or with their friends in unsupervised activities?'

'Is it best for young people to go out with a variety of persons before marriage in order to become experienced at intimate relationships? Or is it better if young people do not go out on dates before marriage and instead allow their parents to arrange a partner for them when it comes time for them to marry?'

'Is it acceptable for young people to become sexually active prior to marriage? Is the acceptability of premarital sexual activity any different for girls than for boys?'

You probably have opinions about each of these issues, and your particular view on these issues is probably typical of the people in your culture. However, whatever views your culture holds on these issues, it is certain that there are other cultures whose beliefs are considerably different. Cultures vary greatly in their views about the proper standards of behaviour for adolescents and emerging adults. Each culture is characterised by **cultural beliefs** that provide the basis for opinions about issues such as the ones presented above (Arnett, 2008).

Throughout this book, we emphasise the cultural approach to understanding development in adolescence and emerging adulthood. Adolescence and emerging adulthood are culturally constructed periods of life. As we have seen in Chapters 2 and 3, even biological and cognitive development in adolescence and emerging adulthood are shaped profoundly by cultural influences. Every chapter of this book emphasises the cultural basis of development and presents a variety of examples of differences and similarities among adolescents and emerging adults in various cultures.

Why is it important to examine cultural beliefs as part of gaining a full understanding of development in adolescence and emerging adulthood? One reason is that cultural beliefs form the foundation for every aspect of socialisation that takes place in a culture (Nelson and Chen, 2007; Boman, 2006; Pierik, 2004). The kinds of rules and responsibilities parents have for adolescents, the materials schools teach and the way schools are run, the kinds of laws cultures make to restrict young people's behaviour – all these practices and more are founded on cultural beliefs about what is morally right and what is morally wrong, which behaviours should be rewarded and which punished, and what it means to be 'a good person' (Shweder et al., 2006).

A second reason for focusing on cultural beliefs is that in many cultures adolescence and emerging adulthood are times when knowledge of these beliefs is communicated with special intensity (King and Boyatzis, 2004). As we saw in the previous chapter, adolescence brings changes in cognitive development that allows people to grasp abstract ideas and concepts in a way they could not when they were younger. Cultural beliefs are abstract; they typically include ideas about good and evil, right and wrong, vice and virtue, and so on. The fact that cultures often choose adolescence as a time for more intensively teaching these beliefs reflects a widespread intuitive awareness that this period is ripe for learning and for embracing cultural beliefs.

WHAT ARE CULTURAL BELIEFS?

Cultural beliefs are the commonly held norms and moral standards of a culture, the standards of right and wrong that set expectations for behaviour. These beliefs are usually rooted in the culture's **symbolic inheritance**, which is a set of 'ideas and understandings, both implicit and explicit, about persons, society, nature and divinity' (Shweder et al., 2006, p. 868). So, cultural beliefs include both the beliefs that constitute a culture's symbolic inheritance and the norms and moral standards that arise from these beliefs. See the upcoming *Cultural Focus* feature for an example of beliefs represented in a culture's symbolic practices.

Cultural belief systems include the **roles** that are appropriate for particular persons. All cultures have **gender roles**, that is, beliefs about the kinds of work, appearance, and other aspects of behaviour that distinguish women from men. Cultures may also have age-related roles – a man may be expected to be a warrior in his youth, for example, but to give up that role by middle adulthood and become part of a council of elders. Cultures may also have roles related to social status or social class. For example, in Britain, working-class young men have historically been characterised as having a distinctive kind of dress (leather and denim – probably now including football shirts (Skeggs, 2004)), language – slang and profanity – and behaviour – fighting and drinking (Wells et al., 2005). Young people everywhere become more aware of their culture's beliefs about such roles in the course of adolescence. This is partly because of increasing cognitive capacities for abstract thinking and self-reflection, and partly because reaching adolescence means that the threshold of adulthood is approaching and young people will soon be expected to adapt themselves to the role requirements for adults in their culture.

A culture's symbolic inheritance is the basis for its norms and standards (Kopelman and Kopelman, 2007; Alas, 2006). The symbolic inheritance usually includes beliefs about the ultimate meaning of human life and the place of an individual's life in the vast scheme of things. Sometimes these beliefs are religious and include ideas about where the soul of the individual came from and where it goes after death. (The idea of the soul – an intangible, individual human identity that is distinct from our bodily natures – is nearly universal in cultures' religious beliefs.) Sometimes these beliefs are political, with ideas about how the individual is part of a great historical movement heading toward an inevitable conclusion. The communist beliefs that were so influential in the twentieth century are an example of this. Sometimes these beliefs are familial and communal, whereby the significance of an individual life is derived from its place in a larger organisation that existed before the individual was born, and will continue to exist after the individual has passed on. Adolescence is a time of particular importance for cultures to communicate these beliefs about the ultimate meaning of things and to encourage young people to embrace them wholeheartedly.

In this chapter, we will first discuss the role that cultural beliefs play in the socialisation of adolescents. Following this we will consider specific aspects of cultural beliefs, including religious beliefs, moral beliefs and political beliefs.

CULTURAL BELIEFS AND SOCIALISATION

An important aspect of cultural beliefs is the set of beliefs that specifically concerns standards of right and wrong for raising children, adolescents and emerging adults. Should young people be taught that individuals should be independent and self-sufficient, following their own desires rather than complying with the norms of the group; or should they be taught that the group comes first, that the needs and requirements of the family and community should have higher priority than the needs and desires of the individual? Should young people be allowed and encouraged to express themselves, even when what they say or do may offend other people; or should each person be pressed – and, if necessary, coerced – to conform to the accepted standards of the culture?

All cultures have answers to these questions as part of their cultural beliefs, but the kinds of answers cultures devise vary widely. At the heart of these answers are cultural beliefs about **socialisation**, the process by which people acquire the behaviours and beliefs of the culture

CULTURAL FOCUS

The Bar and Bat Mitzvah

In Jewish tradition, an important event at age 13 signifies the adolescent's new responsibilities with respect to Jewish beliefs. The event is a ceremony called the **Bar Mitzvah**, and it has existed in some form for over 2000 years. The details have changed over the centuries, and today the ceremony differs in some respects from one synagogue to another. Until recently, for example, only boys participated in the Bar Mitzvah. However, today many girls participate as well (although it is still more common for boys). For girls, the ceremony is called the **Bat Mitzvah**. Although these ceremonies vary among synagogues, Bar and Bat Mitzvahs share some common elements (Marcus, 2004; Davis, 1988):

The Bar Mitzvah.

- Prayers are recited stating belief in the one and only God and promising allegiance to God's commandments. Further prayers praise God and reaffirm the sacredness of the Sabbath.

- The Torah is passed from one generation to the next, literally and figuratively. (The Torah consists of the first five books of the Hebrew Bible. These are also the first five books of what Christians call the Old Testament.) The initiate and the parents and grandparents come to the front of the synagogue. The Torah is taken from the ark (where it is normally kept) and passed from the grandparents to the parents to the initiate.

- The initiate carries the Torah around the room so that people may touch it with their hands or with a prayer book or prayer shawl, which they then kiss. The congregation remains standing as it is taken around the room.

- The Torah is returned to the front and unwrapped. Often younger children perform the unwrapping.

- The initiate recites a portion of the Torah, and then reads from the Haftorah, which consists of the teachings of Jewish prophets.

- The initiate receives the blessings of the parents and rabbi.

- The initiate gives a brief talk on some aspect of Jewish teachings. Often, the talk focuses on some of the implications that might be drawn from the portions of the Torah and the Haftorah the initiate has just recited.

- The initiation is celebrated with a festive meal.

In Jewish tradition, completing the Bar/Bat Mitzvah means that the young person can now participate fully in the religious activities of the community. For example, after their Bar/Bat Mitzvah, young people can be counted toward the minimum of ten persons required for holding religious services. Also, they are now obliged to carry out the same religious rituals as adults, and their word is valid in sessions determining violations of Jewish law.

Furthermore, they are now 'subject to the commandments'. That is, they are now responsible for their own actions, as children are not. (Recall from Chapter 1 the importance of 'responsibility for one's actions' in contemporary views of the transition to adulthood.) In fact, the Bar Mitzvah sometimes includes a part where the parents declare, 'Blessed is He who has freed me from responsibility for this child's conduct.' Perhaps this declaration reflects an intuitive awareness in Jewish tradition of the cognitive advances of adolescence, which make young people capable of a new level of self-reflection and decision making.

Notice how the ceremony works to inculcate cultural beliefs. The beliefs are passed, quite literally, from one generation to the next during the ceremony, as the grandparents and parents pass the Torah to the initiate. The initiate's new responsibility for carrying on those beliefs is signified by taking the Torah around the room to be blessed. The initiate also reads from the holy books, and this act – declaring aloud before the community a portion of their shared beliefs – is crucial to attaining full status as a member of the community.

CONNECT AND EXTEND

To learn more about cultural initiation in a very different context read 'Rites of passage to adulthood: traditional initiation schools in the context of HIV/AIDS in the Limpopo Province' by Lutendo Malisha, Pranitha Maharaj and Michael Rogan in South Africa. *Health, Risk & Society*, Volume 10, Number 6 (December 2008), pp. 585–598

The three goals of socialisation.

they live in (Bugental and Grusec, 2006). Three outcomes are central to this process (Grusec, 2002). **Self-regulation** is the capacity for exercising self-control in order to restrain one's impulses and comply with social norms. This includes the development of a conscience, which is the internal monitor of whether you are complying adequately with social norms; when your conscience determines that you are not, you experience guilt. **Role preparation** is a second outcome of socialisation. This includes preparation for occupational roles, gender roles and roles in institutions such as marriage and parenthood. The third outcome of socialisation is the cultivation of **sources of meaning**, which indicate what is important, what is to be valued, and what is to be lived for. Human beings are uniquely existential creatures. Unlike other animals, we are capable of reflecting on our mortality and on what our lives mean in light of the inescapable fact that we will all die some day (Bastion and Stately, 2009). Sources of meaning provide consolation, guidance, and hope to people in confronting existential questions.

These three outcomes of socialisation are shared by all cultures. To survive and thrive and perpetuate themselves from one generation to the next, cultures must teach these things to their members. However, this does not mean that cultures express these goals explicitly, or that cultural members are even consciously aware of them as outcomes of socialisation. Much of what cultures teach about what people should believe and value is taught implicitly, through the practices and behaviours young people are encouraged to adopt (Shweder et al., 2006). For example, requiring students to wear uniforms in schools teaches that conformity to the group standards and behaviours of schooling is more important than individual expression.

Adolescence and emerging adulthood are important periods of development with respect to each of these outcomes of the process of socialisation. Self-regulation begins to be learned in infancy, but a new dimension is added to it in adolescence as regulation of sexual impulses rises in importance with puberty and the development of sexual maturity. Also, as puberty progresses

and young people reach their full size and strength, it becomes more important for cultures to ensure that youngsters have learned self-regulation so that they will not disrupt or endanger the lives of others. Role preparation also becomes more urgent in adolescence. These years are crucial for young people to prepare themselves for the occupational and social roles they will soon be expected to take on as adults. Adolescence and emerging adulthood are also key times for the development of sources of meaning because adolescents are newly capable of grasping and understanding the abstract ideas about values and beliefs that are part of the meanings of life that cultures teach.

THINKING CRITICALLY

Do you think that the beliefs of all cultures are equally good and true, or do you think that the beliefs of some cultures are better and truer than the beliefs of others? Give an example of an issue that illustrates your view. If you believe that some cultural beliefs are better and truer than others, on what standard would you base your evaluation, and why?

Cultural Values: Individualism and Collectivism

Although all cultures share similar socialisation *outcomes*, cultures differ widely in their socialisation *values*. A central issue with respect to cultural values about socialisation concerns whether cultures place more value on independence and self-expression or, alternately, on obedience and conformity as the characteristics they wish to promote in their children. This issue is sometimes portrayed as a contrast between individualism and collectivism, with individualistic cultures giving priority to independence and self-expression and collectivist cultures placing a higher value on obedience and conformity (Triandis, 2001).

A great deal of research has taken place on individualism and collectivism in the past 30 years (Brewer and Chen, 2007; Oyserman and Lee, 2008), especially focusing on cultural contrasts between the majority cultures of the Eastern cultures such as those in China, Japan and Korea and the West (defined in Chapter 1 and elsewhere as much of Europe, North America, Australia and New Zealand). Scholars have examined differences in values and beliefs among people in a wide range of cultures and have consistently found people in the West to be more individualistic and people in Eastern cultures to be more collectivistic (e.g. Marshall, 2008; Kim & Markus, 1999). Scholars have also discussed the development of the self in individualistic and collectivistic cultures (Markus and Kitayama, 2003; Shweder et al., 2006). Collectivistic cultures promote the development of an **interdependent self**, such that people place a strong value on cooperation, mutual support, harmonious social relations and contributions to the group. In contrast, individualistic cultures promote the development of an **independent self**, such that people place a strong value on independence, individual freedoms and individual achievements.

Several points should be kept in mind regarding individualism and collectivism. First, the belief systems of most cultures are not 'pure types' of individualism or collectivism but a combination of the two in various proportions. Although the contrast between the individualistic West and the collectivistic East holds up quite well in research, some scholars have pointed out that most Western cultures, too, have elements of collectivism, and most Eastern cultures have elements of individualism (Tamis-Lemonda et al., 2008; Matsumoto, 2002; Killen and Wainryb, 2000). In Eastern cultures, this blend is increasingly complex as they are influenced by the West through globalisation (Chang, 2008; Naito and Gielen, 2003; Matsumoto, 2002).

A second point is that individualism and collectivism describe overall tendencies for the values of cultures as a whole, but individual differences exist in every culture (Tamis-Lemonda et al., 2008; Killen and Wainryb, 2000). A culture that is individualistic overall is likely to have some people who are more collectivistic than individualistic, and a culture that is collectivistic overall is likely to have some people who are more individualistic than collectivistic.

A third point is that diversity also exists within individuals. Most people are probably not purely individualistic or purely collectivistic in their beliefs and behaviour but have some combination of the two tendencies, which they may use in different settings (Killen and Wainryb, 2000). For example, a person may be relatively individualistic at work or in school, striving for individual achievement and recognition, but relatively collectivistic at home, seeking to cooperate and maintain harmony with family members. Individualism and collectivism are not necessarily mutually exclusive and can coexist within individuals.

Keep these qualifiers in mind as we discuss individualism and collectivism in this chapter and throughout the book. As long as you remember these limitations, the concepts of individualism and collectivism remain highly useful and valid as a 'shorthand' way of describing the general patterns and contrasts in beliefs among various cultures. Also bear in mind that youngsters are, to some extent 'products' of the culture in which they are raised. Understanding what characterises the culture in which adolescents grow and develop helps to explain their behaviour in relation to their community.

Collectivism is especially strong in Asian cultures.

CONNECT AND EXTEND

Examine collectivism and individualism in the context of religious belief in 'Individualism and collectivism in Israeli society: comparing religious and secular high-school students' by Shifra Sagy, Emda Orr and Dan Bar-On in *Human Relations*, Volume 52, Number 3 (1999), pp. 327–348

Broad and Narrow Socialisation

We like to discuss the contrast in socialisation patterns between individualistic and collectivistic cultures in terms of broad and narrow socialisation (Arnett, 2006d) Cultures characterised by **broad socialisation** favour individualism. They encourage individual uniqueness, independence and self-expression. Cultures characterised by **narrow socialisation** favour collectivism. They hold obedience and conformity to be the highest values and discourage deviation from cultural expectations. *Individualism* and *collectivism* describe the general differences in values and beliefs among cultures; *broad* and *narrow socialisation* describe the *process* by which cultural members come to adopt the values and beliefs of an individualistic (broad) or collectivistic (narrow) culture.

The terms *broad* and *narrow* refer to the range of individual differences cultures allow or encourage – relatively broad in broad socialisation, relatively narrow in narrow socialisation. All socialisation involves some degree of restrictiveness on individual preferences and inclinations. As early as 1993, psychology professor Sandra Scarr noted 'cultures set a range of opportunities for development; they define the limits of what is desirable, "normal" individual variation' (p.1335) and 'Cultures define the *range* and *focus* of personal variation that is acceptable and rewarded' (p.1337; emphasis in the original). We agree. Socialisation inevitably means the establishment of limits, but cultures differ in the *degree* of restrictiveness they impose, and the degree of cultures' restrictiveness is the central contrast between broad and narrow socialisation.

Because Western cultural beliefs emphasise individualism, Western cultures tend toward broad socialisation. The West has a long history of emphasising individualism in a variety of aspects of life (Deets, 2006), and this includes cultural beliefs about socialisation. In contrast, socialisation in non-Western cultures tends to be narrower, with a greater emphasis on promoting the well-being of the family and community rather than the individual, and often including hierarchies of authority based on gender,

age, and other characteristics (Kim and Markus, 1999).

Most cultures with narrow socialisation are less economically developed than those in the West. Narrow socialisation is emphasised in cultures of the developing world partly because young people's work is necessary for families' survival; conformity and obedience are demanded to ensure that young people will make their necessary contributions (Brown and Johnson, 2008). However, narrow socialisation is also characteristic of some highly industrialised Asian cultures, such as Japan, although socialisation in these societies may be becoming broader in response to globalisation (Noguchi, 2007; Naito and Gielen, 2003; Stevenson and Zusho, 2002).

The same qualifiers that apply to individualism and collectivism also apply to broad and narrow socialisation. All cultures have a considerable amount of variability, based on individuals' personalities and preferences. If we say socialisation in a particular culture is broad, that does not mean that everyone in the culture has the same beliefs about the desirability of individualism. It simply means that the culture as a whole can be described as tending towards broad socialisation, although individuals within the culture may vary in their beliefs. Think of the concepts of broad and narrow socialisation as a simple, shorthand way of referring to an essential contrast in socialisation, not as absolute categories that every culture in the world fits into cleanly.

It is important, too, to state explicitly that the concepts of individualism–collectivism and broad–narrow socialisation are not meant to imply moral evaluations. With each general type of socialisation there are 'trade-offs'. Under broad socialisation, because individualism is encouraged there is likely to be more creativity and more innovation, but also a higher degree of loneliness, social problems and disorder (Rego and Cunha, 2009; Kaylor, 1999). Under narrow socialisation, there may be a stronger sense of collective identity and greater social order, but at the cost of greater suppression of individual uniqueness (Jetten et al., 2006). Each form of socialisation has its costs as well as its benefits.

CONNECT AND EXTEND

A 'socialisation approach' through vocational training is described in 'Youth transitions and employment in Germany' by Walter R. Heinz in the *International Social Science Journal*, Volume 52, Number 164 (June 2000), pp. 161–170

THINKING CRITICALLY

Do you agree or disagree with the view that there are 'pros and cons' to both broad and narrow socialisation? Explain your view.

Sources of Socialisation

Socialisation involves many aspects of a culture. You may think most readily of parents when you think of socialisation, and parents usually are central to the socialisation process (Bugental and Grusec, 2006). However, socialisation involves other sources as well. The sources of socialisation include *family* (not just parents but also siblings and extended family), *peers and friends, school, community, the workplace, media, the legal system* and *the cultural belief system* (Wahlstrom and Ponte, 2005; Lawrence and Valsiner, 2003). In general, the family's influence on socialisation diminishes in adolescence (Aquilino, 2006), whereas the influences of peers/friends, school, community, media and the legal system increase. Family influence in Western majority cultures diminishes further in emerging adulthood, when most emerging adults move out of their family household (Aquilino, 2006). Nevertheless, the family remains a powerful influence on socialisation in adolescence and emerging adulthood, even if its influence is not as powerful as earlier in development.

Later in this text, a specific chapter will be devoted to each of several socialisation sources, including family, peers and friends, school and the workplace. Information on socialisation in the community and the legal system will be presented in a variety of chapters. Table 4.1 provides a summary description of broad and narrow socialisation.

Cultures can vary in their socialisation from these different sources – a culture may be relatively broad in family socialisation, for example, and relatively narrow in socialisation through the school. However, usually a culture's sources are consistent in their socialisation, because the cultural belief system is the foundation for the socialisation that takes place through the other sources. Parents, teachers, community leaders and other socialisation agents in a culture carry out common socialisation practices because of their shared beliefs about what is best for children and adolescents (Tamis-LeMonda et al., 2008).

An Example of Socialisation for Cultural Beliefs

So far, our discussion of cultural beliefs and the different forms of socialisation has been abstract, describing the nature of cultural beliefs and distinguishing two general cultural approaches to socialisation. Now let us look at a specific example of socialisation for cultural beliefs, as an illustration of the ideas we have introduced.

We can draw on a number of ethnographic studies of adolescence among the indigenous people of Australia (sometimes called Aborigines) to support a very particular and illuminating illustration of socialisation for cultural beliefs (Healy, 2006; Piquemal, 2005). Until about 70 years ago, the Aborigines were nomadic hunters and gatherers. They had no settled residence but moved their small communities from one place to another according to the seasons and the availability of food such as fish and sea turtles. They had few possessions; shelters and tools were manufactured easily from materials that were widely available.

A key part of traditional adolescent socialisation among the Aborigines involves the ritual teaching of a set of cultural beliefs known as the Law. The Law includes an explanation of how the world began and instructions for how various ritual ceremonies should be performed, such as the circumcision ritual that is one of the rites of passage initiating adolescent boys into manhood. The Law also includes moral precepts for how interpersonal relations should be conducted. For example, there are complex rules about who may have sex with whom and who may marry whom, depending on the family and clan to which persons belong. Also, it is viewed as best if marriages are arranged by parents rather than by the young people themselves.

The Law is presented in a series of three public ceremonies, with each ceremony representing a stage in the initiation of adolescent boys into manhood. (Although both boys and girls learn the Law, only boys participate in the rituals of initiation.) In the ceremonies, various aspects of the Law are taught. Songs, dances and the painted bodies of the performers present stories that illustrate the Law. The whole community attends. Following the ceremonies, the adolescent boys experience an extended period of seclusion in which they are given little to eat and have almost no contact with others. After learning the Law and experiencing this period of seclusion, they have a new, higher status in the community.

Table 4.1 Broad and Narrow Socialisation

Broad socialisation	
Source	**Description**
Family	Few restrictions on adolescents' behaviour; adolescents spend considerable time away from family in unsupervised leisure. Parents encourage independence and self-sufficiency in adolescents.
Peers/Friends	Adolescents are allowed to choose their own friends. Adolescents make friends of different ethnic groups and social classes, based on their similar interests and attractions as individuals.
School	Teachers promote students' individuality and attempt to adapt the curriculum to each student's individual needs and preferences. Low emphasis is placed on order and obedience to teachers and school authorities. No uniforms or dress code are required.
Community	Community members do not know each other well, and adult community members exercise little or no social control over adolescents. Independence and self-expression of the individual are valued more highly than conformity to the expectations and standards of the community.
Workplace	Young people are allowed to choose for themselves among a wide range of possible occupations. Workplaces generally promote creativity and individual achievement.
Media	Media are diverse, and media content is mostly unregulated by governmental authorities. Media promote gratification of individual desires and impulses.
Legal system	Legal restrictions on behaviour are minimal. The rights of the individual to a wide range of self-expression are highly valued. Punishments for most offences are light.
Cultural beliefs	Individualism, independence, self-expression.
Narrow socialisation	
Source	**Description**
Family	Duty and obligation to family are valued highly. Adult family members command respect and deference. Responsibility to family is considered more important than the individual's autonomy or achievements.
Peers/Friends	Adults exercise control over adolescents' friendship choices, in part by disapproving of friendships between adolescents of different ethnic groups and social classes.
School	Emphasis is on learning the standard curriculum rather than on independent or critical thinking. Firm discipline is used in the classroom. Uniforms or conformity to strict dress code may be required.
Community	Community members know each other well and share common cultural beliefs. Adherence to the standards and expectations of the community is highly valued. Nonconformity is viewed with suspicion and treated with ostracism.
Workplace	Young people's job choices are constrained by the decisions of adults (e.g. parents, governmental authorities). Workplaces promote conformity and discourage innovative thinking that might challenge the status quo.
Media	Media are tightly controlled by governmental authorities. Media content is generally restricted to socially acceptable themes that do not threaten common moral standards.
Legal system	Legal restrictions are placed on a wide range of behaviour, including sexuality and political views, and are backed by swift and severe punishment.
Cultural beliefs	Collectivism, obedience, conformity.

In this dance ceremony, young Australian Aborigines act out tenets of the Law.

In the traditional teaching of the Law, we can see illustrations of the principles of socialisation and cultural beliefs we have discussed. The Law is at the centre of the symbolic inheritance of the Aborigines; it contains ideas about relations between the individual, society, and divine forces. The Law stresses self-regulation, especially with regard to sexual desire, by specifying rules for sexual contact. Information about roles is taught as part of the Law; adolescent boys learn the expectations for behaviour that they must follow in their role as adult men. The Law also provides a source of meaning by explaining the origin of the world and by providing adolescents with a clear and secure place in their communities.

The cultural beliefs expressed in the Law are collectivistic. Adolescents are taught that they have obligations to others as part of the Law and that they must allow others to make important decisions which affect them, such as whom they shall marry. As their beliefs are collectivistic, socialisation among the Aborigines is narrow; conformity and obedience to the Law and to elders are emphasised. Adolescent boys do not decide for themselves whether to take part in the ceremonies of the Law; they *must* take part, or be ostracised.

However, like so many of the practices of traditional cultures, the relationship between adolescents and the Law has been dramatically affected by tensions in global legal practice in relation to family law and globalisation (Watson, 2009; Robinson, 1997). The ceremonies still exist, and adolescents still take part. However, the period of boys' seclusion that follows, which used to last about two months, now lasts only a week. Furthermore, adolescents are showing increasing resistance to learning and practising the beliefs and rules of the Law at all. To many of them, the Law seems irrelevant to the world they live in, which is no longer a world of nomadic hunting and gathering but of schools, a complex economy and modern media.

Adolescents now develop beliefs based not just on the Law but on their other experiences as well, and these experiences have made their beliefs more individualistic. Learning about the rest of the world through school and the media has led many of them to question their native cultural practices, such as arranged marriages. Australian psychology professor Victoria Burbank (1988) observes in an early text about the control of female reproduction in an Australian Aboriginal community:

'Today the Law must compete with the lessons of school, church, movies, and Western music. Initiation may no longer be viewed by the initiate himself as a means to a desired end – the achievement of adult male status. Rather, it may be seen as a nonsensical ordeal of pain and privation. Under these circumstances, its ability to affect subsequent behaviour may be minimized' (pp. 37–38).

In recent years, young Aborigines have also begun to display many of the modern problems of adolescence and emerging adulthood, such as unmarried pregnancy in their teens, substance use and crime (Senior and Chenhall, 2008). The power of the Law has diminished as a source of self-regulation, roles and meaning, and for young Aborigines their new problems signify that nothing has yet arisen to take its place.

CONNECT AND EXTEND

Schooling can be used as a method of political socialising of minority indigenous groups. Read 'Knowing their place: the political socialisation of Maori women in New Zealand through schooling policy and practice, 1867–1969' by Kuni Jenkins and Kay Morris Matthews in *Women's History Review*, Volume 7, Number 1 (1998), pp. 85–105

Socialisation for Cultural Beliefs in the West

Can you think of anything in your own community comparable to the Aborigines' teaching of cultural beliefs for adolescents? If you grew up in Europe or North America, it may be difficult. Most industrial countries of the Northern hemisphere have no formal, ritual teaching of individualism. In a way, that would be contrary to the whole spirit of individualism because ritual implies a standard way of doing things and individualism stresses independence from standard ways. You could find evidence of implicit teaching of individualism in adults' practices with regard to adolescence, such as the kinds of freedoms parents allow adolescents, or the range of choices adolescents are allowed for the courses they take at school. We will discuss these and other practices reflecting individualism in future chapters; but what about *beliefs*? What evidence do we have of cultural beliefs that reflect individualism?

One interesting piece of evidence comes from 'across the pond' in a famous and historical study conducted by Helen and Robert Lynd in the 1920s (Lynd and Lynd, 1929), describing life in a typical American community they called 'Middletown' (actually Muncie, Indiana). The Lynds studied many aspects of life in Middletown, including women's beliefs about the qualities they considered most important to promote in their children. Fifty years later, another group of researchers (Caplow et al., 1982) returned to Middletown and asked the residents many of the same questions, including the ones about child-rearing beliefs.

As you can see from Table 4.2, the results indicate that the child-rearing beliefs of the majority culture changed dramatically over the twentieth century (Alwin, 1988). Narrow socialisation values such as obedience and loyalty to church declined in importance, whereas broad socialisation values such as independence and tolerance became central to their child-rearing beliefs. This change was reflected in

Table 4.2 Child-rearing Values of Women in Middletown, 1928–1978

	1928 %	1978 %
Loyalty to church	50	22
Strict obedience	45	17
Good manners	31	23
Independence	25	76
Tolerance	6	47

The table indicates the percentage of women in 1928 and 1978 who listed each of the indicated values as one of the three most important for their children to learn, out of a list of 15 values.

Source: Alwin, D. F. (1988) 'From obedience to autonomy: changes in traits desired in children, 1924–1978', *Public Opinion Quarterly*, 52, pp. 33–52

behavioural differences in Middletown adolescents, particularly girls.

In more recent times, adolescents have become substantially more independent from their parents, spending more of their time away from home and depending less on their parents (Hay and Ashman, 2003), including for information about sex (Somers and Surmann, 2005). Other studies have confirmed this trend in cultural beliefs during the twentieth century, away from obedience and conformity and toward individualism (Jetten et al., 2002; Cohn, 1999). Even though Britain and many other European countries – particularly in the context of post-communist freedom – have a long tradition of valuing individualism (Marková et al., 1998; Deets, *ibid.*), individualistic beliefs have evidently grown stronger during the past century, and adolescents in most European cultures today are growing up at a time when individualism is more highly valued and protected than in the past (Fredman, 2001).

CONNECT AND EXTEND

For a fascinating example of comparing parents' cultural beliefs about child rearing in Israel read 'Child maltreatment: differences in perceptions between parents in low income and middle income neighbourhoods' by R. Shor in *The British Journal of Social Work*, Volume 30, Number 2 (April 2000), pp. 165–178

CONNECT AND EXTEND

Does increased independence apply to young people with disabilities? Read 'Sexuality in children and adolescents with disabilities' by Nancy Murphy and Paul C. Young in *Developmental Medicine & Child Neurology*, Volume 47, Number 9 (September 2005), pp. 640–644

THINKING CRITICALLY

Have you experienced any direct teaching of cultural beliefs, such as in the Scouts, preparation for Bar or Bat Mitzvah, Sunday School or confirmation lessons? Perhaps you attended skūla, szkoła, shule or ysgol. If so, did these experiences form the basis for your current beliefs? If not, how do you think you developed your current beliefs?

THINKING CRITICALLY

Give an example of a custom complex you have experienced in your own culture. Describe how the behaviour or practice reflects cultural beliefs.

CULTURAL BELIEFS AND THE CUSTOM COMPLEX

The examples of the Aborigines and Middletown portray the cultural beliefs that adults hold explicitly and teach intentionally to their young people. However, cultural beliefs are also reflected in people's everyday practices, even when they are not conscious of it. Every aspect of development is influenced by the cultural context in which it takes place, and every pattern of behaviour reflects something about cultural beliefs.

This means that every aspect of development and behaviour in adolescence and emerging adulthood can be analysed as a **custom complex** (Shweder et al., 2006). This term was coined more than half a century ago by Whiting and Child (1953), who stated that a custom complex 'consists of a customary practice and of the beliefs, values, sanctions, rules, motives and satisfactions associated with it' (p. 27). More recently, scholars have placed the custom complex at the centre of the growing field of cultural psychology (Embree, 2003; Laungani, 2002), which examines human development from a perspective that combines psychology and anthropology.

To put it simply, a custom complex consists of typical practice in a culture and the cultural beliefs that provide the basis for that practice. We will use this term at various points in the book, but for illustration here let us briefly consider dating as an example of a custom complex.

Dating is something you may be used to thinking about as something that is **ontogenetic**; when adolescents reach the ages of 13, 14 or 15, it is 'natural' for them to begin dating.

However, analysing dating as a custom complex shows that dating is not simply a natural part of development but a custom complex that reflects certain cultural beliefs. We can begin by noting that dating is by no means a universal practice. It is less common in Europe than in the United States (Alsaker and Flammer, 1999), and it is discouraged in most non-industrialised cultures – although the practice is growing in response to globalisation (Schlegel, 2001). Furthermore, dating is a recent practice. Before the last third of the twentieth century, young people in Britain and Northern Europe typically engaged not in dating but in courtship, which was structured and monitored by adults (Mumm et al., 2007). The move from courting to dating in Southern and Eastern Europe occurred somewhat later and courtship has survived in some cultures.

Dating is not universal but is part of the custom complex that reflects certain cultural beliefs.

HISTORICAL FOCUS

The Origin of the Scouting Movement

One of the points discussed in this chapter is that, for the most part, Western cultures do little in the way of formal teaching of cultural beliefs. All adolescents in the United Kingdom receive some formal instruction in religious beliefs as Religious Education is specifically part of the statutory National Curriculum, but in other Western cultures religion is much less a part of the education of adolescents. Even in the United States, only about half of adolescents take part regularly in religious activities (Smith and Denton, 2005).

The absence of formal moral training was discussed with particular intensity in British and European public forums in the early and middle twentieth century (Jackson, 2004; Conroy, 2001). Adults worried greatly that, with the decline of religion, young people would grow up without a moral orientation strong enough to guide them through an increasingly complex and dangerous world.

In the UK, Robert Baden-Powell had an idea for how to address this perceived danger of moral decline among young people. In 1908, he started an organisation called the Boy Scouts that would be dedicated to teaching moral precepts to adolescent boys aged 11 to 17 (Pryke, 2001). Boy Scouts would learn how to do woodcraft, swim, set up a camp, cook outdoors and perform various other out-door survival skills. However, Baden-Powell made it clear that these activities were all intended to have a moral purpose: to socialise boys so that they would become good citizens with a high moral character (Rosenthal, 1986).

This purpose is reflected explicitly in two key parts of the Scout programme: the Scout Oath and the Scout Law, which all are required to learn (by memory) to become Scouts. The UK Scout Oath is as follows:

The Scout Promise is as follows:

On my honour, I promise that I will do my best
– To do my duty to God and the Queen;
– To help other people;
– and to keep the Scout Law.

The Scout Law is as follows:

1 A Scout is to be trusted.
2 A Scout is loyal.
3 A Scout is friendly and considerate.
4 A Scout belongs to the worldwide family of Scouts.
5 A Scout has courage in all difficulties.
6 A Scout makes good use of time and is careful of possessions and property.
7 A Scout has self-respect and respect for others.

Notice that these are mostly collectivistic rather than individualistic values. There's nothing here about self-esteem or individual achievement. Instead, values such as being trustworthy, loyal, helpful, courteous, kind and obedient are all oriented toward consideration for and service to others. In a sense, the creation of the Scouts can be seen as an attempt to create an organisation that would maintain some elements of collectivism in Western cultures that were becoming increasingly individualistic.

Baden-Powell's idea was instantly and phenomenally successful. A few years after the origin of the Boy Scouts in 1908 the organisation had spread all over the world and involved millions of adolescent boys. In 1912 the Girl Scouts was created on the basis of similar principles and quickly spread around the world to include millions of adolescent girls. Parallel organisations were created for pre-adolescent boys (Cub Scouts) and pre-adolescent girls (Junior Girl Scouts) as well as for older adolescents (Venturing for boys and girls and Senior Girl Scouts for girls only).

The Scouting movement continues to thrive today. Membership in the Boy Scouts has remained more or less steady for the past two decades at a total of over 28 million boys in virtually every country in the world (World Organization of the Scout Movement, 2008). The country with the largest number of Boy Scouts is Indonesia, which has nearly 10 million. Membership in the Girl Scouts is about half the size of the Boy Scouts. Boy Scouts and Girls Scouts are the largest voluntary organisations of adolescent boys and girls in the world. Many troops are now mixed and the movement is increasingly referred to simply as The Scouts.

Of course, Scouting has changed considerably from its early days when, as one scholar described it, the organisation stressed 'glorification of discipline' and had an 'obsession . . . with inculcating obedience' (Rosenthal, 1986, pp. 8, 112). The Scouting movement has adapted to the broadening of socialisation in the twentieth century in Western cultures by becoming less strict and focusing more on each Scout's individual development.

For example:

The mission of Scouting (2010) is to contribute to the education of young people, through a value system based on the Scout Promise and Law, to help build a better world where people are self-fulfilled as individuals and play a constructive role in society. This is achieved by:

1 Involving them throughout their formative years in a non-formal educational process

2 Using a specific method that makes each individual the principal agent of his or her development as a self-reliant, supportive, responsible and committed person

3 Assisting them to establish a value system based upon spiritual, social and personal principles as expressed in the Promise and Law.

Note that Scouting was originally created for young people reaching adolescence, the same period that cultures such as the Australian Aborigines choose for their own socialisation rituals communicating cultural beliefs. As suggested earlier, this may be because people in many cultures have intuitively realised that adolescence is the period of life when the time is ripe for such socialisation, because the young person's cognitive capacities have matured to a point capable of grasping abstract ideas such as duty and obligation. The initiation practices of many cultures seem to reflect a view that when young people reach adolescence, it is imperative to ensure that they have understood and embraced the beliefs of their culture before they take on the responsibilities of adult life.

Source: **http://www.scout.org/en/about_scouting/mission_vision/the_mission** accessed 21 April 2010

THINKING CRITICALLY

Look at the mission statement of the Scouting Movement in 2010. How would you use the main concepts of socialisation: broad and narrow socialisation; individualism and collectivism to characterise the different elements of the mission statement?

A custom complex involves both a typical practice and the cultural beliefs that underlie that practice. What cultural beliefs underlie the Western practice of dating? First, dating reflects a cultural belief that adolescents and emerging adults should be allowed to have a substantial degree of independent leisure time. This is in contrast to cultures that believe young people should spend their leisure time with their families. Second, dating reflects a cultural belief that young people should

Scouting was begun with the explicit purpose of teaching values to young people.

have a right to choose for themselves the persons with whom they wish to have intimate relationships. This is in contrast to cultures whose beliefs specify that young people should allow their parents to make those decisions for them. Third, dating reflects a cultural belief that some degree of sexual experience before marriage is acceptable and healthy for young people. This is in contrast to cultures that believe young people's sexual experiences should begin only after they are married.

All aspects of development in adolescence and emerging adulthood can be analysed in this way. Family relationships, peer relations, school experiences, and more – all of them consist of a variety of custom complexes that reflect the beliefs of the cultures in which young people live. Thus, in the chapters to come, we will use the idea of the custom complex as a way of revealing and exploring the cultural beliefs that underlie socialisation.

CULTURAL BELIEFS IN MULTICULTURAL SOCIETIES

In describing cultural beliefs, cultures should not be confused with countries. Many countries contain a variety of cultures with a variety of different cultural beliefs. For this reason, in this book we speak not of a British cultural belief system but of the cultural beliefs of the British majority culture, as well as the cultural beliefs of minority cultures within British society. Even then, care must be taken, for within a particular society, neighbourhood or locality a head count might show an ethnic minority to be

in the majority, yet they can still be characterised as a minority because the wider cultural images and entertainments, particularly present in the mass media, may reflect the custom complexes of the national majority culture.

Many studies have shown that the cultural beliefs of British minority cultures tend to be less individualistic and more collectivistic than the cultural beliefs of the British majority culture. Among British Pakistanis, obedience to parents and obligations to family are strongly emphasised. Adolescents in British Pakistani families generally accept the authority of the parents and express a strong sense of obligation and attachment to their families (Dwyer et al., 2008; Crozier and Davies, 2006 Hussain and Bagguley, 2005). British Chinese adolescents are also considerably more collectivistic and less individualistic than adolescents in the British majority culture. They spend much more time carrying out family chores, and they express a strong sense of duty and obligation to

British minority families tend to be more collectivistic than families in the British majority culture. Here, a British Pakistani family enjoying a day out.

CONNECT AND EXTEND

'In contemporary media and policy debates young British Muslim men are frequently described as experiencing cultural conflict, as alienated, deviant, underachieving, and as potential terrorists' (p. 117). Read 'From cricket lover to terror suspect: challenging representations of young British Muslim men' by Claire Dwyer, Bindi Shah and Gurchathen Sanghera in *Gender, Place and Culture: A Journal of Feminist Geography*, Volume 15, Number 2 (2008), pp. 117–136

their families (Sham and Woodrow, 1998). In their conceptions of what it means to be an adult, nearly all Chinese emerging adults hold to the two major premises of Chinese behaviour – 'filial piety' and 'respect for elders'; striking aspects of their collectivism (Nelson and Chen, 2007; Chen, 2001). With respect to British Caribbean, little research has been conducted on the individualism–collectivism dimension. However, there is some evidence that British Caribbean young people are more individualistic than young people in other British minority groups but less individualistic than young people in the majority British white culture (Reynolds, 2006).

Most other European countries also have substantial minority populations whose cultural beliefs tend to be considerably more collectivistic and less individualistic than the European majority culture. Further afield, Canada has a substantial Inuit (or 'First Nations') population; Australia has a Chinese immigrant population; New Zealand has a substantial number of Maoris. There is a Turkish minority culture in Germany, an Algerian minority culture in France, and a substantial Latino minority culture in the US – many other examples could be given. In every case, the cultural beliefs of the minority culture tend to be more collectivistic and less individualistic than those in the majority culture.

As noted earlier, because cultural beliefs typically provide the foundation for socialisation from all other sources, usually there is a great deal of consistency of socialisation across sources. What happens when the socialisation young people experience is not consistent across sources? What happens when young people are part of a minority culture whose beliefs differ from those of the majority culture? When this is the case, youngsters may find themselves being exposed to a kind of socialisation within the family that is different from the socialisation they experience from sources such as school, the media and the legal system because the majority culture tends to control sources of socialisation outside the family (Pels, 2003).

For example, many first- and second-generation Chinese adolescents embrace the individualistic beliefs of the Western culture they live in rather than the culture from which they and their families have come. Other studies also demonstrate this and show that the differences in beliefs between immigrant parents and their adolescent children can be a source of parent–adolescent conflict, as adolescents resist their parents' beliefs and parents feel frustrated and threatened when their adolescents adopt beliefs different from their own (Qin, 2009a; Zontini, 2007; Bornstein and Cote, 2004; Farver et al., 2002; Phinney et al., 2000; Zhou, 1997). More generally, these studies provide good examples of the importance of conceptualising socialisation as a cultural process that has a variety of sources – not only the family but also peers, school, community and media – with all of these sources ultimately rooted in cultural beliefs. Even though Chinese adolescents continue to live with their families in their new country, their beliefs and values change because they are exposed daily to contrary socialisation influences outside the family.

CONNECT AND EXTEND

British Chinese adolescents are high attainers in British schools. Are there cultural beliefs driving this success story? Read 'British-Chinese pupils' and parents' constructions of the value of education' by Becky Francis and Louise Archer in *British Educational Research Journal,* Volume 31, Number 1 (2005), pp. 89–108

CONNECT AND EXTEND

To read about several different 'boundaries of Britishness' that operate in the popular imagination of people in Britain read 'Perceptions of Britishness'

by Jessica Jacobson in *Nations and Nationalism*, Volume 3, Number 2 (July 1997), pp. 181–199

In the last 30 years Britain has developed what is termed a 'multicultural society', and in those 30 years many adolescents throughout British history have experienced this kind of contrasting socialisation environment. In the last decade, a new surge of immigration has steeply increased the proportion of people from minority cultures living in Britain, especially British Somali and migrant workers from new members of the European Union. In other Western countries as well, immigration from non-Western countries has increased in recent decades and is expected to increase further in the decades to come. The Netherlands has a large and growing Turkish and Surinamese population (Troe et al., 2007) and Canada has been especially open to immigrants and has received many people from Asian nations in the past decade (Sears et al., 2006). All over Europe, North America and Australasia, the status and well-being of people in minority cultures is likely to be one of the most important issues of the twenty-first century.

THINKING CRITICALLY

In Chinese culture, ageing parents often live with their adult children. How is this an example of a custom complex? What is the effect of this on adolescents living in the same household?

RELIGIOUS BELIEFS

'God's a father. Like, I learned, even though you may not have a dad, he's still a father, he disciplines like a father, he's a good friend, he's a provider, he cares. It's kind of, you know he's there, you know he's watching over you, it's great but you also know that there are going to be hard times and that he's still there then.'
– Kristen, age 16 (from Smith and Denton, 2005, p. 19)

'I don't think going to Mass really does anything. Sometimes I agree with what they're saying in

church, but other times I'm like, "What time is it? I wanna go home." It doesn't really feel interesting.'
– Heather, age 15 (from Smith and Denton, 2005, p. 197)

'My parents put me through Sunday School, and I was baptized and stuff. But I like the theory that all these religions, Mohammed and Buddha and Jesus, all the patterns there are very similar. And I believe that there's a spirit, an energy. Not necessarily a guy or something like that, but maybe just a power force. Like in *Star Wars – The Force*. The thing that makes it possible to live.'
– Jared, age 24 (from Arnett, 2004, p. 171)

In most cultures throughout human history, cultural beliefs have essentially taken the form of religious beliefs. Although the content of cultures' religious beliefs is extremely diverse, virtually all cultures have religious beliefs of some kind. These beliefs typically include explanations for how the world began and what happens to us when we die.

Religious belief systems also typically contain prescriptions for socialisation related to the three main outcomes: self-regulation, role preparation and sources of meaning. Religions typically specify a code for behaviour, and these codes usually contain various rules for self-regulation. For example, the Ten Commandments that are part of the Jewish and Christian religions state explicit rules for self-regulation – thou shalt not kill, steal, covet thy neighbour's wife, and so on. For role preparation, gender roles in particular are emphasised in religious belief systems. Most religious belief systems contain ideas about distinct roles for males and females. For example, the Roman Catholic Church allows men but not women to become priests. Finally, with respect to sources of meaning, most religious belief systems contain ideas about the significance of each individual's life in relation to an eternal supernatural world containing gods, supernatural forces or the souls of one's ancestors.

In general, adolescents and emerging adults in industrialised societies are less religious than their counterparts in traditional cultures. Industrialised societies of Europe tend to be highly **secular**; that is, they are based on non-religious beliefs and values. In every industrialised country, the influence of religion has gradually faded over the past two centuries (Eatwell and Wright, 2003) Adherence to religious beliefs and practices is especially

CONNECT AND EXTEND

Read more about the Penguin Books Survey results: **http://www.dailymail.co.uk/news/article-1194711/**

low among adolescents in Europe. For example, in Belgium only 8 per cent of 18-year-olds attend religious services at least once a month (Goossens and Luyckx, 2007). In Spain, traditionally a Roman Catholic country, only 18 per cent of adolescents attend church regularly (Gibbons and Stiles, 2004).

In 2009 a report commissioned by Penguin Books showed that 66 per cent of the British teenagers (13–18) surveyed did not believe a deity exists, while 50 per cent had never prayed and 16 per cent had never been to church. The respondents rated everything from family and friends to music and even reality TV shows, as more 'important' than religious faith. Furthermore:

- 59 per cent of children believed religion has had a negative influence on the world;

- 60 per cent only go to church for a wedding or christening;

- only 30 per cent of teenagers think there is an afterlife …

- while 10 per cent believe in reincarnation;

- 47 per cent said organised religion had no place in the world; and

- 60 per cent don't believe religious studies should be compulsory in schools.

Source: Penguin Books Survey reported in the *Daily Mail* newspaper, 2 June 2009; **http://www.dailymail.co.uk/news/article-1194711/**.

Contrast the British figures with those of the USA. Americans are more religious than people in virtually any other industrialised country, and this is reflected in the lives of American adolescents and emerging adults.

In 2005, the largest and most extensive study ever conducted on American adolescents' religious beliefs was completed (Smith and Denton, 2005). This study, called the National Survey of Youth and Religion (NSYR), involved over 3000 adolescents ages 13–17 in every part of the United States, from all major ethnic groups, and included qualitative interviews with 267 of the adolescents. The results of the NSYR show that for a substantial proportion of American adolescents, religion plays an important part in their lives.

According to the NSYR, 84 per cent of American adolescents aged 13 to 17 believe in God (or a universal spirit), 65 per cent pray at least once a week, and 51 per cent say religious faith is important in shaping their daily lives. Seventy-one per cent feel at least somewhat close to God, 63 per cent believe in the existence of angels, and 71 per cent believe in a judgement day when God will reward some and punish others.

THINKING CRITICALLY

Why do you think Americans generally are more religious than people in other industrialised countries?

Fifty-two per cent of American adolescents report attending religious services at least twice a month. Fifty-one per cent say they attend Sunday School at least once a month, and 38 per cent report being involved with a church youth group. Even if their actual participation may not be quite as high as the participation they report (see the *Focus on Research* box), these figures indicate a strikingly positive view of religion among American adolescents.

CONNECT AND EXTEND

There are fascinating age differences in religious beliefs across the adolescent age range (13–20) for those young people diagnosed with cancer. Read 'Relationships of age and gender to hope and spiritual well-being among adolescents with cancer' by Verna Hendricks-Ferguson in *Journal of Pediatric Oncology Nursing*, Volume 23, Number 4 (July 2006), pp. 189–199

Many American adolescents are religious, some are not; many British adolescents are not religious, some are. What explains differences among adolescents in their religiosity? It will not surprise you to read that family characteristics are one important influence (Smith and Denton, 2005). Adolescents are more likely to embrace religion when their parents talk about religious issues and participate in religious activities (Ream and Savin-Williams, 2003; King et al., 2002). Adolescents are less likely to be religious when their parents disagree with each other about religious beliefs (Rew et al., 2007) and when their parents are divorced (Lawton and Bures, 2001). Ethnicity is another factor. In European societies, religious faith and religious practices tend to be stronger among ethnic minorities than among the white European majority (King et al., 2006) and sometimes there are extreme examples of this phenomenon – e.g. honour killing (Korteweg and Yurdakul, 2009).

CONNECT AND EXTEND

Is antisocial behaviour in teenage (12–17) footballers socially desirable, or just part of the game? Read Maria Kavussanu's 'Motivational predictors of prosocial and antisocial behaviour in football' in *Journal of Sports Sciences*, Volume 24, Number 6 (2006), pp. 575–588

RESEARCH FOCUS Ⓡ

Religious Practices and Social Desirability

According to an important and illuminating survey (Smith and Denton, 2005) presented in this chapter, a substantial proportion of American adolescents are actively involved in religious practices. The numbers are strikingly high, if valid. But are they valid? There is some debate among scholars on religion over the accuracy of people's self-reported religious behaviour. Polls conducted by the Gallup organisation over the past half-century have indicated that the proportion of adults reporting weekly attendance at religious services has remained remarkably stable during that time, at about 40 per cent (Gallup and Lindsay, 1999). However, other scholars have questioned the accuracy of those self-reports. In an earlier 1993 study, a team of sociologists measured religious participation by counting people at services and concluded that the actual rate of weekly attendance was 20 per cent rather than 40 per cent (Hardaway et al., 1993).

Another study took the approach of investigating people's religious behaviour through examining their time-use diaries (Presser and Stinson, 1998). The diaries were not kept for the purposes of recording religious practices, but the daily record of activities over several months revealed, among other things, the extent of people's attendance at religious services. Thousands of diaries were available from 1965 to 1994. Analysis of the diaries showed that the rate of weekly attendance dropped from 42 per cent in 1965 to 26 per cent in 1994. Although similar analyses have yet to be conducted for adolescents, the results of these studies suggest that current self-reports of religious participation among adolescents may also be inflated.

Why would people report their behaviour inaccurately? Perhaps because they respond to what scholars call **social desirability** (Salkind, 2003). Socially desirable behaviour is conduct and expressed attitudes of which you believe others would approve. Adolescents and adults may exaggerate the extent to which they attend religious services because they believe that other people would approve of them if they did attend religious services. It can be argued that most people believe going to church is a good thing and, when surveyed, often say they go to church, even when they don't (Chaves, 2004). Given the British survey results of low attendance, would it be fair to suggest that going to church and believing in God is not a socially desirable behaviour amongst British adolescents?

Social desirability is a research issue not just for religious practices but for many other types of behaviour we will examine in this book. Drug use is generally stigmatised; for this reason, young people may not always report the full extent of their drug use. Having numerous sexual partners tends to be more socially desirable for boys than for girls; perhaps for this reason, boys often report more sexual partners than girls in surveys of young people's sexual behaviour. Each time you read about a study, ask yourself: Is there any reason why the young people in this study may have reported their behaviour inaccurately to make it appear more socially desirable?

Religious faith and religious practices tend to be especially strong among young British Muslims.

It is not only among minority groups that religiosity is associated with favourable adolescent outcomes. In the Western majority cultures, adolescents who are more religious report less depression and lower rates of pre-marital sex, drug use and delinquent behaviour (Good et al., 2009; Kerestes et al., 2004; Lefkowitz et al., 2003; Pullen et al., 1999). The protective value of religious involvement is especially strong for adolescents living in the most challenging neighbourhoods (Bridges and Moore, 2002). Religious adolescents tend to have better relationships with their parents, both with mothers and fathers (Wilcox, 2008). Also, adolescents who value religion are more likely than other adolescents to give volunteer service to their community (Hart and Atkins, 2004; Kerestes et al., 2004; Youniss et al., 1999). In non-European cultures, too, religious involvement has been found to be related to a variety of positive outcomes, for example among Indonesian Muslim adolescents (French et al., 2008).

Both religious participation and religious beliefs decline throughout the teens, and are lower in the late teens and early 20s than at any other period of the lifespan. Emerging adults may feel they need to make a break with their parents' religious beliefs and practices to establish that they are making their own decisions about their beliefs and values (Berg et al., 2009). One earlier longitudinal study found that parents' frequency of church attendance when their children were in early adolescence was unrelated to their children's religiosity 11 years later, as emerging adults (Willits and Crider, 1989). Another reason religiosity declines in emerging adulthood may be that by the time they reach their late teens young people are no longer pressured by their parents to attend church, and they resume attendance (if at all) only when they have young children of their own (Putnam, 2000).

Despite the decline in religiosity from adolescence to emerging adulthood, a majority of emerging adults remain religious in some respects. As Table 4.3 shows, a strong majority of them believe in God or a higher power and about half state that their religious beliefs play an important part in their daily lives. Just as among adolescents, religious beliefs are more important to emerging adults than attending religious services.

Religious Beliefs and Cognitive Development

Cognitive development from childhood and adolescence leads to changes in how young people think about religion. Specifically, adolescents' ideas about religious faith tend to be more abstract and less concrete, compared with younger children. In a historic and landmark study, psychologist and educator David Elkind (1978) interviewed several hundred Jewish, Catholic and Protestant children from ages 5 to 14. They were asked various questions about religion, such as 'What is a Catholic?' and 'Are all boys and girls in the world Christians?' They were also asked various questions about their own and their families'

Table 4.3 Religiosity of Emerging Adults Ages 21–28

	Per cent
How often do you attend religious services?	
About 3–4 times a month	19
About 1–2 times a month	10
Once every few months	20
About 1–2 times a year, or less	50
How important is religious faith in your daily life?	
Very important	27
Quite important	20
Somewhat important	21
Not at all important	32
To what extent do you believe that God or some higher power watches over you and guides your life?	
Strongly believe this	52
Somewhat believe this	22
Somewhat sceptical of this	16
Definitely do not believe this	10

Source: Arnett and Jensen (2002)

religious beliefs. By the time they reached their early teens and the beginning of formal operations, children's responses were more abstract and complex than at younger ages. Younger children tended to emphasise external behaviour in explaining what it means to be a member of a particular faith – people are Catholic if they go to Mass regularly. In contrast, the adolescents emphasised internal and abstract criteria, such as what people believe and their relationship with God.

Developmental psychologist Professor James Fowler has proposed a theory of stages of religious development from birth through adulthood that is linked to cognitive development (Fowler and Dell, 2006; 2004). According to Fowler, early adolescence is a stage of **poetic-conventional faith**, in which people become more aware of the symbolism used in their faith. In this stage, according to Fowler, religious understanding becomes more complex in the sense that early adolescents increasingly believe there is more than one way of knowing the truth. Late adolescence and emerging adulthood are a stage of **individuating-reflective faith**, in which people rely less on what their parents believed and develop a more individualised faith based on questioning their beliefs and incorporating their personal experience into their beliefs. Of course, movement into this stage could also reflect an integration of religious faith with the individualistic values of the majority culture. Fowler's theory is based on studies of people in a white majority culture, and people in less individualistic cultures may not go through the 'individuating' process Fowler describes.

One contrast to the individuating process of religious development in Western majority cultures can be found in cultures where Islam is the dominant religion. In Islam, the most important change that occurs at adolescence involves the holy month that Muslims call **Ramadan** (Maughan et al., 2008; Al-Mateen and Afzal, 2004). Ramadan commemorates the revelation of the Muslim holy book, the **Koran**, from God to the prophet Muhammad. During this month each year, Muslims are forbidden from taking part in any indulgences, and they are required to fast (that is, refrain from eating, drinking and sexual activity) from sunrise to sunset every day. The final day of Ramadan is celebrated with a great feast. It is estimated that there are a billion Muslims in the world's population, and Muslims all over the world observe Ramadan. (Most of the world's Islamic population is not in the Middle East but in Asia – Indonesia has the largest Muslim population of any country in the world, with India and Pakistan second and third.)

Before puberty, young Muslims have no obligation to participate in fasting. Girls are supposed to fast for the first time after they reach menarche. The judgement of whether a boy is old enough to be expected to fast is based on signs such as beard growth and changes in body shape (Meckel et al., 2008). Preadolescent children sometimes fast for a day or a few days, especially around the time they are nearing puberty. They are commended for doing so by older children and adults, but they are not obligated. However, once they have reached puberty young people are expected to fast during Ramadan (Erol et al., 2008). In fact, it is considered shameful for a person who has clearly reached physical maturity not to fast. Thus, in adolescence, religious practices among Muslims become less open to individual choice and more guided by social pressures. Socialisation for their religious behaviour becomes narrower; less individual variability is tolerated in whether they observe the fast.

CONNECT AND EXTEND

British families from minority ethnic groups with strong religious ties are said to observe more family rituals and routines. Are there any therapeutic benefits? Read 'Relationships between family rituals, family routines and health' by Sharon A. Denham in *Journal of Family Nursing*, Volume 9, Number 3 (1 August 2003), pp. 305–330

When they reach adolescence, Muslims are expected to participate in the month-long fast of Ramadan.

In some urban areas there have been earlier reports that some Muslim adolescents are rebelling by refusing to observe the fast, but in the smaller rural communities the narrow socialisation pressures of family and community can be intense, and few adolescents resist (Carolan et al., 2000; Ghuman, 1998). Or, more accurately, because they have been raised in a culture that values fasting at Ramadan, by the time young people reach adolescence nearly all of them eagerly take part in the fast. They have accepted the beliefs of their culture as their own beliefs, and they do not usually have to be coerced or pressured into participating.

THINKING CRITICALLY

Is it possible to apply Fowler's theory of changes in religious beliefs in adolescence to the beliefs and practices of Muslim adolescents with respect to Ramadan, or not?

CULTURAL BELIEFS AND MORAL DEVELOPMENT

Religious beliefs are usually learned from one's culture, although the development of adolescents' religious thinking is also based in part on their cognitive development. What about moral development? To what extent are adolescents' moral beliefs dependent on their culture's beliefs, and to what extent are adolescents' moral beliefs a result of cognitive processes common to adolescents everywhere?

Scholars who have studied and theorised adolescents' moral development have largely viewed it as rooted in universal cognitive processes. This is true of the theories of the two most influential scholars on adolescent moral development, Jean Piaget and Lawrence Kohlberg. However, their views have recently begun to be challenged by scholars who emphasise the role of cultural beliefs in moral development. We will first consider Piaget's and Kohlberg's ideas, then other points of view, including the cultural approach.

Piaget's Theory

Piaget (1932) developed his ideas about moral development using several different methods. He watched children play games (such as marbles) to see how they discussed the rules. He played games with them himself and asked them questions during the games (e.g., 'Can the rules be changed?' 'How did the rules begin?') in order to investigate how they would explain the origin of rules and how they would react to violations of the rules. Also, he presented children with hypothetical situations involving lying, stealing and punishment to see what kinds of judgements they would make about how to determine whether an action was right or wrong.

On the basis of his research, Piaget concluded that children have two distinct approaches to reasoning about moral issues, based on the level of their cognitive development. **Heteronomous morality**, which corresponds to the pre operational stage, from about age 4 to about age 7: moral rules are viewed as having

CONNECT AND EXTEND

For further ideas about social services suiting provision to the target culture read 'Assimilation, control, mediation or advocacy? Social work dilemmas in providing anti-oppressive services for Traveller children and families' by S. Cemlyn in *Child & Family Social Work*, Volume 5, Number 4 (1 November 2000), pp. 327–341

a sacred, fixed quality. They are believed to be handed down from figures of authority (especially parents) and can be altered only by them. **Autonomous morality** is reached at the beginning of adolescence with the onset of formal operations at about age 10–12 and involves a growing realisation that moral rules are social conventions that can be changed if people decide they should be changed. (From age 7 to age 10 there is a transitional stage between heteronomous and autonomous moral thinking, with some properties of each.)

The stage of autonomous morality also involves growing complexity in moral thinking in the sense that autonomous moral thinkers take into account people's motivations for behaviour rather than focusing only on the consequences. For example, a child who breaks several dishes by accident is seen as less guilty than a child who breaks a single dish while doing something wrong such as stealing food.

Piaget's interest in the rules of children's games reflected his belief that personal moral development is promoted by interactions with peers. In Piaget's view, peers' equal status requires them to discuss their disagreements, negotiate with one another, and come to a consensus. This process gradually leads to an awareness of the rules of games and from there to a more general awareness of moral rules. According to Piaget, parents are much less effective than peers in promoting children's moral development because parents' greater power and authority make it difficult for children to argue and negotiate with them as equals.

Kohlberg's Theory

Social psychologist Lawrence Kohlberg (1958) was inspired by Piaget's work and sought to extend it by examining moral development through adolescence and into adulthood. Like Piaget, he viewed moral development as based on cognitive development, such that moral thinking changes in predictable ways as cognitive abilities develop, regardless of culture. Also like Piaget, Kohlberg presented people with

hypothetical moral situations and had them indicate what behaviour they believed was right or wrong in those situations, and why.

Kohlberg began his research by studying the moral judgements of 72 boys aged 10, 13 and 16 from middle-class and working-class families (Kohlberg, 1958). He presented the boys with a series of fictional dilemmas, each of which was constructed to elicit their moral reasoning. Here is one of the dilemmas:

'During [World War II], a city was often being bombed by the enemy. So each man was given a post he was to go to right after the bombing, to help put out the fires the bombs started and to rescue people in the burning buildings. A man named Diesing was made the chief in charge of one fire engine post. The post was near where he worked so he could get there quickly during the day but it was a long way from his home. One day there was a very heavy bombing and Diesing left the shelter in the place he worked and went toward his fire station. But when he saw how much of the city was burning, he got worried about his family. So he decided he had to go home first to see if his family was safe, even though his home was a long way off and the station was nearby, and there was somebody assigned to protect the area where his family was. Was it right or wrong for him to leave his station to protect his family? Why?' (Kohlberg, 1958, pp. 372–373)

In each interview, the participant would be asked to respond to three stories such as this one. To Kohlberg, what was crucial for understanding the level of people's moral development was not whether they concluded that the actions of the persons in the dilemma were right or wrong but how they explained their conclusions. Kohlberg (1976) developed a system for classifying their explanations into three levels of moral development, with each level containing two stages, as follows:

FOCUS ON PROFESSIONAL PRACTICE

Community Workers: Why do Traveller Adolescents drop out of Schooling and what are the Consequences?

Elizabeth Jordan (University of Edinburgh) begins her 2001 report *'From interdependence, to dependence and independence'* with a ringing indictment of effects of cultural mismatch between Traveller cultures and schooling:

'Travellers are the most discriminated against group within the European Union. Empirical research on their situation within schools is minimal, yet policy, supported by substantial funds, has been developed throughout Europe, largely focused on issues of ethnicity and anti-racist approaches. This article, based on 10 years research in Scotland and in the analysis of the UK and EU approaches, reviews the mismatch between Traveller cultures and their schooling experience. Schools ignore and devalue the children's home learning of interdependence and independence and offer only learned dependence and institutional exclusion, leading to lowered self-esteem, high absenteeism and early drop-out.' (p. 57)

Research methods were threefold:

1 Traveller enrolments and attendance records covering a five-year period.

2 Case studies of five disparate schools with regular enrolments of Travellers.

3 Face-to-face interactions with 100 Gypsy and Occupational Travellers of all generations and both sexes.

Findings included:

1 The significant high rates of absenteeism in both primary and secondary schooling.

2 The significantly high rates of early drop-out (around age 14 years) of Travellers.

3 The presence in schools of groups of Traveller children is 'at odds' with a curriculum and delivery that assumes regular attendance and dependence upon the school.

4 That the cultural strengths of Traveller children are not recognised or encouraged in formal school settings. There is a profound mismatch in cultural beliefs, moral frameworks and lifespan aspirations.

Community workers need to recognise that Travellers will continue to remain marginalised within the education system; parents will need considerable support as they strive to educate their children as best they can with minimal appropriate help from the state. Assimilation and control approaches are increasingly seen as counter-productive. Therefore, innovative approaches involving joint health, social work and education initiatives involving advocacy through *individual family plans* may represent a way forward.

Source: Jordan, E. (2001) 'From interdependence, to dependence and independence: home and school learning for traveller children', *Childhood*, Volume 8, Number 1, pp. 57–74

Level 1: **Preconventional reasoning.** At this level, moral reasoning is based on perceptions of the likelihood of external rewards and punishments. What is right is what avoids punishment or results in rewards.

• Stage 1: *Punishment and obedience orientation.* Rules should be obeyed to avoid punishment from those in authority.

• Stage 2: *Individualism and purpose orientation.* What is right is what satisfies one's own needs and occasionally the needs of others, and what leads to rewards for oneself.

Level 2: **Conventional reasoning.** At this level, moral reasoning is less egocentric and the person advocates the value of conforming to the moral expectations of others. What is right is whatever agrees with the rules established by tradition and by authorities.

- Stage 3: *Interpersonal concordance orientation.* Care of and loyalty to others is emphasised in this stage, and it is seen as good to conform to what others expect in a certain role, such as being a 'good husband' or a 'good girl'.

- Stage 4: *Social systems orientation.* Moral judgements are explained by reference to concepts such as social order, law and justice. It is argued that social rules and laws must be respected for social order to be maintained.

Level 3: **Postconventional reasoning**. Moral reasoning at this level is based on the individual's own independent judgements rather than on what others view as wrong or right. What is right is derived from the individual's perception of objective, universal principles rather than the subjective perception of either the individual (as in Level 1) or the group (as in Level 2).

- Stage 5: *Community rights and individual rights orientation.* The person reasoning at this stage views society's laws and rules as important, but also sees it as important to question them and change them if they become obstacles to the fulfilment of ideals such as freedom and justice.

- Stage 6: *Universal ethical principles orientation.* The person has developed an independent moral code based on universal principles. When laws or social conventions conflict with these principles, it is seen as better to violate the laws or conventions than the universal principles.

THINKING CRITICALLY

What's your judgement about the firefighter's dilemma? Was it right or wrong for him to leave his station to protect his family? Why? Where would you place your judgement on the Kohlberg classification scale?

Kohlberg followed his initial group of adolescent boys over the next 20 years (Colby et al., 1983), interviewing them every three or four years, and he and his colleagues also conducted numerous other studies on moral reasoning in adolescence and adulthood. Results of these studies (e.g. Gilligan, 1982) verified Kohlberg's theory of moral development in a number of important ways:

- Stage of moral reasoning tended to increase with age. At age 10, most of the participants were in Stage 2 or

in transition between Stage 1 and Stage 2; at age 13, the majority were in transition from Stage 2 to Stage 3; by ages 16 to 18, the majority were in Stage 3 or in transition to Stage 4; and by ages 20 to 22, 90 per cent of the participants were in Stage 3, in transition to Stage 4, or in Stage 4. However, even after 20 years, when all of the original participants were in their 30s, few of them had proceeded to Stage 5, and none had reached Stage 6 (Colby et al., 1983). Kohlberg eventually dropped Stage 6 from his coding system (Kohlberg, 1986).

- Moral development proceeded in the predicted way, in the sense that the participants did not skip stages but proceeded from one stage to the next highest.

- Moral development was found to be cumulative, in the sense that the participants were rarely found to slip to a lower stage over time. With few exceptions, they either remained in the same stage or proceeded to the next highest stage.

The research of Kohlberg and his colleagues also indicated that moral development was correlated with socio-economic status (SES), intelligence and educational level. Middle-class boys tended to be in higher stages than working-class boys of the same age, boys with higher IQs tended to be in higher stages than boys with lower IQs, and boys who received a university education tended to reach higher stages than boys who did not (Mason and Gibbs, 1993; Weinreich, 1974).

For a quarter of a century, research based on Kohlberg's theory has also included cross-cultural studies in countries all over the world such as Turkey, Japan, Taiwan, Kenya, Israel and India (Gibbs et al., 2007). Many of these studies have focused on moral development in adolescence and emerging adulthood. In general, the studies confirm Kohlberg's hypothesis that moral development as classified by his coding system progresses with age. Also, as in the earlier studies, participants in longitudinal studies in other cultures have rarely been found to regress to an earlier stage or to skip a stage of moral reasoning. However, Stage 5 postconventional thinking has been found to be even rarer in non-Western cultures than in Western cultures (De Mey et al., 1999; Kohlberg, 1981).

Does this mean that people in non-Western cultures tend to engage in lower levels of moral reasoning than people in the West, perhaps because of lower educational levels? Or does the absence of Stage 5 reasoning in non-Western cultures reflect a cultural bias built into Kohlberg's classification system, a bias in favour of Western secularism and individualism? These questions have been the source of some controversy, as we will see in more detail when the cultural approach is described shortly.

CONNECT AND EXTEND

This study focuses on children ages 7–16 and uses Kohlberg's classification system. 'A comparative study of moral development of Korean and British children' by Hye-Jeong Baek in *Journal of Moral Education*, Volume 31, Number 4 (2002), pp. 373–391

Critiques of Kohlberg

It would be difficult to overstate the magnitude of Kohlberg's influence on the study of moral development in adolescence. Not only was he highly productive himself and in his collaborations with colleagues, but he also inspired many other scholars over many years to investigate moral development according to the stage theory he proposed (e.g. Gibbs et al., 2007). However, his theory has also been subject to diverse criticisms. The critiques can be divided into two main types: the gender critique and the cultural critique.

The Gender Critique

Did you notice that Kohlberg's original research sample included only males? Later, when he began to study females as well, he initially found that in adolescence females tended to reason at a lower moral level than males of the same age. This finding inspired a former student of his, Carol Gilligan, to develop a critique that claimed his theory was biased toward males, undervaluing the perspective of females, whom she viewed as having a different moral 'voice' than males.

According to Gilligan (1982), Kohlberg's theory of moral development is biased in favour of a **justice orientation**. This orientation places a premium on abstract principles of justice, equality and fairness when judgements are made about moral issues. The primary consideration is whether these principles have been followed. For example, in the sample dilemma described earlier, a person reasoning with the justice orientation would focus on whether the firefighter was being fair in checking on his family first, and on whether justice would be better served if he went to his post instead. Gilligan argued that males are more likely than females to approach moral issues with a justice orientation, with the result that males tend to be rated as more 'advanced' morally in Kohlberg's system.

However, according to Carol Gilligan, the justice orientation is not the only legitimate basis for moral reasoning. She contrasted the justice orientation with what she termed the **care orientation**, which involves focusing on relationships with others as the basis for moral reasoning. For example, in the sample dilemma above,

someone reasoning from the care orientation would focus on the relationships between the firefighter and his family and community, viewing the dilemma in terms of the relationships involved and the needs of each person rather than in terms of abstract principles. Gilligan claimed that the care orientation is more likely to be favoured by females and that Kohlberg's system would rate moral reasoning from this perspective as lower than moral reasoning from the justice orientation.

Gilligan particularly focused on early adolescence as a period when girls come to realise that their concerns with intimacy and relationships are not valued by a male-dominated society, with the result that girls often 'lose their voice'; that is, they become increasingly insecure about the legitimacy of their ideas and opinions (Gilligan, 2008).

Furthermore, Gilligan criticised Kohlberg's theory of moral development, as well as other prominent theories of human development by Freud, Piaget and Erikson, for being too male oriented in presenting the independent, isolated individual as the paragon of mental health, thus undervaluing females' tendencies toward interdependence and relational thinking.

Gilligan's gender critique has inspired a great deal of attention and research since she first articulated it in 1982. What does the research say about her claims? For the most part, early studies seemed to support Gilligan's contention that males and females tend to emphasise somewhat different moral concerns (Skoe and Gooden, 1993; Galotti et al., 1991; Galotti, 1989). For example, when adolescents are asked to recall their personal moral dilemmas, girls are more likely than boys to report dilemmas that involve interpersonal relationships. However, when reasoning about hypothetical moral issues, a later study showed there are no differences between adolescent boys and girls in their use of 'care' reasoning (Pratt et al., 2004).

THINKING CRITICALLY

From your experience, do you think there are overall differences between males and females in the basis of their moral reasoning (justice vs. care)? Give an example.

Carol Gilligan has proposed that adolescent girls' moral reasoning is based on a care orientation.

The Cultural Critique

Although Kohlberg did not deny that culture has some influence on moral development, in his view the influence of culture is limited to how well cultures provide opportunities for individuals to reach the highest level of moral development (Jensen, 2008b). To Kohlberg, cognitive development is the basis for moral development. Just as cognitive development proceeds on only one path (given adequate environmental conditions), so moral development has only one natural path of maturation. As development proceeds and individuals' thinking becomes progressively more developed, they rise inevitably along that one and only path. Thus, the highest level of moral reasoning is also the most rational. With an adequate education that allows for the development of formal operations, the individual will realise the inadequacies and irrationality of the lower levels of moral reasoning and embrace the highest, most rational way of thinking about moral issues. By becoming able to take the perspective of each party involved in a moral situation, a person can learn to make postconventional moral judgements that are objectively and universally valid.

Recently, these assumptions have been called into question by scholars taking a cultural approach to moral development. The most cogent and penetrating critique has been presented by cultural psychologist Richard Shweder (2003; Shweder et al., 2006). According to Shweder, the postconventional level of moral reasoning described by Kohlberg is not the only rational moral code and is not higher or more developed than other kinds of moral thinking. In Shweder's view, Kohlberg's system is biased in favour of the individualistic thinking of 'Western elites' of the highest social classes and highest levels of Western education. Like Gilligan, Shweder objects to Kohlberg's classification of detached, abstract individualism as the highest form of moral reasoning.

This bias makes it difficult for people in most cultures to be classified as reaching the highest level of rationality, Level 3, because people in most cultures outside the

West invoke principles of tradition or a religious authority. However, Shweder argues, it is no less rational to believe in objective principles established by a religiously based divine authority and handed down through tradition than to believe in objective principles that have a secular, individualistic basis. To argue otherwise would be to assume that all rational thinkers must be atheists or that it is irrational to accept an account of truth from beings believed to have superior powers of moral understanding, and to Shweder neither of these assertions is defensible.

THINKING CRITICALLY

Having read about Kohlberg's theory and Shweder's cultural critique of it, which do you find more persuasive, and why?

The Worldviews Approach to Moral Development

As we have seen, Richard Shweder and his colleagues presented an alternative to Kohlberg's theory of moral development. Shweder's alternative theory has been developed mostly by a former student of Shweder's, Lene Jensen (2008b; 2007). According to Jensen, the ultimate basis of morality is a person's **worldview**. A worldview is a set of cultural beliefs that explain what it means to be human, how human relations should be conducted, and how human problems should be addressed. Worldviews provide the basis for *moral reasoning* (explanations for *why* a behaviour is right or wrong). The outcome of moral reasoning is *moral evaluations* (judgements as to *whether* a behaviour is right or wrong), which in turn prescribe *moral behaviours*. Moral behaviours reinforce worldviews. An illustration of the worldviews theory of moral development is shown in Figure 4.1.

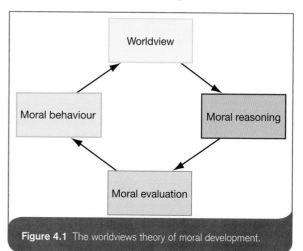

Figure 4.1 The worldviews theory of moral development.

CONNECT AND EXTEND

Radical environmentalists often decry and dismiss as dangerous the ethic of autonomy, of individual rights. Read 'New ethics for old? Or, how (not) to think about future generations' by Terence Ball in *Environmental Politics*, Volume 10, Number 1 (2001), pp. 89–110

In her research, Jensen codes people's responses to moral issues according to three types of 'ethics' based on different worldviews:

1 The *Ethic of Autonomy* defines the individual as the primary moral authority. Individuals are viewed as having the right to do as they wish as long as their behaviour does no direct harm to others.

2 The *Ethic of Community* defines individuals as members of social groups to which they have commitments and obligations. In this ethic, the responsibilities of roles in the family, community and other groups are the basis of one's moral judgements.

3 The *Ethic of Divinity* defines the individual as a spiritual entity, subject to the prescriptions of a divine authority. This ethic includes moral views based on traditional religious authorities and religious texts (e.g. the Koran, the Bible).

There are few There are very few studies of the extent to which the 'ecology' of the three ethic types of worldview reflects in a cultural analysis. This is perhaps in part because there was no published scale to measure the endorsement of different moral codes. However, in 2010 Valeschka Guerra and Roger Giner-Sorolla of the University of Kent (UK) reported the development of the Community, Autonomy and Divinity Scale (CADS), based on Shweder's moral codes, as a means to measure cross-cultural, sub-cultural and individual differences in the contents of morality. They applied CADS in two studies across British and Brazilian cultural contexts (Guerra and Giner-Sorolla, 2010). Guerra and Giner-Sorolla found the CADS to be a reliable and valid scale, thereby enabling the future cross-cultural quantitative study of similarities and differences in endorsement of moral codes. However, it remains to be seen how the three ethics change in different cultures from childhood through emerging adulthood and the extent to which worldview is a powerful and authentic analysis of cultural and development differences in moral perspectives.

Morality in Everyday Life

In his research on moral development, Kohlberg used only hypothetical dilemmas such as the firefighter dilemma described earlier. The hypothetical dilemmas concern unusual, life-and-death issues that most people would be unlikely to experience in their own lives, such as stealing in order to save a life, the mercy killing of a terminally ill person, and a soldier's sacrifice of his life for his fellow soldiers. Kohlberg believed that this lack of connection to everyday experience was a strength of his dilemmas because people would reason about them without preconceptions or pre-existing tendencies based on personal experience, so that only their moral reasoning competence would be tested (Walker et al., 1999). As Kohlberg put it, what matters is the *structure* of moral reasoning – the underlying cognitive basis of how a person reasons about moral issues – and not the *content*; that is, the actual topic

CONNECT AND EXTEND

It is worth looking at the original paper exploring the three ethic types. Read 'The Community, Autonomy and Divinity Scale (CADS): a new tool for the cross-cultural study of morality' by V. M. Guerra and R. Giner-Sorolla in *Journal of Cross-Cultural Psychology*, Volume 41, Number 1 (2010), pp. 35–50

or issue they are reasoning about (Kohlberg, 1981). By responding to the dilemmas, people would reveal the structure of their moral reasoning without being distracted by the content. Using hypothetical dilemmas also makes it easier to compare people in their moral development.

The fact that the dilemmas are hypothetical or (perhaps) more extreme examples than the experiences of most people does not mean they are unrelated to how people reason about morality in real life. The stage of moral reasoning people apply to Kohlberg's hypothetical dilemmas tends to be similar to the moral reasoning they apply to moral dilemmas they describe from their own lives (Walker et al., *ibid.*). Also, the stage of moral reasoning on Kohlbergian dilemmas is related to people's moral behaviour. Adolescents and emerging adults who rate relatively high in Kohlberg's coding system are also less likely to engage in antisocial behaviour, less likely to engage in cheating, and more likely to assist others who are in need of help (Hart et al., 2005; 2003).

However, like other aspects of Kohlberg's approach to studying moral development, the use of hypothetical dilemmas has been increasingly criticised, even by scholars who have used Kohlberg's approach. Lawrence Walker, a top scholar on moral development who has frequently used Kohlberg's dilemmas in his research, argues that 'Kohlberg's cognitive-developmental paradigm [has] led to a somewhat restricted view of morality and moral functioning' (Walker et al., 1999, p. 371). By using only hypothetical dilemmas, according to Walker, 'we may be ignoring some, or perhaps even much, of what is important in people's moral functioning – in particular, how they understand the moral domain and handle everyday moral issues' (*ibid.*, p. 373).

In response to this concern, Walker and others have begun expanding research on morality to include the moral issues of everyday life (e.g. Walker, 2004; Jensen and Williams, 2001; Killen and Hart, 1999). In one study in 1999, Walker and his colleagues (*ibid.*) studied real-life moral dilemmas among adolescents (16–19), those in emerging adulthood (18–25), middle adulthood (35–48) and late adulthood (65–84).

The participants discussed a recent real-life moral dilemma and their most difficult moral dilemma. In contrast to the life-and-death hypothetical dilemmas, the kinds of dilemmas people reported from everyday life most often had to do with personal relationships – with parents and friends for adolescents and emerging adults, and with spouse, children and colleagues for older participants.

One striking difference from studies of hypothetical dilemmas was that in reasoning about real-life moral issues people of all ages often relied on practical costs (e.g. losing one's job) and benefits (e.g. having a pleasurable experience). In Kohlberg's system such considerations are rated at the lowest level, 'preconventional' moral reasoning, but as one emerging adult in the study observed, 'It's a lot easier to be moral when you have nothing to lose' (Walker et al., 1999, pp. 381–382) – that is, when the consequences are only hypothetical.

Also notable was that people of all ages frequently invoked religious justifications for their moral judgements. According to Walker, this calls into question Kohlberg's attempts to separate morality from religion. The pervasiveness of religious justifications was especially striking because in the area where the study took place (Vancouver, British Columbia) formal religious participation was very low (5 per cent regular religious attendance). Thus, in many ways, Walker's study demonstrated that studying morality in everyday life situations (moral reasoning involving religious justifications) greatly expands our understanding of moral behaviour.

THINKING CRITICALLY

Think of a recent moral dilemma from your own life. What did you decide, and why did you decide it that way? How would your moral reasoning on that dilemma be scored according to Kohlberg's system? How would it be classified according to Jensen's three ethics?

CONNECT AND EXTEND

This article analyses the results of a study of conceptions of justice among Italian teenagers. Read '"Right" and "Not right": representations of justice in young people' by Roberta Bosisio in *Childhood*, Volume 15, Number 2 (May 2008), pp. 276–294

Studying real-life moral issues allows for the expression of culturally distinct moral views. In an earlier study of Chinese adults, Walker and Moran (1991) found that asking about real-life moral dilemmas revealed moral concepts based on Chinese culture, such as the importance of maintaining 'face' (respect) and the belief in the traditional Confucian idea that a hierarchy of authority is valuable for social order. However, and as we have noted in relation to the theoretical work of Lene Jensen, there is a need for much more research that explores moral judgements in cultural context.

POLITICAL BELIEFS

Cultural beliefs include political beliefs about desirable and undesirable features of political institutions, about what kind of political arrangements are fair or unfair, and about the extent to which human rights such as free speech and freedom of the press should be allowed. As political thinking often involves a consideration of abstract ideas such as justice, human rights, and the distribution of wealth, it seems reasonable to expect that political thinking develops in adolescence toward greater abstraction and complexity, in a manner similar to religious thinking and moral thinking. Research on the development of political thinking seems to support this expectation. However, research in this area is limited, and it provides few insights into the cultural basis of political thinking.

One scholar who did important early work on political development in adolescence was Joseph Adelson (1991; 1971). Adelson's research was in the classic methodological tradition of Piaget and Kohlberg. He used hypothetical situations to elicit adolescents' thinking about political arrangements and ideas, and he explained political development in terms of the cognitive changes of adolescence.

Adelson's main hypothetical situation was as follows: 'Imagine that a thousand men and women, dissatisfied with the way things are going in this country, decide to purchase and move to an island in the Pacific where they must devise laws and modes of government.' (Adelson, 1971, p. 1040). Based on this hypothetical situation, the researchers asked adolescents numerous questions about their political views. Each adolescent was asked about the merits of different possible forms of government for the island (democracy, monarchy, etc.), and about the purpose and enforcement of laws. Adolescents were asked to consider what should be done if the government wanted to build a road across the island and a person who owned part of the land where the road was to be built refused to sell; if a law was passed to forbid smoking and people continued to smoke; and what to do about the rights of minority citizens on the island.

Adelson and his colleagues examined political development in relation to age, gender, social class and IQ, but the only variable found to be related to political thinking was age. Studying adolescents aged 11 to 18, they found a profound shift in political thinking beginning at ages 12 to 13 and completed by ages 15 to 16. The shift involved three key changes: a change in what Adelson called 'cognitive mode'; a sharp decline in support for authoritarian political systems; and the development of the capacity for **ideology.**

Political Ideas as Evidence of Development

The change in cognitive mode included several changes related to the development of formal operations, such as increased use of abstract ideas and increased tendency to see laws as human constructions rather than as absolute and unchangeable. Older adolescents were more likely than younger adolescents to use abstract ideas instead of concrete examples. For example, when asked about the purpose of laws, a typical older adolescent responded, 'to ensure safety and enforce the government', whereas a typical younger adolescent said laws are necessary 'so people don't steal or kill'. Similarly, when asked questions about the nature of government, older adolescents were more likely to refer to abstract ideas such as community or society, whereas younger adolescents' statements were more concrete and specific, referring, for example, to the president or the mayor.

Changes in cognitive mode also led to changes in adolescents' views of laws. The youngest adolescents viewed laws as eternal and unchangeable. However, by about age 15, adolescents were more likely to see laws as social constructions that could be changed if the people governed by them wished to change them. In Adelson's view, this reflected the development of formal operations and a growing tendency to see laws less as concrete objects and more as social arrangements subject to change. This is similar to what Kohlberg described in moral development as the development from Level 1 thinking, emphasising a fixed moral code, to Level 2 thinking, emphasising the changeable, socially created quality of moral and legal rules. Kohlberg and Adelson found a similar change at a similar time, from age 10 to 15.

The second key change observed by Adelson and his colleagues between early and late adolescence was a sharp decline in authoritarian political views. Younger adolescents tended to be remarkably authoritarian. For example, to enforce a law prohibiting cigarette smoking, they approved of procedures such as hiring police informers and hiding spies in the cupboards of people's homes! 'To a large and various set of questions on crime and punishment,' noted Adelson, 'they consistently propose one form of solution: punish, and if that does not suffice, punish harder' (1971, p. 1023). Older adolescents' thinking was, again, more complex. They tried to balance the goal of the law with considerations such as individual rights and long-term versus short-term costs and benefits. On an index of authoritarianism used in the study, 85 per cent of the youngest participants were rated in the highest category, compared with only 17 per cent of the 17- and 18-year-olds.

The third key change involved the capacity to develop an ideology. This means that the older adolescents had developed a set of beliefs that served as the basis for their political attitudes. In addressing Adelson's questions, they spoke of principles reflecting a belief in some combination of individual and community rights, rather than being limited to a focus on immediate and concrete solutions as the younger adolescents were.

More recent studies of the development of political thinking in adolescence have confirmed many of Adelson's findings that authoritarianism declines in adolescence (e.g. Flanagan and Botcheva, 1999). Furthermore, Professor of Human Development Judith Torney-Purta (2004) has described how political thinking becomes increasingly abstract and complex during adolescence, progressing from the concrete, simple views of pre-adolescence to the more coherent, abstract ideology of late adolescence. Tolerance of opposing or offensive views increases from childhood to adolescence and peaks in late adolescence (Witenberg, 2007) with girls being found to be more tolerant than boys at the same age (H. R. Gordon, 2008; Sotelo, 1999). Recent studies on political development have also touted the promise of the Internet as a source of international knowledge, which, under a teacher's guidance, could promote tolerance and perspective taking in adolescents' political views (e.g. Lupia and Philpot, 2005).

THINKING CRITICALLY

How do you think political thinking might differ (if at all) between adolescents and emerging adults? State a hypothesis and explain how you would test it.

Political Ideas as Cultural Beliefs

Like Piaget and Kohlberg, Adelson was seeking to establish a path of development through stages that would apply to young people everywhere. However, neither Adelson nor others have attempted to apply his ideas to cultures other than a Western majority culture, so it is difficult to say how similar the developmental path of political thinking he described would be to the path followed by adolescents in very different cultures. However, if we borrow a little from the research and critiques on moral development, we can state two likely hypotheses. One hypothesis is that there would be some common changes in political thinking with age from early adolescence to late adolescence across cultures because the abstract ideas invoked by the older adolescents in Adelson's studies reflect their more advanced cognitive abilities. The second hypothesis is that it is also likely that the pattern observed by Adelson reflects adolescents' socialisation into the political ideas that are part of the beliefs of a particular culture.

Adelson and his colleagues studied adolescents in three different countries, but they were similar countries – Great Britain, Germany and the United States, countries with similar laws and political institutions. What would they find if they asked similar questions of adolescents in China, in Saudi Arabia, or among the Australian Aborigines? It seems likely that the political ideas of adolescents in those cultures would reflect the dominant political ideas of their societies and would differ accordingly from European adolescents. Aristotle, the ancient Greek philosopher, who some would argue was one of the most brilliant persons who ever lived, yet he believed that dictatorship was superior to democracy; that some men were born to be slaves; and that women were inferior to men in virtually every respect. Was he less

Emerging adults are more likely than older adults to participate in political demonstrations.

developed or less logical than the typical 16-year-old of our time? Not likely. What is more likely is that he, like us, reflected the cultural beliefs of his time and place.

Emerging Adults' Political Involvement

Little research has been done on political thinking in emerging adulthood, but in Western Europe the political participation of emerging adults is strikingly low by conventional measures such as voting rates and involvement in political parties (e.g. Barrio et al., 2007; Botcheva et al., 2007; Meeus, 2006). Emerging adults tend to have lower conventional political participation in comparison not only to adults but also to previous generations of young people. They tend to be sceptical of the motivations of politicians and to see the activities of political parties as irrelevant to their lives. One recent study of young people in eight European countries found that low levels of trust in political authorities and political systems were consistent from adolescence through emerging adulthood (Hooghe and Wilkenfeld, 2008).

However, the rejection of conventional politics should not be construed as a lack of interest in improving the state of their communities, their societies and the world (Arnett, 2002b). On the contrary, emerging adults in the West are more likely than older adults to be involved in organisations devoted to particular issues, such as environmental protection and efforts against war and racism (e.g. Goossens and Luyckx, 2007; Meeus, 2006). It could be argued that emerging adults today live in a world where they are increasingly expected to rely on themselves, and so they may seem to be oriented more towards their own self-achievement rather than to broader social commitments. Yet there is evidence from a range of countries which highlights that young people hold strong opinions and views about distributive justice and public politics (Jonsson and Flanagan, 2000). However, often frustrated by and alienated from conventional political processes, emerging adults choose instead to direct their energies towards specific areas of importance to them, where they believe they are more likely to see genuine progress (Vaizey, 2005).

Furthermore, emerging adults have often been involved in movements at the political extremes, including protests, revolutionary movements and terrorism. The leaders of politically extreme groups are usually in mid-life or later, but many of their most zealous followers are often emerging adults. There are many recent historical examples. The 'Cultural Revolution' that took place in China from 1966 to 1975 and involved massive destruction and violence towards anyone deemed to be a threat to the 'purity' of Chinese communism was instigated by Chairman Mao and his wife Jiang Ching but carried out almost entirely by fervent Chinese emerging adults (MacFarquhar and Schoenhals, 2006). Terrorist attacks by Muslim extremists against Western targets have been planned by older men but executed almost entirely by young men in the 18–29 age range (Sen and Samad, 2007).

These examples involve destruction and violence, but emerging adults have been prominent in peaceful political movements as well. When the collapse of communism began in Eastern Europe in 1989, it was initiated by emerging adults: the 'Velvet Revolution' in Czechoslovakia began with a massive but non-violent student-led strike and demonstration (Macek et al., 2007). When some of the students were beaten, shot and killed, the rest of Czechoslovakian society rose up in outrage. The communist government soon resigned in the face of the massive protests, and from there 'the dominoes' fell all across Eastern Europe as communist governments resigned or were thrown out. Young people played a prominent role in the revolutions that led to the fall of communism in many of these countries (Flanagan and Botcheva, 1999). In Hungary, young people organised demonstrations agitating for independence, and the first new political party after the fall of communism was an explicitly youth-centred party with membership restricted to persons under age 35. In Bulgaria, young people were active in the strikes and demonstrations that led to the fall of the communist government, and representatives of student movements took a prominent role in the new parliament (Botcheva et al., 2007).

CONNECT AND EXTEND

If you are interested in politics as it relates to aspects of human development (such as the formation of identity, values and social ties to others) read 'Developmental roots of political engagement' by Constance Flanagan in *PS: Political Science and Politics*, Volume 36, Number 2 (April 2003), pp. 257–261

Why are emerging adults especially likely to be involved in extreme political movements? One reason is that they have fewer social ties and obligations than people in other age groups (Arnett, 2005b). Children and adolescents can be restrained from involvement by their parents. Young, middle and older adults can be deterred from involvement by their commitments to others who depend on them, especially a spouse and children. However, emerging adulthood is a time when social commitments and social control are at their nadir. Emerging adults have more freedom than people at other age periods, and this freedom allows some of them to become involved in extreme political movements.

Another possibility is that their involvement is identity related. Recall that one of the key developmental features of emerging adulthood is that it is a time of identity explorations. Emerging adulthood is a time when people are looking for an ideological framework for explaining the world, and some emerging adults may be attracted to the definite answers provided by extreme political movements. Embracing an extreme political ideology may relieve the discomfort that can accompany the uncertainty and doubt of ideological explorations. Still, these explanations beg the question: since only a small minority of emerging adults are involved in these extreme movements, why them and not the others?

FOCUS ON YOUTH IN THE MEDIA

Images of Extremism

The main focus of this chapter has been the cultural framework for social, moral, political and religious development during adolescence and emerging adulthood. We might argue that there is no more vivid image in the media than in the actions and outcomes of young extremists who are led to believe that the only way to express their views and be heard is to kill and to be killed themselves in the process.

Hasib Hussain detonated a bomb on a bus in Tavistock Square during the 7 July 2005 London bombings, killing 13 of the 52 people killed on that day, and himself. At the age of 18, he was the youngest of a group of four young suicide bombers. Unlike one of the other bombers, Germaine Lindsay, Hussain had no history of serious crime; he was not, as Lindsay was reported to be in much of the media at the time, a 'violent, racist drug dealer'. Rather Hussain was a 'gentle giant' who had a pretty typical upbringing in Holbeck, Yorkshire.

It was reported that Hussain became more religious in the latter half of 2003, after visiting Pakistan; and that he started wearing traditional Muslim dress, grew a beard – viewed by many Muslim teachers as one of the essential signs of Islamic faith for a man – and made the haj – the pilgrimage to Mecca (Bulley, 2008). Most pertinent in Hussain's case was his friendship with two of the other bombers, Kahn and Tanweer, which grew from attending the Stratford Street Mosque in Beeston and particularly from the three friends frequenting the Hamara Youth Access Point, a drop-in centre for teens. We can only conjecture about the different motives of the four young men involved in these horrific and callous crimes. However, in the case of Hussain, my reading (MH) of the media at the time, and since, suggests to me that it was

The Tavistock Square bus bombing.

more the power of peer pressure and friendship that drove Hasib Hussain to take lives, and to lose his own, rather than vengeance (Rosenberger, 2003) or to prove a point (Kiras, 2007).

Hussain and the other three bombers are labelled many things, but perhaps their most disturbing legacy is to put fear into the minds of other members of our largely successful British multi cultural society (Rubin et al., 2005). In particular, it is the fear that any young Muslim with a rucksack travelling on the London Underground, or on a bus anywhere, is a likely suicide bomber (Handley et al., 2009). More broadly it is the suspicion that any young British Muslim is a likely extremist who has embraced a potentially violent anti-Western understanding of Islam and is probably a member of al-Qaeda (Osler, 2009). It is the fear that adolescents are indoctrinated into anti-Western beliefs and groomed for self-destruction as a form of terrorist destruction (Sivanandan, 2006).

Often in the media it is polarisation of political, religious or moral thought among our young people – extremism – that we find most frightening and disturbing (Davies, 2009). Let's look at another example, that of the far-right anti-Muslim group the English Defence League (EDL). On 10 August 2010 Jon Cruddas, the Labour MP for Dagenham and Rainham, wrote in the *Guardian* newspaper about a then-recent spate of anti-Muslim demonstrations and picketing across the English North and Midlands, and in London. For example 40 EDL followers protested for three days outside a KFC restaurant in Blackburn that was trialling halal meat. Cruddas concludes:

'The [EDL] has regional organisers and units emerging in most towns and cities. They bring together a dangerous cocktail of football hooligans, far-right activists and pub racists. Yet there is no national strategy to deal with this group and little understanding of what the EDL is about, its appeal and how it is just one component, albeit a violent one, of a growing cultural, religious and political battle that is emerging across western Europe and is supported by rightwing [anti-Muslim] religious groups in the US.'

What do young people make of these violent rifts in British society? How does music and art react to extremism? Heavy metal band, Machine Head, includes these lyrics in their track 'Clenching the fists of dissent' from their 2007 album *The Blackening,* which includes a reference to 'the threat of patriotic brute':

Look for the lyrics of *Clenching the Fists of Dissent*
using a web search.
You will find the section that speaks of an ugly truth.
What is that ugly truth?
Why should it cause us to feel rage?

And in The Frontlines
(Look for the lyrics
of *Clenching the Fists of Dissent*
using a web search)
Why does he feel bitter?

Where are the cracks?
What is the burning effigy?
What is being worshipped?

The whole track appears to be anti-religious extremism and some bloggers have thought reference to the 'sacred oil' to be anti-Arabic and anti-Muslim. Well, anti-Muslim sentiment in Britain has been likened to anti-Semitism that at times has haunted many European societies (Meer, 2008). Or is this too sensitive an interpretation? What do you think of acrylic satire on Edvard Munch's *The Scream,* poking fun at religious fundamentalists such as the

'The Real Terror' by Darren Stein.

artist characterises as the Taliban's fear of Western or independent women? *The Real Terror* is an example of 'extremism art' by Darren Stein, an Australian artist and poet who worked in the townships and squatter camps around Johannesburg and Soweto, South Africa, during the transition to democracy. As one consequence he suffered from post-traumatic stress disorder caused by his exposure to the violence of the period.

Do young people fear extremism? Scholars have researched the views of young people (e.g. Burdsey, 2007; Weissman, 2007; Iannaccone and Berman, 2006) and find their attitudes informed by graphic reports in the news media (Shaftoe et al., 2007) and further 'fuelled' by the anti-extremist views of popular music of all genres (see also the Chapter 10 *Focus on Youth in the Media* feature). Research and read more about the proselytisation – to convert to or to win over – of extreme political and religious views among young people and the backlash of those who fear the long-term effects of extremism among adolescents and emerging adults. It is an extremely important topic.

SUMMING UP

In this chapter, we have examined various aspects of the cultural beliefs underlying the socialisation of adolescents and emerging adults, and you have been introduced to many of the ideas that are part of the cultural approach that will be taken in the chapters to come. The key points of the chapter are as follows:

- Socialisation is the process by which people acquire the behaviours and beliefs of the culture they live in. Three outcomes central to this process are self-regulation, role preparation and the cultivation of sources of meaning.
- Cultural beliefs usually tend toward either individualism or collectivism, with individualistic cultures giving priority to independence and self-expression and collectivist cultures placing a higher value on obedience and conformity. *Broad socialisation* and *narrow socialisation* are the terms for the process by which cultural members come to adopt the values and beliefs of an individualistic or a collectivistic culture. Sources of socialisation include family, peers and friends, school, community, media, the workplace, the legal system and cultural beliefs.

- A custom complex consists of a distinctive cultural practice and the cultural beliefs that are the basis for that practice. Many aspects of development and behaviour in adolescence and emerging adulthood can be understood as custom complexes.
- Cultural beliefs are often based on religious beliefs. Most industrialised countries today tend to be secular rather than religious, and religiosity is weaker in Northern Europe than in Southern Europe or the USA. Ideas about religious faith tend to become more abstract and less concrete in adolescence, compared with pre-adolescence.
- Kohlberg's theory of moral development proposed that moral development occurs in a universal sequence regardless of culture. However, Shweder has disputed this assumption and Jensen has proposed a worldviews theory as a culturally based alternative to Kohlberg's theory.
- As with religious and moral beliefs, political beliefs become more abstract and complex in the course of adolescence. Emerging adults are often disengaged from conventional politics, but many of them are involved in organisations working towards change in a specific area, and some are attracted to extreme political movements.

The ideas about cultural beliefs presented in this chapter form a foundation for understanding development in adolescence and emerging adulthood using a cultural approach. Individualism and collectivism provide a useful way of distinguishing between two general types of cultural beliefs, although these are rough categories and cultures do not necessarily fit neatly into one or the other. Broad socialisation and narrow socialisation describe the process through which individualism and collectivism become beliefs that are held by adolescents and emerging adults. The idea of the custom complex is useful for directing our attention to the cultural beliefs that lie behind everything that people in a culture do as a customary practice. Religious, moral and political beliefs are different kinds of cultural beliefs that people use for guiding their behaviour and making sense of the world around them.

The development of ideas about cultural beliefs has mostly proceeded separately from research on adolescence and emerging adulthood. Only in recent years have scholars on adolescence and emerging adulthood begun to recognise cultural beliefs as an essential part of understanding these age periods. This new melding of the cultural approach with research on adolescence and emerging adulthood is producing a great deal of illuminating and exciting research, which we will be examining in the chapters to come.

INTERNET RESOURCES

http://www.submission.org/teenagers/
Nothing provokes misunderstanding more than lack of knowledge about other cultures – their religious, moral and political values and beliefs. This site provides information for Muslim teenagers about Islam. It is worth exploring the site to see the range of ideas presented. How does the website differ from those written for teenagers from other cultures? For example:

http://www.gypsy-traveller.org/cyberpilots/
Try the website for 'Gypsy, Traveller, Barge and Showmen young people'.

http://www.catholic-ew.org.uk/
The Catholic Church is the largest Christian denomination in the world. It has more than 1 billion members worldwide – that means one in every six people walking the earth is a baptised Catholic. Around 5 million live in England. Here is just one example of how the Internet is being used by Christian churches and other religions for information, education and evangelism. For another example try:

http://www.islamreligion.com/

FURTHER READING

A. Bennett, *After Subculture: Critical Studies in Contemporary Youth Culture* London: Palgrave Macmillan (2004)
What is the difference between a culture and a subculture? It is often asserted that adolescents and emerging adults have their own youth subculture which in multi-ethnic societies becomes more important than the cultures of minority ethnic groups. This book is an up-to-date account of new developments in youth culture research that sometimes reject, refine or reinvent the concept of subculture. It includes analyses of particular aspects of youth culture – popular music, clubbing, body modification, the Internet, etc. – this is an ideal introduction to a diverse and wide-ranging field.

Martin J. Gannon and Rainandini Pillai, *Understanding Global Cultures: Metaphorical Journeys through 29 Nations, Clusters of Nations, Continents, and Diversity* London: Sage (2009)
In the 4th edition of this book authors Gannon and Pillai present a method for understanding the cultural mindsets of individual nations, clusters of nations and even continents, and present guidelines to help outsiders quickly understand what members of a culture consider important. A book for a multitude of audiences, including scholars, practitioners, students and all those who are simply interested in culture. It is also an ideal reference tool to 'dip into'.

L. Kohlberg and C. Gilligan, The adolescent as a philosopher: the discovery of the self in a post-conventional world. *Daedalus,* 100, 1051–1086 (1971)
It is good to read the original work of significant thinkers and theorists rather than only at second hand. This historic work is an engaging statement of Kohlberg's conception of moral development in adolescence. Written with his student, Carol Gilligan, before she developed her critique of his theory.

Another example of an original text is

J. Piaget, *The Moral Judgement of the Child*. Abingdon: Routledge and Kegan Paul (1932)

A. Waller, *Constructing Adolescence in Fantastic Realism*. Abingdon: Routledge (2009)
This is an 'off-the-wall' read exploring the adolescent culture of reading and books. Alison Waller examines themes that inform our understanding of 'the teenager' through the fiction published for teenagers over the last 40 years, which merge fantasy and realism. A different and refreshing view of how we construct a culture of adolescence.

For more reviews, responses to the *Thinking Critically* features, case studies, web links and practice tests, log on to **www.pearsoned.co.uk/arnett**.

CHAPTER 5
GENDER

OUTLINE

Terry undresses, feeling nervous and apprehensive, and then feels silly. After all, the photographer is a professional and has probably seen a thousand naked bodies, so what is one more? All that work in the gym, the aerobics – why not show off, after all the work it took to get such an attractive body? 'I should be proud,' Terry thinks, slipping into the robe thoughtfully provided by the photographer. Once exposed to the lights of the studio, Terry gets another pang of doubt but dismisses it and drops the robe. The photographer suggests a seated pose, and Terry sits down, but he drops his hands to cover himself. 'Move your hands to your knees, please,' the photographer says gently. After all, she is a professional and knows how to put her models at ease (adapted from Carroll and Wolpe, 1996, p. 162).

THE PURPOSE OF THIS STORY, AS YOU HAVE probably guessed, is to show how readily our minds slip into assumptions about male and female roles and how surprised we are when our gender stereotypes turn out to be wrong. Thinking about the world in terms of gender comes so easily to most of us that we do not even realise how deeply our assumptions about gender shape our perceptions. The first thing most people ask when they hear someone they know has had a baby is, 'Is it a boy or a girl?' From birth onwards – and these days, with pre-natal testing, even before birth – gender organises the way we think about people's traits and abilities and how people behave. At adolescence, when sexual maturity arrives,

consciousness of gender and social pressures related to gender become especially acute.

In every chapter of this book gender is an important theme; in family relationships, in school performance and in sexuality. Many questions need to be addressed. What sorts of gender-specific requirements do different cultures have for young people when they reach adolescence? In what ways does gender become especially important to socialisation in adolescence, and how is gender socialisation expressed in the family and other settings? What are the consequences for adolescents of conforming or refusing to conform to cultural expectations for gender role behaviour?

Because information on gender is relevant to all the chapters of this book, here we present especially extensive sections on cultural and historical patterns of gender socialisation in adolescence, as a foundation for the chapters to come. These sections will be followed by an examination of gender socialisation in modern, particularly European societies. Then we will consider gender stereotypes in young adulthood and reasons for the persistence of gender stereotypes even when the evidence supporting them is weak. Finally, we will consider the ways globalisation is changing gender expectations for adolescents and young adults in traditional cultures.

Before we proceed, however, let's clarify the difference between gender and **sex**. In general, social scientists use the term sex to refer to the *biological status of being male or female*. **Gender**, in contrast, refers to the *social categories of male and female* (Tobach, 2004; Helgeson, 2002). Use of the term *sex* implies that the characteristics of males and females have a biological basis. Use of the term *gender* implies that characteristics of males and females may be due to cultural and social beliefs, influences and perceptions. For example, the fact that males grow more muscular at puberty and females develop breasts is a sex difference. However, the fact that girls tend to have a more negative body image than males in adolescence is a gender difference. In this chapter, our focus will be on gender.

ADOLESCENTS AND GENDER IN TRADITIONAL CULTURES

For adolescents in traditional cultures, gender roles and expectations infuse virtually every aspect of life, even more so than in Northern Europe or North America. Adolescent boys and girls in traditional cultures often have very different lives and spend little time in each other's presence. The expectations for their behaviour as adolescents and for the kinds of work they will do (see Chapter 11) as adults are sharply divided, and as a result their daily lives do not often overlap (Cole et al., 2001).

Furthermore, for both males and females the gender requirements tend to intensify at adolescence and to allow for very little deviation from normal expectations. In cultures where socialisation is narrow, it tends to be narrowest of all with regard to gender expectations. Let's look first at the gender expectations for girls in traditional cultures, then at the gender expectations for boys.

From Girl to Woman

Girls in traditional cultures typically work alongside their mothers from an early age. Usually by age 6 or 7, they help take care of younger siblings and cousins (DeLoache and Gottlieb, 2000). By 6 or 7 or even earlier, they also help their mothers obtain food, cook, make clothes, gather firewood, and perform all of the other activities that are part of running a household. By adolescence, girls typically work alongside their mothers as near-equal partners (Lloyd, 2005). The authority of mothers over their daughters is clear, but by adolescence daughters have learned the skills involved in childcare and running a household so well that they can contribute an amount of work that is more or less equal to their mothers' work.

One important gender difference that occurs at adolescence in traditional cultures is that boys typically have less contact with their families and considerably more contact with their peers than they did before adolescence, whereas girls typically maintain a close relationship with their mothers and spend a great deal of time with them on a daily basis (Lloyd, *ibid.*). This difference exists partly because girls are more likely to work alongside their mothers than boys are to work alongside their fathers, but even when adolescent boys work with their fathers they have less contact and intimacy with them

By adolescence, girls in traditional cultures often work alongside their mothers as near equals. Here, a mother and daughter capture fish with a Kanga cloth.

than adolescent girls typically have with their mothers. This interdependence between mothers and daughters does not imply that girls remain suppressed in a dependent, childlike way. As a father of two now older women I (MH) can confirm that adolescent girls can be exceptionally confident and assertive.

Nevertheless, in traditional cultures socialisation becomes broader for boys in adolescence and stays narrow or becomes even narrower for girls. In the words of one team of commentators, 'During adolescence, the world expands for boys and contracts for girls. Boys enjoy new privileges reserved for men; girls endure new restrictions observed for women' (Mensch et al., 1998, p. 2). In the company of their mothers and often with other adult women as well, adolescent girls' daily lives remain within a hierarchy of authority. Girls are subject to the authority of all adult women because of the women's common experience as wives and mothers and their status as wise and knowing adults (Helson and Srivastava, 2002).

Another reason for the narrower socialisation of girls at adolescence is that the budding sexuality of girls is more likely to be tightly restricted than is the budding sexuality of boys (see Chapter 9). Typically, adolescent boys in traditional cultures are allowed and even expected to gain some sexual experience before marriage. Sometimes this is true of girls as well but for girls more variability exists across cultures, from cultures that allow or encourage them to become sexually active before marriage to cultures that punish girls' loss of virginity before marriage with death, and every variation in between. When adolescent girls are expected to be virgins and adolescent boys are expected not to be, boys sometimes gain their first sexual experience with prostitutes or with older women who are known to be friendly to the sexual interests of adolescent boys. However, this double standard also sets up a great deal of sexual and personal tension between adolescent girls and boys, with boys pressing for girls to relax their sexual resistance and girls fearful

of the shame and disgrace that will fall on them (and not on the boy) if they should give in (Imtoual and Hussein, 2009).

During adolescence, girls' activities in traditional communities mainly involve learning how to run a household. Middle childhood is a time of learning how to care for children (usually the girls' younger siblings), but by adolescence other girls in middle childhood take over some of the childcare, and adolescent girls spend their time learning household skills such as cooking, sewing and embroidery. School is not usually a part of the adolescent girl's experience. If she had the opportunity to go to school at all, it would have been for just long enough to become literate. Boys, in contrast, are much more likely to be allowed to attend school until age 12 or older.

From about age 10 to about age 16 girls are provided few opportunities to interact with boys. Talking to boys at these ages is strongly discouraged, and in small communities a girl's behaviour can be monitored almost constantly, if not by her parents or her brothers than by other adults who know her. However, around age 16 girls are considered to be reaching marriageable age, and they are allowed to attend public occasions under the watchful eye of an older female relative – a mother, aunt or grandmother. This provides a rare chance for young people to look each other over and maybe even exchange a few words. Vestiges of these differences in gender expectations remain in European countries that have strong traditional cultural roots and in the more traditional cultures within our multicultural societies (Kelly et al., 2004)

THINKING CRITICALLY

Compare the gender expectations for adolescent girls in many traditional cultures with the gender expectations for adolescent girls in your own culture. What are the similarities and differences?

CONNECT AND EXTEND

To read about the 'double standard' find 'Gender, belief in the sexual double standard, and sexual talk in heterosexual dating relationships' by Kathryn Greene and Sandra Faulkner in *Sex Roles*, Volume 53, Numbers 3–4 (August 2005), pp. 239–251

From Boy to Man

One striking difference between gender expectations for girls and gender expectations for boys in traditional cultures is that for boys manhood is something that has to be *achieved*, whereas girls reach womanhood inevitably, mainly through their biological changes. It is true that girls are required to demonstrate various skills and character qualities before they can be said to have reached womanhood. However, in most traditional cultures womanhood is seen as something that girls attain naturally during adolescence, and their readiness for womanhood is viewed as indisputably marked when they reach menarche (see Chapter 2). Adolescent boys have no comparable biological marker of readiness for manhood. For them, the attainment of manhood is often fraught with peril and carries a definite and formidable possibility of failure (Harnischfeger, 2003).

It is striking to observe how many cultures have a term for a male who is a failed man. In Spanish, for example, a failed man is *flojo* (a word that also means flabby, lazy, useless). Similar words exist in a wide variety of other languages. (You can probably think of more than one example in your own language.) In contrast, although there are certainly many derogatory terms applied to women, none of them have connotations of *failure at being a woman* the way *flojo* and other terms mean *failure at being a man*.

So, what must an adolescent boy in traditional cultures do to achieve manhood and escape the stigma of being viewed as a failed man? The anthropologist David Gilmore analysed this question across traditional cultures around the world in his classic book *Manhood in the Making: Cultural Concepts of Masculinity* (1990). He concludes that in most cultures an adolescent boy must demonstrate three capacities before he can be considered a man: *provide, protect* and *procreate*. He must *provide* in the sense that he must demonstrate that he has developed skills that are economically useful and that will enable him to support the wife and children he is likely to have as an adult man. For example, if adult men mainly fish, the adolescent boy must demonstrate that he has learned the skills and face the dangers involved in fishing adequately enough to provide for a family.

Second, the adolescent boy must *protect*, in the sense that he must show he can contribute to the protection of his family, kinship group, tribe and other groups to which he belongs, from attacks by human enemies or animal predators. He learns this by acquiring the skills of warfare and the capacity to use weapons. Conflict between human groups has been a fact of life for most cultures throughout human history, so this is a pervasive requirement. Finally, he must learn to *procreate*, in the sense that he must gain some degree of sexual experience before marriage. He gains this experience not in order to demonstrate his sexual attractiveness but so that he can prove that in marriage he will be able to perform well enough sexually to produce children.

Manhood requirements in traditional cultures typically involve not just the acquisition of specific skills in these three areas but also the development of certain *character qualities* that must accompany these skills to make them useful and effective (Arnett, 1998a). Learning to provide involves developing not just economic skills but also the character qualities of diligence and stamina. Learning to protect involves not just learning the skills of warfare and weapons but also cultivating the character qualities of courage and fortitude. Learning to procreate involves not just sexual performance but also the character qualities of confidence and boldness that lead to sexual opportunities.

David Gilmore (*ibid.*) gives many fine examples of the manhood requirements of different cultures in his book. For example, the *Mehinaku* live in the remotest part of the world's largest rain forest in central Brazil. Their location is so remote that they are one of the few remaining cultures that have been little affected by globalisation. Other than the occasional visit from a missionary or an anthropologist, they have been (so far) left alone.

For an adolescent male among the Mehinaku, learning to provide means learning to fish and hunt, which are the two main male economic activities (the females tend vegetable gardens, care for children and run the household). Depending on the local food supply, fishing and hunting might involve going on long expeditions to promising territory, sometimes for days or weeks at a time. Learning to provide means not only learning the skills involved in fishing and hunting, but also developing the character qualities of diligence, stamina and courage (because the expeditions are sometimes dangerous). Adolescent boys who fail to accompany their fathers on these trips out of laziness or weakness or fear are ridiculed as 'little girls' and told that women will find them undesirable.

THINKING CRITICALLY

Do you think the manhood requirements common in traditional cultures – provide, protect and procreate – also exist in a modified form for adolescent boys in your society? Are there other qualities that are part of the requirements for manhood – not just adulthood, but manhood specifically – in your society?

CULTURAL FOCUS

Male and Female Circumcision in Adolescence

Circumcision, which involves cutting some portion of the genitals so that they are permanently altered, is an ancient practice. We know that male circumcision goes back at least 2500 years among the ancient Jews and other cultures in what is now known as the Middle East (Henerey, 2004). For many Jews then and now, circumcision has had great religious and communal significance, serving as a visible sign of the covenant between God and the Jewish people and as a permanent marker of a male's membership in the Jewish community. Among Jews, circumcision takes place in infancy, eight days after birth.

Circumcision may also be performed shortly after birth for hygienic reasons, as a way of preventing certain diseases that are more likely to develop in uncircumcised males. However, in several parts of the world, circumcision takes place not in infancy but in adolescence, and not just among boys but among girls as well. Cultures with adolescent circumcision exist in the Middle East and Asia but are most prevalent in Africa (Hatfield and Rapson, 2006). In most cultures that have circumcision in adolescence, it takes place for both boys and girls. However, the nature of it and the consequences of it are quite different for males and females.

Male circumcision in adolescence typically involves cutting away the foreskin of the penis. This procedure is intensely painful, and no anaesthetic of any kind is used. Boys are supposed to demonstrate their courage and fortitude by enduring the circumcision without resisting, crying or flinching (Ragnarsson et al., 2008). There is a great deal of social pressure to be stoic. Circumcision usually occurs as a public ritual, observed by the community, and if a boy displays resistance or emotion he will be disgraced permanently before his community, and his family will be disgraced as well.

Although male circumcision is painful and traumatic, and the emotional and social effects of failure can be great, the physical effects of male circumcision are not harmful in the long run. Once the cut heals, the boy will be capable of experiencing the same pleasurable sensations in his penis as he did before the circumcision. Also, if a boy endures the circumcision without visible emotion, his status in the community will rise, for he will now be considered to have left childhood and entered adolescence.

For adolescent girls, the procedure and consequences of circumcision are considerably different. Female circumcision takes a variety of forms, but nearly always involves the clitoris, where female sexual sensations are concentrated. In some cultures the hood of the clitoris is cut off, in some the entire clitoris is cut off, and in yet others the clitoris is cut off along with parts of the labia minora and the labia majora (Hatfield and Rapson, 2006). Figure 5.1 shows the rates of female circumcision in various African countries.

Although the circumcision of adolescent girls is not performed publicly as it usually is for boys, and although girls are not expected to remain silent and stoic during the procedure, the physical consequences of circumcision are much more severe for them (Sedgh et al., 2005). Typically, a great deal of bleeding occurs, and the possibility of infection is high. Afterward many girls have chronic pain whenever they menstruate or urinate, and their risks of urinary infections and childbirth complications are heightened. Furthermore, the operation makes sexual intercourse less pleasurable.

Why would cultures sustain a tradition such as this? One reason lies in the inertia surrounding cultural practices. In general, people grow up believing that the practices and beliefs of their culture are good and right, and do not often question the ultimate ethical foundation for them. Another motivation for males may be that if it lowers females' enjoyment of sex, their wives may be less likely to have sex with other men (Hatfield and Rapson, 2006). Female circumcision is one way for men to exercise control over women's sexuality (Kalev, 2004).

Why would women submit to circumcision? One reason is that they have no choice. If they do not submit willingly, they may be held or tied down (Hatfield & Rapson, *ibid.*). Another reason is that girls in these cultures grow up knowing that a man will not marry a girl who is uncircumcised, and they also know

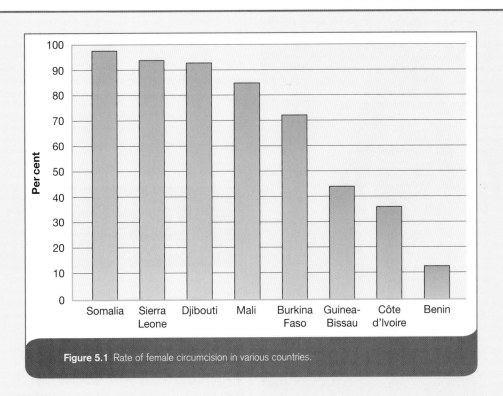

Figure 5.1 Rate of female circumcision in various countries.

that they must marry to have an accepted social place in their culture (Hayford, 2005). So, the girls usually submit voluntarily, and many even value the practice as a way of gaining higher status in their community and becoming acceptable to men as a potential marriage partner (Shweder, 2002).

In recent years, female circumcision has become an extremely controversial issue of global concern. Critics have termed it female genital mutilation (FGM) and have waged an international campaign against it (Kalev, *ibid.*; Sedgh et al., *ibid.*). International organisations such as the United Nations have issued reports condemning it (UNDESA, 2005). Some defenders have argued that the evidence of physical and sexual consequences is exaggerated and that the developed world should not impose its values on the cultures that practise female circumcision (Shweder, *ibid.*). The critics respond that respect for cultural differences can go only so far and that practices which cause suffering to large numbers of people should be condemned and abolished in whatever culture they take place (Hatfield and Rapson, 2006). Nevertheless, at the time of writing, female circumcision continues to be the norm for adolescent girls in many African cultures.

Learning to protect means learning to fight and wield weapons against men of neighbouring tribes. The Mehinaku themselves prefer peace and are not aggressive towards their neighbours, but their neighbours attack them on a regular basis and the men are required to defend themselves and their women and children. The men must also learn to defend themselves on their food-finding trips, which often require travelling through the territory of more aggressive tribes.

As part of their preparation for protecting, Mehinaku boys and men engage in almost daily wrestling matches. These matches are fiercely competitive, and

each time a male wins he elevates his status in the community, whereas repeatedly losing is deeply humiliating and a threat to his manhood status. This puts considerable pressure on adolescent boys, because boys who cannot compete well at these matches find their progress toward legitimate manhood called into question, and they find themselves considerably less attractive to adolescent girls as potential husbands.

With regard to learning to procreate, sex is the most popular topic of conversation among Mehinaku adolescent boys and men. They joke and brag about it, but they are also deeply concerned about potential failures

In traditional cultures, adolescent boys must learn to provide, protect, and procreate. Here, Mbuti boys in central Africa learn to hunt.

illustrates the intense gender socialisation pressure that often exists for adolescent boys in traditional cultures and the dire social consequences for boys who fail to measure up to culturally prescribed norms for manhood. For both boys and girls in traditional cultures, adolescence is a time when gender roles are clarified and emphasised. As we will see in the next section, emphasis on gender roles in adolescence has long been practised in modern societies as well.

ADOLESCENTS AND GENDER IN EUROPEAN HISTORY

In the same way that looking at adolescence in traditional cultures reveals sharp disparities in the socialisation of males and females, looking at adolescence in European history reveals a similar pattern. As in traditional cultures, what it means to grow from girl to woman in the history of our societies has been very different from what it means to grow from boy to man.

From Girl to Woman

Adolescent girls growing up in the British middle class in the nineteenth and first half of the twentieth centuries faced expectations that both constricted and supported them more than adolescent girls experience today. They were narrowly constricted in terms of the occupational roles they were allowed to study or enter. Few professions other than teacher, nurse or seamstress were considered appropriate for a woman. In fact, no profession at all was considered best, so that a young woman could focus on her future roles of wife and mother.

Adolescent girls were also constricted by cultural perceptions of females, especially young females, as fragile and innocent. One key reason they were discouraged from pursuing a profession was that intellectual work was considered 'unhealthy' for women. This view was connected to beliefs about menstruation, specifically the belief that intellectual work would draw a woman's energy towards her brain and away from her ovaries, thus disrupting her menstrual cycle and endangering her health (Taylor, 2006). This is a good example of something that was claimed to be a sex difference – women were viewed as biologically less capable of intellectual work – but that turned out to be a gender difference instead (rooted in cultural beliefs). Girls were also viewed as too weak to do any important physical work.

because in their small community any failures to 'perform' quickly become public knowledge. Because impotence is such a formidable prospect, they use numerous magical rituals to prevent or cure it, such as rubbing the penis with various animal or plant products. As with providing and protecting, adolescent boys are under considerable pressure to show they can perform sexually, and they are ridiculed and ostracised if they cannot.

One other aspect of Mehinaku manhood bears mentioning, because it is quite common in other cultures as well. Men and adolescent boys are supposed to spend their leisure time with each other, not at home with their mothers or wives and children. Adolescent boys and men gather daily in public places to talk, wrestle and make collective decisions, whereas girls and women are generally supposed to keep out of any central public place. A male who prefers the company of women, even his wife, is ridiculed as a 'trash yard man' – a man who is not truly a man. (This is a good example of a term for a failed man, as described earlier.) Again, the pressure on adolescent boys to conform to this norm is intense. Whatever his own inclinations may be, this narrow socialisation for the male role demands his conformity.

The themes of providing, protecting and procreating can be seen clearly in adolescent boys' gender socialisation among the Mehinaku. This example also

CONNECT AND EXTEND

The results of a study in 2004 support the view that people perceive psychometric intelligence (IQ) as a primarily masculine attribute in contrast with emotional intelligence (EI), which they perceive as a primarily feminine attribute. Read 'Estimates of emotional and psychometric intelligence: evidence for gender-based stereotypes' by V. Petrides, Adrian Furnham and G. Neil Martin in *The Journal of Social Psychology*, Volume 144, Number 2 (April 2004), pp. 149–162

The view of adolescent females as incapable of strenuous work is in sharp contrast to the expectations we have seen in traditional cultures, where adolescent girls work alongside their mothers with near-adult responsibilities. However, this exclusion from work applied mainly to adolescent girls in the growing middle class. Until the mid-nineteenth century many families were small-scale farmers or farm workers (Cinnirella, 2008), and in those families the lives of adolescent girls were very much like the lives of their counterparts in traditional cultures, working alongside their mothers doing useful and necessary work every day. Also, – and as noted in Chapter 11 – throughout the nineteenth and early twentieth centuries many adolescent girls worked in the factories that were springing up in the course of industrialisation (Sass, 1999).

Sexuality is a third area where the lives of middle-class girls were narrowly constricted historically in British and many other European societies. Until the 1920s, virginity until marriage was considered essential for adolescent girls. The word **hymen** was rarely used, but adolescent girls were taught that they possessed a 'jewel' or 'treasure' that they should surrender only on the night of their wedding (Saharso, 2003). Until marriage, young women were kept as innocent as possible in body and in mind.

The goal of keeping girls innocent was taken so far that many adolescent girls were not even told about menarche. Historians estimate that before the mid-twentieth century the majority of adolescent girls were entirely unprepared for menarche (Teitelman, 2004) – and we have seen, in Chapter 2, how shocking it can be to girls who do not know it is coming. Mothers believed that by saying nothing about it they were shielding their girls for as long as possible from the dark mysteries of sex. It was only in the 1920s, sometimes called the decade of the first sexual revolution, that virginity began to lose its near-sacred status. It was only in the late 1940s that a majority of girls learned about menstruation from school, their mothers, or other sources before menarche actually arrived (Brumberg, 1997).

A fourth area of constriction for adolescent females historically was physical appearance. We discussed in Chapter 2 how the current slim ideal of female appearance can be difficult for girls when their bodies reach puberty, but irrational ideals of female appearance are not new. Until the early twentieth century, most middle-class adolescent girls and women in Britain and elsewhere wore some version of the corset, which was designed to support the breasts and pinch the waist tightly to make it look as small as possible. By the 1920s, corsets were rarely used, replaced by bras, but the 1920s also witnessed new requirements for female appearance – shaving the legs and underarms became the convention for women, and dieting became a common practice in an effort to attain a slim, boyish figure.

By the 1950s, boyishness was out and big breasts were in. Adolescent girls' diaries from the 1950s show a preoccupation with bras and breasts and a variety of

Until the 1920s, middle-class girls wore corsets once they reached puberty.

CONNECT AND EXTEND

'Cars, corsets, and cigarettes occupied a prominent place in British (and US) editions of *Vogue* in the interwar years. All three products were presented as quintessentially modern and possessing the capacity to modernize the women who used them' – from the abstract. There is more to read in 'Feminine modernity in interwar Britain and North America: corsets, cars, and cigarettes' by Penny Tinkler and Cheryl Krasnick Warsh in the *Journal of Women's History*, Volume 20, Number 3 (October 2008), pp. 113–143

dubious techniques for increasing breast size, from exercise programmes and creams to exposing them to moonlight (Brumberg, *ibid.*). In each era, adolescent girls have striven for the female ideal they have been socialised to desire, and have often experienced the normal course of their biological development during puberty as a great source of frustration.

Yet developing from girl to woman also had some advantages historically as compared to the present, according to Joan Jacobs Brumberg, a social historian and the author of a thoughtful book called *The Body Project: An Intimate History of American Girls* (1997). Brumberg acknowledges, and describes in detail, how girls in the eighteenth and nineteenth centuries were constricted and left largely ignorant of the workings of their own bodies. However, she argues that girls of those times also benefited from the existence of a wide range of voluntary organisations, such as the Young Women's Christian Association (YWCA) and the Girl Guides, in which adult women provided a 'protective umbrella' for the nurturing of adolescent girls. In these organisations, the focus was not on girls' physical appearance but on service projects in the community, building relationships between adolescent girls and adult women, and developing character qualities, including self-control, service to others, and belief in God. Brumberg (1997) observes:

'Whether Christian or Jew, black or white, volunteer or professional, most women in this era shared the ethic that older women had a special responsibility to the young of their sex. This kind of mentoring was based on the need to protect all girls, not just one's own daughters, from premature sexuality and manipulation at the hands of men. Although the ethic generated all kinds of censorious directives about sexual behaviour and its consequences . . . it also gave a cooperative and expansive tone . . . middle-class matrons and young adult women performed countless mundane acts of guidance and supervision, such as showing girls how to sew, embroider, or arrange flowers, or helping them to organise collections of food and clothing for impoverished families. In all of these settings, there were chattering girls along with concerned adults, bound together by both gender and common projects.' (pp. 19–20)

Today, in Brumberg's view, adolescent girls are less constricted but also more vulnerable and less integrated into the lives of adult women outside their families.

THINKING CRITICALLY

Would it be possible today to reconstruct the 'protective umbrella' provided for adolescent girls by adult women in previous times, or would today's adolescent girls find such protection patronising and overly restrictive?

From Boy to Man

Like gender expectations for adolescent girls, gender expectations for adolescent boys have changed markedly in the past two centuries but have also retained some consistent features. Historian Anthony Rotundo (1993) describes the transformations that have taken place in the last couple of centuries in how we view the passage from boyhood to manhood.

In Rotundo's account, the seventeenth and eighteenth centuries were characterised by communities that were small, tightly knit and strongly based in religion. In this phase of what Rotundo terms **communal manhood**, the focus of gender expectations for adolescent boys was on preparing to assume adult role responsibilities in work and marriage. Rotundo calls this *communal manhood* because preparing for community and family responsibilities was considered more important than striving for individual achievement and economic success. Preparing to become 'head of the household' was seen as especially important for adolescent boys because as adult men they would be expected to act as provider and protector of wife and children. Note the striking resemblance to the requirements of manhood in traditional cultures, with the common emphasis on learning to provide and protect.

During the nineteenth century, as many societies became more urbanised, young men became more likely to leave home in their late teens for the growing cities to make it on their own without much in the way of family ties. Rotundo calls the nineteenth century the era of **self-made manhood**. This was a time in history when individualism was growing in strength and males were increasingly expected to become independent from their families in adolescence and young adulthood as part of becoming a man, rather than remaining closely interdependent with other family members. Although becoming a provider and protector remained important, an explicit emphasis also developed on the importance of developing the individualistic character qualities necessary for becoming a man. *Decision of character* became a popular term to describe a young man's passage from high-spirited but undisciplined youth to a manhood characterised by self-control and a strong will for carrying out independent decisions (Hunter et al., 2006).

One interesting historical similarity between gender expectations for young males and females was the creation during the nineteenth century of a wide range of voluntary organisations that brought young people of the same sex together. The organisations for girls were described above. For males, the organisations were The Scouts, The Boys Brigade, military cadet groups and the Young Men's Christian Association (YMCA). Like the organisations for girls, the boys' organisations stressed the importance of developing self-control, service to others and belief in God. However, the male organisations were less likely to be run by matronly adults and more likely to be run by the young adults themselves. Perhaps for this reason the male organisations tended to involve not just sober camaraderie but occasional boisterous play, rowdy competition and (in some organisations) fighting and drinking alcohol, in

For both boys and girls, voluntary organisations were popular in the nineteenth century. Shown here are young Girl Guides.

spite of the professed commitment to self-control (Enyeart, 2003).

Organisations for young males also emphasised strenuous physical activity. Populations in the big cities were growing rapidly, but many men voiced concerns that growing up in a city made boys soft and weak. They advocated activities such as military training, competitive sports and outward-bound for young males because they believed that becoming a man meant becoming tough and strong. As discussed in Chapter 4, the creation of the Boy Scouts arose from this belief.

Rotundo calls the twentieth century the era of **passionate manhood**, during which individualism increased still further. Although individualism grew more important in nineteenth-century society, adolescent boys were nevertheless expected to learn self-control and self-denial as part of becoming a man, so that they would maintain control over their impulses. In contrast, during the twentieth century passionate emotions such as anger and sexual desire became regarded as part of the manhood ideal. Self-expression and self-enjoyment replaced self-control and self-denial as the paramount virtues young males should learn in the course of becoming a man.

CONNECT AND EXTEND

What about men in traditionally female dominated occupations? Are they good examples of what is meant by 'passionate manhood'? For research based on interviews with male workers from four occupational groups, librarians, cabin crew, nurses and primary school teachers, read 'Masculinity at work: the experiences of men in female dominated occupations' by Ruth Simpson in *Work, Employment & Society,* Volume 18, Number 2 (1 June 2004), pp. 349–368

THINKING CRITICALLY

Now that you know something about the history of gender expectations for adolescents, how do you think they are likely to change (if at all) in the course of the twenty-first century, and why?

SOCIALISATION AND GENDER TODAY

So far we have looked at gender socialisation in traditional cultures and in history. What about today's majority cultures and similar cultures in Europe and other developed parts of the world? What sort of socialisation for gender goes on during adolescence? We address this question by looking first at how gender socialisation changes from childhood to adolescence. Then we examine cultural beliefs about gender and gender socialisation with respect to family, peers, school and the media.

The Gender Intensification Hypothesis

Psychologists John Hill and Mary Ellen Lynch (1983; Lynch, 1991) proposed that adolescence is a particularly important time in gender socialisation, especially for girls. According to their **gender intensification hypothesis**, psychological and behavioural differences between males and females become more pronounced in the transition from childhood to adolescence because of intensified socialisation pressures to conform to culturally prescribed gender roles. Hill and Lynch believe that it is this intensified socialisation pressure, rather than the biological changes of puberty, that results in increased differences between males and females as adolescence progresses. Furthermore, they argue that the intensity of gender socialisation in adolescence is greater for females than for males and that this is reflected in a variety of ways in adolescent girls' development.

In support of their hypothesis, Hill and Lynch offer several arguments and sources of evidence. During adolescence, girls become notably more self-conscious than boys about their physical appearance because looking physically attractive becomes an especially important part of the female gender role. Girls also become more interested and adept than boys in forming intimate friendships. To Hill and Lynch this is because adolescents have been socialised to believe that having intimate friendships is part of the female gender role but is inconsistent with the male gender role. Since Hill and Lynch (1983) proposed this hypothesis, several supporting studies have been presented (e.g. Shanahan et al., 2007; Galambos, 2004; Wichstrom, 1999).

In one early study, boys and girls (11 to 13) filled out a questionnaire on gender identity each year (Galambos et al., 1990). Over this two-year period, girls' self-descriptions became more 'feminine' (e.g. gentle, affectionate) and boys' self-descriptions became more 'masculine' (e.g. tough, aggressive). However, in contrast to Hill and Lynch's earlier claim that gender intensification is strongest for girls, the pattern in this study was especially strong for boys and masculinity. A more recent study found that among both boys and girls, adolescents embraced gender stereotypes more than younger children did (Rowley et al., 2007). Another earlier study found that increased conformity to gender roles during early adolescence took place primarily for adolescents whose parents influenced them toward gender conformity (Crouter et al., 1995). This study indicates that gender intensification does not occur equally for all adolescents, but is especially strong among adolescents exposed to family socialisation pressures to conform to traditional gender roles.

Cultural Beliefs About Gender

What sort of cultural beliefs about gender exist for adolescents and young adults currently growing up in our societies? The results of an annual national survey show a clear trend towards more egalitarian gender attitudes in recent decades, as Figure 5.2 shows (Cotter et al., 2009). Compared to 1977, many adults today are less likely to believe men are better politicians, less likely to see women as the ones who should take care of the home, more likely to believe working mothers can have warm relationships with their children, and less likely to believe under-5s would suffer if mothers work.

However, the results of the GSS also show that a considerable proportion of adults questioned – from about a quarter to over one-third, depending on the question – continue to harbour beliefs about gender roles not unlike those we have seen in traditional

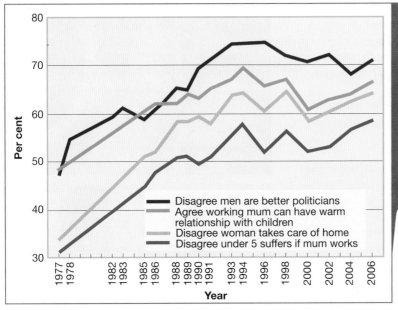

Figure 5.2 Changes in gender attitudes, 1977–2006.

Source: General Social Survey (GSS), 1977–2006.

cultures: men should hold the power and be out in the world doing things, and women should focus on caring for children and running the household. The persistence of traditional gender role beliefs in society is also indicated in studies of gender socialisation and gender stereotypes, as we shall see in the following sections.

Gender Socialisation: Family, Peers and School

The previous chapter described cultural differences in socialisation. However, differences in socialisation also occur within cultures, especially in the socialisation of boys and girls. **Differential gender socialisation** is the term for socialising males and females according to different expectations about the attitudes and behaviour appropriate to each gender (Bussey and Bandura, 2004). We have seen in this chapter how intense differential socialisation can be in traditional cultures and how intense it has been in history. It also continues to exist in more subtle but nevertheless effective forms. We will consider differential gender socialisation with respect to family, peers and school in detail in future chapters, but this section will serve as an introduction.

Differential gender socialisation begins early, in virtually every culture. Parents dress their boys and girls differently, give them different toys, and decorate their bedrooms differently. One early study found that 90 per cent of the infants observed at a shopping centre were wearing clothing that was gender specific in colour and/or style (Shakin et al., 1985). In a classic experimental study (Sidorowicz and Lunney, 1980), adults were asked to play with a 10-month-old infant they did not know. All adults played with the same infant, but some were told it was a girl, some were told it was a boy, and some were given no information about its gender. There were three toys to play with: a rubber football, a doll and a teething ring. When the adults thought the child was male, 50 per cent of the men and 80 per cent of the women played with the child using the football. When they thought the child was female, 89 per cent of the men and 73 per cent of the women used the doll in play.

In the course of growing up, children get encouragement from parents, peers and teachers to conform to gender roles. Numerous studies attest that parents encourage gender-specific activities in their children and discourage activities they see as inconsistent with their child's gender (Bussey and Bandura, *ibid.*; Bronstein, 2006). In early childhood, most children play almost exclusively with same-sex peers, and children (especially boys) who deviate from gender norms in play suffer peer ridicule and are less popular than children who conform to gender roles (Maccoby, 2002).

During middle childhood, gender rules often become temporarily more flexible (Basow and Rubin, 1999). However, with the gender intensification of adolescence, differential socialisation becomes more pronounced. Parents tend to monitor and restrict adolescent girls more tightly than adolescent boys with respect to where they are allowed to go and with whom (McHale et al., 2003). Peers continue to punish with ridicule and unpopularity the adolescents who deviate from gender role expectations (Pascoe, 2007) – the boy who takes up the flute, the girl who wears unbranded clothes and no make-up.

With regard to school, research has found that teachers – both males and females – generally reinforce the traditional cultural messages regarding gender (Basow, 2004; Spencer et al., 2003). Specifically, teachers often assume that boys and girls are inherently different, with different interests and abilities; that boys are more aggressive and dominant; and that girls are more silent and compliant. Girls have made remarkable gains in academic achievement in recent decades and now exceed boys in nearly every area of school performance (Sommers, 2000). However, the educational and occupational interests and choices of adolescent and young adult males and females remain different in some gender-specific ways, with girls more likely to go into traditionally female professions such as nursing and childcare, and boys more likely to pursue traditionally male professions such as engineering and scientific research (Basow, 2004).

Why do pressures to conform to traditional gender roles intensify in adolescence?

CONNECT AND EXTEND

To examine the role of the school, and of the peer group culture in particular, in constructing male and female identity among adolescents read 'Learning to be violent: the role of the school in developing adolescent gendered behaviour' by Fiona Leach in *Compare*, Volume 33, Number 3 (2003), pp. 385–400

These differences are at least partly a result of gender socialisation in the school. Teachers pay more attention to boys in maths lessons and are more demanding (Amit and Fried, 2005). Girls tend to have less peer support for their science interests than boys do (Stake and Nickens, 2005), which may partly explain why girls are less likely to pursue science education in school and university. One study found that the gender difference in self-perceptions of possible future occupations became wider in secondary school and college (Lips, 2004). We will discuss school and gender in more detail in Chapter 10.

The findings about differential socialisation at home and at school do not mean that parents and teachers consciously and intentionally treat adolescent girls and boys differently. Sometimes they do, but often differential socialisation simply results from the different expectations that parents and teachers have for males and females as a consequence of their own gender socialisation (Bronstein, *ibid.*). In their differential gender socialisation of adolescent girls and boys, parents and teachers reflect their culture's beliefs about gender, often without even thinking consciously about what they are doing.

THINKING CRITICALLY

Based on your experience, think through examples of differential gender socialisation in childhood, adolescence and young adulthood.

FOCUS ON YOUTH IN THE MEDIA

Magazines and Gender

'"What guys love to hate" [pointing to an article she read in *YM*] just their opinions on things, what they like about girls or they didn't like. You would be able to tell if they liked you, or if they didn't like what you were doing, or something like that … [We] just thought it was helpful, kind of helpful. Just to know what we should do, or shouldn't do. I don't know. It's kind of bad to follow a magazine article, but it gives some [good] advice. [Points to] "What guys love and hate on the first date". Tips on what to wear, what to do, what to talk about and how to act.'

– Erica, age 16 (in Currie, 2001, p. 5)

The television shows, films and music most popular with adolescents promote many stereotypes about gender; check out the *Focus on Youth in the Media* feature in many of the chapters. However, magazines are worth focusing on here because they are the media form with the most obvious focus on gender socialisation, especially the magazines read by adolescent girls. Some boys read magazines, too, but their favourite magazines are not as clearly gender focused. For girls, every issue of their favourite magazine is packed with gender-specific messages about how to be an adolescent girl (Massoni, 2004).

What sort of gender messages do adolescent girls get when they read these magazines? Several analyses of the content of girls' magazines have reported highly similar findings (Ballentine and Ogle, 2005; Massoni, 2004; Currie, 1999). One early study (Evans et al., 1991) analysed the content in ten issues of three magazines for adolescent girls. The analysis showed that the magazines relentlessly promote the gender socialisation of adolescent girls towards the traditional female gender role. Physical appearance is of ultimate importance, and there is an intense focus on how to be appealing to boys. Figure 5.3 shows the proportion of articles devoted to each of six topics. Fashion was the most common topic in all three magazines, occupying 27 to 41 per cent of the articles. Another 10 to 13 per cent of the articles were devoted to beauty, and most of the articles on 'health' (3 to 6 per cent) were about weight reduction and control. Altogether, for each of the magazines, from 44 to 60 per cent of the content focused directly on physical appearance.

This percentage actually understates the focus on physical appearance because it does not include the advertisements. In the three magazines taken together, 46 per cent of the space was devoted to advertisements. The advertisements were almost exclusively for clothes, cosmetics and weight-loss programmes.

In contrast to the plethora of articles and advertisements on physical appearance, there were few articles on political or social issues. The main topic of 'career' articles was modelling. There were virtually no articles on possible careers in business, the sciences, law, medicine or any other high-status profession in which the mind would be valued more than the body. Of course, no doubt the magazine publishers would carry an abundance of articles on social issues and professional careers if they found they could sell more magazines that way. They pack the magazines with articles and adverts on how to enhance physical attractiveness because that is the content to which adolescent girls respond most strongly.

Why? Perhaps adolescent girls no longer get much direct instruction from older females about becoming a woman (Brumberg, *ibid.*). With the gender intensification of adolescence, girls become acutely aware that others expect them to look like a girl is supposed to look and act like a girl is supposed to act – but how is a girl supposed to look and act? These magazines promise to provide the answers. The message to adolescent girls is that if you buy the right products and strive to make your appearance conform to the ideal presented in the magazines, you will look and act like a girl is supposed to look and act and you will attract all the boys you want (Ballentine and Ogle, 2005). But you will not necessarily be happy. One summary of 47

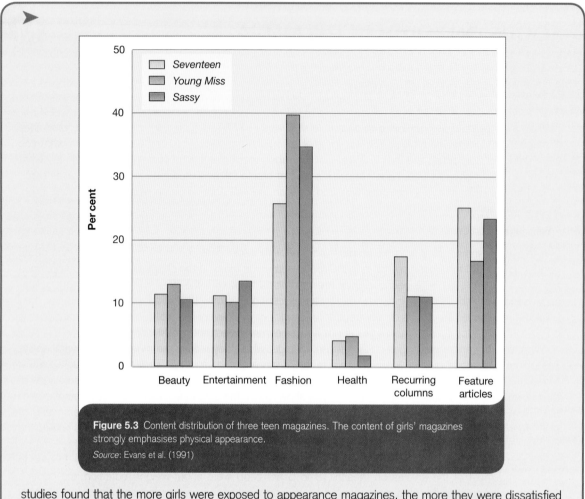

Figure 5.3 Content distribution of three teen magazines. The content of girls' magazines strongly emphasises physical appearance.
Source: Evans et al. (1991)

studies found that the more girls were exposed to appearance magazines, the more they were dissatisfied with their own appearance (Murnen and Levine, 2007). In summary, recent analyses of the most popular magazines for girls show little change in content over time, with physical appearance and boy catching still predominant (Olson, 2007; Ballentine and Ogle, *ibid.*; Massoni, 2004).

Gender Socialisation as a Source of Problems

For both girls and boys, the intensified gender socialisation they experience in adolescence can be a source of problems. For girls, the focus on physical appearance that is the heart of the female gender role can produce many kinds of distress. For example, girls are more likely than boys to develop a negative body image in adolescence (Grabe et al., 2008; Siegel, 2002); hardly surprising, given the magazine ideals to which they compare themselves. The emphasis on thinness that is part of the female ideal

of physical appearance leads the majority of girls to diet in adolescence (Mackey and La Greca, 2007), and at the extreme, some girls develop serious eating disorders (discussed in more detail in Chapter 12) that threaten their health and even their lives (Krauth et al., 2002). Adolescent girls who are overweight or regarded by their peers as physically unattractive suffer merciless ridicule (Thompson et al., 2007). This ridicule comes not only from boys but from other girls (LópezGuimerà et al., 2008). Even long after adolescence, close to half of adult women are dissatisfied with their physical appearance (Grabe et al., *ibid.*).

CONNECT AND EXTEND

What part do perceptions of the need to diet, health status and social isolation have in adolescent eating disorders? Read 'Perception of overweight and obesity among Portuguese adolescents: an overview of associated factors' by Helena Fonseca and Margarida Gaspar de Matos in *The European Journal of Public Health*, Volume 15, Number 3 (June 2005), pp. 323–328

For boys, the problem at the core of their gender role in adolescence is aggressiveness (Keltikangas-Järvinen, 2002). Boys are more aggressive than girls from infancy onwards, partly for biological reasons (see Chapter 2) but also because of their gender socialisation (Baillargeon et al., 2007; Maccoby, 2002). During adolescence, boys are expected by their peers to be verbally aggressive, directing half-joking insults at other boys on a regular basis (Pascoe, 2007). Often these insults involve manhood itself; adolescent boys commonly use insults such as 'wimp', 'girl', 'scaredy-cat' and 'yeller', calling the manhood of other boys into question. From this we can see that it is not just in traditional cultures that adolescent boys face the intimidating prospect of being regarded as a failed man. They defend themselves by using verbal aggressiveness in return and by being physically aggressive when necessary. Boys who demonstrate physical aggressiveness successfully in sports frequently have the highest status among their peers (Pascoe, 2007; 2003).

A variety of problems stem from this emphasis on aggressiveness in the male role. Aggressiveness is used as a way of establishing social hierarchies among adolescent boys, and low-status boys suffer frequent insults and humiliations from other boys (Pascoe, 2007). Furthermore, aggressiveness contributes to problem behaviours in adolescence and young adulthood such as vandalism, risky driving, fighting and crime (van Lier et al., 2009). Adolescents who value aggressiveness as part of the male gender role are especially likely to engage in problem behaviour (Keltikangas-Järvinen, *ibid.*). Boys who agreed with statements such as 'A young man should be tough, even if he is not big' were more likely than other boys to report school difficulties, alcohol and drug use, and risky sexual behaviour (Ma, 2005).

Cognition and Gender

We have already noted that socialisation interacts with cognitive development to produce adolescents' ideas about gender (Bussey and Bandura, *ibid.*). Lawrence Kohlberg, whose ideas about moral development were discussed in Chapter 4, also proposed an influential

Why does aggressiveness become more of a problem for boys in adolescence?

theory of gender development known as the **cognitive-developmental theory of gender** (1966). Kohlberg based this theory on Piaget's ideas about cognitive development, applied specifically to gender. According to Kohlberg's theory, gender is a fundamental way of organising ideas about the world.

By the time children are about 3 years old, they understand **gender identity**; that is, they understand themselves as being either male or female (Renk et al., 2006). Once children possess gender identity, they use gender as a way of organising information obtained from the world around them. Certain toys become 'toys that girls play with', whereas others are 'toys that boys play with'. Certain clothes become 'clothes that boys wear' and others become 'clothes that girls wear'. By age 4 or 5, children identify a wide range of things as appropriate for either males or females, including toys, clothing, activities, objects and occupations (Kulik, 2000; Bussey and Bandura, *ibid.*). Furthermore, according to cognitive-developmental theory, children seek to maintain consistency between their categories and their behaviour. Kohlberg called this process **self-socialisation**. Boys become quite insistent about doing things they regard as boy things and avoiding things that girls do; girls become equally intent on avoiding boy things and doing things they regard as appropriate for girls (Rasmussen, 2006). All of this can also get mixed up in early childhood with the development of ethnic identities, and as always we should recognise that developing identity is a multifaceted dynamic process (Barron, 2007).

During middle childhood, from about age 6 to 10, children's perceptions of gender roles become more flexible (P. R. Carver et al., 2003; Basow and Rubin, 1999). Boys and girls alike enjoy sports, music, toys and games with less concern about whether the activity is appropriate for their gender. Why this change takes place is not clear, but it appears to be due in part to the way adults and peers also become less concerned with enforcing gender norms during this period (Helgeson, 2002). It may be, too, that once gender identity is well established children no longer find violations of gender norms so unsettling.

However, expectations become more rigid again in early adolescence, as part of the gender intensification process (Basow and Rubin, 1999). In one earlier but useful study, views of gender roles were examined among children and adolescents aged 9 to 17 years (Alfieri et al., 1996). Students were presented with 12 gender-related terms, 6 'masculine' and 6 'feminine', and asked to indicate whether they thought the items described males, females or both. The 'both' response was defined as indicating greater gender role flexibility. The results indicated that gender role flexibility increased in the younger years and peaked when the participants were aged

12 and 13, but then became steadily more rigid from that point on, through to the end of secondary schooling. Boys had especially rigid views of gender roles, particularly for masculine traits.

How can cognitive-developmental theory explain these changes? The hallmark of cognitive development in adolescence is formal operations, which includes the development of self-reflection and idealisation. As a consequence, reaching adolescence leads to asking oneself questions about what it means to be a woman or a man, and to making judgements about how one measures up to cultural gender expectations. As adolescents become more capable of reflecting on these issues they become more concerned with compliance to gender norms, for themselves and others. Also contributing to greater gender role rigidity in adolescence is the development of sexual maturity, which makes adolescents more conscious of the gender of themselves and others in social interactions. Furthermore, parents and peers exert increased pressure to conform to gender norms (Williams et al., 2008; Williams et al., 2007; Huebner and Mancini, 2003).

Another cognitive theory of gender that uses Piaget's ideas is **gender schema theory**. Like Kohlberg's cognitive-developmental theory, gender schema theory views gender as one of the fundamental ways that people organise information about the world. (Recall from Chapter 3 that *scheme* is Piaget's term for a structure for organising and processing information. *Scheme* and **schema** are used interchangeably.)

According to gender schema theory, gender is one of our most important schemas from early childhood onward. By the time we reach adolescence, on the basis of our socialisation we have learned to categorise an enormous range of activities, objects and personality characteristics as 'female' or 'male'. This includes not just the obvious – vaginas are female, penises are male – but many things that have no inherent 'femaleness' or 'maleness' and are nevertheless taught as possessing gender – the moon as 'female' and the sun as 'male' in traditional Chinese culture, or long hair as 'female' and short hair as 'male' in many cultures, for example.

CONNECT AND EXTEND

To judge the extent to which parents' education and occupation can have an impact on the choice of male- and female-dominated subjects at university, read 'Women's and men's choice of higher education: what explains the persistent sex segregation in Norway?' by Liv Anne Støren and Clara Åse Arnesen in *Studies in Higher Education*, Volume 32, Number 2 (2007), pp. 253–275

HISTORICAL FOCUS

The Women's Movement of the 1960s

The women's movement, seeking equality of rights and opportunities for women, has a long history, dating back over a century to the time when women first organised together in an effort to gain the right to vote. One especially important period in the history of the women's movement was the 1960s. The 1960s were a time of dramatic social changes in many ways – the civil rights movement in America, the 'War on Poverty' and the sexual revolution are examples – and the women's movement was one of these changes. The greatly expanded range of opportunities in education and employment that exist for adolescent girls and young adult women today are rooted in the changes in gender role attitudes that were inspired by the women's movement in the 1960s.

The roots of the second-wave feminist movement in Britain (the first wave, to win the right to vote, was the suffragette campaign much earlier in the century) were in the late 1960s when women were very low paid, were expected to become at best either a nurse or a secretary, and most women workers were in low paid jobs (Orazem et al., 2003; Warren et al., 2001) such as cleaners. The 1960s was a period of huge social and political change and the authors of change stressed progress, liberalisation and egalitarianism.

The context for political/social action was exciting, almost 'heady': the civil rights movement in Northern Ireland and the black civil rights and women's movements in the USA; the 'Ban the Bomb' and anti-war demonstrations in America and Europe; and the availability of oral contraceptives, pop music, pop fashion and youth culture. In this context, British women took to the streets and organised public meetings. The feminist movement in Britain became known as 'women's lib' and the 'popular persona' of women's lib was 'burning your bra' – destroying the strictures of being a woman; the one requirement of a woman's shape for which there was no male equivalent.

The first ever National Women's Liberation Conference took place at Ruskin College, Oxford, in 1970 and that is pretty much how things were organised to start off: small, local, groups, linked through newsletters (McIntosh, 2001). The emphasis was on groups operating in a non-hierarchical way, giving space for all women to demonstrate and to take action on sexuality, reproduction and relationships – all hugely important issues for women (Cullen and Gotell, 2002) but all too often the locus of the oppression and subordination of women (Sharp et al., 2003)

Early campaigns of the Women's Liberation Movement included action against sexism in public institutions; supporting women at work, in trades unions and in industrial action; speaking out against domestic violence and against attempts to restrict women's abortion rights. These campaigns resulted in a focus for the Women's Liberation Movement on four demands:

'Burn your bra' became synonymous with the 'Women's Lib' movement.

➤

equal pay (Fredman, 2008); equal education and opportunity (Unterhalter, 2008); 24-hour nurseries (Brown, 2004); and free contraception and abortion on demand (Free et al., 2005; Medoff, 2007).

What else was happening? Germaine Greer's hugely influential *The Female Eunuch* and Kate Millett's *Sexual Politics* were both published in 1970, and there was a major demonstration at the Miss World contest that year. Feminist activists flour-bombed the stage in protest at what was considered the competition's 'objectification' of women. (What was the reaction of the host, Bob Hope? 'Pretty girls don't have these problems.') In 1975, *The Times* newspaper reported that there were more than 1500 groups of women meeting regularly around Britain. That same year, the Equal Pay Act came into force – an iconic moment. During the 1970s there was tumultuous amounts of activism around rape and male violence against women – in 1979, for instance, the Southall Black Sisters acted against domestic violence and legal injustice (Charanji, 2008; Patel, 2008).

By the end of the decade, the tumult was dying down. When Margaret Thatcher became prime minister in 1979, the political climate of the country shifted radically (King, 2002) and although **feminism** continued – the activism surrounding violence against women and the continuation of unequal pay has never died away – the defining moments of the 1970s became matters of history. Nevertheless, for feminists today there's a sense of being part of a worldwide movement; something that wasn't as clear in 1970. There are women's rights campaigns across the globe (Zwingel, 2005). In certain parts of Africa for example, it's about political emancipation and reforms to the law around violence against women – not unlike but even more vivid than the British campaigns of the 1970s (Dauer and Gomez, 2006).

However, the importance of the women's lib movement of the 1970s for adolescents and young adults is not only that young people played a part in it but that young women growing up today have far more opportunities and are far less restricted by gender roles than any generation of girls before them, due substantially to the changes that began during the 1970s. Sexism is still strong in many ways in our society and adolescent girls continue to experience sexism (Leaper and Spears-Brown, 2008), but young women growing up today have many opportunities in education, employment and leisure that their predecessors could only imagine.

Gender schemas influence how we interpret the behaviour of others and what we expect from them. This well-known story provides an example: 'A little boy and his father were in a terrible car accident. The father died, but the boy was rushed to the hospital. As the boy was rushed into surgery, the doctor looked down at him and said, 'I cannot operate on this boy – he is my son!''

How could the boy be the doctor's son, if the father died in the accident? The answer, of course, is that the doctor is the boy's *mother*. But people reading this story are often puzzled by it because their gender schemas have led them to assume the doctor was male. (This story is less effective than it used to be because many more women today are physicians. Try it on someone.) The story that began this chapter is another example. People typically assume the model is female and the photographer is male because their gender schemas lead them to this assumption, then they are surprised when they are wrong. We tend to notice information that fits within our gender schemas and ignore or dismiss information that is inconsistent with them (Helgeson, 2002).

Sandra Bem (1993; 1981), one of the foremost early proponents of gender schema theory, stresses that people apply gender schemas not just to the world around them but to themselves. Once they have learned gender schemas from their culture, they monitor their own behaviour and attitudes and shape them so that they conform to cultural definitions of what it means to be male or female. In this way, according to Bem, 'cultural myths become self-fulfilling prophecies' (1981, p. 355). Thus, Sandra Bem, like Lawrence Kohlberg, sees gender development as taking place in part through self-socialisation, as people strive to conform to the gender expectations they perceive in the culture around them.

THINKING CRITICALLY

Give an example of a custom complex – a cultural practice that reflects cultural beliefs – related to gender roles in your culture.

Masculinity, Femininity and Androgyny

'In our class, the guys and the girls had to switch roles for a day. We were supposed to try to imagine what it's like to be the other one and act that way. The guy I switched with said he thought it would be so much easier to be a girl, because you wouldn't have to worry about knowing what to do or have to be smooth and cool and all that crap . . . I just couldn't believe he was saying those things, because I always thought how much easier it would be to be a guy. You wouldn't have to worry about how you looked or how you acted. You could do whatever you felt like doing without worrying about your reputation. But he said, of course guys worry about their reputation, but it's the opposite kind of reputation. He said they have to put on this big act about how experienced they are … He worries that he won't do the right thing or say the right thing.'

– Penny, 17, (in Bell, 1998, p. 106)

The gender intensification of adolescence means that adolescents increasingly think of themselves and others in terms of what is masculine and what is feminine. But what sort of characteristics and behaviour do adolescent boys and girls see as being feminine or masculine? How is their evaluation of their own femininity and masculinity related to their overall sense of self?

Traits regarded by most members of majority cultures as masculine or feminine are shown in Table 5.1. These traits are taken from Sandra Bem's (Bem, 1974) Sex Role Inventory (BSRI), the most widely used measure of gender role perceptions. The BSRI was originally developed on the basis of university students' ratings of the traits most desirable for a man or woman but since it was developed similar responses have been obtained in studies of other age groups, including adolescents. A later cross-national study of young people in 30 countries found similar gender role perceptions across the countries, with remarkable consistency (Williams and Best, 1990).

The items in the scale show a clear pattern. In general terms, femininity is associated with being nurturing (sympathetic, compassionate, gentle, etc.) and compliant (yielding, soft-spoken, childlike, etc.). In contrast, masculinity is associated with being independent (self-reliant, self-sufficient, individualistic, etc.) and aggressive (assertive, forceful, dominant, etc.). The difference in traits associated with each gender role has been described by commentators as a contrast between the **expressive traits** ascribed to females and the **instrumental traits** ascribed to males (Yaremko and Lawson, 2007).

What adolescents view as masculine or feminine is also reflected in their gender ideals, that is, their views of what their ideal man or woman would be like. Psychologist Judith Gibbons has done cross-cultural studies of adolescents' gender ideals, indicating that adolescents in many different parts of the world have similar views. Gibbons and her colleagues (e.g. Gibbons and Stiles, 2004) have surveyed over 12,000 adolescents aged 11 to 19 in 20 countries around the world, including countries in Europe, Central America, Asia and Africa. In their survey, adolescents rate the importance of ten qualities as characteristics of the ideal man or woman.

In nearly all the countries, the most important and least important qualities for the ideal man and the ideal woman were not gender specific after all. The most important quality was being 'kind and honest'. In contrast, having a lot of money and being popular were rated low as ideal qualities, for both the ideal man and the ideal woman. However, some differences were seen in male and female gender ideals. In all countries it was considered more important for the ideal man to have a good job than for the ideal woman to have one. Also, in nearly all countries being good looking was viewed as more important for the ideal woman than for the ideal man. Generally, adolescent boys and girls had similar views of the ideal man and the ideal woman, but there were some differences. Girls were more likely than boys to think it was important for the ideal man to like children. Girls were also more likely to think it was important for the ideal woman to have a good job. In

CONNECT AND EXTEND

This paper investigates aspects of British-Chinese pupils' constructions of learning, focusing particularly on subject preferences and their constructions of themselves as pupils. Becky Francis and Louise Archer, 'British-Chinese pupils' constructions of gender and learning', *Oxford Review of Education*, Volume 31, Number 4 (2005), pp. 497–515

contrast, boys were more likely than girls to think it was important for the ideal woman to be good looking. Both the similarities and differences in adolescent girls' and boys' views of gender ideals are paralleled in cross-cultural findings of adults' gender ideals (e.g. Buss, 2001). But must we think of people as being either masculine or feminine? If an adolescent girl possesses 'feminine' traits, does that mean that she must be low on 'masculine' traits, and vice versa for boys? Some scholars have argued that the healthiest human personalities contain both masculine and feminine traits. **Androgyny** is the term for the combination of masculine and feminine traits in one person.

The idea of androgyny first became popular in the 1970s (e.g. Spence and Helmreich, 1978; Bem, 1977). The **women's movement** of the 1960s (see *Historical Focus* box) had led people in some European and North American cultures to reconsider ideas about male and female roles, and one outcome of this thinking was that it might be best to transcend the traditional opposition of masculine and feminine traits and instead promote the development of the best of each. In this view, there is no reason why a man could not be both independent ('masculine') and nurturing ('feminine'), or why a woman could not be both compassionate ('feminine') and ambitious ('masculine'). Androgynous persons would rate themselves highly on traits from both the 'feminine' column and the 'masculine' column in Table 5.1.

Advocates of androgyny have argued that being androgynous is better than being either masculine or feminine because androgynous persons have a greater repertoire of traits to draw on in their daily lives (Leszczynski and Strough, 2008). In a given situation, it might be better on some occasions to be gentle ('feminine') and on other occasions to be assertive ('masculine'). More generally, it might be best to be ambitious ('masculine') at work and affectionate ('feminine') at home. One study found that androgynous men and women tend to have higher 'emotional intelligence' than men and women who are more stereotypically masculine or feminine (Guastello and Guastello, 2003).

Table 5.1 Masculine and Feminine Traits (from Sandra Bem's Sex Role Inventory)

Masculine	Feminine
Self-reliant	Yielding
Defends own beliefs	Cheerful
Independent	Shy
Athletic	Affectionate
Assertive	Open to flattery
Strong personality	Loyal
Forceful	Feminine
Analytical	Sympathetic
Has leadership abilities	Sensitive to others
Willing to take risks	Understanding
Makes decisions easily	Compassionate
Self-sufficient	Eager to soothe hurt feelings
Dominant	Soft-spoken
Masculine	Warm
Willing to take a stand	Tender
Aggressive	Gullible
Acts as a leader	Childlike
Individualistic	Does not use harsh language
Competitive	Loves children
Ambitious	Gentle

Source: Bem (1974)

CONNECT AND EXTEND

What about ethical orientation? 'Girls and individuals high in femininity are higher on the ethic of care than are boys and individuals high in masculinity' – from the abstract. For a report of studies conducted to examine questions regarding the development of an ethic of care versus an ethic of justice, read 'Caring, gender role orientation and volunteering' by Rachel Karniol, Efrat Grosz and Irit Schorr in *Sex Roles*, Volume 49, Number 1–2 (2003), pp. 11–19

But what about adolescents? Is being predominantly androgynous best for them? Here the answer is more complex. In general, research evidence indicates that in adolescence, androgyny is more likely to be related to a positive self-image for girls than for boys. Androgynous girls generally have a more favourable self-image than girls who are either highly feminine or highly masculine, but highly masculine boys have more favourable self-images than boys who are feminine or androgynous (Strough et al., 2007; Karniol et al., 2003).

Why would this be the case? Probably because adolescents' views of themselves are a reflection of how they measure up to cultural expectations. Due in large part to the women's movement, people have become more favourable towards females who are androgynous. It is regarded more favourably now than it was 40 years ago for females to be ambitious, independent and athletic, and to possess other 'masculine' traits (Hicks, 1999; Coney and Mackey, 1997). However, males are still expected to avoid being soft-spoken and tender, or to exhibit other 'feminine' traits. Adolescents view themselves, and others, in terms of how they fit these cultural gender expectations. It is revealing that not only self-image but also peer acceptance is highest in adolescence among androgynous girls and masculine boys (Leszczynski and Strough, *ibid.*). Among young adults, too, androgynous females and masculine males are viewed favourably by peers, whereas males who violate gender norms are viewed negatively (Sirin et al., 2004). For both adolescents and young adults, their evaluations of gender-related behaviour reflect the expectations and values of their culture.

PROFESSIONAL FOCUS

Supporting Transgender Young People

Mirrors

Each time I look into a mirror,
I see a face look back at me.
Sometimes it's the face of a girl,
And sometimes it's a boy. Each face shows its sadness,
Each one shows its pain.
Both of them have their sorrow,
But one has room for Joy. I know some day that I must choose a face,
And live with it forever more.
But which one can joy live in?
Which one can I scorn?

– By Naimh, age 16 (Mermaids UK – Young Voices)

That's a heart-rending poem, but what is it about? Well, Aoife is identifying herself as transgender and it doesn't sound a comfortable experience. Transgender is a term used to describe those who self-identity their gender as a woman, man, neither or both that does not match the gender assigned at birth. It does not imply any form of sexual orientation but relates to combining or moving between conventional ideas of male and female gender characteristics and roles. Transgender is an umbrella term, popularly used by those and about those (particularly in the media, the academic world and the law – Sharpe, 2002) whose gender identity is not congruent with their gender assigned at birth (Monro and Warren, 2004).

It is worth noting that when referring to a transgender person it is better to use the person's preferred name and male/female noun regardless of their legal gender status; i.e. 'transgender' should be used as an adjective rather than a noun. For example, 'John is transgender' or 'John is a transgender man' rather than 'John is *a* transgender' (Monro, 2003).

This sounds straightforward enough but there remains a good deal of misunderstanding and suspicion about transgender. So much so that as many young people begin to form gender identities which are not compatible with their assigned gender, they feel unable to talk about their feelings with family or

From the *Mermaids* website. *Mermaids* is for children and teenagers under 19 years of age, who have gender identity issues. Note the label 'Me, I wish' for the middle person.

friends (Docter and Fleming, 2001). When adolescents feel unable to talk, then feelings of isolation and internal conflict are never far behind (Bosacki et al., 2007). Sometimes transgender youngsters will wait to 'come out' to their families until they are adults because they fear that if they come out earlier their parents will disapprove, will form a bad opinion of them, kick them out or take privileges away from them (Fiese and Skillman, 2000). It should be noted that some parents may be fully aware of their child's transgenderism because of the way she or he acts as they grow up, yet do not understand why their children are transgender. In an effort to make their children 'normal' they will often send them to therapy, as 'such things are just a phase' (Tasker and McCann, 1999). Of course, most mental health professionals recommend some form of therapy for those who suffer from internal conflicts regarding their gender identity or those who feel discomfort in their assigned gender role. However, research on gender identity is relatively new to psychology and clinical psychology practice (Hird, 2003).

Transgender people may be diagnosed as having **gender identity disorder** (GID) if being transgender causes particular forms of distress or disability (à Campo et al., 2003). This distress is referred to as **gender dysphoria** and may present to a clinician as depression related to an inability to work and form robust relationships with others. Such a diagnosis can be misinterpreted by parents or other family that being transgender means a person will necessarily suffer from GID (Wilson et al., 2002). This is not the case as transgender people who are comfortable with their gender, whose gender does not directly cause inner frustration, or impair their functioning, are much less likely to suffer from GID. Moreover, GID is not necessarily permanent, and is often resolved through therapy and/or undergoing a gender transition with hormone and surgical treatment (Weyers et al., 2012). Neither does a diagnosis of GID imply any moral dimension – any kind of mental or emotional problem is not a matter of moral judgement and the solution for GID is whatever will alleviate suffering and restore functionality (Manners, 2009).

Professionals working in the children's and young people's workforce will generally follow the foregoing advice and information and provide ongoing support and affirmation to young people who are in the process of 'coming out'. Adolescents and young people are often more open to advice, reassurance and social contact available online and can be safely directed to appropriate websites such as Mermaids. Mermaids is for children and teenagers under 19 years of age who have gender identity issues. The URL is **http://www.mermaidsuk.org.uk**.

Day by Day
I dread the next day
I have come to dread everyday
for each one I live
the life of another not mine
I can never live
the life that first meant for me
this life I now live
is a prison unfamiliar
my soul is now trapped
in bones it never knew and foreign flesh the torture never dies and my hopeless cries cover my smile now and forever

– by Brigitte, aged 17 (Mermaids UK – Young Voices)

CONNECT AND EXTEND

Adolescence is (hopefully) part of a much longer lifespan for most people. For a greater understanding of lifespan gender development read the excellent paper 'From adolescence to later adulthood: femininity, masculinity and androgyny in six age groups' by JoNell Strough, Jennifer Leszczynski, Tara Neely, Jennifer Flinn and Jennifer Margrett in *Sex Roles*, Volume 57, Numbers 5–6 (September 2007), pp. 385–396

These patterns of gender-related behaviour may also indicate that for boys, as for their counterparts in traditional cultures, manhood is a status that is more insecure and fraught with potential failure than womanhood is for girls, so that any mixing of masculine and feminine traits in their personalities is viewed as undesirable and threatening, by themselves and others. Some commentators have also argued that, despite the changes inspired by the women's movement, males continue to have higher status than females. Consequently, for a girl to act more 'like a boy' means that her self-image and status among peers improves because she associates herself with the higher-status group – males – whereas for a boy to act more 'like a girl' means that his self-image and peer status decline because he is associating himself with the lower-status group – females (Merten et al., 2008).

Gender Roles in Minority Groups

'In terms of the guys, one of the hardest things I see is they need to become tough. You have to save face, you have to argue it out. The lack of tolerance is much more pronounced [than among girls]. The readiness to fight has a lot to do with the environment of our schools and cities.'
– Teacher (Suarez-Orozco and Qin-Hilliard, 2004)

Gender roles in minority cultures differ in important ways from gender roles in the majority culture. What kinds of gender role socialisation takes place for young people in these cultures? Black adolescent girls tend to have higher self-esteem and less concern with physical appearance than do white girls (Basow and Rubin, 1999; Vasquez and de las Fuentes, 1999). One study found that black adolescent girls often critique and reject the ideals of female attractiveness presented in teen magazines (Duke, 2002), perhaps because female attractiveness in these magazines is predominantly white.

Two-thirds of British Muslims are ethnically Pakistani, Indian and Bangladeshi, but one-third come from diverse European, African, North African, Middle Eastern and other Asian sources. Despite this ethnic mix, Muslim gender roles as a whole emerge as an important factor of socio-economic vulnerability. Taken as a whole, the female Muslim population is young and rapidly growing; its socio-economic profile is depressed, marked by the exceptionally low participation rate of women in the formal labour market, and by high concentration in areas of social and economic deprivation (Peach, 2006).

According to some commentators, a consequence of historic humiliations of slavery and servitude – and the discrimination they experience today – is that many young black men adopt extreme characteristics of the male role in order to declare their masculinity (Stevenson, 2004). These characteristics include physical toughness, risk taking and aggressiveness. Some time ago Richard Majors (1989) described the 'cool pose' common to young black men in many city areas. The 'cool pose' is a set of language and behaviour intended to display strength, toughness and detachment. Behaviour can be both 'cool' and 'hot' – with hot behaviour leading to arguing and fighting, but also public performance (Hoggett, 2006). Cool behaviour can be demonstrated in creative, sometimes flamboyant dance, hip-hop or other forms of performance in a variety of settings, from the street corner to the classroom (Budasz, 2007). Of course, it is not just among young blacks that street performance is a sign of growing masculinity; this is also true of other young men including those from the Chinese and South Asian communities. These performances are meant to convey pride and confidence. According to Majors, this sometimes aggressive assertion of masculinity helps young black men – and those from other ethnic groups who wish to associate with the 'cool pose' – guard their self-esteem and their dignity. Majors (*ibid.*) refers to this in the title of his paper: 'Cool pose: the proud signature

Young black males sometimes adopt the 'cool pose' as a way of guarding against threats to their manhood.

of black survival'. However, the cool pose can be damaging to their relationships because it requires a refusal to express emotions or needs, which they fear would make them appear vulnerable.

Among Mediterranean cultures, gender roles have been highly traditional until recently, much along the lines of the traditional cultures described earlier in this chapter (Rivadeneyra and Ward, 2005; Vasquez and de las Fuentes, 1999). The role of women was concentrated on caring for children, taking care of the home and providing emotional support for the husband (Ortega, 2008). The Catholic Church has been very strong historically, and women have been taught to emulate the Virgin Mary by being submissive and self-denying (Cuffel, 2005); based upon Eve's (all women) 'responsibility' for leading Adam (all men) astray and the subsequent expulsion from the Garden of Eden (Clifton, 1999). The role of men, in contrast, has been guided by the ideology of **machismo**, which emphasises males' dominance over females. Men have been expected to be the undisputed head of the household and to demand respect and obedience from their wives and children. The traditional aspects of manhood have been strong in Mediterranean cultures – providing for a family, protecting the family from harm and procreating a large family (Arciniega et al., 2008).

However, in recent years evidence has emerged that gender expectations in the Mediterranean have begun to change, at least with respect to women's roles. Women are now employed outside the home at rates similar to Northern Europeans (Stickney and Konrad, 2007), and a feminist movement has emerged (Taylor et al., 2007; Denner and Guzman, 2006). This movement does not reject the traditional emphasis on the importance of the role of wife and mother, but seeks to value these roles while also expanding the roles available to all women. A recent study found that although adolescent girls are aware of the traditional gender expectations of their culture, they often strive to negotiate a less traditional and more complex and personal form of the female gender role in their relationships with family, peers and teachers (Denner and Dunbar, 2004). In rural and isolated communities such negotiation is not always easy, particularly when the goats need milking, feeding, breeding and grazing; the milk processing, the barn cleaning, stubble and pasture preparation – all activities performed by young women (Davran et al., 2009).

Like those from Mediterranean cultures, Asian adolescents have often received traditional gender role socialisation that their parents brought to Europe from their culture of origin (Francis and Archer, 2005). In addition, British Asians are subjected to media stereotypes of Asian women as submissive and 'exotic' (Lee and Vaught, 2003), and of Asian men as high in intelligence but poor at sports and less overtly masculine than other men. As a result of these stereotypes, Asian adolescent boys often experience a sense of gender role inferiority (Qin, 2009b; Sue, 2005).

Adolescents and young adults who are members of minority cultures are exposed not only to the gender roles of their own culture but also to the gender roles of the majority culture, through school, the media, and friends and peers who may be part of the majority culture. This may make it possible for young people in minority cultures to form a variety of possible gender concepts based on different blends of the gender roles in their minority culture and the gender roles of the larger society. However, moving towards the gender roles of the majority culture often results in conflict with parents who have more traditional views, especially for girls and especially concerning issues of independence, dating and sexuality (de las Fuentes and Vasquez, 1999; Qin, *ibid.*). We will discuss this issue further in the chapter on sexuality (Chapter 9).

CONNECT AND EXTEND

Adolescent 'voice' is defined by some writers as a function of ethnicity, attachment and gender role socialisation.' Intrigued? Then read 'Predictors of level of voice in adolescent girls: ethnicity, attachment and gender role socialization' by Sally Theran in the *Journal of Youth and Adolescence*, Volume 38, Number 8 (2009), pp. 1027–1037

Gender Stereotypes in Young Adulthood

Given the differential gender socialisation that people in society experience in childhood and adolescence, it should not be surprising to find that by the time they reach young adulthood they have different expectations for males and females. Most research on gender expectations in adulthood has been conducted by social psychologists, and because social psychologists often use university undergraduates as their research participants – a 'captive audience' – much of this research pertains to young adults' views of gender. Social psychologists have especially focused on gender stereotypes. A **stereotype** occurs when people believe others possess certain characteristics simply as a result of being a member of a particular group. Gender stereotypes, then, attribute certain characteristics to others simply on the basis of whether they are male or female (Kite et al., 2008). Gender stereotypes can be viewed as one aspect of gender schemas. Gender schemas include beliefs about objects (dresses are 'female') and activities (football is 'male') as well as people, but gender stereotypes are beliefs specifically about people.

One area of particular interest with regard to young adulthood is research on university students' gender stereotypes involving work. Generally, this research indicates that students often evaluate women's work performance less favourably than men's. In one classic and now historic study, Philip Goldberg (1968) asked women to evaluate the quality of several articles supposedly written by professionals in a variety of fields. Some of the articles were in stereotypically female fields such as diet, some were in stereotypically male fields such as city planning, and some were in gender-neutral fields. There were two identical versions of each article, one supposedly written by, for example, 'John McKay' and the other written by 'Joan McKay.' The results indicated that the women rated the articles more highly when they thought the author was a man. Even articles on the 'female' fields were judged as better when written by a man. Other studies have found similar results with samples of both male and female students (e.g. Cejka and Eagly, 1999). Recent studies have continued to find strong gender stereotypes related to work (S. K. Johnson et al., 2008; White and White, 2006).

THINKING CRITICALLY

Do you think your lecturers evaluate your work without regard to your gender? Does it depend on the subject area?

However, some studies have also found that when a person's behaviour violates stereotypical gender expectations, the result may be a 'boomerang effect' that works in their favour (Granato et al., 2008; Perkinson, 2004). In one early study, university students were presented with photographs supposedly taken by finalists in two photography contests, one for football and one for tennis (Heilman et al., 1988). Some students were told the photographs were taken by a female finalist, and some were told they were taken by a male finalist; actually, both groups of students were shown the same photographs. In the football photography contest, photos supposedly taken by females were evaluated more highly than photos supposedly taken by males, whereas in the tennis photography contest no gender-related difference in evaluations was found. Because football (unlike tennis) is strongly associated with the male gender role, the researchers concluded that the females in the football contest were **over evaluated** because they had violated gender role expectations. These findings show that gender-related evaluations of performance can be complicated, and often depend on the specific characteristics of the person and on the specific area in which the person is being evaluated.

Gender-related evaluations may also depend on the age of the evaluator. As noted, most studies in this area have been done exclusively on university students, but one more recent study compared males who were early adolescents, late adolescents or university students (Lobel et al., 2004). Participants were given a description of either an average or outstanding male election candidate behaving gender stereotypically or counter-stereotypically and were asked to indicate their personal election choice, the likelihood that others would choose each candidate, and how successful the candidate would be if he were elected. Adolescents were more likely than the young adult students to favour the gender-stereotypical candidate. No differences were found between the two stages of adolescence. This suggests that gender stereotypes may wane from adolescence to young adulthood.

The Persistence of Beliefs About Gender Differences

Although some gender differences exist in adolescence and young adulthood with respect to various aspects of development, for the most part the differences are not large. Even when a statistically significant difference exists between males and females, for most characteristics there is nevertheless more similarity than difference between the genders. For example, even if it is true overall that adolescent girls are emotionally closer to their parents than adolescent boys,

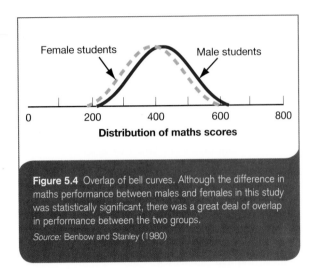

Figure 5.4 Overlap of bell curves. Although the difference in maths performance between males and females in this study was statistically significant, there was a great deal of overlap in performance between the two groups.

Source: Benbow and Stanley (1980)

there are nevertheless many adolescent boys who are closer to their parents than the typical adolescent girl.

Most human characteristics fall into something resembling what is called a **normal distribution** or a **bell curve**; that is, a small proportion of people rate much higher than most other people, a small proportion rate much lower than most people, but most people fall somewhere in the middle, somewhere around average. Think of height as an example. You may have a friend who is 4 foot 10 inches and another friend who is 6 feet 10 inches, but most of the people you know are probably between 5 foot 2 inches and 6 feet tall.

The point, with regard to gender, is that even when gender differences exist between males and females, for most characteristics the portion of the two bell curves which overlaps is much greater than the portion that is distinctive to either gender. (The same is true for children and adults as well as adolescents.) For example, Figure 5.4 shows the distribution of male and female adolescents from a famous study that found a significant gender difference in mathematics performance (Benbow and Stanley, 1980). As you can see, the two distributions overlap far more than they differ. When people hear that 'adolescent boys do better at maths than adolescent girls', they tend to think of the two distributions as mostly or entirely separate, without realising that the similarity between the genders is actually greater than the difference between them. Indeed, whenever you read about studies reporting gender differences (including in this textbook), keep in mind that the distributions of males and females usually overlap a great deal (e.g. Escriche, 2007; Itakura and Tsui, 2004; Wodarz et al., 2003).

Why, then, do so many stereotypes about gender persist? Why do so many people continue to think of the genders as radically different in many ways, as 'opposite' sexes? Two reasons can be offered. One reason stems from the development of gender schemas. Gender

schemas tend to shape the way we notice, interpret and remember information according to our expectations about the genders. Once we have formed ideas about how males and females are different, we tend to notice events and information that confirm our expectations and disregard or dismiss anything that does not. In several studies (building on an early study by social psychologist Carol Martin, 1987) subjects recalled gender-stereotyped people and activities better than those that were non-stereotyped, and this tendency was strongest for those who already possessed the strongest gender stereotypes (e.g. Klauer et al., 2002; Bell, 2001; Coats and Smith, 1999). Also, studies have found that when adolescents and young mothers are shown girls and boys performing an equal number of gender-stereotyped and non-gender-stereotyped play behaviours, they consistently overestimate the number of gender-stereotyped behaviours performed (Yu et al., 2010; Wilansky-Traynor and Lobel, 2008). These studies illustrate how our gender schemas draw our attention to examples that confirm our expectations, so that we perceive the behaviour of others to be more gender consistent than it actually is.

A second reason for the persistence of our beliefs about gender differences in capabilities is that the social roles of men and women seem to confirm those beliefs. According to **social roles theory**, social roles for males and females enhance or suppress different capabilities (Eagly et al., 2004). Differential gender socialisation leads males and females to develop different skills and attitudes, which leads to different behaviours. The differences in behaviour seem to confirm the appropriateness of the different roles (Davies-Netzley, 2002).

For example, caring for children is seen as part of the female gender role in most European majority cultures: girls are given dolls as children, and many are given some responsibility for caring for younger siblings. When they reach early adolescence, girls learn that babysitting is one of the options available to them as a way to earn money; boys, in contrast, learn that babysitting is something girls do but not boys. When they reach young adulthood, women are more likely than men to enter childcare as a profession, perhaps including studying early childhood education at university. When they have children of their own, young women are also more likely than young men to devote themselves to full-time care of their own children.

Thus, as a consequence of differential gender socialisation, and because girls grow up seeing childcare as a possible future role but boys do not, girls are more likely to develop skills and attitudes that involve caring for children. As a result of developing these skills and attitudes, they are more capable of and more interested in devoting themselves to childcare in their personal and professional lives as adolescents and

CONNECT AND EXTEND

To explore the association between early adolescents' gender-role identity and sense of peer group acceptance, read 'Gender-role identity and perceived peer group acceptance among early adolescents in Belgian mixed and single-sex schools' by Herman Brutsaert in *Gender and Education*, Volume 18, Number 6 (2006), pp. 635–649

young adults. The different behaviour of women and men regarding childcare confirms cultural beliefs that women are 'naturally' more loving and nurturing than men. So, we see males and females doing different things, and we conclude that it must be because they are inherently different, overlooking the way their behaviour has been shaped by differential gender socialisation and by the social roles offered by their culture. It could be argued that young men, even if drawn to studying early childhood education at university with a view to professional engagement in the future, would find such a decision less acceptable to their peer group, as this may have been their experience at school.

THINKING CRITICALLY

Consider the overlapping bell curves of mathematics scores in adolescence. Then use social roles theory to explain why so few women are in fields such as engineering and architecture.

GENDER AND GLOBALISATION

As today's adolescents grow into adulthood, what kind of world will they face in terms of gender roles? In most of Europe adolescent girls today have opportunities that were unknown to women in previous eras of 'Western' history. Formal prohibitions no longer exist to women becoming doctors, lawyers, professors, engineers, accountants, athletes or anything else they wish. However, as we have seen in this chapter, it is not quite that simple. Direct and indirect gender role socialisation often steers adolescent girls away from maths- and science-oriented careers. Nevertheless, statistics show definite signs of change. The proportion of females in fields such as medicine, business and law is considerably higher than 20 years ago (Soethout et al., 2008; Umans et al., 2008; Worthington and Higgs, 2003) and is remarkable compared with 50 or 100 years ago. Whether similar changes will occur in male-dominated fields such as engineering and architecture is difficult to predict. However, women tend to earn less money than men even when they are doing similar work (see Chapter 11), which shows that gender equality has a way to go.

For the most part adolescent girls in traditional cultures have much less in the way of educational and occupational opportunities, not only compared with boys in their own countries but compared with girls in the West. In most developing countries, adolescent girls are considerably less likely than adolescent boys to go to secondary school (UNDP 2009; Mensch et al., 1998) because adolescents' education requires families to sacrifice the labour of an otherwise potentially productive adolescent (and sometimes families must also pay for the schooling). Families tend to be less willing to make this sacrifice for adolescent girls than for adolescent boys, in part because girls tend to leave the household after marriage, whereas boys

CONNECT AND EXTEND

'While the process of "learning to think like a lawyer" retains traditionally male attributes, women students clearly learn this cognitive style competently.' Read 'Thinking like a lawyer: gender differences in the production of professional knowledge' by Debra Schleef in *Gender Issues*, Volume 19, Number 2 (March 2001), pp. 69–86

RESEARCH FOCUS

R

Meta-analyses of Gender Differences

Conducting research on adolescence and young adulthood usually means collecting data through methods such as questionnaires or interviews. However, sometimes a scholar will approach a research question by taking data that other scholars have collected in a variety of studies and combining it into one analysis to obtain an overview of studies in an area. **Meta-analysis** is the term for the statistical technique that integrates the data from many studies into one comprehensive statistical analysis. This technique has been used frequently in research on gender differences (e.g. White and Gardner, 2009; Grabe et al., 2008; Geer and Robertson, 2005; Lanvers, 2004) including gender differences in adolescence (e.g. Stams et al., 2006). Meta-analysis is used more often in research on gender than in most other areas, partly because so many studies have been published on gender differences. However, it can be used on any topic for which numerous studies exist.

A meta-analysis indicates whether a difference exists between groups (e.g. males and females) and also indicates the size of the difference. The difference between the groups is called the **effect size**, and it is usually represented by the letter d. In a meta-analysis, the effect size is computed for each study by subtracting the mean of one group (e.g. females) from the mean of the other group (e.g. males) and then dividing the result by the within-group standard deviation for the two groups combined (e.g. Yost et al., 2005). The within-group standard deviation is a measure of how much variability exists within each group. The convention in these analyses is that $d \leq 0.2$ indicates a small effect size, d of around 0.5 a medium effect size, and $d \geq 0.8$ a large effect size (Cohen et al., 2007). First, d is calculated for each study, and then the ds are mean averaged across all the studies included in the meta-analysis.

Table 5.2 shows the results of an early but important meta-analysis of gender differences on mathematics achievement tests for 13-year-old adolescents in 19 countries. As you can see, for the most part the effect sizes are very small – only three of the studies found an effect size above 0.2 in favour of males, and only one found an effect size above 0.2 in favour of females. Overall, the average effect size for the seven countries where boys' performance was significantly better than girls was 0.18, and the average effect size for the four countries where girls' performance was significantly better than boys was 0.16. Thus, the meta-analysis provides a useful overview of cross-national gender differences on maths performance and shows that, overall, the differences between boys' and girls' performance in mathematics at 13 are small and inconsistent.

Table 5.2 National Sex Differences on Mathematics Test of 13-year-olds

Country	Mean for boys	Mean for girls	X_M–X_F difference	Effect Size
Superior performance of boys				
France	17.02	14.18	2.84*	.37
Israel	18.79	17.74	1.05*	.11
Luxembourg	13.34	11.74	1.60*	.25
Netherlands	22.00	20.23	1.77*	.17
New Zealand	14.60	13.51	1.09*	.10
Ontario, Canada	17.72	16.94	.78*	.08
Swaziland	9.29	7.89	1.40*	.21

Table 5.2 *Continued*

Country	Mean for boys	Mean for girls	X_M–X_F difference	Effect Size
Equal performance				
British Columbia	19.55	19.27	.28	.03
England & Wales	15.38	14.92	.46	.04
Hong Kong	16.59	16.09	.50	.05
Japan	23.84	23.80	.04	.004
Nigeria	9.50	9.05	.45	.07
Scotland	16.83	16.68	.15	.01
Sweden	10.70	11.18	−.48	−.06
United States	14.98	15.12	−.14	−.01
Superior performance of girls				
Belgium (French)	19.44	20.54	−1.10*	−.12
Finland	13.24	14.87	−1.63*	−.17
Hungary	22.36	23.62	−1.26*	−.13
Thailand	12.09	14.16	−2.07*	−.22

*Indicates female and male scores were significantly different according to an *F* test, p < .01 (a test of how well different data fits into the meta data set). Note effect sizes, which are all in the small range.

Source: Baker and Perkins-Jones (1993)

often remain within the household or nearby as part of a close extended family.

However, such discrimination against girls may change as globalisation proceeds and traditional cultures become increasingly industrialised and connected to the global economy. Traditional gender roles are often rooted partly in biological differences that determine the kind of work that men and women can perform in a pre-industrial economy. Men's greater size and strength gives them advantages in work such as hunting and fishing. Women's biological capacity for childbearing restricts their roles mainly to childbearing and childrearing. When they are unable to control their reproductive lives through contraception, they spend most of their late teens, 20s and 30s either pregnant or nursing.

As economies become more developed and complex, brain matters more than brawn and men's physical advantage does not apply to work that involves analysing and processing information. Economic development

In traditional cultures, boys are more likely than girls to be able to attend secondary school. Here is a school in Pakistan.

also usually includes increased access to contraception; in turn, access to contraception makes women's adult roles less focused on childbearing and childrearing alone. Because traditional cultures are likely to continue to move further in the direction of economic development, their gender roles are likely to become more egalitarian as well. There is some evidence that this change is taking place internationally, although it is happening slowly (UNDP, *ibid.*). Yet there is evidence over the last 15 years that adolescents may lead the way. Studies report that adolescents in developing countries have fewer conservative perceptions of gender roles than adults do (e.g. UNDP, *ibid.*; Mensch et al., 1998).

SUMMING UP

In this chapter we have examined theories and research concerning the significance of gender in development during adolescence and young adulthood. The information in this chapter provides an introduction to many issues concerning gender that will be explored in more detail in the chapters to come. The main points of the chapter are as follows:

- In traditional cultures gender roles tend to be sharply divided, and during adolescence boys' and girls' daily lives are often separate. Girls spend their time with adult women learning skills important for childcare and running a household, whereas boys learn the skills necessary for the requirements of the male role: provide, protect and procreate.

- In earlier periods of European history, adolescent girls were constricted in many ways, but they also benefited from a 'protective umbrella' of involvement and concern by adult women. Ideals of manhood have also changed in the course of history, from 'communal manhood' to 'self-made manhood' to the 'passionate manhood' that is the current ideal.

- In European society today, boys and girls receive differential gender socialisation from birth, and gender-related socialisation pressures intensify at adolescence. Research shows that pressures to conform to gender expectations come from the family, peers and teachers. For girls, the magazines they like best relentlessly emphasise physical appearance.

- The cognitive-developmental theory of gender and gender schema theory state that we tend to organise our perceptions of the world according to schemas of male and female, and we categorise a wide range of behaviour and objects on this basis.

- Research indicates that there is a widespread tendency across cultures to classify some traits as 'feminine' and others as 'masculine'. Androgyny is the term for combining 'feminine' and 'masculine' traits within one person. Among adolescents, androgyny tends to be acceptable for girls but not for boys.

- Among young adults, gender stereotypes sometimes lead them to evaluate women's work less favourably than men's. However, gender stereotypes appear to be weaker in young adulthood than in adolescence.

- Although research generally finds few substantial differences between males and females in most respects, perceptions of gender differences persist, partly because gender schemas are resistant to change once established and partly because males' and females' social roles seem to confirm stereotypes about gender differences in some respects.

- Views of gender have changed substantially in the past century and are likely to change in developing countries in the future as a result of economic development and globalisation.

Theories and research have established quite well how gender socialisation takes place and have identified the specific influences in adolescence that promote conformity to gender expectations. The evidence also portrays quite vividly the costs that gender expectations exact from adolescents and young adults. For girls, the emphasis on physical appearance in adolescence is a frequent source of anxiety and distress. Also, girls are sometimes dissuaded from pursuing certain high-status, high-paying educational and occupational paths because they learn to regard these paths as incompatible with being female; as young adults, their work may be regarded less favourably simply because they are female. In traditional cultures, girls are often excluded even from opportunities to attend secondary school.

Adolescent boys face different sorts of gender-based restrictions and obstacles, no less daunting. Boys in traditional cultures have to achieve manhood by developing the required skills for providing, protecting and procreating. The price of failing to meet these requirements is humiliation and rejection. In the West, gender socialisation pressures on boys are less formal but nevertheless formidable. Whatever their personal inclinations, adolescent boys must learn to use verbal and physical aggressiveness to defend themselves against insults to their manhood from other boys. Adolescent boys who cross the gender divide and display 'feminine' traits such as sensitivity to the feelings of others risk ridicule and rejection, like their counterparts in traditional cultures.

You might wonder, given the negatives associated with gender socialisation in adolescence and young adulthood, and given the limitations that gender roles place on the development of young people's potentials, why gender socialisation is so highly emphasised and why conformity to gender roles is so highly valued across virtually all cultures and across history as well. Perhaps the answer lies in the ways that gender roles provide us with schemas, with frameworks for understanding how the world works. As they reach sexual maturity, adolescents and young adults are especially eager for information about what their potential mates may find attractive. Gender schemas and gender roles provide them with that information.

Although beliefs about gender may be useful in some ways for making sense of the world, they can also be misleading because they oversimplify the complexity of real life. Remember that any statement about gender differences involves comparing 3 billion of the world's people to the other 3 billion. Although overall differences exist between males and females, there is also a tremendous amount of variability within each group on nearly every characteristic. As you think about gender issues in your own life, as you read social science research, and as you read this book, any time you find broad statements about gender characteristics – males are more [fill in the blank] than females, females are more [fill in the blank] than males – it would be wise to keep this in mind and approach such statements with a critical eye.

At this point, we know relatively little about how young people themselves perceive the gender socialisation process. Future studies may investigate this question and it would be especially interesting to investigate this question with both adolescents and young adults. We have discussed young adulthood as a period when explorations of worldviews are common and when critical-thinking skills are more developed than in adolescence. Does this mean that some young adults may begin to question the gender expectations of their culture? Do young adults feel less constricted by gender roles and more comfortable with androgyny? Or is this true of only some young adults, in some peer groups, in some cultures?

INTERNET RESOURCES

www.unece.org
Contains the Gender Statistics Database for the United Nations Economic Commission for Europe. Provides gender-related statistics on topics such as education and family.

http://www.un.org/esa/socdev/unyin/wyr07.htm
Contains the 2009 *World Youth Report* published by the United Nations Department of Economic and Social Affairs, which includes abundant information on gender issues concerning adolescents in developing countries.

http://www.transgenderzone.com/transpanic.htm
Weblinks and emergency phone numbers to many UK-based organisations working to support transgender people who doubt themselves or suffer low self-esteem and moments of panic.

FURTHER READING

J. L. Gibbons, and D. A. Stiles, *The Thoughts of Youth: An International Perspective on Adolescents' Ideal Persons*. Greenwich, CT: IAP Information Age Publishing (2004).

Presents results of the author's 21-country study of adolescents' view of the ideal man and woman. The authors' methods included the creative approach of having the adolescents draw pictures of their ideal man and woman, and they present many of those drawings in the book.

D. Gilmore, *Manhood in the Making: Cultural Concepts of Masculinity.* New Haven, CT: Yale University Press (1990).

Gilmore's superb account of the gender expectations for adolescent boys in a variety of traditional, non-industrialised cultures.

For more reviews plus practice tests, case studies and responses to the *Critical Thinking* features, log on to **www.pearsoned. co.uk/arnett.**

CHAPTER 6
THE SELF

OUTLINE

The Catcher in the Rye (1951/1964) by J. D. Salinger is probably the best-known classic novel of adolescence and continues to be widely read and studied in schools and colleges. It consists entirely of one long self-reflective monologue by the main character, Holden Caulfield. Holden is talking to someone, but we never learn who the person is – a psychologist, perhaps? He gives a long narrative about a dramatic 24-hour period of his life. It begins when he abruptly leaves the school where he had been enrolled, feeling alienated from his schoolmates, sick to death at what he perceives as their hypocrisy and shallowness. Afraid to go home – this is not the first time he has had trouble at school – he instead goes into the city, where he has a series of misadventures, culminating in a physical and psychological collapse.

Holden tells the whole complicated (and often hilarious) story to the reader through the course of the book. However, it is not really the events that are the focus of Holden's tale but Holden himself. It is about his attempts to understand who he is and how he fits into the world around him, a world he finds confusing, bruising, and sad. He is reluctant to move towards entering the adult world, because nearly all adults seem to him to be pathetic or corrupt. He much prefers the world of children. Throughout the book he expresses his tender and perhaps romanticised view of their innocence and sweetness. His growing self-awareness has come as an unpleasant shock, because in his view it has jarred him out of the Eden of his childhood innocence.

HOLDEN IS NOT A TYPICAL ADOLESCENT. it is his atypical sensitivity and wit that make him such a compelling character in *The Catcher in the Rye*. Nevertheless, he provides a good example of how issues of the self come to the forefront of development in adolescence. He engages in self-reflection about his maturity, or lack of it ('I act quite young for my age . . . '). He evaluates himself, sometimes negatively ('I'm a terrific liar . . .'). He has moments of elation, but more moments of loneliness and sadness, in which he broods about death and the cruelties of life. He tries to work out issues of identity, of who he is and what he wants out of life, concluding – at least for now – that the only future which appeals to him is the imaginary one of being the 'catcher in the rye', the guardian of playing children.

The issues Holden confronts in his monologue are the kinds of issues we will address in this chapter on 'the self'. As we saw in Chapter 3 on cognitive development, moving into adolescence results in new capacities for self-reflection. Adolescents can think about themselves in a way that younger children cannot. The ability for abstract thinking that develops in adolescence includes asking abstract questions about one's self, such as 'What kind of person am I? What characteristics make me who I am? What am I good at, and not so good at? How do other people perceive me? What kind of life am I likely to have in the future?' Younger children can ask these questions, too, but only in a rudimentary way. With adolescents' growing cognitive capacities, they can now ask these questions of themselves more readily, and they can come up with answers that are more complex and insightful.

This enhanced cognitive capacity for self-reflection has a variety of consequences. It means that adolescents change in their *self-conceptions*, that is, in their answers to the question 'What kind of person am I?' It means that adolescents change in their *self-esteem*, that is, in their capacity for evaluating their fundamental worth as a person. It means that adolescents change in their *emotional understanding*, as they become more aware of their own emotions and as their enhanced understanding of themselves and others affects their daily emotional lives. It also means that adolescents change in their *identities*, that is, in their perceptions of their capacities and characteristics and how these fit into the opportunities available to them in their society. All of these changes continue through emerging adulthood, but identity issues are especially central to emerging adulthood, even more than in adolescence in many respects.

We will discuss each of these aspects of the self in this chapter, and end with a look at young people's experiences and states of mind when they are alone. First, however, we consider the cultural approach to concepts of the self. Although self-reflection increases in adolescence as a part of normal cognitive development, the culture young people live in has profound effects on how they experience this change.

CULTURE AND THE SELF

The general distinction introduced in Chapter 4, between individualistic and collectivistic cultures, and between broad socialisation values and narrow socialisation values, comes into play in considerations of the self, and perhaps especially on this topic. As noted in Chapter 4, in discussing cultural differences in conceptions of the self, scholars typically distinguish between the *independent self* promoted by individualistic cultures and the *interdependent self* promoted by collectivistic cultures (Shweder et al., 2006; Cross and Gore, 2003).

Cultures that promote an independent, individualistic self also promote and encourage reflection about the self. In such cultures it is seen as a good thing to think about yourself, to consider who you are as an independent person, and to think highly of yourself (within certain limits, of course – no culture values selfishness or egocentrism). This outlook is most common in the West where it is considered that all that exists consists of genuinely separate individuals – referred to as *dualism* by some writers (Chimisso, 2003; Ramp, 2003), although the term dualism is also used to conceptualise two distinct aspects of one idea (e.g. Gimenez, 2007; King, 2007). Many European countries continue to be known to the rest of the world as a place where the independent self is valued and promoted (Green et al., 2005).

However, not all cultures look at the self in this way, and value the self to the same extent. In collectivistic cultures – non-dualist (Chimisso, *ibid.*) characterised by narrow socialisation, an interdependent conception of the self prevails. In these cultures, the interests of the group – the family, the kinship group, the ethnic group, the nation, the religious institution – are supposed to come first, before the needs of the individual. This means that it is not necessarily a good thing, in

CONNECT AND EXTEND

For a comprehensive survey of differences in cultural individualism – and a reminder of the issues raised in Chapter 4 – read 'Variation of individualism and collectivism within and between 20 countries: a typological analysis' by E. G. T. Green, Jean-Claude Deschamps and D. Páez, in the *Journal of Cross-Cultural Psychology*, Volume 36 (2005), 321–339

these cultures, to think highly of yourself. People who think highly of themselves, who possess a high level of self-esteem, threaten the harmony of the group because they may be inclined to pursue their personal interests regardless of the interests of the groups to which they belong.

Thus, children and adolescents in these cultures are socialised to mute their self-esteem and to learn to consider the interests and needs of others to be at least as important as the interests and needs of themselves (Lalonde and Chandler, 2004). By adolescence, the 'self' is thought of not so much as a separate, independent being, essentially apart from others, but as *defined by* relationships with others, to a large extent (Kundu and Adams, 2005). This is what it means for the self to be interdependent rather than independent (Nishikawa et al., 2007). In the perspective of these cultures, the self cannot be understood apart from social roles and obligations.

We will learn in more detail about different ways of thinking about the self as we move along in this chapter. Throughout the chapter, keep in mind that cultures vary in the way their members are socialised to think about the self.

THINKING CRITICALLY

Based on what you have learned so far in this book, what would you say are the economic or political reasons traditional cultures would promote an interdependent self?

SELF-CONCEPTIONS

Adolescents think about themselves differently than younger children do, in a variety of respects. The changes in self-understanding that occur in adolescence have their foundation in the more general changes in cognitive functioning discussed in Chapter 3. Specifically, adolescent self-conceptions, like adolescent cognitive development overall, become more *abstract* and more *complex*.

More Abstract

'The hardest thing is coming to grips with who you are, accepting the fact that you're not perfect – but then doing things anyway. Even if you are really good at something or a really fine person, you also know that there's so much you aren't. You always know all the things you don't know and all the things you can't do. And however much you can fool the rest of the world, you always know how much bullshit a lot of it is.'
– Nan, age 17 (in Bell, 1998, p. 78)

According to psychologist Susan Harter (1999; 2006), with increasing age children describe themselves less in concrete terms ('I have a dog named Buster and a sister named Carrie') and more in terms of their traits ('I'm quite clever, but also a bit shy'). For adolescents, self-conceptions become still more trait-focused, and the traits become more abstract, as they describe themselves in terms of intangible personality characteristics. For example, one 15-year-old girl in an earlier study by Dr Harter on self-conceptions described herself as follows:

'What am I like as a person? Complicated! I'm sensitive, friendly, outgoing, popular, and tolerant, though I can also be shy, self-conscious, even obnoxious. . . . I'm a pretty cheerful person, especially with my friends. . . . At home I'm more likely to be anxious around my parents.
(Harter, 1990, p. 352)

Notice the use of all the abstractions. 'Sensitive'. 'Outgoing'. 'Cheerful'. 'Anxious'. Adolescents' capacity for abstraction makes these kinds of descriptions possible.

One aspect of this capacity for abstraction in adolescents' self-conceptions is that they can distinguish between an **actual self** and **possible selves** (Oyserman and Fryberg, 2006; Whitty, 2002). Scholars distinguish two kinds of possible selves, an ideal self and a feared self (Westenberg et al., 2004; Knox et al., 2000). The **ideal self** is the person the adolescent would like to be (for example, an adolescent may have an ideal of becoming highly popular with peers or highly successful in sport or music). The **feared self** is the person the adolescent imagines it is possible to become but dreads becoming (for example, an adolescent might fear becoming a 'loner' or victim, or fear becoming like a disgraced relative or friend). Both kinds of possible selves require adolescents to think abstractly. That is, possible selves exist only as abstractions, as *ideas* in the adolescent's mind.

The capacity for thinking about an actual, an ideal and a feared self is a cognitive achievement, but this capacity may be troubling in some respects. If you can imagine an ideal self, you can also become aware of the discrepancy between your actual self and your ideal self, between what you are and what you wish you were. If the discrepancy is large enough, it can result in feelings of failure, inadequacy and depression. Studies over a decade or so found that the size of the discrepancy between the actual and ideal self is related to depressed mood in both adolescents and emerging adults (e.g. Romens et al., 2009; Moretti and Wiebe, 1999). Furthermore, the discrepancy between the actual and the ideal self is greater in mid-adolescence than in either early or late adolescence (Sweeting et al., 2006). This helps explain why depression is very rare before adolescence, but rates of depressed mood rise in early adolescence (Broderick and Korteland, 2004) and peak in middle adolescence (Kosunen et al., 2003).

However, awareness of actual and possible selves provides some adolescents with a motivation to strive towards their ideal self and avoid becoming the feared self (Oyserman and Fryberg, 2006; Cota-Robles et al., 2000). One study of an intervention, designed to encourage adolescents to develop an academic possible self, found that among the adolescents in the intervention academic initiative and grades improved while depression and school misbehaviour declined, compared to the control group (Oyserman et al., 2006).

Emerging adults, too, are often inspired by the vision of a possible self. In fact, one of the distinctive features of emerging adulthood mentioned in Chapter 1 is that it is the 'age of possibilities' (Arnett, 2004). In one Australian study (Whitty, 2002), early emerging adulthood (ages 17–22) was found to be a time of 'grand dreams' of being wealthy and having a glamorous occupation, but beyond emerging adulthood (ages 28–33) the visions of a possible self became more realistic, if still optimistic.

Most scholars who have studied this topic see it as healthiest for adolescents to possess both an ideal self and a feared self. Studies that compared delinquent adolescents to other adolescents found that the non-delinquent adolescents tended to have this balance between an ideal self and a feared self. In contrast, the delinquent adolescents possessed a feared self but were less likely than other adolescents to have a clear conception of an ideal self to strive for (Horne, 2004).

More Complex

A second aspect of adolescents' self-understanding is that it becomes more complex. Again, this is based on a more general cognitive attainment, the formal operational ability to perceive multiple aspects of a situation or idea. Self-conceptions become more complex especially from early adolescence to middle adolescence as 'new' aspects of self image, particularly body image, attain greater importance (Meland et al., 2007) and middle adolescents become subject to programmes of social and emotional training (Kimber et al., 2008; Spence, 2003).

Contradictions in personalities and behaviour can be confusing to adolescents, as they try to sort out 'the real me' from the different aspects of themselves that appear in different situations (Kroger, 2004). However, adolescents' contradictory descriptions do not necessarily mean that they are confused about which of the

CONNECT AND EXTEND

To examine gender differences between adolescents' *possible selves* read the appropriately entitled paper 'Gender differences in adolescents' possible selves' by M. Knox, J. Funk, R. Elliott and E.G. Bush in *Youth & Society*, Volume 31, Number 3 (March 1, 2000), pp. 287–309

Adolescents are more likely than children to show a false self to new friends.

two contradictory descriptions apply to their actual selves. To some extent, the contradictions indicate that adolescents, more than younger children, recognise that their feelings and their behaviour can vary from day to day and from situation to situation (Samuels and Casebeer, 2005). Rather than simply saying 'I'm shy' as a younger child might, an adolescent might say 'I'm shy when I'm around people I don't really know, but when I'm with my friends I can go crazy.'

A related aspect of the increasing complexity of self-conceptions is that adolescents become aware of times when they are exhibiting a **false self**, a self that they present to others while realising that it does not represent what they are actually thinking and feeling (Holinger, 2009; Harter, 2002). With whom would you think adolescents would be most likely to exhibit their false selves – friends, parents or boy/girlfriends? Susan Harter's research indicates that adolescents are most likely to put on their false selves with dating partners, and least likely with their close friends, with parents in between. Most adolescents in Harter's research indicate that they sometimes dislike putting on a false self, but many also say that some degree of false self behaviour is acceptable and even desirable, to impress someone or to conceal aspects of the self they do not want others to see.

THINKING CRITICALLY

Why do you think a false self is most likely to be shown to dating partners? Would the false self be gradually discarded as the dating partner becomes a more long-term boyfriend or girlfriend, or not?

SELF-ESTEEM

Self-esteem is a person's overall sense of worth and well-being. **Self-image**, **self-concept** and **self-perception** are closely related terms, referring to the way people view and evaluate themselves. A great deal has been written and discussed about self-esteem in the past 50 years in developmental psychology texts, especially concerning adolescents. In the 1960s and 1970s, self-esteem enhancement programmess for young people became popular, based on the idea that making children and adolescents 'feel better about themselves' would have a variety of positive effects on other aspects of functioning, such as school achievement and relationships with peers (DuBois, 2003; DuBois and Tevendale, 1999). Over the last 30 years, particular concern has developed about self-esteem among girls and about abundant evidence showing that girls often experience a drop in self-esteem as they enter adolescence (e.g. Currie et al., 2006; Wills et al., 2006; Mahaffy, 2004; Knox et al., 2000).

As previously discussed in Chapter 4 and at the start of this chapter, there is a cultural focus on self-esteem in Western society (Green et al., 2005) that has led to a considerable amount of research on adolescent self-esteem by European and American scholars in recent decades. This research has shed light on a number of issues, including changes in self-esteem in pre-adolescence and adolescence, different aspects of self-esteem, self-esteem and physical appearance, and influences on self-esteem.

Self-esteem in Pre-adolescence and Adolescence

Several longitudinal studies of self-esteem (e.g. Robins et al., 2002; Harter, 2006) have followed groups of youngsters during pre-adolescence and adolescence or from adolescence throughout emerging adulthood, and these studies generally find that self-esteem declines in early adolescence, then rises through late adolescence and emerging adulthood. A number of developmental reasons explain why self-esteem might follow this pattern. The 'imaginary audience' that we have discussed as part of adolescents' cognitive development can make them self-conscious in a way that decreases their self-esteem when they first experience it in early adolescence (Rose et al., 2008; J. R. Chambers et al., 2003). That is, as adolescents develop the capacity to imagine that others are especially conscious of how they

CONNECT AND EXTEND

In a study of adolescents M. Knox, J. Funk, R. Elliott and E. G. Bush found it was more acceptable for girls to work hard and still be part of the 'in crowd', while boys were under greater pressure to conform to a 'cool', masculine image, and were more likely to be ridiculed for working hard. Read 'Student attitudes, image and the gender gap', *British Educational Research Journal*, Volume 26, Number 3 (2000), pp. 393–407

look and what they say and how they act, they may suspect or fear that others are judging them harshly.

They may be right. Adolescents in Western cultures tend to be strongly peer oriented and to value the opinion of their peers highly, especially on day-to-day issues such as how they are dressed and what they say in social situations (Piehler and Dishion, 2007). However, as discussed in Chapter 3, their peers have developed new cognitive capacities for sarcasm and ridicule, which tend to be dispensed freely towards any peer who seems odd or awkward or uncool (Rosenbloom and Way, 2004). So, the combination of greater peer orientation, greater self-consciousness about evaluations by peers, and peers' potentially harsh evaluations contributes to declines in self-esteem in early adolescence. Self-esteem rises in late adolescence and emerging adulthood as peers' evaluations become less important (Galambos et al., 2006).

On the other hand, the degree of decline in early adolescents' self-esteem should not be exaggerated. Although a substantial proportion of adolescents experience a decline in self-esteem during early adolescence, many others do not. One earlier study (Zimmerman et al., 1997) followed a sample of youngsters from 11-years-old to 15-years-old and showed that different children have different patterns of change in self-esteem as they move through adolescence. Figure 6.1 shows the patterns. Self-esteem across the total sample declined only slightly, and only about one-third of adolescents (the 'high to low' and 'low and decreasing' groups) followed a pattern of decline. The majority of adolescents were either consistently high or increased slightly in self-esteem during the period of the study. More recent studies have reported similar patterns (e.g. Le et al., 2007; Pahl and Way, 2006; Gerard and Buehler, 2004; Baranowski et al., 2003; Pahl et al., 2000).

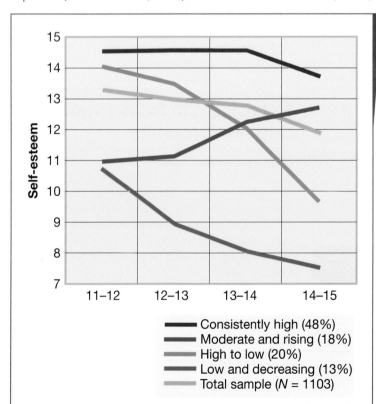

Figure 6.1 Trajectories of self-esteem throughout adolescence.
Source: Zimmerman et al. (1997).

CONNECT AND EXTEND

When studying self-perception Feyishola Apena found that ten key themes emerged, which included: the importance of black history; ability to define their ethnic background; negative representations of black people and lack of a role model. Read 'Being black and in trouble: the role of self-perception in the offending behaviour of black youth' in *Youth Justice*, Volume 7, Number 3 (December 2007), pp. 211–228

Diversity in self-esteem also exists among different ethnic groups; however, evidence for making too broad or sweeping generalisations about this important matter is in short supply. There have been a large number of studies in the USA (Gaylord-Harden et al., 2007; Greene and Way, 2005; Bracey et al., 2004; Rosenbloom and Way, 2004; Twenge and Crocker, 2002) and comparisons of groups in Europe and the Far East (e.g. Nishikawa et al., 2007) which have found that differences in adolescents' self-esteem are broadly in accord with the individualism–collectivism difference between Eastern and Western cultures.

Research in Europe has focused on specific aspects of any difference in self-esteem that might exist between adolescents from different ethnic backgrounds. Psychologists Hanna Zagefka and Rupert Brown (2005) looked at differences between how Turkish adolescents from minority groups in London and Germany identified with the majority cultures and what effects this had on measures of self-esteem – the greater the identification, the higher the self-esteem. Maykel Verkuyten and Jochem Thijs (2004) checked how ethnic minority adolescents in The Netherlands disengaged academic achievement and self-esteem when they met prejudice in school settings – a kind of self-esteem protection strategy. A particularly interesting study reported in 2007 by Feyishola Apena looks at the role of self-perception in the offending behaviour of British black youth. This research is the subject of a nearby *Connect and Extend* feature.

Earlier, at the turn of the century, Yiu Man Chan reported on a cross-cultural comparison of British-Chinese, white British and Hong Kong Chinese young people that confirmed the East–West divide on the effect of cultural individualism/collectivism on self-esteem and, therefore, the findings of many of the earlier American studies. It was also a precursor to Hanna Zagefka and Rupert Brown's (2005) study, mentioned earlier, which found an association between levels of self–esteem among an ethnic minority and identification with the majority culture. In a more recent study (2006) Félix Neto aimed to find out the degree of perceived discrimination among adolescents with an immigrant background in Portugal, and the effect of embracing the majority culture.

Researchers are also very interested, not surprisingly, in how valid their measurements of self-esteem are in different cultural settings and for both genders, and studies in the last ten years are positive about the kinds of measures used (e.g. Robins et al., 2001) – more on this next.

THINKING CRITICALLY

What hypothesis would you propose to explain the ethnic differences in adolescent self-esteem explored above? How would you test your hypothesis?

Different Aspects of Self-esteem

As developmental psychologists have studied self-esteem, they have concluded that it has different aspects in addition to overall self-esteem. For example, the social learning theorist Morris Rosenberg, who developed the widely used – and still widely used – *Rosenberg Self-Esteem Scale* (1965), distinguished between baseline self-esteem and barometric self-esteem (Rosenberg, 1986). **Baseline self-esteem** is a person's stable, enduring sense of worth and well-being. People with high baseline self-esteem might have an occasional bad day in which they feel incompetent or self-critical, but still have high baseline self-esteem because most days they evaluate themselves positively. In contrast, people with low baseline self-esteem might continue to have a poor opinion of themselves even though they have some days when things go well and they have positive feelings about themselves.

Barometric self-esteem is the fluctuating sense of worth and well-being people have as they respond to different thoughts, experiences and interactions in the course of a day. According to Rosenberg, early adolescence is a time when variations in barometric self-esteem are especially intense. An adolescent might have a disagreement with a parent over breakfast and feel miserable, then go to school and have some fun with friends before class and feel good, then get back a test in biology with a poor mark and feel miserable again, then get a smile from an attractive potential love interest and feel great – all in just a few hours.

Experience Sampling Method (ESM) studies (e.g. Nica and Links, 2009) in which, for example, adolescents wear beeper watches and record their moods and activities when beeped at random times, confirm Rosenberg's insights, by showing just this kind of rapid fluctuation of moods among adolescents in a typical day. ESM studies find that adults (Adam et al., 2006) and pre-adolescents (Fernyhough, 2009) experience changes in their moods as well, but not with the same frequency or intensity as adolescents. Other studies confirm that adolescents' self-esteem varies depending on who they are with (e.g. Harter et al., 1996). Furthermore, adolescents vary in how much their barometric self-esteem fluctuates, with some relatively stable across time and contexts and some highly variable (Harter and Whitesell, 2003). The more enjoyable and secure their social relationship, the more stable is their self-esteem.

From other aspects of research into adolescent self-esteem that have been investigated by Susan Harter (e.g. 2006; 2003; 2001), her *Self-Perception Profile for Adolescents* identifies the following eight domains of adolescent self-image:

- scholastic competence
- social acceptance
- sporting competence
- physical appearance
- job competence
- romantic appeal
- behavioural conduct
- close friendship.

Examples of items from each subscale are provided in the *Focus on Research* feature, along with more information about the scale. In addition to the eight subscales on specific domains of self-esteem, Harter's scale also contains a subscale for global (overall) self-esteem.

Susan Harter's research, among other research we have discussed and cited, indicates that adolescents do not need to have a positive self-image in all domains to have high global self-esteem. Each domain of self-image influences global self-esteem only to the extent that the adolescent views that domain as important. For example, some adolescents may view themselves as having poor sporting ability, but that would influence their global self-esteem only if it was important to them to be good at sport. Nevertheless, some domains of self-esteem are more important than others to most adolescents, as we will see in the next section.

Self-esteem and Physical Appearance

Which of Susan Harter's eight aspects of self-image would you expect to be most important in adolescence? OK, the title gives it away! Research by Harter and others has found that physical appearance is most strongly related to global self-esteem, followed by social acceptance from peers (Harter, 2006a; 2006b; 2003; 2001; Shapka and Keating, 2005; Bizman and Yinon, 2004; Patrick et al., 2004). A similar link between physical appearance and self-esteem was found for emerging adults (Mendelson et al., 2000).

Adolescent girls are more likely than boys to emphasise physical appearance as a basis for self-esteem. This gender dissimilarity largely explains the gender difference in self-esteem that occurs at adolescence in most Western cultures. Girls have a more negative body image than boys in adolescence and are more critical of their physical appearance. They are less satisfied with the shape of their bodies than boys are, and the majority of them believe they weigh too much and have attempted to diet (Berger et al., 2009; Friestad and Rise, 2004). As girls tend to evaluate their physical appearance negatively, and because physical appearance is at the heart of their global self-esteem, girls' self-esteem tends to be lower than boys' during adolescence (Shapka and Keating, 2005; Frost and McKelvie, 2004; Klomsten et al., 2004).

CONNECT AND EXTEND

'Self-esteem and body image play quite different roles in the prediction of dieting among girls and boys.' Read 'A longitudinal study of the relationship between body image, self-esteem and dieting among 15–21 year olds in Norway' by Christine Friestad and Jostein Rise in *European Eating Disorders Review: The Journal of the Eating Disorders Association*, Volume 12, Number 4 (July 2004), pp. 247–255

FOCUS ON RESEARCH

Harter's Self-perception Profile for Adolescents

The most widely used measure of the self in adolescence is Susan Harter's (1999) *Self-perception Profile for Adolescents*. The scale consists of nine subscales of five items each, for a total of 45 items. Eight of the subscales assess specific domains of self-image, and the ninth subscale assesses overall ('global') self-worth. The format of the items is to present two statements about 'teenagers'. The adolescent then selects which of the statements most applies to him or her, and whether the statement is 'sort of true for me' or 'really true for me'. Examples of items from each subscale are shown in Table 6.1.

In each item there is a positive statement and a negative statement. Look closely at each of the nine elements. What do you notice? Yes, that's right! For some items, the response that signifies high self-esteem comes first (before the 'BUT'), whereas for other items the high self-esteem response comes

Table 6.1 Sample Items From the *Self-perception Profile for Adolescents*

Scholastic competence

Some teenagers have trouble working out the answers in school BUT Other teenagers can almost always work out the answers.

Social acceptance

Some teenagers are popular with others their age BUT Other teenagers are not very popular.

Athletic competence

Some teenagers do not feel that they are very athletic BUT Other teenagers feel that they are very athletic.

Physical appearance

Some teenagers think that they are good looking BUT Other teenagers think that they are not very good looking.

Job competence

Some teenagers feel that they are ready to do well at a part-time job BUT Other teenagers feel that they are not quite ready to handle a part-time job.

Romantic appeal

Some teenagers feel that other people their age will be romantically attracted to them BUT Other teenagers worry about whether people their age will be attracted to them.

Behavioural conduct

Some teenagers often get into trouble for the things they do BUT Other teenagers usually don't do things that get them into trouble.

Close friendship

Some teenagers are able to make really close friends BUT Other teenagers find it hard to make really close friends.

Global self-worth

Some teenagers are happy with themselves most of the time BUT Other teenagers are often not happy with themselves.

> second (after the 'BUT'). The reason for this variation is to avoid a **response bias**, which is the tendency to choose the same response for all items. If the high self-esteem response came first for all items, after a few items an adolescent might start simply checking the first box without reading the item closely. Altering the arrangement of the items helps to avoid this response bias.
>
> Reliability and validity are two qualities sought in any questionnaire. To establish the reliability of the subscales, Harter calculated the **internal consistency** of each one. Internal consistency is a statistic that indicates the extent to which the different items in a scale or subscale are answered in a similar way. Harter's subscales showed high internal consistency, which means that adolescents who reported a positive self-perception on one item of a subscale also tended to report a positive self-perception on the other items of the subscale, and adolescents who reported a negative self-perception on one item of a subscale also tended to report a negative self-perception on the other items.
>
> What about the validity of the scale? Recall from Chapter 1 that the validity of a scale is the extent to which it really measures what it claims to measure. One way to establish validity is to see whether findings using the scale are consistent with findings using other methods. Research using the Harter scale has found that girls rate themselves lower than boys on physical appearance and global self-worth, but higher than boys on close friendships (Harter, 2006). As these results are consistent with findings from other studies, the findings appear to support the validity of the Harter scale. However, Harter's research has taken place mostly on adolescents in the American middle class. The measure may not be as valid for adolescents in other cultures, especially in Eastern cultures such as Japan and China, in which, as we have discussed, it is socially disapproved of to evaluate yourself positively (Nishikawa et al., 2007).

The prominence of physical appearance as a source of self-esteem also helps explain why girls' self-esteem is especially likely to decline as they enter early adolescence. As we have seen in Chapter 2, girls are often highly ambivalent about the changes that take place in their physical appearance when they reach puberty. Reaching puberty means becoming more womanly, which is good, but becoming more womanly means gaining weight in certain places, which is not good in some cultures. As the physical ideal for Western females is so thin, reaching an age where nature promotes rounder body development makes it difficult for adolescent girls to feel good about themselves (Frost and McKelvie, *ibid.*). The focus on physical attractiveness as a source of self-esteem is further promoted by the fact that reaching adolescence also means facing evaluations from others as a potential romantic/sexual partner – as we shall see in Chapter 9. It should be emphasised that the research that has found a decline in girls' self-esteem in adolescence and a gender difference in perceived physical appearance has been mainly on white adolescents. However, some evidence suggests that black and Asian young women evaluate themselves according to skin colour, with those having relatively dark skin also having negative perceptions of their attractiveness (Kiang and Fuligni, 2009; Spencer-Rodgers et al., 2004; Kang et al., 2003; Thompson and Keith, 2001).

Causes and Effects of High and Low Self-esteem

What leads some adolescents to have high self-esteem and others to have low self-esteem? Feeling accepted and approved by others – especially parents and peers – is the influence identified by theorists and researchers as the most important (Harter, 2006; Greene and Way, 2005; Farruggia et al., 2004; DuBois, 2003). As noted earlier, peers gain considerable power over self-esteem in adolescence compared with earlier ages because others of the same age become especially prominent in the social world of adolescents; but parents are important as well. Although adolescents often spend less time with their parents and experience more conflict with them than before adolescence, adolescents' relationships with parents remain crucial (Cohen et al., 2008; Slicker et al., 2004; Feinberg et al., 2000a). If parents provide love and encouragement, adolescent self-esteem is enhanced; if parents are denigrating or indifferent, adolescents respond with lower self-esteem (Berenson et al., 2005). Approval from adults outside the family, especially teachers, contributes to self-esteem as well (Miller and Moran, 2005; Veenman et al., 2000).

CONNECT AND EXTEND

How can parenting style effect self-esteem among adolescents who have serious health problems? Read 'Perceived parenting style, self-esteem and psychological distress in adolescents with heart disease' by Miri Cohen, Daniela Mansoor, Roni Gagin and Avraham Lorber in *Psychology, Health & Medicine*, Volume 13, Number 4 (2008), pp. 381–388

School success has also been found to be related to self-esteem in adolescence (Hein and Haggar, 2007; Croker et al., 2002), especially for ethnic minorities in European schools (Verkuyten and Thijs, 2004); but which comes first? Do adolescents gain in self-esteem when they do well in school, or does self-esteem directly influence adolescents' performance in school? In the 1970s and 1980s the predominant belief was that self-esteem is more of a cause of school success than a consequence.

Therefore, many programmes were developed to try to enhance students' self-esteem by praising them and teaching them to praise themselves, in the hopes that this would raise their school performance. However, researchers eventually concluded that these short courses did not work (Gendron et al., 2004; DuBois, 2003) rather that school success tends to be a cause rather than a consequence of self-esteem (Hein and Haggar, 2007). In fact, adolescents who have inflated self-esteem – that is, they rate themselves more favourably than parents, teachers and peers rate them – tend to have greater conduct problems in the classroom compared with their peers (DuBois, 2003). The best way to improve adolescents' school-related self-esteem is to teach them knowledge and skills that can be the basis of real achievements in the classroom (Hascher et al., 2004; DuBois, 2003).

In other areas of functioning, the question of the effects of self-esteem is controversial, with some scholars claiming that self-esteem has a wide range of effects whereas others argue that, like the findings regarding school performance, functioning in other areas is a cause of self-esteem rather than an effect (see Donnellan et al., 2005, for a discussion of this issue). One study indicates that the effects of self-esteem may depend on which domains are high and which are low (Wild et al., 2004). *Low* self-esteem in the family and school domains and *high* self-esteem in the peer domain were associated with multiple risk behaviours in adolescents of both sexes. In a longitudinal study of early adolescents (DuBois and Silverthorn, 2004) low self-esteem at the start of the study predicted associations with deviant peers at a later time, which was in turn related to risk behaviour, but there

was no direct association between low self-esteem and risk behaviour. The foregoing discussion reflects the complexity of the relations between self-esteem and adolescents' behaviour.

THINKING CRITICALLY

In Europe we generally consider it healthy to have high self-esteem. However, is it possible for self-esteem to be too high? If so, how would you be able to tell when that point is reached? Is it subjective, based simply on each person's opinion, or can you define that point more objectively?

Self-esteem in Emerging Adulthood

Although self-esteem tends to decline from pre-adolescence to adolescence, for most people it rises during emerging adulthood (Galambos et al., 2006; Schulenberg and Zarrett, 2006; Roberts et al., 2001). Figure 6.2 shows this pattern. There are a number of reasons why self-esteem increases over this period. Physical appearance is important to adolescents' self-esteem, and by emerging adulthood most people have passed through the awkward changes of puberty and may be more comfortable with how they look. Also, feeling accepted and approved by parents contributes to self-esteem, and during emerging adulthood relationships with parents generally improve while conflict diminishes (Galambos et al., 2006; Arnett, 2003). Peers and friends are also important to self-esteem, and entering emerging adulthood means leaving the social 'pressure cooker' of secondary school, where peer evaluations are a part of daily life and can be harsh (Pascoe, 2007).

Also, reaching emerging adulthood usually means having more control over the social contexts of everyday life, which makes it possible for emerging adults to emphasise the contexts they prefer and avoid the contexts they find

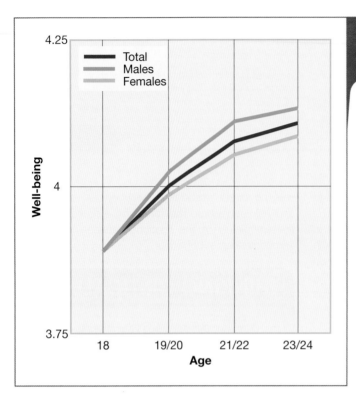

Figure 6.2 Self-esteem rises during emerging adulthood.
Source: Monitoring the Future (2003).

disagreeable, in a way that adolescents cannot. For example, adolescents who dislike school and do poorly have little choice but to attend school, where poor results may repeatedly undermine their self-esteem. However, in emerging adulthood young people can leave school and instead engage in full-time work that they may find more gratifying and enjoyable, thus enhancing their self-esteem.

THE EMOTIONAL SELF

Among the issues of the self that adolescents confront is how to understand and manage their emotions. One of the most ancient and enduring observations of adolescence is that it is a time of heightened emotions. Over 2000 years ago, the Greek philosopher Aristotle observed that youth 'are heated by Nature as drunken men by wine'. About 250 years ago, the French philosopher Jean-Jacques Rousseau made a similar observation: 'As the roaring of the waves precedes the tempest, so the murmur of rising passions announces the tumultuous change' of puberty and adolescence. Around the same time that Rousseau was writing, a type of German literature was developing that became known as *'sturm und drang'* literature – German for 'storm and stress'. In these stories, young people in their teens and early 20s experienced extreme emotions of angst, sadness and romantic passion. Today, too, most parents see adolescence as a time of heightened emotional fluctuations (McEwen and Flouri, 2009; Rissanen et al., 2008).

CONNECT AND EXTEND

Adolescents' emotional symptoms appear to be directly linked to fathers' psychological control and number of adverse life events experienced. Read 'Fathers' parenting, adverse life events and adolescents' emotional and eating disorder symptoms: the role of emotion regulation' by Ciara McEwen and Eirini Flouri in *European Child & Adolescent Psychiatry*, Volume 18, Number 4 (April 2009), pp. 206–216

Negative moods become more common in adolescence.

What does contemporary research tell us about the validity of these historical and popular ideas about adolescent emotionality? Probably the best sources of data on this question are the ESM studies already referred to (e.g. Nica and Links, 2009), in which people record their emotions and experiences when they are 'beeped' at random times during the day. What makes the ESM method especially valuable for addressing the question of adolescent emotionality is that it assesses emotions at numerous specific moments, rather than having adolescents make an overall judgement of their emotional fluctuations. Remember that ESM studies have also been conducted on pre-adolescents and adults. Thus, if we compare the patterns of emotions reported by the different age groups, we can get a good sense of whether adolescents report more extremes of emotions than pre-adolescents or adults.

The results indicate that they do (e.g. Delaney, 2006). Adolescents report feeling 'self-conscious' and 'embarrassed' two to three times more often than their parents and are also more likely than their parents to feel awkward, lonely, nervous and ignored. Adolescents are also moodier when compared to pre-adolescents. In an earlier but telling study comparing pre-adolescent 10-year-olds to adolescent 13-year-olds, Reed Larson and Maryse Richards (1994) describe the emotional 'fall from grace' that occurs during that time, as the proportion of time experienced as 'very happy' declines by 50 per cent, and similar declines take place in reports of feeling 'great,' 'proud' and 'in control.' The result is an overall 'deflation of childhood happiness'

(p. 85) as childhood ends and adolescence begins. This finding is consistent with the decline in self-esteem described previously.

More recent research indicates that brain development may contribute to adolescents' emotionality (Giedd, 2002) – see Chapter 3. In one study comparing adolescents (ages 10–18) to emerging adults and young adults (ages 20–40), participants were shown pictures of faces displaying strong emotions (Baird et al., 1999). When adolescents processed the emotional information from the photos, brain activity was especially high in the amygdala, a primitive part of the brain involved in emotions, and relatively low in the frontal lobes, the part of the brain involved in higher functions such as reasoning and planning. The reverse was true for adults. This seems to indicate that adolescents often respond to emotional stimuli more 'with the heart' than with the head, whereas adults tend to respond in a more controlled and rational way. Studies also indicate that the hormonal changes of puberty contribute to increased emotionality in early adolescence (Susman and Rogol, 2004). However, some psychologists see these emotional changes as due to environmental factors more than to biological changes (e.g. Susman and Rogol, 2004).

How does emotionality change during the course of adolescence? Larson and Richards assessed their original ESM sample of 10- to 13-years-olds four years later, as 14- to 18-year-olds (Larson et al., 2002). As Figure 6.3 shows, they found that the decline in positive emotional states continued as 14- and 15-year-olds and then levelled out. Also, the older adolescents were less volatile in their emotions; that is, the changes in their emotions from one time to the next were less extreme.

THINKING CRITICALLY

Adolescent girls have lower overall self-esteem than adolescent boys, yet boys have lower average emotional states than girls do. Is this a contradiction, or is it possible that both these findings could be true?

What about other cultures? Is adolescent emotionality especially a Western phenomenon, or does it take place in other cultures as well? Only limited evidence is available to answer this question. However, in one study the ESM method was used with adolescents and their parents in India (Verma and Larson, 1999). The results indicated that, in India as in the West, adolescents reported more extremes of emotion than their parents did.

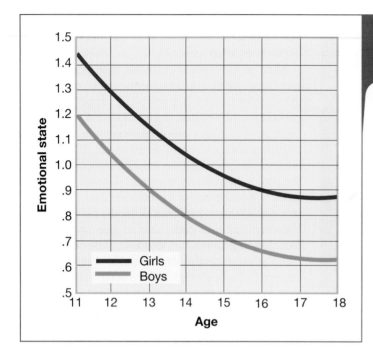

Figure 6.3 Decline in average emotional state from age 11–16.
Source: adapted from Larson et al. (2002).

Few studies have examined emotionality in emerging adulthood, but one recent longitudinal study found that from age 18 to 25 negative emotions (such as feeling depressed or angry) decrease (Galambos et al., 2006). This finding fits well with the research on self-esteem in showing that for most people the self becomes happier by the end of adolescence and continues during emerging adulthood (Arnett, 2004).

Gender and the Emotional Self: Do Adolescent Girls Lose Their 'Voice'?

One of the most influential theorists on the self-development of girls in adolescence has been feminist and psychologist Carol Gilligan. In Chapter 4 we discussed how Gilligan and her colleagues have proposed that adolescent girls and boys tend to think differently about moral issues, with girls emphasising care and boys emphasising justice. Gilligan argues that there are gender differences in the development of self in adolescence; early adolescence is a crucial turning point in self-development, in which boys learn to assert their opinions, whereas girls lose their 'voice' and become reticent and insecure (Gilligan, 2008).

In Gilligan's view, from early childhood onwards girls and boys differ in their emotional responses to social relationships. She sees girls as more sensitive to the nuances of human relationships from an early age, more observant of the subtleties of social interactions, and more interested in cultivating emotional intimacy in their relationships with others. Girls have a 'different voice' from boys, not just in their views of moral issues but in their views of human relationships more generally.

CONNECT AND EXTEND

For research that challenges the notion that adolescent boys are less interested in close personal peer relationships than girls read 'The development of adolescents' emotional stability and general self-concept: the interplay of parents, peers and gender' by Ian Hay and Adrian Ashman in the *Ashman International Journal of Disability, Development and Education*, Volume 50, Number 1 (2003), pp. 77–91

Early adolescence is crucial, according to Gilligan, because it is at this point that girls become aware of an irreconcilable conflict in the gender expectations that the majority culture has for females. On the one hand, girls perceive that independence and assertiveness are valued in their culture, and that people who are ambitious and competitive are most likely to be rewarded in their education and in their careers. On the other hand, they perceive that their culture values females mainly for their physical appearance and for feminine traits such as nurturing and care for others, and rejects girls and women as selfish when they show the traits the culture rewards most, such as independence and competitiveness. As a result, girls in early adolescence typically succumb to the gender socialisation of their culture and become more insecure and tentative about their abilities, more likely to mute their voices in an effort to be socially accepted. At the extreme, according to Gilligan, the muting of girls' voices is reflected in an escalation in such problems as depression and eating disorders when girls reach adolescence.

In her views of adolescent girls' emotional development, Gilligan's influence over the last 20 years has been profound. Her writings have received a wide audience, not just in the social sciences but also among the general public. A clinical psychologist, Mary Pipher, wrote a book called *Reviving Ophelia* (1994), drawing heavily on Gilligan's early ideas about the emotional selves of adolescent girls, and it became a best-seller. One of the schools in which Gilligan has conducted her research, a private girls' school, was so impressed by Gilligan's findings that the school management revised the entire school curriculum in an effort to preserve girls' voices in adolescence by emphasising cooperation over competition and making special efforts to encourage girls to express themselves.

However, here as in her research in moral development, Gilligan has attracted as many critics as admirers. Much of the criticism, that Gilligan exaggerates the differences between boys and girls in adolescence, has come from philosopher Christina Sommers (Sommers, 2001; 2000). For example, it is true that girls' self-esteem declines in early adolescence, but boys' self-esteem declines as well, something Gilligan rarely acknowledges. A related criticism is of Gilligan's research methods. As in her studies of moral development, her research of gender differences in the self in adolescence has rarely included boys. The allegation is that she studies girls and then makes assumptions about how they differ from the patterns that might be found among boys. Also, she typically presents the results of her research only in the form of excerpts from the interviews she and her colleagues have

conducted, and commentaries on those excerpts. Sommers find this approach weak methodologically and difficult to judge for reliability and validity.

Although Gilligan's research methods may have certain flaws, other researchers began to explore the issues she has raised, using more rigorous methods. In one study, over a decade ago now, Susan Harter and her colleagues examined Gilligan's idea of losing one's voice in adolescence, but they included boys as well as girls (Harter et al., 1998; Harter et al., 1997). Harter and her colleagues gave the adolescents a questionnaire to measure the degree of their 'voice' (expressing an opinion, disagreeing, etc.), and another questionnaire to measure the degree of their self-reported masculinity and femininity. The results indicated some support for Gilligan's theory, in that 'feminine' girls reported lower levels of 'voice' than boys. In contrast, androgynous girls – those who reported having both masculine and feminine traits – were equal to boys in 'voice'. However, Susan Harter's research does not support Gilligan's claim that girls' 'voice' declines as they enter adolescence (Harter, 1999). Only the more 'feminine' girls were lower than boys in 'voice', not girls in general.

THINKING CRITICALLY

Based on your experience and observation, do you agree or disagree with Carol Gilligan's view that girls lose their 'voice' in adolescence? Is there any difference between boys and girls in this respect?

IDENTITY

One of the most distinctive features of adolescence is that it is a time of thinking about who you are, where your life is going, what you believe in, and how your life fits into the world around you. These are all issues of **identity**. It is the adolescent's **nascent capacity** for self-reflection that makes consideration of identity issues possible. Adolescents are able to consider themselves in the abstract, in the 'third person', in a way that younger children cannot. During adolescence and continuing through emerging adulthood, explorations are made into various aspects of identity, culminating in commitments that set the foundation for adult life.

CONNECT AND EXTEND

For an example of using developmental theory to assist adolescents in constructing positive life stories that can influence their identity formation read 'Accessing self-development through narrative approaches in child and adolescent psychotherapy' by Janiece E. DeSocio in the *Journal of Child and Adolescent Psychiatric Nursing*, Volume 18, Number 2 (April 2005), pp. 53–61

Because adolescence and emerging adulthood are crucial periods for identity development, theorists and researchers have devoted a considerable amount of attention to this topic. In this section, we will look first at developmental psychologist Erik Erikson's theory of the adolescent identity crisis, then at the research that has been conducted to explore Erikson's theory. After that, we will consider the roles of gender and culture in adolescent identity development, with a special focus on ethnic identity.

Erikson's Theory

Erik Erikson (1902–1994) is one of the most influential scholars in the history of the study of adolescent development. Indeed, he has had a substantial influence on the study of human development from infancy to old age. Drawing on his diverse experience as a teacher, psychoanalyst, ethnographer and therapist of second World War veterans, he developed a comprehensive theory of human development across the lifespan. However, the primary focus of Erikson's work was on adolescence, and adolescent development is where he has had his greatest influence.

In Erikson's theory of human development, each period of life is characterised by a distinctive developmental issue or 'crisis', as he described in his classic book *Childhood and Society* (1950). Each of these crises holds the potential for a healthy path of development and an unhealthy path. For example, Erikson views infancy as a period of *trust versus mistrust*; infant development follows a healthy path when the infant establishes a secure sense of trust with at least one person who can be counted on to provide protection and loving care. The unhealthy path is mistrust, which results from a failure to establish that secure sense of trust.

Each stage of life has a central crisis of this kind, according to Erikson. In adolescence, the crisis is **identity versus identity confusion**. The healthy path in adolescence involves establishing a clear and definite sense of who you are and how you fit into the world around you. The unhealthy alternative is identity confusion, which is a failure to form a stable and secure identity. Identity formation involves reflecting on what your traits, abilities and interests are, and then sifting through the range of life choices available in your culture, trying out various possibilities, and ultimately making commitments. The key areas in which identity is formed are love, work and ideology – beliefs and values. In Erikson's view, a failure to establish commitments in these areas by the end of adolescence reflects identity confusion.

Erikson did not assert that adolescence is the only time when identity issues arise and that once adolescence is over identity issues have been resolved, never to return. Identity issues exist early in life, from the time children first realise they have an existence separate from others, and continue far beyond adolescence as adults continue to ask themselves questions about who they are and how they fit into the world around them. As Erikson observed, 'A sense of identity is never gained nor maintained once and for all. . . . It is constantly lost and regained' (1959, p. 118).

Nevertheless, Erikson saw adolescence as the time when identity issues are most prominent and most crucial to development. Furthermore, Erikson argued that it is important to establish a clear identity in adolescence as a basis for initial commitments in adult life and as a foundation for later stages of development. Erikson viewed this as true of all his stages; developing via the healthy path provides a stable foundation for the next stage of development, whereas developing via the unhealthy path is problematic not only in that stage but as an unreliable foundation for the stages to come.

How does an adolescent develop a healthy identity? In Erikson's view, identity formation is founded partly in the **identifications** the adolescent has accumulated in childhood. Children *identify* with their parents and other loved ones as they grow up – that is, children love and admire them and want to be like them. When adolescence comes, adolescents reflect on their identifications, rejecting some and embracing others. The ones that remain are integrated into the adolescent self, combined of course with the adolescent's own individual characteristics. Thus, adolescents create an identity

HISTORICAL FOCUS

Young Man Luther

Among Erik Erikson's many innovative contributions to the field of human development were his studies in **psychohistory**, which is the psychological analysis of important historical figures. His most extensive works of psychohistory were his analyses of the development of Mohandas K. Gandhi, the leader of the independence movement in India in the mid-twentieth century, and Martin Luther, the theologian and leader of the Protestant Reformation in the sixteenth century. His study of Luther is of particular interest for our purposes because he focused on Luther's development during adolescence and emerging adulthood. In fact, the title of his book on Luther is *Young Man Luther* (1958).

According to Erikson, two events were especially important in Luther's identity formation. The first event took place in 1505, when Luther was 21. He was about to begin studying law. Since his childhood, his father had decreed that he would become a lawyer, and he was on the verge of fulfilling his father's dream. However, shortly before beginning his first semester of law school, as he was travelling to the college where he was to be enrolled, he was caught in a severe thunderstorm. A bolt of lightning struck the ground close to where he was taking shelter from the storm and may even have thrown him to the ground. In his terror, he cried out to St Anne for protection from the storm and promised that he would become a monk if he survived. The storm abated, and a few days later Luther entered a monastery in accordance with his promise to St Anne – without informing his father, who was enraged when he learned what Luther had done.

The second event took place two years later, when Luther was 23. He was with his fellow monks in the choir of the monastery, listening to a reading from the Bible that described Jesus's cure of a man who was possessed by a demon (Mark 9:17). Suddenly, Luther threw himself to the ground, raving and roaring 'It isn't me! It isn't me!' Erikson (and others) interpreted this event as indicating the depth of Luther's fear that he could never eradicate his sense of moral and spiritual inadequacy, no matter what he did, no matter how good a monk he was. By shouting 'It isn't me!' Luther 'showed himself possessed even as he tried most loudly to deny it' (Erikson, 1958, p. 23). Erikson and others have seen this event as pivotal in Luther's identity development. His sense that nothing he could do would be good enough to make him holy in the eyes of God eventually led him to reject the Roman Catholic Church's emphasis on doing good works to earn entry into heaven. Luther created a new religious doctrine based on the idea that faith, and faith alone, was enough to make a person worthy and saved before God.

Erikson's study of Luther illustrates several aspects of his theory of identity formation. First, Erikson viewed identity formation as centring on an identity crisis. More recent theorists and researchers tend to use the term *exploration* rather than *crisis* to describe the process of identity formation, but Erikson used the term *crisis* deliberately. As he wrote in *Young Man Luther*:

'Only in ill health does one realise the intricacy of the body; and only in a crisis, individual or historical, does it become obvious what a sensitive combination of interrelated factors the human personality is – a combination of capacities created in the distant past and of opportunities divined in the present; a combination of totally unconscious preconditions developed in individual growth and of social conditions created and recreated in the precarious interplay of generations. In some young people, in some classes, at some periods in history, this crisis will be minimal; in other people, classes and periods, the crisis will be clearly marked off as a critical period, a kind of "second birth," apt to be aggravated either by widespread neuroticisms or by pervasive ideological unrest. . . . Luther, so it seems, was a rather endangered young man, beset with a syndrome of conflicts.' (pp. 14–15)

Thus, Erikson viewed Luther's youth, including the two crisis events described above, as an extreme example of the identity crisis that all adolescents go through in one form or another.

➤

Second, Erikson's study of Luther shows his sensitivity to the cultural and historical context of identity development. Throughout the book Erikson emphasises the match between Luther's unusual personality and the historical and cultural circumstances in which he lived. Had Luther grown up in a different time

and place, he would have developed a much different identity. In analysing Luther, Erikson shows the importance in identity development of the person looking inward and assessing his or her individual abilities and inclinations, then looking outward to possibilities available in the social and cultural environment. Successful identity development lies in reconciling the individual's abilities and desires with the possibilities and opportunities offered in the environment.

Third, in describing Luther's development Erikson shows that identity formation reaches a critical point during the identity crisis, but it begins before that time and continues well after. In explaining Luther, Erikson describes not only his adolescence and emerging adulthood but also his childhood, particularly his relationship with his loving but domineering father. Also, Erikson describes how Luther's identity continued to develop through his adulthood. The two key crises took place in his early 20s, but it was not until his early 30s that he broke away from the Catholic Church and established a new religious denomination. In the decades that followed, his identity developed further as he married, had children, and continued to develop his religious ideas.

Martin Luther as a young man.

in part by modelling themselves on parents, friends and others they have loved in childhood, not simply imitating them but integrating parts of their loved ones' behaviour and attitudes into their own personality.

The other key process that contributes to identity formation, according to Erikson, is exploring various possible life options. Erikson described adolescence as often including a **psychosocial moratorium**, a period when adult responsibilities are postponed as young people try on various possible selves. Thus, falling in love is part of identity formation because during this process you get a clearer sense of yourself through intimate interactions with other persons. Trying out various possible jobs or selecting different subjects to study are part of identity formation, too, because these explorations give you a clearer sense of what you are good at and what you truly enjoy. Erikson saw ideological exploration as part of identity formation as well. 'Trying out' a set of religious or political beliefs by learning about them and participating in organisations centred around a particular set of beliefs serves to clarify for adolescents what they believe and how they wish to live. In Erikson's view, the psychosocial moratorium is not characteristic of all societies but only those

with greater individualistic values, in which individual choice is supported (1968).

Most young people in Western societies go through the explorations of the psychosocial moratorium and then settle on more enduring choices in love, work and ideology as they enter adulthood. However, some young people find it difficult to sort out the possibilities that life presents to them, and they remain in a state of identity confusion after their peers have gone on to establish a secure identity. For many of these adolescents, according to Erikson, this may be a result of unsuccessful adaptation in previous stages of development. Just as identity formation provides the foundation for further development in adulthood, development in childhood provides the basis for development in adolescence. If development in any of the earlier stages has been unusually problematic, then identity confusion is more likely to be the outcome of adolescent development. For other adolescents, identity confusion may be the result of an inability to sort through all the choices available to them and decide among them.

At the extreme, according to Erikson, such adolescents may develop a **negative identity**, 'an identity perversely based on all those identifications and roles

CONNECT AND EXTEND

Read more about the Goth youth subculture in: 'Prevalence of deliberate self-harm and attempted suicide within contemporary Goth youth subculture: longitudinal cohort study' by Robert Young, Helen Sweeting and Patrick West in the *BMJ* (*British Medical Journal*), Volume 332, Number 7549 (May 2006), pp. 1058–1061

which, at critical stages of development, had been presented to them as most undesirable or dangerous' (1968, p. 174). Such adolescents reject the range of acceptable possibilities for love, work and ideology offered by their society, and instead deliberately embrace what their society considers unacceptable, strange, contemptible and offensive. Youth subcultures such as skinheads (Varga, 2008) and metalheads – fans of heavy metal music – (Patton and McIntosh, 2008) and Goths (Young et al., 2006) have been formed by adolescents who share a negative identity.

Research on Identity

Erikson was primarily a theoretical writer and a therapist rather than a researcher, but his ideas have inspired a wealth of research over the past 30 years. One of Erikson's most influential interpreters has been developmental psychologist James Marcia (e.g. 1999; Marcia and Carpendale, 2004). Marcia constructed a measure called the 'Identity Status Interview' that classified adolescents into one of four identity statuses: *diffusion, moratorium, foreclosure*, or *achievement*. As shown in Table 6.2, each of these classifications involves a different combination of *exploration* and *commitment*. This system of four categories, known as the **identity status model**, has also been used by other researchers who, rather than using Marcia's interview, have constructed their own questionnaires to investigate identity development in adolescence (e.g. Kroger, 2007; Adams, 1999). Why is this? Well,

Erikson used the term **identity crisis** (1968) to describe the process through which young people construct their identity, but Marcia and other current researchers prefer the term *exploration* (Kroger, 2007; Waterman, 2007; Marcia and Carpendale, 2004). Crisis implies that the process inherently involves anguish and struggle, whereas exploration implies a more positive investigation of possibilities.

Identity diffusion is a status that combines no exploration with no commitment. For adolescents in identity diffusion, no commitments have been made among the choices available to them. Furthermore, no exploration is taking place. The adolescent at this stage is neither seriously attempting to sort through potential choices nor make enduring commitments.

Identity moratorium involves exploration but no commitment. This is a stage of actively trying out different personal, occupational and ideological possibilities. This classification is based on Erikson's idea of the psychosocial moratorium, discussed earlier. Different possibilities are being tried on, sifted through, some discarded and some selected, in order for adolescents to be able to determine which of the available possibilities are best suited to them.

Adolescents who are in the **identity foreclosure** classification have not experimented with a range of possibilities but have nevertheless committed themselves to certain choices – commitment, but no exploration. This is often a result of their parents' or others' strong influence. Marcia and most other researchers tend to see exploration as a necessary part of forming a healthy identity, and therefore see foreclosure as unhealthy. We will discuss this important issue further in a moment or two.

Finally, the classification that combines exploration and commitment is **identity achievement**. Identity achievement is the classification for young people who have made definite personal, occupational and ideological choices. By definition, identity achievement is preceded by a period of identity moratorium in which exploration takes place. If commitment takes place without exploration, it is considered identity foreclosure rather than identity achievement.

Table 6.2 The Four Identity Statuses

		Commitment	
		Yes	**No**
Exploration	**Yes**	Achievement	Moratorium
	No	Foreclosure	Diffusion

Two findings stand out from the many studies that have been conducted using the identity status model. One is that adolescents' identity status tends to be related to other aspects of their development (Kroger, 2007; 2003; Seaton et al., 2006; Swanson et al., 1998). The identity achievement and moratorium statuses are notably related to a variety of favourable aspects of development. Adolescents in these categories of identity development are more likely than adolescents in the foreclosure or diffusion categories to be self-directed, cooperative, and good at problem solving. Adolescents in the achievement category are rated more favourably in some respects than adolescents in the moratorium category. As you might expect, 'moratorium adolescents' are more likely than 'achievement adolescents' to be indecisive and unsure of their opinions (Abu-Rayya, 2006; Knafo and Schwartz, 2004).

In contrast, adolescents in the diffusion and foreclosure categories of identity development tend to have less favourable development in other areas as well (Waterman, 2007; Abu-Rayya, 2006; Kroger, 2003). Diffusion is considered to be the least favourable of the identity statuses and is viewed as predictive of later psychological problems (Meeus et al., 1999). Compared with adolescents in the achievement or moratorium statuses, adolescents in the diffusion status are lower in self-esteem and self-control. Diffusion status is also related to high anxiety, apathy, and disconnected relationships with parents.

We return to the foreclosure status – a kind of premature closing down of the possibilities and choices available. The foreclosure status is more complex in its relation to other aspects of development (Phinney, 2000). Adolescents in the foreclosure status tend to be higher on conformity, conventionality and obedience to authority than adolescents in the other statuses (Kroger, 2003). These are generally considered negative outcomes by researchers from Western majority cultures, although they are virtues in many non-Western cultures (Shweder et al., 2006). Also, adolescents with the foreclosure status tend to have especially close relationships with their parents, which may lead them to accept their parents' values and guidance without going through a period of exploration, as adolescents with the achievement status have done (Phinney, 2000). Again, this is sometimes portrayed as negative by psychologists who believe it is necessary to go through a period of exploration in order to develop a mature identity, but this view rests partly on values that favour individualism and independent thinking.

The other prominent finding in research on identity formation is that it takes longer to reach identity achievement than scholars had expected. In fact, for most young people this status is reached – if at all – in emerging adulthood or beyond, rather than in adolescence. Studies that have compared adolescents from ages 12 to 18 have found that, although the proportion of adolescents in the diffusion category decreases with age and the proportion of adolescents in the identity achievement category increases with age, even by early emerging adulthood less than half are classified as having reached identity achievement (Kroger, 2003; van Hoof, 1999). An example of this pattern (Waterman, 1999), is shown in Figure 6.4. Similar findings were also reported in a study of 12- to 27-year-olds in The Netherlands (Meeus et al., 1999).

Studies of university students find that progress towards identity achievement also takes place during the university years, but mainly in the specific area of occupational or racial identity rather than for identity more generally (Carson, 2009). Some studies indicate that identity achievement may come faster for emerging adults who do not attend university, perhaps because in the university environment young people's ideas about themselves are challenged and they are encouraged to question previously held ideas (Kur et al., 2008; Star and Hammer, 2008; Lytle et al., 1997). However, even for non-university emerging adults, the majority have not reached identity achievement by age 21 (Kroger, 2003; Waterman, 1999).

CONNECT AND EXTEND

For a different view of the adolescent culture of experiment and self-exploration and its developmental potential, read 'Narcissism: an adolescent disorder?' by Margot Waddell in the *Journal of Child Psychotherapy*, Volume 32, Number 1 (2006), pp. 21–34

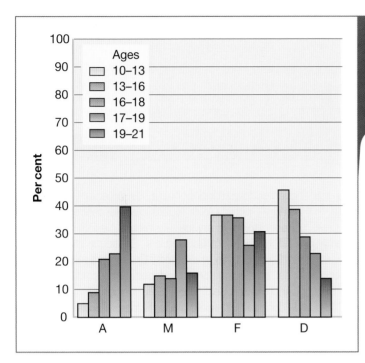

Figure 6.4 Changes in identity status with age. The numbers indicate the percentage of people in each identity status category at each age.
A = Achievement, M = Moratorium,
F = Foreclosure, D = Diffusion.
Source: Meesus et al. (1999).

Emerging adulthood is now regarded by many identity researchers as an especially important time for identity development (Coté, 2006). Even 40 years ago, Erik Erikson observed that it was taking longer and longer for young people in industrialised societies to achieve identity formation. He commented on the 'prolonged adolescence' that was becoming increasingly common in such societies and how this was leading to a prolonged period of identity formation, 'during which the young adult through free role experimentation may find a niche in some section of his society' (1968, p. 156).

Considering the changes that have taken place since Erikson made this observation in the late 1960s – including much higher ages of marriage and parenthood and longer education (Coté, 2006; 2000) – Erikson's observation applies to far more young people today than it did even then. Indeed, the conception of emerging adulthood as a distinct period of life is based to a considerable extent on the fact that, over recent decades, the late teens and early 20s have become a period of 'free role experimentation' for an increasing proportion of young people (e.g. Arnett, 2007a). The achievement of an adult identity comes later, compared with earlier generations, as many emerging adults use the years of their late teens and early 20s for identity explorations in love, work and ideology.

Critiques and Elaborations of Identity Theory and Research

Erikson's theory has dominated identity theory and research for over half a century, and like any long-standing theory it has been critiqued and modified over time. Specifically, three important elaborations of identity theory and research have been the study of gender, of ethnic identity among minority groups and the analysis of how globalisation influences identity development. The following sections explore these topics.

The Identity Status Model: A Postmodern Perspective

In recent years, the identity status model has come under increasing criticism from scholars who view it as a narrow and outdated model of identity formation (Schachter, 2005a, 2005b; Schwartz, 2005; van Hoof and Raaijmakers, 2003; Coté, 2000; van Hoof, 1999). According to these critics, identity is neither nearly as stable and unitary as the identity status model portrays it, nor does identity development proceed through a predictable set of stages that culminate in identity achievement some time in late adolescence or emerging adulthood. On the contrary, according to this view, the most common form of identity today is the **postmodern identity**, which is

CONNECT AND EXTEND

Adolescents seem to make continual reference to a mobile phone. How does the possession and unfettered use of a mobile phone change the self? Read 'Changes in the self resulting from the use of mobile phones' by José M. García-Montes, Domingo Caballero-Muñoz and Marino Pérez-Álvarez in *Media, Culture & Society*, Volume 28, Number 1 (January 2006), pp. 67–82

composed of diverse elements that do not always form a unified, consistent self.

The postmodern identity changes across contexts, so that people may show a different identity to friends, family, co-workers and others. It also changes continuously, not just in adolescence and emerging adulthood but throughout the life course, as people add new elements to their identities and discard others. As noted in Chapter 1, a similar theme has been sounded by globalisation theorists, who have argued that young people around the world increasingly develop a complex identity that combines elements from their culture and the global media culture, and that this complex identity changes as these cultures change (Giddens, 2000). Even though the identity status model continues to dominate research on identity development in adolescence and emerging adulthood, the postmodern critique can lead to new methods that will expand our understanding of identity issues.

THINKING CRITICALLY

Which better fits your own sense of identity, the identity status model or the postmodern identity theory? How would you devise a study to test the claims of the postmodern identity theorists?

Gender and Identity

Another critique of identity theory and research concerns the role of gender. Erikson has been the subject of theoretical critiques for being biased toward male development (Sorell and Montgomery, 2001). Erikson believed that to some extent 'anatomy is destiny', meaning that there are sex differences in psychological development, including identity development, that are based on biological sex differences. Specifically, he believed that women's biology, represented by the 'inner space' of the uterus and the capacity for bearing children, makes them oriented towards relationships with others, whereas men's biology, represented by the penis, makes them oriented toward independent, instrumental – a means to an end – activity. With regard to adolescence in Erikson's theory, forming an identity means becoming separate and independent from others. Consequently, according to Carol Gilligan and others, Erikson presents the male goal of striving for an independent identity in adolescence as the healthy standard for normal development. In contrast, Erikson's presentation of females' emphasis on relationships rather than independent activity is a less desirable deviation from normal development (Archer, 2002; Sorell and Montgomery, 2001).

However, defenders of Erikson, and even many of his feminist critics, argue that in his descriptions of females as relational and males as active and instrumental achievers he was simply reflecting the social conditions of the time when he first developed his ideas: the mid-twentieth century (Kroger, 2002; Sorell and Montgomery, 2002; 2001). Also, scholars now agree that independence and connectedness are often balanced differently in males' and females' sense of identity – that is, more towards independence for males, more towards connectedness for females – not because of biological sex differences, as Erikson believed, but because of culturally based differences in gender role socialisation, beginning at birth and continuing throughout life (Sorell and Montgomery, 2002: 2001).

What does the research say? Some studies have found gender differences in identity formation, especially in relation to occupational exploration (e.g. Kroger, 2007) – how youngsters can be guided when exploring different careers is exemplified in the *Focus on Professional Practice* feature in Chapter 11. There is some evidence to suggest that females are more willing than males to constrain their occupational exploration to maintain their relationships (Hoobler, 2007). For example, females might be less willing than males to take advantage of an educational or occupational opportunity that would require them to move a great distance because that would mean leaving their parents, their friends, and perhaps their romantic partner (van der Klis and Mulder, 2008).

FOCUS ON PROFESSIONAL PRACTICE

Psychoanalysis: Psychology or Psychiatry?

In Chapter 1 we focused on paediatric psychology, particularly the professional roles of educational psychologists, clinical psychologists and researchers. Specific reference was made to the distinction between psychology and psychiatry. You may remember that Logan Wright – who first coined the term *paediatric psychology* – specifically excluded psychiatry from his definition of paediatric psychology because he considered psychiatry to be a highly specialist study in the treatment of mental disease and very much about understanding *self*. Psychology on the other hand concentrates on the relationship between behaviour, mental functioning, health and relationships. The most obvious demonstration of clinical psychiatry is psychoanalysis – the name given to the *theory of mind* developed originally by Sigmund Freud – a theory that continues to have a huge impact on clinical practice, particularly in consultative practice with adolescents and emergent adults. Theory of mind is a psychodynamic theory and all such theories have their roots in the work of Sigmund Freud, often hailed as one of the greatest thinkers of the twentieth century; whose views on personality and motivation continue to invite controversy even today.

The **theory of psychosexual development** (Freud, 1940/64) states that behaviour is governed by unconscious (the brain working while your 'back is turned') as well as conscious processes (deliberate thinking about something). Freud argued that some processes are present at birth, while others emerge in later development. A second key idea is that many facets of our personality such as aggression and sexuality originate in early childhood drives, for example to hold on to waste products in the body until a time when it will give greater pleasure to release them. These early childhood drives sometimes conflict with external pressures – we would probably call them forces environmental or social – such as those exerted by parents, family or other significant others to adjust behaviour to social norms and expectations. Freud's daughter Anna, argues that for some adolescents conflict between their drives and social expectations remain unresolved and so become internalised conflicts affecting thoughts and emotions, and directly affecting behaviour (Freud, A., 1969; 1968; 1958).

Sigmund Freud

Freud's theories of development are characterised by instinctive drives of pleasure that are usually mitigated by the development of social conscience and moral judgement. However, the conflict between pleasure taking and socialisation is not always appropriately resolved. Any lack of opportunities to have needs of self appropriately met have negative consequences on personal feelings of self-worth, self-image and self-esteem – *self* really – and the ability to form relationships (as covered in Chapters 7, 8 and 9). Despite Freud valuing family influences and early childhood experiences in personality development, there are few strong advocates of Freud's theory today. Thomas Keenan (2002), senior lecturer in psychology at the University of Canterbury, New Zealand, summarises criticisms of Freud's theory, including that the theory is culture bound, that it relies on boys for study and that many of Freud's claims have not been substantiated in more recent studies.

So, although there has been considerable improvement in the theory and practice of psychoanalysis since Freud's day,

➤

some of his original and key ideas have retained their locus and vigour within the practice of psychoanalysis. These include the following:

- understanding that there are major aspects of our psychological functioning which are largely hidden, that is, they are *unconscious*;

- recognition of the omnipresence of unconscious *conflict*;

- notion that early relationships form 'templates' which transfer into the adolescent and adult situations, that is they form *transferences*;

- recognition of the importance of sexuality and aggression in cognition.

Psychoanalysis therefore, is a method of psychiatric and psychological help based on the theory that early childhood experiences of love, loss and sexuality all lay down patterns in the mind which provide, as mentioned above, unconscious 'templates' or patterns. These patterns have lasting effects on our psychological functioning. Psychoanalysis provides a clinical setting within which these unconscious patterns can be brought into consciousness, creating the possibility for a patient of being able to understand her or himself at a deep level and so be free to live their lives in a richer and more fulfilling way.

Psychoanalysts may work with patients intensively (50 minutes a day, five days a week) or less intensively (50 minutes a day, once or twice a week). They work in public organisations as well as in private practice. Over 250 psychoanalysts work in the UK National Health Service; and many hold distinguished positions in psychiatry, paediatric psychotherapy, social work and family therapy. Psychoanalysts inhabit a very influential role in the team of paediatric professionals who attempt to provide clinical support for those many adolescents and emergent adults who exhibit mental disorders such as anorexia nervosa; obsessive-compulsive disorder; Asperger's syndrome; selective mutism; attention deficit-hyperactivity disorder; Tourette's syndrome; autistic disorder; stuttering; bipolar disorder; sleepwalking disorder; bulimia nervosa; paranoid personality disorder; Munchausen's syndrome; and dissociative identity disorder.

Source: **http://www.psychoanalysis.org.uk/**

In Erikson's theory, intimacy is often a higher priority than identity for females, whereas for males identity tends to come before intimacy. Remember that according to Erikson, **intimacy versus isolation** is the central issue of young adulthood. Establishing intimacy means uniting your newly formed identity with another person in an intimate relationship. The alternative is isolation, characterised by an inability to form an enduring intimate relationship. Research on the relation between identity and intimacy has often focused on gender differences. Most studies indicate that developmental processes of forming an identity and establishing intimacy take place simultaneously for females, whereas males tend to achieve identity before intimacy (e.g. Phillips, 2006; Lytle et al., 1997). This is an important idea.

Culture and Identity

Erik Erikson's cultural background was diverse – he was the son of Danish parents, raised in Germany, and spent most of his adult life in the United States – and he was acutely aware of the relation between culture and identity formation. He spent time as an ethnographer among the Sioux and Yurok tribes of Native Americans, and he devoted a chapter in *Childhood and Society* (1950) to adolescent identity development in these tribes. Nevertheless, virtually all of the research inspired by Erikson's theory has taken place among white middle-class adolescents in the United States. What can we say about identity development among adolescents in other cultures?

One observation that can be made is that, although Erikson sought to ground his theory in historical and cultural context (Erikson, 1968; 1950; Kroger, 2002), his discussion of identity development nevertheless assumes an independent self that is allowed to make free choices in love, work and ideology. The focus of Erikson's identity theory is on how young people develop an understanding of themselves as unique individuals. However, as we have discussed, this

Opportunities for exploring identity are often limited in traditional cultures, especially for girls. Here, young girls in Bangladesh collect water for their family.

conception of the self is distinctively Western and is historically recent. In most cultures until recently the self has been understood as interdependent, defined in relation to others, rather than as independent. Even today, Erikson's assertions of the prominence of identity issues in adolescence may apply more to modern Western adolescents than to adolescents in other cultures.

A related cultural observation is that the psychosocial moratorium, the period of exploration that Erikson viewed as a standard part of identity formation, is considerably more possible in some cultures than others. In today's industrialised societies, there are few pressures on young people to become economic contributors in childhood or adolescence. Young people in industrialised societies are generally allowed a long psychological moratorium in adolescence and emerging adulthood to try out various possible life choices in love, work and ideology. However, the experience of adolescence is often much different in traditional cultures. Explorations in love are clearly limited or even non-existent in cultures where dating is not allowed and marriages are either arranged by parents or strongly influenced by

them (Jacobs, 2010). Explorations in work were historically limited in European cultures where trades were passed from parents to children, and continue to be limited in cultures where the economy is simple and offers only a limited range of choices (Patnaik, 2005) – though care should be taken not to make sweeping generalisations in this context (Abdi, 2008)

THINKING CRITICALLY

Were you allowed a long moratorium in adolescence (and perhaps still in emerging adulthood) to try out various possible life choices in love, work and ideology? Perhaps pursuing this course and reading this book is part of your exploration in terms of work and ideology – probably not love! Do you have a cultural aspect to your answer? You might like to provide a case study for the partner website at **www.pearsoned.co.uk/arnett**.

CONNECT AND EXTEND

Erik Erikson is an important figure in issues of identity and the formation of the self. Read an excellent biography of Erik Erikson at **http://**

webspace.ship.edu/cgboer/erikson.html accessed 1 September 2010

CONNECT AND EXTEND

In Roma cultures men have great sexual freedom before and during marriage. In contrast, women are expected to maintain virginity before marriage and then sexual exclusivity to their husbands. Read 'Gender roles and HIV sexual risk vulnerability of Roma (Gypsies) men and women in Bulgaria and Hungary: an ethnographic study' by J. A. Kelly, Y. A. Amirkhanian, E. Kabakchieva, P. Csepe, D. W. Seal, R. Antonova, A. Mihaylov and G. Gyukits in *AIDS Care*, Volume 16, Number 2 (2004), pp. 231–245

Limitations on exploration in both love and work are narrower for girls in traditional cultures than for boys. With regard to love, as noted in Chapter 4, some degree of sexual experimentation is encouraged for adolescent boys in most cultures, but for girls sexual experimentation is more likely to be restricted or forbidden (Kelly et al., 2004). With regard to work, in most traditional cultures today and for most of human history in every culture, adolescent girls have been designated by their cultures for the roles of wife and mother, and these were essentially the only choices open to them (Kelly et al., *ibid*.; Mensch et al., 1998).

In terms of ideology, too, a psychosocial moratorium has been the exception in human cultures rather than the standard. In most cultures, young people have been expected to grow up to believe what adults teach them to believe, without questioning it. It is only in recent history, and mainly in industrialised Western countries, that these expectations have changed and that it has come to be seen as desirable for adolescents and emerging adults to think for themselves, decide on their own beliefs, and make their life choices independently (Darling et al., 2008; Elias and Lemish, 2008; Witenberg, 2007).

For modern young people in the West, then, identity development is a longer and more complex process than in the past and compared with traditional cultures. As we will see later in this chapter, this is increasingly true for the rest of the world as well, as industrialisation increases worldwide and as Western values of individualism influence traditional cultures through globalisation (Suárez-Orozco, 2004; Schlegel, 2000).

Ethnic Identity

In discussing identity, we have noted that in Erikson's theory the three key areas of identity formation are love, work and ideology. For a large and growing proportion of adolescents in industrialised societies, one aspect of ideology is beliefs about what it means to be a member of an ethnic minority within a society dominated by the majority culture. Scholarly attention to this topic has increased in recent years as immigration from developing countries to industrialised societies has grown and as scholars have begun to devote greater attention to cultural issues in development (Berry et al., 2006; Phinney, 2006; 2000).

Like other identity issues, issues of ethnic identity come to the forefront in adolescence because of the cognitive capacities that adolescents develop (Pahl and Way, 2006; Portes et al., 2000). One aspect of the growing capacity for self-reflection among adolescents who belong to ethnic minorities is likely to be a sharpened awareness of what it means for them to be a member of their minority group. Group terms such as *British-Asian, Chinese-Canadian* and *Turkish-Dutch* take on new meanings as adolescents think about what these terms mean and how the term for their ethnic group applies to themselves. Also, as a consequence of their growing capacity to think about what others think about them, adolescents become more acutely aware of the prejudices and stereotypes that others may hold about their ethnic group.

Because adolescents and emerging adults who are members of ethnic minorities have to confront such issues, identity development is likely to be more complex for them than for those who belong to the majority culture (Phinney, 2006; 2000). Consider, for example, identity development in the area of love. Love – along with dating and sex – is an area where cultural conflicts are especially likely to arise for adolescents who are members of ethnic minorities. Part of identity development in Western majority cultures means trying out different possibilities in love by forming emotionally intimate relationships with different people and gaining sexual experience. However, this model is in sharp conflict with the values of many ethnic minority groups. These ideas will be fully explored in Chapter 9 but for

Table 6.3 Four Possible Ethnic Identity Statuses

		Identification with ethnic group	
		High	**Low**
Identification with	**High**	Bicultural	Assimilated
majority culture	**Low**	Separated	Marginal

Examples
Assimilation: 'I don't really think of myself as British Asian, just as British.'
Separation: 'I am not part of two cultures. I am just black.'
Marginality: 'When I'm with my Indian friends, I feel white, and when I'm with my white friends, I feel Indian. I don't really feel like I belong with either of them.'
Biculturalism: 'Being both Turkish and Dutch means having the best of both worlds. You have different strengths you can draw from in different situations.'

Source: Based on Phinney and Devich-Navarro (1997)

the time being it is important to note that young people in these ethnic groups face a challenge in achieving identity. This often means reconciling the values of their ethnic group on sex and marriage with the values of the majority culture, to which they are inevitably exposed through school, the media and peers (Qin, 2009b).

How, then, does identity development take place for young people who are members of minority groups within Western societies? To what extent do they develop an identity that reflects the values of the majority culture, and to what extent do they retain the values of their minority group? One scholar who has done extensive work on these questions among minorities is psychologist Professor Jean Phinney – who we have frequently cited during this chapter. On the basis of her research, Phinney has concluded that adolescents who are members of minority groups have four different ways of responding to their awareness of their ethnicity (Table 6.3).

Assimilation is the option that involves leaving behind the ways of one's ethnic group and adopting the values and way of life of the majority culture. This is the path that is reflected in the idea of society as a 'melting pot' which blends people of diverse origins into one national culture. **Marginality** involves rejecting one's culture of origin but also feeling rejected by the majority culture. Some adolescents feel little identification with the culture of their parents and grandparents, nor do they feel accepted and integrated into society. **Separation** is the approach that involves associating only with members of one's own ethnic group and rejecting the ways of the majority culture. **Biculturalism**

Adolescents with a bicultural ethnic identity are able to alternate their identities depending on the group they are with.

CONNECT AND EXTEND

Although reviews have been published on acculturation and mental health in adolescents, far less is known about how acculturation influences adolescent interpersonal and self-directed violence. Read 'Acculturation and violence in minority adolescents: a review of the empirical literature' by Paul Smokowski, Corinne David-Ferdon and Nancy Stroupe in *The Journal of Primary Prevention*, Volume 30, Numbers 3–4 (July 2009), pp. 215–263

involves developing a dual identity, one based in the ethnic group of origin and one based in the majority culture. Being bicultural means moving back and forth between the ethnic culture and the majority culture; and alternating identities as appropriate.

Which of these ethnic identity statuses is most common among minority adolescents? The bicultural status is the most common status among some European minority groups such as Turkish adolescents in The Netherlands (Verkuyten, 2002). However, separation is the most common ethnic identity status among Somali adolescents (Kia-Keating and Ellis, 2007), and marginality remains a threat among female British Sikh and Muslim adolescents (Brown, 2008; Ramji, 2007; Jakobsh, 2006; Dwyer, 1999). Of course, each ethnic group is diverse and contains adolescents with a variety of different ethnic identity statuses and this more complex notion is explored in the upcoming *Cultural Focus* feature.

Recently, Phinney (e.g. 2008) has proposed that emerging adulthood may be an especially important time for developing ethnic identity because emerging adults often enter new contexts (new schools, new jobs, perhaps new living situations) that may involve greater contact with people outside their ethnic group and thus sharpen their awareness of their ethnic identity. Is a strong ethnic identity related to other aspects of development in adolescence and emerging adulthood? Some studies have found that adolescents who are bicultural or assimilated have higher self-esteem (e.g. Farver et al., 2002a). Furthermore, research has found that having a strong ethnic identity is related to a variety of other favourable aspects of development, such as overall well-being, academic achievement and lower rates of risk behaviour (Giang and Wittig, 2006; St. Louis and Liem, 2005; Yasui et al., 2004; McMahon and Watts, 2002; Yip and Fuligni, 2002).

Some scholars have argued that cultivating pride in adolescents' ethnic identity is an important part of overall identity formation, especially in a society where they are likely to experience unfair discrimination because of the colour of their skin (Santana et al., 2007) even when that discrimination is not explicit (Kobayashi, 2006). However, others argue that promoting ethnic identity may lead adolescents to adopt a separation identity that cuts them off from the majority culture in a way that inhibits their personal growth (Ascherson, 2004). These scholars express concern that some minority adolescents may come to define themselves in opposition to the majority culture – developing, in Erikson's terms, a negative identity – in a way that may interfere with developing a positive identity of their own. Two 'big ideas' are working to break down the idea of majorities and ethnic minorities, of separation and marginalisation, and particularly of integration and 'the great melting pot'. The first big idea is globalisation and the second is the development of a multicultural society. We will look at identity and globalisation first.

Identity and Globalisation

One identity issue that has risen in prominence in recent years is how globalisation influences identity, especially for adolescents and emerging adults. Two aspects of identity stand out as issues related to globalisation. First, as noted in Chapter 1, because of globalisation more young people around the world now develop a bicultural identity, with one part of their identity rooted in their local culture while another part stems from an awareness of their relation to the global culture. For example, India has a growing, vigorous high-tech economic sector, led largely by young people. However, even the better-educated young people, who have become fully fledged members of the global economy, still express a preference for an arranged marriage, in accordance with Indian tradition (Das et al., 2008; Nijman, 2006; Plüss, 2005; Kamat, 2004;

Young people in traditional cultures may develop a bicultural or hybrid identity in response to globalisation. Here, a young man in India is enjoying Harry Potter.

Ganguly-Scrase, 2003; Verma and Saraswathi, 2002). They also generally expect to care for their parents in old age, again in accordance with Indian tradition. Thus they have one identity for participating in the global economy and succeeding in the fast-paced world of high technology, and another identity, rooted in Indian tradition, that they maintain with respect to their families and their personal lives.

Although developing a bicultural identity means retaining a local identity alongside a global identity, there is no doubt that many cultures are being modified by globalisation, specifically by the introduction of global media, free market economics, democratic institutions, increased length of formal schooling and delayed entry into marriage and parenthood (Larson et al., 2010; Jensen, 2008a). These changes often alter traditional cultural practices and beliefs, and may lead less to a bicultural identity than to a **hybrid identity**, integrating local culture with elements of the global culture (Hermans and Dimaggio, 2007).

Increasing immigration is one of the forces promoting globalisation (Jensen, 2008a; Hermans and Dimaggio, 2007) and identities become even more complicated for young people who are immigrants. They may develop identities that combine their native culture, the local culture to which they have immigrated, and the global culture, along with various hybrids, leading to a multicultural identity or a complex hybrid identity. Furthermore, people living in a culture to which immigrants have come may incorporate aspects of the immigrants' culture into their own identities. Thus for an increasing number of the world's young people, as Dutch psychologists Hubert Hermans and Harry Kempen (1998) observe, 'Different and contrasting cultures can be part of a repertoire of collective voices playing their part in a multi-voiced self' (p. 1118).

A second identity-related consequence of globalisation is that it seems to be leading to an increase in identity confusion – a marginalised identity, in Jean Phinney's scheme – among young people in traditional cultures. As local cultures change in response to globalisation, most young people manage to adapt to the changes and develop a bicultural or hybrid identity that provides the basis for living in their local culture and also participating in the global culture. For some young people, however, adapting to the rapid changes taking place in their cultures is more difficult. The images, values and opportunities they perceive as being part of the global culture undermine their belief in the value of local cultural practices. At the same time, the ways of the global culture seem out of reach to them, too foreign to everything they know from their direct experience. Rather than becoming bicultural, they may experience themselves as marginalised, excluded from both their local culture and the global culture, truly belonging to neither.

Identity confusion among young people may be reflected in problems such as depression, suicide and substance use. A variety of cultures have experienced an increase in problems of mental health, suicide

CULTURAL FOCUS

The Multicultural Society

Since the beginning of the twentieth century, a flow of immigrants has entered the United Kingdom, Western Europe, Canada, Australia, the United States and many other developed countries. Many immigrants left their homelands to escape famine and abject poverty, or to seek safety from war, disaster and oppression. These new immigrants were expected to assimilate – that is, to enter the cultural 'melting pot' and become like those who had arrived earlier. New immigrant children and adolescents who spoke different languages and had diverse religious and cultural heritages were expected to master English – if necessary to forget their mother tongue, and learn to become mainstream citizens. Of course, schooling for adolescents was designed to prepare them to contribute to a communication revolution and specifically to prepare adolescents for entry to the professions through an expansion in higher education. Immigrant adolescents rather than secondary schools were expected to do the adapting and changing, and so gain access to mainstream citizenship and the professions.

In the 1960s and 1970s, some educators suggested that coloured adolescents and adolescents from low-income backgrounds had problems aspiring to entry to the professions because they were 'culturally disadvantaged' or 'culturally handicapped'. From these suggestions developed a cultural deficit model, a model that attempts to explain the achievement problems of adolescents from ethnic minority groups. The assumption of this cultural deficit model is that these adolescents' home culture is inferior because it had not prepared them to 'fit' into schools and universities. Today, social psychologists and European scholars and researchers reject the idea of cultural deficits. They believe that no culture is deficient, but rather that they wish to explore incompatibilities between the student's home culture and the expectations of the wider society (E. Gregory et al., 2001; Lemmer, 2002) and how those incompatibilities are best handled within the larger society.

Also during the 1960s and 1970s, there was growing concern for civil and human rights in Western developed nation states and an increasing sense among many ethnic groups in those countries that they did not want to assimilate completely into mainstream society. Rather, members of ethnic groups wanted to maintain their culture and identity while still being a respected part of the larger society. There remain many different cultures within every modern country. In the United Kingdom, adolescents growing up in a small rural town in central Scotland are part of a cultural group that is very different from that of youngsters in a large urban centre such as Liverpool or Leeds. In The Netherlands, teenagers living in the leafy suburbs of The Hague certainly differ in a number of ways from those growing up in a Rotterdam apartment block or on a farm in Dokkum. Within the small towns in Northern Netherlands, the son or daughter of a *kleine winkel* (small shop) owner grows up in a different culture from the child of a city doctor or dentist.

Adolescents of African, Asian, Hispanic, Arabic or European descent have distinctive histories and traditions. The experiences of males and female adolescents are different in most ethnic and economic groups, yet everyone living within a particular country shares many common experiences and values, especially because of the influence of the mass media, while other aspects of their lives are shaped by differing cultural backgrounds. In Britain and much of Europe there is an accepted desire to build a multicultural society but tensions remain. Such tensions can 'boil over' into interracial mistrust and conflict. When this happens the ideal of multiculturalism comes under attack and has to be defended.

In Britain and much of Europe, multiculturalism remains the goal for our adolescents, for our emerging adults and for all our communities.

Professor Tariq Modood (of Bristol University) in his response to the London bombings of 7 July 2005 (see the *Focus on Youth* in the media feature in Chapter 4), and in defence of a developing 'multicultural Britishness', makes a useful distinction between the following:

- 'assimilation,' where the preferred result is one where newcomers 'become as much like their new compatriots as possible';

- 'integration', where members of the majority community as well as immigrants and ethnic minorities are required to become more like each other; and

- 'multiculturalism', where processes of integration work differently for different groups.

Modood defines multiculturalism in this way:

'Multiculturalism is where processes of integration are seen both as two-way and as working differently for different groups. In this understanding, each group is distinctive, and thus integration cannot consist of a single template (hence the "multi"). The "culturalism" – by no means a happy term either in relation to "culture" or "ism" – refers to the understanding that the groups in question are likely to not just be marked by newness or phenotype or socio-economic location but by certain forms of group identities. The latter point indeed suggests that a better, though longer, term might be "pluralistic integration"'. (2005; webpage)

Furthermore he says: 'Multiculturalism can be defined as the challenging, the dismantling, the remaking of public identities in order to achieve an equality of citizenship' (webpage). In the pursuit of equality of citizenship, widespread aspiration for assimilation (represented by the melting pot idea) is now dead in Britain and much of Europe – although it remains an aspiration in the USA for historical and political reasons. In Britain and much of Europe multiculturalism – where integration is negotiated and facilitated by the political and social structures of the nation and the European community – remains the goal for our adolescents, for our emerging adults and for all in our communities.

Source: Woolfolk (2006)

CONNECT AND EXTEND

'Adolescence, as experienced by girls of immigrant diaspora groups, is complicated by issues of race, culture and nation that intersect with discourses of sex and gender' (from the abstract). Read 'Constructing the "new ethnicities": media, sexuality and diaspora identity in the lives of South Asian immigrant girls' by Meenakshi Gigi Durham in *Critical Studies in Media Communication*, Volume 21, Number 2 (2004), pp. 140–161

and substance use among their young people since their rapid move towards joining the global culture (Bynner, 2005; Durham, 2004; Griffin, 2001; Luke and Luke, 2001). This increase in these problems seems to indicate the difficulty that some young people in traditional cultures experience in forming a stable identity in the context of the rapid social changes caused by globalisation. Whether this means that young people in traditional cultures are more likely than young people in the West to experience identity confusion remains to be studied.

THE SELF, ALONE

One of the reasons that adolescents are able to engage in the frequent self-reflection which allows them to consider their self-conceptions, self-esteem, emotional states and identity is that they are often by themselves. Studies of time use among adolescents indicate that they spend about a quarter of their time alone, which is more time than they spend with either their families or

Adolescents spend more time by themselves than with family or friends.

their friends (Lewis et al., 2008; Engström and Norring, 2001).

Two historical and important ESM – experience sampling method – studies provide some interesting data on adolescents' experiences of being alone (Larson and Richards, 1994; Larson et al., 1982). These studies find that a substantial proportion of adolescents' time alone is spent in their bedrooms, with the door closed. Is this a lonely time for them? Yes, but it also has benefits. During their time alone their moods tend to be low – they are more likely than at other times to report feeling weak, lonely and sad. However, after a period alone their mood tends to rise. Larson and Richards concluded that adolescents use their time alone for self-reflection and mood management. They listen to music, they lie on their beds, they groom themselves in the mirror, they brood, they fantasise. When their time alone is done, they tend to feel restored, ready to face the 'slings and arrows' of daily life again.

Larson and Richards provide a revealing example of one adolescent girl's experience of being alone. She was alone about a quarter of the times she was beeped, the typical rate. Often, she reported feeling lonely during her times alone. She brooded over her looks, she brooded over how all the girls except herself seemed to have a boyfriend. Yet, she wrote, 'I like to be by myself. I don't have to be worried or aggravated by

my parents. I have noticed that when I'm alone I feel better sometimes.' Then she added, in large print, '*!NOT ALWAYS!,*' reflecting her ambivalence (1994, p. 102).

Being alone can be constructive, then, as long as an adolescent does not have too much of it. Studies have found that adolescents who spend an unusually high proportion of their time alone tend to have higher rates of school problems, depression, and other psychological difficulties (Peter and Vaulkenberg, 2006). However, the same studies have found that adolescents who are rarely alone also have higher rates of school problems and depression. A moderate amount of time alone can be healthy for adolescents because, as Larson and Richards observe, 'After a long day in which their emotions are played upon by peers, teachers, and family members, a measured period of time by themselves, to reflect, regroup, and explore, may be just what they need' (1994, p. 103).

Just as being alone does not necessarily mean being lonely, a person can be lonely even when among others. Robert Weiss – one of the first researchers into loneliness to make the connection between loneliness and attachment theory (see Chapter 7) – made an important and seminal distinction between two types of loneliness: social loneliness and emotional loneliness (1973). **Social loneliness** occurs when people feel that they lack a sufficient number of social contacts and relationships. In contrast, **emotional loneliness** occurs when people feel that the relationships they have lack sufficient closeness and intimacy. Thus, social loneliness reflects a deficit in the *quantity* of social contacts and relationships, whereas emotional loneliness reflects a deficit in the emotional *quality* of a person's relationships (Mcwhirter et al., 2002; Qualter and Munn, 2002; Green et al., 2001). Young people may experience either or both of these types of loneliness in their teens and early 20s.

Emerging adulthood is a period when time alone is especially high (Iacovou, 2002). Emerging adults have also been found to report greater feelings of loneliness than either adolescents or adults (Rokach, 2000), and there are good reasons why these years would be lonelier. Most emerging adults move out of the home by

CONNECT AND EXTEND

'Low self-esteem and low social coping significantly predicted high social loneliness'. Read 'Loneliness in high-risk adolescents: the role of coping, self-esteem, and empathy' by Benedict Mcwhirter, Tricia Besett-Alesch, Jarrett Horibata and Irit Gat in the *Journal of Youth Studies*, Volume 5, Number 1 (2002), pp. 69–84

FOCUS ON YOUTH IN THE MEDIA

Apples by Richard Milward

The Times Magazine

'Apples is an astonishing debut . . . *Catcher in the Rye* meets Arctic Monkeys.'

Financial Times

'A wonderful take on amoral youth . . . *Apples* is unlike any other novel I've read. Who knows? We may have discovered our J. D. Salinger early.'

We started this chapter by highlighting the way in which Holden Caufield, the 'narrator' of *Catcher in the Rye* provides a good example of how issues of the self come to the forefront of development in adolescence. Both the *Times Magazine* and *Financial Times* reviews of *Apples* – published in 2007 and quoted above – make reference back 60 years or more to the iconic *Catcher in the Rye* and its author J. D. Salinger. You may remember that it is Holden's growing self-awareness that comes as an unpleasant shock, because in his view coming to know his self – himself – has jarred him out of the Eden of his childhood.

The reference to Eden is mirrored in both the title and substance of *Apples*. The two main characters are Adam and Eve and their 'Eden' is a **council estate** in Middlesbrough, UK. To continue the biblical metaphor, Eve has completely fallen from grace; she has swallowed Satan's offered apple whole and spat out the pips. She is beautiful and she knows it. She binge drinks, does drugs and sleeps around. She may only be just 16, but she's been doing it all for much of her adolescence. Her mum is dying of lung cancer, but Eve is not about to give up one night out to be with her. Eve epitomises the self-obsession of youth.

In contrast there is Adam, though he too is shockingly self-obsessed. Adam is a socially useless, a 'Billie No-mates' loner beaten up by his father and ignored by almost everybody, including Eve, of whom he endlessly and hopelessly fantasises. His obsessive, compulsive behaviour includes opening and closing doors a precise number of times to avoid some possible, but unknown, disaster.

Adam and Eve inhabit a book set in a real council estate in Middlesbrough, UK; an area of high deprivation and poverty. Although the book is shocking, gritty, harrowing and sometimes heartbreaking it is also real; an honest depiction of urban adolescence and how the self has to be formed in what is graphically depicted in this novel as a heady and chaotic whirlwind of self-determination and gratification without obligation.

Yes, the council estate and secondary school used as the backdrop of *Apples* are real. Many readers who know the area are keen to confirm on online review sites such as that provided by Amazon Books that the book is an honest reflection of daily life for youngsters on this estate and in many similar council estates in the UK. How adolescents and emerging adults on council estates are characterised and depicted in the media is almost as shocking as the 'goings-on' in *Apples*. Let's take an example.

In the Benchill Estate, Manchester, a teenager was photographed making a gun gesture behind the back of the then Conservative Party leader, now prime minister, David Cameron. Ryan Florence, 17, became the nation's most notorious **hoodie** in 2007 when he made the gun gesture during Mr Cameron's visit to a Wythenshawe estate. Florence later told reporters he was in a gang called the Benchill Mad Dogs, and bragged about his cannabis habit and criminal activities. Benchill is one of the most deprived estates in the country and news reporters and television crews were quick to seize on the incident as a symbol of the lawlessness of young hoodies on the estate and their association with guns.

A gun gesture from a hoodie in the Wythenshawe area of Manchester, UK.

In the weeks that followed the 'gun' incident many of the follow-up newspaper and television reports highlighted the presence on the Benchill Estate of new generations of young hoodies more than happy to take over the streets. It was regularly reported that during the day boys in their late teens and 20s rode around the streets on bikes and some walked around with menacing-looking dogs. Though many local politicians and community workers were keen to point out the work being done in Benchill to mitigate the worst outcomes of poverty and social fragmentation – 'Broken Britain' David Cameron went on to call it – many reporters highlighted the fact that in 2000 Benchill came bottom in the 'Index of Multiple Deprivation' – a meta measure of poverty. This made Benchill officially the most deprived of all 8414 council areas in England and Wales.

What pictures form in your mind of Benchill? What is it like to live or work there? What about the estate gangs, the car and gun crime, the burglaries and prostitution? Hold it! Are we all falling into believing that the images and impressions the media reports or, perhaps, creates are true or are typical of all urban council estates? Try some web surfing including **http://www.youtube.com/** to test out your impressions of the Benchill estate. Which estate in Middlesbrough is the setting for *Apples* and what are the similarities with and differences from Benchill?

age 18 or 19 (Goldscheider and Goldscheider, 1999) to go to university or just to live independently. This move may have many advantages, such as giving emerging adults more independence and requiring them to take on more responsibility for their daily lives, but it also means that they are no longer wrapped in the relative security of the family environment. They may be glad to be on their own in many ways, but nevertheless they may find themselves lonely more often than when they had lived at home (DiTommaso and Spinner, 1997). Most young people in industrialised societies do not enter marriage – and the emotional support and companionship that usually go along with it – until their mid- to late 20s (Douglass, 2007). For many young people emerging adulthood is a period between the companionship of living with family and the companionship of marriage or some other long-term partnership.

In the university environment, emerging adults rarely experience social loneliness but emotional loneliness is common (Garcia-Montes et al., 2009; Löfström and Nevgi, 2007). The first year of university has been found to be an especially lonely period for emerging adults (Larose and Boivin, 1998), even though they are meeting many new people. A first-year undergraduate living on campus may have people around virtually every moment of the day – while sleeping, eating, studying, working and going to lectures – but still feel lonely if those social contacts are not emotionally rewarding.

THINKING CRITICALLY

Compared with young people in Western cultures, do you think young people in traditional cultures would be more or less likely to experience loneliness? Think through the reasons.

SUMMING UP

In this chapter we have addressed a variety of aspects of the self in adolescence and emerging adulthood, including self-conceptions, self-esteem, the emotional self, identity and being alone. The main points of the chapter are as follows:

- Cultures differ greatly in their views of the self, with some promoting an independent self that is high in self-esteem and others promoting an interdependent self that is defined by relations with others.
- Self-conceptions become more abstract in adolescence. This includes the development of the capacity to distinguish between an actual self and two types of possible selves, an ideal self and a feared self. Self-conceptions in adolescence also become more complex, with an increased awareness that different aspects of the self might be shown to different people and in different situations. This includes awareness that one may show a false self to others at times.
- Research indicates that self-esteem tends to decline in early adolescence and rise through late adolescence and emerging adulthood. Self-esteem does not decline among all adolescents, but is more likely to decline for girls than for boys. The most influential aspects of self-esteem in adolescence are physical appearance and peer acceptance.
- The ESM studies show that adolescents tend to experience more extremes of emotions, especially negative ones such as feeling embarrassed or awkward, compared with pre-adolescents or adults. Carol Gilligan has argued that gender differences exist in emotional self-development during adolescence, as girls 'lose their voice' in the course of conforming to cultural pressures for the female role, rather than asserting their authentic selves. However, research has provided limited support for this claim.

- According to Erik Erikson, the key issue in adolescent development is identity versus identity confusion, and the three principal areas of identity formation are love, work and ideology. The identity status model has guided most research in this area by classifying adolescents into one of four statuses: foreclosure, diffusion, moratorium and achievement. For young people in Western societies, identity formation usually involves a psychosocial moratorium (a period of exploration of various life possibilities) that continues through emerging adulthood.
- Adolescents who are members of ethnic minorities face the challenge of developing an ethnic identity in addition to an identity in the areas of love, work and ideology. Four possible alternatives of ethnic identity formation are assimilation, marginality, separation and biculturalism.
- Globalisation is influencing identity issues in adolescence and emerging adulthood. Specifically, it is leading to the development of multiculturalism in some countries more bicultural and hybrid identities that combine elements of the local culture with elements of the global culture, and it appears to be leading to greater identity confusion among young people in some traditional cultures.
- The ESM studies find that adolescents are alone about a quarter of the time. Although their moods tend to be low during these times, they often use these times for reflection and regeneration. Emotional loneliness tends to be high among university first-year undergraduates.

Studies of the self in adolescence and emerging adulthood are especially common in Western society. Because of Western traditions of individualism, issues of the self have been of more interest and concern to Europeans than to people in other societies, and this is reflected in the interests of scholars and researchers. The distinction between the independent self and the interdependent self is an important one, but so far this idea has not been applied much to research on adolescence and emerging adulthood.

INTERNET RESOURCES

http://www.psychology.soton.ac.uk/research/divhumanwellbeing/crsi/home.php

The mission of the Centre for Research on Self and Identity (CRSI) is to carry out programmatic research on themes surrounding the topics of self and identity. The CRSI aspires to transform empirically derived knowledge (academic research) into interventions that will benefit society, i.e. improving interpersonal relationships, boosting psychological and physical health, enhancing the quality of group relations.

http://www.gires.org.uk/

Information on gender variance for trans people, their families and the professionals who care for them.

http://www.ssc.uwo.ca/sociology/identity/links.htm

The website for the journal *Identity*. Many of the articles in the journal pertain to adolescence or emerging adulthood. The site also contains information on conferences and membership of the Society for Research on Identity Formation.

http://www.psych.neu.edu/ISSI/

The website for the International Society for Self and Identity. The site contains information about publications and conferences related to the self.

FURTHER READING

E. Erikson, *Identity: Youth and Crisis*. New York: Norton (1968).

It is good to read the original work by the great historic figures. This is Erikson's classic book on the development of identity during adolescence and emerging adulthood.

A. Giddens, *Runaway World: How Globalisation is Reshaping our Lives*. London: Routledge (2002 rev. edn).

Giddens is a major theorist and was an adviser to Tony Blair and Bill Clinton on globalisation. In this book he ponders its effects on the self and relationships.

Anita Jones Thomas and Sara E. Schwarzbaum, *Culture and Identity: Life Stories for Counsellors and Therapists*. London: Sage Publications (2006).

A collection of autobiographical stories that explores themes of race/ethnicity, immigration/acculturation, religion, and social class. These are engaging personal accounts.

For more reviews, responses to the *Thinking Critically* features, case studies, web links and practice tests, log on to **www.pearsoned.co.uk/arnett**.

PART 2

CONTEXTS

CHAPTER 7
FAMILY RELATIONSHIPS

OUTLINE

'I've wanted to play [the bass guitar] for quite a while but have never really mentioned it seriously to mum and dad because I know what will come next . . .

'You're not having a bass guitar. You've already got a guitar. You're so spoilt.'

Ellie, age 15 (Jellyellie, 2007, p. 28)

'I used to hate [my brother] when we were younger, so it's a lot better now he's older. I don't really know why I hated him; he was just so annoying.'

Kevin, age 12 (Jellyellie, 2007, p. 132)

'I'd respect my parents if they stop thinking they know best, and perhaps treat me like I'm 17 not 12. And I'm sick to death of being told to cut my hair.'

Kev, age 17 (Jellyellie, 2007, p. 36)

FAMILY LIFE! IT CAN BE THE SOURCE OF OUR deepest attachments as well as our most bitter and painful conflicts. For young people and their parents, frequent adjustments are required in their relationships as new adolescents and emerging adults gain more autonomy; moving away from their families towards the larger world and new attachments outside the family. These adjustments are not always made smoothly, and conflicts often result when young people and their parents have different perceptions of the speed and scope of this growing autonomy. For many adolescents and emerging adults in Western societies, family life is further complicated by their parents' divorce and perhaps remarriage, both of which make adjusting family relationships to growing personal autonomy even more complex.

Despite these complications, for most young people the family remains a crucial source of love, support, protection and comfort (Blum and Rinehart, 2000). Family members, especially parents, are the people admired most by the majority of adolescents and emerging adults and are among the people to whom they have the closest attachments (Halvor et al., 2000; Allen and Land, 1999; Claes, 1998). For example, in one study, over 80 per cent of adolescents aged 12–14 reported that they think highly of their parents, nearly 60 per cent stated that their parents are people they want to be like, and about 75 per cent reported that their parents are always there to help them with what is important to them (Moore et al., 2002). Adolescents and emerging adults also typically attribute their core moral values to the influence of their parents (Wyatt and Carlo, 2002).

In this chapter, we will explore many aspects of the family lives of adolescents and emerging adults. We will begin with a look at various aspects of the family system in which adolescents develop, including parents' development at mid-life, sibling relationships and relationships with extended family members. Then we will focus on the central relationships in adolescents' family systems, their relationships with their parents. This will include a discussion of the effects of various parenting styles on adolescents' development and an examination of adolescents' and emerging adults' attachments to parents.

In the second half of the chapter we will turn to challenges and difficulties in young people's relationships with parents. We will examine the basis for conflict with parents in adolescence. We will also look at the historical context of adolescents' family lives, including changes in family life over the past 200 years as well as more recent family changes – rising rates of divorce, remarriage, single-parent households and dual-earner families – and how these changes have influenced adolescents' development. The chapter will close with a look at the causes and effects of physical and sexual abuse in the family and the problems faced by adolescents who live on the streets, in Europe and around the world.

THE ADOLESCENT IN THE FAMILY SYSTEM

One useful framework for making sense of the complex ways family members interact with each other is the **family systems approach**. According to this approach, to understand family functioning one must understand how each relationship within the family influences the family as a whole (Goldenberg and Goldenberg, 2005; Minuchin, 2002; Steinberg and Silk, 2002). The family system is composed of a variety of subsystems. For example, in a family consisting of two parents and an adolescent, the subsystems would be mother and adolescent, father and adolescent, and mother and father. In families with more than one child, or with extended family members who are closely involved in the family, the family system becomes a more complex network of subsystems, consisting of each **dyadic relationship** – a relationship of two persons – as well as every possible combination of three or more persons.

The family systems approach is based on two key principles. One is that each subsystem influences every other subsystem in the family. For example, a high level of conflict between the parents affects not only the relationship between the two of them but also the relationship that each of them has with the adolescent (Bradford et al., 2004).

A second, related principle of the family systems approach is that a change in any family member or family subsystem results in a period of **disequilibrium** – or imbalance – until the family system adjusts to the change. When a child reaches adolescence, the changes that accompany adolescent development make a certain amount of disequilibrium normal and inevitable. A key change, as we saw in Chapter 2, is the advent of puberty and sexual maturity, which typically results in disequilibrium in relationships with each parent. Changes also take place as a result of adolescents' cognitive development, which may lead to disequilibrium because of the way cognitive changes affect adolescents' perceptions of their parents. When emerging adults leave home, the disequilibrium caused by their leaving often changes relationships with their parents for the better (Aquilino, 2006). Parents change, too, and the changes they experience may result in disequilibrium in their relationships with their children (Steinberg and Silk, 2002). Other, less normative changes that may take place in adolescence or emerging adulthood can also be a source of disequilibrium – the parents' divorce, for example, or psychological problems in the adolescent or in one or both parents. For both normative and non-normative changes, adjustments in the family system are required to restore a new equilibrium.

THINKING CRITICALLY

Think of an example of disequilibrium that occurred in your family during your adolescence or emerging adulthood. How did the various family members adapt?

In the following sections, we will examine three aspects of the family system that have implications for adolescents' development: changes in parents at mid-life, sibling relationships and extended family relationships.

Parents' Development during Mid-life

'Each time another one left I was able to try something new, such as getting fitter, home improvements and going to concerts. Life seems so much more balanced now, . . . I go to Pilates class every week and I've taken up Nordic walking – a type of cross-country hiking using ski poles.'

– Paul Jenkins, age 55 (quoted in The *Observer*, 8 August 2010)

For most parents, their children's development during adolescence and emerging adulthood overlaps with their own development during mid-life. As noted in Chapter 1, the mean average age of marriage and first childbirth in industrialised societies today is quite high, usually in the mid- to late 20s. If adolescence begins at about age 10, this means that most parents in industrialised societies are nearing age 40 when their first child enters adolescence, and age 40 is usually considered the beginning of mid-life (Brim et al., 2004). Of course, a great deal of variability exists in most industrialised societies, and a substantial proportion of people have their first child in their teens or in their 30s or 40s. But even for people who have their children relatively early or relatively late, their children's development in adolescence and emerging adulthood is likely to overlap at least in part with changes during their own mid-life development; if it can be said that mid-life lasts roughly from age 40 to 60.

What kinds of developmental changes take place during mid-life that may have an impact on the family system? Studies have consistently found that, for most people in most respects, mid-life is an especially satisfying and enjoyable time of life (Brim et al., 2004; Lachman, 2004). Although most people do perceive a decline in energy, physical health, creativity and physical attractiveness when they reach mid-life, they perceive increases in wisdom, competence, psychological health and respect from others. Despite popular beliefs that mid-life is typically a time to experience a **mid-life crisis**, for most people mid-life is in many ways the prime of life.

This is true in a variety of ways. Job satisfaction peaks in middle adulthood, as does the sense of having job status and power (Feldman, 2003). Earning power tends to increase, so that many couples who struggled financially when their children were younger find themselves during mid-life financially secure for the first time (Whitbourne and Willis, 2006). Gender roles become less restrictive and more flexible for both men and women, not only in the West but in non-Western cultures as well (Etaugh and Bridges, 2006).

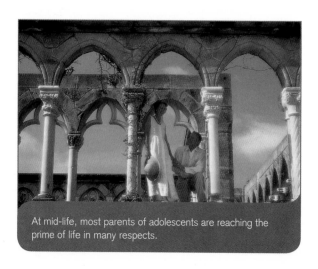

At mid-life, most parents of adolescents are reaching the prime of life in many respects.

CONNECT AND EXTEND

The roots of mid-life problems may lie in adolescence. To examine the association between recall of bullying at school and depression in mid-life read 'Exposure to bullying at school and depression in adulthood: a study of Danish men born in 1953' by Rikke Lund, Karoline Kragelund Nielsen, Ditte Hjorth Hansen, Margit Kriegbaum, Drude Molbo, Pernille Due and Ulla Christensen in *The European Journal of Public Health*, Volume 19, Number 1 (January 2009), pp. 111–116

People's personalities also tend to become more flexible and adaptive when they reach mid-life. For example, in one large study of German adults at mid-life, during their 40s and 50s most people reported a steady rise in what the researchers called 'flexible goal adjustment', as defined by affirmative responses to items such as 'I can adapt quite easily to changes in a situation' (Brandtstädter, 2006). It appears, then, that as their children reach adolescence, most parents are likely to be flexible enough to adapt their parenting to adolescents' changing development and growing autonomy. The results of studies on mid-life adults also suggest that adolescents' growing autonomy may be welcomed by most parents, because it gives parents more time to enjoy their own lives (Osler et al., 2008; Thompson et al., 2002). Before their children reach adolescence, there are many challenges for mum and dad to find *couple time* (Dyck and Daly, 2006). Women in particular emphasise the importance of changing social relationships with partners, children and parents, and that therefore the 'change of life' is about the multiplicity of biological and social changes that occur during mid-life, of which menopause – and the freedom from menstruation – is one part (Ballard et al., 2001).

One change that has been much discussed in popular culture is the *empty-nest syndrome*, referring to the adjustments that parents must make in mid-life when their youngest or only child leaves home. Although popular stereotypes suggest that this is a difficult time for parents, in fact most parents handle it easily. In general, parents' marital satisfaction and overall life satisfaction improve when their adolescent children enter emerging adulthood and leave the nest (Campbell et al., 2007;

Whitbourne and Willis, 2006). Disequilibrium is not necessarily negative, and for most parents the disequilibrium in the family system that results from children leaving home is often experienced as positive.

THINKING CRITICALLY

Why do you think many parents respond favourably when their children leave home?

Although reaching mid-life is positive for most adults, there is variability at mid-life as there is at other ages (Lachman, 2004). For men in blue-collar professions that require physical strength and stamina, such as construction or factory work, job performance becomes more difficult to sustain in middle adulthood and job satisfaction declines (Claes and Van de Ven, 2008). Only about a quarter of divorces take place after age 40, but mid-life divorces tend to be even more emotionally and financially difficult than divorces at younger ages, especially for women (Etaugh and Bridges, 2006; McDaniel and Coleman, 2003). Also, although most adults do not experience a mid-life crisis, for the minority of adults who undergo an unusually intense period of re-evaluation and reappraisal at mid-life, their relationships with their adolescent children tend to be negatively affected by it (Polden, 2002). In short, evaluating the influence of parents' mid-life development on the family systems that adolescents and emerging adults experience requires taking into account the specific characteristics of the parents' lives.

CONNECT AND EXTEND

For an interesting European study read 'The reproduction of gender: housework and attitudes towards gender equality in the home among Swedish boys and girls' by Marie Evertsson in the *British Journal of Sociology*, Volume 57, Number 3 (September 2006), pp. 415–436

RESEARCH FOCUS

The Daily Rhythms of Adolescents' Family Lives

In nearly every chapter of this book we refer to research using the Experience Sampling Method (ESM), which involves having people carry wristwatch beepers and then beeping them randomly during the day so that they can record their thoughts, feelings and behaviour. This method is an exceptionally creative and unusual approach to studying adolescents' lives. Some of the most interesting and important findings so far using this method concern the interactions and relationships between adolescents and their families. Here, let's look at ESM research in greater detail.

Reed Larson and Maryse Richards are two researchers who, arguably, have done most to apply the ESM to adolescents and their families. In their classic and influential book *Divergent Realities: The Emotional Lives of Mothers, Fathers, and Adolescents* (1994), they described the results of an American study that included a sample of 483 adolescents aged 11 to 14, and another sample of 55 11- to 13-year-olds and their parents. All were two-parent, white families. All three family members (adolescent, mother and father) were beeped at the same times, about 30 times per day between 7:30 in the morning and 9:30 at night, during the week of the study. Importantly, Larson and Richards have published more recent articles that follow up this sample at age 17; see Larson et al., (2002); Richards et al., (2002). They have also begun to publish results of ESM research with families from ethnic minority groups; see Bohnert et al., (2008).

When beeped, the family members in the original and follow-up studies paused from whatever they were doing and recorded a variety of information in the notebooks that the researchers had given them for the study. The notebooks contained items about their objective situation when beeped: where they were, who they were with, and what they were doing. There were also items about their subjective situation. They rated the degree to which they felt happy to unhappy, cheerful to irritable, and friendly to angry, as well as how hurried, tired and competitive they were feeling. The results provide 'an emotional photo album…a set of snapshots of what [adolescents] and [their] parents go through in an average week' (Larson and Richards, 1994, p. 9).

What do the results tell us about the daily rhythms of adolescents' family lives? One striking finding of the original study was how little time adolescents and their parents actually spent together on a typical day. Mothers and fathers each averaged about an hour a day spent in shared activities with their adolescents, and their most common shared activity was watching television. The amount of time adolescents spent with their families dropped by 50 per cent between 11 and 14 and declined even more sharply between 14 and 17, as you can see in Figure 7.1. In turn, there was an increase from 11 to 14 in the amount of time adolescents spent alone in their bedrooms (as noted in Chapter 6).

The study also revealed some interesting gender differences in parent–adolescent relationships. Mothers were more deeply involved than fathers with their adolescents, both for better and for worse. The majority of mother–adolescent interactions were rated positively by both of them, especially experiences such as talking together, going out together, and sharing a meal. Adolescents, especially girls, tended to be closer to their mothers than to their fathers and had more conversations with them about relationships and other personal issues. However, adolescents' negative feelings towards their mothers increased sharply from 11 to 14, and certain positive emotions decreased. For example, the proportion of interactions with the mother in which adolescents reported feeling 'very close' to her fell from 68 per cent at 11 to just 28 per cent at 14. Also, adolescents reported more conflicts with their mothers than with their fathers – although fathers were often called in if Mum's authority failed to achieve the results she desired – and, not surprisingly, the total number of conflicts between mothers and adolescents increased between the ages of 11 and 14.

As for fathers, they tended to be only tenuously involved in their adolescents' lives, a 'shadowy presence', as Larson and Richards put it. For most of the time they spent with their adolescents, the mother was there as well, and the mother tended to be more directly involved with the adolescent when the three

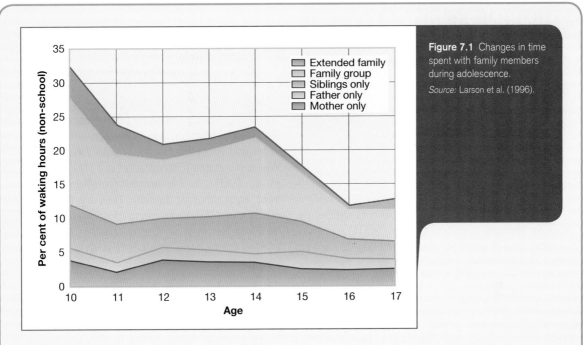

Figure 7.1 Changes in time spent with family members during adolescence.
Source: Larson et al. (1996).

of them were together. Mums were usually on the 'front lines' of parenting, whereas for fathers parenting was more of a voluntary, leisure-time activity. Fathers averaged only 12 minutes per day alone with their adolescents, and 40 per cent of this time was spent watching TV together. Fathers and their adolescents did not talk much, and when they did, sport was the most common topic.

Fathers usually reported being in a good mood during the rare times they and their adolescents were doing something together. In contrast, adolescents' enjoyment of their time with their fathers decreased between 11 and 14, especially for girls. Fathers tended to dominate when they were with their adolescents, and adolescents often resented it. Dad may have been enjoying their time together, but by age 14 the adolescent usually was not. The 'divergent realities' experienced in adolescents' families seem to be especially sharp between fathers and adolescents.

Larson and Richards coined the term *the Six O'Clock Crash* to describe what happens when Mum and Dad come home from work in the early evening and face a barrage of demands – greeting each other, making dinner, taking care of household chores, and dealing with the emotions each has piled up during the day. The burden of household tasks fell mostly on mothers rather than fathers, even when both parents worked an equal number of hours. Adolescents were even less help than fathers (ouch!). They did only half as much household work as fathers, who already did a lot less than mothers. Even when adolescents helped with housework, cooking or laundry, they often did so grudgingly and resentfully; they interpreted requests for help as harassment. As the authors put it, 'Many of these adolescents, especially boys, felt little responsibility for their family's needs, and were therefore annoyed when asked to do their part' (1994, p. 100).

At the same time, however, the studies by Larson and Richards showed that parents are often important sources of comfort and security for adolescents. Adolescents brought home to the family their emotions from the rest of the day. If their parents were responsive and caring, adolescents' moods improved and their negative emotions were relieved. In contrast, if adolescents felt their parents were unavailable or unresponsive, their negative feelings deepened. However not all is what it seems. For many young people the 'tables are turned' and the carer relationship is reversed. See the upcoming *Focus on Professional Practice* feature.

In summary, the original study and follow-up studies by Larson and Richards demonstrate the enduring importance of parents in the lives of adolescents. Also, because the studies included the perspectives of fathers and mothers as well as adolescents, interacting in dyadic relationships as well as all together, the results provide a vivid sense of the interconnected emotions and perspectives within the family system.

THINKING CRITICALLY

Why do you think fathers tend to be less involved than mothers in the lives of their adolescents? Do you think this will remain true when the current generation of adolescents grows up and becomes parents?

Sibling Relationships

For about 73 per cent of young people in Great Britain (Office for National Statistics, *Census*, 2001) and similar proportions in other European societies (European Commission Eurostat, statistics for 2001), the family system – whether couple families or lone parent – also includes relationships with at least one **sibling**. The proportion of families with siblings is even higher in developing countries, where birth rates tend to be higher and families with only one child are rare (Population Reference Bureau, 2009).

In Great Britain, Muslim families tend to have the largest number of children, compared with families of other religions. Apart from the younger age structure of the Muslim population, other cultural factors may also have an influence. Many Muslims have a Pakistani or Bangladeshi background and, in 2001, the average number of children among women of these ethnic groups was 3.4 and 3.6 respectively, compared with 2.1 children among white women (see Table 7.1).

A decade or so ago five common patterns in adolescents' relationships with their siblings were identified (Stewart et al., 2001). In the **caregiver relationship**, one sibling serves parental functions for the other. This kind of relationship is most common between an older sister and younger siblings, in both Western and non-Western cultures (Stoneman et al., 1999; Slomkowski et al., 2001). In the **amicus relationship**, siblings treat each other as friends. They try to be like one another, and they enjoy being together. A **critical relationship** between siblings is characterised by a high level of conflict and teasing. In a **rival relationship**, siblings compete against each other and measure their success against one another. Finally, in a **casual relationship** between siblings, the relationship between them is not emotionally intense, and they may have little to do with one another.

Adolescents' relationships with their siblings can take any one of these forms, or any combination of them (Noller, 2005; Zukow-Goldring, 2002). A critical relationship between siblings is common. In fact, in studies that compare adolescents' relationships with siblings to relationships with parents, grandparents, teachers and friends, adolescents report more frequent

Table 7.1 Dependent Children in Family:[1] by Number and Religion, 2001, Great Britain

	Percentages		
	None	**1 or 2**[2]	**3 or more**[2]
Christian	59.8	33.5	6.7
Jewish	59.4	31.3	9.3
Not stated	58.3	34.5	7.2
Other	53.8	39.6	6.6
Buddhist	47.0	45.3	7.8
No religion	46.1	45.0	8.9
Hindu	43.9	48.1	8.0
Sikh	40.4	45.8	13.8
Muslim	27.2	45.5	27.3

1 A family consists of a couple (married or cohabiting, including same-sex couples) with or without children, or a lone parent and their children.
2 Dependent children.
Source: Census, Office for National Statistics; Census, General Register Office for Scotland accessed 19 September 2010

Adolescents tend to have more conflict with siblings than with anyone else.

THINKING CRITICALLY

Thus far, little research has been reported on sibling relationships in emerging adulthood. Based on your own observations and experience, what would you expect research to indicate about how sibling relationships change from adolescence to emerging adulthood?

conflicts with their siblings than with anyone else. Common sources of conflict include teasing, possessions (e.g. borrowing a sibling's clothes without permission), responsibility for chores, name calling, invasions of privacy, and perceived unequal treatment by parents (Updegraff et al., 2005).

However, even though adolescents tend to have more conflicts with siblings than in their other relationships, conflict with siblings is lower in adolescence than at younger ages (Noller, 2005; Brody, 2004). From childhood to adolescence, relationships with siblings become more casual and less emotionally intense, partly because adolescents gradually spend less time with their siblings (Hetherington et al., 1999). Adolescents' involvement in friendships and employment takes them outside the family environment for an increasing amount of time (Updegraff et al., 2006) resulting in less time together and less opportunity for conflict with siblings.

Nevertheless, many adolescents have an amicus relationship with their siblings and feel close to them. When asked to list the most important people in their lives, most adolescents include their siblings, often as an important source of emotional support (Noller, 2005; Seginer, 1998). Adolescents who have two or more siblings may be closer to one sibling than to the others. With respect to their 'favourite' brother or sister, adolescents rate the level of closeness as similar to their relationship with their best friend (Cutting and Dunn, 2006; Updergaff et al., 2000). However, for sibling relationships in general, adolescents rate the level of closeness as lower than in their relationships with parents or friends (Updegraff et al., 2002).

Adolescent siblings in divorcing families often experience a heightened intensity in both hostility and warmth in their relationship (Sheehan et al., 2004). They report greater conflict than adolescents in non-divorced families during the period when the divorce is occurring, but they also report greater closeness because of the support they provide each other during that stressful time, and the closeness tends to endure after the conflict subsides (Bush and Ehrenberg, 2003). This is a good example of how one subsystem in the family, the dyadic relationship between the parents, affects other subsystems in the family, the relationship between siblings.

CONNECT AND EXTEND

To investigate the relationship between parental perceptions of family functioning and school-aged siblings' social skills, and problem behaviours in families raising a child with a disability, read 'The relationship between family and sibling functioning in families raising a child with a disability' by Barbara Mandleco, Susanne F. Olsen, Tina Dyches and Elaine Marshall in the *Journal of Family Nursing*, Volume 9, Number 4 (1 November 2003), pp. 365–396

More recently, some research has been published on sibling relationships in emerging adulthood (e.g. Aquilino, 2006). One study of adolescents and emerging adults in Israel found that emerging adults spent less time with their siblings than adolescents did but also felt more emotional closeness and warmth towards their siblings (Scharf et al., 2005). Conflict and rivalry were also reported to be less intense by emerging adults than by adolescents. Qualitative analyses of the data collected in this study showed that emerging adults had a more mature perception of their relationship with their siblings than adolescents did, in the sense that they were better able to understand their siblings' needs and perspectives – an increased capacity for **empathy** and **altruism**.

FOCUS ON PROFESSIONAL PRACTICE

The Child Carers

What do you think about the idea of children, some quite young, having to shoulder responsibility for a seriously ill or disabled relative? Many people may think of this as a 'bad thing', but caring for older relatives does dominate the lives of many of our young people.

'Start thinking about those children caring for someone with a chronic condition, for instance, and you quickly realise that unless the children are given some help, these responsibilities may end not when the child turns 18 or 21, but with the death of the person they look after, or with the child's own death. It is the very definition of a no-win situation'.

In 2007 the 'problem' of children as carers was spotlighted in the UK media with the story of a 13-year-old girl who helped care for her terminally ill mother for four years before taking a fatal overdose of her mother's morphine tablets. Following the inquest, the coroner wrote to the [then] children's minister, Beverley Hughes, demanding an inquiry into the situation for young carers. This highlights some frightening statistics: in 2007, there were 175,000 children caring for sick or disabled relatives; one in ten caring for more than one adult; 13,000 spent more than 50 hours a week on their caring responsibilities. There is no suggestion that these figures have changed much in the last five years.

'Child carers report many of the same health problems as their adult counterparts – depression, anxiety, stress, extreme tiredness – and there is concern about high levels of self-harm. Speaking to the charity Carers UK, Sam, 15, who cares for her mother, described breaking down when her mother's illness suddenly got worse. I was cooking the dinner, doing five or six pieces of homework a night, and looking after my sister. That was it. I had a nervous breakdown and became very withdrawn. I was constantly crying'.

Identifying which adolescents have caring responsibilities is difficult. Ill parents and their children do not want to advertise how much caring is needed because they are understandably very worried that the children will be taken from the family and placed in care. Also, who is responsible for identifying and supporting these families? Is it children's services who are responsible for the carer-child, or adult social services responsible for the cared-for parent? What are the outcomes of not identifying families who need support and for there being a lack of support for families that have been identified? What about the effect upon the caring child's schooling?

'There is supposed to be a person dedicated to helping young carers in every school, but often there isn't one. In fact, many child carers report that their tiredness or absence is misread as truancy. It is vital that we help these youngsters achieve, but basic mistakes are being made. For instance, 16- and 17-year-olds are allowed to claim the (paltry) weekly carer's allowance of £48.65 if they look after someone for at least 35 hours a week, but only if they give up full-time education. If they're in education for 21 hours or more a week – however many hours they happen to spend caring – the financial help is unavailable. Who wouldn't be tempted to give up school?'

Matthew, 16, has been a carer for his father these past five years, since he lost the use of his left side. 'I wash him, bath him, put him in bed, dress him,' he says. 'I won't go nowhere until my dad passes away.' We can admire Matthew for the love and care he gives, for his selfless support of his father and the maturity of how he understands his own situation. However, where is the support for Matthew? What can we do to support him and make sure he has time to be an adolescent and to explore his emerging adulthood? What should the professionals do in this situation?

Source: Adapted from Kira Cochrane, 'The hidden burden on young shoulders: The apalling plight of Britain's child carers', *New Statesman*, Volume 136, Number 4845 (21 May 2007), pp. 20.2–20.2

The Only Child

I think it's affected my confidence in myself
I was so isolated
It's narrowed my experience of being a child in
the way I feel –
I very much lived in an adult world,
A lost, lonely figure is the image I now see
No one to be a child with.
Something that I really valued about being an
only child is
I've kept some continuity of dreaming experiences and imagination into my adult life –
I didn't have to test it against other kids
I never had to lose it.

A guest writing on **http://www.onlychild.org.uk**.

Swingball. A great present for an only child?

'When we were young a stint at only-child treatment was such a treat. One of us would be taken out by ourselves by Mum or Dad to get a new pair of football boots or something else we needed, or we would go shopping with them and be bought treats in the supermarket. But it was never about what was bought for us, it was about getting that uninterrupted time with one of your parents and feeling for just a short time that it was all about you. Not that family times weren't special too, but it was so nice to have your parent or parents to yourself. This lasted into our teens and now I'm 27 it's still a much sought-after treat.'

– Becca, aged 27 (Hughes, unpublished data)

The first quotation above displays an ambivalent attitude to being bought up as a single or only child: some pain of loneliness remembered, some celebration of dreams unshattered by the hurly-burly of family life. At one time we used to call single children living with one or two parents or guardians 'the Swingball children' because it seemed that this was an outdoor game that was in every garden at the time and could be played by one person as well as by two. This typified the impression that only children were lonely children (as the guest writer above says), and that only-child adolescents in particular spent (as we noted in Chapter 6) a lot of time by themselves, perhaps playing Swingball.

There are increasing numbers of single-child-households in Britain and elsewhere in the industrialised world (Parr, 2007), either as a result of social and economic pressures (Bornstein et al., 2006; Lorensen et al., 2004) or national political policies; for example, and most notably, in China (Zhu et al., 2009).

Spending time alone – perhaps playing Swingball – is a personal choice where adolescents have one or more siblings living in the same household. For only children, however, it is normal for them to spend even more time alone than those who have siblings but elect to spend some time alone. Of course it's not just about spending time alone, being an only child can change the relationship between adolescents and parents or carers.

One of the reasons why Becca and her siblings loved spending time as an 'only child' was that it made them feel special; their sense of self as being, and being treated as, special. Would this be even more true for only children who have never shared their parents' or carers' attention; who have been the only focus of socialisation; the centre of attention? Are these spoiled children and therefore spoiled teenagers? Does the 'little emperor' become a selfish adolescent (Evans, 2005)?

Writers on the subject of family (e.g. Hoffman, 2006; Luoma et al., 1999) identify a number of potential problems for only children that become more apparent when youngsters are faced with the enforced social interactions of school and the increasing opportunities for spending leisure time away from the family home during adolescence (see Chapter 8). Only children, according to some observers (e.g. Jablonska and Lindberg, 2007), are not used to sharing bedrooms, time, attention, clothes, food, treats; everything that goes for defining our experience of family, and of being a child or teenager. Only children can also exhibit odd social behaviours, acting in 'old-fashioned ways' (Bongers et al., 2008; Ray, 1990) and talking like a 'little adult' (Paglieri, 2005), which makes them stand out from their peers.

Those youngsters who remain only children throughout their childhood and adolescence will not experience what some psychologists have termed **dethronement** when the appearance of a new sibling makes the youngster learn to accept a relative 'abandonment' by the parents and engenders a sense of self as belonging to a family unit but no longer being the centre of attention. In the view of some psychologists, going through dethronement is an important developmental experience and those who miss out on such an episode are more likely to exhibit emotional and behavioural disorders in school and other 'enforced' social situations (Marlowe et al., 2004).

However the good news is that these effects, though continuing through adolescence, become attenuated by emergent adulthood and have little transgenerational effect (Heard et al., 2008). There is no suggestion in the research literature that only children become lone parents or are less likely to form larger family units in their future lives. Perhaps other social forces such as those in the different systems of Urie Bronfenbrenner's ecological theory (see Chapter 1) provide the appropriate checks and balances to overly self-centred attitudes and behaviours; a kind of dethronement occurs outside of the immediate family and a bit later.

What are some of the plusses of being an only child? Well, some might point to a lack of sibling rivalry or conflict that, in certain situations, can result in sibling bullying (Wolke and Samara, 2004). Others point to potential advantages to the household finances, to parental career trajectories or to possible benefits from increased time and the quality of attachments with parents or caregivers (Volling et al., 2002; Feinberg et al., 2003; Hesketh et al., 2003). One possible approach to considering the impacts of only-child status is to think about the decisions made by fostering and adoptive agencies. Are those tasked with placing children in new care arrangements more willing to place them in established multisibling family households than to single applicants with no children or childless couples? See the nearby *Connect and Extend* feature for some ideas.

CONNECT AND EXTEND

Search out these three articles:

1 'Developmental attachment psychotherapy with fostered and adopted children' by David Howe in *Child and Adolescent Mental Health*, Volume 11, Number 3 (September 2006), pp. 128–134

2 'Adopted foster youths' psychosocial functioning: a longitudinal perspective' by Cassandra Simmel, Richard P. Barth and Devon Brooks in *Child & Family Social Work*, Volume 12, Number 4 (November 2007), pp. 336–348

3 'Genealogy's desire: practices of kinship amongst lesbian and gay foster-carers and adopters' by Stephen Hicks in *The British Journal of Social Work*, Volume 36, Number 5 (July 2006), pp. 761–776

Adolescents in traditional cultures often take care of younger siblings. Here's an adolescent girl and her younger sibling in Kenya.

In traditional cultures, where multisibling households are the norm, the caregiver relationship between siblings is the most common form, mainly because adolescents in traditional cultures often have childcare responsibilities. In anthropologists Alice Schlegel and Herbert Barry's much-quoted and influential analysis of adolescence in traditional cultures (1991), over 80 per cent of adolescent boys and girls had frequent responsibility for caring for younger siblings. This responsibility promotes close attachments between siblings. Time together and closeness are especially high between siblings of the same gender, mainly because in traditional cultures daily activities are often separated by gender.

Conflict tends to be low between adolescent siblings in traditional cultures, because age serves as a powerful determinant of status. Older siblings are understood to have authority over younger ones simply by virtue of being older. This lessens conflict because it is accepted that the older sibling has the right to exercise authority – although of course sometimes younger siblings resist their older siblings' authority. Also, siblings in traditional cultures often rely on one another economically throughout life, which means that they all have an interest in maintaining harmony in the relationship (Schlegel and Barry, *ibid.*).

What about members of traditional cultures living in European societies? There isn't too much research available at the moment but what there is shows that first-generation immigrant or transnational families find traditional parent and sibling responsibilities and relationships in tension with the new majority culture in which they live, but that by the second and third generations many of these tensions have been resolved (McGregor, 2008; Dale et al., 2002).

Extended Family Relationships

Alice Schlegel and Herbert Barry also reported that in traditional cultures, young men generally remain in their family home after marriage, and young women move into their new husband's home. This practice has been remarkably resistant to the influence of globalisation so far. It remains the typical pattern, for example, in the majority cultures of India and China, the two most populous countries in the world, as well as in most other traditional cultures in Asia and Africa. Consequently, children in these cultures and in ethnic minority groups in Western societies typically grow up in a household that includes not only their parents and siblings but also their grandparents, and often their uncles, aunts and cousins as well (Ho and Bedford, 2008; Crozier and Davies, 2006; Luke, 2003).

These living arrangements promote closeness between adolescents and their extended family. Schlegel and Barry's cross-cultural analysis showed that daily contact was as high with grandparents as with parents for adolescents in traditional cultures, and adolescents were usually even closer to their grandparents than to their parents. Perhaps this is because in all cultures parents typically exercise authority over adolescents, which may add ambivalence to adolescents' relationships with their parents, whereas grandparents are less likely to exercise authority and may focus more on nurturing and supporting adolescents (Gauthier, 2002).

Even if this phenomenon is found in all cultures, especial closeness to grandparents has been found among adolescents in minority Asian cultures established in the West. Asian adolescents typically grow up with grandparents either in the home or living nearby, and they report high levels of nurturing and support from their grandparents (Fuligni et al., 1999).

Extended family members are also important figures in the lives of adolescents in Western majority cultures. About 80 per cent of adolescents in another American study list at least one member of their extended family among the people most important to them, and closeness to grandparents is positively related to adolescents' well-being (Ruiz and Silverstein, 2007). However, in the British majority culture, adolescents' contact with extended

Grandparents tend to be important figures in the lives of adolescents living in minority Asian cultures.

family members is relatively infrequent, in part because extended family members often live many miles away. British adolescents of the majority culture have significantly less contact with their extended family members compared with adolescents in other European countries because members of European extended families are more likely to live in closer proximity (Crozier and Davies, 2006; Chang et al., 2003; Guglani et al., 2000).

An exception to this pattern occurs among adolescents in divorced families, who tend to have increased rather than decreased contact with their grandparents during adolescence, especially with their maternal grandfather (Douglas and Ferguson, 2003). This suggests that the maternal grandfather fills the father's role in these families, to some extent, by spending more time with his grandchildren than he would if the father were present. Mothers and adolescents in divorced families may have greater need for the grandfather's support and assistance, given the economic and emotional strains that often occur in divorced families (Smart, 2004).

PARENTING STYLES

'Well, they wouldn't care if I started going out till God knows what time (they'd probably be glad to get rid of me!), and they aren't bothered that I sit

here all day and night till whatever time I want (probably because I've left school).'
– Kev, age 17 (Jellyellie, 2007, p. 19)

'I stayed out last night until one. When I came back, Dad wouldn't stop shouting at me, so I left. He thinks I'm still a little kid.'
– Jasmine, age 14 (NSPCC, 2007, p. 4)

Because parents are so important in the development of children, social scientists have devoted a great deal of research to the quality of parent–child relationships and to the effects of parenting. One branch of this research has involved the study of **parenting styles** and results are consistent across historic and more recent research (e.g. Collins and Laursen, 2004; Steinberg, 2001). Virtually all of the prominent scholars who have studied parenting have described it in terms of two dimensions: **demandingness** and **responsiveness** (also known by other terms such as *control* and *warmth*). Parental demandingness is the degree to which parents set down rules and expectations for behaviour and require their children to comply with them. Parental responsiveness is the degree to which parents are sensitive to their children's needs and express love, warmth and concern.

Many researchers have combined these two dimensions to describe different kinds of parenting styles. For many years, the best-known and most widely used conception of parenting styles was the one articulated by Diana Baumrind (1991a; 1991b; 1971; 1968). Her research on middle-class families, along with the research of many other scholars inspired by her ideas, has identified four distinct parenting styles, and their effects upon adolescents (e.g. Keller, 2008; Aunola and Nurmi, 2005) and emerging adults (e.g. Manzeske and Stright, 2009) – see Table 7.2.

Authoritative parents are high in demandingness and high in responsiveness. They set clear rules and expectations for their children. Furthermore, they

Table 7.2 Parenting Styles and the Two Dimensions of Parenting

		Demandingness	
		High	**Low**
Responsiveness	**High**	Authoritative	Permissive
	Low	Authoritarian	Disengaged

make clear what the consequences will be if their children do not comply, and apply the consequences if necessary. However, authoritative parents do not simply 'lay down the law' and then enforce it rigidly. A distinctive feature of authoritative parents is that they *explain* the reasons for their rules and expectations to their children, and they willingly engage in discussion with their children over issues of discipline, sometimes leading to negotiation and compromise. Authoritative parents are also loving and warm towards their children, and they respond to what their children need and desire.

Authoritarian parents are high in demandingness but low in responsiveness. They require obedience from their children, and they punish disobedience without compromise. None of the verbal give-and-take common with authoritative parents is allowed by authoritarian parents. They expect their commands to be followed without dispute or dissent. Also, they show little in the way of love or warmth toward their children. Their demandingness takes place without responsiveness, in a way that shows little emotional attachment and may even be hostile.

Permissive parents are low in demandingness and high in responsiveness. They have few clear expectations for their children's behaviour, and they rarely discipline them. Instead, their emphasis is on responsiveness. They believe that children need love that is truly 'unconditional'. They may see discipline and control as having the potential to damage their children's healthy tendencies for developing creativity and expressing themselves however they wish. They provide their children with love and warmth and give them a great deal of freedom to do as they please.

Disengaged parents are low in both demandingness and responsiveness. Their goal may be to minimise the amount of time and emotion they devote to parenting. Thus, they require little of their children and rarely bother to correct their behaviour or place clear limits on what they are allowed to do. They also express little in the way of love or concern for their children.

They may seem to have little emotional attachment to them.

Parenting Styles as Custom Complexes

These four parenting styles can be understood as custom complexes as described in Chapter 4. What custom complexes are reflected in the parenting styles described above? An ongoing theme of research on parents' child-rearing goals shows that parents in Western cultures tend to value independence highly as a quality they wish to promote in their children (De Groof, 2008; Mottram and Hortaçsu, 2005). Authoritarian parenting clearly discourages independence, but the other three parenting styles – authoritative, permissive and disengaged – reflect parents' custom complex that it is good for adolescents to learn **autonomy** –that is, to learn to be independent and self-sufficient, to learn to think for themselves and be responsible for their own behaviour (Zimmer-Gembeck and Collins, 2003).

Authoritative parents promote autonomy in positive ways through encouraging discussion and give-and-take that teaches adolescents to think independently and make mature decisions. Permissive and disengaged parents promote this outcome in a negative way – that is, through the absence of restraint that allows adolescents a great deal of autonomy without parental guidance. As we will see in the next section, the differences in how these parenting styles promote autonomy result in different effects on adolescents' development. Nevertheless, in combination the prominence of these parenting styles in the families of adolescents in Western cultures reflects the prominence of individualism in cultural beliefs (Lewis, 2007). This is an example of how cultural beliefs form the basis for the socialisation that occurs in the family and elsewhere, as discussed in Chapter 4.

CONNECT AND EXTEND

For a study that investigates behavioural autonomy in a multi-ethnic context in The Netherlands, read 'Connectedness with parents and behavioural autonomy among Dutch and Moroccan adolescents' by Annemarie Huiberts, Annerieke Oosterwegel, Inge Vandervalk, Wilma Vollebergh and Wim Meeus in *Ethnic and Racial Studies*, Volume 29, Number 2 (2006), pp. 315–330

The Effects of Parenting Styles on Adolescents

A great deal of research has been conducted on how parenting styles influence adolescents' development. In general, authoritative parenting is associated with the most favourable outcomes, at least by Western standards. Adolescents who have authoritative parents tend to be independent, self-assured, creative and socially skilled (Collins and Laursen, 2004). They also tend to do well in school and to get along well with their peers and with adults (Spera, 2005). Authoritative parenting helps adolescents develop characteristics such as optimism and self-regulation that in turn have positive effects on a wide range of behaviours (Jackson et al., 2005; Purdie et al., 2004).

All the other parenting styles are associated with some negative outcomes, although the type of negative outcome varies depending on the specific parenting style. Adolescents with authoritarian parents tend to be dependent, passive and conforming. They are often less self-assured, less creative and less socially adept than other adolescents. Adolescents with permissive parents tend to be immature and irresponsible. They are more likely than other adolescents to conform to the behaviour of peers. Adolescents with disengaged parents tend to be impulsive. Partly as a consequence of their impulsiveness, and partly because disengaged parents do little to monitor their activities, adolescents with disengaged parents tend to have higher rates of problem behaviours (see Chapter 12) such as delinquency, early sexual involvement and use of drugs and alcohol (Goldstein et al., 2005).

Authoritative parenting tends to do better for adolescents for a number of reasons. First, adolescents are at a point in their lives when they have become capable of exercising more autonomy and self-regulation than when they were younger (Zimmer-Gembeck and Collins, 2003). In order to be able to move into adult roles after adolescence, they need to be given a greater amount of autonomy and be required to exercise a greater amount of responsibility (Hallam et al., 2006). At the same time, they lack the experience with the world and with their own impulses and abilities that adults have; consequently, an excess of autonomy may leave them aimless or even lead them into harm (Huiberts et al., 2006). Authoritative parenting achieves a balance between allowing enough autonomy for adolescents to develop their capacities and at the same time requiring them to exercise their increased autonomy in a responsible way. All the other parenting styles either fail to allow as much autonomy or allow it without requiring the kind of responsibility that is associated with healthy development.

Most studies of parenting in adolescence assess one parent or combine ratings for the two parents into one rating, but studies that examine differences have produced interesting results. Inconsistency between parents also tends to be related to negative outcomes for adolescents. Specifically, adolescents who perceived inconsistency between their parents are lower on self-esteem and school performance compared not only with those who perceived both parents as authoritative but also with those who perceived both parents as permissive (Sheppard, 2007; Gould et al., 2004).

THINKING CRITICALLY

How would you categorise the parenting style of your parents when you were in adolescence? Was it the same for you as for your siblings (if you have any)? To what extent did their parenting influence you, and – if you are already a parent – to what extent did you learn certain parenting behaviours from them?

A More Complex Picture of Parenting Effects

Although parents undoubtedly affect their adolescents profoundly by their parenting, the process is not nearly as simple as the cause-and-effect model just described. Sometimes discussions of parenting make it sound as though an authoritative parenting style automatically and inevitably produces a perfect, well-balanced emerging adult. However, enough research has taken place by now to indicate that the relationship between parenting styles and adolescent development is considerably more complex than that (e.g. J. E. Gregory et al., 2001; Collins et al., 2000). Adolescents also affect their parents in return. Developmental scholars refer to this principle as **reciprocal effects** or bi-directional effects between parents and children (Collins and Laursen, 2004; Crouter and Booth, 2003; Patterson and Fisher, 2002).

Recall our discussion of evocative genotype-environment interactions in Chapter 2. Adolescents are not like billiard balls that head predictably in the direction they are propelled. They have personalities and desires of their own that they bring to the parent–adolescent relationship. Thus, adolescents may evoke certain behaviours from their parents. An especially aggressive adolescent may evoke authoritarian parenting, perhaps because the parents find that authoritative explanations of the rules are simply ignored, and their responsiveness diminishes as a result of the adolescent's repeated violations of their trust. An especially mild-tempered adolescent may evoke indulgent parenting because parents may see no point in laying down specific rules for an adolescent who has no inclination to do anything outrageous anyway.

An interesting finding of some studies is that adolescent siblings *within the same family* often give very different accounts of what their parents are like towards them. For example, one early study investigated families with two adolescents aged 11 to 17 and found that these siblings perceived significant differences in their parents' love for them, their parents' closeness to them, their parents' use of discipline, and the degree to which their parents involved them in family decisions (Daniels et al., 1985). These findings have been borne out in more recent research (Kowal et al., 2004).

Thus, one adolescent may see her parents as admirably demanding and responsive, the epitome of the authoritative parent, whereas her brother describes the same parents as dictatorial and unresponsive. These differences in how adolescents perceive their parents' behaviour are in turn related to differences in the adolescents: the ones who perceive their parents as authoritative tend to be happier and to be functioning better in a variety of ways (Chao, 2001). Overall, little similarity in personality exists between adolescent siblings (Wright et al., 2008; Neiderhiser et al., 2007), which suggests that whatever effect parents have it is different for different adolescents within the same family.

Does this research discredit the claim that parenting styles influence adolescents? No, but it modifies this claim. Parents do have beliefs about what is best for their adolescents, and they try to express those beliefs through their behaviour towards their adolescents (Kerr and Stattin, 2003). However, parents' actual behaviour is affected not only by what they believe is best but also by how their adolescents behave towards them and how their adolescents seem to respond to their parenting. Being an authoritative parent is easier if an adolescent responds to the demandingness and responsiveness provided, and not so easy if love is rejected and the rules, and the reasons provided for them, are ignored. Parents whose efforts to persuade their adolescents through reasoning and discussion fall 'on deaf ears' may be tempted either to demand compliance (and become more authoritarian) or to give up trying (and become permissive or disengaged).

Recently, an ambitious research project has gone deeper than previous research into the complexities of adolescents' family lives (Neiderhiser et al., 2007; Reiss et al., 2000). This project studied 720 families from various areas of the United States with two same-sex siblings within each family, including identical twins, fraternal twins, full siblings, half-siblings, and biologically unrelated step-siblings. The research design enabled the researchers to examine questions of genetic and environmental family influences on adolescents, as well as the different experiences of siblings within the same family. The research methods used in the study included not only questionnaires but interviews, videotaped family interactions and information on the adolescents' social world outside the family. The average ages of the siblings when the study began were 12 and 15, and the families were followed over a three-year period.

In terms of dimensions of *warmth* and *negativity,* there was evidence for **differential parenting**, which resulted in **non-shared environmental influences**. The consequences of these differences were evident in adolescents' behaviour and psychological functioning. Also, the influence of genetics seemed to be especially strong for parental negativity, in the sense that the more alike two siblings were genetically, the more alike parents' behaviour was towards siblings with respect to more negative parental behaviours. This seems to suggest that the parents' negativity (overly authoritarian or permissive behaviours) was evoked by the adolescents' genetically based behaviour.

Furthermore, parents and adolescents often differed in their reports of parenting behaviour (Feinberg et al., 2001), with parents reporting more warmth and less negativity for themselves than their adolescents reported for them. For younger adolescents, the more different their reports were from their parents' reports, the more likely they were to be functioning poorly (Feinberg et al., 2000b). This suggests that it is important to include multiple reports of parenting behaviour rather than only the adolescents' reports, as most studies do.

Adolescent siblings within the same family often report different experiences with their parents.

CONNECT AND EXTEND

Hearing directly from adolescents is always enlightening, particularly when exploring the fighting behaviour of an inner-city population of adolescent girls before and after becoming pregnant! For a fascinating insight read 'Fighting and depression among poor pregnant adolescents' by Arielle Shanok and Lisa Miller in the *Journal of Reproductive and Infant Psychology*, Volume 23, Number 3 (2005), pp. 207–218

Parenting in Other Cultures

Almost all the research on parenting styles has taken place in western society, and most of it has centred on families in Western majority cultures. What do parent–adolescent relationships look like if we look around the world, especially towards non-Western cultures? There may be some lessons for us about traditional cultures now living in multi-ethnic European communities.

Probably the most striking difference is how rare the authoritative parenting style is in non-Western cultures. Remember, a distinctive feature of authoritative parents is that they do not rely on the authority of the parental role to ensure that adolescents comply with their commands and instructions. They do not simply lay down the law and expect to be obeyed. On the contrary, authoritative parents explain the reasons for what they want adolescents to do and engage in discussion over the guidelines for their adolescents' behaviour.

Outside of the West, however, this is an extremely rare approach to adolescent socialisation. In traditional cultures – as we have already noted – parents expect that their authority will be obeyed, without question and without requiring explanation. This is true not only of non-industrial traditional cultures but also of industrialised traditional cultures outside the West, most notably Asian cultures such as China, Japan, Vietnam and South Korea (Zhang and Fuligni, 2006; Tseng, 2004). As noted in Chapter 1, Asian cultures have a tradition of filial piety, meaning that children are expected to respect, obey and revere their parents throughout life (Lieber et al., 2004). In other traditional cultures as well, the *role of parent* carries greater inherent authority than it does in the West. Parents are not supposed to provide reasons why they should be respected and obeyed. The simple fact that they are parents and their children are children is viewed as sufficient justification for their authority (the *Cultural Focus* feature provides an important example that transfers into multi-ethnic contexts).

Does this mean that the typical parenting style in traditional cultures is authoritarian? No, although sometimes

Most traditional cultures emphasise respect and obedience toward parents. Here, an African adolescent and his father.

writers have come to this erroneous conclusion. Keep in mind that authoritarian parenting combines high demandingness with *low responsiveness*. Parents in traditional cultures are indeed high in demandingness, and their demandingness is often of a more uncompromising quality than is typical in the West. However, it is not true that parents in traditional cultures are typically low in responsiveness. On the contrary, parents and adolescents in non-industrialised traditional cultures often develop a closeness that is nearly impossible in Western families because – as we have previously observed – families in traditional cultures spend virtually all of their days together, working side by side (boys with their fathers, girls with their mothers) in a way that the economic structure of industrialised societies does not allow. Parents and adolescents in industrialised traditional cultures such as Asian

CULTURAL FOCUS

Young People and Their Families in India

India is currently the second most populous country in the world, with a population of over 1 billion people. By the middle of the twenty-first century it will reach a population of 1.5 billion. India is an astonishingly diverse country, with a wide variety of religions, languages and regional cultures. Nevertheless, developmental and anthropological scholars generally believe that a common Indian culture can be identified (Sabat, 2008; Segal, 1998), including with regard to young people and their families. The features of the Indian family provide a good illustration of young people's family lives in a traditional culture and how that culture translates to being a minority culture living as part of a Western nation state.

Indian families have many features in common with other traditional cultures discussed in this book. Collectivistic values are strong, and the well-being and success of the family are considered more important than the well-being and success of the individual (Saraswathi, 2006; 1999). There is a strong emphasis on personal sacrifice, and children are taught from an early age to relinquish their own desires for the sake of the family as a whole. Interdependence among family members is stressed throughout life; emotionally, socially and financially (Chaudhary and Sharma, 2007).

As in most traditional cultures, the Indian family has a clear hierarchy based on age (Saraswathi, 2006; Laungani, 2005). Respect for elders is strongly emphasised. Even in childhood, older children are understood to have definite authority over anyone younger than they are; even in adulthood, older adults merit respect and deference from younger adults simply on the basis of being older. Because it is common for young married couples to live with the husband's parents rather than establishing a separate residence, many households with children contain grandparents and often uncles, aunts and cousins as well. This pattern is changing because Indian society is becoming increasingly urbanised, and extended family households are less common in urban areas than in rural areas. Nevertheless, recent studies show that around 80 per cent of India's population is rural and tends to live according to traditional family arrangements (Prokopy, 2009; Chaudhary and Sharma, 2007).

One feature that is distinctive to the traditional Indian family is the idea that the parents, especially the father, are to be regarded by their children as a god would be regarded by a devotee. The Hindu religion, which most Indians believe, has many gods of varying degrees of power, so this is not like stating that the father is like 'God' in a Western sense. Nevertheless, the analogy of a father being like a god to his children effectively symbolises and conveys the absolute nature of his authority within the family.

These features of the Indian family have important implications for the development of

Adolescents in India benefit from close family relationships.

➤

adolescents and emerging adults. The inherent authority of parents and the emphasis on respect for elders mean that parents expect obedience even from adolescents and emerging adults. Traditional Indian families include little of the explanation of rules and discussion of decisions that characterise the relationships between adolescents and parents in authoritative Western families. For parents to explain the reasons for their rules, or for young people to demand to take part in family decisions, would be considered an offence to the parents' inherent authority. This does not mean the parents are 'authoritarian', in the scheme of parenting styles described by Western social scientists. On the contrary, warmth, love and affection are known to be especially strong in Indian families (Larson et al., 2000; Chaudhary and Sharma, 2007). Indian parenting is better described by the 'traditional' parenting style discussed in this chapter.

The authority of parents in Indian families also means that there are not the same expectations of autonomy for adolescents and emerging adults as there are in Western families (Vijayakumar et al., 2006; Larson et al., 2000). Indian adolescents spend most of their leisure time with their families, not with their friends. Dating and sexual relationships before marriage are almost non-existent (Chaudhary and Sharma, 2007). Most marriages are arranged by the parents, not chosen independently by the young people themselves. Emerging adults usually remain in their parents' homes until marriage.

What are the consequences of these family practices for the development of Indian adolescents and emerging adults? A Western reader may be tempted to regard the practices of Indian families as 'unhealthy' because of their hierarchical, patriarchal quality and because of the way that the autonomy of young people is suppressed. However, it is probably more accurate to view Indian family socialisation as having both costs and benefits, like other cultural forms of socialisation. For young people in India there are clearly costs in terms of individual autonomy. To be expected to be obedient to your parents even in your teens and 20s (and beyond), to be discouraged from ever questioning your parents' authority and judgement, and to have your parents control crucial life decisions in love and work clearly means that young people's autonomy is restricted in Indian families.

However, Indian family practices have clear benefits as well. Young people who grow up in a close, interdependent Indian family have the benefit of family support and guidance as they enter adult roles. Because they respect their parents' experience, they value the advice their parents provide about what occupation to pursue and whom to marry (Saraswathi, 2006). Having a strong sense of family interdependence also provides Indian young people with a strong family identity, which may make them less lonely and vulnerable as they form an individual identity. Indian adolescents have low rates of delinquency, depression and suicide compared with Western adolescents (Chaudhary and Sharma, 2007; Vijayakumar, 2005).

The influence of globalisation can be seen in Indian culture as in other traditional cultures. Western styles of dress, language and music are popular among young Indians. In urban middle-class families the traditional Indian pattern of parental authority is changing, and parents' relationships with their adolescents increasingly involve discussion and negotiation (Patel-Amin and Power, 2002; Larson et al., 2000; Scrase, 2000). Nevertheless, young Indians remain proud of the Indian tradition of close families, and they express the desire to see that tradition endure (Sin, 2006; Jones, 2004; Selvan et al., 2001).

The traditions, beliefs and practices of family life in India transfer when Indian families become part of ethnic minority subcultures in European countries. Young people's attitudes and actions in relation to the family, to aspirations of autonomy and independence, towards the selection of a marriage partner, an occupation or a place to live continue to be profoundly affected by the fundamental belief in the importance of family and the ways in which family is central to the protection of cultural identity. With all the tensions and dilemmas, young Indian people in Britain and other western countries remain proud and protective of their origins and beliefs (Sin, 2006; Uddin, 2006; Basu and Altinay, 2002).

cultures also maintain a strong degree of closeness that is reflected in a sense of interdependence and in shared activities and mutual obligations (Hardaway and Fuligni, 2006; Lim and Lim, 2004; Fuligni et al., 1999).

However, parental responsiveness may be expressed quite differently in non-Western cultures. For example, parents in non-Western cultures rarely use praise with their children (Paiva, 2008), and in many Asian cultures open expressions of affection and warmth between parents and adolescents are uncommon (Jeffries, 2004). But are typical parents of adolescents in non-Western cultures responsive; do they have deep emotional attachments to their adolescents; do they love them; are they deeply concerned with their well-being? Unquestionably, the answer is yes.

If parents in non-Western cultures cannot be called authoritarian, what *are* they? The fact is, they do not fit very well into the parenting scheme presented earlier. They are generally closest to authoritative parents because, like them, they tend to be high in demandingness and high in responsiveness. However, as noted, their demandingness is very different from the demandingness of the authoritative Western parent.

Diana Baumrind, the developmental researcher who originally invented the terminology for the parenting styles we have been discussing, has recognised the problem of fitting traditional cultures into her scheme. Accordingly, she has proposed the term **traditional parenting style** (1991b; 1987) to describe the kind of parenting typical in traditional cultures – high in responsiveness and high in a kind of demandingness that does not encourage discussion and debate but rather expects compliance by virtue of cultural beliefs supporting the inherent authority of the parental role.

For example, in recent years, some Asian psychologists have argued that designations of authoritative and authoritarian cannot be easily applied to parents from Asian minority groups (Lim and Lim, 2004). They suggest that researchers – particularly those from the majority ethnic culture may misunderstand immigrant, second or multigeneration Asian parenting and mislabel it as authoritarian because it involves a degree and type of demandingness that is typical of Asian families. Yet Asian British adolescents show none of the negative effects typically associated with authoritarian parenting. On the contrary, they have higher educational achievement, lower rates of behavioural problems, and lower rates of psychological problems, compared with white adolescents (Ghuman, 2002). Furthermore, family attitudes of interdependence among Asian adolescents and emerging adults are related to their high rates of academic achievement and their low rates of problems (Tseng, 2004). This suggests that cultural context is crucial to predicting the effects parenting will have on adolescents.

ATTACHMENTS TO PARENTS

'It's like if I get in some really, really bad trouble then my friends might get afraid, you know, and go away. But my parents will always be there.'
– Devon (Jeffries, 2004, p. 120)

We have noted that adolescents consistently state that their parents are among the most important figures in their lives, and that most young people maintain a sense of emotional closeness to their parents throughout adolescence and emerging adulthood. An influential theory describing emotional relationships between parents and children is **attachment theory**. This theory was originally developed in the second half of the twentieth century by British psychiatrist John Bowlby (1980; 1973; 1969), who argued that among humans, as among other primates, attachments between parents and children have an evolutionary basis in the need for vulnerable young members of the species to stay in close proximity to adults who will care for and protect them. Bowlby's colleague, psychologist Mary Ainsworth (1982), observed interactions between mothers and infants and described two general types of attachment: **secure attachment**, in which infants use the mother as a 'secure base from which to explore' when all is well, but seek physical comfort and consolation from her if frightened or threatened; and **insecure attachment**, in which infants are wary of exploring the environment and resist or avoid the mother when she attempts to offer comfort or consolation.

Although most of the early research and theory on attachment focused on infancy, both Bowlby and Ainsworth believed that the attachment formed with the **primary caregiver** in infancy (usually but not necessarily the mother) forms the foundation for attachments to others throughout a person's life. Bowlby quoted a phrase from Sigmund Freud (see the *Focus on Professional Practice* feature in Chapter 6) to describe this concept, in which Freud stated that the relationship with the mother is 'the prototype of all [future] love relations' (Freud, 1940/1964, p. 188). According to Bowlby, in the course of interactions with the primary caregiver, the infant develops an **internal working model** that shapes expectations and interactions in relationships

CONNECT AND EXTEND

The fundamentals of attachment theory and family systems theory are outlined in 'Systemic attachment theory and therapeutic practice: a proposal' by Kirsten von Sydow in *Clinical Psychology & Psychotherapy*, Volume 9, Number 2 (March/April 2002), pp. 77–90

with others throughout life. This implies that during adolescence and emerging adulthood the quality of relationships with others – parents, friends, teachers, romantic partners – will all be shaped, for better or worse, by the quality of the attachments to parents experienced in infancy.

This is a provocative and intriguing claim. How well does it hold up in research? First, abundant research continues to indicate that a secure attachment to parents *in adolescence* is related to favourable outcomes – aspects of adolescents' well-being, including self-esteem and psychological and physical health (Dashiff et al., 2009; Laghi et al., 2009; Roisman et al., 2002; Granqvist, 2002; Allen and Land, 1999; Lieberman et al., 1999). Adolescents who have secure attachments to

Secure attachments to parents are related to adolescents' well-being in a variety of respects.

parents tend to have closer relationships with friends and romantic partners (Roisman et al., 2001; Laible et al., 2000). Security of attachment to parents in adolescence has also been found to predict a variety of outcomes in emerging adulthood, including educational and occupational attainment, psychological problems, quality of romantic relationships and drug use (Mayseless and Scharf, 2007; Allen et al., 2006; Cooper et al., 2004).

Another prediction of attachment theory involves the compatibility between autonomy and **relatedness** in adolescence. According to attachment theory, autonomy (being capable of self-direction) and relatedness should be compatible, not opposing dynamics in relations with parents. That is, in infancy as well as in adolescence, if children feel close to their parents and confident of their parents' love and concern, they are likely to be able to develop a healthy sense of autonomy from parents as they grow up (Zimmer-Gembeck and Collins, 2003). Rather than promoting prolonged dependence on parents, a secure attachment gives children the confidence to go out into the world, using the comfort of that attachment as a 'secure base from which to explore'.

Adolescents who have trouble establishing autonomy in adolescence also tend to have more difficulty maintaining a healthy level of relatedness to parents. An imbalance between autonomy and relatedness (i.e., too little of one or both) tends to be related to a variety of negative outcomes, such as difficulties at school, psychological problems and drug use (Gillison et al., 2008; Allen et al., 2007).

However, what about the claim that attachments in infancy form the basis for all later relationships, including those in adolescence and emerging adulthood? What do studies indicate on this crucial issue? Several longitudinal studies on attachment have by now followed samples from infancy to adolescence, and they provide mixed support for the predictions of attachment theory (e.g. Grossman et al., 2005). On one hand, psychologist Everett Waters and his colleagues (2000) reported that 72 per cent of the children in their sample received the same attachment classification at age 21 as they did at 1 year of age. On the other hand, other studies found that a prolonged separation from parents during infancy or early childhood predicted a less secure attachment to parents in adolescence, in accord with attachment theory, which asserts that early separation from parents can result in long-term difficulties in emotional development (e.g. Woodward et al., 2000).

An earlier but informative study found that attachment classification in infancy was able to predict the quality of interactions with others at ages 10 and 15 (Sroufe et al., 1993). When the children in the original infancy study reached age 10, the researchers invited them to attend a summer camp where their relations with peers could be observed. At age 10, the children who had been securely attached in infancy were judged to be more skilled socially, more self-confident, and less dependent on other campers. Five years later, the researchers arranged a camp reunion where the children could again be evaluated. At age 15, adolescents who had been securely attached in infancy were more open in expressing their feelings and were more likely to form close relationships with peers (Weinfield et al., 2000). However, in a more recent follow-up, these researchers found no continuity between security of attachment to parents in infancy and at age 19 (Sroufe et al., 2005). Similar results were reported in a longitudinal study by Michael Lewis and colleagues (2000) where there was no continuity in how the quality of attachment to parents was classified from 1 to 18 years of age and – importantly – no relation between infant attachment status and adolescent maladjustment.

Based on this mixed bag of results, most attachment researchers have modified the claim that infant attachment is the foundation of all later relationships (Grossman et al., 2005; Egeland and Carlston, 2004). Instead, they view infant attachment as establishing tendencies and expectations that may then be modified by later experiences in childhood, adolescence, and beyond. This view of attachment is also more bi-directional, viewing the quality of attachment as due not only to the behaviour of the parent but also to the temperament and behaviour of the child as well.

PARENT–ADOLESCENT CONFLICT

'This is a dangerous world, what with all the drugs and drunk drivers and violent crime and kids disappearing and you name it. I know my kids are pretty responsible, but can I trust all their friends?

Are they going to end up in some situation they can't get out of? Are they going to get in over their heads? You can never be sure, so I worry and set curfews and make rules about where they can go and who they can go with. Not because I want to be a tough dad, but because I want them to be safe.'

– John, father of a 16-year-old son and a 13-year-old daughter (Bell, 1998, p. 54)

'My father is very strict and had a great deal of rules when I was in high school, which usually could not be bent for anything. My father was very worried about the fact that I was getting older and interested in boys so much. This worrying led him to lay down strict rules which led to many arguments between us. He would hardly let me go anywhere.'

– Danielle, age 19 (Arnett, unpublished data)

Although children and adolescents typically develop attachments to their parents, the course of family life does not always run smoothly, and this seems to be especially true for families with adolescents. For a variety of reasons, adolescence can be a difficult time for relationships with parents.

The degree of parent–adolescent conflict should not be exaggerated. Early theories of adolescence, such as those of G. Stanley Hall (1904) and Anna Freud (1946), claimed that it was universal and inevitable that adolescents rebel against their parents, and that parents and adolescents experience times of intense conflict for many years. Anna Freud even asserted that adolescents would not develop normally without this kind of turmoil in their relationships with their parents.

Few developmental experts on adolescence believe this anymore. Over the past few decades, numerous studies (e.g. Smetana, 2005; Moore et al., 2002)

Conflict in adolescence is especially frequent and intense between mothers and daughters.

have shown that it is simply not true. In fact, adolescents and their parents agree on many of the most important aspects of their views of life and typically have a great deal of love and respect for one another. Of course, adolescents and their parents frequently disagree, but the arguments are usually over relatively minor issues such as curfews, clothes, grooming and use of the family car. These arguments usually do not seriously threaten the attachments between parents and their adolescents.

However, let's not get carried away with the rosy portrait of family harmony, either. Conflict with parents increases sharply in early adolescence, compared with pre-adolescence, and remains high for several years before declining in late adolescence (Dworkin and Larson, 2001). Figure 7.2 shows the pattern of conflict across adolescence, from a longitudinal study that observed mothers and sons in videotaped interactions on five occasions over eight years (Granic et al., 2008). Conflict in adolescence is especially frequent and intense between mothers and daughters (Collins and Laursen, 2004). Another study found that 40 per cent of adolescents reported arguments with their parents at least once a week (Sears et al., 2006). By mid-adolescence, conflict with parents tends to become somewhat less frequent but more intense (De Goede et al., 2009). It is only in late adolescence and emerging adulthood that conflict with parents diminishes substantially (Cui et al., 2008; C. Gordon, 2008).

Perhaps as a consequence of these conflicts, parents tend to perceive adolescence as the most difficult stage of their children's development. In a recent study in The Netherlands, 56 per cent of Dutch parents viewed adolescence as the most difficult time to be a parent, compared to 5 per cent for infancy and 14 per cent for the toddler period (Meeus, 2006). Although mid-life tends to be an especially fruitful and satisfying time for adults, for many of them their satisfaction with their relationships with their children diminishes when their children reach adolescence (Gladding, 2002) because as times and intensity of conflict rise between parents and adolescents, closeness declines (Laursen and Collins, 2004).

THINKING CRITICALLY

Conflict in adolescence is especially frequent and intense between mothers and daughters (Collins and Laursen, 2004). Why is that?

Sources of Conflict with Parents

'One minute my mother treats me like I'm old enough to do this or this – like help her out at home by doing the marketing or making dinner or babysitting my little brother. And she's always telling me, "You're thirteen years old now, you should know better than that!" But then the next minute, when there's something I really want to do, like there's a party that everyone's going to, she'll say, "You're too young to do that." '
– Elizabeth, age 13 (Bell, 1998, p. 55)

Why do parents and adolescents argue more than they did earlier? Why would early adolescence be a time when conflict with parents is especially high? Part of the explanation may lie in the physical and cognitive changes of adolescence. Physically, adolescents become bigger and stronger during puberty, making it more difficult for parents to impose their authority by virtue of their greater physical presence. Also, puberty means sexual maturity, which means that sexual issues may be a source of conflict – at least indirectly – in a way they would not have been in childhood. Early-maturing adolescents tend to have more conflict with parents than adolescents

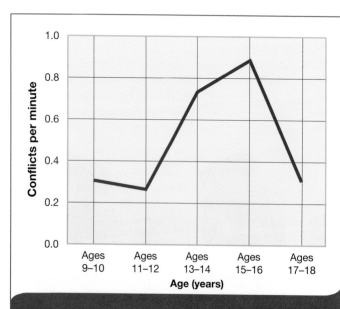

Figure 7.2 Observed conflicts per minute between mother and son in 30-minute videotaped interactions over an 8-year period.
Source: Granic, et al. (2008).

CONNECT AND EXTEND

Of course family conflict is better avoided in some circumstances. Read 'Conflict avoidance in anorexia nervosa: an observational study of mothers and daughters' by P. J. Lattimore, H. L. Wagner and S. Gowers in *European Eating Disorders Review: The Journal of the Eating Disorders Association*, Volume 8, Number 5 (October 2000), pp. 355–368

who mature 'on time', perhaps because sexual issues arise earlier (Collins and Laursen, 2004).

Cognitively, increased abilities for thinking abstractly and with more complexity make adolescents better arguers than pre-adolescents and make it more difficult for parents to prevail quickly in arguments with their children (Sigfusdottir et al., 2004). According to psychologist Judith Smetana, conflict may also reflect the different ways adolescents and their parents perceive and define the range of adolescents' autonomy (Smetana, 2005). Parents frequently view issues of conflict as matters of desirable social convention, whereas adolescents regard these issues as matters of personal choice. Smetana's research indicates that, especially in early adolescence, parents and adolescents often disagree about who should have the authority over issues such as dress and hairstyles, choice of friends, and the state of order (or disorder) in the adolescent's bedroom.

Parents tend to see these as issues they should decide, or at least influence and set boundaries for; adolescents, however, tend to see the issues as matters of personal choice that should be theirs to decide by now. Perhaps the peak of conflict occurs in early adolescence because that is the time when adolescents are first pressing for a new degree of autonomy, and parents are adjusting to their adolescents' new maturity and struggling over how much autonomy they should allow. In the view of Smetana and other scholars on adolescents and families, conflict can be constructive and useful because it promotes the development of a new equilibrium in the family system that allows adolescents greater autonomy (Collins and Laursen, 2004).

Although most parent–adolescent conflict is over apparently minor issues, some issues that seem trivial on the surface may in fact be substitutes for more serious underlying issues. For example, most parents and adolescents have limited communication about sexual issues. Especially in the era of AIDS and other sexually transmitted diseases (STDs), it would be surprising indeed if most parents did not have some concerns about their adolescents' sexual behaviour, yet they find it difficult to speak to their adolescents directly about sexual issues. As a result, they may say 'You can't wear that to school' when they mean 'That's too sexually provocative.' They may say 'I don't know if it's a good idea for you to go out with him' when they really mean 'He looks like a gland on legs to me. He's after sex and I worry that you'll like the idea.' They may say 'You have to be home by 11:00' which might mean 'The film ends at ten, and I don't want you to have time to have sex between the time the film ends and the time you come home.'

Sexual issues are not the only issues that may be argued about in this indirect way. 'I don't like that crowd you're hanging around with lately' could mean 'They look like the type who might use drugs, and I worry that they might persuade you to use them, too.' Arguments about curfews may reflect parents' attempts to communicate that 'The sooner you come in, the less likely it is that you and your friends will have drunk enough beer to put yourselves at risk for a terrible car accident.'

Seen in this light, these arguments are not necessarily over trivial issues but may be proxies for arguments over serious issues of life and death (Ruschena et al., 2005). Parents have legitimate concerns about the safety and well-being of their adolescents, given the high rates of adolescents' risky behaviour (as we will see in Chapter 12), but they also know that in most European majority cultures they are expected to loosen the reins substantially when their children reach adolescence. The result may be that they express their concerns indirectly, through what seem to be less serious issues.

Culture and Conflict with Parents

Although the physical and cognitive changes of adolescence may provide a basis for parent–adolescent conflict, this does not mean that such conflict is universal and 'natural'. Physical and cognitive changes take place among adolescents in all cultures, yet parent–adolescent conflict is not typical in all cultures (Ortega, 2001). Cultures can take the raw material of nature and shape it in highly diverse ways. This is no less true for parent–adolescent conflict than for the other topics addressed in this book.

In traditional cultures, it is rare for parents and adolescents to engage in the kind of frequent, petty conflicts typical of parent–adolescent relationships in most European majority cultures (Smokowski et al., 2009). Part of the reason is economic. In traditional cultures, family members tend to rely on each other economically. In many of these cultures, family members spend a great deal of time together each day, working on family economic enterprises. Children and adolescents depend on their parents for the necessities of life, parents depend on children and adolescents for the contribution of their labour, and all family members are expected to assist one another routinely and help one another in times of need. Under such conditions, the pressure to maintain family harmony is intense because the economic interdependence of the family is so strong (Sin, 2006).

However, more than economics and the structure of daily life are involved in the lower levels of parent–adolescent conflict in traditional cultures. Levels of conflict are low in parent–adolescent relationships not only in non-industrialised traditional cultures but also in highly industrialised traditional cultures, such as Japan and Taiwan (Zhou, 1997), as well as in the Asian cultures that are part of European society (Harwood et al., 2002). This indicates that even more important than economics are cultural beliefs about parental authority and the appropriate degree of adolescent independence. As discussed earlier, the role of parent carries greater authority in traditional cultures than in the West, and this makes it less likely that adolescents in such cultures will express disagreements and resentments towards their parents (Phinney et al., 2005).

THINKING CRITICALLY

How would you predict parent–adolescent conflict in traditional cultures will be affected by globalisation?

This does not mean that adolescents in traditional cultures do not sometimes feel an inclination to resist or defy the authority of their parents. Like Western adolescents, they undergo physical and cognitive

changes at puberty that may incline them towards such resistance. But cultural socialisation shapes not only the way people behave but their beliefs – their whole way of looking at the world. Someone who has been raised in a culture where the status and authority of parents and other elders are taught to them and emphasised constantly and consistently is unlikely at adolescence to question their parents' authority, regardless of their new physical and cognitive maturity. Such questioning is simply not part of their cultural beliefs about the way the world is and the way it should be. Even when they disagree with their parents, they are unlikely to say so because of their feelings of duty and respect (Phinney and Ong, 2002).

A key point in understanding parent–adolescent relationships in traditional cultures – and minority traditional cultures living within multi-ethnic European nation states – is that the independence which is so important to Western adolescents is not nearly as prized in non-Western cultures. In the West, as we have seen, regulating the pace of adolescents' autonomy is often a source of parent–adolescent conflict. However, parents and adolescents in the West agree that independence is the ultimate goal for adolescents as they move into adulthood (Aquilino, 2006). Individuals in the West are supposed to reach the point, during emerging adulthood, where they no longer live in their parents' household, no longer rely on their parents financially, and have learned to stand alone as self-sufficient individuals (Mulder and Clark, 2002). The pace of the adolescent's growing autonomy is a source of contention between parents and adolescents not because parents do not want their adolescents to become independent, but because the ultimate goal of self-sufficiency that both of them value requires continual adaptations and adjustments in their relationship as they move towards that goal. Increasing autonomy prepares adolescents for life in a culture where they will be expected to be capable of independence and self-sufficiency. The discussion, negotiation and arguments typical of parent–adolescent relationships in the West may also help prepare adolescents for participation in a politically diverse and democratic society.

As previously observed, outside of the West, independence is not highly valued as an outcome of adolescent development. Financially, socially, and even psychologically, interdependence is a higher value than independence, not only during adolescence but throughout adulthood (Phinney et al., 2005; Markus and Kitayama, 2003). Just as a dramatic increase in autonomy during adolescence prepares Western adolescents for adult life in an individualistic culture, learning to suppress disagreements and submit to the authority of one's parents prepares adolescents in traditional cultures for an adult life in which interdependence is among the highest values and throughout life each person has a clearly designated role and position in a family hierarchy.

Leaving Home

In most Western majority cultures, most young people move out of their parents' home sometime during emerging adulthood. In Europe the timing of home leaving and its key determinants have been studied across the enlarged EU. Social researcher Srna Mandic (2008) of the University of Ljubljana noted three clusters of countries: the north-western, characterised by the earliest home leaving and best opportunities for independent housing; the south-western cluster, marked by the latest leaving of the parental home and only a little less favourable opportunities, but highest family support; the north-eastern cluster, characterised by late, yet not extremely late, home leaving, combined with poor housing opportunities and strikingly low family support.

When a young person leaves home, a disruption in the family system takes place that requires family members to adjust. As we have seen, parents generally adjust very well, and in fact report improved marital satisfaction and life satisfaction once their children leave (Campbell et al., 2007; Whitbourne and Willis, 2006). What about the relationship between parents and emerging adults? How is it influenced by the young person's departure?

Typically, relationships between parents and emerging adults improve once the young person leaves home. In this case, at least, absence does make the heart grow fonder. Many studies have confirmed that emerging adults report greater closeness and fewer negative feelings towards their parents after moving out (e.g. Aquilino, 2006; Smetana et al., 2004). Furthermore, emerging adults who move out tend to get along better with their parents than those who remain at home. For example, in an earlier (1996) study specifically about geographical distance between parents and emerging adults psychologists Judith Dubas and Andreas Petersen followed a sample of 246 young people from age 13 to age 21. At age 21, the emerging adults who had moved at least an hour away (by car) from their parents reported the highest levels of closeness to their parents and valued their parents' opinions most highly. Emerging adults who remained home had the poorest relations with their parents in these respects, and those who had moved

Relationships with parents tend to improve when emerging adults leave home.

out, but remained within an hour's drive were in between the other two groups.

What explains these patterns? Some scholars have suggested that leaving home leads young people to appreciate their parents more (Holdsworth, 2004). Another factor may be that it is easier to be fond of someone you no longer live with. Once emerging adults move out, they no longer experience the day-to-day friction with their parents that inevitably results from living with others. They can now control the frequency and timing of their interactions with their parents in a way they could not when they were living with them. They can visit their parents for the weekend, for a holiday, or for dinner, enjoy the time together, and still maintain full control over their daily lives.

As previously noted emerging adults in Southern and Eastern Europe tend to live with their parents longer than in other parts of Europe (Douglass, 2005; 2007). Figure 7.3 shows the patterns in various European countries (Iacovou, 2002). A number of practical reasons explain why some European emerging adults stay home longer. Southern and Eastern European university students are more likely than Northern European students to continue to live at home while they attend university. Eastern European emerging adults who do not attend university may have difficulty finding or affording accommodation of their own. Also important are Southern European cultural values that emphasise mutual support within the family while also allowing young people substantial autonomy. Young Southern Europeans find that they can enjoy a higher standard of living by staying at home rather than living independently, and at the same time enjoy substantial autonomy. Italy provides a good case in point (Krause, 2005). Ninety-four per cent of Italians aged 15 to 24 live with their parents, the highest percentage in the European Union. However, only 8 per cent of

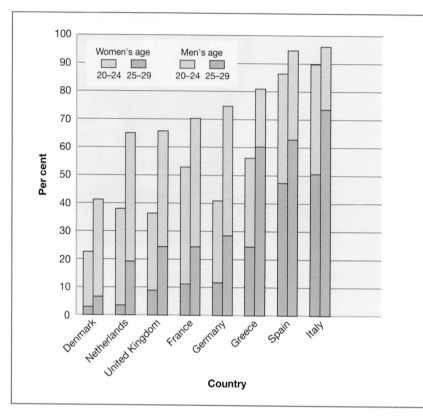

Figure 7.3 Percentage of emerging adults living at home in Europe
Source: Iacovou (2002).

them view their living arrangements as a problem – the lowest percentage among EU countries. Many Southern European emerging adults remain at home contentedly through their early 20s, by choice rather than necessity.

In summary, research studies show that young people can maintain or enhance the closeness they feel to their parents even as they become more autonomous. For both adolescents and emerging adults, autonomy and relatedness are complementary rather than opposing dimensions of their relationships with their parents.

HISTORICAL CHANGE AND THE FAMILY

To gain a complete understanding of adolescents' and emerging adults' family relationships today, it is necessary to understand the historical changes that are the basis for current patterns of family life. Many of the changes that have taken place in Western societies over the past two centuries have had important effects on families. Let's take a look briefly at these changes, considering how each has affected adolescents' and emerging adults' family lives. We will focus on British

examples, but similar changes have taken place in other industrialised countries in the past two centuries and are taking place today in economically developing countries. We will first examine changes over the past two centuries, then focus on changes during the past 50 years.

Patterns Over Two Centuries

Three of the changes that have influenced family life over the past two centuries are a lower birth rate, longer life expectancy, and a movement from predominantly rural residence to predominantly urban residence. In the nineteenth century, Britain became the world's first industrial and urban society; by 1851 more than half the population lived in towns. The population of Britain boomed during the nineteenth century. In 1801 it was about 9 million but by 1901 it had risen to about 41 million.

In contrast to young people today, young people of 200 years ago tended to grow up in large families; in 1800, women in Northern Europe gave birth to an average of seven children (Parker, 2009). It was much more common then for children to die in infancy or early childhood, but nevertheless, adolescents were much more likely to have responsibility for younger children than they are today, when the average number

Between 1830 and the present, the proportion of farm families fell from about 70% to less than 2%.

of births per mother is just two – actually a mean average of 1.96 in 2009 (Office for National Statistics, 2009a). In this respect, adolescents' family lives 200 years ago in the West were like the lives of adolescents in many traditional cultures today (Lloyd, 2005).

Longer life expectancy is another change that has affected the way young people experience family life. Up until about 1900, the average human life expectancy was about 45; in 1901 baby boys were expected to live for 45 years and girls 49 years (House of Commons Library, 1999). Now it is well over 75 and in Britain is still rising. In 2006–08 life expectancy at birth for males was highest in the South East of England – 79.2 years – and lowest in Scotland – 75.0 years. For females, life expectancy was highest in the South West of England – 83.1 years – and lowest in Scotland – 79.9 years (Office for National Statistics, 2009b). Because of the lower life expectancy in earlier times, marriages frequently ended in the death of a spouse in young or middle adulthood (Ruschena et al., 2005). Thus, adolescents frequently experienced the death of a parent and the remarriage of their widowed parent.

Increased urbanisation has also resulted in changes in family life. Up until about 200 years ago, most European people lived and worked on a family farm; nearly 90 per cent of children lived in farm families (Sperber, 2008). Today in Britain this figure is less than half of one percent. (Office for National Statistics, 2009c). This means that the majority of adolescents 200 years ago would have grown up in a rural area in a farm family, with their daily lives structured around farm work and spent almost entirely with their families. As people moved off the farms, they migrated increasingly to the cities. Emerging adults often led the way, leaving their farm families to head for the 'bright lights of the big city'. This meant new opportunities for education and employment, as well as greater opportunities for premarital sex, alcohol use, and other temptations of urban life (Jayne et al., 2006).

Each of these changes has had effects not just on young people but on young people's family lives. Overall, we can say that the range of functions the family serves has been greatly reduced, many of them taken over by other social institutions (Dillen, 2007; King et al., 2005; Nelson, 2004; Sykorova, 2002). Table 7.3 shows some of the functions the family once served and the institutions that now serve those functions, although the family also contributes in the other areas. The family in our time has mainly emotional or **affective functions**. So, most

Table 7.3 The Changing Functions of the Family

Function	Performing institution, 1800	Performing institution, 2000
Educational	Family	School
Religious	Family	Church/ Synagogue/ Temple/Mosque
Medical	Family	Medical profession
Economic support	Family	Employer
Recreational	Family	Entertainment industry
Affective	Family	Family

young people living in industrialised countries do not rely on their parents to educate them, treat their medical problems, make a place for them in the family business, or provide recreation. Rather, young people look to their parents mainly for love, emotional support, and some degree of moral guidance (Allen and Land, 1999).

The Past 50 Years

Family life today is not only very different from that of 200 years ago, but has also changed dramatically in the past 50 years. During this time, the most notable changes have been: the rise in the divorce rate and family separation; the rise in the proportion of children in single-parent households; and the rise in the prevalence of dual-earner families. Once again, let's look at each of these changes with an eye to their implications for development in adolescence and emerging adulthood.

Rise in the Divorce Rate

Fifty years ago divorce was relatively rare in Europe compared with the present. In the United Kingdom the divorce rate increased almost four and a half times between 1957 and 2007 affecting six times as many dependent children now as then (Office for National Statistics, 2010c). However, in the last decade the annual divorce rate in the UK has declined by 15 per cent, bucking the trend across the 27 states of Europe that have seen a 16 per cent increase during the same period (Eurostat, 2010). Rates remain low in Italy and Ireland – both Catholic countries – and only a third of the rate in Spain (another Catholic country) which has seen a trebling of divorces over the same period. The Czech Republic has the highest mean average rates of divorce at 3 divorces a year for every thousand Czech citizens (the usual measure for divorce rates) but even the European 'champion' is nothing compared with the United States, which has a divorce rate of 4.5. The current rate is so high in the US (see Figure 7.4) that nearly half of the current generation of their young people are projected to experience a parents' divorce by the time they reach their late teens (Hetherington and Kelly, 2002). Furthermore, between 1981 and 2008 although the total number of marriages each year in England and Wales fell by a third (Office for National Statistics, 2010d) the proportion of 'remarriages' – where one or both of the couple have been married before – rose by over a third (37 per cent). With more people remarrying, adolescents have became more likely to experience new family arrangements in what are sometimes referred to as blended families (C. Gordon, 2008; Rigg and Pryor, 2007; Kaganas and Diduck, 2004) – but more of this later.

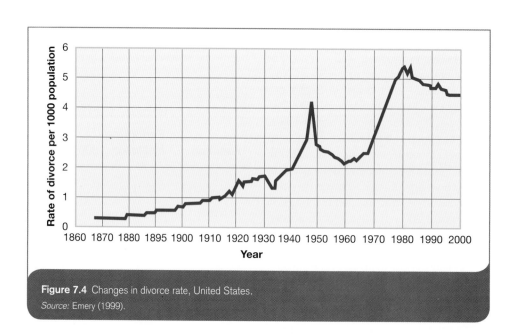

Figure 7.4 Changes in divorce rate, United States.
Source: Emery (1999).

CONNECT AND EXTEND

For a study that investigated supporting children's school career among parents in divorced lone-parent and stepfamilies, read: 'Supporting the educational career of children from divorced families: parents' experiences and the role of the school' by H. Colpin, L. Vandemeulebroecke and P. Ghesquière in the *British Journal of Sociology of Education*, Volume 25, Number 3 (2004), pp. 275–289

Rise in the Rate of Single-Parent Households

The rise in the divorce rate and the breakup of long-term relationships causing family separation has contributed to a simultaneous rise in the rate of single-parent households. Although most divorced parents remarry, they have a period between marriages as single parents. In the majority of divorces (up to 90 per cent) it is the mother who is the **custodial parent** and this is generally the case in different cultural contexts (Miller, 2006; Colpin et al., 2004; Skevik, 2004; Liu, 2001; Emery, 1999).

In addition to the rise in single-parent households, there has been an increase in the proportion of children born outside of marriage. During 1964 in England and Wales there were 63.3 thousand live births outside of marriage out of a total of 875,972 live births, some 7.25 per cent of the total (National Archives, 2010). By 2004 this had risen to just over 269 thousand out of almost 640 thousand, over 42 per cent of live births were taking place outside of marriage – an almost five-fold increase in the proportion of the population being born outside of civil or religious marriage (Office for National Statistics, 2010). A word of warning.

Any discussion of factors that might impact on the social ecology of development during adolescence and emerging adulthood is – as we discussed in Chapter 1 – open to two main charges. First that selection for discussion of factors such as single-parent households, rates of divorce or birth out of wedlock appears to position the writer as making a judgement that these factors may have a deleterious effect. Second that there is, therefore, a moral dimension to the discussion. It is important for you to check as you study that empirical research is used in all such discussions to show some association between the social factors and any effects described. Does the experience of your parents' divorcing have a deleterious effect upon the youngsters in the family? Does being born outside of marriage or stable long-term relationship change how you will experience the world and therefore impact on your development? These are important questions and deserve your attention. Some of these matters lie at the heart of the upcoming *Historical Focus* feature.

HISTORICAL FOCUS

The Problem of Lone-mother Families in the Twentieth Century

In this feature we want to examine the changes during the twentieth century in national policy solutions to the perceived problem of lone mothers – a family structure that we have already discussed in the main text. The sociopolitical context chosen is that of Britain but similar changes are reflected in many northern countries of the EU. During the last century major policy solutions to the 'problem' did not focus on social problems associated with the additional pressures on lone parents or on *family processes* (Klaff, 2007) – the quality of relationships and family interactions – but were defined primarily in terms of the cost of the financial support provided by the state. There were four main policy turning points during the century:

➤

1. The period just before and after the First World War

Prior to the First World War, widowed, deserted and unmarried mothers were expected to turn to poor law relief for financial support, but such was the practice of the charity organisations which worked in tandem with the poor law that some or all of her children were often removed from a mother who applied for financial support. One extreme case was a widow so fearful that all or some of her children would be removed by poor law authorities that she left her children uncared for while she went to work. She was convicted of child cruelty.

There were many campaigns, some from newly formed socialist, women's and trades unions groups, for the right to non-stigmatised support from the state to enable poor lone mothers to combine paid employment – often only sweated labour was available – with the work of caring for children.

At this time the vast majority of lone mothers were widows and following the First World War – a tragic widow-making war on a huge scale – there was a call for paying pensions to widows, and those women whose husbands were imprisoned or incapacitated. This pension was to be sufficient to allow them to care full time for their children. To the list of intended recipients was added divorced women with custody of children, all separated and deserted women and unmarried mothers. Not everybody agreed. The Local Government Board (responsible for administering poor law benefit to lone mothers) said 'Ten shillings is not transmuted into fifteen by calling it a pension, nor is a shiftless mother converted into a model of care and forethought by a grant of money' (LGB, 1918: iii). Despite such views the British government enacted the right to widows' pensions for women whose husbands had paid National Insurance. Deserted, separated and divorced wives, and unmarried mothers, remained the responsibility of (ex-) husbands, other members of the family or the local board for poor law relief.

2. Beveridge's 1942 Plan for Social Security Reform

The *Beveridge Report* of 1942 was the report of a UK Government Committee chaired by an economist, William Beveridge. The report identified five 'giant evils' in society that must be tackled on the way to reconstruction of a fair society: squalor, ignorance, want, idleness and disease, and went on to address these evils by proposing widespread reform to social welfare in the United Kingdom. The report formed the basis for the post-war reforms known as the Welfare State, including expansion of National Insurance (a prerequisite for payment of the Widow's Pension) and the creation of a National Health Service.

War widows with children.

Beveridge was opposed to 'means-tested' benefits. His proposal was for a flat rate contribution rate for everyone and a flat rate benefit for everyone. However in the end, marital status – once-married women – remained the determinate of access to social insurance monies and unmarried mothers 'were never serious contenders' (Lewis et al., 1998; p. 265).

Rather, the one hope for all lone mothers was another of William Beveridge's recommendations, the universal family allowance, which offered some support as long as all children were covered and the allowance was set at a high enough rate. However, when the reforms of the *Beveridge Report* passed into legislation and were enacted, the allowance did not apply to the first child and was set at 60 per cent of that recommend by Beveridge. The vast majority of lone mothers still had to depend upon national assistance to support themselves and their children.

William Beveridge.

3. The 1974 *Finer Report* on One-parent Families

The Finer Committee on One-parent Families was appointed in 1969 at a time when illegitimate births were beginning to rise dramatically and 1969 divorce legislation had made the grounds for divorce not dependent upon finding fault – the principle of 'irretrievable breakdown' – thus enshrining the unfettered right to divorce and remarry. The report preserved the responsibility of absent husbands and fathers to pay maintenance while establishing that the burden of support should fall upon the state. The report committee recommended replacing magistrate and higher courts' jurisdiction with a new family court to rule on matters of separation and divorce, and to set and manage maintenance orders, guaranteed by a non-contributory government-funded maintenance allowance (GMA) for all lone mothers. Maintenance was to be collected by the court and offset against the GMA so all lone mothers would receive the same support irrespective of their marital status.

Despite debate in the House of Commons the *Finer Report* was not implemented, yet it made a significant contribution to subsequent changes:

- A benefit for the first child was introduced in 1976 and a permanent one-parent benefit in 1981.

- The earnings disregard (allowing working mothers to be employed without any detriment to their benefits) was doubled in 1975 and combined with an increase in the Additional Personal (tax) Allowance for lone mothers.

- There was an automatic entitlement to free milk for under-5s and free school meals for lone mothers on supplementary benefit or family income supplement.

- Housing benefit was extended to lone parents who worked part time.

By 1978 a review of social security found that with the extension of benefits and rights to part-time work, one-parent families had a higher income than two-parent families in the same economic grouping. Much of this burden fell on the state as family courts struggled to administer the maintenance orders on absent fathers. It had become acceptable (some argued desirable) to be or to become a lone mother, for state benefits to be an expectation of right, and for absent fathers to contribute little or nothing to the upkeep and upbringing of their children.

➤

Mother leaving child with child minder.

4. Developments in the 1990s

By the end of the 1980s, there developed a desire shared across the political spectrum to shift the balance of support for lone mothers away from the state to the absent fathers and to the earnings of lone mothers. The 1991 Child Support Act established the Child Support Agency (CSA) to take over the judgements and enforcement of maintenance payments from the family courts and made the way clear for the new New Labour Government of 1997 to abandon the special benefits and premiums paid to lone mothers. It soon became clear that the CSA had failed to make the major shift to support from absent fathers that government wanted so attention again turned to the remaining source of income for lone mothers: earnings.

In 1997, the British government piloted a 'welfare to work' scheme which included all lone mothers, and gave assistance with job search and training to take advantage of job opportunities that were already available. The weight of expectation had shifted again from dependence upon charity at the start of the century through access to universal benefits – no matter how inadequate – in the post-Second World War period through the 'boom years' for lone mothers of the 1970s and 1980s, and to the new reality of the 1990s where unsuccessful attempts to make absent fathers fully financially responsible gave way to shifting the balance of financial support for lone mothers, largely now divorced and never-married mothers rather than widows, to the lone mothers themselves. This state of affairs continues into the first two decades of the twenty-first century and shapes the socio-economic context for many of today's adolescents and emerging adults.

Source: Jane Lewis (University of Nottingham) 'The problem of lone-mother families in twentieth-century Britain', *Journal of Social Welfare and Family Law*, Volume 20, Number 3 (1998), pp. 251–283

Rise in the Rate of Dual-earner Families

In the nineteenth and early twentieth centuries, the rise of industrialisation took most employment outside of the home and farm into factories, larger businesses, shops, civic and domestic services and the offices of government. It was almost exclusively men who obtained this employment; women were rarely employed in the economic enterprises of industrialisation. During the nineteenth century, their designated sphere became the home, and their designated role was the cultivation of a family life that their husband and children would experience as a refuge from the complex and sometimes bruising world of industrialised societies (Matud et al., 2002; Murphy-Lawless, 2000).

This trend changed about 50 years ago with the rise of **dual-earner families**, as mothers followed fathers out of the home and into the workplace. Over the past 50 years, employment among women with school-aged children has increased steadily. Mothers of adolescents are more likely than mothers of younger children to be employed outside of the home – see Figure 7.5. In the second quarter of 2008 more than two-thirds

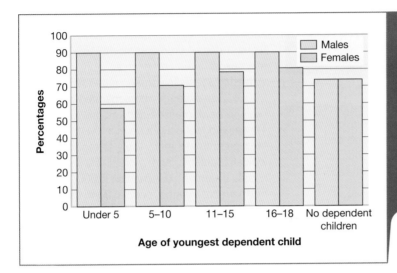

Figure 7.5 Adolescents in the UK are more likely to have a working mum than mums of younger children or those with no dependent children.

Source: http://www.statistics.gov.uk/cci/nugget.asp?id=1655

(68 per cent) of working-age women in the UK with dependent children were in employment; over the same period women without children were more likely to be in employment, at 73 per cent. The age of the youngest child affects the employment rate of mothers. Of working-age women with children aged under five, 57 per cent were in employment. This compared with 71 per cent for those whose youngest child was aged 5 to 10 and 78 per cent whose youngest child was aged 11 to 15 – more than those with no dependent children (Office for National Statistics, 2008).

Part of the increase in working mums is related to the increase in rates of divorce, family separation and single parenthood discussed earlier, which have often left the mother as the only source of the family's income. Mothers in non-divorced or separated families may also work to help the family maintain an adequate income (Schneider and Waite, 2005).

Across Europe, proportions of dual-earner families do vary, but there is an interesting association between employment rates for men and women and educational attainment. Almost double the women work who have high educational qualifications and attainment as those women with no or low educational attainment – see Table 7.4.

Table 7.4 Employment Rates of Women and Men, by Level of Educational Attainment, 2005

Educational attainment	Employment rate	
	Women	**Men**
Low	43.8	69.7
Medium	65.6	79.7
High	80.4	87.4

Source: Eurostat, 2007, pp. 3–4

Of course, non-economic reasons are often involved as well. Many educational and occupational opportunities have opened up to women in the past 50 years that had been denied to them before. Research indicates that most employed mothers would continue to work even if they had enough money (Schneider and Waite, 2005; Hochschild, 2001). Women in professional careers, in the restaurant trade and factory workers generally report that they are committed to their jobs, enjoy having a work role as well as family roles, and desire to continue to work.

CONNECT AND EXTEND

To study changes in female labour force behaviour around childbirth read 'Changing dynamics in female employment around childbirth: evidence from Germany, The Netherlands and the UK' by Jan Dirk Vlasblom and Joop Schippers in *Work, Employment & Society*, Volume 20, Number 2 (June 2006), pp. 329–347

EFFECTS OF FAMILY CHANGE

Now that we have reviewed the historical background of the current Western family, let's take a look at how divorce or parental separation, remarriage and reconstitution of families, single parenthood, and dual-earner families are related to young people's behaviour and to their perceptions of their family lives.

Divorce and Parental Separation

'When I was 15 my parents separated. I continued to live with my mother but would visit my father on Sunday. During that time we would do something "entertaining", like go to a movie, which relieved the pressure from us to actually interact … My parents are now divorced and my father calls me every Sunday night. We talk about school, my job, and things in the news. But when I need advice or just want to talk, I always call my mother. She is more aware of my everyday life and I feel very comfortable with her. With my father, on the other hand, our relationship is more forced because he is not up to date on my life and hasn't been for some time.'

– Marilyn, age 21 (Arnett, unpublished data)

'My parents were divorced, so the money was pretty thin … I wanted everything that the other kids had – designer clothes, etc. I would pester my mother for money constantly, sometimes to the point where she would be in tears because she wanted to give me things but couldn't afford to do so.'

– Dawn, age 20 (Arnett, unpublished data)

Because the rate of divorce and parental separation is so high and has risen so dramatically in the past 50 years in many countries, scholars have devoted a great deal of attention to investigating the effects. Across a wide range of countries, studies consistently find that young people whose parents have divorced or separated are at higher risk for a wide variety of negative outcomes compared with young people in non-separated families, in areas including behaviour problems, psychological distress and academic achievement (Breivik and Olweus, 2006; Hetherington

and Kelly, 2002). With regard to behaviour problems, adolescents whose parents have separated have higher rates of drug and alcohol use and tend to initiate sexual intercourse at an earlier age, compared with adolescents in non-separated families (Buchanan, 2000). Adolescents with separated parents are more likely to be depressed and withdrawn (Meeus, 2006). Those who feel caught up in a loyalty conflict between their parents are more likely to report having psychological problems and more likely to receive mental health treatment (Buchanan, 2000; Cherlin, 1999). Furthermore, young people from separated families tend not to do as well in school as their peers (Jeynes, 2002), and are less likely to go to university than young people from non-separated families (Aquilino, 2006).

In general, adolescents show fewer negative effects of parental separation than younger children do (Klaff, 2007; Buchanan, 2000), perhaps because adolescents are less dependent on their parents, spend more time with their peers outside of the family household, and have greater cognitive capacities to understand and adapt to what is happening. However, even many years after the separation, the painful memories and feelings linger for many adolescents and emerging adults (Cartwright, 2006; Laumann-Billings and Emery, 2000). In emerging adulthood, the effects of parental separation are evident in greater problems in forming close romantic relationships (Aquilino, 2006; Herzog and Cooney, 2002; Wallerstein et al., 2000). As they anticipate a possible marriage of their own, emerging adults from divorced families tend to be somewhat wary of entering marriage, but especially determined to avoid having a divorce of their own (Kelly, 2007; Hetherington, 2003; Darlington, 2001; Hansagi et al., 2000). Nevertheless,

Exposure to conflict between parents leads to a variety of problems in children and adolescents.

the risk of divorce is higher for young people from divorced families (Amato, 2000).

Although the findings on the effects of divorce or separation are consistent, a great deal of variability exists in how adolescents and emerging adults respond to and recover from their parents' separation (Cherlin, 1999). To say that a young person's parents are separated tells us only about **family structure**. *Family structure* is the term researchers and writers use to refer to the outward characteristics of the family – whether or not the parents are married, how many adults and children live in the household, whether or not there is a biological relationship between the family members and so on. However, in recent years scholars studying divorce and separation have focused primarily on **family process** (Klaff, 2007) – that is, the quality of family members' relationships, the degree of warmth or hostility between them, and so on. So it is important to go beyond the simple question such as 'Why does parental separation have negative effects on children and adolescents?' to the more complex and potentially enlightening question – 'How does parental separation influence family process in ways that, in turn, influence children and adolescents?'

Perhaps the most important aspect of family process with regard to the effects of parental separation on children and adolescents is exposure to conflict between parents (Sbarra and Emery, 2008; Emery, 1999). Divorce and separation involve the dissolution of a relationship that is, for most adults, at the heart of their emotional lives and their personal identities. Because the beginning of long-term partnership commitments carry such a weight of hopes and dreams, they rarely end without numerous explosions occurring along the way. Living in a household where separation is taking place, children and adolescents are likely to be exposed to their parents' hostility and recriminations before, during, and after the separation, which is often painful, stressful and potentially damaging (Hetherington and Kelly, 2002; Kelly, 2000).

In non-separated families too, conflict between parents has potentially damaging effects on children's development (Bradford et al., 2004; Kelly, 2000; Emery, 1999). In fact, many studies have found that adolescents and emerging adults in high-conflict non-divorced households have poorer adjustment than adolescents and adults in low-conflict divorced households (Amato, 2000; Emery, 1999). Longitudinal studies which include data before and after separation indicate that adolescents' problems after divorce and separation often began long before the separation, as a consequence of high conflict between their parents (Peris and Emery, 2004; Buchanan, 2000;

Kelly, 2000). Thus, it is exposure to parents' conflicts, not simply the specific event of separation that can be especially damaging to children and adolescents.

A second important aspect of family process to consider with regard to the effects of parental separation is that separation affects parenting practices. Separation is highly stressful and painful to most of the adults who experience it (Mack, 2001), and not surprisingly it affects many aspects of their lives, including how they carry out their role as parents. The burdens fall especially on mothers. As the sole remaining parent in the household, the mother has to take on all the parenting that was previously shared with the father, and often has increased employment responsibilities now that the father's income no longer comes directly into the family – not to mention handling by themselves the leaky roof, the sick pet, the broken-down car and all the other typical stresses of daily life.

So it is understandable that mothers' parenting tends to change following separation, usually for the worse. In the first year following family separation mothers tend to be less affectionate, more permissive and less consistent in their parenting than they were before the divorce took place or than they will be after a few years have passed (Hetherington and Kelly, 2002; Buchanan, 2000). Adolescents in separated families have greater freedom than adolescents in non-separated families in matters such as how to spend their money and how late to stay out, but younger adolescents especially may find it to be more freedom than they can handle wisely.

Another way parenting may change after separation is that the mother may rely on the adolescent as a confidant (Afifi et al., 2007; Silverberg-Koerner et al., 2004). This is a mixed blessing for adolescents. They may enjoy becoming closer to their mothers while at the same time finding it difficult to hear about their parents' marital troubles and their mothers' difficulties in the aftermath of the separation (Cookston et al., 2007). Emerging adults may be able to handle this role better. Some studies find that emerging adults who experience their parents' separation become closer to their mothers after the separation (Kielty, 2006) and feel closer to their mothers than emerging adults in non-separated families (Smetana et al., 2004).

As for relations with fathers, in most families children's contact with their father declines steadily in the years following separation because adolescents in separated families may live many miles away from their fathers, and almost half have not seen their father in over a year (Hetherington and Kelly, 2002). Even when separated fathers and adolescents remain in close proximity, fathers complain that it often becomes difficult to arrange

CONNECT AND EXTEND

Mediation can offer a viable alternative to adversarial separation or divorce because couples are helped to speak directly to each other as they move towards separate lives. Read 'A family therapy perspective on mediation' by Elena Katz in *Family Process*, Volume 46, Number 1 (March 2007), pp. 93–107

meetings as adolescents become increasingly involved in activities of their own (Kielty, 2006). Also, separated fathers are frequently the target of young people's resentment and blame following separation (Brown et al., 2009). Children often feel pressured to take sides when their parents separate, and because mothers are usually closer to their children before the separation, children's sympathies and loyalties are more often with the mother than with the father (Dowling and Gorell-Barnes, 1999). Thus, young people in separated households tend to have more negative feelings and fewer positive feelings towards their fathers compared with young people in non-separated families (Wells and Johnson, 2001).

A third factor in considering the effects of parental separation on young people is the increase in economic stress that typically results from separation (Klaff, 2007; Jeynes, 2002). With the father's income no longer coming directly into the household, money is often tight in mother-headed households following separation. In the aftermath of parental separation, the income in mother-headed families decreases significantly (Chambaz, 2001). Some studies claim that the problems children and adolescents exhibit following separation are due largely to these economic problems (Gram-Hanssen and Bech-Danielsen, 2008; Sheehan et al., 2008).

Several factors help to ameliorate the negative effects of separation on adolescents. Adolescents who maintain a good relationship with their mothers tend to function well in the aftermath of separation (Emery, 1999). Also, when separated parents are able to maintain a civil relationship and communicate without hostility, their children and adolescents are less likely to exhibit the negative effects of separation (Sbarra and Emery, 2008). A related factor of importance is consistency of parenting between the separate households of the mother and the father. If parents maintain consistency with each other in parenting – which they are more likely to do if they are communicating well – their adolescents benefit (Bream and Buchanan, 2003).

Of course, maintaining communication and consistency is not easy between two parents who have experienced a divorce or separation and often harbour hostile feelings towards one another (Hetherington and Kelly, 2002). In recent decades, relationship and **divorce mediation** has grown as a way of minimising the damage to children and adolescents that may result from heightened parental conflict during and after separation (Sbarra and Emery, 2008; Emery et al., 2005). In divorce mediation, a professional mediator meets with separating parents to help them negotiate an agreement that both will find acceptable. Research has shown that mediation can settle a large percentage of cases otherwise headed for court and lead to remarkably improved relationships between separated parents and their children, as well as between separated parents, even 12 years after divorce or permanent parental separation (Emery et al., 2005).

Remarriage and Reconstituted Families

'For a while [my stepfather] tried, I always call it "tried to be my dad", you know, but it wasn't in a good way, it was in a bad way. I felt like he was trying to boss me around or something, and I didn't feel he had any right to. So I guess right from the beginning we just never really got along. We kind of avoided each other as much as possible.'
– Leanne, age 23 (Arnett, 2004, p. 69)

'[My stepfather] is a very wonderful man. He always has been, but we just didn't appreciate him. But I think that would be the same for any

THINKING CRITICALLY

In addition to the factors mentioned here, can you think of other things that might influence adolescents' responses to family separation, for better or worse?

kid. Really, I don't know that you appreciate your parents until you're older and can look back and think "Wow. They were pretty incredible."'

—Lillian, age 24 (Arnett, 2004, p. 70)

In the light of the factors that seem to be most strongly related to adolescents' problems following parental separation – parental conflict, disruptions in parenting and economic stress – you might think that the mother's remarriage – including beginning a new long-term commitment with another partner – would greatly improve the well-being of adolescents in separated families. (We focus here on mothers' remarriage because it is usually the mother who has custody of the children.) The mother and her new husband or partner have just chosen to get married or move in together, so presumably they are getting along well. The mother's parenting could be expected to become more consistent now that she is happier in her personal life. She is not on her own as a parent anymore now that she has her new partner to help her with parenting and daily household tasks. As for economic stress, presumably it eases now that the stepfather's income comes into the family.

Despite these favourable prospects, studies find that adolescents typically take a turn for the worse when their mothers remarry. In general, adolescents in stepfamilies have a greater likelihood of a variety of problems compared with their peers in non-separated families, including depression, anxiety and conduct disorders (Hetherington and Stanley-Hagan, 2002). The academic achievement of adolescents in stepfamilies tends to be lower than in non-separated families, and in some studies lower than in separated families, too (Jeynes, 2007; 1999). Adolescents in stepfamilies are also more likely to be involved in delinquent activities, not only compared with adolescents in non-separated families but also compared with adolescents in separated families (Ruschena et al., 2005; Pagani et al., 1998).

Furthermore, although following separation adolescents tend to have fewer problems than younger children, following remarriage the reverse is true – adolescents have more problems adjusting to remarriage compared with younger children (Hetherington and Kelly, 2002; Hetherington and Stanley-Hagan, 2000). Adolescent girls tend to have an especially negative reaction to their mothers' remarriage (Ahrons, 2007). The reasons for this are not clear, but one possibility is that the girls develop a closer relationship with their mothers following divorce, and this closeness is disrupted by the mother's remarriage (Stoll et al., 2005; Hetherington and Kelly, 2002).

Why do adolescents often respond unfavourably to their mother's remarriage? Family researchers who have studied remarriage emphasise that, although remarriage may seem as though it should be positive for children and adolescents, it also represents another disruption of the family system, another stressful change that requires adjustment (Hetherington and Stanley-Hagan, 2000). Remember that the toughest time for families after separation tends to be one year following the separation. After that, family members usually begin to adjust, and their functioning typically improves substantially after two years have passed. Any remarriage or new relationship disrupts this new equilibrium.

With reconstituted families, all nuclear family members have to adapt to a new extended family structure and integrate one, maybe more new person(s) into a family system that has already been stressed and strained by separation. The precarious quality of this integration is illustrated by the fascinating finding in one earlier study that many stepfathers and adolescents did not mention each other when listing their family members, even two years following the remarriage (Hetherington, 1991). Adolescents and their mothers often experience 'divergent realities' when the stepfather enters the family, with the mother happier because of her new partner's love and support but the adolescent regarding him as an unwelcome intruder (Stoll et al., 2005; Silverberg-Koerner et al., 2004).

With remarriage as with separation, adolescents' responses are diverse, and the influence of family process as well as family structure must be recognised. A key family process issue is the extent to which the stepfather attempts to exercise authority over the adolescent (Moore and Cartwright, 2005). A stepfather who attempts to remind an adolescent that the curfew hour is ten o'clock, or that it is the adolescent's turn to do the hoovering may well receive the withering retort, 'You're *not* my father!' Younger children are more likely to accept a stepfather's authority, but adolescents tend to resist or reject it.

Relationships between parents and adolescents must overcome a number of other hazards in addition to the issue of the stepfather's authority (Ganong and Coleman, 2004). Establishing an attachment to a stepparent can be difficult at an age when adolescents are spending less time at home and becoming more peer oriented. Adolescents (and younger children as well) may also have divided loyalties and may fear that establishing an attachment to the stepfather amounts to a betrayal of their father. Also, because adolescents are reaching sexual maturity, they may find it difficult to welcome their mother's new partner into the household. They are more likely than younger children to be aware of the sexual relationship between mother and stepfather, and they may be uncomfortable with this awareness.

All of these considerations present a formidable challenge for stepfathers and adolescents as they attempt to establish a good relationship. However, many stepfathers and adolescents do meet these challenges successfully and establish a relationship of warmth and mutual respect (Ganong and Coleman, 2004; Hetherington and Stanley-Hagan, 2000). Also, in emerging adulthood relationships with step-parents often improve substantially (Hans et al., 2009; Jones et al., 2006; Clawson and Ganong, 2002). Just as with parents, emerging adults come to see a step-parent more as a person than simply as step-parent. Just as with biological parents, emerging adults and step-parents get along much better once they do not live in the same household and can control (and limit) the amount of contact they have.

Single Parenthood

Just as in separated families, adolescents in never-married, single-parent households are at greater risk of a variety of problems, including low school achievement, psychological problems such as depression and anxiety, and behavioural problems such as substance use and early initiation of sexual activity (Lichter et al., 2002). However, just as in separated families, family process is at least as important as family structure. Many never-married single parents have relationships with their adolescent children that are characterised by love, mutual respect and mutual support, and adolescents in these families tend to do as well as or better than adolescents in two-parent families.

Also, looking at family structure only in terms of the parents can be misleading. As noted earlier in the chapter, extended family households, in which one or more grandparents, uncles, aunts or cousins also live in the household, have been found to provide important assistance to single-parent nuclear families, through the sharing of emotional and financial support and parenting responsibilities. Extended family members not only provide direct support to adolescents, but also help adolescents indirectly by supporting the single parent, which enhances her parenting effectiveness (Oberlander et al., 2007).

Dual-earner Families

With both parents gone from the household for at least part of a typical day in most Western families, and with parents so important in the socialisation of their children and adolescents, scholars have turned their attention to the questions: 'What happens when both parents are employed?' 'What are the consequences for adolescents' development? For the most part, few substantial effects have been found on adolescents from living in a dual-earner family as compared with a family where only one parent is employed (Crouter and McHale, 2005; Galambos, 2004).

However, the effects of dual-earner families depend on the gender of the adolescent and on whether both parents are working full time. The effects of being in a dual-earner family are often quite positive for adolescent girls. These girls tend to be more confident and have higher career aspirations than girls whose mothers are not employed (Crouter and McHale, 2005), perhaps because of the model the mother provides through her participation in the workplace.

THINKING CRITICALLY

Describe how living in a dual-earner family influences adolescents, in terms of the ideas of the mesosystem in Bronfenbrenner's ecological theory (introduced in Chapter 1).

In contrast, several studies have found that adolescent boys in dual-earner families do not function as well as boys in families with only one employed parent. Adolescent boys (but not girls) in dual-earner families have more arguments with their mothers and siblings compared with boys whose mothers are not employed (Crouter and McHale, 2005). Apparently, these conflicts result from the greater household responsibilities required of adolescents when the mother is employed, and from the fact that boys resist these responsibilities more than girls do. Having two full-time working parents is also associated with poorer school performance for boys in middle-class and upper-middle-class families, although not for boys in lower social classes (Ransford et al., 2008). However, boys' school performance is not affected if one parent works part time.

The number of hours worked by the parents is an important variable in other studies as well. Adolescents, both boys and girls, are at higher risk for various problems if both parents work full time than if one parent works just part time. The risks are especially high for adolescents who are unsupervised by parents or other adults on a daily basis for several hours between the time school ends and the time a parent arrives home from work – sometimes referred to as the 'latch-key kids'. These adolescents tend to have higher rates of social isolation, depression, and drug and alcohol use (Voydanoff, 2004; Jacobson and Crockett, 2000).

Another key variable in considering the effects of dual-earner families is the quality of the relationships between the parents and the adolescent. Adolescents in dual-earner families are more likely to function well if parents maintain monitoring from a distance, for example by having their children 'check in' with them by phone (Waizenhofer et al., 2004). If parents can manage to maintain adequate levels of demandingness and responsiveness even when both of them are working, their adolescents generally function well.

PHYSICAL, EMOTIONAL AND SEXUAL ABUSE IN THE FAMILY

Although most adolescents and emerging adults generally have good relationships with their parents, some young people are subject to physical, sexual or emotional abuse. Rates of abuse in Western society are difficult to establish because this is an area in which social desirability is especially strong – abuse involves behaviours that most families would not readily disclose to others. However, numerous studies indicate that physical and emotional abuse is more likely to be inflicted on adolescents than on younger children and that sexual abuse typically begins just before adolescence and then continues into adolescence (Gance-Cleveland et al., 2008; Christoffersen et al., 2003; Tims et al., 2002; Kilpatrick et al., 2000; Kaplan et al., 1999). In the following sections we look first at physical and emotional abuse, then at sexual abuse.

Physical and Emotional Abuse

What leads parents to inflict physical and emotional abuse on their adolescent children? One well-established finding is that abusive parents are more likely than other parents to have been abused themselves as children (Donald and Jureidini, 2004; McEwen, 2003; Martin et al., 2002; Timmer et al., 2002; Doyle, 2001). They are also more likely to have experienced parental conflict, harsh discipline, or the loss of a parent as they were growing up (Nevid et al., 2003).

This does not mean that children who are abused are destined to grow up to abuse their own children; in fact, the majority of them will not (Herrenkohl et al., 2007; Littlechild, 2003). It does mean, however, that being abused is a strong risk factor for becoming an abusive parent, perhaps because some children who are abused learn the wrong lessons about how to parent their own children (Skuja and Halford, 2004; Nevid et al., 2003).

Other factors that are related to parents' physical and emotional abuse of their children and adolescents tend to involve family stresses or problems in the parents' lives. Abuse is more likely to occur in poor than in middle-class families, in large than in small families, and in families in which parents have problems such as depression, poor health or alcohol abuse (Anderson et al., 2005; Elkins et al., 2004; McCloskey and Lichter, 2003).

Physical and emotional abuse is related to a variety of difficulties in the lives of adolescents. Abused adolescents tend to be more aggressive in interactions with peers and adults (Wolfe et al., 2001). This may occur as a result of modelling their behaviour after the aggressive behaviour displayed by their parents, although it is also possible that passive genotype–environment interactions are involved (i.e. that abusing parents may pass down genes to their children that contribute to aggressiveness). Abused adolescents are more likely than other adolescents to engage in anti-social behaviour and substance use (Kilpatrick et al., 2000). They are also more likely than other adolescents to be depressed and anxious, to perform poorly in school, and to have difficulty in their peer relationships (Naar-King et al., 2002; Shonk and Cicchetti, 2001). However, these consequences are not inevitable; many abused adolescents are surprisingly resilient and grow up to be normal adults and non-abusive parents (Barber and del Fabbro, 2000).

CONNECT AND EXTEND

What is physical punishment to some, is physical abuse to others! How do the professionals make judgements about interventions in families? Read 'Professionals' decision making in cases of physical punishment reported to child welfare authorities: does family poverty matter?' by Sabrina Moraes, Joan E. Durrant, Douglas Brownridge and Grant Reid in *Child & Family Social Work*, Volume 11, Number 2 (May 2006), pp. 157–169

Sexual Abuse

The causes of sexual abuse by parents are quite different from the causes of physical abuse. Physical abuse is more commonly inflicted on boys than on girls, whereas sexual abuse is usually inflicted on girls by their brothers, fathers or stepfathers (Cyr et al., 2002). Unlike physically or emotionally abusive parents, sexually abusive fathers are usually not aggressive, but rather tend to be insecure and socially awkward around adults (Nevid et al., 2003). Because they feel inadequate in their relationships with adults – usually including their wives – they prefer to seek sexual satisfaction from children, who are easier for them to control (Reinemann et al., 2003). Sexual abuse is more likely to be committed by stepfathers than by fathers, perhaps because there is no biological incest taboo between stepfathers and their stepdaughters (Cyr et al., 2002).

The effects of sexual abuse tend to be even more profound and pervasive than the effects of physical and emotional abuse. Parental sexual abuse constitutes an ultimate breach of trust – rather than providing care and protection, the parent has exploited the child's need for nurturance and protection for the sake of his own needs. Consequently, many of the effects of parental sexual abuse are evident in the victim's social relationships. Adolescents who have been sexually abused tend to have difficulty trusting others and forming stable intimate relationships (Cherlin et al., 2004).

During the period of sexual abuse and for many years afterwards, many victims of sexual abuse experience depression, high anxiety and social withdrawal (Bergen et al., 2003). Adolescent victims may react with one extreme or the other in their sexual behaviour, becoming either highly avoidant of sexual contacts or highly promiscuous (Kendall-Tackett et al., 2001). Other consequences of sexual abuse include substance abuse, higher risk for a variety of psychological disorders, and suicidal thoughts and behaviour (Bergen et al., 2003; Bensley et al., 1999).

THINKING CRITICALLY

Explain the effects of sexual abuse in terms of attachment theory.

Although sexual abuse is among the most harmful things a parent can do to a child, one-third of sexually abused children demonstrate few or no symptoms as a result (Kendall-Tackett et al., 2001). Support from the mother after a father's or stepfather's sexual abuse has been disclosed is especially important to girls' recovery from sexual abuse; daughters cope far better if their mothers believe their account of the abuse and comfort and reassure them, rather than rejecting or blaming them (McNab and Kavner, 2001).

CONNECT AND EXTEND

It's not only about abuse in all its forms; many adolescents are neglected, which sometimes leads to the abuse. Access these four important and recent papers to extend your thinking about family-based maltreatment of adolescents.

1 'Which came first, the chicken or the egg? Examining the relationship between child neglect and poverty' by Dominic McSherry in *The British Journal of Social Work*, Volume 34, Number 5 (July 2004), pp. 727–733

2 'Prevention of child abuse and neglect and improvements in child development' by Mogens Nygaard Christoffersen and Diane DePanfilis in

Child Abuse Review, Volume 18, Number 1 (January 2009), pp. 24–40

3 'Stress generation in adolescent depression: the moderating role of child abuse and neglect' by Kate Harkness, Margaret Lumley and Alanna Truss in the *Journal of Abnormal Child Psychology*, Volume 36, Number 3 (April 2008), pp. 421–432

4 'Defining the boundaries of child neglect: when does domestic violence equate with parental failure to protect?' by Glenda Kaufman Kantor and Liza Little in the *Journal of Interpersonal Violence*, Volume 18, Number 4 (1 April 2003), pp. 338–355

FOCUS ON YOUTH IN THE MEDIA

Can Parents Control Family Access to the Media?

We have seen in this feature in foregoing chapters that media use is a big part of the lives of most adolescents and that it is becoming a global phenomenon. This prominence is even more striking when we think about it in historical perspective. At the beginning of the twentieth century, adolescents' exposure to media even in the countries traditionally designated as the West would have been limited to print media such as books, magazines and newspapers. Television, radio, MP3 players, DVDs, smart phones, computer games and the Internet did not even exist. In less than a century, all these media have become a central part of the cultural environment of fully, newly and partly industrialised societies.

Adolescence and emerging adulthood are times when important aspects of socialisation are taking place, especially with regard to identity-related issues such as beginning occupational preparation, learning gender roles and developing a set of values and beliefs. It is also a time when the presence and influence of parents diminishes relative to childhood, as we have discussed in this chapter.

Most Western societies value free speech highly, so a diverse range of media content is allowed. However, this is not a total 'free for all'. For example, Germany has a legal prohibition against music lyrics that express hatred or advocate violence towards minorities. In Norway, one person in the government reviews all films before they are allowed to be shown and prohibits the showing of those judged to be too violent. In Britain, the British Board of Film Classification regulates, restricts and advises on the age suitability of all forms of moving image (especially film, video/DVD and video games), and also provides guidance for new and developing media – see **http://www.bbfc.co.uk** for more information.

However, the enforcement of these guidelines and restrictions requires substantial parental involvement (for the most part they are guidelines, not legal requirements). Because parents are often either unaware of the media their adolescents are using or hesitant to place restrictions, most adolescents easily gain access to whatever media they like (Curtis and Hunt, 2007; Lo and Wei, 2005; Strasburger, 1999).

An important difference exists between media and the socialising influence of parents. Typically, parents have a deep and abiding interest in encouraging their adolescent to accept their attitudes, beliefs and values in order to pass the family culture on from one generation to the next. In contrast, media are typically presented by people whose primary concern is the economic success of the media enterprise. As a result, the content of media consumed by adolescents is driven not by a desire to promote a successful adolescence but by the uses adolescents themselves can make of media. Because the media are largely market driven, media providers are likely to provide adolescents with whatever it is they believe adolescents want – mostly within the limits imposed on media providers by legal authorities.

This means that adolescents have greater control over their choice of media than they do over socialisation from parents or school. This has two important consequences (Arnett, 2006c). First, it results in a great deal of diversity in the media available to adolescents as media providers try to cover every potential niche of the market for media products. Adolescents can choose from among this diversity whatever media materials best suit the circumstances and their emotional state.

Second, to some extent this socialisation goes *over the heads* of their parents as in many cases the content of music videos, for example, doesn't appear on the 'parental radar' (Strasburger, 2006; Taillon, 2004). Parents may try to impose restrictions on the music, television shows, films and electronic games their adolescents consume, but these restrictions are unlikely to be successful if an adolescent is determined to avoid them. The limited time parents and adolescents spend in each other's company makes it difficult for parents to enforce such restrictions (Barnes et al., 2007). In any case, few parents in many Western cultures now even attempt to impose restrictions (Kalenkoski and Foster, 2012; Sanders et al., 2000).

➤

> As a source of adolescent socialisation, media bear the greatest similarity to peers. With media as with peers, adolescents have substantial control over their own socialisation, as they make choices with only limited influence from their parents. With media as with peers, adolescents sometimes make choices that adults find troublesome. Indeed, media scholars have proposed that the media function as a **super peer** for adolescents, meaning that adolescents often look to media for information (especially concerning sexuality) that their parents may be unwilling to provide, in the same way they might look to a friend (Strasburger, *ibid.*; Brown et al., 2005). In the upcoming chapter you will read of many examples where media is a super peer to young people, despite parental concerns and parents' attempts to regulate what their youngsters see and hear.

LEAVING EARLY: RUNAWAYS AND 'STREET CHILDREN'

Running Away From Home

'Mum chucked me out,' said 14-year-old Serena. 'She says she wishes I hadn't been born and that it was my fault she and Dad split up. She's insane – I was only seven when he left. She threw all my stuff out into the street and was screaming at me in front of everybody. I was really ashamed.'
NSPCC Childline casenotes Running Away and Homelessness (2007, p. 7)

For some adolescents, family life becomes unbearable to them for one reason or another, and they run away from home. Eleven per cent of children (one in nine) in the UK run away from home or are forced to leave, and stay away overnight, on one or more occasion before the age of 16. It is estimated that 100,000 young people run away each year in the UK (Rees and Lee, 2005). Adolescents who stay away from home for weeks or months, or who never return at all, are at high risk of experiencing a wide variety of problems (Rosenthal and Rotheram-Borus, 2005; Whitbeck and Hoyt, 1999). Not surprisingly, adolescents who run away from home have often experienced high conflict with their parents, many have experienced physical, emotional or sexual abuse from their parents (Chen et al., 2004) and running away may be no escape. In the UK, one in eight young people are physically hurt and one in nine sexually assaulted while they are away from home (Biehal et al., 2003)

Other family factors related to running away from home include low family income, parental alcoholism, high conflict between parents, and parental neglect of the adolescent (Christoffersen, 2000; Whitbeck and Hoyt, 1999). Characteristics of the adolescent also matter. Adolescents who run away are more likely than other adolescents to have been involved in criminal activity, to use illegal drugs, and to have had problems at school (Mallett et al., 2005). They are also more likely to have had psychological difficulties such as depression and emotional isolation (Rohde et al., 2001; Whitbeck and Hoyt, 1999). They are also more likely to be gay or lesbian (Noell and Ochs, 2001).

'I ran away seven weeks ago,' said 16-year-old Leah. 'Sometimes I sleep on the streets, but mostly I've been staying with guys I've met. I meet them out drinking and stay the night with them. I don't want to go home – Mum beats me.'
NSPCC Childline casenotes Running Away and Homelessness (2007, p. 9)

Although leaving home often represents an escape from a difficult family life, running away is likely to lead to other problems. Adolescents who run away from home tend be highly vulnerable to exploitation. Many of them report being robbed, physically assaulted, sexually assaulted, and malnourished (Tyler et al., 2004; Tyler et al., 2000; Whitbeck and Hoyt, 1999). In their desperation they may seek money through 'survival sex', including trading sex for food or drugs, or becoming involved in prostitution or pornography (Tyler et al., 2004). An earlier American study of 390 runaway adolescent boys and girls demonstrated the many problems they may have. Nearly half had stolen food and over 40 per cent had stolen other expensive items. Forty-six per cent had been jailed at least once, and 30 per cent had provided sex in exchange for money. Fifty-five per cent had used hallucinogenic drugs, and 43 per cent had used cocaine or crack (McCarthy and Hagan, 1992). More recent studies have found that depression and suicidal behaviour are common among runaway adolescents (Votta and Manion, 2004; Whitbeck et al., 2004; Yoder et al., 1998). In one study that compared homeless adolescents to other adolescents, the homeless adolescents were 13 times as likely to report feeling depressed, and 38 per cent of them had attempted suicide at least once (Rohde et al., 2001).

'Some callers [to Childline] had been placed in hostels or B&Bs, but had since been evicted and had nowhere else to go. "Both my parents got arrested last week," said 16-year-old Samantha. "I've been in a hostel since. But last night they chucked me out 'cos I had someone in my room."'
NSPCC Childline casenotes Running Away and Homelessness (2007, p. 11)

Many larger towns and cities have shelters for adolescent runaways. Typically, these shelters provide adolescents with food, protection and counselling (Dekel et al., 2003). They may also assist adolescents in contacting their families, if the adolescents wish to do so and if it would be safe for them to go home. However, many of these shelters lack adequate funding and have difficulty providing services for all the runaway adolescents who come to them.

CONNECT AND EXTEND

Many of the world's wealthiest nations have a large homeless population. People at all stages of development are affected by this problem, but adolescents who are homeless face a unique set of challenges. Read 'Homelessness and health in adolescents' by Amy M. Haldenby, Helene Berman and Cheryl Forchuk in *Qualitative Health Research*, Volume 17, Number 9 (November 2007), pp. 1232–1244

SUMMING UP

In this chapter, we have explored a wide range of topics related to the family lives of adolescents and emerging adults. The following are the main points of the chapter:

- The family systems approach is based on two key principles: that each subsystem influences the other subsystems in the family and that a change in any family member or subsystem – such as when parents reach mid-life, adolescents reach puberty or emerging adults leave home – results in a period of disequilibrium that requires adjustments.
- Adolescents in industrialised countries generally have higher conflict with siblings than in their other relationships, but most adolescents have a casual relationship with siblings in which their contact is limited. In traditional cultures, a caregiver relationship between siblings is the most common form. Adolescents in traditional cultures tend to be as close to their grandparents

as to their parents because grandparents often live in the same household as their children and grandchildren.
- The two key dimensions of parenting styles focused on by family researchers are demandingness and responsiveness. Authoritative parenting, which combines high demandingness with high responsiveness, has generally been found to be related to positive outcomes for adolescents in many majority cultures. Studies of non-Western cultures indicate that the 'traditional' parenting style that combines responsiveness with a stricter form of demandingness is most common in those cultures.
- According to attachment theory, attachments formed in infancy are the basis for relationships throughout life. Although sufficient evidence is not yet available to test this claim, studies of attachment involving adolescents and emerging

➤

adults indicate that attachments to parents are related to young people's functioning in numerous ways and that autonomy and relatedness in relationships with parents are compatible rather than competing qualities.

- Research shows that conflict between parents and children tends to be highest during early adolescence, and many parents experience their children's adolescence as a difficult time. Parent–adolescent conflict tends to be lower in traditional cultures because of the greater economic interdependence of family members and because the role of parent in those cultures holds greater authority.

- Emerging adults who move away from home tend to be closer emotionally to their parents and experience less conflict with them than those who remain at home. Most emerging adults get along better with their parents than they did as adolescents.

- Profound social changes in the past two centuries have influenced the nature of adolescents' family lives, including decreasing family size, lengthening life expectancy and increasing urbanisation. Changes over the past 50 years include increases in the prevalence of divorce and family separation, single-parent households and dual-earner families.

- Parents' separation tends to be related to negative outcomes for adolescents, including behavioural problems, psychological distress, problems in intimate relationships and lower academic performance. However, there is considerable variation in the effects of separation, and the outcomes for adolescents depend not just on family structure but on family process.

- Adolescents tend to respond negatively to their parents' remarriage and the reconstitution of the nuclear families, but again a great deal depends on family process, not just family structure.

- Dual-earner families have become much more common since the Second World War. For today's adolescents, having two parents who work tends to be unrelated to most aspects of their functioning. However, some studies have found some negative effects for boys and for adolescents in families where both parents work full time.

- Adolescents who are physically abused tend to be more aggressive than other adolescents, more likely to engage in criminal behaviour, and more likely to do poorly in school, among other problems.

- Sexual abuse in families takes place most commonly between daughters and their fathers or stepfathers, who are often incompetent in their relationships with adults. Sexual abuse has a variety of negative consequences, especially in girls' abilities to form intimate emotional and sexual relationships.

- Running away from home is most common among adolescents who have experienced family problems such as physical, emotional or sexual abuse, high conflict, neglect or parents' addictions. Adolescents who stay away from home for more than a week or two are at high risk for problems such as physical assault, substance use and suicide attempts.

Even though adolescents spend considerably less time with their families than they did when younger and even though emerging adults typically move out of the family household, family relationships play a key role in development during adolescence and emerging adulthood, both for better and for worse. Home is where the heart is, and where a part of it remains; adolescents and emerging adults continue to be attached to their parents and to rely on them for emotional support, even as they gain more autonomy and move away from their families literally and figuratively.

The power of the family on development is considerable, but family life is not always a source of happiness. Conflict with parents is higher in adolescence than prior to adolescence. Adolescents and emerging adults often experience pain and difficulties when their parents separate, divorce or remarry, although the effects vary widely. The family is sometimes the setting for neglect, for physical or sexual abuse, and some adolescents find their family lives so unbearable that they run away from home.

The many cultural changes of the past two centuries have resulted in profound changes in the kinds of family lives young people experience. Rates of family separation, single-parent households and dual-earner families all rose dramatically in Western societies during the second half of the twentieth century. In many ways, the family's functions in the lives of adolescents and emerging adults have been reduced in the past century, as new institutions have taken over functions that used to be part of family life. Still, the family endures as the emotional touchstone of young people's lives all over the world.

INTERNET RESOURCES

http://www.nspcc.org.uk

Website for the National Society for the Prevention of Cruelty to Children (NSPCC). Contains information on their reports, journals and conferences. The society does not focus on adolescence alone, but does conduct research on adolescence and families.

http://www.instituteoffamilytherapy.org.uk/

Website for the UK Institute for Family Therapy, which provides training and accreditation for family therapists. The institute supports three research centres: the Centre for Child Studies; the Centre for Cross Cultural Studies; and the Centre for Mediation and Conflict Resolution.

FURTHER READING

K. E. Grossman, K. Grossman and E. Waters (eds), *Attachment from Infancy to Adulthood: The Major Longitudinal Studies.* New York: Guilford (2005).

Presents the results of several attachment studies beginning in infancy and extending into adolescence and emerging adulthood.

K. S. Ng (ed.), *Cultural Perspectives in Family Therapy: Development, Practice, Trends.* Hove: Routledge (2003).

This text provides an overview of the development of family therapy in 14 countries and addresses the issues and concerns families are faced with in different cultural contexts.

This book explores the diverse cultural approaches to family therapy and suggests various clinical interventions that are helpful to clinicians dealing with families from different countries. It includes case studies, vignettes and research outcomes of family therapy.

S. T. Trask and R. R. Hamon (eds), *Cultural Diversity and Families: Expanding Perspectives.* London: Sage Publications (2007).

Provides an excellent, insightful and vivid portrayal of adolescents' family lives in a range of multicultural contexts.

For more reviews, responses to the *Thinking Critically* features, case studies, web links and practice tests, log on to **www.pearsoned.co.uk/arnett**

CHAPTER 8
FRIENDS AND PEERS

OUTLINE

'Do I value my friends over my parents? Yup. I don't think anyone's life would be worth living without good friends.'

Freddie, age 12 (Jellyellie, 2007, p. 155)

'I'd say friends are very important. They're the only people who will offer you honest opinions about your life, whilst actually caring about what you're doing with it; this isn't really something you can get from your family, since they generally don't always see every side of your personality. Your parents also often have particular expectations that you perhaps do not necessarily agree with.'

Rich, age 20 (Jellyellie, 2007, p. 155)

'I value my friends more than my parents because they are more like me and easier to talk to.'

Jordy, age 16 (Jellyellie, 2007, p. 155)

THESE STATEMENTS ARE ELOQUENT EXPRES-SIONS of the value of friendship in adolescence – or at any age, for that matter. At all ages, we value friends as people we can both have fun with and be serious with. We look for friends who understand us, in part based on common interests and experiences. We rely on friends to be gentle with us when we make mistakes and to support us and prop up our confidence when we are in doubt or afraid.

Friendship is of special value and importance during adolescence and emerging adulthood. These are periods of life in which the emotional centre of young people's lives is shifting from their immediate families to persons outside the family (Crosnoe et al., 2002). This does not mean that parents cease to be important. As described in the previous chapter, the influence of parents remains prominent in many ways throughout adolescence, and attachments to parents remain strong for most emerging adults as well. Nevertheless, in many cultures the influence of parents diminishes as young people become more independent and spend less and less of their time at home. Eventually, most young people in Western societies move away from home and, at some point, form an enduring romantic partnership. However, during their teens and early 20s few adolescents or emerging adults have yet formed a romantic partnership that will endure into adulthood. Friends provide a bridge between the close attachments young people have to their family members and the close attachment they will eventually have to a romantic partner.

During adolescence, it is not only close friends who become important but also the larger world of peers.

In industrialised societies, adolescents typically attend large secondary or high schools with a complex peer culture. These schools are usually much larger than the primary schools they attended as children. In these much larger schools, group hierarchies are established, with some adolescents clearly understood to be high in status and others clearly viewed as having low status. Being an adolescent in Western societies means, in part, learning to navigate through this school-based peer culture.

In this chapter we will consider both close relationships with friends and social relationships in the larger peer culture. We will begin by examining friendships. First, adolescents' relationships with friends and family will be compared and contrasted. Then we will explore various developmental changes that take place in friendships from middle childhood through adolescence, with a special focus on intimacy as a key quality of adolescent friendships. We will also examine the factors involved in choosing friends, particularly the similarities that draw adolescent friends to one another. This will be followed by a discussion of 'peer pressure', or 'friends' influence' as it will be discussed here. There will also be a section on friends and leisure activities in emerging adulthood.

In the second half of the chapter we will examine larger peer social groups, including cliques and crowds. This section will feature a discussion of popularity and unpopularity in adolescence, including bullying. Finally, we will explore the idea of a common 'youth culture' with values and styles that set it apart from the ways of adults.

PEERS AND FRIENDS

Before we proceed, we need to distinguish **peers** from **friends** because the two terms are sometimes erroneously believed to be the same. Peers are simply people who have certain aspects of their status in common. For example, Louis Armstrong and Dizzy Gillespie are peers because they are generally considered to be two of the greatest trumpet players who ever lived. When social scientists use the term *peers* they are usually referring to the more concrete aspects of status, especially age. So, for our purposes, peers are people who are about the same age. For adolescents, peers consist of the large network of their same-age classmates, community members and co-workers.

Friendships are especially important during adolescence and emerging adulthood.

Friends, of course, are something quite different. For adolescents, their friends tend also to be peers – people who are about their age. However, not all their peers are friends. Friends are people with whom they develop a valued, mutual relationship. This is clearly different from simply being in the same age group.

FAMILY AND FRIENDS

In the previous chapter we talked about how, in Western majority cultures, the amount of time spent with family decreases from childhood to adolescence, while the amount of conflict with parents increases (De Goede et al., 2009). Parents remain important figures in the lives of adolescents, but the level of warmth and closeness between parents and their children typically declines (Collins and Laursen, 2004). As they move through their teens Western adolescents, who are not part of traditional cultures move steadily away from the social world of their families.

As they move away from their parents, adolescents become increasingly involved with their friends. We have noted that from the age of 6 or 7, all children in industrialised societies spend the better part of a typical day in school with their peers. However, during adolescence, young people increasingly spend time with other young people their age not only at school but in their leisure time after school, in the evenings, at weekends, and during the summer and other holiday breaks from school.

Experience Sampling Method (ESM) studies testify to the change in proportion of time spent with friends and parents that occurs during adolescence. In one example we quoted in Chapter 7, the amount of time spent with family decreases by about half from age 11 to 14, then declines even more steeply from age 14 to 17 (Larson et al., 2002). In contrast, time spent with same-sex friends remains stable, and time with other-sex friends increases (Richards et al., 2002).

Relationships with family and friends during adolescence change not only in quantity but also in quality. Adolescents indicate that they depend more on friends than on their parents or siblings for companionship and intimacy (Nickerson and Nagle, 2005); Updegraff et al., 2002; French et al., 2001. Friends become increasingly important during adolescence – the source of adolescents' happiest experiences, the people with whom they feel most comfortable, the ones they feel they can talk to most openly (Richards et al., 2002). A Dutch study that we have previously cited found that 82 per cent of adolescents named spending free time with friends as their favourite activity (Meeus, 2006).

One earlier classic study comparing the quality of adolescents' relationships with friends and parents was carried out by James Youniss and Jacqueline Smollar in 1985, who surveyed over a thousand American adolescents aged 12 to 19. Over 90 per cent of these adolescents indicated that they had at least one close friend 'who means a lot to me'. In addition, the majority (about 70 per cent) agreed with each of these statements:

'My close friend understands me better than my parents do.'

'I feel right now in my life that I learn more from my close friends than I do from my parents'.

'I'm more myself with my close friends than with my parents'.

Youniss and Smollar also asked adolescents to indicate whether they would prefer parents or friends as the ones they would go to for discussion of various issues. The results are shown in Figure 8.1. Parents were preferred for issues related to education and future occupation, but for more personal issues friends were preferred by large margins.

CONNECT AND EXTEND

For an example of how Experience Sampling Method was applied to a research project read 'Reflecting on the Experience Sampling Method in the qualitative research context' by Mirka Koro-Ljungberg, Regina Bussing, Pamela Williamson and Fredline M'Cormack-Hale in *Field Methods*, Volume 20, Number 4 (November 2008), pp. 338–355

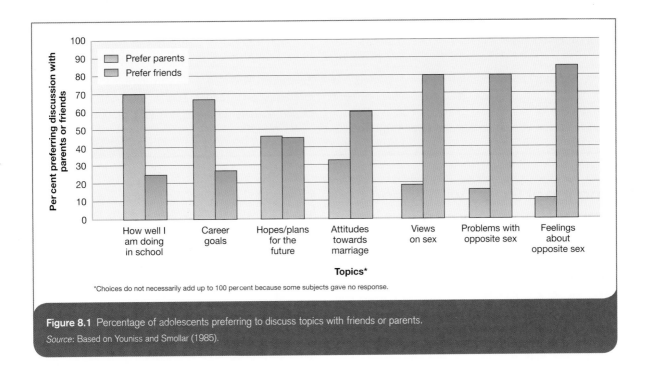

Figure 8.1 Percentage of adolescents preferring to discuss topics with friends or parents.
Source: Based on Youniss and Smollar (1985).

THINKING CRITICALLY

Why do you think many adolescents find it more difficult to be close to their parents than to their friends? Is this phenomenon cultural or developmental, or both?

A study of Dutch adolescents aged 15 to 19 (Zeijl et al., 2000) asked them with whom they 'communicate about themselves, about their personal feelings, and about sorrows and secrets'. Nearly half of the adolescents named their best friend or their romantic partner, whereas only 20 per cent named one or both parents (only 3 per cent their fathers – ouch that hurts – MH). Studies in other European countries (e.g. Farrand et al., 2007; Thompson et al., 2007) confirm that adolescents tend to be happiest when with their friends and that they tend to turn to their friends for advice and information on social relationships and leisure; and to parents for advice about education and career plans (Spencer-Dawe, 2005; Wikeley and Stables, 1999).

The results of the studies comparing relationships with parents and friends suggest that not only are friends highly important in young people's lives, but in many ways they are even more important than parents (Branje et al., 2004; Crosnoe et al., 2002; Prinstein et al., 2001b). However, this does not necessarily mean that close relationships with parents are incompatible with having close friendships. On the contrary, studies indicate that adolescents who have secure attachments to their parents are also more likely to develop secure attachments to friends (Liu, 2008; Ducharme et al., 2002; Furman et al., 2002). The more adolescents are able to trust and confide in their parents, the more likely they are to identify the same qualities in their relationships with their friends.

Although the direct influence of parents diminishes during adolescence, parents shape their adolescents' peer relationships in a variety of indirect ways: through parents' choices of where to live; where to send their adolescents to school (e.g. state versus private school); and where to attend religious services (or whether to attend at all). Parents influence the peer networks their adolescents are likely to experience and the pool of peers from which adolescents are likely to select their friends (Keresztes et al., 2008; Wills et al., 2005). It will not surprise you to hear that parents often engage in active management of their adolescents' friendships by encouraging the friendship or communicating disapproval (Mounts, 2004; Tilton-Weaver and Galambos, 2003). Furthermore, parents influence adolescents' personalities and behaviour through their parenting practices, which in turn affect adolescents' friendship choices (Laird et al., 2008).

CONNECT AND EXTEND

For a study about the influence of parents on adolescents' alcohol use, read 'The impact of peer and parental norms and behaviour on adolescent drinking: the role of drinker prototypes' by Renske Spijkerman, Regina J. J. M. Van den Eijnden, Geertjan Overbeek and Rutger Engels in *Psychology and Health*, Volume 22, Number 1 (2007), pp. 7–29

Emotional States with Friends: Higher Highs, Lower Lows

Experience Sampling Method studies of adolescents report that their happiest moments take place with friends, and even pre-adolescent children are generally much happier with friends than with family (Holder and Coleman, 2009). In an important and often-quoted earlier ESM study, researchers Reed Larson and Maryse Richards describe two principal reasons for this. One is that in a close friend adolescents find someone who mirrors their own emotions. One 13-year-old girl described her friend by saying, 'She feels the same about the same things, and she understands what I mean. Mostly, she is feeling the same things . . . And if she doesn't, she'll say "Yeah, I understand what you're talking about"' (Larson and Richards, 1994, p. 92). This girl and her friend both took part in this ESM study, and when they were 'beeped' while together their moods were usually the same, usually highly positive. This is in sharp contrast to adolescents' moods with parents, as we saw in the previous chapter. Adolescents often experience negative moods when with parents, and there is often a deep split in moods between the parent who is enjoying their time together and the adolescent who feels 'low' and would like to be somewhere else – anywhere else!

A second reason that adolescents enjoy their time with friends so much more than their time with parents, according to Larson and Richards, is that adolescents feel free and open with friends in a way they rarely do with parents. Perhaps this is the essence of friendship – friends accept and value you for who you really are. For adolescents, sometimes this means being able to talk about their deepest feelings, especially about their budding romantic relationships. Sometimes it means being able to go a little crazy, letting loose with adolescent exuberance. Larson and Richards described an escalating dynamic of manic joy they sometimes captured in 'beeped' moments, when adolescents would be feeding on each other's antics to their increasing delight. In one episode, a group of boys were hanging around in one of their back gardens when they started spraying each other with a hose, taunting each other and laughing. In another episode, adolescent girls at a sleepover were 'discovered' dancing on the table, laughing and hugging each other. As Figure 8.2 shows, shared enjoyment among adolescent friends is especially high on weekend nights, which Larson and Richards call 'the emotional high point of the week' for adolescents (1998, p. 37).

Of course, adolescent friendships are not only about emotional support and good times. In ESM studies, friends are also the source of adolescents' most negative emotions – anger, frustration, sadness and anxiety. Adolescents' attachments to friends and their strong reliance on friends leave them vulnerable emotionally. They worry a great deal about whether their friends like them

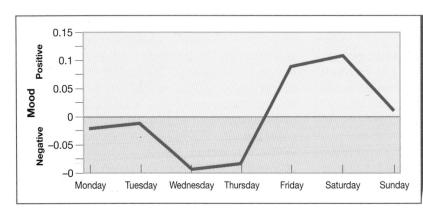

Figure 8.2 This graph of mood changes among adolescents aged 14 to 17 years shows that their moods are most positive on the weekends, when they are most likely to be spending leisure time with friends.
Source: Larson and Richards (1998).

and about whether they are popular enough. In the same study, Larson and Richards observed that: 'Triangles, misunderstandings, and conflicting alliances were a regular part of the social lives of the [adolescents] we studied' (p. 94). For example, when one boy showed up an hour and a half late to meet his friend, the friend angrily rejected him and avoided him for days. During this time the boy spent much of his time alone, feeling guilty – 'I'll just think about it and I'll get upset' (p. 95) – until they reconciled. Overall, however, positive feelings are much more common with friends than with family during adolescence, and enjoyment of friends increases steadily through the adolescent years (Richards et al., 2002).

Family and Friends in Traditional Cultures

As in the West, adolescence in traditional cultures entails less involvement with family and greater involvement with peers. However, even in traditional cultures where most adolescents attend school, the social and emotional balance between friends and family remains tilted more towards family than it does for adolescents in the West. For example, adolescents in India tend to spend their leisure time with family rather than friends, not because they are required to do so but because of collectivistic Indian cultural values and because they enjoy their time with family (Larson et al., 2000; Saraswathi, 1999). Among Brazilian adolescents, emotional support is higher from parents than friends (Van Horn and Cunegatto, 2000). In one study, Indonesian adolescents rated their family members higher and their friends lower on companionship and enjoyment (French et al., 2001). Nevertheless, friends were the primary source of intimacy. Thus, it may be that adolescents in non-Western countries remain close to their families even as they also develop greater closeness to their friends during adolescence, whereas in the West closeness to family diminishes as closeness to friends grows.

DEVELOPMENTAL CHANGES IN FRIENDSHIPS

We have seen that friends become more important in adolescence than they have been prior to adolescence. So what is it about development from late childhood to adolescence that makes friends increasingly important? How is friendship quality different in adolescence than in late childhood?

Intimacy in Adolescent and Emerging Adult Friendships

'I feel close to my friends when I've had troubles and stuff. I've been able to go to them and they'll help me. Last spring I let my friend know all about me, how my family was having trouble and stuff. I felt close to her and like she would keep this and not tell anyone else about it.'
– 13-year-old girl (Radmacher and Azmitia, 2006, p. 428)

'There was one night, my friend and I were in our hotel room just hanging out and smoking a Cuban cigar. And we ended up talking about a lot of stuff, our lives, our plans, what we hoped for the future. I felt especially close to him because I don't usually open up. Sharing is difficult for me.'
– Young man, age 19 (Radmacher and Azmitia, 2006, p. 440)

Probably the most distinctive feature of adolescent friendships, compared with friendships in late childhood, is intimacy. **Intimacy** is the degree to which two people share personal knowledge, thoughts and feelings. Adolescent friends talk about their thoughts and feelings, confide hopes and fears, and help each other understand what is going on with their parents, their teachers and peers to a far greater degree than younger children do.

Harry Stack Sullivan (1953) was the first theorist to develop ideas on the importance of intimacy in adolescent friendships. In Sullivan's view, the need for intimacy with friends intensifies in early adolescence.

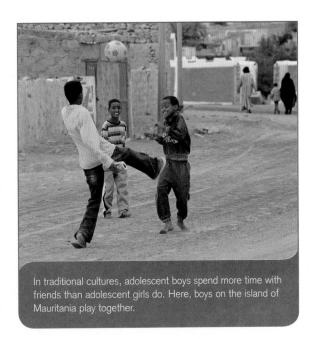

In traditional cultures, adolescent boys spend more time with friends than adolescent girls do. Here, boys on the island of Mauritania play together.

Around age 10, according to Sullivan, most children develop a special friendship with 'a *particular* member of the same sex who becomes a chum or close friend' (Sullivan, 1953, p. 245, emphasis in original). Children at this age become cognitively capable of a degree of perspective taking and empathy they did not have earlier in childhood, and this new capacity enables them to form friendships in which they truly care about their chums as individuals rather than simply as play partners.

Over the next few years, during early adolescence, a relationship with one close friend enhances development in a variety of ways. Best friends promote further development of perspective taking, as they share their thoughts. Their mutual attachment gives one-to-one friends the motivation to try to see things from one another's point of view. Also, they provide honest evaluations of each other's merits and faults. This contributes to identity formation, as adolescents develop a more accurate self-evaluation of their abilities and personalities.

Since Sullivan described his theory, many writers have presented research supporting his assertion of the importance of intimacy in adolescent friendships (e.g. Berndt, 2004). We have already noted how adolescents tend to rely more on their friends than on their parents for confiding important personal information, especially as it pertains to romantic and sexual issues. Also, adolescents are more likely than younger children to disclose personal information to their friends (Radmacher and Azmitia, 2006). When adolescents are asked (as they often are in numerous studies – see below for an example of numerous studies) what they would want a friend to be like or how they can tell that someone is their friend, they tend to mention intimate features of the relationship. They state, for example, that a friend is someone who understands you, someone you can share your problems with, someone who will listen when you have something important to say (Lavallee and Parker, 2009; Selfhout et al., 2009; Durkin and Conti-Ramsden, 2007; Piehler and

Dishion, 2007; Helgeson et al., 2006; Bhui et al., 2005; Hendry et al., 2002). In contrast, younger children are less likely to mention these kinds of features and more likely to stress shared activities – 'We both like to play football', 'We ride, our bikes together', 'We play computer games', and so on. Adolescents also describe their friends as the ones who help them work through personal problems (such as conflicts with parents or the end of a romance) by providing emotional support and advice (Branje et al., 2004; Steca et al., 2007).

Adolescents rate trust and loyalty as more important than younger children do (Smetana et al., 2006; Leets, 2005; Jonsson and Flanagan, 2000). Adolescents describe their friends as the ones who won't talk behind their backs or say nasty things to others about them. This is related to the emphasis on intimacy. If you are going to open up your heart to someone and reveal things you would not reveal to anyone else, you want to be especially sure that they would not use that knowledge against you. In fact, when adolescents explain why a close friendship has ended, they most often mention some form of breaking trust as the reason – failing to keep a secret, breaking promises, lying or competing over a romantic partner (Beneson and Christakos, 2003; Bleske-Rechek and Buss, 2001).

Let's take a closer look at one study that shows the development of intimacy from early adolescence to emerging adulthood. Researchers Kimberley Radmacher and Margarita Azmitia (2006) asked early adolescents (ages 12–13) and emerging adults (ages 18–20) to describe a time when they felt especially close to a friend. Emerging adults' accounts contained more self-disclosure and fewer shared activities compared to early adolescents. Among the emerging adults (but not the early adolescents) there was a gender difference. Self-disclosure promoted emotional closeness for young women, whereas for young men shared activities were usually the basis of feeling emotional closeness. We explore gender differences in more detail in the next section.

CONNECT AND EXTEND

To examine the ways that adolescent boys (ages 12–15 years) manage certain features of 'heterosexuality' in peer interactions read 'Positioning a "mature" self in interactive practices: how adolescent males negotiate "physical attraction" in group talk' by Neill Korobov and Michael Bamberg in the *British Journal of Developmental Psychology*, Volume 22, Number 4 (November 2004), pp. 471–492

Friendships in late childhood tend to be based on shared activities, whereas adolescents are more likely to rely on friends for intimacy and support.

Intimacy and Adolescent Development

One way of explaining the increased importance of intimacy in adolescents' friendships is in terms of cognitive changes. Recall from Chapter 3 that thinking becomes more *abstract* and *complex* during adolescence. As we discussed, these advances influence not only how adolescents solve problems but also how they understand their social relationships, that is, their social cognition. Greater ability for abstract thinking makes it possible for adolescents to think about and talk about more abstract qualities in their relationships – loyalty, trust and affection (Dumont, 2008). Greater ability for complex thinking can also be applied to adolescents' social relationships. Adolescents are newly aware of all the complex social webs, alliances and rivalries that exist in human relationships, and friends are the ones they can talk to about it all: who just broke up with whom; who had a really embarrassing moment in a maths class; how to get a 'good effort' grade out of the new music teacher. Talking about these social cognitive topics promotes the kind of exchange of personal knowledge and perspectives that constitutes intimacy.

Also consider that many events are taking place as part of puberty and sexual maturity which lend themselves to the development of intimacy between friends.

We have seen how much difficulty adolescents have talking to their parents about sexual issues. Friends are much preferred. Momentous things are happening – changes in the body, first romances, first kisses (see the start of Chapter 9), and so on. Sharing personal thoughts and feelings about these topics promotes intimacy between friends.

Gender is also important in the development of intimacy in adolescent friendships. Although both boys and girls go through the cognitive changes of adolescence to a similar degree, and both go through puberty and sexual maturity, there are consistent gender differences in the intimacy of adolescent friendships, with girls tending to have more intimate friendships than boys (Bauminger et al., 2008a; Roy et al., 2000; McNelles and Connolly, 1999). Girls spend more time than boys talking to their friends (Spreckels, 2008) and they place a higher value on talking together as a component of their friendships (Pichler, 2006). Girls also rate their friendships as higher in affection, helpfulness and nurturance, compared with boys' ratings of their friendships (Efrati-Virtzer and Margalit, 2009), and are more likely than boys to say they trust and feel close to their friends (Helgeson et al., 2006). In contrast, boys are more likely – like younger children – to emphasise shared activities, such as sports or hobbies, as the basis of friendship (Radmacher and Azmitia, 2006).

CONNECT AND EXTEND

Perhaps boy adolescents stress shared activities more because they are more active than girls. Read 'Physical activity levels of secondary school Spanish adolescents' by Miguel Angel Cantera-Garde and José Devís-Devís in *Physical Education and Sport Pedagogy*, Volume 5, Number 1 (2000), pp. 28–44

What explains these gender differences? Thus far, not many studies have looked for the reasons behind gender differences in the intimacy of adolescent friendships. However, there is ample research on gender differences in socialisation that has implications here. From early in life, girls are more likely than boys to be encouraged to express their feelings openly (Bussey and Bandura, 2004). Boys who talk openly about how they feel risk being called a 'wimp', a 'gay' or some other (in some contexts) unflattering term. This is even more true in adolescence than earlier because with puberty and sexual maturity both males and females become more conscious of what it means to be a male and what it means to be a female. Engaging in intimate conversation is usually associated with being female, so adolescent girls may cultivate their abilities for it, whereas adolescent boys may be wary of moving too much in that direction.

Nevertheless, intimacy does become more important to boys' friendships in adolescence, even if not to the same extent as for girls. In one study of boys from poor and working-class families, researcher Niobe Way (2004) reported themes of intimacy that involved sharing secrets, protecting one another physically and emotionally, and disclosing feelings about family and friends.

CHOOSING FRIENDS

Why do people become friends? For adolescents, as for children and adults, one of the key reasons identified in many studies is *similarity*. People of all ages tend to make friends with people who are similar to them in age, gender and other characteristics (Rubin et al., 2008; Rose, 2002). Similarities important in adolescent friendships include educational orientation, media and leisure preferences, participation in risky behaviour, and ethnicity.

'To like and dislike the same things, that is indeed true friendship.'
– Sallust, *c.* 50 BC

Adolescent friends tend to be similar in their educational orientations, including their attitudes towards school, their levels of educational achievement, and their educational plans (Crosnoe et al., 2003). During emerging adulthood in the university setting, there are often groups of friends who study a lot together and seem very serious about getting a good degree, and other groups of friends who party a lot together and seem very intent on having a good time. You may have friends who expect you to study with them the night before the big psychology exam, or you may have friends who expect you to join them at the local nightclub and 'Who cares?' about the psychology exam. Both adolescents and emerging adults tend to prefer as friends people who would make the same choice as they would in this kind of situation (Popp et al., 2008) – a useful idea to remember.

Another common similarity in adolescent friendships is in preferences for media and leisure activity. Adolescent friends tend to like the same kinds of music, wear the same styles of clothes, and prefer to do the same things with their leisure time (Mathur and Berndt, 2006). These similarities make relations between friends smoother and help them avoid conflict. An adolescent who is a devoted fan of hip-hop is likely to be more interested in becoming friends with another adolescent who also loves hip-hop than with

In adolescence and emerging adulthood, friends tend to be similar in educational goals.

an adolescent who considers hip-hop to be obnoxious noise (we couldn't possibly comment!). If one adolescent likes to play computer games during leisure time and another prefers to do sports, the two are unlikely to become friends.

A third common similarity among adolescent friends is in risky activities. Adolescent friends tend to resemble each other in the extent to which they drink alcohol, smoke cigarettes, try drugs, drive dangerously, get in fights, shoplift, vandalise and so on (Hoffman et al., 2007; Stone et al., 2000). Adolescents engage in these risky behaviours to varying degrees – some on a regular basis, some now and then, some not at all. Because adolescents usually take part in risky behaviour with friends, they tend to choose friends who resemble themselves in willingness to participate. We will talk in more detail about this aspect of adolescent friendships in the next section.

'Our minds and feelings are trained by the company we keep, and perverted by the company we keep. Thus good or bad company trains or perverts respectively.'

– Blaise Pascal, *Pensées* (1670)

Although ethnic similarity between friends is typical at all ages, adolescence is a time when ethnic boundaries in friendships often become sharper. During childhood ethnicity is related to friendship, but not strongly. However, as children enter adolescence friendships become less inter-ethnic, and by late adolescence they are generally more ethnically segregated (Kao and Joyner, 2004). This has been found to be true in Europe and Israel as well as the United States (Titzmann et al., 2007).

Why would this be so? One factor may be that as they grow into adolescence, young people become increasingly aware of inter-ethnic tensions and conflict in their societies, and this awareness fosters mutual suspicion and mistrust. Similarly, as adolescents form a more complex and profound ethnic identity, they may begin to see the divisions between ethnic groups as sharper than they had perceived them before. As noted in Chapter 6, for some adolescents part of forming an ethnic identity is rejecting associations with people of other ethnicities (Phinney, 2000).

Ethnic similarity in adolescent friendships also reflects ethnic segregation in schools and neighbourhoods. The peers that adolescents meet in their schools and neighbourhoods tend to be from their own ethnic group, so this is the group from which they draw their friends (Mouw and Entwistle, 2008).

Because ethnic segregation tends to exist throughout societies, ethnic segregation in friendships does not end when adolescence ends. In emergent (and throughout) adulthood, inter-ethnic friendships are fairly uncommon (Oliver and Ha, 2008). Therefore, the ethnic segregation in adolescents' friendships reflects the patterns of the society they live in. Nevertheless, as shown in the *Cultural Focus* box, some young people do form inter-ethnic friendships.

CULTURAL FOCUS

Inter-ethnic Friendships among British Girls

In Europe a considerable proportion of young people's interactions with peers takes place through youth clubs (Alsaker and Flammer, 1999). Time in school is not focused solely on academic education. Extra-curricular activities such as sports teams, dancing and music performance are sponsored by schools and youth clubs. In many Western European countries, a majority of young people belong to at least one youth club (Alsaker and Flammer, 1999).

In the mid-1990s, Helena Wulff studied interracial friendships among adolescent girls in a youth club in a working-class area of London, England. Wulff, a Swedish anthropologist, used interviews as the main method of her research, along with observations of the girls in the youth club. She focused especially on the friendships among 20 black and white girls aged 13 to 16. The black girls were the English-born daughters of immigrants from former British colonies such as Jamaica and Nigeria. Wulff was especially interested in exploring the inter-ethnic friendships among the girls, which she noticed were very common at the club.

In many ways, the friendships among the girls had little to do with ethnicity and were similar to the friendships already described among adolescent girls in other countries. Their most common activity together was talking, mostly about boys and about male celebrities they admired (e.g. singers, actors). They also talked a great deal about aspects of appearance – the latest hairstyles, clothes, cosmetics and

➤

jewellery. Other favourite shared activities were listening to recorded music and dancing in their bedrooms, at parties and teen nightclubs. They occasionally took part in risky activities together such as shoplifting or smoking marijuana.

Although they spent a great deal of time together enjoying shared activities, when they spoke to Wulff about their friendships the girls emphasised not shared activities but the importance of intangible qualities, especially trust. A friend, they told Wulff, is 'someone you can share things with, like problems, and also someone you can trust', as well as 'someone you can talk to, tell secrets and all that and you know they won't . . . tell anybody else' (Wulff, 1995, p. 68).

Interethnic friendships are common among British girls.

However, the girls were also conscious of ethnic issues and explicitly addressed those issues in their friendships. They were well aware that racism and ethnic inequality are present in some areas of British society. In reaction to this, and in resistance to it, they deliberately emphasised black elements in their youth styles, taking 'an interesting revenge against the low-class position of most Blacks' (Wulff, 1995, p. 71). Thus, they listened especially to predominantly black forms of music such as reggae, ska and 'jazzfunk'. Some – whites as well as blacks – wore their hair in a mass of thin plaits most often worn by blacks. They mixed black and white components in their clothing and their jewellery. In the various aspects of their common style, according to Wulff (1995), 'the concern with and the search for ethnic equality runs through them all . . . they cultivated their own aesthetic of ethnic equality through their youth styles' (pp. 72–73).

For an exciting update on driving forces in our social lives read Helena Wulff's 2007 book *The Emotions: A Cultural Reader*, which applies a cross-cultural perspective. It examines classic essays and chapters from anthropology, sociology and psychology with important contributions from philosophy and neuroscience to provoke interdisciplinary debate on cross-cultural friendships and emotional intelligence.

CONNECT AND EXTEND

For an investigation of pre-adolescent (10–12) popularity and friendship in multi-ethnic schools – the impact on early adolescence – read 'The impact of a cooperative learning experience on pupils' popularity, non-cooperativeness and inter-ethnic bias in multi-ethnic elementary schools' by Michiel Bastiaan Oortwijn, Monique Boekaerts, Paul Vedder and Janna Fortuin in *Educational Psychology*, Volume 28, Number 2 (2008), pp. 211–221

FRIENDS' INFLUENCE AND PEER PRESSURE

'OK, I've always been really against smoking – it stinks, and I hate it when my mates smoke. I've slagged off so many of them for doing it. So the other night, I was at this party, sitting on a bench playing my guitar – slightly drunk (how drunk can be left to your imagination, you've seen me drunk, not pretty). Anyway, my friends were smoking (grr) and somehow, in my drunkenness, they shoved a rollie in my mouthy, which I happily smoked. Then I really did turn into a hypocrite – later when my friend had another fag, I asked him for one. I happily smoked that too, and felt pretty darn cool. I wouldn't consider myself to be the sort of person that'd do something like that just to look cool, but I guess I'm wrong.'

– Emily, age 17 (Jellyellie, 2007, p. 141)

'If the kids in my group are smoking marijuana they say, 'You want to try it?' If you say no, they say 'Fine.' That's all there is to it. No one forces you. And no one puts you down.'

– Aaron, age 14 (Bell, 1998, p. 76)

One of the topics involving adolescents' peer relationships that has received the most attention, is 'peer pressure'. Writers on adolescence have devoted considerable theoretical and research attention to it, and the general public believes that peer pressure is a central part of adolescence, something all adolescents have to learn to deal with in the course of growing up (Brown et al., 2008).

Some would argue that *friends' influence* is a more accurate term than *peer pressure* for the social effects adolescents experience. Remember the difference between friends and peers: peers are simply the more or less anonymous group of other people who happen to be the same age as you are; friends are emotionally and socially important in a way that peers are not. When people talk about peer pressure, what they might really mean is friends' influence. When we think of an adolescent girl standing around with a group of other adolescents as they pass around a joint, and we imagine them handing it to her expecting her to take a puff, we assume that the people she is hanging around with are her friends, not merely her peers. If we overhear an argument between an adolescent boy who wants to get his navel pierced and his parents who regard that as a bizarre notion, and he says 'Everybody else is doing it!' we can probably guess he means every one of his friends, not everybody else in his entire school. Friends can have a substantial influence on adolescents, but the effects of the entire peer group are weaker and friends can be a protection against adverse peer protection (Singer and Doornenbal, 2006). Nevertheless *peer pressure* is a widely accepted term to encompass friends' influence and we will use it; particularly in the upcoming *Focus on Youth in the Media* feature.

What do you think of first when you think of how adolescents are influenced by their friends? Often, the assumption is that the influences of adolescent friends are negative. The influence of friends is often blamed for adolescents' involvement in a wide range of risky behaviours, including alcohol and other drug use, cigarette smoking, and delinquent behaviour (Brown et al., 2008; Dishion et al., 2008).

However, evidence suggests that the influence of friends is important not only in encouraging adolescents to participate in risky behaviour but also in *discouraging* risky behaviour, as well as in supporting them emotionally and helping them cope with stressful life events (Brown, 2004). Both types of friends' influence – the

type that pertains to risky behaviour and the type that pertains to support – appear to follow a similar developmental pattern, rising in strength in early adolescence and peaking in the mid-teens, then declining in late adolescence (Allen et al., 2006). Let's take a look at the research on each of these aspects of friends' influence.

THINKING CRITICALLY

What has been your experience with friends' influence? Has it ever led you to do something you wish you had not done? To what extent has friends' influence been positive or negative?

Friends' Influence: Risky Behaviour

A correlation exists between the rates of risky behaviours that adolescents report for themselves and the rates they report for their friends. This is true for alcohol use, cigarette use, use of illegal drugs, sexual behaviour, risky driving practices and criminal activity (Dishion et al., 2008; Gaughan, 2006; Unger, 2003; Prinstein et al., 2001a; Sieving et al., 2000).

What does this mean exactly? Because a correlation exists between the behaviour adolescents report and the behaviour they report for their friends, can we conclude that adolescents' participation in these behaviours is *influenced* by their friends? Not on the basis of a correlation alone. As we discussed in Chapter 1, one of the simplest and most important principles of statistics is that *correlation is not the same as causation*. Just because two events happen together does not mean that one causes the other. Unfortunately, this principle is often overlooked in the conclusions drawn from studies of similarities among adolescent friends.

There are two good reasons to question whether the correlations in these studies reflect causation. One is that, in most studies, reports of both the adolescents' behaviour and the behaviour of their friends come from the adolescents themselves. However, studies that have obtained separate reports of behaviour from adolescents and their friends indicate that adolescents, perhaps because of **egocentrism**, generally perceive their friends as more similar to themselves than they actually are (according to the friends' reports) in their alcohol use, cigarette use, use of illegal drugs and sexual attitudes (e.g. Prinstein and Wang, 2005). Perhaps because of egocentrism, adolescents perceive more similarity between themselves and their friends than is actually the case, which inflates the correlations in the risky behaviour they report for themselves and their friends.

The second and perhaps even more important reason for doubting that correlation can be interpreted as causation in studies of risky behaviour among adolescents and their friends is **selective association**, the principle, already discussed, that most people (including adolescents) tend to choose friends who are similar to themselves (Popp et al., 2008; Rose, 2002). Remember that friends tend to be similar to one another in a variety of ways, and this is in part because people *seek out* friends who are similar to themselves. Thus, the correlation between adolescents' risky behaviour and their friends' risky behaviour might exist partly or even entirely because they have selected each other as friends on the basis of the similarities they have in common, including risky behaviour, not because they have influenced each other in their risky behaviour. In friendships, the old cliché is true – birds of a feather flock together (Hamm, 2000; Urberg et al., 1998).

Friends Online: the Social Networking Sites

The opening scene of David Fincher and Aaron Sorkin's 2010 film on the making of Facebook, *The Social Network,* takes place in a pub near Harvard in the autumn of 2003 – Facebook was originally designed for the college students at Harvard. In 2003, the Internet had been around for the better part of 25 years, but MySpace, Wikipedia and Friendster had barely begun, and YouTube and Twitter were still to be conceived.

This was grabbed from a blog by Telly Davidson on 16 October 2010 at **http://www.frumforum.com/how-facebook-changed-the-world**

'I am whatever I want you to think I am online, or whatever you want to think of me. You only see my good (or funny) pictures; you only know about me what I want you to know.'

Is this true: 'You only know about me what I want you to know'? How risky is joining in a social networking site (SNS)? What can happen if you make a few enemies, as the poster for *The Social Network* explains? The explosion in SNS such as MySpace, Facebook, Bebo and Friendster was widely regarded as an exciting opportunity for young people but researchers have started to explore connections between online opportunity and risk (e.g. Livingstone, 2008).

For example Facebook – the market leader by a country mile – is a networking site that mainly depends upon the power of the visual image. Therefore an

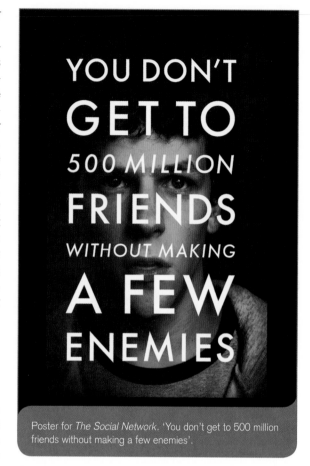

Poster for *The Social Network*. 'You don't get to 500 million friends without making a few enemies'.

embarrassing photograph can be winged into hundreds and thousands of personal *newsfeed* pages. The opportunity for ridicule and (very) public humiliation can be taken – a common 'weapon' and experience of young people within the non-virtual networks of school, club and even family; unfettered by place and time as almost all mobile phones now contain browser software for web access.

Such opportunities for publicly humiliating others didn't really exist when Facebook was developed. In 2003 most online communication was in chat rooms without some of the privacy features – despite the risks of embarrassing photographs – of access to personal profiles that Facebook and other social networking sites (SNS) offer. It is worth noting that confidence in the privacy features of Facebook was not always rock-solid. Many Facebook users distrusted the launch in September 2006 of the 'newsfeeds' feature. Users were concerned about privacy implications, and thousands of them expressed their discontent through the site itself, forcing the company to implement privacy tools (Boyd, 2008).

It's worth noting that another 'safe' feature of the use of Facebook is that it is mainly used for taking existing friendships and family relationships online rather than making new friends or engineering social contact. In contrast, chat rooms pre-Facebook were a most convenient and continuous set of chances for threatening and potentially dangerous activities when young people were often at their most vulnerable and yet felt safe. Being approached by a stranger online at midnight, and in the security of your bedroom, seemed a lot less threatening than the same experience on the street.

In an article based on the 'UK Children Go Online' survey, Professor Sonia Livingstone of the London School of Economics and Ellen Helsper, Senior Research Fellow at the Oxford Internet Institute, sought to explore the online communication of 9- to 19-year-olds. The 'UK Children Go Online' survey was conducted via multimedia computer-assisted questionnaire, together with a paper questionnaire completed by one of the parents of the 9- to 17-year-olds and took place between 12 January and 7 March 2004 – note that this is early research in terms of social networking sites and mainly concerns how teenagers use online chat rooms. However some of the findings about the association between offline characteristics and risky uses of online social websites has subsequently been found to be relevant to SNS (Livingstone, *ibid.*).

Livingstone and Helsper (2008) explored teenagers offline socio-psychological characteristics of shyness, life satisfaction, risk taking, of family communication patterns and online behaviour/skills. The most sensitive questions in the young people's questionnaire (e.g. those relating to viewing pornographic and hate websites, and meeting people through the Internet) were contained in a self-completion section in the questionnaire.

Findings show that older teens engage in more online communication than younger children and therefore encounter more communication risks. Even though girls communicate more on the Internet, they seem to be at no more risk. Young people's offline social psychological characteristics, particularly their levels of life satisfaction and risk taking, have a particular influence; different online communication activities are predicted by different patterns of offline characteristics. Teens in families that have a more conversational style of communication may take fewer risks online, including a lower likelihood of meeting online friends offline. It was also found that teens who were less satisfied with their lives and who became more frequent and skilled Internet users were more likely to feel more confident than they do offline, particularly in relation to the potential for anonymous communication leading to risky activities. Despite the contrast with today's SNS where anonymous communication is far less common, research is showing that Facebook users can encounter some detrimental psychological consequences. These include: fear of victimisation (Higgins et al., 2008); opportunities of overly narcissistic expression (Buffardi and Campbell, 2008); the mix of social function and pro-anorexia constructs of body image (Ringwood, 2008); and potential involvement in inappropriate quasi-political or campaigning groups (Utz, 2009).

How do parents regulate teenagers' online activities? Recent research (e.g. Choi and Berger, 2009; Roche and Skinner, 2009; Sharples et al., 2009) is showing that parents favour active co-use and home rules over using filters or monitoring software, but also shows that co-use and home rules are not necessarily effective in reducing risk. Parental restriction of online peer-to-peer interactions are associated with reduced risk but other strategies, including active co-use, are not (Livingstone, *ibid.*; Eastin et al., 2006). There is some evidence starting to emerge that parents want to add themselves to their children's profiles (Sharples et al., *ibid.*). For example, I (MH) am networked into all five of my children's Facebook profiles, although they are young adults and not adolescents! How do adolescents react? Do they see adding their parents to their profile as a healthy inclusion of their parents into their social lives, or as an unwelcome intrusion and an opportunity for parental surveillance? There are now increasingly urgent calls for researchers and professionals supporting families to identify effective strategies for parents to mitigate risk without impeding teenagers' freedom to interact with their peers online (Livingstone, *ibid.*).

CONNECT AND EXTEND

For a discussion of some of the dangers of risky online social contact read 'Online aggressor/targets, aggressors, and targets: a comparison of associated youth characteristics' by Michele L. Ybarra and Kimberly J. Mitchell in the *Journal of Child Psychology and Psychiatry* (formerly *Journal of Child Psychology and Psychiatry and Allied Disciplines*), Volume 45, Number 7 (October 2004), pp. 1308–1316

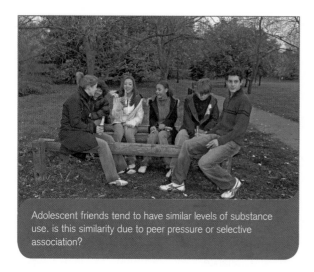

Adolescent friends tend to have similar levels of substance use. is this similarity due to peer pressure or selective association?

Several longitudinal studies have been conducted that help to unravel the correlation between adolescents' risky behaviour and their friends' risky behaviour. These studies indicate that both selection and influence contribute to similarities in risky behaviour among adolescent friends. That is, adolescents are similar in risky behaviour before they become friends, but if they stay friends they tend to become even more similar, increasing or decreasing their rates of participation in risky behaviour so that they more closely match one another. This pattern has been found to be true for cigarette use (Hoffman et al., 2007), alcohol use (Popp et al., 2008), other drug use (Parker, 2002), delinquency (Lonardo et al., 2009) and aggressive behaviour (Leach, 2003).

As previously noted, evidence also suggests that friends can influence each other not only towards participation in risky behaviour but also *against* it (Maxwell, 2002). It depends on who your friends are, and some adolescents are adamantly against risky behaviour. In one study, adolescents who did not smoke indicated that they believed their friends would disapprove if they started smoking (V. Carver et al., 2003). Some studies find adolescents are also more likely to report that their friends pressured them *not* to use alcohol than to use it (Makela, 1997); *not* to engage in risky sexual behaviour (Zwane et al., 2004); *not* to inject drugs (Rácz et al., 2007).

This is not meant to dismiss entirely the role of friends' influence in encouraging risky behaviour in adolescence. No doubt, friends' influence does occur for some adolescents for some types of risky behaviour on some occasions. However, we must not exaggerate this influence, and we should interpret the research on this topic carefully. Friends' influence is one part of the story of some adolescents' participation in risky behaviour, but it is only one part, and the closer you look at it the smaller it seems.

Friends' Influence: Support and Nurturance

'Julie was on the swimming team with me, and she was scared to compete because she thought she wouldn't beat the other person. I was trying to tell her, "Come on, you can do it." But she always thought she wasn't good enough. And that was the way she felt about everything, not just swimming. Since I was her best friend, I really talked to her. "You can do it. You're great. Do it for our team." I kept boosting her confidence, and you know, after a while she did do it. We all cheered for her and she was terrific.'
– Marlianne, age 18 (Bell, 1998, p. 81)

Harry Stack Sullivan – mentioned earlier – tended to emphasise the positive over the negative aspects of adolescents' friendships. In Sullivan's view, intimate friendships in adolescence are important for building self-esteem. These friendships also help adolescents develop their social understanding, according to Sullivan, as they compare their own perspective with their friends' perspective. More recently, Thomas Berndt (2004) has specified four types of support that friends may provide to each other in adolescence:

- **Informational support** is advice and guidance in solving personal problems, such as those involving friends, romantic relationships, parents or school. Because of their similar ages, adolescents are often going through similar experiences. This is particularly true of friends because they tend to choose one another partly on the basis of their similarities. Intimate friendships give adolescents a source of support because they can talk about their most personal thoughts and feelings with someone they believe will accept and understand them.

- **Instrumental support** is help with tasks of various kinds. Adolescent friends support each other by helping with homework, assisting with household jobs, lending money, and so on.

- **Companionship support** is being able to rely on each other as companions in social activities. Did you ever experience the anxiety, in your teens, of having no friend to invite for a birthday treat, or the big football game, or a much-discussed party? Adolescent friends support each other by being reliable companions for these kinds of events, as well as for more routine daily events – having someone to eat with at lunch or someone to sit with on the bus, and so on.

- **Esteem support** is the support adolescent friends provide by congratulating their friends when they succeed and encouraging them or consoling them when they fail. Adolescents support their friends by being 'on their side' whether things go well or badly.

THINKING CRITICALLY

Think about an example, from your own experience, of each of the four types of friendship support described in this section.

What sort of effects do these kinds of support have on adolescents' development? Cross-sectional studies have found that support and nurturance in adolescents' friendships are positively associated with psychological health (Urberg et al., 2004) and negatively associated with depression and psychological disturbance (Way and Chen, 2000). However, because these studies are cross-sectional, it could be that adolescents with more favourable characteristics attract support and nurturance from friends, rather than that friends' support and nurturance cause the favourable characteristics. Recent longitudinal studies in this area have found supportive friendships lead to higher self-esteem and lower depressive symptoms as well as improvements in academic performance (Altermatt and Pomerantz, 2005; Crosnoe et al., 2003). However, longitudinal studies have also found that supportive friendships have a mixed relation to risky behaviour, sometimes decreasing risky behaviour (Laird et al., 2005) and sometimes increasing it (Wills et al., 2004; Miller-Johnson et al., 2003) when friends participate in risky behaviour as one of the activities they enjoy together.

Although adolescent friendships are usually with members of their own gender, platonic (non-romantic) friendships among adolescent boys and girls may be of special importance as sources of support in some cultures. Adolescents often rely on their friends to cope with emotionally challenging situations (Stanton-Salazar and Spina, 2005) and adolescent boys especially benefit from having a girl as a source of emotional support, perhaps because the boys could express their feelings more openly in a friendship with a girl. Platonic friendships are becoming more common in many cultures as gender roles become less rigid, so this is an area that may draw more research attention in years to come (Grover et al., 2007).

CONNECT AND EXTEND

For an exploration of attachment theory in the relationship domains of family, platonic friendships and romantic partners read: 'Mapping the intimate relationship mind: comparisons between three models of attachment representations' by Nickola C. Overall, Garth J. O. Fletcher and Myron D. Friesen in *Personality and Social Psychology Bulletin*, Volume 29, Number 12 (1 December 2003), pp. 1479–1493

FOCUS ON YOUTH IN THE MEDIA

Friendship: Not a Laughing Matter?

One of the most popular TV series of the last 20 years is the American situation comedy (sitcom) programme *Friends,* which was first broadcast in 1994. After ten series and 236 episodes, *Friends* reached its final broadcast in 2004. However, the series continues to be broadcast today in syndication worldwide and is an omnipresent feature of primetime schedules of smaller channels in the UK, particularly those appealing to younger audiences (e.g. E4). Why mention an increasingly 'dated' series that, although immensely popular worldwide at the time, now feels more culturally situated back in white 'picture postcard' New York (Sadler and Haskins, 2005) than in multi-ethnic Britain of the present decade?

Emergent adults. The cast of *Friends* in the early days of the series.

More importantly, this series was about young people in their 20s, who might have been termed emergent adults in 1994 but certainly not adolescents. The point about *Friends* was that the six main characters formed a kind of nuclear family to replace, perhaps, the childhood families they had 'lost' by leaving home. We got to know them as (often very) funny and attractive individuals but the 'chemistry' between them was what sold the show; perhaps because we wanted to have a group of attractive and funny friends just like them and to feel that kind of supportive bond. Much of that chemistry was about the different relationships, many romantic, between the main characters. It was friendship that was the strongest tie and the most powerful influence on their actions and attitudes; and the show was very funny.

Humour and friendship are often woven together in books, films, animations and programmes directed at young people (see the nearby *Connect and Extend* feature). Recent examples are the friendship groups in the *Ice Age* animation series and the Dreamworks Pixar animation series, *Shrek*. Both of these film series blend the forming and testing of unlikely friendship groups – and many adult-oriented jokes and themes – with a simple enough plot and humour to appeal to children. In *Shrek* and *Ice Age* both groups of friends overcame adversity, danger and internal rifts; emerging as friendships made closer and more supportive through the hilarious happenings. More realistically and directly relevant to British adolescents is the sitcom series, *The Inbetweeners*.

The Inbetweeners series broadcast on the UK digital terrestrial network E4 from 2008 until 2010. Three series, each of six episodes, follows four friends, Will, Simon, Jay and Neil, as they negotiate their way through their sixth form (16 to 18) at a suburban comprehensive school.

All they think and talk about is sex and booze without the emotional maturity, money or ID to get them. There is a good deal of toilet humour, swearing for effect, name calling, poking fun at sisters, mums, dads and old people in general. It's worth taking a moment or two to web surf some video clips of the show to get a feel for this representation of adolescence, and at the same time forming a view of why the series is called *The Inbetweeners*.

The plot and the dialogue contains many intensely embarrassing and brilliantly observed moments that are difficult to capture here on the page but we can provide some not-too colourful but indicative quotes. Will's ability for self-mockery establishes itself from the outset:

The Inbetweeners (from left to right: Will, Neil, Jay and Simon).

Will: 'A few years ago I went to see *King Kong* at the cinema, now I'm on a date with her!'

The four boys share some of the vicissitudes of the common experiences of adolescence, like a parent moving out; sympathy is in short supply and there is no opportunity missed for making fun of the older generation:

Will: 'Your dad's moved out?'

Simon: 'It's no biggie, they've not been getting on lately so he's moved out for a few weeks while they sort stuff out.'

Jay: [talking about Simon's mum] 'What like her face? It's gonna take more than a few weeks to sort that mess out!'

Finally, Simon's dad tries to shame the friends into facing up to their behaviour:

Simon's Dad: 'You've had an eventful day bunking off school, buying alcohol illegally, defacing Carly's drive and insulting Neil's dad. Have I missed anything?'

Will: 'We also hit a spastic with a Frisbee!'

This is very funny dialogue, which captures the feel of white, male, middle-class British suburban adolescence quite perfectly, but TV aimed at young people also contains representations of a contrasting experience of adolescence. For example, *Skins* is a British teen drama, again from the UK digital terrestrial network E4, that follows a group of teenagers in Bristol, south-west England, through – like *The Inbetweeners* – the two years of sixth form. The plot line explores issues such as dysfunctional families, mental illness (including eating disorders), sexual orientation identity, substance abuse and death.

The show has a cast or eight or nine young, mainly amateur actors who are entirely replaced every two series when they 'leave the sixth form' and begin their emergent adult lives. Additionally, the show has traditionally cast well-known British comic actors as the parents of the central cast. The 'parents' often provide the overtly comedic aspect of the show. It is as if the business of the teenagers is taken seriously whereas parents (as in *The Inbetweeners*) are embarrassing figures of fun. The series does depict teenagers in extreme and 'gritty' storylines and therefore clearly not a reflection of typical teenage life. However, it is entertainment, which though thoroughly believable – what is less believable is how E4 gets away with broadcasting some of the content – is open to the accusation of also being stereotypical. Again, if you have not seen any of *Skins*, then a web search for clips should prove a fruitful enterprise.

The *Skins* 5 cast; five of them chosen from the 7000 hopefuls at the open auditions for the 2011 series.

In all the foregoing examples, comedy is layered with the ideas and influences of friendship in sometimes complex and demanding ways. I (MH) remember my adolescence as a time of laughing (a lot) at other people and learning to laugh at myself. Perhaps exposure to more modern representations of adolescence and emergent adulthood helps today's teenagers to also develop a healthy and 'humourful' self-image. A knowledge of self that doesn't take itself too seriously, and so builds emotional resilience (see Stallard et al., 2005) to combat anxiety and promote successful adjustment to life-changing events (Greeff and van der Merwe, 2004; Barrett et al., 2003).

CONNECT AND EXTEND

Friendship is not just a common theme on television. To explore the theme in fiction aimed at adolescents and young adults read 'Best mates: an exploration of male adolescent friendships in contemporary young adult fictions' by Michele Gill in the *New Review of Children's Literature and Librarianship*, Volume 14, Number 1 (2008), pp. 1–17

CLIQUES AND CROWDS

So far, we have focused on close friendships. Now we turn to larger groups of friends and peers. Social researchers generally make a distinction between two types of adolescent social groups: cliques and crowds. **Cliques** are small groups of friends who know each other well, do things together, and form a regular social group. They have no precise size – 3 to 12 is a rough range – but they are small enough so that all the members of the clique feel they know each other well, and they think of themselves as a cohesive group (Brown and Klute, 2003). Sometimes cliques are defined by distinctive shared activities – for example, working on bikes, playing music, playing football, surfing the Internet – and sometimes simply by shared friendship (a group of friends who eat lunch together every school day, for example).

Crowds, in contrast, are larger, reputation-based groups of adolescents who are not necessarily friends and do not necessarily spend much time together (Brown et al., 2008; Horn, 2003). A recent review of 44 studies on adolescent crowds concluded that five major types of crowds are found in many schools (Sussman et al., 2007). Such groups are called by different names in different cultures, but studies in different contexts – some of which we will talk about – confirm the types that social psychologist Steve Sussman and his colleagues identify, such as Populars, Brains and Toughies, but there were also one or two clear differences, a noticeable absence of Jocks and Outcasts in a British study by Crispin Thurlow (2001). Therefore the following names are only indicative:

- *Elites* (populars, the posse). The crowd recognised as having the highest social status in the school.

- *Athletes* (sporties). Sports-oriented students, usually members of at least one sports team.

- *Academics* (brains, boffs, nerds, geeks). Known for striving for good grades and for being socially inept.

- *Deviants* (druggies, smokers, Goths). Increasingly alienated from the school social environment, suspected by other students of using illicit drugs and engaging in other risky activities.

- *Others* (normals, nobodies). Students who do not stand out in any particular way, neither positively nor negatively; mostly ignored by other students.

Within each of these crowds, of course, there are cliques and close friends (Urberg et al., 2000). However, the main function of crowds is not to provide a setting for adolescents' social interactions and friendships. Crowds mainly serve the function of helping adolescents to locate themselves and others within the secondary school social structure. In other words, crowds help adolescents to define their own identities and the identities of others. Knowing that others think of you as a brain has implications for your identity – it means you are the kind of person who likes school, does well in school, and perhaps has more success in school than in social situations. Thinking of someone else as a druggie tells you something about that person (whether or not it is accurate) – he or she uses drugs, of course, probably dresses unconventionally, and does not seem to care too much about school.

Members of both cliques and crowds tend to be similar to each other in the same way that friends are – age, gender and ethnicity, as well as educational attitudes, media and leisure preferences, and participation in risky activities (Brown et al., 2008; Meeus, 2006; Miller-Johnson and Costanzo, 2004; Brown and Klute, 2003). Crowds, however, are not so much groups of friends as social categories, so their characteristics differ in important ways from friendships and cliques, as we will explore later. First, we examine one of the distinctive characteristics of adolescent cliques.

Sarcasm and Ridicule in Cliques

Recall from Chapter 3 that the cognitive changes of adolescence, particularly the increased capacity for complex thinking, make adolescents capable of appreciating and using sarcasm more than they did prior to adolescence. Sarcasm – and a sharper form of sarcasm, ridicule – plays a part in adolescent friendships and clique interactions (Eisenberger et al., 2004; Janes and Olson, 2000). Critical evaluations of one another are a typical part of the social interactions in adolescent cliques – one of the reasons why young people diagnosed as being on the autistic spectrum (see the upcoming *Focus on Professional Practice* feature) find being part of a clique very difficult (Papp, 2006). Sarcasm and ridicule are included in what are sometimes called 'antagonistic interactions'. Antagonistic interactions are directed both at members within the group and at those outside the group, and are more common in early and middle adolescence than in late adolescence (Platt, 2008; Warrington et al., 2000).

There are number of possible reasons for these kinds of interactions. One function of antagonistic interactions is that they promote the establishment of a dominance hierarchy – higher-status members dish out more sarcasm and ridicule than they take. Also, antagonistic interactions serve to bring non-conformist group members into line and reinforce clique conformity, which helps to buttress the cohesiveness of the group (Knowles and Gardner, 2008; Wong, 2008). If an adolescent boy comes to school wearing a shirt with monkeys on it (as a friend of Jeff Arnett's once did), and all his clique friends laugh at him all day (as they did), he will know better than to wear that shirt again (which he didn't) if he wants to remain part of their clique (which he did!).

Sarcasm and ridicule of people outside the clique also serve to strengthen clique identity by clarifying the boundaries between 'us' and 'them'. Psychologist Erik Erikson remarked on this tendency among adolescents:

'They become remarkably clannish, intolerant, and cruel in their exclusion of others who are "different," in skin colour or cultural background, in tastes and gifts, and often in entirely petty aspects of dress and gesture arbitrarily selected as the signs of an in-grouper or an out-grouper.' (Erikson, 1959, p. 97)

To Erikson, the motive was mainly psychological – sarcasm and ridicule are used by adolescents at a time when they are unsure of their identities, as part of the process of sorting through who they are and who they are not. Antagonistic interactions are a way of easing their anxiety about these issues by drawing attention to others who are implied to be both inferior to and very different from themselves.

In a historical example, Gillis (1974) describes how in various parts of Europe in the sixteenth and seventeenth centuries, groups of unmarried males in their teens and early 20s had an unwritten responsibility for enforcing social norms. Using profane songs and mocking pantomimes, they would publicly mock violators of social norms – the adulterer, the old man who had married a young bride, the widow or widower who had remarried a bit hastily following the death of a spouse. In Gillis's description, 'a recently remarried widower might find himself awakened by the clamour of the crowd, an effigy of his dead wife thrust up to his window and a likeness of himself, placed backward on an ass, drawn through the streets for his neighbours to see' (Gillis, 1974, p. 30).

Thus, in some culturally approved circumstances, young people are given permission to do what under other circumstances would be seen by adults as intolerable, even criminal behaviour. Allowing young people to use sarcasm and ridicule in a socially constructive way enforces community standards and saves the adults the trouble of doing so.

Relational Aggression

'I happened to kiss a boy that one of my friends had a crush on. By the next day it was all over school and Emily, my friend who had the crush, had ordered all of the other girls not to talk to me. They made a web page about me that said mean, untrue things, such as that I was a lesbian, that I had had sex with at least 20 guys, and that I was pregnant. My mother dismissed the problem as "girls being girls" and figured that … the girls would grow out of this "phase" and become more mature. They didn't. The name calling and slandering and spreading of rumours went on as my eating disorder grew progressively worse. At last my mother realised the seriousness of the situation and allowed me to transfer to a Catholic school'.

– Simmons (2004), pp. 24–25

Among cliques of adolescent girls, a phenomenon related to sarcasm and ridicule has been identified in recent years. **Relational aggression** is the term for

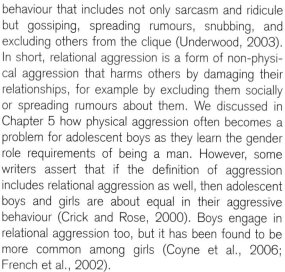

CONNECT AND EXTEND

To mark reported increases in violence among European youth, the topic of aggression, and more specifically relational aggression, has gained in interest. Read 'A concept analysis of relational aggression' by M. M. Gomes in *Journal of Psychiatric* *& Mental Health Nursing*, Volume 14, Number 5 (August 2007), pp. 510–515

behaviour that includes not only sarcasm and ridicule but gossiping, spreading rumours, snubbing, and excluding others from the clique (Underwood, 2003). In short, relational aggression is a form of non-physical aggression that harms others by damaging their relationships, for example by excluding them socially or spreading rumours about them. We discussed in Chapter 5 how physical aggression often becomes a problem for adolescent boys as they learn the gender role requirements of being a man. However, some writers assert that if the definition of aggression includes relational aggression as well, then adolescent boys and girls are about equal in their aggressive behaviour (Crick and Rose, 2000). Boys engage in relational aggression too, but it has been found to be more common among girls (Coyne et al., 2006; French et al., 2002).

Why do girls exhibit more relational aggression than boys? According to researchers in this area, girls resort to relational aggression because their gender role prohibits more direct expressions of disagreement and conflict (Underwood, 2003; Simmons, 2002; Crick and Rose, 2000). They *experience* anger, but they are not allowed to *express* it openly, even in a verbal form. Consequently, for girls aggression often takes the more covert and indirect form of relational aggression. Relational aggression can also be a way of asserting dominance. Studies have shown that high-status adolescent girls are more likely than other girls to be high in relational aggression (Cillessen and Rose, 2005; Rose et al., 2004).

Being the target of relational aggression is associated with feelings of depression and loneliness (Underwood, 2003; Prinstein et al., 2001a). Relational aggression is also associated with negative outcomes for the aggressors. Adolescents and emerging adults who use relational aggression are prone to problems such as depression and eating disorders (Storch et al., 2004; Simmons, 2002).

Developmental Changes in Crowds

'As for choosing friends, it is natural that we graduate towards peers who have common interests and values. This is probably the most important reason why friends are so important to us'.
– Jellyellie, age 15, *How Teenagers Think*, P. 155

If you think back, you can probably remember the different crowds that existed in your secondary school. Now think of your primary school, say when you were 10. Most likely you find it harder to name any crowds from primary school. Crowd definition and membership seem to become important in adolescence, and not before. This may be partly because of the cognitive changes of adolescence (Sussman et al., 2007; Brown and Klute, 2003). Crowd labels are abstract categories, each with some abstract defining characteristics – degree of popularity, attitudes towards school, and so on – and the capacity for abstract thinking is one of the cognitive advances of adolescence. As noted earlier, crowds may also become more important in adolescence because identity issues become important in adolescence. Adolescents are more concerned than younger children with asking questions about who they are, and who others are. Crowds help adolescents ascribe definite characteristics to themselves and to others as they grow through the process of identity formation in adolescence.

Although the focus on crowds in adolescence reflects developmental characteristics such as cognitive changes and identity formation, the cultural basis of crowds is also important. In industrialised societies, most adolescents remain in school at least until their late teens and that these schools are almost always strictly age grouped makes crowd definition especially important. Spending so much time around peers on a daily basis elevates the importance of peers as social reference groups – that is, as groups which influence how adolescents think about how they compare to others (Brown et al., 2008). Also, crowds are especially likely to exist in large secondary schools where a crowd structure is useful in helping adolescents make sense of a complex social context (Brown and Klute, 2003). In the many cultures around the world where adolescents spend most of their time with family members or with groups of mixed ages, crowds have no relevance to their lives (Brown et al., 2008a).

For adolescents in Western society, however, crowds are an important part of their social lives, especially in early to middle adolescence. Social psychologists Bradford Brown and David Kinney and their colleagues (Sussman et al., 2007; Brown and Klute, 2003; Kinney, 1999) have described how crowd structure changes during adolescence, becoming more differentiated and more influential from early to mid-adolescence, then less hierarchical and less influential from mid- to late adolescence. In David Kinney's (1999) longitudinal research on adolescent crowds in America he found that early adolescents (ages 12 and 13) perceived only two distinct crowds – a small group of popular, high-status adolescents and a larger group composed of everybody else. By mid-adolescence (ages 14 and 15), however, the adolescents identified five crowds in their school. The high-status crowd were still on top, followed in status by normals and headbangers (heavy metal music fans), with *grits* (known for their rural attire, e.g. overalls) and punkers (known for liking punk music) on the bottom of the status hierarchy. Among late adolescents (ages 16 and 17), the same crowds were identified, but two others, skaters (skateboard enthusiasts) and hippies, had been added to the mix – notice the crowd names reflect the American origin of the research.

Kinney and Brown also noted changes during adolescence in the role and importance of crowds. As crowds become more differentiated in mid-adolescence, they also become more central to adolescents' thinking about their social world. Among Kinney's 14-year-olds,

nearly all agreed about their school's crowd structure, and their perceptions of the influence of these crowds was very high. By 16, however, the significance of crowds had begun to diminish, and the adolescents saw them as less important in defining social status and social perceptions. This finding parallels studies of friends' influence, which report friends' influence to be most intense during mid-adolescence, diminishing in the later secondary school years (Brown et al., 2008).

Social and developmental psychologists generally see this pattern as reflecting the course of identity development (refer back to Chapter 6). During early to mid-adolescence, identity issues are especially prominent and crowd structures help adolescents define themselves. The distinctive features of the crowd they belong to – the clothes they wear, the music they like best, the way they spend their leisure time, and so on – are ways for adolescents to define and declare their identities. By late adolescence, when their identities are better established, they no longer feel as great a need to rely on crowds for self-definition, and the importance of crowds diminishes. By that time, they may even see crowds as an impediment to their development as individuals. As they grow to adopt the individualism of a Western majority culture, membership in any group – even a high-status one – may be seen as an infringement on their independence and uniqueness (Brown and Klute, 2003).

One reflection of this resistance to crowd identification is that adolescents do not always accept the crowd label attributed to them by their peers. According to one early study by Bradford Brown (1989), only 25 per cent of the students classified by other students as jocks or druggies classified themselves that way, and only 15 per cent of those classified as nobodies and loners by their peers also picked this classification for themselves. Thus, adolescents may readily sort their fellow students into distinct crowds, but they may be more likely to see themselves as the kind of person who is too distinctively individual to fit neatly into a crowd classification. Subsequent studies have confirmed Brown's findings in different cultural contexts (e.g. Thurlow, 2001).

CONNECT AND EXTEND

Football hooliganism was called the 'English Disease'. For a fascinating study of collective crowd behaviour and identity read 'Variability in the collective behaviour of England fans at Euro2004: "Hooliganism", public order policing and social change' by Clifford Stott, Otto Adang, Andrew Livingstone and Martina Schreiber in *European Journal of Social Psychology*, Volume 37, Number 1 (January 2007), pp. 75–100

THINKING CRITICALLY

Why do you think some adolescents resist identifying themselves as part of a particular crowd, even though they routinely apply crowd labels to others?

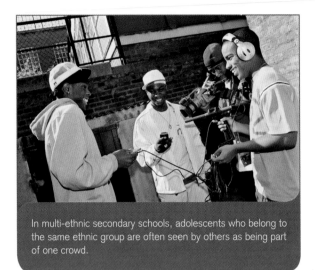

In multi-ethnic secondary schools, adolescents who belong to the same ethnic group are often seen by others as being part of one crowd.

Nevertheless, both self-reported and other-reported crowd membership relate to a variety of other characteristics observed in many studies over the last ten years (Delsing et al., 2007; Sussman et al., 2007; Verkooijen et al., 2007; Prinstein and La Greca, 2004; La Greca et al., 2001). 'Deviants' tend to be highest in risky behaviours (such as substance use and delinquency) and lowest in school performance and social acceptance; 'Academics' tend to be lowest in risky behaviour and (of course) highest in school performance; and 'Elites' tend to be highest in social acceptance and in between the other groups on risky behaviours and school performance.

There is also evidence that adolescents use their beliefs about the characteristics of specific crowds to make judgements about the adolescents in that crowd. In one study (Horn et al., 1999), 14-year-olds were asked whether it was acceptable to punish an entire group of students for a transgression (e.g. damaging school property at a disco or hacking into the school computer system). The results showed that, even when there was no evidence of who had actually committed the transgression, students were more likely to believe it was acceptable to punish the entire group if the transgression was consistent with stereotypical perceptions of the group being blamed. For example, it was more acceptable to punish the jocks or sporties for damaging school property than to punish them for hacking into the school computer system. This indicates that adolescents' crowd beliefs influence their social and moral judgements regarding the people they perceive to be part of these groups.

Crowds in Minority Cultures

Research on crowds in minority cultures has revealed some interesting similarities and differences compared with the patterns in the majority culture (Brown et al., 2008a). With respect to similarities, scholars have found that in secondary schools with mostly non-white students, the same kinds of crowds exist as among white adolescents – Elites, Athletes, Academics and so on. This makes sense because students in these schools would experience the same age grouping, the same cognitive changes, and the same identity issues that contribute to the formation of crowds among white adolescents. For minority adolescents, too, crowds serve as reference groups and as a way to establish a status hierarchy.

An interesting difference applies, however, to secondary schools that have multi-ethnic populations. In these high schools, adolescents tend to see fewer crowd distinctions in other ethnic groups than they do in their own. To non-Asians, for example, all Asian students are part of the Asian crowd, whereas the Asian students themselves distinguish among Asian Elites, Asian Athletes, and so on. Also of interest is that in multi-ethnic high schools there tends to be little crossing of ethnic boundaries in crowd membership, just as with clique membership and friendships. However, one exception to this rule is that adolescent boys with a common interest in sports – the Athletes – are more likely than other adolescents in secondary school to form a multi-ethnic crowd. Sometimes it is difficult to define the most influential crowd (Cross and Fletcher, 2009; Brown et al., 2008a; Hendry et al., 2002).

In industrialised societies, the end of formal education marks a key transition in friendships and peer relationships, usually at some point in the late teens or early 20s. The school is the main arena for adolescents' relationships, and the end of schooling removes young people from a setting where most of

RESEARCH FOCUS

Participant Observation of Adolescent Crowds

One fruitful way that adolescent crowds have been studied is through **participant observation** (Hodkinson, 2005). This research method involves taking part in various activities with the people you are interested in studying. As the scholar, you participate in the activities, but you also use that participation as an opportunity to observe and record the behaviour of others.

Participant observation is related to the ethnographic method we discussed in Chapter 1, which is typically used by anthropologists. However, anthropologists using ethnographic methods usually live among the people they are studying. Participant observation does not go quite that far – the scholar takes part in many activities with the group of interest, but without actually living among them on a daily basis. Nevertheless, participant observation shares many of the strengths of the ethnographic method. Both methods allow the scholar to observe the behaviour of people in action, as it actually occurs, rather than relying on later memories of behaviour, as do questionnaires and interviews.

One of the early researchers who did participant observation of adolescent crowds is the American sociologist David Kinney. For several years, Kinney's research involved blending in with adolescent crowds in secondary schools and observing their behaviour. He also conducts interviews with adolescents to supplement his observations. Of course, Kinney obtained permission from head teachers.

Kinney's participant observation research has provided some of the early information we have on the composition of adolescent crowds and how they change during secondary schooling (e.g. Kinney, 1999; 1993). For example, as explained earlier, he observed how crowds in early adolescence tend to be divided simply into the popular crowd and the unpopular crowd, whereas later on the crowds tend to be more diverse and defined by common interests and styles (e.g. skaters, headbangers). Kinney's interviews, too, provide valuable data on adolescent peer groups, for example on the sometimes brutal process of establishing social hierarchies among peers through sarcasm and ridicule, as exemplified in this quotation:

'[In middle school] you were afraid of getting laughed at about anything you did because if you did one thing that was out of the ordinary, and you weren't expected to do anything out of the ordinary, then you were laughed at and made fun of, and you wouldn't fit the group at all, and then, of course, you were excluded and then you didn't even exist.' (Kinney, 1993, p. 27)

For the most part, the adolescents know he is not 'one of them', and he does not attempt to hide that fact. However, effective participation does require blending into the social setting as thoroughly as possible, and Kinney takes steps to achieve that goal:

'I attempted to carve out a neutral identity for myself at the school by making and maintaining connections with students in a wide variety of peer groups and by being open to their different viewpoints . . . I also distanced myself from adult authority figures by dressing in jeans and casual shirts and by emphasising my status as a college student writing a paper about teenagers' high school experiences.' (Kinney, 1993, p. 25)

Of course, participant observation of adolescents is easier for someone who looks young, as Kinney did when he began his research as a graduate student. An older researcher, grey-haired and clearly a long way from adolescence, would be more conspicuous and would have a more difficult time being accepted by adolescents as a participant in their activities – perhaps one of the reasons why the authors of this text no longer engage in participant observation of this age group. As a young scholar, Kinney was able to 'hang out' with various adolescent crowds, not just in school but at sports events, dances and parties, and have them accept and even enjoy his presence.

their daily social interactions are with people their own age. In the workplaces most young people enter following the end of their education, age grouping either does not exist or is much less intense. Also, a hierarchy of social authority already exists in workplaces, so the anxiety adolescents experience about finding a place in a highly ambiguous and unstructured social hierarchy of crowds is no longer as much of an issue.

In a classic study now almost 50 years old, Australian sociologist Dexter Dunphy (1963) described developmental changes in the structure of adolescent cliques and crowds. In the first stage, during early adolescence, according to Dunphy, adolescents' social lives mostly take place within same-sex cliques. Boys hang around other boys and girls hang around other girls, each of them enjoying their separate activities apart from the other sex. In the second stage, a year or two later, boys and girls become more interested in one another, and boys' and girls' cliques begin to spend some of their leisure time near each other, if not actually doing much interacting across the gender gap. Picture the setting of a party, or a school disco, or the food court of a shopping centre with small groups of adolescent boys and adolescent girls watching each other, checking each other out, but rarely actually speaking to members of the other clique.

In the third stage, the gender divisions of cliques begin to break down as the clique leaders begin to form romantic relationships. The other clique members soon follow, in the fourth stage (around the mid-teens), and soon all cliques and crowds are mixed-gender groups. In the fifth and final stage, during the late teens, males and females begin to pair off in more serious relationships, and the structure of cliques and crowds begins to break down and finally disintegrates.

Does Dunphy's model still work 50 years later? Yes, but probably more at the early stages than at the later stages. Recent research does confirm that early adolescents spend most of their time with same-sex friends and that gradually these cliques of same-sex friends begin to spend time together in larger mixed-sex cliques and crowds (Resnick, 2008; O'Brien, 2007; Carroll, 2002; Connolly et al., 2000). However, whether the model holds beyond these early stages is questionable. In industrialised countries 50 years ago, the median marriage age was in the very early 20s but is now much later, typically 27 or 28 in many European countries (Douglass, 2007). Up-to-date data from the British Office for National Statistics (ONS) show that the average age of first-time brides reached 30 years in spring 2009, and 30.1 by the summer. By contrast, in 1966 the average age of first-time brides in England and Wales was 22.5 and in 1991, it was 25.5 years (Office for National Statistics, 2010d).

Thus, Dunphy's model of ending up in committed intimate pairings – preparing for marriage – by the end of secondary school probably applies more to his time, when marriage took place relatively early, than to our time, when most people marry much later. Most young people in the West have a series of romantic relationships, not just in secondary school but for many years after. Although many of them will have had at least one romantic relationship by the end of secondary school, they are likely to maintain membership in a variety of same-sex and mixed-sex groups not just during secondary school but well into emerging adulthood. As Figure 8.3 illustrates, early ESM studies have found that the amount of time adolescents spend in other-sex groups or pairs increases from between 14 and 17, but even at 17 more time is spent with same-sex friends than with other-sex friends (e.g. Csikszentmihalyi and Larson, 1986).

CONNECT AND EXTEND

'It is young adults' lifestyle options and choices . . . that are responsible for the fall in marriage and fertility rates' (in the former Soviet Union). For a comparative study read 'Economic conditions, and the family and housing transitions of young adults in Russia and Ukraine' by Ken Roberts, Galina Osadchaya, Khasan Dsuzev, Victor Gorodyanenko and Jochen Tholen in the *Journal of Youth Studies*, Volume 6, Number 1 (2003), pp. 71–88

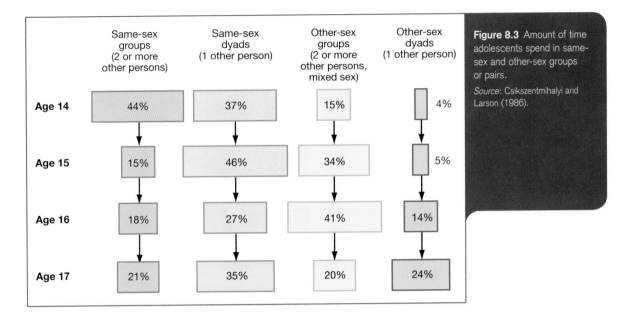

Figure 8.3 Amount of time adolescents spend in same-sex and other-sex groups or pairs.

Source: Csikszentmihalyi and Larson (1986).

THINKING CRITICALLY

Little research has taken place on clique and crowd composition after secondary school. Based on your observations and experience, what hypothesis would you propose about peer group relations in emerging adulthood?

POPULARITY AND UNPOPULARITY

'When I got to school the first day, everyone looked at me like I was from outer space or something. It was like, "Who's that? Look at her hair. Look at what she's wearing." That's all anybody cares about around here: what you look like and what you wear. I felt like a total outcast. As soon as I got home, I locked myself in my room and cried for about an hour.'

– Tina, age 14 (Bell, 1998, p. 78)

A consistent finding in studies on peer crowds is that adolescents agree that certain of their peers are popular and certain others are unpopular. As we have discussed, the popular, high-status crowds go by various names, including sporties, trendies and (naturally) populars. The unpopular, low-status crowds have their characteristic names, too: chavs, nerds, geeks, loners and druggies (Sussman et al., 2007; Horn, 2003).

In addition to this research on crowd popularity, a great deal of research has been done at the individual level, investigating what makes some adolescents popular and others unpopular. Typically, this research has used a method known as **sociometry**, which involves having pupils rate the social status of other pupils (e.g. McElhaney et al., 2008). Pupils in a classroom or a school are shown the names or photographs of other pupils and asked about their attitudes towards them. They may be asked directly who is popular and who is unpopular, or whom they like best and whom they like least. Another approach is more indirect, asking pupils whom they would most like and least like to be paired with on a school project or to have as a companion for social activities. In addition to the popularity ratings, pupils may rate the other pupils on characteristics hypothesised to be related to popularity and unpopularity, such as physical attractiveness, intelligence, friendliness and aggressiveness.

Sociometric research has revealed some aspects of adolescent popularity that are consistent with popularity at other ages and some aspects that are especially prominent in adolescence. Physical attractiveness and social skills are factors related to popularity at all ages (Becker and Luthar, 2007). High intelligence also tends to be related to popularity, not to unpopularity, in spite of the negative crowd labels applied to nerds and geeks. What stigmatises the nerds and geeks and makes them unpopular is not high intelligence but the perception that they lack social skills and focus on academic work to the exclusion of, or as a substitute for a social life (Nevgi et al., 2006). Overall, however, social intelligence and general intelligence are correlated – being intelligent usually goes along with being better at working out what people want and how to make them like you.

The Importance of Social Skills

At all ages, including adolescence, the qualities most often associated with popularity and unpopularity can be grouped under the general term **social skills** (Nangle et al., 2002). People who are well liked by others tend to be friendly, cheerful, good-natured and humorous (Becker and Luthar, 2007). They treat others with kindness and are sensitive to others' needs. They listen well to others (that is, they are not simply wrapped up in their own concerns) and communicate their own point of view clearly (Hunter et al., 2005; Gilmour et al., 2004). They participate eagerly in the activities of their group and often take the lead in suggesting group activities and drawing others in to participate (Martinek et al., 2006). They manage to be confident without appearing conceited or arrogant (Due et al., 2003). In all of these ways, they demonstrate the skills that contribute to social success.

Unpopular adolescents, by contrast and not surprisingly, tend to lack social skills. Psychologists who have studied popularity and unpopularity in childhood and adolescence tend to distinguish between two types of unpopularity, reflecting different types of deficiencies in social skills. **Rejected adolescents** are actively disliked by their peers, usually because others find them to be excessively aggressive, disruptive and quarrelsome. They tend to ignore what others want and respond to disagreements with selfishness and belligerence (Prinstein and LaGreca, 2004). These are the adolescents mentioned in sociometric ratings as peers who are disliked and who other adolescents do *not* want as team members or companions. **Neglected adolescents** do not make enemies the way rejected adolescents do, but they do not have many friends either. They are the nobodies, the ones who are barely noticed by their peers. They have difficulty making friendships or even normal peer contacts, usually because they are shy and withdrawn, and they avoid group activities. In sociometric ratings, they are rarely mentioned as either liked or disliked – other adolescents have trouble remembering

Neglected adolescents lack the social skills necessary for making friends.

who they are (Draucker, 2005; Frydenberg and Lewis, 2004). Both types of unpopular adolescents lack the social skills necessary to be accepted by others and to establish durable relationships.

Social Skills and Social Cognition

One interesting line of research indicates that rejected adolescents' deficits in social skills are based on a deficit of social cognition, at least for males. According to the findings of this research, aggressive boys have a tendency to interpret other boys' actions as hostile even when the intention is ambiguous. Social psychologist Kenneth Dodge and his colleagues came to this conclusion after showing videotapes to children and adolescents depicting ambiguous situations (Prinstein and Dodge, 2008; Lansford et al., 2006; Dodge et al., 2003). For example, one boy would be shown bumping into another boy who was holding a drink, causing the boy to drop the drink. Boys who had been named as aggressive by their teachers and peers were more likely to see the bump as a hostile act intended to spill the

CONNECT AND EXTEND

Poor social skills – and resultant status as neglected – are associated with a range of adolescent psychiatric disorders, with deficits being particularly marked in autistic spectrum disorders (ASDs). Read 'The Social Aptitudes Scale: an initial validation' by

Elizabeth Liddle, Martin Batty and Robert Goodman in *Social Psychiatry and Psychiatric Epidemiology*, Volume 44, Number 6 (June 2009), pp. 508–513

drink, whereas other boys were more likely to see it as an accident. According to Dodge, this is a problem of **social information processing**. Part of lacking social skills, for rejected boys, is seeing the world as filled with potential enemies and being too quick to retaliate aggressively when events take place that could be interpreted as hostile. To put it another way, having social skills means, in part, giving others the benefit of the doubt and avoiding the tendency to interpret their actions as hostile when they may not be hostile after all.

Aggressiveness is not always a source of unpopularity in adolescence, however. Researchers have noted that some adolescents are high in aggressiveness but also high in social skills (de Bruyn and Cillessen, 2006; Pakaslahti et al., 2002; Demir and Tarhan, 2001). They are classified as **controversial adolescents**, because they tend to generate mixed responses among their peers. Rather than being consistently popular or unpopular, they may be strongly liked as well as strongly disliked, by different people and by the same people on different occasions. One relatively recent study found that friendships with controversial adolescents were high in intimacy and fun but also in physical and relational aggression (Hawley et al., 2007). Another earlier study reported that controversial adolescents were more likely than popular adolescents to be the leader of a deviant peer group (Miller-Johnson et al., 2003).

The Continuity of Popularity and Unpopularity

Popularity and unpopularity tend to be consistent from childhood and throughout adolescence. Exceptions do exist, of course, but in general popular children become popular adolescents and unpopular children remain unpopular as adolescents. This may be partly because of stability in the qualities that contribute to popularity and unpopularity, such as intelligence and aggressiveness. We have seen, in Chapter 3, that intelligence in childhood is highly correlated with intelligence in adolescence. Aggressiveness, which is such a distinguishing quality of rejected children, also tends to be consistent from childhood to adolescence (Fanti et al., 2009; Thomaes et al., 2008; Raine, 2002). The quality of the family environment influences the development of social skills, and this is true in adolescence as well as childhood (Engels et al., 2002; Engels et al., 2001).

In addition, social psychologists emphasise that both popularity and unpopularity in adolescence have a certain self-perpetuating quality (e.g. Dodge et al., 2003). Children who are popular are reinforced every day in

THINKING CRITICALLY

Would you expect popularity and unpopularity to be more important or less important among adolescents in traditional cultures compared with adolescents in industrialised societies? Why?

their popularity. Other kids like them, are glad to see them, and want to include them in what they are doing. This kind of reinforcement strengthens their confidence in their popularity and also gives them daily opportunities to continue to develop the kinds of social skills that made them popular in the first place. Thus, it makes sense that popular children tend to become popular adolescents.

Unfortunately, unpopularity is also self-perpetuating (Prinstein and LaGreca, 2004). Children and adolescents who are unpopular develop a reputation with their peers as unpleasant and hard to get along with (in the case of rejected children) or submissive and weak (in the case of neglected children). These reputations, once developed, can be hard to break. Children and adolescents who have learned to see certain peers as unpopular may continue to view them negatively even if their behaviour changes. Why? Because they are used to thinking of them that way (Pitner et al., 2003). For both rejected and neglected children, being unpopular makes it less likely that they will be included in the kinds of positive social exchanges that would help them develop better social skills.

THINKING CRITICALLY

Would you expect popularity and unpopularity to be more important or less important in emerging adulthood compared with adolescence? Why?

Interventions for Unpopularity

Although unpopularity is often self-perpetuating, this is not always the case. Many of us can remember a period in childhood or adolescence when we felt unpopular – rejected or neglected, or both. If we are lucky, we 'grow out of it'. We develop social skills, or new interests and abilities that lead to new social contacts with others who have similar interests. Perhaps

CONNECT AND EXTEND

This article examines the process of engagement within group work with adolescents identified as having anger problems. Read 'The rules of engagement' a case study of a group with "angry" adolescents' by John Sharry and Conor Owens in

Clinical Child Psychology and Psychiatry, Volume 5, Number 1 (1 January 2000), pp. 53–62

we move to a new class or a new school where we can start fresh. Whatever the reasons, many of the young people who are unpopular during late childhood and early adolescence go on to have more satisfying friendships in adolescence and beyond (Kinney, 1993).

Adolescents who remain unpopular, however, suffer a number of negative consequences. Overall, a correlation exists between unpopularity and depression, behaviour problems and under-achievement (Nolan et al., 2003). Rejected children and adolescents are at greater risk of experiencing such problems than neglected children and adolescents (Colman et al., 2009; Dickson et al., 2005). For rejected children, the aggressiveness that is often the basis of their rejection is also the basis of their other problems (Prinstein and LaGreca, 2004). They tend to end up becoming friends with other aggressive adolescents, and they have higher rates of aggression-related problems including violent conflicts with peers, teachers and parents (McCrory et al., 2008). Rejected adolescents are also more likely than their peers to drop-out of school (Zettergren, 2003). Neglected children tend to have a different set of problems in adolescence, such as low self-esteem, loneliness, depression and alcohol abuse (Laukkanen et al., 2009).

Responding to the problems associated with unpopularity, educators and psychologists have devised a variety of intervention programmes intended to ameliorate unpopularity and its effects. Because social skills are the primary basis of both popularity and

unpopularity, interventions for unpopularity tend to focus on learning social skills (Ladd et al., 2002; Nangle et al., 2002). For rejected children and adolescents, this means learning how to control and manage anger and aggressiveness.

In this intervention, the adolescents who took part improved their abilities to generate constructive solutions to problem situations, and their teachers reported improvement in their social relations in the classroom following the intervention.

For *neglected adolescents*, interventions are designed to teach the social skills involved in making friends. Typically, adolescents are taught (through instruction, modelling and role playing) how to enter a group, how to listen in an attentive and friendly way, and how to attract positive attention from their peers (Harrell et al., 2009). These programmes generally report some degree of success in improving adolescents' relations with their peers.

However, most of these interventions with rejected and neglected adolescents (and university students – see the nearby *Connect and Extend* feature) have not included long-term follow-up studies to see if the effects last. A variety of programmes have demonstrated success in improving social skills during and immediately following the programme, but whether such interventions result in long-term changes in unpopularity is currently unknown.

CONNECT AND EXTEND

'Rather, [university students] experienced isolation, loneliness and the lack of practical ICT usability to be the main obstacles to learning.' Read 'From strategic planning to meaningful learning: diverse perspectives on the development of web-based

teaching and learning in higher education' by Erika Löfström and Anne Nevgi in the *British Journal of Educational Technology*, Volume 38, Number 2 (March 2007), pp. 312–324

FOCUS ON PROFESSIONAL PRACTICE

Autistic Spectrum Disorder and Asperger's Syndrome

Being popular or unpopular is not really an issue for adolescents on the autistic spectrum. It is making and maintaining any kind of friendship that often proves difficult or impossible for an adolescent with autism (Bauminger et al., 2008b). Autism is usually diagnosed in childhood and while some autistic behaviours can improve during the teenage years, some get worse (McGovern and Sigman, 2005). Remember that the teenage years are a time when children become more sensitive about body shape, acne, popularity, exam grades, family relationships and friendships. Adolescents with autism may become painfully aware that they are different from their peers: they lack friends; aren't 'going out with anyone' or planning for a career (MacLeod and Johnston, 2007).

Swiss psychologist Eugen Bleuler (1910) first used the term autism about 100 years ago, while defining signs of schizophrenia. Autism comes from the Greek word αὐτός (autós), meaning self. Perhaps, because the word refers to a kind of overdeveloped egocentric thinking, Bleuler defined autism as 'autistic withdrawal of the patient to his fantasies, against which any influence from outside becomes an intolerable disturbance' (p. 625).

Although it is acceptable to use the phrase 'children with autism' it does rather sound as if these children have some kind of communicable disease such as measles, but this is not the case. You cannot catch autism. Instead, autism has a strong genetic basis, although the genetics are complex. It is unclear whether ASD is explained by rare combinations of variations in genes, particularly in relation to the X chromosome, or is associated with substances experienced during pregnancy that are suspected of causing birth defects (Freitag, 2008). So, rather than 'children with autism', we generally refer to children as being on the autistic spectrum. Psychologists may also diagnose a specific condition as part of the more general diagnosis of being autistic (see below). The five specific diagnoses that form the autistic spectrum are:

1 **Classical autism** is a disorder of neural development characterised by a complete range of impairments to social interaction and communication, and by restricted and repetitive behaviour (Baieli et al., 2003).

2 **Asperger syndrome** is characterised by significant difficulties in social interaction, with restricted and repetitive patterns of behaviour and interests, but with no evidence of any diminution of linguistic and cognitive ability (Ritvo et al., 2008).

3 **Atypical autism**, sometimes called PDD-NOS, is sometimes considered milder than typical autism; this is not always true. While some characteristics may be milder, others may be more severe. It is probably safer to consider that the complete range of impairments is not observable (de Bruin et al., 2006).

4 **Rett syndrome** is a developmental disorder of the grey matter of the brain. Although the causes of Rett are different from those of other conditions on the autistic spectrum, many of the signs of Rett are similar to autism: screaming fits; panic attacks; inconsolable crying; avoidance of eye contact; lack of social or emotional give-and-take; a general lack of interest; and loss of speech (Young et al., 2008).

5 **Childhood Disintegrative Disorder** (CDD) is also known as Heller's syndrome and disintegrative psychosis. It is a rare condition characterised by developmental regression, usually between the age of 2 and 10, of language and social functions and motor skills. Some children describe or appear to be reacting to hallucinations (Tordjman, 2008), but the most obvious symptom is that skills already mastered are lost (Carter and Wheeler, 2007).

➤

Treatment for autism is a very comprehensive undertaking that involves an adolescent's entire family and a team of professionals including specially trained classroom support staff in schools (Hewett, 2007). Some programmes take place in the adolescent's home with trained therapists (Johnson and Hastings, 2002) and may include parent training (Weiskop et al., 2005). Treatment can include:

- applied behaviour analysis (ABA) by teachers and others (Grey et al., 2005);

- differently structured teaching in mainstream schools (Glashan et al., 2004);

- time away from the home in a special school (de Bildt et al., 2005);

- speech and language therapy (Sharpe and Baker, 2007);

- social skills therapy (Aldred et al., 2004; Tse et al., 2007); and

- occupational therapy (Schaaf and Miller, 2005).

The main goals of treatment are to lessen social deficits and family distress, and to increase quality of life and independence from parents, who are, sometimes, the only consistent source of social contact for adolescents with ASD. Parents are so important to the successful therapeutic treatment of children and adolescents with an ASD and therefore need to have access to unbiased, scientifically validated information about treatments for autism (Green, 2007). This is an ongoing and demanding challenge for all teachers, classroom support staff and family healthcare practitioners working with youngsters diagnosed as autistic.

Bullying

An extreme form of peer rejection in adolescence is **bullying**. There are three components to bullying (Wolak et al., 2007; Olweus, 2000): *aggression* (physical or verbal); *repetition* (not just one incident but a pattern over time); and *power imbalance* (the bully has higher peer status than the victim). The prevalence of bullying rises through middle childhood and peaks in early adolescence, then declines substantially by late adolescence (Pepler et al., 2006). Bullying is an international phenomenon, observed in many countries in Europe (Dijkstra et al., 2008; Gini et al., 2008), Asia (Hokoda et al., 2006; Ando et al., 2005) and North America (Pepler et al., 2008; Volk et al., 2006). In a landmark study of bullying among over 100,000 adolescents aged 11 to 15 in 28 countries around the world, self-reported prevalence rates of being a victim of bullying ranged from 6 per cent among girls in Sweden to 41 per cent among boys in Lithuania, with rates in most countries in the 10 per cent to 20 per cent range (Due et al., 2005). Across countries, in this study and many others, boys are consistently more likely than girls to be bullies as well as victims.

Bullying in adolescence is common in many countries.

Bullying has a variety of negative effects on adolescents' development. In the 28-country study of adolescent bullying, victims of bullying reported higher rates of a wide range of problems, including physical symptoms such as headaches, backaches and difficulty sleeping, as well as psychological symptoms such as loneliness, helplessness, anxiety and unhappiness. Many other studies have reported similar results (e.g. Due et al.,

CONNECT AND EXTEND

To explore possible culture differences related to bullying and cyberbullying read 'A cross-cultural comparison of adolescents experience related to cyberbullying' by Qing Li in *Educational Research*, Volume 50, Number 3 (2008), pp. 223–234

2005; Bond et al., 2001; Natvig et al., 2001; Olweus, 2000). Not only victims but bullies are at high risk of encountering other problems (Klomek et al., 2007). A Canadian study of bullying that surveyed adolescents for seven years beginning at ages 10 to 14 found that bullies reported more psychological problems and more problems in their relationships with parents and peers than did non-bullies (Pepler et al., 2008).

Who bullies, and who is bullied? Victims tend to be low-status adolescents who are rejected by their peers (Sentse et al., 2007; Veenstra et al., 2007; Perren and Hornung, 2005). Other adolescents are reluctant to come to their defence because of their low status. The social status of bullies is more complex. Sometimes they are high-status adolescents who bully as a way of asserting and maintaining their high status – the 'controversial' adolescents described earlier in the chapter (Dijkstra et al., 2008). Sometimes they are middle-status adolescents who go along with bullying by high-status adolescents to avoid being targeted as a victim (Olthof and Goossens, 2008) and sometimes they are low-status adolescents who look for a victim so there will be someone who is even lower in status than they are (Juvonen and Galván, 2006). About a quarter of bullies are also victims (Solberg et al., 2007).

A recent variation on bullying is **cyberbullying** (also called electronic bullying), which involves bullying behaviour via e-mail, the Internet or mobile phones (Kowalski, 2008). A Swedish study of 12- to 20-year-olds found an age pattern of cyberbullying similar to what has been found in studies of 'traditional' bullying, with the highest rates in early adolescence and a decline through late adolescence and emerging adulthood (Slonje and Smith, 2008). In another recent study of nearly 4000 adolescents aged 11 to 13, 11 per cent reported being victims of a cyberbullying incident at least once in the past two months; 7 per cent indicated that they had been cyberbullies as well as victims during this time period; and 4 per cent reported committing a cyberbullying act (Kowalski and Limber, 2007). Notably, half of the victims did not know the bully's identity, a key difference between cyberbullying and other bullying. However, researcher

Janis Wolak and her colleagues (2007) assert that cyberbullying usually involves only a single incident, so it does not meet the criterion of repetition required in the standard definition of traditional bullying and might be better termed *online harassment*. This is an area that has just begun to be researched, so it will be worth watching for further developments.

YOUTH CULTURE

So far in this chapter we have looked at various aspects of friendship and at peer groups such as cliques and crowds, including issues of popularity and unpopularity. In addition to research in these areas, sociologists have written extensively on **youth culture**. This is the idea that, along with their smaller social groups (one-to-one friendships, cliques and crowds) young people also constitute a group as a whole, separate from children and separate from adult society, with their own distinct culture (Steinberg et al., 2005). The analysis of youth culture has a long history in the field of sociology. More detail on the rise of youth culture is provided in the *Historical Focus* box.

What are the distinctive features of youth culture? What qualifies it as a culture? Recall from Chapter 1 that a culture is a group's distinctive way of life, including its beliefs and values, its customs, and its art and technologies. According to Talcott Parsons (1964), the sociologist who first used the term *youth culture*, the values that distinguish youth culture are *hedonism* (which means the seeking of pleasure) and *irresponsibility* (that is, the postponement of adult responsibilities). He argued that the values of youth culture are the inverse of the values of adult society. Adult society emphasises a regular routine, delay of gratification and acceptance of responsibilities; youth culture turns these values upside down and prizes hedonism and irresponsibility instead. More recent sociologists have also emphasised the pursuit of adventure in youth culture (Beames and Brown, 2005; Pais, 2000).

HISTORICAL FOCUS

The 'Roaring Twenties' and the Rise of Youth Culture

The idea of a youth culture arose in Western countries during the 1920s (Hodkinson and Deicke, 2009). Previous historical periods may have had some small-scale youth cultures, but the 1920s were the first time that youth culture became a widespread social phenomenon. Then as now, the participants in youth culture were mainly emerging adults in their late teens and 20s.

The youth culture values of hedonism, leisure, and the pursuit of adventure and excitement were vividly displayed in the youth culture of the 1920s. This was especially evident in sexual behaviour (Soland, 2000). The sexual code of previous eras was highly restrictive, especially for girls. Adolescent girls were taught to keep themselves pure and virginal until the right man came along to lead them to the altar. This meant not only no sexual intercourse but no petting, no kissing even, until the right man appeared. There was no such thing as dating (Capellanus, 2010); instead, there was courtship, in which a young man would visit a young woman in her home – only if he had serious marriage intentions, of course.

This standard changed dramatically in the 1920s. In *This Side of Paradise* (1920), one of F. Scott Fitzgerald's novels depicting the lives of young people during the 1920s, the narrator observed that 'None of the Victorian mothers – and most of the mothers were Victorian – had any idea how casually their daughters were accustomed to being kissed.' One of the heroines brazenly confessed, 'I've kissed dozens of men. I suppose I'll kiss dozens more.'

Jazz was also part of the hedonism and leisure of 1920s youth culture. The 1920s are sometimes referred to as the 'Jazz Age' because jazz was so popular then and because that was when jazz first became recognised as a distinct musical form. Jazz music was regarded by many as stimulating sexual desire, a quality the participants in youth culture found exciting but many adults considered dangerous. Jazz dancing, too, was regarded as sexually provocative (Cotgrove, 2009).

Numerous aspects of the style of youth culture in the 1920s reflected the changes in sexual norms. The hems of women's dresses, previously considered improper if they rose any higher than 7 inches off the ground, now rose steadily until they reached the knee, a height many older people considered scandalous. Flesh-coloured stockings became popular to enhance the now-exposed knee and calf. Short, bobbed hair became the most popular hairstyle for young women. Cosmetics became widely used for the first time – rouge and lipstick, wrinkle creams, and methods for plucking, trimming and colouring the eyebrows.

The language of 1920s youth culture was also distinctive. There was '23-skiddoo' and 'the bee's knees' to describe something young people today would call 'cool'; 'rumble seat' for the back seat of a car, where sexual encounters frequently took place; and 'spooning' for what today would be called 'making out' or 'hooking up.'

What historical influences led to the rise of youth culture in the 1920s? One important influence was the end of the First World War, which had just preceded the 1920s. Millions of young people in their late teens and 20s had been shipped to and moved around the European mainland as part of the war effort. Participation in the war removed many young people from the narrow strictures of socialisation in the families and communities from which they had come, and when they returned home they resisted returning to the old restraints and taboos.

Another influence were the ideas of Sigmund Freud, which became popularised after the war (Thomas, 2007; Holton, 1993). In the popularised version of Freud's theories, an uninhibited sex life was viewed as promoting psychological health. To many, this made self-control seem not just prudish but harmful. Terms that had formerly been regarded as compliments became terms of reproach and even ridicule: *Victorian, puritan, virginal, innocent*. The values reflected in these terms became regarded by many young people as old-fashioned and incompatible with a modern and healthy (sex) life.

A third factor in the rise of youth culture was the changing status of women. The emancipation of women was achieved in many European countries during the 1920s, and this both reflected and promoted a new status for women as more equal – if not entirely equal – to men (Williams, 2008; Childs, 2006; Lefebvre, 2003). During the 1920s, women also became substantially more likely to enter the workplace as emerging adults, although most of them left paid employment after marriage or after their first child was born. Nevertheless for some, having their own income gave young women independence and social opportunities that had been unavailable to them in the past.

Not all young people take part in youth culture, and this was no less true in the 1920s than today. Many (perhaps even most) adolescents and emerging adults continued and continue to abide by the traditional rules of morality and behaviour with regard to friendship, sexual behaviour, rights and obligations as well as many other aspects of life (Yu, 2008; Bromnick and Swallow, 2001; Jonsson and Flanagan, 2000). Youth culture then and now appeals most to young people who have sensation-seeking personalities (McGregor, 2008) and who live in conditions affluent enough to allow them to pursue the allurements of hedonism and adventure that youth culture offers (Botterill, 2007; Jackson et al., 2000).

According to scholars, a distinct youth culture first developed during the 1920s.

This inversion of values is, of course, temporary. According to Talcott Parsons participation in youth culture is a 'rite of passage' in Western societies. Young people enjoy a brief period in which they live by hedonism and irresponsibility before entering the adult world and accepting its responsibilities. This period lasts only from the time young people become relatively independent of their parents – especially after they leave home – until they marry. Marriage represents, for Parsons, the formal entry into adulthood and thus the departure from youth culture. Of course, Parsons was writing at a time when the typical age of marriage was much lower than it is now (discussed earlier). This means that the years available for participation in youth culture have expanded dramatically and are mainly experienced in emerging adulthood rather than adolescence.

It is not only values that distinguish youth culture. Early in the identification of youth culture, British sociologist Michael Brake (1985) proposed that there are three essential components to the **style of youth culture**:

1 **Image** refers to dress, hairstyle, jewellery and other aspects of appearance. An example would be jewellery worn by some young people in piercings of the nose, tongue, navel or eyebrow.

2 **Demeanour** refers to distinctive forms of gesture, gait and posture. For example, certain ways of shaking hands (e.g. a 'high five') have sometimes distinguished youth cultures.

3 **Argot** (pronounced *ar-go*) is a certain vocabulary and a certain way of speaking. Examples include 'well-bad' to refer to something desirable or considered very good, and 'chill will' to mean relax or calm down.

One useful way to look at these aspects of style is that each of them constitutes a custom complex as discussed in Chapter 4. That is, each distinctive form of image, demeanour and argot in youth culture symbolises certain values and beliefs that distinguish youth culture from adult society. For example, dressing in tattered jeans and T-shirts signifies the emphasis on leisure and hedonism in youth culture and resistance to the more formal dress requirements of adult society. Using a youthful argot – think back to *The Inbetweeners* and *Skins* earlier in this chapter – considered obscene

1920s (a)

1950s (b)

1960s (c)

1990s (d)

The changing styles of youth cultures.

and objectionable by adults signifies resistance to the manners and expectations of adults in favour of something more down-to-earth and authentic (Botterill, 2007; Moran, 2006). More generally, all aspects of style in youth culture serve to mark the boundaries between young people and adults.

Why do youth cultures develop? Sociologists have offered a variety of explanations. One condition necessary for the development of a youth culture is a pluralistic society (Durante, 2009), in other words, a society which is broad enough in its socialisation that it condones a high degree of variability among individuals and groups, including many forms of behaviour and belief that depart from the norms of society as a whole. A related view has been proposed by sociologists who see youth culture as arising in modern societies as a

CONNECT AND EXTEND

For a review of social divisions in the making of young people's leisure and cultural identities read 'In defence of subculture: young people, leisure and social divisions' by Tracy Shildrick and Robert MacDonald in the *Journal of Youth Studies*, Volume 9, Number 2 (2006), pp. 125–140

result of increasing individualism and the weakening of personal ties (Rantala and Sulkunen, 2003). In this view, youth culture is a way of constructing a coherent and meaningful worldview in a society that fails to provide one.

There is also Talcott Parsons' original view, as we have noted, that youth cultures arise in societies that allow young people an extended period between the time they gain substantial independence from parents and the time they take on adult responsibilities. Similarly, Michael Brake proposed that youth culture provides opportunities for young people to experiment with different possible identities (see Chapter 6). According to Brake:

'Young people need a space in which to explore an identity which is separate from the roles and expectations imposed by family, work and school. Youth culture offers a collective identity, a reference group from which youth can develop an individual identity. It provides cognitive material from which to develop an *alternative script* . . . It represents a free area to relax with one's peers outside the scrutiny and demands of the adult world.' (1985, p. 195)

Youth culture does not necessarily exist in opposition or rebellion to adult society. As mentioned in Chapter 7, adolescents and their parents generally share many common values, such as the value of education, honesty and hard work. This is not inconsistent with believing that the teens and early 20s represent a unique opportunity to pursue pleasure and leisure. Both young people and their parents know that this period is temporary and that the responsibilities of adult life will eventually be assumed.

Of course, one could argue that there is not just one youth culture but many youth subcultures (Brown and Klute, 2003). The crowds we discussed earlier in this chapter represent different youth subcultures – sporties, geeks and Goths all have their distinctive styles, and not all of these crowds are part of the larger youth culture just described. Crowds such as geeks and normals are conventional in style and do not participate in the pursuit of pleasure and leisure that defines youth culture. In contrast, crowds such as Goths and druggies clearly have styles that represent resistance to the routine and conventions of adult life. Youth subcultures have also developed around certain distinctive musical forms such as heavy metal (Patton and McIntosh, 2008) and hip-hop (Clay, 2003) loved by some adolescents and hated by others.

Some scholars have observed that youth culture is breaking worldwide into traditional cultures (Maira,

2004; Griffin, 2001). Driven by globalisation and worldwide media, new youth styles make their way quickly around the world. Of course, in all countries, young people vary in how much they take part in youth culture. Nevertheless, the image, argot and media popular among adolescents in Western youth cultures have been influential among many adolescents in non-Western countries (Schlegel, 2001). Western countries also influence one another, and although the youth culture of the United States is dominant in the West, youth cultures in other Western countries, particularly the music of the United Kingdom, also influence some American adolescents.

THINKING CRITICALLY

Nearly all the scholarly work on youth culture has been theoretical rather than empirical (research based). How would you design a study to examine the validity of the theoretical ideas about youth culture presented here?

Technological Change and the Power of Youth Culture

Michael Brake also draws our attention to the idea that youth culture is largely created and spread by young people themselves. To learn the latest styles of dress, hair and argot, and the hot new forms of music and other media, young people look mainly to each other for cues. Adults may try to control or monitor this process – to make youth culture less disruptive or to profit from selling the items popular in youth culture – but young people learn the ways of youth culture from one another, not from adults (DeGennaro and Brown, 2009; Portes et al., 2005). According to the influential anthropologist Margaret Mead (1928), in times of rapid technological change – which was as true an observation in the 1920s as it is today – young people tend to look to one another for instruction in a variety of aspects of life.

Writing during the time youth culture was first forming, Mead described how the rate of technological change in a culture influences the degree to which adolescents receive teachings from adults or from each other. In cultures where the rate of technological change is very slow, which Mead called **post-figurative cultures**, what children and adolescents need to learn to function as adults changes little from one generation to the next. As a result, children and adolescents can

In a co-figurative culture, adolescents learn a great deal from one another, not just from adults.

learn all they need to know from their elders. For example, if a culture's economy is based on the same methods of farming for many generations, the elders will be the authorities young people look to for instruction in how to plant, cultivate and harvest their crops.

Most cultures through most of human history have been post-figurative cultures. However, since the Industrial Revolution began about 250 years ago, the pace of technological change has increased with each decade. Particularly in the past 100 years in industrialised countries, technological change has occurred with such speed that the skills most important in the economy change with each generation. The result is what Mead called **co-figurative cultures**, where young people learn what they need to know not only from adults but also from other young people. Learning about the styles and media of youth culture would be one example of this kind of learning. Another example would be the use of computers. An adolescent who wanted to learn how to make charts and graphs on her computer might be more likely to ask a computer-savvy

friend for advice than to ask her grandparents, who may have reached retirement age before personal computers became popular.

Traditional cultures are likely to move from post-figurative to co-figurative status as globalisation proceeds. For example, we could look to changing views among adolescent Aborigines in Australia. In the present generation of adolescents, the traditional Law describing relations between adults and children and between men and women has become viewed by many adolescents as obsolete (Singleton et al., 2009; Dawes 2002). The world they are growing up in has changed too much in recent decades for the traditions of their elders to be relevant to their lives. Consequently, they are rejecting these traditions in favour of the global media of youth culture that they share with their friends and peers. These media seem to many young Aborigines to show where their futures lie, and with their peers they share a desire to look forwards to the world shaped by globalisation rather than backwards to their cultural traditions. However this is not the whole story. See the nearby *Connect and Extend* feature.

CONNECT AND EXTEND

For a case study of how Aboriginal youth cultures use information and communication technologies (ICTs) to communicate, archive cultural knowledge, empower their communities, develop skills and generate income, read 'Youth empowerment and information and communication technologies: a case study of a remote Australian Aboriginal community' by Guy Singleton, Maria Rola-Rubzen, Kado Muir, Deeva Muir and Murray McGregor in *GeoJournal*, Volume 74, Number 5 (October 2009), pp. 403–413

The use of *post-figurative* and *co-figurative* describe levels of technological change and orientations to peers and adults in two kinds of cultures. Mead believed that in the future, as the pace of technological change continues to accelerate, a third type may emerge. In **pre-figurative cultures**, the direction of learning would come full circle – young people would teach adults how to use the latest technology. Mead proposed this theory in 1928, long before the computer age, and in many ways her prediction has come to pass in our lifetime. Children and adolescents in industrialised societies now grow up with computers and the Internet, and many of them soon achieve a level of skill far beyond that of their elders. Many newspaper articles in the last decade contain profiles of adolescents in their teens who have thriving and lucrative businesses creating websites and developing computer software, with much of their business coming from adults much older than themselves.

THINKING CRITICALLY

Margaret Mead wrote her prediction of the arrival of pre-figurative cultures in 1928. Would you say the culture you live in has reached a pre-figurative state by now, at least in some respects? What other examples could you give of the pre-figurative pattern?

The history of the personal computer provides many other examples of revolutionary developments led by adolescents and emerging adults. Bill Gates, founder of Microsoft, developed the DOS operating system that is now the basis of most personal computer operations when he was still in his 20s. Steve Jobs started the Apple Computer Corporation by making a personal computer in his garage when he was still in his teens. Many of the older, more experienced executives and inventors at more established companies such as IBM have borrowed many of their ideas from Gates, Jobs and other young people – one sign that the pre-figurative culture predicted by Mead may have begun to arrive.

Still, it is difficult to believe that the day will ever come when *most* knowledge will be conveyed from adolescents to adults. Inevitably, adults have more experience than adolescents and have had more years to accumulate knowledge. Even now, the computer examples described above are the exception, not the rule. Most knowledge remains communicated from adults to young people rather than the other way around; the schools, colleges and universities that adolescents and emerging adults attend are created for this purpose. Furthermore, although young people learn a great deal about youth culture from their peers during adolescence and emerging adulthood, youth culture is largely left behind after emerging adulthood ends and the responsibilities of adult life begin.

SUMMING UP

In this chapter we have covered diverse topics related to friends and peers, including developmental changes in friendships, how adolescents choose friends, friends' influence or 'peer pressure', cliques and crowds, and youth culture. The following are the key points of this chapter:

- Friends become increasingly important during adolescence. The amount of time spent with friends increases (and time spent with family decreases), and friends become increasingly significant as confidants and as sources of personal advice and emotional support.
- A key change in friendships from preadolescence to adolescence is the increased importance of intimacy, with a focus on qualities such as trust and loyalty and an increased amount of time together spent in conversation about significant issues rather than on shared activities.
- The most important basis for friendships in adolescence is similarity, particularly in ethnicity, educational orientation, media and leisure preferences, and participation in risky behaviour.
- Although *peer pressure* is often used as a negative term to describe how adolescent friends encourage each other to participate in risky behaviour, studies indicate that the extent of this influence may be exaggerated because of

➤

selective association; adolescent friends may influence each other against risky behaviour as well as towards it.

- Emerging adults take part frequently in leisure activities with friends, such as attending festivals, going to the cinema, and getting together for no particular purpose. However, participation in leisure activities with friends declines during emerging adulthood.

- Cliques are small groups of close friends. Sarcasm and ridicule are common in adolescent cliques, to establish a dominance hierarchy and to enforce conformity to clique norms.

- Relational aggression includes sarcasm and ridicule as well as gossip and exclusion. It is especially common among adolescent girls, evidently because more direct forms of disagreement and conflict are prohibited in the female gender role.

- The age-grouped school setting of Western societies lends itself to the development of reputation-based crowds as a way of defining and organising a social structure. Traditional cultures sometimes have a version of a peer crowd, with a separate dormitory where adolescents hang out, relax and engage in sexual play.

- The most important determinant of popularity and unpopularity in adolescence is social skills. Other qualities related to popularity are intelligence and physical attractiveness. Interventions for unpopular adolescents have shown some short-term success, but their long-term effectiveness is unknown.

- Bullying has three components: aggression, repetition and power imbalance. Studies show that bullying in adolescence is a worldwide phenomenon. An electronic form of bullying, cyberbullying, has arisen in recent years.

- A distinctive youth culture first appeared in the West during the 1920s. According to sociologists, youth cultures are characterised by subterranean values of hedonism and irresponsibility and by a distinctive style consisting of image, demeanour and argot. Late adolescents and emerging adults are the main participants in youth culture, but the degree of their participation varies from highly intense to not at all.

A common thread running through all the topics we have considered in this chapter is that the influence of peers on development during adolescence and emerging adulthood is substantial and has grown in the past century. Because of economic and social changes during the twentieth century, adolescents in the second decade of the twenty-first century spend considerably more time with their peers on a typical day, in school and in play, and considerably less time with parents. Although peers are also important to young people in traditional cultures, the influence of peers is enhanced in industrialised societies because school brings peers together for many hours each day, away from their parents. Also, by adolescence many young people become part of a media-driven youth culture in which what is viewed as most valued, most desirable, most 'cool' is based on the preferences of peers and friends, not adults.

Although we have examined a wide range of issues on peers and friends in this chapter, one crucial area we have not discussed fully is romantic relationships. We will examine this in detail in the following chapter on love and sex.

INTERNET RESOURCES

http://www.educational-psychologist.co.uk/social.htm

Tim Francis, educational psychologist, provides a 'Social Skills' package that details how to form and run a small group where the focus of the work is the development of social skills. There are a number of ready-made group sessions as an aid to starting in this type of work and the approach includes advice on how to plan and run a group using information gained from the context in which adolescents live and by identifying the particular difficulties the group may be experiencing. The website includes a free download of the materials. Very useful in a youth group or educational setting.

http://www.anti-bullyingalliance.org.uk/pdf/aba_tackling_bullying_in_schools2.pdf

A summary of approaches for tackling bullying by the Anti-Bullying Alliance research group at Goldsmiths College, University of London. Its purpose is both to inform and to connect those most closely involved in preventing and responding to bullying with the range of approaches that exist and which may be of further interest to them in their work.

http://www.direct.gov.uk/en/YoungPeople/index.htm

A UK government website that provides information and advice for young people on how to stay healthy, on eating disorders, bullying, coping with divorce; help and advice for disabled teenagers moving into adulthood; and some ideas on how to fill up spare time with social activities.

FURTHER READING

Maarten van Zalk-Selfhout, *Me, Myself, and You: Friendships in Adolescence – the Experience of Close Friendship in Adolescence.* Lambert Academic Publishing (2009)

　　Maarten van Zalk-Selfhout was born 1981 in Hengelo, Twente, The Netherlands. He gained his PhD with honours – 'cum laude' – in 2009 at Utrecht University. He currently lives and works at Orebro University, Sweden.

Niobe Way and Jill V. Hamm, *Child and Adolescent Development.* San Francisco, CA: Josey Bass (2005)

　　The authors address the following questions: *How* do adolescents experience trust and intimacy in their friendships? *Why* are these relational experiences critical for emotional adjustment? And *how* does the social and cultural context shape the ways in which adolescents experience their close friendships?

G. Weisfeld, *Evolutionary Principles of Human Adolescence (Lives in Context).* Boulder, CO: Westview Press (1999)

　　An exploration of human adolescence, this book is unique because of its ethological perspective in a comprehensive treatment of adolescent development from an evolutionary point of view, providing a research-based description of human adolescence. He also offers a comparative perspective, describing adolescence in other species, human cultures and historical periods.

For more reviews, responses to the *Thinking Critically* features, case studies, web links and practice tests, log on to **www.pearsoned.co.uk/arnett.**

CHAPTER 9
LOVE AND SEXUALITY

OUTLINE

Do you remember your first kiss? I know that I will never forget mine even though it was over 40 years ago. Yes, this is a personal anecdote from one of the authors, Mal Hughes. My first kiss was with the younger sister of the man who was engaged to my sister. I was 14 (I guess that makes me a late developer by today's 'norms') and Andrea was about the same age. We had been holding hands in the back of her brother's car on a day trip around North Wales and later, back at my house I asked her to come with me to take the dog – a black Labrador called Boswell – for a walk. Away from the house we held hands and on a dark path we stopped as if by some unspoken agreement. I held both of her hands and leaned towards her. We bumped noses a bit but the sensation of softly pressing my lips against hers was incredibly exciting and we adjusted all the angles to keep the kiss going. Afterwards we found we could talk even more easily; as if the embarrassing bit of a first kiss had been successfully negotiated and we could now settle for a comfortable friendship without the anxiety of wondering what to do and what it would be like.

I HOPE YOUR FIRST KISS WAS AS EXCITING AND delightful as mine. As we will see in this chapter, the beginnings of love and sexuality can be a source of many emotions for adolescents – pleasure, delight and wonder, but also fear, anxiety and confusion. The chapter is divided into just two sections: love and sexuality. In all cultures, developing into sexual maturity in adolescence and emerging adulthood involves forming close relationships with persons outside the family. Most young people eventually form a relationship in which they experience love. We begin the section on love by discussing love in its cultural context, as well as the developmental progression that adolescent love tends to follow in most European cultures and the different love scripts that adolescent boys and girls learn.

We will also consider psychologist Robert Sternberg's theory of love and how it applies to adolescents and young adults. The emphasis on the cultural context of love continues with an examination of how various cultures allow or discourage adolescent passion. This is followed by a discussion about the reasons young people select a specific partner, and a section on breaking up a love relationship.

Love in adolescence and emerging adulthood often includes sexuality, but sexual activity among young people may also take the form of sexual play or experimentation, not necessarily including love. In the second section of this chapter, we look at the statistics of various kinds of sexual activity among adolescents and emerging adults. Then we examine the wide variety in cultural standards with regard to sex before marriage, as well as the different sexual scripts for adolescent

boys and girls in European societies. Next is the development of sexuality among gay, lesbian and bisexual adolescents, and the difficulties they face in societies that mostly disapprove – or are wary – of young people with different sexual orientations.

In many societies, sexuality in adolescence and emerging adulthood is considered problematic in a number of ways. Towards the close of the chapter we address those problems, including contraceptive use and non-use; pregnancy, abortion and parenthood in adolescence; and sexually transmitted diseases.

LOVE

The Changing Forms of Adolescent Love

In recent decades, the forms of early romantic relations among adolescents have changed. Before the 1960s, adolescent love in Western cultures was structured by 'dating', which usually followed more or less formal rules (Furman and Hand, 2006). Boy asked girl to accompany him to some well-defined event – for example a film, the Saturday home game or the local dance hall. In the 1950s and 1960s, a boy picked up a girl at her house, where he would meet her parents and tell them what time he would bring her home. It was not unusual in some British households for the girl's family to insist that a younger brother or sister accompany the pair as a kind of chaperone, which is how I (MH) got to see the film *Lawrence of Arabia* before most of my friends!

Today, adolescent romantic relations tend to be much less formal. Even the terms 'date' and 'dating' have fallen out of fashion, replaced by 'going out with' or 'hanging out with' or 'seeing' someone (Furman and Hand, *ibid*.). Adolescent boys and girls still go together to the cinema, sports events and clubs, of course, but they are much more likely than before to spend time together informally. As we saw in Chapter 5, before the women's movement of the 1960s gender roles were much more sharply drawn in many European societies, and adolescent boys and girls were less likely simply to spend time together as friends. Now teenagers often know each other as friends before they become involved romantically (Selfhout et al., 2009; Kuttler et al., 1999), perhaps by meeting or more likely developing a new friendship on a social networking website (Arvidsson, 2006).

The back row of the cinema was a favourite place for early romantic 'experiences' despite the presence of a younger chaperone!

Since the 1980s adolescent love also tends today to be much more informal as the concept of 'a date' hardly exists any more in European countries (Alsaker and Flammer, 1999). Of course, adolescents and young adults do pair up and become boyfriend and girlfriend. However, they rarely date in a formal way, by designating a specific event at a specific time and going out in order to explore what they would be like as a couple. More typically, they go out in mixed-gender groups, without any specific pairing up. Or a boy and a girl may go out simply as friends, without thinking of themselves as potential boyfriend and girlfriend, without the boy having the responsibility to pay the expenses, and without the implication of possible sexual activity as the evening progresses. In traditional cultures, dating is also rare as we will see in more detail later in the chapter. Dating and even informal male–female social contact in adolescence are forbidden in many traditional cultures because of religious or cultural values emphasising female chastity before marriage and because adults wish to control whom their adolescents end up marrying. Where traditional cultures are embedded in multicultural societies these constraints on dating come under some pressure (Uddin, 2006; Bhopal, 2000).

The Developmental Course of Adolescent Love

The prevalence of involvement in romantic relationships increases gradually over the course of adolescence. According to one relatively recent national study the percentage of adolescents reporting a current love relationship is 17 per cent for 12-year-olds, 32 per cent of 14-year-olds and 44 per cent by 16 (Furman and Hand, *ibid*.). By 16, 80 per cent of adolescents questioned in this study report having had a romantic relationship at some point, even if they do not have one currently. Not surprisingly but of interest is that the quality of these early romantic relationships can be predicted from early high-quality maternal parenting and peer social competence throughout childhood (Roisman et al., 2009).

Adolescents with an Asian cultural background tend to have their first romantic relationship later than adolescents with a European cultural background because Asian cultural beliefs discourage early involvement in romantic relationships and encourage minimal or no sexual involvement before marriage (Connolly et al., 2004; Regan et al., 2004; K. Carver et al., 2003).

Love relationships among many adolescents tend to follow a developmental sequence of four steps (Connolly et al., 2004). In the first step, adolescents in same-gender groups go to places where they hope to find other-gender groups (shopping centres and fast-food restaurants are popular spots for today's adolescents). In the second step, adolescents take part in social gatherings arranged by adults, such as parties and school discos, which include interactions between boys and girls. In the third step, mixed-gender groups arrange to go to some particular event together, such as going to see a new film. In the final step, adolescent couples begin to date as pairs in activities such as going to the cinema, shopping, rock concerts or just spending time together. This pattern of couple dating continues through to young adulthood.

Although studies agree that heterosexual love relationships rarely begin before adolescence, actual biological maturity has little to do with when love relationships begin among adolescents. One especially interesting historical analysis exploring this question was carried out by researcher and author Sanford Dornbusch and his colleagues (Dornbusch et al., 1981). They used data from a large American study of adolescents (aged 12 to 17) that included family doctors' ratings of the adolescents' physical maturity, using the Tanner stages described in Chapter 2. They used the term 'dating' to refer to love relationships because at the time of the study this term was still widely used.

In two ways they demonstrated that physical maturation did not predict whether adolescents had begun dating. First, they looked at adolescents who were of different ages (12 to 15) but who were all at Tanner's Stage 3 of physical maturity and found that the older adolescents were more likely to have begun dating even though all the adolescents were at the same level of physical maturity. Second, they showed that adolescents of a particular age were more or less equally likely to have begun dating regardless of their level of physical maturity. For example, few of the 12-year-olds had begun dating, even though they varied widely in their level of physical maturation.

Over the last 25 years, adolescents' reports of the reasons they form love relationships include the following (refer for example to: Bisson and Levine, 2009; Furman et al., 2002; Connolly et al., 2000):

- recreation – fun and enjoyment

- learning – becoming more skilled at dating interactions

- status – impressing others by how often one dates and whom one dates

CONNECT AND EXTEND

Yet another forgotten minority? Read 'Social and sexual relationships of adolescents and young adults with cerebral palsy: a review' by Diana J. H. G. Wiegerink, Marij E. Roebroeck, Mireille Donkervoort, Henk J. Stam and Peggy T. Cohen-Kettenis in *Clinical Rehabilitation*, Volume 20, Number 12 (December 2006), pp. 1023–1031

- companionship – sharing pleasurable activities with another person

- intimacy – establishing a close emotional relationship with another person

- courtship – seeking someone to have as a steady partner.

THINKING CRITICALLY

Given that sexual contact in some form is often part of adolescent love relationships, why do you suppose sex was not mentioned among adolescents' and emerging adults' reasons for forming love relationships in the studies described here?

Adolescents' reasons for forming love relationships tend to change as they enter young adulthood. Psychologist Marilyn Montgomery (2005) – building on earlier studies – investigated views of the functions of love relationships among early adolescents (11-year-olds), late adolescents (16-year-olds) and university students. The early and late adolescents expressed similar views. Both considered recreation to be the most important function, followed by intimacy and then status. In contrast, among university students, intimacy ranked highest, followed by companionship, with recreation a bit lower and status much lower.

Montgomery also found that what adolescents look for in a romantic partner also changes with age, at least for boys. During middle adolescence, boys mention physical attractiveness prominently as a quality they prefer, whereas girls emphasise interpersonal qualities such as support and intimacy. By late adolescence, however, both males and females emphasise interpersonal qualities, and what they seek is highly similar: support, intimacy, communication, commitment and passion (Montgomery, 2005; Shulman and Scharf, 2000).

Although adolescent girls have become a lot more assertive over the past 25 years in their relationships with boys, this does not mean that the old standards have expired entirely. Evidence indicates that **dating scripts**, the cognitive models that guide interactions in adolescents' love relationships, are still highly influenced by gender, with the dynamic control mostly on the side of the boys (Connolly et al., 2004). In general, males still follow a **proactive script**, and females a **reactive script**. The male script includes initiating the love relationship – calling the girl on the phone, suggesting they do something together, deciding where they will go, controlling the public domain (e.g. driving the car) and initiating sexual contact. The female script focuses on the private domain (spending considerable time on dress and grooming), responding to the male's gestures in the public domain (being picked up at her home) and responding to his sexual initiatives. Most adolescent girls are reluctant to be the initiator, although they are more likely to do so than in past generations (Furman and Hand, *ibid*.).

If adolescent romantic relationships often begin as friendships today, what distinguishes a friendship from a romantic relationship? Adolescents see romantic relationships as different from friendships in positive as well as negative ways (Giordano et al., 2006). Romantic relationships tend to involve more intense emotions, including positive feelings of love and happiness as well as feelings of anxiety and discomfort. Romantic relationships are also more likely to involve sexual activity, although sex sometimes spills into adolescent friendships, as we will see later in the chapter. Having a romantic relationship is also valued for the feeling of being cared for by the romantic partner and for having a social companion in leisure activities. On the other hand, adolescents see romantic relationships as constraining their social freedom, as making them emotionally vulnerable, and as more likely than friendships to involve conflict. Frequently, the boundary between friendship and romantic relationship is not clear, with one adolescent seeing it as a friendship and the other as a romantic relationship, with misunderstandings and hurt feelings as a result (Furman and Hand, *ibid*.).

CONNECT AND EXTEND

To examine the links among adolescents' representations of their relationships with parents, friends and romantic partners read 'Adolescents' working models and styles for relationships with parents, friends, and romantic partners' by Wyndol Furman, Valerie A. Simon, Laura Shaffer and Heather A. Bouchey in *Child Development*, Volume 73, Number 1 (January 2002), pp. 241–255

FOCUS ON YOUTH IN THE MEDIA

Television, Film and Sex

Sex is second only to violence as a topic of public concern with respect to the possible effects of media on adolescents. A high proportion of prime-time television shows contain sexual themes. What sort of information about sexuality does prime-time television present to adolescents?

Sexual behaviour is more frequent than sexual talk and tends to take place between partners who were not married but who have an established relationship. Usually, the sexual behaviour is limited to kisses and hugs – intercourse is depicted or strongly implied in fewer than 10 per cent of the programmes – and nudity is also infrequent (Eyal et al., 2007).

What uses do adolescents make of the portrayals of sexuality on television? With sexuality, as with aggressiveness, it is difficult to establish causality, but most scholars in this area agree that through TV programmes adolescents learn cultural beliefs about how male and female roles differ in sexual interactions and what is considered physically attractive in males and females (Pardun et al., 2005). Television also informs adolescents about appropriate sexual scripts (Rivadeneyra and Ward, 2005) that is, the expected patterns of sexual interactions based on cultural norms of what is acceptable and desirable. For adolescents, who are just beginning to date, this information may be eagerly received, especially if their culture provides little in the way of explicit instruction in male and female sexual roles.

Of course, the 'information' adolescents receive about sexual scripts from TV may not be the kind most adults would consider desirable. Television shows portray strong gender stereotypes, with the message that 'boys will be boys and girls better be prepared', that is, that boys seek sex actively and aggressively and girls act as 'sexual gatekeepers' who are supposed to attract boys' sexual interest but also resist their advances (Hust et al., 2008; Kim et al., 2007). Often, the sexual scripts in TV shows portray a 'sniggering attitude' (Bing, 2007) and a 'recreational orientation' toward sex (Attwood, 2007). However, this may be mainly because most of the TV shows popular among adolescents are situation comedies – remember *Friends, The Inbetweeners* and *Skins* in Chapter 8 (Cope-Farrar and Kunkel, 2002), and they rely on standard comedic devices such as sexual innuendo, double entendre (that is, words or phrases that have two meanings), irony and exaggeration. Most adolescents are cognitively capable (see Chapter 3) of separating what is intended to be humorous from what is intended to be a true portrayal of sexuality (Ward et al., 2002). Nevertheless, watching TV depictions of sexual interactions may affect adolescents' own sexual scripts (Tolman et al., 2007).

Films or movies are another medium in which adolescents witness portrayals of sexual behaviour. Like TV shows, films provide adolescents with sexual scripts, but in a more explicit way than TV does (Freeman, 2006; Pardun, 2002; Steele, 2002). Many films aimed at adolescents are explicit about themes of love and 'innocent' sexuality, for example *Angus, Thongs and Perfect Snogging* (2008) starring Georgia Groomer and Liam Hess.

Equally innocent are *She's All That* and *Pretty in Pink*, but a more explicit and darker side of teenage and adult sexuality is observed in *American Pie*. Also on the darker side is the *Twilight Saga*; a series of supernatural romance fantasy films based on the four Twilight novels by the American author Stephenie Meyer. The combination of sexual tension, teenage feelings of alienation and the eroticism of the vampire myth is a successful mix for both the books and the three films released to date.

A recent splendid spoof on the genre of teenage films is *Not Another Teen Movie,* which is deemed suitable by the UK certification authorities for those aged 15 years or older. Of course adolescents have always sneaked into cinemas to watch films with older age certificates and it is worth noting that film censors have always been more alert to depictions of sexual violence than explicit scenes of sexual activities. However, the last decade has seen the growth of DVD releases of films and unfettered access to films

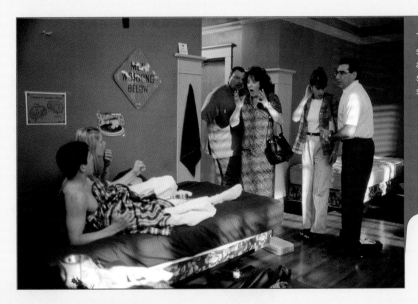

The movies and television shows most popular among adolescents often contain sexual content. Here, a scene from *American Pie*.

on the Internet that do depict sexual violence, for example the compelling but disturbing 2010 film *The Girl with the Dragon Tattoo*; and it's not just mainstream films!

Now that pornographic films are easily accessible on the Internet, more adolescents may be exposed to them and have their sexuality shaped by them. One recent study of Dutch adolescents concluded that boys who watched sexually explicit online films were more likely than other boys to view women as sex objects (Peter and Valkenburg, 2007). There was no effect for exposure to pornographic magazines, only films.

Sex on Music Websites

Early attempts to create a medium that combines television and music were (and some would argue remain) very successful: music television was referred to by the initials of the most popular music television network available in the last 30 years – MTV. MTV began in 1981 and was instantly popular among adolescents (Hansen, 2006). MTV is still broadcast to more than 1 billion people in 164 countries worldwide, making it a significant force towards globalisation (J. L. Roberts, 2005). Some studies in the mid-noughties indicated that most adolescents watch music videos for about 15 to 30 minutes per day (e.g. Roberts et al., 2005). What has subsequently changed is the growth of online sites for viewing music videos, e.g. YouTube – see *Focus on Youth in the Media* feature in Chapter 2 – on which music videos are uploaded and shared. This move to viewing online was identified and studied by a number of scholars working in the area (e.g. Hargittai and Walejko, 2008; Webb, 2007; Demers, 2006).

What uses are made of music videos by adolescents? Music videos can be divided into two general categories *performance videos*, which show an individual performer or a group singing a song in a concert setting or a studio, and *concept videos*, which enact a story to go along with the lyrics of the song. For the most part, performance videos simply convey the songs and have generated no more (or less) controversy than the songs themselves. Most research attention has been directed at the concept videos and the stories they depict. The targets of concern among critics are the same as for television more generally: violence and sex.

➤ Personal experience at the gym tells me (MH) that sexual themes appear in the vast majority of current music videos but for the most part the sexuality is implied rather than shown – that is, the videos are more likely to contain provocatively dressed women than actually to show people kissing, fondling and so forth. Rap or hip-hop videos have been found to be especially high in sexual content, compared to other videos (Peterson et al., 2007). Content analyses indicate that the characters in music videos tend to be highly gender stereotyped, with the men aggressive and the women sexual and subservient (Arnett, 2002c). Do these gender stereotypes influence adolescents' own views of gender? There is the usual correlation-causation problem of media research here. Does watching music videos make young people's views of gender more stereotyped, or are adolescents with stronger gender stereotypes more attracted to music videos, or both? It should be noted that studies show considerable diversity in how adolescents interpret the content of concept videos (Hansen, 2006). Adolescents may watch the same music video or film, or TV show, yet the messages they perceive in it and the uses they make of it may be quite variable.

Romantic experiences are also associated with both positive and negative outcomes in adolescence (Furman et al., 2007). Adolescents who have a romantic relationship tend to be more popular and have a more positive self-image (La Greca and Harrison, 2005). However, this association with positive qualities depends partly on the age of the adolescents. In particular, for early adolescent girls, participating in mixed-gender group activities such as parties and discos may be positive, but a serious love relationship tends to be related to negative outcomes such as depressed mood (Kaltiala-Heino et al., 2003). An important reason for their depression appears to be that early adolescent girls in a serious relationship often find themselves under their boyfriends' pressure to participate in sexual activity before they feel ready (Haavet et al., 2006)

A recent American longitudinal study suggests that having romantic experiences may have mixed effects for other adolescents, too, not just early adolescent girls (Furman et al., 2009). The study surveyed 14- to 16-year-olds on the degree of their romantic experience, ranging from romantic interest to a serious relationship, then followed them up one

Intimacy becomes more important in dating by late adolescence and emerging adulthood.

year later. The amount of adolescents' romantic experience was associated with higher reports of social acceptance, friendship competence and romantic competence. However, romantic experience was also associated with greater substance use and more delinquent behaviour. The amount of romantic experience predicted increased substance use one year later.

CONNECT AND EXTEND

Do shorter adolescents find it more difficult to form love relationships? Read: 'Personality functioning: the influence of stature' by F. Ulph, P. Betts, J. Mulligan and R. J. Stratford in *Archives of Disease in Childhood*, Volume 89, Number 1 (January 2004), pp. 17–21

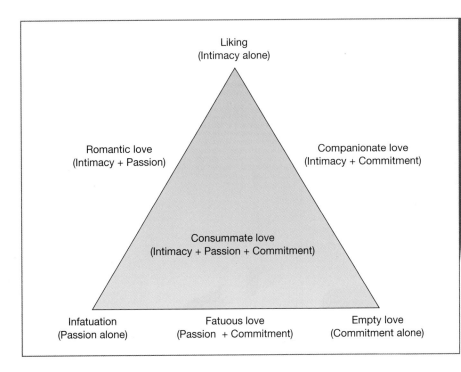

Figure 9.1 Sternberg's Triangular Model of Love.
Source: Sternberg (1988), p. 122.

Sternberg's Theory of Love

After two adolescents share romantic experiences, the relationship sometimes develops into love. The best-known theory of love was developed some 25 years ago by psychologist Robert Sternberg (1988, 1987, 1986). Sternberg proposed that different types of love involve combining three fundamental qualities of love in different ways (Figure 9.1). These three qualities are passion, intimacy and commitment. *Passion* involves physical attraction and sexual desire. It is emotional as well as physical and may involve intense emotions such as anxiety, delight, anger and jealousy. *Intimacy* involves feelings of closeness and emotional attachment. It includes mutual understanding, mutual support and open communication about issues not discussed with anyone else. *Commitment* is the pledge to love someone over the long run, through the ups and downs that are often part of love. Commitment is what sustains a long-term relationship through fluctuations in passion and intimacy.

These three qualities of love are combined in different ways into seven different forms of love in Sternberg's theory, as follows:

- **Liking** is intimacy alone, without passion or commitment. This is the type of love that characterises most friendships. Friendships often involve some level of intimacy, but without passion and without an enduring commitment. Most people have many

friendships that come and go in the course of their lives.

- **Infatuation** is passion alone, without intimacy or commitment. Infatuation involves a great deal of physiological and emotional arousal, and a heightened level of sexual desire, but without emotional closeness to the person or an enduring commitment.

- **Empty love** is commitment alone, without passion or intimacy. This might apply to a couple who have been married for many years and who have lost the passion and intimacy in their relationship but nevertheless remain together. It could also apply to the early stage of marriage in cultures where marriages are arranged by the parents rather than chosen by the young people themselves (Hatfield and Rapson, 2005). However, arranged marriages that begin as empty love may eventually develop both passion and intimacy.

- **Romantic love** combines passion and intimacy, but without commitment. This is the kind of love people mean when they talk about being 'in love'. It is often experienced as intense and joyful, but it rarely lasts long.

- **Companionate love** combines intimacy and commitment, but without passion. It may be applied to married or long-term couples whose passion for each other has gradually waned but who have maintained the other qualities of their love. It could also be applied to unusually close friendships as well as to close family relationships.

- **Fatuous love** (which means 'silly' or 'foolish') involves passion and commitment without intimacy. This kind of love would apply to a 'whirlwind' courtship where two people meet, fall passionately in love, and get married, all within a few weeks, before they even have time to know each other well.

- **Consummate love** integrates all three aspects of love into the ultimate love relationship. Of course, even if consummate love is reached in a relationship, in time passion may fade, intimacy may falter, or commitment may be betrayed. However, this is the kind of love that represents the ideal for many people.

THINKING CRITICALLY

Do you think most people are capable of consummate love by the time they reach emerging adulthood? Do you think adolescents are ever capable of it?

Infatuation and romantic love are the most common types of love in adolescence.

How does Sternberg's theory of love apply to adolescence? Certainly in most adolescent love relationships commitment is either missing or highly tentative (Feldman and Cauffman, 1999). Most adolescent relationships last only a few weeks or months; few of their relationships last a year or longer, although their relationships tend to get longer as they get older (K. Carver et al., 2003). This does not mean that adolescents are incapable of commitment; it simply reflects the fact that in industrialised countries today most people are not likely to get married until they are in their mid- to late 20s. Under these circumstances, it is understandable that adolescents' love relationships would involve commitment much less than passion or intimacy. Commitment tends to develop in emerging adulthood, when young people begin looking more seriously for someone with whom they may have a lifelong love relationship.

The absence of long-term commitment in adolescence means that there are two principal types of adolescent love: infatuation and romantic love. (We do not include liking because it applies mainly to friends – Chapter 8 – not lovers.) Infatuation is common among adolescents; partly because they are new to love and the first few times they 'fall in love' they may take passion alone, with its intensity of feeling and sexual desire, as enough evidence of love. For example,

imagine two adolescents who sit next to one another in maths class, exchange occasional smiles, and maybe flirt a little before and after class. She finds herself day-dreaming of him as she lies in her bedroom and listens to love songs; he starts writing her name surreptitiously in the margins of his exercise book when his mind drifts during class. It feels like love to both of them, and it is a certain kind of love, but it lacks the element of intimacy that people come to desire and expect from love once they become more experienced in it.

Adolescents can experience intimacy in their relationships, too, and combine passion and intimacy to create romantic love (Collins and Sroufe, 1999). The passion is there, with its heightened emotions and sexual desire, but now it is combined with intimacy, as two adolescents spend time together and come to know each other, and they begin to share thoughts and feelings that they share with no one else. The prominence of intimacy in romantic relationships tends to grow through adolescence and into emerging adulthood (Montgomery, 2005).

Adolescents could even experience consummate love, combining passion, intimacy and commitment. Some 'school sweethearts' continue their relationship long after secondary school, and perhaps marry and stay together their whole lives. However, this is rare

CONNECT AND EXTEND

To study 'child marriage' in the context of international women's rights and children's rights. read 'Stages of development: marriage of girls and teens as an international human rights issue' by Annie Bunting in *Social and Legal Studies*, Volume 14, Number 1 (March 2005), pp. 17–38

among adolescents, especially in the current generation. With the typical marriage age so high, only in emerging adulthood do most young people begin thinking about committing themselves to someone for years to come (Jamieson et al., 2002). For this reason, adolescent love relationships rarely progress past infatuation and romantic love to consummate love.

Adolescent Passion in Non-Western Cultures

It is not only in the West, and not only in industrialised countries, that adolescents experience infatuation and romantic love. On the contrary, feelings of passion appear to be a virtually universal characteristic of young people. Twenty years ago, in an important and comprehensive international study, anthropologists William Jankowiak and Eugen Fischer (1992) investigated this issue systematically by analysing the *Standard Cross-cultural Sample*, a collection of data provided by anthropologists on 186 traditional cultures representing six distinct geographical regions around the world. They concluded that there was evidence that young people fell passionately in love in *all but one* of the 186 cultures studied. Although the other 185 cultures differed widely in geographical region, economic characteristics, and many other ways, in all of them young lovers experienced the delight and despair of passionate love, told stories about famous lovers, and sang love songs.

However, this does not mean that young people in all cultures are allowed to act on their feelings of love. On the contrary, romantic love as the basis for marriage is a fairly new cultural idea (Hatfield and Rapson, 2005). As we will see in more detail later in this chapter, in most cultures throughout most of history marriages have been arranged by parents, with little regard for the passionate desires of their adolescent children. Consequently, many cultures also have some version of Shakespeare's Romeo and Juliet tragedy, about a tragic young couple whose love was

thwarted by adults forbidding them to marry, and who defied this prohibition by committing suicide together. These stories are commemorated and passed down through poems, songs, plays and legends. Although these tales of dual suicide for love have a powerful appeal to adolescents all over the world, in real life eloping is a more popular strategy for evading the obstacles to love erected by adults and by cultural customs.

Falling in Love

'I would like to marry someone the same age and ethnicity mainly due to tradition but I am open to other religions and would not discount someone for their religion as a potential partner'
– Alexander, aged 16

How do adolescents and emerging adults choose romantic partners? Do 'opposites attract', or do 'birds of a feather flock together'? The bird metaphor prevails for adolescents and emerging adults and throughout adulthood (Furman and Simon, 2008). Just as we have seen with friendships, people of all ages tend to be most likely to have romantic relationships with people who are similar to them in characteristics such as intelligence, social class, ethnic background, religious beliefs, personality and physical attractiveness (Luo and Klohnen, 2005). Of course, sometimes opposites *do* attract, and partners fall in love even though (and perhaps because) they may differ widely in their characteristics. For the most part, however, people are attracted to others who are like themselves. Social scientists attribute this to **consensual validation**, meaning that people like to find in others an agreement, or consensus, with their own characteristics. Finding this consensus supports, or validates, their own way of looking at the world.

For example, if you have a partner who shares your religious beliefs, the two of you will validate each other in the beliefs that you possess and in the

Adolescents usually choose love partners whose peer crowd status is similar to their own.

they go out to face the challenges in the world, the way children use their parents as a secure base. Furthermore, whether the attachment is to a lover or a parent, extended separation is experienced as a source of distress and the loss of the person is deeply painful. Of course, there are differences as well between attachments to lovers and attachments to parents, most notably that attachments between lovers include a sexual element that attachments to parents do not.

Specifically, attachment styles between lovers have been found to resemble the secure and insecure parent–child attachment styles we have already discussed in Chapter 7 (Braungart-Rieker et al., 2001). Secure attachments in romantic relationships are characterised by emotional support and concern for the partner's well-being. Insecure attachments take the form of either an excess of dependence on the partner or an excess of distance. It has been suggested that these attachment styles to romantic partners may be based on earlier attachments to parents (Creasey and Hesson-McInnis, 2001). However, as noted in Chapter 7, this hypothesis has not yet been truly tested in long-term longitudinal studies.

One way that romantic relationships tend to be different in adolescence than in emerging adulthood or adulthood is that in adolescence the peer context of romantic relationships tends to be especially important (Brown, 2004). We have noted, especially in the previous chapter, that adolescence is a time when responsiveness to the opinions of friends and peers reaches its peak. Adolescents tend to be highly aware of and concerned about the social worlds of friendships, cliques and crowds, and consequently friends and peers exercise considerable power over their love lives. A substantial amount of the conversation among friends, especially in early adolescence, involves questions of who likes whom and who is 'going out with' whom; questions often explored with much joking and teasing. So, adolescent friends often monitor each other's romantic interests and are quick to offer inspiration, guidance, support or scorn (Perlstein, 2003).

In 2003, German social psychologist Inge Seiffge-Krenke (building on work by psychologist Bradford Brown) confirmed a developmental model of adolescent love that recognises the important role played by peers and friends. The model contains four phases: the **initiation phase**, the **status phase**, the **affection phase** and the **bonding phase**. The initiation phase usually takes place in early adolescence, when the first

prescriptions for behaviour that follow from those beliefs. However, if one of you is devout and the other is an atheist, you are likely to find that your different ways of looking at the world lead to conflicts of beliefs and behaviour. One of you wants to go to religious services, the other scoffs that it is a waste of time. Most people find this kind of regular collision of preferences disagreeable, so they seek people who are like themselves to minimise the frequency of collisions (Laursen and Jensen-Campbell, 1999).

After the initial attraction, how does love develop? One promising line of theory and research has explored similarities between attachments to romantic partners and attachments to parents (Furman, 2002). Romantic partners try to maintain regular proximity to each other, the way children try to maintain proximity to parents. Romantic partners seek each other out for comfort and protection in times of crisis, as children do their parents. Romantic partners also use one another as a 'secure base', a source of psychological security, as tentative explorations of romantic interests begin. These explorations are usually superficial and brief, and are often fraught with anxiety and fear, in addition to excitement. The anxiety and fear result in part from the novelty of romantic feelings and behaviours, but also from adolescents' awareness that these new feelings and behaviours are subject to scrutiny and potential ridicule from their friends and peers.

In the status phase, adolescents begin to gain confidence in their skills at interacting with potential romantic partners, and they begin to form their first romantic relationships. In forming these relationships they remain acutely aware of the evaluations of their friends and peers. In considering a potential romantic partner, they assess not just how much they like and are attracted to the person but how their status with friends and peers would be influenced. Peer crowds represent a clear status hierarchy, and adolescents usually date others who have similar crowd status, but lower-status adolescents often fantasise about and may attempt a romantic relationship with someone of higher status – 'nerd loves popular girl/boy' is a popular premise for many a film and television show involving adolescents. Friends may act as messengers in the status phase, enquiring on behalf of a friend to see if a potential love partner might be interested. This is a way of gaining information without risking the direct humiliation – and loss of status – that may result from enquiring oneself.

In the affection phase, adolescents come to know each other better and express deeper feelings for each other, as well as engaging in more extensive sexual activity. Relationships in this phase tend to last several months rather than weeks or days as in the previous two phases. Because intimacy is greater in this phase, romantic relationships become more emotionally charged, and adolescents face greater challenges in managing these strong emotions. The role of peers and friends changes, too. Peers become less important as the relationship grows and the importance of status diminishes, but friends become even more important as *private eyes* who keep an eye on the friend's romantic partner to monitor faithfulness, as *arbitrators* between romantic partners when conflicts occur, and as *support systems* who provide a sympathetic ear when romantic difficulties or complexities arise. Issues of jealousy may also arise, if friends begin to resent the amount of time and closeness the adolescent devotes to the romantic partner at the expense of the friendship.

In the bonding phase, the romantic relationship becomes more enduring and serious, and partners

begin to discuss the possibility of a lifelong commitment to each other. This phase usually occurs in emerging adulthood rather than adolescence. The role of friends and peers recedes in this phase, as the question of others' opinions becomes less important than issues of compatibility and commitment between the romantic partners. Nevertheless, friends may continue to provide guidance and advice, as someone to talk with about whether the romantic partner is the right person with whom to form a lifelong commitment.

When Love Goes Bad: Breaking Up

Love in adolescence and emerging adulthood is not only about affection and bonding. On the contrary, love is often the source of anxiety and distress as well. Because most young people have a series of love relationships, most of them experience 'breaking up', the dissolution of a relationship, at least once (Battaglia et al., 1998).

What is breaking up like for adolescents and emerging adults? For adolescents, egocentrism may contribute to the intensity of the unhappiness following a breakup. Egocentrism's personal fable can contribute to adolescents' feelings that their suffering in the aftermath of a breakup is something that no one has ever experienced as deeply as they are experiencing it and that the pain of it will never end. 'I just feel like my life's over, like there's never going to be anything to smile about again,' one 17-year-old girl lamented after breaking up (Bell, 1998, p. 71). Broken-up couples appear to lack the consensual validation that most people find attractive in an intimate relationship (Felmlee, 2001).

The emotions involved in love are intense, and breaking up often provokes sadness and a sense of loss. Increased alcohol and drug use is common following a breakup (Davis et al., 2003). Furthermore, breaking up can inspire 'romantic harassment' that involves unwanted pursuit of the ex-partner (Langhinrichsen-Rohling et al., 2002). In one study of female university students (K. A. Roberts, 2005), two-thirds reported romantic harassment following the breakup of a relationship. Of these, half were classified as mild harassment (such as persistent unwanted telephone calls) and half as 'stalking' (being followed and threatened by the ex-partner). The young women who experienced romantic harassment also recalled more controlling behaviour by their ex-partner during the relationship.

CONNECT AND EXTEND

Some victims of stalking blame themselves. Read 'The role of cognitive coping in female victims of stalking' by Vivian Kraaij, Ella Arensman, Nadia Garnefski and Ismay Kremers in the *Journal of Interpersonal Violence*, Volume 22, Number 12 (December 2007), pp. 1603–1612

The experience was highly stressful for the women. They reported feeling acute fear, anxiety and depression during the harassment and experienced nervous physical symptoms such as stomach aches and nervous tics. The women tried a variety of strategies to deter their harassers, from ignoring them to trying to reason with them, to being rude to threatening them. Some changed their phone number or moved accommodation; some had a parent or boyfriend talk to or threaten them. None of these strategies worked very well in the short term. The best defence was simply time – eventually the harassers gave up.

Choosing a Marriage Partner

Although love has a potential dark side, for most young people experiencing feelings of love and being loved, rather than 'wreaking havoc' with adolescent emotions is a source of joy and contentment, and the positive emotions experienced with love become steadily stronger and more stable during adolescence and young adulthood (Larson et al., 1999). Eventually about 90 per cent of people in most societies marry (King, 2005). So how do young people choose a marriage partner?

In Chapter 5, on gender, we discussed the characteristics adolescents use to describe the ideal man and the ideal woman. The most important qualities considered ideal for both genders were personal qualities such as being kind and honest, whereas qualities such as having a lot of money and being popular ranked quite low (Gibbons and Stiles, 2004).

The same kinds of results have been found in studies that ask young people about the qualities they consider most important in the person they marry. Psychologist David Buss carried out a historic and influential study of over 10,000 young people in 37 countries on the qualities they consider most important in the person they marry (1989). The questionnaire had to be translated into 37 languages, with great care taken to make the meanings of words such as 'love' as similar as possible in every country. In many of the countries, a high proportion of the young people were illiterate, so the questions had to be read aloud to them.

Despite all of these challenges, the results showed impressive consistencies across countries and across genders (see Table 9.1). 'Mutual attraction – love' ranked first among marriage criteria across countries, followed by 'dependable character', 'emotional stability and maturity' and 'pleasing disposition'. Similarity in religious and political background ranked very low, which is surprising given that (as noted earlier) people tend to marry others who are similar to them in these ways. 'Good financial prospects' also ranked fairly low, as 'having a lot of money' did in the studies of adolescents' views of the ideal man and the ideal woman.

Although the cross-cultural similarities were strong and striking, some cross-cultural differences were also notable. The sharpest cross-cultural division was on the issue of chastity (marrying someone who has never had sex before). In Eastern cultures (e.g. China, India, Indonesia) and Middle Eastern cultures (Iran, Palestinian Arabs in Israel), chastity was rated as highly important. However, in the West (e.g. Finland, France, Norway, Germany), chastity was generally considered unimportant.

CONNECT AND EXTEND

Roma men have great sexual freedom before and during marriage. In contrast, women are expected to maintain virginity before marriage. Read 'Gender roles and HIV sexual risk vulnerability of Roma (Gypsies) men and women in Bulgaria and Hungary: an ethnographic study' by J. A. Kelly, Y. A. Amirkhanian, E. Kabakchieva, P. Csepe, D. W. Seal, R. Antonova, A. Mihaylov and G. Gyukits in *AIDS Care*, Volume 16, Number 2 (2004), pp. 231–245

HISTORICAL FOCUS

They're Playing Our Song

Love relationships begin (initiation phase), develop (status phase and affection phase) and deepen (the bonding phase) all with a 'backing soundtrack' that means so much at the time and remains with us long after the relationship has broken up. Go on, think about one of your early loves and remember the love song that became your song, something that 'spoke' to you both about what you felt, how you began or perhaps what signalled the beginning of the end. You may have a personal history of love songs that can recapture for you the thrilling and perhaps still painful feelings that a love song can reawaken.

Of course there is an ancient history of love songs. The poems/songs of Sumeria still speak to us of sexual pleasure and romantic encounters. In the biblical 'Song of Songs' physical delights of lovemaking are described in such detail it seems unlikely that it was written as praise to the God of the Israelites. The Greek poet Sappho wrote yearning words to both men and women but her most sensual lines are addressed to a female lover. Even Sappho is restrained in comparison to Roman love songs, which are full of orgiastic pleasure and sexual excess.

The European troubadours of a thousand years ago set sensuous poetry to common melodies and their lyrics were expressions of passionate love and desire. Sexual puns, allusions and bawdy language were quite common in the love songs of the Renaissance, thinly disguised by employing the metaphor of dancing. Of course, love songs were few and far between during the European Reformation and the centuries of religious fervour that followed. This remained true until songs of love were reawakened in the Victorian parlours of the European aristocracy and growing middle classes. Sheet music of the 1890s to 1930s sold by the million and was 'enjoyed' by courting couples around the piano or harmonium on a Sunday afternoon. However, it was the widespread rise of radio and recordings in the 1930s that changed everything. Lovers could could enjoy 'their song' at home, not just in the dance hall or music hall. The heart-throb singer was singing just for them and the song became an intimate and personal emotional experience.

The high emotions, tragedies and triumphs of the Second World War produced a generation of love songs that reflected the enhanced romanticism of super-heated, temporary love affairs and bittersweet, fearful partings. The rebuilding of the post-war years and the birth of youth culture set the scene for the rise of rock and roll, for the ballad love song, as the 'last dance' took over from the last waltz. It was not just a personal love song that young people yearned for; it was the rebirth of sexuality in popular music. The scene was set for *The King*; for Elvis Presley.

Elvis the Pelvis

In the spring of 1953, an 18-year-old delivery truck driver named Elvis Presley walked into a recording studio in Memphis, Tennessee, and paid $4 for the opportunity to record two songs as a birthday present for his mother. Three years later, Elvis Presley was 21 years old, a multimillionaire entertainer and, arguably, the most famous person on the planet.

How did this happen? Part of the explanation, of course, lies in Elvis's extraordinary talents. He had a uniquely rich, expressive and versatile singing voice, and he sang with an extraordinary sensual intensity. He had grown up in the South listening to rhythm-and-blues songs performed by black musicians, and he incorporated the sensuality and power of their styles into his own. Many people recognised the black influence in his singing, and Elvis himself acknowledged it.

Not only his singing but his performing was influenced by black musicians he had seen, as he developed a performance style of bracing himself against the microphone stand and thrusting his pelvis back and forth in a distinctly sexual way (leading to the nickname 'Elvis the Pelvis'), his legs pumping rhythmically, his body shaking all over. He made black rock-and-roll music and styles popular to white audiences at a time in history when racist beliefs about black people possessing an uncontrolled sexuality would have made it difficult for a black person singing in that style to be accepted by the majority culture.

However, in addition to Elvis's talents, four media forms interacted to fuel his fame: radio, newspapers, television and film. His career got its initial burst through radio, when a Memphis radio station played a recording of him singing 'That's All Right (Mama)' and within days thousands of adolescents were storming Memphis record stores seeking copies of the record (which had not actually been released yet). Soon, radio stations all over the South were playing 'That's All Right' and every other Elvis song as he recorded more of them.

Next, newspapers came into the mix. A Memphis newspaper printed a front-page story with the title 'He's Sex!' and it was reprinted in newspapers all over the South. This, along with increasingly widespread exposure on radio stations, gave Elvis a hot reputation as he and his band began to tour and perform in cities throughout the South. Everywhere he performed, newspapers covered his concerts, mostly with rave reviews, further enhancing his popularity.

But it was television that made Elvis a world-famous star. Following his first television appearance on *The Ed Sullivan Show* early in 1956, when he was still relatively unknown outside the South, CBS was flooded with phone calls and letters from aroused adolescent fans. He appeared several more times on television in 1956, each time to an enormous national audience.

As he became increasingly popular, his critics grew louder and more numerous, calling his performances 'lewd' and 'obscene'. Jackie Gleason, a popular TV performer of the day, sneered, 'The kid has no right behaving like a sex maniac on a national show' (Lichter, 1978, p. 22). A newspaper critic was one of many to express concern about the potential effects on young people: 'When Presley executes his bumps and grinds, it must be remembered by [CBS] that even the twelve-year-old's curiosity may be overstimulated' (Lichter, 1978, p. 34). By the time Elvis appeared on *The Ed Sullivan Show* again in September 1956, CBS executives decided he would be shown only from the waist up, so as not to provoke any unruly sexual impulses among the young.

Elvis's first performance on *The Ed Sullivan Show* still ranks as the highest-rated television show ever broadcast in the United States, with an astonishing 83 per cent of the television sets in the country tuned in. It is worth noting that the rise of Elvis coincided fortuitously with the rise of TV. Television propelled Elvis into unprecedented national fame. His fame became international as his performances and stories of his performances were distributed in newspapers, on radio stations and television networks all over the world.

Soon Elvis added movies to his media machine. His first film, *Love Me Tender,* was released near the end of 1956. Neither this film nor any of his 32 other films was highly regarded by movie critics, but Elvis's adolescent fans worldwide had a different opinion. They made this film and many of the others huge box office hits. Even in the mid-1960s, after Elvis's musical career had been eclipsed by the Beatles and other new performers, his movies continued to bring in millions of dollars (Lichter, *ibid.*).

These four interacting media contributed substantially to Elvis's fame, but from the beginning the explosion of his fame was driven by the responses of his adolescent fans – their calls to radio stations demanding to hear his songs again and again, the raucous screaming crowds at the concerts covered by newspaper reporters, the rapt and enormous television audiences, and a devoted film-going audience even for Elvis movies that were (to put it mildly) less than memorable. Although corporate businesspeople have tried hard ever since Elvis to control the highly lucrative business of popular music, the enthusiasms of adolescents have usually proven difficult to predict (Selfhout et al., 2008; Huntsinger and Jose, 2006) and ultimately it is adolescents who drive the direction of popular music, as you may have already read about in Chapters 4 to 6.

(For those of you who have not heard of Elvis or for whom the foregoing *Historical Focus* feature was just a bit too historic then you can look to Michael Jackson as a comparable pop icon. If Elvis was an icon of male sexuality, and therefore an object of suspicion among some, then Jackson, who had an ungendered quality to his sexuality and his image, was also a figure of controversy amidst the worldwide adulation from young fans.)

Table 9.1 The Importance of Various Traits in Mate Selection Throughout the World

Men's ranking of various traits[a]	Women's ranking of various traits[a]
1 Mutual attraction – love	1 Mutual attraction – love
2 Dependable character	2 Dependable character
3 Emotional stability and maturity	3 Emotional stability and maturity
4 Pleasing disposition	4 Pleasing disposition
5 Good health	5 Education and intelligence
6 Education and intelligence	6 Sociability
7 Sociability	7 Good health
8 Desire for home and children	8 Desire for home and children
9 Refinement, neatness	9 Ambitious and industrious
10 Good looks	10 Refinement, neatness
11 Ambitious and industrious	11 Similar education
12 Good cook and housekeeper	12 Good financial prospect
13 Good financial prospect	13 Good looks
14 Similar education	14 Favourable social status or rating
15 Favourable social status or rating	15 Good cook and housekeeper
16 Chastity (no previous experience in sexual intercourse)	16 Similar religious background
17 Similar religious background	17 Similar political background
18 Similar political background	18 Chastity (no previous experience in sexual intercourse)

[a]The lower the number, the more important men and women throughout the world consider this trait to be (using the arithmetic mean average).

Source: based on Hatfield and Rapson (2005)

Arranged Marriages

As noted earlier, although romantic love is found in all cultures, it is not considered the proper basis of marriage in all cultures. In fact, the idea that romantic love should be the basis of marriage is only about 300 years old in the West and is even newer in most of the rest of the world (Hatfield and Rapson, 2005). Marriage has more often been seen by cultures as an alliance between two families rather than as the uniting of two individuals (Buunk et al., 2008). Parents and other adult kin have often held the power to arrange the marriages of their young people, sometimes with the young person's consent, sometimes without it. The most important considerations in an **arranged marriage** did not usually include the prospective bride and groom's

love for one another – often they did not even know each other – or even their personal compatibility. Instead, the desirability of marriage between them was decided by each family on the basis of the other family's status, religion and wealth. Economic considerations have often been of primary importance.

A cultural tradition of arranged marriage implies different expectations for the marriage relationship. In the West, young people expect marriage to provide intimacy as well as passion and commitment. They leave their homes and families well before marriage, and they expect their closest attachment in adulthood to be with their marriage partner. For example, in one national survey, 94 per cent of single people in their 20s agreed that 'when you marry you want your spouse to be your soul mate, first and foremost' (Popenoe and Whitehead, 2001).

Arranged marriages are still common in countries such as India.

However, in the East, where many cultures have a tradition of arranged marriage, much less has been demanded of marriage. Commitment comes first, and passion is welcomed if it exists initially or develops eventually, but expectations of intimacy in marriage are modest. On the contrary, people expect to find intimacy mainly with their family of origin – their parents and their siblings – and eventually with their own children.

Currently, even cultures with a tradition of arranged marriage are beginning to change in their marriage expectations through the influence of globalisation. India, for example, has a history of arranged marriage that has existed for 6000 years. By the first decade of the twenty-first century, however, nearly 40 per cent of adolescent Indians said they intended to choose their own mates (Saraswathi, 2006). This still left the majority (60 per cent) who expected an arranged marriage, but for 40 per cent to prefer choosing their own spouse is high compared with any time in the past, when the percentage would have been close to zero. A similar pattern is taking place in many other cultures with a tradition of arranged marriage (Oprea, 2005; Stevenson and Zusho, 2002). Increasingly, young people in these cultures believe that they should be free to choose their mate or at least to have a significant role with their parents in choosing the right person (Batabyal and Beladi, 2002). Globalisation has increased the extent to which young people value individual choice and the individual's pursuit of happiness, and these values are difficult to reconcile with the tradition of arranged marriage.

Consequently, in many cultures the tradition of arranged marriage has become modified. For example, in most Eastern cultures, the 'semi-arranged marriage' is the most common practice (Naito and Gielen, 2003). This means that parents influence the mate selection of their children but do not simply decide it without the children's consent. Parents may introduce a potential mate to their child. If the young person has a favourable impression of the potential mate, they date a few times. If they agree that they are compatible, they marry. In another variation of semi-arranged marriage, young people meet a potential mate on their own but seek their parents' approval before proceeding to date the person or to consider marriage.

It is difficult to say if semi-arranged marriage will be an enduring form or if it is a transitional stage on the way to the end of the tradition of arranged marriage. Although semi-arranged marriages are now common in Eastern cultures, it is also increasingly common for young people to choose their own marriage partner without any involvement from their parents (Stevenson and Zusho, 2002). Match-making services, including some through the Internet, have also become increasingly popular. Recreational dating remains rare in Asian cultures, but it is more common than in the past, and it may grow in the future.

Even though some argue that the tradition of arranged marriage has operated successfully within many communities and countries over a long period of time (Uddin, 2006) this tradition has come under challenge because of the increasing incidence of forced marriages taking place both in Indian and Pakistani communities in Europe and through families in the Indian subcontinent. There is a clear distinction between forced and arranged marriage. Arranged marriage takes place only with the full agreement and consent from both bride and groom, whereas in forced marriage, one or both spouses do not consent to the marriage, and an element of physical and or emotional duress is sometimes involved.

Confusion between arranged and forced marriages has led to increased tension between Northern European and Asian cultures. For example, even though during the last decade the UK government considered proposals to make forcing someone to marry a specific criminal offence, they concluded that criminalisation would not provide an effective intervention into this problem. Instead, government ministers advocated the use of existing laws with improved support for victims from health and social care professionals. The nearby *Connect and Extend* feature provides a more detailed examination of the problem of forced marriage in minority ethnic communities.

CONNECT AND EXTEND

This paper supports a better-informed discussion about the reportedly 'increasing problem' of forced marriage. Read 'Arranged marriage: a dilemma for young British Asians' by Mohammad Shams Uddin in *Diversity in Health and Social Care*, Volume 3, Number 3 (September 2006), pp. 211–219

Cohabitation

'I agree that you should live with the person before you get married. However not in case they don't put the lid back on the toothpaste. It should be because you love them and you want to see if you can live together in harmony before you give each other your life.'

Beth, aged 15 (Hughes, unpublished data)

Increasingly in industrialised countries, marriage no longer marks the beginning of living with a romantic partner. In many northern European countries, **cohabitation** before or instead of marriage is now experienced by at least two-thirds of emerging adults (Kiernan, 2004; Wu, 1999). The percentage is highest in Sweden, where nearly all young people cohabit before marriage (Duvander, 1999). Cohabitation can be a brief and unstable experience for young people. One American study found that half of cohabiting relationships lasted less than a year, and only one in ten couples were together five years later (Bumpass and Liu, 2000). In contrast, cohabiting couples in European countries tend to stay together as long as married couples (Hacker, 2002a).

However, in Europe there are distinct differences in cohabitation between north and south (Kiernan, 2004; 2002). Emerging adults in Southern Europe are considerably less likely than their counterparts in the north to cohabit; most emerging adults in Southern Europe live at home until marriage (Douglass, 2005), especially females. Perhaps because of the Catholic religious tradition in the south, cohabitation carries a moral stigma in Southern Europe that it does not have in the north.

Young people choose to cohabit in part because they wish to enhance the likelihood that when they marry, it will last. Indeed, in a large survey of 20 to 29-year-olds, 62 per cent agreed that 'living together with someone before marriage is a good way to avoid eventual divorce' (Popenoe and Whitehead, 2001). Emerging adults from divorced families are especially likely to cohabit because they are especially determined to avoid their parents' fate (Cunningham and Thornton, 2007). However, cohabitation before marriage is related to a higher likelihood of later divorce (Kiernan, 2004; 2002; Cohan and Kleinbaum, 2002).

This may be because cohabiting couples become used to living together while maintaining separate lives in many ways, especially financially, so that they are unprepared for the compromises required by marriage. Also, even before cohabitation begins, emerging adults who cohabit tend to be different from emerging adults who do not, in ways that are related to higher risk of divorce: they tend to be less religious, more sceptical of the institution of marriage, and more accepting of divorce (Stanley et al., 2004; Cohan and Kleinbaum, 2002). However, one recent analysis concluded that cohabitation itself increases the risk of divorce because it leads some couples who are not compatible to marry anyway, out of 'the inertia of cohabitation' (Stanley et al., 2006).

THINKING CRITICALLY

Why do *you* think cohabitation before marriage is related to higher likelihood of divorce?

SEXUALITY

As we have discussed throughout this book, puberty and the development of sexual maturation are central to adolescence. We have seen how reaching sexual maturity has multiple effects on young people's development, from relationships with parents to the intensification of gender differences. However, like other aspects of development in adolescence, sex cannot be understood apart from its cultural context. Because human beings are shaped so much by their cultural and social environment, when considering sexual issues we have to think not just of sex but of **sexuality**, that is, not just biological sexual development but also sexual values, beliefs, thoughts, feelings, relationships and behaviour. Thus, our focus in this section will be not just on sex but on sexuality.

Rates of Adolescent Sexual Activity

Most of the research on adolescent sexuality focuses on sexual intercourse, perhaps because of concerns about problems such as adolescent pregnancy and sexually transmitted diseases. However, intercourse is only one part of adolescent sexuality, and it is not the most widespread or the most frequent part of adolescent sexual activity. Most 'Western' adolescents have a considerable amount of other kinds of sexual experience before they have intercourse for the first time, and for most, intercourse is reached through a progression of stages lasting many years (K. Carver et al., 2003). The progression often begins with masturbation, followed by extended bouts of kissing, petting and oral sex before full sexual intercourse.

Masturbation

'Through school life every teenager jokes about having a wank and most who joke about it are generally the ones who do it the most. Students don't see this subject as private as it used to be.'
– Alexander, age 16 (Hughes, unpublished data)

'Masturbation, like your sex life, etc. is a personal thing – why would you advertise that about yourself? A lot of teenagers do it, some don't: it might be something that you talk about with your close friends, but why would it be something that you brag about?'
– Alexandra (Alex), age 15 (Hughes, unpublished data)

For many adolescents, especially boys, their first sexual experiences take place alone – private sexual behaviour. Consistently for over a half century, Western studies have found that the majority of boys begin masturbating by age 13 and that about 90 per cent of boys masturbate by age 19 (King, 2005; Halpern et al., 2000). Masturbation among adolescent boys tends to occur frequently, about five times a week on average (Bockting and Coleman, 2003).

For girls, the picture is quite different. In studies a half-century ago, only about 15 per cent of females reported masturbating by age 13 and only about 30 per cent by age 20 (Kinsey et al., 1953). In more recent studies, these percentages have increased, but it remains true that girls report considerably lower rates of masturbation than boys (Ginsberg et al., 2005). For both boys and girls, masturbation is not just a sexual release for adolescents who are not having intercourse. On the contrary, adolescents who have had sexual intercourse are more likely to masturbate than adolescents who have not (Bockting and Coleman, 2003).

The recent increase in adolescent girls' reports of masturbation is related to changes in cultural attitudes toward more acceptance of female sexuality and more acceptance of masturbation. By the late 1970s, over 70 per cent of adolescents in their mid-teens agreed that 'It's okay for a boy/girl my age to masturbate' (Hass, 1979). However, this is one of those areas where it is useful to ask about the validity of people's self-reports of their behaviour. It could be that part of the increase in reported rates of girls' masturbation is due to girls' greater willingness to report it. For reasons of social desirability, they may have been less willing to report it 50 years ago than they are today. Even today, masturbation may be a particularly problematic topic in terms of self-report. Sex researchers find that both adolescents and adults are more reluctant to discuss masturbation than any other topic (Halpern et al., 2000). Although masturbation is both normal and harmless, many young people still feel guilty and frightened by it (Shand, 2007). There is a long and bizarre cultural history of masturbation in the West, including claims that it causes a wide variety of ills, from pimples to epilepsy; from insanity to death (Laqueur, 2004). Part of that anxious legacy endures today despite the sexual revolutions of the twentieth century.

CONNECT AND EXTEND

How do staff respond to incidents of public masturbation and other sexual acts by teenagers with severe learning difficulties? Read 'Experiences of staff in dealing with client sexuality in services for teenagers and adults with intellectual disability' by R. McConkey and D. Ryan in *Journal of Intellectual Disability Research*, Volume 45, Number 1 (February 2001), pp. 83–87

Kissing and Petting

'When I was with my boyfriend and we were all alone for the first time .... We were French-kissing real long kisses, so sometimes I had to pull away to catch my breath. He was rubbing my back and I was rubbing his.'
– Jennifer, age 14 (in Bell, 1998, p. 115)

'I think [kissing and stroking] is fine because you're doing something you want to with the person you love and obviously you won't do anything you don't want to with them if you feel uncomfortable.'
– Beth, age 15 (Hughes, unpublished data)

After masturbation, sexual experience for adolescents tends to follow a sequence (see Table 9.2) from kissing through stroking and petting to intercourse and oral sex (Feldman et al., 1999). Kissing and stroking (mutual touching and stroking above the waist) are the first sexual experiences most adolescents have with a sexual partner. Little research has been done on this early stage of adolescent sexual experience. We have to look to one early study which found that of those questioned, 73 per cent of 13-year-old girls and 60 per cent of 13-year-old boys had kissed at least once (Coles and Stokes, 1985). The same study found that 35 per cent of the girls reported having their breasts touched by a boy, and 20 per cent of the boys reported touching a girl's breast. By age 16, a majority of boys and girls had engaged in this breast-touching aspect of necking. The next step in the sequence is usually petting (mutual touching and stroking below the waist). By age 18, 60 per cent of adolescent boys reported vaginal touching and 77 per cent of adolescent girls reported penile touching. A more recent study that asked young adults to recall their earlier sexual behaviour reported a similar sequence at similar ages, as shown in Table 9.2 (Feldman et al., 1999).

Recent research by Dutch researcher Hanneke de Graaf and colleagues in The Netherlands (2009) attempted to identify a typical and successful 'sexual trajectory' during adolescence. The Dutch researchers defined the 'sexual trajectory' as an age-graded set of various new sexual experiences, defined by three key dimensions: sequence, duration and timing. A representative Dutch sample of 1263 males and 1353 females (M = 20.46 years; range, 12–25) who had engaged in sexual intercourse completed a questionnaire about sexual behaviour. About three-quarters of participants had followed a progressive and common sexual trajectory from less intimate (e.g. kissing) to more intimate behaviour (e.g. stroking and petting). Immigrant groups and less educated youth were more likely to follow a non-linear trajectory, 'jumping' to oral sex and anal intercourse. A progressive trajectory was associated with a higher likelihood of consistent contraceptive use and, for girls, with a lower likelihood of having unprotected anal intercourse.

Table 9.2 Average Age at First Experience of Various Sexual Behaviours

	Average Age at First Experience	
	Males	**Females**
Kissing	13.9	15.0
Touch breast	14.9	16.2
Touch penis	15.7	16.6
Touch vagina	15.4	16.4
Sexual intercourse	16.3	17.3
Oral sex	16.9	17.8

Source: Feldman et al., (1999)

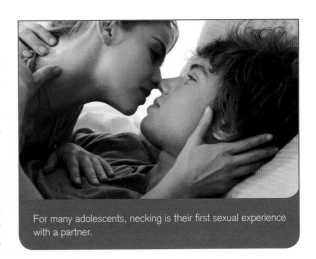

For many adolescents, necking is their first sexual experience with a partner.

Sexual Intercourse and Oral Sex

'When I had intercourse for the first time it was because I really wanted to do it. We talked about it and sort of planned when we would do it … The actual intercourse wasn't as great for me as I thought it would be, but the part leading up to it and the part being together afterwards was really nice.'
– Serena, age 19 (Bell, 1998, p. 124)

'I think it's good to talk about it with your partner and plan it out so that you know you're both ready and prepared to make this big step.'
– Nadine, age 16 (Hughes, unpublished data)

'I think everyone has high expectations and when it actually happens it's not as good as you thought it would be.'
– Amy, age 15 (Hughes, unpublished data)

'When I first experienced sexual intercourse, I was ready, and I knew that it was my choice and I didn't feel pressured at all. It was lovely feeling so close to my boyfriend and it was a magical experience. He had waited more than a year: I love him and him me, it just felt right.'
– Alexendra (Alex), aged 15 (Hughes, unpublished data)

The most researched topic on adolescent sexuality is the timing of adolescents' first episode of sexual intercourse. For example, two 'National Surveys of Sexual Attitudes and Lifestyles' (Natsal) were conducted in Britain, one in 1990 (Johnson et al., 1994) and one in 2000 (Johnson et al., 2001). Northern Ireland was excluded from both studies. By 2004, comparable data about sexual attitudes and lifestyles of young people (14- to 25-year-olds) in Northern Ireland was collected through self-administered questionnaires, one-to-one interviews and focus-group discussions. A total of 1013 young people in the target age group completed the self-administered questionnaire. Young people in Northern Ireland did not differ significantly from their counterparts in Britain. Some 26.7 per cent of all respondents said they had sex before age 16. Respondents who first had sex when they were 15 or

16 years of age were more likely than other respondents to say that 'being drunk' was the main reason why intercourse occurred, and peer pressure to engage in sex was more prevalent among males than females. The average age of first intercourse was similar to that in most European countries – around age 17 (Avery and Lazdane, 2008).

Are there any 'causes' of earlier than average experience of sexual intercourse? It should not surprise you that parenting styles (discussed earlier in Chapter 7) have a considerable effect upon emerging personality types, and different personalities act differently! Social researchers Robert Atkins and Daniel Hart (2008) categorised child participants at 5 or 6 years of age in a longitudinal survey of youth into one of three personality types: under-controlled, resilient (those who can accurately estimate risks and can resist stressors, pressure and adversity) and over-controlled. Those categorised as under-controlled at 5 or 6 years of age were more likely than those resilient or over-controlled to have sexual intercourse before the age of 16. Three early adolescent factors – team or club membership, church attendance and peer influence, particularly peer influence at the age of 11 and 12, were found to mediate the association of childhood personality type to the timing of first sexual intercourse. These are important findings for all practitioners interested in improving the health and well-being of young people.

Are there differences between ethnic groups in a multicultural society? Researchers Lester Coleman and Adrienne Testa (2007) looked for evidence about the sexual health knowledge, attitudes and behaviours of an ethnically diverse sample of young people in school Years 11 to 13 (aged 15–18 years), in 16 secondary/high schools in London where the black and minority ethnic (BME) population exceeded two-thirds of the intake. Questionnaires were completed by 2602 students aged 15 to 18, who self-defined their ethnicity as follows: 559 white British; 256 white other; 710 black and 1077 Asian. The pupils completed 30-minute questionnaires distributed and collected by a team of ethnically diverse fieldworkers. This questionnaire recorded sociodemographic information, sexual health

CONNECT AND EXTEND

Read the original paper referred to in the nearby text 'The under-controlled do it first: childhood personality and sexual debut' by Robert Atkins and Daniel Hart in *Research in Nursing & Health*, Volume 31, Number 6 (December 2008), pp. 626–639

knowledge, sexual health attitudes, experience of sexual intercourse, and sexual risk behaviour and outcomes.

With 65 per cent of black Caribbean males reporting experience of sexual intercourse, and 48 per cent reporting first intercourse under the age of 16, this group is possibly the most at risk of poor sexual health. Although less likely to report early sexual intercourse than black Caribbeans, black African females and Asian males and females also reported early sexual behaviour in contrast to adolescents in Asian countries who maintain conservative sexual norms (Naito and Gielen, 2003a).

CONNECT AND EXTEND

For a study of the associations of early sexual activity and self-reported depression in a school survey in Finland read 'Risk-taking sexual behaviour and self-reported depression in middle adolescence: a school-based survey' by E. Kosunen, R. Kaltiala-Heino, M. Rimpelä and P. Laippala in *Child: Care Health & Development*, Volume 29, Number 5 (1 September 2003), pp. 337–344

FOCUS ON RESEARCH

R

Sex, Lies and Methodology

For obvious reasons, studies of adolescent sexuality are based almost entirely on self-report. This raises the question of how truthful people are about what they report. Sex involves many sensitive and private issues, and people may be unwilling to disclose information on these issues accurately even if they are promised that their responses will be anonymous.

One way around this problem involves having adolescents respond on a computer to prerecorded questions given through headphones. In a national study of sexual behaviour among 1600 adolescent males aged 15 to 19 (Harmon, 1998), adolescents who listened to questions on the headphones and answered them on a computer screen were far more likely to report high-risk sexual behaviour than adolescents who answered the questions in the traditional questionnaire format. The computer group was 4 times as likely to report having had sex with another male (5.5 to 1.5 per cent), 14 times as likely to report sex with an intravenous drug user (2.8 to 0.2 per cent), and 5 times as likely to report that they were 'always' or 'often' drunk or high when they had sex (10.8 to 2.2 per cent). These differences remained after the researchers controlled statistically for ethnic background and school performance. The gap between computer answers and questionnaire answers was greatest among adolescents who did well in school, indicating that these adolescents felt they had more of an image to maintain and so were more influenced by social desirability.

Other studies of sensitive topics such as illegal drug use and online gambling have also found that use of a computer results in higher reports of the behaviour (McBride and Derevensky, 2009; Supple et al., 1999). One most interesting project (Martin, 1998) was with 30 youths aged 18/19 from child welfare contexts who constructed self-narratives using notebook computers about how they conceptualised and managed their adolescent transition, including leaving care homes. Research reported in 2006 by psychologist Alison Bryant and colleagues working in the area of computer-mediated communication and adolescent development raised issues regarding adolescent use of socially interactive technologies (SITs). Network data collection and analysis were integrated with more traditional questionnaire methodology and statistical analysis. The research explored the friendship patterns of those taking part – a potentially sensitive issue. These research projects and others you will read about in this chapter and others suggest that youngsters generally experience a decrease in their inhibitions when a computer mediates their communication and makes it easier for adolescents (and others) to disclose their participation in behaviour they perceive to be disapproved by their society, in risky behaviour or matters about which they may feel sensitive.

Having sexual intercourse once does not necessarily initiate a pattern of frequent intercourse from that point onward. The average length of a sexual relationship among adolescents is six months, and only one-third last more than seven months. In between relationships, adolescents may have periods when they are not sexually active. Why might this be?

Most adolescent sexual activity, especially sexual intercourse, takes place within the context of a romantic relationship (Furman et al., 2009). According to a national study of adolescents who had had sex, 77 per cent indicated that their most recent sexual partner was also their romantic partner (Manlove et al., 2006). However, many adolescents also have occasional episodes of recreational sex, sometimes known today as 'hooking up' (a one-time sexual experience between uncommitted partners, which may or may not include intercourse). In another American study, over 60 per cent of sexually active adolescents reported having at least one episode of sexual intercourse with an uncommitted partner (Giordano et al., 2006). However, partners in 'hooking up' were not usually strangers. In fact, in 70 per cent of hooking up episodes, the partner was a friend, acquaintance, or ex-boyfriend/girlfriend, and only 6 per cent were with a partner the adolescent had just met. Sexual activity between friends sometimes serves as a bridge towards building a romantic relationship (Furman and Hand, ibid.).

One other area for which rates of sexual behaviour should be mentioned is oral sex. Most studies find that, for most young people, their first episode of oral sex comes at a later age than their first episode of sexual intercourse. According to one recent study of 15- to 19-year-olds, 54 per cent of girls and 55 per cent of boys reported ever having oral sex (Lindberg et al., 2008). Sexual intercourse experiences predicted oral sex; within six months of their first episode of sexual intercourse, 82 per cent of the participants had engaged in oral sex.

Pornography

'I'm not going to say I've never watched porn. I mean, what can you do? It's part of life. If you're going to look at it and you're going to watch it, that's your decision, I guess. I don't watch it on a regular basis. Every now and then, of course, but ... it doesn't affect me.'

– Luke, age 16 (in Regnerus, 2007, p. 177)

'I know that people of my age have watched porn and I have been asked if I have – I haven't, but I'm not going to say it's because I don't agree

with it. The men and women that [take part] are not generally forced to, it's a choice and the people that watch it choose to.'

– Alexandra (Alex), age 15 (Hughes, unpublished data)

Because adolescence is a time of reaching sexual maturity, interest in sexual topics and sexual issues is high. Yet, as we have seen, actual participation in sexual activity during adolescence is mixed, and in many cases low or non-existent. Many adolescents are not sexually active, and even those who are sexually active have long periods when they have no regular partner. Even in emerging adulthood, when sexual activity is more common than in adolescence, it is substantially lower than among typical married adults. Some cultures strongly prohibit sexual activity of all kinds before marriage, as we shall see in the next section.

Perhaps for these reasons, pornography has long been appealing to many adolescents and emerging adults, especially males. For many decades, pornographic magazines have shown naked women in sexual poses, and pornographic movies have depicted various sex acts. In recent years, with the invention of the Internet, pornographic material has suddenly become much easier to obtain. In fact, of all the many uses of the Internet, the number one use above all is accessing pornography (Carroll et al., 2008).

What do we know about the viewing of pornographic materials among adolescents specifically? A survey of 10- to 17-year-olds found that 8 per cent of 10- to 13-year-olds and 20 per cent of 14- to 17-year-olds had viewed pornography, with about half of this exposure taking place on the Internet (Ybarra and Mitchell, 2005). Viewing pornography was far more common among boys; only 5 per cent of pornography viewers were girls. Pornography viewers were more likely than non-viewers to report delinquency and substance use, but of course this is a correlation, not causation. It does not mean that viewing pornography causes delinquency and substance use in adolescence.

A study of Internet pornography use among Chinese adolescents showed much higher rates of use, despite (or perhaps because of) the more restrictive and conservative sexual attitudes of Chinese culture (Lo and Wei, 2005). In this study, 38 per cent of secondary school students had ever viewed Internet pornography. Viewing pornography was related to more favourable attitudes toward premarital sex and greater likelihood of reported sexual activity. Once again, however, this is a correlation and does not show causation.

CONNECT AND EXTEND

For an important examination of the existence of a causal link between possessing child pornography and the act of committing child sexual abuse read 'Children at risk: legal and societal perceptions of the potential threat that the possession of child pornography poses to society' by S. Ost, *Journal of Law and Society*, Volume 29, Number 3 (September 2002), pp. 436–460

Pornography use appears to be far higher among emerging adults than among adolescents. In a study of university students 87 per cent of the young men and 31 per cent of the young women reported viewing Internet pornography (Carroll et al., 2008). Notably, 67 per cent of the young men and 49 per cent of the young women agreed that viewing pornography is acceptable, which means that many of the young men who reported viewing pornography did not view this behaviour as acceptable, whereas many young women who did not view pornography believed it was acceptable to do so. Here as in the other studies, viewing pornography was related to risky behaviours, specifically sexual risk behaviours and substance use, but here again this is a correlation rather than causation. As we will see in more detail in Chapter 12 on media use, it is often difficult to establish causality in media research because people make choices about media consumption that reflect their pre-existing personal qualities and behaviour patterns.

A study of emerging adults in Sweden found high rates of viewing Internet pornography among both men and women (Häggström-Nordin et al., 2005). Ninety-eight per cent of young men and 72 per cent of young women in this study had ever viewed pornography. Viewing pornography was related to reported experiences of having sexual intercourse with a friend and to earlier timing of first episode of sexual intercourse. Swedish emerging adults expressed mixed feelings about pornography viewing. They described it as interesting and pleasurable to view, but also expressed concerns about the submissive and degrading ways women are depicted in pornography and the separation of sex from intimacy.

Cultural Beliefs and Adolescent Sexuality

Even though adolescents in all cultures experience similar biological processes in reaching sexual maturity, cultures vary enormously in how they view adolescent sexuality. The most complete description of this variation remains a book that is now over 50 years old, *Patterns of Sexual Behavior* by Clellan Stearns Ford and Frank Beach (1951). These two anthropologists compiled information about sexuality from over 200 cultures. On the basis of their analysis, they described three types of cultural approaches to adolescent sexuality: restrictive, semi-restrictive and permissive.

Restrictive cultures place strong prohibitions on adolescent sexual activity before marriage. One way of enforcing this prohibition is to require strict separation of boys and girls from early childhood through adolescence. In several parts of the world, from East Africa to the rainforests of Brazil, from about age 7 until marriage boys and girls live mostly separate lives; boys with fathers and other men, or with each other; girls with their mothers and other women. In other restrictive cultures the prohibition on premarital sex is enforced through strong social norms. Young people in Asia tend to disapprove strongly of premarital sex (Rydstrøm, 2006; Morrison, 2004; Ip, 2001), reflecting the view they have been taught by their cultures.

In some countries the sanctions against premarital sex even include the threat of physical punishment and

Female virginity before marriage is highly valued in North African countries. Here, adolescent girls in Saudi Arabia.

public shaming. A number of North African countries take this approach, including Jordan, Algeria, Syria and Saudi Arabia. Premarital female virginity is a matter of not only a bride's honour but the honour of her family, and if she is known to lose her virginity before marriage the males of her family may punish her, beat her, or even kill her – honour killing (Faqir, 2001). Although many cultures also value male premarital chastity, no culture punishes violations of male premarital chastity with such severity. Thus, restrictive cultures are usually more restrictive for girls than for boys. A **double standard** in cultural views of adolescent sexuality is common worldwide (Hatfield and Rapson, 2005; Crawford and Popp, 2003).

THINKING CRITICALLY

What do you think explains the gender double standard regarding young people's sexuality that exists in so many cultures?

Semi-restrictive cultures also have prohibitions on premarital adolescent sex. However, in these cultures the formal prohibitions are not strongly enforced and are easily evaded. Adults in these cultures tend to ignore evidence of premarital sexual behaviour as long as young people are fairly discreet. However, if pregnancy results from premarital sex the adolescents are often forced to marry. The Samoans studied by Margaret Mead (1928) are an example of this kind of culture. Adolescent love affairs were common among the Samoans when Mead studied them, but pregnant girls were expected to marry.

Finally, **permissive cultures** encourage and expect adolescent sexuality. In fact, in some permissive cultures sexual behaviour is encouraged even in childhood, and the sexuality of adolescence is simply a continuation of the sex play of childhood. One example of this type of culture are the people of the Trobriand Islands in the South Pacific. In Ford and Beach's historic (1951) description:

'Sexual life begins in earnest among the Trobrianders at six to eight years for girls, ten to twelve for boys. Both sexes receive explicit instruction from older companions whom they imitate in sex activities … At any time an [adolescent] couple may retire to the bush, the bachelor's hut, an isolated yam house, or any other convenient place and there engage in prolonged sexual play with full approval of their parents.' (pp. 188–191)

It should be noted that these descriptions are from the past. In recent decades, the Trobrianders as well as many other permissive cultures have become less permissive in response to globalisation and the censure of Christian missionaries (Hatfield and Rapson, 2005).

Which of these categories best applies to the current norms in the Western majority culture? When Ford and Beach published *Patterns of Sexual Behavior* in 1951 they classified mainstream society as restrictive. However, a great deal has changed in adolescent sexuality in society over the past 50 years. Adolescent sexual activity has become far more prevalent during this time, and the attitudes of both adults and adolescents toward adolescent sexuality have become much less restrictive (Isler et al., 2009; Chia, 2006). Semi-restrictive is probably a better classification of European majority cultures today. For the most part, parents look the other way with respect to their adolescents' sexuality, especially by the time their adolescents reach the late teens. Even though they may not approve of their adolescents' having sexual intercourse, they allow dating and romantic relationships to flourish during adolescence, knowing that at least some expression of adolescent sexuality is likely under these circumstances.

In recent years, other social scientists have conducted surveys in numerous countries that demonstrate the wide variability in cultural approaches to adolescent sexuality around the world. Table 9.3 shows some examples. Premarital sex is common in Western European countries, and African countries such as Nigeria and Kenya report rates of premarital sex similar to the West. Premarital sex is somewhat less common in South America, although the large differences in reported premarital sex by male and female adolescents in countries such as Brazil and Chile suggest that males exaggerate their sexual activity or females under-report theirs (or both). Finally, premarital sex is least common in Asian countries such as Japan and South Korea, where the emphasis on female virginity before marriage is still very strong. Missing from the table are figures from the North African countries (no 'Arab' country allows social scientists to ask adolescents about their sexual behaviour), but ethnographic studies indicate that rates of premarital sex in those countries are even lower than in Asia because of the potential severe penalties – discussed earlier – for girls who violate the prohibition.

CULTURAL FOCUS

Young People's Sexuality in The Netherlands

Young people's sexuality is viewed quite differently in Northern Europe than in Southern European countries. Northern Europeans tend to be considerably more liberal about sexuality than those in the Mediterranean and other more traditional cultures, and much more tolerant of sexual involvements by late adolescents and young adults. However, this does not mean that young people's sexuality in these countries is uncomplicated. Earlier research by Manuela du Bois-Reymond and Janita Ravesloot (1996) provides interesting insights into young people's sexuality in Northern Europe.

Bois-Reymond and Ravesloot interviewed 60 young people (aged 15 to 22) and their parents in a city in The Netherlands, a country that has long had liberal attitudes toward sexuality. The data collected in the study were mostly qualitative, based on interviews that were coded in various ways. The interviews focused on communication about sexual issues with peers and parents.

With regard to peers, most young people reported little pressure from peers to engage in sex. However, there was social pressure on girls – but not boys – to avoid changing sexual partners frequently. It was socially approved among peers for both boys and girls to be sexually active and to have intercourse with a steady partner, but girls experienced peer disapproval for having numerous partners. As one 18-year-old girl remarked, 'My best friends do not allow me to date every boy ... we think that's stupid' (p. 181). Thus, liberal attitudes toward sexuality among peers had limits, and a double standard was applied to the sexual behaviour of boys and girls.

As for parents, most of them accepted sexual involvements by their adolescents and emerging adults. The authors noted that in The Netherlands as in most other Northern European countries, 'Parents are prepared to either permit or tolerate premarital sexual behaviour in their children, under one main condition: sexual relationships must be monogamous and serious, based on feelings of true love' (p. 182). However, this attitude did not mean that communication about sexuality was easy for young people and their parents. On the contrary, the authors observed 'a certain embarrassment about communicating about sexuality among the parents. Their children feel this embarrassment and therefore refrain from confidential communication about their sexual lives' (p. 193). Fathers were particularly unlikely to be involved in discussions about sexual issues with their children.

Because of their mutual discomfort in discussing sexuality, Dutch young people and their parents often seemed to misunderstand each other. In particular, parents often perceived themselves as more permissive about sexual behaviour and more open about sexual communication than their children perceived them to be. For example, one father described himself as lenient: 'I do not interfere with anything ... I am not able to do that ... it's not my business' (p. 191); however, his 19-year-old daughter saw him much differently: 'I am not allowed to go upstairs for a few hours [with my boyfriend] ... I'm using the pill in secret and that's annoying ... He badgers the life out of me to come home early ... always restrictions' (p. 191).

The authors – Bois-Reymond and Ravesloot – interpreted this conflict in perspectives as stemming from the fact that the parents had grown up in a much more sexually restrictive time. They viewed themselves as liberal and as tolerant of their children's sexual behaviour – and by the standards of the previous generation they were, but not by the standards of their children, who had become still more liberal about sexuality. Parents worried about their children having sex too early, about sexually transmitted diseases (STDs) and about premarital pregnancy. They liked to see themselves as allowing their children a great deal of freedom and autonomy, but given these concerns, many of them attempted to manage their children's sex lives in ways the parents viewed as subtle and indirect but the children saw as overbearing.

In summary, although Dutch society was more permissive about young people's sexuality than societies of Southern Europe, Bois-Reymond and Ravesloot's research indicates that in Dutch society, too, communication about sexuality is fraught with ambiguity. Young people must deal with the double standard that exists among their peers regarding males' and females' sexual behaviour. In their families, young people and their parents have difficulty discussing sexuality openly and often differ in how they perceive the parents' attitudes and behaviour. The 'divergent realities' that have been found to be common in relationships between young people and their parents in the other Western societies appear to exist in The Netherlands as well.

Table 9.3 Percentage of Young Men and Women who have Engaged in Premarital Sexual Relations

Country	Age	Men (%)	Women (%)
United States	20	84	61
Norway	20	78	86
United Kingdom	19–20	84	85
Germany	20	78	83
Mexico	15–19	44	13
Brazil	15–19	73	28
Chile	15–19	48	19
Colombia	20	89	65
Liberia	18–21	93	82
Nigeria	19	86	63
Hong Kong	27	38	24
Japan	16–21	15	7
Republic of Korea	12–21	17	4

Source: Hatfield and Rapson (2005).

CONNECT AND EXTEND

To explore reasons given by youth for refraining from or engaging in sexual intercourse, and their perceptions regarding the advantages and disadvantages of premarital intercourse read. '"It's a choice, simple as that": youth reasoning for sexual abstinence or activity' by Douglas Abbott and Rochelle Dalla in the *Journal of Youth Studies*, Volume 11, Number 6 (December 2008), pp. 629–649

Gender and the Meanings of Sex

'In our school, if you don't go around bragging about how far you got and what you did with the girl you were out with, well, then they start calling you gay or queer or something like that ... I think most guys lie about how far they go and what they do just to keep their image up.'
— Henry, age 15 (in Bell, 1998, p. 105)

'You know how it's okay for a guy to go around telling everybody about how horny he is and bragging about how he's going to get some this weekend? Well if a girl ever said those things, everybody would call her a slut.'
— Diana, age 16 (in Bell, 1998, p. 105)

Although few people advocate a punishment of death for adolescent girls who engage in premarital sex, even in majority European cultures some degree of gender double standard exists in cultural attitudes toward adolescent sexuality (Moore and Rosenthal, 2006; Crawford and Popp, 2003). Just as in dating, adolescent girls and boys learn different **sexual scripts** (Frith and Kitzinger, 2001) that is, different cognitive frameworks for understanding how a sexual experience is supposed to proceed and how sexual experiences are

Males and females tend to interpret their sexual experiences differently.

friends (Kontula and Pötsönen, 1999). This seems to indicate that the sexual script for girls is more fraught with ambivalence than the script for boys, as a result of cultural attitudes that view girls (but not boys) who engage in premarital sex as morally wrong.

The fact that girls can get pregnant and boys cannot may partly explain why girls are more ambivalent about premarital sex, especially premarital sex in the absence of a committed relationship. If pregnancy results, the consequences are likely to be much more serious for her than for him – physically, socially and emotionally. However, cultural attitudes also reinforce the tendencies that arise from biological differences in consequences, and may in fact be more important than the biological differences. As previously observed, many investigators of sexual attitudes have observed that adolescent sex is more disapproved of for girls than for boys (Moore and Rosenthal, 2006; Hird and Jackson, 2001). Because of this double standard, adolescent girls who are engaging in sexual intercourse are more likely than boys to be seen as bad by themselves as well as by others (Crawford and Popp, 2003; Jackson and Cram, 2003).

Characteristics of Sexually Active Adolescents

As noted earlier, different ethnic groups have quite different rates of sexual intercourse in adolescence. What other characteristics distinguish adolescents who are having sex from adolescents who are not, and what factors are related to the timing of adolescents' first episodes of sexual intercourse?

At secondary school age, adolescents who remain virgins and adolescents who are non-virgins are similar in some ways and different in others. Any differences in levels of self-esteem and overall life satisfaction are more likely to be related to body image, gang membership and social standing rather than between those who have sexual intercourse in late adolescence and those who remain virgins (Currie et al., 2006; Friestad and Rise, 2004; Esbensen et al., 1999). However, adolescents who remain virgins throughout secondary schooling tend to have higher levels of academic performance and academic aspirations, to be politically conservative and to participate in religious activities (Smith and Denton, 2005).

Sharper differences exist between adolescents who have their first episode of sexual intercourse relatively early in adolescence (age 15 or younger) and other adolescents. Adolescents who have early sexual intercourse are more likely than other adolescents to be

to be interpreted. In general, both girls and boys expect the boy to 'make the moves' (i.e. to be the sexual initiator), whereas the girl is expected to set the limits on how far the sexual episode is allowed to progress. Studies have also found that girls are more likely than boys to have sexual scripts that include romance, friendship and emotional intimacy, whereas for boys sexual attraction tends to outweigh emotional factors (Hatfield and Rapson, 2005; Eyre and Millstein, 1999).

Evidence of differing sexual scripts for adolescent girls and boys can also be found in studies of adolescents' responses to their first sexual intercourse (Moore and Rosenthal, 2006). Boys' responses to first intercourse are generally highly positive. They most commonly report feeling excitement, satisfaction and happiness (Chambers et al., 2004), and they take pride in telling their friends about it. In contrast, girls tend to be considerably more ambivalent. Almost half of them indicate that the main reason for having first intercourse was affection/love for their partner, compared with only a quarter of males (Sears et al., 2006). However, they are less likely than boys to find the experience either physically or emotionally satisfying. Although many report feeling happy and excited about it, they are much more likely than boys to report feeling afraid, worried, guilty, and concerned about pregnancy, and they are much less likely than boys to tell their

CONNECT AND EXTEND

For an importtant discussion of the influence of peer pressure on decision making about first sex read 'The first time: young people and sex in Northern Ireland' by Bill Rolston, Dirk Schubotz and Audrey Simpson in the *Journal of Youth Studies*, Volume 7, Number 2 (2004), pp. 191–207

early users of drugs and alcohol as well. They are also more likely than other adolescents to be from single-parent families and to have grown up in poverty (Crockett et al., 2003).

Perhaps surprisingly, few differences exist in family relationships between early sexually active adolescents and other adolescents. Most studies find no differences between adolescents in these groups in parental monitoring – the extent to which parents know where their adolescents are and what they are doing (Blum, 2002). However, one study in an ethnic minority group did find that higher levels of parental monitoring were associated with lower likelihood of having sexual intercourse in adolescence and fewer partners for adolescents who did have intercourse (Miller et al., 1999). This suggests that the effect of parental monitoring on adolescents' sexual behaviour may depend on the cultural context.

Research is also mixed regarding the role that communication between parents and adolescents about sexual issues plays in the timing of adolescents' first intercourse. According to one small study, girls whose mothers talk to them frequently about sex have their first sexual intercourse at a younger age than their peers do ('Mum's Not the Word', 1999). However, another larger study reported that adolescents' perceptions of parents' disapproval of sexual intercourse in the teen years was associated with later age of first intercourse (Blum, 2002). Broadly speaking, adolescents who have closer relationships with their mothers are less likely to report having sex, more likely to use contraception if they do have sex, and less likely to become pregnant (Claes et al., 2005; Dittus and Jaccard, 2000).

With respect to the influence of peers, when most of the adolescents in a clique are sexually active, they establish a norm within the clique that having sex is acceptable. The remaining virgins in the clique may be influenced toward sexual involvement through their exposure to that norm and to experienced potential sex partners. Of course, selective association may also be involved here. Adolescent virgins who are hanging around a group of non-virgins are likely to have characteristics in common with the non-virgins that also contribute to decisions of whether to become sexually active, such as lower academic goals and lower religiosity.

Also, girls who mature early tend to attract attention from older boys, which tends to result in the girls' becoming sexually active earlier than other girls (Petersen, 1993). More generally, girls with older boyfriends (three or more years older) are more likely to be sexually active and more likely to be subject to sexual coercion (Young and d'Arcy, 2005; Gowen et al., 2002; Darroch et al., 1999) Older boys are more likely to expect sex as part of a romantic relationship, and they have more power and status in relationships with younger girls. Consequently, girls with older boyfriends are more likely to accept their sexual demands, in an effort to maintain a relationship that gives them status. However, girls with older boyfriends also tend to be more interested in sex than other girls their age are (Compian et al., 2004).

Sexual Harassment and Date Rape

Like love, sex has its dark side. Sexual interactions among adolescents and emerging adults are not always enjoyable or even voluntary. Two of the problems that arise in sexual interactions are **sexual harassment** and **date rape**.

Sexual Harassment

During adolescence, sexual harassment is a pervasive part of peer interactions. Sexual harassment is usually defined as including a wide range of behaviours, from name calling, jokes and leering looks to unwanted touching or sexual contact (Uggen and Blackstone, 2004; Connolly and Goldberg, 1999).

Table 9.4 Exposures of 540 Swedish Female Pupils to Various Verbal Behaviours

Verbal behaviours	(%)
Demeaning comments about gender, e.g. 'All boys are immature'	77 (32*)
Sexualised conversations	77 (44*)
Students publicly 'rating' other students' attractiveness	71 (28*)
Sexual personal comments	65 (23*)
Demeaning comments about sexuality, e.g. 'All girls are whores'	56 (23*)
Name calling, e.g. slut, whore, bitch, etc.	37 (16*)
Pressuring for sexual favours	26 (14*)
Students spreading sexual rumours about other students	25 (9*)
'Homophobic' name calling, e.g. dyke, lesbian, gay, etc.	17 (13*)

*Exposed repeatedly: monthly, weekly, daily (proportion of all exposed students).

Source: Eva Witkowska and Ewa Menckel, 'Perceptions of sexual harassment in Swedish high schools: experiences and school-environment problems', *The European Journal of Public Health*, Volume 15, Number 1 (February 2005), pp. 78–85

Rates of sexual harassment in adolescence are strikingly high (Timmerman, 2005). Among early adolescents, research indicates that the incidence of sexual harassment increases from 9 to 13, with over 40 per cent of 13-year-olds reporting that they have been victims of sexual harassment from their peers (Connolly and Goldberg, 1999), with more recent research confirming these rates of incidence (e.g. Renold, 2003; 2002). From early adolescence into adulthood, females are more likely than males to be the victims of sexual harassment, and males are more likely than females to be the harassers (Timmerman, 2005; Uggan and Blackstone, 2004).

Rates of sexual harassment (see Figure 9.2) for older adolescents in the school environment are even higher, as reported in a 2005 snapshot of 540 Swedish 17- and 18 year-old girls (see Table 9.4). Rates of the kinds of harassment typified in Table 9.4 (and abuse by peers) are even higher in residential children's care homes (Gibbs and Sinclair, 2000). As noted earlier, early-maturing girls are especially likely to be targeted for sexual harassment – from both boys and girls (Goldstein et al., 2007).

Sexual and romantic joking and teasing are a common part of adolescents' peer interactions, making it difficult to tell where the border is between relatively harmless and enjoyable joking and harmful harassment. Indeed, the majority of adolescents who report being sexually harassed also report sexually harassing others (K. Robinson, 2005; Hemmings, 2002; Luster et al., 2002). Teachers who witness adolescents' interactions may be reluctant to intervene, unsure of what might qualify as harassment (Meyer, 2008). However vigilance by practitioners is important because being the victim of persistent harassment can be extremely unpleasant for adolescents, and can result in anxiety, depression and social exclusion as well as declining school performance and absenteeism (Gruber and Fineran, 2008).

CONNECT AND EXTEND

Read 'Perceptions of sexual harassment in Swedish high schools: experiences and school-environment problems' by Eva Witkowska and Ewa Menckel in *The European Journal of Public Health*, Volume 15, Number 1 (February 2005), pp. 78–85

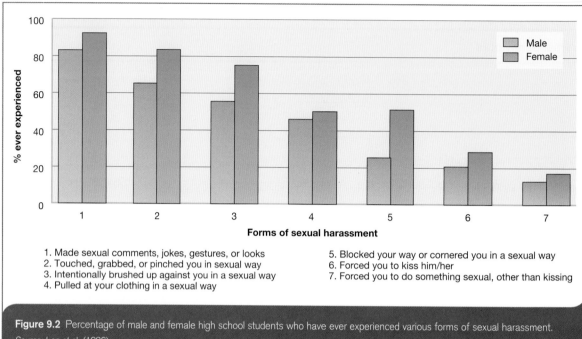

1. Made sexual comments, jokes, gestures, or looks
2. Touched, grabbed, or pinched you in sexual way
3. Intentionally brushed up against you in a sexual way
4. Pulled at your clothing in a sexual way

5. Blocked your way or cornered you in a sexual way
6. Forced you to kiss him/her
7. Forced you to do something sexual, other than kissing

Figure 9.2 Percentage of male and female high school students who have ever experienced various forms of sexual harassment.
Source: Lee et al. (1996).

Date Rape

Date rape takes place when a person, usually a woman, is forced by a romantic partner, date or acquaintance to have sexual relations against her will. Some studies indicate that up to 15 per cent of adolescent girls (e.g. Schubot, 2001) are victims of date rape. Indeed 16- to 19-year old women were over four times as likely to have reported being raped than women from any other age group (Myhill and Allen, 2002). Girls and women are most often sexually assaulted by men they know. Some studies (e.g. Harris and Grace, 1999) suggest that only 12 per cent of rapes recorded by the police are categorised as 'stranger' rapes, and some national crime surveys suggest the percentage figure may be as little as 8 per cent (see Figure 9.3).

The definition used to categorise the police cases as 'stranger' rapes was 'where the suspect had had no contact with the complainant prior to the attack'. Younger adolescents are rarely raped by strangers and rates of date rape are highest of all for girls who have sex at an early age; nearly three-quarters of girls who have intercourse before age 14 report having had intercourse against their will with somebody known to them (Alan Guttmacher Institute, 2002). More recent comparative annual statistics show an alarming trend

for an increase in rape overall of both girls and boys under the age of 13, very little of which is assault by a stranger (see Table 9.5).

Alcohol and drugs play a big part in date rape (King, 2005). This accounts for a more narrow definition of date rape adopted elsewhere that date rape is rape

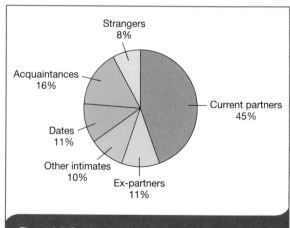

Figure 9.3 Relationship to perpetrator, last incident of rape experienced since age 16

Source: Andy Myhill and Jonathan Allen (2002) Rape and sexual assault of women: the extent and nature of the problem. Findings from the British Crime Survey. Home Office Research Study 237

Table 9.5 Recorded Crime Statistics – England and Wales 2004/05–2009/10

Year	Rape of a female aged 16 and over	Rape of a female child under 16	Rape of a female child under 13	Rape of a male aged 16 and over	Rape of a male child under 16	Rape of a male child under 13
2004/05	8192	3014	970	444	322	297
2005/06	8725	3153	1388	438	292	364
2006/07	8222	2853	1524	413	261	458
2007/08	7586	2413	1485	333	237	428
2008/09	7780	2538	1652	317	218	407
2009/10	9102	2926	1963	372	241	561

Source: **http://rds.homeoffice.gov.uk/rds/pdfs10/recorded-crime-2002-2010.xls** accessed 19 November 2010

that occurs as a result of a victim (usually female) being deliberately intoxicated or drugged (Girard and Senn, 2008; Moore and Valverde, 2000) in a pub or club in order to render her defenceless. Being intoxicated makes women less effective in communicating reluctance to have sex and makes men more likely to ignore or overpower a woman's resistance. When intoxicated, men are more likely to interpret women's behaviour, such as talking to them or dancing with them, as indicating sexual interest (Fisher et al., 2000).

However, even when sober, young men and women often interpret date rape incidents differently (Yamawaki, 2007; Monson et al., 2000; Miller and Benson, 1999). In their accounts of rape, men (including husbands and partners) often deny they forced sex on the woman and say they interpreted the way the woman dressed or offered affection as cues that she wanted sex. In contrast, women describing the same incident deny that their dress or behaviour was intended to be sexually alluring and say that the men were coercive and ignored their verbal or non-verbal resistance to sex. There will be a further examination of both risky behaviour in relation to alcohol/drug abuse and sexual violence in Chapter 12, Problems and problem behaviours.

Lesbian, Gay, Bisexual and Transgender Adolescents

'After people at school found out I was gay, a lot of them kind of kept a distance from me. I think they were scared that I was going to do something to them … I guess that was one of the reasons I didn't come out sooner, because I was afraid that they would be scared of me. It's stupid and crazy, but a lot of people feel that way.'
– Jamie, age 17 (in Bell, 1998, p. 141)

So far we have discussed adolescent dating, love and sexuality in terms of the attractions and relationships between males and females. But what about young people who are sexually attracted to other persons of the same sex, unsure of their sexual preferences or of their gender identity? What is it like for them to reach the age where issues of dating, love and sex become more prominent? Why haven't these issues already arisen as part of our foregoing discourse on love, marriage, cohabitation and adolescent sexuality?

There is an argument that lesbian, gay, bisexual and transsexual (LGBT) identities are so much part of our mainstream social psychology that it would be far more natural to have included same-sex relationships and transgender throughout this chapter, as the development of, and changing forms of adolescent love apply to all forms of sexual and gender preference. Our view is that, although much of what we have said so far applies to a greater or lesser extent to all adolescents, the heady whirl of new sexual excitement, the highs and lows of adolescent emotions and the psychological and social forces that apply are particularly powerful for young people who come to understand their lesbian, gay, bisexual or transgender identity. Simply, there is more to learn here.

First, important distinctions between same-sex attractions, same-sex sexual behaviour and homosexual

Adolescence is usually the time when homosexuals become fully aware of their orientation.

identity should be noted. A quite recent large-scale longitudinal study included several questions about same-sex and other-sex attractions and sexual behaviour (Savin-Williams and Ream, 2007). Questionnaire data were collected at ages 16, 17 and 22. As shown in Table 9.6, at each age considerably more adolescents and young adults experienced same-sex romantic attractions than engaged in same-sex sexual behaviour. At age 22, more young adults reported same-sex romantic attractions than reported same-sex sexual behaviour or a lesbian, gay or bisexual (LGB) identity, especially among women. Other studies have reported slightly higher levels of LGB attractions, sexual behaviour and sexual identity, but there is a consistent pattern across studies that prevalence of same-sex attractions is higher than same-sex behaviour, which is in turn higher than prevalence of LGB identity (Savin-Williams and Ream, 2007).

Here is an example of the complex relations between sexual attraction, behaviour and identity. At age 15, Stephanie and Lolita were best friends. Stephanie recalled,

'Lolita would sleep over a lot and one night she was talking about her boyfriend Juan and talking about sex … We had been very affectionate, like most girlfriends. I asked her how he kissed her, and so she kissed me like her Juan did. This was quite a shocker. From then on we kissed a lot when we got together, and began touching and

Table 9.6 Same-sex Romantic Attractions, Sexual Behaviour and Sexual Identity

Sexual domain	Females			Males		
	Age 16	Age 17	Age 22	Age 16	Age 17	Age 22
Same-sex romantic attractions	5%	4%	13%	7%	5%	5%
Same-sex sexual behaviour	1%	1%	4%	1%	1%	3%
Sexual identity:						
Gay/Lesbian			1%			2%
Bisexual			3%			1%

Source: Savin-Williams and Ream (2007) The question about sexual identity was asked only at age 22.

caressing. To make it "okay", one of us would be the boy … She's straight as far as I know … I was the only girl she did anything with. We never said we were lesbians.'

– Savin-Williams, (2006, p. 212)

Transgender is self-defining 'gender identity' as a woman, man, both or neither. For many transgender people the genetic and biological gender identity ascribed to them at birth is not adequate. It is important to note that self-identification as transgender does not point to any specific form of sexual orientation. Transgender people may also identify themselves as heterosexual, homosexual or bisexual. This means that it is sometimes not appropriate to talk about transgender youngsters in the same way as we often 'lump' together LGB identities; something to think about during the remainder of this section.

Adolescence is an especially important period with respect to establishing an LGBT identity. In the past in almost all cultures, and still today in many of the world's cultures, people would keep this knowledge to themselves all their lives because of the certainty that they would be stigmatised and ostracised if they disclosed the truth. Today in many cultures, however, LGBTs commonly engage in a process of **coming out**, which involves a person's recognising his or her own sexual or transgender identity and then disclosing this to friends, family, and others (Flowers and Buston, 2001; Savin-Williams, 2001). Awareness of an LGBT identity usually begins in early adolescence, with disclosure to others coming in late adolescence or young adulthood (Floyd and Bakeman, 2006). The average age of coming out has declined in recent decades, from 21 in the 1970s to 16 in the present, perhaps because of growing acceptance of homosexuality and transgender selfhood (Savin-Williams, 2006).

LGBTs usually disclose their sexual or gender identity first to a friend; fewer than 10 per cent tell a parent first (Savin-Williams, 2001; 1998) and families can be tricky places to negotiate new or 'different'

identities (Valentine et al., 2003) although supportive families can make all the difference (Gorman-Murray, 2008). Coming out is often a long process, as information is disclosed gradually to others. For many LGBTs the coming-out process is never complete, and they withhold information about their sexual orientation or gender identity to some degree until mid-life (Rickards and Wuest, 2006) or throughout their lives. According to a number of studies, the coming-out process takes longer for those in ethnic minority groups than those in white majority cultures of Northern Europe, North America, Australia and New Zealand, perhaps because of stronger anti-homosexual views in these cultures (Tawake, 2006; Rosario et al., 2004).

Given the **homophobia** (fear and hatred of homosexuals) that remains to some extent in many societies (Baker, 2002), coming to the realisation of an LGBT identity can be traumatic for many adolescents. Studies indicate that about one-third of LGBT adolescents have attempted suicide, a much higher rate than among other adolescents (Bobrow, 2002; D'Augelli, 2002). Rates of substance abuse, school difficulties and running away from home are also higher among LGBT adolescents (D'Augelli and Patterson, 2002). All these problems tend to increase after the adolescent comes out to parents, because parents' responses, as we have already argued, can be highly negative (Heatherington and Lavner, 2008).

Adolescents and emerging adults who are LGBT also face potential mistreatment from their peers, including harassment, verbal abuse, and even physical abuse (Horn, 2006). In one study, more than three-quarters of LGBT adolescents reported that they had been verbally abused because of their sexual orientation, and 15 per cent reported physical attacks (D'Augelli, 2002). More than one-third said they had lost friends because of their sexual orientation. Given the unpleasant reception that often awaits them if they come out, it is not surprising that many LGBT adolescents hide their feelings, behaviour and identities (D'Augelli et al., 2005; Davis and Stewart, 1997).

CONNECT AND EXTEND

Kristinn Hegna, 'Coming out, coming into what? Identification and risks in the "coming out" story of a Norwegian late adolescent gay man' in *Sexualities*, Volume 10, Number 5 (December 2007), pp. 582–602

Nevertheless, in recent years there has been a noticeable change in attitudes toward LGBs, constituting 'a dramatic cultural shift' towards more favourable and tolerant perceptions. A national survey of 13- to 19-year-olds (Savin-Williams, 2006) shows that the percentage who 'don't have any problem' with homosexuality tripled over the past decade, to 54 per cent. Of course, 54 per cent is barely half and leaves plenty of room for continued homophobia and abuse, but it does show that public attitudes toward LGBTs are becoming less hostile.

Young LGBT people are increasingly resistant to being labelled with a stable sexual or gender identity as gay, lesbian, bisexual or transgender. Lisa Diamond interviewed 'non-heterosexual' young women at ages 18–25, then every two years for the next ten years (Diamond, 2008). She found that over this time the young women who engaged in same-sex sexual behaviour became increasingly reluctant to categorise themselves as lesbian or even bisexual, 'because they are still engaged in the process of sexual questioning or because they find the existing range of sexual identity categories, and the process of categorisation altogether, to be limiting and restrictive' (p. 7).

In summary, fear and misunderstanding of LGBTs is still pervasive, and the problems faced by LGBT adolescents and young adults are formidable. However, young people today seem to be developing a more flexible and tolerant view of sexual and gender variability than their parents or grandparents had.

CONNECT AND EXTEND

For current interpretations of Islam, sexuality and same-sex relationships among British Muslims who identify as lesbian, gay, bisexual and transgendered read 'Sexual ethics, marriage and sexual autonomy: the landscapes for Muslim and lesbian, gay, bisexual and transgendered Muslims' by Dervla Shannahan in *Contemporary Islam*, Volume 3, Number 1 (April 2009), pp. 59–78

FOCUS ON PROFESSIONAL PRACTICE

A History of 'Coming Out' – No!

A history of 'coming out' in most majority European cultures would be a very short history, which is one reason why this is a *Focus on Professional Practice* feature rather than a *Historical* one. Why such a short history? Well, 'coming out' – telling family, friends and the wider community that your sexual preference is partly or wholly for people of your own gender – would have been quite impossible until relatively recently because homosexual behaviour was unlawful in many European countries.

Take a look at the information in Table 9.7.

According to the International Lesbian, Gay, Bisexual, Trans and Intersex Association, five of these countries legalised same-sex sexual activity in the eighteenth and nineteenth centuries and six more countries in the two decades following 1931. Most European countries, including the UK, made same-sex sexual activity legal in the two decades after 1962 and the last five between 1992 and 1998. So in most European countries, active LGBT activity has only been legal for 50 years or so. It's also worth noting that, according to available data in Table 9.7, same-sex partnerships are still not recognised in nine of these countries and that discrimination on the basis of sexual orientation is not wholly unlawful in 15 of these European states. This might mean that in some parts of Europe 'coming out' remains a potentially uncomfortable business and those who do have none of the legal rights of heterosexuals or protections of other equality groups.

Table 9.7 Legalisation of Same-sex Sexual Activity In Europe

Country	Same-sex sexual activity legalised	Same-sex parnerships recognised	Anti-discrimination made unlawful
Austria	1971	2010	
Belgium	1795	2000	All
Croatia	1977	2003	All
Cyprus	1998		
Czech Republic	1962	2006	
Denmark	1933	1989	All
Estonia	1992		
Finland	1971	2002	
France	1791	1999	All
Germany	1968(E) 1969(W)	2001	
Greece	1951		
Hungary	1962	2009	
Iceland	1940	1996	All
Ireland	1993	2011	All
Italy	1890		
Latvia	1992		
Lithuania	1993		All
Luxembourg	1795	2004	
Netherlands	1811	1998	All
Norway	1972	1993	All
Poland	1932		
Portugal	1983	2001	All
Slovakia	1962		
Slovenia	1977	2006	
Spain	1979		All
Sweden	1944	1995	All
Switzerland	1798/1942	2007	
UK England	1967	2005	All
UK Northern Ireland	1982	2005	All
UK Scotland	1981	2005	All
UK Wales	1967	2005	All

Source: 'State-sponsored homophobia: a world survey of laws prohibiting same-sex activity between consenting adults', an ILGA report by Daniel Ottosson © 2010 ILGA, the International Lesbian, Gay, Bisexual, Trans and Intersex Association – **www.ilga.org**

➤

In the UK there are now well-established rights and protections in terms of education, terms and conditions of employment, personal dignity and well-being. Yet self-identification as being lesbian, gay, bisexual, trans or intersex can still meet with a mixed response from parents, family, friends and employers. There are added pressures for teenagers needing to self-identify, particularly younger adolescents. The average coming-out age has fallen by over 20 years in Britain, according to *Stonewall's* – the UK lesbian, gay and bisexual charity – 2010 online poll. The poll was conducted through Stonewall's social media pages and some observers do question the validity and reliability of the information. Nevertheless the poll had 1536 respondents, and of those Stonewall found that lesbian, gay and bisexual people aged 60 and over 'came out' at 37 on average, whereas people aged 18 and under are coming out at 15 on average; which means that some adolescents are claiming – online – to coming out during younger adolescence.

This is a professional focus, as we need to identify how counsellors and others involved more widely in the welfare of young people can best support young people during their telling us what it is like to grow up and identify oneself as 'gay'. Researcher Lindsay Cooper (2008), of the University of Nottingham, sets out a framework for understanding the development of LGBT identity and for supporting the process of coming out, based largely on what she learned during face-to-face interviews with young people who had already identified themselves as 'gay'.

Cooper suggests a broad framework: the RAC Model, comprising *realisation, activation* and *consolidation*. These are broad phases against which it is possible to explore an individual's life story – and important idea for those working with young people. *Realisation* is the first phase, which originates in a child – often not yet an adolescent – feeling 'different', often alienated in some respects from peers and sometimes alone either physically or with his/her thoughts. This difference may or may not be accompanied by homoerotic desire at this point. Eventually information is received from the social context that allows the individual to attach the label 'gay' to these feelings of difference; for example, the presence of gay characters in television soap operas and other dramas, name calling at school and many other sources. However, this does not necessarily resolve the discomfiture at feeling odd or different.

Activation occurs when individuals acknowledge their homosexual feelings (it may mean simply acknowledging a thought or a specific or recurring fantasy). It is at this point that first disclosures take place and they finally give themselves permission to become sexual with members of their own sex. This is a time of experimenting with a new sexual identity.

Consolidation represents the fusion of the private identity ('I am gay and no one else must know') with a public identity where one is out of the closet, albeit to selected audiences, into one self-image ('I am gay and I don't mind [some] people knowing it'). This element of self-definition leads to a need for intimacy and relationships begin. Sometimes these become stable, committed relationships but the ability (or inability) to sustain these is no different to that of heterosexual peers.

Cooper concludes that:

'Coming out is most crucial at the transition from realisation to activation where the affective dimension is key. At this transition a gay person, whatever their age, is likely to feel the effects of anti-homosexual prejudice whether verbalised or not. The combination of internalised homophobia, structural pressures of the closet and lack of positive role models are important influences that together with shame are powerful motivations for "staying in". I believe it is the most important point at which counsellors can intervene.' (Cooper, 2008, p. 433)

Cooper further suggests that a first step for counsellors is to adopt the model of gay affirmative therapy that very clearly locates the problems facing their clients in homophobia, not homosexuality. Gay affirmative therapy requires the counsellor to be knowledgeably and affectively aware of homosexuality as a normal and natural kind of human sexual expression. Cooper asserts that the RAC Model provides a memorable template to offer respectful and knowledgeable support in individual work with clients. By focusing on the transition and the timing of moving between one broad phase and the next, counsellors and helpers can assist the young person to examine and understand the personal impact of their journey.

CONNECT AND EXTEND

For a discussion on supporting young Islamic people read 'Should educators accommodate intolerance? Mark Halstead, homosexuality, and the Islamic case' by Michael Merry in the *Journal of Moral Education*, Volume 34, Number 1 (2005), pp. 19–36

THINKING CRITICALLY

What do you think explains the homophobia that exists in many cultures? Why does homosexuality make many people uncomfortable and even angry?

Contraceptive Use and Non-use

Just as cultures have a variety of ways of viewing adolescent sexuality, from encouraging it to strictly prohibiting it, adolescent pregnancy is viewed by different cultures in a variety of ways. In most of the 186 traditional cultures described by Schlegel and Barry (1991 – there have been and will be numerous references to this seminal study during *Adolescence and Emerging Adulthood*), girls usually marry by the time they reach age 18. Thus, they tend to marry within two years of reaching menarche because menarche tends to take place later in most traditional cultures – age 15 or 16 – than in industrialised societies. Furthermore, as discussed in Chapter 2, in the first two years after menarche girls tend to ovulate irregularly and are less likely to become pregnant during this time than later, after their cycle of ovulation has been established (Finkelstein, 2001a). This means that for most adolescent girls in traditional cultures, even if they begin having sexual intercourse before marriage, their first child is likely to be born in the context of marriage. Remember that in some traditional cultures, even if a girl has a child before marriage it may be viewed positively, as an indication that she is fertile and will be able to have more children once she has married (Schlegel and Barry, 1991).

Clearly, the situation is quite different for adolescent girls in most European countries. Generally, they reach menarche much earlier, usually around age 12 or 13, and they tend to marry much later, usually in their mid- to late 20s. Because the majority of adolescent girls in European countries begin having sexual intercourse at some time in their mid- to late teens, this leaves a period of a decade or more for many girls between the time they begin having intercourse and the time they enter marriage. Furthermore, it remains true that for adolescent girls, having a child while unmarried and in their teens has serious detrimental effects on their future prospects. Unlike in traditional cultures, the late teens and early 20s are crucial years for educational and occupational preparation. For girls who have a child outside of marriage during those years, their educational and occupational prospects are often severely impeded, as we will see in the next section.

Of course, unlike girls in some traditional cultures, most adolescents in industrialised societies also have available various methods of contraception to prevent pregnancy. It is at least theoretically possible that adolescents who have begun having sexual intercourse and do not yet want to produce a child could use one of the highly effective methods of contraception available to them.

However, this theoretical possibility does not always match reality, especially in Britain. The reality is that many British adolescents who are having sex do not use contraception responsibly and consistently. Although condom use among adolescents increased substantially during the 1980s and early 1990s, in an international study only a little more than 60 per cent of sexually active adolescents reported using contraception 'always' in their most recent sexual relationship, whereas about 20 per cent responded 'sometimes' and 20 per cent 'never' (Avery and Lazdane, 2008). These results are similar to other national and local studies carried out in the last decade (e.g. Manlove et al., 2006).

If young people know how to obtain and use contraception, why do they so often fail to use it consistently? One of the best analyses of this question is an early classic article by Diane Morrison (1985), in which she reviewed dozens of articles on this topic. She concluded that the core of the answer is that most adolescent

Girls in traditional cultures often marry by age 18, about 2 or 3 years after reaching menarche. Here, a young bride in Nepal.

sexual activity is *unplanned* and *infrequent*. Adolescents typically do not anticipate that they will have sex on a given occasion. The opportunity is there – they start kissing, they start taking their clothes off – and 'it just happens'. If contraception is available at that moment, they may use it, but if it is not, they sometimes simply take their chances. Also, the fact that adolescent sex tends to be infrequent – only once or twice a month, much less often than for adults – means that they may

never get into the habit of preparing for sex as something they take part in on a regular basis. These early findings are confirmed more recently (Breheny and Stephens, 2004) in other European countries (Kosunen et al., 2003; Kontula and Pötsönen, 1999) including post-communist societies (Agadjanian, 2002). Also, the personal fable of adolescence makes it easy for adolescents to believe that getting pregnant 'won't happen to me' (Kershaw et al., 2003), especially when they are caught up in the heat of the moment.

Other scholars have identified a variety of other factors related to the likelihood that adolescents will use contraception. Both male and female adolescents are more likely to use contraception if they are in their late rather than early teens, involved in an ongoing relationship with their partner, and doing well in school (Civic, 1999; Cooper et al., 1999). Cultural factors are also involved in contraceptive use. The United States has a higher rate of teenage pregnancy than any other industrialised country (Teitler, 2002; Alan Guttmacher Institute, 2001), as Figure 9.4 shows. This is not because adolescents in the United States have more sex than those in other countries. Adolescents in European countries such as Sweden and Denmark are as likely as adolescents in the United States to be sexually active but much less likely to become pregnant (Avery and Lazdane, 2008; Teitler, 2002). What explains these differences? In part, high rates of adolescent pregnancy are due to high rates of poverty. Numerous studies have found that adolescents who are from low-income families are less likely than other adolescents to use contraception (e.g. Boyle, 2000).

Most analyses of cross-national differences have concluded that the core of the problem of

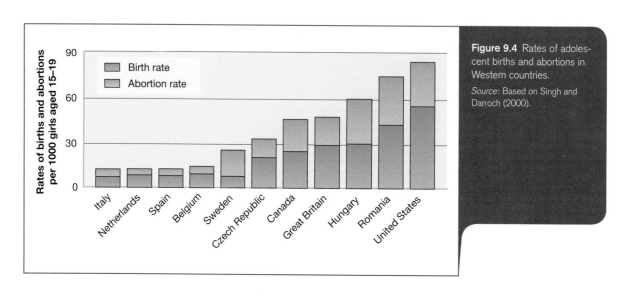

Figure 9.4 Rates of adolescent births and abortions in Western countries.

Source: Based on Singh and Darroch (2000).

inconsistent contraceptive use is the mixed messages that adolescents receive about sexuality (Alan Guttmacher Institute, 2002). Earlier we stated that many European societies have a semi-restrictive approach to adolescent sex. What this means, in practice, is that adolescents are not strongly prohibited from having sex, but neither is adolescent sex widely accepted (Graber et al., 1999). Adolescents receive different messages from different socialisation sources, and few clear messages from any source, about the morality and desirability of premarital sex.

The media are often blamed for stoking adolescent sexual desires in a simplistic and irresponsible way (Brown et al., 2002). A recent analysis of sexual content in four media (television, magazine, music and flim) found that sexual health information was found to be frequently inaccurate and to promote gender stereotypes that 'boys will be boys and girls better be prepared' (Hust et al., 2008). In school, most adolescents receive sex education, but this 'education' rarely includes an explicit discussion (or demonstration) of contraceptive use (L. M. Wallace et al., 2007; Schubotz et al., 2004). Also, communication between parents and adolescents about contraceptive methods tends to be low, in part because of the discomfort both parents and adolescents feel about discussing such issues (Crockett et al., 2003).

Two types of countries have low rates of teenage pregnancy: those that are permissive about adolescent sex and those that adamantly forbid it. Countries such as Denmark, Sweden and The Netherlands have low rates of adolescent pregnancy, perhaps because the majority ethnic group are permissive about adolescent sex (Avery and Lazdane, 2008;

Countries with permissive views of adolescent sex, such as the Scandinavian countries, have low rates of adolescent pregnancy. Here, two adolescents in Norway.

Boyle, 2001). There are explicit safe-sex campaigns in the media. Adolescents have easy access to all types of contraception. Parents accept that their children will become sexually active by their late teens. It is not uncommon for adolescents in these countries to have a boyfriend or girlfriend spend the night in their bedroom in their parents' home, a practice barely imaginable to many traditional cultures and ethnic minority households.

At the other end of the spectrum, more socially 'restrictive countries' such as Japan, South Korea and Morocco strictly forbid adolescent sex (Hatfield and Rapson, 2005; Stevenson and Zusho, 2002). Adolescents in these countries are even strongly discouraged from dating until they are well into young adulthood and are seriously looking for a marriage partner. It is rare for an adolescent boy and girl even to spend any time alone together, much less have sex. Some adolescents follow the 'call of nature' anyway and violate the taboo, but violations are rare because the taboo is so strong and the shame of being exposed for breaking it is so great.

Pregnancy, Parenthood and Abortion in Adolescence

The Consequences of Early Parenthood

The concern over adolescent pregnancy is not only moral, based on the view of many that adolescents should not be having sex. The concern is also based on the practical consequences for the adolescent mother and her child (Chen et al., 2007). For the unmarried adolescent mother, having a child means that she will be twice as likely as her peers to drop-out of school and less likely to become employed or to go on to higher education after secondary school, even compared to peers who come from a similar economic background (Miller et al., 2003). Furthermore, adolescent mothers are less likely than their peers to get married and more likely to get divorced if they do marry (Moore and Brooks-Gunn, 2002). In addition, many adolescent mothers are still a long way from maturity in their emotional and social development, and they feel overwhelmed by the responsibilities of motherhood (Leadbeater and Way, 2001). Adolescent mothers often had problems even before becoming pregnant, such as poor school performance, discipline problems and psychological problems, and becoming a parent only deepens their difficulties (Miller-Johnson et al., 1999).

CONNECT AND EXTEND

For information about the international variation in rates of teenage pregnancy investigate and follow leads from **http://www.statistics.gov.uk/pdfdir/con1110.pdf**.

You will also find important leads from 'Why do we measure teenage pregnancy but do not count teenage mothers?' by Mary Shaw and Debbie Lawlor in *Critical Public Health*, Volume 17, Number 4 (2007), pp. 311–316; and 'Factors associated with teenage pregnancy in the European Union countries: a systematic review' by Mari Imamura et al. in *The European Journal of Public Health*, Volume 17, Number 6 (December 2007), pp. 630–636

Do adolescent mothers eventually get back on track and catch up with their peers? A classic American study by Furstenberg and colleagues (1987) began with a sample of 300 urban, mostly black, low-SES (Social and Economic Status) teenage mothers in 1966 when they first had their children, and followed both mothers and children every few years until 1984, when the children were 18 years old. Five years after giving birth, the mothers lagged behind their peers in their educational, occupational and economic progress. By the final follow-up, however, 18 years after the study began, the life situations of the mothers were striking in their diversity. A quarter of the mothers were still on social security payments and had remained there for most of the 18-year period. In contrast, another quarter had succeeded, gaining enough education and job experience to make substantial progress economically. A majority of the mothers had eventually completed secondary school, and a third had completed at least some higher education. Accessing higher education and getting married were related to the most favourable economic outcomes.

Not nearly as many studies have been conducted on adolescent fatherhood as on adolescent motherhood, but the available studies indicate that becoming a father as a teen is also related to a variety of negative outcomes. Adolescent fathers are more likely than their male peers to become divorced, to have a lower level of education, to have a lower-paying job, be prone to the use of drugs and alcohol, violations of the law, and feelings of anxiety and depression (Miller-Johnson and Constanzo, 2004). For the most part, adolescent fathers are unlikely to be heavily involved in the life of their child. One earlier study found that only a quarter of adolescent fathers were viewed by the adolescent mother as having a 'close' relationship with the child by the time the child was 3 years old (Leadbeater and Bishop, 1994). Teenage fathers tend to be from low socio-economic backgrounds, experience lower educational attainment and fewer employment opportunities than their childless peers. Similarly they tend to experience greater psychological and emotional difficulties and may have a history of delinquent behaviour (Bunting and McAuley, 2004).

What are the consequences for the children born to adolescent mothers? These children face a higher likelihood of difficulties in life, beginning even before they are born (Miller et al., 2003). Only one in five adolescent mothers receives any prenatal care during the first three months of pregnancy. Partly for this reason, babies born to adolescent mothers are more likely to be born prematurely and to have a low birth weight. Prematurity and low birth weight in turn predict a variety of physical and cognitive problems in infancy and childhood. Children of adolescent mothers also face a greater likelihood of behavioural problems throughout childhood, including school misbehaviour, delinquency and early sexual activity (Moore and Brooks-Gunn, 2002).

However, researchers have stressed that the children's problems are due not just to the young age of their mothers but also to the fact that most adolescent mothers are

Having a baby in adolescence puts both mother and baby at risk for a variety of difficulties.

poor as well (Levine et al., 2007; Boyle, 2000). Having a mother who is young, unmarried or poor puts children at greater risk for a variety of developmental problems. Children whose mothers have all three characteristics – as many adolescent mothers do – face an environment in which it will be difficult for them to thrive.

Abortion

If having a child in adolescence often results in dire consequences for adolescent mothers and their babies, what about adolescent girls who have an abortion? Studies have consistently found little evidence of serious physical or psychological harm for adolescents who abort an unwanted pregnancy (Russo, 2008; Adler et al., 2003). Nevertheless, many girls do experience guilt and emotional stress, and feel highly ambivalent about their decision to abort (Miracle et al., 2003). The right and practice of abortion remains tremendously controversial, especially with respect to adolescents, and arguments about abortion are profoundly culturally situated.

Sexually Transmitted Diseases

'I don't think I would ever have unprotected sex, meaning without a condom. I've always known a lot about AIDS. I certainly wouldn't want to put my life in jeopardy for something like that.'

– Gabriela, age 22 (in Arnett, 2004, p. 91)

'we actually didn't use anything, and I don't know why. We were both being stupid … [After my next test] they called me and said I was positive for chlamydia. That just shook me up because I couldn't believe that would happen to me.'

– Holly, age 23 (in Arnett, 2004, p. 93)

In addition to the problem of unwanted pregnancy, sex in adolescence and emerging adulthood carries a relatively high risk of sexually transmitted diseases (STDs). Few young people have sex with numerous partners, but as we have seen, occasional sex with a temporary partner is quite common among adolescents and young adults. Even where sex takes place in a committed relationship, most youthful love relationships do not endure for long. Young people typically get involved in a relationship, it lasts for a few months, sometimes sexual intercourse is part of it, and then they break up and move on. In this way, young people gain experience with love and sex. Unfortunately, having sex with a variety of people at any age carries with it a risk of STDs.

A World Health Organization (WHO) report, *Global Prevalence and Incidence of Selected Curable Sexually Transmitted Infections: Overview and Estimates* (2001) provides estimates of the extent of the world's STD epidemics As there are no more recent international estimates, this report forms the basis of the data in Table 9.8. The WHO estimates that 340 million new cases of syphilis, gonorrhea, chlamydia and trichomoniasis occurred throughout

Table 9.8 Estimated Prevalence and Annual Incidence of Curable STDs by Region

Region	Adolescent and adult population (millions)	Infected (millions)	Infected per 1000 population	New infections in (millions)
North America	156	3	19	14
Western Europe	203	4	20	17
North Africa & Middle East	165	3.5	21	10
Eastern Europe & Central Europe	205	6	29	22
Sub-Saharan Africa	269	32	119	69
South & South-east Asia	955	48	50	151
East Asia & Pacfic	815	6	7	18
Australia & New Zealand	11	0.3	27	1
Latin America & Carribean	260	18.5	71	38
Total	3039	121.3	–	340

Source: World Health Organization (2001) *Global Prevalence and Incidence of Selected Curable Sexually Transmitted Infections: Overview and Estimates.* Geneva: WHO

CONNECT AND EXTEND

'Average age of first intercourse was 15 years, and most visited the clinic after having sex rather than before' (from the abstract). Read 'No worries!: Young people's experiences of nurse-led drop-in sexual health services in South West England' by Jenny Ingram and Debra Salmon in the *Journal of Research in Nursing*, Volume 12, Number 4 (July 2007), pp. 305–315

the world in men and women aged 15 to 49 years. The largest number of new infections occurred in the region of South and South-east Asia, followed by sub-Saharan Africa and Latin America and the Caribbean. The highest rate of new cases per 1000 population occurred in sub- Saharan Africa. Infection rates can vary enormously between countries in the same region and between urban and rural populations. In general, however, the prevalence of STDs tends to be higher in urban residents, in unmarried individuals and in young adults.

New diagnoses of STDs, sometimes also called sexually transmitted infections (STI), in a genito-urinary medicine (GUM) clinic have on the whole increased for males and females in the UK since 2000 (Office for National Statistics, 2010e). Rates of newly diagnosed STIs are on the whole higher in England than in any other UK country; however, it is not clear whether this is due to higher rates of screening or incidence. Chlamydia in 2009 remained the most common newly diagnosed bacterial STI in the UK (Office for National Statistics, 2010).

The symptoms and consequences of STDs vary widely, from the merely annoying (pubic lice or 'crabs') to the deadly (HIV/AIDS). In between these extremes, many other STDs leave young women at higher risk for later infertility because the female reproductive system is much more vulnerable than the male reproductive system to most STDs and their consequences (King, 2005).

Two other general characteristics of STDs bear mentioning before we discuss specific STDs. One is that many people who have STDs are **asymptomatic**, meaning that they show no symptoms of the disease. Under these circumstances, they are especially likely to infect others because neither they nor others realise that they are infected. Second, some STDs (such as herpes and HIV) have a **latency period** that can last for years. This means that there may be years between the time people are infected and the time they begin to show symptoms, and during this time they may be infecting others without either themselves or their partners being aware of it.

THINKING CRITICALLY

Do you think adolescents and emerging adults would be more likely to use condoms if they knew that many people who have STDs are asymptomatic? Why or why not?

Remember that chlamydia in 2009 remained the most common newly diagnosed bacterial STI in the UK and chlamydia is highly infectious, with 70 per cent of women and 25 per cent of men contracting the disease during a single sexual episode with an infected partner. Seventy-five per cent of women and 25 per cent of men with the disease are asymptomatic (Cates, 1999). When symptoms occur, they include pain during urination, pain during intercourse, and pain in the lower abdomen. Chlamydia can usually be treated effectively with antibiotics, but in recent years antibiotics have become less effective because widespread use has led to evolutionary adaptations in chlamydia that make it more resistant (King, 2005).

HIV/AIDS

'It's a really scary thing right now. If for some reason you're not careful or you forget to use protection, you're like paranoid for a long time, until you get tested. Nobody that I know has [HIV] right now, but everybody's scared about it. You never know for sure.'
– Holly, age 18 (in Bell, 1998, p. 119)

Many STDs have been around for a long time, but HIV/AIDS appeared comparatively recently, first diagnosed in 1981 (King, *ibid*.). In this STD, the human immunodeficiency virus (HIV) causes acquired immune deficiency syndrome (AIDS), which strips the body of its ability to fend off infections. Without this ability, the body is highly vulnerable to a wide variety of illnesses and diseases.

HIV is transmitted through bodily fluids, including semen, vaginal fluid and blood. The virus typically enters the body through the rectum, vagina or penis, during anal or vaginal intercourse. Another common form of transmission is through shared needles among intravenous drug users, but in traditional cultures HIV/AIDS is spread mainly between heterosexual partners. As with most other STDs, women are more vulnerable than men to the transmission of HIV/AIDS (Ashford, 2002).

HIV/AIDS has an unusually long latency period. After the HIV virus is acquired, people who contract it tend to be asymptomatic for at least five years before the symptoms of AIDS appear, and in some cases as long as ten years (King, 2005). Thus, few adolescents have AIDS, but the incidence of AIDS rises sharply in the early 20s, and cases of AIDS that appear in these years occur mostly in people who contracted the HIV virus in their teens (Arthur et al., 2005; Fenton and Lowndes, 2004). The incidence of AIDS has risen dramatically since it was first diagnosed in 1981, and by the mid-1990s it was a leading cause of death among some groups of adolescents, especially homeless adolescents (Rosenthal and Rotheram-Borus, 2005; Whitbeck and Hoyt, 1999a). AIDS has been most devastating in Southern Africa, where 10 of every 11 new HIV infections worldwide take place and where more than a quarter of young people are infected in some countries, as Figure 9.5 shows (Bankole et al., 2004).

HIV/AIDS is having a devastating effect on life in Africa, especially for young people. Already 10 million African children under age 15 have lost their mother or both parents to AIDS, and 90 per cent of the world's total of AIDS orphans are in Africa (Bankole et al., 2004). This AIDS epidemic will affect young Africans mainly in three ways (Nsamenang, 2002; Bartholet, 2000).

First, many of them will be required to assume the leadership of their families due to their parents' deaths. Second, many of them will be forced into even deeper poverty by their parents' deaths and may end up joining the millions of AIDS orphans who have already become street children in African cities, where they are vulnerable to illness, malnutrition and sexual exploitation. Third, many young Africans will become AIDS victims themselves in the twenty-first century if vast changes are not made soon in the prevalence of safe sex practices.

HIV infection also remains of major public health importance in the European Union. In 2009, nearly 26,000 HIV-diagnosed cases were reported by the 28 countries. In Europe, certain population groups suffer from high infection rates, e.g. men who have sex with men, individuals from countries with generalised HIV epidemics, and injecting drug users (IDUs), with the largest increase in HIV infections among practising homosexual and bisexual men. Not surprisingly therefore, additional groups at risk in Europe are prisoners, commercial sex workers and people with other sexually transmitted infections. In 2009, more than 4500 newly diagnosed AIDS cases were reported by 27 EU/EEA countries (ECDC, 2005–2009).

No symptoms are evident when a person first contracts HIV, but evidence of HIV can be identified in a blood test about six weeks after infection. Later during the HIV latency period a person may experience flu-like symptoms including fever, sore throat, fatigue and swollen lymph nodes in the neck and armpits. After this initial outbreak of symptoms, no further evidence of the disease may appear until years later. Once AIDS does appear, it is usually in the form of symptoms of unusual diseases that people rarely get unless there is something seriously wrong with their immune system. AIDS-specific symptoms include wasting syndrome, in which the person loses a great deal of body weight and becomes extremely emaciated.

AIDS has proven to be extremely difficult to treat because the virus has the ability to change itself and thus render medications ineffective. However, in recent years effective drug treatments for prolonging the lives of AIDS sufferers have begun to be

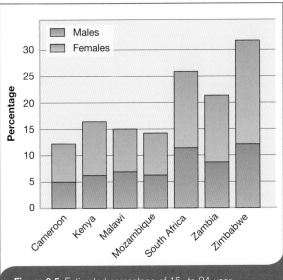

Figure 9.5 Estimated percentage of 15- to 24-year-olds with AIDS in selected African countries.
Source: Bankole et al. (2004).

CONNECT AND EXTEND

Do personality traits influence motives for having risky sex among 18- to 21-year-old British university students? Did that get your attention? Read 'Personality and riskier sexual behaviour: motivational mediators' by David Ingledew and Eamonn Ferguson in *Psychology and Health*, Volume 22, Number 3 (2007), pp. 291–315

developed. Nevertheless, the mortality rate for people who have AIDS remains extremely high. In Africa, where the prevalence of AIDS is greatest, the most effective drugs are rarely available. Intervention programmes to reduce HIV risk among adolescents have now been conducted in many developing countries but with limited effectiveness (Bankole et al., 2004; Magnussen et al., 2004).

After this information about STDs and their consequences, are you feeling concerned? Well, if you are a sexually active young adult, you should be.

Young adulthood is the age period when the risks of contracting STDs are greatest because young adults are so much more likely than others to have sex with a variety of partners (King, *ibid*.). Hopefully, the information presented here will be enough to inspire you to have regular medical examinations if you are sexually active. Young women in particular should receive regular pelvic exams and STD smears because, as we have already noted from the research, they are at higher risk than young men for virtually all STDs.

SUMMING UP

In this chapter we have covered a variety of topics related to dating, love and sexuality. Here are the main points we have discussed:

- Romantic relationships tend to begin with mixed-sex groups in early adolescence and develop into romantic partnerships by late adolescence. Most adolescents have their first romantic relationships in their early teens. In majority European cultures dating has been replaced in recent years by more informal ways of meeting potential romantic partners and establishing a relationship. Young people in traditional communities tend to be discouraged from dating until they are looking seriously for a marriage partner.
- Sternberg's theory of love describes a variety of types of love derived from combinations of passion, commitment and intimacy. Adolescent love usually lacks long-term commitment, so it is most often characterised by infatuation or romantic love. Adolescents in traditional cultures and communities also experience passion, but many cultures restrict adolescents' expressions of passionate love because some believe that marriage should be based on family interests rather than individual choice.
- With respect to their views on adolescent sexuality, cultures can be generally classified as restrictive, semi-restrictive or permissive. Much of Northern Europe today is probably best classified as semi-restrictive, with a great deal of ambivalence and divided opinions about adolescent sexuality.
- Adolescent sexual activity tends to follow a progression that begins with masturbation, followed by kissing and necking, sexual intercourse and oral sex. Having first intercourse at age 15 or younger tends to be associated with problems such as higher rates of drug and alcohol use. Adolescents tend to use contraceptives inconsistently, owing to deep ambivalence about adolescent sexuality.
- Gay, lesbian and bisexual (GLB) adolescents often have difficulty coping with their sexual orientation in a culture that stigmatises homosexuality.

Consequently they are more likely than other adolescents to have problems of suicide, substance abuse, school difficulties and running away from home. However, acceptance of homosexuality has risen substantially in recent years, especially among young people.

• Most sex in young adulthood takes place between romantic partners, but recreational sex or 'hooking up' is also common, frequently involving alcohol use.

• Sexually transmitted diseases contracted by adolescents and emerging adults include chlamydia, HPV, herpes simplex and HIV/AIDS. Rates of all these STDs are especially high in young adulthood.

One striking characteristic of research on sexuality in adolescence and young adulthood is that it is so heavily weighted towards the problems that can arise from premarital sexual contact, such as unwanted pregnancies and STDs. This emphasis is understandable, given the profound effects that these problems can have on young people's lives. Still, such an emphasis can leave a distorted impression of how young people experience sexuality. If you knew nothing about sex except what you read in academic studies of adolescents, you would never guess that sex can be pleasurable. It is true that young people's sexuality can be a source of difficulties and problems, but what about sexuality as a source of enjoyment? What positive feelings and thoughts do adolescents have as they experience kissing, necking, petting and intercourse? How are love and sex related in young people's relationships? In what ways does sexual contact enhance emotional intimacy between young people in love? We need to learn much more about these questions in order to have a complete picture of love and sexuality among young people.

INTERNET RESOURCES

http://www.childrenfirst.nhs.uk/teens/

A very comprehensive teenage health website for 12–18s from Great Ormond Street Hospital, London.

http://www.fpa.org.uk/professionals/factsheets/teenagers

Website for the Family Planning Association. This page is a very useful factsheet about teenagers' sexual health and behaviour. The site has links to training courses, FPA awards for professionals, publications and resources.

http://www.nhs.uk/Livewell/TeenGirls/Pages/teengirlshome.aspx

The National Health Service website with specific information on and for teenage health issues including ten questions you should ask yourself to test if you are ready for sex. There are plenty of links to a wealth of information and advice.

http://www.relate.org.uk/home/index.html

The website for Relate, a UK national federated charity to support relationships. Relate offers advice, relationship counselling, sex therapy, courses and workshops, mediation, consultations and support face to face, by phone and through this website.

FURTHER READING

E. Hatfield and R. L. Rapson, *Love and Sex: Cross-cultural Perspectives*. **Boston: Allyn & Bacon (2005)**

A lively, fascinating account of beliefs and behaviour on love and sex around the world, including material related to adolescents and young adults.

Paul Pedersen, Hugh Crethar and Jon Carlson, *Inclusive Cultural Empathy: Making Relationships Central in Counseling and Psychotherapy.* **Washington DC: American Psychological Association (2008)**

This text provides procedural, theoretical and practical lessons to bring readers a model for how counsellors might infuse their work with inclusion and multicultural sensitivity.

Gill Jones, *Youth (Key Concepts)*. **Cambridge: Polity Press (2009)**

Individual chapters are organised around the themes of action, identity, transition, inequality and dependence – conceptual themes that cross–cut young people's lives. The book uncovers notions which are erroneously attributed to young people and acts as an antidote to some of the generalisations that might sneak into texts on adolescence and youth studies.

Roger Penn, *Children of International Migrants in Europe: Comparative Perspectives*. **Basingstoke: Palgrave Macmillan (2009)**

This book provides a comparative analysis of the situation of over 2500 children of international migrants in Europe. Focusing on Britain, France and Germany, it examines nine ethnic/nationality groups including Pakistanis and Indians in Britain, Maghrebians in France and Turks in Germany. The book includes new empirical material on the cultural behaviour of young adults in these three countries based upon a unique comparative international survey.

For more reviews, responses to the *Thinking Critically* features, case studies, web links and practice tests, log on to **www.pearsoned.co.uk/arnett.**

CHAPTER 10
SCHOOL

OUTLINE

At Drayton School near Banbury, Oxfordshire, a part-time French teacher, Jane Wright, isn't looking forward to teaching a modern foreign languages class of 11- and 12-year-olds. The children enter the classroom and Jane is at the door to greet them 'Bonjour. Ça va?' She is largely ignored and some pupils have to be cajoled into coming in from the corridor. As the classroom fills up an atmosphere grows of constant low-level disruption, shouting out, swinging on seats, moving places and chatting. Five minutes in and some of the pupils haven't opened their books. A group of four girls pick arguments with the teacher, turn their chairs away, call out; almost anything goes to gain attention to their rude behaviour . . . .

http://www.teachers.tv/videos/attention-seekers *(see the note on Teachers TV in the Preface)*

At Hove Park School near Brighton, Spanish teacher Mirella Jerez-Rios divides her classes into competing teams where 'points mean prizes'. A Year 10 (14- and 15-year-olds) class play the 'Star Game', 'Pass the Envelope' and 'Spanish Catch' and the classroom bubbles over with good humour and excitement. Mirella is an expert at making the most creative use of simple resources, and she reinforces her pupils' learning through a varied series of games and activities, making one PowerPoint slide and a page of a textbook the starting point for a diverse, energetic and challenging double lesson. Using a games playing approach, Mirella encourages the pupils to practise their Spanish without realising they're being taught.

http://www.teachers.tv/videos/points-mean-prizes

THESE SCENES, TAKEN FROM A SERIES OF video clips on teachers TV (UK) provide an illustration of the diversity of experiences that can occur in a typical British **secondary school**. The general term secondary school is used in many parts of Britain to include academies, community and sixth form colleges, grammar and high schools, comprehensive and upper schools. Secondary schools contain all sorts of pupils, with a vast range of interests and abilities. With nearly all of them, teachers wage a daily struggle to keep them engaged in learning, some with only intermittent success. School competes for adolescents' attention with family problems, part-time work, media stimulation and the many allurements of leisure with friends. Schools also struggle against the ambivalence of beliefs about adolescence. Many parents want adolescents to succeed in school and learn what they need to prepare themselves for work (or at least for further or higher education), but many parents also want adolescence to be a time when young people are free to enjoy life to the fullest before the responsibilities of adulthood arrive.

In this chapter we examine young people's school experiences in the past and present in secondary schools and in colleges and universities in Britain and in other countries. The chapter begins with a short historical account of the rise of secondary schooling. This history is important because secondary schooling is relatively recent as a normal part of adolescence and because it would be difficult to understand secondary schools today without knowing how they developed.

Following this history, we look at secondary education around the world, including international comparisons of academic performance.

Although the overall quality of British secondary education is troubling in some ways, many schools do succeed, and we spend part of this chapter celebrating the characteristics of effective schools. We also examine adolescents' school achievement in the context of the rest of their lives. Educationalists have concluded that adolescents' academic performance is related in crucial ways to their family relationships, friendships, and work and leisure patterns. We also consider the role of cultural beliefs in what is required from adolescents academically.

Just as schools vary in their effectiveness, adolescents vary in their academic achievement. We focus especially on ethnic differences and gender differences in achievement, two areas that have been the focus of much research. We also consider the characteristics of adolescents with disabilities, adolescents who are in lower academic groupings, adolescents who are considered gifted or talented and adolescents who drop-out of secondary schooling. At the end of the chapter we turn our attention to the way schooling is organised in Denmark and compare this provision with what we have explored in the British system. The potential scope of this chapter is enormous and so much of the detailed discussion of adolescents' experience of schooling and the outcomes of those experiences can be found in the *Connect and Extend* features.

A British secondary school.

THE RISE OF SCHOOLING FOR ADOLESCENTS

Compulsory secondary school education in Britain is relatively recent. It was only from April 1900 that higher elementary schools were recognised, providing education from the age of 10 to 15. Yet it wasn't until The Elementary Education (School Attendance) Act of 1893 was amended in 1905 that the school minimum leaving age went up to 12 years of age; the first time that a minimum age for leaving – now considered a feature of secondary schooling policy – was made compulsory. The Fisher Education Act 1918 made secondary education compulsory up to age 14 and gave responsibility for secondary schools to the state, rather than churches or charitable foundations. Under the Act, many higher elementary (primary) schools and charitable (endowed) grammar schools sought to become state-funded secondary schools. However, most children attended primary (elementary) school up until age 14, rather than going to a separate school for secondary education. This is an interesting fact and one that could be usefully recalled towards the end of this chapter.

The Education Act 1944 – sometimes known as 'the Butler Act' – relating to England and Wales defined the modern dichotomy between primary education and secondary education at age 11, and provided for the raising of the minimum school leaving age to 15; the rise to 15 was enforced in 1947. The minimum school leaving age was raised again, this time to 16, from September 1973 onwards and, finally, in January 2007, HM Government announced plans to extend the school leaving age in England to 18 by 2013.

Britain now has a 'mosaic' of secondary school provision that includes publicly funded schools and independent schools. An independent school in the United Kingdom is a school that is not financed through the taxation system by the state and is instead funded by private sources (mainly fees paid by the parents of those attending) and charitable endowments. Many independent schools are called 'public schools' because they were founded for public use and subject to public management; private schools (also referred to by many people as public schools) are run for the profit of the owners. Most of the larger independent schools are either full or partial boarding schools where pupils live at the school during term-time or during the week. Some independent schools are called preparatory schools, or 'prep schools', designed to prepare a pupil for fee-paying, secondary independent school. The age range is normally 8 to 11 or 13, although it may include younger pupils as well. There are now more than 2500 independent schools in the UK, educating some 615,000 children, or some 7 per cent of children throughout the country (ISC, 2010).

The outcomes for the United Kingdom of having such a variety of state-funded, public and private education provision are potentially politically contentious and socially controversial, particularly in relation to access to higher education. There are private schools in many other parts of Europe and in other countries but they do not serve such a significant proportion of the population, nor, arguably, do they have the same political, social and economic influence as the public schools of the United Kingdom.

Between 1980 and the end of the century almost all British 15- and 16-year-olds remained at school (Chitty, 2004). In other countries (see Table 10.1), a similar trend occurred during the final quarter of the last century. Schooling became the normal experience for middle adolescents, and an increasing proportion of young adults also remained in full-time education or training. For example, in Norway, as recently as 1950 only 20 per cent of adolescents continued school past age 15; today education is compulsory until age 16, and 90 per cent of 17- and 18-year-olds are still in school (Hansen and Wold, 2007).

Table 10.1 shows that even recently adolescents often do not attend school in societies that are not

Table 10.1 Changes in Secondary School Enrolment in Selected Countries, 1980–2000

	% (14- to 17-year-olds) enrolled in 1980		% (14- to 17-year-olds) enrolled in 2000	
	Males	Females	Males	Females
Germany	93	87	99	99
Italy	73	70	94	95
Poland	75	80	98	97
Argentina	53	62	73	81
Egypt	66	41	83	73
China	54	37	74	67
Turkey	44	24	68	48
Mexico	51	46	64	64
India	39	20	59	39
Nigeria	25	13	36	30

Note: Percentages reflect the proportion of pupils enrolled in secondary school in the applicable age group in each country.

Source: Population Reference Bureau (2000)

CONNECT AND EXTEND

For an overview of the main approaches that have been taken to measure adult literacy within and across countries read 'Adult literacy: monitoring and evaluation for practice and policy' by Daniel Wagner in the *International Review of Education/Internationale* *Zeitschrift für Erziehungswissenschaft/Revue internationale l'éducation*, Volume 54, Numbers 5–6 (November 2008), pp. 651–672

fully industrialised. In those societies, education beyond childhood is only for the elite (just as it was in developed countries a century ago). Adolescents are usually engaged in productive work rather than attending school. Their labour is needed by their families, and they can best learn the skills needed for adult work by working alongside adults rather than by attending school. However, these patterns are changing in many countries due to growing economic development. Virtually everywhere in the world, countries and cultures that were economically underdeveloped 50 or more years ago are now becoming more industrialised and entering the global economy. One consequence of economic development in these countries is that adolescents are increasingly likely to remain in school. Economic development introduces agricultural technologies that make children's and adolescents' labour less necessary to the family, while staying in school brings increasing economic benefits because more jobs become available that require knowledge, skills and understanding usually gained at school.

The developing world is making progress in literacy but the challenge remains. It has been estimated that the number of adults who are not literate has fallen from 871 million between 1985 and 1994 to 774 million between 2000 and 2006 (UNESCO, 2008). Comparing these two periods, the world adult literacy rate rose accordingly from 76 per cent to 83.6 per cent, with the largest increase occurring in developing countries – from 68 per cent to 79 per cent. However, the figure of 774 million is believed to be an underestimation. (See the nearby *Connect and Extend* feature.) It is widely believed that there exist many more adults in 'developing countries' who do not have an adequate level of literacy to meet the demands of their work and to engage in social networks through more widely available information and communication technologies.

Changes in Schooling for Adolescents

Not only has the proportion of adolescents attending secondary school in Britain and the rest of Europe changed dramatically in the past century, but the kinds of things adolescents learn in school have changed as well. An examination of these changes is useful for understanding the requirements that exist for adolescents today. The following *Historical Focus* feature is based upon policy in the UK – during the period responsibility for education and training was increasingly devolved to the four countries of the United Kingdom. Alternative patterns of policy and provision from across Europe will be explored in later sections of this chapter and the *Connect and Extend* features.

CONNECT AND EXTEND

For a discussion of European trends in secondary vocational curriculum, read *Young People in Europe:* *Labour Markets and Citizenship* by H. Bradley and J. van Hoof (eds) (2005), Bristol, Policy Press

HISTORICAL FOCUS

Secondary Education for All?

In the nineteenth century, when few adolescents attended school, secondary education was mainly for the wealthy. The curriculum was constructed to provide young people (mainly males) with a broad liberal arts education – history, art, literature, science, philosophy, Latin and Greek – with no specific economic purpose (Chitty, *ibid*.). By 1918, there was a widespread consensus that educational reform was needed. The year 1918 saw the introduction in the UK of the Education Act 1918 – the Fisher Act. The act enforced compulsory full-time education from 5–14 years, but also included provision for compulsory part-time education for all 14- to 18-year-olds. The 1918 Act was not implemented immediately, instead waiting until an act in 1921 before coming into effect.

The composition of the pupil population in secondary schools changed from the privileged few to a broad cross-section of the population, and it was necessary to adapt the content of secondary education to respond to this change. Thus, the central goal of secondary education shifted from education for its own sake to more practical goals focusing on training for work and citizenship. It was in the 1920s that the post-elementary curriculum framework for secondary schooling as we know it today was established, designed to educate a diverse population of adolescents for life in society. Rather than being restricted to the liberal arts, education in the higher elementary schools or central schools included classes in general education and vocational training.

Between the 1920s and the middle of the twentieth century, the proportion of young people attending secondary school continued to expand, and the diversity of the secondary school curriculum continued to expand as well. The curriculum was enlarged to include preparation for family life and leisure, with courses available on music, art, health, parenting and physical education.

Since the 1950s, periodic cries of alarm have been sounded over the ineffectiveness of schools, with much of the alarm focusing on the education of adolescents in secondary schools. In the early 1960s, concern focused on the perceived deficiencies of science education in the schools (the 1968 Council for Scientific Policy 'the Dainton Report' – *Inquiry into the Flow of Candidates into Science and Technology in Higher Education* – prompted by reduction in numbers of science students) and for 13–16-year-olds of below average ability (the 1963 Central Advisory Council for Education 'the Newsom Report' – *Half Our Future*). In the early 1970s, the social upheaval of the previous decade led various committees of educational commentators to heap blame on secondary schools for the growing alienation and disillusionment of young people. The problem, according to these committees, was that the education provided by secondary schools was too far removed from real life and was based on progressive rather than traditional teaching methods (e.g. 1976 Neville Bennett's report, *Teaching Styles and Pupil Progress*).

Relevance became a new buzzword and, in pursuit of relevance, secondary schools were encouraged to develop programmes or provide access that would involve less time in the traditional classroom and more time learning skills in the workplace, obtaining direct occupational training and experience. In 1969, the Haslegrave Report promoted technical and business education, the 1973 Education (Work Experience) Act allowed local education authorities (LEAs) to organise work experience for final-year school students and the 1980 White Paper *A New Training Initiative: A Programme for Action* set out the first plans for the Youth Training Scheme (YTS). This led in the next 30 years to a plethora of initiatives in training, curriculum and qualifications.

What does all this mean? The foregoing information led to and derives from the UK Labour government aspiration (Blair, 1999) to support 50 per cent of young people of 16 to 18 years, to prepare for higher education. The then government wanted 16- to 19-year-olds predominantly but not quite exclusively to study academic courses in science, mathematics, engineering and technology and the remaining 50 per cent (this time targeted at 14 to 19 years) in full-time vocational education including employment-based training and qualification. Why? Well, by 1999 politicians had recognised the rising phenomenon of large numbers of young NEETs (those young people 'Not in Employment, Education or Training'), particularly in UK inner cities (Maguire, 2008; Pemberton, 2008; Simmons, 2008; Furlong, 2006; Yates and Payne, 2006; Maguire and Rennison, 2005).

THINKING CRITICALLY

In your view, should secondary school courses focus on academic subjects such as maths and English, on vocational subjects such as engineering or childcare, or on courses in music, art and physical education? Justify your view.

Secondary Education around the World

There is a great deal of diversity worldwide in the kinds of secondary schools adolescents attend, and world regions also vary in how likely adolescents are to attend secondary school at all. There is an especially sharp contrast between fully industrialised countries and economically developing countries. As we observed earlier with middle and older adolescents, virtually all adolescents are enrolled in secondary school in industrialised countries. In contrast, only about 50 per cent of adolescents in economically developing countries attend secondary school (Figure 10.1). Furthermore, tertiary education (college and university) is obtained by about half of emerging adults in industrialised countries but is

only for the elite (and wealthy) 10 per cent in developing countries. In this section we look at secondary education first in industrialised countries and then in developing countries.

Secondary Education in Industrialised Countries

Canada and Japan are examples of countries with single-model comprehensive high schools as the norm, but most other industrialised countries (as we have seen in the example of the UK) have several different kinds of schools that adolescents may attend. Most European countries have three types of secondary schools (Arnett, 2002b). One type is similar in many ways to a single-model **comprehensive school** in that it offers a variety of academic courses and the goal is general education rather than education for any specific profession. In most European countries, about half of adolescents attend this type of school. A second type of secondary school is the *vocational school*, where adolescents learn the skills involved in a specific occupation such as plumbing or auto mechanics. Usually, about a quarter of adolescents in European countries attend this type of school. Some European countries also have a third type of secondary school, a *professional school* devoted to the arts or some other specific

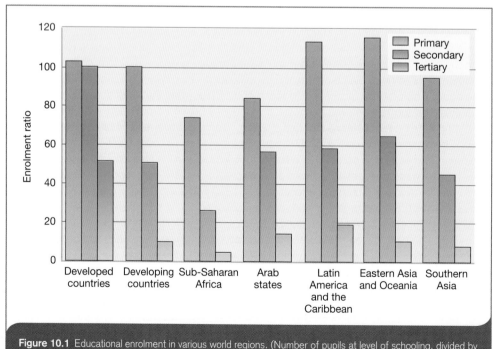

Figure 10.1 Educational enrolment in various world regions. (Number of pupils at level of schooling, divided by number of people of appropriate age for that level of schooling, times 100.)
Source: Fussell and Greene (2002), p. 32.

purpose (Flammer and Alsaker, 2001). About a quarter of European adolescents usually attend this type of school. Some European countries, such as Germany and Switzerland, also have extensive apprenticeship systems, in which adolescents can attend a vocational or professional school part of the time and also spend time learning a profession in the workplace under the supervision of adults. We will discuss apprenticeships in more detail in the next chapter.

One consequence of the system adopted in many parts of Europe is that adolescents must decide at a relatively early age what direction to pursue for their education and occupation. In some countries adolescents at age 13 or 14 decide which type of secondary school they will enter, and this decision is likely to have an enormous impact on the rest of their lives. Usually, the decision is made by adolescents in conference with their parents and teachers, based on the adolescents' interests as well as on their school performance (e.g. Motola et al., 1998). Although adolescents sometimes change schools after a year or two, and adolescents who attend a vocational school sometimes attend university, these switches are rare. However, in recent years most countries have begun to offer professional colleges that pupils can attend after pursuing a vocational education in secondary school (Flammer and

Alsaker, 2001). In addition to providing professional training, graduation from professional colleges also allows entrance to university. This has added flexibility to the system by providing young people with an alternative route to university even if they did not attend a comprehensive or academic secondary school.

Nevertheless, in general these school systems tend to require early decision making about career directions. An earlier study (Motola et al., 1998) demonstrated how the timing of streaming – ability grouping across all curriculum areas – into different types of schooling influences the timing of adolescents' decisions about which occupational path to pursue. They compared adolescents in France and Finland. French adolescents are formally assessed beginning at age 13, and at age 16 they must choose a 'stream' from 5 academic and 16 technical programmes, or enter a vocational high school or apprenticeship. In contrast, Finnish adolescents are in one comprehensive school until age 16, then choose either an upper secondary school or a vocational school. However, they don't need to make a decision about a specific occupation until they enter university or leave vocational school. French adolescents were three times as likely as Finnish adolescents (58 per cent to 19 per cent) to have a clear idea of their chosen future occupation.

About a third of adolescents in Europe attend a vocational school or vocational courses in Further Education Institutions. Here a British student learns to paste wallpaper.

Secondary Education in Developing Countries

In contrast to industrialised countries, where attending secondary school is virtually universal for adolescents and the schools are well funded, in developing countries secondary education is often difficult to obtain and relatively few adolescents stay in school until the end of adolescence. Here we take a short comparative look at secondary education in the 'Arab' countries of North Africa, sub-Saharan Africa, India, China and Latin America.

In the Arab countries of North Africa there are high rates of illiteracy among parents and grandparents – over 50 per cent in most countries – but adolescents are much more likely than their parents or grandparents to be literate (Booth, 2002). Until recent decades, most education was oriented around the study of the Koran, the Muslim holy book, but now virtually all countries in the region have a secular educational system. Nevertheless, the influence of Islam remains very strong, and most of the secondary schools are segregated by sex, in the belief that this conforms to Islamic values. Girls are considerably less likely than boys to attend secondary school or to go to university because their household labour is needed and because they are

Ability Grouping

One explanation for the lower achievement of many pupils' low social and economic status (SES) backgrounds is that these pupils experience teaching in low-ability groups and therefore have a different academic experiences; that is, they are actually taught differently (Venkatakrishnan and Wiliam, 2003).

Forty years ago it was common in Britain for adolescents of different abilities to attend different schools. At age 10 or 11 primary school pupils took a test, the '11-plus' and were then awarded places either at a grammar school for an academic education or sent to a secondary modern or secondary technical school for a more vocational type of education. This was called the selective system. In the late 1960s comprehensive schools were introduced in many parts of Britain, particularly England and Wales. Some local authorities did keep some or all of their selective schools and so in Britain there is now a mixed system of secondary provision (Haydn, 2004).

One of the benefits that was argued for a new system of comprehensive secondary schooling was that such schools would allow for greater flexibility; movement between ability groups as pupils developed at different rates; and provide a mixture of academic and vocational courses according to individual interest and aptitude. With the exception of adolescents who are directed into lower-ability streams, all adolescents in a comprehensive school can choose from a broad range of courses. Because all adolescents attend the same secondary school, for the majority of them little about their occupational direction is decided by the time they leave. At that point, they may decide to enter work full time, pursue training at a vocational college, attend a two-year college course, enrol in a three- or four-year university course, or pursue some combination of work and training. To allow for this flexibility, to be comprehensive of all abilities and to provide a wide range of courses for all ability groups, it was thought that comprehensive schools needed to be large schools and so schools often doubled or trebled in size to 1000 or 1500 pupils (Oxlery and Kassissieh, 2008). As we will see later in the chapter, the development of these supersized schools has led to some difficulty for pupils, particularly those from low SES backgrounds.

Another potential drawback of the comprehensive school is that adolescents are all in the same school and – without streaming – in many of the same classes, even though by their mid-teens they may have widely divergent educational and occupational interests and abilities. This makes it difficult for teachers to find a level of teaching that will appeal to all adolescents. It can also be frustrating for adolescents who would prefer to be obtaining job-specific skills but are forced instead to take further years of more general education (Salmela-Aro et al., 2008a).

Remember the key difference is that streaming groups pupils by ability for all subjects (usually based on ability in mathematics and/or English) whereas setting systems group pupils for just some subjects. Not all secondary schools use streaming and schools do vary in the number and types of streams. Of course, streaming – and to a lesser extent setting – has been a target of fierce debate among educators for many years (e.g. Eccles and Roeser, 2003; Wong and Watkins, 2001; Crozier et al., 1999). Advocates argue that streaming is the best way to ensure that all students are engaged in the schoolwork that is best suited to their varying levels of ability and achievement (Barrow, 2007). According to this perspective, placing all pupils in the same classes makes no sense. The brightest and most advanced ones will be bored to death, and the slowest will be not only bored but humiliated that all the other students seem to be more advanced than they are. Also, not all pupils plan to attend university. Advocates of streaming argue that it would be better to give these students some useful vocational preparation as part of their secondary education, instead of alienating them by forcing them to sit through courses on topics that do not interest them or appear not to be of any use. However, students in the lower streams are often labelled as slow or stupid by their peers, often come to see themselves that way as well (Eccles and Roeser, *ibid.*), and is one of the causes of pupils disengaging with secondary schooling and dropping out. Why is this?

A substantial literature (e.g Pecek et al., 2008; Ireson and Hallam, 2005; De Fraine et al., 2003; Hallam and Ireson 2003; Myklbust, 2002; Boaler et al., 2000) shows a tendency for teaching in lower-ability groups to be different from that provided for high-ability groups. Some differences are to be expected, such as a slower pace and smaller steps, but there is concern that instruction in low-ability groups is over simplified with more highly structured written work. Tasks for higher-ability classes tend to include more critical thinking tasks and high-ability groups are also allowed more independence and choice, more opportunities are provided for discussion and pupils are allowed to take responsibility for their own work. Lower streams tend to undertake work that is more tightly structured. There is a concentration on basic skills, work sheets and repetition with fewer opportunities for independent learning, discussion and activities that promote critique and creativity. Researchers have also found that when high-stream pupils gave incorrect answers, teachers required correct answers, while low-stream pupils' incorrect responses were ignored (Gådin and Hammarström, 2003). It seems that based on past experience and a 'proven' set of stereotypes, teachers hold low expectations for low-ability pupils (Rubie-Davies et al., 2006). Perceiving these teachers' views in the learning tasks they were offered, the pupils lowered their self-image, in turn confirming the low teacher expectations (Mistry et al., 2009).

Furthermore, pupils in the lower streams tend to fall further and further behind their peers with each year of school. If pupils who are placed in a low stream receive a lower academic level of resources and a lower level of challenge compared with pupils in the higher streams, this makes it very difficult for students ever to get out of a low stream once they are placed in one (Akos et al., 2007). Over time, streaming increases the gap in learning between high-stream and low-stream students; ultimately, streaming influences students' achievement in secondary school and how much education they go on to obtain after secondary school (O'Connell et al., 2006). Finally, research has shown that pupils from many ethnic minorities are more likely to be placed in a lower stream than white or some Asian students of similar abilities (Strand and Winston, 2008; McDonald et al., 2007; Leventhal et al., 2006), raising the question of whether streaming decisions may be made in a way that is unfair and discriminatory, or whether teaching is culturally relevant (Durden, 2008; Eccles and Roeser, 2003). Is there a connection between ability grouping, low SES, some ethnic minority groups and school drop-out? Watch out for the *Connect and Extend* features later in the chapter.

often subject to an early marriage arranged by their parents. Education for girls is becoming more available as the marriage age rises and cultural values change in response to globalisation (Arnett, 2002a). Still, it remains true that the long-term benefits of education go mainly to men, as few women continue to work after marriage (Booth, *ibid.*).

Sub-Saharan Africa has the lowest rates of secondary school enrolment of any world region. However, rates of secondary school enrolment vary widely among countries, from 94 per cent in Zimbabwe (though a good deal has changed in Zimbabwe in the last few years) to just 3 per cent in Rwanda and Tanzania (Population Reference Bureau, 2000). Reasons for low rates include poverty and civil war. Furthermore, the economy is not industrialised in many areas, and consequently school-based knowledge is of limited use, whereas the labour of adolescents is needed for agricultural work, animal care, household work and childcare. Rates of secondary school enrolment are especially low among girls because girls are generally not expected to enter the workplace, and they have more responsibility than do boys for household work and for younger siblings.

Critics of the African educational system such as Bame Nsamenang (2002) of Cameroon argue that it is based on a model developed when European powers ruled Africa. The textbooks used are usually foreign and include little about African cultures. Rote learning is the main method of teaching. This method is not grounded in African cultures and fails to take into account their strengths. In Nsamenang's view, African educational systems should be remodelled so that they are based on indigenous African cultural practices. Adolescents should be taught not mainly in school but by working alongside adults in their daily economic activities. He believes this method would be truer to African traditions and values and would also be better suited to the current state of Africa's mostly rural and agricultural economy.

CONNECT AND EXTEND

For an article examining the expansion of vocational education at junior and higher secondary schools in Gujarat, India, read 'Vocational teachers in higher secondary schools in developing countries: a case study of Gujarat' by Govind Desai and Tom Whiteside in *Research in Post-compulsory Education*, Volume 4, Number 3 (1999), pp. 249–259

In India the educational system is similar to Africa's in that it was devised by a colonial government, in this case the British (Verma and Saraswathi, 2002). The schools were designed on the British model – textbooks, rote learning and exams – and English remains the main language of government and higher education. Secondary educational enrolment has grown in recent decades (see Table 10.1), but even now only about half of Indian adolescents receive secondary education. There are sharp differences in enrolment by gender, social class and rural/urban residence. Poor girls in rural areas are the most disadvantaged. They rarely attend secondary school, and nearly 40 per cent of them cannot read and write (Verma and Saraswathi, *ibid.*). However, India has a high-quality and growing system of higher education that is producing graduates with growing influence in the world economy, especially in computers and information technology (Arnett, 2002a).

The Chinese and Japanese secondary education systems are similar in many ways, although China is a newly developed country and Japan has one of the most advanced economies in the world (Stevenson and Zusho, 2002). In both countries, admission to university is restricted to the very highest-performing pupils, and consequently there is intense pressure at the high school level as pupils compete to prepare for the university entrance exam. Both countries also emphasise rote learning and memorisation in the classroom. Both have long school days that include extensive after-school activities such as martial arts, calligraphy and team sports. However, there are distinct differences between the two countries in educational attainment. In Japan virtually all adolescents graduate from high school, but in China less than three-quarters of adolescents even attend high school (Stevenson and Zusho, 2002; Population Reference Bureau, 2000). Nevertheless, in China as in much of the rest of the world, enrolment in secondary school is said to be rising, although it is difficult to obtain dependable statistics.

Latin America, like the other developing regions we have discussed, has experienced a rise in enrolment rates in secondary education in recent decades (Welti, 2002). However, the gender gap that exists in most regions outside the West does not exist in most countries in Latin America; in fact, in countries such as Argentina, enrolment in secondary school is higher among girls, as Table 10.1 shows. Despite the impressive gender equality in access to secondary school, there are stark differences by social class in many Latin American countries. State-funded secondary schools are often overcrowded and underfunded. Consequently, most wealthy families send their adolescents to private secondary schools, which are much higher in quality. Among adolescents who attend public secondary schools there is a high drop-out rate, 50 per cent in urban areas and 75 per cent in rural areas.

In most developing and recently developed countries, boys are more likely than girls to attend secondary school, but the gap is shrinking. Here, girls in Johannesburg, South Africa.

THE CHARACTERISTICS OF EFFECTIVE SCHOOLING

A number of common themes recur in accounts of secondary education in developing countries (Lloyd et al., 2008; Lloyd, 2005). Most have gender differences (favouring boys) in secondary education enrolment, but the gender gap is decreasing, and all have rising rates of enrolment for both genders. That's about where the good news ends. Many of the schools are poorly funded and overcrowded. Many countries have too few teachers, and the teachers they have are insufficiently trained. Often families have to pay for secondary education, a cost they find difficult to afford, and it is typical for families to have to pay for books and other educational supplies. There tends to be one education for the elite – in exclusive private schools and well-funded universities – and a much inferior education for everyone else.

Comparing secondary education in industrialised countries and developing countries, what is most striking is how unequal educational opportunities are between the two. If you happen to be born in a developing country, you are likely to get an education through primary school but unlikely to have the resources to finish secondary school, and your chances of attending university are very small – especially if you are a girl. In contrast, if you happen to be born in an industrialised country, it is extremely likely that you will finish secondary school, and it is quite likely that you will have the opportunity to attend university or college if you wish – especially if you are a girl. In all parts of the world, education is the basis of many of the good things in life, from income level to physical and mental health (Lloyd et al., 2008; Stromquist, 2007; Lloyd, 2005). Yet for the majority of the world's adolescents and emerging adults, their educational fate was already largely determined at birth, simply on the basis of where they were born.

International Comparisons

For about 30 years, international studies have been published comparing adolescents on academic performance. For example, Table 10.2 shows some results from a 2006 (NCES) report of the performance of young adolescents in various countries around the world on achievement tests. The pattern of results is similar across reading, maths and science. In all three

Table 10.2 International Rankings of 12- to 13-year-olds in Reading, Maths and Science

Reading		Maths		Science	
Country	Score	Country	Score	Country	Score
Finland	546	South Korea	589	South Korea	558
Canada	534	Japan	570	Japan	552
New Zealand	529	Belgium	537	Hungary	543
South Korea	523	The Netherlands	536	United Kingdom	538
United Kingdom	523	Canada	531	The Netherlands	536
Japan	522	Hungary	529	Canada	533
Austria	507	Russian Federation	508	United States	527
France	505	United States	504	Belgium	516
United States	504	United Kingdom	496	Russian Federation	514
				Italy	491
INTERNATIONAL AVERAGE	500	INTERNATIONAL AVERAGE	466	INTERNATIONAL AVERAGE	473
Denmark	497	Italy	484	Iran	453
Italy	487	Iran	411	Egypt	421
Poland	479	Indonesia	411	Indonesia	420
Russian Federation	462	Egypt	406	Chile	413
Mexico	422	Chile	387	Morocco	396
Brazil	396	Morocco	387	South Africa	244
		South Africa	264		

Source: National Center for Education Statistics (2006)

areas, the countries that tend to perform best are the industrialised countries of the West, along with Japan and South Korea. The performance of young adolescents in the United Kingdom tends to be above the international average, higher than developing countries but lower than Japan and South Korea. The countries below the international average are mostly countries in Africa, Latin America and Asia. What about results for middle adolescents? Are the comparative results for different countries stable for development during the teenage years?

Some of the largest-scale international comparative testing of schoolchildren is reported in the findings of the Organization for Economic Co-operation and Development (OECD) Programme for International Student Assessment (PISA). It is a three-yearly collaborative effort on the part of member countries (42 countries in 2003 with an additional 11 countries in 2006) of the OECD to measure how well pupils at age 15 are prepared to meet the challenges of today's societies. Take a look at the chart in Figure 10.2 that is taken from the 2009 results of tests completed by up to 10,000 pupils in each country taking part. Are there any surprises? More importantly, what questions spring to mind when looking at these results?

THINKING CRITICALLY

Based on what you have read so far about British and European secondary schools, what do you think explains the performance of young British adolescents in international comparisons?

In some ways Figure 10.2 begs some knotty questions. For example, it seems odd that results for different parts of China are reported separately. Is this to reflect the newly developed status of China, which is hugely industrialised in parts but also has areas that remain underdeveloped, agricultural communities?

Also, in Table 10.2, South Korea also did very well but the country is referred to as Korea in the OECD 2009 results – why is this?

Anyway, what is clear is that 15-year-olds in the United Kingdom are not statistically different from the OECD mean averages for reading and mathematics and are above average for science, which all seems reassuring. Although it should be noted that from age 12 to 15 there is some fall-off in scores for reading, leaving those in middle adolescence in the United Kingdom performing less well against their international comparators than at the age of 15. However, many young people do very well in our secondary schools, have high standards of achievement and go on to university or alternative routes of vocational training. Although this is a cause for some confidence in the work of our teachers and the organisation of our schools, it is not quite the whole story.

In 2007, a report for the Rowntree Foundation found that over 20,000 British teenagers each year gave up going to school by the age of 14, over 35,000 left school at 16 with no educational qualifications whatsoever and a staggering 140,000 (25 per cent of the age group) left with no qualifications recognised as being at a pass standard (Cassen and Kingdon, 2007). Nearly half of these low achievers were white British males, boys outnumbered girls as low achievers by three to two, and low achievement was linked to economic status (much more on this later) and to poor reading and writing skills at primary school.

The Rowntree report, drawing on other contemporaneous reports (e.g. Thomson and Russell, 2007) also highlighted how exclusions (temporary or permanent withdrawal of the right to attend a school) contribute to the complexity of the problem. The report showed that 12 young people in every 10,000 were permanently excluded from mainstream schools in England, 80 per cent of these from secondary schools. Of these, young people with special educational needs were overrepresented at the rate of 8:1 and the ratio of boys to girls

CONNECT AND EXTEND

What is the impact of the Programme for International Student Assessment (PISA) results on national education systems in Europe? This paper gives three examples of the impact of PISA in Finland, Germany and the UK and then looks beyond. Read

'Governing by numbers: the PISA "effect" in Europe' by Sotiria Grek in the *Journal of Education Policy*, Volume 24, Number 1 (January 2009), pp. 23–37

Rank Order of Average Scores in Reading, Mathematics and Science					
Reading	Mean	Mathematics	Mean	Science	Mean
Shanghai-China	556	Shanghai-China	600	Shanghai-China	575
Korea	539	Singapore	562	Finland	554
Finland	536	Hong Kong-China	555	Hong Kong-China	549
Hong Kong-China	533	Korea	546	Singapore	542
Singapore	526	Chinese Taipei	543	Japan	539
Canada	524	Finland	541	Korea	538
New Zealand	521	Liechtenstein	536	New Zealand	532
Japan	520	Switzerland	534	Canada	529
Australia	515	Japan	529	Estonia	528
Netherlands	508	Canada	527	Australia	527
Belgium	506	Netherlands	526	Netherlands	522
Norway	503	Macao-China	525	Chinese Taipei	520
Estonia	501	New Zealand	519	Germany	520
Switzerland	501	Belgium	515	Liechtenstein	520
Poland	500	Australia	514	Switzerland	517
Iceland	500	Germany	513	United Kingdom	514
United States	500	Estonia	512	Slovenia	512
Liechtenstein	499	Iceland	507	Macao-China	511
Sweden	497	Denmark	503	Poland	508
Germany	497	Slovenia	501	Ireland	508
Ireland	496	Norway	498	Belgium	507
France	496	France	497	Hungary	503
Chinese Taipei	495	Slovak Republic	497	United States	502
Denmark	495	Austria	496	Czech Republic	500
United Kingdom	494	Poland	495	Norway	500
Hungary	494	Sweden	494	Denmark	499
Portugal	489	Czech Republic	493	France	498
Macao-China	487	United Kingdom	492	Iceland	496
Italy	486	Hungary	490	Sweden	495
Latvia	484	Luxembourg	489	Austria	494
Slovenia	483	United States	487	Latvia	494
Greece	483	Ireland	487	Portugal	493
Spain	481	Portugal	487	Lithuania	491
Czech Republic	478	Spain	483	Slovak Republic	490
Slovak Republic	477	Italy	483	Italy	489
Croatia	476	Latvia	482	Spain	488

Figure 10.2 PISA results 2009

Source: PISA 2009 at a Glance, OECD Publishing (2011), **http://dx.doi.org/10.1787/9789264095298-en** Copyright OECD, 2009 Accessed 27.12.2010.

Rank Order of Average Scores in Reading, Mathematics and Science

Reading	Mean	Mathematics	Mean	Science	Mean
Israel	474	Lithuania	477	Croatia	486
Luxembourg	472	Russian Federation	468	Luxembourg	484
Austria	470	Greece	466	Russian Federation	478
Lithuania	468	Croatia	460	Greece	470
Turkey	464	Dubai (UAE)	453	Dubai (UAE)	466
Dubai (UAE)	459	Israel	447	Israel	455
Russian Federation	459	Turkey	445	Turkey	454
Chile	449	Serbia	442	Chile	447
Serbia	442	Azerbaijan	431	Serbia	443
Bulgaria	429	Bulgaria	428	Bulgaria	439
Uruguay	426	Romania	427	Romania	428
Mexico	425	Uruguay	427	Uruguay	427
Romania	424	Chile	421	Thailand	425
Thailand	421	Thailand	419	Mexico	416
Trinidad &Tobago	416	Mexico	419	Jordan	415
Colombia	413	Trinidad & Tobago	414	Trinidad & Tobago	410
Brazil	412	Kazakhstan	405	Brazil	405
Montenegro	408	Montenegro	403	Colombia	402
Jordan	405	Argentina	388	Montenegro	401
Tunisia	404	Jordan	387	Argentina	401
Indonesia	402	Brazil	386	Tunisia	401
Argentina	398	Colombia	381	Kazakhstan	400
Kazakhstan	390	Albania	377	Albania	391
Albania	385	Tunisia	371	Indonesia	383
Qatar	372	Indonesia	371	Qatar	379
Panama	371	Qatar	368	Panama	376
Peru	370	Peru	365	Azerbaijan	373
Azerbaijan	362	Panama	360	Peru	369
Kyrgyzstan	314	Kyrgyzstan	331	Kyrgyzstan	330

Statistically significantly above the OECD average

Not statistically significantly different from the OECD average

Statistically significantly below the OECD average

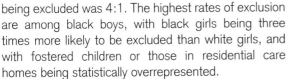

CONNECT AND EXTEND

School exclusion and violence are defined with boys as the reference point and relatively little attention is given to the various forms of exclusion to which girls are subject: disciplinary exclusion; self-exclusion; and withdrawal from learning. Read 'Excluded girls: interpersonal, institutional and structural violence in schooling' by Audrey Osler in *Gender and Education*, Volume 18, Number 6 (2006), pp. 571–589

being excluded was 4:1. The highest rates of exclusion are among black boys, with black girls being three times more likely to be excluded than white girls, and with fostered children or those in residential care homes being statistically overrepresented.

The Rowntree report's assessment of educational achievement in the UK shows the increasing numbers of young people who leave or who are forced to leave our schools with few qualifications. The Office for National Statistics reports that between 1997 and 2007 the numbers of young people aged between 15 and 24 who are not in education, in employment or on a training scheme (known as NEETs), rose by 15 per cent. Specifically, the rise in 16- and 17-years-olds who are not in education, training or employment has increased over the same period by 30 per cent. See Table 10.3 for some regional differences across the United Kingdom. What might account for these differences?

In August 2009 a British newspaper headline (The *Daily Telegraph*, 23 February 2009) announced 'One in six long-term young jobless "dead within ten years".' The article claims that there had been a surge in the number of British NEETs aged 16 to 24. In 2009 there were 935,000 young people in this position – almost 16 per cent of their age group. Jon Coles, the director of schools for England, at the Department for Children, Schools and Families, quoted anecdotal research from the north of England in a BBC News Report, stating that he considered there were social consequences when young people failed to engage with society. He said:

'Those who had been outside the system for a long time, whether because they were perma-nently excluded or simply because they had dropped out at the end of compulsory schooling and had not got into anything else, 15 per cent of those young people of ten years ago were dead by the time the research was done . . . For those of us who sometimes console ourselves with the thought that education is not a matter of life and death, actually for the most vulnerable children and young people in our society it really is.'

Table 10.3 Percentage of Young People aged 16 and 17 not in Employment, Education or Training (NEET), 2007

	Percentages
United Kingdom	6
North-east	7
North-west	7
Yorkshire and The Humber	6
East Midlands	5
West Midlands	9
East	9
London	5
South-east	9
South-west	7
England	7
Wales	7
Scotland	3
Northern Ireland	5

Source: Annual Population Survey, Office for National Statistics (2007)

Is there a different impact of these trends – hinted at in the Rowntree report of 2007 – on minority ethnic young people in Britain? The last comprehensive report was in 2006 (Department for Education and Skills), which we will now draw on and add to, to assemble the most up-to-date information available. (Again, we note that at the time of writing the awaited results of the UK-wide 2011 Census are not yet available.)

In 2001, 4.9 million (8.3 per cent) of the total popu-lation of the UK were born overseas, more than double the 2.1 million (4.2 per cent) in 1951. Compared with the UK-born population, the foreign-born population has a greater mix of ethnic groups. While 92 per cent of people born in the UK identified themselves as white in 2001, 53 per cent (2.6 million) of the foreign-born population was white. The next largest ethnic groups for people born overseas were Indian – 569,800, and Pakistani 336,400 (Office for National Statistics, 2011). As we noted in Chapter 4, many different cultures are represented in Britain and the range and variety of those cultures continues to increase as the enlarged European Union provides for right of economic migration across much of the continent.

Ethnic and Racial Differences in School Achievement

A major concern in British and other European schools is that some minority ethnic groups consistently achieve below the average for all pupils (Uline and Johnson, 2005). This pattern of results tends to hold for all kinds of tests and examinations, but the gaps have been narrowing over the past two to three decades and in some cases have been turned around, as you can see in

Figure 10.3. Non-British readers should note that the General Certificate of Secondary Education (GCSE) is taken by pupils in England and Wales at the academic age of 15 (the year in which they become 16). Opportunities for continuing formal schooling after this age are associated with passing at least five subjects at grades A* to C – considered the pass grades.

Figure 10.3 shows that black Caribbean and black 'Other' boys are two of the lowest attaining groups at GCSE. Only a third of boys in these groups achieved five or more A*–C grades at GCSE in 2005, compared to 50 per cent of white British boys.

Although there are consistent differences among ethnic groups on tests of academic achievement we would assert that these differences are mainly as follows: the legacy of past discrimination, which we will explain a little later; the product of cultural mismatches; or a result of growing up in a low social and economic status (SES) environment, as many pupils from minority groups are also economically disadvantaged. Importantly, when we compare pupils from different ethnic and racial groups who are all at the same SES level, then their achievement differences diminish (Andriessen and Phalet, 2002).

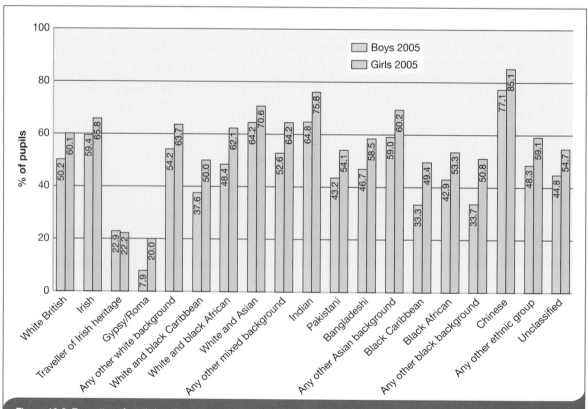

Figure 10.3 Proportion of pupils by ethnic group and gender achieving 5+ A* to C GCSEs (and equivalent) in 2005

Source: Department for Education and Skills (2006). *Ethnicity and Education: the Evidence on Minority Ethnic Pupils aged 5–16*. Research topic paper 0208-2006DOM-EN.

CONNECT AND EXTEND

In 'Stereotype accuracy: estimating the academic performance of ethnic groups' M. C. Ashton and V. M. Esses investigate the accuracy of stereotypes of the academic performance of ethnic groups. Read

Personality and Social Psychology Bulletin, Volume 25, Number 2 (1 February 1999), pp. 225–236

For example, in an analysis of National Assessment of Educational Progress (NAEP) mathematics test results, researcher James Byrnes (2003) found that less than 5 per cent of the variance in maths test scores was associated with race. About 50 per cent of the variance came from differences in SES, in levels of personal motivation to learn and exposure to learning opportunities (coursework, calculator use, homework, etc.). Hungarian psychologist Anikó Zsolnai (2002) concluded that parental motivation explained only 8 per cent of the variance in subject grades, while the effect of teacher and peer motivation accounted only for 2 per cent. Remarkably, 44 per cent of the variance of intrinsic motivation (the key to success at school) is explained by Zsolnai as the social factors of the personality in relation to learning motivation (e.g. self-image, conscientiousness and friendliness).

The Legacy of Discrimination

Why do pupils with low SES have trouble succeeding in school? We might suggest some possible 'culprits' such as low expectations and biases of teachers and fellow pupils, and that this is the experience of many ethnic minority pupils. Nearby *Connect and Extend* features explore the connection between low expectation and educational underachievement but we can also explore the issues through a case study. Imagine that 'Zoe's story' on the next page (reported in a number of UK national newspapers in September 2004) is your story. How well would you have done at school?

What about post-compulsory education and higher education? Only 8 per cent of black British population have university degrees and only 7 per cent of British Pakistanis/Bangladeshis have degrees. Although some ethnic groups were more likely than the white population to have degrees, they were also more likely to have no qualifications at all. In particular British Pakistani and Bangladeshis were most likely to be unqualified. In 2001/2 nearly half (48 per cent) of British Bangladeshi women and 40 per cent of British

Bangladeshi men had no qualifications. Among British Pakistanis, 40 per cent of women and 27 per cent of men had no qualification (Office for National Statistics, 2002), and unemployment rates for ethnic minority groups were up to five times higher than for the white British population.

In school, children from ethnic minorities are chosen less often for gifted classes and acceleration or enrichment programmes. They are more likely to be streamed into 'basic skills' classes. As they progress through secondary school or college their paths take them further and further out of the 'academic pipeline' that produces our scientists, mathematicians and engineers. (If they do persist and become scientists or engineers they, along with women, will still be paid less than white male employees for the same work – TUC, 2002). Why then do many young people from our minority ethnic communities fail at school and not progress to vocational training and higher education? Social psychologists tell us that much of the cause of dis-identification with success at school ('Me and success have nothing common!') is the amount of stereotype threat that youngsters experience who then subsequently fail or drop-out of secondary school.

Stereotype Threat

Stereotype threat, 'is defined as the risk of confirming a negative stereotypic expectation about one's group' (Keller and Dauenheimer, 2003, p. 371). The basic idea, first described by social psychologist Claude Steele and colleagues (1995), is that when individuals are in situations in which a stereotype applies, they bear an extra emotional and cognitive burden. The burden is the possibility of confirming a stereotype of their own group, either in the eyes of others or in their own eyes. Thus, when girls are asked to solve complicated mathematics problems, for example, they are at risk of confirming widely held stereotypes that girls are inferior to boys in mathematics. Psychologists Laurie O'Brien and Christian Crandall (2003) say it is not necessary

ZOE'S STORY

'My smart school still failed me': Zoe reveals the reality of education when your face doesn't fit

'It wasn't exactly racism. No one called me "nigger". But I can't remember anything we did about black history. The only black people we came across were in English Literature and they were slaves. No one taught me about Marcus Garvey. No one said, "You'll do great things"'.

I don't come from a disadvantaged background. Nor do I fit any of the other stereotypes that commentators cite as the reasons for black children under performing. My parents were keen to take an active role in my education. However, in the Eighties mentioning phrases such as "positive racial identity" and the "self-confidence of black children" was not welcomed by the staff at my school.

My mother soon earned a reputation as being "difficult". Talking with my parents now, we laugh about my early experiences. When it came to school plays, Nativity or otherwise, black children were either donkeys or devils. When my sister, who went to the school four years later, got to play a wise man in the Christmas play, it was considered ground breaking by black parents at the school.

At secondary school I remember being made to stand in front of my English Literature class while an irate teacher shouted: "Who do you think you are? You'll never amount to anything!" Those were pretty harsh words for a 13-year-old whose only crime was to forget her dictionary.

At 13, I was preparing to sit exams that would be used to decide which set I would be in for my GCSEs. I was predicted a very low grade for maths. My father, a former maths lecturer, was convinced that I could do much better and subjected me to hours of extra tuition after school. When I received my results, my maths teacher told me I had got the highest mark possible. Yet she looked at me as if I had cheated.

When I was 14, my headmistress recommended to my parents that I repeat the year. Since primary school, I had been a year ahead, but my teachers at my secondary school seemed to think this was a mistake. They believed I wouldn't achieve five GCSE passes. The option of encouraging me to work harder or giving me extra help was never offered. Instead, that role fell to my parents, who were adamant that I was more than capable of passing my exams without repeating the year. With extra tuition from my father and family friends who were teachers, I achieved 10 GCSE passes, all grade A* to C. While I was pleased to have done well, what gave me the greatest satisfaction was proving my teachers wrong.

The general lesson I learned from my school years was that people's expectations of me were going to be zero and that I would have to prove myself and dispel their stereotyped views. Race is a problem in education as much as it is in any other part of life. Unfortunately, because school is an environment where children are subjected to the power of adults, the impact of any prejudice is much more intense.'

(The *Guardian*, 12 September 2004)

that the individual even believes the stereotype. They continue:

'For a person to experience stereotype threat, she or he need only to have knowledge that some people hold a negative stereotype about their group. This knowledge can make a person worried about being viewed stereotypically, even when she or he does not endorse the stereotype.' (p. 782)

What are the results of stereotype threat? Recent research provides answers that should interest all who work with young people. In the short term, the fear that you might confirm a negative stereotype of yourself can induce test anxiety and undermine performance. Jean-Claude Croizet, Gérard Després and a group of colleagues

CONNECT AND EXTEND

One of the main tenets of Claude Steele's stereotype threat is that stereotype threat serves to increase individual anxiety levels, thus hurting performance. This was tested by Jason Osborne and reported in his article 'Linking stereotype threat and anxiety' in *Educational Psychology*, Volume 27, Number 1 (2007), pp. 135–154

at the Université Blaise Pascal, Clermont-Ferrand, tested a group of healthy science and psychology students using computer-mediated exercises of analytical intelligence. It was a widely held view among the students that the science students were more academically able than the students of psychology. (An idea at total variance to our observations over many years!) Half the students were told this was a test of their intellectual ability and the other half that it was a laboratory test *not* diagnostic of their ability. Results of the tests led Croizet et al. (2004) to observe:

'Evidence is accumulating that stereotypic reputations of intellectual inferiority, which usually target ethnic group members and people from lower social classes, can undermine performance on intellectual testing beyond any actual differences in cognitive ability.' (p. 721)

All groups, not just minority-group pupils, can be susceptible to stereotype threat. The work of Croizet and his colleagues draws heavily upon studies by other psychologists, particularly Joshua Aronson. In one study by Aronson the subjects were white male university students who were very strong in mathematics. One group was told that the test they were taking would help experimenters determine why Asian students performed so much better than white students on that particular test. Another group just took the test. The group that faced the stereotype threat of confirming that 'Asians are better in maths' scored significantly lower on the test (Aronson et al., 1999).

Long-term Effects: Dis-identification

Pupils often develop self-defeating strategies to protect their self-esteem. They withdraw, claim not to care, exert little effort, or even drop out of school. They psychologically disengage from success in the context and claim 'maths is for nerds' or 'school is for losers'. Once pupils define academic attainment as 'uncool' it is unlikely they will exert the effort needed for real learning. There is some evidence that black male pupils are more likely than black female pupils and white pupils to *dis-identify* with academic attainment – that is, to separate their sense of self-esteem from their academic achievement (Cokley, 2002). However, other studies have questioned any straightforward connection between dis-identification and British ethnic communities.

For example, psychology professor Paul Singh Ghuman (2002) makes it quite clear that South Asian young people in the UK (with the exception of Bangladeshis) are achieving as well as their white counterparts. Indeed, the rate of entry (particularly among girls) to universities is higher than that of whites. However, what emerges from his analysis is that there remain two main areas for concern; namely, the teaching of the mother tongue within the school curriculum and the entrenched negative attitudes (prejudice) of some teachers against South Asians.

A backward glance at the 'leader board' provided in Figure 10.3 will show that Chinese girls and pupils from other far eastern cultures such as Japan do very well in the British school system. There are a number of 'Japanese Schools' in British and other European education systems (Sato, 2007) that provide a culturally specific style of teaching which expects all children in the school to achieve very high standards. The Japanese education culture transfers well into many European settings and children from Japanese families do very well in mainstream state secondary schools (McPake and Powney, 1998). Why is this?

Improving the School Experience of Adolescents

As previously argued, many teenagers do very well at school; schooling for many is part of a successful, well-managed and thoroughly enjoyable adolescence that provides its own rewards as well as leading to all the educational, employment, leisure and relationship opportunities of young adulthood. Many teenagers cope well with the additional pressures of public examinations, homework, course choices, complex social interactions with many different groups of peers and many (very) different teachers and teaching styles. Successful

CULTURAL FOCUS

Japanese High Schools and Colleges

Japan has been a frequent focus of international educational comparisons for British policy makers in recent decades, partly because Japan is a major economic competitor to Britain and partly because Japan is often at or near the top in international comparisons of academic achievement. Especially in maths and science, Japanese children and adolescents consistently outperform young Britons, and the gap grows larger with age from childhood through adolescence (National Center for Education Statistics, 2005). Furthermore, 98 per cent of Japanese adolescents finish secondary school, a percentage higher than in any Western country, and levels of university attendance and graduation are similar to levels in Britain and Germany (Yoshimoto et al., 2007; Stevenson and Zusho, 2002).

What are the characteristics of the Japanese educational system with regard to adolescents and emerging adults? One notable feature of the Japanese system is the length of the school year. Japanese adolescents attend their high schools for 243 days a year, more than British adolescents (typically about 190 days), or adolescents in any Western European country. Japanese secondary education is also notable for how seamlessly the parts of the curriculum fit together. Japanese adolescents at 14 or 16 have fewer courses to choose from than British pupils (Okada, 2002; Mason et al., 2000; Schumer, 1999), and a more structured ordering of courses from one level to the next. The curriculum and the textbooks for each course are chosen on a national basis by the Ministry of Education, so that all Japanese pupils in a particular grade are learning the same things at the same time (Stevenson and Zusho, 2002). The curriculums are connected. For example, in maths courses, pupils who have completed Maths I have learned what they will need to know at the beginning of Maths II. As a result, Japanese teachers spend much less time than British teachers reviewing material from previous levels before presenting fresh material for the current level. In the past, Japanese high schools focused almost exclusively on rote learning and memorisation, with little time or encouragement for critical thinking.

Cultural beliefs are also important to the practices of Japanese schools. Teachers, adolescents and parents believe that all children are capable of learning the material that teachers present (Stevenson and Zusho, *ibid.*). The Japanese (as well as people in other Asian countries) generally believe that success or failure in school depends on effort, in contrast to the belief that ability is what matters most. When pupils do poorly in school, these beliefs result in intense socialisation pressure to try harder, pressure that comes from teachers, parents, peers and the struggling pupils themselves.

The major underlying source of pressure on Japanese adolescents was the national system of entrance exams to secondary school and university, which the anthropologist Thomas Rohlen (1983), in his classic ethnography of Japanese high schools, called Japan's 'national obsession'. These two exams essentially determined young people's occupational fate for the rest of their lives because in Japanese society obtaining a job is based primarily on the status of the schools a person has attended.

To prepare for the entrance exams the majority of Japanese pupils not only apply themselves seriously at school and in their homework, but also from middle childhood through adolescence they attend 'cram schools' after school or receive instruction from private tutors (Takahashi and Takeuchi, 2007). This system goes a long way towards explaining the high level of performance of Japanese children and adolescents. They work intensely on their schoolwork because the stakes are so high, much higher than in Britain where both the higher education system and the job market are much more open and much less about people's occupational future is determined by the time they leave secondary school.

Is there a cost for the high performance of Japanese adolescents? Surprisingly, most evidence indicates that the intense academic pressure does not make Japanese children and adolescents any more unhappy or psychologically disturbed. Japanese adolescents do not show higher rates of stress, depression or psychosomatic ailments than British adolescents, and rates of suicide are lower for Japanese than for British adolescents (Taylor, 2003).

Nevertheless, many Japanese view the exam system as a problem for young people. There is a constant debate in Japanese society about the exam system, with many people objecting that it places too much pressure on young people and takes virtually all the fun out of childhood. With longer school days, a longer school year, cram schools and private tutors, Japanese adolescents have far less time for after-school leisure and informal socialising with friends than British adolescents do and this can cause problems (Nishizono-Maher et al., 2004). Reforms in the 1990s reduced the length of the school day and cut the number of school days per week from six to five, but the average school day remains long and cram schools continue to be the norm (Takahashi and Takeuchi, 2007). Also, because Japan has one of the lowest birth rates in the world (1.2 children per woman), competition for places at university is steadily decreasing as the number of 18-year-olds in the population decreases, although it is still intense with respect to the top universities (Fackler, 2007).

It should be noted that Japanese society is in the process of dramatic change, and the schools are changing as part of this process (Takahashi and Takeuchi, 2006; French, 2002; Matsumoto, 2002). Nearly two decades of economic stagnation have led many Japanese to begin to doubt whether their educational system is well suited to today's economy. Critics hold up the British system in favourable contrast for encouraging independent and creative thinking, particularly in science and technology (Taniguchi, 2006), even though the British system is less successful than the Japanese system at teaching facts. Globalisation has made Japan more individualistic than in the past, and pupils in Japanese classrooms are no longer as orderly and obedient as they once were. The prospect of a lifelong job with a stable, well-paying company is not as certain as it was in the days when the Japanese economy was booming. Nor is that prospect as attractive to today's more individualistic adolescents and young adults. Nevertheless, Japanese adolescents continue to be near the top of international rankings of academic performance, indicating that the educational system is one of the chief assets of Japanese society (Motani, 2005; Fuwa, 2001).

In Japan, pressure for academic achievement is much greater in secondary school than in university.

adolescents are resilient to social pressures, cultural pressures, temporary periods of isolation, failure or confusion, and this success is not culturally situated. Successful adolescents have secure attachments to a number of key people in their lives and, despite challenging the authority of influential adults, are able to form different 'adult' relationships with others including parents, teachers and other carers.

Although differences can be observed among different groups of young people (remember Figure 10.2), ethnicity and gender are not the key ideas here. What we have demonstrated is that it is young people from low SES families and communities who are far less likely to succeed at secondary school despite making good progress and achieving well at primary school. Let's explore this important idea.

Holding Children in Mind over Time

In 2006, James Wetz – former British secondary head teacher and now policy researcher – published a regional report, *Holding Children in Mind over Time*. The report was based on a study of the 10 per cent of young people leaving secondary school in the City of Bristol (UK) in 2005 without any GCSE qualifications. These young people had become disengaged from and disaffected with their secondary schooling – many had demonstrated disruptive or violent behaviour and had been permanently excluded from at least one school. The report suggested that

'a significant number of the disaffected young might well be those who have lacked affection and are acting out a remembered hurt of separation, loss, neglect, abuse, or less than secure attachment, which schools as they are currently designed and organised have neither the expertise or resource to recognise and attend to.' (p. 1)

Wetz suggested that some young people disengage from school out of boredom, refusing to 'play the school game' that they find increasingly dull or irrelevant. Or worse, that school makes them feel inadequate and a failure by giving little opportunity for developing a resilient self-image. For some youngsters, their disruptive behaviour may also be a reflection of disrupted lives over which they have little control. For others, a rejection of what secondary schools offer may be their own route to adulthood outside of the school setting and demonstrates not a lack of resilience but a strong need to practise self-determination.

Whether the issues are caused by disaffection, disengagement or determination, this Bristol research highlighted a particular concern: 40 per cent of those who left Bristol's state-funded secondary schools without a single GCSE qualification had achieved expected or above expected results in English, mathematics or science at primary school. At 11 years, these pupils might reasonably have expected to look forward to achieving at least five good GCSE qualifications, to securing places in post-16 courses and gaining access to further or higher education. However, five years or less after achieving at least the expected results, they left with nothing.

Holding Children in Mind over Time also revealed that those who left the school system with no GCSE qualifications were young people who had to manage complex, emotional and social changes in their lives. For example, many had:

- experienced periods of isolation at home and at school;

- undergone myriad changes in family and school settings between the ages of 5 and 16;

- experienced significant early loss and separation, particularly from absent fathers; and/or

- felt that the reliability of personal attachments, care, safety and consistency which they had enjoyed at primary school were not available to them at secondary school.

As a result, many adolescents had effectively excluded themselves from learning in school before they had reached the age of 14. Wetz argues that those who arrive at secondary school needing the most enrichment of their learning experience and the best of adult advocacy – arguably what they have received in primary schooling – routinely leave secondary schooling having received the least enrichment and the most inadequate of adult advocacy. Furthermore, Wetz concludes that there is a compelling case for reconsidering the organisation and particularly the size of British secondary schools so that these less resilient young people can stay safe, enjoy good mental health, achieve qualifications and take delight in their own learning.

Before looking at how practitioners and parents can help and support adolescents through their secondary schooling and looking at the evidence of what makes for effective schooling for young people we need to explore some of the areas of potential difficulty that young people can experience. Let's start with the transition from primary schooling to secondary schooling. Considerable evidence suggests that the reason for difficulties with school transitions from primary to secondary schooling in early adolescence lay not so much in the timing of the transition as in the nature of adolescents' school experiences in many secondary schools (Barber and Olsen,

CONNECT AND EXTEND

It's not just school size. What about class size? For a study of class size research and classroom processes that might mediate class size effects on pupils' learning, read 'Are small classes better? Understanding relationships between class size, classroom processes and pupils' learning' by David Pedder in *Oxford Review of Education*, Volume 32, Number 2 (2006), pp. 213–234

2004). Jacquelynne Eccles, a researcher who has conducted several studies on early adolescents' school experiences, attributes the difficulties of these transitions to the fact that many adolescents find the environment of secondary schools alienating and oppressive (Eccles and Roeser, 2003; Eccles et al., 1997). Compared with primary schools, secondary schools tend to have less consistent individual contact between pupils and teachers and less opportunity for close relationships with teachers, in part because pupils are taught by many teachers rather than just one or two. Also, there is a greater emphasis on teacher control. According to Eccles and her colleagues, this increased emphasis on control is especially mismatched with early adolescents' increased abilities and desires for autonomy, and consequently undermines their motivation and self-esteem.

Eccles and Roeser (*ibid.*) also argue that early adolescents' difficulties with school transitions are due to secondary teachers' beliefs about adolescents. Eccles and her colleagues found that secondary teachers are considerably more negative in their views of adolescents. They are less likely to trust their pupils and more likely to see adolescents as inherently troublesome and unruly. When compared with primary school teachers, secondary teachers report less confidence in their understanding of the development and psychologies of young people, perhaps because the majority of them have not had any specialised training on adolescence – something this text attempts to provide for all those, including teachers, who work with young people.

A number of researchers now report that for the last decade secondary teacher training in England is pretty much limited to preparation for the examination of professional classroom competencies and the packaging of subject knowledge (Beck, 2009; Poulou, 2005; Hamilton, 2002; Hockly, 2000) rather than understanding the cognitive, social, emotional and developmental needs of adolescents and young adults. This trend towards professional competence models is also noted by commentators in other European countries (Karila et al., 2005; Kárpáti, 2004; Kirschner et al., 1997;) and in other professional contexts, for example social work (Gregory and Holloway, 2005). If the findings of researchers and commentators, including Jacquelynne Eccles that we discussed earlier, are widely true of British secondary schools and teachers, it could go a long way towards explaining the difficulties adolescents have with school transitions from primary to secondary schooling in early adolescence. What are the difficulties and who most experiences difficulty with the timing of and outcome transitions to secondary schooling at the start of adolescence?

Some commentators think that school transfer acts like a prism, diffracting – breaking up into different bands – children's social and learning trajectories. To explain – it is thought that primary schooling is more likely to converge pupils' achievement and social experience, whereas the diffraction that occurs as a result of moving to the secondary style of schooling exaggerates the differences in social, economic and educational experience and achievement. Let's look at some examples from the research literature. Andrew Noyes of the University of Nottingham (2006) explored two case studies of children moving from primary to secondary school. Noyes' analysis explained that the economically and culturally more well-endowed pupils make the most of moving school, a finding borne out more recently by researchers at the University of Bristol (Burgess et al., 2008), who examined the transitions from primary to secondary school for a cohort of children moving between state schools in England. The researchers used data on over 12,000 primary schools, over 2000 secondary schools and around 400,000 pupils. The results suggest that the experiences of poor pupils at age 11 and at transfer to secondary schools were quite different, on average, to their non-poor peers. Poor pupils tended to find themselves more concentrated within lower-performing secondary schools. The Bristol large-scale research also found that pupils from low SES families were much less able to deal well with the challenge of changes to the style of schooling (Lucey and Reay, 2002). This finding has also been observed in other European countries (Pietsch and Stubbe, 2007).

What about children of different abilities, specifically the experiences of young people with special educational needs prior to and following moves from primary to secondary school? Pam Maras and Emma-Louise Aveling of the University of Greenwich, London (2006) used interviews to focus on the transition process. Findings suggested that schools differed in the quality and efficacy of the support systems they provided. Some difficulties arise because of the more exacting academic and environmental demands of secondary schools, particularly in relation to the difficulties commonly faced by children with **attention deficit-hyperactivity disorder** (ADHD) – Chapter 3 – during the transition from primary to secondary school (Thompson et al., 2003). What did appear to be beneficial was continuity of support throughout the transition to a new school, and the provision of a dedicated space within the school, such as a special needs or behavioural unit. Several of the young people adapted easily alongside their peers without special educational needs, while others required more structured support based on effective communication between support services, the young person and their parents.

CONNECT AND EXTEND

Read a technical paper about prevalence and diagnosis of ADHD. 'How often are German children and adolescents diagnosed with ADHD? Prevalence based on the judgment of health care professionals: results of the German health and examination survey (KiGGS)' by Michael Huss, Heike Hölling, Bärbel-Maria Kurth and Robert Schlack in *European Child & Adolescent Psychiatry*, Volume 17, Supplement 1 (December 2008), pp. 52–58

CONNECT AND EXTEND

A longitudinal study was conducted to follow children, in a city in Scotland, to understand their experiences of primary–secondary transition. Read 'A holistic approach to primary–secondary transitions' by D. Jindal-Snape and J. Foggie in *Improving Schools*, Volume 11, Number 1 (March 2008), pp. 5–18

Finally in this section it should be noted that the transition from primary to secondary school can be a period of anxiety for many young people. Although many schools have developed processes and systems to ease this process, it has been argued that the emphasis is often on administrative and organisational procedures (Jindal-Snape and Miller, 2010). In contrast it can be argued that young adolescents and parents are typically more concerned with personal and social issues and it may be that such concerns have received insufficient attention in the past. Dr Divya Jindal-Snape and colleagues at the University of Dundee (2008) argue that for some children at least, transition should be considered a particular challenge because of the range of experiences within a concentrated period of time. Jindal-Snape is among others who continue to argue that in order to help vulnerable individuals cope with, and even benefit from, the period of transition, we need to focus more on their social and personal experiences and less on the passing on of school records or curriculum continuity.

School Climate

Although many studies indicate that school size and the timing and handling of school transitions can be important influences on adolescents' school experience, most researchers and commentators agree that these factors are important only insofar as they influence the kinds of interactions that pupils and pupils, and pupils and teachers, have in the classroom and around the school. **School climate** is the term for the quality of these interactions (Way et al., 2007; Brand et al., 2003) and specifically for the sort of expectations and standards schools have for pupils, and what kinds of teaching methods are used in classrooms.

The term *school climate* was coined by Michael Rutter (Rutter et al., 1983; 1979), a British psychiatrist who did extensive research on adolescents and schools. Rutter and his colleagues studied several thousand young adolescents in British secondary schools. Their study included observations in the classrooms as well as pupils' attendance records, achievement test scores, and self-reports of participation in delinquent behaviour.

The results indicated that the most important differences among the schools were related to school climate. Pupils were better off in schools where teachers tended to be supportive and involved with pupils but also applied firm discipline when necessary and held high expectations for pupils' conduct and academic performance. Specifically, pupils in schools with this kind of school climate had higher attendance and achievement test scores and lower rates of delinquency compared with pupils in the schools where the school climate was not as favourable.

This was true even after taking into account statistically the differences in the pupils' IQ and socio-economic background. So, it was not simply that the pupils in the better schools also came from more advantaged backgrounds. The schools themselves made a substantial difference in pupils' performance, based on differences in school climate.

CONNECT AND EXTEND

This paper argues that religious fundamentalism, as well as state terrorism, needs to be addressed in schools. It explores identity formation and radicalisation; religious belief, faith schools and the myth of equal value; justice, revenge and honour; and free speech, humour and satire. Read 'Educating against extremism: towards a critical politicisation of young people' by Lynn Davies in the *International Review of Education/ Internationale Zeitschrift für Erziehungswissenschaft/ Revue internationale l'éducation*, Volume 55, Numbers 2–3 (May 2009), pp. 183–203

School climate is an important indicator of adolescents' school experiences.

for behaviour and a moderate level of control seems to work as well in the classroom as it does in the home (see the section Parenting styles in Chapter 7 and refer to Zedd et al., 2002). However, as with parenting, the practices that take place in schools are often rooted in a particular set of cultural or religious beliefs. Researchers have concluded that one of the key reasons for the success of faith schools is that a common set of religious beliefs was held by parents, teachers and pupils (Worsley, 2008; Colson, 2004). These beliefs included respect for authority (including teachers), consideration for and cooperation with others, and the importance of striving to make the most of one's abilities. Schools did not have to introduce these beliefs to pupils and persuade them to accept them. The religious beliefs and cultural norms were taught to the children from an early age, at home and in church, and school simply reinforced the values and attitudes shaped in those settings (Flint, 2007; Moti Gokulsing, 2006).

More recent research has confirmed and expanded the findings of the Rutter studies, showing that a favourable school climate is related to lower levels of depression and behaviour problems (Loukas and Robinson, 2004) as well as higher levels of motivation and participation (Anderson et al., 2004). One study of over 100,000 pupils in over 100 middle schools found that school climate was favourably related to academic, behavioural and socio-emotional outcomes (Brand et al., 2003).

THINKING CRITICALLY

Imagine that you have just become the principal of a secondary school. What could you do to assess the school climate in your school? How would you go about improving it if it were less than satisfactory?

We can conclude from these studies that successful teaching looks a lot like successful parenting in that both combine demandingness and responsiveness. A combination of warmth, clear communication, high standards

ENGAGEMENT AND ACHIEVEMENT IN SECONDARY SCHOOL: BEYOND THE CLASSROOM

The studies by Rutter and others show that a favourable school climate succeeds in promoting adolescents' engagement while they are in school. **Engagement** is the quality of being psychologically committed to learning (Guthrie, 2008; Sirin and Rogers-Sirin, 2005). It means being alert and attentive in the classroom, and approaching educational tasks and assignments with the aim of deeply learning and understanding the material, not just scraping by with minimal effort.

Unfortunately, engagement is the exception rather than the norm in the school experience of many adolescents. Research indicates that a remarkably high proportion of adolescents not only fall short of an ideal

RESEARCH FOCUS

Two Approaches to Research on Adolescents' School Experiences

Two of the most important studies of adolescents' school experiences published in the past 20 years provide a striking contrast in research methods. The American study by Laurence Steinberg (1996) is a classic of quantitative, questionnaire-focused research. Consider some of the features of this study:

- 20,000 pupils participated in the study.

- The pupils were from nine different schools in urban, rural and suburban communities.

- Forty per cent of the sample was from ethnic minority groups.

- Data were collected from the adolescents each year for four years, so that patterns of change over time could be investigated.

- Before the collection of any data, planning and **pilot testing** of the measures – the methods used to find data – took two years.

- Questionnaire measures were included on adolescents' academic attitudes and beliefs, academic performance, psychological functioning and problem behaviour, among other topics. Questionnaires were also included on adolescents' views of their parents' parenting practices, on their views of their peers' attitudes and behaviour with regard to education and other areas, and on adolescents' work and leisure attitudes and behaviour.

The study has yielded an enormous amount of useful and interesting information on school engagement, academic performance, and many other topics, summarised in a book by Steinberg (1996) and in numerous articles in academic journals. We cite the book and the articles often in this chapter.

In contrast, Niobe Way (1998) interviewed 24 adolescents of various ethnic backgrounds at one city school over a three-year period. Although her study was much smaller in scale than the Steinberg study, she got to know the adolescents and their school extremely well. Her interviews yielded many insights into their experiences in school and the intersection between school and the rest of their lives. For example, take this comment from Chantel:

'I was coming to school for a while and doing no work. I just sat there and was like I didn't want to deal with nothing. When I was having problems with my father, and then I had broke up with my boyfriend. . . . I just didn't care any more.' (p. 192)

Or this comment from Sonia:

'It gets boring sometimes. . . . I fall asleep sometimes. . . . I was working every night 'til 10 o'clock [at a local chemist]. So I would come home so tired that I wouldn't even think about homework.' (p. 195)

In addition, Way's (1998) own **ethnographic** experience within the school gave her vivid and disturbing insights into the quality of education the adolescents received:

'During my time working and conducting research at this school, I have repeatedly seen teachers spend entire [lessons] having their pupils fill out worksheets rather than actively engaging with them about class materials. I have heard about and seen teachers arrive fifteen or twenty minutes late to their fifty-minute classes. . . . I have watched teachers reading a book or a newspaper during class while the pupils slept, threw notes, or chatted among themselves. I have heard pupils and teachers yelling at each other, calling one another 'animals,' 'fat slob,' 'slut,' or 'bitch' in the classroom or in the stairwells. . . . I have witnessed some teachers – especially the new ones – put tremendous efforts into trying to create cohesive and supportive environments for their colleagues and pupils only to be met with hostile and resentful responses from the school [managers], teaching staff, and the pupils themselves' (pp. 201–202).

Steinberg's information is of the kind that can only be obtained with a large-scale study; Way's insights can be obtained only through the kind of qualitative, ethnographic research she conducts. Both kinds of research are valuable, and the combination is essential to attempt to build a more complete understanding of adolescent development.

of engagement, but are strikingly disengaged during their time in school, 'physically present but psychologically absent' (Steinberg, 1996, p. 67). In a landmark and historic study of secondary schools by Steinberg and colleagues (Steinberg, 1996; see the *Focus on Research* feature), more than one-third of the pupils in the study indicated that they rarely try hard, and a similar proportion indicated that they rarely pay attention in class. Over two-thirds admitted they had cheated on a test at least once in the past year, and *nine out of ten* said they had copied someone else's homework within the past year.

It seems clear that school climate makes a difference. A favourable school climate enhances pupils' engagement, which in turn results in higher levels of achievement (Zedd et al., 2002). The structure of the classroom environment matters, too, with pupils more engaged when they are working on individual or group tasks rather than listening to a teacher or watching a video (Shernoff and Csikszentmihalyi, 2003). Nevertheless, there is substantial evidence that the main problems with secondary education lie 'beyond the classroom' (Luthar and Ansary, 2005), in the family environments, peer relations, work and leisure patterns, and cultural beliefs experienced by, and adopted or rejected by adolescents. The following sections address each of these in turn.

Family Environments and School

We saw in Chapter 7 that parenting styles are related to a variety of important aspects of adolescent development. Parenting affects not only the quality of the

relationship between parents and adolescents but also a variety of other aspects of adolescents' lives, including their attitudes towards and performance in school.

THINKING CRITICALLY

Think back to some of the research cited in this text and highlighted in the *Connect and Extend* feature. Can you identify another large-scale, largely quantitative survey on a similar scale to Steinberg's? Contrast that with a smaller-scale qualitative ethnographic study like that of Niobe Way. Is all ethnographic research necessarily small scale? What are some of the problems with questionnaire-based approaches?

One way parents influence adolescents' academic performance is through their expectations for achievement. Adolescents whose parents expect them to do well tend to live up to those expectations, as reflected in their achievements in secondary school; adolescents whose parents have lower expectations for their school performance tend to perform less well (Juang and Silbereisen, 2002; Schneider and Stevenson, 1999). Parents who have high expectations also tend to be more involved in their adolescents' education, assisting with exam options, attending school open days and parents' evenings, and keeping abreast of their adolescents' performance. This involvement contributes to adolescents' school success (Abd-El-Fattah, 2006; Driessen et al., 2005; Catsambis, 2001).

CONNECT AND EXTEND

To examine the relationship between dislike of school, teenage pregnancy and educational disengagement read '"I hated everything about school": an examination of the relationship between dislike of school, teenage pregnancy and educational disengagement' by Alison C. S. Hosie in *Social Policy and Society*, Volume 6, Number 3 (July 2007), pp. 333–347

However, it is useful to keep in mind the possibility of passive genotype – environment interactions here. That is, it is likely to be true that parents with higher intellectual abilities not only have high expectations for their adolescents' education but also provide their children with a genetic contribution to higher intelligence and high academic performance. Studies on parents' expectations in relation to adolescents' academic performance generally do not control for this possibility.

Parents' involvement in their adolescents' education tends to reflect their overall parenting style (Juang and Silbereisen, 2002). For school as for other areas, authoritative parenting has the most favourable associations with adolescents' development. Adolescents whose parents combine high demandingness with high responsiveness have the highest levels of engagement in school and the highest levels of school success (Shek and Lee, 2007). Authoritative parents contribute to adolescents' school success directly by being more involved than other parents in their adolescents' education (Shek, 2005). Such parents also have a variety of favourable indirect effects on their adolescents' school performance. Adolescents with authoritative parents are more likely than other adolescents to develop personal qualities such as self-reliance, persistence and responsibility, which in turn lead to favourable school performance (Steinberg, 1996).

Adolescents with authoritarian, permissive or neglectful parents all tend to perform worse in school than adolescents with authoritative parents (Ang and Goh, 2006; Kaufmann et al., 2000). Adolescents' academic achievement tends to be worst when they have neglectful parents – low levels of both demandingness and responsiveness (Eastin et al., 2006). These are adolescents whose parents know little about how they are doing in school and who also know little or nothing about how the adolescent's time is spent outside of school. Adolescents with such parents have the lowest estimation of their abilities, the weakest engagement to school, and the poorest academic achievement (Hoeve et al., 2008; McGinn et al., 2005).

Of course, here as with other parenting research, the direction of effects is not clear and the results should be interpreted carefully. It could be that authoritative parenting helps adolescents do well in school, or it could be that adolescents who do well in school are easier to parent with an admirable combination of demandingness and responsiveness. Nevertheless, research similar to and including that which we cited earlier shows some disturbing findings regarding parents' involvement in their adolescents' education.

However, other studies have shown that schools can design effective programmes to increase parents' involvement in their adolescents' education (Hallam et al., 2006; Blanksby, 1999), particularly in the area of special educational needs (Stroggilos and Xanthacou, 2006; Lingard, 2001) and school dropout (Graeff-Martins et al., 2006). When parents become or stay engaged, their adolescents' engagement and academic achievement tend to improve. The development of these programmes in secondary schools is especially important in the light of studies showing that, in general, parents tend to be less involved in their adolescents' education than they were when their children were younger (Gonzalez-DeHass et al., 2005; Holden, 2004; Brain and Reid, 2003).

Family Social Class and School

We have already identified that one particular aspect of adolescents' families which has been found to be strongly related to academic achievement is the family's social class or socio-economic status (SES). Numerous studies have found a positive association between family SES and adolescents' examination grades, as well as between family SES and the highest level of education that adolescents or emerging adults ultimately attain (Kelly, 2004; Zedd et al., 2002). These SES differences appear long before adolescence. Even before entering school, children from families with middle SES score higher than children from low SES families on tests of basic academic

CONNECT AND EXTEND

Schools are still falling some way short of providing parents with the kind of information they need to be able to participate actively in their children's education. Read 'The right to know: parents, school reports and parents' evenings' by Sally Power and Alison Clark in *Research Papers in Education*, Volume 15, Number 1 (2000), pp. 25–48

skills. By middle childhood, these class differences are clearly established, and class differences in academic achievement remain strong through secondary school (Kelly, 2004). Young adults from middle SES families are also more likely than young adults from low SES families to attend university following secondary school (Titus, 2006).

What makes social and economic status so important in predicting academic achievement? Social and economic status represents many other family characteristics that contribute to achievement. Parents from middle SES backgrounds tend to have higher IQs than those from low SES backgrounds and they pass this advantage on to their children through both genes and the early learning environment they create; in turn, IQ is related to academic achievement (see Chapter 3). Children from middle SES families also tend to receive better nutrition and health care than low SES children, beginning prenatally and continuing through adolescence; for children from low SES families, health problems may interfere with their ability to perform academically (Davies et al., 2008; Steptoe and Feldman, 2001). Low SES families tend to be subject to more stresses than middle SES families, with respect to major stresses such as family violence (Thompson and Massat, 2005) as well as day-to-day minor stresses such as the car breaking down, and these stresses are negatively related to adolescents' school performance (Rogers et al., 2009). One recent longitudinal study of adolescents found that across ethnic groups, family stressors predicted academic problems (Flook and Fuligni, 2008).

Remember that parents' parenting behaviour also varies by social class in ways that are related to adolescents' academic achievement. However, social classes are large categories, and substantial variability exists within each social class. In the low SES as well as the middle SES, adolescents' academic performance benefits from authoritative parents and from parents who are involved in their education and have high expectations for their academic achievement (Annunziata et al., 2006).

Peers, Friends and School

'You'd be stoned in class and sit back and make a fool of yourself and everybody would laugh and you'd be considered fun. Like you'd be entertaining everyone. And if you didn't get caught, you were cool.'
– Annie, age 17 (in Bell, 1998, p. 76)

'OMG! I can relate to this too much! I love the feeling of being popular among my peers and I like the attention.'
– Nadine, age 15 (Hughes, unpublished data)

'It's stupid skipping school. Why do it? You are only putting your career on the line. At school, people try and be cool and hard, so they may bunk off school because they have an exam or have to hand in homework. Why?'
– Sam, age 16 (Hughes, unpublished data)

Although the influence of friends tends to be strongest in relatively less important areas such as dress, hairstyle and music (see Chapter 8), school is one important area in which the influence of friends is in some respects greater than the influence of parents. Several studies have found that in secondary school, friends' influence is greater than the influence of parenting practices in a variety of school-related ways: how consistently adolescents attend school, how much time they spend on homework, how hard they try in school, and the exam grades they achieve (Ryan, 2001; Woodward and Fergusson, 2000).

Of course, as we have seen in Chapter 8, the influence of peers is not necessarily negative and may in fact be quite positive. Adolescent friends with high educational achievements and aspirations tend to give each other support and encouragement for doing well in school (Van Ryzin et al., 2009; Holfve-Sabel, 2006; Stake and Nickens, 2005). This is true even taking into account selective association (the fact that adolescents tend to choose friends who are similar to themselves). When low-achieving adolescents have high-achieving friends, over time the high achievers

CONNECT AND EXTEND

'Widening access to further and higher education does not reach those most in need. This is nowhere more true than in the case of people who have spent all or part of their childhood in the care of local authorities, and who appear to be the most excluded category of all'. Is this a case of low academic self-

concept? Read more in 'Academic underachievement and exclusion of people who have been looked after in local authority care' by James Mallon in *Research in Post-compulsory Education*, Volume 10, Number 1 (2005), pp. 83–104

tend to have a positive influence, so that the low achievers' grades improve (Zedd et al., 2002). Low-achieving adolescents with high-achieving friends are also more likely to plan to attend university, compared with low achievers whose friends are not high achievers (Brusling and Pepin, 2003).

However, the influence of having high-achieving *friends* appears to be different from the influence of being in a school of high-achieving *peers*. (Remember the distinction made in Chapter 8 between friends and peers.) Adolescents in schools where their peers have lower average levels of school achievement tend to have better academic self-concepts and higher expectations for academic attainment than adolescents surrounded by high-achieving classmates (Zedd et al., 2002). Social psychologists (and many others in everyday life!) call this the 'big fish in a little pond effect' (Marsh and Hau, 2003). Adolescents naturally compare themselves to their classmates. If classmates mostly seem to be doing fairly or poorly in their schoolwork, the slightly above-average adolescent is likely to feel pretty good about how school is going – like a 'big fish', in other words. However, in a school of high achievers, the same adolescent may well feel inferior to others in academic abilities and prospects. One study of over 100,000 adolescents in 26 countries found that the 'big fish' effect existed in all 26 countries: adolescents in less selective schools had a significantly higher academic self-concept than adolescents in more selective schools (Marsh and Hau, *ibid.*).

Studies suggest other reasons for concern about the influence of friends and peers on adolescents' school performance. By the time they reach the middle years, many adolescents become concerned with concealing their high achievement from their peers. For example, in one early study 13-year-old pupils indicated that they wanted their teachers to know that they worked hard in school – but not their peers, because they feared that their peers would disapprove (Juvonen and Murdock, 1995). Also, adolescents who are more concerned than

other adolescents about what their friends think of them tend to perform worse in school (Boehnke, 2008)

In school as in other areas, the influences of parents and peers are often intertwined. On the one hand, parents influence adolescents' choices of friends, which can in turn influence school performance, beliefs and attitudes (Castrucci et al., 2002). On the other hand, having friends who denigrate school tends to be related to lower school success, even for adolescents with authoritative parents (Vitaro et al., 2001).

Work, Leisure and School

Part-time work in high school (which we look at in the next chapter) tends to be damaging to school performance in a variety of ways, especially for adolescents who work more than ten hours per week (Dustmann and Soest, 2007). Beyond ten hours a week the more adolescents work, the lower their grades, the less time they spend on homework, the more they 'bunk off' school, the more they cheat on their schoolwork, the less committed they are to school, and the lower their educational aspirations (Marsh and Kleitman, 2005). Of course, some degree of self-selection is involved here – pupils may decide to work more because they do not care about school (Zierold et al., 2005). Nevertheless, evidence indicates that working more than 10 hours a week has effects beyond self-selection. In Steinberg's (1996) study, one-third of adolescents said they took easier courses because of their jobs, and the same proportion said they were frequently too tired from their jobs to do their homework. In the course of the three-year study, pupils who increased the number of hours they worked also reported declines in school commitment, whereas those who decreased the number of hours they worked reported increased school commitment.

Abundant leisure also interferes with adolescents' attention to school and schoolwork. Steinberg (1996)

British adolescents from South Korean, Chinese, Indian and Japanese heritages tend to have high levels of academic achievement.

the highest levels of academic achievement of any ethnic group, including whites (Qin et al., 2008; Department for Education and Skills, 2006) in part because they spend less time on part-time employment, less time on socialising, and more non-school time on homework.

Cultural Beliefs and School

The practices of schools and the attitudes of parents, peers and adolescents themselves towards school are ultimately rooted in cultural beliefs about what is valuable and important (Wu, 2006; Wubbels et al., 2006). Although some policy makers and commentators do a lot of public hand wringing about the state of the British educational system, the truth is that education – at least at the secondary school level – is not as highly valued by some British parents as it is by people of many other industrialised countries (Attwood and Croll, 2006; Vulliamy and Webb, 2003). Of course, parents would like to see their adolescents perform better in international comparisons with adolescents from other countries – the sort of league tables presented in the media – but would most parents support a law restricting employment for persons under age 18 to no more than ten hours a week? Would parents support restricting participation in gymnastic and swimming clubs to a similar time commitment, no more than ten hours a week? Would parents of British adolescents be pleased if secondary school teachers began assigning homework that routinely required three or four hours per day after school and began handing out failing report grades and comments to adolescents who did not measure up to an inappropriately high and inflexible standard of performance?

found that socialising with friends was adolescents' most common daily activity. Adolescents reported socialising – activities such as 'hanging out with friends' and 'partying' – an average of 20 to 25 hours per week, more than the average time they worked and more than the amount of time they spent in school. In turn, amount of time spent socialising was negatively associated with performance in school (Fischer and Barkley, 2006). However, it should be noted that adolescents who participate in extra-curricular activities (such as sports and music) have better academic performance and are less likely to drop-out of secondary school (Zedd et al., 2002). So unstructured socialising is negatively related to academic performance, but structured leisure in extra-curricular activities appears to have positive effects.

For both work and leisure, the ethnic comparisons are striking, especially with respect to those from Chinese, Japanese, Indian and south-east Asian minority ethnic cultures. According to Steinberg (1996), adolescents from these Asian cultures are less likely than other adolescents to have a part-time job and less likely to work 20 or more hours per week if they are employed. On average, Asian youngsters spend only half as much time socialising, compared with adolescents in other ethnic groups. Asians have

THINKING CRITICALLY

A parent once accused me (MH) of expecting too much of her son. 'Not everybody can be brilliant and he needs the space and time to grow up happy,' she asserted. If we have universally high expectations of all our pupils, many parents would have to change their beliefs about what should be required of adolescents. Do you think more should be required of adolescents in secondary school in your country? Why? Or why not?

CONNECT AND EXTEND

Which children are gifted? Who is talented? Investigate the definitions used at **http://www. nagcbritain.org.uk/**, the website for gifted children and their families or web search for other sites that support the development of gifted children

The contrast we have drawn between much of black and white British culture and minority Asian cultural beliefs regarding education is striking and informative. Remember that Asian cultures have a long tradition of valuing education. In India, South Korea, China and Japan (see the earlier *Cultural Focus* feature), for example, the high value on education is a tradition thousands of years old. Today's educational systems for adolescents in Asian countries are built on this tradition. The value placed on education is so high that the focus on school performance often comes first in adolescents' lives, and other aspects of life are expected to be given a much lower priority, including time with friends, romantic involvements and extra-curricular activities (Lee and Larson, 2000; Asakawa and Csikszentmihalyi, 1999). This thought contributes to the discussion on individual differences in the next section, specifically with respect to Asian adolescents.

ACADEMIC ACHIEVEMENT IN SECONDARY SCHOOL: INDIVIDUAL DIFFERENCES

Adolescents' academic achievement is related not only to characteristics of their environments but also to characteristics of the adolescents themselves. In this area, ethnic differences and gender differences in achievement are two issues that have been of particular interest to scholars. We will examine these two issues first, then look at adolescents who drop out of secondary school. We will also point you to recent research that examines the characteristics of pupils who are **gifted**, have general or specific **learning difficulties**, adolescents with disabilities or with behaviour difficulties.

Ethnic Differences

'You don't have to go to school to necessarily become successful. You can go about it another way. . . . If you do drop-out, you can still make it in life, because I know people who dropped out at an early age like 14 and they're still making it.'
– Tony (in Figueira-McDonough, 1998)

Although looking at the overall academic performance of British adolescents provides interesting insights and information, the overall patterns obscure the sharp differences that exist between different ethnic groups. We have established that Asian (Chinese, Indian, South Korean and Japanese) British adolescents have the best academic performance of all the ethnic groups in British society, followed by whites, with the performance of Caribbean, African British, Pakistani and Bangladeshi adolescents below whites (Department for Education and Skills, 2006; Qin et al., 2008). These differences exist even in early primary school, but they become more pronounced in adolescence.

CONNECT AND EXTEND

'The social origins of students identified as gifted and talented in England: a geo-demographic analysis' by R. J. Campbell, R. D. Muijs, J. G. A. Neelands, W. Robinson, D. Eyre and R. Hewston in the *Oxford Review of Education*, Volume 33, Number 1 (2007), pp. 103–120

What explains these differences? To some extent, the explanation lies in ethnic group differences in the factors we have already discussed as important in school success, such as social class, parenting practices and friends' influences. With regard to social class, Caribbean, African British and Pakistani British are more likely than other British Asian or British white to live in poverty, and living in poverty is negatively associated with academic performance regardless of ethnicity (Gillock and Reyes, 1999; Gutman and Eccles, 1999).

We have also seen the importance of parental expectations in adolescents' educational achievement, and ethnic differences exist here as well. As noted previously, although the majority of parents in all ethnic groups say they value education highly, the emphasis on education is especially strong in Asian cultures (Lee and Larson, 2000; Asakawa and Csikszentmihalyi, 1999), and British Asian parents tend to have higher educational expectations than parents in other ethnic groups (Abbas, 2007). Furthermore, as previously noted, Asian parents and adolescents tend to believe that academic success is due mainly to *effort*; in contrast, parents and adolescents in other ethnic groups are more likely to believe that academic success is due mainly to *innate ability* (Ouwerkerk and Ellerners, 2002; Elliott et al., 2001). Consequently, British Asian parents are less likely than parents in the other ethnic groups to accept mediocre or poor academic performance as due to fixed limitations in their adolescents' academic abilities, and are more likely to insist that their adolescents address academic difficulties by trying harder and spending more time on their schoolwork.

One ethnic difference that does not correspond to other findings on adolescents' academic performance concerns parenting styles. Asian parents are less likely than white parents to be classified by researchers as authoritative, and more likely to be classified as

Educational performance among black adolescents has improved in recent years but remains well below that of whites.

authoritarian (see Parenting styles in Chapter 7); British Asian adolescents excel even though authoritative parenting is more likely than authoritarian parenting to be associated with academic success in adolescence. However, as we discussed in the chapter on families, it makes more sense to view most British Asian parents as 'traditional' rather than authoritarian because they tend to combine a high level of demandingness with strong attachments to their adolescents and intense involvement in their lives (Lim and Lim, 2004; Chao and Tseng, 2002; Chao, 2001).

With all this in mind (and nevertheless) every ethnic group has a substantial amount of individual differences. Not all British Asian adolescents do well in school; many British Caribbean and African, Pakistani and Bangladeshi British adolescents excel. The kinds of parenting practices that we have discussed as important to academic achievement – high expectations, high involvement, and so on – make a difference within every ethnic group, as do the differences we might observe in the educational achievement of boys and girls.

CONNECT AND EXTEND

The inclusion of students with disabilities in the mainstream of general education remains one of the most contested topics in education today. Pupils in inclusive settings can be more restricted in their choice of programme and actual educational situation than their peers in segregated secondary schools. Read 'Adjusted school environment for students with severe motor disabilities' by Eva Heimdahl Mattson in the *International Journal of Inclusive Education*, Volume 2, Number 3 (1998), pp. 237–253

Gender Differences

As we discussed in Chapter 5, few differences in intellectual abilities exist between males and females. However, gender differences do exist in academic achievement. For the most part, these differences favour females. From the first year of primary school to the last year of secondary school, girls tend to achieve higher test and examination results than boys and have higher educational aspirations (Van Houtte, 2004; Sommers, 2000). Girls are also less likely to have learning disabilities and less likely to drop out of secondary school. The female advantage continues into young adulthood. Young women are more likely to attend university and more likely to graduate (Draper and Gittoes, 2004; Longden, 2006; Clark et al., 2008; Mottarella et al., 2009). From pre-school through to university, the female advantage in academic achievement exists not only in Britain but also across all developed and newly developed countries (van Langen et al., 2006).

What explains girls' superior performance in school and the relatively poorer performance of boys? One reason is that girls tend to enjoy the school environment more. Adolescent girls report more positive experiences and interactions in the classroom than adolescent boys and have more favourable relationships with their teachers (Davis and Lease, 2007; Tsouroufli, 2002; Sommers, 2000). Teresa Tinklin of the University of Edinburgh suggests (2003) that 'The only factor which offers any explanation for gender differences in attainment is the evidence that girls took school more seriously than boys' (p. 307), but there

is also research evidence that girls get more praise – positive attention – in the classroom and boys get more reprimands – negative attention (Burnett, 2002). A second reason for girls' superior performance lies 'beyond the classroom'. Adolescent girls are more likely than adolescent boys to feel supported by their parents, academically as well as in other areas, and are more likely to have supportive relationships with adults outside the family as well (Rueger et al., 2010; Hay and Ashman, 2003; Sommers, 2000). Boys also do less homework, watch more TV, and read fewer books on their own (Hacker, 2002b).

What about areas of the school curriculum in which traditionally boys have 'done better' than girls? In the area of maths and science, where males once had greater levels of achievement in adolescence and beyond, more recent evidence indicates that gender differences in maths and science achievement have nearly disappeared (Georgiou et al., 2007; Watt, 2006; Zedd et al., 2002). Although women continue to be less likely than men to choose university courses in engineering and the physical sciences, female representation has grown in all traditionally male-dominated fields in the past two decades, as we will see in more detail later in the chapter. These trends indicate that progress is being made in eroding the gender biases that have kept females out of traditionally male fields emphasising maths and science skills.

The initial premise and purpose of *Adolescence and Emerging Adulthood* was our own concern that a successful adolescence includes successful schooling. Many commentators consider that British boys increasingly find their schooling irrelevant, threatening and a context for personal failure (Booher-Jennings, 2008; Keddie, 2007; Francis, 2006; Jackson, 2003), and this judgement is also being made elsewhere in Europe (e.g. Livaditis et al., 2003). Gender differences in school performance have been the subject of considerable research and heated debates among scholars and in the public arena. One search of an online database of research articles, using the search terms *gender*, *differences* and *schools* created a list of 837 relevant results, the majority reporting research from the last 15 years and from around the world. A general web search on boys' underachievement will illicit many thousands of 'hits' promoting texts, conferences, government programmes and local initiatives. For many years now boys' underachievement has been a matter of deeply felt concern for parents, for teachers and for all practitioners in the children's workforce (Sommers, 2000). See the nearby *Connect and Extend* features for more information.

Girls generally perform better academically than boys at all levels.

CONNECT AND EXTEND

A group of 12 pupils from an emotional and behavioural difficulties (EBD) school were transferred to a mainstream comprehensive school. What happened? Read 'Including emotional and behavioural difficulties pupils in a mainstream comprehensive: a study of the behaviour of pupils and classes' by Jeremy Swinson, Catherine Woof and Richard Melling in *Educational Psychology in Practice*, Volume 19, Number 1 (2003), pp. 65–75

However, for this topic as for others, it is important to keep in mind that gender comparisons involve comparing half of the population to the other half, and there is a great deal of variability within each group. Girls generally do better academically than boys, but many boys excel and some girls struggle. Although the gender differences are genuine, we should avoid stereotypes that might lead us to prejudge the abilities and performance of any individual boy or girl.

THINKING CRITICALLY

Boys generally do worse than girls on virtually every measure of academic achievement. What hypotheses would you propose to explain why this is the case? What can parents and practitioners do?

A final point before we move on. Girls are not as likely to be excluded from full-time mainstream secondary education or to 'voluntarily' drop-out of schooling as boys; it is not as likely, but still a common happening in some neighbourhoods with low SES. We have already touched on the problem of the non-completion of secondary schooling when looking at the problems recounted by some young people in Bristol, UK. Now we will take a longer look at the causes and likely outcomes for young people of non-completion of schooling; a significant problem for them, their parents, teachers, and all who work with families and young people.

Dropping Out of Secondary Schooling

There are two kinds of 'dropping out' from secondary schooling. The first is the pupil electing not to go to school, sometimes choosing not to go to particular lessons or on days when they know they will have a negative experience. Finally, pupils drop out altogether.

'I had a problem with authority. They'd try and say, I'm the adult and you're a child, and say shut up, and you will do this, and don't talk. The teachers would swear and bully and shout in your face. I couldn't take this and at the end of Year 8 I sort of stopped going. I know I was only about 12 years old but I was independent.'
– Kirsten, (in Wetz, 2009, p. 28)

'I didn't like school. I just didn't like it. There was nothing I liked about it. Having to do all this reading and writing, and all that stuff. I had better things to do. I didn't want to be tied down with some schoolwork that I wasn't even going to remember in six weeks, or six days. I just found it all pointless. I'd rather go out in real life and learn real-life things than sit in a classroom and read a book, and answer questions from a teacher.'
– Rich, age 17 (in Arnett, 1996, p. 120)

Another reason for non-completion or dropping out of secondary schooling is exclusion by a school or schools. Exclusion can be temporary or permanent and although local authorities in England and Wales, for example, remain responsible for the schooling of youngsters up to the age of 16, some excluded pupils appear to 'drop below the radar'.

'By the time [my learning mentor] returned I had already been excluded . . . this time I was pushed into [the teacher's] desk. She pulled me and I pushed her and she hit her wrist on the door handle and in the end I went completely mad and just started hitting her and things. I was angry . . . with her for putting me out of the class. She bruised her rib on the door and she had a cut on her face . . . for the rest of the summer term in Year 10 and all through Year 11, I did no schooling at all.'
– Devlin (in Wetz, 2009, p. 34)

FOCUS ON YOUTH IN THE MEDIA

Rap: Protesting about Schools

Some kinds of music have been criticised for promoting morally questionable tendencies in adolescents and the criticism does not only apply to adolescent sexuality (Chapter 9). Jazz was criticised in the 1920s for promoting promiscuity and alcohol use. Rock-and-roll performers were accused throughout the 1950s and 1960s of promoting rebellion through songs of protest. However, in recent decades, the criticism has focused on two particular genres of popular music: rap and heavy metal. Let's explore the contribution of rap as a means of protesting about schools and schooling.

Rap music (also called hip-hop) began in the late 1970s as street music in New York City. It grew from the African Caribbean tradition of 'toasting' – talking or chanting over a rhythm or drum beat. Disc jockeys began 'rapping' (speaking or shouting rhythmically) spontaneous lyrics to a background of a lively beat and perhaps a repeated line of music. Only gradually did it develop into 'songs' that were recorded. By the 1990s, a wide range of rap groups were appearing on lists of the highest-selling albums.

Rap is highly popular among young people in Europe, the United States and in many other places around the world (Motley and Henderson, 2008), at least partly because of the high-sensation quality of the stimulation. Adolescent boys also dominate the audiences for the high-sensation musical forms of rap and heavy metal and the protests that many rap songs contain (Rawlings et al., 2000). What are common causes of protest in rap songs? Schools and schooling certainly feature.

Being excluded from school is a common theme of many of these protest songs. There's a good example from Masta Killa, 'School' on the album *No Said Date* (2004).

Look for the lyrics of *School* by Masta Killa using a web search.
You will find the section where he is asked
why he is home early from school
It is because he has been suspended
For being black

Why was he suspended?
A friend was thrown out of class and suspended
For challenging the teacher's account of early American history
What might the story be that the teacher is telling?
Why might that account offend his friend?
Why might it 'brain numb' the class?

In turn the singer (Diggs) challenges the teacher
About the accounts of various historical periods and events
Europe during the Dark Ages
And The Inquisition

The challenge is an accusation of racisim
And for that, in turn, Diggs is suspended

Dropping out of school is associated with gaining freedom and freedom, as we have noted in this and earlier chapters, is a common aspiration of adolescence. Dead Prez in 'They schools' on the album *Let's Get Free* (2000) asks and answers the question 'Why haven't you learned anything?'

Why haven't you learned anything?

Look for the lyrics of '*Why haven't you learned anything*' using a web search.
It is about boring history classes where only European history is taught
And Africans are not treated as fully human

Then a brilliant bit about if you argue you get expelled
(Permanent exclusion from the school)
Friends will understand even if the school thinks you are a failure
Active learning is best
Book learning doesn't reach the kids

Even if pupils stay at school and 'do well', they may still be culturally consigned to low-level employment as Kanye West declares in '*School spirit*' on the album *The College Dropout* (2004).

Look for the lyrics of '*School Spirit*' using a web search.
The singer says he left school to start up a business

Because he hadn't graduated he went back to school
For another year of waiting

A clever black friend came top of the class
But still ended up waiting on tables

So what's the problem with school? Already in your study related to this chapter you will have read some important academic papers that address many of the themes complained about by MC Paul Barman from the stream '*School anthem*' on the album *It's Very Stimulating* (2000).

Look for the lyrics of '*School Anthem*' using a web search.
The track is a challenge to much of schooling practice
Schools are about babysitting
Copying chunks out text for homework
And over-testing that means pupils can't explore ideas
History classes come in for particular attention
And a novel way of entertaining yourself.

Fellow pupils who conform and engage with the lesson
Are called 'trimmed poodles'

The singer demands doing away
With publishing class lists in rank order of grades
An A grade isn't much of an aspiration
And restricts ambition
Car mechanics should be as important
as studying other academic subjects

One way of getting better teachers
Is to reward them properly – who could argue with that?

What leads adolescents to drop out of school? The nearby *Focus on Youth in the Media* is packed full of ideas and possibilities! For most, dropping out is not a sudden event but the culmination of many years of school problems (Barton, 2005). Adolescents who drop out are more likely to have had a history of other school difficulties, including behaviour problems, separation anxiety disorder, and low scores on achievement and intelligence tests (Pellegrini, 2007; Stroobant and Jones, 2006). Given the difficulties they have in school, it is not surprising that drop-out often report that they disliked school and found it boring, or frightening and alienating (Janosz et al., 2008).

Personal characteristics and problems are also related to adolescents' risk of dropping out. Drop-outs sometimes have aggressive, active, high-sensation-seeking personalities that make it difficult for them to endure the typical classroom environment, which often involves working alone quietly or listening to someone else talk (Fisher and Larkin, 2008). Adolescents who have learning disabilities of various kinds are more likely than other adolescents to drop out, in part because their difficulties in learning may have left them hopelessly behind their peers by the time they reach secondary school. For girls, having a child while of school age puts them at high risk of dropping out, although such girls often report lower school engagement even before becoming pregnant (McGaha-Garnett, 2008; Leadbeater and Way, 2001).

A variety of family factors also predict adolescents' risk for dropping out of school. Parents' education and income are strong predictors. Adolescents with parents who have dropped out of school are at high risk of dropping out themselves, as are adolescents whose families are in poverty (Barton, 2005). The two often go together, of course – parents who have dropped out often have low incomes. Parents who have dropped out provide a model of dropping out to their adolescents and often have lower educational expectations for their children (McIntyre-Bhatty,

2008). Also, families with low incomes often live in low-income neighbourhoods where schools find it difficult to respond to the individual needs of pupils (Pérez et al., 2007). In addition, the stresses of living in a low-income family make it more difficult for parents to support their children's education, for example by helping them with their homework or attending parent–teacher evenings. Rates of dropping out are higher for adolescents in single-parent families, largely because of the lower incomes and higher stresses experienced in such families (Barton, 2005; Buchanan, 2000). Among ethnic minorities difficulty using English is an important contributor to dropping out (Johnston et al., 2004).

School characteristics also predict adolescents' risk of dropping out. Here, as in other areas we have discussed, school climate is of primary importance. Drop-out rates are lower in schools where teachers are supportive of pupils and dedicated to teaching and where the classroom environment is orderly (Salmelo-Aro et al., 2008b). Drop-out rates are higher in larger schools, at least partly because it appears to be more difficult to sustain a healthy school climate in large schools (Wetz, 2009).

Dropping out of secondary school is related to a variety of present and future problems. Rates of substance use are considerably higher among drop-outs than among adolescents who stay in school (Wu et al., 2003). Drop-outs are also at high risk for depression and other psychological problems. Job prospects for drop-outs are limited, both in the short and long term (Stearns and Glennie, 2006). Even for those who do obtain a job, it is likely to be a low-paying one. Drop-outs earn less in adolescence, emerging adulthood and beyond than their peers who obtain more education (Jarvinen and Vanttaja, 2001). High-paying manufacturing jobs are no longer widely available, and as a result one research project found that wages for school drop-outs *declined* by 35 per cent over the past 30 years, adjusted for inflation (Hamilton and Hamilton, 2006).

CONNECT AND EXTEND

From the analysis of comparative data in Nigeria, it was found that financial, home, societal values and personal characteristics of adolescents predispose pupils to drop-out of school. However, peer influence and school factors were found not to predispose adolescents to drop out. Would this hold true for Britain and other European countries? Read 'Analysis of the variables that predispose adolescents to drop out of schools' by Oyaziwo Aluede and B. N. Ikechukwu in the *International Journal for the Advancement of Counselling*, Volume 25, Number 2 (September 2003), pp. 181–192

Because dropping out predicts a variety of future problems, intervention programmes have been designed to assist adolescents who drop out or who are at risk of dropping out because of poor school performance or because of attending a school where the drop-out rate is high. In general, these programmes have concluded that because the problems that lead to dropping out are diverse, programmes to prevent dropping out need to be adapted to adolescents' individual needs and problems (Prevatt and Kelly, 2003). Promising approaches include the establishment of alternative schools for pupils who are at risk for dropping out (McIntyre-Bhatty, 2008; Franklin et al., 2007; Barton, 2005) and the use of learning mentors (Rose and Doveston, 2008). Evaluations of these programmes have shown that pupils in the alternative schools or with the support of learning mentors are half as likely to drop-out as pupils in control groups who were similarly at risk but did not participate in the programmes (Bottrell, 2007) – although evidence is patchy (Hilton, 2006).

What sense can we now make out of the school experience of adolescents in countries such as Britain? For some young people, their teenage youth remains an exciting and vivid opportunity to explore their world and all it offers, in part through the learning and social experiences of schools. For others, as we have seen, their school experience not only fails to contribute to a successful adolescence but becomes a barrier to personal fulfilment. Why is this? You will have some ideas from your own experience, the accounts of others you have spoken to or read, and from reading this chapter and the associated *Connect and Extend* features. Is there a different, perhaps more effective way for us to organise our secondary schooling that can better take account of the needs and aspirations of adolescents? Some European countries claim that there is a better way, and so to finish the chapter let's explore secondary schooling in one of those countries and see if there are lessons that can be learned for how we school our adolescents.

COMPARING SCHOOLING IN DENMARK AND BRITAIN

In preparation for this chapter one of the authors (MH) travelled to Denmark and spent a week visiting schools, lecturing, questioning and discussing in an education training college in Skarup. The following account looks at the way that the Danish authorities have attempted to engage with the national aspiration for a kind of schooling less likely to exclude adolescents. We have interwoven a comparative commentary on equivalent British provision, drawing on ideas that have emerged in this chapter.

A review of schooling in Denmark arose out of a national 'conversation' in the early 1990s. The review's findings were enacted in legislation (the Folkeskole Act of 1994) that emphasised a national shared responsibility for the education and well-being of its young people. In England, the link between education and children's well-being was one formally adopted in 2002 in response to the tragic case of Victoria Climbie, and enshrined in the report *Every Child Matters* (Department for Education and Skills, 2003). However, a number of commentators have argued that, so far, *Every Child Matters* seems to have had little effect upon secondary schools or education policy about the nature of schooling in England (George and Clay, 2008; Payne, 2007; Hudson, 2006).

The Folkeskole Act required the design of a 12-year inclusive school experience for all children, with a curriculum built on ideas of social relevance in schools that should be accountable to the local community. Setting by ability was made unlawful. All schools are well resourced and have status. In Britain (and elsewhere) – as we have already noted – schools are labelled 'good schools' and 'failing schools'. Different levels of resourcing are provided in private and state schools, and between areas where parents and local organisations – e.g. churches and business – contribute to school funds in formal and informal ways (Gillard, 2008; Walford, 2001). In impoverished areas, school rolls (the headcount of pupils attending) fall as parents try to move their children into schools reported as being good (Gorard et al., 2002) or move area to 'win' places at good schools during the transition from primary to secondary schooling (Leech and Campos, 2003).

In Denmark there are no transition difficulties, as primary and secondary provision is integrated into one *Folkeskole* (people's school) for all children aged from 6 to 16, with no more than 500 students in a school. In practice this means a two-form entry throughout. There are nine years of compulsory education with an optional additional year at age 16; children are divided into groups by age, but not by ability; and progression from one year to the next is automatic.

Most UK primary schools are one- or two-form entry but after transition most pupils enter a secondary school of typically 1000 pupils or more, indeed there are a growing number of super-sized schools of pupil roles between 1500 and 3000 (Gillard, 2008; Spielhofer et al., 2004; Power and Prasad, 2003). The contrast between primary and secondary schooling in Britain is stark and, as noted earlier in the section on transfer and transition, can be a significant ordeal for children (Jindal-Snape and Foggie, 2008) many of whom make negative progression in educational attainment and social development (Capel et al., 2004).

Teaching practice throughout Danish schools is based on group work and learning together that leads to ways of working required for the completion of a significant final-year project. Assessment is continuous and contributes to planning for what comes next, and teachers are not required to give their students grades until they are 14 years of age. School status is not linked to examination results but to school ambience, the well-being of pupils, the quality of attachment relationships between teachers and pupils, and the quality of learning experiences.

Much of the teaching practice at British secondary schools and elsewhere in Europe is didactic – based on instruction of large classes – (Meyer, 2007; Veugelers and Vedder, 2003) and 'skewed' by teaching to the statutory tests and public examinations taken in Britain at 16 and 18 years (Greatorex and Malacova, 2006). Assessments form the basis for reports to parents that include attainment grades and relative examination mark positions with other pupils of the same age (Power and Clark, 2000).

In Denmark, the class group remains the same throughout so that students have continuity both with their subject teachers (who have undertaken a four-year training programme in child development and are expected to teach three or four subjects) and their class group. The key person for all students is the *Klasslaerer* (class teacher or tutor), who stays with the group all the way, providing a consistent attachment for pupils (and families) through school to young adulthood. In Britain the class teacher or form tutor usually changes every year in both primary and secondary

Teaching practice throughout Danish schools is based on group work and learning together.

schools. Although the primary school class teacher will teach his or her class for almost the whole curriculum, at secondary school the form tutor may not teach his or her tutor group for any subject (Reid, 2006; Marland, 2002; Lodge, 2002; Osborn, 2001). It is not out of the ordinary for teenagers to be taught by 11 or 12 different teachers in a week and for a teacher to teach 400 different pupils in a week (Wetz, 2009).

The foregoing comparative descriptions demonstrate that the Danish *Folkeskoles* represent very different kinds of schools, delivering different kinds of teaching and learning experiences, and programmes of study. These schools in Denmark contrast sharply with current provision in secondary schooling in the United Kingdom, and in other parts of Europe and the USA. There are now increasingly urgent and powerful calls for the development of small, 'different' secondary schools, particularly in areas of social and economic deprivation (Rainey and Murova, 2004; Papatheodorou, 2002; Tasker, 2008).

SUMMING UP

In this chapter we have discussed a variety of topics related to adolescents' and young adults' school experiences and performance. Here is a summary of the main points:

- Over the past century, the secondary school curriculum has changed from a focus on liberal arts to a curriculum intended to prepare pupils for work and citizenship; to a curriculum that

includes a wide range of courses from mathematics and English to music and physical education. These changes have taken place partly in response to the changing characteristics of the young people attending secondary school, and partly in response to changes in cultural beliefs about what adolescents need to learn.
- Secondary education around the world varies greatly in terms of availability and quality.

- Industrialised countries tend to provide relatively high-quality secondary education for most adolescents. Adolescents in developing countries are less likely to complete secondary school and the quality of secondary education available to them is often poor, but the proportion of adolescents enrolled in secondary school is increasing.

- In international comparisons, industrialised countries rank higher than developing countries in academic performance, and the average academic performance of British secondary school pupils tends to be towards the upper end compared with the average performance of pupils in many other industrialised countries. However, that contrasts with the performance of British youngsters from low SES backgrounds.

- School climate – the quality of the classroom interactions between teachers and pupils – affects pupils' academic performance and their participation in delinquency. The same qualities of warmth and moderate control that are effective in parenting are also effective in schools.

- Adolescents' school performance is influenced not only by factors within the school but also by many influences beyond the classroom, including family, friends, work and leisure, and cultural beliefs.

- Ethnic differences in adolescents' academic performance are explained in part by social class differences and in part by different influences from family and friends.

- Girls perform better than boys on nearly all measures of academic performance, and in recent years they have become increasingly likely to pursue mathematics and science.

- Streaming is a controversial practice in British secondary schooling, with advocates arguing that it results in a better fit between pupils' abilities and interests and their curriculum, and critics maintaining that it relegates pupils in lower streams to a second-rate education in which they fall steadily further behind other pupils.

- Dropping out of secondary school is predicted by a variety of factors, including previous problems in school, personality characteristics and family difficulties. Successful programmes to prevent dropping out have focused on providing alternative schools or smaller learning communities within larger institutions.

- There is much that Britain and other countries can learn from Danish schooling about the importance of relationships and group working, particularly for lower-ability pupils and those from low SES backgrounds.

The practice of having adolescents spend many hours each day in school is fairly recent historically and has developed in response to economic changes that require young people to have academic skills in order to fulfil the requirements of jobs in an increasingly information-based economy. As the material in this chapter shows, to some extent industrialised societies are still struggling with how best to teach their young people. We do understand that adolescents need and deserve teachers of the highest calibre (such as Mirella Jerez-Rios whom we met in the opening scenarios of this chapter). However, the issues affect the structures of schooling, not just the training and development of outstanding practitioners. Some European societies allow young people to begin specialised education by the time they are just 14 or 15 years old. This may make young people more engaged in their education because they will be studying topics in areas they have chosen themselves, but such a system makes it difficult for them to change directions in their later teens or early 20s. Perhaps many of the European systems involve different but inevitable trade-offs, or perhaps all our current systems will eventually be seen as early experiments on the way to other educational forms that will prove more effective.

For adolescents in economically developing countries, secondary school and access to higher education are currently restricted mainly to the elite, just as they were in fully industrialised countries a century ago. The proportion of young people in secondary school and beyond in developing countries is growing and is likely to continue to grow as a consequence of globalisation and the requirements of the global economy. Currently, however, the focus of daily activity for adolescents in developing countries is not school but work. In the next chapter, we will explore in depth the nature of their work experiences and discuss the work experiences of young people in industrialised countries as well.

INTERNET RESOURCES

http://www.statistics.gov.uk/hub/children-education-skills/index.html

Website for Education Statistics, a British government agency. The site contains useful information on education from nursery school through to university, including a great deal of social information that pertains to adolescents and young adults.

http://www.ofsted.gov.uk/

The website of the British government's Office for Standards in Education in England. There is a wealth of information and research on these pages and access to inspection reports on every school in England. Of particular interest is 'The Annual Report of Her Majesty's Chief Inspector of Education, Children's Services and Skills'.

http://www.tda.gov.uk/

The website of the Training and Development Agency for Schools (TDA) is the national agency and recognised sector body responsible for the training and development of the school workforce. A useful starting point when considering any career in schools.

FURTHER READING

Michael Adewale, *Class Dismissed: A Guide Book for Teens in Secondary School & Sixth Form* Published by author (2009).

A guide for adolescents that is much more than how to get by in maths, English and science. In *Class Dismissed*, adolescents are taught about self-image and attachment, about nurturing healthy relationships and building resilience, all in the context of their daily experience of secondary schooling.

C. Lloyd (ed.), *Growing up Global: The Changing Transitions to Adulthood in Developing Countries*. Washington, DC: National Research Council and Institute of Medicine (2005).

This book contains excellent chapters on a variety of topics, including the diversity of adolescents' school experiences worldwide and how schooling for adolescents is becoming more widespread due to globalisation.

Molly Potter, *A Parent's Survival Guide to Starting Secondary School: Ease the Transition for You and Your Child!* London: A & C Black Publishers (2011).

Not just a guide for parents, as this very readable guide gets into many of the issues we have raised in this chapter and is well researched and supported.

Michael Rutter, Barbara Maughan, Peter Mortimore and Janet Ouston, *Fifteen Thousand Hours. Secondary Schools and their Effects on Children*. London: Open Books (1979).

This now historic book gives a remarkable account of what (still) goes on in schools and what the effects are likely to be. The Conclusions chapter makes for a valuable comparison with some of the themes of this chapter and the more recent research you have read in the *Connect and Extend* features

For more reviews, responses to the *Thinking Critically* features, case studies, web links and practice tests, log on to **www.pearsoned.co.uk/arnett.**

CHAPTER 11
WORK

OUTLINE

'At 16 I left school as my mum needed me to help out with the cost of running the home. I worked as a stockroom assistant and then in the evenings restacked the shelves at a supermarket. Neither of these seemed promising. I went into retail and by the time I was 17 I was a superviser but the company went into liquidation and I was out of a job. I quickly found a job as a bartender in a night club and then I started as a chef in the kitchen. I have now been stuck in the kitchen with no prospect of going anywhere and no life as the hours are very demanding. I work for below minimum wage and see no escape. A job is a job and the way the economy is now I am grateful that I am in work but I earn barely enough to live on and have no savings. I am waiting for that big break but I doubt it will come anytime soon.'

Andy, 25 (Hughes, unpublished data)

'I have been teaching for nearly four years now and I can say without a doubt that I have found each day to be as fulfilling as the last. I particularly enjoy teaching Literacy as I have always loved reading and I love sharing great books with the children I teach. It is a joy to see the pleasure they get from books that I have always enjoyed myself as well as feeling the thrill of discovering a new book together. I have particularly relished the challenge of taking on the coordinator role for Literacy. I find it so rewarding to work with the teachers in my school to plan exciting developments for the subject and the best part is seeing the end results with the children when they achieve in reading and writing. The look on a child's face when they are enjoying a story is the most wonderful sight in the world.'

Becca, age 26 (Hughes, unpublished data)

'LOVE AND WORK' WAS SIGMUND FREUD'S succinct response when he was asked what a person should be able to do well in order to be considered psychologically healthy. Work is, in all cultures and in all historical times, one of the most important areas of human activity. Earlier, we discussed preparation for adult roles as one of the three principal goals of socialisation during adolescence. All cultures expect their members to contribute some kind of work, whether it be paid employment; cooperative hunting, fishing or farming; or taking care of children and running a household. Adolescence is often a key time of preparation for adult work roles. Whatever work young people may have contributed as children, adolescence is the time when work expectations grow more serious, as adolescents prepare to take their place as full members – which always means working members – of their culture.

In this chapter, we begin by discussing adolescent work in traditional cultures. This is a good place to start because work has a special prominence for adolescents in traditional cultures as part of the preparation for the responsibilities of adulthood. Engagement in work from an early age also helps to define and develop family loyalties and relationships, and there are vestiges of this important role for work in family enterprises of post-traditional cultures. Unlike adolescents in fully industrialised societies, most adolescents in traditional cultures are no longer in school, and most of their day is devoted to work. As noted in earlier chapters, in traditional cultures adolescents typically work alongside adults, doing the kind of work that adults do. So we begin this chapter by taking a look at the types of work that occupy adolescents and adults in most traditional cultures: hunting, fishing and gathering; farming; and childcare. Then we look at how the economies of traditional cultures are changing with globalisation and how adolescents in these cultures increasingly work in new industries that offer them economic opportunities but also, all too often, exploit them.

Adolescents in traditional cultures are now in a position, with regard to work, that is similar to what was experienced by adolescents in industrialised societies a century ago. In both cases, prolonged schooling was rarely available or useful to adolescents, given the jobs available in their economy. In both cases, industrialisation left adolescents vulnerable to exploitation in unhealthy and unsafe working conditions. Both cases involve an economy rapidly becoming industrialised. In the second part of this chapter, we examine these issues in the history of adolescent work in industrialised societies.

Following this discussion, we take a look at various issues related to adolescent work as it currently takes place in industrialised societies. This will include a look at what adolescents typically do in their jobs and at how work influences various aspects of their development. We will also look at the transition from school to work, both for young adults who enter further and higher education and for those who do not. This will include an examination of the occupational choices that young people make and of how young adults view work. At the end of the chapter we will examine the characteristics and experiences of young people who undertake volunteer work.

ADOLESCENT WORK IN TRADITIONAL CULTURES

For much of human history before industrialisation, most human work involved the same basic activities: hunting, fishing, and gathering edible fruits and vegetables; farming and caring for domestic animals; and caring for children while doing household work. These kinds of work are still common in many traditional cultures, and we will first look at adolescents' participation in such work. However, because virtually all traditional cultures are in the process of industrialising, it will be important to look at adolescents' experiences in industrial settings as well.

Hunting, Fishing and Gathering

Hunting and fishing in traditional cultures are typically undertaken by men, and adolescent boys learn how it is done by accompanying their fathers and other men on hunting or fishing expeditions (León and Mantiel, 2008; Jørgensen et al., 2006; C. Robinson, 2005). Females are rarely the principal hunters, but they sometimes assist in the hunting enterprise by holding nets, setting traps or beating the bushes to flush out game.

Hunting often provides not only food but also materials for tools, clothing and other purposes. As such, it serves many important functions in cultures that rely on it, and success at hunting may be required of adolescent boys as a way of showing that they are ready for

CONNECT AND EXTEND

For a vivid record of family fishing businesses in Yarmouth and the experiences and hardships of young people working in such a demanding environment, read *The Great Yarmouth herring industry* by Colin Tooke, The History Press Limited (2006).

Contrast Tooke's account with 'Occupational risks, safety and masculinity: Newfoundland fish harvesters' experiences and understandings of fishery risks' by Nicole Gerarda Power in *Health, Risk & Society*, Volume 10, Number 6 (December 2008), pp. 565–583

manhood. For example, among the nomadic Bushmen of the Kalahari Desert in south-west Africa, an adolescent boy is not considered a man – and is not allowed to marry – until he has successfully killed his first antelope. Doing so is a way of demonstrating that he will be able to provide for a family as part of his adult role.

Fishing is another form of work that adolescent boys learn through observing and assisting their fathers and other men. The skills required for success at fishing include not only fishing itself but boating and navigation. For example, adolescents in the South Sea Islands in the Pacific Ocean traditionally learned complex systems of night-time navigation from their fathers, using a 'star compass' through which they set their course – rather like many animals (Grocott, 2003) – according to the

Adolescent boys in traditional cultures learn the work of adult men. Here, a boy in the Abouri Tribe of West Africa learns to carve a dugout canoe.

positions of the constellations (Nunn, 2003). Of course, there remain the vestiges of similar kindred enterprise in the family-owned trawlers, drifters and dories moored in the fishing ports of fully – industrialised countries across the world. It is still the case, though less and less as the years go on, that many sons leave school on Friday and go full time on the family boat on Saturday.

Often in cultures where males have the responsibility for hunting or fishing, women have a complementary responsibility for gathering. This means that they find edible wild fruit and vegetables growing in the surrounding area and collect them to contribute to their families' food supply. This can be a substantial contribution. Anthropologists have observed that in cultures that rely on a combination of hunting and gathering, women contribute as much or more to the family food supply through gathering as men do through hunting (Hames and Draper, 2004).

Hunting and gathering cultures have rapidly changed in the past half-century in response to globalisation, and only a few such cultures exist in the present (Schlegel, 2009; 2008; 2001). The nomadic way of life typical of hunting and gathering cultures – moving from place to place, following the food supply – is not well suited to the global economy, with its stable communities and its property boundaries. Fishing, too, has largely disappeared as a central basis for a culture's economy. Even in cultures that have a long tradition of fishing, such as Norway and Japan, modern fishing techniques are so advanced that a very small proportion of people engaged in fishing can provide more than enough fish to feed the entire population.

Farming and Care of Domestic Animals

Farming and care of domestic animals often go together in the same way that hunting and gathering tend to go together – one for providing meat, the other for providing grains, vegetables and fruit. Adolescents in cultures with economies based on farming and care of domestic animals often provide useful work to their families. Care of domestic animals is a frequent responsibility of adolescents and even pre-adolescents all over the world – cattle in southern Africa, sheep and goats in Northern Africa and Southern Europe, small livestock in Asia and Eastern Europe – perhaps because such work requires little in the way of skill or experience. Farming often requires a higher level of training and skill, particularly if the amount of land to be farmed is large. This enterprise is typically carried out by fathers and sons working together, with the sons not only contributing to their families in the present but also learning how to manage the land they will eventually inherit.

Even today, farming remains the main occupation of a substantial proportion of the world's population. In newly-developed countries such as Brazil, India, and the Philippines, over half of the adult males are employed in agricultural work (UNDP, 2009; Lloyd, 2005). However, in all newly developed and developing countries, the proportion of people in farming is declining in the course of industrialisation. Just as with fishing, advanced technology and equipment make it possible for a few people to do work that once required hundreds.

Childcare and Household Work

When it comes to childcare, women and girls have the main responsibility in most traditional cultures, with men and boys occasionally providing support. The work of childcare usually begins quite early in life for girls. If they have younger siblings, girls often become at least partly responsible for taking care of them as early as age 6 or 7 (Edmonds, 2006). By the time she reaches adolescence, the oldest girl in a family may have several younger siblings to care for, and perhaps frail or ill older relatives. Of course these kinds of caring responsibilities are adopted by youngsters, usually girls in fully industrialised countries, which accounts sometimes for attendance problems at school – but more of this later.

Along with childcare, working alongside her mother often means household work for an adolescent girl living in a traditional culture. A great deal of household work needs to be done in a traditional culture that has no access to electricity and the many conveniences that go with it. Chores such as collecting firewood, starting and tending the fire and fetching water must be done on a daily basis. Preparing food is also heavily labour intensive in such cultures. Want chicken for dinner? You have to kill it, pluck it and trim it before you can cook it. All we have to do is unwrap it and zap it in

Adolescent girls in traditional cultures typically have responsibility for household work such as food preparation. Here, a girl of the Sahelian culture of northern Africa prepares a meal.

the microwave (or stop by the drive-through window at KFC).

With so much work to be done, women in these cultures often enlist the help of their daughters from an early age, and by adolescence daughters typically work alongside their mothers and other women of the family as near-equal partners (Lloyd, 2005). By doing this kind of work the adolescent daughter prepares herself for her adult work role and also demonstrates to others, including potential marriage partners, that she is capable of fulfilling the expectations for running a household that are typically required of women in traditional cultures.

Globalisation and Adolescent Work in Traditional Cultures

Adolescents and adults in traditional cultures have been doing the kinds of work described above for thousands of years. However, as we have seen in previous chapters, all traditional cultures today are being influenced by globalisation. An important aspect of globalisation is economic integration, including increasing trade between countries and increasingly large-scale agriculture and manufacturing in many cultures that have known only small, local, family-based economic activity until very recently. Globalisation has certainly conferred some economic benefits on the people in these cultures. Pre-industrial economic life can be hard. Simply providing the everyday necessities of life is a lot of work without industrialisation, as the chicken example above illustrates. Entry into the global economy is usually accompanied by increased access to electricity, which often makes food preparation, clothes washing, heating and other tasks considerably easier. Entry into the global economy is also usually accompanied by increased access to education and medical care.

The globalisation of economic life thus holds the promise of making life better for people in the many cultures around the world. Adolescents and their families derive several benefits when adolescents work (Larson et al., 2010). Poor families in developing countries often depend on adolescents' contributions to the family income for basic necessities such as food and clothing. Adolescents gain status and respect within the family by being able to bring money into the family. Although jobs in industrial settings are often difficult and may even be hazardous, the alternative of agricultural work is just as hard, and working in an industrial setting is often seen as a way for adolescents to gain skills and contacts that will eventually lead to a better job and a higher income.

However, the transition from a pre-industrial economy to the global economy is proving to be problematic in many places. Currently, many people are not experiencing increased comfort and opportunity but brutal work in terrible conditions for miserable pay. The burden of much of this work is falling on the shoulders of adolescents, mainly those between 10 and 15 years of age, who are more capable than children of doing useful industrial work and less capable than adults of asserting their rights and resisting maltreatment.

The **International Labour Organization (ILO)** has estimated that about *200 million* children and adolescents are employed worldwide and that 95 per cent of them are in developing countries (ILO, 2008; 2006; 2004a). They are numerous in Latin America and Africa, but the greatest number of adolescent workers and the worst working conditions are found in Asia (including countries such as India, Bangladesh, Thailand, Indonesia, the Philippines and Vietnam). Agricultural work is the most common form of employment for adolescents, usually on commercial farms or plantations, often working alongside their parents but for only a third or half the pay (ILO, 2002).

In addition, many adolescents in these countries work in factories and workshops where they perform labour such as weaving carpets, sewing clothes, gluing shoes, curing leather and polishing gems. The working conditions are often horrific – crowded garment factories where the doors are locked and the adolescents (and adults) work 14-hour shifts, small poorly lit huts where they sit at a loom weaving carpets for hours on end, glass factories where the temperatures are unbearably hot and adolescents carry hot rods of molten glass from one station to another (ILO, 2004b). Other adolescents work in cities in a wide variety of jobs, including domestic service, grocery shops, tea stalls, road construction and the sex industries.

In India, a common and particularly brutal system for exploiting adolescent labour is called **debt bondage** (Basu and Chau, 2007). Debt bondage begins when a person needs a loan and has no money to offer for security, so instead pledges his labour or that of his children. The poor of India are most often the ones desperate enough to accept this kind of loan. Because many of them are illiterate, they are easily exploited by lenders who manipulate the interest and the payments in such a way that the loan becomes virtually impossible to pay back. In desperation, parents sometimes offer the labour of their children in an effort to pay off the debt.

Adolescents are especially valuable for bonded labour because they are more productive than children.

CONNECT AND EXTEND

How could you get involved in the debate about sweatshops and the anti-sweatshop movement? For an analysis of the place of sweatshops in the process of globalisation, and efforts to end sweatshop abuse, read 'Teaching about sweatshops and globalization' by John Miller in the *Review of Radical Political Economics*, Volume 36, Number 3 (1 September 2004), pp. 321–327

According to the ILO, adolescents most often end up as bonded labourers in agriculture, domestic service, prostitution, and industries such as the manufacture of hand-knitted carpets. Once adolescents have been committed by their parents to debt bondage, it is extremely difficult for them to free themselves of it; the United Nations has condemned debt bondage as a modern form of slavery (ILO, 2004b).

Perhaps the worst form of exploitation of adolescents' work is prostitution. Estimates of the number of adolescent prostitutes in developing countries vary, but it is widely agreed that adolescent prostitution is a pervasive and growing problem, especially in Asia, and within Asia especially in Thailand (Basu and Chau, 2007; ILO, 2002). Of course, there are adolescent prostitutes in industrialised countries as well, but the problem is much more widespread in developing countries.

Adolescent girls in these countries become prostitutes in several ways. Some are kidnapped and exported to a different country. Isolated in a country where they are not citizens and where they do not know the language, they are highly vulnerable and dependent on their kidnappers. Some are rural adolescent girls who are promised jobs in restaurants or domestic service, then forced to become prostitutes once the recruiter takes them to their urban destination. Sometimes parents sell the girls into prostitution, out of desperate poverty or simply out of the desire for more consumer goods (ILO, 2004b). A large proportion of the customers in Asian brothels are Western tourists. The proportion is large enough that the UK and several other European countries now have laws permitting prosecution of their citizens for sexually exploiting young adolescent girls in other countries. The demand is increasingly for younger adolescent girls, partly because they are perceived to be less likely than older girls to be carrying the HIV virus.

Although the exploitation of adolescents in developing countries is widespread and often brutal, signs of

Many adolescent girls in developing countries have been forced into prostitution. Here, a young prostitute at a rehabilitation centre in Brazil.

positive change can be seen. According to the ILO, from 2002 to 2006 the number of child and adolescent labourers fell 11 per cent worldwide, and the number engaged in hazardous work fell even more, by 26 per cent (ILO, 2006). This decline has taken place because the issue of child and adolescent labour has received increased attention from the world media, governments, and international organisations such as the ILO and the United Nations Children's Fund (UNICEF). Furthermore, many countries have taken legislative action to raise the number of years children and adolescents are legally required to attend school and to enforce the often-ignored laws in many countries against employing children younger than their

CONNECT AND EXTEND

'In Thailand, there appears to be a long history of child prostitution, and this article explores the factors that underpin the Thai child sex industry and the lessons and implications that can be drawn for health care and nursing around the world.' Read 'Child prostitution in Thailand' by Carmen Lau in the *Journal of Child Health Care*, Volume 12, Number 2 (June 2008), pp. 144–155

Table 11.1 Child Employment in Mining 1851–1881

Age cohort	1851	1861	1871	1881
Males 10–14	37,300	45,100	43,100	30,400
Females 10–14	1,400	500	900	500
Males 15–20	50,100	65,300	74,900	87,300
Females 15–20	5,400	4,900	5,300	5,700
Total 10–14 as % of workforce	13	12	10	6
Total 15–20 as % of workforce	18	18	18	18
Total 10–20 as % of workforce	31	30	28	24

Source: Booth (1886, pp. 353–399)

could lead to serious injury, and crushed hands and fingers were common. Dust and residue from the spinning process damaged their lungs and caused stomach illnesses and eye infections.

The first attempts at government regulation of the mills were tentative, to say the least. Because the British economy depended so heavily on the young millworkers, even reformers were reluctant to advocate an end to their labour. There was also little public support for abolishing child and adolescent labour, and labour restrictions were fiercely resisted by parents who depended on their income. Thus, the first law, the Health and Morals of Apprentices Act of 1802, simply limited young workers to 12 hours of labour a day! The act also mandated minimum standards of ventilation and sanitation in the mills, but mill owners widely ignored these provisions.

In addition, the act required employers to provide daily schooling to young workers. Employers generally complied with this requirement because they believed that educated children would be more compliant and more valuable as workers. The result was a significant increase in literacy among young workers. The schooling requirement spread to other industries over the following decades and became the basis of the *half-time system,* in which young workers in factories received schooling for a half day and worked for a half day. This system survived in Britain until the end of the nineteenth century.

In the 1830s, regulatory attention turned to mining. Just as changes in textile production had created a boom in jobs in the late 1700s, an increase in the need for coal in the early 1800s created a mining boom. Once again, children and adolescents were sought as workers because they were cheap, manageable, and could do some jobs better than adults. Once again, parents urged their children to become labourers as early as possible to contribute to the family income, even though the work in the mines was especially hazardous.

Like those in the factories, a workday of 12 to 14 hours per day, six days a week was common for young miners. Many of them descended into the mine before sunrise and came up again after sunset, so that they never saw daylight for weeks at a time except on Sundays. Accidents were common, and coal dust damaged young miners' lungs. The first reforms, in the 1842 Mines Act, prohibited boys under age 10 from working in mines and required boys over age 10 to be provided with schooling by the mine owners, but did nothing about the working conditions in the mines. As this law and others restricted the employment of children, employment among adolescents became even more widespread.

Over the second half of the nineteenth century legal regulations on child and adolescent labour slowly and gradually reduced the exploitation of young workers in British industrial settings. Regulations increased concerning the work young workers could be required to do. The half-time system, once celebrated as a way of protecting young workers from exploitation, became viewed as an obstacle to their educational opportunities. Public schools were established, and attendance at school became legally required for all children in the 1880s. This essentially marked the end of child labour in Great Britain, and in the following decades more and more adolescents attended secondary school rather than working.

Before industrialisation, most children in the West grew up on a family farm.

patterns of child and adolescent labour took place slowly. Even as recently as 1970 the majority of British adolescents – particularly those from low- or middle-socio-economic neighbourhoods left school by age 15 to become full-time workers (Flouri and Ereky-Stevens, 2008). Most families viewed the labour of their adolescents as an important contributor to the family income, and only relatively affluent families could afford the luxury of keeping their adolescents in school in their mid-teens.

This pattern changed dramatically towards combining school with part-time work. From 1950 through the 1990s, the fastest-growing sectors of the British economy were the retail trade and services (Lee and Wolpin, 2006). In the late twentieth century, jobs became numerous for young people who were willing to work part time for relatively low

wages in doorstep delivery, restaurants or retail; or who could combine schooling with entrepreneurial activity in IT business services (Chadwick et al., 2008). By the end of the twentieth century, part-time employment outside of family businesses during secondary school had changed from the rare exception to the typical experience for those in relatively prosperous neighbourhoods.

In Western Europe, rates of work in late adolescence vary among countries from about 30 to 50 per cent (Bonino et al., 2007; Meeus, 2006). In Canada, the proportion of adolescents who work by their late teens (45 per cent) is higher than in Japan, but still substantially lower than in the United States. American adolescents are more able to work part time because their schools make relatively lower demands on them. In turn, pervasive employment among adolescents makes it difficult for secondary schools to require more academic work from them because many adolescents have little time or energy left over for homework after school and work (Sears et al., 2006). In many European countries, adolescents have a longer school day and more homework on a typical evening, leaving less time for part-time jobs.

THE ADOLESCENT WORKPLACE

We have seen what kind of work adolescents do in traditional cultures, and what kind of work they did in European countries in the nineteenth and most of the twentieth century. What kinds of jobs are held by today's adolescents?

You won't find many British adolescents these days whose work involves hunting, fishing, farming – a few perhaps combined with schooling – or factory work. Interestingly enough, however, British girls in early adolescence have something in common with girls in traditional cultures in that their first kind of work involves childcare. Babysitting is the most common first job for girls (Mortimer, 2003). For boys, the most common first job is delivering newspapers or doing occasional gardening work for neighbours. However, the work done in these kinds of jobs is more or less informal and does not require a substantial commitment of time. An adolescent girl may babysit for Mr and Mrs Jones on Saturday night every couple of weeks, and for Mr and Mrs Peabody on the occasional afternoon until they get home from work. An adolescent boy may mow a couple of neighbours' lawns once a week. Typically, these jobs are unlikely to interfere much with the rest of an adolescent's life.

For older adolescents, the work is different, and the amount of time involved tends to be greater. The majority of jobs held by adolescents in secondary school involve restaurant work (waiting on tables, washing up or simple food preparation) or retail sales (Staff et al., 2004; Loughlin and Barling, 1999). These jobs involve a more formal commitment. You are assigned a certain number of hours a week, and you are expected to be there at the times you are assigned. Typically, this does not mean simply a few hours one week and a few the next. Some employed 'sixth formers' (17- and 18-year-olds) can work as many as 15 hours per week, and

By 1980, part-time work had become typical for many secondary school pupils.

even 20 hours a week in countries such as the USA and Canada (Barling and Kelloway, 1999).

That is a substantial number of weekly hours. What are adolescents typically doing during that time? One important source of information on this topic comes from a classic book by researchers Ellen Greenberger and Laurence Steinberg (1986), who studied over 200 16- and 17-year-olds. Rather than relying only on adolescents' reports of what goes on in the places where they work, the research team observed adolescents directly in their work settings, recording the behaviour of the adolescents, the things they said, and the people with whom the adolescents interacted. The researchers also interviewed the adolescents and had them fill out questionnaires about their work experiences.

The kind of work performed by the adolescents fell into five general categories: restaurant work, retail, clerical (e.g. secretarial work), manual labour (e.g. working for a moving company), and skilled labour (e.g. carpenter's apprentice). With the exception of the jobs involving skilled labour, the work performed by the adolescents tended to be repetitive and monotonous, involving little that would challenge them or help them develop new skills. Twenty-five per cent of their time on the job was spent cleaning or carrying things – not exactly work that entails much of a cognitive challenge. Furthermore, the work was almost never connected to anything the adolescents were learning or had previously learned in school. Again, if you think about the work – cooking burgers, taking food orders, answering the phone, helping people find their size in clothes – this is hardly surprising.

With respect to the people they interacted with at work, adolescents spent about an equal proportion of their time interacting with other adolescents and with adults. However, their relationships with adult bosses and co-workers were rarely close. For the most part they did not see these adults except at work, they were reluctant to speak to them about personal issues, and they felt less close to them than they felt to the other people in their lives, such as parents and friends.

You can see how different the work experience of school pupils is, compared with adolescents in traditional cultures (before industrialisation) or adolescents in European countries who work in apprenticeships. Unlike these other adolescents, school pupils rarely do work that involves a close partnership with an adult who teaches them and provides a model. Unlike these other adolescents the work done by school pupils does little to prepare them for the kind of work they are likely to be doing as adults. Consequently, few adolescents see their secondary school jobs as the basis for a future career (Mortimer et al., 2008).

CONNECT AND EXTEND

'There was no significant difference between the individuals with SCI and the control participants in chores or volunteer work experiences, but the individuals with SCI were significantly less likely to have paid work experience than peers without disabilities' (from the abstract). For a study to compare the work experiences of adolescents with spinal cord injuries (SCI) to peers without disabilities, read 'Work experience in adolescents with spinal cord injuries' by Caroline J. Anderson and Lawrence C. Vogel in *Developmental Medicine & Child Neurology*, Volume 42, Number 8 (August 2000), pp. 515–517

WORK AND ADOLESCENT DEVELOPMENT

You might expect that, given the dreary work they do and lack of connection between this work and their futures, the work done by adolescents does little to promote their development in favourable ways. There is some evidence that this is true, as we will see in this section, although the connection between cause and effect is not always clear. In the previous chapter, we discussed the relationship between part-time work and school performance. Now let's look at the relationships between work and two other aspects of development: psychological functioning and problem behaviour.

Work and Psychological Functioning

'I sometimes do find it difficult to cope with the amount of schoolwork we receive and balancing it with activities outside of school and some free time. As a keen amateur dramatist, I am involved with a lot of in-school and out of school productions, and these are extremely time consuming. I know that in Year 11, the work we are set is generally revision, coursework and exam preparations, so it is difficult for teachers to limit the work; however, some teachers don't always understand how difficult it is to balance the excessive amount of work we get and outside of school activities. I had to drop my waitressing job because of schoolwork, which means I can't always join in going out with friends at weekends! The balance is very difficult and sometimes I crumble, but it is possible.'

– Alexandra, age 16 (Hughes, unpublished data)

Both for psychological functioning and for problem behaviour, the amount of time worked per week is an important variable. Most studies find that working up to 10 hours a week at a part-time job has little effect on adolescents' development. However, beyond 10 hours a week problems arise, and beyond 20 hours a week the problems become considerably worse.

Working up to 10 hours a week is not related to increased psychological symptoms such as anxiety and depression (Lee and Staff, 2007; Frone, 1999). However, reports of psychological symptoms jump sharply for adolescents working more than 10 hours a week and continue to rise among adolescents working 20 hours a week or more (see Chapter 10).

Up to 10 hours a week, working has little effect on the amount of sleep adolescents get. However, beyond 10 hours a week, amount of sleep per night declines steadily as work hours increase. Studies also show that working more than 10 hours a week can be disruptive to eating and exercise habits. When adolescents take on demanding jobs they reduce their sleep by an hour a night and eliminate nearly all sports activities (Sears et al., 2006).

Some studies report positive findings concerning work and psychological functioning. Working at a job that involves learning new skills is positively related to psychological well-being and self-esteem (Mortimer, 2003). Also, learning new skills on the job is related to higher life satisfaction (Dabic, 2008; McNess et al., 2003). We will consider the case in favour of adolescent work in more detail shortly.

Work and Problem Behaviour

One strong and consistent finding in research on adolescents and work is that adolescents who work are more likely to use alcohol (as noted in the nearby *Research Focus* feature), cigarettes and other drugs, especially if they work more than 10 hours a week

RESEARCH FOCUS

R

A Longitudinal Study and a Cross-sectional Study of Adolescents and Work

One of the most ambitious and long-lasting studies of adolescents and work has been conducted by Jeylan Mortimer and her colleagues (Mortimer et al., 2008; Mortimer and Staff, 2004; Mortimer, 2003; Mortimer et al., 1999; Mortimer and Johnson, 1998; Mortimer and Finch, 1996; Mortimer et al., 1996). The focus of this longitudinal study was on work in relation to mental health and post-secondary school education and employment. The study began in 1987 with a sample of 1000 adolescents who were randomly selected from a list of 14-year-olds attending urban state schools. The adolescents completed questionnaires each year of secondary school and each year after leaving school – every year from age 14 to 30. Their parents also completed questionnaires when the adolescents were 14 and again when they were 18.

One of the impressive features of this study is the **retention rate**, which means the percentage of participants who continued to take part in the study after the first year. Retention rates are sometimes a problem in longitudinal studies because people move, change phone numbers or fail to return the questionnaire. This would be especially likely to be a problem in a study such as this, in which young people are being followed through young adulthood, a time that involves frequent changes of residence for many people. In Mortimer's study, the retention rate was 93 per cent after four years of secondary schooling and 78 per cent over eight years (Mortimer et al., 1999). Normally, 50 per cent would be considered adequate after eight years. They were able to keep the retention rate so high in this study by maintaining regular contact with the participants to see whether they had moved or were planning to move.

The longitudinal design of the study enabled Mortimer and her colleagues to provide insights into important aspects of the influences of work on adolescent development. One of the key questions in this area is, does working influence adolescents' problem behaviour, especially substance use? It is well established that adolescents who work report higher rates of problem behaviour, especially if they work more than 20 hours a week, but this leaves open the question: does working long hours cause adolescents to engage in problem behaviour, or do adolescents who engage in problem behaviour also choose to work more? Mortimer and her colleagues (1999), focusing on alcohol use, found that adolescents who work long hours while at school already have higher rates of alcohol use by age 14, before they start working long hours. However, they also found that working long hours contributed to even greater alcohol use.

A second, related question is, does the higher rate of alcohol use among adolescents working long hours in high school establish a pattern that continues beyond high school? Again, the answer to this question could only be determined through a longitudinal study that follows adolescents from high school to several years beyond. Mortimer and Johnson (1998) found that, four years after high school, the young adults who had worked long hours in high school had rates of alcohol use in their early 20s which were no higher than for young adults who had worked less in high school. It was not that the high-working adolescents had decreased their use of alcohol as young adults, but that the other adolescents had 'caught up', reporting higher rates of alcohol use by the time they reached their early 20s.

By way of comparison with longitudinal studies, cross-sectional studies take a 'snapshot' of a behaviour or set of attitudes for example, at a particular point in time. An example of using cross-sectional survey data is provided by researchers Anne Kouvonen and Tomi Lintonen (2002), who examined the relationship between part-time work and heavy drinking among Finnish adolescents. The data was collected as part of the School Health Promotion Survey, which was adminstered to 47,568 secondary school pupils aged 14–16 years. The survey instrument (self-administered questionnaires) included questions on work intensity, work type and the frequency of heavy drinking.

➤

Mortimer's longitudinal study involved at best 1000 pupils and, even with good retention rates, the validity and reliability of the methodology and the findings owe much to the period of time over which the study ranged. In comparison Kouvonen and Lintonen's study owes much to the ability to access almost 50,000 sets of data – a very large snapshot indeed! Let's get back to what Kouvenan and Lintonen found out about part-time work and heavy drinking.

Compared with non-workers, adolescents working more than 10 hours a week had an increased risk of heavy drinking, and also the frequency of heavy drinking was connected with this intensive working. When gender, grade level, parental education, the employment status of the parents, family structure, economic situation of the family, the degree of urbanisation, parental control, steady dating and disposable allowance were adjusted for, reports of weekly drunkenness of 'intensive part-time workers' were almost three times that of pupils not involved in intensive work. The researchers concluded that work does not seem to protect adolescents from heavy drinking.

Both cross-sectional and longitudinal studies require a great deal of effort – not to mention a considerable amount of money – but both kinds of study can provide results that help unravel complex questions of cause and effect with respect to development among adolescents and young adults. With longitudinal studies you also need a good deal of patience!

(Longest and Shanahan, 2007; Brame et al., 2004; Bachman et al., 2003; Wu et al., 2003; Kouvonen and Lintonen, 2002; Frone, 1999; Mortimer et al., 1999). However, scholars disagree on whether this means that working leads to greater substance use or whether adolescents who work already have a tendency towards substance use. Some scholars have argued that the relationship is merely correlational. In this view, adolescents who work more than 10 hours a week also have a tendency towards substance use, but this tendency was evident even before they began working long hours (Bachman et al., 2003; Bachman and Schulenberg, 1993). In contrast, other researchers report that increases in work hours *precede* increases in drug and alcohol use, suggesting that working long hours causes an increase in substance use. These explanations are not incompatible, and both may be valid. Adolescents who work relatively long hours may already have a tendency towards substance use, and that tendency may be further amplified by working long hours.

Another Finnish study (Kouvonen and Kivivuori, 2001), using data from the nationally representative sample of 15- to 16-year-olds discussed in the *Research Focus* feature, found that working more than 20 hours a week was associated with a variety of types of problem behaviour, including vandalism, driving while intoxicated and beating someone up. Adolescents who worked more than 20 hours a week were two to three times as likely as other adolescents to commit these acts. However, remember that because the study was cross-sectional rather than longitudinal this does not necessarily show that working intensively caused them to engage in problem behaviour. They may have had a propensity for problem behaviour even before they became employed.

Not only is working related to problem behaviour outside of work, but there is also a considerable amount of on-the-job deviance among adolescents who work. Greenberger and Steinberg investigated a variety of behaviours they called **occupational deviance** as part of a classic and still referred to piece of

CONNECT AND EXTEND

To see how unstable employment records, no vocational training, occasional work or long-term unemployment are significant risk factors for violent criminal behaviour among adolescents and young men aged between 15 and 27 years, read 'An upbringing to violence? Identifying the likelihood of violent crime among the 1966 birth cohort in Denmark' by Mogens Nygaard Christoffersen, Brian Francis and Keith Soothill in the *Journal of Forensic Psychiatry and Psychology*, Volume 14, Number 2 (2003), pp. 367–381

research on adolescents and work (Ruggiero et al., 1982). First-time adolescent workers indicated on a confidential questionnaire how often they had engaged in each of nine behaviours that involved some kind of occupational deviance, such as falsely calling in sick and stealing things at work. Altogether, over 60 per cent of the working adolescents had engaged in at least one type of occupational deviance after being employed for nine months.

That may seem like a lot, and it is, but keep in mind that the study included only adolescents. Adults have also been known to call in sick when they were not, take things from work that did not belong to them, and so on. We have no way of knowing, from this study alone, whether adolescents tend to do these things more than adults do.

Nevertheless, the combination of studies clearly indicates a relationship between intensive part-time work while at school and problem behaviour in adolescence. Why would this be the case? The answer seems to be different for occupational deviance than it is for other types of problem behaviour. For occupational deviance, the characteristics of the typical adolescent workplace offer likely explanations (Mortimer and Staff, *ibid.*). The work is often boring and tedious, and adolescents do not see the jobs as leading to anything they plan to be doing in the future, so they rarely have much of a feeling of personal investment in the job. If you get caught doing something wrong, you might get fired, but who cares? There are plenty of other jobs of the same type (i.e. low skilled and low paying) readily available. Also, the adolescent workplace often has little adult supervision, and adolescents do not feel close to the adults they work with, so they may feel they have little obligation or responsibility to behave ethically.

With regard to higher rates of substance use among adolescents who work, as we have noted, some scholars believe that this tendency exists among adolescents who work even before they start working. However, other scholars have found that adolescents who work in jobs with a high level of stress are more likely to use drugs and alcohol than adolescents who work in lower-stress jobs (Mortimer and Staff, *ibid.*). This suggests that substance use may be serving as a stress reliever, and provides further evidence that the role of work in problem behaviour is causal, not just 'correlational'.

Also important is that having a part-time job gives adolescents more money to spend on leisure. Very little of the money they make goes to their family's living expenses or saving for future education (Mortimer,

Adolescents who work are more likely to use substances, including tobacco.

2003). Instead, it goes towards purchases for themselves, here and now: designer clothes, downloads, mobile contracts, fuel and insurance for a car, concert tickets, films, eating out – and alcohol, cigarettes and other drugs (Mortimer and Staff, *ibid.*). Adolescents tend to spend the money they make at their jobs in pursuit of good times, and for some of them the pursuit of good times includes substance use.

The Case in Favour of Adolescent Work

You'll see that Jeylan Mortimer's name comes up a lot to cite as evidence for conclusions drawn or theories about the relationship between school, part-time work and problem behaviours (2003). You may even think that, after finding some correlations and perhaps causes of problem behaviour related to part-time work, Mortimer is anti part-time work for secondary school pupils. In fact, Jeylan Mortimer and her colleagues argue that the case against adolescent work has been overstated, and that in fact a strong case can be made in favour of adolescent work. Although some of Mortimer's own research has revealed certain problems associated with adolescent work, she argues that, on the whole, the benefits outweigh the problems.

According to her research, adolescents see many benefits from their work. As Table 11.2 shows, far more of them see benefits in their work than see

Table 11.2 Percentages of Adolescents Indicating Benefits and Costs of Employment

	Girls	Boys
Benefits		
Responsibility	90	80
Money management	66	57
Learned social skills	88	78
Work experience/skill development	43	42
Work ethics	73	68
Independence	75	78
Time management	79	75
Learned about life/shaped future	26	29
Problems		
Less leisure time	49	49
Lower school grades	28	25
Less time for homework	48	49
Think about work during class	78	11
Fatigue	51	45

Source: adapted from Table 2.10 in Aronson et al. (1996)

problems. They believe they gain a sense of responsibility from working, improve their abilities to manage money, develop better social skills and learn to manage their time better. Over 40 per cent believe that their jobs have helped them develop new occupational skills, in contrast to the portrayal of adolescent work as involving nothing but dreary tasks (although we might note that 40 per cent, while substantial, is still a minority). Mortimer (2003) also argues that good relationships with the adults they meet in the workplace can be a protective factor for adolescents from difficult and stressful family situations.

Mortimer and her colleagues (1999) concede that nearly half of adolescents report that working gives them less time for homework, and over a quarter believe that working has negatively affected their grades, as you can see in Table 11.2. However, Mortimer argues that the main activity working adolescents spend less time on is watching television. According to her argument, adolescents simply spend too little time on homework for part-time working to make much difference in their school performance. She claims that no consistent relationship exists across studies between working and school performance in adolescence, even among adolescents who work 20 or more hours a week.

Our judgement is that the case against adolescents working over 20 hours or even 10 hours per week is strong. Problems consistently develop across a wide range of areas beyond 10 hours a week of work. Even Mortimer's data indicate that adolescents perceive negative effects of working on their school performance, and enough studies find a relationship between adolescents and young adults working long hours and poor grades to make this case convincingly (e.g. Dustmann and van Soest, 2007; Marriott, 2007; Stern and Briggs, 2001). Also, there is little dispute that working over 20 hours per week leads to higher substance use. However, Mortimer's research is a useful reminder that the effects of work on adolescent development are complex and that doing some part-time work does offer certain benefits to many adolescents.

CONNECT AND EXTEND

There is a view that part-time work limits participation in more developmentally beneficial activities and confronts teenagers with stressors for which they are not yet ready. However, the analysis provided by Jeylan Mortimer and Jeremy Staff in 'Early work as a source of developmental discontinuity during the transition to adulthood' in *Development and Psychopathology*, Volume 16, Number 4 (October 2004), pp. 1047–1070, indicates that the character of their teenage work experience is a source of resilience as young adults make the transition from school to work. Check out the argument.

THINKING CRITICALLY

Many adolescents clearly prefer to work, even though the work is often boring and is frequently related to negative outcomes (although to some positive outcomes as well). Given this situation, would you be for or against legislation to limit adolescents' work (under age 16 or perhaps 18) to 10 hours a week? Justify your answer in terms of development in adolescence and in young adulthood.

FROM SCHOOL AND PART-TIME WORK TO A 'REAL JOB'

Teaching skills to adolescents directly in the workplace tends to be effective.

As we have observed, few adolescents see their part-time jobs as the beginning of the kind of work they expect to be doing as adults. Waiting on tables, washing dishes, mowing lawns, retail sales and the like are fine for bringing in enough money to finance an active leisure life, but generally these are jobs that adolescents view as temporary and transient, not as forming the basis of a long-term career. Full-time work in a 'real job' comes only after adolescents have completed their education – the end of secondary schooling for some, the end of college or university for others. Let's take a look at the transition to work, first for those who take on full-time work immediately after high school, then for those who make the transition to full-time work following college or university.

Apprenticeships in Western Europe

The focus of work preparation programmes in Western Europe is on apprenticeships (Vazsonyi and Snider, 2008; Hamilton and Hamilton, 2006; 2000). In an **apprenticeship**, an adolescent 'novice' serves under contract to a 'master' who has substantial experience in a profession, and through working under the master the novice learns the skills required to enter the profession successfully. Although apprenticeships originally began centuries ago in craft professions such as carpentry and blacksmithing, today they are undertaken to prepare for a wide range of professions, from car mechanics and carpenters to police officers, computer technicians and childcare workers (Fuller et al., 2005). Apprenticeships are common in Western Europe, especially in Central and Northern Europe. For example, Germany's apprenticeship programme includes over 60 per cent of all 16- to 18-year-olds (Heckhausen and Tomasik, 2002), and Switzerland's includes about one-third of the adolescents who do not attend college after secondary school (Vazsonyi and Snider, ibid.). The *Cultural Focus* box in this chapter provides more detail about Germany's apprenticeship programme.

Common features of apprenticeship programmes are as follows (Hamilton and Hamilton, 2006; 2000):

- entry at age 16, with the apprenticeship lasting two to three years;

- continued part-time schooling while in the apprenticeship, with the college curriculum closely connected to the training received in the apprenticeship;

- training that takes place in the workplace, under authentic working conditions; and

- preparation for a career in a respected profession that provides an adequate income.

This kind of programme requires close coordination between colleges and employers, so that what adolescents learn at college during their apprenticeships will complement and reinforce what is being learned in the workplace. This means that schools consult employers with respect to the skills required in the workplace, and employers make opportunities available for adolescent apprentices and provide masters for them to work under. The employers see this effort as worth their trouble because apprenticeships provide them with a reliable supply of well-qualified entry-level employees (Dustmann and Schoenberg, 2008).

THINKING CRITICALLY

Apprenticeships in Europe appear to work quite well, but they require that adolescents make career decisions by their mid-teens, much earlier than is typical in other countries, for example in America. Do you think the benefits of apprenticeships outweigh the fact that they require these early decisions, or do you prefer the American system of allowing for a longer period of exploration – well into young adulthood – before such decisions are made? Is it a question of what is best developmentally, or is it just a question of different values?

Apprenticeships are common in some European countries. Here an apprentice learns to become a car mechanic.

Although the European school-to-work system has some advantages over the American system, it has some disadvantages as well. Educational psychologist Stephen Hamilton, in comparing the American and European systems, makes a useful distinction between *transparency* and *permeability* (Hamilton and Hamilton, 2006). Transparency is Hamilton's term for how clearly the path is marked through the educational system leading to the labour market. In a transparent system, the educational and training requirements for various occupations are clearly laid out and young people are well informed about them from an early age. Permeability refers to how easy it is to change directions within the educational system. A permeable system makes it easy to drop one educational/career path and move to another.

The American system is low in transparency and high in permeability. Even in young adulthood, most Americans have only a limited understanding of how to obtain the education or training that will lead to the job they want, but it is easy to enter college and easy to switch paths once they get there. In contrast, the European system is high in transparency but low in permeability. European adolescents know which education and training path leads to which job, but once they choose a path – as they are required to do at the age of just 15 or 16 – the system makes it difficult for them to change their minds. Currently, the European system is becoming more permeable because young adults are pushing for more choices and because the traditional system is increasingly viewed as too inflexible to respond to today's rapidly changing information-based economy (Hamilton and Hamilton, 2006).

CONNECT AND EXTEND

For a discussion of the importance of apprenticeship systems in the UK and Germany, read 'Does the concept of apprenticeship still have relevance as a model of skill formation and vocational learning in contemporary society?' by Suwimon Pattayanunt in *Transition Studies Review*, Preprint (January 2012), pp. 1–13

OCCUPATIONAL CHOICE

'In talking to my peers, I realise increasingly that there is no one place to find your passion. For myself, like many others, my career decisions included a mix of all these reasons: a lifelong interest in working with people, a need for a sustainable career that will pay the bills, and a feeling of accomplishment at the end of the day. A friend, paraphrasing the words of novelist Frederick Buechner, once said to me, "Your place is where the world's greatest need meets your greatest love." While the needs of the world are infinite, and how we find our interests takes a number of different paths, this formula is the best and most universal advice I've heard for making career decisions.'

— Emily, third-year university student (in Spengler, 2002, p. C10)

As we saw at the outset of the chapter, adolescents in pre-industrial traditional cultures (and in Northern European cultures historically) work alongside their parents – boys with their fathers and other men, girls with their mothers and other women – doing the kind of work adults do. Because the economies in such cultures are usually not diverse, there are few 'occupations' to choose from. Boys learn to do what men do, whether it is hunting or farming or something else, and girls learn to do what women do, which is usually childcare and running the household, and perhaps some gathering or gardening work. There is a certain security in this arrangement; you grow up knowing that you will have useful and important work to do as an adult, and you grow up gradually learning the skills required for it. On the other hand, there is a narrowness and limitation to it as well – if you are a boy, you must do the work that men do whether you care for it or not; and if you are a girl, your role is to learn childcare and running a household regardless of what your individual preferences or talents might be.

Adolescents in cultures with industrialised economies face a different kind of trade-off. Industrialised economies are astonishingly complex and diverse. This means that, as an adolescent or young adult, you can choose from a tremendous range of possible occupations. However, every adolescent has to find a place among all of that fabulous diversity of choice. And even once you make your choice, you have to hope that the occupation you decide you want will be achievable for you. More young people would like to be medical doctors, veterinarians, musicians or professional athletes than is possible (Schneider and Stevenson, 1999).

Let us take a look now at the developmental pattern in how adolescents make occupational choices and at the various influences that play a part in their choices.

The Development of Occupational Goals

Although children and adolescents may have occupational dreams – fantasies of being a famous footballer, singer or film star – adolescence and especially young adulthood are times when more serious reflection on occupational goals often begins (Arnett, 2004). For young adults, decisions must be made about educational and occupational preparation that will have potential long-term effects on their adult lives.

One influential theory of the development of occupational goals, by Donald Super (1992; 1980; 1976; 1967; Tracey et al., 2005), begins with adolescence and continues through five stages into adulthood, as follows:

- *Crystallisation*, ages 14 to 18. In this initial stage, adolescents begin to move beyond fantasising and start to consider how their talents and interests match up with the occupational possibilities available to them. During this time, they may begin to seek out information about careers that are of interest to them, perhaps by talking over various possibilities with family and friends. Also, as adolescents begin to decide on their own beliefs and values, this helps to guide their occupational explorations as they consider how various job possibilities may confirm or contradict those values.

- *Specification*, ages 18 to 21. During this stage, occupational choices become more focused. For example, a young person who decided during the crystallisation stage to seek an occupation that involves working with children may now decide whether that means being a child psychologist, a teacher, a child centre care worker or a paediatrician. Making this choice usually involves seeking information about what is involved in these occupations, as in the crystallisation stage, but with more of a focus on specific occupations rather than a general field. It also usually involves beginning to pursue the further or higher education or training required to obtain the desired occupation.

- *Implementation*, ages 21 to 24. This stage involves completing the education or training that began in the specification stage and entering the job itself. This may mean that young people must reconcile any discrepancy between what they would like to do and what is available in the work world. For example, you may have been trained to be a teacher but find out after graduation that there are more teachers than available jobs, so that you end up working in a social service agency or a shop.

- *Stabilisation*, ages 25 to 35. This is the stage in which young adults establish themselves in their careers. The initial period of 'getting their feet wet'

in a job comes to an end, and they become more stable and experienced in their work.

- *Consolidation*, age 35 and up. From this point onwards, occupational development means continuing to gain expertise and experience and seeking advancement into higher-status positions as expertise and experience grow.

CULTURAL FOCUS

Germany's Apprenticeship Programme

'Anna is only a few months away from the completion of her apprenticeship in a large [German] manufacturing firm. At age 17, Anna has worked in the firm's accounting, purchasing, inventory, production, personnel, marketing, sales and finance departments, and studied those functions in school. She is very enthusiastic about the recent news that the company will give her an additional 18 months of training in electronic data processing before taking her on as a full-time employee. She is already skilled and reliable enough to have substituted for two weeks in cost accounting during her supervisor's vacation.'

This example is taken from a book by the developmental psychologist Stephen Hamilton (1990) of Cornell University about Germany's apprenticeship system. Hamilton describes Germany's system and suggests how a similar system might be established elsewhere in the world.

Germany's apprenticeship system has existed in various forms for several hundred years (Dustmann and Schoenberg, 2008). In the present, more than 60 per cent of all 16- to 18-year-olds are apprentices, making apprenticeships the most common form of education in the final years of secondary school and the main way of passage from school to work (Hamilton and Hamilton, 2000). As Anna's example illustrates, the apprenticeships train young people not just for trades or skilled labour, but for professional and managerial positions as well. Young people are usually in the programme for three years, and during that time they spend one day a week in a vocational school and the other four in their apprenticeship placement. More than half of apprentices remain with the company that trained them for at least two years after they complete the apprenticeship.

Employers pay all the costs of training their apprentices and in addition pay them a modest salary during the apprenticeship. About 10 per cent of industrial and commercial businesses (e.g. insurance or banking) and 40 per cent of craft businesses take part in the apprenticeship programme. What is the incentive for employers? They participate partly out of German cultural traditions and partly because, once an apprentice learns to do useful work, the employer will have relatively cheap labour during the rest of the apprenticeship and a well-trained employee after the apprenticeship is completed (Dustmann and Schoenberg, 2008).

Hamilton's ethnographic research demonstrates the effectiveness of the German apprenticeship system. Apprentices have numerous opportunities for learning on the job, and what they learn on the job is coordinated with and reinforced by what they learn in school or college. Motivation for learning in college is enhanced by the awareness that the knowledge they gain in school will have a direct and immediate application in the workplace. Adolescents work closely with adults who are in charge of instructing them and providing them with learning opportunities, and typically they have a variety of different positions during the apprenticeship so that they learn a variety of skills. Furthermore, Hamilton notes, 'Germany's apprenticeship system is more than a training programme intended to teach the knowledge and skills related to a specific job. In addition to fulfilling that function, it is a form of general education and an institution for socialising youth to adulthood' (1990, p. 63).

Could a system like this work elsewhere? In some places it already does, but it is not as common as in Germany. A vast government-sponsored system is required to coordinate schools with employers. It also requires earlier decisions about what road to take occupationally; this decision would have to be made by age 15 or 16, rather than putting it off until well after secondary schooling.

However, the benefits are great. Young people leave their teens much better prepared for the workplace than is often the case. School would be less 'boring' to them and more clearly related to their futures. If the benefit of these programmes can be demonstrated, increased enthusiasm may be seen for many more national apprenticeship systems.

CONNECT AND EXTEND

The career choices of both girls and boys still reflect a deeply embedded gender dichotomy. Read 'Is the future really female? The impact and implications of gender for 14–16 year olds' career choices' by Becky Francis in the *Journal of Education and Work*, Volume 15, Number 1 (2002), pp. 75–88

Although this theory remains important in shaping the way commentators think about occupational development and career counsellors provide advice to young people, not everyone fits the pattern prescribed by the theory, and certainly not according to these precise ages. Because education is stretching out further and further into the 20s for more and more people, it is not unusual for the implementation stage to begin in the mid-20s rather than the early 20s. Perhaps more important, it is less and less common for occupational development to follow the kind of linear path through the life course that is described in Super's theory. Increasingly, people have not just one career or occupation, but two or more in the course of their working lives. Most of today's adolescents and young adults will change career directions at least once (Donohue, 2007). Also, for women and increasingly for men, balancing work and family goals may mean taking time off or at least working fewer hours during the years when they have to care for young children.

The occupational development theories of Super and others do not take into account the kinds of considerations often faced by women. Traditional theories assume that occupational development follows a single path. However, this assumption ignores the fact that most women in Northern European societies lead a dual-career life, with their role as homemaker and mother as a 'second career' in addition to the out-of-home occupation they hold (Cinamon,

2006). Most women have a period of their lives, during the time they have one or more young children, when they spend as much or more time in the homemaker-mother role as they do in the role of their paid occupation. Throughout the years their children are growing up, women face the challenge of integrating these two roles, more so than men because even now in Northern European cultures (as in Eastern and traditional cultures), women have the main responsibility for child care (van der Lippe et al., 2006). For this reason, theories of career development that neglect the challenge of this integration do not fit the career paths that today's young adult women are likely to follow.

Influences on Occupational Goals

Theories of occupational development provide a general outline of how adolescents and young adults may progress through their working lives. But how do adolescents and young adults make choices among the great variety of occupations available to them? What influences enter into their decisions? A great deal of research has been conducted on these questions, especially focusing on the influence of personality characteristics and gender.

Personality Characteristics

One influence on occupational choice in cultures where people are allowed to choose from a wide range of possible occupations is the individual's judgement of how various occupations would be suited to his or her personality. It makes sense that people seek occupations they judge to be consistent with their interests and talents. One influential theorist, John Holland (1996), investigated the personality characteristics typical of people who hold various jobs and of adolescents who aspire to those jobs. Holland's theory describes six personality categories to consider when matching a person with a prospective occupation:

- *Realistic.* High physical strength, practical approach to problem solving, and low social understanding. Best occupations: those that involve physical activity and practical application of knowledge, such as farming, truck driving and construction.

- *Intellectual.* High on conceptual and theoretical thinking. Prefer thinking problems through rather than applying knowledge. Low on social skills. Best occupations: scholarly fields such as mathematics and science.

- *Social.* High in verbal skills and social skills. Best professions: those that involve working with people, such as teaching, social work and counselling.

- *Conventional.* High on following directions carefully, dislike of unstructured activities. Best occupations: those that involve clear responsibilities but require little leadership, such as bank clerk or secretary.

- *Enterprising.* High in verbal abilities, social skills and leadership skills. Best occupations: sales, politics, management, running a business.

- *Artistic.* Introspective, imaginative, sensitive, unconventional. Best occupations: artistic occupations such as painting or writing fiction.

You can probably see the potential for overlap in some of these categories. Obviously, they are not mutually exclusive. A person could have some *Artistic* qualities as well as some *Social* qualities, or some *Intellectual* qualities as well as some *Enterprising* qualities. Holland does not claim that all people fall neatly into clear types. However, he and other researchers believe that most people will be happiest and most successful in their careers if they are able to find a match between their personality qualities and an occupation that allows them to express and develop those qualities (Vondracek and Porfelli, 2003). Career counsellors use Holland's ideas to help adolescents gain insights into the fields that might be best for them to pursue. The widely used Strong-Campbell Vocational Interest Inventory is based on Holland's ideas.

Keep in mind the limitations of this approach to understanding occupational choice. Within any particular profession, you are likely to find persons with a considerable variety of personality traits. If you think of teachers you have known, for example, you will probably find that they varied considerably in their personalities, even if they may have had some characteristics in common. Their different personalities may have allowed each of them to bring a different combination of strengths to the job. So, there probably is not just one personality type that is potentially well suited to a particular type of job.

In the same way, any one person's personality could probably fit well with many of the jobs available in a diverse economy. Because most people's personalities are too complex to fall neatly into one type or another, different occupations may bring out different combinations of strengths in a particular person. For this reason, assessing your personality traits may narrow somewhat the range of fields that you think are suitable for you, but for most people in industrialised countries that would still leave a considerable number of possible occupations to choose from.

Gender

Gender has a substantial influence on job choice. In Chapter 10 we observed the relation between gender and choice of subject to study at college or university. This relation holds in the workplace as well. Although the proportion of young women who are employed rose steeply in the twentieth century, and although women aged 16 to 24 are now more likely than young men to be employed – see Figure 11.1 – (Labour Force Survey, 2010) it remains true that some jobs are held mainly by men and some jobs are held mainly by women (Porfelli et al., 2008; Vondracek and Porfeli, *ibid.*). Jobs held mainly by women are concentrated in the service sector – for example teacher, nurse, secretary, childcare worker. Jobs held mainly by men include engineer, chemist, surgeon, computer software designer. In general, 'women's jobs' tend to be low paying and low status, whereas 'men's jobs' tend to be high paying and high status. These patterns have changed somewhat in recent years; for example, women are now nearly as likely as men to become lawyers and medical doctors. However, for many jobs the gender differences have proven to be remarkably stable. Even within high-status professions, women tend

Occupations such as nursery nursing continue to be highly gender segregated.

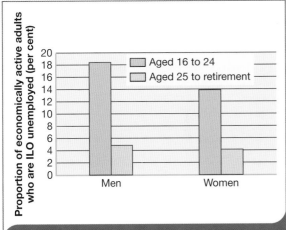

Figure 11.1 The unemployment rate is higher for young men than for young women

Source: Adapted from Labour Force Survey, ONS; the data is the average for 2007 to 2009; UK; updated May 2010

to have the lower-status and lower-paying positions; for example, women who are physicians are more likely to be general practice doctors than surgeons.

Why do these gender differences in job choice persist, despite the fact that women now exceed men in terms of overall educational attainment? Gender socialisation is certainly part of it. Children learn early on that some jobs are appropriate for either males or females, in the same way that they learn other aspects of gender roles (Maccoby, 2002). By the time young people reach the age when it is time for them to choose an occupational direction, their gender identities are well established and constitute a powerful influence on their job selection (Desmairis and Curtis, 1999). One study of young adult women found that even mathematically talented young women often avoid information technology (IT) fields because they view IT as male dominated,

a perception that in turn perpetuates the male domination of IT (Messersmith et al., 2008). Similarly, a study in The Netherlands found that adolescent girls avoid going into computer science because they believe that others view women in computer science as sexually unattractive (Rommes et al., 2007).

Another important influence is that, already in young adulthood, young women anticipate the difficulties they are likely to face in balancing their work and family roles, and this too influences their job selection. It has long been true that wives spend considerably more time on family tasks than husbands do, especially when the couple has young children. Although men now handle more of the childcare than in previous generations, wives still do more housework than their husbands, even when both of them work full time (Strandh and Nordenmark, 2006; van der Lippe et al., 2006; Gershury et al., 2005). Sociologists have called this the **second shift** (Craig, 2007; Hochschild, 1998), referring to the domestic work shift that women must perform after they complete their shift in the workplace.

THINKING CRITICALLY

How would you explain the fact that wives usually end up doing most of the household work and childcare even when they work as many hours as their husbands? Do you think this is likely to change in the current generation of young adults?

While they are still young adults, young women often anticipate the tensions they are likely to face with their roles as worker, spouse and mother (Cinamon, 2006). This realisation affects their occupational choices, making them less likely to choose jobs that will be highly demanding and time consuming, even if the job is high paying and is in an area they enjoy and for which they have talent (Hochschild, 1998). They anticipate, too, that they will leave the workplace at some point to focus on caring for their young children. For example, one study asked university students reading business studies about their future work and family plans (Dey and Hurtado, 1999). The young women expected to work a total of 29 years full time, nearly 8 years less than their male classmates. Even though these young women were studying business, an area that is traditionally 'male,' they too expected to take time away from the workplace to care for their young children.

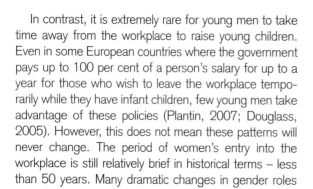

CONNECT AND EXTEND

Career choices depend upon gender, school success, ethnicity and social class. For example the situation of girls from ethnic minorities is better than expected, while that of indigenous boys from low socio-economic backgrounds is worse when compared to similar boys from ethnic minorities.

Read 'Complex inequalities of educational opportunities: a large-scale longitudinal study on the relation between gender, social class, ethnicity and school success' by Hetty Dekkers, Roel Bosker and Geert Driessen in *Educational Research and Evaluation*, Volume 6, Number 1 (2000), pp. 59–82

In contrast, it is extremely rare for young men to take time away from the workplace to raise young children. Even in some European countries where the government pays up to 100 per cent of a person's salary for up to a year for those who wish to leave the workplace temporarily while they have infant children, few young men take advantage of these policies (Plantin, 2007; Douglass, 2005). However, this does not mean these patterns will never change. The period of women's entry into the workplace is still relatively brief in historical terms – less than 50 years. Many dramatic changes in gender roles have already taken place that could not have been anticipated a half century ago. The changes appear to be continuing. Young men at the turn of the century said they give time with family a higher priority than prestigious or high-paying work, more than older men and similar to young women (Grimsley, 2000). Furthermore, technologically driven changes in work that are likely to allow an increasing proportion of work to be done at home or in flexible shifts may make it easier for both men and women to balance successfully – and more equally – the demands of work and family.

FOCUS ON YOUTH IN THE MEDIA

Punk on Career Direction, Aspiration and Unemployment

Examples of how adolescents may use media in developing their personal and professional aspirations can be of concern to their parents and other adults in their immediate social environment. Young people can develop admiration for media stars who seem to reject the work or behaviour values of the adult world; media stars who may in fact ostentatiously scorn the very idea of striving towards a good steady job as part of 'growing up' and therefore to become a responsible and self-sufficient adult (Steele and Brown, 1995). Adolescents can be attracted to popular media that promotes 'get rich quick' through overnight celebrity status, some of which adults find disagreeable for precisely the reason it is so appealing to adolescents – the social intensity and prevalence of reality TV (Lachlan, 2006). Adolescents may seclude themselves in their rooms and use media in coping with their problems about deciding what to be and where to go in a way that seems to shut out their parents (Larson, 1995). Finally, adolescents may become involved in a media-based youth subculture that actively and explicitly rejects the future that adult society holds out to them. In all of these ways, socialisation from the media may be subversive to the socialisation promoted by part-time work and **community service**.

It's not all bad news for the media. Adolescents do not come to media as blank slates, but as members of a family, community and culture that have socialised them from birth and from whom they have learned ideals and principles that are likely to influence their career choices; the amount and nature of their part-time work; and whether or not to engage in voluntary community service. Second, their learned socialisation also influences how adolescents and young adults interpret the media they consume. Adolescents perceive much of the mass media as reinforcing conventional values such as 'honesty is the best policy' and, particularly in the context of this chapter, 'hard work yields rewards' (Brown et al., 2002). Or try 'Make the most of your life everyday, and every opportunity that comes your way'. Surprisingly (perhaps) these are lyrics from the track 'Wake Up' by an English punk band of the 1980s, The Neurotics:

Wake Up

Look for the lyrics of '*School Anthem*' using a web search.
Failure at school leads to poor self-image
And dead-end jobs
Confirm the lie that you mess up every chance you get
The singer exhorts the listener to change mindset
In language that all can understand

Of course it is worth continuing to try
To just enjoy life
By taking every chance
Or you could just give in and agree that you're no good at anything
Express yourself and your feelings
And don't give in to indifference.

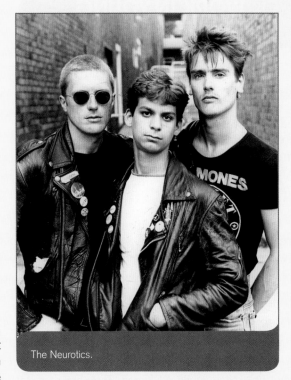

The Neurotics.

Another Neurotics track, 'Living with Unemployment', was covered by The Oppressed, an anti-fascist punk band that formed in 1981 in Cardiff as an outlet for Roddy Moreno, an outspoken advocate for racial unity in the skinhead and Oi! (working-class protest) scenes. Most of the musicians in the band's various line-ups were skinheads who openly voiced opposition to racism – in their lyrics, interviews and on stage. The band split in 2006, but re-formed in 2009, and performed around Europe in 2011:

Living with unemployment

Look for '*Living with Unemployment*' using a web search.
The track talks of a move to London and a lonely bedsit
With no job
And just a television for company

The lack of work is blamed on what?
Who, in the words of the singer
Is responsible for the lack of work?

In his neighbourhood the only way out of unemployment
Is to join the army

Unemployment is a lonely existence
And very inhibiting
It means Loneliness for everybody affected.

Check out some great performances of these tracks on **www.youtube.com**. Could young people today identify with these lyrics; the lack of career direction, lack of aspiration, and the loneliness and despair of unemployment?

WORK IN YOUNG ADULTHOOD

'I didn't really choose my job [as a bank clerk]. It chose me. I needed the money. I was so broke! And they pay well. But I hate my job! There's no opportunity for growth there. I want to do something in maybe the health care field or fashion industry.'

—Wendy, age 25 (in Arnett, 2004, p. 151)

'At first [I studied] journalism. Then I got a part-time job at a preschool. They asked me to teach a three-year-old classroom and I did it and I loved it and I thought "You know, this is what I need to do." So I changed to education. I love teaching. I can't imagine doing anything else.'

– Kim, age 23 (in Arnett, 2004, p. 147)

Because many adolescents start part-time work beginning in their mid-teens, work is nothing new to them when they reach young adulthood. They are used to applying for a job, learning the ropes of a new job, and being paid. What changes in young adulthood is that it is no longer enough to have just any job. As we have already observed, most secondary school pupils do not expect their jobs to provide them with skills that will be the basis for the kinds of work they will be doing as adults. They simply want to find a job that will bring in enough cash to allow them to pursue an active leisure life. In contrast, most young adults are looking for a job that will turn into a career, a long-term occupation, something that will not only bring in a good income but provide personal fulfilment (Taylor, 2005).

Work in young adulthood focuses on identity questions: What do I really want to *do?* What am I best at? What do I enjoy the most? How do my abilities and desires fit in with the kinds of opportunities that are available to me? In asking themselves what kind of work they want to do, it could be argued that young adults are also asking themselves what kind of person they are. In the course of young adulthood, as they try out various jobs they begin to answer their identity questions, and they develop a better sense of who they are and what work suits them best.

Many adolescents have an idea, while they are still at school, of what kind of career they want to go into (Schneider and Stevenson, 1999). Often that idea dissolves in the course of young adulthood, as they develop a clearer identity and discover that their secondary school aspiration does not align with it. In place of their school notions, many seek another career that does fit their identity, something they really enjoy and really want to do (Vaughan, 2005).

Some young adults engage in systematic exploration as they go about looking for a career path they wish to settle into for the long term. They think about what they want to do, they try a job or a college course in that area to see if the fit is right, and if it is not they try another path until they find something they like better. But for many others, 'exploration' is a bit too lofty a word to describe their work history during their late teens and early 20s (Mortimer et al., 2002). Often it is not nearly as systematic, organised and focused as 'exploration' implies. 'Meandering' might be a more accurate word, or maybe 'drifting' or even 'floundering' (Hamilton and Hamilton, 2006). Their eventual goal is to find a job they love and that fits their interests and abilities, but virtually all of them have many jobs in their late teens and early 20s that have little or nothing to do with this goal. For many young adults, working in young adulthood simply means finding a job, any job that will pay the bills until something better comes along. In Western Europe job changes and periods of unemployment and part-time employment are common during young adulthood (Sneeding and Phillips, 2002).

Many young adults express a sense that they did not really choose their current job; one day they just found themselves in it, like a ball that rolls randomly on a

CONNECT AND EXTEND

What factors are relevant to the linked process of forming identities and choosing careers? Read 'Constructing identities and making careers: young people's perspectives on work and learning' by Helen Stokes and Johanna Wyn in the *International Journal of Lifelong Education*, Volume 26, Number 5 (2007), pp. 495–511

pitted surface until it lands in one of the holes. For the most part, young adults who got their jobs in this random fashion are looking for something else. Falling into a job rarely results in the kind of fit with one's identity that makes a job fully satisfying. Most young adults want to find that kind of fit, and any job that does not provide it is viewed as a way station on the road to that goal.

Even for young adults who meander or drift through various jobs in their early 20s rather than exploring their options in a systematic way, the process of trying various jobs often serves the function of helping them sort out what kind of work they want to do. When you are in a dead-end job, at least you find out what you do *not* want to do. You may also find out that a job has to be about more money; that you are not willing to do something boring and pointless in the long run even if it pays the bills; that you are willing to keep looking until you find something interesting and enjoyable. There is also the possibility that as you drift through various jobs you may happen to drift into one you enjoy; one that unexpectedly clicks.

UNEMPLOYMENT

'I feel trapped. When you work hard and you're motivated, they should give you a chance. They don't.'

– Stephanie, age 25, unemployed young adult in Paris (in Swardson, 1999)

Although the majority of young people in industrialised countries are able to find a job once they leave high school or college, this is not true for all of them. In both Europe the unemployment rate for young adults is consistently at least twice as high as for adults beyond age 25 (Wolbers, 2007). We have already noted – Figure 11.1 – that unemployment rates for 16- to 24-year-olds in the United Kingdom are four times higher than adult rates (25 to retirement age). Most European countries have similar unemployment rates, especially for young people (Hämäläinen et al., 2005; Sneeding and Phillips, 2002). Unemployment has been found to be associated with higher risk of depression, especially for young adults who lack strong parental support (Bjarnason and Sigurdardottir, 2003; Axelsson and Ejlertsson, 2002). The relation between unemployment and depression has also been found in longitudinal studies (Dooley et al., 2000), which indicates that unemployment leads to depression more often than being depressed makes it hard to find a job.

A large proportion of young people from 16 to their early 20s are attending school, college or university – in full-time education – but they are not classified as unemployed because education is considered to be the focus of their efforts, not whatever part-time work in which they might engage. People whose time is devoted mainly to caring for their own children also would not be classified as unemployed. In Britain a comparatively new term is now applied to young people who are **n**ot in **e**mployment, **e**ducation or **t**raining – **NEETs**.

How many NEETs are there? Well, Figure 11.2 shows that the overall average of about 12 per cent of young people in England are NEETs in both 2005 and 2008 – well over three times the number of 'adult' unemployed – and that the trend for 18- to 24-year-olds to have higher proportions of NEETs (up to 16 per cent in 2008) is worsening.

Furthermore, more recent analysis by the EU's Eurostat (2011) provides evidence that Britain has now one of the worst NEET figures in Europe at around

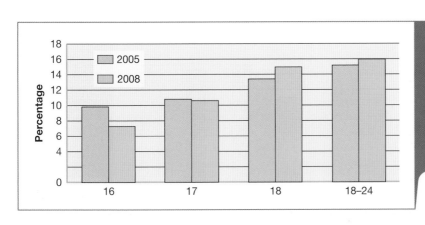

Figure 11.2 16–24-year-olds not in education, employment or training (NEET) in England, by age, 2005 and 2008.

Source: Adapted from DCSF (2007). NEET Statistics Quarterly Brief.

CONNECT AND EXTEND

Early in 2011, the British government proposed doing away with the Education Maintenance Allowance (EMA). The EMA was designed to encourage more young people from lower-income households to participate in post-compulsory education – to stay on at school or college. Was it a success or a failure? Read 'Paying young people to learn: does it work?' by Sue Maguire in *Research in Post-compulsory Education*, Volume 13, Number 2 (2008), pp. 205–215

1 million; one in five 18-year-old boys and one in six girls. The study also shows that the number of NEETs has risen dramatically, making the UK worse than countries such as Lithuania and Slovakia and just above Italy and Spain. The last figures to be published in February 2011 (DFE) showed that 1,026,000 16- to 24-year-olds were 'NEETs' in the third quarter of 2010, the highest number since records began in 1992.

The regional picture (Figure 11.3) on 16–18 NEETs is taken from English Local Authorities' Client Caseload Information System (CCIS), so is not directly comparable with statistics from the Department for Education quoted earlier. CCIS data shows a lower percentage NEET as it is based on calendar age and young people taking a formal gap year or in custody are not counted as NEET in this regional data. Nevertheless it shows that some regions of England, notably the ex-heavy industrial regions of the North West, Yorkshire, Humberside and the North East have higher densities of NEETs than more affluent London and the South West. What about other parts of the United Kingdom?

There is an annual survey of all leavers from state schools in Wales to obtain their destinations as at end of October. The results from this survey can be used to provide estimates of NEET rates by unitary authority

for 16-year-olds. Figure 11.4 shows the proportion of 2008 16-year-old school leavers who were NEET by the local unitary authority based upon the counties, towns and cities of Wales.

The proportion of NEETs in post-heavy industrial Cardiff and Newport are almost four times that of the rural county of Powys. Even within regions and authorities there are 'pockets' of very high densities of unemployed young people. These pockets are often to be found on large council estates – defined areas of almost exclusively 'social housing', houses, and blocks – sometimes high-rise – of flats, built and owned by local authorities, and rented to people living in or moving into the local authority. Though a much more complex picture than can be painted here, such estates are often described as areas of low socio-economic status containing many 'problem families' and schools working in very challenging circumstances. Many of these estates are considered centres of problem behaviours including delinquency, domestic and street violence, and social exclusion.

Does being NEET present a major risk for young people of becoming socially excluded? This danger is reflected in the practices of the Connexions service (see the upcoming *Focus on Professional Practice*

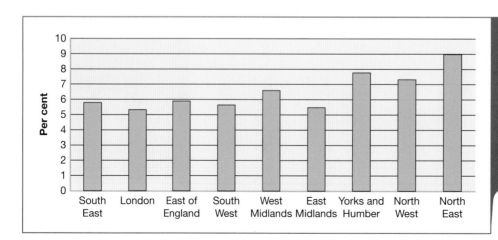

Figure 11.3
Regional averages for NEETs aged 16 to 18 in England (November 2009 to January 2010).

Source: Adapted from CCIS data.

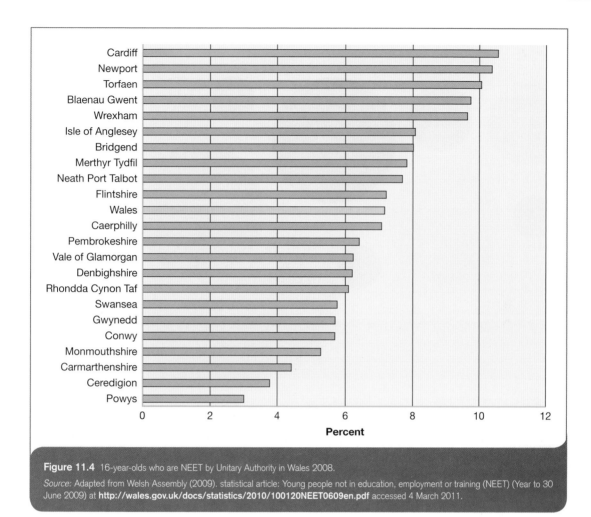

Figure 11.4 16-year-olds who are NEET by Unitary Authority in Wales 2008.

Source: Adapted from Welsh Assembly (2009). statistical article: Young people not in education, employment or training (NEET) (Year to 30 June 2009) at **http://wales.gov.uk/docs/statistics/2010/100120NEET0609en.pdf** accessed 4 March 2011.

feature), whose effectiveness is measured by meeting targets for reducing the numbers of NEET young people. However, being NEET defines young people by what they are not, rather than as a mix of young people whose varied regional situations and local difficulties are not thoroughly understood (Yates and Payne, 2006).

What accounts for these regional and local authority differences? Changes that have taken place in urban areas in recent decades have resulted in a combination of dire conditions that are proving difficult to reverse.

The changes began with the decline in high-paying, low-skilled manufacturing jobs (Wilson, 2006; Quillian, 2003). As economic activity in the inner cities declined, many people followed the movement of jobs out of the cities into the suburbs. The people who took the initiative to move were often the most able, the most educated and the most ambitious, including community leaders who had been important in building and sustaining institutions such as churches, businesses, social clubs and political organisations.

CONNECT AND EXTEND

Andy Furlong argues that to represent vulnerable youth effectively we must use a set of definitions that are narrower than that represented by NEET. Read 'Not a very NEET solution: representing problematic labour market transitions among early school-leavers' by Andy Furlong in *Work, Employment & Society*, Volume 20, Number 3 (September 2006), pp. 553–569

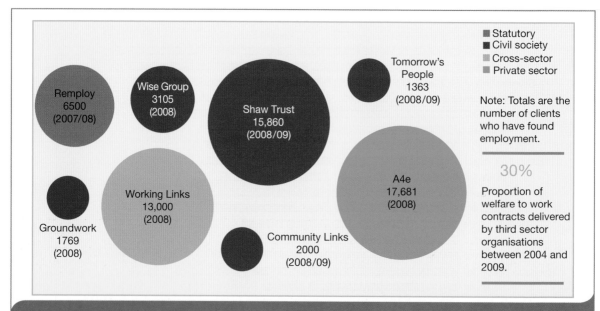

Figure 11.5 Getting the disadvantaged back to work: examples of major providers.

Source: Adapted from The UK Civil Society Almanac 2010: Workforce **http://www.skills-thirdsector.org.uk/documents/NC652_Workforce_mini_almanac_03.pdf** accessed 4 March 2011.

With the departure of these community leaders, the downward spiral of life in the cities accelerated. Neighbourhoods eroded and crime increased, giving the businesses that had remained more incentive to join the exodus (Wilson, *ibid.*). As the financial base of the cities and towns declined with the departure of businesses and the more affluent citizens, the quality of schools also declined from lack of adequate funding to deal with the problems they faced – though there were many notable exceptions. By the early 1980s, many young people living in large estates in our towns and cities lacked the basic skills of reading and arithmetic necessary even for low-paying, entry-level jobs. With few jobs available and with many of the young people lacking the skills to qualify for the available jobs, rates of crime, drug use and gang violence among young people in urban areas climbed steadily higher.

What can be done about this complex and so far intractable situation? Most commentators and policy makers now agree that, given the number and seriousness of the problems in our towns and cities, simply offering job-training programmes will not be enough. William Wilson (*ibid.*), one of the most prominent sociologists on this topic, has proposed an approach with the following elements:

• *Upgrade education.* The current system of funding of schools perpetuates inequality because schools in poor areas such as the inner cities need more financial support to deal with the additional

challenges they face. Also, the quality of teachers in the inner cities could be enhanced through scholarships to attract promising young people to teach in urban schools and through reforms in teacher training and qualification that require teachers to demonstrate thorough going understanding of not only the subjects they teach but also the development and psychology of the youngsters they will teach.

• *Improve school-to-work programmes.* Young people in urban areas are especially harmed by the lack of effective school-to-work programmes, as shown in their high rates of unemployment. The programmes currently available with payments to stay on in education to the age of 18 and the Future Jobs Fund are planned to be scrapped and in their stead the current UK government (at the time of writing in March 2011) plans to target unemployment benefits as a way of encouraging young people to take available jobs. However there are many statutory crosssector and private sector organisations that work with disadvantaged youngsters (and others) to get back to work, although numbers of the young unemployed helped back to work is low in comparison with the large number of NEETs. It could be argued that more support for this sector could be a major way of strengthening this element of Wilson's approach to youth unemployment.

• *Improve access to employment.* Because most new jobs are opening up in suburban rather than urban locations, young people in the inner cities are at a disadvantage because few own cars and public transportation between cities and suburbs is inadequate. Also, because newly available jobs are most often filled not through widely accessible advertisements but through personal contacts, young people in urban areas with high concentrations of unemployment have less information about available jobs. Creating better job information and the placement of more job centres in areas of high NEET density would help to address this problem. Again, see the upcoming *Focus on Professional Practice* feature:

Building on Connexions: Advice and Guidance for those aged 13–19.

- *Provide government-funded public service jobs.* Urban areas have many needs that less skilled workers could help to address in public service jobs. Having young people serve in jobs such as nursing assistants, playground supervisors, bridge painters, pothole fillers and library shelf-fillers would not only give them useful work experience – and provide a substitute for unemployment benefits – but would also enhance the quality of life in the areas where they live, both for themselves and for others.

FOCUS ON PROFESSIONAL PRACTICE

Building on Connexions: Advice and Guidance for those aged 13–19

The Connexions service was established in 2001 by the British government with the aim of providing an all-round service to meet young people's needs for information, advice and support, and so ensure young people made a smooth transition to adulthood and working life. Through multi-agency working, Connexions was tasked to provide impartial information, advice and guidance (including careers advice and guidance) and access to personal development opportunities to help remove barriers to learning.

Connexions was designed to help all young people aged 13 to 19 regardless of need, and those aged up to 24 with a learning difficulty or disability. However, there was a particular focus on those at risk of not being in education, employment or training (termed NEETs), or of being socially excluded.

As part of the service, a dedicated website, *Connexions Direct*, remains available for young people who can contact Connexions Direct by telephone, adviser online, email and text, and advisers are available 18 hours a day. The website provides information on careers, learning, health, housing, free time, travel, young people's rights, relationships and money. Let's focus on careers.

Connexions Direct contains links to advice on school course options at 14 and 16 and the implications of course selection for future careers. The website also gives access to downloadable publications, a *jobs4U* careers database – online access to up-to-the minute list of local job vacancies and a searchable database of courses of vocational training.

A key element of Connexions was the provision of information, advice and guidance by a workforce of personal advisers. Local authorities must provide all 13- to 19-year-olds, and all those up to 25 years old with a learning difficulty or disability, with reasonable, face-to-face access to a personal adviser to provide information, advice, guidance, advocacy and brokerage (including brokering access to targeted youth support services). As a minimum, each personal adviser must have, or be actively working towards, an appropriate qualification, and have undertaken relevant appropriate training. The Connexions service had particular responsibility for coordinating transition planning for students with learning difficulties. In one study Bob Grove and Alison Giraud-Saunders (2003) reported on the development of the personal adviser role in two special schools and an FE college as part of the Lewisham Connexions pilot.

The introduction of Connexions services emphasised the integration of service provision by sponsoring the creation of the new professional roles of personal adviser and by promoting closer inter-agency links. The current Connexions service aspires to high levels of integration; however, it has been argued that the process of integration in Connexions has been limited because of the lack of influence by Connexions workers (sometimes the 'wrong person for the job' – Artaraz, 2006), and what is termed the unbalanced power relations between schools and the Connexions service (Artaraz, 2008). ➤

> Furthermore it is argued that in supporting educational expansion (more young people extending their school and college careers) the Connexions service is failing to see that such expansion may be part of the problem rather than an actual or potential solution to young people's transition difficulties (Roberts, 2004). Perhaps adding more rungs to educational ladders will only exacerbate school-leavers' difficulties and personal advisers should focus on connections into work rather then extensions to schooling; 'the effective transfer and integration of learning from education to the workplace' (Oliver, 2004 p. 109).

> (At the time of writing some Connexions services are being assimilated into Integrated Youth Support Services (IYSS) to integrate youth work and Connexions based on a single role – youth support worker with a focus on specialised services. The IYSS will itself be part of an all-age careers service to be known as the National Careers Service. It does look as if Connexions Direct may remain the name of the online service, so a web search will connect you to the changing picture of careers advice for young people.)

CONNECT AND EXTEND

To access research undertaken within Greater Merseyside (UK), which has relatively high levels of young NEET and where a 'culture of worklessness' has developed within the poorest areas read 'Tackling the NEET generation and the ability of policy to generate a "NEET" solution: evidence from the UK' by Simon Pemberton in *Environment and Planning C: Government and Policy*, Volume 26, Number 1 (2008), pp. 243–259

VOLUNTARY WORK – COMMUNITY SERVICE

In addition to the paid work that adolescents and young adults do, some youngsters also do voluntary work. Scholars sometimes refer to such work as community service because it involves volunteering to serve members of the young person's community without monetary reward (McIntosh et al., 2005; McLellan and Youniss, 2003; Youniss and Yates, 2000).

Many people choose to become more involved in the community through activities such as fundraising, serving on committees, organising or helping to run clubs or groups (such as Brownies or Scouts) or by giving advice. In 2001 the Omnibus Survey (Table 11.3) asked adults aged 16 and over in Great Britain about the sorts of volunteering activities they had undertaken during the previous 12 months. Personally raising or collecting money was found to be the most common community service for both men and women. Organising or helping to run clubs or groups was more common among people aged between 16 and 24, and this declined with age.

There are clearly a growing number of opportunities to engage in voluntary activities and we can get some more detail of the types of activities from a survey for the UK NCVO (National Council for Voluntary Organisations) published in the *Civil Society Almanac* (2010) and presented in Table 11.4.

Community Service and Adolescent Development

Research on adolescents and community service has focused on two main questions: What are the distinctive characteristics of adolescents who do volunteer work? What effects does volunteer work have on adolescents who take part in it?

Adolescents who volunteer tend to have a high sense of personal competence, and they tend to have higher educational goals and performance than other adolescents (Pancer et al., 2007; Bloom, 2000). They tend to have high ideals and to perceive a higher degree of similarity between their 'actual selves' and their 'ideal selves' than do other adolescents (McIntosh et al., 2005). Adolescents who participate in community service often report that one or both parents do so as well (Pancer et al., 2007). By their participation, parents provide both a model for community service and concrete opportunities for adolescents to participate (Law et al., 2003).

Table 11.3 Volunteering (16- to 24- year-olds) in Great Britain by Type of Activity carried out and Gender, 2001

Great Britain	Percentages	
	Males	Females
Personally raising or collecting money	12	19
Organising or helping a club or group	10	11
Serving on committees	8	9
Giving non-professional advice	5	4
Giving professional advice	5	3
Giving other kinds of practical help	4	7
Providing administrative/ clerical help	4	3
Any other type of voluntary activity	3	4

By adults aged 16 and over. In 12 months prior to interview.

Source: Office for National Statistics (2001a) Omnibus Survey

Table 11.4 Type of Activity Volunteers were most likely to participate in, England 2007

	(%)
Helping in schools	31
Religion	24
Sports, exercise	22
Health, disability	22
Children, young people	18
Local community, neighbourhood, citizens' group	17
Hobbies, recreation, social clubs	13
Overseas aid, disaster relief	11
Animal welfare	10
Elderly people	8
Arts, museums	8
Conservation, the environment, heritage	8
Social welfare	7
Politics	4
Safety, first aid	4
Justice, human rights	4
Trade unions	3
Other	3

Source: NCVO (2010)

For most adolescents, their community service is motivated by both individual and collectivist values. Often, of course, they are motivated by collectivist values such as wanting to help others or a concern for those who have been less fortunate than themselves. However, perhaps less obviously, studies have found that individualist values are equal to collectivist values as a motivation for adolescents' community service. In addition to wanting to help others, adolescents also volunteer because it gives them a sense of personal satisfaction and they enjoy doing the work. As Yates and Youniss (1996) suggested in some of their earlier writing, performing community service 'requires a personal investment in which the action of helping others becomes part of one's identity and, thus, is understood and articulated in terms of what makes one feel good' (p. 91).

CONNECT AND EXTEND

The British National Citizen Service (NCS) was launched and piloted during the summer of 2011. It is a voluntary eight-week summer programme for 16-year-olds that aims to mix participants of different backgrounds; support the transition into adulthood for young people; and create social action projects in local communities. Read more about the scheme at: **http://www.education.gov.uk/** and follow the links to National Citizen Service

CONNECT AND EXTEND

People from black ethnic minorities have little to do with the voluntary sector services because of lack of knowledge of their existence and because of invisible cultural barriers. What are those barriers? Read 'Reaching out to black ethnic minorities: a voluntary sector perspective on mental health' by Clare Lai in *Practice: Social Work in Action*, Volume 12, Number 1 (2000), pp. 17–28

With regard to the effects of community service, commentators have observed that such service is often part of adolescents' political socialisation. Through their participation, adolescents become more concerned about social issues and develop an understanding of themselves as members of their society (Pancer et al., 2007; Reinders and Youniss, 2006; McIntosh et al., 2005; Metz et al., 2003). In one example of this effect Youniss and Yates (2000; 1997) studied adolescents who were volunteering in a soup kitchen for homeless people. Through the course of the year of their service, the adolescents began to reassess themselves, not only reflecting on their fortunate lives in comparison to the people they were working with but also seeing themselves as potential activists in working for the reforms needed to address the problem of homelessness. Furthermore, the adolescents began to raise questions about characteristics of a political system in relation to homelessness, such as government policies on affordable housing and job training. Thus, their participation not only made them more conscious of themselves as citizens but also led them to be more critical of political policies and more aware of their own responsibility in addressing social problems in society.

Studies have also examined the long-term effects of taking part in volunteer work in adolescence. In general, these studies indicate that people who take part in volunteer work in adolescence are also more likely to be active in political activities and volunteer organisations as adults (Hart et al., 2007; Sherrod et al., 2002). Of course, these studies do not show that community service in adolescence causes people to volunteer in adulthood as well. As we have seen, adolescent volunteers already differ from their peers in ways that explain their greater participation in community service in adolescence and beyond.

Nevertheless, the study by Youniss and Yates (2000) and other studies (e.g. McIntosh et al., 2005; Metz et al., 2003; Flanagan et al., 1999) indicate that community service does have a variety of favourable effects on the young people who take part in it. One longitudinal study found that adolescents who were required to perform community service as part of their school curriculum, and who indicated that they would have served anyway, showed no changes resulting from their participation (Metz and Youniss, 2005). However, those who would not have volunteered to serve without the requirement showed an increase on measures of civic attitudes and behaviours, such as interest in political and social issues and interest in participating in civic organisations. This indicates positive effects of community service even on – in fact, especially on – those adolescents who might not have been inclined to serve.

THINKING CRITICALLY

Does the incidence of community service indicate that adolescents and young adults have stronger collectivist values than commentators may have realised – or not, since only a relatively small proportion of young people take part in community service on a frequent basis? Has the introduction of the British National Citizen Service increased the number of young people taking part in voluntary service? How would you find out?

SUMMING UP

In this chapter we have discussed work in traditional cultures, the history of young people's work in developing and developed countries, and current patterns of work among adolescents and young adults in Northern Europe. The main points we have discussed are as follows:

- Adolescents in traditional cultures have typically worked alongside their parents, the boys in work such as hunting, fishing and farming, the girls in work such as gathering, childcare and household work. However, because of globalisation, virtually all traditional cultures are moving toward industrialisation. The result in many countries is that people in traditional cultures, especially adolescents, are being subjected to hard work in terrible conditions for very low pay, such as on commercial farms and plantations, in factories, and in prostitution.

- Before industrialisation, adolescents in the West typically worked alongside their parents, boys with their fathers mostly in farming, girls with their mothers mostly in childcare and household work. During the nineteenth century, adolescents made up a substantial proportion of the workforce in factories.

- Since the Second World War, the proportion of adolescents in part-time work has risen steeply. Research results on the effects of working part time during high school are complex, but evidence is quite strong that working more than ten hours per week has a variety of negative effects.

- Prospects have dimmed over the past 30 years as high-paying jobs for low-skilled workers have become scarcer in the economy and secondary schools have failed to provide all young people with the skills necessary for obtaining the best jobs available in the new technological economy.

- Most European countries have a national school-to-work programme that coordinates secondary education with the needs of employers, for example through apprenticeships.

- Super's widely used theory of occupational development focuses on adolescence and young adulthood as an important period containing stages of crystallisation, specification and implementation.

- Holland's theory describes six personality types and the jobs to which they are likely to be best suited. However, most people have personality characteristics that fit into more than one type, and most occupations can be performed with success and satisfaction by persons with a variety of personality characteristics.

- Most young adults spend several years changing jobs frequently as they seek work that will not only pay well but will also fit their identity and provide personal fulfilment. Their work explorations are often haphazard and unsystematic.

- Voluntary work (community service) is quite common among adolescents and young adults and there is an association between developing political and civic awareness and community service even where that service is part of a school's curriculum.

Because school extends for so many years for most adolescents in industrialised countries, work plays less of a role in their lives than it does for young people in developing countries. The work that most adolescents do in their jobs is not work that many of them expect or want to be doing beyond adolescence. Still, it is striking that some adolescents spend 10 or even 20 hours or more per week in employment, especially since their employment as adolescents does little to help them develop skills for adult work. They work in adolescence to finance an active leisure life, and their leisure is important enough to them that they are willing to spend a considerable number of hours a week in employment to be able to pay for it. It is a paradox – they give up leisure hours for employment, in order to be able to spend more money on their remaining leisure. In doing so, they often sacrifice something of their school performance, which can have real effects on the success they are likely to have in their future occupations.

Young adults face different kinds of work challenges. Work becomes more serious for young adults as a foundation for their occupations as adults. The central challenge for young adults in industrialised countries is to sort through the sometimes daunting range of possible occupations available to them and choose one occupational path they will find reasonably fulfilling and well paid. They have to hope, too, that the path they choose will be open to them and that they will succeed in the pursuit of the work they want.

For young people in developing countries, work is especially a problem. The economy of their parents' and grandparents' generations is disappearing under the influence of globalisation, so they may feel that learning the skills that were central to work in their culture in the past is now pointless. However, the alternatives open to them right now in their industrialising economies are grim for the most part and often involve arduous work under dangerous, unhealthy, exploitative conditions. The history of work experience of adolescents in Northern Europe suggests that for young people in developing countries, changes in the twenty-first century will be in the direction of better work conditions, higher pay and an increasing number of years in adolescence and young adulthood devoted to education and preparation for meaningful work that they choose for themselves. However, this will not happen through some inevitable mechanism of history – if it happens at all – but through the activism of committed people in their own countries as well as in industrialised countries.

INTERNET RESOURCES

http://www.ilo.org

Website for the International Labour Organization, a United Nations agency dedicated to collecting information about work conditions around the world and working to improve them. Among their top priorities are eliminating child labour and improving working conditions for adolescents.

http://www.eu-employment-observatory.net/

In July 2010, 33 national articles on the theme of youth employment measures were commissioned from the European Employment Observatory (EEO) network of national experts. This document summarises key messages on: vocational education and training; measures to link work and school; traineeship programmes; apprenticeship; and basic skills. Further detail on the national-level developments discussed in this report can be found in the national articles, which are available on the EEO website.

http://www.hcsprovek.co.uk/

For a more local UK 'picture' see how the Connexions initiative – the *Professional Focus* of this chapter – is implemented on a local authority basis by Hertfordshire County Council. 'Youth Connexions Hertfordshire is a service for young people that provides information and advice, guidance and support, and personal development opportunities for all 13–19-year-olds (up to 25 years for young people with learning difficulties and/or disabilities). Personal advisers will discuss the things which are important to you and to help you plan your next steps.' (Home page of the website.)

FURTHER READING

Jenny Kidd, *Understanding Career Counselling: Theory, Research and Practice*. London: Sage (2006).

'The career counselling profession has been under some pressure in the UK. This text outlines the base of theory, research and practice upon which this professional activity is built. It provides a resource for those thinking about career counselling and related fields, as well as for established practitioners'.

Christopher Perry, *Vulnerable Youth and Employment Issues*. Nova Science Publishers (2011).

Challenges in the economy and among certain youth populations have heightened concern that some young people may not be prepared to fill these roles. The employment levels for youth under age 25 have declined markedly, and the current recession may cause these levels to decrease further. This book explores the vulnerable youth population with regard to schooling, employment and job training programmes.

Robin Simmons and Ron Thompson, *NEET Young People and Training for Work: Learning on the Margins*. Staffordshire: Trentham Books (2011)

'This book examines the experiences of youth in post-industrial England attending a work-based learning programme for those who are not in education or employment or risk becoming so. It critically appraises the social, economic and political context and challenges conventional stereotypes of "the NEETs" as dysfunctional and lacking aspiration'.

For more web links, further reading; plus practice tests, case studies, PowerPoint presentations and discussion of the *Critical Thinking* features, log on to **www.pearsoned.co.uk/arnett.**

PART 3

PROBLEMS AND RESILIENCE

PROBLEMS AND PROBLEM BEHAVIOURS

You do not have to look very far to find evidence of young people's problems in most societies. Your local newspaper is likely to provide plenty of examples on a daily basis. A typical story appeared recently in my (JJA) local newspaper. Four young men aged 17–22 were killed when the driver, a 17-year-old boy, lost control of his car while rounding a curve. The car veered off the road and slammed into a telephone pole. The driver and his three passengers died at the scene after being thrown from the car. None of them had been wearing seat belts, and the car had been travelling at an estimated 75 miles per hour in a 40-mile-per-hour speed limit. 'Speed was definitely a factor,' said the police officer who was called to the scene. 'They could have had seat belts on. This crash was so horrific there was no chance of survival.'

TERRIBLE STORIES LIKE THIS ARE PROBABLY familiar to you, and you may have noticed that these stories frequently involve young people in their teens and early 20s. Commentators sometimes complain that such stories promote stereotypes about young people, especially the stereotype that adolescence is inherently a time of 'storm and stress' and that adolescents are disproportionately the cause of social problems such as crime (e.g. Irwin, 2004). To the extent that such a stereotype exists, applying it to all adolescents and young adults would be unfair. In examining many aspects of development in the various chapters of this book, we have seen that the teens and early 20s are years of many changes, some of them profound and dramatic. However, for most young people these changes are manageable, and they navigate their way through adolescence and young adulthood without suffering any serious or enduring problems.

Nevertheless, the teens and 20s remain the period of life when various problems are *more likely* to occur than at other times (Eskin et al., 2008). Most adolescents and young adults do not develop serious problems, but the risk of a wide range of problems is higher for them than it is for children or adults. These problems range from car accidents to criminal behaviour to eating disorders to depressed mental states. We will explore all of these problems in this chapter.

Before we examine specific problems, you should be introduced to some of the ideas that provide a context for understanding the problems. These ideas will be the topic of the next section.

TWO TYPES OF PROBLEM

Those who study young people's problems often make a distinction between *internal problems* and *external problems* (e.g. Ollendick et al., 2008). Internal problems are problems that primarily affect a person's internal world. This includes problems such as depression, anxiety and eating disorders. Internal problems tend to go together. For example, adolescents who have an eating disorder are more likely than other adolescents to be depressed. Adolescents who are depressed are more likely than other adolescents to have an anxiety disorder. Young people who have internal problems are sometimes referred to as *over-controlled* (Van Leeuwen et al., 2004; Asendorpf and van Aken, 1999). They tend to come from families in which parents exercise tight psychological control (Barber, 2002). As a result, their own personalities are often overly controlled and self-punishing. Internal problems are more common among females than among males (Ollendick et al., 2008).

External problems are difficulties in a person's external world. Types of external problems include delinquency, fighting, substance use, risky driving and unprotected sex. Like internal problems, external problems tend to go together (Frick and Kimonis, 2008). For example, adolescents who fight are more likely than other adolescents to commit crimes; adolescents who have unprotected sex are more likely than other adolescents to use substances such as alcohol and marijuana. Young people with external problems are sometimes referred to as *under-controlled* (Van Leeuwen et al., *ibid.*; Asendorpf and van Aken, *ibid.*). They tend to come from families where parental monitoring and control is lacking (Arim and Shapka, 2008). As a result, they tend to lack self-control themselves, which then leads to their external problems. External problems are more common among males than among females (Frick and Kimonis, 2008; Bongers et al., 2004).

Another key difference between internal and external problems is that young people with internal problems usually experience distress, whereas young people with external problems often do not (Maggs, 1999). The majority of young people in Western societies take part in external behaviours from time to time (Arnett, 2002b). Although external behaviours may be a manifestation of problems with family, friends or school, many young people who take part in external behaviours have no such problems. External behaviours are often motivated not by underlying unhappiness or psychopathology but by the desire for excitement and intense experiences (Falkin et al., 2007; Zuckerman, 2003), and can be viewed as cementing friendships (Maggs, *ibid.*). External behaviours are almost always viewed as problems by adults, but young people themselves may not see it that way.

The distinction between internal and external problems is useful in terms of understanding the causes of problems and problem behaviours, but it should not be taken to be absolute. In general, the problems within each category occur together, but some young people have both kinds of problem. For example, delinquent adolescents are sometimes depressed as well (Beyers and Loeber, 2003), and depressed adolescents sometimes abuse drugs and alcohol (Saluja et al., 2004). Some studies have found that adolescents with both external and internal problems have had especially difficult family backgrounds (Sears, 2004). For the moment let's keep the types of problem separate and examine external problems first, then internal problems.

EXTERNAL PROBLEMS

External problems in adolescence have been intensively studied by social scientists, especially in the past 30 years. Scholars have used various terms in studying this topic, including not only external problems but also risk behaviour and problem behaviour. Regardless of the terms used, these behaviours generally include risky sexual behaviour, risky driving behaviour, substance use and crime. We will discuss each of these types of behaviour (except for risky sexual behaviour, which was discussed in Chapter 9), and for each type we will discuss interventions designed to prevent the problem. Then we will discuss the various factors that have been found to be related to these behaviours.

Risky Car Driving

'I just enjoyed the feeling of acceleration, speeding through corners and flat out to speed. I liked testing my driving skill and the car in different conditions. You get a minor buzz from the fact its breakin' the law, but I did it so often then, I didn't really think it, even when you're over 105 mph, which is rare these days cos now I drive a diesel. If there's a journey that you and friends did often you could compare journey times, but I always won so I didn't really bother with that. Getting 105 out of my metro was great. Not only was it an amazing speed for the metro, but I got caught and got away with it. So I got the buzz of going fast, got a great story to tell, and had mates in the car so people can't say I was making it up.'

— Christopher, now aged 28 (Hughes, unpublished data)

Across industrialised countries, the most serious threat to the lives and health of adolescents and young adults is driving cars (Heuveline, 2002). The UK government Department for Transport reports that in Great Britain the number of deaths among all car users in 2009 was 1059 and the number seriously injured in accidents reported to the police was 10,053. Total reported casualties among car users were 143,412 (DFT, 2010). What proportion of these were young drivers? Well, UK national statistics by age group are curiously difficult to get hold of but one example may give us some clues. In 2004, 17- to 25-year-olds made up an estimated 13 per cent of the Greater London population. When calculated in relation to the potential number of drivers on the road and the percentage of the population, the number of young car drivers involved in collisions is 18 per cent, which is disproportionate but not wildly so (TfL, 2005).

Statistics from the USA evidence much higher proportions of young people involved in serious car collisions but this may be due to a younger driving age and cars being made more available to younger people; particularly among some parts of American society where car ownership and access to cars from an early age is very common. More generally, road traffic accidents kill more people aged 10–24 than any other single cause, according to research accounting in many studies for up to 30 per cent of male deaths and 17 per cent of female deaths (e.g. Patton et al., 2009; Pan et al., 2007; Twisk and Stacey, 2007).

What is responsible for these grim statistics? Is it young drivers' inexperience or their risky driving behaviour? Inexperience certainly plays a large role. Rates of accidents and fatalities are extremely high in the early months of driving but fall dramatically by one year after gaining a full licence (McNight and Peck, 2002; Williams, 1998). Studies that have attempted to disentangle experience and age in young drivers have generally concluded that inexperience is partly responsible for young drivers' accidents and fatalities.

However, these studies and others have also concluded that inexperience is not the only factor involved. Equally important is the way young people drive and the kinds of risk they take (Ferguson, 2003). Compared to older drivers, young drivers (especially males) are more likely to drive at excessive speeds, follow other vehicles too closely, ignore traffic signs and signals, take more risks when changing lane and overtaking and fail to give way to pedestrians (Bina et al., 2006; Williams and Ferguson, 2002). They are also

CONNECT AND EXTEND

The male-to-male driver–passenger combination has higher fatal crash risk than the female-to-female driver–passenger combination. As age progresses, fatal crash risk differences between male and female young drivers also increase. For a full discussion read

'Effect of passenger age and gender on fatal crash risks of young drivers' by Haoqiang Fu and Chester Wilmot in *Transportation Research Record*, Volume 2078, Number 1 (December 2008), pp. 33–40

more likely than older drivers to drive under the influence of alcohol. Specifically drivers aged 21 to 24 involved in fatal accidents are more likely to have been intoxicated at the time of the accident than persons in any other age group (Huckle et al., 2005), although researcher Taisia Huckle and colleagues report a worrying trend for an increasing number of 16- to 19-year-olds to be involved in accidents while above legal limits for alcohol. Young people are also less likely than older drivers to wear seat belts (Williams and Ferguson, 2002), and in serious car crashes those not wearing seat belts are twice as likely to be killed and three times as likely to be injured, compared with those wearing seat belts (NHTSA, 2002).

In addition to inexperience and specific driving behaviours, a variety of other factors are involved in young drivers' risk of crashing. For example, parental involvement and monitoring of adolescents' driving behaviour has been shown to be especially important in the early months of driving, and interventions to increase parental involvement have been shown to be effective (Simons-Morton, 2007; Simons-Morton et al., 2006; Simons-Morton et al., 2002). In contrast, friends' influence has been found to promote risky driving. Young drivers are more likely than older drivers to believe their friends would approve of risky driving behaviour such as speeding, closely following another vehicle, and overtaking in dangerous circumstances (Chen and Chang, 2007).

Driver characteristics matter, too. Personality characteristics such as sensation seeking and aggressiveness promote risky driving and subsequent crashes, and these characteristics tend to be highest in young male drivers (Arnett, 2002c). The optimistic bias leads people to believe that they are less likely than others to be in a crash, and this bias is especially strong in younger drivers (Mayhew and Simpson, 2002). Driver characteristics and the driving environment interact with the socialisation environment to result in driving behaviour that leads to crashes, and seat belt use plays a large part in determining whether a crash results in injuries or fatalities.

Preventing Automobile Accidents and Fatalities

What can be done to reduce the rates of car accidents and fatalities among young drivers? On the face of it, driving lessons in preparation for taking a test would seem promising as a way to improve adolescents' driving practices. It seems logical that if beginning drivers were taught by professional instructors, they would become more proficient more quickly and therefore be

Young drivers tend to take more risks than older drivers, with sometimes fatal consequences.

safer drivers. However, studies that have compared adolescents who have taken lessons from a professional to adolescents who have not have found that crash involvement tends to be as high or *higher* for the adolescents who have taken driving lessons (Mayhew, 2007; Hirsch, 2003; Mayhew and Simpson, 2002). Perhaps professional driving lessons generally fail to teach the knowledge and skills necessary for safe driving, in part because the adolescents who take the courses have little interest in learning those skills – what they want is to get their licence and drive.

An alternative approach, one favoured strongly by most commentators on adolescent driving, is engaging young drivers in driving courses aimed at new drivers. For those who successfully complete the course it can mean much lower car insurance premiums, which are otherwise set very high for young drivers in the first two years of driving. The UK government supports a scheme – Pass Plus – which teaches new drivers to anticipate, plan for and deal with all kinds of hazards they meet when driving in town, in all weathers, at night and on motorways. Another current scheme in the UK is the P Plate scheme. Beginner drivers display green P plates on their vehicles which warn other road users that the vehicle is being driven by an inexperienced driver and so encourage them to give the beginner a little more space and time to complete manoeuvres such as changing lanes or turning right. Even with the best of schemes, young drivers remain subject to greater risk of accident, injury and fatality than older and more experienced drivers. This is especially the case when youngsters engage in racing, in 'joy riding' – stealing cars and 'competing 'against the police to drive wildly so as not to get caught; and in drink driving or driving while under the influence of other drugs. Look to the nearby *Connect and Extend* features for research into these kinds of risky and problem behaviours.

CONNECT AND EXTEND

To examine the motivations of indigenous youth who steal cars for the purpose of joy riding, read 'Figure eights, spin outs and power slides: Aboriginal and Torres Strait Islander youth and the culture of joy riding' by Glenn Dawes in the *Journal of Youth Studies*, Volume 5, Number 2 (2002), pp. 195–208. Compare that with 'The key to auto theft' by Heith Copes and Michael Cherbonneau in *The British Journal of Criminology*, Volume 46, Number 5 (September 2006), pp. 917–934

Substance Use

Another common form of risk behaviour in adolescence and young adulthood is the use of alcohol and other drugs. Scholars often use the term **substance use** to refer to this topic, with 'substances' including alcohol, cigarettes, and illegal drugs such as marijuana, LSD, Ecstasy and cocaine.

Current and Past Rates of Substance Use

Rates of substance use vary across Western countries. A recent study by the World Health Organization (WHO) investigated rates of using alcohol, cigarettes and marijuana among 15-year-olds in 41 Western countries (WHO, 2008). A summary of the results is shown in Figures 12.1, 12.2 and 12.3. As you can see,

Marijuana is one of the most common types of substances used by young people.

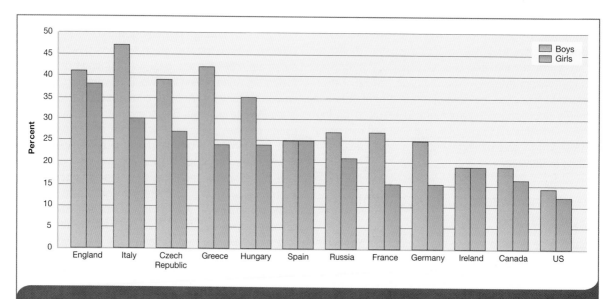

Figure 12.1 Alcohol use among 15-year-olds, weekly use.
Source: WHO (2008).

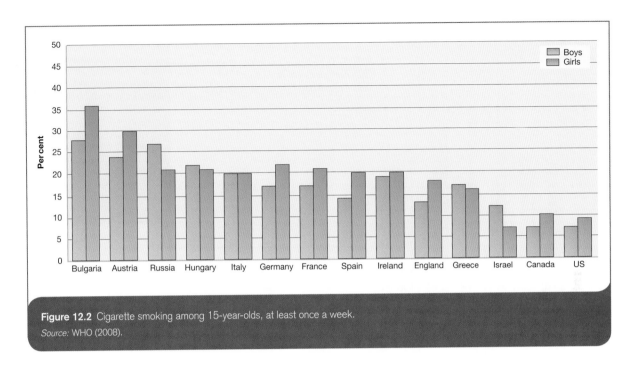

Figure 12.2 Cigarette smoking among 15-year-olds, at least once a week.
Source: WHO (2008).

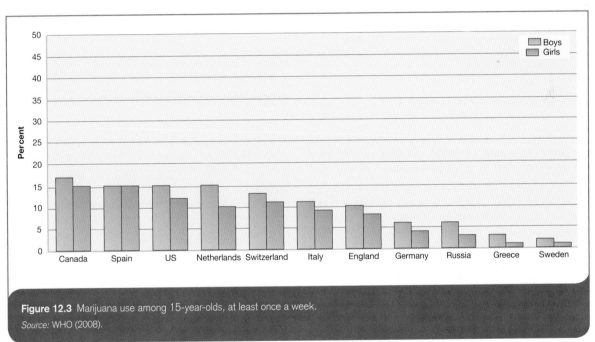

Figure 12.3 Marijuana use among 15-year-olds, at least once a week.
Source: WHO (2008).

rates of substance use depended on the substance. For example, English adolescents were relatively high in alcohol use but relatively low in marijuana use and cigarette smoking. More details on the reasons for national differences will be presented later in the chapter.

The peak of substance use actually comes not in adolescence but in young adulthood (Schulenberg and Maggs, 2000). Research show that substance use of all kinds continues to rise through the late teens and peaks in the early 20s before declining in the late 20s. Figure 12.4 shows the results of a national survey of drug use and binge drinking – five or more drinks in a row – from age 18 to 45 (Johnston et al., 2008). Substance use, especially alcohol use, is highest among young adults who are university students (Okie, 2002; Wechsler and Nelson, 2001; Schulenberg, 2000).

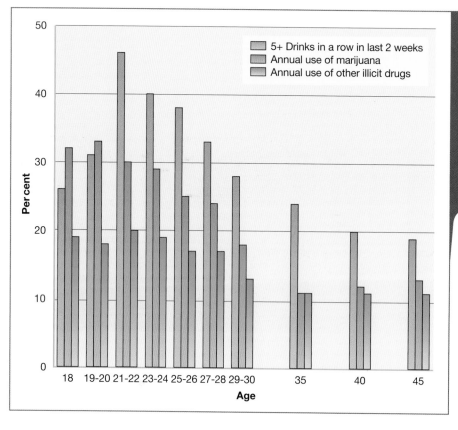

Figure 12.4 Substance abuse by age.
Source: Johnston et al. (2008).

Some evidence shows that substance use is high among young adults in many Western countries. A study of Spanish adults reported that among 18- to 24-year-olds, rates of binge drinking in the past 30 days were 31 per cent for men and 18 per cent for women, far higher than in any other age group (Valencia-Martín et al., 2007). A peak in binge drinking in young adulthood has been found in other European countries as well (Kuntsche et al., 2004). Among female college students in Scotland, most regarded binge drinking as 'harmless fun' (Guise and Gill, 2007).

What explains the higher rates of substance use among young adults? Wayne Osgood has proposed a useful answer to this question. Osgood (Osgood et al., 2005) borrows from a sociological theory that explains all deviance on the basis of *propensity* and *opportunity* (see origins of this idea in Gottfredson and Hirschi, 1990). People behave deviantly when they have a combination of sufficient propensity (that is, sufficient motivation for behaving deviantly) along with sufficient opportunity. In his explanation, Osgood especially focuses on the high degree of opportunity that young adults have for engaging in substance use and other deviant behaviour, as a result of spending a high proportion of their time in unstructured socialising.

Osgood uses the term unstructured socialising to include behaviour such as riding around in a car for fun, going to parties, going shopping and going out with friends. He shows that unstructured socialising is highest in the late teens and early 20s, and that within this age period young adults who 'score' highest in unstructured socialising are also highest in the use of alcohol and marijuana (Osgood et al., *ibid.*). Rates of most types of substance use are especially high among young adults who are college students because they have so many opportunities for unstructured socialising. Substance use declines in the mid- to late 20s, as role transitions such as marriage, parenthood and full-time work cause a sharp decline in unstructured socialising (Monitoring the Future, 2002).

The Sequence of Substance Use

Substance use in adolescence and young adulthood has been found to follow a typical sequence of four stages: (1) drinking beer and wine; (2) smoking cigarettes and drinking hard liquor; (3) smoking marijuana; and (4) using 'hard' drugs (e.g. cocaine, heroin). Almost all adolescents who begin to smoke cigarettes or use hard liquor have already tried beer and wine; almost all adolescents who try marijuana have already tried cigarettes and hard liquor; and almost all adolescents who use hard drugs have already tried marijuana (Kandel, 2002; 1975). Beer, wine, cigarettes and marijuana have been called **gateway drugs** because most adolescents who try hard drugs have already passed through the 'gates' of these substances (Kandel, 2002).

Of course, this does not mean that all or even most of the people who try one type of substance will go on to try the next substance in the sequence. It simply means that young people who try one type of substance are *more likely* than young people who have not tried it to move along the sequence to the next substance. So, for example, most young people who try marijuana will never try hard drugs, but among young people who try hard drugs almost all of them have used marijuana first.

An excellent critique and exposition of the gateway hypothesis – the sequence of substance use – comes from the classic study by health researchers Denise Kandel and Richard Faust (1975). The study assessed secondary school pupils' substance use on two occasions six months apart. At the six-month follow-up, 27 per cent of the pupils who had smoked or used alcohol at the time of the original study had subsequently tried marijuana, compared with only 2 per cent of the pupils who had not smoked or used alcohol. Similarly, 26 per cent of the pupils who had used marijuana at the time of the original study had subsequently tried hard drugs, compared with only 1 per cent of the pupils who had never used marijuana. From these statistics we can see both that young people who use one substance in the sequence are more likely to use the next one and that most young people who use one substance do not proceed right away to use the next one in the sequence. More recent longitudinal studies continue to support the gateway drug hypothesis, showing that use of cigarettes and alcohol predicts entry to marijuana use and that use of marijuana predicts use of hard drugs (Fergusson

et al., 2006; Tarter et al., 2006). In a book summarising research on the 'gateway drug' hypothesis, Denise Kandel (2002) concluded that the hypothesis accurately describes the sequence of substance use, but using earlier drugs in the sequence does not necessarily cause young people to use the later drugs.

THINKING CRITICALLY

Some people have interpreted the 'gateway drug' hypothesis as indicating that if adolescents could be prevented from using alcohol and cigarettes, they would also be less likely to use marijuana and hard drugs. Do you think this is true, or would they be more likely to use other drugs if their access to alcohol and cigarettes were curtailed?

Substance Use and Abuse

Young people use substances for a variety of purposes; purposes that were classified in 1992 by psychologist Irving Weiner as *experimental, social, medicinal* and *addictive*. Young people who take part in experimental substance use try a substance once or perhaps a few times out of curiosity and then do not use it again. A substantial proportion of substance use in adolescence and young adulthood is experimental. 'To see what it was like' has been found to be the most common motivation given by young people when asked why they used an illicit drug (Botvin and Griffin, 2007; Davis, 2006; R. A. Chambers et al., 2003). Social substance use involves the use of substances during social activities with one or more friends – unstructured socialising. Parties and nightclubs are common settings for social substance use in adolescence and young adulthood (Chen et al., 2004; Lindsay, 2003).

CONNECT AND EXTEND

Research results suggest that the pattern of drug use interpreted as the 'gateway effect' might be better conceptualised as a 'genetically influenced developmental trajectory'. This is an important idea. Read 'Understanding the association between adolescent marijuana use and later serious drug use: gateway effect or developmental trajectory?' by Harrington Cleveland and Richard Wiebe in *Development and Psychopathology*, Volume 20, Number 2 (January 2008), pp. 615–632

Medicinal substance use is undertaken to relieve an unpleasant emotional state such as sadness, anxiety, stress or loneliness (Woodward and Fergusson, 2001). Using substances for these purposes has been described as a kind of self-medication (Miranda et al., 2002). Young people who use substances for this purpose tend to use them more frequently than those whose purposes are mainly social or experimental. Frequent substance users are three times as likely as other adolescents to be depressed, which suggests the importance of self-medication as a motivation for frequent substance use (Repetto et al., 2004; Saluja et al., 2004).

Finally, addictive substance use takes place when a person has come to depend on regular use of substances to cope physically or psychologically. Addictive substance users experience withdrawal symptoms such as high anxiety and physical cramps, pain and tremors when they stop taking the substance to which they are addicted. Addictive substance use involves the most regular and frequent substance use of the four categories described here.

All substance use in adolescence and young adulthood is considered 'problem behaviour' in the sense that it is something that adults generally view as a problem if young people engage in it. However, the four categories described here indicate that young people may use substances in very different ways, with very different implications for their development. Frequent substance users are much more likely than other adolescents to have problems in school, to be withdrawn from peers, to have problems in their relationships with their parents, and to engage in delinquent behaviour (Tubman et al., 2004).

Preventing Substance Use

Efforts to prevent or reduce substance use among young people have generally been delivered through schools (Coggans, 2006). A variety of approaches have been tried. Some programmes attempt to raise pupils' self-esteem, in the belief that the main cause of substance use is low self-esteem. Some programmes present information about the health dangers of substance use in the hope that becoming more knowledgeable about the effects of substance use will make pupils less likely to use them. Other programmes have focused on teaching students to resist 'peer pressure', in the belief that peer pressure is the main reason young people use drugs. None of these approaches has worked very well (Coggans, *ibid.*; Triplett and Payne, 2004).

More successful programmes have focused on family functioning, addressing family problems that may be motivating adolescents' substance use (Austin et al., 2005) or teaching parents how to enhance skills such as parental monitoring, the extent to which parents know where their adolescents are and what they are doing at any given time (Mason et al., 2003). Other successful programmes have combined a variety of strategies and have been implemented not only in school but through families, peers and neighbourhoods as well (Horn et al., 2005; Swenson et al., 2005). We will discuss this *multisystemic approach* in more detail below. The most successful programmes also start young, in early adolescence, and continue on a yearly basis through secondary school (Stockwell et al., 2004).

With regard to young adults, prevention of substance use has focused especially on university students and on binge drinking in particular. Approaches include providing first-year workshops on alcohol use and abuse, handing out alcohol awareness pamphlets, sponsoring alcohol-free events, and pressuring student union bars to limit offers of cheap drinks. However, overall, these programmes have had little effect on college students' drinking behaviour. Binge drinking – in particular – is so much a part of the culture of university and college campuses that it is difficult for an intervention programme to fight it (Okie, 2002).

Delinquency and Crime

Because criminal acts are so disruptive to societies, and because crime became increasingly pervasive with the development of modern cities, crime is one of the oldest and most intensively studied topics in the social sciences. In more than 150 years of research on crime, one finding stands out prominently with remarkable consistency: the great majority of crimes are committed by young people – mostly males – who are between the ages of 12 and 25 (Eisner, 2002).

Before proceeding further, some definitions are necessary. Crimes, of course, are acts that violate the law. When violations of the law are committed by persons defined by the legal system as **juveniles**, these violations are usually considered acts of **delinquency**. Legal systems in most countries define juveniles as persons under 18 years of age.

Age-related offences – sometimes called status offences – are defined as violations of the law only because they are committed by juveniles. For example, adults can leave home any time they wish, but juveniles who leave home without their parents' consent commit the offence of running away from home. Other examples of status offences include truancy (failure to attend school), consensual under-age sex and purchasing alcohol.

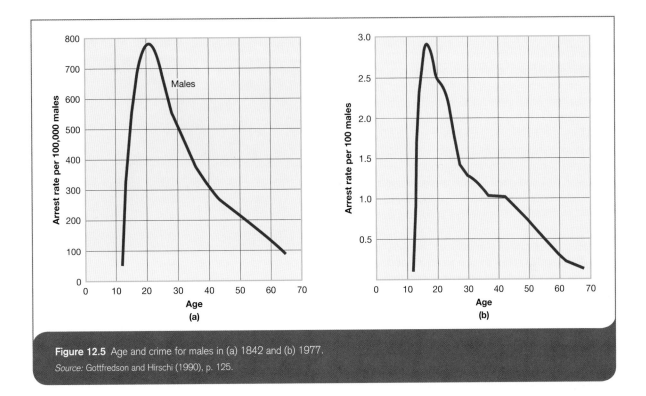

Figure 12.5 Age and crime for males in (a) 1842 and (b) 1977.
Source: Gottfredson and Hirschi (1990), p. 125.

Crimes are offences that would be considered viola-tions of the law if committed by a person of any age, juvenile or adult. Serious offences include two sub-categories, *violent crimes*, such as rape, assault and murder, and *property crimes*, such as robbery, motor vehicle theft and arson. There are also less serious offences such as disorderly conduct.

By definition, status offences are committed entirely by adolescents – they are acts that would not be crimi-nal if performed by someone who is legally an adult. However, the dramatic relationship between age and crime – the finding that criminal acts are committed mostly by males aged 12 to 25 – is true for crimes as well. In the West, this finding is remarkably consistent over a period of more than 150 years. Figure 12.5 is a striking depiction of the age – crime relationship at two points, one in 1842 and one 135 years later. It can be argued that at any point before, after or in between

these times, in most countries, the pattern would look very similar (Eisner, 2002). Adolescent and young adult males are not only more likely than children or adults to commit crimes but also more likely to be the victims of crimes (Eisner, 2002; Cohen and Potter, 1999).

What explains the strong and consistent relationship between age and crime? One theory suggests that the key to explaining the age–crime relationship is that adolescents and young adults combine increased inde-pendence from parents and other adult authorities with increased time with peers and increased orientation towards peers (Barnes et al., 2007). A consistent find-ing of research on crime is that crimes committed by young men in their teens and early 20s usually take place in a group, much more so than among adult offenders (Dishion and Dodge, 2005). Crime is an activity that in some adolescent cliques is encouraged and admired (Dishion et al., 1999).

CONNECT AND EXTEND

To examine the crime–age profiles of two groups: those who leave school at 16 and those who stay on past the compulsory school leaving age read 'Education and the crime–age profile' by Kirstine Hansen in the *The British Journal of Criminology*, Volume 43, Number 1 (1 January 2003), pp. 141–168

Of course, as we noted in Chapter 8, peers and friends can influence each other in a variety of ways, including towards conformity to adult standards, not just towards deviance and norm breaking. However, adolescence and young adulthood appear to be the times of life when peer groups that value and reinforce norm breaking are most likely to form (Dishion and Dodge, 2005; Gifford-Smith et al., 2005). In their search for excitement and sensation-seeking adventure, young men in these peer groups may engage in activities that violate the law. Their motives are rarely economic – even when their activities involve theft; they (the thefts) tend to be for small amounts. When they reach their mid-20s, these antisocial peer groups break up as young adults enter the various roles of young adulthood, and participation in crime subsequently declines (Moffitt, 2003).

Life-course-persistent delinquents have problems from an early age.

Two Kinds of Delinquency

Breaking laws of various kinds is quite common in the teens and early 20s, especially for males. Most surveys find that over three-quarters of adolescents commit at least one criminal act some time before the age of 20 (Moffitt, 2003). However, there are obvious differences between committing one or two acts of minor crime – vandalism or minor 'shop-lifting' theft, for example – and committing crimes frequently over a long period, including more serious crimes such as rape and assault. What are the differences between adolescents who commit an occasional minor violation of the law and adolescents who are at risk of more serious, long-term criminal behaviour?

Psychology professor Terrie Moffitt (2007; 2003; 1993), has proposed a provocative theory in which she distinguishes between 'adolescence-limited' delinquency and 'life-course-persistent' delinquency. In Moffitt's view, these are two distinct types of delinquency, each with different motivations and different sources. However, the two types may be hard to distinguish from one another in adolescence, when criminal offences are more common than in childhood or adulthood. The way to tell them apart, according to Moffitt, is to look at behaviour before adolescence.

Life-course-persistent delinquents (LCPDs) show a pattern of problems from birth onwards. Moffitt believes their problems originate in neuropsychological deficits that are evident in a difficult temperament in infancy and a high likelihood of attention deficit-hyperactivity disorder (ADHD) and learning disabilities in childhood. Children with these problems are also more likely than other children to grow up in a high-risk environment (e.g. low-income or single-parent family), with parents who have a variety of problems of their own. Consequently, their neurological deficits tend to be made worse rather than better by their environments. When they reach adolescence, children with the combination of neurological deficits and a high-risk environment are highly prone to engage in criminal activity. Furthermore, they tend to continue their criminal activity long after adolescence has ended, well into adulthood.

Adolescence-limited delinquents (ALDs) follow a much different pattern. They show no signs of problems in infancy or childhood, and few of them engage in any criminal activity after their mid-20s. It is just during adolescence – actually, adolescence and young adulthood, from about age 12 to about age 25 – that they have a period of occasional criminal activity, breaking the law with behaviour such as vandalism, theft and use of illegal drugs.

Moffitt's theory is supported by her research on young people in New Zealand (Moffitt, 2007; 2003; Moffitt and Caspi, 2005; 2001; Moffitt et al., 2002; also see Piquero and Brezina, 2001). Known as the Dunedin longitudinal study, it began when the participants were in infancy and has followed them through to ages approaching 30 (so far). The results show that, as predicted by the theory, LCPDs exhibited problems of neurological functioning, temperament and behaviour from an early age, whereas ALDs did not. In young adulthood, LCPDs continued to have difficulties such as mental health problems, financial problems, work problems, substance use and criminal behaviour. The risk behaviour of ALDs mostly diminished by age 26, although they continued to have more substance use and financial problems than young adults who did not engage in delinquent behaviour in adolescence.

Participation in delinquency is common during adolescence, especially for boys.

THINKING CRITICALLY

LCPDs' problems have deep roots in early development, but what explains delinquency among ALDs? Perhaps read the upcoming *Cultural Focus* feature to help shape your ideas.

CULTURAL FOCUS

'Mind the Man Gap' (between innocence and responsibility)

External problems such as fighting, stealing and substance use are far more common among males than among females, everywhere in the world and in every era of the historical record. The reasons for this may be partly biological, but they are also clearly connected to gender role socialisation. In a wide range of cultures, what we have been calling 'external problems' are often part of the requirements for demonstrating an adolescent male's readiness for manhood (Lam and McBride-Chang, 2007; Lyons et al., 2006; Smiler, 2006). Here we are not talking about the rites of passage such as those referred to in many of the *Cultural Focus* features in earlier chapters. Formal rites of passage such as the Bar and Bat Mitzvah serve to signal a move to a time of change in a young person's life – leaving behind the innocence of childhood and looking forward to the responsibilities of full adulthood, employment, marriage and a new family.

What fills this gap between innocence and responsibility for young men in particular, and in many cultures, is an opportunity to 'kick over the traces'; to 'sow a few wild oats'; to join up with others of the same age in non-adult-structured social groups, usually referred to as gangs, in some of our towns and cities. Fraternisation with older boys provides abundant opportunities for young and mid-adolescents to explore new physical strength, to test their courage and to engage in new and exciting sensation-seeking behaviours that help define their new masculinity; where learning to be a man is associated with external problems such as fighting, stealing and substance use.

One vivid example of this interaction between external problems and manhood requirements can be found among the people of Truk Island, an island that is part of a string of small islands in the South Pacific known as Micronesia. The culture of Truk Island has been vividly described by the anthropologist Mac Marshall (1979) and summarised by David Gilmore (1990). Their accounts provide an excellent demonstration not only of the importance of gender role socialisation in the external behaviour of young males but also of the effect of globalisation on young people even in cultures in the remotest parts of the world.

The globalisation of the Trukese culture goes back more than 100 years. Even long before that, the Trukese were known far and wide as fierce warriors who fought frequently among themselves and made short work of any Western sailors unlucky enough to drift nearby. However, in the late 1800s, German colonists arrived and took control of the islands and of the Trukese people. They stamped out local warfare, introduced Christianity, and also brought in alcohol, which soon became widely and excessively used by young men. Much has changed on Truk Island during the century of Western influence, but the emphasis on strictly defined gender roles remains strong. When they reach puberty, girls learn the traditional female role of cooking, sewing and performing other household duties. Meanwhile, boys are expected to demonstrate their manhood principally in three ways: fighting, drinking large quantities of alcohol and taking daredevil risks.

Fighting among young Trukese men is a group activity. It takes place in the context of rivalries between clans (extended family networks). Young men fight not just for their own prestige but for the honour and prestige of their clan. On weekend evenings, they roam the streets in clan groups looking for other groups to challenge and taking part in brawls when they find them.

Drinking alcohol is also part of the weekend group activities of young males. By the time they are 13, getting drunk with their clan pals is a regular part of weekend evenings for adolescent boys. The drinking contributes to the fighting because it diminishes any trepidation a boy might have over becoming injured. Also, on weekend days groups of young men sometimes take risky trips in motorboats. They take long trips with limited fuel, a small motor, and nothing for sustenance except beer, risking the open sea in order to demonstrate their bravery and thereby prove their readiness for manhood.

Although nearly all Trukese males in their teens and 20s engage in these activities, their external escapades are limited to the weekends, and they rarely drink or fight during the week. In fact, Marshall's (1979) book on them is entitled *Weekend Warriors*. Also, when they reach about age 30, the expectations for manhood change. At that point, they are expected to marry and settle down. They rarely fight after reaching that age, and most stop drinking alcohol entirely. The external behaviour of males in adolescence and young adulthood is not viewed as a social problem but, rather, as an accepted behaviour during a limited period of their lives, when their culture demands it as part of fulfilling the expectations for becoming a man.

Preventing Crime and Delinquency

The seriousness of crime as a social problem has drawn a great deal of attention to preventing young people from committing crimes and trying to rehabilitate young offenders so that they will not commit further crimes. For most young people, as we have discussed, criminal acts are limited to adolescence and young adulthood, and once they grow beyond their early 20s they no longer have any inclination to offend. The real focus of concern is the life-course-persistent offenders, who have problems from early childhood onwards, become chronic delinquents in adolescence, and are at high risk for a life of continued crime in adulthood.

Prevention programmes to help children who show signs of being headed for trouble in adolescence or to help adolescents who have become involved in serious delinquency are enormously varied. They include individual therapy, group therapy, vocational training, 'Outward Bound' kinds of programmes that involve group activities in the outdoors, 'Scared Straight' programmes that take young offenders into a prison to show them the grim conditions of prison life, and many, many, many others. Unfortunately, few of these types of programmes have worked very well (Greenwood, 2006; Dishion and Dodge, 2005). The overall record of delinquency prevention and intervention programmes

CONNECT AND EXTEND

In recent years there has been a profusion of laws that punish parents for their children's offences. To consider whether parental responsibility laws are an effective means of tackling youth crime read 'Punishing parents for the crimes of their children' by Raymond Arthur in *The Howard Journal of Criminal Justice*, Volume 44, Number 3 (July 2005), pp. 233–253

is frustratingly poor, despite the best intentions of the many dedicated and highly skilled people who have undertaken them. Some interventions have even been found to increase delinquency because they bring together high-risk adolescents who then form a delinquent clique, a phenomenon known as **peer contagion** (Dishion et al., 2006; 1999; Dishion and Dodge, 2005).

Two problems seem to be at the heart of the failure of these programmes. One is that delinquents rarely welcome the opportunity to participate in them (Heilbrun et al., 2005). Typically, they are required to participate in the programmes against their will, often because the legal system commands them to participate or face incarceration. They do not see themselves as having a problem that needs to be 'cured', and their resistance makes progress extremely difficult.

A second problem is that prevention programmes typically take place in adolescence, after a pattern of delinquency has already been clearly established, rather than earlier in childhood when signs of problems first appear (Moffitt, 2007). This is due partly to the limited resources for addressing these problems. The money tends to go to where the problems are most obvious and serious – current offenders rather than possible future offenders. Furthermore, the problems of children frequently originate at least partly in the family and, in many developed societies, the state or local authorities have limited authority to intervene in family life until a clear and serious problem is established.

Nevertheless, some programmes do show definite success (Greenwood, 2006) including 'standalone' programmes involving summer camps that evidence a change in behaviour for the period immediately following the camp and beyond (Hanes et al., 2005). Another successful approach has been to intervene at several levels, including the home, the school, and the neighbourhood. This is known as the *multisystemic approach* (Henggeler et al., 2007; Saldana and Henggeler, 2006; Swenson et al., 2005; Borduin et al., 2003). Programmes based on this approach include parent training, job training and vocational counselling, and the development of neighbourhood institutions such as youth centres and sports clubs. The goal is to direct the energy of delinquents into more socially constructive directions (Daly et al., 2009).

Multisystemic programmes have been shown to be effective in reducing arrests and out-of-home placements among delinquents (Henggeler et al., 2007; Ogden and Haden 2006; Alexander, 2001). Furthermore, multisystemic programmes have been found to be cheaper than other programmes, primarily because they reduce the amount of time that delinquent adolescents spend in foster homes and detention centres (Alexander, 2001). It could be argued that the use of multisystemic approaches is likely to grow in the future because of this combination of proven effectiveness and relatively low cost per person.

Factors Involved in Risk Behaviour

As mentioned earlier, the various types of risk behaviour tend to be correlated. Adolescents who have one kind of external problem tend to have others as well. For this reason it makes sense to look at the factors involved in risk behaviours as a group of behaviours rather than separately. At the same time, it will be important to mention factors that are distinctive to one type of risk behaviour but not others. We will focus on various sources of socialisation, including family, friends/peers, school, neighbourhood/community and religious beliefs. Then we will consider individual characteristics such as sensation seeking and aggressiveness that are related to participation in risk behaviour. A summary model is presented in Figure 12.6. We will focus mostly on substance use and crime/delinquency because the sources of risky driving were discussed earlier in the chapter.

As we discuss the factors involved in risk behaviour, keep in mind that the *majority* of adolescents and young adults take occasional risks of the kind that have been described in this chapter. Many of them have no evidence of problems in their socialisation environment. Thus, although problems in the environment tend to be *related* to degree of participation in risk behaviour, this does not mean that such problems necessarily exist among all or even most young people who engage in risk behaviour. In general, the more serious a young person's involvement in risk behaviour, the more likely these problems are to exist in the socialisation environment. Keep in mind, too, that adolescents are active participants in their socialisation environment, as Figure 12.6 shows. They are influenced by socialisation agents, but they make choices about their environment (e.g. with respect to friends, media and religious participation) and they respond to their socialisation environments in different ways, depending on their individual characteristics.

Family

A great deal of research has focused on the ways that family characteristics are related to risk behaviour. This research is mainly on adolescents rather than young adults because many young adults leave home, so parents' control and influence over them diminishes.

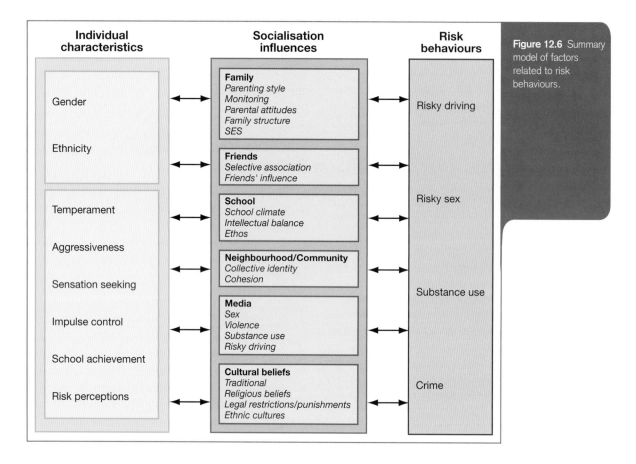

Figure 12.6 Summary model of factors related to risk behaviours.

Consistently, this research supports a relationship between parenting styles (Chapter 7) and risk behaviour. Specifically, adolescents who have authoritative parents – parents who combine warmth and control in their relationships with their adolescents – take part in risk behaviour to a lesser extent than other adolescents. In contrast, adolescents whose parents are authoritarian (harshly controlling but not warm), permissive (high warmth, low control) or disengaged (low in both warmth and control) tend to have higher rates of participation in risk behaviour.

Thus, adolescents with substance abuse problems are more likely than other adolescents to have parents who are permissive, disengaged or hostile (Barrera et al., 2001). In contrast, adolescents in families where closeness and warmth are high are less likely to have substance abuse problems (Kiesner and Kerr, 2004; Bogenschneider et al., 1998). Other family factors related to adolescent substance abuse are high levels of family conflict and family disorganisation (Austin et al., 2005). As noted in Chapter 7, adolescents in divorced families are more likely to use substances, due in part to the high levels of family conflict that often precedes and accompanies divorce (Peris and Emery, 2004).

Adolescents are also more likely to use substances when one or more other family members use substances or have a lenient attitude towards substance use (Luthar et al., 2007; Barrett and Turner, 2006). A good relationship with a parent or an adult outside the family can also act as a protective factor, making substance use and other risk behaviour less likely (Beam et al., 2002).

A similar pattern of family factors has been found in studies of delinquency. Half a century ago, McCord and McCord (1959) found that delinquents were about twice as likely as non-delinquents to come from homes where discipline was inconsistent or lenient, and this finding has been confirmed numerous times since then. An especially important concept in research on delinquency has been parental monitoring (Kerr and Stattin, 2000), which was mentioned earlier in the chapter. Parental monitoring is one reflection of the control dimension of parenting, and when parental monitoring is lacking adolescents are considerably more likely to engage in delinquent acts (Dishion et al., 2003; Jacobson and Crockett, 2000). Adolescents in divorced families have higher rates of delinquency (Buchanan, 2000) partly because monitoring is more difficult when there is only one parent.

CONNECT AND EXTEND

Adolescent gang members report more delinquent behaviour than their counterparts who do not affiliate with gangs: a) adolescents who commit more crimes join gangs (selection hypothesis); b) gang membership facilitates deviant behaviour (facilitation hypothesis); c) selection and facilitation work interactively (enhancement hypothesis). To test this out, read 'Youth gangs, delinquency and drug use: a test of the selection, facilitation and enhancement hypotheses' by Uberto Gatti, Richard E. Tremblay, Frank Vitaro and Pierre McDuff in the *Journal of Child Psychology and Psychiatry* Volume 46, Number 11 (November 2005), pp. 1178–1190

Parental monitoring tends to weaken as adolescents get older, so parents are often unaware of their older adolescents' involvement in risk behaviour. In one study of secondary school pupils, over 50 per cent of the adolescents reported engaging in sexual intercourse and alcohol use, even though over 98 per cent of their parents thought they had not (Strasburger and Wilson, 2002). Parental monitoring is especially likely to be low once older adolescents move out of their parents' household and enter young adulthood. Young adults have neither parents nor spouses to provide social control and this relative freedom makes risk behaviour more likely. This may help to explain why young adults consistently have higher rates of risk behaviour than adolescents (Schulenberg and Zarrett, 2006).

THINKING CRITICALLY

Passive gene–environment interaction refers to the association between the characteristics a child inherits from his/her parents (their genotype) and the home environment parents create – an environment that is influenced by their own inherited characteristics. Is it possible that passive genotype–environment interactions are involved in crime and delinquency? Explain how you would test this possibility. After attempting the task you can access a sample answer on the companion website **www.pearsoned.co.uk/arnett.**

Friends' Influence

Because of the widespread belief that peers play a strong role in risk behaviour, risk behaviour has been the most common focus of research on the influence of peers and friends in adolescence. However, as we saw in Chapter 8, this research has shown that the role of friends' influence in adolescents' risk behaviour is considerably more complicated than originally supposed. In particular, studies have shown that similarity between friends in their risk behaviour is due both to selective association and to friends' influence. That is, young people tend to seek out friends who are like themselves – in their tendencies for risk behaviour as well as in other respects – but if they remain friends, they tend to influence each other; that is, they become more alike in their levels of risk behaviour (Jaccard et al., 2005; Brown, 2004; Rose, 2002).

In studies of delinquency, friends' influence has been argued to play an especially strong role in **socialised delinquency** (Dishion and Dodge, 2005), which involves committing acts of delinquency as part of a group or gang. Socialised delinquents rarely commit crimes alone, and other than their criminal activity they are very similar to non-delinquent adolescents in their psychological functioning and family relationships. In contrast, **unsocialised delinquents** usually have few friends and commit their crimes alone.

Socialised delinquents commit offences, despite being similar in many ways to adolescents who do not, because their friendship group or gang both supports and rewards illegal behaviour (Dishion and Dodge, 2005). Although they may be alienated from school and other adult institutions, they tend to form close interpersonal relationships within their delinquent friendship group. They see their delinquent behaviour not as immoral or deviant but as a way of finding excitement, proving their (usually) manly bravery, and demonstrating their support and loyalty to one another. Adolescents who are gang members often fit this profile of socialised delinquents (Taylor et al., 2003).

A number of studies have explored the connections between family factors and peer factors in relation to risk behaviour. Social psychologist Judith Brook and her colleagues (e.g. Brook et al., 2006) have argued that the path to drug abuse in adolescence begins in early childhood with a lack of warmth from parents and a high level of conflict in the family. Children who experience this kind of family environment develop alienation and low self-control, which are expressed in adolescence through drug use and affiliation with drug-using peers. In contrast, experiencing close and supportive relationships with parents in childhood makes substance use less likely even in a peer environment where drug use is common. Other studies have also found that close relationships to parents in adolescence tend to be related to lower orientation to peers, which is in turn related to lower substance use (Kiesner and Kerr, 2004).

Psychologist Gerald Patterson and his colleagues have developed a similar model to explain delinquency (Dishion and Patterson, 2006; Granic and Patterson, 2006; Snyder et al., 2003). In their extensive longitudinal research, Patterson and colleagues have found that the first risk factors for delinquency begin in infancy, with an infant temperament that is aggressive and difficult. This kind of temperament is especially challenging for parents, and some respond not with the extra measure of love and patience that would be required to ameliorate the challenging behaviour but with harsh, inconsistent or permissive parenting. This family environment leads by middle childhood to the development of personality characteristics such as impulsiveness and low self-control, which makes friendships with most other children problematic. Children with these characteristics are often left with no one to have as friends but each other, and associations in friendship groups of aggressive and rejected children lead in turn to delinquency in adolescence.

Other Socialisation Influences

Family and peer factors have been the areas studied most in relation to risk behaviour in adolescence, but some research also exists on the ways that other aspects of socialisation are related to risk behaviour,

including school, neighbourhood/community and religious beliefs. School has been of interest because of the consistent finding that poor school performance is associated with a variety of types of risk behaviour, especially substance use and delinquency (e.g. Bryant et al., 2003). However, problems in school have fared poorly as an explanation for risk behaviour because tendencies towards the most serious and enduring involvement in risk behaviour begin before children enter school (Moffitt, 2007; 2003).

Nevertheless, some studies have found that the overall school environment can have an influence on adolescents' risk behaviour. The classic study of British schools described in Chapter 10, by Michael Rutter and his colleagues (Rutter, 1983; Rutter et al., 1979), showed the influence of the school environment on delinquency. They studied early adolescents in 12 schools in London, beginning at age 10 and following them for four years. The results indicated that school climate (refer back for a reminder of what this means) had a significant effect on rates of delinquency, even after controlling for such influences as social class and family environment.

In addition to school climate, two other qualities of the school environment stood out as having the most positive effects. One was having an intellectual balance of pupils in the school that included a substantial proportion of bright and achievement-oriented youngsters who identified with the aims and rules of school. These pupils tended to be leaders and discouraged misbehaviour by setting norms of behaviour that other pupils copied. The other important quality was what Rutter and his colleagues called the **ethos** of the school, meaning the school's prevailing belief system. A favourable ethos – one that emphasised the value of schoolwork, rewarded good performance and established fair but firm discipline – was related to lower rates of delinquency through early adolescence.

CONNECT AND EXTEND

Adolescents who report higher teacher support and regard for pupils are more likely to see their schools as having respectful climates associated with lower levels of personal drug use. Some interesting perspectives in 'Teachers as builders of respectful school climates: implications for adolescent drug use norms and depressive symptoms in high school' by Maria LaRusso, Daniel Romer and Robert Selman in the *Journal of Youth and Adolescence*, Volume 37, Number 4 (April 2008), pp. 386–398

Neighbourhood and community factors have also been studied in relation to risk behaviour in adolescence, particularly in relation to delinquency (Swenson et al., 2005). A number of classic and now historic studies in sociology focused on the ways that neighbourhood factors promote or discourage delinquency (e.g. Whyte, 1943). These studies described how a sense of neighbourhood identity and cohesion has the effect of discouraging delinquency. More recent studies on neighbourhood and community factors have noted that high rates of residential mobility tend to be related to high rates of crime and delinquency, perhaps because when people move in and out of a neighbourhood frequently, residents tend to have weaker attachments to their neighbours and less regard for neighbourhood opinion (Fell and Piper, 2001). Also, neighbourhood and community norms regarding drug use and the availability of drugs in a community have been found to be related to substance use in adolescence (Diamond et al., 2009).

Community norms regarding substance use can influence adolescents.

Finally, in recent years religious beliefs have become a topic of interest in relation to risk behaviour. Numerous studies have found that religiosity is inversely related to participation in risk behaviour in adolescence and young adulthood (Smith and Denton, 2005; Steinman and Zimmerman, 2004; Nonnemaker et al., 2003). It may be that religious beliefs and religious participation, like good schools and authoritative parents, act as a *protective factor* which makes participation in risk behaviour less likely. However, unlike with schools or family, with religious beliefs self-selection has to be considered as a possible explanation. That is, it may be that it is not so much that religious involvement causes adolescents and young adults to be less likely to take part in risk behaviour, but rather that young people who strive for a high standard of moral behaviour are both less likely to be interested in risk behaviour and more likely to be interested in structured social involvement such as clubs, organisations and volunteering.

Individual Factors in Risk Behaviour

We have examined various aspects of socialisation that have been found to promote or discourage risk behaviour. Within any particular socialisation context, what makes some young people more likely than others to participate in risk behaviour? Given the same or similar types of family, peer, school and community environments, some adolescents take part in risk behaviour and others do not. Thus, in addition to socialisation influences, a variety of individual factors need to be considered in relation to various types of risk behaviour in adolescence and young adulthood.

One individual factor related to a variety of risk behaviours is aggressiveness. Aggressiveness is obviously related to delinquency and crime because many delinquent and criminal acts – destroying property, assault, rape – inherently involve aggressiveness. However, aggressiveness is also related to reckless driving behaviour in the teens and 20s. Risky driving is often an expression of anger and hostility (Begg and Langley, 2004). Aggressiveness has also been found to be related to substance use, for reasons that are not clear (Hayatbakhsh et al., 2008). Perhaps some adolescents use substances as self-medication for aggressiveness, just as they do for anxiety and depression.

Another characteristic consistently related to risk behaviour is sensation seeking. Sensation seeking is a personality trait characterised by the degree to which a person seeks out *novelty* and *intensity* of experience (Zuckerman, 2007). Many types of risk behaviour provide novelty and intensity of experience – for example, substance use leads to novel mental states, and breaking the law in delinquent and criminal acts is often described in terms of the intensity of the experience (Turnbull and Beese, 2000). For this reason, young people who are high in sensation seeking are also more likely to engage in a variety of risk behaviours, including substance use, risky driving, delinquency and risky sexual behaviour (van Beurden et al., 2005;

Hartos et al., 2002; Comeau et al., 2001; Hansen and Breivik, 2001). Sensation seeking, fuelled by the vicarious experiences of media – see the upcoming *Focus on Youth in the Media* feature – rises at puberty (C. A. Martin et al., 2002) and tends to be higher in the teens and early 20s than in adulthood. This enthusiasm for sensation seeking helps explain why risk behaviour is most common among the young (Romer and Hennessy, 2007; Zuckerman, 2003).

FOCUS ON YOUTH IN THE MEDIA

Suicide, Sensation Seeking and Imitation

In 1774, the great German writer Johann Wolfgang von Goethe published *The Sorrows of Young Werther*, about a young man who kills himself in despair over his unrequited love for a married woman. The novel immediately became immensely popular all over Europe, inspiring poems, plays, operas, songs, even jewellery and an 'Eau de Werther' scent for ladies. At the same time, the novel inspired immense controversy. It was banned in some parts of Germany for fear that impressionable young readers might interpret it as recommending suicide, and in Denmark a proposed translation was prohibited for the same reason. Although claims that Werther caused an epidemic of suicide in Europe are now regarded as unfounded (Hulse, 1989), in one verified case a young woman who had been deserted by her lover drowned herself in the river behind Goethe's house in Weimar, Germany; a copy of *Werther* in her pocket. Goethe was sufficiently disturbed by the controversy over the book to add an epigraph to the 1775 edition of the novel urging his readers not to follow Werther's example.

In Goethe's time as well as our own, the question of media effects has been a source of public debate and concern, often with a particular focus on the lives of adolescents. A more recent example took place in the autumn of 1993, concerning a film called *The Program* released by the Walt Disney Company. The film, about the players and coach of a football team, quickly became controversial because of a scene in which one of the players demonstrates his manly toughness by lying down in the middle of a busy motorway at night as cars and HGVs whoosh by him. Some adolescents who had seen the film proceeded to try the stunt for themselves. An 18-year-old boy was killed and two other boys were critically injured, one of them paralysed. In response to the resulting outcry, Disney hastily recalled the film and deleted the scene in question, while strenuously denying responsibility for the boys' reckless acts.

This is about as definite an example of media effects as it is possible to find. There can be little doubt that the boys were imitating the behaviour they had witnessed in the film. They had seen it just days before, and friends who accompanied them on the night of the accidents testified later that they were imitating the stunt they had seen in the film.

At the same time, this example illustrates why drawing a simple cause-and-effect relationship between the media consumed by adolescents and their subsequent behaviour is problematic. Literally hundreds of thousands of people (mostly adolescents) saw the film with the controversial scene. It was playing in 1220 cinemas at the time, and even estimating modestly at 100 persons per cinema would put the total number of viewers over 100,000. Yet the total number of reported incidents that resulted from adolescents imitating the scene was *three*. Evidently, then, the adolescents who imitated the scene had traits or circumstances that led them to imitate it, even though the vast majority of the people who watched it did not.

Finally, an even more up-to-date example of how 'reverse psychology' is being used to dissuade teenagers from imitating that which they see in, arguably, the most persuasive of media productions, the advertisement. Anti-smoking ads in France show a teen boy and a teen girl on their knees mimicking oral sex on a man. The ads from the 'Non-Smokers' Rights Association' display the two adolescents kneeling at the waist of a businessman, each with a cigarette in their mouth. The ads are meant to link smoking to submission and have a caption that reads: 'Smoking means being a slave to tobacco'.

The director for the Non-Smoker's Rights Association, Remi Parola, defends the ads in an interview with Associated Press:

'Traditional advertisements targeting teens don't affect them. Talking about issues of health, illness or even death, they don't get it. However, when we talk about submission and dependence, they listen. The visuals have a sexual connotation, that I can't deny, but it's really a way to start a discussion with young people to get them to understand the dangers of smoking.' (Associated Press, 2010)

Intriguingly, I (MH) captured this story from a hip-hop video magazine website **http://hiphopwired. com**, which publishes hip-hop videos, features, news, politics and forums (accessed 21 February 2011). The website presents this media story about the power of advertising for a perceived good cause using strong visual images showing young people in subservient and demeaning roles; the antithesis of cool, sensation-seeking empowered personas found in most media aimed at young people. We could not get permission to reproduce the image here, but you should have enough information to find the image yourself.

A third individual factor often related to risk behaviour is *poor school achievement*. Although we have noted that future delinquents often exhibit problems even before they begin school, it has been a long-standing and consistent finding that poor school achievement is also a predictor of delinquency (Moffitt, 2007; 2003). Poor school achievement has also been found in numerous studies to be related to substance use (Bryant et al., 2003). To some extent, poor school achievement is a reflection of other characteristics such as sensation seeking and aggressiveness, both related to poor school achievement, as well as to risk behaviour. Attention deficit-hyperactivity disorder (ADHD) is related to poor school achievement and to delinquency (Loeber et al., 2001) as is low performance on intelligence tests (Meijer, 2007). Although poor school achievement may not directly cause risky behaviour, the fact that poor school achievement represents such a wide range of other problems makes it an especially strong predictor of risk behaviour in adolescence.

Low impulse control, which means difficulty in exercising self-control, is another characteristic related to risk behaviours in adolescence such as substance use and delinquency (De Li, 2004; Cooper et al., 2003; Loeber et al., 2001). Low impulse control is often a reflection of a family environment that is either too harsh or too permissive (Moffitt, 2003). Finally, the *optimistic bias* also contributes to a variety of risk behaviours. As discussed in Chapter 3, adolescents have a tendency to assume that accidents, diseases and other misfortunes are more likely to happen to other people than to themselves. Thus, young people who participate in risky behaviour tend to be more likely than others to believe that nothing bad will happen to them as a result of such behaviour (Reyna and Farley, 2006). You will find a further examination of some of

CONNECT AND EXTEND

A little dated now but still worth a read. Try 'Childhood conduct problems, hyperactivity-impulsivity, and inattention as predictors of adult criminal activity' by Leslie M. Babinski, Carolyn S. Hartsough and Nadine M. Lambert in the *Journal of Child Psychology and Psychiatry* (formerly *Journal of Child Psychology and Psychiatry and Allied Disciplines*), Volume 40, Number 3 (March 1999), pp. 347–355

the factors involved in delinquency in the upcoming *Research Focus* feature.

For every one of the individual factors described here, males are more at risk than females. Males tend to be higher in aggressiveness (Bongers et al., 2004), higher in sensation seeking (Zuckerman, *ibid.*), lower in school achievement (Bryant et al., *ibid.*), lower in impulse control (De Li, 2004), and higher in optimistic bias (Reyna and Farley, *ibid.*). Together, these gender differences in individual risk factors largely explain why males are more likely than females to engage in risk behaviour during adolescence and young adulthood.

Culture and Risk Behaviour

So far we have been focusing on majority cultures because that is the population which has been the focus of most research on risk behaviour among young people. To what extent is young people's risk behaviour a problem in cultures worldwide, and to what extent is it peculiar to European societies? Remember the classic study by anthropologists Alice Schlegel and Herbert Barry (1991), and their analysis of 186 traditional cultures which concluded that 'for boys but not for girls, adolescence tends to be the stage during which

antisocial behaviour most often occurs, if it occurs at all' (p. 39). (By 'antisocial behaviour' they meant behaviour such as fighting and stealing.) However, Schlegel and Barry found notable evidence of adolescent antisocial behaviour in fewer than half of the traditional cultures they studied. Thus, traditional cultures have less of a problem with antisocial behaviour than cultures in the developed world, and antisocial behaviour is especially rare among adolescent girls in traditional cultures, in part because young girls are usually closely monitored by adults.

THINKING CRITICALLY

The Gluecks' longitudinal study has been criticised on methodological grounds. The criticism is about interviewers' interpretations being affected by prior knowledge of the delinquency status of each of the boys. Do you think it matters whether or not the interviewers know the 'status' of the boys before the interviews took place? What are the arguments as to whether or not it matters?

RESEARCH FOCUS   R

A Longitudinal Study of Delinquency

Longitudinal studies of crime and delinquency go back far enough into the early part of the twentieth century that the boys who originally took part in them have long since become men, and we have information on what became of their lives in adulthood. One of the most influential and informative of these now classic studies was conducted by Sheldon and Eleanor Glueck, a husband-and-wife team of scholars who followed delinquent and non-delinquent boys from their teens until their early 30s. The study provides rich information on the factors involved in delinquency as well as the implications of delinquency for adult development.

The Gluecks' study began in the early 1940s with 1000 boys aged 10 to 17, including 500 delinquents and 500 non-delinquents (Glueck and Glueck, 1950). The delinquent boys were in residential care for delinquents. The non-delinquent boys were recruited from state schools, and they were not randomly selected but were matched case by case with the delinquent boys for age, ethnic group, IQ and neighbourhood socio-economic status. The Gluecks chose this method because they wanted to be able to show that any differences between the two groups were not due to these pre-existing characteristics. Boys in both groups grew up in family and neighbourhood environments that were characterised by poverty and high exposure to delinquency and crime.

The Gluecks' study lasted 18 years, and their research team collected data on the boys at three times: adolescence (ages 10 to 17), during young adulthood (ages 21 to 28), and during established adulthood (ages 28 to 35). Each time, an abundance of information was collected. In adolescence, information was collected from the boys themselves as well as from parents, teachers, social workers and local police. In the two follow-ups, information was collected from the young men and their families as well as from employers, neighbours, and officials in criminal justice and social welfare agencies. Ninety-two per cent of the participants remained in the study through all three times of data collection, an exceptionally high rate across an 18-year period.

An enormous amount of information was collected in the study, and only the outlines of the results can be described here (see Sampson and Laub, 1994; Glueck and Glueck, 1968; 1950). Briefly, the Gluecks found that the key to delinquency lay in an interaction between constitutional factors and family environments. By 'constitutional factors' they meant biological predispositions. The constitutional factors they found to be related to delinquency were body type and temperament. Delinquent adolescent boys were more likely than non-delinquents to have a 'mesomorphic' body type, that is, a body that was stocky and muscular rather than rounded (endomorphic) or tall and slim (ectomorphic). Also, delinquents were more likely than non-delinquents to have had a difficult temperament as children. That is, their parents more often reported that as infants and children they cried often, were difficult to soothe when upset, and had irregular patterns of eating and sleeping.

With regard to family environment, delinquent boys were more likely to be from families in which one or both parents were neglectful or hostile towards them. Parents' discipline in the families of delinquents tended to be either permissive or inconsistent, alternating periods of neglect with outbursts of punishment. This is now a familiar pattern to researchers, but the Gluecks were among the first to establish systematically the relationship between parenting and outcomes in adolescence.

And how did the boys 'turn out' once they reached their 20s and early 30s? For the most part, their behaviour in adolescence was highly predictive of their later development. By age 25, the 500 boys in the delinquent group had been arrested for 7 murders, 100 robberies, 172 burglaries, 225 larcenies – the theft of personal property – and numerous other offences (Wilson and Herrnstein, 1985). These rates were more than five times as high as for the non-delinquent group. However, it was not just crime that was predicted by delinquent status in adolescence. In young adulthood, those who had been adolescent delinquents were four times as likely as non-delinquents to abuse alcohol, seven times as likely to have a pattern of unstable employment, three times as likely to be divorced, and far less likely to have completed secondary schooling (Sampson and Laub, 1990).

In sum, delinquent status in adolescence was a strong predictor of a wide range of serious future problems. However, not all of the adolescent delinquents went on to have difficulties in adulthood. For those who did not, job stability and attachment to spouse were the best predictors of staying out of trouble in adulthood (Sampson and Laub, 1990). Income itself was a poor predictor, but job stability made a difference. Similarly, simply getting married was a poor predictor by itself, but a close emotional attachment to a spouse made a positive difference.

The Gluecks' study has been criticised on methodological grounds. The most serious criticism is that the persons collecting data on the boys and their environments were not blind to the boys' 'status' as delinquent or non-delinquent. This means that researchers who interviewed the boys' parents or conducted psychological interviews with the boys knew in advance whether a boy was part of the delinquent or the non-delinquent group. Because the conclusions for much of the study were based on interpretations from interviews rather than questionnaires or objective tests, the interpretations may have been biased by what the researchers knew about the boys in advance. However, the Gluecks' conclusions have stood the test of time quite well, and their study continues to be regarded as a classic of social science research.

CONNECT AND EXTEND

We can make a connection with some of the themes of Chapter 9. Do you think that earlier age at first sex predicts higher levels of delinquency in early adulthood? For a surprising set of findings read 'Rethinking timing of first sex and delinquency' by K. Harden, Jane Mendle, Jennifer Hill, Eric Turkheimer and Robert Emery in the *Journal of Youth and Adolescence*, Volume 37, Number 4 (April 2008), pp. 373–385

INTERNAL PROBLEMS

So far we have been discussing external problems. Now we turn to the class of problems known as internal problems. We will focus on two of the most common types of these problems in adolescence and young adulthood: depression and eating disorders.

Depression

Depression, as a general term, means an enduring period of sadness. However, psychologists make distinctions between different levels of depression (Bjerkeset et al., 2008). **Depressed mood** is a term for an enduring period of sadness by itself, without any related symptoms. **Depressive syndrome** means an enduring period of sadness along with other symptoms such as frequent crying, feelings of worthlessness, and feeling guilty, lonely or worried. The most serious form of depression is **major depressive disorder**. An episode of major depressive disorder includes the following specific symptoms (Muris et al., 2009):

1 Depressed or irritable mood for most of the day, nearly every day.

2 Reduced interest or pleasure in all or almost all activities, nearly every day.

3 Significant weight loss or gain, or decrease in appetite.

4 Insomnia or oversleeping.

5 Psychomotor agitation or retardation, observable by others.

6 Low energy or fatigue.

7 Feelings of worthlessness or inappropriate guilt.

8 Diminished ability to think or concentrate.

9 Recurrent thoughts of death, recurrent suicidal thoughts.

For a diagnosis of a major depressive episode, five or more of these symptoms must be present during a two-week period and must represent a change from previous functioning. At least one of the symptoms must be depressed mood or reduced interest/pleasure.

Depressed mood is the most common kind of internal problem in adolescence. Several studies find that adolescents have higher rates of depressed mood than adults or children (e.g. Muris et al., 2009; Smith et al., 2009; Saluja et al., 2004). Episodes of depressed mood before adolescence are relatively rare (Curry and Reinecke, 2003), although they do sometimes occur. The beginning of adolescence marks a steep increase in the pervasiveness of depressed mood. Studies of rates of depressed mood at different ages have concluded that there is a 'mid-adolescence peak' in depressed mood (Murray et al., 2006; Soloman et al., 2006; Beyers and Lober, 2003) so that rates of depressed mood rise steeply from age 10 to about ages 15 to 17, then decline in the late teens and 20s.

A variety of studies have shown that the proportion of adolescents who report experiencing depressed mood within the past six months is about 35 per cent (e.g. Saluja et al., 2004). In contrast, rates of depressive syndrome and major depressive disorder among adolescents range in various studies from 3 to 7 per cent (e.g. Emslie et al., 2008; Park et al., 2005; Cheung et al., 2005; Tamplin and Gooyer, 2001), which is about the same rate found in studies of adults.

Causes of Depression

The causes of depression in adolescence and young adulthood differ somewhat depending on whether the diagnosis is depressed mood or the more serious forms of depression (depressive syndrome and depressive disorder). The most common causes of depressed mood tend to be common experiences among young people – conflict with friends or family members, disappointment or rejection in love, and poor performance in school (Costello et al., 2008).

THINKING CRITICALLY

Few studies have been conducted on depressed mood among young adults. How would you expect the sources of depressed mood in young adulthood to be similar to or different from the sources of depressed mood in adolescence?

Depressed mood peaks in mid-adolescence.

The causes of the more serious forms of depression are more complicated and less common. Studies have found that both genetic and environmental factors are involved (e.g. Glowinski et al., 2003). Of course, both genetic and environmental influences are involved in most aspects of development, but the interaction of genes and environment is especially well established with respect to depression. One useful model of this interaction that has been applied to depression as well as to other mental disorders is the **diathesis-stress model** (Ingram and Smith, 2008). The theory behind this model is that mental disorders such as depression often begin with a diathesis, meaning a pre-existing vulnerability. Often, this diathesis will have a genetic basis, but not necessarily. For example, being born prematurely is a diathesis for many physical and psychological problems in development, but it is not genetic. However, a diathesis is only a vulnerability, a potential for problems. Expression of that vulnerability requires the existence of a stress as well, meaning environmental conditions that interact with the diathesis to produce the disorder.

The role of a genetic diathesis in depression has been established in twin studies and in adoption studies. Identical twins have a much higher **concordance rate** for depression – meaning the probability that if one gets the disorder, the other gets it as well – than fraternal twins do (Glowinski et al., *ibid.*). This is true even for identical twins who are raised in different homes and who thus have different family environments. Also, adopted children whose biological mothers have experienced depression are more likely than other adopted children to develop depression themselves (Ong and Caron, 2010; Smith and Brodzinsky, 2002).

There is also evidence that the diathesis for depression may be stronger when the onset of depressive disorder occurs in childhood or adolescence rather than adulthood (Zalsman et al., 2006). In Moffitt's Dunedin study, described earlier in the chapter, people who were diagnosed with depressive disorder in adolescence (ages 11 to 15) were more likely than those

diagnosed in young adulthood (ages 18 to 26) to have experienced prenatal difficulties and early deficits in the development of motor skills (Jaffee et al., 2002). Such early difficulties suggest that they had a neurological diathesis for depression which was expressed when the stresses of adolescence arrived.

What sort of stresses bring out the diathesis for depression in adolescence? A variety of family and peer factors have been found to be involved. In the family, factors contributing to depression in adolescence include emotional unavailability of parents, high family conflict, economic difficulties and parental divorce (Hammack et al., 2004; Forkel and Silbereisen, 2001). With respect to peers, less contact with friends and more experiences of rejection contribute to depression over time (Bosacki et al., 2007). Unfortunately, poor peer relationships tend to be self-perpetuating for depressed adolescents because other adolescents tend to avoid being around adolescents who are depressed (Zimmer-Gembeck et al., 2009). Some studies on depression in adolescence have also taken the approach of calculating an overall stress score, which usually includes stress in the family and in peer relationships as well as stresses such as changing schools and experiencing pubertal changes. These studies find that overall stress is related to depression in adolescence (e.g. Hampel and Petermann, 2005; Sund et al., 2003; Mathiesen et al., 2002).

CONNECT AND EXTEND

To examine whether and how parental gender role influences children's own gender development and mental health read 'Children and adolescents with transsexual parents referred to a specialist gender identity development service: a brief report of key developmental features' by David Freedman, Fiona Tasker and Domenico di Ceglie in *Clinical Child Psychology and Psychiatry*, Volume 7, Number 3 (1 July 2002), pp. 423–432

Gender Differences in Depression

One of the factors that constitutes the highest risk for depression in adolescence is being female. In childhood, when depression is relatively rare, rates are actually higher among boys. However, in adolescence the rates become substantially higher among females, and they remain higher among females throughout adulthood, for depressed mood as well as major depressive disorder (Hammack et al., 2004; Hoffman et al., 2003; Curry and Reinecke, 2003). What explains the gender difference in adolescent depression?

A variety of explanations have been proposed. There is a little evidence that biological differences (such as the earlier entry of females into puberty) can explain it (Petersen, 2000). However, some scholars have suggested that the female gender role itself leads to depression in adolescence. As we have discussed in earlier chapters, because of the gender intensification that takes place in adolescence (Lobel et al., 2004; Watt, 2004), concerns about physical attractiveness become a primary concern, especially for girls. There is evidence that adolescent girls who have a poor self-body image are more likely than other girls to be depressed (Marcotte et al., 2002).

A turn of the century study of adolescents and young adults in Norway is especially enlightening on this issue (Wichstrom, 1999). The study was on a representative national sample of young people aged 12 to 20. At age 12 no gender difference in depressed mood was found. However, by age 14 girls were more likely to report depressed mood, and this gender difference remained stable through age 20. Statistical analyses showed that the gender difference could be explained by girls' responses to the physical changes of puberty. As their bodies changed, they became increasingly dissatisfied with their weight and their body shape, and that dissatisfaction was linked to depressed mood. Depressed mood in girls was also related to an increase in describing themselves in terms of feminine gender role traits of the kind we discussed in Chapter 5:

shy, soft-spoken, tender, and so on. In contrast, depressed mood was not related to masculine gender role identification in boys. Another more recent study reported similar findings, indicating that girls' body shame in early adolescence preceded an increase in the prevalence of depressed mood (Grabe et al., 2007). Just as in the Norwegian study, there was no gender difference in depressed mood in early adolescence, but girls' greater body shame led to greater prevalence of depressed mood by mid-adolescence.

Other explanations have also been offered. Stress is related to depression in adolescence, and adolescent girls generally report experiencing more stress than adolescent boys do (Cyranowski et al., 2003). Also, when faced with the beginning of a depressed mood, males are more likely to distract themselves (and forget about it), whereas females have a greater tendency to brood on their depressed feelings and thereby amplify them (Jose and Brown, 2008; Nolen-Hoeksema et al., 2008; Grant et al., 2004). Adolescent girls are more likely than adolescent boys to devote their thoughts and feelings to their personal relationships and these relationships can be a source of distress and sadness (Agosto, 2004; Hay and Ashman, 2003; Leach, 2003).

Males and females generally differ in their responses to stress and conflict, which helps explain both the greater tendency towards external problems in boys – discussed earlier – and the greater tendency towards internal problems in girls. Remember that in adolescence as well as in childhood and adulthood, males tend to respond to stress and conflict by directing their feelings *outwards* – in the form of external behaviour. Females, in contrast, tend to respond to these problems by turning their distress *inwards*, in the form of critical thoughts *towards themselves* (Calvete and Cardeñoso, 2005). In summary, then, studies have found that even when exposed to the same amount of stress as adolescent boys, adolescent girls are more likely to respond by becoming depressed (Bearman and Stice, 2008).

CONNECT AND EXTEND

Sexual minority adolescents report more externalising behaviours and depression symptoms than heterosexual youth. For a study examining links between sexual orientation and adjustment in a sample of 97 sexual minority (gay male, lesbian, bisexual and questioning) secondary school students, read 'Peer victimisation, social support and psychosocial adjustment of sexual minority adolescents' by Trish Williams, Jennifer Connolly, Debra Pepler and Wendy Craig in the *Journal of Youth and Adolescence*, Volume 34, Number 5 (October 2005), pp. 471–482

Treatments for Depression

Just because depression in adolescence is common does not mean that it should be ignored or viewed as something that will go away eventually, especially when it persists over an extended period or reaches the level of depressive syndrome or major depressive disorder. Depressed adolescents are at risk for a variety of other problems, including school failure (Frydenburg et al., 2004) delinquency (Rowe et al., 2006) and suicide (Fergusson et al., 2005). Therefore, symptoms of depression in adolescence should be taken seriously, and treatment provided when necessary.

For adolescents as for adults, the two main types of treatment for depression are antidepressant medications and psychotherapy. Studies of the effectiveness of antidepressant medications typically use a **placebo design**, meaning that all of the depressed adolescents take pills but only the pills taken by adolescents in the treatment group contain the drug. Adolescents in the control group take a *placebo*, that is, a pill which does not contain any medication, although the adolescents do not know this.

Studies in the last decade indicate that relatively newly developed antidepressants such as Prozac are often effective in treating adolescent depression (Bostic et al., 2005; Brent, 2004; Cohen et al., 2004; Michael and Crowley, 2002). For example, in one study, adolescents diagnosed with major depressive disorder were randomly assigned to take either Prozac or a placebo for eight weeks (Emslie et al., 2002). At the end of this period, symptoms of depression were significantly improved in 41 per cent of the treatment group but only 20 per cent of the control (placebo) group.

However, there is also disturbing evidence that antidepressant medications, including Prozac, may increase suicidal thinking and behaviour among some depressed adolescents (Cheung et al., 2004). Researchers in this area agree that when antidepressants are used with depressed adolescents, parents and adolescents should be fully informed of the possible risks, and the adolescents should be monitored closely for evidence of adverse effects (Bostic et al., 2005; Brent, 2004; Cheung et al., 2004). Suicidal thinking and behaviour are lower among depressed adolescents when antidepressants are combined with psychotherapy than when they are used alone (TADS, 2007).

Psychotherapy for adolescent depression takes a variety of forms, including individual therapy, group therapy and skills training. Studies that have randomly assigned depressed adolescents to either a treatment group (which received psychotherapy) or a control group (which did not) have found that therapy tends to be effective in reducing the symptoms of depression (e.g. Bostic et al., 2005).

Psychotherapy is often effective in treating young people's depression.

CONNECT AND EXTEND

Cognitive behaviour therapy (CBT) is now a widely accepted and effective form of psychotherapy for the learning disability population. However, the model needs to be applied differently! To see how CBT can contribute to addressing the emotional needs of people with learning disabilities read

'Cognitive behaviour therapy and people with learning disabilities: implications for developing nursing practice' by M. Brown and K. Marshall in the *Journal of Psychiatric & Mental Health Nursing*, Volume 13, Number 2 (April 2006), pp. 234–241

One especially effective type of therapy for depression is **cognitive behaviour therapy (CBT)** (Gaynor et al., 2003). This approach describes depression as characterised by **negative attributions,** that is, negative ways of explaining what happens in one's life. Typically, young people who are depressed believe their situation is *permanent* ('It's never going to get better') and *uncontrollable* ('My life is awful and there's nothing I can do about it'). Depressed adolescents also have a tendency for *rumination*, which means they dwell on the things that are wrong with their lives and brood about how worthless they feel and how pointless life seems. As noted earlier, one of the explanations for the gender difference in depression is that girls and women tend to ruminate in this way more than boys and men.

The goal of CBT, then, is to help the young person recognise the cognitive habits that are promoting depression and work to change those habits (Kaufman et al., 2005; Persons et al., 2001). The therapist actively challenges the negative attributions, so that the client will examine them critically and begin to see them as distortions of reality. In addition to changing cognitive habits, CBT works on changing behaviour. For example, the therapist and client might engage in role playing, where the therapist pretends to be the client's parent, or spouse, or colleague at work. Through role playing the client is able to practise new ways of interacting. People who have received CBT are less likely than those who have received antidepressant drugs to relapse when the treatment is over, indicating that the new ways of thinking and interacting endure beyond the therapeutic period (Rohde et al., 2005; Persons et al., 2001).

Suicide

'When Sandy told me she wanted to break up, I thought there was no point in going on. I loved her so much. I wanted to spend the rest of my life with her. So I started thinking about killing myself. I imagined how I could do it and what kind of note I'd leave my parents. Then I started thinking about my parents and my little sister, and I thought of them at the funeral crying and being so sad, and I knew I couldn't go through with it. I realised I didn't really want to die; I just wanted everything to be okay again.'
– Donnie, age 16 (in Bell, 1998, p. 176)

One reason for taking young people's depression seriously is that it is a risk factor for suicide. Suicide attempts are usually preceded by symptoms of depression (Pfeffer, 2006; Spirito and Overholser, 2003). However, often young people's suicide attempts take place as the symptoms of depression appear to be abating. At the depths of depression, young people are often too dispirited to engage in the planning required to commit suicide. As they improve slightly, they remain depressed but now have enough energy and motivation to make a suicide attempt. Making a plan to commit suicide may also raise the mood of deeply depressed young people because they may believe that the suicide will mean an end to all the problems they feel are plaguing them.

Suicide rates in those aged 10–19 in the UK declined by 28 per cent in the seven-year period from 1997 to 2003 (Windfuhr et al., 2008). The study, carried out by researchers at the University of Manchester, showed that the decline was particularly marked in young males, where rates declined by 35 per cent yet, suicide remains more common among young males (75 per cent of suicides) than young females. The majority of young people were aged 15–19 (93 per cent of the sample), and overall, the most common methods of suicide were hanging, followed by self-poisoning. The study also revealed that over the seven-year period, only 14 per cent of young people who committed suicide were in contact with mental health services in the year prior to their death, compared to 26 per cent of adults. Again, there was a marked difference between males and females, with 20 per cent of young females in contact with mental health services compared to only 12 per cent of young males.

It is important to note that suicide rates for teenagers and young adults is lower both for males and females than for other age groups. Compare Figures 12.7 and 12.8 for rates of suicide and open verdicts in England and Wales, 1968 to 2008.

Sharp gender differences also exist in rates of suicide attempts. Females are about four times as likely

THINKING CRITICALLY

A critical comparison of Figures 12.7 and 12.8 raises a lot of questions, not least of which is how can you make a straightforward reconciliation of the scales used on the two vertical axes? How do you account for the differences between the age groups and the trends in rates of suicide over time? Even more intriguing is, how do you account for the gender difference between males and females despite higher rates among females for depressed mood and major depressive disorder?

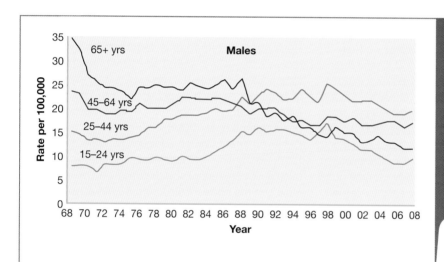

Figure 12.7 Rates of suicide and open verdicts in England and Wales, 1968–2008: males. (Data are for registrations of death in each calendar year.)

Source: The Oxford University Centre for Suicide Research at: **http://cebmh.warne. ox.ac.uk/csr/msui6808.html** accessed 19 February 2011. Hawton et al. (2009)

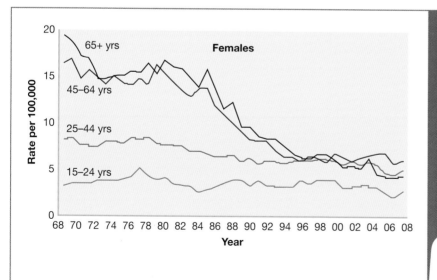

Figure 12.8 Rates of suicide and open verdicts in England and Wales, 1968–2008: females. (Data are for registrations of death in each calendar year.)

Source: The Oxford University Centre for Suicide Research at: **http://www.mind. org.uk/help/research_ and_policy/statistics_2_ suicide#whichage** accessed 19 February 2011. Hawton et al. (2009)

Suicide rates among young people are highest in countries where guns are easy to obtain.

as males to attempt suicide in adolescence and young adulthood, but males are about four times as likely as females actually to kill themselves (Oltmanns and Emery, 2001). These gender differences exist in adulthood as well. The higher rate of attempts among females is probably a consequence of their higher rates of depression (Wichstrom and Rossow, 2002). The reason for the higher rate of completed suicides among males seems to be due mainly to gender differences in the methods used. Males are more likely to use guns (particularly where guns are relatively easy to get hold of) or hang themselves, and these methods are more deadly than the method of taking poison or pills that is more commonly used by females in their suicide attempts (Chung et al., 2008; Hawton et al., 2007; Shenassa et al., 2003; Hultén et al., 2000). In a study comparing suicide rates among young people in 34 countries (Johnson et al., 2000), rates were highest in countries where guns were most easily available.

Other than depression, what are the risk factors for suicide? One major factor for adolescents is *family disruption*. Attempted and completed suicide has frequently been found to be related to a family life that is chaotic, disorganised, high in conflict and low in warmth (Brent and Mann, 2003; Breton et al., 2002). Furthermore, an adolescent's suicide is often preceded by a period of months in which family problems have worsened (Zhang et al., 2006; Rosario et al., 2005; Lowe, 2003). Adoption and twin studies indicate that families also contribute genetic vulnerability to suicide, via susceptibility to major depression and other mental illnesses (Brent and Melhem, 2008).

In addition to family risk factors, suicidal adolescents often have substance abuse problems (Wolpert et al., 2006), perhaps as an attempt at self-medication for distress over their family problems and their depression. Also, suicidal adolescents have usually experienced problems in their relationships outside the family. Because they often come from families where they receive little in the way of emotional nurturance, suicidal adolescents may be more vulnerable to the effects of experiences such as school failure, loss of a boyfriend or girlfriend, or feelings of being rejected by their peers (Herba et al., 2008).

Nevertheless, most adolescents who experience family disruption or substance use problems never think about or attempt suicide (Brent and Mann, 2006). How can the adolescents at most serious risk be identified? One group of researchers used interviews with family members and friends to identify three different pathways among adolescents who had committed suicide (Fortune et al., 2007). The largest group had experienced years of difficulty in relations with family, friends and teachers. They had attempted suicide previously and had communicated their suicidal intentions and plans to friends and family. A second group had struggled with severe mental illness such as major depression or bipolar disorder. The third and smallest

CONNECT AND EXTEND

This article proposes four revolutions in psychotherapy: therapists should focus on building strengths rather than patching up weaknesses; translate symptoms into gifts; consider alternative goals rather than returning to previous functioning; and, finally, giving fish, not just teaching how to fish. Intrigued? Read 'Psychotherapy revolution: translating symptoms into gifts' by Lara Honos-Webb in the *Journal of Contemporary Psychotherapy*, Volume 39 (January 2008), pp. 65–71. In this paper several case studies are offered focusing on those diagnosed with major depression and attention deficit-hyperactivity disorder.

group consisted of young people who had previously been functioning well but experienced an acute crisis that led to the suicide, without apparent mental illness or previous suicidal intention. However, and importantly, even in this group two out of five youngsters communicated specific suicidal intent in the weeks before their death.

The effect of an attempted or completed suicide by a peer or friend can be a very traumatic and shocking experience for young people (Melhem et al., 2004). I remember (MH) a boy at my school, Martin, who hanged himself early one Saturday morning. I think we were about 13. The story going around school first thing on Monday morning was that he had been caught shoplifting and that the police were going to call round to talk to his mother. He had ridden his bike to The Duke's Drive (part of our school cross-country running route), a most impressive driveway leading up to the Duke of Westminster's estate in Chester. He threw a rope over a branch of one of the trees that lined the drive, leaned his bike against the tree, balanced on the cross bar and saddle then kicked the bike away. There was a hushed and shocked reverence to the whispered conversations in the playground and on our way into school assembly; the head teacher, John Scott, took the opportunity for a moving tribute, a minute of silence and a warning that there was no problem that couldn't be faced up to. By the end of the day some boys were re-enacting what we thought had happened right from the shoplifting through to the final awful seconds for Martin, alone and miserable in a cold dawn. Perhaps those play actors were coming to terms in some way with the enormity of what had now become a personal experience for us all. Even now, when I meet old school friends from 50-plus years ago we still talk about Martin and why he 'did it'. What effect did it have on us?

A relationship has been established between friends' suicide attempt and adolescent's own attempt to commit suicide, and the extent to which there are gender differences in this interrelationship. Ruth Liu (2006) found that friends' suicide attempt and adolescent depression each predicts adolescent's own attempt to commit suicide, and these effects are similar for both boys and girls. Second, and perhaps surprisingly given that suicidal thoughts are one of the symptoms of depression, highly depressed adolescents are less likely than low- or non-depressed adolescents to attempt suicide when their friends attempt suicide. Finally Lui found that, for adolescent girls, depression reduces the relationship between friends' suicidal attempt and adolescent's own attempt. As far as I know, there were no copycat attempted suicides by Martin's friends and peers in the 1960s. For us, Martin's suicide remained an enormously powerful event in our lives that stood as a lesson. In our headmaster's words, 'Boys, there is no problem that cannot be faced up to.'

Despite stories like my own of Martin, many studies concur that in almost all cases, adolescent suicide takes place not in response to a single stressful or painful event but only after a series of difficulties extending over months or even years (e.g. Spirito and Overholser, 2003). It is rare for suicidal adolescents to show no warning signs of emotional or behavioural problems prior to attempting suicide (see Table 12.1). Often, they have made efforts to address the problems in their lives, and the failure of these efforts has sent them on a downward spiral that deepened their hopelessness and led them to attempt suicide.

Adolescents who attempt suicide are at high risk for future attempts and for completed suicide (Pfeffer, 2006). In one study of attempters, at a three-month follow-up assessment 45 per cent reported continued suicidal thoughts and 12 per cent reported a repeat attempt (Spirito et al., 2003). As with depression, the most effective treatments for suicidal adolescents combine CBT with antidepressants (Donaldson et al., 2003).

CONNECT AND EXTEND

This paper set out to explore the cultural context of youth suicide and more specifically any connections between sexual identity and self-destructive behaviour. 'Lesbian, gay, bisexual and transgender young people's experiences of distress: resilience, ambivalence and self-destructive behaviour' by Jonathan Scourfield, Katrina Roen and Liz McDermott in *Health & Social Care in the Community*, Volume 16, Number 3 (May 2008), pp. 329–336

Table 12.1 Early Warning Signs of Adolescent Suicide

1   Direct suicide threats or comments such as 'I wish I were dead'; 'My family would be better off without me'; 'I have nothing to live for'.

2   A previous suicide attempt, no matter how minor. Four out of five people who commit suicide have made at least one previous attempt.

3   Preoccupation with death in music, art and personal writing.

4   Loss of a family member, pet, or boy/girlfriend through death, abandonment or breakup.

5   Family disruptions such as unemployment, serious illness, relocation or divorce.

6   Disturbances in sleeping and eating habits and in personal hygiene.

7   Declining grades and lack of interest in school or hobbies that had previously been important.

8   Drastic changes in behaviour patterns, such as a quiet, shy person becoming extremely gregarious.

9   Pervasive sense of gloom, helplessness and hopelessness.

10   Withdrawal from family members and friends and feelings of alienation from significant others.

11   Giving away prized possessions and otherwise 'getting their affairs in order'.

12   Series of 'accidents' or impulsive, risk-taking behaviours. Drug or alcohol abuse, disregard for personal safety or taking dangerous 'dares'.

Sources: Brent and Melhem (2008); Pfeffer (2006).

THINKING CRITICALLY

In 2008 there was a spate of teenage suicides in Bridgend, South Wales, linked to social networking websites. We found the story at: **http://www.telegraph.co.uk/news/uknews/1577672/New-teenage-suicide-in-Bridgend.html**. What was happening there, and why?

Eating Disorders

'At 102 pounds I thought I would be happy. But when I lost another two pounds, I was even happier. By the time I was down to 98 pounds, I stopped getting my period. . . . Also, my hair, which was normally healthy and shiny, became very brittle and dull, and it started falling out. . . . [My skin] took on a yellowish tone that on me looked sick, but I didn't care. I thought I looked better than I ever had in my whole life.'
– Alicia (in Bell, 1998, p. 191)

Adolescents find that people in their environment, such as peers and parents, respond differently to them as they show outward signs of reaching sexual maturity. These responses from others, along with their own self-reflection, lead to changes in the way adolescents think about their bodies.

For many adolescents, changes in the way they think about their bodies are accompanied by changes in the way they think about food. Girls, in particular, pay more attention to the food they eat once they reach adolescence, and worry more about eating too much

Even when they are so thin they risk serious medical problems, anorexic girls see themselves as 'too fat'.

CONNECT AND EXTEND

'Overall, adolescents' body image has little to do with how others perceive them, but once developed remains constant through much of adolescence.' A little dated but still 'on the button'. Read 'The relations among body image, physical attractiveness, and body mass in adolescence' by Gianine D. Rosenblum and Michael Lewis in *Child Development*, Volume 70, Number 1 (January 1999), pp. 50–64

and getting 'fat' (Nichter, 2001). Presented with a cultural ideal that portrays the ideal female body as slim, at a time when their bodies are biologically tending to become less slim and more rounded, many of them feel distressed at the changes taking place in their body shape, and they attempt to resist or at least modify those changes.

This dissatisfaction exists far more often among girls than among boys (Vincent and McCabe, 2000). Boys are much less likely to believe they are overweight and much more likely to be satisfied with their bodies (Walcott et al., 2003). Even long before adolescence, girls are more likely to worry about becoming overweight and to desire to be thinner than they are (McKnight Investigators, 2003). Body dissatisfaction among girls increases during the teens and continues through young adulthood and beyond (Rosenblum and Lewis, 1999). In fact, extreme weight-loss behaviours among adolescent girls, such as fasting, 'crash dieting' and skipping meals are related to their mothers' own extreme weight-loss behaviour (Nichter, 2001). Exposed to this cultural emphasis on slimness as part of social and sexual attractiveness for women, some girls go to extremes in controlling their food intake and develop eating disorders. About 90 per cent of eating disorders occur among females (Reijonen et al., 2003).

The two most common eating disorders are **anorexia nervosa** (intentional self-starvation) and **bulimia** (binge eating combined with purging [intentional vomiting]). The British mental heath charity Mind (2010) reports that as many as 1 female in 20 will have eating habits that give cause for concern, and most will be aged 14 to 25 years. A sister charity, Beat (Beating Eating Disorders), believes the number of people in the UK receiving treatment for anorexia or bulimia to be close to 90,000, while many more people have eating disorders undiagnosed, in particular those with bulimia nervosa (Beat, 2010). About half of anorexics are also bulimic, meaning that they avoid food except for episodes of binge eating and purging

(Polivy et al., 2003). Most cases of eating disorders have their onset among females in their teens and early 20s (Reijonen et al., 2003), and eating disorders are more prevalent among white girls than in other ethnic groups (CQC, 2010; Hoek, 2006). What are the traditional cultural pressures that might apply to explain these differences? Check out the upcoming *Historical Focus* feature.

Far more prevalent than fully fledged eating disorders are eating disordered symptoms (including fasting for 24 hours or more, use of diet products, purging and use of laxatives). In a national study of German 11- to 17-year-olds, one-third of girls and 15 per cent of boys reported eating disorder symptoms (Herpetz-Dahlmann et al., 2008). In Finland, a large study of 14- to 15-year-olds found eating disordered behaviour among 24 per cent of girls and 16 per cent of boys (Hautala et al., 2008).

For a diagnosis of anorexia nervosa, food intake is reduced so much that the person loses at least 15 per cent of body weight (Roberto et al., 2008). As weight loss continues, it eventually results in **amenorrhea**, which means that menstruation ceases. Hair becomes brittle and may begin to fall out, and the skin develops an unhealthy, yellowish pallor. As anorexics become increasingly thin, they frequently develop physical problems that are symptoms of their starvation, such as constipation, high sensitivity to cold and low blood pressure.

One of the most striking symptoms of anorexia is the cognitive distortion of body image (Striegel-Moore and Franko, 2006; Bowers et al., 2003). The reduction in food intake is accompanied by an intense fear of gaining weight, a fear that persists even when the person has lost so much weight as to be in danger of literally starving to death. Young women with anorexia sincerely believe themselves to be too fat, even when they have become so thin that their lives are threatened. Standing in front of a mirror with them and pointing out how emaciated they look does no good – the

HISTORICAL FOCUS

From Fasting Saints to Anorexic Girls

Scholars generally view anorexia nervosa as a modern disorder, resulting primarily from current cultural pressures for young women to be thin. However, the phenomenon of young women voluntarily, wilfully reducing their food intake, even to the point of self-starvation, has a surprisingly long history in the West, extending back many centuries. An examination of that history, with its illuminating similarities to and differences from present-day anorexia, is provided by Dutch scholars Walter Vandereycken and Ron Van Deth (1994) in their book *From Fasting Saints to Anorexic Girls: The History of Self-Starvation*.

Fasting, involving partial or total abstinence from food, has long been a part of both Eastern and Western religions. It has been undertaken for a variety of purposes – to purify the body while engaging in prayer, to demonstrate the person's elevation of spiritual concerns over bodily needs, or as a sign of penance and remorse for sins. Fasting has been a part of the religious ideal in the Eastern religions of Hinduism and Buddhism for millennia. In ancient Egypt, Pharaohs fasted for days before important decisions and religious celebrations. In the Bible, Moses and Jesus undertake periods of fasting. Fasting was required for all believers during the first millennium of the Christian Church at various times of the year, including the period prior to Christmas. It remains a requirement of Islam during the annual holy period of Ramadan.

It was only from the twelfth century onwards that religious fasting in the West became associated mainly with young women. Why this happened when it did is not entirely clear, but it appears to be linked to females being allowed greater participation in Church life. For both males and females during the medieval period religious faith was demonstrated in ways that seem extreme from the modern perspective. Men would often demonstrate their piety by such practices as self-flagellation; piercing their tongues, cheeks or other body parts with iron pins; or sleeping on beds of thorns or iron points. For women, in contrast, extreme fasting became the characteristic path to holiness.

Young women who engaged in extreme fasting often gained great fame and were regarded by their contemporaries with reverence and awe. For example, in the thirteenth century an English girl became known far and wide as 'Joan the Meatless' for reputedly abstaining from all food and drink except on Sundays, when she fed only on the morsel of bread distributed as part of the communion ritual. Many of these young women became anointed as saints by the Church, although official Church policy discouraged extreme fasting as detrimental to physical and mental well-being. In the sixteenth and seventeenth centuries, Catholic officials sharply tightened the rules for proving fasting 'miracles' in response to exposed cases of fraud as well as concern over the health of girls seeking sainthood, and extreme fasting lost its religious allure.

Extreme fasting as a commercial spectacle now arose in place of extreme religious fasting. From the sixteenth through the nineteenth centuries, young women who had supposedly fasted for months or even years were exhibited at fairs. Their renown now came not from the piety their fasting demonstrated but from the way their fasting supposedly enabled them to transcend the requirements of nature. When these 'miraculous maidens' were put to the test in conditions where they could be monitored closely, some starved to death trying to prove their legitimacy, whereas others were exposed as frauds – one such young woman was found to have sewn a substantial quantity of gingerbread into the hem of her dress!

During this same period, cases of self-starvation received increasing attention from physicians. The first medical description of anorexia nervosa was made by the British physician Richard Morton in 1689. All of the characteristics of Morton's clinical description of the disorder remain part of the clinical diagnosis of anorexia nervosa in the present, over three centuries later:

1   occurs primarily in females in their teens and 20s;

2   characterised by striking emaciation as a consequence of markedly decreased intake of food;

3   often accompanied by constipation and amenorrhea (absence of menstruation);

4 affected persons usually lack insight into the illness (that is, they do not believe anything is wrong with them); consequently, treatment is resisted;

5 no physical cause is responsible for the symptoms; they are psychological in origin.

Although these symptoms still characterise anorexia nervosa, it was only from the early nineteenth century onwards that the disorder became motivated by a desire to conform to cultural standards of female attractiveness. In the early nineteenth century, the standard of beauty for young women in the West became the 'hourglass figure', characterised by a substantial bosom and hips and the slimmest waist possible. In pursuit of this figure young women had themselves laced tightly into corsets (often made of whalebone or some other unforgiving material), ignoring the physicians who warned against the 'unhealthiness' of the fashion. By the early twentieth century, corsets had gone out of fashion, but in their place came an ideal of the female form as slim all over, not just the waist but the bosom and hips as well – not unlike the ideal that exists today.

That this thin ideal motivated self-starvation among girls is evident from clinical reports of the time, for example by this late-nineteenth-century physician who, while examining an anorexic patient, 'found that she wore on her skin, fashioned very tight around her waist, a rose-colored ribbon. He obtained the following confidence: the ribbon was a measure which the waist was not to exceed. "I prefer dying of hunger to becoming as big as mamma"' (Vandereycken and Van Deth, 1994, p. 171).

Although fasting saints may seem a long way from anorexic girls, Vandereycken and Van Deth point out the striking similarities. In both cases the self-starvers were striving for an elusive perfection – the fasting girls for sainthood and the anorexic girls for the feminine ideal, a kind of secular sainthood – and typically their perfectionism extended into all aspects of their lives, not just their eating habits. In both cases, their abnormal eating patterns were often evident in childhood before developing into a fixed pattern in adolescence; and in both cases, the phenomenon reached its peak in the late teens and early 20s, sometimes with fatal consequences.

anorexic looks in the mirror and sees a fat person, no matter how thin she is.

Bulimia is an eating disorder characterised by *binge eating* and *purging* (Striegel-Moore and Franko, 2006). Like anorexics, bulimics have strong fears that their bodies will become big and fat (Bowers et al., 2003). Bulimics engage in binge eating, which means eating a large amount of food in a short time. Then they purge themselves; that is, they use laxatives or induce vomiting to get rid of the food they have just eaten during a binge episode. Bulimics often suffer damage to their teeth from repeated vomiting. Unlike anorexics, bulimics typically maintain a normal weight because they have more or less normal eating patterns in between their episodes of bingeing and purging. Another difference from anorexics is that bulimics do not regard their eating patterns as normal. Bulimics view themselves as having a problem and often hate themselves in the aftermath of their binge episodes.

CONNECT AND EXTEND

Adolescents' involvement in either some kind of sports activity or ballet is sometimes blamed as a factor in the development of eating disorders in adolescence. Contrast: 'Psychopathology in elite rhythmic gymnasts and anorexia nervosa patients' by Nora Klinkowski, Alexander Korte, Ernst Pfeiffer, Ulrike Lehmkuhl and Harriet Salbach-Andrae in *European Child & Adolescent Psychiatry*, Volume 17, Number 2 (March 2008), pp. 108–113 with 'Eating disorders in ballet dancing students: problems and risk factors' by Josep Toro, Marta Guerrero, Joan Sentis, Josefina Castro and Carles Puértolas in *European Eating Disorders Review: The Journal of the Eating Disorders Association*, Volume 17, Number 1 (January 2009), pp. 40–49

Studies of anorexics and bulimics provide evidence that these eating disorders have cultural roots. First, eating disorders are more common in cultures that emphasise slimness as part of the female physical ideal, especially Western countries (Walcott et al., 2003; Gowen et al., 1999). Next, eating disorders are most common among females who are part of the middle to upper socio-economic classes, which place more emphasis on female slimness than do lower classes. Third, most eating disorders occur among females in their teens and early 20s, which is arguably when gender intensification and cultural pressures to comply with a slim female physical ideal are at their strongest. Finally, girls who read magazines that contain numerous ads and articles featuring thin models are especially likely to strive to be thin themselves and to engage in eating disordered behaviour (Utter et al., 2003).

Although many girls in cultures that emphasise a thin female ideal strive for thinness themselves, only a small percentage actually have an eating disorder. What factors lead some young females but not others to develop an eating disorder? In general, the same factors are involved for both anorexia and bulimia (Shisslak and Crago, 2001). One factor appears to be a general susceptibility to 'internal' disorders. Females who have an eating disorder are also more likely than other females to have other internal disorders, such as depression and anxiety disorders (Swinbourne and Touyz, 2007; Striegel-Moore et al., 2003; Johnson et al., 2002) and eating disordered behaviour is also related to substance use, especially cigarette smoking, binge drinking and use of inhalants (Pisetsky et al., 2008).

Eating disorders are highest in cultures that prize thinness as attractive in females.

THINKING CRITICALLY

What other causes of eating disorders would you hypothesise from your reading in the *Connect and Extend* features, besides the ones explicitly stated here?

Treatments for Eating Disorders

Because anorexia is eventually life threatening, a hospital-based programme is usually recommended as a first step to begin to restore the person's physical functioning (Cleaves and Latner, 2008). In addition to physical treatment, a variety of approaches have been found to be effective for anorexia and bulimia, including family therapy (to address family issues that may contribute to or be caused by the problem) and individual therapy (Polivy et al., 2003). There is some evidence that, for adolescents, family therapy is more effective than individual treatment (Paulson-Karlsson et al., 2009; Le Grange et al., 2003) particularly those using a variety of drug therapies, which have been found to be mostly ineffective (Crow et al., 2009).

Cognitive behaviour therapy (CBT) promises to be an especially appropriate treatment because cognitive distortions often accompany eating disorders (Lock, 2002). In this context, CBT focuses on changing beliefs that the person is 'too fat' despite being emaciated, and on changing patterns of eating behaviour (Bowers et al., 2003; Gore et al., 2001). However, remember that many adolescents with eating disorders deny they have a problem and resist attempts to help them (Fisher et al., 2001). Perhaps for this reason CBT has been found to be no more effective than other types of individual therapy in treating eating disorders (Bulik et al., 2007). Many adolescents get no treatment at all; in one study, only 22 per cent of the adolescents with eating disorders had received treatment within the past year (Johnson et al., 2002).

Even for adolescents who do receive treatment, the success of treating anorexia and bulimia is often limited. About two-thirds of anorexics treated in hospital programmes improve, but one-third remain chronically ill despite treatment and remain at high risk for chronic health problems or even death from the disorder (Steinhausen et al., 2003). Similarly, although treatments for bulimia are successful in about 50 per cent of cases, there are repeated relapses and recovery is often slow (Oltmanns and Emery, 2006). Young adult women with a history of adolescent eating disorders often continue to show significant impairments in mental and physical health, self-image and social functioning even after their eating disorder has faded (Berkman et al., 2007; Striegel-Moore et al., 2003). About 10 per cent of anorexics eventually die from physical problems caused by their weight loss, the highest mortality rate of any psychiatric disorder (Striegel-Moore and Franko, 2006; Polivy et al., 2003).

We have been looking at 'the dark side' of developmental and social psychology, the problems, the pitfalls and the potential for tragic outcomes in young people's lives. Yet incidences of many of the problems we have discussed are comparatively rare in comparison with the majority of adolescents and young adults, who experience a successful childhood and adolescence, revelling in new-found freedoms and taking advantage of the burgeoning opportunity of youth. If the pressures and dangers are common to all young people, what makes the difference? Psychologists tell us one difference lies in the amount of personal 'resilience' that any individual has – this is an important idea and will provide a fitting conclusion to this chapter.

RESILIENCE

'Hopefully with what I've got behind me and the experiences I've had, I'm equipped to make better judgments to push my life in a better direction. . . . There's a lot of bad things that have happened in my life, and I just kind of feel like, anymore, they kind of roll off.'
– Jeremy, age 25 (in Arnett, 2004, p. 193)

'Mum was good at verbal abuse, and Dad was good at the physical . . . It's always been bad, and now that I've moved out it's just not there, which I guess is good. I don't have to deal with it on a daily basis . . . There's been a lot of pain and a lot of hurt, but I've really grown from it. It's made me the person who I am today.'
– Bridget, age 23 (in Arnett, 2004, pp. 198, 200)

This chapter has covered a wide range of problems that adolescents and young adults may have, together with the risk factors related to their problems, such as poverty, poor family relationships and inadequate schools. However, there are also many adolescents and young adults who face dire conditions and yet manage to adapt and function well. Resilience is the term for this phenomenon, and has been defined as 'good outcomes in spite of serious threats to adaptation and development' (Masten, 2001, p. 228). Sometimes 'good outcomes' are measured as notable academic or social achievements, sometimes as internal conditions such as well-being or self-esteem, and sometimes as the absence of notable problems. Young people who are resilient are not necessarily high achievers who have some kind of extraordinary ability. More often they display what resilience researcher Ann Masten calls the 'ordinary magic' of being able to function reasonably well despite being faced with unusually difficult circumstances (Masten, *ibid.*).

CONNECT AND EXTEND

'Early intervention programmes aimed at increasing resilience may enable young people to manage negative peer relationships in childhood and adolescence.' Read 'Peer relationships in adolescents experiencing a first episode of psychosis' by L. Mackrell and T. Lavender in the *Journal of Mental Health*, Volume 13, Number 5 (2004), pp. 467–479

Resilience is promoted by **protective factors** that enable adolescents and young adults to overcome the risk factors in their lives. Some of the most important protective factors identified in resilience research are high intelligence, parenting that provides an effective balance of warmth and control, and a caring adult 'mentor' outside the family. For example, high intelligence may allow an adolescent to perform well academically despite going to a poor performing school with low expectations and living in a disorderly household (Masten et al., 2006). Effective parenting may help an adolescent have a positive self-image and avoid antisocial behaviour despite growing up in poverty and living in a rough neighbourhood (Leschied et al., 2005). A mentor outside the immediate family may foster high academic goals and good future planning in an adolescent whose family life is characterised by abuse or neglect (Rhodes and DuBois, 2008). Some 'mentors' are appointed to supervisory roles of young people who have engaged in problem behaviours, most notably those trained officers of the UK Probation Service.

FOCUS ON PROFESSIONAL PRACTICE

The Probation Service

In the UK there are now a number of agencies including local authority social services, the police service, schools, health services and the Probation Service that are jointly responsible for protecting young people during the period when they are most likely to engage in problem behaviours. Specifically, the Youth Offending Service and officers provide a mentoring service for young people under the age of 18.

Sometimes ways of making joint responsibility work fall short of statutory obligations to care for young people at risk. Here is one story of Carly Townsend, who died in May 2007. A report was commissioned into her death by the Swansea Safeguarding Children Board (SSCB), which found that Carly's needs 'were not adequately considered and there was a lack of effective engagement between probation and other agencies'.

Carly had been staying at a secure unit in Neath, South Wales, when she was released back to the family home in Swansea. The report said: 'It is now known that on the day of her release [Carly] took heroin. The next day she breached her curfew and her mother gave a false explanation to protect her.' Her mother, Andrea Townsend, and her half-sister, Gemma Evans, put her to bed despite her suffering ill-effects from the drug, and then watched television rather than calling an ambulance.

The serious case review identified that at several key points information sharing between key agencies involved with her in the report was 'inadequate'. The report said: 'The review found that the decisions made and actions taken in [Carly's] case were not based on careful assessments. Over the whole period of the scope of the review, the Probation Service had considerable involvement with Child B's mother and sister, who both had chronic involvement in criminal activity and drug dependence.' (All quotations David Spicer, author of the report into Carly Townsend's death; SSCB, 2010)

In this case very serious questions are asked about the work of professional agencies, particularly the Probation Service. The Probation Service aims to provide a 'significant other' outside of the family: a mentor, guardian, counsellor and supervisor for young people such as Carly to help build resilience and empower young people to make the changes in their lives that are needed. Many probation officers specialise in working with young people through the Youth Courts system, Young Offenders Centres and Services.

'The National Probation Service works within England and Wales to provide supervision of offenders, primarily in the community. It also assists in doing reports for the courts which aid in sentencing of individuals. The history of how the probation service actually came about has its roots in religion. The Church of England Temperance Society, as well as a few other voluntary organisations, appointed a selection of missionaries to the London Police Courts in the latter part of the 18th century. It was around this time that

Probation officers help support young offenders in Community Payback schemes such as this one for Kent Criminal Justice Board.

offenders began to be released into the community, but only on the understanding that they kept in touch with an appointed missionary and accepted the guidance that they were given by this missionary. In 1907 this practice became a matter of statute and the courts were able to employ "probation officers" to fulfil this role.' (NPS, 2011)

It might be interesting to ask our current probation officers the extent to which they might consider themselves to be missionaries. Certainly the 'worlds' into which officers necessarily enter are sometimes alien and daunting. Providing counselling/mentoring and supervisory services can be onerous, yet the opportunity of helping young people to make the changes they need to must be enormously rewarding. Of course, as Carly's tragic case exemplifies, our agencies, including the Probation Service, do not always cope well with the demands of the work. Reoffending rates among juvenile offenders (one important marker of the success of the Probation Service) remain high, but they are falling. Between 2000 and 2008 the proportion of offenders in England and Wales who reoffended decreased by 7.3 per cent (2.9 percentage points) from 40.2 per cent to 37.3 per cent (Ministry of Justice, 2010). Taking more and more young people 'out of crime' is and remains an important aim.

One classic study of resilience followed a group of infants from birth through adolescence (Werner and Smith, 2001; 1992; 1982). The Kauai (kow'ee) study focused on a high-risk group of children who had four or more risk factors by age 2, such as problems in physical development, parents' marital conflict, parental drug abuse, low maternal education and poverty. Out of this group there was a resilient subgroup that showed good social and academic functioning and few behaviour problems by ages 10–18. Compared with their less resilient peers, adolescents in the resilient group were found to benefit from several protective factors, including one well-functioning parent, higher intelligence and higher physical attractiveness.

More recent studies have supported the Kauai findings but also broadened the range of protective factors (Gardner et al., 2008; Masten, 2007). One study of adolescents with high levels of family adversity, such as poverty and parental alcohol abuse – in this study only 38 per cent of the adolescents were classified as living in low-adversity households – found adolescents with a relatively strong ethnic identity were higher in pro-social behaviour and lower in risk behaviours (LaFromboise et al., 2006). Religiosity has become recognised as an especially important protective factor. Adolescents who have a strong religious faith are less likely to have problems such as substance abuse, even when they have grown up in a high-risk environment (Howard et al., 2007; J. M. Wallace et al., 2007).

CONNECT AND EXTEND

For a study examining the impact of terrorism where resilience was observed in adolescents' ability to make a coherent narrative of 11 September and to focus on their daily living, read 'Terrorism and resilience: adolescents' and teachers' responses to September 11, 2001' by Illene Noppe, Lloyd Noppe and Denise Bartell in *Death Studies*, Volume 30, Number 1 (2006), pp. 41–60. How valid an example is this?

Unlike children and adolescents, young adults have the ability to leave an unhealthy, high-risk family environment. Unlike older adults, young adults have not yet made the commitments that structure adult life for most people. Consequently, young adulthood is a period when there is an unusually high scope for making decisions that could turn life in a new and better direction. New experiences and work opportunities provide turning points; opportunities for changing the course of life during young adulthood (Masten et al., 2006). In the Kauai study, a surprise finding was that many of the participants who had been placed in the non-resilient category in adolescence turned out to be successful after all in young adulthood (Werner and Smith, 2001). The experiences that helped them change their lives for the better included participation in further or higher education, learning new occupational skills through military service, and conversion to a religious faith that provided a community of support. Whatever future research may teach us about why some young people take advantage of and benefit from turning point opportunities (whereas others do not) the stories of resilient young people revealed in our research to date are fascinating and inspiring, and there is much more to be learned from them.

SUMMING UP

In this chapter we have discussed a wide range of problems in adolescence and young adulthood, including both external and internal problems. The main points we have discussed are as follows:

- The two main classes of adolescent problems are external problems (such as delinquency and risky driving) and internal problems (such as depression and eating disorders).
- Car accidents are the leading cause of death among young people in their late teens and early 20s in industrialised societies, and young people at these ages have the highest rates of car accidents and fatalities of any age group. These high rates appear to be due to the risks they take while driving as well as their inexperience.
- With regard to substance use, young people in Europe use alcohol and cigarettes more than Americans and Canadians but are less likely to use marijuana. Across countries, young adults have higher rates of substance use than adolescents do, partly because they spend more time in unstructured socialising.
- Alcohol and cigarettes have been called 'gateway drugs' because they typically precede use of illegal drugs. Patterns of substance use can be classified as experimental, social, medicinal and addictive.
- Studies over the past 150 years have found consistently that crime rates peak in the late

teens and that crimes are committed mainly by males. Crime is highest in adolescence and young adulthood because these periods combine independence from parents with a high amount of time spent with peers, and peer groups sometimes seek out crime as a source of excitement. Among programmes to deter delinquents from committing further crimes, the most promising are multisystemic programmes that intervene in a variety of contexts, including family, peer group and neighbourhood.

- Family factors that contribute to adolescent risk behaviour include high conflict and parents who are neglectful, harsh or inconsistent. Parental monitoring has been found to be an especially important predictor of adolescent delinquency. Other factors involved in risk behaviour include friends' influence, school qualities, neighbourhood cohesion and religious beliefs. Individual factors that predict involvement in risk behaviour include aggressiveness, sensation seeking, poor school achievement, low impulse control and optimistic bias.
- Depressed mood is more common in adolescence than in adulthood. Rates of depression in adolescence are considerably higher among girls than among boys. Explanations for this difference include gender differences in coping with problems, girls' greater concern with body image and an internal response to stress among girls. Major depression is most effectively

treated with a combination of cognitive behaviour therapy and antidepressant medications.

- Female adolescents attempt suicide four times as often as males, but males are about four times as likely to kill themselves. Family disruptions and substance abuse are among the strongest predictors of suicide among adolescents.
- Anorexia nervosa and bulimia are most common among females in their teens and early 20s. Factors proposed to explain eating disorders include a tendency toward internal disorders and a cultural emphasis on slimness. Treatment for anorexia generally requires hospitalisation

and relapse rates are high for both anorexia and bulimia.

- Many adolescents exhibit resilience despite growing up in high-risk conditions. Some of the key protective factors that promote resilience are high intelligence, high religiosity and a supportive relationship with one person within or outside of the family. Young adulthood may be an especially important period for the expression of resilience, as it is a time when people are most likely to have the scope of individual choice that may enable them to make decisions that change their lives for the better.

We have focused on young people's tendencies for risk behaviour as a source of problems in this chapter. In most societies, it is adolescents and young adults who are most likely to break the rules and violate social norms for behaviour. This tendency can be disruptive and threatening to others, whether it be expressed in fighting, stealing, substance use, risky driving or many other behaviours. Adolescence and (especially) young adulthood are times that are relatively free from the constraints of social roles. In childhood, behaviour is restrained by parental control; in adulthood, obligations and expectations as spouse, parent and employer/employee include restraints. It is in between, during adolescence and young adulthood, that social control is most lenient, and increased risk behaviour is one consequence.

However, not all risky or norm breaking behaviour is negative. Young people have often been the ones willing to take risks for political and social changes by defying oppressive authorities. As we have seen in Chapter 4, young people are often at the forefront of political changes. Their relative freedom from role obligations provides the opportunity not just for socially disruptive behaviour but for socially constructive risks as well. They are often the explorers, the creative thinkers, the innovators, in part because they have fewer roles that structure and constrict their daily thoughts and behaviour.

In the course of many years of studying young people, conducting hundreds of interviews and spending countless hours in informal conversations with them, we have been struck again and again by how adolescence and young adulthood are times of life when hopes for the future tend to be high. There are exceptions, of course, but for the most part even if their lives have so far been difficult and filled with problems, young people tend to see their futures as bright and filled with promise. Adolescents and young adults are setting the foundation for their adult lives and making decisions that will affect their futures. But for now, while they remain adolescents and young adults, the fate of their dreams has yet to be determined, the possible lives lying before them have yet to harden into accomplished facts. For the most part, they still believe their dreams will be fulfilled and they will ultimately achieve the kind of life they envision.

Given the formidable problems that lie before today's young people, should we conclude that their high hopes are misplaced, that such hopes constitute a distortion of the realities they face? Perhaps it is rather that their hopes provide them with the motivation and energy to proceed with confidence in a world that can be fraught with peril.

INTERNET RESOURCES

http://www.crimestatistics.org.uk and

UK Criminal Statistics, which includes an 'Interactive Crime Map' tool that allows users to create maps showing counts and rates of police recorded crime at local authority level for England and Wales. This tool provides access to data since 2002/03.

http://www.britsoc.co.uk/specialisms/RiskandSociety.htm

Risk Society. The concept of risk is now established as one of the main ideas of adolescence and youth studies. This study group aim to provide a forum in which the diverse range of researchers in the field of risk research might work together at mapping out our current 'risk society'.

http://www.prisonstudies.org

Based at King's College, London, The International Centre for Prison Studies assists governments and other relevant agencies to develop appropriate policies on prisons and the use of imprisonment including the detention of young people.

http://www.nya.org.uk

The National Youth Agency is an independent UK charity and a partner for government, local authorities, businesses and the third sector, delivering with them, and advising and supporting them in the development of programmes and policies for young people.

http://www.un.org/esa/socdev/unyin/index.html

Youth at the United Nations. The UN Programme on Youth is the focal point on youth within the United Nations. It aims to build an awareness of the global situation of young people, as well as promote their rights and aspirations. The Programme also works towards greater participation of young people in decision making as a means of achieving peace and development.

FURTHER READING

E. Burton-Phillips, *Mum Can You Lend Me Twenty Quid? What Drugs Did to My Family*. London: Piatkus Books (2008)

    'Heartbreaking … a story that encapsulates every mother's nightmare' (Review from The *Mail on Sunday*)

A. Millie, *Anti-social Behaviour*. Maidenhead: OUP. (2008)

    This book provides an overview of antisocial behaviour, including the theory, main ideas and alternative approaches to tackling the problem. It includes plenty of case study material from research in the United Kingdom.

T. E. Moffitt, *Life-course-persistent and adolescence-limited antisocial behavior: A 10-year research review*

and a research agenda. In B. B. Lahey and T. E. Moffitt (eds), *Causes of Conduct Disorder and Juvenile Delinquency* (pp. 49–75). New York: Guilford (2003)

    An update of Moffitt's influential theory of antisocial behaviour.

G. Parker and K. Eyers, *Navigating Teenage Depression: A Guide for Parents and Professionals*. Hove: Routledge (2010)

    The author writes: 'After many years as a clinician, I formally detail here a model that I have found useful for dealing with mood disorders, and invite you into the world of clinical assessment. This book presents some of the reasoning that takes place on my side of the desk' (Preface, p. ix)

For more reviews plus practice tests, case studies, responses to *Critical Thinking* and more, log on to **www.pearsoned.co.uk/arnett**.

GLOSSARY

absolute performance In IQ tests, performance results compared to other persons, regardless of age.

abstract thinking Thinking in terms of symbols, ideas and concepts.

accommodation The cognitive process that occurs when a scheme is changed to adapt to new information.

active genotype–environment interactions Occur when people seek out environments that correspond to their genotypic characteristics.

actual self A person's perception of the self as it is, contrasted with the possible self.

adolescence A period of the life course between the time puberty begins and the time adult status is approached, when young people are in the process of preparing to take on the roles and responsibilities of adulthood in their culture.

adolescence-limited delinquents (ALDs) In Moffitt's theory, delinquents who engage in criminal acts in adolescence and/or young adulthood but show no evidence of problems before or after these periods.

adolescent egocentrism Type of egocentrism in which adolescents have difficulty distinguishing their thinking about their own thoughts from their thinking about the thoughts of others.

adolescent growth spurt The rapid increase in height that takes place at the beginning of puberty.

adrenocorticotropic hormone (ACTH) The hormone that causes the adrenal glands to increase androgen production.

affection phase In Brown's developmental model of adolescent love, the third phase, in which adolescents come to know each other better and express deeper feelings for each other, as well as engaging in more extensive sexual activity.

affective functions Emotional functions of the family, pertaining to love, nurturance and attachment.

age norms Technique for developing a psychological test, in which a typical score for each age is established by testing a large random sample of people from a variety of geographical areas and social class backgrounds.

Alfred Binet French psychologist who developed the first intelligence test in the early twentieth century, which later became known as the Stanford-Binet.

altruism Acting with a selfless concern for others.

amenorrhea Cessation of menstruation, sometimes experienced by girls whose body weight falls extremely low.

amicus relationship Between siblings, a relationship in which they treat each other as friends.

androgens The sex hormones that have especially high levels in males from puberty onwards and are mostly responsible for male primary and secondary sex characteristics.

androgyny A combination of 'male' and 'female' personality traits.

anorexia nervosa Eating disorder characterised by intentional self-starvation.

apprenticeship An arrangement, common in Europe, in which an adolescent 'novice' serves under contract to a 'master' who has substantial experience in a profession, and through working under the master, learns the skills required to enter the profession.

areola Area surrounding the nipple on the breast; enlarges at puberty.

argot (pronounced *ar-go*) In youth culture, a certain vocabulary and a certain way of speaking.

arranged marriage A marriage in which the marriage partners are determined not by the partners themselves but by others, usually the parents or other family elders.

assimilation (chapter 3) The cognitive process that occurs when new information is altered to fit an existing scheme.

assimilation (chapter 6) In the formation of an ethnic identity, the approach that involves leaving the ethnic culture behind and adopting the ways of the majority culture.

asymptomatic A condition common with STDs in which an infected person shows no symptoms of the disease but may potentially infect others.

asynchronicity Uneven growth of different parts of the body during puberty.

attachment theory Theory originally developed by British psychiatrist John Bowlby, asserting that among humans as among other primates, attachments between parents and children have an evolutionary basis in the need for vulnerable young members of the species to stay in close proximity to adults who will care for and protect them.

attention deficit-hyperactivity disorder (ADHD) Disorder characterised by difficulty in maintaining attention on a task along with a high activity level that makes self-control problematic.

authoritarian parents Parenting style in which parents are high in demandingness but low in responsiveness, i.e. they require obedience from their children and punish disobedience without compromise, but show little warmth or affection towards them.

authoritative parents A parenting style in which parents are high in demandingness and high in responsiveness, i.e. they love their children but also set clear standards for behaviour and explain to their children the reasons for those standards.

automaticity A facility for the fast, seemingly instant recall of information requiring little cognitive effort and therefore allowing for simultaneous attention to other matters.

autonomous morality Piaget's term for the period of moral development from about age 10 to age 12, involving a growing realisation that moral rules are social conventions that can be changed if people decide they should be changed.

autonomy The quality of being independent and self-sufficient, capable of thinking for one's self.

Bar Mitzvah Jewish religious ritual for boys at age 13 that signifies the adolescents' new responsibilities with respect to Jewish beliefs.

barometric self-esteem The fluctuating sense of worth and well-being people have as they respond to different thoughts, experiences and interactions in the course of a day.

baseline self-esteem A person's stable, enduring sense of worth and well-being.

Bat Mitzvah Jewish religious ritual for girls at age 13 that signifies the adolescents' new responsibilities with respect to Jewish beliefs.

behavioural decision theory Theory of decision making that describes the decision-making process as including: (1) identifying the range of possible choices; (2) identifying the consequences that would result from each choice; (3) evaluating the desirability of each consequence; (4) assessing the likelihood of each consequence; and (5) integrating this information.

bell curve See normal distribution.

bicultural Having an identity that includes aspects of two different cultures.

biculturalism In the formation of ethnic identity, the approach that involves developing a dual identity, one based in the ethnic group of origin and one based in the majority culture.

bonding phase In Brown's developmental model of adolescent love, the final phase, in which the romantic relationship becomes more enduring and serious and partners begin to discuss the possibility of a lifelong commitment to each other.

breast buds The first slight enlargement of the breast in girls at puberty.

broad socialisation The process by which persons in an individualistic culture come to learn individualism, including values of individual uniqueness, independence and self-expression.

bulimia An eating disorder characterised by episodes of binge eating followed by purging (self-induced vomiting).

bullying In peer relations, the aggressive assertion of power by one person over another.

burka See chador.

cardiac output A measure of the quantity of blood pumped by the heart.

care orientation Carol Gilligan's term for the type of moral orientation that involves focusing on relationships with others as the basis for moral reasoning.

caregiver relationship Between siblings, a relationship in which one sibling serves parental functions for the other.

caste system Hindu belief that people are born into a particular caste based on their moral and spiritual conduct in their previous life. A person's caste then determines their status in Indian society.

casual relationship Between siblings, a relationship that is not emotionally intense, in which they have little to do with one another.

central executive The area of the brain that controls cognition.

cerebellum A structure in the lower brain, well beneath the cortex, now known to be important for many higher functions as well, such as mathematics, music, decision making and social skills.

chador (or burka) A garment that covers the hair and most of the face, worn by many girls and women in Muslim societies.

child study movement Late nineteenth-century group, led by G. Stanley Hall, that advocated research on child and adolescent development and the improvement of conditions for children and adolescents in the family, school and workplace.

chronosystem In Bronfenbrenner's ecological theory, changes that occur in developmental circumstances over time, both with respect to individual development and to historical changes.

cliques Small groups of friends who know each other well, do things together, and form a regular social group.

clitoris Part of vulva in which females' sexual sensations are concentrated.

closed question Questionnaire format that entails choosing from specific responses provided for each question.

co-figurative cultures Cultures in which young people learn what they need to know not only from adults but also from other young people.

cognitive behaviour therapy (CBT) An approach to treating psychological disorders that focuses on changing negative ways of thinking and practising new ways of interacting with others.

cognitive development Changes over time in how people think, how they solve problems, and how their capacities for memory and attention change.

cognitive-developmental approach Approach to understanding cognition that emphasises the changes that take place at different ages.

cognitive-developmental theory of gender Kohlberg's theory, based on Piaget's ideas about cognitive development, asserting that gender is a fundamental way of organising ideas about the world and that children develop through a predictable series of stages in their understanding of gender.

cohabitation Living with a romantic partner outside of marriage.

collectivism A set of beliefs asserting that it is important for persons to mute their individual desires in order to contribute to the well-being and success of the group.

coming out For homosexuals, the process of acknowledging their homosexuality and then disclosing the truth to their friends, family and others.

commitment Cognitive status in which persons commit themselves to certain points of view they believe to be the most valid while at the same time being open to re-evaluating their views if new evidence is presented to them.

communal manhood Anthony Rotundo's term for the norm of manhood in the seventeenth and eighteenth centuries, in which the focus of gender expectations for adolescent boys was on preparing to assume adult male role responsibilities in work and marriage.

community service Volunteer work provided as a contribution to the community, without monetary reward.

companionate love In Sternberg's theory of love, the type of love that combines intimacy and commitment, but without passion.

companionship support Between friends, reliance on each other as companions in social activities.

complex thinking Thinking that takes into account multiple connections and interpretations, such as in the use of metaphor, satire and sarcasm.

componential approach Description of the information-processing approach to cognition, indicating that it involves breaking down the thinking process into its various components.

comprehensive school The typical form of secondary school in the UK – mostly opened in the late 1960s and 1970s – that encompasses a wide range of curriculum in general education and vocational training.

concordance rate A quantitative statistical expression for the coincidence of a given genetic trait particularly among identical and fraternal twins.

concrete operations Cognitive stage from age 7 to 11 in which children learn to use mental operations but are limited to applying them to concrete, observable situations rather than hypothetical situations.

consensual validation In social science studies of interpersonal attraction, the principle that people like to find in others an agreement or consensus with their own characteristics and view of life.

consent form Written statement provided by a researcher to potential participants in a study, informing them of who is conducting the study, the purposes of the study, and what their participation would involve, including potential risks.

conservation The cognitive ability to logically determine that a certain quantity will remain the same despite adjustment of the arrangement, container, shape or apparent size.

consummate love In Sternberg's theory of love, the form of love that integrates passion, intimacy and commitment.

context The environmental settings in which development takes place.

continuous A view of development as a gradual, steady process rather than as taking place in distinct stages.

control group In experimental research, the group that does not receive the treatment.

controversial adolescents Adolescents who are aggressive but who also possess social skills, so that they evoke strong emotions both positive and negative from their peers.

conventional reasoning In Kohlberg's theory of moral development, the level of moral reasoning in which the person advocates the value of conforming to the moral expectations of others. What is right is whatever agrees with the rules established by tradition and by authorities.

correlation versus causation A correlation is a predictable relationship between two variables, such that knowing one of the variables makes it possible to predict the other. However, just because two variables are correlated does not mean that one causes the other.

council estate An area of a city in which there are houses and apartments owned by local housing associations or local councils and available for rent. These properties are now normally referred to as social housing.

critical relationship Between siblings, a relationship characterised by a high level of conflict and teasing.

critical thinking Thinking that involves not merely memorising information but analysing it, making judgements about what it means, relating it to other information and considering ways in which it might be valid or invalid.

cross-sectional study Study that examines individuals at one point in time.

crowds Large, reputation-based groups of adolescents.

crystallised intelligence Accumulated knowledge and enhanced judgement based on experience.

cultural beliefs The predominant beliefs in a culture about right and wrong, what is most important in life, and how life should be lived. They may also include beliefs about where and how life originated and what happens after death.

cultural psychology Approach to human psychology emphasising that psychological functioning cannot be separated from the culture in which it takes place.

custodial parent The parent who lives in the same household as the children following a divorce.

custom complex A customary practice and the beliefs, values, sanctions, rules, motives and satisfactions associated with it; that is, a normative practice in a culture and the cultural beliefs that provide the basis for that practice.

cyberbullying Bullying via new communication technologies, mainly through the Internet.

date rape An act of sexual aggression in which a person, usually a woman, is forced by a romantic partner, date or acquaintance to have sexual relations against her will.

dating scripts The cognitive models that guide dating interactions.

debt bondage Arrangement in which a person who is in debt pledges his labour or the labour of his children as payment.

delinquency Violations of the law committed by juveniles.

'I would that there were no age between ten and three-and-twenty, or that youth would sleep out the rest; for there is nothing in between but getting wenches with child, wronging the ancientry, stealing, fighting . . .'
– William Shakespeare, 1610, *The Winter's Tale,* Act III, Scene 3

demeanour In Brake's description of youth cultures, refers to distinctive forms of gesture, gait and posture.

demandingness The degree to which parents set down rules and expectations for behaviour and require their children to comply with them.

depressed mood An enduring period of sadness, without any other related symptoms of depression.

depression An enduring period of sadness.

depressive syndrome An enduring period of sadness along with other symptoms such as frequent crying, feelings of worthlessness, and feeling guilty, lonely or worried.

dethronement A description of what happens when a first sibling comes into the household and the original only-child comes to accept that they are no longer the centre of attention, but one member of a larger family unit.

dialectical thought Type of thinking that develops in emerging adulthood, involving a growing awareness that most problems do not have a single solution, that problems must often be addressed by reconciling contradictions and combining opposing perspectives, and that problems have to be solved without all the relevant information.

diathesis-stress model A theory that mental disorders result from the combination of a diathesis (biological vulnerability) and environmental stresses.

differential gender socialisation The term for socialising males and females according to different expectations about what attitudes and behaviour are appropriate to each gender.

differential parenting When parents' behaviour differs towards siblings within the same family.

discontinuous A view of development as taking place in stages that are distinct from one another rather than as one gradual, continuous process.

disengaged parents Parenting style in which parents are low in both demandingness and responsiveness and relatively uninvolved in their children's development.

disequilibrium In the family systems approach, this term is used in reference to a change that requires adjustments from family members.

divided attention The ability to focus on more than one task at a time.

divorce mediation An arrangement in which a professional mediator helps divorcing parents negotiate an agreement that both will find acceptable.

dizygotic (DZ) twins Twins with about half their genotype in common, the same as for other siblings; also known as fraternal twins.

double standard Two different sets of rules for sexual behaviour, one applying to males and the other females, with rules for females usually being more restrictive.

dual-earner families A family in which both parents are employed.

dualistic thinking Cognitive tendency to see situations and issues in polarised, absolute, black-and-white terms.

dyadic relationship A relationship between two persons.

early adolescence Period of human development lasting from about age 10 to about age 14.

ecological theory Urie Bronfenbrenner's sociocultural theory of human development, with five interrelated systems: the microsystem (the immediate environment), the mesosystem (connections between microsystems), the exosystem (institutions such as schools and community organisations), the macrosystem (the overarching system of cultural beliefs and values), and the chronosystem (the changes in the individual and the cultural environment over time).

effect size The difference between two groups in a meta-analysis, represented by the letter *d*. ≤ is less than or equal to ≥ is more than or equal to.

egocentrism An approach to thinking about self which emphasises which self is more important, and so more thought about, than others.

emerging adulthood Period from roughly ages 18 to 25 in industrialised countries during which young people become more independent from parents and explore various life possibilities before making enduring commitments.

emotional loneliness Condition that occurs when people feel that the relationships they have lack sufficient closeness and intimacy.

empathy The ability to understand different emotions, to take another person's perspective or to respond similarly.

empty love In Sternberg's theory of love, the type of love that is based on commitment alone, without passion or intimacy.

endocrine system A network of glands in the body. Through hormones, the glands coordinate their functioning and affect the development and functioning of the body.

engagement The quality of being psychologically committed to learning, including being alert and attentive in the classroom and making a diligent effort to learn.

esteem support The support friends provide each other by providing congratulations for success and encouragement or consolation for failure.

estradiol The oestrogen most important in pubertal development among girls.

ethnographic Study is first-hand observation of daily behaviour as an observer or as a participant in the group behaviour. Another common method is interviewing.

ethnographic research Research in which researchers spend a considerable amount of time among the people they wish to study, usually living among them.

ethnography A book that presents an anthropologist's observations of what life is like in a particular culture.

ethos The beliefs about education that characterise a school as a whole.

evocative genotype–environment interactions Occur when a person's inherited characteristics evoke responses from others in their environment.

exosystem In Bronfenbrenner's ecological theory, societal institutions such as schools, religious institutions, systems of government and media.

experimental group In experimental research, the group that receives the treatment.

experimental research method A research method that entails assigning participants randomly to an experimental group that receives a treatment and a control group that does not receive the treatment, then comparing the two groups in a post test.

expressive traits Personality characteristics such as gentle and yielding, more often ascribed to females, emphasising emotions and relationships.

extremities The feet, hands and head.

exuberance See overproduction.

false self The self a person may present to others while realising that it does not represent what he or she is actually thinking and feeling.

family process The quality of relationships among family members.

family structure The outward characteristics of a family, such as whether or not the parents are married.

family systems approach An approach to understanding family functioning that emphasises how each relationship within the family influences the family as a whole.

fatuous love In Sternberg's theory of love, the type of love that involves passion and commitment without intimacy.

'Fall in love, fall into disgrace.'
– Chinese proverb

feared self The self a person imagines it is possible to become but dreads becoming.

feedback loop System of hormones involving the hypothalamus, the pituitary gland and the gonads, which monitors and adjusts the levels of the sex hormones.

feminism A political ideology and social philosophy that advocates women's rights on the grounds of the equality of the sexes.

filial piety Confucian belief, common in many Asian societies, that children are obligated to respect, obey and revere their parents, especially the father.

fluid intelligence Mental abilities that involve speed of analysing, processing and reacting to information.

fMRI A technique for measuring brain functioning during an ongoing activity.

follicle-stimulating hormone (FSH) Along with LH, stimulates the development of gametes and sex hormones in the ovaries and testicles.

formal operations Cognitive stage from age 11 onwards in which people learn to think systematically about possibilities and hypotheses.

friends Persons with whom an individual has a valued, mutual relationship.

frontal lobes The part of the brain immediately behind the forehead. Known to be involved in higher brain functions such as planning ahead and analysing complex problems.

gametes Cells, distinctive to each sex, that are involved in reproduction (egg cells in the ovaries of the female and sperm in the testes of the male).

gateway drugs Term sometimes applied to alcohol, cigarettes and marijuana because young people who use harder drugs usually use these drugs first.

gender The social categories of male and female, established according to cultural beliefs and practices rather than being due to biology.

gender dysphoria The distress and depression caused by inability to form robust relationships with others as a result of being transgender.

gender identity Children's understanding of themselves as being either male or female, reached at about age 3.

gender identity disorder A diagnosis of distress or disability caused by being transgender.

gender intensification hypothesis Hypothesis that psychological and behavioural differences between males and females become more pronounced at adolescence because of intensified socialisation pressures to conform to culturally prescribed gender roles.

gender roles Cultural beliefs about the kinds of work, appearance and other aspects of behaviour that distinguish women from men.

gender schema theory Theory in which gender is viewed as one of the fundamental ways that people organise information about the world.

generalisable Characteristic of a sample that refers to the degree to which findings based on the sample can be used to make accurate statements about the population of interest.

gifted Pupils are those who have unusually high abilities in academic subjects.

globalisation Increasing worldwide technological and economic integration, which is making different parts of the world increasingly connected and increasingly similar culturally.

gonadotropin-releasing hormone (GnRH) Hormone released by the hypothalamus that causes gonadotropins to be released by the pituitary.

gonadotropins Hormones (FSH and LH) that stimulate the development of gametes.

gonads The ovaries and testicles. Also known as the sex glands.

grey matter The outer layer of the brain, where most of the growth in brain cells occurs.

guided participation The teaching interaction between two people as they participate in a culturally valued activity.

Harvard Adolescence Project Project initiated by Beatrice and John Whiting of Harvard University in the 1980s, in which they sent young researchers to do ethnographic research in seven different cultures in various parts of the world.

heteronomous morality Piaget's term for the period of moral development from about age 4 to about age 7, in which moral rules are viewed as having a sacred, fixed quality, handed down from figures of authority and alterable only by them.

homophobia Fear and hatred of homosexuals.

hoodie A person who wears a sweatshirt with a hood – the garment also called a hoodie – which is an article of street clothing associated with teenage gangs and wanting to hide identity.

hormones Chemicals, released by the glands of the endocrine system, that affect the development and functioning of the body, including development during puberty.

hybrid identity An identity that integrates elements of various cultures.

hymen The thin membrane inside a girl's vagina that is usually broken during her first experience of sexual intercourse. Tested in some cultures before marriage to verify the girl's virginity.

hypothalamus The 'master gland', located in the lower part of the brain beneath the cortex, which affects a wide range of physiological and psychological functioning and stimulates and regulates the production of hormones by other glands, including the ones involved in the initiation of puberty.

hypotheses Ideas, based on theory or previous research, that a researcher wishes to test in a scientific study.

hypothetical–deductive reasoning Piaget's term for the process by which the formal operational thinker systematically tests possible solutions to a problem and arrives at an answer that can be explained and defended.

ideal self The person an adolescent would like to be.

identifications Relationships formed with others, especially in childhood, in which love for another person leads one to want to be like that person.

identity Individuals' perceptions of their characteristics and abilities, their beliefs and values, their relations with others, and how their lives fit into the world around them.

identity achievement The identity status of young people who have made definite personal, occupational and ideological choices following a period of exploring possible alternatives.

identity crisis Erikson's term for the intense period of struggle that adolescents may experience in the course of forming an identity.

identity diffusion An identity status that combines no exploration with no commitment. No commitments have been made among the available paths of identity formation, and the person is not seriously attempting to sort through potential choices and make enduring commitments.

identity foreclosure An identity status in which young people have not experimented with a range of possibilities but have nevertheless committed themselves to certain choices – commitment, but no exploration.

identity moratorium An identity status that involves exploration but no commitment, in which young people are trying out different personal, occupational and ideological possibilities.

identity status model An approach to conceptualising and researching identity development that classifies people into one of four identity categories: foreclosure, diffusion, moratorium or achievement.

identity versus identity confusion Erikson's term for the crisis typical of the adolescent stage of life, in which individuals may follow the healthy path of establishing a clear and definite sense of who they are and how they fit into the world around them, or follow the unhealthy alternative of failing to form a stable and secure identity.

ideology A set of beliefs that affects attitudes and actions.

image In Brake's description of the characteristics of youth culture, refers to dress, hairstyle, jewellery and other aspects of appearance.

imaginary audience Belief that others are acutely aware of and attentive to one's appearance and behaviour.

incest taboo The prohibition on sexual relations between family members. Believed to be biologically based, as children born to closely related parents are at higher risk for genetic disorders.

independent self A conception of the self typically found in individualistic cultures, in which the self is seen as existing independently of relations with others, with an emphasis on independence, individual freedoms and individual achievements.

individual differences Approach to research that focuses on how individuals differ within a group, for example in performance on IQ tests.

individualism Cultural belief system that emphasises the desirability of independence, self-sufficiency and self-expression.

individuating–reflective faith Fowler's term for the stage of faith most typical of late adolescence and emerging adulthood, in which people rely less on what their parents believed and develop a more individualised faith based on questioning their beliefs and incorporating their personal experience into their beliefs.

infatuation In Sternberg's theory of love, the type of love that is based on passion alone, without intimacy or commitment.

information-processing approach An approach to understanding cognition that seeks to delineate the steps involved in the thinking process and how each step is connected to the next.

informational support Between friends, advice and guidance in solving personal problems.

informed consent Standard procedure in social scientific studies that entails informing potential participants of what their participation would involve, including any possible risks.

initiation phase In Brown's developmental model of adolescent love, the first phase, usually in early adolescence, when the first tentative explorations of romantic interests begin, usually superficial and brief, often fraught with anxiety, fear and excitement.

insecure attachment Type of attachment to caregiver in which infants are timid about exploring the environment and resist or avoid the caregiver when she attempts to offer comfort or consolation.

instrumental support Between friends, help with tasks of various kinds.

instrumental traits Personality characteristics such as self-reliant and forceful, more often ascribed to males, emphasising action and accomplishment.

intelligence quotient A measure of a person's intellectual abilities based on a standardised test.

interdependence The web of commitments, attachments and obligations that exist in some human groups.

interdependent self A conception of the self typically found in collectivistic cultures, in which the self is seen as defined by roles and relationships within the group.

internal consistency A statistical calculation that indicates the extent to which the different items in a scale or subscale are answered in a similar way.

internal working model In attachment theory, the term for the cognitive framework, based on interactions in infancy with the primary caregiver, that shapes expectations and interactions in relationships to others throughout life.

International Labour Organization (ILO) An organisation that seeks to prevent children and adolescents from being exploited in the workplace.

interventions Programmes intended to change the attitudes and/or behaviour of the participants.

intimacy The degree to which two people share personal knowledge, thoughts and feelings.

intimacy versus isolation Erikson's term for the central issue of young adulthood, in which persons face alternatives between committing themselves to another person in an intimate relationship or becoming isolated as a consequence of an inability to form an enduring intimate relationship.

Jean Piaget Influential Swiss developmental psychologist, best known for his theories of cognitive and moral development.

justice orientation A type of moral orientation that places a premium on abstract principles of justice, equality and fairness.

juveniles Persons defined by the legal system as being younger than adult status.

Koran The holy book of the religion of Islam, believed by Muslims to have been communicated to Muhammad from God through the angel Gabriel.

labia majora Part of vulva; Latin for 'large lips'.

labia minora Part of vulva; Latin for 'small lips'.

Lamarckian Reference to Lamarck's ideas, popular in the late nineteenth and early twentieth centuries, that evolution takes place as a result of accumulated experience such that organisms pass on their characteristics from one generation to the next in the form of memories and acquired characteristics.

late adolescence Period of human development lasting from about age 15 to about age 18.

latency period A period, common with STDs, between the time a person is infected with a disease and the time symptoms appear.

learning difficulties In schools, a diagnosis made when a child or adolescent has difficulty in one or more academic areas and the difficulty cannot be attributed to any other disorder.

leptin A protein, produced by fat cells, that signals the hypothalamus to initiate the hormonal changes of puberty.

life-course-persistent delinquents (LCPDs) In Moffitt's theory, adolescents who show a history of related problems both prior to and following adolescence.

life-cycle service A period in their late teens and 20s in which young people from the sixteenth to the nineteenth century engaged in domestic service, farm service or apprenticeships in various trades and crafts.

liking In Sternberg's theory of love, the type of love that is based on intimacy alone, without passion or commitment.

longitudinal study A study in which data is collected from the participants on more than one occasion.

long-term memory Memory for information that is committed to longer-term storage, so that it can be drawn upon after a period when attention has not been focused on it.

low impulse control Difficulty in exercising self-control, often found to be related to risk behaviour in adolescence.

luteinising hormone (LH) Along with FSH, stimulates the development of gametes and sex hormones in the ovaries and testicles.

machismo Ideology of manhood, common in Latin cultures, that emphasises males' dominance over females.

macrosystem In Bronfenbrenner's ecological theory, the broad system of cultural beliefs and values, and the economic and governmental systems that are built on those beliefs and values.

major depressive disorder Psychological diagnosis that entails depressed mood or reduced interest or pleasure in all or almost all activities, plus at least four other specific symptoms. Symptoms must be present over at least a two-week period and must involve a change from previous functioning.

marginality In the formation of ethnic identity, the option that involves rejecting one's culture of origin but also feeling rejected by the majority culture.

maturation Process by which abilities develop through genetically based development with limited influence from the environment.

maximum oxygen uptake (VO2 max) A measure of the ability of the body to take in oxygen and transport it to various organs; peaks in the early 20s.

median In a distribution of scores, the point at which half of the population scores above and half below.

menarche A girl's first menstrual period.

mental operations Cognitive activity involving manipulating and reasoning about objects.

mental structure The organisation of cognitive abilities into a single pattern, such that thinking in all aspects of life is a reflection of that structure.

mesosystem In Bronfenbrenner's ecological theory, the network of interconnections between the microsystems.

meta-analysis A statistical technique that integrates the data from many studies into one comprehensive statistical analysis.

metacognition The capacity for 'thinking about thinking' that allows adolescents and adults to monitor and reason about their own thought processes.

microsystem Bronfenbrenner's term for the settings where people experience their daily lives, including relationships with parents, siblings, peers/friends, teachers and employers.

mid-life crisis The popular belief, largely unfounded according to research, that most people experience a crisis when they reach about age 40, involving intensive re-examination of their lives and perhaps sudden and dramatic changes if they are dissatisfied.

mikveh Among Orthodox Jews, the traditional ritual bath taken by a woman seven days after her menstrual period was finished, as a way of ridding herself of the uncleanness believed to be associated with menstruation.

mnemonic devices Memory strategies.

monozygotic (MZ) twins Twins with exactly the same genotype; also known as identical twins.

multiple thinking Cognitive approach entailing recognition that there is more than one legitimate view of things and that it can be difficult to justify one position as the true or accurate one.

mutual perspective taking Stage of perspective taking, often found in early adolescence, in which persons understand that their perspective-taking interactions with others are mutual, in the sense that each side realises that the other can understand their perspective.

myelination Process by which myelin, a blanket of fat wrapped around the main part of the neuron, grows. Myelin serves the function of keeping the brain's electrical signals on one path and increasing their speed.

narrow socialisation The process by which persons in a collectivistic culture come to learn collectivism, including values of obedience and conformity.

nascent capacity A personal capability that is just being formed so is particularly reactive to what is happening.

national survey Questionnaire study that involves asking a sample of persons in a country to respond to questions about their opinions, beliefs or behaviour.

natural experiment A situation that occurs naturally but that provides interesting scientific information to the perceptive observer.

nature–nurture debate Debate over the relative importance of biology and the environment in human development.

NEETs Those young people in the 16 to 24 age groups who are **n**ot in **e**mployment, **e**ducation or **t**raining.

negative attributions Beliefs that one's current unhappiness is permanent and uncontrollable.

negative identity Erikson's term for an identity based on what a person has seen portrayed as most undesirable or dangerous.

neglected adolescents Adolescents who have few or no friends and are largely unnoticed by their peers.

neurons Cells of the nervous system, including the brain.

non-shared environmental influences Influences experienced differently among siblings within the same family, e.g. involvement of grandparents; financial ability to provide recreational opportunities.

normal distribution (or bell curve) The bell-shaped curve that represents many human characteristics, with most people around the average and a gradually decreasing proportion towards the extremes.

occupational deviance Deviant acts committed in relation to the workplace, such as stealing supplies.

oestrogens The sex hormones that have especially high levels in females from puberty onwards and are mostly responsible for female primary and secondary sex characteristics.

ontogenetic Something that occurs naturally in the course of development as part of normal maturation; that is, it is driven by innate processes rather than by environmental stimulation or a specific cultural practice.

open-ended question Questionnaire format that involves writing in responses to each question.

optimistic bias The tendency to assume that accidents, diseases and other misfortunes are more likely to happen to other people than to one's self.

over evaluated Evaluating persons more favourably because they violate gender expectations.

overproduction (or exuberance) A rapid increase in the production of synaptic connections in the brain.

ovum Mature egg that develops from follicle in ovaries about every 28 days.

parenting styles The patterns of practices that parents exhibit in relation to their children.

participant observation A research method that involves taking part in various activities with the people being studied, and learning about them through participating in the activities with them.

passionate manhood Anthony Rotundo's term for the norm of manhood in the twentieth century, in which self-expression and self-enjoyment replaced self-control and self-denial as the paramount virtues young males should learn in the course of becoming a man.

passive genotype–environment interactions Situation in biological families that parents provide both genes and environment for their children, making genes and environment difficult to separate in their effects on children's development.

patriarchal authority Cultural belief in the absolute authority of the father over his wife and children.

peak height velocity The point at which the adolescent growth spurt is at its maximum rate.

peer contagion Term for the increase in delinquent behaviour that often takes place as an unintended consequence of bringing adolescents with problems together for an intervention, because in the intervention setting they reinforce each other's delinquent tendencies and find new partners for delinquent acts.

peer reviewed When a researched article or book is evaluated by a researcher's peers (i.e. other researchers) for scientific credibility and importance.

peers People who share some aspect of their status, such as being the same age.

pendulum problem Piaget's classic test of formal operations, in which persons are asked to figure out what determines the speed at which a pendulum sways from side to side.

performance subtests In the Wechsler IQ tests, subtests that examine abilities for attention, spatial perception and speed of processing.

permissive cultures Cultures that encourage and expect sexual activity from their adolescents.

permissive parents Parenting style in which parents are low in demandingness and high in responsiveness. They show love and affection towards their children but are permissive with regard to standards of behaviour.

personal fable A belief in one's personal uniqueness, often including a sense of invulnerability to the consequences of taking risks.

perspective taking The ability to understand the thoughts and feelings of others.

PET scans A technique for assessing ongoing brain functioning, in which a chemical that emits positrons is injected into the body and detectors measure their activity levels in various parts of the brain.

pheromones Airborne chemicals, secreted by the sweat glands, that have effects on other mammals of the same species.

phonological loop A short-term store and retrieval system for sounds and words.

pilot testing Trying out the research measures on a small number of potential participants before the larger study begins to make sure the measures have adequate reliability and validity.

pituitary gland A gland about a centimetre long located at the base of the brain that releases gonadotropins as part of the body's preparation for reproduction.

placebo design Research design in which some persons in a study receive medication and others receive placebos, which are pills that contain no medication.

poetic-conventional faith Fowler's term for the stage of faith development most typical of early adolescence, in which people become more aware of the symbolism used in their faith, and religious understanding becomes more complex in the sense that early adolescents increasingly believe there is more than one way of knowing the truth.

population The entire group of people of interest in a study.

possible selves A person's conception of the self as it potentially may be. May include both an ideal self and a feared self.

postconventional reasoning In Kohlberg's theory of moral development, the level in which moral reasoning is based on the individual's own independent judgements rather than on egocentric considerations or considerations of what others view as wrong or right.

post-figurative cultures Cultures in which what children and adolescents need to learn to function as adults changes little from one generation to the next, and therefore children and adolescents can learn all they need to know from their elders.

postformal thinking Type of thinking beyond formal operations, involving greater awareness of the complexity of real-life situations, such as in the use of pragmatism and reflective judgement.

postmodern identity A conception of identity as complex and as highly variable across contexts and across time.

pragmatism Type of thinking that involves adapting logical thinking to the practical constraints of real-life situations.

preconventional reasoning In Kohlberg's theory of moral development, the level in which moral reasoning is based on perceptions of the likelihood of external rewards and punishments.

predictive validity In longitudinal research, the ability of a variable at Time 1 to predict the outcome of a variable at Time 2.

pre-figurative cultures Cultures in which young people teach knowledge to adults.

premenstrual syndrome (PMS) The combination of behavioural, emotional and physical symptoms that occur in some females the week before menstruation.

preoperational stage Cognitive stage from age 2 to 7 during which a child becomes capable of representing the world symbolically – for example, through the use of language – but with limited ability to use mental operations.

primary caregiver The person mainly responsible for caring for an infant or young child.

primary sex characteristics The production of eggs and sperm and the development of the sex organs.

proactive script A dating script, more common for males than for females, which includes initiating the date, deciding where they will go, controlling the public domain (e.g. driving the car and opening the doors) and initiating sexual contact.

procedure Standards for the way a study is conducted. Includes informed consent and certain rules for avoiding biases in the data collection.

prosocial behaviour Promoting the well-being of others.

protective factor Characteristics of young people that are related to lower likelihood of participation in risk behaviour.

psychohistory The psychological analysis of important historical figures.

psychometric approach Attempt to understand human cognition by evaluating cognitive ability differences using intelligence tests.

psychosocial moratorium Erikson's term for a period during adolescence when adult responsibilities are postponed as young people try on various possible selves.

puberty The changes in physiology, anatomy and physical functioning that develop a person into a mature adult biologically and prepare the body for sexual reproduction.

qualitative Data that is collected in verbal rather than numerical form, usually in interviews.

quantitative Data that is collected in numerical form, usually on questionnaires.

Ramadan A month in the Muslim year that commemorates the revelation of the Koran from God to the prophet Muhammad, requiring fasting from sunrise to sunset each day and refraining from all sensual indulgences.

random sample Sampling technique in which the people selected for participation in a study are chosen randomly, meaning that no one in the population has a better or worse chance of being selected than anyone else.

reaction range Term meaning that genes establish a range of possible development and environment determines where development takes place within that range.

reactive script A dating script, more common for females than males, that focuses on the private domain (e.g. spending considerable time on dress and grooming prior to the date), responding to the date's gestures in the public domain (e.g. being picked up at her home, waiting for him to open the doors) and responding to his sexual initiatives.

recapitulation Now-discredited theory which held that the development of each individual recapitulates the evolutionary development of the human species as a whole.

reciprocal effects In relations between parents and children, the concept that children not only are affected by their parents but affect their parents in return; also called bi-directional effects.

reductionism Breaking up a phenomenon into separate parts to such an extent that the meaning and coherence of the phenomenon as a whole becomes lost.

reflective judgement The capacity to evaluate the accuracy and logical coherence of evidence and arguments.

rejected adolescents Adolescents who are actively disliked by their peers.

relatedness The quality of being emotionally close to another person.

relational aggression A form of non-physical aggression that harms others by damaging their relationships, for example by excluding them socially or spreading rumours about them.

relative performance In IQ tests, performance results compared to other persons of the same age.

relativism Cognitive ability to recognise the legitimacy of competing points of view but also compare the relative merits of competing views.

reliability Characteristic of a measure that refers to the extent to which results of the measure on one occasion are similar to results of the measure on a separate occasion.

representative Characteristic of a sample that refers to the degree to which it accurately represents the population of interest.

resilience Overcoming adverse environmental circumstances to achieve healthy development.

response bias On a questionnaire, the tendency to choose the same response for all items.

responsiveness The degree to which parents are sensitive to their children's needs and express love, warmth and concern for them.

restrictive cultures Cultures that place strong prohibitions on adolescent sexual activity before marriage.

retention rate In a longitudinal study, the percentage of participants who continued to take part in the study after the first year.

rival relationship Between siblings, a relationship in which they compete against each other and measure their success against one another.

role preparation An outcome of socialisation that includes preparation for occupational roles, gender roles, and roles in institutions such as marriage and parenthood.

roles Defined social positions in a culture, containing specifications of behaviour, status and relations with others. Examples include gender, age and social class.

romantic love In Sternberg's theory of love, the type of love that combines passion and intimacy, but without commitment.

sample The people included in a given study, who are intended to represent the population of interest.

sampling Collecting data on a subset of the members of a group.

scaffolding The degree of assistance provided to the learner in the zone of proximal development, gradually decreasing as the learner's skills develop.

schema A mental structure for organising and interpreting information.

schemes Mental structures for organising and interpreting information.

school climate The quality of interactions between teachers and students, including how teachers interact with students, what sort of expectations and standards they have for students, and what kinds of methods are used in the classroom.

scientific method A systematic way of finding the answers to questions or problems that includes standards of sampling, procedure and measures.

second shift The domestic work shift performed in the household by women after they complete their 'first shift' in the workplace.

secondary school The schools attended by pupils aged 11/12 to 18/19 years.

secondary sex characteristics Bodily changes of puberty not directly related to reproduction.

secular Based on non-religious beliefs and values.

secular trend A change in the characteristics of a population over time.

secure attachment Type of attachment to caregiver in which infants use the caregiver as a 'secure base from which to explore' when all is well, but seek physical comfort and consolation from her if frightened or threatened.

selective association The principle that most people tend to choose friends who are similar to themselves.

selective attention The ability to focus on relevant information while screening out information that is irrelevant.

self-concept Persons' views of themselves, usually including concrete characteristics (such as height and age) as well as roles, relationships and characteristics of personality.

self-esteem A person's overall sense of worth and well-being.

self-image A person's evaluation of his or her qualities and relations with others. Closely related to self-esteem.

self-made manhood Anthony Rotundo's term for the norm of manhood in the nineteenth century, in which males were increasingly expected to become independent from their families in adolescence and young adulthood as part of becoming a man.

self-perception A person's view of his or her characteristics and abilities. Closely related to self-esteem.

self-regulation The capacity for exercising self-control in order to restrain one's impulses and comply with social norms.

self-socialisation In gender socialisation, refers to the way that children seek to maintain consistency between the norms they have learned about gender and their behaviour.

semenarche A male's first ejaculation.

semi-restrictive cultures Cultures that have prohibitions on premarital adolescent sex, but the prohibitions are not strongly enforced and are easily evaded.

sensorimotor stage Cognitive stage in first two years of life that involves learning how to coordinate the activities of the senses with motor activities.

sensory register The sensory register experiences memories that last for no more than about a second.

separation In the formation of ethnic identity, the approach that involves associating only with members of one's own ethnic group and rejecting the ways of the majority culture.

set point Optimal level of sex hormones in the body. When this point is reached, responses in the glands of the feedback loop cause the production of sex hormones to be reduced.

sex The biological status of being male or female.

sex hormones Androgens and oestrogens that cause the development of primary and secondary sex characteristics.

sexual harassment A wide range of threatening or aggressive behaviours related to sexuality, from mild harassment such as name calling, jokes and leering looks to severe harassment involving unwanted touching or sexual contact.

sexual scripts Cognitive frameworks, often different for males and females, for understanding how a sexual experience is supposed to proceed and how sexual experiences are to be interpreted.

sexuality Biological sexual development as well as sexual values, beliefs, thoughts, feelings, relationships and behaviour.

short-term memory Component of memory system that holds information for about 20 seconds.

sibling Each of two or more children having one or both parents in common.

social and conventional system perspective taking Realising that the social perspectives of self and others are influenced not just by their interaction with each other but by their roles in the larger society.

social cognition How people think about other people, social relationships and social institutions.

social desirability The tendency for people participating in social science studies to report their behaviour as they believe it would be approved by others rather than as it actually occurred.

social information processing The interpretation of others' behaviour and intentions in a social interaction.

social loneliness Condition that occurs when people feel that they lack a sufficient number of social contacts and relationships.

social roles theory Theory that social roles for males and females enhance or suppress different capabilities, so that males and females tend to develop different skills and attitudes, which leads to gender-specific behaviours.

social skills Skills for successfully handling social relations – getting along well with others.

socialisation The process by which people acquire the behaviours and beliefs of the culture in which they live.

socialised delinquency Delinquents who commit crimes in groups and are similar to non-delinquents in psychological functioning and family relationships.

sociometry A method for assessing popularity and unpopularity that involves having students rate the social status of other students.

sources of meaning The ideas and beliefs that people learn as part of socialisation, indicating what is important, what is to be valued, what is to be lived for, and how to explain and offer consolation for the individual's mortality.

spermarche Beginning of development of sperm in boys' testicles at puberty.

stage A period in which abilities are organised in an identifiable, distinctive, coherent, interrelated way.

Stanford-Binet Widely used IQ test developed by Alfred Binet and revised by scholars at Stanford University.

status phase In Brown's developmental model of adolescent love, the second phase, in which adolescents begin to gain confidence in their skills at interacting with potential romantic partners and begin to form their first romantic relationships, assessing not just how much they like and are attracted to the person, but also how their status with friends and peers would be influenced.

stereotype A belief that others possess certain characteristics simply as a result of being a member of a particular group.

storm and stress Theory promoted by G. Stanley Hall asserting that adolescence is inevitably a time of mood disruptions, conflict with parents and antisocial behaviour.

stratified sampling Sampling technique in which researchers select participants so that various categories of people are represented in proportions equal to their presence in the population to which the results can be generalised.

style of youth culture The distinguishing features of youth culture, including image, demeanour and argot.

substance use Use of substances that have cognitive and mood-altering effects, including alcohol, cigarettes, and illegal drugs such as marijuana, LSD and cocaine.

super peer One of the functions of media for adolescents, meaning that adolescents often look to media for information (especially concerning sexuality) which their parents may be unwilling to provide, in the same way they might look to a friend.

survey A questionnaire study that involves asking a large number of people questions about their opinions, beliefs or behaviour.

symbolic inheritance The set of ideas and understandings, both implicit and explicit, about persons, society, nature, and divinity that serve as a guide to life in a particular culture; expressed symbolically through stories, songs, rituals, sacred objects and sacred places.

synapse The point of transmission between two nerve cells.

synaptic pruning Following overproduction, the process by which the number of synapses in the brain are reduced, making brain functioning faster and more efficient but less flexible.

test-retest reliability Type of reliability that examines whether or not persons' scores on one occasion are similar to their scores on another occasion.

testosterone The androgen most important in pubertal development among boys.

theory of genotype–environment interactions Theory that both genetics and environment make essential contributions to human development but are difficult to unravel because our genes actually influence the kind of environment we experience.

theory of mind The ability to attribute mental states to one's self and others, including beliefs, thoughts and feelings.

theory of multiple intelligences Howard Gardner's theory that there are eight separate types of intelligence.

traditional parenting style The kind of parenting typical in traditional cultures, high in responsiveness and high in a kind of demandingness that does not encourage discussion and debate but rather expects compliance by virtue of cultural beliefs supporting the inherent authority of the parental role.

transracial adoption The adoption of children of one race by parents of a different race.

unsocialised delinquents Delinquent adolescents who have few friends and commit their crimes alone.

validity The truthfulness of a measure, that is, the extent to which it measures what it claims to measure.

verbal subtests In the Wechsler IQ tests, subtests that examine verbal abilities.

vital capacity The amount of air that can be exhaled after a deep breath, which increases rapidly during puberty, especially for boys.

vulva External female sex organs, including the labia majora, the labia minora, and the clitoris.

Vygotsky Russian psychologist who emphasised the cultural basis of cognitive development.

Wechsler Adult Intelligence Scale (WAIS-IV) Intelligence test for persons aged 16 and over, with six Verbal and five Performance subtests.

Wechsler Intelligence Scale for Children (WISC-IV) Intelligence test for children aged 6 to 16, with six Verbal and five Performance subtests.

women's movement Organised effort in the twentieth century to obtain greater rights and opportunities for women.

working memory An aspect of short-term memory that refers to where information is stored as it is comprehended and analysed.

worldview A set of cultural beliefs that explain what it means to be human, how human relations should be conducted, and how human problems should be addressed.

youth Prior to the late nineteenth century, the term used to refer to persons in their teens and early 20s.

youth culture The culture of young people as a whole, separate from children and separate from adult society, characterised by values of hedonism and irresponsibility.

zone of proximal development The gap between how competently a person performs alone and when guided by an adult or more competent peer.

REFERENCES

Abbas, T. (2007). British South Asians and pathways into selective schooling: social class, culture and ethnicity. *British Educational Research Journal*, *33*(1), 75–90.

Abd-El-Fattah, S. (2006). Effects of family background and parental involvement on Egyptian adolescents' academic achievement and school disengagement: A structural equation modelling analysis. *Social Psychology of Education*, *9*(2), 139–157.

Abdi, A. (2008). Europe and African thought systems and philosophies of education. *Cultural Studies*, *22*(2), 309–327.

Abu-Rayya, H. M. (2006). Ethnic identity, ego identity, and psychological well-being among mixed-ethnic Arab-European adolescents in Israel. *British Journal of Developmental Psychology*, *24*(4), 669–679.

à Campo, J., Nijman, H., Merckelbach, H. & Evers, C. (2003). Psychiatric comorbidity of gender identity disorders: a survey among Dutch psychiatrists. *The American Journal of Psychiatry*, *160*(7), 1332–1336.

Adam, E. K., Hawkley, L. C., Kudielka, B. M. & Cacioppo, J. T. (2006). Day-to-day dynamics of experience–cortisol associations in a population-based sample of older adults. *Proceedings of the National Academy of Sciences of the United States of America*, *103*(45), 17058–17063.

Adamo, S. (2004). An adolescent and his imaginary companions: from quasi-delusional constructs to creative imagination. *Journal of Child Psychotherapy*, *30*(3), 275–295.

Adams, G. R. (1999). *The objective measure of ego identity status: A manual on test theory and construction*. Guelph, Canada: Author.

Adegoke, A. (1993). The experience of spermarche (the age of onset of sperm emission) among selected adolescent boys in Nigeria. *Journal of Youth and Adolescence*, *22*, 201–209.

Adelson, J. (1991). Political development. In R. M. Lerner, A. C. Petersen, & J. Brooks-Gunn (Eds.), *Encyclopedia of adolescence* (Vol. 2, pp. 792–793). New York: Garland.

Adelson, J. (1971). The political imagination of the young adolescent. *Daedalus*, *100*, 1013–1050.

Adler, N. E., Ozer, E. J. & Tschann, J. (2003). Abortion among adolescents. *American Psychologist*, *58*, 211–217.

Afifi, T. D., McManus, T., Hutchinson, S. & Baker, B. (2007). Inappropriate parental divorce disclosures, the factors that prompt them, and their impact on parents' and adolescents' well-being. *Communication Monographs*, *74*(1), 78–102.

Agadjanian, V. (2002). Adolescents' views on childbearing, contraception, and abortion in two post-Communist societies. *Journal of Youth Studies*, *5*(4), 391–406.

Agosto, D. E. (2004). Design vs. content: A study of adolescent girls' website design preferences. *International Journal of Technology and Design Education*, *14*(3), 245–260.

Ahrons, C. (2007). Family ties after divorce: long-term implications for children. *Family Process*, *46*(1), 53–65.

Ainsworth, M. D. S. (1982). Attachment: Retrospect and prospect. In C. M. Parkes & J. Stevenson-Hinde (Eds.), *The place of attachment in human behavior*. New York: Basic Books.

Akos, P., Lambie, G. W., Milsom, A. & Gilbert, K. (2007). Early adolescents' aspirations and academic tracking: An exploratory investigation. *Professional School Counseling* *11*(1), 57–64.

Alan Guttmacher Institute (2002). *Policy analysis: Issues in brief*. New York: Author.

Alan Guttmacher Institute (AGI) (2001). *Teenage sexual and reproductive behaviour in developed countries: Can more progress be made?* New York: Author. Available: www.agi-usa.org.

Alas, R. (2006). Ethics in countries with different cultural dimensions. *Journal of Business Ethics*, *69*(3), 237–247.

Alberts, A., Elkind, D. & Ginsberg, S. (2007). The personal fable and risk-taking in early adolescence. *Journal of Youth and Adolescence*, *36*(1), 71–76.

Aldred, C., Green, J. & Adams, C. (2004). A new social communication intervention for children with autism: pilot randomised controlled treatment study suggesting effectiveness. *Journal of Child Psychology and Psychiatry* (formerly *Journal of Child Psychology and Psychiatry and Allied Disciplines*), *45*(8), 1420–1430.

Alexander, B. (2001, June). Radical idea serves youth, saves money. *Youth Today*, 1, 42–44.

Alfieri, T., Ruble, D. N. & Higgins, E. T. (1996). Gender stereotypes during adolescence: Developmental changes and the transition to junior high school. *Developmental Psychology*, *32*, 1129–1137.

Allen, J., & Land, P. (1999). Attachment in adolescence. In J. Cassidy & P. R. Shaver (Eds.), *Handbook of attachment: Theory, research, and clinical applications*. New York: Guilford.

Allen, J. P., Porter, M. R. & McFarland, F. C. (2006). Leaders and followers in adolescent close friendships: Susceptibility to peer influence as a predictor of risky behavior, friendship instability and depression. *Development and Psychopathology*, *18*(1), 155–172.

Allen, J. P., Porter, M. R., McFarland, F. C., Marsh, P. & McElhaney K. B. (2005). The two faces of adolescents' success with peers: adolescent popularity, social adaptation, and deviant behavior. *Child Development*, *76*(3), 747–760.

Allen, J. P., Porter, M., McFarland, C., McElhaney, K. B. & Marsh, P. (2007). The relation of attachment security to adolescents' paternal and peer relationships, depression, and externalizing behavior. *Child Development*, *78*(4), 1222–1239.

Al-Mateen, C. S. & Afzal, A. (2004). The Muslim child, adolescent, and family. *Child and Adolescent Psychiatric Clinics of North America*, *13*, 183–200.

Alriksson-Schmidt, A.I., Wallander, J. & Biasini, F. (2007). Quality of life and resilience in adolescents with a mobility disability. *Journal of Pediatric Psychology*, *32*(3), 370–370.

Alsaker, F. D. & Flammer, A. (2006) Pubertal maturation. In S. Jackson & LucGoossens (Eds.), *Handbook of adolescent development* (pp. 30–50). New York: Psychology Press.

Alsaker, F. D. & Flammer, A. (1999). Cross-national research in adolescent psychology: The Euronet project. In F. D. Alsaker & A. Flammer (Eds.), *The adolescent experience: European and American adolescents in the 1990s* (pp. 1–14). Mahwah, NJ: Erlbaum.

Altermatt, E. R. & Pomerantz, E. M. (2005). The implications of having high-achieving versus low-achieving friends: A longitudinal analysis. *Social Development*, *14*, 61–81.

Alwin, D. F. (1988). From obedience to autonomy: Changes in traits desired in children, 1924–1978. *Public Opinion Quarterly*, *52*, 33–52.

Amato, P. (2000). The consequences of divorce for children and adults. *Journal of Marriage and the Family*, *62*, 1269–1287.

Ametller, L., Castro, J., Serrano, E., Martínez, E. & Toro, J. (2005) Readiness to recover in adolescent anorexia nervosa: prediction of hospital admission. *Journal of Child Psychology and Psychiatry* (formerly *Journal of Child Psychology and Psychiatry and Allied Disciplines*), *46*(4), 394–400.

Amit, M. & Fried, M. N. (2005). Authority and authority relations in mathematics education: A view from an 8th grade classroom. *Educational Studies in Mathematics*, *58*(2), 145–168.

Anderson, A., Hamilton, R. J. & Hattie, J. (2004). Classroom climate and motivated behavior in secondary schools. *Learning Environments Research*, *7*, 211–225.

Anderson, C. A., Duffy, D. L., Martin, N. G. & Visscher, P. M. (2007). Estimation of variance components for age of menarche in twin families. *Behavior Genetics*, *37*, 668–677.

Anderson, L., Vostanis, P. & O'Reilly, M. (2005). Three-year follow-up of a family support service cohort of children with behavioural problems and their parents. *Child: Care Health & Development*, *31*(4), 469–477.

Ando, M., Asakura, T. & Simons-Morton, B. (2005). Psychosocial influences in physical, verbal and indirect bullying among Japanese early adolescents. *Journal of Early Adolescence*, *25*(3), 268–297.

Andriessen, I. & Phalet, K. (2002). Acculturation and school success: a study among minority youth in the Netherlands. *Intercultural Education*, *13*(1), 21–36.

Ang, R. & Goh, D. (2006). Authoritarian parenting style in asian societies: A cluster-analytic investigation. *Contemporary Family Therapy*, *28*(1), 131–151.

Annunziata, D., Hogue, A., Faw, L. & Liddle, H. A. (2006). Family functioning and school Success in at-risk, inner-city adolescents. *Journal of Youth and Adolescence*, *35*(1), 105–113.

Apena, F. (2007). Being black and in trouble: the role of self-perception in the offending behaviour of black youth. *Youth Justice*, *7*(3), 211–228.

Aquilino, W. S. (2006). Family relationships and support systems in emerging adulthood. In J. J. Arnett and J. Tanner (Eds.), *Coming of age in the 21st century: The lives and contexts of emerging adults* (pp. 193–218). Washington, DC: American Psychological Association.

Archer, S. L. (2002). Commentary on 'Feminist perspectives on Erikson's theory: Their relevance for contemporary identity development research.' *Identity*, *2*, 267–270.

Archibald, A. B., Graber, J. A. & Brooks-Gunn, J. (2003). Pubertal processes and physiological growth in adolescence. In G. Adams & M. Berzonsky (Eds.), *Blackwell handbook of adolescence*. Malden, MA: Blackwell.

Arciniega, G. M., Anderson, T. C., Tovar-Blank, Z. G. & Tracey, T. J. G. (2008). Toward a fuller conception of machismo: Development of a traditional machismo and caballerismo Scale. *Journal of Counseling Psychology*, *55*(1), 19–33.

Arim, R. & Shapka, J. (2008). The impact of pubertal timing and parental control on adolescent problem behaviors. *Journal of Youth and Adolescence*, *37*(4), 445–455.

Arnett, J. J. (2010). *Adolescence and Emerging Adulthood: A Cultural Approach* (4th edition). Boston: Prentice Hall

Arnett, J. J. (2008). The neglected 95%: Why American psychology needs to become less American. *American Psychologist*, *63*(7), 602–614.

Arnett, J. J. (2007a). Emerging adulthood: What is it, and what is it good for? *Child Development Perspectives*, *1*, 68–73.

Arnett, J. J. (2007b). The myth of peer influence in adolescent smoking initiation. *Health Education & Behavior*, *34*, 594–607.

Arnett, J. J. (2006a). G. Stanley Hall's *Adolescence: Brilliance and nonsense. History of Psychology*, *9*, 186–197.

Arnett, J. J. (2006b). Emerging adulthood: Understanding the new way of coming of age. In J. J. Arnett and J. L. Tanner (Eds.), *Emerging adults in America: Coming of age in the 21st century*, (pp. 3–20). Washington, DC: American Psychological Association Press.

Arnett, J. J. (2006c). The case for emerging adulthood in Europe. *Journal of Youth Studies*, *9*, 111–123.

Arnett, J. J. (2006d). Socialization in emerging adulthood: From the family to the wider world, from socialization to self-socialization. In J. Grusec and P. Hastings (Eds.), *Handbook of socialization*. New York: Guilford.

Arnett, J. J. (2005b). The developmental context of substance use in emerging adulthood. *Journal of Drug Issues*, *35*, 235–253.

Arnett, J. J. (2004). *Emerging adulthood: The winding road from the late teens through the twenties*. New York: Oxford University Press.

Arnett, J. J. (2003). Conceptions of the transition to adult-hood among emerging adults in American ethnic groups. *New Directions in Child and Adolescent Development*, *100*, 63–75.

Arnett, J. J. (2002a). The psychology of globalization. *American Psychologist*, *57*, 774–783.

Arnett, J. J. (2002b). Adolescents in Western countries in the 21st century: Vast opportunities—for all? In B. B. Brown, R. W. Larson, & T. S. Saraswathi (Eds.), *The World's Youth: Adolescence in Eight Regions of the Globe* (pp. 307–343). New York: Cambridge University Press.

Arnett, J. J. (2002c). Developmental sources of crash risk in young drivers. *Injury Prevention*, *8*(Suppl. 2), ii17–ii21.

Arnett, J. J. (2001). Adolescents' responses to ciga-rette advertisements for five 'youth brands' and one 'adult brand.' *Journal of Research on Adolescence*, *11*, 425–443.

Arnett, J. J. (2000a). Emerging adulthood: A theory of development from the late teens through the twenties. *American Psychologist*, *55*, 469–480.

Arnett, J. J. (2000b). Optimistic bias in adolescent and adult smokers and nonsmokers. *Addictive Behaviors*, *25*, 625–632.

Arnett, J. J. (1998a). Learning to stand alone: The contem-porary American transition to adulthood in cultural and his-torical context. *Human Development*, *41*, 295–315.

Arnett, J. J. (1998b). Risk behavior and family role transitions during the twenties. *Journal of Youth & Adolescence*, *27*, 301–320.

Arnett, J. J. (1996). *Metalheads: Heavy metal music and adolescent alienation*. Boulder, CO: Westview Press.

Arnett, J. J., Hendry, L., Kloep, M. & Tanner, J. L. (2009). *Diverging perspectives on emerging adulthood: Stage or process?* London: Psychology Press.

Arnett, J. J. & Jensen, L. A. (2002). A congregation of one: Individualized religious beliefs among emerging adults. *Journal of Adolescent Research*, *17*, 451–467.

Aronson, J., Steele, C. M., Salinas, M. F. & Lustina, M. J. (1999). The effect of stereotype threat on the standard-ized test performance of college pupils. In E. Aronson (Ed.), *Readings about the social animal* (8th ed.). New York: Freeman.

Aronson, P. J., Mortimer, J. T., Zierman, C. & Hacker, M. (1996). Generational differences in early work experi-ences and evaluations. In T. J. Mortimer & M. D. Finch (Eds.), *Adolescents, work, and family: An intergenera-tional developmental analysis*. Thousand Oaks, CA: Sage.

Artar, M. (2007). Adolescent egocentrism and theory of mind: In the context of family relations. *Behaviour and Personality*, *35*(9), 1211–1220.

Artaraz, K. (2008). Going full circle? Integrating provision for young people in the Connexions service. *Social Policy and Society*, 7(2), 173–183.

Artaraz, K. (2006). The wrong person for the job? Professional habitus and working cultures in Connexions. *Critical Social Policy*, 26(4), 910–931.

Arthur, G., Lowndes, C. M., Blackham, J., Fenton, K. A., and the European Surveillance of Sexually Transmitted Infections (ESSTI) Network (2005). Divergent approaches to partner notification for sexually transmitted infec-tions across the European Union. *Sexually Transmitted Diseases*, *32*(12), 741–764.

Arvidsson, A. (2006). 'Quality singles': Internet dating and the work of fantasy. *New Media & Society*, *8*(4), 671–690.

Asakawa, K. & Csikszentmihalyi, M. (1999). The quality of experience of Asian American adolescents in activities related to future goals. *Journal of Youth & Adolescence*, *27*, 141–163.

Ascherson, N. (2004). 'Better off without them'? Politics and ethnicity in the twenty-first century. *International Affairs*, *80*(1), 99–106.

Asendorpf, J. B. & van Aken, M. A. (1999). Resilient, over-controlled, and undercontrolled personality prototypes in childhood: Replicability, predictive power, and the trait-type issue. *Journal of Personality and Social Psychology*, *77*, 815–832.

Ashcraft, M. H. (2002). *Cognition*. Upper Saddle River, NJ: Prentice Hall.

Ashford, L. (2002). Young women in sub-Saharan Africa face a high risk of HIV infection. *Population Today* (pp. 3, 6). Washington, DC: Population Reference Bureau.

Associated Press (2010). *Sexual Anti-smoking Ads Spark Scandal* accessed 21.02.2011 at http://www.msnbc. msn.com/id/35565815/ns/health-kids_and_parenting/

Atkins, R. & Hart., D (2008). The undercontrolled do it first: Childhood personality and sexual debut. *Research in Nursing & Health*, *31*(6), 626–639.

Attree, P. (2005). Parenting support in the context of poverty: A meta-synthesis of the qualitative evidence. *Health & Social Care in the Community*, *13*(4), 330–337.

Attwood, F. (2007). No money shot? Commerce, pornog-raphy and new sex taste cultures. *Sexualities*, *10*(4), 441–456.

Attwood, G. & Croll, P. (2006). Truancy in secondary school pupils: prevalence, trajectories and pupil perspectives. *Research Papers in Education*, *21*(4), 467–484.

Aunola, K. & Nurmi, J-E. (2005). The role of parenting styles in children's problem behavior. *Child Development*, *76*(6), 1144–1159.

Austin, A. M., Macgowan, M. J. & Wagner, E. F. (2005). Effective family-based interventions for adolescents with substance use problems: A systematic review. *Research on Social Work Practice*, *15*, 67–83.

Avery, L. & Lazdane, G. (2008). What do we know about sexual and reproductive health among adolescents in Europe? *European Journal of Contraception and Reproductive Health*, *13*, 58–70.

Axelsson, L. & Ejlertsson, G. (2002). Self-reported health, self-esteem and social support among young unemployed people: A population-based study. *International Journal of Social Welfare*, *11*, 111–119.

Ayman-Nolley, S. & Taira, L. (2000). Obsession with the dark side of adolescence: A decade of psychological studies. *Journal of Youth Studies*, *3*(1), 35–48.

Bachman, J. G., Safron, D. J., Sy, S. R. & Schulenberg, J. E. (2003). Wishing to work: New perspectives on how adolescents' part-time work intensity is linked to educational disengagement, substance use, and other problem behaviours. *International Journal of Behavioral Development*, *27*(4), 301–315.

Bachman, J. G. & Schulenberg, J. (1993). How part-time work intensity relates to drug use, problem behavior, time use, and satisfaction among high school seniors: Are these consequences or just correlates? *Developmental Psychology*, *29*, 220–235.

Baddeley, A. (2000). Short-term and working memory. In E. Tulving & F. I. M. Craik (Eds.), *The Oxford handbook of memory*. New York: Oxford University Press.

Baddeley, A. D. & Larsen, J. D. (2007). The phonological loop unmasked? A comment on the evidence for a 'perceptual-gestural' alternative. *The Quarterly Journal of Experimental Psychology*, *60*(4), 497–504.

Badouraki, M., Christoforidis, A., Economou, I., Dimitriadis, A. S. & Katzos, G. (2008). Sonographic assessment of uterine and ovarian development in normal girls aged 1 to 12 years. *Journal of Clinical Ultrasound*, *36*(9), 539–544.

Baieli, S., Pavone, L., Meli, C., Fiumara, A. & Coleman, M. (2003). Autism and phenylketonuria. *Journal of Autism and Developmental Disorders*, *33*(2), 201–204.

Baillargeon, R. H., Zoccolillo, M., Keenan, K., Côté, S., Pérusse, D., Wu, H., Boivin, M. & Tremblay, R. E. (2007). Gender differences in physical aggression: A prospective population-based survey of children before and after 2 years of age. *Developmental Psychology*, *43*(1), 13–26.

Bain, S. K. & Allin, J. D. (2005). Stanford-Binet intelligence scales, fifth edition. *Journal of Psychoeducational Assessment*, *23*, 87–95.

Baird, A. A., Gruber, S. A., Cohen, B. M., Renshaw, R. J. & Yureglun-Todd, D. A. (1999). FMRI of the amygdala in children and adolescents. *American Academy of Child and Adolescent Psychiatry*, *38*, 195–199.

Baker, D. P. & Perkins-Jones, D. (1993). Creating gender equality: Cross-national gender stratification and mathematical performance. *Sociology of Education*, *66*, 91–103.

Baker, J. M. (2002). *How homophobia hurts children: Nurturing diversity at home, at school, and in the community*. New York: Haworth Press.

Ball, C. (2010). *Ritual: Perspectives & dimensions* (reissue edition). Oxford. OUP

Ballard, K. D., Kuh, D. J. & Wadsworth, M. E. J. (2001). The role of the menopause in women's experiences of the 'change of life'. *Sociology of Health and Illness*, *23*(4), 397–424.

Ballentine, L. W. & Ogle, J. P. (2005). The making and unmaking of body problems in *Seventeen magazine* 1992–2003. *Family & Consumer Sciences Research Journal*, *33*, 281–307.

Bamberger, M. (2004) *Wonderland: A year in the life of an American high school*. New York: Atlantic Monthly Press.

Bangsbo, J., Iaia, F. & Krustrup, P. (2008). The yo-yo intermittent recovery test: A useful tool for evaluation of physical performance in intermittent sports. *Sports Medicine*, *38*(1), 37–51.

Bankole, A., Singh, S., Woog, V. & Wulf, D. (2004). *Risk and protection: Youth and HIV/AIDS in sub-Saharan Africa*. Washington, DC: Alan Guttmacher Institute.

Baranowksi, M. J., Jorga, J., Djordjevic, I., Marinkovic, J. & Hetherington, M. M. (2003). Evaluation of adolescent body satisfaction and associated eating disorder pathology in two communities. *European Eating Disorders Review: The Journal of the Eating Disorders Association*, *11*(6), 478–495.

BARB (2010). *2010 Weekly Viewing Summary* (26½ hours-week ending 18th July 2010) http://www.barb.co.uk/ accessed 29 July 2010.

Barber, B. K. (2002). *Intrusive parenting: How psychological control affects children and adolescents*. Washington, DC: American Psychological Association.

Barber, B. K. & Olsen, J. A. (2004). Assessing the transitions to middle and high school. *Journal of Adolescent Research*, *19*, 3–30.

Barber, J. G. & del Fabbro, P. (2000). The assessment of parenting in child protection cases. *Research on Social Work Practice*, *10*(2), 243–256.

Barling, J. & Kelloway, E. K. (1999). *Young workers: Varieties of experience*. Washington, DC: American Psychological Association.

Barnes, G., Hoffman, J., Welte, J., Farrell, M. & Dintcheff, B. (2007). Adolescents' time use: Effects on substance use, delinquency and sexual activity. *Journal of Youth and Adolescence*, *36*(5), 697–710.

Barrera, M., Biglan, A., Ary, D. & Li, F. (2001). Replication of a problem behavior model with American Indian, Hispanic, and Caucasion youth. *Journal of Early Adolescence*, *21*, 133–157.

Barrett, A. E. & Turner, R. J. (2006). Research Report: Family structure and substance use problems in adolescence and early adulthood: examining explanations for the relationship. *Addiction*, *101*(1), 109–120.

Barrett, P. M., Sonderegger, R. & Xenos, S. (2003). Using friends to combat anxiety and adjustment problems among young migrants to Australia: A national trial. *Clinical Child Psychology and Psychiatry*, *8*(2), 241–260.

Barrio, C., Morena, A. & Linaza, J. L. (2007). Spain. In J. J. Arnett, R. Ahmed, B. Nsamenang, T. S. Saraswathi, & R. Silbereisen (Eds.), *International encyclopedia of adolescence*. New York: Routledge.

Barron, I. (2007). An exploration of young children's ethnic identities as communities of practice. *British Journal of Sociology of Education*, *28*(6), 739–752.

Barrow, R. (2007). Common schooling and the need for distinction. *Journal of Philosophy of Education*, *41*(4), 559–573.

Barsalou, L. W. (1992). *Cognitive psychology: An overview for cognitive scientists*. Hillsdale, NJ: Erlbaum.

Bartholet, J. (2000). The plague years. *Newsweek*, January 17, 32–37.

Barton, P. E. (2005). *One-third of a nation: Rising dropout rates and declining opportunities*. Princeton, NJ: Educational Testing Service.

Barzilai, S. & Zohar, A. (2008). Is information acquisition still important in the information age? *Education and Information Technologies*, *13*(1), 35–53.

Basow, S. (2004). The hidden curriculum: Gender in the classroom. In M. A. Paludi, (Ed.), *Praeger guide to the psychology of gender* (pp. 117–131). Westport, CT: Praeger/Greenwood Publishing Group.

Basow, S. A. & Rubin, L. R. (1999). Gender influences on adolescent development. In N. B. Johnson, M. C. Roberts, & J. Worell (Eds.), *Beyond appearance: A new look at adolescent girls* (pp. 25–52). Washington, DC: American Psychological Association.

Basseches, M. (1989). Dialectical thinking as an organized whole: Comments on Irwin and Kramer. In M. L. Commons, J. D. Sinnott, F. A. Richards, & C. Armon (Eds.), *Adult development, Vol. 1: Comparisons and applications of developmental models* (pp. 161–178). New York: Praeger.

Basseches, M. (1984). *Dialectical thinking and adult development*. Norwood, NJ: Ablex.

Bastion, E. W. & Stately, T. L. (2009). *Living fully dying well*. Boulder: Sounds True.

Basu, A. & Altinay, E. (2002). The interaction between culture and entrepreneurship in London's immigrant businesses. *International Small Business Journal*, *20*(4), 371–393.

Basu, A. K. & Chau, N. H. (2007). An exploration of the worst forms of child labor: Is redemption a viable option? In K. A. Appiah & M. Bunzl (Eds.), *Buying freedom: The ethics of economics of slave redemption* (pp. 37–76). Princeton, NJ: Princeton University Press.

Batabyal, A. & Beladi, H. (2002). Arranged or love marriage? That is the question. *Applied Economics Letters*, *9*(13), 893–897.

Battaglia, C., Regnani, G., Mancini, F., Iughetti, L., Venturoli, S. & Flamigni, C. (2002). Pelvic sonography and uterine artery color Doppler analysis in the diagnosis of female precocious puberty. *Ultrasound in Obstetrics & Gynecology*, *19*(4), 386–391.

Battaglia, D. M., Richard, F. D., Datteri, D. L. & Lord, C. G. (1998). Breaking up is (relatively) easy to do: A script for the dissolution of close relationships. *Journal of Social and Personal Relationships*, *15*, 829–845.

Bauminger, N., Finzi-Dottan, R., Chason, S. & Har-Even, D. (2008a). Intimacy in adolescent friendship: The roles of attachament, coherence and self-disclosure. *Journal of Social and Personal Relationships*, *25*(3), 409–428.

Bauminger, N., Solomon, M., Aviezer, A., Heung, K., Gazit, L., Brown, J. & Rogers, S. (2008b) Children with autism and their friends: A multidimensional study of friendship in high-functioning autism spectrum disorder. *Journal of Abnormal Child Psychology*, *36*(2), 135–150.

Baumrind, D. (1991a). Effective parenting during the early adolescent transition. In P. A. Cowan & E. M. Hetherington (Ed.), *Advances in family research* (vol. 2, pp. 111–163). Hillsdale, NJ: Erlbaum.

Baumrind, D. (1991b). The influence of parenting style on adolescent competence and substance use. *Journal of Early Adolescence*, *11*, 56–95.

Baumrind, D. (1987). A developmental perspective on adolescent risk taking in contemporary America. *New Directions for Child Development*, *37*, 93–125.

Baumrind, D. (1971). Current patterns of parental authority. *Developmental Psychology Monographs*, *4(1, Pt.2)*.

Baumrind, D. (1968). Authoritative vs. authoritarian parental control. *Adolescence*, *3*, 255–272.

Bayley, N. (1968). Behavioural correlates of mental growth: Birth to thirty-six years. *American Psychologist*, *23*, 1–17.

Beam, M. R., Gil-Rivas, V., Greenberger, E. & Chen, C. (2002). Adolescent problem behavior and depressed mood: Risk and protection within and across social contexts. *Journal of Youth & Adolescence*, *31*, 343–357.

Beames, S. & Brown, A. (2005). Outdoor education in Hong Kong: Past, present and future. *Journal of Adventure Education & Outdoor Learning*, *5*(1), 69–82.

Bearman, S. & Stice, E. (2008). Testing a gender additive model: The role of body Image in adolescent depression. *Journal of Abnormal Child Psychology*, *36*(8), 1251–1263.

Beat (Beating Eating Disorders) (2010). The Incidence of eating disorders accessed 20.02.2011 at http://www.b-eat.co.uk/Home/PressMediaInformation/Somestatistics

Beausang, C. & Razor, A. (2000). Young Western women's experiences of menarche and menstruation. *Health Care for Women International*, *21*(6), 517–528.

Beck, J. (2009). Appropriating professionalism: restructuring the official knowledge base of England's 'modernised' teaching profession. *British Journal of Sociology of Education*, *30*(1), 3–14.

Becker, B. E. & Luthar, S. S. (2007). Peer-perceived admiration and social preference: Contextual correlates of positive peer regard among suburban and urban adolescents. *Journal of Research on Adolescence*, *17*(1), 117–144.

Beckett, C., Maughan, B., Rutter, M., Castle, J., Colvert, E., Groothues, C., Hawkins, A., Kreppner, J., O'Connor, T., Stevens, S. & Sonuga-Barke, E. (2007). Scholastic attainment following severe early institutional deprivation: A study of children adopted from Romania. *Journal of Abnormal Child Psychology*, *35*(6), 1063–1073.

Begg, D. J. & Langley, J. D. (2004). Identifying predictors of persistent non-alcohol or drug-related risky driving behaviors among a cohort of young adults. *Accident Analysis & Prevention*, *36*, 1067–1071.

Bell, J. (2001). Investigating gender differences in the science performance of 16-year-old pupils in the UK. *International Journal of Science Education*, *23*(5), 469–486.

Bell, R. (1998). *Changing bodies, changing lives* (3rd ed.). New York: Times Books.

Bell, S. & Lee, C. (2008). Transitions in emerging adulthood and stress among young Australian women. *International Journal of Behavioral Medicine*, *15*(4), 280–288.

Belsky, J., Steinberg, L. D., Houts, R. M., Friedman, S. L., DeHart, G., Cauffman, E., Roisman, G. I, Halpern-Felsher, B. & Susman, E. (2007). Family rearing antecedents of pubertal timing. *Child Development*, *78*, 1302–1321.

Bem, S. L. (1993). *The lenses of gender: Transforming the debate on sexual inequality*. New Haven: Connecticut University Press.

Bem, S. L. (1981). Gender schema theory: A cognitive account of sex-typing. *Psychological Review, 88*, 354–364.

Bem, S. L. (1977). On the utility of alternative procedures for assessing psychological androgyny. *Journal of Consulting and Clinical Psychology, 45*, 196–205.

Bem, S. L. (1974). The measurement of psychological androgyny. *Journal of Consulting and Clinical Psychology, 42*, 155–162.

Bembo, S. A. & Carlson, H. E. (2004). Gynecomastia: Its features, and when and how to treat it. *Cleveland Clinic Journal of Medicine, 71*(6), 511–517.

Ben-Amos, I. K. (1994). *Adolescence and youth in early modern England.* New Haven, CT: Yale University Press.

Benbow, C. P. & Stanley, J. C. (1980). Sex differences in mathematical ability: Fact or artifact? *Science, 210*, 1262–1264.

Benenson, J. F. & Christakos, A. (2003). The greater fragility of females' versus males' closest same-sex friendships. *Child Development, 74*(4), 1123–1129.

Bennett, N. (1976). *Teaching Styles and Pupil Progress.* London: Open Books.

Bensley, L. S., Van Eeenwyk, J., Spieker, S. J. & Schoder, J. (1999). Self-reported abuse history and adolescent problem behaviors. I: Antisocial and suicidal behaviors. *Journal of Adolescent Health, 24*, 163–172.

Berenson, K. R., Crawford, T. N., Cohen, P. & Brook, J. (2005). Implications of identification with parents and parents' acceptance for adolescent and young adult self-esteem. *Self & Identity, 4*, 289–301.

Berg, C., Choi, W., Kaur, H., Nollen, N. & Ahluwalia, J. (2009). The roles of parenting, church attendance, and depression in adolescent smoking. *Journal of Community Health, 34*(1), 56–63.

Bergen, H. A., Martin, G, Richardson, A. S., Allison, S. & Roeger, L. (2003). Sexual abuse and suicidal behavior: A model constructed from a larger community sample of adolescents. *Journal of the American Academy of Child & Adolescent Psychiatry, 42*, 1301–1309.

Berger, U., Weitkamp, K. & Strauss, B. (2009). Weight limits, estimations of future BMI, subjective pubertal timing and physical appearance comparisons among adolescent girls as precursors of disturbed eating behaviour in a community sample. *European Eating Disorders Review: The Journal of the Eating Disorders Association, 17*(2), 128–136.

Berndt, T. J. (2004). Children's friendships: Shifts over a half-century in perspectives on their development and their effects. *Merrill-Palmer Quarterly, 50*, 206–223.

Berry, J. W., Phinney, J. S., Sam, D. L. & Vedder, P. (Eds.). (2006). *Immigrant youth in cultural transition: Acculturation, identity, and adaptation across national contexts.* Mahwah, NJ: Lawrence Erlbaum.

Beveridge, W. (1942) *Social Insurance and Allied Services.* London: HMSO.

Beyers, J. M. & Loeber, R. (2003). Untangling developmental relations between depressed mood and delinquency in male adolescents. *Journal of Abnormal Child Psychology, 31*(3), 247–266.

Bhattacharya, K. (2007). Consenting to the consent form: What are the fixed and fluid understandings between the researcher and the researched? *Qualitative Inquiry, 13*(8), 1095–1115.

Bhopal, K. (2000). South Asian women in East London: The impact of education. *The European Journal of Women's Studies, 7*(1), 35–52.

Bhui, K., Stansfeld, S., Head, J., Haines, M., Hillier, S., Taylor, S., Viner, R. & Booy, R. (2005). Cultural identity, acculturation, and mental health among adolescents in east London's multiethnic community. *Journal of Epidemiology & Community Health, 59*(4), 296–302.

Biehal, N., Mitchell, F. & Wade, J. (2003). *Lost from view: Missing persons in the UK* (p. 32). Bristol: Policy Press.

Biehl, M. C., Natsuaki, M. N. & Ge, X. (2007). The influence of pubertal timing on alcohol use and heavy drinking trajectories. *Journal of Youth and Adolescence, 36*(2), 153–167.

Bina, M., Graziano, F. & Bonino, S. (2006). Risky driving and lifestyles in adolescence. *Accident Analysis & Prevention, 38*(3), 472–481.

Bing, J. (2007). Liberated jokes: Sexual humor in all-female groups. *Humor - International Journal of Humor Research, 20*(4), 337–366.

Bird, C. M., Papadopoulou, K., Ricciardelli, P., Rossor, M. N. & Cipolotti, L. (2004). Monitoring cognitive changes: Psychometric properties of six cognitive tests. *British Journal of Clinical Psychology, 43*(2), 197–210.

Bishop, D. V. M. (2000). How does the brain learn language? Insights from the study of children with and without language impairment. *Developmental Medicine & Child Neurology, 42*(2), 133–142.

Bisson, M. & Levine, T. (2009). Negotiating a friends with benefits relationship. *Archives of Sexual Behavior, 38*(1), 66–73.

Bizman, A. & Yinon, Y. (2004). Social self-discrepancies from own and other standpoints and collective self-esteem. *The Journal of Social Psychology, 144*(2), 101–113.

Bjarnason, T. & Sigurdardottir, T. J. (2003). Psychological distress during unemployment and beyond: Social support and material deprivation among youth in six Northern European countries. *Social Science & Medicine, 56*, 973–985.

Bjerkeset, O., Nordahl, H., Larsson, S., Dahl, A. & Linaker, O. (2008). A 4-year follow-up study of syndromal and sub-syndromal anxiety and depression symptoms in the general population. *Social Psychiatry and Psychiatric Epidemiology, 43*(3), 192–199.

Blacher, J. & McIntyre, L. L. (2006). Syndrome specificity and behavioural disorders in young adults with intellectual disability: Cultural differences in family impact. *Journal of Intellectual Disability Research, 50*(3), 184–198.

Blair, A. (1999). Speech to the Annual Conference of the Labour Party.

Blanchard-Fields, F. (1986). Reasoning on social dilemmas varying in emotional saliency: An adult development perspective. *Psychology and Aging, 1*, 325–332.

Blanksby, D. (1999). Not quite eureka: Perceptions of a trial of cluster grouping as a model for addressing the diverse range of student abilities at a junior secondary school. *Educational Studies*, *25*(1), 79–88.

Bleske-Rechek, A. L. & Buss, D. M. (2001). Opposite-sex friendship: Sex differences and similarities in initiation, selection, and dissolution. *Personality and Social Psychology Bulletin*, *27*(10), 1310–1323.

Bleuler, E. (1910). Die Psychanalyse Freuds. Verteidigung und kritische Bemerkungen, *Jahrbuch für Psychoanalytische une Psychopathologische Forschungen*, *2*, 623–730.

Bloom, M. (2000). The uses of theory in primary prevention practice: Evolving thoughts on sports and other after-school activities as influences on social competency. In S. J. Danish & T. P. Gullotta (Eds.), *Developing competent youth and strong communities through after-school programming* (pp. 17–66). New York: Child Welfare League of America.

Blum, R. & Rinehart, P. (2000). *Reducing the risk: Connections that make a difference in the lives of youth*. University of Minnesota, Division of General Pediatrics and Adolescent Health.

Blum, R. W. (2002). *Mothers' influence on teen sex: Connections that promote postponing sexual intercourse*. University of Minnesota: Center for Adolescent Health and Development.

Boaler, J., Wiliam, D. & Brown, M. (2000). Students' experiences of ability grouping – Disaffection, polarisation and the construction of failure. *British Educational Research Journal*, *26*(5), 631–648.

Bobrow, R. S. (2002). Sexual orientation and suicide risk among teenagers. *JAMA: Journal of the American Medical Association*, *287*, 1265–1266.

Bockting, W. O. & Coleman, E. (2003). *Masturbation as a means of achieving sexual health*. New York: Haworth.

Boehnke, K. (2008). Peer pressure: a cause of scholastic underachievement? A cross-cultural study of mathematical achievement among German, Canadian, and Israeli middle school students. *Social Psychology of Education*, *11*(2), 149–160.

Bogenschneider, K., Wu, M., Raffaelli, M. & Tsay, J. C. (1998). Parent influences on adolescent peer orientation and substance use: The interface of parenting practices and values. *Child Development*, *69*, 1672–1688.

Bohnert, A. M., Richards, M. H., Kolmodin, K. E. & Lakin, B. L. (2008). Young urban African American adolescents' experience of discretionary time activities. *Journal of Research on Adolescence*, *18*(3), 517–539.

Bois-Reymond, M. & Ravesloot, J. (1996). The roles of parents and peers in the sexual and relational socialization of adolescents. In K. Hurrelmann & S. Hamilton (Eds.), *Social problems and social contexts in adolescence: Perspectives across boundaries* (pp. 175–197). Hawthorne, NY: Aldine de Gruyter.

Boman, Y. (2006). The struggle between conflicting beliefs: on the promise of education. *Journal of Curriculum Studies*, *38*(5), 545–568.

Bond, L., Carlin, J. B., Thomas, L., Rubin, K. & Patton, G. (2001). Does bullying cause emotional problems? A prospective study of young teenagers. *BMJ (British Medical Journal)*, *323*(7311), 480–4.

Bond, L., Toumbourou, J. W., Thomas, L., Catalano, R. F. & Patton, G. (2005). Individual, family, school, and community risk and protective factors for depressive symptoms in adolescents: A comparison of risk profiles for substance use and depressive symptoms. *Prevention Science*, *6*(2), 73–88.

Bongers, I. L., Koot, H. M., van der Ende, J. & Verhulst, F. C. (2008). Predicting young adult social functioning from developmental trajectories of externalizing behaviour. *Psychological Medicine*, *38*(7), 989–999.

Bongers, I. L., Koot, H. M., van der Ende, J. & Verhulst, F. C. (2004). Developmental trajectories of external behaviors in childhood and adolescence. *Child Development*, *75*, 1523–1537.

Bonino, S., Cattelino, E. & Ciairano, S. (2007). Italy. In J. J. Arnett, R. Ahmed, B. Nsamenang, T. S. Saraswathi, & R. Silbereisen (Eds.), *International encyclopedia of adolescence*. New York: Routledge.

Booher-Jennings, J. (2008). Learning to label: socialisation, gender, and the hidden curriculum of high-stakes testing. *British Journal of Sociology of Education*, *29*(2), 149–160.

Booth, C. (1886). Occupations of the People of the United Kingdom, 1801–81. *Journal of the Royal Statistical Society (J.S.S.)*, *XLIX*, 314–436.

Booth, M. (2002). Arab adolescents facing the future: Enduring ideals and pressures for change. In B. B. Brown, R. Larson, & T. S. Saraswathi (Eds.), *The World's Youth: Adolescence in Eight Regions of the Globe* (pp. 207–242). NY: Cambridge University Press.

Borduin, C. M., Schaeffer, C. M. & Ronis, S. T. (2003). Multisystemic treatment of serious antisocial behavior in adolescents. In C. A. Essau (Ed.), *Conduct and oppositional defiant disorders: Epidemiology, risk factors, and treatment*. (pp. 299–318). Mahwah, NJ: Lawrence Erlbaum.

Bornstein, M. H. & Cote, L. R. (2004). Mothers' parenting cognitions in cultures of origin, acculturating cultures, and cultures of destination. *Child Development*, *75*(1), 221–235.

Bornstein, M. H., Putnick, D. L., Suwalsky, J. T. D. & Gini, M. (2006). Maternal chronological age, prenatal and perinatal history, social support, and parenting of infants. *Child Development*, *77*(46), 875–892.

Boromisza-Habashi, D. & Rappoport, L. (2007). Punchlines: The case for racial, ethnic, and gender humor. *Language in Society*, *36*(5), 808–809.

Bosacki, S., Dane, A. & Marini, Z. (2007). Peer relationships and internalizing problems in adolescents: mediating role of self-esteem. *Emotional and Behavioural Difficulties*, *12*(4), 261–282.

Bostic, J. Q., Rubin, D. H., Prince, J. & Schlozman, S. (2005). Treatment of depression in children and adolescents. *Journal of Psychiatric Practice*, *11*, 141–154.

Botcheva, L., Kalchev, P. & Leiderman, P. H. (2007). Bulgaria. In J. J. Arnett, R. Ahmed, B. Nsamenang, T. S. Saraswathi, & R. Silbereisen (Eds.), *International encyclopedia of adolescence*. New York: Routledge.

Botterill, J. (2007). Cowboys, outlaws and artists: The rhetoric of authenticity and contemporary jeans and sneaker advertisements. *Journal of Consumer Culture*, *7*(1), 105–125.

Bottrell, D. (2007). Resistance, resilience and social identities: Reframing 'problem youth' and the problem of schooling. *Journal of Youth Studies*, *10*(5), 597–616.

Botvin, G. & Griffin, K. (2007). School-based programmes to prevent alcohol, tobacco and other drug use. *International Review of Psychiatry*, *19*(6), 607–615.

Bowers, W. A., Evans, K., LeGrange, D. & Andersen, A. E. (2003). Treatment of adolescent eating disorders. In M. A. Reinecke & F. M. Dattilio (Eds.), *Cognitive therapy with children and adolescents: A casebook for clinical practice* (2nd ed., pp. 247–280). New York: Guilford Press.

Bowlby, J. (1980). *Attachment and loss, Vol. 3: Loss, sadness, and depression*. New York: Basic Books.

Bowlby, J. (1973). *Attachment and loss, Vol. 2: Separation, anxiety, and anger*. New York: Basic Books.

Bowlby, J. (1969). *Attachment and loss, Vol. 1: Attachment*. New York: Basic Books.

Bowman, S. (2004). Effects of fast-food consumption on energy intake and diet quality among children in a national household survey. *Pediatrics*, *113*(1), 112–118.

Boyd, C., Abraham, S. & Luscombe, G. (2007). Exercise behaviours and feelings in eating disorder and non-eating disorder groups. *European Eating Disorders Review: The Journal of the Eating Disorders Association*, *15*(2), 112–118.

Boyd, D. (2008). Facebook's privacy trainwreck: Exposure, invasion, and social convergence. *Convergence*, *14*(1), 13–20.

Boyle, P. (2004). Snack attacks. *Youth Today*, *13*(4), 1, 31–33.

Boyle, P. (2001). Why are Dutch teens so sexually safe? *Youth Today*, *10*, 1, 34.

Boyle, P. (2000). Latinas' perplexing lead in teen births. *Youth Today*, *9*, 1, 47–49.

Bracey, J. R., Bámaca, M. Y. & Umaña-Taylor, A. J. (2004). Examining ethnic identity and self-esteem among biracial and monoracial adolescents. *Journal of Youth & Adolescence*, *33*, 123–132.

Bradford, K., Barber, B. K., Olsen, J. A., Maughan, S. L., Erickson, L. D., Ward, D. & Stolz, H. E (2004). A multinational study of interparental conflict, parenting, and adolescent functioning: South Africa, Bangladesh, China, India, Bosnia, Germany, Palestine, Columbia, and the United States. *Marriage & Family Review*, *35*, pp. 107–137.

Brain, K. & Reid, I. (2003). Constructing parental involvement in an education action zone: Whose need is it meeting? *Educational Studies*, *29*(2–3), 291–305.

Brake, M. (1985). Comparative youth culture: *The sociology of youth cultures and youth subcultures in America, Britain, and Canada*. London: Routledge and Kegan Paul.

Brame, R., Bushway, S. D., Paternoster, R. & Apel, R. (2004). Assessing the effect of adolescent employment on involvement in criminal activity. *Journal of Contemporary Criminal Justice*, *20*, 236–256.

Bramwell, R. & Zeb, R. (2006). Attitudes towards and experience of the menstrual cycle across different cultural and religious groups. *Journal of Reproductive and Infant Psychology*, *24*(4), 314–322.

Brand, S., Felner, R., Shim, M., Seitsinger, A. & Dumas, T. (2003). Middle school improvement and reform: Development and validation of a school level assessment of climate, culture pluralism, and school safety. *Journal of Educational Psychology*, *95*, 570–588.

Brandtstädter, J. (2006). Adaptive resources in later life: Tenacious goal pursuit and flexible goal adjustment. In M. Csikszentmihalyi & I. S. Csikszentmihalyi, (Eds.), *A life worth living: Contributions to positive psychology*. (pp. 143–164). New York: Oxford University Press.

Branje, S. J. T., van Lieshout, C. F. M., van Aken, M. A. G. & Haselager, G. J. T. (2004). Perceived support in sibling relationships and adolescent adjustment. *Journal of Child Psychology and Psychiatry* (formerly *Journal of Child Psychology and Psychiatry and Allied Disciplines*), *45*(8), 1385–1396.

Braungart-Rieker, J. M., Garwood, M. M., Powers, B. P. & Wang, X. (2001). Relationships and interactions parental sensitivity, infant affect, and affect regulation: Predictors of later attachment. *Child Development*, *72*(1), 252–270.

Bream, V. & Buchanan, A. (2003). Distress among children whose separated or divorced parents cannot agree arrangements for them. *The British Journal of Social Work*, *33*(2), 227–238.

Breheny, M. & Stephens, C. (2004). Barriers to effective contraception and strategies for overcoming them among adolescent mothers. *Public Health Nursing*, *21*(3), 220–227.

Breivik, K. & Olweus, D. (2006). Adolescents' adjustment in four post-divorce family structures: Single mother, stepfather, joint physical custody and single father families. *Journal of Divorce & Remarriage*, *44*(3–4), 99–124.

Brent, D. A. (2004). Antidepressants and pediatric depression: The risk of doing nothing. *New England Journal of Medicine*, *35*, 1598–1601.

Brent, D. A. & Mann, J. J. (2006). Familial pathways to suicidal behavior: Understanding and preventing suicide among adolescents. *New England Journal of Medicine*, *355*(26), 2719–2721.

Brent, D. A. & Mann, J. J. (2003). Familial factors in adolescent suicidal behavior. In R. A. King & A. Apter (Eds.), *Suicide in children and adolescents* (pp. 86–117). New York, NY: Cambridge University Press.

Brent, D. & Melhem, N. (2008). Familial transmission of suicidal behavior. *Psychiatric Clinics of North America*, *31*(2), 157–177.

Breton, J. J., Tousignant, M., Bergeron, L. & Berthiaume, C. (2002). Informant-specific correlates of suicidal behavior in a community survey of 12–14 year olds. *Journal of the*

American Academy of Child & Adolescent Psychiatry, 41, 723–730.

Brewer, M. B. & Chen, Y-R. (2007). Where (who) are collectives in collectivism? Toward conceptual clarification of individualism and collectivism. *Psychological Review, 114*(1), 133–151.

Bridges, L. & Moore, K. (2002). Religious involvement and children's well-being: What research tells us (and what it doesn't). *Child Trends Research Brief*. Washington, DC: Author. Available: www.childtrends.org

Briggs, C. L. (1989). *Learning how to ask: A sociolinguistic appraisal of the role of the interview in social science research*. New York: Cambridge University Press.

Brim, O. G., Ryff, C. D. & Kessler, R.C. (Eds.) (2004). *How healthy are we? A national study of well-being at midlife*. Chicago: University of Chicago Press.

Broderick, P. C. & Korteland, C. (2004). A prospective study of rumination and depression in early adolescence. *Clinical Child Psychology and Psychiatry, 9*(3), 383–394.

Brody, G. H. (2004). Siblings' direct and indirect contributions to child development. *Current Directions in Psychological Science, 13*(3), 124–126.

Brody, N. (1992). *Intelligence* (2nd ed). San Diego, CA: Academic Press.

Bromley, P. D., Hodges, L. D. & Brodie, D. A. (2006). Physiological range of peak cardiac power output in healthy adults. *Clinical Physiology and Functional Imaging, 26*, 240–246.

Bromnick, R. & Swallow, B. (2001). Parties, lads, friends, love and Newcastle United: A study of young people's values. *Educational Studies, 27*(2), 143–158.

Bronfenbrenner, U. (Ed.) (2005). *Making human beings human: Bioecological perspectives on human development*. Thousand Oaks, CA: Sage.

Bronfenbrenner, U. (2000). Ecological theory. In A. Kazdin (Ed.), *Encyclopedia of psychology*. Washington, DC: American Psychological Association.

Bronfenbrenner, U. & Morris, P. A. (1998). The ecology of developmental processes. In W. Damon (Series Ed.) and R. Lerner (Vol. Ed.), *Handbook of child psychology, Vol. 1: Theoretical models of human development* (pp. 993–1028). New York: Wiley.

Bronstein, P. (2006). *The family environment: Where gender role socialization begins*. Oxford: Oxford University Press

Brook, J. S., Brook, D. W. & Pahl, K. (2006). The developmental context for adolescent substance abuse intervention. In H. A. Liddie, & C. L. Rowe (Eds.), *Adolescent substance abuse: Research and clinical advances* (pp. 25–51). New York: Cambridge University Press.

Brooks-Gunn, J. & Ruble, D. (1982). The development of menstrual-related beliefs and behaviors during early adolescence. *Child Development, 53*, 1567–1577.

Brown, B. B. (2004). Adolescent relationships with peers. In R. Lerner & L. Steinberg (Eds.), *Handbook of adolescent psychology*. New York: Wiley.

Brown, B. B. (1989). The role of peer groups in adolescents' adjustment to secondary school. In T. J. Berndt & G. W.

Ladd (Eds.), *Peer relationships in child development* (pp. 188–215). New York: Wiley.

Brown, B. B., Bakken, J. P. Ameringer, S. W. & Mahon, S. D. (2008). A comprehensive conceptualization of peer influence process in adolescence. In M. J. Prinstein & K. A. Dodge (Eds.), *Understanding peer influence in children and adolescents: Duke series in child development and public policy* (pp. 72–93). New York: Guilford Press.

Brown, B. B., Herman, M., Hamm, J. V. & Heck, D. K. (2008a). Ethnicity and image: Correlates of crowd affiliation among ethnic minority youth. *Child Development, 79*(3), 529–546.

Brown, B. B. & Klute, C. (2003). Friendships, cliques, and crowds. In R. G, Adams., & D. M, Berzonsky (Eds.), *Blackwell handbook of adolescence* (pp. 330–348). Malden, MA: Blackwell.

Brown, J. & Johnson, S. (2008). Childrearing and child participation in Jamaican families. *International Journal of Early Years Education, 16*(1), 31–40.

Brown, J. D., Halpern, C. T. & L'Engle, K. L. (2005). Mass media as a sexual super peer for early maturing girls. *Journal of Adolescent Health, 36*, 420–427.

Brown, J. D., Steele, J. & Walsh-Childers, K. (Eds.) (2002). *Sexual teens, sexual media*. Mahwah, NJ: Erlbaum.

Brown, K. (2008). The promise and perils of women's participation in UK mosques: the impact of securitisation agendas on identity, gender and community. *The British Journal of Politics & International Relations, 10*(3), 472–491.

Brown, L., Callahan, M., Strega, S., Walmsley, C. & Dominelli, L. (2009). Manufacturing ghost fathers: the paradox of father presence and absence in child welfare. *Child & Family Social Work, 14*(1), 25–34.

Brown, L. S. & Wright, J. (2001). Attachment theory in adolescence and its relevance to developmental psychopathology. *Clinical Psychology & Psychotherapy, 8*(1), 15–32.

Brown, S. (2004). Celebrating childhood: Research to inform improvement in provision. *European Early Childhood Education Research Journal, 12*(1), 5–14.

Brumberg, J. J. (1997). *The body project: An intimate history of American girls*. New York: Random House.

Brusling, C. & Pepin, B. (2003). Introduction: Inclusion in Schools: who is in need of what? *European Educational Research Journal, 2*(2), 197–202.

Bryant, A. L., Schulenberg, J. E., O'Malley, P. M., Bachman, J. G. & Johnston, L. D. (2003). How academic achievement, attitudes, and behaviors relate to the course of substance use during adolescence: A 6 year, multiwave national longitudinal study. *Journal of Research on Adolescence, 13*, 361–397.

Bryant, J. A., Sanders-Jackson, A. & Smallwood, A. M. K. (2006). IMing, text messaging, and adolescent social networks. *Journal of Computer-Mediated Communication. 11*(2), 577–592.

Buchanan, C. M. (2000). The impact of divorce on adjustment during adolescence. In R. D. Taylor & M. Weng (Eds.), Resilience across contexts: *Family, work, culture, and community*. Mahwah, NJ: Erlbaum.

Buckley, T. & Gottlieb, A. (1988). *Blood magic: The anthropology of menstruation*. Berkeley: University of California Press.

Budasz, R. (2007). Black guitar-players and early African-Iberian music in Portugal and Brazil. *Early Music*, *35*(1), 3–22.

Buffardi, L. E. & Campbell, W. K. (2008). Narcissism and social networking web sites. *Personality and Social Psychology Bulletin*, *34*(10), 1303–1314.

Bugental, D. B. & Grusec, J. E. (2006). Socialisation processes. In N. Eisenberg, W. Damon, & R. M. Lerner (Eds.), *Handbook of child psychology: Vol. 3. Social, emotional, and personality development* (6th ed., pp. 366–428, xxiv, 1128). Hoboken, NJ: John Wiley & Sons

Bulik, C. M., Berkman, N. D., Brownley, K. A., Sedway, J. A. & Lohr, K. N. (2007). Anorexia nervosa treatment: A systematic review of randomized controlled trials. *International Journal of Eating Disorders*, *40*(4), 310–320.

Bulley, D. (2008). 'Foreign' terror? London bombings, resistance and the failing state. *The British Journal of Politics & International Relations*, *10*(3), 379–394.

Bumpass, L. & Liu, H. H. (2000, March). Trends in cohabitation and implications for children's family contexts in the United States. *Population Studies*.

Bunting, L. & McAuley, C. (2004). Research review: Teenage pregnancy and parenthood: the role of fathers. *Child & Family Social Work*, *9*(3), 295–303.

Burbank, V. K. (1988). *Aboriginal adolescence: Maidenhood in an Australian community*. New Brunswick, NJ: Rutgers University Press.

Burdsey, D. (2007). Role with the punches: the construction and representation of Amir Khan as a role model for multi-ethnic Britain. *The Sociological Review*, *55*(3), 611–631.

Burgess, S., Johnston, R., Key, T., Propper, C. & Wilson, D. (2008). The transition of pupils from primary to secondary school in England. *Transactions of the Institute of British Geographers*, *33*(3), 388–403.

Burnett, P. (2002). Teacher praise and feedback and students' perceptions of the classroom environment. *Educational Psychology*, *22*(1), 5–16.

Burrow, A. L. & Finley, G. E. (2004). Transracial, same-race adoptions, and the need for multiple measures of adolescent adjustment. *American Journal of Orthopsychiatry*, *74*, 577–583.

Burrows, M., Baxter-Jones, M., Mirwald, R., Macdonald, H. & McKay, H. (2009). Bone mineral accrual across growth in a mixed-ethnic group of children: Are Asian children disadvantaged from an early age? *Calcified Tissue International*, *84*(5), 366–378.

Bush, J. E. & Ehrenberg, M. F. (2003). *A Journal of Divorce & Remarriage*, *39*, 1–35.

Buss, D. M. (2001). The strategies of human mating. In P. W. Sherman & J. Alcock (Eds.), *Exploring animal behavior: Readings from American Scientist* (3rd ed., pp. 240–251).

Buss, D. M. (1989). Sex differences in human mate preferences: Evolutionary hypothesis tested in 37 cultures. *Behavioral and Brain Sciences*, *12*, 1–49.

Bussey, K. & Bandura, A. (2004). Social cognitive theory of gender development and functioning. In A. H. Eagly, A. Beall, & R. Sternberg (Eds.). *The psychology of gender* (2nd ed., pp. 92–119) New York: Guilford

Buunk, A. P., Park, J. H. & Dubbs, S. L. (2008). Parent–offspring conflict in mate preferences. *Review of General Psychology*, *12*(1), 47–62.

Bynner, J. (2005). Rethinking the youth phase of the life-course: The case for emerging adulthood? *Journal of Youth Studies*, *8*(4), 367–384.

Byrnes, J. P. (2003). Factors predictive of mathematics achievement in White, Black, and Hispanic 12th graders. *Journal of Educational Psychology*, *95*, 316–326.

Byrnes, J. P., Miller, D. C. & Reynolds, M. (1999). Learning to make good decisions: A self-regulation perspective. *Child Development*, *70*, 1121–1140.

Calcaterra, V., Sampaolo, P., Klersy, C., Larizza, D., Alfei, A., Brizzi, V., Beneventi, F. & Cisternino, M. (2009). Utility of breast ultrasonography in the diagnostic workup of precocious puberty and proposal of a prognostic index for identifying girls with rapidly progressive central precocious puberty. *Ultrasound in Obstetrics and Gynecology*, *33*, 85–91.

Caldas, S. J. (2008). Changing bilingual self-perceptions from early adolescence to early adulthood: Empirical evidence from a mixed-methods case study. *Applied Linguistics*, *29*(2), 290–311

Caldwell, M. S., Rudolph, K. D., Troop-Gordon, W. & Kim, D.-Y. (2004). Reciprocal influences among relational self-views, social disengagement, and peer stress during early adolescence. *Child Development*, *75*(4), 1140–1154.

Calvete, E. & Cardeñoso, O. (2005). Gender differences in cognitive vulnerability to depression and behavior problems in adolescents. *Journal of Abnormal Child Psychology*, *33*, 179–192.

Campbell, E. R., Devries, H. M., Fikkert, L., Kraay, M. & Ruiz, J. N. (2007). *Trajectory of marital satisfaction through the empty-nest transition.* Paper presented at the annual meeting of the American Psychological Association, Washington, DC.

Capel, S., Zwozdiak-Myers, P. & Lawrence, J. (2004). Exchange of information about physical education to support the transition of pupils from primary and secondary school. *Educational Research*, *46*(3), 283–300.

Capellanus, A. (2010) *The art of courtly love (Records of Western Civilization Series)*. Columbia: Columbia University Press

Caplow, T., Bahr, H. D. M. & Chadwick, B. E. A. (1982). *Middletown families: Fifty years of change and continuity*. Minneapolis: University of Minnesota Press.

Carson, L. (2009). 'I am because we are:' collectivism as a foundational characteristic of African American college student identity and academic achievement. *Social Psychology of Education*, *12*(3), 327–344.

Carolan, M. T., Bagherinia, G., Juhari, R., Himelright, J. & Mouton-Sanders, M. (2000). Contemporary Muslim families: Research and practice. *Contemporary Family Therapy*, *22*(1), 67–79.

Carr, J. (2005). Stability and change in cognitive ability over the life span: a comparison of populations with and without Down's syndrome. *Journal of Intellectual Disability Research*, *49*(12), 915–928.

Carroll, A. (2002). At-risk and not at-risk adolescent girls in single-sex and mixed-sex school settings: An examination of their goals and reputations. *International Journal of Research & Method in Education*, *25*(2), 147–162.

Carroll, J. L. & Wolpe, P. R. (2005). *Sexuality now: Embracing diversity*. Pacific Grove, CA: Wadsworth.

Carroll, J. L. & Wolpe, P. R. (1996). *Sexuality and gender in society*. Reading, MA: Addison-Wesley.

Carroll, J. S., Padilla-Walker, L. M., Nelson, L. J., Olson, C. D., Barry, C. M., & Madsen, S. D. (2008) Generation XXX: Pornography acceptance and use among emerging adults. *Journal of Adolescent Research*, *23*(1), 6–30.

Carter, S. L. & Wheeler, J. J. (2007). Analysis of behavioural responding across multiple instructional conditions for a child with childhood disintegrative disorder. *Journal of Research in Special Educational Needs*, *7*(3), 137–141.

Cartwright, C. (2006). You want to know how it affected me? Young adults' perceptions of the impact of parental divorce. *Journal of Divorce & Remarriage*, *44*(3–4), 125–143.

Carver, K., Joyner, K. & Udry, J. R. (2003). National estimates of adolescent romantic relationships. In P. Florsheim (Ed.), *Adolescent romantic relations and sexual behaviour: Theory, research, and practical implications* (pp. 23–56). Mahwah, NJ: Lawrence Erlbaum.

Carver, P. R., Yunger, J. L. & Perry, D. G. (2003). Gender identity and adjustment in middle childhood. *Sex Roles*, *49*(3–4), 95–109.

Carver, V., Reinert, B., Range, L. M. & Campbell, C. (2003). Adolescents' attitudes and self-perceptions about anti-tobacco advocacy. *Health Education Research*, *18*(4), 453–460.

Case, A. & Deaton, A. S. (2005). *Broken down by work and sex: How our health declines in analyses in the economics of aging*. Chicago: University of Chicago Press.

Casey, B. J., Getz, S. & Galvan, A. (2008). The adolescent brain. *Developmental Review*, *28*(1), 62–77.

Cassen, R. & Kingdon, D. (2007). *Tackling low educational achievement*. York: Joseph Rowntree Foundation.

Castrucci, B. C., Gerlach, K. K., Kaufman, N. J. & Orleans, C. T. (2002). The association among adolescents' tobacco use, their beliefs and attitudes, and friends' and parents' opinions of smoking. *Maternal and Child Health Journal*, *6*(3), 159–167.

Cates, W. (1999). Chlamydial infections and the risk of ectopic pregnancy. *JAMA: Journal of the American Medical Association*, *281*, 117–118.

Catsambis, S. (2001). Expanding knowledge of parental involvement in children's secondary education: Connections with high school seniors' academic success. *Social Psychology of Education*, *5*(2), 149–177.

Cauffman, E. & Woolard, J. (2005). Crime, competence, and culpability: Adolescent judgment in the justice system. In

E. J. Jacobs & P. A. Klaczynski (Eds.), *The development of judgment and decision making in children and adolescents* (pp. 279–302). Mahwah, NJ: Erlbaum.

Cejka, M. A. & Eagly, A. H. (1999). Gender-stereotypic images of occupations correspond to the sex segregation of employment. *Personality and Social Psychology Bulletin*, *25*, 413–423.

Central Advisory Council for Education (England) (1963). *Half our future (The Newsom Report)*. London: HMSO.

Cesario, S. K. & Hughes, L. A. (2007). Precocious puberty: A comprehensive review of literature. *Journal of Obstetric, Gynecologic & Neonatal Nursing*, *36*(3), 263–274.

Chadwick, A., Glasson, J. & Lawton Smith, H. (2008). Employment growth in knowledge-intensive business services in Great Britain during the 1990s – variations at the regional and sub-regional level. *Local Economy*, *23*(1), 6–18.

Chambaz, C. (2001). Lone-parent families in Europe: A variety of economic and social circumstances. *Social Policy & Administration*, *35*(6), 658–671.

Chambers, D., van Loon, J. & Tincknell, E. (2004). Teachers' views of teenage sexual morality. *British Journal of Sociology of Education*, *25*(5), 563–576.

Chambers, J. R., Windschitl, P. D. & Suls, J. (2003). Egocentrism, event frequency, and comparative optimism: When what happens frequently is 'more likely to happen to me.' *Personality and Social Psychology Bulletin*, *29*(11), 1343–1356.

Chambers, R. A., Taylor, J. R. & Potenza, M. N. (2003). Developmental neurocircuitry of motivation in adolescence: A critical period of addiction vulnerability. *The American Journal of Psychiatry*, *160*(6), 1041–52.

Chan, Y. M. (2000). Self-esteem: A cross-cultural comparison of British-Chinese, White British and Hong Kong Chinese children. *Educational Psychology*, *20*(1), 59–74.

Chang, C-O., Chen, S-M. & Somerville, T. (2003). Economic and social status in household decision-making: Evidence relating to extended family mobility. *Urban Studies*, *40*(4), 733–746.

Chang, L. T. (2008). *Factory girls: From village to factory in changing China*. New York: Spiegel & Grau.

Chao, R. K. (2001). Extending research on the consequences of parenting style for Chinese Americans and European Americans. *Child Development*, *72*(6), 1832–1843.

Chao, R. & Tseng, V. (2002). Parenting of Asians. In M. H. Bornstein (Ed.), *Handbook of parenting, Vol. 4: Social conditions and applied parenting* (pp. 59–93). Mahwah, NJ: Erlbaum.

Charanji, A. (2008). Save the sisters. *New Statesman*, *137*(4888), 19.1.

Chaudhary, N. & Sharma, N. (2007). India. In J. J. Arnett (Ed.), *International encyclopedia of adolescence* (pp. 442–459). New York: Routledge.

Chaves, M. (2004). *Congregations in America*. Cambridge, Massachusetts: Harvard University Press.

Chen, C-Y., Dormitzer, C. M., Gutiérrez, U., Vittetoe, K., González, G. B. & Anthony, J. C. (2004). Research

Report: The adolescent behavioral repertoire as a context for drug exposure: behavioral autarcesis at play. *Addiction, 99*(7), 897–906.

Chen, X. & Chang, L. (2007). China. In J. J. Arnett (Ed.), *International encyclopedia of adolescence*. New York: Routledge.

Chen, X., Tyler, K. A., Whitbeck, L. B. & Hoyt, D. R. (2004). Early sexual abuse, street adversity, and drug use among female homeless and runaway adolescents in the Midwest. *Journal of Drug Issues, 34*, 1–21.

Chen, X-K., Wen, S. W., Fleming, N., Demissie, K., Rhoads, G. G. & Walker, M. (2007). Teenage pregnancy and adverse birth outcomes: a large population based retrospective cohort study. *International Journal of Epidemiology, 36*(2), 368–368.

Chen, Y-C. (2001). Chinese values, health and nursing. *Journal of Advanced Nursing, 36*(2), 270–273.

Cherlin, A. J. (1999). Going to extremes: Family structure, children's well-being, and social science. *Demography, 36*, 421–428.

Cherlin, A. J., Burton, L. M., Tera, R. & Purvin, D. M. (2004). The influence of physical and sexual abuse on marriage and cohabitation. *American Sociological Review, 69*, 768–789.

Cheung, A. H., Emslie, G. J. & Mayes, T. (2005). Review of the efficacy and safety of antidepressants in youth depression. *Journal of Child Psychology & Psychiatry, 46*, 735–754.

Cheung, A., Emslie, G. J. & Maynes, T. L. (2004). Efficacy and safety of antidepressants in youth depression. *Canadian Child & Adolescent Psychiatry Review, 13*, 98–104.

Chia, S. (2006). How peers mediate media influence on adolescents' sexual attitudes and sexual behavior. *Journal of Communication, 56*(3), 585–606.

Childs, S. (2006). The complicated relationship between sex, gender and the substantive representation of women. *The European Journal of Women's Studies, 13*(1), 7–21.

Chimisso, C. (2003) *Exploring European identities*. Milton Keynes: OUP.

Chinas, B. (1992). *The Isthmus Zapotecs: A matrifocal culture of Mexico*, 2nd ed. New York: Harcourt Brace Jovanovich College Publishers.

Chitty, C. (2004). *Education policy in Britain*. Basingstoke: Palgrave Macmillan.

Cho, G. J., Park, H. T., Shin, J. H., Hur, J. Y., Kim, Y. T., Kim, S. H., Lee, K. W. & Kim, T. (2010). Age at menarche in a Korean population: secular trends and influencing factors. *European Journal of Pediatrics, 169*(1), 89–94.

Choi, C. & Berger, R. (2009). Ethics of global Internet, community and fame addiction. *Journal of Business Ethics, 85*(2), 193–200.

Christoffersen, M. N. (2000). Growing up with unemployment: a study of parental unemployment and children's risk of abuse and neglect based on national longitudinal 1973 birth cohorts in Denmark. *Childhood, 7*(4), 421–438.

Christoffersen, M. N., Francis, B. & Soothill, K. (2003). An upbringing to violence? Identifying the likelihood of violent crime among the 1966 birth cohort in Denmark.

Journal of Forensic Psychiatry and Psychology, 14(2), 367–381.

Chung, K-H., Lee, H-C., Kao, S. & Lin, H-C. (2008). Urbanicity and methods of suicide: A nationwide population-based study. *Journal of Urban Health, 85*(1), 136–145.

Cillessen, A. H. N. & Rose, A. J. (2005). Understanding popularity in the peer system. *Current Directions in Psychological Science, 14*, 102–105.

Cinamon, R. H. (2006). Anticipated work-family conflict: Effects of gender, self-efficacy, and family background. *Career Development Quarterly, 54*(3), 202–215.

Cinnirella, F. (2008). Optimists or pessimists? A reconsideration of nutritional status in Britain, 1740–1865. *European Review of Economic History, 12*(3), 325–354.

Civic, D. (1999). The association between characteristics of dating relationships and condom use among heterosexual young adults. *AIDS Education and Prevention, 11*, 343–352.

Claes, M. (1998). Adolescents' closeness with parents, siblings, and friends in three countries: Canada, Belgium, and Italy. *Journal of Youth & Adolescence, 27*, 165–184.

Claes, M., Lacourse, E., Ercolani, A. P., Pierro, A., Leone, L. & Presaghi, F. (2005) Parenting, peer orientation, drug use, and antisocial behaviour in late adolescence: A cross-national study. *Journal of Youth and Adolescence, 34*(5), 401–411.

Claes, R. & Van de Ven, B. (2008). Determinants of older and younger workers' job satisfaction and organisational commitment in the contrasting labour markets of Belgium and Sweden. *Ageing and Society, 28*(8), 1093–1112.

Clark, M., Thompson, P. & Vialle, W. (2008). Examining the gender gap in educational outcomes in public education: Involving pre-service school counsellors and teachers in cross-cultural and interdisciplinary research. *International Journal for the Advancement of Counselling, 30*(1), 52–66.

Clawson, J. & Ganong, L. (2002). Adult stepchildren's obligations to older stepparents. *Journal of Family Nursing, 8*(1), 50–72.

Clay, A. (2003). Keepin' it real: Black youth, hip-hop culture, and black identity. *American Behavioural Scientist, 46*, 1346–1358.

Cleaves, D. H. & Latner, J. D. (2008). Evidence-based therapies for children and adolescents with eating disorders. In R. G. Steele, T. D. Elkin, & M. C. Roberts (Eds.), *Handbook of evidence-based therapies for children and adolescents: Bridging science and practice: Issues in clinical child psychology* (pp. 335–353). New York: Springer Science + Business Media.

Clifton, J. (1999). Gender and shame in Masaccio's *Expulsion from the Garden of Eden*. *Art History, 22*(5), 637–655.

Coats, S. & Smith, E. R. (1999). Perceptions of gender subtypes: Sensitivity to recent exemplar activation and in-group/out-group differences. *Personality and Social Psychology Bulletin, 25*(4), 515–526.

Coggans, N. (2006). Drug education and prevention: Has progress been made?. *Drugs: Education, Prevention & Policy, 13*(5), 417–422.

Cohan, C. L. & Kleinbaum, S. (2002). Toward a greater understanding of the cohabitation effect: Premarital cohabitation and marital communication. *Journal of Marriage & the Family*, *64*, 180–192.

Cohen, D., Gerardin, P., Mazet, P., Purper-Ouakil, D. & Flament, M. F. (2004). Pharmacological treatment of adolescent major depression. *Journal of Child and Adolescent Psychopharmacology 14*(1), 19–31.

Cohen, L., Manion, L. & Morrison, K. (2007). *Research Methods in Education* (6th Edition). London: Routledge.

Cohen, L. R. & Potter, L. B. (1999). Injuries and violence: Risk factors and opportunities. *Adolescent Medicine: State of the Art Reviews*, *10*, 125–135.

Cohen, M., Mansoor, D., Gagin, R. & Lorber, A. (2008). Perceived parenting style, self-esteem and psychological distress in adolescents with heart disease. *Psychology, Health & Medicine*, *13*(4), 381–388.

Cohn, D. (1999). Parents prize less a child's obedience. *Washington Post*, (Nov 24) p. A8.

Cokley, K. O. (2002). Ethnicity, gender, and academic self-concept: A preliminary examination of academic disidentification and implications for psychologists. *Cultural Diversity and Ethnic Minority Psychology*, *8*, 378–388.

Colby, A., Kohlberg, L., Gibbs, J. & Lieberman, M. (1983). A longitudinal study of moral judgment. *Monographs of the Society for Research in Child Development*, *48*.

Cole, D. A., Maxwell, S. E., Martin, J. M., Peeke, L. G., Seroczynski, A. D., Tram, J. M., Hoffman, K. B., Ruiz, M. D., Jacquez, F. & Maschman, T. (2001). The development of multiple domains of child and adolescent self-concept: A cohort sequential longitudinal design. *Child Development*, *72*(6), 1723–1746.

Cole, M. (1996). *Cultural psychology: A once and future discipline*. Cambridge, MA: Harvard University Press.

Coleman, L. & Testa, A. (2007). Sexual health knowledge, attitudes and behaviours among an ethnically diverse sample of young people in the UK. *Health Education Journal*, *66*(1), 68–81.

Coles, R. & Stokes, G. (1985). *Sex and the American teenager*. New York: Harper & Row.

Collins, W. A. & Laursen, B. (2004). Parent–adolescent relationships and influences. In R. M. Lerner & L. Steinberg (Eds.), *Handbook of adolescent psychology* (pp. 331–361). Hoboken, NJ: John Wiley & Sons.

Collins, W. A., Maccoby, E. E., Steinberg, L., Hetherington, E. M. & Bornstein, M. H. (2000). Contemporary research on parenting: The case for nature and nurture. *American Psychologist*, *55*, 218–232.

Collins, W. A. & Sroufe, L. A. (1999). Capacity for intimate relationships: A developmental construction. In W. Furman, B. B. Brown, & C. Feiring (Eds.), *The development of romantic relationships in adolescence* (pp. 125–147). New York: Cambridge University Press.

Colman, I., Murray, J., Abbott, R. A., Maughan, B., Kuh, D., Croudace, T. J. & Jones, P. B. (2009) Outcomes of conduct problems in adolescence: 40 year follow-up of national cohort. *BMJ (British Medical Journal)*, *338*(1), a2981–a2981.

Colom, R., Flores-Mendoza, C. & Rebollo, I. (2003). Working memory and intelligence. *Personality & Individual Differences*, *34*, 33–39.

Colpin, H., Vandemeulebroecke, L. & Ghesquie're, P. (2004). Supporting the educational career of children from divorced families: Parents' experiences and the role of the school. *British Journal of Sociology of Education*, *25*(3), 275–289.

Colson, I. (2004). 'Their churches are at home': the communication and definition of values in four aided Church of England secondary schools. *British Journal of Religious Education*, *26*(1), 73–83.

Comeau, N., Stewart, S. H. & Loba, P. (2001). The relations between trait anxiety, anxiety sensitivity, and sensation seeking to adolescents' motivations for alcohol, cigarette, and marijuana use. *Addictive Behaviors*, *26*, 803–825.

Compian, L., Gowen, L. K. & Hayward, C. (2004). Peripubertal girls' romantic and platonic involvement with boys: Association with body image and depression symptoms. *Journal of Research on Adolescence*, *14*(1), 23–47.

Condon, R. G. (1987). *Inuit youth: Growth and change in the Canadian Arctic*. New Brunswick, NJ: Rutgers University Press.

Coney, N. & Mackey, W. (1997) A re-examination of Gilligan's analysis of the female moral system. *Human Nature*, *8*(3), 247–273.

Conklin, H. M., Luciana, M., Hooper, C. J. & Yarger, R. S. (2007). Working memory performance in typically developing children and adolescents: Behavioural evidence of protracted frontal lobe development. *Developmental Neuropsychology*, *31*(1), 103–128.

Connolly, J., Craig, W., Goldberg, A. & Pepler, D. (2004). Mixed-gender groups, dating, and romantic relationships in early adolescence. *Journal of Research on Adolescence*, *14*, 185–207.

Connolly, J., Furman, W. & Konarski, R. (2000). The role of peers in the emergence of heterosexual romantic relationships in adolescence. *Child Development*, *71*, 1395–1408.

Connolly, J. & Goldberg, A. (1999). Romantic relationships in adolescence: The role of friends and peers in their emergence and development. In W. Furman, B. B. Brown, & C. Feiring (Eds.), *The development of romantic relationships in adolescence* (pp. 266–290). New York: Cambridge University Press.

Conroy, J. (2001). A very Scottish affair: Catholic education and the state. *Oxford Review of Education*, *27*(4), 543–558.

Constable, P. (2000, May 8). In Pakistan, women pay the price of 'honor.' *Washington Post*, pp. A1–A14.

Cookston, J., Braver, S., Griffin, W., Delusé, S. & Miles, J. (2007). Effects of the dads for Life intervention on interparental conflict and coparenting in the two years after divorce. *Family Process*, *46*(1), 123–137.

Cooper, L. (2008). On the other side: supporting sexual minority students. *British Journal of Guidance & Counselling*, *36*(4), 425–440.

Cooper, M. L., Albino, A. W., Orcutt, H. K. & Williams, N. (2004). Attachment styles and intrapersonal adjustment: A longitudinal study from adolescence into young adulthood. In S. W. Rholes & J. A. Simpson (Eds.), *Adult attachment: Theory, research, and clinical implications* (pp. 438–466). New York: Guilford.

Cooper, M. L., Bede, A. V. & Powers, A. M. (1999). Motivations for condom use: Do pregnancy prevention goals undermine disease prevention among heterosexual young adults? *Health Psychology, 18*, 464–474.

Cooper, M. L., Wood, P. K., Orcutt, H. K. & Albino, A. (2003). Personality and the predisposition to engage in risky or problem behaviors during adolescence. *Journal of Personality & Social Psychology, 84*, 390–410.

Cope-Farrar, K. & Kunkel, D. (2002). Sexual messages in teens' favorite prime-time television programs. In J. D. Brown, J. R. Steele, & K. Walsh-Childers (Eds.), *Sexual teens, sexual media: Investigating media's influence on adolescent sexuality* (pp. 59–78). Mahwah, NJ: Erlbaum.

Corrado, S. P., Patashnick, B. S. & Rich, M. (2004). Factors affecting change among obese adolescents. *Journal of Adolescent Health, 23*, 112–120.

Costello, D. M., Swendsen, J., Rose, J. S. & Dierker, L. C. (2008). Risk and protective factors associated with trajectories of depressed mood from adolescence to early adulthood. *Journal of Consulting and Clinical Psychology, 76*(2), 173–183.

Cota-Robles, S., Neiss, M. & Hunt, C. B. (2000, April). *Future selves, future scholars: A longitudinal study of adolescent 'possible selves' and adult outcomes*. Poster presented at the biennial meeting of the Society for Research on Adolescence, Chicago.

Côté, J. (2006). Emerging adulthood as an institutionalized moratorium: Risks and benefits to identity formation. In J. J. Arnett and J. L. Tanner (Eds.), *Emerging adults in America: Coming of age in the 21st century* (pp. 85–116). Washington, DC: American Psychological Association Press.

Coté, J. (2000). *Arrested adulthood: The changing nature of maturity and identity in the late modern world*. New York: New York University Press.

Cotgrove, M. (2009). *From jazz funk & fusion to acid jazz: The history of the UK jazz dance scene*. Milton Keynes: Authorhouse.

Cotter, D. A., Hermsen, J. M., Kendig, S. M. & Vanneman, R. (2009) *The end of the U.S. gender revolution: Changing attitudes from 1974 to 2004*. Paper presented at the annual meeting of the American Sociological Association, Montreal, Canada. Retrieved August 21, 2009, from http://www.allacademic.com/meta/p103486_index.html

Council for Scientific Policy (1968). *Inquiry into the flow of candidates into science and technology in Higher Education (the Dainton report)*. London: HMSO.

Cowan, N., Saults, J. S. & Elliot, E. M. (2002). The search for what is fundamental in the development of working memory. In R. V. Kail & H. W. Reese (Eds.), *Advances in child development and behaviour* 29, pp. 1–49. San Diego, CA: Academic Press.

Coyne, S. M., Archer, J. & Eslea, M. (2006). 'We're not friends anymore! Unless...': The frequency and harmfulness of indirect, relational and social aggression. *Aggressive Behaviour, 32*(4), 294–307.

CQC (Care Quality Commission) (2010). *Count me in, Results of the 2009 national census of inpatients on supervised community treatment in mental health and learning disability services in England and Wales*. London: Care Quality Commission.

Craig, L.L.C. (2007). Is there really a second shift, and if so, who does it? A time-diary investigation. *Feminist Review, 86*(1), 149–170.

Crawford, M. & Popp, D. (2003). Sexual double standards: A review and methodological critique of two decades of research. *Journal of Sex Research, 40*, 13–26.

Crawford, S., Channon, S. & Robertson, M. M. (2005). Tourette's syndrome: performance on tests of behavioural inhibition, working memory and gambling. *Journal of Child Psychology and Psychiatry* (formerly *Journal of Child Psychology and Psychiatry and Allied Disciplines*), *46*(12), 1327–1336.

Creasey, G. & Hesson-McInnis, M. (2001). Affective responses, cognitive appraisals, and conflict tactics in late adolescent romantic relationships: Associations with attachment orientations. *Journal of Counseling Psychology, 48*, 85–96.

Crick, N. R. & Rose, A. J. (2000). Toward a gender-balanced approach to the study of social-emotional development: A look at relational aggression. In P. H. Miller & E. K. Scholnick (Eds.), *Toward a feminist developmental psychology* (pp. 153–168). New York: Routledge.

Crocker, J., Sommers, S. R. & Luhtanen, R. K. (2002). Hopes dashed and dreams fulfilled: Contingencies of self-worth and graduate school admissions. *Personality and Social Psychology Bulletin, 28*(9),1275–1286.

Crockett, L., Brown, J., Iturbide, M., Russell, S. & Wilkinson-Lee, A. (2009). Conceptions of good parent–adolescent relationships among Cuban American teenagers. *Sex Roles, 60*(7–8), 575–587.

Crockett, L. J., Rafaelli, M. & Moilanen, K. L. (2003). Adolescent sexuality: Behavior and meaning. In G. Adams & M. Berzonsky (Eds.), *Blackwell handbook of adolescence* (pp. 371–392). Malden, MA: Blackwell.

Croizet, J-C., Després, G. Gauzins, M-E., Huguet, P., Leyens, J-P. & Méot, A. (2004). Stereotype threat undermines intellectual performance by triggering a disruptive mental load. *Personality and Social Psychology Bulletin, 30*(6), 721–731.

Crone, E. A., Wendelken, C., Donohue, S., van Leijenhorst, S. L. & Bunge, S. A. (2006) Neurocognitive development of the ability to manipulate information in working memory. *Proceedings of the National Academy of Sciences of the United States of America, 103*(24), 9315–9320.

Crosnoe, R., Cavanagh, S. & Elder G. H., Jr. (2003). Adolescent friendships as academic resources: The intersection of friendship, race, and school disadvantage. *Sociological Perspectives, 46*, 331–352.

Crosnoe, R., Erickson, K. G. & Dornbusch, S. M. (2002). Protective functions of family relationships and school factors on the deviant behavior of adolescent boys and girls: Reducing the impact of risky friendships. *Youth & Society*, *33*(4), 515–544.

Cross, J. & Fletcher, K. (2009). The challenge of adolescent crowd research: Defining the crowd. *Journal of Youth and Adolescence*, *38*(6), 747–764.

Cross, S. E. & Gore, J. S. (2003). Cultural models of the self. In E. S. Cross., S. J. Gore, & R. M. Leary (Eds.), *Handbook of self and identity* (pp. 536–564). New York: Guilford Press.

Crouter, A. C. & Booth, A. (Eds.) (2003). *Children's influence on family dynamics: The neglected side of family relationships*. Mahwah, NJ: Lawrence Erlbaum.

Crouter, A. C., Manke, B. A. & McHale, S. M. (1995). The family context of gender intensification in early adolescence. *Child Development*, *66*, 317–329.

Crouter, A. C. & McHale, S. M. (2005). The long arm of the job revisited: Parenting in dual-earner families. In T. Luster & L. Okagaki (Eds.). *Parenting: An ecological perspective* (2nd ed., pp. 275–296). *Monographs in parenting*. Mahwah, NJ: Lawrence Erlbaum.

Crow, S. J., Mitchell, J. E., Roerig, J. D. & Steffen, K. (2009). What potential role is there for medication treatment in anorexia nervosa? *International Journal of Eating Disorders*, *42*(1), 1–8.

Crozier, G. & Davies, J. (2006). Family matters: A discussion of the Bangladeshi and Pakistani extended family and community in supporting the children's education. *The Sociological Review*, *54*(4), 678–695.

Crozier, W. R., Rees, V., Morris-Beattie, A. & Bellin, W. (1999). Streaming, self-esteem and friendships within a comprehensive school. *Educational Psychology in Practice*, *15*(2), 128–134.

Csikszentmihalyi, M. & Larson, R. W. (1986). *Being adolescent: Conflict and growth in the teenage years*. New York: Basic Books.

Cuffel, A. (2005). From practice to polemic: shared saints and festivals as 'women's religion' in the medieval Mediterranean. *Bulletin of the School of Oriental and African Studies*, *68*(3), 401–419.

Cui, M., Fincham, F. D. & Pasley, B. K. (2008). Young adult romantic relationships: The role of parents' marital problems and relationship efficacy. *Personality and Social Psychology Bulletin*, *34*(9), 1226–1235.

Cukrowicz, K. C., Taylor, J., Schatschneider, C. & Iacono, W. G. (2006). Personality differences in children and adolescents with attention-deficit/hyperactivity disorder, conduct disorder, and controls. *Journal of Child Psychology and Psychiatry* (formerly *Journal of Child Psychology and Psychiatry and Allied Disciplines*), *47*(2), 151–159.

Cullen, D. & Gotell, L. (2002). From orgasms to organizations: Maslow, women's sexuality and the gendered foundations of the needs hierarchy. *Gender, Work and Organization*, *9*(5), 537–555.

Cunningham, M. & Thornton, A. (2007). Direct and indirect influences of parents' marital instability on children's attitudes toward cohabitation in young adulthood. *Journal of Divorce & Remarriage*, *46*(3–4), 125–143.

Currie, D. (2001). Dear Abby: Advice pages as a site for the operation of power. *Feminist Theory*, *2*(3), 259–281.

Currie, D. (1999). *Girl talk: Adolescent magazines and their readers*. Toronto, Canada: University of Toronto Press.

Currie, D., Kelly, D. & Pomerantz, S. (2006). 'The geeks shall inherit the earth': Girls' agency, subjectivity and empowerment. *Journal of Youth Studies*, *9*(4), 419–436.

Curry, J. F. & Reinecke, M. A. (2003). Modular therapy for adolescents with major depression. In A. M. Reinecke., M. F. Dattilio., et al. (Eds.), *Cognitive therapy with children and adolescents: A casebook for clinical practice* (2nd ed., pp. 95–128). New York: Guilford Press.

Curtis, B. & Hunt, A. (2007). The fellatio 'epidemic': Age relations and access to the erotic arts. *Sexualities*, *10*(1), 5–28.

Cutting, A. L. & Dunn, J. (2006). Conversations with siblings and with friends: Links between relationship quality and social understanding. *British Journal of Developmental Psychology*, *24*(1), 73–87.

Cyr, M., Wright, J., McDuff, P. & Perron, A. (2002). Intrafamilial sexual abuse: Brother-sister incest does not differ from father-daughter and stepfather-stepdaughter incest. *Child Abuse & Neglect*, *26*, 957–973.

Cyranowski, J. M., Frank, E., Young, E. & Shear, M. K. (2003). Adolescent onset of the gender difference in lifetime rates of major depression: A theoretical model. In E. M. Hertzig & A. E. Farber (Eds.), *Annual progress in child psychiatry and child development: 2000–2001* (pp. 383–398). New York: Brunner-Routledge.

Czudková, L. & Musilová, J. (2000). The pendulum: A stumbling block of secondary school mechanics. *Physics Education*, *35*(6), 428–435.

Dabic, S. (2008) The alchemy of learning and work: Negotiating learner knowledge in a global society. *International Journal of Lifelong Education*, *27*(6), 613–624.

Dadds, M., Hunter, K., Hawes, D., Frost, A., Vassallo, S., Bunn, P., Merz, S. & Masry, Y. (2008). A measure of cognitive and affective empathy in children using parent ratings. *Child Psychiatry and Human Development*, *39*(2), 111–122.

Dale, A., Fieldhouse, E., Shaheen, N. & Kalra, V. (2002). The labour market prospects for Pakistani and Bangladeshi women. *Work, Employment & Society*, *16*(1), 5–25.

Daley, A. (2008). Exercise and primary dysmenorrhoea: A comprehensive and critical review of the literature. *Sports Medicine*, *38*(8), 659–670.

Dalheim-Englund, A-C., Rydström, I., Rasmussen, B. H., Möller, C. & Sandman, P-O. (2004). Involving parents and families in clinical nursing. Having a child with asthma – quality of life for Swedish parents. *Journal of Clinical Nursing*, *13*(3), 386–395.

Daly, B., Shin, R., Thakral, C., Selders, M. & Vera, E. (2009). School engagement among urban adolescents of color: Does perception of social support and neighborhood safety really matter? *Journal of Youth and Adolescence*, *38*(1), 63–74.

Dandy, J. & Nettelbeck, T. (2002). The relationship between IQ, homework, aspirations and academic achievement for Chinese, Vietnamese and Anglo-Celtic Australian school children. *Educational Psychology*, *22*(3), 267–275.

Daniels, D., Dunn, J. Furstenberg, F., Jr. & Plomin, R. (1985). Environmental differences within the family and adjustment differences within pairs of adolescent siblings. *Child Development*, *56*, 764–774.

Daniels, H., Cole, M. & Wertsch, J. V. (Eds.) (2007). *The Cambridge companion to Vygotsky.* New York: Cambridge University Press.

Darling, N., Cumsille, P. & Martínez, M. L. (2008). Individual differences in adolescents' beliefs about the legitimacy of parental authority and their own obligation to obey: A longitudinal investigation. *Child Development*, *79*(4), 1103–1118.

Darlington, Y. (2001). 'When all is said and done': The impact of parental divorce and contested custody on young adults' relationships with their parents and their attitudes to relationships and marriage. *Journal of Divorce & Remarriage*, *35*, 23–42.

Darroch, J. E., Landry, D. J. & Oslak, S. (1999). Age differences between sexual partners in the United States. *Family Planning Perspectives*, *31*, 160–167.

Das, D., Dharwadkar, R. & Brandes, P. (2008). The importance of being 'Indian': Identity centrality and work outcomes in an off-shored call center in India. *Human Relations*, *61*(11), 1499–1530.

Dashiff, C. (2001). Data collection with adolescents. *Journal of Advanced Nursing*, *33*(3), 343–9.

Dashiff, C., Vance, D., Abdullatif, H. & Wallander, J. (2009). Parenting, autonomy and self-care of adolescents with Type 1 diabetes. *Child: Care Health & Development*, *35*(1), 79–88,

Dauer, S. & Gomez, M. (2006). Violence against women and economic, social and cultural rights in Africa. *Human Rights Review*, *7*(2), 49–58.

D'Augelli, A. R. (2002). Mental health problems among lesbian, gay, and bisexual youths ages 14 to 21. *Clinical Child Psychology & Psychiatry*, *7*, 433–456.

D'Augelli, A. R., Grossman, A. H. & Starks, M. T. (2005). Parents' awareness of lesbian, gay, and bisexual youths' sexual orientation. *Journal of Marriage & the Family*, *67*, 474–482.

D'Augelli, A. R. & Patterson, C. J. (2002). *Lesbian, gay, and bisexual identities in youth: Psychological perspectives* (pp. 126–152).

Daurignac, E., Houdé, E. O. & Jouvent, R. (2006). Negative priming in a numerical Piaget-like task as evidenced by ERP. *Journal of Cognitive Neuroscience*, *18*(5), 730–736.

Davies, B., Davis, E., Cook, K. & Waters, E. (2008). Getting the complete picture: Combining parental and child data to identify the barriers to social inclusion for children living in low socio-economic areas. *Child: Care Health & Development*, *34*(2), 214–222.

Davies, H. D. & Fitzgerald, H. E. (Eds.) (2008). *Obesity in childhood and adolescence, Vol. 1: Medical, biological, and social issues.* New York: Praeger.

Davies, L. (2009). Educating against extremism: Towards a critical politicisation of young people. *International Review of Education/Internationale Zeitschrift für Erziehungswissenschaft/Revue internationale l'éducation*, *55*(2–3), 183–203.

Davies-Netzley, S. A. (2002). Gender-stereotypic images of occupations correspond to the sex-segregation of employment. In A. E. Hunter & C. Forden (Eds.), *Readings in the psychology of gender: Exploring our differences and commonalities* (pp. 281–299). Needham Heights, MA: Allyn & Bacon.

Daving, Y. D., Andrén, E. A., Nordholm, L. N. & Grimby, G. G. (2001). Reliability of an interview approach to the Functional Independence Measure. *Clinical Rehabilitation*, *15*(3), 301–310.

Davis, D., Shaver, P. R. & Vernon, M. L. (2003). Physical, emotional, and behavioural reactions to breaking up: The roles of gender, age, emotional involvement, and attachment style. *Personality & Social Psychology Bulletin*, *29*, 871–884.

Davis, H. & Lease, A. (2007). Perceived organizational structure for teacher liking: the role of peers' perceptions of teacher liking in teacher–student relationship quality, motivation, and achievement. *Social Psychology of Education*, *10*(4), 403–427.

Davis, J. (2006). The London drug scene and the making of drug policy, 1965–73. *Twentieth Century British History*, *17*(1), 26–49.

Davis, J. (1988). Mazel tov: The bar mitzvah as a multigenerational ritual of change and continuity. In E. Imber-Black & J. Roberts (Eds.), *Rituals in families and family therapy*. New York: Norton.

Davis, L. & Stewart, R. (1997, July). *Building capacity for working with lesbian, gay, bisexual, and transgender youth*. Paper presented at the conference on Working with America's Youth, Pittsburgh, PA.

Davis, S. S. & Davis, D. A. (2007). Morocco. In J. J. Arnett, R. Ahmed, B. Nsamenang, T. S. Saraswathi, & R. Silbereisen (Eds.), *International encyclopedia of adolescence*. New York: Routledge.

Davis, S. S. & Davis, D. A. (1995). 'The mosque and the satellite': Media and adolescence in a Moroccan town. *Journal of Youth & Adolescence*, *24*, 577–594.

Davis, S. S. & Davis, D. A. (1989). *Adolescence in a Moroccan town*. New Brunswick, NJ: Rutgers.

Davran, M., Ocak, S. & Secer, A. (2009). An analysis of socio-economic and environmental sustainability of goat production in the Taurus Mountain Villages in the Eastern Mediterranean Region of Turkey, with consideration of gender roles. *Tropical Animal Health and Production*, *41*(7), 1151–1155.

Dawes, G. (2002). Figure eights, spin outs and power slides: Aboriginal and Torres Strait Islander youth and the culture of joyriding. *Journal of Youth Studies*, *5*(2), 195–208.

DCSF (Department for Children, Schools and Families) (2007). NEET Statistics Quarterly brief. http://www.education.gov.uk (accessed 27 February 2012).

de Bildt, A., Sytema, S., Kraijer, D., Sparrow, S. & Minderaa, R. (2005). Adaptive functioning and behaviour problems in relation to level of education in children and adolescents with intellectual disability. *Journal of Intellectual Disability Research*, *49*(9), 672–681.

de Bruin, A. K., Woertman, L., Bakker, F. & Oudejans, R. (2009). Weight-related sport motives and girls' body image, weight control behaviors, and self-esteem. *Sex Roles*, *60*(9–10), 628–641.

de Bruin, E., Verheij, F. & Ferdinand, R. (2006). WISC-R subtest but no overall VIQ–PIQ difference in Dutch children with PDD-NOS. *Journal of Abnormal Child Psychology*, *34*(2), 254–262.

de Bruyn, E. H. & Cillessen, A. H. N. (2006). Popularity in early adolescence: Prosocial and antisocial subtypes. *Journal of Adolescent Research*, *21*(6), 607–627.

De Fraine, B., Van Damme, J., Van Landeghem, G., Opdenakker, M-C. & Onghena, P. (2003). The effect of schools and classes on language achievement. *British Educational Research Journal*, *29*(6), 841–859.

DeGennaro, D. & Brown, T. (2009). Youth voices: Connections between history, enacted culture and identity in a digital divide initiative. *Cultural Studies of Science Education*, *4*(1), 13–39.

De Goede, I., Branje, S. & Meeus, W. (2009). Developmental changes in adolescents' perceptions of relationships with their parents. *Journal of Youth and Adolescence*, *38*(1), 75–88.

de Graaf, H., Vanwesenbeeck, I., Meijer, S., Woertman, L. & Meeus, W. (2009). Sexual trajectories during adolescence: Relation to demographic characteristics and sexual risk. *Archives of Sexual Behavior*, *38*(2), 276–282.

De Groof, S. (2008). And my Mama said: The (relative) parental influence on fear of crime among adolescent girls and boys. *Youth & Society*, *39*(3), 267–293.

De Guzman, M. R. T. (2006). Understanding the physical changes of puberty. *Adolescent Worlds Newsletter*, Lincoln, NE: University of Nebraska–Lincoln.

de las Fuentes, C. & Vasquez, M. J. T. (1999). Immigrant adolescent girls of color: Facing American challenges. In N. B. Johnson, M. C. Roberts, & J. Worell (Eds.), *Beyond appearance: A new look at adolescent girls* (pp. 131–150). Washington, DC: American Psychological Association.

De Li, S. (2004). The impacts of self-control and social bonds on juvenile delinquency in a national sample of mid-adolescents. *Deviant Behavior*, *25*, 351–373.

De Lisi, R. (2005). A lifetime of work using a developmental theory to enhance the lives of children and adolescents. *Journal of Applied Developmental Psychology*, *26*, 107–110.

DeLoache, J. & Gottlieb, A. (2000). *A world of babies: Imagined childcare guides for seven societies*. New York: Cambridge University Press.

De Mey, L., Baartman, H. M. & Schultze, H. J. (1999). Ethnic variation and the development of moral judgment of youth in Dutch society. *Youth & Society*, *31*, 54–75.

De Ridder, I., Vangehuchten, L. & Seseña Gómez, M. (2007). Enhancing automaticity through task-based language learning. *Applied Linguistics*, *28*(2), 309–315.

Dean, B. B., Borenstein, J. E., Knight, K. & Yonkers, K. (2006). Evaluating the criteria used for identification of PMS. *Journal of Women's Health*, *15*(5), 546–555.

Deets, S. (2006). Reimagining the boundaries of the nation: Politics and the development of ideas on minority rights. *East European Politics and Societies*, *20*(3), 419–446.

Dekel, R., Peled, E. & Spiro, S. E. (2003). Shelters for houseless youth: A follow-up evaluation. *Journal of Adolescence*, *26*, 201–212.

Delaney, K. (2006). Following the affect: Learning to observe emotional regulation. *Journal of Child and Adolescent Psychiatric Nursing*, *19*(4), 175–181.

Delsing, M. J. M. H., ter Bogt, T. F. M., Engels, R. C. M. E. & Meeus, W. H. J. (2007). Adolescents' peer crowd identification in the Netherlands: Structure and associations with problem behaviours. *Journal of Research on Adolescence*, *17*(2), 467–480.

Demers. J. (2006). Dancing machines: 'Dance Dance Revolution', cybernetic dance, and musical taste. *Popular Music*, *25*(3), pp. 401–414.

Demir, A. & Tarhan, N. (2001). Loneliness and social dissatisfaction in Turkish adolescents. *Journal of Psychology*, *135*, 113–123.

Demorest, A., Meyer, C., Phelps, E., Gardner, H. & Winner, E. (1984). Words speak louder than actions: Understanding deliberately false remarks. *Child Development*, *55*, 1527–1534.

Denner, J. & Dunbar, N. (2004). Negotiating femininity: Power and strategies of Mexican American girls. *Sex Roles*, *50*, 301–314.

Denner, J. & Guzman, B. L. (Eds.) (2006). *Latina girls: Voices of adolescent strength in the United States*. New York: New York University Press.

Department for Education and Skills (DES) (2006). *Ethnicity and education: The evidence on minority ethnic pupils aged 5–16*. Nottingham: DES

(DfES) Department for Education and Skills (2003). *Every child matters*. London: TSO.

Der, G. & Deary, I. J. (2006). Age and sex differences in reaction time in adulthood: Results from the United Kingdom Health and Lifestyle Survey. *Psychology and Aging*, *21*(1), 62–73.

DeRose, L. M. & Brooks-Gunn, J. (2006). Transition into adolescence: The role of pubertal processes. In L. Balter & C. S. Tamis-LeMonda (Eds.), *Child psychology: A handbook of contemporary issues* (2nd ed., pp. 385–414). New York: Psychology Press.

Desmairis, S. & Curtis, J. (1999). Gender differences in employment and income experiences among young people. In J. Barling & E. K. Kelloway (Eds.), *Youth workers: Varieties of experience* (pp. 59–88). Washington, DC: American Psychological Association.

Dey, E. L. & Hurtado, S. (1999). Students, colleges, and society: Considering the interconnections. In P. G. Altbach, R. O. Berndahl, & P. J. Gumport (Eds.), *American higher education in the twenty-first century: Social, political, and economic challenges* (pp. 298–322). Baltimore: Johns Hopkins University Press.

DFE (Department for Education) (2011). *NEET statistics Quarterly Brief February 2011* http://www.education.gov.uk/rsgateway/DB/STR/d000987/osr05–2011.pdf London, DfE

DFT (Department for Transport) (2010). *Reported road casualties Great Britain main results: 2009* accessed 21.01.2011 at http://www.dft.gov.uk/pgr/statistics/

Diamond, L. M. (2008). Female bisexuality from adolescence to adulthood: Results from a 10-year longitudinal study 2008. *Journal of Personality and Social Psychology 44*(1), 5–14.

Diamond, S., Schensul, J., Snyder, L., Bermudez, A., D'Alessandro, N. & Morgan, D. (2009). Building Xperience: A multilevel alcohol and drug prevention intervention. *American Journal of Community Psychology, 43*(3–4), 292–312.

Dickson, K., Emerson, E. & Hatton, C. (2005). Self-reported anti-social behaviour: prevalence and risk factors amongst adolescents with and without intellectual disability. *Journal of Intellectual Disability Research, 49*(11), 820–826.

Dijkstra, J. K., Lindenberg, S. & Veenstra, R. (2008). Beyond the class norm: Bullying behaviour of popular adolescents and its relation to peer acceptance and rejection. *Journal of Abnormal Child Psychology, 36*(8), 1289–1299.

Dillen, A. (2007). Religious participation of children as active subjects: toward a hermeneutical-communicative model of religious education in families with young children. *International Journal of Children's Spirituality, 12*(1), 37–49.

Dillen, L., Fontaine, J. & Verhofstadt-Deneve, L. (2009). Confirming the distinctiveness of complicated grief from depression and anxiety among adolescents. *Death Studies, 33*(5), 437–461.

Dishion, T. J. & Dodge, K. A. (2005). Peer contagion in interventions for children and adolescents: Moving towards an understanding of the ecology and dynamics of change. *Journal of Abnormal Child Psychology, 33*, 395–400.

Dishion, T. J., Dodge, K. A. & Lansford, J. E. (2006). Findings and recommendations: A blueprint to minimize deviant peer influence in youth interventions and programs. In K. A. Dodge, T. J. Dishion, & J. E. Lansford (Eds.), *Deviant peer influences in programs for youth: Problems and solutions* (pp. 366–394). New York: Guilford Press.

Dishion, T. J., McCord, J. & Poulin, F. (1999). When interventions harm: Groups and problem behavior. *American Psychologist, 54*, 755–764.

Dishion, T. J., Nelson, S. E. & Kavanagh, K. (2003). The family check-up with high-risk young adolescents: Preventing early-onset substance use by parent monitoring. *Behavior Therapy, 34*, 553–571.

Dishion, T. J. & Patterson, G. R. (2006). The development and ecology of antisocial behavior in children and adolescents. In D. Cicchetti & D. J. Cohen (Eds.), *Developmental psychopathology, Vol. 3: Risk, disorder, and adaptation* (2nd ed., pp. 503–541). Hoboken, NJ: John Wiley & Sons.

Dishion, T. J., Piehler, T. F. & Myers, M. W. (2008). Dynamics and ecology of adolescent peer influence. In M. J. Prinstein & K. A. Dodge (Eds.), *Understanding peer influence in children and adolescence: Duke series in child development and public policy* (pp. 72–93). New York: Guilford Press.

DiTommaso, E. & Spinner, B. (1997). Social and emotional loneliness: A re-examination of Weiss' typology of loneliness. *Personality and Individual Differences, 22*, 417–427.

Dittus, P. & Jaccard, J. (2000). Adolescents' perceptions of maternal disapproval of sex: Relationship to sexual outcomes. *Journal of Adolescent Health, 26*, 268–278.

Dobson, M. J. (2008). *Disease: The extraordinary stories behind history's deadliest killers*. London: Quercus Publishing Plc.

Docter, R. F. & Fleming, J. S. (2001). Measures of transgender behavior. *Archives of Sexual Behavior, 30*(3), 255–271.

Dodge, K. A., Lansford, J. E., Burks, V. S., Bates, J. E., Pettit, G. S., Fontaine, R. P. & Joseph M. (2003). Peer rejection and social information-processing factors in the development of aggressive behaviour problems in children. *Child Development, 74*, 374–393.

Doherty, J. & Hughes, M. (2009). *Child development theory and practice 0–11*. Harlow, England: Pearson Education.

Donald, T. & Jureidini, J. (2004). Parenting capacity. *Child Abuse Review, 13*(1), 5–17.

Donaldson, D., Spirito, A. & Overholser, J. (2003). In A. Spirito & J. C. Overholser (Eds.), *Evaluating and treating adolescent suicide attempters: From research to practice.* (pp. 295–321). San Diego, CA: Academic Press.

Donfield, S. M., Lynn, H. S., Lail, A. E., Hoots, W. K., Berntorp, E. & Gomperts, E. D. (2007). Delays in maturation among adolescents with hemophilia and a history of inhibitors. *Blood, 110*(10), 3656–3661.

Donnellan, M. B., Trzesniewski, K. H., Robins, R. W., Moffitt, T. E. & Caspi, A. (2005). Low self-esteem is related to aggression, antisocial behavior, and delinquency. *Psychological Science, 16*, 328–335.

Donohue, R. (2007). Examining career persistence and career change intent using the career attitudes and strategies inventory. *Journal of Vocational Behavior, 70*(2), 259–276.

Dooley, D., Prause, J. & Ham-Rowbottom, K. A. (2000). Underemployment and depression: Longitudinal relationships. *Journal of Health and Social Behavior, 41*, 421–436.

Dorey, E. & McCool, J. (2009). The role of the media in influencing children's nutritional perceptions. *Qualitative Health Research, 19*(5), 645–654.

Dorn, L. D., Kolko, D., Huang, B., Susman, E. J. & Burkstein, O. (2009). Salivary gonadal and adrenal hormone differences in boys and girls with and without disruptive behavior disorders: Contextual variants. *Biological Psychology, 80*, 31–39.

Dornbusch, S. M., Carlsmith, J. M., Gross, R. T., Martin, J. A., Jennings, D., Rosenberg, A. & Duke, P. (1981). Sexual development, age, and dating: A comparison of biological and social influences upon one set of behaviors. *Child Development, 52*, 179–185.

dos Santos Silva, I., de Stavola, B.L., Mann, V., Kuh, D., Hardy, R. & Wadsworth, M.E. (2002). Prenatal factors, childhood growth trajectories and age at menarche. *International Journal of Epidemiology, 31*(2), 405–412.

Douglas, G. & Ferguson, N. (2003). The role of grandparents in divorced families. *International Journal of Law, Policy and the Family, 17*(1), 41–67.

Douglass, C. B. (2007). From duty to desire: Emerging adulthood in Europe and its consequences. *Child Development Perspectives, 1*, 101–108.

Douglass, C. B. (2005). *Barren states: The population 'implosion' in Europe.* New York: Berg.

Dowda, M., Ainsworth, B. E., Addy, C. L., Saunders, R. & Riner, W. (2001). Environmental influences, physical activity, and weight status in 8 to 16 year-olds. *Archives of Pediatric and Adolescent Medicine, 155,* 711–717.

Dowling, E. & Gorell-Barnes, G. (1999). Children of divorcing families: A clinical perspective. *Clinical Child Psychology and Psychiatry, 4*(1), 39–50.

Downing, K., Ho, R., Shin, K., Vrijmoed, L. & Wong, E. (2007). Metacognitive development and moving away. *Educational Studies, 33*(1), 1–13.

Doyle, C. (2001). Surviving and coping with emotional abuse in childhood. *Clinical Child Psychology and Psychiatry, 6*(3), 387–402.

Draper, D. & Gittoes, M. (2004). Statistical analysis of performance indicators in UK higher education. *Journal of the Royal Statistical Society: Series A (Statistics in Society), 167*(3), 449–474.

Draucker, C. B. (2005). Interaction patterns of adolescents with depression and the important adults in their lives. *Qualitative Health Research, 15*(7), 942–963.

Driessen, G., Smit, F. & Sleegers, P. (2005). Parental involvement and educational achievement. *British Educational Research Journal, 31*(4), 509–532.

Dubas, J. S. & Petersen, A. C. (1996). Geographical distance from parents and adjustment during adolescence and young adulthood. *New Directions for Child and Adolescent Development, 71,* 3–19.

DuBois, D. L. (2003). Self-esteem, adolescence. In T. P. Gullotta & M. Bloom (Eds.) and T. P. Gullotta & G. Adams (Section Eds.), *Encyclopedia of primary prevention and health promotion* (pp. 953–961). New York: Kluwer Academic/Plenum.

DuBois, D. L., & Silverthorn, N. (2004). Do deviant peer associations mediate the contributions of self-esteem to problem behavior during early adolescence? A 2-year longitudinal study. *Journal of Clinical Child & Adolescent Psychology, 33,* 382–388.

DuBois, D. L. & Tevendale, H. D. (1999). Self-esteem in childhood and adolescence: Vaccine or epiphenomenon? *Applied & Preventive Psychology, 8,* 103–117.

Ducharme, J., Doyle, A. B. & Markiewicz, D. (2002). Attachment security with mother and father: Associations with adolescents' reports of interpersonal behaviour with parents and peers. *Journal of Social and Personal Relationships, 19,* 203–231.

Due, P., Holstein, B. E., Lunch, J., Diderichsen, F., Gabhain, S. N., Scheidt, P. & Currie, C. (2005). The health behaviour in school-aged children bullying working group. *European Journal of Public Health, 15*(2), 128–132.

Due, P., Lynch, J., Holstein, B. & Modvig, J. (2003). Socioeconomic health inequalities among a nationally representative sample of Danish adolescents: the role of different types of social relations. *Journal of Epidemiology & Community Health, 57*(9), 692–698.

Duke, L. (2002). Get real! Cultural relevance and resistance to the mediated feminine ideal. *Psychology & Marketing, 19,* 211–233.

Dumont, R. H. (2008). Drawing a family map: An experiential tool for engaging children in family therapy. *Journal of Family Therapy, 30*(3), 247–259.

Dunlop, R., Burns, A. & Bermingham, S. (2001). Parent–child relations and adolescent self-image following divorce: A 10 year study. *Journal of Youth and Adolescence, 30*(2), 117–134.

Dunphy, D. (1963). The social structure of urban adolescent peer groups. *Sociometry, 26,* 230–246.

Du Pasquier-Fediaevsky, L., Chwalow, A. J. & Tubiana-Rufi, N. (2005). Is the relationship between adherence behaviours and glycaemic control bi-directional at adolescence? A longitudinal cohort study. *Diabetic Medicine, 22*(4), 427–433.

Durante, C. (2009). Bioethics in a pluralistic society: Bioethical methodology in lieu of moral diversity. *Medicine, Health Care and Philosophy, 12*(1), 35–47.

Durden, T. (2008). Do your homework! Investigating the role of culturally relevant pedagogy in comprehensive school reform models serving diverse student populations. *The Urban Review, 40,* 403–419.

Durham, M. G. (2004). Constructing the 'new ethnicities': media, sexuality, and diaspora identity in the lives of South Asian immigrant girls. *Critical Studies in Media Communication, 21*(2), 140–161.

Durkin, K. & Conti-Ramsden, G. (2007). Language, social behavior, and the quality of friendships in adolescents with and without a history of specific language impairment. *Child Development, 78*(5), 1441–1457.

Dustmann, C. & Schoenberg, U. (2008). Why does the German apprenticeship system work? In K. U. Mayer & H. Solga (Eds.), *Skill information: Interdisciplinary and cross-national perspective* (p. 85–108). New York: Cambridge University Press.

Dustmann, C. & van Soest, A. (2007). Part-time work, school success and school leaving. *Empirical Economics, 32*(2–3), 277–299.

Duthie, J. K., Nippold, M. A., Billow, J. L. & Mansfield, T. C. (2008). Mental imagery of concrete proverbs: A developmental study of children, adolescents and adults. *Applied Psycholinguistics, 29*(1), 151–173.

Duvander, A. E. (1999). The transition from cohabitation to marriage: A longitudinal study of the propensity to marry in Sweden in the early 1990s. *Journal of Family Issues, 20,* 698–717.

Duyme, M., Dumaret, A. C. & Tomkiewicz, S. (1999). How can we boost IQs of 'dull children'?: A late adoption study. *Proceedings of the National Academy of Sciences of the United States of America, 96*(15), 8790–4.

Dworkin, J. B. & Larson, R. (2001). Age trends in the experience of family discord in single-mother families across adolescence. *Journal of Adolescence, 24,* 529–534.

Dwyer, C. (1999). Contradictions of community: questions of identity for young British Muslim women. *Environment and Planning A*, *31*(1), 53–68.

Dwyer, C., Shah, B. & Sanghera, G (2008). 'From cricket lover to terror suspect' – challenging representations of young British Muslim men. *Gender, Place and Culture: A Journal of Feminist Geography*, *15*(2), 117–136.

Dyck, V. & Daly, K. (2006). Rising to the challenge: Fathers' role in the negotiation of couple time. *Leisure Studies*, *25*(2), 201–217.

Eagly, A. H. (1987). *Sex differences in social behavior: A social-role interpretation*. Hillsdale, NJ: Erlbaum.

Eagly, A. H., Wood, W. & Johannesen-Schmidt, M. C. (2004). Social role theory of sex differences and similarities: Implications for the partner preferences of women and men. In A. H. Eagly, A. E. Beall, & R. A. Sternberg (Eds.), *The psychology of gender* (2nd ed., pp. 269–295). New York: Guilford Press.

Eastin, M., Greenberg, B. & Hofschire, L. (2006). Parenting the Internet. *Journal of Communication*, *56*(3), 486–504.

Eatwell, R. & Wright, A. (2003). *Contemporary political ideologies* (2nd ed.). London: Continuum.

Eaves, L., Silberg, J. & Erkanli, A. (2003). Resolving multiple epigenetic pathways to adolescent depression. *Journal of Child Psychology and Psychiatry* (formerly *Journal of Child Psychology and Psychiatry and Allied Disciplines*), *44*(7), 1006–1014.

Ebling, F. J. P. (2005). The neuroendocrine timing of puberty. *Reproduction*, *129*(6), 675–683.

Eccles, J. S., Lord, S. E., Roeser, R. W., Barber, B. L. & Hernandez Jozefowicz, D. M. (1997). The association of school transitions in early adolescence with developmental trajectories through high school. In J. Schulenberg, J. L. Maggs, & K. Hurrelmann (Eds.), *Health risks and developmental transitions during adolescence* (pp. 283–320). New York: Cambridge University Press.

Eccles, J. S. & Roeser, R. W. (2003). Schools as developmental contexts. In G. Adams & M. Berzonsky (Eds.), *Blackwell handbook of adolescence* (pp. 129–148). Malden, MA: Blackwell.

ECDC (European Centre for Disease Prevention and Control) (2005–2009). http://ecdc.europa.eu/en/healthtopics/ aids accessed 01.12.2010.

Edmonds, E. (2006). Understanding sibling differences in child labor. *Journal of Population Economics*, *19*(4), pp. 795–821.

Efrati-Virtzer, M. & Margalit, M. (2009). Students' behaviour difficulties, sense of coherence and adjustment at school: risk and protective factors. *European Journal of Special Needs Education*, *24*(1), 59–73.

Egeland, B. & Carlston, E. A. (2004). Attachment and psychopathology. In L. Atkinson & S. Goldberg (Eds.), *Attachment issues in psychopathology and intervention* (pp. 27–48). Mahwah, NJ: Erlbaum.

Eiðsdóttir, S. P., Kristjánsson, Á. L., Sigfúsdóttir, I. D. & Allegrante, J. P. (2008). Trends in physical activity and participation in sports clubs among Icelandic adolescents. *The European Journal of Public Health*, *18*(3), 289–289.

Eisenberg, N., Zhou, Q. & Koller, S. (2001). Brazilian adolescents' prosocial moral judgment and behaviour: Relations to sympathy, perspective taking, gender-role orientation, and demographic characteristics. *Child Development*, *72*, 518–534.

Eisenberger, R., Lynch, P., Aselage, J. & Rohdieck, S. (2004). Who takes the most revenge? Individual differences in negative reciprocity norm endorsement. *Personality and Social Psychology Bulletin*, *30*(6), 787–799.

Eisner, M. (2002). Crime, problem drinking, and drug use: Patterns of problem behavior in cross-national perspective. *Annals of the American Academy of Political and Social Science*, *580*, 201–225.

Elias, N. & Lemish, D. (2008). Media uses in immigrant families: Torn between 'inward' and 'outward' paths of integration. *International Communication Gazette*, *70*(1), 21–40.

Elkind, D. (2001). Cognitive development. In J. V. Lerner & R. M. Lerner (Eds.), *Adolescence in America: An encyclopedia*, (pp. 127–134). Santa Barbara, CA: ABC-CLIO.

Elkind, D. (1985). Egocentrism redux. *Developmental Review*, *5*, 218–226.

Elkind, D. (1978). Understanding the young adolescent. *Adolescence*, *13*, 127–134.

Elkind, D. (1967). Egocentrism in adolescence. *Child Development*, *38*, 1025–1034.

Elkins, I. J., McGue, M., Malone, S. & Iacono, W. G. (2004). The effect of parental alcohol and drug disorders on adolescent personality. *The American Journal of Psychiatry*, *161*(4), 670–6.

Elliott, J., Hufton, N., Illushin, L. & Willis, W. (2001). 'The Kids are Doing All Right': Differences in parental satisfaction, expectation and attribution in St Petersburg, Sunderland and Kentucky. *Cambridge Journal of Education*, *31*(2), 179–204.

Ellis, B. J. & Garber, J. (2000). Psychosocial antecedents of variation in girls' pubertal timing: Maternal depression, stepfather presence, and marital and family stress. *Child Development*, *71*, 485–501.

Embree, L. (2003). Aron Gurwitsch's Theory of Cultural-Scientific Phenomenological Psychology. *Husserl Studies*, *19*(1), 43–70.

Emery, R. E. (1999). *Marriage, divorce, and children's adjustment* (2nd ed.). Newbury Park, CA: Sage.

Emery, R. E., Sbarra, D. & Grover, T. (2005). Divorce mediation: Research and reflections. *Family Court Review*, *43*, 22–37.

Emslie, G. J., Heiligenstein, J. H. & Wagner, K. D. (2002). Fluoxetine for acute treatment of depression in children and adolescents: A placebo-controlled randomized clinical trial. *Journal of the American Academy of Child & Adolescent Psychiatry*, *41*, 1205–1214.

Emslie, G. J., Kennard, B. D., Mayes, T. L., Nightingale-Teresi, J., Carmody, T., Hughes, C. W., Rush, A. J., Tao,

R. & Rintelmann, J. W. (2008). Fluoxetine versus placebo in preventing relapse of major depression in children and adolescents. *The American Journal of Psychiatry*, *165*(4), 459–467.

Engeland, A., Bjorge, T., Tverdal, A. & Sogaard, A. J. (2004). Obesity in adolescence and adulthood and the risk of adult mortality. *Epidemiology*, *15*, 79–85.

Engels, R. C. M. E., Dekovic, M. & Meeus, W. (2002). Parenting practices, social skills, and peer relationships in adolescence. *Social Behaviour and Personality*, *30*, 3–18.

Engels, R. C. M. E., Finkenauer, C., Meeus, W. & Dekovic, M. (2001). Parental attachment and adolescents' emotional adjustment: The associations with social skills and relational competence. *Journal of Counseling Psychology*, *48*, 428–439.

Engström, I. & Norring, C. (2001). Risk for binge eating in a nonclinical Swedish adolescent sample: A repeated measure study. *European Eating Disorders Review: The Journal of the Eating Disorders Association*, *9*(6), 427–441.

Enyeart, J. (2003). Making men, making class: The YMCA and workingmen, 1877–1920. By Thomas Winter. Chicago: The University of Chicago Press, 2002. pp. vii, 208. *The Journal of Economic History*, *63*(1), 279–280.

Ephron, N. (2000). *Crazy Salad* (pp. 2–4). New York: Random House.

Erikson, E. H. (1968). *Identity: Youth and crisis*. New York: Norton.

Erikson, E. H. (1959). Identity and the life cycle. *Psychological Issues*, *1*, 1–171.

Erikson, E. H. (1958). *Young man Luther*. New York: Norton.

Erikson, E. H. (1950). *Childhood and society*. New York: Norton.

Ernst, J. & Monroe, M. (2004). The effects of environment-based education on students' critical thinking skills and disposition toward critical thinking. *Environmental Education Research*, *10*(4), 507–522.

Erol, A., Baylan, G. & Yazici, F. (2008). Do Ramadan fasting restrictions alter eating behaviours? *European Eating Disorders Review: The Journal of the Eating Disorders Association*, *16*(4), 297–301.

Esbensen, F-A., Deschenes, E. P. & Winfree Jr., L. T. (1999). Differences between gang girls and gang boys: Results from a multisite survey. *Youth & Society*, *31*(1), 27–53.

Escriche, L. (2007). Persistence of occupational segregation: The role of the intergenerational transmission of preferences. *The Economic Journal*, *117*(520), 837–857.

Eskin, M., Ertekin, K. & Demir, H. (2008). Efficacy of a problem-solving therapy for depression and suicide potential in adolescents and young adults. *Cognitive Therapy and Research*, *32*(2), 227–245.

Etaugh, C. A. & Bridges, J. S. (2006). Midlife transitions. In J. Worell, J. & C. D. Goodheart (Eds.), *Handbook of girls' and women's psychological health: Gender and well-being across the lifespan. Oxford series in clinical psychology* (pp. 359–367). Oxford: Oxford University Press.

European Commission Eurostat (2001). At http://appsso.eurostat.ec.europa.eu/nui/show.do accessed 19/09/2010.

Eurostat (2011). *Unemployment by sex, age groups and nationality* accessed 1 March 2011 at http://appsso.eurostat.ec.europa.eu/nui/show.do?dataset=lfsq_ugan&lang=en

Eurostat (2010). Population Divorces at http://epp.eurostat.ec.europa.eu accessed 23.09.2010.

Eurostat (2007). The narrowing education gap between women and men (160Kb PDF), *Statistics in Focus*, *Population and social conditions 130/2007*, Luxembourg, Office for Official Publications of the European Communities

Evans, E. D., Rutberg, J., Sather, C. & Turner, C. (1991). Content analysis of contemporary teen magazines for adolescent females. *Youth & Society*, *23*, 99–120.

Evans, H. (2005). The little emperor grows selfish. *New Statesman*, *134*(4719), 21–21.

Evans, J. St. B. T. (2008). Dual-processing accounts of reasoning, judgment, and social cognition. *Annual Review of Psychology*, *59*, 255–278.

Evans, W. D., Renaud, J. & Kamerow, D. (2006). News media coverage, body mass index, and public attitudes about obesity. *Social Marketing Quarterly*, *12*(4), 19–33.

Eveleth, P. B. & Tanner, J. M. (1990). *Worldwide variation in human growth. Cambridge*, MA: Cambridge University Press.

Eyal, K., Kunkel, D., Biely, E. N. & Finnerty, K. L. (2007). Sexual socialization messages on television programs most popular among teens. *Journal of Broadcasting & Electronic Media*, *51*(2), 316–336.

Eyre, S. L. & Millstein, S. G. (1999). What leads to sex? Adolescent preferred partners and reasons for sex. *Journal of Research on Adolescence*, *9*, 277–307.

Facio, A. & Micocci, F. (2003). Emerging adulthood in Argentina. In J. J. Arnett & N. Galambos (Eds.), *New Directions in Child and Adolescent Development, Vol. 100*, 21–31.

Fackler, M. (2007). As Japan ages, universities struggle to fill classrooms. *New York Times*, June 22, p. A3.

Falkin, G. P., Fryer, C. S. & Mahadeo, M. (2007). Smoking cessation and stress among teenagers. *Qualitative Health Research*, *17*(6), 812–823

Fanti, K., Frick, P. & Georgiou, S. (2009). Linking callous-unemotional traits to instrumental and non-Instrumental forms of aggression. *Journal of Psychopathology and Behavioral Assessment*, *31*(4), 285–298.

Faqir, F. (2001). Intrafamily femicide in defence of honour: The case of Jordan. *Third World Quarterly*, *22*(1), 65–82.

Farrand, P., Parker, M. & Lee, C. (2007). Intention of adolescents to seek professional help for emotional and behavioural difficulties. *Health & Social Care in the Community*, *15*(5), 464–473.

Farruggia, S. P., Chen, C., Greenberger, E., Dmitrieva, J. & Macek, P. (2004). Adolescent self-esteem in cross-cultural perspective: Testing measurement equivalence and a mediation model. *Journal of Cross-Cultural Psychology*, *35*, 719–733.

Farver, J. A. M., Narang, S. K. & Bhadha, B. R. (2002). East meets West: Ethnic identity, acculturation, and conflict in Asian Indian families. *Journal of Family Psychology*, *16*, 338–350.

Farver, J. A., Bhadha, B. R. & Narang, S. K. (2002a). Acculturation and psychological functioning in Asian Indian adolescents. *Social Development*, *11*, 11–29.

Feinberg, M., Howe, G. W., Reiss, D. & Hetherington, E. M. (2000a). Relationship between perceptual differences of parenting and adolescent antisocial behavior and depressive symptoms. *Journal of Family Psychology*, *14*, 531–555.

Feinberg, M. E., McHale, S. M., Crouter, A. C. & Cumsille, P. (2003). Sibling differentiation: Sibling and parent relationship trajectories in adolescence. *Child Development*, *74*(5), 1261–1274.

Feinberg, M., Neiderhiser, J., Howe, G. & Hetherington, E. M. (2001). Adolescent, parent, and observer perceptions of parenting: Genetic and environmental influences on shared and distinct perceptions. *Child Development*, *72*, 1266–1284.

Feinberg, M. E., Neiderhiser, J. M., Simmens, S., Reiss, D. & Hetherington, E. M. (2000b). Personality and social development sibling comparison of differential parental treatment in adolescence: Gender, self-esteem, and emotionality as mediators of the parenting-adjustment association. *Child Development*, *71*(6), 1611–1628.

Feldman, R. S. (2003). *Development across the lifespan (5th ed.)*. Upper Saddle River, NJ: Prentice Hall.

Feldman, S. S. & Cauffman, E. (1999). Sexual betrayal among late adolescents: Perspectives of the perpetrator and the aggrieved. *Journal of Youth & Adolescence*, *28*, 235–258.

Feldman, S. S., Turner, R. A. & Araujo, K. (1999). Interpersonal context as an influence on the sexual timetables of youths: Gender and ethnic effects. *Journal of Research on Adolescence*, *9*, 25–52.

Fell, P. & Piper, H. (2001). Framing and reframing fears of disorderly youth. *Practice: Social Work in Action*, *13*(2), 43–54.

Felmlee, D. H. (2001). From appealing to appalling: Disenchantment with a romantic partner. *Sociological Perspectives*, *44*, 263–280.

Fenton, K. A. & Lowndes, C. M, for the European Surveillance of Sexually Transmitted Infections (ESSTI) Network (2004). Recent trends in the epidemiology of sexually transmitted infections in the European Union. *Sexually Transmitted Infection*, *80*, 255–263.

Fergusson, D. M., Boden, J. M. & Horwood, L. J. (2006). Cannabis use and other illicit drug use: testing the cannabis gateway hypothesis. *Addiction*, *101*(4), 556–569.

Fergusson, D. M., Horwood, L. J., Ridder, E. M. & Beautrais, A. L. (2005). Suicidal behaviour in adolescence and subsequent mental health outcomes in young adulthood. *Psychological Medicine*, *35*(7), 983–993.

Ferguson, S. A. (2003). Other high-risk factors for young drivers – how graduated licensing does, doesn't, or could address them. *Journal of Safety Research*, *34*, 71–77.

Fernyhough, C. (2009). What can we say about the inner experience of the young child? *Behavioral and Brain Sciences*, *32*(2), 143–144.

Fiese, B. H. & Skillman, G. (2000). Gender differences in family stories: Moderating influence of parent gender role and child gender. *Sex Roles*, *43*(5–6), 267–283.

Fife-Schaw, C. & Barnett, J. (2004). Measuring optimistic bias. In G. M. Breakwell (Ed.), *Doing social psychology research* (pp. 54–74). Leicester, England: British Psychological Society; Blackwell Publishing.

Figueira-McDonough, J. (1998). Environment and interpretation: Voices of young people in poor inner-city neighborhoods. *Youth & Society*, *30*, 123–163.

Finkelstein, J. W. (2001a). Menstrual cycle. In J. V. Lerner & R. M. Lerner (Eds.), *Adolescence in America: An encyclopedia*, pp. 432–433. Santa Barbara, CA: ABC-CLIO.

Finkelstein, J. W. (2001b). Puberty: Physical changes. In J. V. Lerner & R. M. Lerner (eds.), *Adolescence in America: An encyclopedia*, pp. 555–558. Santa Barbara, CA: ABC-CLIO.

Finkelstein, J. W. (2001c). Menstruation. In J. V. Lerner & R. M. Lerner (Eds.), *Adolescence in America: An encyclopedia*, (pp. 434–436). Santa Barbara, CA: ABC-CLIO.

Fischer, K. W. & Pruyne, E. (2003). Reflective thinking in adulthood: Emergence, development, & variation. In J. Demick & C. Andreotti (Eds.), *Handbook of adult psychology* (pp. 169–198). New York: Kluwer.

Fischer, M. & Barkley, R. (2006). Young adult outcomes of children with hyperactivity: Leisure, financial, and social activities. *International Journal of Disability*, *Development and Education*, *53*(2), 229–245.

Fischoff, B. (2005). Afterword: Development of and in behavioural decision research. In E. J. Jacobs & P. A. Klaczynski (Eds.), *The development of judgment and decision making in children and adolescents* (pp. 335–346). Mahwah, NJ: Erlbaum.

Fisher, B. S., Cullen, F. T. & Turner, M. G. (2000). *The sexual victimization of women*. Washington, DC: National Institute of Justice.

Fisher, M., Schneider, M., Burns, J., Symons, H. & Mandel, F. S. (2001). Differences between adolescents and young adults at presentation to an eating disorders program. *Journal of Adolescent Health*, *28*, 222–227.

Fisher, R. & Larkin, S. (2008). Pedagogy or Ideological struggle? An examination of pupils' and teachers' expectations for talk in the classroom. *Language and Education*, *22*(1), 1–16.

Flammer, A. & Alsaker, F. D. (2001). Adolescents in school. In L. Goossens & S. Jackson (Eds.), *Handbook of adolescent development: European perspectives*. Hove, UK: Psychology Press.

Flanagan, C. & Botcheva, L. (1999). Adolescents' preference for their homeland and other countries. In F. D. Alsaker & A. Flammer (Eds.), *The adolescent experience: European and American adolescents in the 1990s* (pp. 131–144). Mahwah, NJ: Erlbaum.

Flanagan, C., Jonsson, B., Botcheva, L., Csapo, B., Bowes, J., Macek, P., Averina, I. & Sheblanova, E. (1999). Adolescents and the 'social contract': Developmental roots of citizenship in seven countries. In M. Yates & J. Youniss, *Roots of civic identity: International perspectives* on community service and activism in youth (pp. 135–155). New York: Cambridge University Press.

Flavell, J. H., Miller, P. A. & Miller, S. A. (2002). Cognitive development (4th ed.). Upper Saddle River, NJ: Prentice-Hall.

Fleming, M. & Towey, K. (Eds.) (2003). Educational forum on adolescent health: Obesity, nutrition, and physical activity. Chicago: American Medical Association.

Flint, J. (2007). Faith schools, multiculturalism and community cohesion: Muslim and Roman Catholic state schools in England and Scotland. Policy & Politics, 35(2), 251–268.

Flook, L. & Fuligni A. J. (2008). Family and school spillover in adolescents' daily lives. Child Development 79(3), 776–787.

Flouri, E. & Ereky-Stevens, K. (2008). Urban neighbourhood quality and school leaving age: Gender differences and some hypotheses. Oxford Review of Education, 34(2), 203–216.

Flowers, P. & Buston, K. (2001). 'I was terrified of being different': Exploring gay men's accounts of growing up in a heterosexist society. Journal of Adolescence, 24, 51–66.

Floyd, F. & Bakeman, R. (2006). Coming-out across the life course: Implications of age and historical context. Archives of Sexual Behaviour, 35(3), 287–297.

Flynn, J. (1991). Asian Americans: Achievement beyond IQ. Hillsdale, NJ: Erlbaum.

Forbes, E. E., Hariri, A. R., Martin, S. L., Silk, J. S., Moyles, D. L., Fisher, P. M., Brown, S. M., Ryan, N. D., Birmaher, B., Axelson, D. A. & Dahl, R. E. (2009). Altered striatal activation predicting real-world positive affect in adolescent major depressive disorder. The American Journal of Psychiatry, 166(1), pp. 64–73.

Ford, C. & Beach, F. (1951). Patterns of sexual behavior. New York: Harper & Row.

Ford, C. A. & Coleman, W. L. (1999). Adolescent development and behavior: Implications for the primary care physician. In M. D. Levine et al. (Eds.) Developmental-Behavioral Pediatrics (4th ed., pp. 69–79). Philadelphia: W.B. Saunders.

Forkel, I. & Silbereisen, R. K. (2001). Family economic hardship and depressed mood among young adolescents in the former East and West Germany. American Behavioral Scientist, 44, 1955–1971.

Fortune, S., Stewart, A., Yadav, V. & Hawton, K. (2007). Suicide in adolescents: Using life charts to understand the suicidal process. Journal of Affective Disorders, 100 (1–3), 199–210.

Fowler, J. W. & Dell, M. L. (2006). Stages of faith from infancy through adolescence: Reflections on three decades of faith development theory. In E. C. Roehlkepartain, P. King, L. Wagener, & P. L. Benson (Eds.), The handbook of spiritual development in childhood and adolescence (pp. 34–45, xvi, 543). Thousand Oaks, CA: Sage.

Fowler, J. W. & Dell, M. L. (2004). Stages of faith and identity: Birth to teens. Child & adolescent psychiatric clinics of North American, 13, 17–33.

Francis, B. (2006). Heroes or zeroes? The discursive positioning of 'underachieving boys' in English neo-liberal education policy. Journal of Education Policy, 21(2), 187–200.

Francis, B. & Archer, L. (2005). British-Chinese pupils' and parents' constructions of the value of education. British Educational Research Journal, 31(1), 89–108.

Frankel, L. (2002). 'I've never thought about it': Contradictions and taboos surrounding American males' experiences of their first ejaculation (semenarche). Journal of Men's Studies, 11, 37–54.

Franklin, C., Streeter, C. L., Kim, J. S. & Tripodi, S. J. (2007). The effectiveness of a solution-focused, public alternative school for drop-out prevention and retrieval. Children & Schools, 29(3), 133–144.

Fraser, S. (1995). The bell curve wars: Race, intelligence, and the future of America. New York: Basic Books.

Frazzetto, G., Keenan, S. & Singh, I. (2007). Bambini e le Droghe?: The right to ritalin vs the right to childhood in Italy. BioSocieties, 2(4), 393–412.

Fredman, S. (2008). Reforming equal pay laws. Industrial Law Journal, 37(3), 193–193.

Fredman, S. (2001). Equality: A new generation? Industrial Law Journal, 30(2), 145–168.

Free, C., Ogden, J. & Lee, R. (2005). Young women's contraception use as a contextual and dynamic behaviour: A qualitative study. Psychology and Health, 20(5), 673–690.

Freeman, S. K. (2006). Facts of life and more: Adolescent sex and sexuality education. In C. Cocca (Ed.), Adolescent sexuality: A historical handbook and guide. Children and youth: History and culture (pp. 45–63). Westport, CT: Praeger Publishers/Greenwood Publishing Group.

Freitag, C. M. (2008). Genetics of autism. Journal of Intellectual Disability Research, 52(10), 817–817.

French, D. C., Eisenberg, N., Vaughan, J., Purwono, U. & Suryanti, T. A. (2008). Religious involvement and the social competence and adjustment of Indonesian Muslim adolescents. Developmental Psychology, 44(2), 597–611.

French, D. C., Jansen, E. A. & Pidada, S. (2002). United States and Indonesian children's and adolescents' reports of relational aggression by disliked peers. Child Development, 73, 1143–1150.

French, D. C., Rianasari, J. M., Pidada, S., Nelwan, P. & Buhrmester, D. (2001). Social support of Indonesian and U.S. children and adolescents by family members and friends. Merrill-Palmer Quarterly, 47, 377–394.

French, H. W. (2002). Educators try to tame Japan's blackboard jungles. New York Times, September 23, p. A6.

Freud, A. (1969). Adolescence as a developmental disturbance. In G. Caplan & S. Lebovici (Eds.), Adolescence: Psychosocial perspectives (pp. 5–10). New York: Basic Books.

Freud, A. (1968). Adolescence. In A. E. Winder & D. Angus (Eds.), Adolescence: Contemporary studies (pp. 13–24). New York: American Book.

Freud, A. (1958). Adolescence. Psychoanalytic Study of the Child, 15, 255–278. New York: International Universities Press, Inc.

Freud, A. (1946). The ego and the mechanisms of defense. New York: International Universities Press.

Freud, S. (1940/64). *An outline of psychoanalysis*. Standard edition of the works of Sigmund Freud. London: Hogarth Press.

Frick, P. J. & Kimonis, E. R. (2008). External disorders of childhood. In J. E. Maddux & B. A. Winstead (Eds.), *Psychopathology: Foundations for a contemporary understanding* (2nd ed., pp. 349–374). New York: Routledge/Taylor & Francis Group.

Friestad, C. & Rise, J. (2004). A longitudinal study of the relationship between body image, self-esteem and dieting among 15–21 year olds in Norway. *European Eating Disorders Review: The Journal of the Eating Disorders Association, 12*(4), 247–255.

Frith, H. & Kitzinger, C. (2001) Reformulating sexual script theory: Developing a discursive psychology of sexual negotiation. *Theory and Psychology, 11*, 209–232.

Frone, M. R. (1999). Developmental consequences of youth employment. In J. Barling & E. K. Kelloway (Eds.), *Youth workers: Varieties of experience* (pp. 89–128). Washington, DC: American Psychological Association.

Frost, J. & McKelvie, S. (2004). Self-esteem and body satisfaction in male and female elementary school, high school, and university students. *Sex Roles, 51*, 45–54.

Fry, A. F. & Hole, S. (1996). Processing speed, working memory, and fluid intelligence: Evidence for a developmental cascade. *Psychological Science, 7*, 237–241.

Frydenberg, E. & Lewis, R. (2004). Adolescents least able to cope: How do they respond to their stresses? *British Journal of Guidance & Counselling, 32*(1), 25–37.

Frydenberg, E., Lewis, R., Bugalski, K., Cotta, A., McCarthy, C., Luscombe-Smith, N. & Poole, C. (2004). Prevention is better than cure: Coping skills training for adolescents at school. *Educational Psychology in Practice, 20*(2), 117–134.

Fuligni, A. J., Tseng, V. & Lam, M. (1999). Attitudes toward family obligations among American adolescents with Asian, Latin American, and European backgrounds. *Child Development, 70*, 1030–1044.

Fuller, A., Beck, V. & Unwin, L. (2005). The gendered nature of apprenticeship: Employers' and young peoples' perspectives. *Education & Training, 47*(4–5), 298–311.

Furlong, A. (2006). Not a very NEET solution: Representing problematic labour market transitions among early school-leavers. *Work, Employment & Society, 20*(3), 553–569.

Furman, W. (2002). The emerging field of adolescent romantic relationships. *Current Directions in Psychological Science, 11*, 177–180.

Furman, W. & Hand, L. S. (2006). The slippery nature of romantic relationships: Issues in definition and differentiation. In A. C. Crouter & A. Booth (Eds.), *Romance and sex in adolescence and emerging adulthood: Risks and opportunities* (pp. 171–178). The Penn State University family issues symposia series. NJ: Lawrence Erlbaum.

Furman, W., Ho, M. J. & Low, S. M. (2007). The rocky road of adolescent romantic experience: Dating and adjustment. In R. C. M. E. Engels, M. Kerr, & H. Stattin (Eds.), *Friends, lovers and groups: Key relationships in adolescence. Hot topics in developmental research* (pp. 61–80). New York: John Wiley & Sons Ltd.

Furman, W., Low, S. & Ho, M. J. (2009). Romantic experience and psychosocial adjustment in early adolescence. *Journal of Consulting and Clinical Psychology.*

Furman, W., & Simon, V. A. (2008). Homophily in adolescent romantic relationships. In M. J. Prinstein & K. A. Dodge (Eds.), *Understanding peer influence in children and adolescents. Duke series in child development and public policy* (pp. 203–224). New York: Guilford Press.

Furman, W., Simon, V. A., Shaffer, L. & Bouchey, H. A. (2002). Adolescents' working models and styles for relationships with parents, friends, and romantic partners. *Child Development, 73*(1), 241–255.

Furstenberg, E. F., Jr., Brooks-Gunn, J. & Morgan, S. P. (1987). *Adolescent mothers in later life*. New York: Cambridge University Press.

Fussell, E. & Greene, M. (2002). Demographic trends affecting adolescents around the world. In B. B. Brown, R. Larson, & T. S. Saraswathi (Eds.), *The world's youth: Adolescence in eight regions of the globe* (pp. 21–60). New York: Cambridge University Press.

Fuwa, K. (2001). Lifelong education in Japan, a highly school-centred society: Educational opportunities and practical educational activities for adults. *International Journal of Lifelong Education, 20*(1–2), 127–136.

Gaddis, A. & Brooks-Gunn, J. (1985). The male experience of pubertal change. *Journal of Youth and Adolescence, 14*, 61–69.

Gådin, K. G. & Hammarström, A. (2003). Do changes in the psychosocial school environment influence pupils' health development? Results from a three-year follow-up study. *Scandinavian Journal of Public Health, 31*(3), 169–178.

Gaines, B. (2009). Designing visual languages for description logics. *Journal of Logic, Language and Information, 18*(2), 217–250.

Galambos, N. (2004). Gender and gender role development in adolescence. In R. Lerner & L. Steinberg (Eds.), *Handbook of adolescent psychology*. New York: Wiley.

Galambos, N., Almeida, D. & Petersen, A. (1990). Masculinity, femininity, and sex role attitudes in early adolescence: Exploring gender intensification. *Child Development, 61*, 1905–1914.

Galambos, N. L., Barker, E. T. & Krahn, H. J. (2006). Depression, anger, and self-esteem in emerging adulthood: Seven-year trajectories. *Developmental Psychology, 42*(2), 350–365.

Galambos, N. & Martinez, M. L. (2007). Poised for emerging adulthood in Latin America: A pleasure for the privileged. *Child Development Perspectives, 1*, 109–114.

Gallup, G., Jr. & Lindsay, D. M. (1999). *Surveying the religious landscape: Trends in U.S. beliefs*. Harrisburg, PA: Morehouse.

Galotti, K. (1989). Gender differences in self-reported moral reasoning: A review and new evidence. *Journal of Youth and Adolescence, 18*, 475–488.

Galotti, K., Kozberg, S. & Farmer, M. (1991). Gender and developmental differences in adolescents' conceptions of moral reasoning. *Journal of Youth and Adolescence*, *20*, 13–30.

Gance-Cleveland, B., Mays, M. Z. & Steffen, A. (2008). Association of adolescent physical and emotional health with perceived severity of parental substance abuse. *Journal for Specialists in Pediatric Nursing*, *13*(1), 15–25.

Ganguly-Scrase, R. (2003). Paradoxes of globalization, liberalization, and gender equality: The worldviews of the lower middle class in West Bengal, India. *Gender & Society*, *17*(4), 544–566.

Ganong, L. H. & Coleman, M. (2004). *Stepfamily relationships: Development, dynamics, and interventions*. New York: Kluwer Academic/Plenum Publishers.

Gao, Y., Griffiths, S. & Chan, E. Y. Y. (2008). Community-based interventions to reduce overweight and obesity in China: A systematic review of the Chinese and English literature. *Journal of Public Health*, *30*(4), 436–436.

García-Montes, J., Zaldívar-Basurto, F., López-Ríos, F. & Molina-Moreno, A. (2009). The role of personality variables in drug abuse in a Spanish university population. *International Journal of Mental Health and Addiction*, *7*(3), 475–487.

Gardiner, H. W. (2001). Child and adolescent development: Cross-cultural perspectives. In L. L. Adler & U. P. Gielen (Eds.), *Cross-cultural topics in psychology* (pp. 63–79). Westport, CT: Praeger Publishers.

Gardner, H. (2006). *Multiple intelligences: New horizons*. New York: Basic Books.

Gardner, H. (1999, February). Who owns intelligence? *Atlantic Monthly*, 67–76.

Gardner, H. (1989). Beyond a modular view of mind. In W. Damon (Ed.), *Child development today and tomorrow*. San Francisco: Jossey-Bass.

Gardner, H. (1983). *Frames of mind*. New York: Basic Books.

Gardner, T. W., Dishion, T. J. & Connell, A. M. (2008). Adolescent self-regulation as resilience: Resistance to antisocial behavior within the deviant peer context. *Journal of Abnormal Child Psychology*, *36*(2), 273–284.

Gary, F. (2005). Stigma: Barrier to mental health care among ethnic minorities. *Issues in Mental Health Nursing*, *26*(10), 979–999.

Gaughan, M. (2006). The gender structure of adolescent peer influence on drinking. *Journal of Health and Social Behaviour*, *47*(1), 47–61.

Gauthier, A. (2002). The role of grandparents. *Current Sociology*, *50*(2), 295–307.

Gaylord-Harden, N. K., Ragsdale, B. L., Mandara, J., Richards, M. H. & Petersen, A. C. (2007). Perceived support and internalizing symptoms in African American adolescents: Self-esteem and ethnic identity as mediators. *Journal of Youth and Adolescence*, *36*(1), 77–88.

Gaynor, S. T., Weersing, V. R., Kolko, D. J., Birmaher, B., Heo, J. & Brent, D. A. (2003). The prevalence and impact of large sudden improvements during adolescent therapy for depression: A comparison across cognitive-behavioral, family, and supportive therapy. *Journal of Consulting & Clinical Psychology*, *71*, 386–393.

Ge, X., Conger, R. D. & Elder, G. H., Jr. (2001). The relation between puberty and psychological distress in adolescent boys. *Journal of Research on Adolescence*, *11*, 49–70.

Ge, X. & Natsuaki, M. N. (2009). In search of explanations for early pubertal timing effects on developmental psychopathology. *Current Directions in Psychological Science*, *18*(6), 327–331.

Ge, X., Natsuaki, M. N., Neiderhiser, J. M. & Reiss, D. (2007). Genetic and environmental influences on pubertal timing: Results from two national sibling studies. *Journal of Research on Adolescence*, *17*(4), 767–788.

Geer, J. & Robertson, G. (2005). Implicit attitudes in sexuality: Gender differences. *Archives of Sexual Behavior*, *34*(6), 671–677.

Gehl, R. (2009). YouTube as archive. *International Journal of Cultural Studies*, *12*(1), 43–60.

Gendron, M., Royer, E., Bertrand, R. & Potvin, P. (2004). Behaviour disorders, social competence and the practice of physical activities among adolescents. *Emotional and Behavioural Difficulties*, *9*(4), 249–259.

General Social Survey (1977–2006). http://www3.norc.org/gss+website (accessed 25 February 2012).

Genereux, R. & McKeough, A. (2007). Developing narrative interpretation: Structural and content analyses. *The British Journal of Educational Psychology*, *77*(4), 849–872.

George, R. & Clay, J. (2008). Reforming teachers and uncompromising 'standards': Implications for social justice in schools. *FORUM: for Promoting 3–19 Comprehensive Education*, *50*(1), 103–112.

Georgiou, S., Stavrinides, P. & Kalavana, T. (2007). Is Victor better than Victoria at maths? *Educational Psychology in Practice*, *23*(4), 329–342.

Gerard, J. M. & Buehler, C. (2004). Cumulative environmental risk and youth maladjustment: The role of youth attributes. *Child Development*, *75*(6), 1832–1849.

Gershuny, J., Bittman, M. & Brice, J. (2005). Exit, voice, and suffering: Do couples adapt to changing employment patterns? *Journal of Marriage and Family*, *67*(3), 656–665.

Ghuman, P. A. S. (2002). South-Asian Adolescents in British schools: A review. *Educational Studies*, *28*(1), 47–59.

Ghuman, P. A. S. (1998). Ethnic identity and acculturation of South Asian adolescents: A British perspective. *International Journal of Adolescence & Youth*, *7*, 227–247.

Giang, M. T. & Wittig, M. A. (2006). Implications of adolescents' acculturation strategies for personal and collective self-esteem. *Cultural Diversity and Ethnic Minority Psychology*, *12*(4), 725–739.

Gibbons, F. X., Gerrard, M. & Lane, D. J. (2003). A social reaction model of adolescent health risk. In J. Suls & K. A. Wallston (Eds.), *Social psychological foundations of health and illness* (pp. 107–136). Malden, MA: Blackwell.

Gibbons, J. L. & Stiles, D. A. (2004). *The thoughts of youth: An international perspective on adolescents' ideal persons*. Greenwich, CT: IAP Information Age Publishing.

Gibbs, I. & Sinclair, I. (2000). Bullying, sexual harassment and happiness in residential children's homes. *Child Abuse Review*, *9*(4), 247–256.

Gibbs, J. C., Basinger, K. S., Grime, R. L. & Snarey, J. R. (2007). Moral judgment development across cultures: Revisiting Kohlberg's universality claims. *Developmental Review, 27*(4), 443–500.

Gibbs, R., Jr., Leggitt, J. & Turner, E. (2002). What's special about figurative language in emotional communication? In S. R. Fussell (Ed.), *The verbal communication of emotion* (pp. 125–149). Mahwah, NJ: Erlbaum.

Giddens, A. (2000). *Runaway world: How globalisation is reshaping our lives*. New York: Routledge.

Giedd, J. (2002, October 15). *The teen brain*. Paper presented at the Medicine for the Public Lecture Series, NIH Clinical Center, Bethesda, MD. Available: www.cc.nih.gov/ccc/mfp/series.html.

Giedd, J. N. (2008). The teen brain: Insights from neuroimaging. *Journal of Adolescent Health, 42*(4), 335–343.

Giedd, J. N., Blumenthal, J. & Jeffries, N. O. (1999). Brain development during childhood and adolescence: A longitudinal MRI study. *Nature Neuroscience, 2*, 861–863.

Gifford-Smith, M., Dodge, K. A., Dishion, T. J. & McCord, J. (2005). Peer influence in children and adolescents: Crossing the bridge from developmental to intervention science. *Journal of Abnormal Child Psychology, 33*, 255–265.

Gilbert, T. (2004). Involving people with learning disabilities in research: issues and possibilities. *Health & Social Care in the Community, 12*(4), 298–308.

Giles, D. C. (2003). Narratives of obesity as presented in the context of a television talk show. *Journal of Health Psychology, 8*(3), 317–326.

Gillard, D. (2008). Blair's academies: the story so far. *FORUM: For Promoting 3–19 Comprehensive Education, 50*(1), 11–22.

Gillies, V. (2000). Young people and family life: Analysing and comparing disciplinary discourses. *Journal of Youth Studies, 3*(2), 211–228.

Gilligan, C. (2008). Exit-voice dilemmas in adolescent development. In D. L. Browning (Ed.), *Adolescent identities: A collection of readings* (pp. 141–156). Relational perspectives book series. New York: Analytic Press/Taylor & Francis Group.

Gilligan, C. (1982). *In a different voice*. Cambridge, MA: Harvard University Press.

Gillis, J. R. (1974). *Youth and history*. New York: Academic Press.

Gillison, F., Standage, M. & Skevington, S. (2008). Changes in quality of life and psychological need satisfaction following the transition to secondary school. *The British Journal of Educational Psychology, 78*(1), 149–162.

Gillock, K. L. & Reyes, O. (1999). Stress, support, and academic performance of urban, low-income Mexican-American adolescents. *Journal of Youth & Adolescence, 28*, 259–282.

Gilmore, D. (1990). *Manhood in the making: Cultural concepts of masculinity*. New Haven: Yale University Press.

Gilmour, J., Hill, B., Place, M. & Skuse, D. H. (2004). Social communication deficits in conduct disorder: a clinical and community survey. *Journal of Child Psychology and Psychiatry* (formerly *Journal of Child Psychology and Psychiatry and Allied Disciplines*), *45*(5), 967–978.

Gimenez, M. (2007). For structure: A critique of ontological individualism. *Journal of Critical Realism, 2*(2), 19–25.

Gini, G., Albierto, P., Benelli, B. & Altoe, G. (2008). Determinants of adolescents' active defending and passive bystanding behaviour in bullying. *Journal of Adolescence, 31*(1), 93–105.

Ginsberg, T. B., Pomerantz, S. C. & Kramer-Feeley, V. (2005). Sexuality in older adults: Behaviours and preferences. *Age and Ageing, 34*(5), 475–480.

Giordano, P. C., Manning, W. D. & Longmore, M. A. (2006). Adolescent romantic relationships: An emerging portrait of their nature and developmental significance. In A. C. Crouter & A. Booth (Eds.), *Romance and sex in adolescence and emerging adulthood: Risks and opportunities* (pp. 127–150). The Penn State University family issues symposia series. NJ: Lawrence Erlbaum.

Girard, A. L. & Senn, C. Y. (2008). The role of the new 'date rape drugs' in attributions about date rape. *Journal of Interpersonal Violence, 23*(1), 3–20.

Gkoltsiou, K., Dimitrakaki, C., Tzavara, C., Papaevangelou, V., Varni, J. & Tountas, Y. (2008). Measuring health-related quality of life in Greek children: Psychometric properties of the Greek version of the Pediatric Quality of Life Inventory™ 4.0 Generic Core Scales. *Quality of Life Research, 17*(2), 299–305.

Gladding, S. T. (2002). *Family therapy: History, theory, and practice*. Upper Saddle River, NJ: Prentice Hall.

Glashan, L., Mackay, G. & Grieve, A. (2004). Teachers' experience of support in the mainstream education of pupils with autism. *Improving Schools, 7*(1), 49–60.

Glowinski, A. L., Madden, P. A. F., Bucholz, K. K., Lynskey, M. T. & Heath, A. C. (2003). Genetic epidemiology of self-reported lifetime *DSM-IV* major depressive disorder in a population-based twin sample of female adolescents. *Journal of Child Psychology & Psychiatry, 44*, 988–996.

Glueck, S. & Glueck, E. (1968). *Delinquents and nondelinquents in perspective*. Cambridge, MA: Harvard University Press.

Glueck, S. & Glueck, E. (1950). *Unraveling juvenile delinquency*. New York: Commonwealth Fund.

Goldberg, P. H. (1968). Are women prejudiced against women? *Transaction, 5*, 28–30.

Goldenberg, H. & Goldenberg, I. (2005). Family therapy. In R. J. Corsini & D. Wedding (Eds.), *Current psychotherapies* (7th ed., instr. ed., 372–404). Belmont, CA: Thomson Brooks/Cole Publishing.

Goldscheider, F. & Goldscheider, C. (1994). *The changing transition to adulthood: Leaving and returning home*. Thousand Oaks, CA: Sage.

Goldstein, S. E., Davis-Kean, P. E. & Eccles, J. S. (2005). Parents, peers, and problem behavior: A longitudinal investigation of the impact of relationship perceptions and characteristics on the development of adolescent problem behavior. *Developmental Psychology, 41*, 401–413.

Goldstein, S. E., Malanchuk, O., Davis-Kean, P. E. & Eccles, J. S. (2007). Risk factors of sexual harassment by peers: A longitudinal investigation of African American and European American adolescents. *Journal of Research on Adolescence, 17*(2), 285–300.

Goleman, D. (1997). *Emotional intelligence*. New York: Bantam.

Gonzalez-DeHass, A. R., Willems, P. P. & Doan Holbein, M. F. (2005). Examining the relationship between parental involvement and student motivation. *Educational Psychology Review, 17*(2), 99–123.

González-Tejera, G., Canino, G., Ramírez, R., Chávez, L., Shrout, P., Bird, H., Bravo, M., Martínez-Taboas, A., Ribera, J. & Bauermeister, J. (2005). Examining minor and major depression in adolescents. *Journal of Child Psychology and Psychiatry* (formerly *Journal of Child Psychology and Psychiatry and Allied Disciplines), 46*(8), 888–899.

Good, M., Willoughby, T. & Fritjers, J. (2009). Just another club? The distinctiveness of the relation between religious service attendance and adolescent psychosocial adjustment. *Journal of Youth and Adolescence, 38*(9), 1153–1171.

Goossens, L. & Luyckx, K. (2007). Belgium. In J. J. Arnett, U. Gielen, R. Ahmed, B. Nsamenang, T. S. Saraswathi, & R. Silbereisen (Eds.), *International encyclopedia of adolescence*. New York: Routledge.

Gorard, S., Taylor, C. and Fitz, J. (2002). Does school choice lead to 'spirals of decline'? *Journal of Education Policy, 17*(3), 367–384.

Gordon, C. (2008). A(p)parent play: Blending frames and reframing in family talk. *Language in Society, 37*(3), 319–349.

Gordon, H. R. (2008). Gendered paths to teenage political participation: Parental power, civic mobility, and youth activism. *Gender & Society, 22*(1), 31–55.

Gore, S. A., Van der Wal, J. S. & Thelen, M. H. (2001). Treatment of eating disorders in children and adolescents. In J. K. Thompson & L. Smolak (Eds.), *Body image, eating disorders, and obesity in youth: Assessment, treatment, and prevention* (pp. 293–311). Washington, DC: American Psychological Association.

Gorman-Murray, A. (2008). Queering the family home: Narratives from gay, lesbian and bisexual youth coming out in supportive family homes in Australia. *Gender, Place and Culture: A Journal of Feminist Geography, 15*(1), 31–44.

Gottfredson, M. & Hirschi, T. (1990). *A general theory of crime*. Stanford, CA: Stanford University Press.

Gould, N., Gould, H. & Brewin, B. (2004). Using repertory grid technique with participants in parenting programmes – A pilot study. *Practice: Social Work in Action, 16*(3), 197–210.

Gould, S. J. (1981). *The mismeasure of man*. New York: Norton.

Gounev, P. & Bezlov, T. (2006). The Roma in Bulgaria's criminal justice system: From ethnic profiling to Imprisonment. *Critical Criminology, 14*(3), 313–338.

Gowen, L. K., Feldman, S. S., Diaz, R. & Yisrael, D. S. (2002). A comparison of the sexual behaviours and attitudes of adolescent girls with older vs. similar-aged boyfriends. *Journal of Youth and Adolescence, 33*(2), 167–175.

Gowen, L. K., Hayward, C., Killen, J. D., Robinson, T. N. & Taylor, C. B. (1999). Acculturation and eating disorder symptoms in adolescent girls. *Journal of Research on Adolescence, 9*, 67–83.

Grabe, S., Hyde, J. S. & Lindberg, S. M. (2007). Body objectification and depression in adolescents: The role of gender, shame, and rumination. *Psychology of Women Quarterly, 31*(2), 164–175.

Grabe, S., Ward, L. M. & Hyde, J. S. (2008). The role of the media in body image concerns among women: A meta-analysis of experimental and correlational studies. *Psychological Bulletin, 134*(3), 460–476.

Graber, J. A., Britto, P. R. & Brooks-Gunn, J. (1999). What's love got to do with it? Adolescent and young adult's beliefs about sexual and romantic relationships. In W. Furman, B. B. Brown, & C. Feiring (Eds.), *The development of romantic relationships in adolescence* (pp. 364–395). New York: Cambridge University Press.

Graber, J. A., Seeley, J. R., Brooks-Gunn, J. & Lewinsohn, P. M. (2004). Is pubertal timing associated with psychopathology in young adulthood? *Journal of the American Academy of Child & Adolescent Psychiatry, 43*, 718–726.

Graeff-Martins, A., Oswald, S., Comassetto, J. O., Kieling, C., Gonçalves, R. R. & Rohde, L. (2006). A package of interventions to reduce school drop-out in public schools in a developing country. *European Child & Adolescent Psychiatry, 15*(8), 442–449.

Graf, C., Koch, B., Falkowski, G., Jouck, S., Christ, H., Staudenmaier, K., Tokarski, W., Gerber, A., Predel, H.-G. & Dordel, S. (2008). School-based prevention: Effects on obesity and physical performance after 4 years. *Journal of Sports Sciences, 26*(10), 987–994.

Graham, M. J., Larsen, U. & Xu, X. (1999). Secular trend in age of menarche in China: A case study of two rural counties in Anhui province. *Journal of Biosocial Science, 31*, 257–267.

Gram-Hanssen, K. & Bech-Danielsen, C. (2008). Home dissolution: What happens after separation? *Housing Studies, 23*(3), 507–522.

Granato, J., Guse, E. A. & Wong, M. C. S. (2008). Learning from the expectations of others. *Macroeconomic Dynamics, 12*(3), 345–377.

Granic, I., Dishion, T. J. & Hollenstein, T. (2008). The family ecology of adolescence: A dynamic systems perspective on normative development. In G. R. Adams & M. D. Berzonsky (Eds.), *Blackwell handbook of adolescence* (pp. 60–91). Malden, MA: Blackwell.

Granic, I. & Patterson, G. R. (2006). Toward a comprehensive model of antisocial development: A dynamic systems approach. *Psychological Review, 113*(1), 101–131.

Granqvist, P. (2002). Attachment and religiosity in adolescence: Cross-sectional and longitudinal evaluations. *Personality and Social Psychology Bulletin, 28*(2), 260–270.

Grant, K. E., Lyons, A. L., Finkelstein, J. S., Conway, K. M., Reynolds, L. K., O'Koon, J. H., Waitkoff, G. R. & Hicks, K. J. (2004). Gender differences in rates of depressive symptoms among low-income, urban, African American Youth: A test of two mediational hypotheses. *Journal of Youth & Adolescence, 33*, 523–533.

Grant, M. & Furstenberg, F. (2007). Changes in the transition to adulthood in less developed countries. *European Journal of population = Revue Européenne de Démographie,* 23(3–4), 415–428.

Gray, G. Z. (2006). *The Children's Crusade; An episode of the thirteenth century.* Researcherly Publishing Office, University of Michigan Library.

Gray, W. M. (1990). Formal operational thought. In W. F. Overton (Ed.), *Reasoning, necessity, and logic: Developmental perspectives* (pp. 227–253). Hillsdale, NJ: Erlbaum.

Greatorex, J. & Malacova, E. (2006). Can different teaching strategies or methods of preparing pupils lead to greater improvements from GCSE to A level performance? *Research Papers in Education,* 21(3), 255–294.

Greeff, A. P. & van der Merwe, S. (2004). Variables associated with resilience in divorced families. *Social Indicators Research,* 68(1), 59–75.

Green, C. D. (2001). Scientific models, connectionist networks, and cognitive science. *Theory & Psychology,* 11(1), 97–117.

Green, D. (2005). Personal construct theory and paediatric health care. *Clinical Child Psychology and Psychiatry,* 10(1), 33–41.

Green, E. G. T., Deschamps, J.-C. & Páez, D. (2005). Variation of individualism and collectivism within and between 20 countries: A typological analysis. *Journal of cross-cultural psychology,* 36, 321–339.

Green, L. R., Richardson, D. S., Lago, T. & Schatten-Jones, E. C. (2001). Network correlates of social and emotional loneliness in young and older adults. *Personality and Social Psychology Bulletin,* 27(3), 281–288.

Green, V. (2007). Parental experience with treatments for autism. *Journal of Developmental and Physical Disabilities,* 19(2), 91–101.

Greenberger, E. & Steinberg, L. (1986). *When teenagers work: The psychological social costs of adolescent employment.* New York: Basic Books.

Greene, M. L. & Way, N. (2005). Self-esteem trajectories among ethnic minority adolescents: A growth curve analysis of the patterns and predictors of change. *Journal of Research on Adolescence,* 15, 151–178.

Greenhalgh, T., Chowdhury, M. & Wood, G. (2005). Big is beautiful? A survey of body image perception and its relation to health in British Bangladeshis with diabetes. *Psychology, Health & Medicine,* 10(2), 126–138.

Greenwood, P. W. (2006). *Changing lives: Delinquency prevention as crime-control policy.* Chicago: University of Chicago Press.

Gregory, E., Williams, A. & Kelly, C. (2001). Home to school and school to home: syncretised literacies in linguistic minority communities. *Language, Culture and Curriculum,* 14(1), 9–25.

Gregory, J. E., Gregory, R. J. & Carroll-Lind, J. (2001). The wisdom of children-in-context. *International Journal of Anthropological Sciences,* 16(2–3), 65–76.

Gregory, M. & Holloway, M. (2005). The debate as a pedagogic tool in social policy for social work students. *Social Work Education,* 24(6), 617–637.

Grey, I. M., Honan, R., McClean, B. & Daly, M. (2005). Evaluating the effectiveness of teacher training in Applied Behaviour Analysis. *Journal of Intellectual Disabilities,* 9(3), 209–227.

Griffin, C. (2001). Imagining new narratives of youth: youth research, the 'new Europe' and global youth culture. *Childhood,* 8(2), 147–166.

Grimsley, K. D. (2000, April 3). Family a priority for young workers: Survey finds change in men's thinking. *Washington Post,* pp. E1–2.

Grisso, T., Steinberg, L., Woolard, J., Cauffman, E., Scott, E., Graham, S., Lexcen, F., Reppucci, N. D. & Schwartz, R. (2003). Juvenile's competence to stand trial: A comparison of adolescents' and adults' capacities as trial defendants. *Law & Human Behaviour,* 27, 333–363.

Grocott, D. F. H. (2003). Maps in mind – How animals get home? Presented at a meeting held in the Royal Geographical Society on 10 October 2002. *Journal of Navigation,* 56(1), 1–14.

Grossman, K. E., Grossman, K. & Waters, E. (Eds.) (2005). Presents the results of several attachment studies beginning in infancy and extending into adolescence and emerging adulthood. *Attachment from infancy to adulthood: The major longitudinal studies.* New York: Guilford.

Grove, B. & Giraud-Saunders, A. (2003). Connecting with connexions: the role of the personal adviser with young people with special educational and support needs. *Support for Learning,* 18(1), 12–17.

Grover, R. L., Nangle, D. W., Serwik, A. & Zeff, K. R. (2007). Girl friend, boy friend, girlfriend, boyfriend: Broadening our understanding of heterosocial competence. *Journal of Clinical Child and Adolescent Psychology,* 36(4), 491–502.

Gruber, J. E. & Fineran, S. (2008). Comparing the impact of bullying and sexual harassment victimization on the mental and physical health of adolescents. *Sex Roles,* 59(1–2), 1–13.

Gruber, S. & Boreen, J. (2003). Teaching critical thinking: Using experience to promote learning in middle school and college students. *Teachers & Teaching: Theory & Practice,* 9, 5–19.

Grumbach, M., Roth, J., Kaplan, S. & Kelch, R. (1990). Hypothalamic-pituitary regulation of puberty in man: Evidence and concepts derived from clinical research. In M. Grumbach, G. Grave, & F. Mayer (Eds.), *Control of the onset of puberty.* New York: Wiley.

Grusec, J. (2002). Parental socialisation and children's acquisition of values. In M. Bornstein (Ed.), *Handbook of parenting* (Vol. 5, pp. 245–281). Mahwah, NJ: Erlbaum.

Guastello, D. D. & Guastello, S. J. (2003). Androgyny, gender role behavior, and emotional intelligence among college students and their parents. *Sex Roles,* 49, 663–673.

Gucray, S. S. (2005). A study of the decision-making behaviours of Turkish adolescents. *Pastoral Care in Education,* 23(1), 34–44.

Guerra, V. M. & Giner-Sorolla, R. (2010). The Community, Autonomy, and Divinity Scale (CADS): A new tool for the cross-cultural study of morality. *Journal of Cross-Cultural Psychology,* 41(1), 35–50.

Guglani, S., Coleman, P. G. & Sonuga-Barke, E. J. (2000). Mental health of elderly Asians in Britain: A comparison of Hindus from nuclear and extended families of differing cultural identities. *International Journal of Geriatric Psychiatry*, *15*(11), 1046–1053.

Guise, J. M. F. & Gill, J. S. (2007). 'Binge drinking? It's good, it's harmless fun': A discourse analysis of accounts of female undergraduate drinking in Scotland. *Health Education Research*, *22*(6), 895–906.

Güre, A., Uçanok, Z. & Sayil, M. (2006). The associations among perceived pubertal timing, parental relations, and self-perceptions in Turkish adolescents. *Journal of Youth and Adolescence*, *35*(4), 541–550.

Guthrie, J. T. (2008). Reading motivation and engagement in middle and high school: Appraisal and intervention. In J. T. Guthrie (Ed.), *Engaging adolescents in reading* (pp. 1–16). Thousand Oaks, CA: Corwin Press.

Gutman, L. M. & Eccles, J. S. (1999). Financial strain, parenting behaviors, and adolescents' achievement: Testing model equivalence between African American and European American single- and two-parent families. *Child Development*, *70*, 1464–1476.

Haavet, O. R., Dalen, I. & Straand, J. (2006). Depressive symptoms in adolescent pupils are heavily influenced by the school they go to. A study of 10th grade pupils in Oslo, Norway. *The European Journal of Public Health*, *16*(4), 400–404.

Hacker, A. (2002a). Gore family values. *New York Review of Books*, pp. 20–25.

Hacker, A. (2002b). How are women doing? *New York Review of Books*, 63–66.

Häggström-Nordin, E., Hanson, U. & Tydén, T. (2005). Associations between pornography and consumption and sexual practices among adolescents in Sweden. *International Journal of STD & AIDS*, *16*(2), 102–107.

Halari, R., Simic, M., Pariante, C. M., Papadopoulos, A., Cleare, A., Brammer, M., Fombonne, E. & Rubia, K. (2009). Reduced activation in lateral prefrontal cortex and anterior cingulate during attention and cognitive control functions in medication-naïve adolescents with depression compared to controls. *Journal of Child Psychology and Psychiatry* (formerly *Journal of Child Psychology and Psychiatry and Allied Disciplines*), *50*(3), 307–316.

Hall, G. S. (1904). *Adolescence: Its psychology and its relation to physiology, anthropology, sociology, sex, crime, religion, and education* (Vols. 1 & 2). Englewood Cliffs, NJ: Prentice-Hall.

Hallam, S. & Ireson, J. (2003). Secondary school teachers' attitudes towards and beliefs about ability grouping. *The British Journal of Educational Psychology*, *73*(3), 343–356.

Hallam, S., Rogers, L. & Shaw, J. (2006). Improving children's behaviour and attendance through the use of parenting programmes: an examination of practice in five case study local authorities. *British Journal of Special Education*, *33*(3), 107–113.

Halpern, C. J. T., Udry, J. R., Suchindran, C. & Campbell, B. (2000). Adolescent males' willingness to report masturbation. *Journal of Sex Research*, *37*, 327–332.

Halvor, N., Hanne-Trine, E. & Bjorkheim, J. O. (2000). Who would you most like to be like? Adolescents' ideals at the beginning and the end of the century. *Scandinavian Journal of Educational Research*, *44*, 5–26.

Hamalainen, J., Poikolainen, K., Isometsa, E., Kaprio, J., Heikkinen, M., Lindermman, S. & Aro, H. (2005). Major depressive episode related to long unemployment and frequent alcohol intoxication. *Nordic Journal of Psychiatry*, *59*(6), 486–491.

Hames, R. & Draper, P. (2004). Women's work, child care, and helpers-at-the-nest in a hunter-gatherer society. *Human Nature*, *15*(4), 319–341.

Hamilton, C. E. (2000). Continuity and discontinuity of attachment from infancy through adolescence. *Child Development*, *71*(3), 690–694.

Hamilton, D. (2002). 'Noisy, fallible and biased though it be' (on the vagaries of educational research). *British Journal of Educational Studies*, *50*(1), 144–164.

Hamilton, S. & Hamilton, M. A. (2006). School, work, and emerging adulthood. In J. J. Arnett & J. L. Tanner (Eds.), *Coming of age in the 21st century: The lives and contexts of emerging adults* (pp. 257–277). Washington, DC: American Psychological Association.

Hamilton, S. F. (1990). *Apprenticeship for adulthood: Preparing youth for the future*. New York: Free Press.

Hamilton, S. F. & Hamilton, M. A. (2000). Research, intervention, and social change: Improving adolescents' career opportunities. In L. J. Crockett & R. K. Silbereisen (Eds.), *Negotiating adolescence in times of social change* (pp. 267–283). New York: Cambridge University Press.

Hamm, J. V. (2000). Do birds of a feather flock together? The variable bases for African American, Asian American, and European American adolescents' selection of similar friends. *Developmental Psychology*, *36*, 209–219.

Hammack, P. L., Robinson, W. LaVome., Crawford, I. & Li, S. T. (2004). Poverty and depressed mood among urban African-American adolescents: A family stress perspective. *Journal of Child & Family Studies*, *13*, 309–323.

Hampel, P. & Petermann, F. (2005). Age and gender effects on coping in children and adolescents. *Journal of Youth and Adolescence*, *34*(2), 73–83.

Handley, R. V., Salkovskis, P. M. & Ehlers, A. (2009). Treating clinically significant avoidance of public transport following the London bombings? *Behavioural and Cognitive Psychotherapy*, *37*(1), 87–93.

Hanes, C. C. H., Rife, E. M. & Laguna, L. B. (2005). The impact of a summer camp program as a secondary prevention measure for at-risk youth. *Crime Prevention and Community Safety: An International Journal*, *7*(3), 37–49.

Hans, J., Ganong, L. & Coleman, M. (2009). Financial responsibilities toward older parents and stepparents following divorce and remarriage. *Journal of Family and Economic Issues*, *30*(1), 55–66.

Hansagi, H., Brandt, L. & Andréasson, S. (2000). Parental divorce: Psychosocial well-being mental health and mortality during youth and young adulthood. A longitudinal study of Swedish conscripts. *The European Journal of Public Health*, *10*(2), 86–92.

Hansen, C. (2006). Music videos, effects. In J. J. Arnett (Ed.), *Encyclopedia of children, adolescents, and the media*. Thousand Oaks, CA: Sage, York: Wiley.

Hansen, E. B. & Breivik, G. (2001). Sensation seeking as a predictor of positive and negative risk behavior among adolescents. *Personality and Individual Differences, 30,* 627–640.

Hansen, F. & Wold, B. (2007). Norway. In J. J. Arnett, R. Ahmed, B. Nsamenang, T. S. Saraswathi, & R. Silbereisen (Eds.), *International encyclopedia of adolescence*. New York: Routledge.

Hansen, L. & Monk, M. (2002). Brain development, structuring of learning and science education: Where are we now? A review of some recent research. *International Journal of Science Education, 24*(4), 343–356.

Hardaway, C. K., Marler, P. L. & Chaves, M. (1993). What the polls don't show: A closer look at U.S. church attendance. *American Sociological Review, 58,* 741–752.

Hardway, C. & Fuligni, A. J. (2006). Dimensions of family connectedness among adolescents with Mexican, Chinese, and European backgrounds. *Developmental Psychology, 42*(6), 1246–1258.

Hargittai, E. & Walejko, G. (2008). The participation divide: Content creation and sharing in the digital age. *Information, Communication & Society, 11*(2), 239–256.

Harkness, S., Super, C. M. & van Tijen, N. (2000). Individualism and the 'Western mind' reconsidered: American and Dutch parents' ethnotheories of the child. In S. Harkness & C. Raeff (Eds.), *Variability in the social construction of the child* (pp. 23–39). San Francisco: Jossey-Bass.

Harley, D. & Fitzpatrick, G. (2009). YouTube and intergenerational communication: The case of Geriatric 1927. *Universal Access in the Information Society, 8*(1), 5–20.

Harmon, A. (1998, May 8). Underreporting found on male teen-age sex. *New York Times*, p. A-14.

Harnischfeger, J. (2003). The Bakassi Boys: fighting crime in Nigeria. *The Journal of Modern African Studies, 41*(1), 23–49.

Harrell, A., Mercer, S. & DeRosier, M. (2009). Improving the social-behavioral adjustment of adolescents: The effectiveness of a social skills group intervention. *Journal of Child and Family Studies, 18*(4), 378–387.

Harries, M. L. L., Walker, J. M., Hawkins, S., Williams, D. M. & Hughes, I. A. (1997). Changes in the male voice at puberty. *Archives of Disease in Childhood, 77*(5), 445–447.

Harris, J. & Grace, S. (1999). *A question of evidence? Investigating and prosecuting rape in the 1990s*. Home Office Research Study 196, London: Home Office.

Hart, D. & Atkins, R. (2004). Religious participation and the development of moral identity in adolescence. In T. A. Thorkildsen & H. J. Walberg (Eds.), *Nurturing morality* (pp. 157–172). New York: Kluwer.

Hart, D., Burock, D., London, B. & Atkins, R. (2003). Prosocial tendencies, antisocial behaviour, and moral development. In A. Slater & G. Bremner (Eds.), *An introduction to developmental psychology* (pp. 334–356). Malden, MA: Blackwell.

Hart, D., Burock, D., London, B., Atkins, R. & Bonilla-Santiago, G. (2005). The relation of personality types to physiological, behavioural, and cognitive processes. *European Journal of Personality, 19*(5), 391–407.

Hart, D., Donnelly, T. M., Touniss, J. & Atkins, R. (2007). High school community service as a predictor of adult voting and volunteering. *American Educational Research Journal, 44*(1), 197–219.

Harter, S. (2006). The development of self-esteem. In M. H. Kernis (Ed.), *Self-esteem issues and answers: A sourcebook of current perspectives* (pp. 144–150). New York: Psychology Press.

Harter, S. (2003). The development of self-representations during childhood and adolescence. In M. R. Leary & J. P. Tagney (Eds.), *Handbook of self and identity* (pp. 610–642). New York: Guilford Press.

Harter, S. (2002). Authenticity. In R. C. Snyder & J. S. Lopez (Eds.), *Handbook of positive psychology* (pp. 382–394). London: Oxford University Press.

Harter, S. (2001). On the importance of importance ratings in understanding adolescents' self-esteem: Beyond statistical parsimony. In R. J. Riding & S. G. Rayner (Eds.), *Self perception: International perspectives on individual differences* (Vol. 2, pp. 3–23). Westport, CT: Ablex.

Harter, S. (1999). *The construction of the self: A developmental perspective*. New York: Guilford.

Harter, S. (1990). Self and identity development. In S. S. Feldman & G. R. Elliott (Eds.), *At the threshold: The developing adolescent* (pp. 352–387). Cambridge, MA: Harvard University Press.

Harter, S., Waters, P. L. & Whitesell, N. R. (1997). Lack of voice as a manifestation of false-self behavior among adolescents: The school setting as a stage upon which the drama of authenticity is enacted. *Educational Psychologist, 32,* 153–173.

Harter, S., Waters, P., Whitesell, N. R. & Kastelic, D. (1998). Predictors of level of voice among high school females and males: Relational context, support, and gender orientation. *Developmental Psychology, 34,* 1–10.

Harter, S. & Whitesell, N. R. (2003). Beyond the debate: Why some adolescents report stable self-worth over time and situation, whereas others report changes in self-worth. *Journal of Personality, 71,* 1027–1058.

Hartos, J., Eitel, P. & Simons-Morton, B. (2002). Parenting practices and adolescent risky driving: A three-month prospective study. *Health Education and Behavior, 29,* 194–206.

Harwood, R., Leyendecker, B., Carlson, V., Asencio, M. & Miller, A. (2002). Parenting among Latino families in the U.S. In M. H. Bornstein (Ed.), *Handbook of parenting, Vol. 4: Social conditions and applied parenting* (2nd ed., 21–46). Mahwah, NJ: Erlbaum.

Hascher, T., Cocard, Y. & Moser, P. (2004). Forget about theory – practice is all? Student teachers' learning in practicum. *Teachers and Teaching: Theory and Practice, 10*(6), 623–637.

Hass, A. (1979). *Teenage sexuality: A survey of teenage sexual behavior*. New York: Macmillan.

Hatfield, E. (2005). *Love and sex: cross-cultural perspectives*. Lanham, MD: University Press of America.

Hatfield, E. & Rapson, R. L. (2005). *Love and sex: Cross-cultural perspectives*. New York: University Press of America.

Hatfield, E. & Rapson, R. L. (2006). Love and sexual health. In J. Kuriansky (Series Ed.), M. S. Teeper & A. F. Owens (Vol. Eds.), *Sex, love and psychology: Sexual health, Vol. 1. Psychological foundations* (pp. 93–97). New York: Praeger Publishing.

Hautala, L. A., Junnila, J., Helenius, H., Vaananen, A.-M., Liuksila, P.-R., Raiha, H., Valimaki, M. & Saarijarvi, S. (2008). Towards understanding gender differences in disordered eating among adolescents. *Journal of Clinical Nursing, 17*(13), 1803–1813.

Hawley, P. H., Little, T. D. & Card, N. A. (2007). The allure of a mean friend: Relationship quality and processes of aggressive adolescents with prosocial skills. *International Journal of Behavioural Development, 31*(2), 170–180.

Hawton, K., Bergen, H., Casey, D., Simkin, S., Palmer, B., Cooper, J., Kapur, N., Horrocks, J., House, A., Lilley, R., Noble, R. & Owens, D. (2007). Self-harm in England: A tale of three cities. *Social Psychiatry and Psychiatric Epidemiology, 42*(7), 513–521.

Hay, I. & Ashman, A. (2003). The development of adolescents' emotional stability and general self-concept: The interplay of parents, peers, and gender. *International Journal of Disability, Development and Education, 50*(1), 77–91.

Hayatbakhsh, M. R., Najman, J. M., Jamrozik, K., Al Mamun, A., Bor, W. & Alati, R. (2008). Adolescent problem behaviors predicting *DSM-IV* diagnoses of multiple substance use disorder: Findings of a prospective birth cohort study. *Social Psychiatry and Psychiatric Epidemiology, 43*(5), 356–363.

Haydn, T. (2004). The strange death of the comprehensive school in England and Wales, 1965–2002. *Research Papers in Education, 19*(4), 415–432.

Hayford, S. R. (2005). Conformity and change: Community effects on female genital cutting in Kenya. *Journal of Health and Social Behavior, 46*(2), 121–140.

Healy, S. (2006). 'Years ago some lived here': Aboriginal Australians and the production of popular culture, history and identity in 1930s Victoria. *Australian Historical Studies, 37*(128), 18–34.

Heard, H., Gorman, B. & Kapinus, C. (2008). Family structure and self-rated health in adolescence and young adulthood. *Population Research and Policy Review, 27*(6), 773–797.

Heatherington, L. & Lavner, J. (2008). Coming to terms with coming out: Review and recommendations for family systems-focused research. *Journal of Family Psychology, 22*(3), 329–343.

Heckhausen, J. & Tomasik, M. J. (2002). Get an apprenticeship before school is out: How German adolescents adjust vocational aspirations when getting close to a developmental deadline. *Journal of Vocational Behavior, 60*, 199–219.

Heilbrun, K., Goldstein, N. E. S. & Redding, R. E. (2005). *Juvenile delinquency: Prevention, assessment and intervention*. New York: Oxford University Press.

Heilman, M. E., Martell, R. F. & Simon, M. C. (1988). The vagaries of sex bias: Conditions regulating the undervaluation, equivaluation, and overvaluation of female job applicants. *Organizational Behavior and Human Decision Processes, 41*, 98–110.

Hein, V. & Hagger, M. (2007). Global self-esteem, goal achievement orientations, and self-determined behavioural regulations in a physical education setting. *Journal of Sports Sciences, 25*(2), 149–159.

Helgeson, V. (2002). *The psychology of gender*. Upper Saddle River, NJ: Prentice Hall.

Helgeson, V. S., Reynolds, K. A., Shestak, A. & Wei, S. (2006). Brief Report: Friendships of adolescents with and without diabetes. *Journal of Pediatric Psychology, 31*(2), 194–199.

Helson, R. & Srivastava, S. (2002). Creative and wise people: Similarities, differences, and how they develop. *Personality and Social Psychology Bulletin, 28*(10), 1430–1440.

Hemmings, A. (2002). Youth culture of hostility: discourses of money, respect, and difference. *International Journal of Qualitative Studies in Education, 15*(3), 291–307.

Hendrick, H. (2007). Optimism and hope versus anxiety and narcissism: Some thoughts on children's welfare yesterday and today. *History of Education, 36*(6), 747–768.

Hendry, L., Kloep, M. & Wood, S. (2002). Young people talking about adolescent rural crowds and social settings. *Journal of Youth Studies, 5*(4), 357–374.

Henerey, A. (2004). Evolution of male circumcision as normative control. *Journal of Men's Studies, 12*(3), 265–276.

Henggeler, S. W., Sheidow, A. J. & Lee, T. (2007). Multisystemic treatment of serious clinical problems in youths and their families. In D. W. Springer & A. R. Roberts (Eds.), *Handbook of forensic mental health with victims and offenders: Assessment, treatments, and research* (pp. 3315–345). Springer series on social work. New York: Springer Publishing Co.

Herba, C. M., Ferdinand, R. F., Stijnen, T., Veenstra, R., Oldehinkel, A. J., Ormel, J. & Verhulst, F. C. (2008). Victimisation and suicide ideation in the TRAILS study: specific vulnerabilities of victims. *Journal of Child Psychology and Psychiatry* (formerly *Journal of Child Psychology and Psychiatry and Allied Disciplines*), *49*(8), 867–876.

Herman-Giddens, M., Wang, L. & Koch, G. (2001). Secondary sexual characteristics in boys. *Archives of Pediatrics and Adolescent Medicine, 155*, 1022–1028.

Hermans, H. J. M. & Dimaggio, G. (2007). Self, identity, and globalisation in times of uncertainty: A dialogical analysis. *Review of General Psychology, 11*(1), 31–61.

Hermans, H. J. M. & Kempen, H. J. G. (1998). Moving cultures: The perilous problems of cultural dichotomies in a globalizing society. *American Psychologist, 53*, 1111–1120.

Herrnstein, R. J. & Murry, C. (1995). *The bell curve: Intelligence and class structure in American life*. New York: Simon & Schuster.

Herpertz-Dahlmann, B., Wille, N., Holling, J., Vloet, T. D., Ravens-Sieberer, U. [BELLA study group (Germany)] (2008). Disordered eating behavior and attitudes, associated psychopathology and health-related quality of life: Results of the BELLA study. *European Child & Adolescent Psychiatry*, *17*(Suppl. 1), 82–91.

Herzog, M. J. & Cooney, T. M. (2002). Parental divorce and perceptions of past interparental conflict: Influences on the communication of young adults. *Journal of Divorce and Remarriage*, *36*, 89–109.

Hesketh, T., Qu, J. D. & Tomkins, A. (2003). Health effects of family size: cross sectional survey in Chinese adolescents. *Archives of Disease in Childhood*, *88*(6), 467–471.

Hetherington, E. M. (2003). Social support and the adjustment of children in divorced and remarried families. *Childhood*, *10*(2), 217–236.

Hetherington, E. M. (1991). Presidential address: Families, lies, and videotapes. *Journal of Research on Adolescence*, *1*, 323–348.

Hetherington, E. M., Henderson, S. & Reiss, D. (1999). Adolescent siblings in stepfamilies: Family functioning and adolescent adjustment. *Monographs of the Society for Research in Child Development*, *64*.

Hetherington, E. M. & Kelly, J. (2002). *For better or worse: Divorce reconsidered*. New York: Norton.

Hetherington, E. M. & Stanley-Hagan, M. (2000). Diversity among stepfamilies. In D. H. Demo & K. R. Allen (Eds.), *Handbook of family diversity* (pp. 173–196). New York: Oxford University Press.

Heuveline, P. (2002). An international comparison of adolescent and young adult mortality. *Annals of the American Academy of Political Social Science*, *580*, 172–200.

Hewett, D. (2007). Do touch: Physical contact and people who have severe, profound and multiple learning difficulties. *Support for Learning*, *22*(3), 116–123.

Hicks, C. (1999). Incompatible skills and ideologies: The impediment of gender attributions on nursing research. *Journal of Advanced Nursing*, *30*(1), 129–139.

Higgins, G., Ricketts, M. & Vegh, D. (2008). The role of self-control in college student's perceived risk and fear of online victimization. *American Journal of Criminal Justice*, *33*(2), 223–233.

Hill, J. & Lynch, M. (1983). The intensification of gender-related role expectations during early adolescence. In J. Brooks-Gunn & A. Petersen (Eds.), *Female puberty*. New York: Plenum.

Hilton, Z. (2006). Disaffection and school exclusion: why are inclusion policies still not working in Scotland? *Research Papers in Education*, *21*(3), 295–314.

Hird, M. J. (2003). A typical gender identity conference? Some disturbing reports from the therapeutic front lines. *Feminism & Psychology*, *13*(2), 181–199.

Hird, M. J. & Jackson, S. (2001). Where 'angels' and 'wusses' fear to tread: Sexual coercion in adolescent dating relationships. *Journal of Sociology*, *37*, 27–43.

Hirsch, P. (2003). Adolescent driver risk taking and driver education: Evidence of a mobility bias in public policymaking. *Journal of Safety Research*, *34*, 289–298.

Ho, E. & Bedford, R. (2008). Asian transnational families in New Zealand: Dynamics and challenges. *International Migration*, *46*(4), 41–62.

Hochschild, A. R. (2001). Emotion work, feeling rules, and social structure. In A. Branaman (Ed.), *Self and society. Blackwell readers in sociology* (pp. 138–155). Malden, MA: Blackwell.

Hochschild, A. R. (1998). *The time bind: When work becomes home and home becomes work*. New York: Henry Holt.

Hockly N. (2000). Modelling and cognitive apprenticeship in teacher education. *ELT Journal*, *54*(2), 118–118.

Hodkinson, P. (2005). 'Insider research' in the study of youth cultures. *Journal of Youth Studies*, *8*, 131–149.

Hodkinson, P. & Deicke, W. (2009). *Youth cultures*. London: Routledge.

Hoek, H. W. (2006). Incidence, prevalence and mortality of anorexia nervosa and other eating disorders. *Current Opinion in Psychiatry*, *19*(4), 389–394.

Hoeve, M., Blokland, A., Dubas, J., Loeber, R., Gerris, J. & van der Laan, P. (2008). Trajectories of delinquency and parenting styles. *Journal of Abnormal Child Psychology*, *36*(2), 223–235.

Hoffman, B. R., Monge, P. R., Chou, C-P. & Valente, T. W. (2007). Perceived peer influence and peer selection on adolescent smoking. *Addictive Behaviours*, *32*(8), 1546–1554.

Hoffmann, J. (2006). Family structure, community context, and adolescent problem behaviors. *Journal of Youth and Adolescence*, *35*(6), 867–880.

Hoffmann, J. P., Baldwin, S. A. & Cerbone, F. G. (2003). Onset of major depressive disorder among adolescents. *Journal of the American Academy of Child & Adolescent Psychiatry*, *42*, 217–224.

Hoggett, P. P. H. (2006). Connecting, arguing, fighting. *Psychoanalysis, Culture & Society*, *11*(1), 1–16.

Hokoda, A., Lu, H-H. A. & Angeles, M. (2006). School bullying in Taiwanese adolescents. *Journal of Emotional Abuse*, *6*(4), 69–90.

Holden, K. (2004). 'Heaven help the teachers!' Parents' perspectives on the introduction of education for citizenship. *Educational Review*, *56*(3), 247–258.

Holder, M. & Coleman, B. (2009). The contribution of social relationships to children's happiness. *Journal of Happiness Studies*, *10*(3), 329–349.

Holdsworth, C. (2004). Family support during the transition out of the parental home in Britain, Spain and Norway. *Sociology*, *38*(5), 909–926.

Holfve-Sabel, M-A. (2006). A comparison of student attitudes towards school, teachers and peers in Swedish comprehensive schools now and 35 years ago. *Educational Research*, *48*(1), 55–75.

Holinger, P. (2009). Winnicott, Tomkins, and the psychology of affect. *Clinical Social Work Journal*, *37*(2), 155–162.

Holland, J. L. (1996). Exploring careers with a typology: What we have learned and some new directions. *American Psychologist*, *51*, 397–406.

Hollos, M. & Leis, P. E. (1989). *Becoming Nigerian in Ijo society*. New Brunswick, NJ: Rutgers University Press.

Holsen, I., Kraft, P. & Vitterso, J. (2000). Stability in depressed mood in adolescence: Results from a 6-year longitudinal panel study. *journal of Youth and Adolescence*, *29*(1), 61–78.

Holton, G. (1993). Can science be at the centre of modern culture?. *Public Understanding of Science*, *2*(4), 291–305.

Hong, T. K., Dibley, M. J., Sibbritt, D., Phan, N. T., Trang, N. H. H. D., & Tran, T. M. (2007). Overweight and obesity are rapidly emerging among adolescents in Ho Chi Minh City, Vietnam, 2002–04. *International Journal of Pediatric Obesity*, *2*, 194–201.

Hoobler, J. M. (2007). On-site or out-of-sight?: Family-friendly child care provisions and the status of working mothers. *Journal of Management Inquiry*, 372–380.

Hooghe, M. & Wilkenfeld, B. (2008). The stability of political attitudes and behaviours cross adolescence and early adulthood: A comparison of survey data on adolescents and young adults in eight countries. *Journal of Youth and Adolescence*, *37*(2), 155–167.

Horn, K., Dino, G., Kalsekar, I. & Mody, R. (2005). The impact of *Not On Tobacco* on teen smoking cessation: End-of-program evaluation results, 1998–2003. *Journal of Adolescent Research*, *20*, 640–661.

Horn, P. (1994). *Children's work and welfare, 1780–1890*. New York: Cambridge University Press.

Horn, S. (2006). Heterosexual adolescents' and young adults' beliefs and attitudes about homosexuality and gay and lesbian peers. *Cognitive Development*, *21*(4), 420–440.

Horn, S. (2003). Adolescents' reasoning about exclusion from social groups. *Developmental Psychology*, *39*(1), 71–84.

Horn, S. S., Killen, M. & Stangor, C. S. (1999). The influence of group stereotypes on adolescents' moral reasoning. *Journal of Early Adolescence*, *19*, 98–113.

Horne, A. (2004). 'Gonnae no' dae that!' The internal and external worlds of the delinquent adolescent. *Journal of Child Psychotherapy*, *30*(3), 330–346.

Horowitz, A. D. & Bromnick, R. D. (2007). Contestable adulthood: Variability and disparity in markers for negotiating the transition to adulthood. *Youth and Society*, *39*, 209–231.

House of Commons Library (1999). Research paper 99/11 A Century of Change: Trends in UK statistics since 1900 at http://www.parliament.uk/ accessed 22/09/2010.

House of Commons Papers (1842). [380]XV *Children's employment (mines)*. R. Com. 1st rep.

Houseman, M. (2007). Menstrual slaps and first blood celebrations. Inference, simulation and the learning of ritual. In Berliner, D. and R. Sarró. *Learning religion: Anthropological approaches*. (pp. 31–48). Oxford and New York: Berghahn Books.

Howard, K. S., Carothers, S. S., Smith, L. E. & Akai, C. E. (2007). Overcoming the odds: Protective factors in the lives of children. In J. G. Borkowski, J. R. Farris, T. L. Whitman, S. S. Carothers, K. Weed, et al. (Eds.), *Risk and Resilience: Adolescent mothers and their children grow up* (pp. 205–232). NJ: Lawrence Erlbaum.

Howie, G. & Shail, A. (Eds.) (2005). *Menstruation: A Cultural History*. New York: Palgrave MacMillan.

Huan, V., See, Y. L., Ang, R. & Har, C. W. (2008). The impact of adolescent concerns on their academic stress. *Educational Review*, *60*(2), 169–178.

Huang-Pollock, C. L., Carr, T. H. & Nigg, J. T. (2002). Development of selective attention: Perceptual load influences early versus late attentional selection in children and adults. *Developmental Psychology*, *38*, 363–375.

Huckle T., Conway K., Casswell S. & Pledger, M. (2005). Evaluation of a regional community action intervention in New Zealand to improve age checks for young people purchasing alcohol. *Health Promotion International*, *20*, 147–155.

Hudson B. (2006). User outcomes and children's services reform: Ambiguity and conflict in the policy implementation process. *Social Policy and Society*, *5*(2), 227–236.

Huebner, A. J. & Mancini, J. A. (2003). Shaping structured out-of-school time use among youth: The effects of self, family, and friend systems. *Journal of Youth and Adolescence*, *32*(6), 453–463.

Huiberts, A., Oosterwegel, A., Vandervalk, I., Vollebergh, W. & Meeus, W. (2006). Connectedness with parents and behavioural autonomy among Dutch and Moroccan adolescents. *Ethnic and Racial Studies*, *29*(2), 315–330.

Hulse, M. (1989). *The sorrows of young Werther, by Johann Wolfgang von Goethe, translated with an Introduction and Notes*. London: Penguin.

Hultén, A., Wasserman, D., Hawton, K., Jiang, G-X., Salander-Renberg, E., Schmidtke A., Bille-Brahe, U., Bjerke, T., Kerkhof, A., Michel, K. & Querejeta, I. (2000). Recommended care for young people (15–19 years) after suicide attempts in certain European countries. *European Child & Adolescent Psychiatry*, *9*(2), 100–108.

Hunter, A. G., Friend, C. A, Murphy, S. Y., Rollins, A., Williams-Wheeler, M. & Laughinghouse, J. (2006). Loss, survival, and redemption: African American male youths' reflections on life without fathers, manhood, and coming of age. *Youth & Society*, *37*(4), 423–452.

Hunter, D., Gambell, T. & Randhawa, B. (2005). Gender gaps in group listening and speaking: issues in social constructivist approaches to teaching and learning. *Educational Review*, *57*(3), 329–355.

Huntsinger, C. S. & Jose, P. E. (2006). A longitudinal investigation of personality and social adjustment among chinese American and European American adolescents. *Child Development*, *77*(5), 1309–1324.

Hussain, Y. & Bagguley, P. (2005). Citizenship, ethnicity and identity: British Pakistanis after the 2001 'riots'. *Sociology*, *39*(3), 407–425.

Hust, S. J. T., Brown, J. D. & L'Engle, K. L. (2008). Boys will be boys and girls better be prepared: An analysis of the rare sexual health messages in young adolescents' media. *Mass Communication and Society*, *11*(1), 3–23.

Hymer, B., Michel, D. & Todd, L. (2002). Dynamic Consultation: Towards process and challenge. *Educational Psychology in Practice*, *18*(1), 47–62.

Iacovou, M. (2002). Regional differences in the transition to adulthood. *Annals of the American Academy of Political Science Studies*, *580*(1), 40–69.

Iannaccone, L. & Berman, E. (2006). Religious extremism: The good, the bad, and the deadly. *Public Choice*, *128*(1–2), 109–129.

Ignatow, G. (2008). Transnational environmentalism at Europe's boundaries: Identity movements in Lithuania and Turkey. *Current Sociology*, *56*(6), 845–864.

ILO (2008). *Global Employment Trends for Youth*. New York: author

ILO (2006). *Global Employment Trends for Youth*. New York: author

ILO (2004a). *Global Employment Trends for Youth*. New York: author

ILO (2004b). Investing in every child. An economic study of the costs and benefits of eliminating child labour. New York: Author.

ILO (2002). *A future without child labour*. New York: Author.

Imtoual, A. & Hussein, S. (2009). Challenging the myth of the happy celibate: Muslim women negotiating contemporary relationships. *Contemporary Islam*, *3*(1), 25–39.

Indredavik, M. S., Vik, T., Heyerdahl, S., Kulseng, S., Fayers, P. & Brubakk, A-M. (2004). Psychiatric symptoms and disorders in adolescents with low birth weight. *Archives of Disease in Childhood. Fetal and Neonatal Edition*, *89*(5), F445–50.

Ingram, R. & Smith, L. T. (2008). Mood disorders. In J. E. Maddux & B. A. Winstead, *Psychopathology: Foundations for a contemporary understanding* (2nd ed., 171–197). New York: Routledge/Taylor & Francis Group.

Inhelder, B. & Piaget, J. (1958). *The growth of logical thinking from childhood to adolescence*. New York: Basic Books.

Ip, W.-Y. (2001). Knowledge and attitudes toward sex among chinese adolescents. *Western Journal of Nursing Research*, *23*(2), 211–223.

Iqbal, Z. (2002). Ethical issues involved in the implementation of a differential reinforcement of inappropriate behaviour programme for the treatment of social isolation and ritualistic behaviour in an individual with intellectual disabilities. *Journal of Intellectual Disability Research*, *46*(1), 82–93.

Ireson, J. & Hallam, S. (2005). Pupils' liking for school: Ability grouping, self-concept and perceptions of teaching. *The British Journal of Educational Psychology*, *75*(2), 297–311.

Irwin, C. E., Shafer, M-A. & Moscicki, A-B. (2003). The adolescent patient. In C. D. Rudolph, A. M. Rudolph (Eds.) *Rudolph's Pediatrics*, (21st ed., 223–270). New York: McGraw-Hill.

Irwin, K. (2004). The violence of adolescent life: Experiencing and managing everyday threats. *Youth & Society*, *35*(4), 452–479.

ISC (2010). Independent Schools Council. *Annual Census 29 April 2010*. London: ISC.

Isler, A., Tas, F., Beytut, D. & Conk, Z. (2009). Sexuality in adolescents with intellectual disabilities. *Sexuality and Disability*, *27*(1), 27–34.

Itakura, H. & Tsui, A. B. M. (2004). Gender and conversational dominance in Japanese conversation. *Language in Society*, *33*(2), 223–248.

Jablonska, B. & Lindberg, L. (2007). Risk behaviours, victimisation and mental distress among adolescents in different family structures. *Social Psychiatry and Psychiatric Epidemiology*, *42*(8), 656–663.

Jaccard, J., Blanton, H. & Dodge, T. (2005). Peer influences on risk behavior: An analysis of the effects of a close friend. *Developmental Psychology*, *41*, 135–147.

Jackson, C. (2003). Motives for 'laddishness' at school: Fear of failure and fear of the 'feminine'. *British Educational Research Journal*, *29*(4), 583–598.

Jackson, L. M., Pratt, M. W., Hunsberger, B. & Pancer, S. M. (2005). Optimism as a mediator of the relation between perceived parental authoritativeness and adjustment among adolescents: Finding the sunny side of the street. *Social Development*, *14*, 273–304.

Jackson, M. C., Hastings, G., Wheeler, C., Eadie, D. & MacKintosh, A. M. (2000). Marketing alcohol to young people: implications for industry regulation and research policy. *Addiction*, *95*(4), 597–608.

Jackson, R. (2004). Intercultural education and recent European pedagogies of religious education. *Intercultural Education*, *15*(1), 3–14.

Jackson, S. M. & Cram, F. (2003). Disrupting the sexual double standard: Young women's talk about heterosexuality. *British Journal of Social Psychology*, *42*, 113–127.

Jackson-Leach, R. & Lobstein T. (2006). Estimated burden of paediatric obesity and co-morbidities in Europe: Part 1. The increase in prevalence of childhood obesity in Europe is itself increasing. *International Journal of Pediatric Obesity*, *1*, 26–32.

Jacobs, J. E. & Klaczynski, P. A. (2005). *The development of judgment and decision making in children and adolescents*. Mahwah, NJ: Erlbaum.

Jacobs, J. E. & Klaczynski, P. A. (2002). The development of judgment and decision making during childhood and adolescence. *Current Directions in Psychological Science*, *11*, 145–149.

Jacobs, S. (2010). *Hinduism today: An introduction*. London: Continuum Publishing Corporation.

Jacobson, K. C. & Crockett, L. J. (2000). Parental monitoring and adolescent adjustment: An ecological perspective. *Journal of Research on Adolescence*, *10*, 65–98.

Jaffee, S. R., Moffitt, T. E., Caspi, A., Fombonne, E., Poulton, R. & Martin, J. (2002). Differences in early childhood risk factors for juvenile-onset and adult-onset depression. *Archives of General Psychiatry*, *59*, 215–222.

Jago, B. J. (2006). A primary act of imagination: An autoethnography of father-absence. *Qualitative Inquiry*, *12*(2), 398–426.

Jakobsh, D. (2006). Sikhism, interfaith dialogue, and women: Transformation and Identity. *Journal of Contemporary Religion*, *21*(2), 183–199.

Jamieson, L., Anderson, M., McCrone, D., Bechhofer, F., Stewart, R. & Li, Y. (2002). Cohabitation and commitment: partnership plans of young men and women. *The Sociological Review*, *50*(3), 356–377.

Janes, L. M. & Olson, J. M. (2000). Jeer pressure: The behavioral effects of observing ridicule of others. *Personality and Social Psychology Bulletin*, *26*(4), 474–485.

Jang, K. L., Vernon, P. A., Livesley, W. J., Stein, M. B. & Wolf, H. (2001). Intra- and extra-familial influences on alcohol and drug misuse: A twin study of gene-environment correlation. *Addiction*, *96*(9), 1307–1318.

Jankowiak, W. R. & Fischer, E. F. (1992). A cross-cultural perspective on romantic love. *Ethology*, *31*, 149–155.

Janosz, M., Archambault, I., Morizot, J. & Pagani, L. S. (2008). School engagement trajectories and their differential predictive relations to drop-out. *Journal of Social Issues*, *64*(1), 21–40.

Järvinen, M. & Østergaard, J. (2009). Governing adolescent drinking. *Youth & Society*, *40*(3), 377–402.

Jarvinen, T. & Vanttaja, M. (2001). Young people, education and work: Trends and changes in Finland in the 1990s. *Journal of Youth Studies*, *4*(2), 195–207.

Jayne, M., Holloway, S. L. & Valentine, G. (2006). Drunk and disorderly: Alcohol, urban life and public space. *Progress in Human Geography*, *30*(4), 451–468.

Jeffries, E. D. (2004). Experiences of trust with parents: A qualitative investigation of African American, Latino, and Asian American boys from low income families. In N. Way., Y. Judy, Chu (Eds.), *Adolescent boys: Exploring diverse cultures of boyhood* (pp. 107–128). New York: New York University Press.

Jellyellie (2007). *How Teenagers Think: An insider's guide to living with a teenager*. Great Ambrook: White Ladder Press.

Jensen, L. A. (2008a). Coming of age in a multicultural world: Globalisation and adolescent cultural identity formation. In D. L. Browning (Ed.), *Adolescent identities: A collection of readings* (pp. 3–17). Relational perspectives book series. New York: Analytic Press/Taylor & Francis Group.

Jensen, L. A. (2008b). Through two lenses: A cultural-developmental approach to moral psychology. *Developmental Review*, *28*, 289–315.

Jensen, L. A. (2007). Coming of age in a multicultural world: Globalization and adolescent cultural identity formation. Reprinted in D. L. Browning (Ed.), *Adolescent identities: A collection of readings* (pp. 3–17). Relational perspectives book series. New York: Analytic Press/Taylor & Francis Group.

Jensen, L. A. & Williams, E. (2001). *The everyday moral life of American emerging adults: A diary study*. Paper presented at the biennial meeting of the Society for Research on Adolescence, New Orleans, LA.

Jetten, J., McAuliffe, B. J., Hornsey, M. J. & Hogg. M. A. (2006). Differentiation between and within groups: the influence of individualist and collectivist group norms. *European Journal of Social Psychology*, *36*(6), 825–843.

Jetten, J., Postmes, T. and McAuliffe, B. J. (2002). 'We're all individuals': Group norms of individualism and collectivism, levels of identification and identity threat. *European Journal of Social Psychology*, *32*(2), 189–207.

Jeynes, W. (2002). *Divorce, family structure, and the academic success of children*. New York: Haworth Press.

Jeynes, W. H. (2007). The impact of parental remarriage on children: A meta-analysis. *Marriage & Family Review*, *40*(4), 75–102.

Jeynes, W. H. (1999). Effects of remarriage following divorce on the academic achievement of children. *Journal of Youth & Adolescence*, *28*, 385–393.

Jindal-Snape, D. & Foggie, J. (2008). A holistic approach to primary—secondary transitions. *Improving Schools*, *11*(1), 5–18.

Jindal-Snape, D. & Miller, D. (2010). A challenge of living? Understanding the psycho-social processes of the child during primary–secondary transition through resilience and self-esteem theories. *Educational Psychology Review*, *20*(3), 217–236.

Joffe, A. (2000). Why adolescent medicine? *Medical Clinics of North America*, *84*(4), 769–785.

Johnson, A., Wadsworth, J., Wellings, K. & Field, J. (1994). *Sexual attitudes and lifestyles*. Oxford: Blackwell.

Johnson, A. M., Mercer, C. H., Erens, B., Copas, A. J., McManus, S., Wellings, K., Fenton, K. A., Korovessis, C., Macdowall, W., Nanchahal, K., Purdon, S. & Field, J. (2001). Sexual behaviour in Britain: Partnerships, practices, and HIV risk behaviours. *Lancet*, *358*(9296),1835–1842.

Johnson, E. & Hastings, R. P. (2002). Facilitating factors and barriers to the implementation of intensive home-based behavioural intervention for young children with autism. *Child: Care Health & Development*, *28*(2), 123–129.

Johnson, F., Cooke, L., Croker, H. & Wardle, J. (2008). Changing perceptions of weight in Great Britain: Comparison of two population surveys. *BMJ (British Medical Journal)*, *337*(7), a494–a494.

Johnson, G. R., Krug, E. G. & Potter, L. B. (2000). Suicide among adolescents and young adults: A cross-national comparison of 34 countries. *Suicide & Life-Threatening Behavior*, *30*, 74–82.

Johnson, J. D., Adams, M. S., Ashburn, L. & Reed, W. (1995). Differential gender effects of exposure to rap music on African American adolescents' acceptance of teen dating violence. *Sex Roles*, *33*, 597–605.

Johnson, J. G., Cohen, P., Kasen, S. & Brook, J. S. (2002). Eating disorders during adolescence and the risk for physical and mental disorders during early adulthood. *Archives of General Psychiatry*, *59*, 545–552.

Johnson, S. K., Murphy, S. R., Zewdie, S. & Reichard, R. J. (2008). The strong, sensitive type: Effects of gender stereotypes and leadership prototypes on the evaluation of male and female leaders. *Organizational Behavior and Human Decision Processes*, *106*(1), 39–60.

Johnston, L. D., O'Malley, P. M., Bachman, J. G., Schulenberg, J. E. & Bethesda, M. D. (2008). *Monitoring the future, national results on adolescent drug Use: Over view of key findings, 2007* (NIH Publication No. 08–6418). Bethesda, MD: National Institutes of Health.

Johnston, R., Wilson, D. & Burgess, S. (2004). School segregation in multiethnic England. *Ethnicities*, *4*(2), 237–265.

Jones, D. (2004). The eloquent sari. *Textile: The Journal of Cloth and Culture, 2*(1), 52–63.

Jones, G., O'Sullivan, A. & Rouse, J. (2006). Young adults, partners and parents: Individual agency and the problems of support. *Journal of Youth Studies, 9*(4), 375–392.

Jonsson, B. & Flanagan, C. (2000). Young people's views on distributive justice, rights, and obligations: A cross-cultural study. *International Social Science Journal, 52*(164), 195–208.

Jordan, E. (2001). Exclusion of travellers in state schools. *Educational Research, 43*(2), 117–132.

Jørgensen, M., Moustgaard, H., Bjerregaard, P. & Borch-Johnsen, K. (2006). Gender differences in the association between westernization and metabolic risk among Greenland Inuit. *European Journal of Epidemiology, 21*(10), 741–748.

Jose, P. E. & Brown, I. (2008). When does the gender difference in rumination begin? Gender and age differences in the use of rumination by adolescents. *Journal of Youth and Adolescence, 37*(2), 180–192.

Juang, L. P. & Silbereisen, R. K. (2002). The relationship between adolescent academic capability beliefs, parenting and school grades. *Journal of Adolescence, 25*, 3–18.

Juvonen, J. & Galván, A. (2008). In M. J. Prinstein & K. A. Dodge (Eds.), *Understanding peer influence in children and adolescents. Duke series in child development and public policy* (pp. 225–244). New York: Guilford Press.

Juvonen, J. & Murdock, T. (1995). Grade-level differences in the social value of effort: Implications for self-presentation tactics of early adolescents. *Child Development, 66*, 1694–1705.

Kaganas, F. & Diduck, A. (2004). Incomplete citizens: Changing images of post-separation children. *The Modern Law Review, 67*(6), 959–981.

Kahn, L. M. (2000). Wage inequality, collective bargaining, and relative employment from 1985 to 1994: Evidence from fifteen OECD countries. *The Review of Economics and Statistics, 82*(4), 564–579.

Kail, R. & Hall, L. K. (2001). Distinguishing short-term memory from working memory. *Memory and Cognition, 29*, 1–9.

Kalenkoski, C. & Foster, G. (2012). The quality of time spent with children in Australian households. *Review of Economics of the Household*, Preprint, 1–24.

Kalev, H. D. (2004). Cultural rights or human rights: The case of female genital mutilation. *Sex Roles, 51*(5–6), 339–348.

Kalman, M. (2003). Taking a different path: Menstrual preparation for adolescent girls living apart from their mothers. *Health Care for Women International, 24*(10), 868–879.

Kaltiala-Heino, R., Kosunen, E. & Rimpelä, M. (2003). Pubertal timing, sexual behaviour and self-reported depression in middle adolescence. *Journal of Adolescence, 26*, 531–545.

Kamat, S. (2004). Postcolonial aporias, or what does fundamentalism have to do with globalization? The contradictory consequences of education reform in India. *Comparative Education, 40*(2), 267–287.

Kandel, D. B. (Ed.) (2002). *Stages and pathways of drug involvement: Examining the gateway hypothesis*. New York: Cambridge University Press.

Kandel, D. B. (1975). Stages in adolescent involvement in drug use. *Science, 190*, 912–914.

Kandel, D. B. & Faust, R. (1975). Sequence and stages in patterns of adolescent drug use. *Archives of General Psychiatry, 32*, 923–932.

Kang, S-M., Shaver, P. R., Sue, S., Min, K-H. & Jing, H. (2003). Culture-specific patterns in the prediction of life satisfaction: Roles of emotion, relationship quality, and self-esteem. *Personality and Social Psychology Bulletin, 29*(12), 1596–1608.

Karniol, R., Grosz, E. & Schorr, I. (2003). Caring, gender role orientation, and volunteering. *Sex Roles, 49*(1–2), 11–19.

Kao, G. & Joyner, K. (2004). Do race and ethnicity matter among friends? Activites among interracial, interethnic, and intraethnic, adolescent friends. *Sociological Quarterly, 45*, 557–573.

Kaplan, S. J., Pelcovitz, D., Salzinger, S., Mandel, F., Weiner, M. & Labruna, V. (1999). Adolescent physical abuse and risk for suicidal behaviors. *Journal of Interpersonal Violence, 14*(9), 976–988.

Karila, K., Kinos, J., Niiranen, P. & Virtanen, J. (2005). Curricula of finnish kindergarten teacher education: Interpretations of early childhood education, professional competencies and educational theory. *European Early Childhood Education Research Journal, 13*(2), 133–145.

Kárpáti, A. (2004). ICT in Hungarian education – A brief overview. *Educational Media International, 41*(1), 19–25.

Kassam, A. (2006). Encounters with the north: Psychiatric consultation with Inuit youth. Journal of the Canadian Academy of Child and Adolescent Psychiatry. *Journal de l'Académie Canadienne de Psychiatrie de l'Enfant et de l'Adolescent, 15*(4), 174–178.

Katz, A. N., Blasko, D. G. & Kazmerski, V. A. (2004). Saying what you don't mean: Social influences on sarcastic language processing. *Current Directions in Psychological Science, 13*, 186–189.

Kaufman, A. S. & Lichtenberger, E. O. (2006). *Assessing adolescent and adult intelligence* (3rd ed.). Hoboken, NJ: John Wiley & Sons.

Kaufman, N. K., Rohde, P., Seeley, J. R., Clarke, G. N. & Stice, E. (2005). Potential mediators of cognitive-behavioral therapy for adolescents with comorbid major depression and conduct disorder. *Journal of Consulting & Clinical Psychology, 73*, 38–46.

Kaufmann, D., Gesten, E., Santa Lucia, R. C., Salcedo, O., Rendina-Gobioff, G. & Gadd, R. (2000). The relationship between parenting style and children's adjustment: The parents' perspective. *Journal of Child and Family Studies, 9*(2), 231–245.

Kaylor, L. (1999). Antisocial Personality Disorder: Diagnostic, ethical and treatment issues. *Issues in Mental Health Nursing, 20*(3), 247–258.

Keage, H. A. D, Clark, C. R., Hermens, D. F., Williams, L. M., Kohn, M. R., Clarke, S., Lamb, C., Crewther, D. &

Gordon, E. (2008). Putative biomarker of working memory systems development during childhood and adolescence. *Neuroreport: For Rapid Communication of Neuroscience Research, 19*(2), 197–201.

Keating, D. (2004). Cognitive and brain development. In L. Steinberg & R. M. Lerner (Eds.), *Handbook of adolescent psychology* (2nd ed.). New York: Wiley.

Keating, D. P. & Sasse, D. K. (1996). Cognitive socialization in adolescence: Critical period for a critical habit of mind. In G. R. Adams, R. Montemayer, & T. Gullotta (Eds.), *Psychosocial development during adolescence* (pp. 232–258). Thousand Oaks, CA: Sage.

Keddie, A. (2007). Issues of power, masculinity, and gender justice: Sally's story of teaching boys. *Discourse, 28*(1), 21–35.

Keenan, T. (2002). *An introduction to child development.* London: Sage.

Keller, J. (2008). On the development of regulatory focus: the role of parenting styles. *European Journal of Social Psychology, 38*(2), 354–364.

Keller, J. & Dauenheimer, D. (2003). Stereotype threat in the classroom: Dejection mediates the disrupting threat effect on women's math performance. *Personality and Social Psychology Bulletin, 29*(3), 371–381.

Kelly, J. (2007). Children's living arrangements following separation and divorce: Insights from empirical and clinical research. *Family Process, 46*(1), 35–52.

Kelly, J. A., Amirkhanian, Y. A., Kabakchieva, E., Csepe, P., Seal, D. W., Antonova, R., Mihaylov, A. & Gyukits, G. (2004). Gender roles and HIV sexual risk vulnerability of Roma (Gypsies) men and women in Bulgaria and Hungary: an ethnographic study. *AIDS Care, 16*(2), 231–245.

Kelly, J. B. (2000). Children's adjustment in conflicted marriage and divorce: A decade review of research. *Journal of the American Academy of Child & Adolescent Psychiatry, 39*, 963–973.

Kelly, S. (2004). Do increased levels of parental involvement account for social class differences in track placements? *Social Science Research, 33*, 626–659.

Keltikangas-Järvinen, L. (2002). Aggressive problem-solving strategies, aggressive behavior, and social acceptance in early and late adolescence. *Journal of Youth and Adolescence, 31*(4), 279–287.

Kendall-Tackett, K. A., Williams, L. M. & Finkelhor, D. (2001). Impact of sexual abuse on children: A review and synthesis of recent empirical studies. In R. Bull (Ed.), *Children and the law: The essential readings* (pp. 31–76). Malden, MA: Blackwell.

Kerestes, M., Youniss, J. & Metz, E. (2004). Longitudinal patterns of religious perspective and civic integration. *Applied Developmental Science, 8*, 39–46.

Keresztes, N., Piko, B. F., Pluhar, Z. F. & Page, R. M. (2008). Social influences in sports activity among adolescents. *Journal of the Royal Society for the Promotion of Health, 128*(1), 21–25.

Kerr, M. & Stattin, H. (2000). What parents know, how they know it, and several forms of adolescent adjustment: Further support for a reinterpretation of parental monitoring. *Developmental Psychology, 36*, 366–380.

Kershaw, T. S., Ethier, K. A., Niccolai, L. M., Lewis, J. B. & Lckovics, J. R. (2003). Misperceived risk among female adolescents: Social and psychological factors associated with sexual risk accuracy. *Health Psychology, 22*, 523–532.

Kett, J. (1977). *Rites of passage: Adolescence in America, 1790 to the present.* New York: Basic Books.

Kia-Keating, M. & Ellis, B. H. (2007). Belonging and connection to school in resettlement: Young refugees, school belonging, and psychosocial adjustment. *Clinical Child Psychology and Psychiatry, 12*(1), 29–43.

Kiang, L. & Fuligni, A. (2009). Ethnic identity in context: variations in ethnic exploration and belonging within parent, same-ethnic peer, and different-ethnic peer relationships. *Journal of Youth and Adolescence, 38*(5), 732–743.

Kielty, S. (2006). Similarities and differences in the experiences of non-resident mothers and non-resident fathers. *International Journal of Law, Policy and the Family, 20*(1), 74–94.

Kiernan, K. (2004). Cohabitation and divorce across nations and generations. In P. L. Chase-Lansdale, K. Kiernan, R. J. Friedman (Eds.), *Human development across lives and generations: The potential for change* (pp. 139–170). New York: Cambridge University Press.

Kiernan, K. (2002). Cohabitation in Western Europe: Trends, issues, and implications. In A. Booth & A. C. Crouter (Eds.), *Just living together: Implications of cohabitation on families, children, and social policy* (pp. 3–31). Mahwah, NJ: Erlbaum.

Kiesner, J. & Kerr, M. (2004). Families, peers, and contexts as multiple determinants of adolescent problem behavior. *Journal of Adolescence, 27*, 493–495.

Killen, M. & Hart, D. (1999). *Morality in everyday life.* New York: Cambridge University Press.

Killen, M. & Wainryb, C. (2000). Independence and interdependence in diverse cultural contexts. In. S. Harkness & C. Raeff (Eds.), *Variability in the social construction of the child* (pp. 5–21). *New Directions for Child Development, No. 87.* San Francisco: Jossey-Bass.

Kilpatrick, D. G., Acierno, R., Saunders, B., Resnick, H. S., Best, C. L. & Schnurr, P. P. (2000). Risk factors for adolescent substance abuse and dependence: Data from a national sample. *Journal of Consulting & Clinical Psychology, 68*, 19–30.

Kim, H. & Markus, H. R. (1999). Deviance or uniqueness, harmony and conformity? *Journal of Personality and Social Psychology, 77*, 785–800.

Kim, J. L., Sorsoli, C. L., Collins, K., Zylbergold, B. A., Schooler, D. & Tolman, D. L. (2007). From sex to sexuality: Exposing the heterosexual script on primetime network television. *Journal of Sex Research, 44*(2), 145–157.

Kim, K. & Smith, P. K. (1999). Family relations in early childhood and reproductive development. *Journal of Reproductive and Infant Psychology, 17*(2), 133–148.

Kimber, B., Sandell, R. & Bremberg, S. (2008). Social and emotional training in Swedish classrooms for the promotion of mental health: results from an effectiveness study in Sweden. *Health Promotion International*, *23*(2), 134–134.

King, A. (2007). Why I am not an Individualist. *Journal for the Theory of Social Behaviour*, *37*, 211–219.

King, A. (2002). The outsider as political leader: The case of Margaret Thatcher. *British Journal of Political Science*, *32*(3), 435–454.

King, B. M. (2005). *Human sexuality today* (5th ed.). Upper Saddle River, NJ: Prentice Hall.

King, G., McDougall, J., DeWit, D., Hong, S., Miller, L., Offord, D., Meyer, K. & LaPorta, J. (2005). Pathways to children's academic performance and prosocial behaviour: Roles of physical health status, environmental, family, and child factors. *International Journal of Disability, Development and Education*, *52*(4), 313–344.

King, M., Weich, S., Nazroo, J. & Blizard, B. (2006). On behalf of the Empiric Team. Religion, mental health and ethnicity. EMPIRIC – A national survey of England. *Journal of Mental Health*, *15*(2), 153–162.

King, P. E. & Boyatzis, C. J. (2004). Exploring adolescent spiritual and religious development: Current and future theoretical and empirical perspectives. *Applied Developmental Science*, *8*, 2–6.

King, P. E., Furrow, J. L. & Roth, N. (2002). The influence of families and peers on adolescent religiousness. *Journal of Psychology and Christianity*, *21*, 109–120.

King, P. M. & Kitchener, K. S. (2004). Reflective judgment: Theory and research on the development of epistemic judgment through adulthood. *Educational Psychologist*, *39*, 5–18.

King, P. M. & Kitchener, K. S. (2002). The reflective judgment model: Twenty years of research on epistemic cognition. In B. K. Hofer & P. R. Pintrich (Eds.), *Personal epistemology: The psychology of beliefs about knowledge and knowing* (pp. 37–61). Mahwah, NJ: Erlbaum.

Kinney, D. (1993). From nerds to normals: The recovery of identity among adolescents from middle school to high school. *Sociology of Education*, *66*, 21–40.

Kinney, D. A. (1999). From 'headbangers' to 'hippies': Delineating adolescents' active attempts to form an alternative peer culture. *New Directions for Child Development*, *84*, 21–35.

Kinsey, A. C., Pomeroy, W., Martin, C. E. & Gebhard, P. (1953). *Sexual behavior in the human female*. Philadelphia: Saunders.

Kipke, M. D. (Ed.) (1999). *Adolescent development and the biology of puberty: Summary of a workshop on new research*. Washington, DC: National Academy Press.

Kiras, J. D. (2007). Dying to prove a point: The methodology of dying to win. *Journal of Strategic Studies*, *30*(2), 227–241.

Kirschner, P., Van Vilsteren, P., Hummel, H. & Wigman, M. (1997). The design of a study environment for acquiring academic and professional competence. *Studies in Higher Education*, *22*(2), 151–171.

Kitchener, K. S., King, P. M. & DeLuca, S. (2006). Development of reflective judgment in adulthood. In

C. Hoare (Ed.), *Handbook of adult development and learning* (pp. 73–98). New York: Oxford University Press.

Kite, M. E., Deaux, K. & Hines, E. (2008). Gender stereotypes. In F. L. Denmark, M. A. Paludi (Eds.), *Psychology of women: A handbook of issues and theories* (2nd ed., 205–236). Women's psychology. Westport, CT: Praeger Publishers/Greenwood Publishing Group.

Kittler, P., Krinsky-McHale, S. J. & Devenny, D. A. (2004). Sex differences in performance over 7 years on the Wechsler Intelligence Scale for Children – Revised among adults with intellectual disability. *Journal of Intellectual Disability Research*, *48*(2), 114–122.

Klaczynski, P. A. (2006). Learning, belief biases, and metacognition. *Journal of Cognition and Development*, *7*(3), 295–300.

Klaczynski, P. A. (2005). Metacognition and cognitive variability: A dual-process model of decision making and its development. In E. J. Jacobs & P. A. Klaczynski (Eds.), *The development of judgment and decision making in children and adolescents* (pp. 39–76). Mahwah, NJ: Erlbaum.

Klaczynski, P. A. (2001). Cognition and language analytic and heuristic processing influences on adolescent reasoning and decision-making. *Child Development*, *72*(3), 844–861.

Klaczynski, P. A. (2000). Motivated scientific reasoning biases, epistemological beliefs, and theory polarization: A two-process approach to adolescent cognition. *Child Development*, *71*(5), 1347–1366.

Klaczynski, P. A., Fauth, J. M. & Swanger, A. (1998). Adolescent identity: Rational vs. experiential processing, formal operations, and critical thinking beliefs. *Journal of Youth and Adolescence*, *27*(2), 185–207.

Klaff, F. (2007). *Children of divorce*. In F. Shaprio, F. W. Kaslow, & L. Maxfield (Eds.), Handbook of EMDR and family therapy processes (pp. 284–305). Hoboken, NJ: John Wiley & Sons Inc. xxxiii, 470.

Klauer, K. C., Wegener, I. & Ehrenberg, K. (2002). Perceiving minority members as individuals: The effects of relative group size in social categorization. *European Journal of Social Psychology*, *32*(2), 223–245.

Klein, C. T. F. & Helweg-Larsen, M. (2002). Perceived control and the optimistic bias: A meta analytic review. *Psychology & Health*, *17*(4), 437–446.

Klomek, A. B., Marrocco, F., Kleinman, M., Schonfeld, I. S. & Gould, M. S. (2007). Bullying, depression and suicidality in adolescents. *Journal of the American Academy of Child & Adolescent Psychiatry*, *46*(1), 40–49.

Klomsten, A. T., Skaalvik, E. M. & Espnes, G. A. (2004). Physical self-concept and sports: Do gender differences still exist? *Sex Roles*, *50*, 119–127.

Knafo, A. & Schwartz, S. H. (2004). Identity formation and parent-child value congruence in adolescence. *British Journal of Developmental Psychology*, *22*(3), 439–458.

Knowles, M. L. & Gardner, W. L. (2008). Benefits of membership: The activation and amplification of group identities in response to social rejection. *Personality and Social Psychology Bulletin*, *34*(9), 1200–1213.

Knox, M., Funk, J., Elliott, R. & Bush, E. G. (2000). Gender differences in adolescents' possible selves. *Youth & Society*, *31*(3), 287–309.

Kobayashi, A. (2006). Why women of colour in geography? Gender, place and culture. *Journal of Feminist Geography*, *13*(1), 33–38.

Kohlberg, L. (1986). A current statement on some theoretical issues. In S. Modgit & C. Modgil (Eds.), *Lawrence Kohlberg*. Philadelphia: Falmer.

Kohlberg, L. (1981). *Essays on moral development Vol. 1: The philosophy of moral development*. New York: Harper & Row.

Kohlberg, L. (1976). Moral stages and moralization: The cognitive-development approach. In T. Lickona (Ed.), *Moral development and behaviour*. New York: Holt, Rinehart and Winston.

Kohlberg, L. (1966). A cognitive-developmental analysis of children's sex role concepts and attitudes. In E. E. Maccoby (Ed.), *The development of sex differences*. Palo Alto, CA: Stanford University Press.

Kohlberg, L. (1958). *The development of modes of moral thinking and choice in the years 10 to 16*. Unpublished doctoral dissertation, University of Chicago.

Kohlstedt, S. G. (2005). Nature, not books: Scientists and the origins of the nature-study movement in the 1890s. *Isis*, *96*(3), 324–352.

Kontula, O. & Pötsönen, R. (1999). How are attitudes towards condoms related to gender and sexual experiences among adolescents in Finland? *Health Promotion International*, *14*(3), 211–219.

Kopelman, L. & Kopelman, A. (2007). Using a new analysis of the best interests standard to address cultural disputes: Whose data, which values? *Theoretical Medicine and Bioethics*, *8*(5), 373–391.

Kornhaber, M. L. (2004). Using multiple intelligences to overcome cultural barriers to identifications for gifted education. In D. Boothe & J. C. Stanley. (Eds.), *In the eyes of the beholder: Critical issues for diversity in gifted education* (pp. 215–225). Waco, TX: Prufrock Press

Korteweg, A. & Yurdakul, G. (2009). Islam, gender, and immigrant integration: Boundary drawing in discourses on honour killing in the Netherlands and Germany. *Ethnic and Racial Studies*, *32*(2), 218–238.

Kosti, R. I. & Panagiotakos, D. B. (2006). The epidemic of obesity in children and adolescents in the world. *Central European Journal of Public Health*, *14*,151–159.

Kosunen, E., Kaltiala-Heino, R., Rimpelä, M. & Laippala, P. (2003). Risk-taking sexual behaviour and self-reported depression in middle adolescence – a school-based survey. *Child: Care Health & Development*, *29*(5), 337–344.

Kouvonen, A. & Kivivuori, J. (2001). Part-time jobs, delinquency and victimization among Finnish adolescents, *Journal of Scandinavian Studies in Criminology and Crime Prevention*, *2*(2), 191–212.

Kouvonen, A. & Lintonen, T. (2002). Adolescent part-time work and heavy drinking in Finland. *Addiction*, *97*(3), 311–318.

Kowal, A. K., Krull, J. L. & Kramer, L. (2004). How the differential treatment of siblings is linked with parent-child relationship quality. *Journal of Family Psychology*, *18*, 658–665.

Kowalski, R. (2008). *Cyberbullying: Bullying in the digital age*. Malden, MA: Blackwell.

Kowalski, R. M. & Limber, S. P. (2007). Electronic bullying among middle school students. *Journal of Adolescent Health*, *41*(6), S22–S30.

Kral, M. J., Burkhardt, K. J. & Kidd, S. (2002). The new research agenda for a cultural psychology. *Canadian Psychology*, *43*, 154–162.

Kramarski, B. (2004). Making sense of graphs: Does meta-cognitive instruction make a difference on students' mathematical conceptions and alternative conceptions? *Learning and Instruction*, *14*, 593–619.

Krause, E. L. (2005). 'Toys and perfumes:' Imploding Italy's population paradox and motherly myths. In C. B. Douglass (Ed.), *Barren states: The population 'implosion' in Europe* (pp. 159–182). New York: Berg.

Krauth, C., Buser, K. & Vogel, H. (2002). How high are the costs of eating disorders - anorexia nervosa and bulimia nervosa – for German society?. *The European Journal of Health Economics*, *3*(4), 244–250.

Kroger, J. (2007). *Identity development: Adolescence through adulthood* (2nd ed.). Thousand Oaks, CA: Sage.

Kroger, J. (2004). *Identity in adolescence: The balance between self and other*. Hove: Routledge.

Kroger, J. (2003). Identity development during adolescence. In G. Adams & M. Berzonsky (Eds.), *Blackwell handbook of adolescence* (pp. 205–225). Malden, MA: Blackwell.

Kroger, J. (2002). Commentary on 'Feminist perspectives on Erikson's theory: Their relevance for contemporary identity development research.' *Identity*, *2*, 257–266.

Kuhn, D. (2002). Metacognitive development. *Current Directions in Psychological Science*, *9*(5), 178–181.

Kuhn, D. (1999). Metacognitive development. In L. Balte & C. S. Tamis-LeMonde (Eds.), *Child psychology: A handbook of contemporary issues* (pp. 259–286). Philadelphia: Psychology Press.

Kuhn D. (1992). Cognitive development. In M. H. Bornstein & M. Lamb (Eds.), *Developmental psychology: An advanced textbook* (3rd ed., 211–272). Hillsdale, NJ: Erlbaum.

Kulik, L. (2000). Gender identity, sex typing of occupations, and gender role ideology among adolescents: Are they related? *International Journal for the Advancement of Counselling*, *22*(1), 43–56.

Kundu, S. & Adams, G. R. (2005). Identity formation, individuality, and connectedness in East Indian and non-East Indian female Canadian emerging adults. *Identity*, *5*, 247–260.

Kuntsche, E., Rehm, J. & Gmel, G. (2004). Characteristics of binge drinkers in Europe. *Social Science & Medicine*, *59*(1), 113–127.

Kur, E., DePorres, D. & Westrup, N. (2008). Teaching and learning action research: Transforming students, faculty and university in Mexico. *Action Research*, *6*(3), 327–349.

Kurdek, L. A. & Krile, D. (1982). A developmental analysis of the relation between peer acceptance, interpersonal understanding and perceived social self-competence. *Child Development*, *53*, 1485–1491.

Kurtz, P. D., Lindsey, E. W., Jarvis, S. & Nackerud, L. (2000). How runaway and homeless youth navigate troubled waters: The role of formal and informal helpers. *Child and Adolescent Social Work Journal*, *17*(5), 381–402.

Kuttler, A. F., La Greca, A. M. & Prinstein, M. J. (1999). Friendship qualities and social-emotional functioning of adolescents with close, cross-sex friendships. *Journal of Research on Adolescence*, *9*, 339–366.

Kwon, H., Reiss, A. L. Menon, V. (2002). Neural basis of protracted developmental changes in visuo-spatial working memory. *Proceedings of the National Academy of Sciences of the United States of America*, *99*(20), 13336–41.

Labour Force Survey (2010). *The Poverty Site Young Adult Unemployment* accessed 27 February 2011 at: http://www.poverty.org.uk/35/index.shtml

Labouvie-Vief, G. (2006). Emerging structures of adult thought. In J. J. Arnett & J. Tanner (Eds.), *Emerging adults in America: Coming of age in the 21st century* (pp. 59–84). Washington, DC: American Psychological Association.

Labouvie-Vief, G. (1998). Cognitive-emotional integration in adulthood. In K. W. Schaie & M. P. Lawton (Eds.), *Annual review of gerontology and geriatrics*, *Vol. 17: Focus on emotion and adult development* (pp. 206–237). New York: Springer.

Labouvie-Vief, G. (1990). Modes of knowledge and the organization of development. In M. L. Commons, J. D. Sinnott, F. A. Richards, & C. Armon (Eds.), *Models and methods in the study of adolescent and adult thought* (pp. 43–62). New York: Praeger.

Labouvie-Vief, G. (1982). Dynamic development and mature autonomy: A theoretical prologue. *Human Development*, *25*, 161–191.

Labouvie-Vief, G. & Diehl, M. (2002). Cognitive complexity and cognitive-affective integration: Related or separate domains of adult development? *Psychology and Aging*, *15*, 490–594.

Lachlan, K. (2006). Sensation seeking. In J. J. Arnett (Ed.), *Encyclopedia of children, adolescents, and the media*. Thousand Oaks, CA: Sage.

Lachman, M. E. (2004). Development in midlife. *Annual review of psychology*, *55*, 305–331.

Ladd, G. W., Buhs, E. & Troop, W. (2002). School adjustment and social skills training. In P. K. Smith & C. H. Hart (Eds.), *Blackwell handbook of childhood social development*. Malden, MA: Blackwell.

LaFromboise, T. D., Hoyt, D. R., Oliver, L. & Whitbeck, L. B. (2006). Family, community, and school influences on resilience among American Indian adolescents in the upper Midwest. *Journal of Community Psychology*, *34*(2), 193–209.

Laghi, F., D'Alessio, M., Pallini, S. & Baiocco, R. (2009). Attachment representations and time perspective in adolescence. *Social Indicators Research*, *90*(2), 181–194.

La Greca, A. M. & Harrison, H. M. (2005). Adolescent peer relations, friendships, and romantic relationships: Do they predict social anxiety and depression? *Journal of Clinical Child and Adolescent Psychology*, *34*(1), 49–61.

La Greca, A. M., Prinstein, M. J. & Fetter, M. D. (2001). Adolescent peer crowd affiliation: Linkages with health-risky behaviours and close friendships. *Journal of Pediatric Psychology*, *26*, 131–143.

Laham, S. M., Gonsalkorale, K. & von Hippel, W. (2005). Darwinian grandparenting: Preferential investment in more certain kin. *Personality and Social Psychology Bulletin*, *31*(1), 63–72.

Laible, D. J., Carlo, G. & Rafaelli, M. (2000). The differential relations of parent and peer attachment to adolescent adjustment. *Journal of Youth & Adolescence*, *29*, 45–60.

Laird, R. D., Criss, M. M., Pettit, G. S., Dodge, K. A. & Bates, J. E. (2008). Parents monitoring knowledge attenuates the link between antisocial friends and adolescent delinquent behaviour. *Journal of Abnormal Child Psychology*, *36*(3), 299–310.

Laird, R. D., Pettit, G. S., Dodge, K. A. & Bates, J. E. (2005). Peer relationship antecedents of delinquent behaviour in late adolescence: Is there evidence of demographic group differences in developmental. *Development & Psychopathology*, *17*, 127–144.

Lakatta, E. G. (1990). Heart and circulation. In E. L. Schneider & J. W. Rowe (Eds.), *Handbook of the biology of aging* (3rd ed., 181–217). San Diego, CA: Academic Press.

Lakshman, R., Forouhi, N., Luben, R., Bingham, S., Khaw, K., Wareham, N. & Ong, K. (2008). Association between age at menarche and risk of diabetes in adults: results from the EPIC-Norfolk cohort study. *Diabetologia*, *51*(5), 781–786.

Lalonde, C. & Chandler, M. (2004). Culture, selves, and time. In C. Lightfoot, C. Lalonde, & M. Chandler (Eds.), *Changing conceptions of psychological life*. Mahwah, NJ: Erlbaum.

Lam, C. & McBride-Chang, C. (2007). Resilience in young adulthood: The moderating influences of gender-related personality traits and coping flexibility. *Sex Roles*, *56*(3–4), 159–172.

Langhinrichsen-Rohling, J., Palarea, R. E., Cohen, J. & Rohlin, M. L. (2002). Breaking up is hard to do: Unwanted pursuit behaviours following the dissolution of a romantic relationship. In K. E. Davis & I. H. Frieze (Eds.), *Stalking: Perspectives on victims and perpetrators* (pp. 212–236). New York: Springer.

Langley, K., Heron, J., O'Donovan, M. C., Owen, M. J. & Thapar, A. (2010). Genotype link with extreme antisocial behavior: The contribution of cognitive pathways. *Archives of General Psychiatry*, *67*(12), 1317–1323.

Lansford, J. E., Malone, P. S., Dodge, K. A., Crozier, J. C., Pettit, G. S. & Bates, J. E. (2006). A 12 year prospective study of patterns of social information processing problems and externalizing behaviours. *Journal of Abnormal Child Psychology*, *34*(5), 715–724.

Lanvers, U. (2004). Original Article Gender in discourse behaviour in parent–child dyads: A literature review. *Child: Care Health & Development*, *30*(5), 481–493.

Lanza, S. T. & Collins, L. M. (2002). Pubertal timing and the onset of substance use in females during early adolescence. *Prevention Science*, *3*, 69–82.

Laqueur, T. W. (2004). *Solitary sex: A cultural history of masturbation*. New York: Zone.

Larose, S. & Boivin, M. (1998). Attachment to parents, social support expectations, and socioemotional adjustment during the high school-college transition. *Journal of Research on Adolescence, 8*, 1–27.

Larson, R. (1995). Secrets in the bedroom: Adolescents' private use of media. *Journal of Youth & Adolescence, 24*, 535–550.

Larson, R., Clore, G. L. & Wood, G. A. (1999). The emotions of romantic relationships: Do they wreak havoc on adolescents? In W. Furman, B. B. Brown, & C. Feiring (Eds.), *The development of romantic relationships in adolescence* (pp. 19–49). New York: Cambridge University Press.

Larson, R., Csikszentmihalyi, M. & Graef, R. (1982). Time alone in daily experience: Loneliness or renewal? In L. A. Peplau & D. Perlman (Eds.), *Loneliness: A sourcebook of theory, research, and therapy* (pp. 40–53). New York: Wiley.

Larson, R. & Richards, M. (1998). Waiting for the weekend: Friday and Saturday nights as the emotional climax of the week. *New Directions for Child and Adolescent Development, 82*, 37–52.

Larson, R. & Richards, M. H. (1994). *Divergent realities: The emotional lives of mothers, fathers, and adolescents*. New York: Basic Books.

Larson, R., Richards, M. H., Moneta, G., Holmbeck, G. & Duckett, E. (1996). Changes in adolescents' daily interactions with their families from ages 10 to 18: Disengagement and transformation. *Developmental Psychology, 32*, 744–754.

Larson, R., Verma, S. & Dworkin, J. (2000, March). *Adolescence without family disengagement: The daily family lives of Indian middle-class teenagers*. Paper presented at the biennial meeting of the Society for Research on Adolescence, Chicago.

Larson, R. W., Moneta, G., Richards, M. H. & Wilson, S. (2002). Continuity, stability, and change in daily emotional experience across adolescence. *Child Development, 73*(4), 1151–1165.

Larson, R. W., Wilson, S. & Rickman, A. (2010). Globalization, societal change, and adolescence across the world. In R. Lerner & L. Steinberg (Eds.), *Handbook of Adolescent Psychology*. Hoboken, NJ: Wiley.

Laukkanen, E., Rissanen, M-L., Honkalampi, K., Kylmä, J., Tolmunen, T. & Hintikka, J. (2009). The prevalence of self-cutting and other self-harm among 13- to 18-year-old Finnish adolescents. *Social Psychiatry and Psychiatric Epidemiology, 44*(1), 23–28.

Laumann-Billings, L. & Emery, R. E. (2000). Distress among young adults from divorced families. *Journal of Family Psychology, 14*, 671–687.

Laungani, P. (2005). Caste, class and culture: A case study. *Counselling Psychology Quarterly, 18*(1), 61–71.

Laungani, P. (2002). Cross-cultural psychology: A handmaiden to mainstream Western psychology. *Counselling Psychology Quarterly, 15*(4), 385–397.

Laursen, B. & Collins, W. A. (2004). Parent-child communication during adolescence. In L. Anita, Vangelisti (Ed.), *Handbook of family communication* (pp. 333–348). Mahwah, NJ: Lawrence Erlbaum.

Laursen, B. & Jensen-Campbell, L. A. (1999). The nature and functions of social exchange in adolescent romantic relationships. In W. Furman, B. B. Brown, & C. Feiring (Eds.), *The development of romantic relationships in adolescence* (pp. 50–74). New York: Cambridge University Press.

Lavallee, K. & Parker, J. (2009). The role of inflexible friendship beliefs, rumination, and low self-worth in early adolescents' friendship jealousy and adjustment. *Journal of Abnormal Child Psychology, 37*(6), 873–885.

Law, M., Hanna, S., King, G., Hurley, P., King, S., Kertoy, M. & Rosenbaum, P. (2003). Factors affecting family-centred service delivery for children with disabilities. *Child: Care Health & Development, 29*(5), 357–366.

Lawrence, J. A. & Valsiner, J. (2003). Making personal sense: An account of basic internalization and externalization processes. *Theory & Psychology, 13*(6), 723–752.

Lawson, A. E. & Wollman, W. T. (2003). Encouraging the transition from concrete to formal operations: An experiment. *Journal of Research in Science Teaching, 40*(Suppl.), S33–S50.

Lawton, L. E. & Bures, R. (2001). Parental divorce and the 'switching' of religious identity. *Journal for the Scientific Study of Religion, 40*(1), 99–111.

Le, T., Tov, W. & Taylor, J. (2007). Religiousness and depressive symptoms in five ethnic adolescent groups. *International Journal for the Psychology of Religion, 17*(3), 209–232.

Leach, F. (2003). Learning to be violent: The role of the school in developing adolescent gendered behaviour. *Compare, 33*(3), 385–400.

Leadbeater, B. J. & Bishop, S. (1994). Predictors of behavior problems in preschool children of Afro-American and Puerto Rican adolescent mothers. *Child Development, 62*(2), 638–648.

Leadbeater, B. J. R. & Way, N. (2001). *Growing up fast: Transitions to early adulthood of inner-city adolescent mothers*. Mahwah, NJ: Erlbaum.

Leaper, C. & Spears-Brown, C. (2008). Perceived experiences with sexism among adolescent girls. *Child Development, 79*(3), 685–704.

Lee, D. & Wolpin, K. I. (2006). Intersectoral labor mobility and the growth of the service sector. *Econometrica: Journal of the Econometric Society, 74*(1), 1–46.

Lee, J. (2009). Bodies at menarche: Stories of shame, concealment, and sexual maturation. *Sex Roles, 60*(9–10), 615–627.

Lee, J. C. & Staff, J. (2007). When work matters: The varying impact of work intensity on high school drop-outs. *Sociology of Education, 80*(2), 158–178.

Lee, K. & Freire, A. (2003). Cognitive development. In A. Slater & G. Bremner (Eds.), *An introduction to developmental psychology* (pp. 359–387). Malden, MA: Blackwell.

Lee, M. & Larson, R. (2000). The Korean 'examination hell': Long hours of studying, distress, and depression. *Journal of Youth & Adolescence*, *29*, 249–271.

Lee M. M. C., Chang K. S. F. & Chan M. M. C. (1963). Sexual maturation of Chinese girls in Hong Kong. *Paediatrics*, *32*(3), 389–398.

Lee, S. J. & Vaught, S. (2003). 'You can never be too rich or too thin': Popular and consumer culture and the Americanization of Asian American girls and young women. *Journal of Negro Education*, *72*, 457–466.

Lee, V., Croninger, R., Linn, E. & Chen, X. (1996). The culture of harassment in secondary schools. *American Educational Research Journal*, *33*(2), 383–417.

Leech, D. & Campos, E. (2003). Is comprehensive education really free?: a case-study of the effects of secondary school admissions policies on house prices in one local area. *Journal of the Royal Statistical Society: Series A (Statistics in Society)*, *166*(1), 135–154.

Leets, L. (2005). Adolescent rules for social exclusion: when is it fair to exclude someone else? *Journal of Moral Education*, *34*(3), 343–362

Lefebvre, E. L. (2003). Belgian citizenship: Managing linguistic, regional, and economic demands. *Citizenship Studies*, *7*(1), 111–134.

Lefkowitz, E. S., Boone, T. L., Au, T. K.-F. & Sigman, M. (2003). No sex or safe sex? Mothers' and adolescents' discussions about sexuality and AIDS/HIV. *Health Education Research*, *18*(3), 341–351.

Le Grange, D., Lock, J. & Dymek, M. (2003). Family-based therapy for adolescents with bulimia nervosa. *American Journal of Psychotherapy*, *57*, 237–251.

Leineweber, M. & Arensman, E. (2003). Culture change and mental health: The epidemiology of suicide in Greenland. *Archives of Suicide Research*, *7*, 41–50.

Lemmer, E. M. (2002). *Schools reaching out: Comprehensive parent involvement in South African primary schools*. Paper presented at the European Conference on Educational Research, University of Lisbon, 11–14 September.

León, P. & Montiel, S. (2008). Wild meat use and traditional hunting practices in a rural Mayan community of the Yucatan peninsula, Mexico. *Human Ecology*, *36*(2), 249–257.

Lerner, R. M. (2006). Developmental science, developmental systems, and contemporary theories of human development. In R. M. Lerner & W. Damon (Eds.), *Handbook of child psychology (6th ed.): Vol 1, Theoretical models of human development* (pp. 1–17). Hoboken, NJ: John Wiley & Sons.

Leschied, A. W., Chiodo, D., Whitehead, P. C. & Hurley, D. (2005). The relationship between maternal depression and child outcomes in a child welfare sample: implications for treatment and policy. *Child & Family Social Work*, *10*(4), 281–291.

Leszczynski, J. P. & Strough, J. (2008). The contextual specificity of masculinity and femininity in early adolescence. *Social Development*, *17*(3), 719–736.

Leventhal, T., Xue, Y. & Brooks-Gunn, J. (2006). Immigrant differences in school-age children's verbal trajectories: A look at four racial/ethnic groups. *Child Development*, *77*(5), 1359–1374.

Levine, J. A., Emery, C. R. & Pollack, H. (2007). The well-being of children born to teen mothers. *Journal of Marriage and Family*, *69*(1), 105–122.

Levorato, M. C. & Cacciari C. (2002). The creation of new figurative expressions: Psycholinguistic evidence in Italian children, adolescents and adults *Journal of Child Language*, *29*(1), 127–150.

Lewis, C. G. (1981). How adolescents approach decisions: Changes over grades seven to twelve and policy implications. *Child Development*, *52*, 538–554.

Lewis, J. (2007). Teenagers and their parents: Parental time and parenting style–what are the issues? *The Political Quarterly*, *78*(2), 292–300.

Lewis, J., Noden, P. & Sarre, S. (2008). Parents' working hours: Adolescent children's views and experiences. *Children & Society*, *22*(6), 429–439.

Lewis, M., Feiring, C. & Rosenthal, S. (2000). Attachment over time. *Child Development*, *71*(3), 707–720.

Lewis, T., Stone, J., Shipley, W. & Madzar, S. (1998). The transition from school to work: An examination of the literature. *Youth & Society*, *29*, 259–292.

LGB (Local Government Board) (1918). *Mothers Pensions in the USA*. London: HMSO.

Lichter, D. T., Shanahan, M. J. & Gardner, E. L. (2002). Helping others? The effects of childhood poverty and family instability on prosocial behavior. *Youth & Society*, *34*(1), 89–119.

Lichter, P. (1978). *The boy who dared to rock: The definitive Elvis*. New York: Dolphin Books.

Lieber, E., Nihira, K. & Mink, I. T. (2004). Filial piety, modernization, and the challenges of raising children for Chinese immigrants: Quantitative and qualitative evidence. *Ethos*, *32*, 324–347.

Lieberman, M., Doyle, A-B. & Markiewicz, D. (1999). Developmental patterns in security of attachment to mother and father in late childhood and early adolescence: Associations with peer relations. *Child Development*, *70*(1), 202–213.

Lien, L., Dalgard, F., Heyerdahl, S., Thoresen, M. & Bjertness, E. (2006). The relationship between age of menarche and mental distress in Norwegian adolescent girls and girls from different immigrant groups in Norway: Results from urban city cross-sectional survey. *Social Science & Medicine*, *63*(2), 285–295.

Lillard, A. (2007). Pretend play in toddlers. In C. A. Brownell & C. B. Kopp (Eds.), *Socioemotional development in the toddler years* (pp. 149–176). New York: Guilford.

Lim, S-L. & Lim, B. K. (2004). Parenting style and child outcomes in Chinese and immigrant Chinese families-current findings and cross-cultural considerations in conceptualization and research. *Marriage & Family Review*, *35*, 21–43.

Lin, M-W. & Bozeman, B. (2006). Researchers' industry experience and productivity in university–industry research centers: A 'scientific and technical human capital' explanation. *The Journal of Technology Transfer*, *31*(2), 269–290.

Lindberg, L. D., Jones, R. & Santelli, J. S. (2008). Noncoital sexual activities among adolescents. *Journal of Adolescent Health*, *43*(3), 231–238.

Lindsay, J. (2003). 'Partying hard', 'partying sometimes' or 'shopping': Young workers' socializing patterns and sexual, alcohol and illicit drug risk taking. *Critical Public Health*, *13*(1), 1–14.

Lingard, T. (2001). Does the Code of Practice help secondary school SENCos to improve learning? *British Journal of Special Education 28*(4), 187–190.

Lips, H. M. (2004). The gender gap in possible selves: Divergence of academic self-views among high school and university students. *Sex Roles*, *50*, 357–371.

Liu, H.-E. (2001). Mother or father: Who received custody? The best interests of the child standard and judges' custody decisions in Taiwan. *International Journal of Law, Policy and the Family*, *15*(2), 185–225.

Liu, R. (2006). Vulnerability to friends' suicide influence: The moderating effects of gender and adolescent depression. *Journal of Youth and Adolescence*, *35*(3), 454–464.

Liu, Y-L. (2008). An examination of three models of the relationships between parental attachments and adolescents' social functioning and depressive symptoms. *Journal of Youth and Adolescence*, *37*(8), 941–952.

Livaditis, M., Zaphiriadis, K., Samakouri, M., Tellidou, C., Tzavaras, N. & Xenitidis, K. (2003). Gender differences, family and psychological factors affecting school performance in Greek secondary school students. *Educational Psychology*, *23*(2), 223–231.

Livingstone, S. (2008). Taking risky opportunities in youthful content creation: Teenagers' use of social networking sites for intimacy, privacy and self-expression. *New Media & Society*, *10*(3), 393–411.

Livingstone, S. & Helsper, E. (2008). Parental mediation of children's Internet use. *Journal of Broadcasting & Electronic Media*, *52*(4), 581–599.

Lloyd, C. (Ed.) (2005). *Growing up global: The changing transitions to adulthood in developing countries*. Washington, DC: National Research Council and Institute of Medicine.

Lloyd, C. B., Grant, M. & Ritchie, A. (2008). Gender differences in time use among adolescents in developing countries: Implications of rising school enrollment rates. *Journal of Research on Adolescence*, *18*(1), 99–120.

Lo, V-H. & Wei, R. (2005). Exposure to Internet pornography and Taiwanese adolescents' sexual attitudes and behavior. *Journal of Broadcasting & Electronic Media*, *49*(2), 221–237.

Lobel, T. E., Nov-Krispin, N., Schiller, D., Lobel, O. & Feldman, A. (2004). Gender discriminatory behavior during adolescence and young adulthood: A developmental analysis. *Journal of Youth & Adolescence*, *3*(6), 535–546.

Lobstein, T., Baur, L. & Uauy, R. (2004). Obesity in children and young people: A crisis in public health. *Obesity Reviews*, *5* (Suppl. 1), 4–85.

Lock, J. (2002). Treating adolescents with eating disorders in the family context: Empirical and theoretical considerations. *Child & Adolescent Psychiatric Clinics of North America*, *11*, 331–342.

Locke, J. L. & Bogin, B. (2006). Language and life history: A new perspective on the development and evolution of human language. *Behavioral and Brain Sciences*, *29*(3), 259–280.

Lodge, C. (2002). Tutors talking. *Pastoral Care in Education*, *20*(4), 35–37.

Loeber, R., Farrington, D. P., Stouthamer-Loeber, M., Moffitt, T. E. & Caspi, A. (2001). The development of male offending: Key findings from the first decade of the Pittsburgh Youth Study. In R. Bull (Ed.), *Children and the law: The essential readings* (pp. 336–378). Malden, MA: Blackwell.

Loehlin, J., Harden, K. & Turkheimer, E. (2009). The effect of assumptions about parental assortative mating and genotype–income correlation on estimates of genotype–environment interaction in the National Merit Twin Study. *Behavior Genetics*, *39*(2), 165–169.

Löfström, E. & Nevgi, A. (2007). From strategic planning to meaningful learning: Diverse perspectives on the development of web-based teaching and learning in higher education. *British Journal of Educational Technology*, *38*(2), 312–324.

Lonardo, R., Giordano, P., Longmore, M. & Manning, W. (2009). Parents, friends, and romantic partners: Enmeshment in deviant networks and adolescent delinquency involvement. *Journal of Youth and Adolescence*, *38*(3), 367–383.

Longden, B. (2006). An institutional response to changing student expectations and their impact on retention rates. *Journal of Higher Education Policy and Management*, *28*(2), 173–187.

Longest, K. C. & Shanahan, M. J. (2007). Adolescent work intensity and substance use: The mediational and moderational roles of parenting. *Journal of Marriage & Family*, *69*(3), 703–720.

Lopez, R. I. (2003). *The Teen Health Book*. New York: Norton.

LópezGuimerà, G., Fauquet, J., Portell, M., SánchezCarracedo, D. & Raich, R. M. (2008). Dieting in Spanish adolescent girls. *European Eating Disorders Review: The Journal of the Eating Disorders Association*, *16*(3), 234–240.

Lorenc, T., Brunton, G., Oliver, S., Oliver, K. & Oakley, A. (2008). Attitudes to walking and cycling among children, young people and parents: A systematic review. *Journal of Epidemiology & Community Health*, *62*(10), 852–857.

Lorensen, M., Wilson, M. & White, M. (2004). Norwegian families: Transition to parenthood. *Health Care for Women International*, *25*(4), 334–348.

Loughlin, C. & Barling, J. (1999). The nature of youth employment. In J. Barling & E. K. Kelloway (Eds.), *Youth workers: Varieties of experience* (pp. 17–36). Washington, DC: American Psychological Association.

Loukas, A. & Robinson, S. (2004). Examining the moderating role of perceived school climate in early adolescent adjustment. *Journal of Research on Adolescence*, *14*, 209–233.

Lowe, E. D. (2003). Identity, activity, and the well-being of adolescents and youths: Lessons from young people in a Micronesian society. *Culture, Medicine and Psychiatry*, *27*(2), 187–219.

Lu, Z.-Y. J. (2001). The relationship between menstrual attitudes and menstrual symptoms among Taiwanese women. *Journal of Advanced Nursing*, *33*(5), 621–628.

Lucey, H. & Reay, D. (2002). Carrying the beacon of excellence: social class differentiation and anxiety at a time of transition. *Journal of Education Policy*, *17*(3), 321–336.

Luciana, M., Conklin, H. M., Hooper, C. J. & Yarger, R. S. (2005). The development of nonverbal working memory and executive control processes in adolescents. *Child Development*, *76*(3), 697–712.

Luke, A. & Luke, C. (2001). Adolescence lost/childhood regained: On early intervention and the emergence of the techno-subject. *Journal of Early Childhood Literacy*, *1*(1), 91–120.

Luke, C. (2003). Global mobilities: Crafting identities in interracial families. *International Journal of Cultural Studies*, *6*(4), 379–401.

Luna, B., Graver, K. E., Urban, T. A., Lazar, N. A. & Sweeney, J. A. (2004). Maturation of cognitive processes from late childhood to adulthood. *Child Development*, *75*, 1357–1372.

Luo, S. Klohnen. E. C. (2005). Assortative mating and marital quality in newlyweds: A couple-centered approach. *Journal of Personality & Social Psychology*, *88*, 304–326.

Luoma, I., Puura, K., Tamminen, T., Kaukonen, P., Piha, J., Räsänen, E., Kumpulainen, K., Moilanen, I., Koivisto, A. & Almqvist, F. (1999). Emotional and behavioural symptoms in 8–9-year-old children in relation to family structure. *European Child & Adolescent Psychiatry*, *8 supp 4*, S29-S40.

Lupia, A. & Philpot, T. S. (2005). Views from inside the net: How websites affect young adults' political interest. *Journal of Politics*, *67*(4), 1122–1142. Lynd, R. S. & Lynd, H. M. (1929). Middletown: *A study in modern American culture*. New York: Harvest Books.

Luster, T., Small, S. A. & Lower, R. (2002). The correlates of abuse and witnessing abuse among adolescents. *Journal of Interpersonal Violence*, *17*(12), 1323–1340.

Luthar, S. S. & Ansary, N. S. (2005). Dimensions of adolescent rebellion: Risks for academic failure among high- and low-income youth. *Development and Psychopathology*, *17*(1), 231–250.

Luthar, S. S., Suchman, N. & Altomore, M. (2007). Relational psychotherapy mothers' group: A randomized clinical trial for substance abusing mothers. *Development and Psychopathology*, *19*(1), 243–2261.

Lynch, M. E. (1991). Gender intensification. In R. M. Lerner, A. C. Petersen, & J. Brooks-Gunn (Eds.), *Encyclopedia of adolescence* (Vol. 1). New York: Garland.

Lynd, R. S. & Lynd, H. M. (1929). Middletown: *A study in modern American culture*. New York: Harvest Books.

Lynn, R. (2006). *Race Differences in Intelligence: An Evolutionary Analysis*. Augusta, GA: Washington Summit Books.

Lynn, R. (2003). The geography of intelligence. In H. Nyborg (Ed.). *The scientific study of general Intelligence*. Amsterdam: Elsevier.

Lynne, S. D., Graber, J. A., Nichols, T. R., Brooks-Gunn, J. & Botvin, G. J. (2007). Links between pubertal timing, peer influences, and externalizing behaviors among urban students followed through middle school. *Journal of Adolescent Health*, *40*(2).

Lyons, A. C., Dalton, S. I. & Hoy, A. (2006). 'Hardcore drinking': Portrayals of alcohol consumption in young women's and men's magazines. *Journal of Health Psychology*, *11*(2), 223–232.

Lytle, L. J., Bakken, L. & Romig, C. (1997). Adolescent female identity development. *Sex Roles*, *37*, 175–185.

Ma, H. K. (2005). The relation of gender-role classifications to the prosocial and antisocial behavior of Chinese adolescents. *Journal of Genetic Psychology*, *166*, 189–201.

Ma, J., Betts, N. M., Horacek, T., Georgiou, C., White, A. & Nitzke, S. (2002). The importance of decisional balance and self-efficacy in relation to stages of change for fruit and vegetable intakes by young adults. *American Journal of Health Promotion*, *16*, 157–166.

Maccoby, E. E. (2002). Gender and group process: A developmental perspective. *Current Directions in Psychological Science*, *11*, 54–57.

Macek, P. (2007). Czech Republic. In J. J. Arnett, R. Ahmed, B. Nsamenang, T. S. Saraswathi, & R. Silbereisen (Eds.), *International encyclopedia of adolescence*. New York: Routledge.

Macek, P., Bejcek, J. & Vanickova, J. (2007). Contemporary Czech emerging adults: Generation growing up in the period of social changes. *Journal of Adolescent Research*, *22*, 444–475.

MacFarquhar, R. & Schoenhals, J. (2006). *Mao's last revolution*. Cambridge, MA: Harvard University Press.

Macias-Cervantes, M., Malacara, J., Garay-Sevilla, M. & Díaz-Cisneros, F. (2009). Effect of recreational physical activity on insulin levels in Mexican/Hispanic children. *European Journal of Pediatrics*, *168*(10), 1195–1202.

Mack, K. Y. (2001). Childhood family disruptions and adult well-being: The differential effects of divorce and parental death. *Death Studies*, *25*(5), 419–443.

Mackey, E. R. & La Greca, A. M. (2007). Adolescents' eating, exercise, and weight control behaviors: Does peer crowd affiliation play a role? *Journal of Pediatric Psychology*, *32*(1), 13–23.

MacLeod, A. & Johnston, P. (2007). Standing out and fitting in: A report on a support group for individuals with Asperger syndrome using a personal account. *British Journal of Special Education*, *34*(2), 83–88.

Maggs, J. L. (1999). Alcohol use and binge drinking as goal-directed action during the transition to post-secondary education. In J. Schulenberg, J. L. Maggs, & K. Hurrelmann (Eds.), *Health risks and developmental transitions during adolescence* (pp. 345–371). New York: Cambridge University Press.

Magnussen, L., Ehiri, J. E., Ejere, H. O. D. & Jolly, P. E. (2004). Interventions to prevent HIV/AIDS among adolescents in less developed countries: Are they effective? *International Journal of Adolescent Medicine & Health*, *16*, 303–323.

Maguire, S. (2008). Paying young people to learn – does it work? *Research in Post-Compulsory Education*, *13*(2), 205–215.

Maguire, S. & Rennison, J. (2005). Two years on: The destinations of young people who are not in education, employment or training at 16. *Journal of Youth Studies*, *8*(2), 187–201.

Mahaffy, K. A. (2004). Girls' low self-esteem: How is it related to later socioeconomic achievements? *Gender & Society*, *18*(3), 309–327.

Mahn, H. (2003). Periods in child development: Vygotsky's perspective. In A. Kozulin, & B. Gindis (Eds.), *Vygotsky's educational theory in cultural context* (pp. 119–137). New York: Cambridge University Press.

Maira, S. (2004). Imperial feelings: Youth culture, citizenship, and globalization. In M. M. Suárez-Oroszco & B. D. Hilliard-Qin (Eds.), *Globalization: Culture and education in the new millennium* (pp. 203–234). Berkeley: University of California Press.

Majors, R. (1989). Cool pose: The proud signature of black survival. In M. S. Kimmel & M. A. Messner (Eds.), *Men's lives* (pp. 83–87). New York: Macmillan.

Makela, K. (1997). Drinking, the majority fallacy, cognitive dissonance and social pressure. *Addiction*, *92*(6), 729–736.

Mallett, S., Rosenthal, D. & Keys, D. (2005). Young people, drug use and family conflict: Pathways into homelessness. *Journal of Adolescence*, *28*, 185–199.

Malouff, J., Rooke, S. & Schutte, N. (2012). The heritability of human behavior: Results of aggregating meta-analyses. *Current Psychology*, Preprint, 1–9.

Mandic, S. (2008). Home-leaving and its structural determinants in Western and Eastern Europe: An exploratory study. *Housing Studies*, *23*(4), 615–637.

Manners, P. J. (2009). Gender identity disorder in adolescence: A review of the literature. *Child and Adolescent Mental Health*, *14*(2), 62–68.

Manlove, J., Franzetta, K., Ryan, S. & Moore, K. (2006). Adolescent sexual relationships, contraceptive consistency, and pregnancy prevention approaches. In A. C. Crouter & A. Booth (Eds.), *Romance and sex in adolescence and emerging adulthood: Risks and opportunities* (pp. 181–212). The Penn State University family issues symposia series. Mahwah, NJ: Lawrence Erlbaum.

Mantzoros, C. S. (2000). The role of leptin in reproduction. *Annals of the New York Academy of Sciences*, *900*, 174–83.

Manzeske, D. & Stright, A. (2009). Parenting styles and emotion regulation: The role of behavioral and psychological control during young adulthood. *Journal of Adult Development*, *16*(4), 223–229.

Maras, P. & Aveling, E-L. (2006). Students with special educational needs: transitions from primary to secondary school. *British Journal of Special Education*, *33*(4), 196–203.

Marcia, J. E. (1999). Representational thought in ego identity, psychotherapy, and psychosocial developmental theory. In I. E. Siegel (Ed.), *Development of mental representation: Theories and applications* (pp. 391–414). Mahwah, NJ: Erlbaum.

Marcia, J. E. & Carpendale, J. (2004). Identity: Does thinking make it so? In C. Lightfoot & M. Chandler (Eds.), *Changing conceptions of psychological life*. Mahwah, NJ: Erlbaum.

Marcotte, D., Fortin, L., Potvin, P. & Papillon, M. (2002). Gender differences in depressive symptoms during adolescence: Role of gender-typed characteristics, self-esteem, body image, stressful life events, and pubertal status. *Journal of Emotional and Behavioral Disorders*, *10*, 29–42.

Marcus, I. G. (2004). *The Jewish life cycle: Rites of passage from biblical times to the modern age.* London: University of Washington Press.

Margolese, S., Markiewicz, D. & Doyle, A. (2005). Attachment to parents, best friend, and romantic partner: Predicting different pathways to depression in adolescence. *Journal of Youth and Adolescence*, *34*(6), 637–650.

Marková, I., Moodie, E., Farr, R. M., Drozda-Senkowska, E., Erös, F., Plichtová, J., Gervais, M-C., Hoffmannová, J. and Mullerová, O. (1998). Social representations of the individual: a post-Communist perspective. *European Journal of Social Psychology*, *28*(5), 797–829.

Markus, H. R. & Kitayama, S. (2003). Culture, self, and the reality of the social. *Psychological Inquiry*, *14*, 277–283.

Marland, M. (2002). From 'form teacher' to 'tutor': The development from the fifties to the seventies. *Pastoral Care in Education*, *20*(4), 3–11.

Marlowe, M., Disney, G. & Wilson, K. J. (2004). Classroom management of children with emotional and behavioral disorders A storied model: Torey Hayden's One Child. *Emotional and Behavioural Difficulties*, *9*(2), 99–114.

Marriott, P. (2007). An analysis of first experience students' financial awareness and attitude to debt in a post-1992 UK university. *Higher Education Quarterly*, *61*(4), 498–519.

Marsh, H. W. & Hau, K. T. (2003). Big fish little pond effect on academic self-concept: A cross-cultural (26-country) test of the negative effects of academically selective schools. *American Psychologist*, *58*, 364–376.

Marsh, H. W. & Kleitman, S. (2005). Consequences of employment during High School: Character building, subversion of academic goals, or a threshold? *American Educational Research Journal*, *42*, 331–369.

Marshall, M. (1979). *Weekend warriors*. Palo Alto, CA: Mayfield.

Marshall, T. C. (2008). Cultural differences in intimacy: The influence of gender-role ideology and individualism-collectivism. *Journal of Social and Personal Relationships*. *25*(1), 143–168.

Marshall, W. A. & Tanner, J. M. (1970). Variations in the pattern of pubertal changes in boys. *Archives of Disease in Childhood*, *45*, 13–23.

Martin, C. A., Kelly, T. H., Rayens, M. K., et al. (2002). Sensation seeking, puberty and nicotine, alcohol, and marijuana use in adolescence. *Journal of the American Academy of Child & Adolescent Psychiatry*, *41*, 1495–1502.

Martin, C. L. (1987). A ratio measure of sex stereotyping. *Journal of Personality and Social Psychology*, *52*, 489–499.

Martin, F. E. (1998). Tales of transition: self-narrative and direct scribing in exploring care-leaving. *Child & Family Social Work*, *3*(1), 1–12.

Martin, S. L., Moracco, K. E., Garro, J., Tsui, A. O., Kupper, L. L., Chase, J. L. & Campbell, J. C. (2002). Domestic violence across generations: findings from northern India. *International Journal of Epidemiology*, *31*(3), 560–572.

Martinek, T., Schilling, T. & Hellison, D. (2006). The development of compassionate and caring leadership among adolescents. *Physical Education and Sport Pedagogy*, *11*(2), 141–157.

Marván, M. L., Vacio, A., García-Yáñez, G. & Espinosa-Hernández, G. (2007). Attitudes toward menarche among Mexican preadolescents. *Women & Health*, *46*(1), 7–23.

Mason, D. J., Humphreys, G. W. & Kent, L. S. (2003). Exploring selective attention in ADHD: visual search through space and time. *Journal of Child Psychology and Psychiatry* (formerly *Journal of Child Psychology and Psychiatry and Allied Disciplines*), *44*(8), 1158–1176.

Mason, M. G. & Gibbs, J. C. (1993). Social perspective taking and moral judgment among college students. *Journal of Adolescent Research*, *8*, 109–123.

Mason, R., Nakase, N. & Naoe, T. (2000). Craft education in lower secondary schools in England and Japan: A comparative study. *Comparative Education*, *36*(4), 397–416.

Mason, W. A., Kosterman, R., Hawkins, J. D., Haggerty, K. P. & Spoth, R. L. (2003). Reducing adolescents' growth in substance use and delinquency: Randomized trial effects of a parent-training prevention intervention. *Prevention Science*, *4*(3), 203–213.

Massoni, K. (2004). Modeling work: Occupational messages in seventeen magazines. *Gender & Society*, *18*, 47–65.

Massy-Westropp, N., Rankin, W., Ahern, M., Krishnan, J. & Hearn, T. C. (2004). Measuring grip strength in normal adults: Reference ranges and a comparison of electronic and hydraulic instruments. *The Journal of Hand Surgery* *29*(3), 514–519.

Masten, A. S. (2007). Competence, resilience, and development in adolescence: Clues for prevention science. In D. Romer & E. F. Walker (Eds.), *Adolescent psychopathology and the developing brain: Integrating brain and prevention science* (pp. 31–52). New York: Oxford University Press.

Masten, A. S. (2001). Ordinary magic: Resilience processes in development. *American Psychologist*, *56*(3), 227–238.

Masten, A. S., Obradovic, J. & Burt, K. B. (2006). Resilience in young adulthood: Developmental perspectives on continuity and transformation. In J. J. Arnett and J. L. Tanner (Eds.), *Young adults in America: Coming of age in the 21st century* (pp. 173–190). Washington, DC: American Psychological Association Press.

Mathiesen, S. G., Cash, S. J. & Hudson, W. W. (2002). The Multidimensional Adolescent Assessment Scale: A validation study. *Research on Social Work Practice*, *12*(1), 9–28.

Mathur, R. & Berndt, T. J. (2006). Relations of friends' activities to friendship quality. *Journal of Early Adolescence*, *26*(3), 365–388.

Matsumoto, D. (2002). *The new Japan: Debunking seven cultural stereotypes of Japan*. New York: Intercultural Press.

Matthews, A. E. (2008). Children and obesity: A pan-European project examining the role of food marketing. *The European Journal of Public Health*, *18*(1), 7–17.

Matud, M. P., Hernández, J. A. & Marrero, R. J. (2002). Work role and health in a sample of spanish women. *Feminism & Psychology*, *12*(3), 363–378.

Maughan, R., Leiper, J., Bartagi, Z., Zrifi, R., Zerguini, Y. & Dvorak, J. (2008). Effect of Ramadan fasting on some biochemical and haematological parameters in Tunisian youth soccer players undertaking their usual training and competition schedule. *Journal of Sports Sciences*, *26*(3), 39–46.

Maxwell, K. A. (2002). Friends: The role of peer influence across adolescent risky behaviours. *Journal of Youth & Adolescence*, *31*, 267–277.

Mayhew, D. R. (2007). Driver education licensing in North America: Past, present, and future. *Journal of Safety Research*, *38*(2), 229–235.

Mayhew, D. R. & Simpson, H. M. (2002). The safety value of driver education and training. *Injury Prevention*, *8*(Suppl 2), ii3–ii8.

Maynard, A. E. & Martini, M. I. (Eds.) (2005). *Learning in cultural context: Family, peers, and school*. New York: Kluwer.

Mayselsss, O. & Scharf, M. (2007). Adolescents' attachment representations and their capacity for intimacy in close relationships. *Journal of Research on Adolescence*, *17*(1), 23–50.

Mayseless, O. & Scharf, M. (2003). What does it mean to be an adult? The Israeli experience. In J. J. Arnett & N. Galambos (Eds.), *New Directions in Child and Adolescent Development* (Vol. 100, 5–20). San Francisco: Jossey-Bass.

McBride, J. & Derevensky, J. (2009). Internet gambling behavior in a sample of online gamblers. *International Journal of Mental Health and Addiction*, *7*(1), 149–167.

McBurnett, K., Raine, A. Stouthamer-Loeber, M., Loeber, R., Kumar, A. M., Kumar, M. & Lahey, B. B. (2005). Mood and hormone responses to psychological challenge in adolescent males with conduct problems. *Biological Psychiatry*, *57*, 1109–1116.

McCarthy, B. & Hagan, J. (1992). Surviving on the street: The experiences of homeless youth. *Journal of Adolescent Research*, *7*, 412–430.

McCloskey, L. A. & Lichter, E. L. (2003). The contribution of marital violence to adolescent aggression across different relationships. *Journal of Interpersonal Violence*, *18*(4), 390–412.

McCord, W. & McCord, J. (1959). *Origins of crime: A new evaluation of the Cambridge-Somerville study*. New York: Columbia University Press.

McCrory, E., Hickey, N., Farmer, E. & Vizard, E. (2008). Early-onset sexually harmful behaviour in childhood: A marker for life-course persistent antisocial behaviour? *Journal of Forensic Psychiatry and Psychology*, *19*(3), 382–395.

McDaniel, A. K. & Coleman, M. (2003). Women's experiences of midlife divorce following long-term marriage. *Journal of Divorce & Remarriage, 38*, 103–128.

McDonald, K., Keys, C. & Balcazar, F. (2007). Disability, race/ethnicity and gender: Themes of cultural oppression, acts of individual resistance. *American Journal of Community Psychology, 39*(1–2), 145–161.

McDowell, M. A., Brody, D. J. & Hughes, J. P. (2007). Has age at menarche changed? Results from the National Health and Nutrition Examination Survey (NHANES) 1999–2004. *Journal of Adolescent Health, 40*(3). 227–231.

McElhaney, K. B., Antonishak, J. & Allen, J. P. (2008). 'They like me, they like me not': Popularity and adolescents' perceptions of acceptance predicting social functioning over time. *Child Development, 79*(3), 720–731.

McEwen, B. S. (2003). Early life influences on life-long patterns of behavior and health. *Developmental Disabilities Research Reviews, 9*(3), 149–154.

McEwen, C. & Flouri, E. (2009). Fathers' parenting, adverse life events, and adolescents' emotional and eating disorder symptoms: The role of emotion regulation. *European Child & Adolescent Psychiatry, 18*(4), 206–216.

McGaha-Garnett, V. (2008). Needs assessment for adolescent mothers: Building resiliency and pupil success towards high school completion. In G. R. Walz, J. C. Bleuer, & R. K Yep (Eds.), *Compelling counseling interventions: Celebrating VISTAS' fifth anniversary* (pp. 11–20). Alexandria, VA: American Counseling Association.

McGinn, L., Cukor, D. & Sanderson, W. (2005). The relationship between parenting style, cognitive style, and anxiety and depression: Does increased early adversity influence symptom severity through the mediating role of cognitive style? *Cognitive Therapy and Research, 29*(2), 219–242.

McGovern, C. W. & Sigman, M. (2005). Continuity and change from early childhood to adolescence in autism. *Journal of Child Psychology and Psychiatry* (formerly *Journal of Child Psychology and Psychiatry and Allied Disciplines), 46*(4), 401–408.

McGregor, J. (2008). Children and 'African values': Zimbabwean professionals in Britain reconfiguring family life. *Environment and Planning A, 40*(3), 596–614.

McGue, M., Keyes, M., Sharma, A., Elkins, I., Legrand, L., Johnson, W. & Iacono, W. (2007). The environments of adopted and non-adopted youth: Evidence on range restriction from the Sibling Interaction and Behavior Study (SIBS). *Behavior Genetics, 37*(3), 449–462.

McHale, S. M., Crouter, A. C. & Whiteman, S. D. (2003). The family contexts of gender development in childhood and adolescence. *Social Development, 12*(1), 125–148.

McIntosh, H., Hart, D. & Youniss, J. (2007). The influence of family political discussion on youth civic development: Which parent qualities matter? *Political Science and Politics, 40*(3), 495–499.

McIntosh, H., Metz, E. & Youniss, J. (2005). Community service and identity formation in adolescents. In J. L. Mahoney, R. W. Larson, & J. S. Eccles (Eds.), *Organized activities as contexts of development: Extracurricular activities, after-school and community programs* (pp. 331–351). Mahwah, NJ: Lawrence Erlbaum.

McIntosh, M. (2001). Engendering economic policy: The Women's Budget Group. *Women: a Cultural Review, 12*(2), 147–157.

McIntyre-Bhatty, K. (2008). Truancy and coercive consent: Is there an alternative? *Educational Review, 60*(4), 375–390.

McKnight, A. J. & Peck, R. C. (2002). Graduated licensing: What works? *Injury Prevention, 8 (Suppl 2)*, ii32–ii38.

McKnight Investigators (2003). Risk factors for the onset of eating disorders in adolescent girls: Results on the McKnight longitudinal risk factor study. *American Journal of Psychiatry, 160*, 248–254.

McLellan, J. A. & Youniss, J. (2003). Two systems of youth service: Determinants of voluntary and required youth community service. *Journal of Youth & Adolescence, 32*, 47–58.

McMahon, S. D. & Watts, R. J. (2002). Ethnic identity in urban African American youth: Exploring links with self-worth, aggression, and other psychosocial variables. *Journal of Community Psychology, 30*, 411–432.

McNab, S & Kavner, E. (2001). When it all goes wrong – challenge to mother blame: forging connections between mother and daughter. *Journal of Family Therapy, 23*(2), 189–207.

McNelles, L. R. & Connolly, J. A. (1999). Intimacy between adolescent friends: Age and gender differences in intimate affect and intimate behaviors. *Journal of Research on Adolescence, 9*, 143–159.

McNess, E., Broadfoot, P. & Osborn, M. (2003). Is the effective compromising the affective? *British Educational Research Journal, 29*(2), 243–257.

McPake, J. & Powney, J. (1998). A mirror to ourselves? The educational experiences of Japanese children at school in the UK. *Educational Research, 40*(2), 169–179.

Mcwhirter, B., Besett-Alesch, T., Horibata, J. & Gat, I. (2002). Loneliness in high risk adolescents: The role of coping, self-esteem, and empathy. *Journal of Youth Studies, 5*(1), 69–84.

Mead, M. (1928). *Coming of age in Samoa*. New York: Morrow.

Meaden, P. M., Hartlage, S. A. & Cook-Karr, J. (2005). Timing and severity of symptoms associated with the menstrual cycle in a community-based sample in the midwestern United States. *Psychiatry Research, 134*, 27–36.

Meckel, Y., Ismaeel, A. & Eliakim, A. (2008). The effect of the Ramadan fast on physical performance and dietary habits in adolescent soccer players. *European Journal of Applied Physiology, 102*(6), 651–657.

Medoff, M. (2007). Price, restrictions and abortion demand. *Journal of Family and Economic Issues, 28*(4), 583–599.

Meer, N. (2008). A sociological comparison of anti-Semitism and anti-Muslim sentiment in Britain. *The Sociological Review, 56*(2), 195–195.

Meeus, W. (2006). Netherlands. In J. J. Arnett, R. Ahmed, B. Nsamenang, T. S. Saraswathi, & R. Silbereisen (Eds.), *International encyclopedia of adolescence*. New York: Routledge.

Meeus, W., Iedema, J., Helsen, M. & Vollebergh, W. (1999). Patterns of adolescent identity development: Review of literature and longitudinal analysis. *Developmental Review, 19*, 419–461.

Meijer, J. (2007). Cross-curricular skills testing in The Netherlands. *The Curriculum Journal, 18*(2), 155–173.

Meinander, H. (2011). *A history of Finland*. London: C Hurst & Co Publishers Ltd.

Meland, E., Haugland, S. & Breidablik, H-J. (2007). Body image and perceived health in adolescence. *Health Education Research, 22*(3), 342–350.

Melhem, N. M., Day, N., Shear, M. K., Day, R., Reynolds, C. F. & Brent, D. F. (2004). Traumatic grief among adolescents exposed to a peer's suicide. *The American Journal of Psychiatry, 161*(8), 1411–6.

Mendelson, M. J., Mendelson, B. K. & Andrews, J. (2000). Self-esteem, body esteem, and body mass in late adolescence: Is a competence* importance model needed? *Journal of Applied Developmental Psychology, 21*, 249–266.

Mendle, J., Turkheimer, E. & Emery, R. E. (2007). Detrimental psychological outcomes associated with early pubertal timing in adolescent girls. *Developmental Review, 27*, 151–171.

Mensch, B. S., Bruce, J. & Greene, M. E. (1998). *The uncharted passage: Girls' adolescence in the developing world*. New York: Population Council.

Mermaids UK – Young Voices Website. Accessed 22 March 2011 at http://www.mermaidsuk.org.uk/New%20Mermaids/youngvoices.htm.

Merten, M., Wickrama, K. & Williams, A. (2008). Adolescent obesity and young adult psychosocial outcomes: Gender and racial differences. *Journal of Youth and Adolescence, 37*(9), 1111–1122.

Messersmith, E. E., Garrett, J. L., Davis-Kean, P. E., Malanchuk, O. & Eccles, J. S. (2008). Career development from adolescence through emerging adulthood: Insights from information technology occupations. Journal of Adolescent Research, 23(2), 206–227.

Metz, E., McLellan, J. & Youniss, J. (2003). Types of voluntary service and adolescents' civic development. *Journal of Adolescent Research, 18*, 188–203.

Metz, E. C. & Youniss, J. (2005). Longitudinal gains in civic development through school-based required services. *Political Psychology, 26*, 413–437.

Meyer, M. A. (2007). Didactics, sense making, and educational experience. *European Educational Research Journal, 6*(2), 161–173.

Meyer, E. (2008). Gendered harassment in secondary schools: understanding teachers' (non) interventions. *Gender and Education, 20*(6), 555–570.

Michael, K. D. & Crowley, S. L. (2002). How effective are treatments for child and adolescent depression? A meta-analytic review. *Clinical Psychology Review, 22*, 247–269.

Miettinen. R. & Peisa, S. (2002). Integrating school-based learning with the study of change in working life: The alternative enterprise method. *Journal of Education and Work, 15*(3), 303–319.

Miller, B. C., Bayley, B. K., Christensen, M., Leavitt, S. C. & Coyl, D. D. (2003). Adolescent pregnancy and childbearing. In R. G. Adams & D. M. Berzonsky (Eds.), *Blackwell handbook of adolescence* (pp. 415–449). Malden, MA: Blackwell.

Miller, B. C. & Benson, B. (1999). Romantic and sexual relationship development during adolescence. In W. Furman, B. B. Brown, & C. Feiring (Eds.), *The development of romantic relationships in adolescence. Cambridge studies in social and emotional development* (pp. 99–121). New York: Cambridge University Press.

Miller, D. & Moran, T. (2005). One in three? Teachers' attempts to identify low self-esteem children. *Pastoral Care in Education, 23*(4), 25–30.

Miller, K., Fasula, A., Dittus, P., Wiegand, R., Wyckoff, S. & McNair, L. (2009). Barriers and facilitators to maternal communication with preadolescents about age-relevant sexual topics. *AIDS and Behavior, 13*(2), 365–374.

Miller, K. S., Forehand, R. & Kotchick, B. A. (1999). Adolescent sexual behavior in two ethnic minority samples: The role of family variables. *Journal of Marriage & the Family, 61*(1), 85–98.

Miller, M. K. (2006). Through the eyes of a father: How PRWORA affects non-resident fathers and their children. *International Journal of Law, Policy and the Family, 20*(1), 55–73.

Miller-Johnson, S. & Costanzo, P. (2004). If you can't beat 'em … induce them to join you: Peer-based interventions during adolescence. In J. G. Kupersmidt & K. A. Dodge (Eds.), *Children's peer relations: From development to intervention* (pp. 209–222). Washington, DC: American Psychological Association.

Miller-Johnson, S., Costanzo, P. R., Cole, J. D., Rose, M. R. & Browne, D. C. (2003). Peer social structure and risky-taking behaviours among African American early adolescents. *Journal of Youth & Adolescence, 32*, 375–384.

Miller-Johnson, S., Winn, D. M., Coie, J., Maumary-Gremaud, A., Hyman, C., Terry, R. & Lochman, J. (1999). Motherhood during the teen years: A developmental perspective on risk factors for childbearing. *Development and Psychopathology, 11*, 85–100.

Miller-Jones, D. (1989). Culture and testing. *American Psychologist, 44*, 360–366.

Mind (2010). *Mental Health Statistics* at http://www.mind.org.uk/help/research_and_policy accessed 20.02.2011.

Ministry of Justice (2010). *Reoffending of juveniles: results from the 2008 cohort. England and Wales* Ministry of Justice Statistics bulletin Published 18 March 2010.

Minuchin, P. (2002). Looking toward the horizon: Present and future in the study of family systems. In J. P. McHale & W. S. Grolinick (Eds.), *Retrospect and prospect in the study of families*. Mahwah, NJ: Erlbaum.

Miracle, T. S., Miracle, A. W. & Baumeister, R. F. (2003). *Human sexuality: Meeting your basic needs*. Upper Saddle River, NJ: Prentice Hall.

Miranda, R., Meyerson, L. A., Long, P. J., Marx, B. P. & Simpson, S. M. (2002). Sexual assault and alcohol use: Exploring the self-medication hypothesis. *Violence & Victims, 17*, 205–217.

Mistry, R., White, E., Benner, A. & Huynh, V. (2009). A longitudinal study of the simultaneous Influence of Mothers' and Teachers' Educational Expectations on Low-income Youth's Academic Achievement. *Journal of Youth and Adolescence, 38*(6), 826–838.

Modell, J. & Goodman, M. (1990). Historical perspectives. In S. S. Feldman & G. Elliott (Eds.), *At the threshold: The developing adolescent*. Cambridge, MA: Harvard University Press.

Modood, T. (2005). In 'Remaking multiculturalism after 7/7' at http://www.opendemocracy.net/conflict-terrorism/multiculturalism_2879.jsp (accessed 28 August 2010).

Moffitt, T. (1993). Adolescence-limited and life-course persistent antisocial behavior: A developmental taxonomy. *Psychological Review, 100*, 674–701.

Moffitt, T., Caspi, A., Harkness, A. & Silva P. (1993). The natural history of change in intellectual performance: Who changes? How much? Is it meaningful? *Journal of Child Psychology and Psychiatry, 34*, 455–506.

Moffitt, T. E. (2007). A review of research on the taxonomy of life-course persistent versus adolescence-limited antisocial behavior. In D. J. Flannery, A. T. Vazsonyi, & I. D. Waldman (Eds.), *The Cambridge handbook of violent behavior and aggression* (pp. 49–74). New York: Cambridge University Press.

Moffitt, T. E. (2003). Life-course-persistent and adolescence-limited antisocial behavior: A 10-year research review and a research agenda. In B. B. Lahey & T. E. Moffitt (Eds.), *Causes of conduct disorder and juvenile delinquency* (pp. 49–75). New York: Guilford.

Moffitt, T. E. & Caspi, A. (2005). Life-course persistent and adolescent-limited antisocial males: Longitudinal follow-up to adulthood. In D. M. Stoff & E. J. Susman (Eds.), *Developmental psychobiology of aggression* (pp. 161–186). New York: Cambridge University Press.

Moffitt, T. E. & Caspi, A. (2001). Childhood predictors differentiate life-course persistent and adolescence-limited antisocial pathways among males and females. *Development & Psychopathology, 13*, 355–375.

Moffitt, T. E., Caspi, A., Harrington, H. & Milne, B. J. (2002). Males on the life-course persistent and adolescence-limited antisocial pathways: Follow-up at 26 years. *Development and Psychopathology, 14*, 179–207.

Moffitt, T. E., Caspi, A., Rutter, M. & Phil, S. (2002). Sex differences in antisocial behavior: *Conduct disorder, delinquency, and violence in the Dunedin longitudinal study*. New York: Cambridge University Press.

Molina, B. & Chassin, L. (1996). The parent-adolescent relationship at puberty: Hispanic ethnicity and parent alcoholism as moderators. *Developmental Psychology, 32*, 675–686.

Monastra, V., Monastra, D. & George, S. (2002). The effects of stimulant therapy, EEG biofeedback, and parenting style on the primary symptoms of attention-deficit/hyperactivity disorder. *Applied Psychophysiology and Biofeedback, 27*(4), 231–249.

Monitoring the Future (2002). *ISR study finds drinking and drug use decline after college*. A. Arbor, MI: Author. at www.umich.edu/newsinfo/releases/2002/Jan02/r013002a.html.

Monro, S. (2003). Transgender politics in the UK. *Critical Social Policy, 23*(4), 433–452.

Monro, S. & Warren, L. (2004). Transgendering citizenship. *Sexualities, 7*(3), 345–362.

Monson, C. M., Langhinrichsen-Rohling, J. & Binderup, T. (2000). Does 'no' really mean 'no' after you say 'yes'? attributions about date and marital rape. *Journal of Interpersonal Violence, 15*(11), 1156–1174.

Montemayor, R. & Flannery, D. J. (1989). A naturalistic study of the involvement of children and adolescents with their mothers and friends: Developmental differences in expressive behavior. *Journal of Adolescent Research, 4*, 3–14.

Montgomery, M. J. (2005). Psychosocial intimacy and identity: From early adolescence to emerging adulthood. *Journal of Adolescent Research, 20*, 346–374.

Moogan, Y. J. & Baron, S. (2003). An analysis of student characteristics within the student decision making process. *Journal of Further and Higher Education, 27*(3), 271–287.

Mooney, G. A., Fewtrell, R. F. & Bligh, J. G. (1999). Cognitive process modelling: Computer tools for creative thinking and managing learning. *Medical Teacher, 21*(3), 277–280.

Moore, D. & Valverde, M. (2000). Maidens at risk: 'date rape drugs' and the formation of hybrid risk knowledges. *Economy and Society, 29*(4), 514–531.

Moore, K. A., Chalk, R., Scarpa, J. & Vandivere, S. (2002, August). Family strengths: Often overlooked, but real. *Child Trends Research Brief*, 1–8.

Moore, M. & Brooks-Gunn, J. (2002). Adolescent parenthood. In M. H. Bornstein (Ed.), *Handbook of parenting, Vol. 3: Being and becoming a parent* (2nd ed., pp. 173–214). Mahwah, NJ: Erlbaum.

Moore, S. & Cartwright, C. (2005). Adolescents' and young adults' expectations of parental responsibilities in stepfamilies. *Journal of Divorce & Remarriage, 43*(1–2), 109–127.

Moore, S. & Rosenthal, D. (2006). *Sexuality in adolescence: Current trends*. New York: Routledge/Taylor & Francis Group.

Moran, J. (2006). Milk Bars, Starbucks, and the uses of literacy. *Cultural Studies, 20*(6), 552–573.

Moreno, L. A., Sarría, A., Fleta, J., Marcos, A. & Bueno, M. (2005). Secular trends in waist circumference in Spanish adolescents, 1995 to 2000–02. *Archives of Disease in Childhood, 90*(8), 818–819.

Moretti, M. M. & Wiebe, V. J. (1999). Self-discrepancy in adolescence: Own and parental standpoints on the self. *Merrill-Palmer Quarterly, 45*, 624–649.

Moriguchi, Y., Ohnishi, T., Mori, T., Matsuda, H. & Komaki, G. (2007). Changes of brain activity in the neural substrates for theory of mind during childhood and adolescence. *Psychiatry and Clinical Neurosciences, 61*(4), 355–363.

Morrison, D. M. (1985). Adolescent contraceptive behavior: A review. *Psychological Bulletin, 98*, 538–568.

Morrison, L. (2004). Traditions in transition: Young people's risk for HIV in Chiang Mai, Thailand. *Qualitative Health Research, 14*(3), 328–344.

Mortimer, J. & Finch, M. (1996). *Adolescents, work, and family: An intergenerational developmental analysis*. Newbury Park, CA: Sage.

Mortimer, J., Finch, M., Ryu, S., Shanahan, M. J. & Call, K. (1996). The effects of work intensity on adolescent mental health, achievement, and behavioral adjustment: New evidence from a prospective study. *Child Development, 67*, 1243–1261.

Mortimer, J. T. (2003). *Working and growing up in America*. Cambridge, MA: Harvard University Press.

Mortimer, J. T., Harley, C. & Aronson, P. J. (1999). How do prior experiences in the workplace set the stage for transitions to adulthood? In A. Booth, A. C. Crouter, & M. J. Shanahan (Eds.), *Transitions to adulthood in a changing economy: No work, no family, no future?* (pp. 131–159). Westport, CT: Praeger.

Mortimer, J. T. & Johnson, M. K. (1998). New perspectives on adolescent work and the transition to adulthood. In R. Jessor (Ed.), *New perspectives on adolescent risk behavior* (pp. 425–496). New York: Cambridge University Press.

Mortimer, J. T. & Staff, J. (2004). Early work as a source of developmental discontinuity during the transition to adulthood. *Development & Psychopathology, 16*, 1047–1070.

Mortimer, J. T., Vuolo, M., Staff, J., Wakefield, S. & Xie, W. (2008). Tracing the timing of 'career' acquisition in a contemporary youth cohort. *Work and Occupations, 35*(1), 44–84.

Mortimer, J. T., Zimmer-Gembeck, M. J., Holmes, M. & Shanahan, M. J. (2002). The process of occupational decision making: Patterns during the transition to adulthood. *Journal of Vocational Behavior, 61*, 439–465.

Motani, Y. (2005). Hopes and challenges for progressive educators in Japan: assessment of the 'progressive turn' in the 2002 educational reform. *Comparative Education, 41*(3), 309–327.

Moti Gokulsing, K. (2006). Without prejudice: An exploration of religious diversity, secularism and citizenship in England (with particular reference to the state funding of Muslim faith schools and multiculturalism). *Journal of Education Policy, 21*(4), 459–470.

Motley, C. M. & Henderson, G. R. (2008). The global hip-hop diaspora: Understanding the culture. *Journal of Business Research, 61*(3), 243–253.

Motola, M., Sinisalo, P. & Guichard, J. (1998). Social habitus and future plans. In J. Nurmi (Ed.), *Adolescents, cultures, and conflicts* (pp. 43–73). New York: Garland.

Mottarella, K., Fritzsche, B., Whitten, S. & Bedsole, D. (2009). Exploration of 'good mother' stereotypes in the college environment. *Sex Roles, 60*(3–4), 223–231.

Mottram, S. A. & Hortaçsu, N. (2005). The effects of social change on relationships between older mothers and daughters in Turkey: A qualitative study. *Ageing and Society, 25*(5), 675–691.

Mounts, N. S. (2004). Adolescents' perceptions of parental management of peer relationships in an ethnically diverse sample. *Journal of Adolescent Research, 19*, 446–467.

Mouw, T. & Entwisle, B. (2008). Residential segregation and interracial friendship in schools. *American Journal of Sociology, 112*(2), 394–441.

Mulder, C. H. & Clark, W. A. V. (2002). Leaving home for college and gaining independence. *Environment and Planning A, 34*(6), 981–999.

Mumm, S., Smith, M. D. & Sears, J. T. (Ed) (2007). *The Greenwood encyclopedia of love, courtship, and sexuality through history*: vols 1–6. Westport CO: Greenwood Press.

Mum's Not the Word. (1999, September). *Population Today*, p. 3.

Muris, P., Fokke, M. & Kwik, D. (2009). The ruminative response style in adolescents: An examination of its specific link to symptoms of depression. *Cognitive Therapy and Research, 33*(1), 21–32.

Murnen, S. K. & Levine, M. P. (2007). *Do fashion magazines promote body dissatisfaction in girls and women?* Paper presented at the annual meeting of the American Psychological Association, San Francisco, CA.

Murphy-Lawless, J. (2000). Changing women's lives: Child care policy in Ireland. *Feminist Economics, 6*(1), 89–94.

Murray, L., Halligan, S. L., Adams, G., Patterson, P. & Goodyer, I. M. (2006). Socioemotional development in adolescents at risk for depression: The role of maternal depression and attachment style. *Development and Psychopathology, 18*(2), 489–516.

Mussen, P. H., Conger, J. J., Kagan, J. & Huston, A. (1990). *Child development and personality* (7th ed.). New York: Harper & Row.

Musso, F., Bettermann, F., Vucurevic, G., Stoeter, P., Konrad, A. & Winterer, G. (2007). Smoking impacts on prefrontal attentional network function in young adult brains. *Psychopharmacology, 191*(1), 159–169.

Myhill, A. & Allen, J. (2002). *Rape and sexual assault of women: the extent and nature of the problem. Findings from the British Crime Survey*. Home Office Research Study, 237.

Myklebust, J. O. (2002). Inclusion or exclusion? Transitions among special needs students in upper secondary education in Norway. *European Journal of Special Needs Education, 17*(3), 251–263.

Naar-King, S., Silvern, V., Ryan, V. & Sebring, D. (2002). Type and severity of abuse as predictors of psychiatric symptoms in adolescence. *Journal of Family Violence, 17*, 133–149.

Nabukera, S., Wingate, M., Salihu, H., Owen, J., Swaminathan, S., Alexander, G. & Kirby, R. (2009). Pregnancy spacing among women delaying initiation of childbearing. *Archives of Gynecology and Obstetrics*, *279*(5), 677–684.

Nader, P. R., Bradley, R. H., Houts, R. M., McRitchie, S. L. & O'Brien, M. (2008). Moderate-to-vigorous physical activity from ages 9 to 15 years. *JAMA: Journal of the American Medical Association, 300*(3), 295–305.

Naito, T. & Gielen, U. P. (2003). The changing Japanese family: A psychological portrait. In J. L. Roopnarine & U. P. Gielen (Eds.), *Families in global perspective*. Boston: Allyn & Bacon.

Naito, T. & Gielen, U. P. (2003a). How can Japanese society be explained from a cross-cultural point of view? *International Psychology Reporter*, *7*(3), 18–19, 43.

Nangle, D. W., Erdley, C. A., Carpenter, E. M. & Newman, J. E. (2002). Social skills training as a treatment for aggressive children and adolescents: A developmental-clinical integration. *Aggression and Violent Behaviour, 7*, 169–199.

National Archives (2010). Population Live Births at http://www.ndad.nationalarchives.gov.uk/CRDA/5/DS/2/1/display.html accessed 23/09/2010.

National Center for Education Statistics (2006). *Highlights from PISA 2006: Performance of U.S. 15-Year-Old Students in Science and Mathematics Literacy in an International Context* at http://nces.ed.gov/surveys/international/report-library.asp accessed 15 January 2011.

National Center for Education Statistics (2005). *The condition of education, 2005*. Washington, DC: U.S. Department of Education. Available: www.nces.gov

Natvig, G. K., Albreksten, G. & Qvarnstrom, F. (2001). Psychosomatic symptoms among victims of school bullying. *Journal of Health Psychology*, *6*(4), 365–377.

Naughton, G., Farpour-Lambert, N., Carlson, J., Bradney, M. & Van Praagh, E. (2000). Physiological issues surrounding the performance of adolescent athletes. *Sports Medicine, 30*(5), 309–325.

NCVO (2010). *Civil Society Almanac* at http://www.ncvo-vol.org.uk/access-tables-behind-almanac accessed 28.02.2011.

Neder, J. A., Nery, L. E., Silva, A. C., Andreoni, S. and Whipp, B. J. (1999). Maximal aerobic power and leg muscle mass and strength related to age in non-athletic males and females. *European Journal of Applied Physiology and Occupational Physiology*, *79*(6), 522–530.

Neiderhiser, J. M., Reiss, D. & Hetherington, E. M. (2007). The nonshared Environment in Adolescent Development (NEAD) project: A longitudinal family study of twins and siblings from adolescence to young adulthood. *Twin Research and Human Genetics, 10*(1), 74–83.

Nelson, J. (2004). Uniformity and diversity in religious education in Northern Ireland. *British Journal of Religious Education*, *26*(3), 249–258.

Nelson, L. J. (2009). An examination of emerging adulthood in Romanian college students. *International Journal of Behavioral Development, 33*(5), 402–411.

Nelson, L. J. (2003). Rites of passage in emerging adulthood: Perspectives of young Mormons. *New Directions in Child and Adolescent Development*.

Nelson, L. J., Badger, S. & Wu, B. (2004). The influence of culture in emerging adulthood: Perspectives of Chinese college students. *International Journal of Behavioral Development, 28*, 26–36.

Nelson, L. J. & Chen, X. (2007). Emerging adulthood in China: The role of social and cultural factors. *Child Development Perspectives, 1,* 86–91.

Neto, F. (2006). Psycho-social predictors of perceived discrimination among adolescents of immigrant background: A Portuguese study. *Journal of Ethnic and Migration Studies*, *32*(1), 89–109.

Nevid, J. S., Rathus, S. A. & Greene, B. (2003). *Abnormal psychology in a changing world*. Upper Saddle River, NJ: Prentice Hall.

Nevgi, A. & Virtanen, P. & Niemi, H. (2006). Supporting students to develop collaborative learning skills in technology-based environments. *British Journal of Educational Technology*, *37*(6), 937–947.

NHTSA (National Highway Traffic Safety Administration) (2002). *Traffic safety facts* Washington, DC: U.S. Department of Transportation.

Nichter, M. (2001). *Fat talk: What girls and their parents say about dieting*. Cambridge, MA: Harvard University Press.

Nickerson, A. B. & Nagle, R. J. (2005). Parent and peer attachment in late childhood and early adolescence. *Journal of Early Adolescence, 25*, 223–249.

Nica, E. & Links, P. (2009). Affective instability in borderline personality disorder: Experience sampling findings. *Current Psychiatry Reports*, *11*(1), 74–81.

Nijman, J. (2006). Mumbai's mysterious middle class. *International Journal of Urban and Regional Research*, *30*(4), 758–775.

Nishikawa, S., Norlander, T., Fransson, P. & Sundbom, E. (2007). A cross-cultural validation of adolescent self-concept in two cultures: Japan and Sweden. *Social Behavior and Personality*, *35*(2), 269–286.

Nishizono-Maher, A., Miyake, Y. & Nakane, A. (2004). The prevalence of eating pathology and its relationship to knowledge of eating disorders among high school girls in Japan. *European Eating Disorders Review: The Journal of the Eating Disorders Association*, *12*(2), 122–128.

Noell, J. W. & Ochs, L. M. (2001). Relationship of sexual orientation to substance use, suicidal ideation, suicide attempts, and other factors in a population of homeless adolescents. *Journal of Adolescent Health, 29*, 31–36.

Noguchi, K. (2007). Examination of the content of individualism/collectivism scales in cultural comparisons of the USA and Japan. *Asian Journal of Social Psychology, 10*(3), 131–144.

Nolan, S. A., Flynn, C. & Garber, J. (2003). Prospective relations between rejection and depression in young adolescents. *Journal of Personality & Social Psychology, 85*, 745–755.

Nolen-Hoeksema, S., Wisco, B. E. & Lyubomirsky, S. (2008). Rethinking rumination. *Perspectives on Psychological Science, 3*(5), 400–424.

Noller, P. (2005). Sibling relationships in adolescence: Learning and growing together. *Personal Relationships, 12*, 1–22.

Nonnemaker, J. M., McNeely, C. A. & Blum, R. W. M. (2003). Public and private domains of religiosity and adolescent health risk behaviors: Evidence from the national longitudinal study of adolescent health. *Social Science & Medicine, 57*, 2049–2054.

Nottelmann, E. D., Susman, E. J., Blue, J. H., Inoff-Germain, G., Dorn, L. D., Loriaux, D. L., Cutler, G. B. & Chrousos, G. P. (1987). Gonadal and adrenal hormone correlates of adjustment in early adolescence. In R. M. Lerner & T. T. Foch (Eds.), *Biological-psychological interactions in early adolescence*. Hillsdale, NJ: Erlbaum.

Noyes, A. (2006). School transfer and the diffraction of learning trajectories. *Research Papers in Education, 21*(1), 43–62.

NPS (National Probationary Service) (2011). *Probation Service* accessed 21 02. 2011 at http://www.national-probationservice.co.uk/page1.html

Nsamenang, A. B. (2010). Issues and challenges to early childhood development professionalism in africa's cultural settings. *Contemporary Issues in Early Childhood, 11*, 20–28.

Nsamenang, A. B. (2002). Adolescence in sub-Saharan Africa: An image constructed from Africa's triple inheritance. In B. B. Brown, R. Larson, & T. S. Saraswathi (Eds.), *The World's Youth: Adolescence in Eight Regions of the Globe* (pp. 61–104). New York: Cambridge University Press.

Nsamenang, A. B. (1998). Work organization and economic management in sub-Saharan Africa: From a Eurocentric orientation toward an Afrocentric perspective. *Psychology and Developing Societies, 10*, 75–97.

Nsamenang, A. B., Fru, F. N. & Browne, M. A. (2007). The roots of community psychology in Cameroon. In S. M. Reich, M. Riemer, I. Prilleltensky, & M. Montero (Eds.), *International community psychology: History and theories* (pp. 394–408). New York: Springer.

NSPCC (2007). Childline casenotes Running Away and Homelessness. London: NSPCC.

Nunn, P. (2003). Fished up or thrown down: The geography of Pacific Island origin myths. *Annals of the Association of American Geographers, 93*(2), 350–364.

Obeidallah, D., Brennan, R. T., Brooks-Gunn, J. & Earls, F. (2004). Links between pubertal timing and neighborhood contexts: Implications for girls' violent behavior. *Journal of the American Academy of Child & Adolescent Psychiatry, 43*, 1460–1468.

Oberlander, S. E., Black, M. M. Starr, R. H., Jr. (2007). African American adolescent mothers and grandmothers: A multigenerational approach to parenting. *American Journal of Community Psychology, 39*(1–2), 37–46.

O'Brien, C. (2007). Peer devaluation in British secondary schools: young people's comparisons of group-based and individual-based bullying. *Educational Research, 49*(3), 297–324.

O'Brien, L. T. & Crandall, C. S. (2003). Stereotype threat and arousal: Effects on women's math performance. *Personality and Social Psychology Bulletin, 29*(6), 782–789.

O'Connell, P. J., McCoy, S. & Clancy, D. (2006). Who went to college? Socio-economic inequality in entry to higher education in the Republic of Ireland in 2004. *Higher Education Quarterly, 60*(4), 312–332.

O'Connor, T. G., Caspi, A., DeFries, J. C. & Plomin, R. (2003). Genotype-environment interaction in children's adjustment to parental separation. *Journal of Child Psychology and Psychiatry (*formerly *Journal of Child Psychology and Psychiatry and Allied Disciplines), 44*(6), 849–856.

OECD (2011) PISA at a Glance database (2009). http://www.oecd.org/document/53/ Copyright OECD, 2009 Accessed 27.12.2010.

Office for National Statistics (2011). *Census Data 1951, 1971, 1981, 1991, 2001* at http://dx.doi.org/10.18787/9789264095298-en/ accessed 15 January 2011.

Office for National Statistics (2010). Population Live Births at http://www.statistics.gov.uk/StatBase/Expodata/Spreadsheets/D9555.xls accessed 23/09/2010.

Office for National Statistics (2010a). Young People. Transport at http://www.statistics.gov.uk/cci/nugget.asp?id=2207 accessed 31st July 2010.

Office for National Statistics (2010b). Social trends. Crime and Justice. at http://www.statistics.gov.uk/CCI/nugget.asp?ID=2133&Pos=5&ColRank=2&Rank=224, accessed 31st July 2010.

Office for National Statistics (2010c). Population Divorces at http://www.statistics.gov.uk/ accessed 22.09.2010.

Office for National Statistics (2010d). Population Marriages at http://www.statistics.gov.uk/ accessed 23.09.2010.

Office for National Statistics (2010e). United Kingdom Health Statistics 2010: Edition No 4. London: ONS at http://www.statistics.gov.uk/downloads/theme_health/ukhs4/ukhs4–2010.pdf accessed 01.12.2010.

Office for National Statistics (2009a). Population Fertility at http://www.statistics.gov.uk/ accessed 22.09.2010.

Office for National Statistics (2009b). Population Life Expectancy at http://www.statistics.gov.uk/ accessed 22.09.2010.

Office for National Statistics (2009c). Population Employee Jobs by Industry at http://www.statistics.gov.uk/ accessed 22.09.2010.

Office for National Statistics (2008). Population Employment at http://www.statistics.gov.uk/cci/nugget.asp?id=1655 accessed 23/09/2010.

Office for National Statistics (2007). *Annual Population Survey* at http://www.ons.gov.uk/ accessed 07.09.2011.

Office for National Statistics (2002). *Annual Local Area Labour Force Survey 2001/02.*

Office for National Statistics (2001). *Census General Household Survey*, accessed 19.9.2010 at http://www.statistics.gov.uk/downloads/theme_social/Social_Trends38/ST38_Ch02.pdf

Office for National Statistics (2001a). Omnibus Survey accessed 28.2.2011 at http://www.statistics.gov.uk/STATBASE/ssdataset.asp?vlnk=6465.

Ogden, T. & Haden, K. A. (2006). Multisystemic treatment of serious behavior problems in youth: Sustainability of effectiveness two years after intake. *Child and Adolescent Mental Health, 11*(3), 142–149.

Okada, A. (2002). Education of whom, for whom, by whom? Revising the Fundamental Law of Education in Japan. *Japan Forum, 14*(3), 425–441.

Okie, S. (2002, April 10). Study cites alcohol link in campus deaths. *Washington Post*, p. A2.

Oliva, J. (2003). The structural coherence of students' conceptions in mechanics and conceptual change. *International Journal of Science Education, 25*(5), 539–561.

Oliver, B. (2004). Professional education as co-inquiry: an evaluation of the learning approach to developing the role of connexions personal adviser. *Assessment & Evaluation in Higher Education, 29*(1), 109–121.

Oliver, J. E. & Ha, S. E. (2008). The segregation paradox: Neighborhoods and interracial contact in multiethnic America. In B. A. Sullivan, M. Snyder, & J. Sullivan (Eds.), *Cooperation: The political psychology of effective human interaction* (p. 161–180). Malden, MA: Blackwell Publishing.

Ollendick, T. H., Shortt, A. L. & Sander, J. B. (2008). Internal disorders in children and adolescents. In J. E. Maddux & B. A. Winstead (Eds.), *Psychopathology: Foundations for a contemporary understanding* (2nd ed., pp. 375–399). New York: Routledge/Taylor & Francis Group.

Olson, E. (2007, May 28). OMG! Cute boys, kissing tips and lots of pics, as magazines find a niche. *New York Times*, 156.

Olthof, T. & Goossens, F. A. (2008). Bullying and the need to belong: Early adolescents' bullying-related behaviour and the acceptance they desire and receive from particular classmates. *Social Development, 17*(1), 24–46.

Oltmanns, T. F. & Emery, R. E. (2006). *Abnormal psychology* (5th ed.). Upper Saddle River, NJ: Prentice Hall.

Oltmanns, T. F. & Emery, R. E. (2001). *Abnormal psychology* (3rd ed.). Upper Saddle River, NJ: Prentice Hall.

Olweus, D. (2000). Bullying. In A. E. Kazdin (Ed.), *Encyclopedia of psychology, Vol. 1* (pp. 487–489). Washington, DC: American Psychological Association, Oxford University Press.

Ong, S. & Caron, A. (2010). Family-based psychoeducation for children and adolescents with mood disorders. *Journal of Child and Family Studies*, Preprint, 1–14.

Oprea, A. (2005). The arranged marriage of Ana Maria Cioaba, intra-community oppression and Romani feminist ideals: Transcending the 'primitive culture' argument. *The European Journal of Women's Studies, 12*(2), 133–148.

Orazem, P. F., Werbel, J. D. & McElroy, J. C. (2003). Market expectations, job search, and gender differences in starting pay. *Journal of Labor Research, 24*(2), 307–321.

Ortega, D. M. (2001). Parenting efficacy, aggressive parenting and cultural connections. *Child & Family Social Work, 6*(1), 47–57.

Ortega, S. (2008). 'Pleading for help': Gender relations and cross-cultural logic in the early modern Mediterranean. *Gender & History, 20*(2), 332–348.

Osborn, M. (2001). Constants and contexts in pupil experience of learning and schooling: Comparing learners in England, France and Denmark. *Comparative Education, 37*(3), 267–278.

Osgood, D. W., Anderson, A. L. & Shaffer, J. N. (2005). Unstructured leisure in the after-school hours. In L. J. Mahoney, W. R. Larson et al. (Eds.), *Organized activities as contexts of development: Extracurricular activities, after-school and community programs* (pp. 45–64). Mahwah, NJ: Lawrence Erlbaum.

Osland, J. S. (2003). Broadening the debate: The pros and cons of globalization. *Journal of Management Inquiry, 12*(2), 137–154.

Osler, A. (2009). Patriotism, multiculturalism and belonging: political discourse and the teaching of history. *Educational Review, 61*(1), 85–100.

Osler, M., Godtfredsen, N. S. & Prescott, E. (2008). Childhood social circumstances and health behaviour in midlife: the Metropolit 1953 Danish male birth cohort. *International Journal of Epidemiology, 37*(6), 1367–1367.

Ouwerkerk, J. W. & Ellemers, N. (2002). The benefits of being disadvantaged: Performance-related circumstances and consequences of intergroup comparisons. *European Journal of Social Psychology, 32*(1), 73–91.

Overton, W. F. & Byrnes, J. P. (1991). Cognitive development. In R. M. Lerner, A. C. Petersen, & J. Brooks-Gunn (Eds.) *Encyclopedia of Adolescence 1, 151–156*. New York: Garland.

Oxlery, D. & Kassissieh, J. (2008). From comprehensive high schools to small learning communities: Accomplishments and challenges. *FORUM: For Promoting 3–19 Comprehensive Education, 50*(2), 199–206.

Oyserman, D., Bybee, D. & Terry, K. (2006). Possible selves and academic outcomes: How and when possible selves impel action. *Journal of Personality and Social Psychology, 91*(1), 188–204.

Oyserman, D. & Fryberg, S. (2006). The possible selves of diverse adolescents: Content and function across gender, race and national origin. In C. Dunkel & J. Kerpelman (Eds.), *Possible selves: Theory, research and applications* (pp. 17–39). Hauppauge: Nova Science Publishers.

Oyserman, D. & Lee, S. W. S. (2008). Does culture influence what and how we think? Effects of priming individualism and collectivism. *Psychological Bulletin, 134*(2), 311–342.

Pagani, L., Tremblay, R., Nagin, D., Zoccolillo, M., Vitaro, F. & McDuff, P. (2009). Risk factor models for adolescent verbal and physical aggression toward fathers. *Journal of Family Violence, 24*(3), 173–182.

Pagani, L., Tremblay, R. E., Vitaro, F., Kerr, M. & McDuff, P. (1998). The impact of family transition on the development of delinquency in adolescent boys: A 9-year longitudinal study. *Journal of Child Psychology and Psychiatry* (formerly *Journal of Child Psychology and Psychiatry and Allied Disciplines*), *39*(4), 489–499.

Page, K. (1999, May 16). The graduate. *Washington Post Magazine*, 18, 20.

Paglieri, F. (2005). Playing by and with the rules: Norms and morality in play development. *Topoi, 24*(2), 149–167.

Pahl, K., Greene, M. & Way, N. (2000, April). *Self-esteem trajectories among urban, low-income, ethnic minority high school students*. Poster presented at the biennial meeting of the Society for Research on Adolescence, Chicago.

Pahl, K. & Way, N. (2006). Longitudinal trajectories of ethnic identity among urban black and Latino adolescents. *Child Development, 77*(5), 1403–1415.

Pais, J. M. (2000). Transitions and youth cultures: Forms and performances. *International Social Science Journal, 52*(164), 219–232.

Paiva, N. D. (2008). South Asian parents' constructions of praising their children. *Clinical Child Psychology and Psychiatry, 13*(2), 191–207.

Pakaslahti, L., Karjalainen, A. & Keltikangas-Jaervinen, L. (2002). Relationships between adolescent prosocial problem-solving strategies, prosocial behaviour, and social acceptance. *International Journal of Behavioural Development, 26*, 137–144.

Pan, S. Y., Desmueles, M., Morrison, H., Semenciw, R., Ugnat, A-M., Thompson, W. & Mao, Y. (2007). Adolescent injury deaths and hospitalization in Canada: Magnitude and temporal trends (1979–2003). *Journal of Adolescent Health, 41*(1), 84–92.

Pancer, S. M., Pratt, M., Hunsberger, B. & Alisat, S. (2007). Community and political involvement in adolescent: What distinguishes the activists from the uninvolved? *Journal of Community Psychology, 35*(6), 741–759.

Papastergiadis, N. (2005). Hybridity and ambivalence: places and flows in contemporary art and culture. *Theory, Culture & Society, 22*(4), 39–64.

Papatheodorou, T. (2002). How we like our school to be ... pupils' voices. *European Educational Research Journal, 1*(3), 445–467.

Papp, S. (2006). A relevance-theoretic account of the development and deficits of theory of mind in normally developing children and individuals with autism. *Theory & Psychology, 16*(2), 141–161.

Pardun, C. J. (2002). Romancing the script: Identifying the romantic agenda in top-grossing movies. In J. D. Brown, J. R. Steele, & K. Walsh-Childers (Eds.), *Sexual teens, sexual media: Investigating media's influence on adolescent sexuality* (pp. 211–225). Mahwah, NJ: Erlbaum.

Pardun, C. J., L'Engle, K. L. & Brown, J. D. (2005). Linking exposure to outcomes: Early adolescents' consumption of sexual content in six media. *Mass Communication & Society, 8*, 75–91.

Park, R. J., Goodyer, I. M. & Teasdale, J. D. (2005). Self-devaluative dysphoric experience and the prediction of persistent first-episode major depressive disorder in adolescents. *Psychological Medicine, 35*(4), 539–548.

Park, S. H., Shim, Y. K., Kim, H. S. & Eun, B. L. (1999). Age and seasonal distribution of menarche in Korean girls. *Journal of Adolescent Health, 25*, 97.

Parker, H. J. (2002). The normalization of 'sensible' recreational drug use: Further evidence from the North West England Longitudinal Study. *Sociology, 36*(4), 941–964.

Parker, M. (2009). *Childbirth: Webster's Timeline History, 82 BC – 2007*. San Diego: ICON Group International.

Parr, N. (2007). Which women stop at one child in Australia? *Journal of Population Research, 24*(2), 207–225.

Parsons, T. (1964). *Essays in sociological theory*. Chicago: Free Press.

Pascoe, C. J. (2007). *Dude, you're a fag: Masculinity and sexuality in high school*. Berkeley: University of California Press.

Pascoe, C. J. (2003). Multiple masculinities? Teenage boys talk about jocks and gender. *American Behavioral Scientist, 46*, 1423–1438.

Patel, P. (2008). Faith in the state? Asian women's struggles for human rights in the U.K. *Feminist Legal Studies, 16*(1), 9–36.

Patel-Amin, N. & Power, T. G. (2002). Modernity and childrearing in families of Gujarati Indian adolescents. *International Journal of Psychology, 37*, 239–245.

Patnaik, N. (2005) *Primitive tribes of Orissa and their development strategies*. London: DK Print World.

Patrick, H., Neighbors, C. & Knee, C. R. (2004). Appearance-related social comparisons: The role of contingent self-esteem and self-perceptions of attractiveness. *Personality and Social Psychology Bulletin, 30*(4), 501–514.

Patterson, G. R. & Fisher, P. A. (2002). Recent developments in our understanding of parenting: Bidirectional effects, causal models, and the search for parsimony. In M. H. Bornstein (Ed.), *Handbook of parenting, Vol. 5: Practical issues in parenting* (pp. 59–88). Mahwah, NJ: Erlbaum.

Patton, D. & McIntosh, A. (2008). Head and neck injury risks in heavy metal: head bangers stuck between rock and a hard bass. *BMJ (British Medical Journal), 337*(12), a2825–a2825.

Patton, G. C., Coffey, C., Sawyer, S. M., Viner, R. M., Haller, D. M., Bose, K., Vos, T., Ferguson, J. & Mathers, C. D. (2009). Global patterns of mortality in young people: a systematic analysis of population health data. *The Lancet, 374*(9693), 881–892.

Paulson-Karlsson, G., Engstrom, I. & Nevonen, L. (2009). A pilot study of a family-based treatment for adolescent anorexia nervosa: 18- and 36-month follow-ups. *Eating Disorders: The Journal of Treatment & Prevention, 17*(1), 72–88.

Paus, T., Zijdenbos, A., Worsley, K., et al. (1999). Structural maturation of neural pathways in children and adolescents: In vivo study. *Science, 283*, 1908–1911.

Payne, L. (2007). A 'children's government' in England and child impact assessment. *Children & Society, 21*(6), 470–475.

Peach, C. (2006). Muslims in the 2001 Census of England and Wales: Gender and economic disadvantage. *Ethnic and Racial Studies, 29*(4), 629–655.

Pecek, M., Cuk, I. & Lesar, I. (2008). Teachers' perceptions of the inclusion of marginalised groups. *Educational Studies, 34*(3), 225–239.

Pellegrini, D. (2007). School non-attendance: Definitions, meanings, responses, interventions. *Educational Psychology in Practice, 23*(1), 63–77.

Pels, T. V. M. (2003). Educational strategies of Moroccan mothers in the Netherlands. *European Early Childhood Education Research Journal, 11*(2), 63–76.

Pemberton, S. (2008). Tackling the NEET generation and the ability of policy to generate a 'NEET' solution – evidence from the UK. *Environment and Planning C: Government and Policy, 26*(1), 243–259.

Peng, K. & Nisbett, R. E. (1999). Culture, dialectics, and reasoning about contradiction. *American Psychologist, 54*, 741–754.

Pepler, D. J., Craig, W. M., Connolly, J. A., Yuile, A., McMaster, L. & Jiang, D. (2006). A developmental perspective on bullying. *Aggressive Behaviour, 32*(4), 376–384.

Pepler, D. J., Jiang, D., Craig, W. M. & Connolly, J. A. (2008). Developmental trajectories of bullying and associated factors. *Child Development, 79*(2), 325–338.

Pérez, R. G., Ezpeleta, L. & Domenech, J. (2007). Features associated with the non-participation and drop-out by socially-at-risk children and adolescents in mental-health epidemiological studies. *Social Psychiatry and Psychiatric Epidemiology, 42*(3), 251–258.

Peris, T. S. & Emery, R. E. (2004). A prospective study of the consequences of marital disruption for adolescents: Predisruption family dynamics and postdisruption adolescent adjustment. *Journal of Clinical Child & Adolescent Psychology, 33*, 694–704.

Perkinson, J. (2004). Reversing the gaze: Constructing European race discourse as modern witchcraft practice. *Journal of the American Academy of Religion, 72*(3), 603–629.

Perlstein, L. (2003). *Not much just chillin': The hidden lives of middle schoolers*. New York: Farrar Straus & Giroux.

Perren, S. & Hornung, R. (2005). Bullying and delinquency in adolescence: Victims' and perpetrators' family and peer relations. *Swiss Journal of Psychology, 64*(1), 51–64.

Perry, W. G. (1999). *Forms of ethical and intellectual development in the college years: A scheme*. San Francisco: Jossey-Bass.

Persons, J., Davidson, J. & Tompkins, M. A. (2001). *Essential components of cognitive behavior therapy for depression*. Washington, DC: American Psychological Association.

Peter, J. & Valkenburg, P. M. (2007). Adolescents' exposure to a sexualized media environment and their notions of women as sex objects. *Sex Roles, 56*(5–6), 381–395.

Peter, J. & Valkenburg, P. M. (2006). Individual differences in perceptions of Internet communication. *European Journal of Communication, 21*(2), 213–226.

Petersen, A. C. (2000, March). *Biology, culture, and behavior: What makes young adolescent boys and girls behave differently?* Paper presented at the biennial meeting of the Society for Research on Adolescence, Chicago.

Petersen, A. C. (1993). Creating adolescents: The role of context and process in developmental trajectories. *Journal of Research on Adolescence, 3*, 1–18.

Peterson, S. H., Wingood, G. M., DiClemente, R. J., Harrington, K. & Davis, S. (2007). Images of sexual stereotypes in rap videos and the health of African American female adolescents. *Journal of Women's Health, 16*(8), 1157–1164.

Petrina, S., Feng, F. & Kim, J. (2012). Researching cognition and technology: how we learn across the lifespan. *International Journal of Technology and Design Education*, Preprint, 1–22.

Pettit, G. S., Laird, R. D., Dodge, K. A., Bates, J. E. & Criss, M. M. (2001). Relationships and interactions antecedents and behavior-problem outcomes of parental monitoring and psychological control in early adolescence. *Child Development, 72*(2), 583–598.

Pexman, P. M. & Glenright, M. (2007). How do typically developing children grasp the meaning of verbal irony? *Journal of Neurolinguistics, 20*(2), 178–196.

Pfeffer, C. R. (2006). Suicide in children and adolescents. In D. J. Stein, D. J. Kupfer, & A. F. Schatzberg (Eds.), *The American Psychiatric Publishing textbook of mood disorders* (pp. 497–507). Arlington, VA: American Psychiatric Publishing.

Phillips, D. (2006). Masculinity, male development, gender, and identity: Modern and postmodern meanings. *Issues in Mental Health Nursing, 27*(4), 403–423.

Phinney, J. S. (2008). Ethnic identity exploration in emerging adulthood. In D. L. Browning (Ed.), *Adolescent identities: A collection of readings* (pp. 47–66). Relational perspectives book series. New York: Analytic Press/Taylor & Francis Group.

Phinney, J. S. (2006). Ethnic identity in emerging adulthood. In J. J. Arnett and J. L. Tanner (Eds.), *Emerging adults in America: Coming of age in the 21st century* (pp. 117–134). Washington, DC: American Psychological Association Press.

Phinney, J. S. (2000, March). *Identity formation among U.S. ethnic adolescents from collectivist cultures*. Paper presented at the biennial meeting of the Society for Research on Adolescence, Chicago.

Phinney, J. S. & Devich-Navarro, M. (1997). Variation in bicultural identification among African American and Mexican American adolescents. *Journal of Research on Adolescence, 7*, 3–32.

Phinney, J. S., Kim-Jo, T., Osorio, S. & Vilhjalmsdottir, P. (2005). Autonomy and relatedness in adolescent–parent disagreements: Ethnic and developmental factors. *Journal of Adolescent Research, 20*(1), 8–39.

Phinney, J. S. & Ong, A.. (2002). Adolescent–parent disagreement and life satisfaction in families from Vietnamese and European American backgrounds. *International Journal of Behavioral Development*.

Phinney, J. S., Ong, A. & Madden, T. (2000). Cultural values and intergenerational value discrepancies in immigrant and non-immigrant families. *Child Development, 71*(2), 528–539.

Piaget, J. (1972). Intellectual evolution from adolescence to adulthood. *Human Development, 15*, 1–12.

Piaget, J. (1967). *Six psychological studies*. New York: Random House.

Piaget, J. (1932). *The moral judgment of the child*. New York: Harcourt Brace Jovanovich.

Piaget, J. & Inhelder, B. (1969). *The psychology of the child*. New York: Basic Books.

Picard, C. L. (1999). The level of competition as a factor for the development of eating disorders in female collegiate athletes. *Journal of Youth & Adolescence, 28*, 583–594.

Pichler, P. (2006). Multifunctional teasing as a resource for identity construction in the talk of British Bangladeshi girls 1. *Journal of Sociolinguistics*, *10*(2), 225–249.

Piehler, T. F. & Dishion, T. J. (2007). Interpersonal dynamics within adolescent friendships: dyadic mutuality, deviant talk, and patterns of antisocial behavior. *Child Development*, *78*(5), 1611–1624.

Pierik, R. (2004). Conceptualizing cultural groups and cultural difference: The social mechanism approach. *Ethnicities*, *4*(4), 523–544.

Pietsch, M. & Stubbe, T. C. (2007). Inequality in the transition from primary to secondary school: School choices and educational disparities in Germany. *European Educational Research Journal*, *6*(4), 424–445.

Pipher, M. (1994). *Reviving Ophelia: Saving the selves of adolescent girls*. New York: Ballantine.

Piquemal, N. (2005). Cultural loyalty: Aboriginal students take an ethical stance. *Reflective Practice*, *6*(4), 523–538.

Piquero, A. R. & Brezina, T. (2001). Testing Moffitt's account of adolescence-limited delinquency. *Criminology, 39*, 901–919.

Pirttilae-Backman, A. M. & Kajanne, A. (2001). The development of implicit epistemologies during early adulthood. *Journal of Adult Development, 8*, 81–97.

Pisetsky, E. M., Chao, Y. M., Dierker, L. C., May, A. M. & Striegel-Moore, R. H. (2008). Disordered eating and substance use in high school students: Results from the Youth Risk Behavior Surveillance System. *International Journal of Eating Disorders 41*(5), 464–470.

Pitner, R. O., Astor, R. A., Benbenishty, R., Haj-Yahia, M. M. & Zeira, A. (2003). The effects of group stereotypes on adolescents' reasoning about peer retribution. *Child Development*, *74*(2), 413–425.

Plantin, L. (2007). Different classes, different fathers?: On fatherhood, economic conditions and class in Sweden. *Community, Work & Family, 10*(1), 93–110.

Platt, T. (2008). Emotional responses to ridicule and teasing: Should gelotophobes react differently? *Humor – International Journal of Humor Research*, *21*(2), 105–128.

Pledger, M. & Casswell, S. (2006). Trends in alcohol-related harms and offences in a liberalized alcohol environment. *Addiction*, *101*(2), 232–240.

Plowman, S. A., Drinkwater, B. L. & Horvath, S. M. (1979). Age and aerobic power in women: A longitudinal study. *Journal of Gerontology, 34*, 512–520.

Plüss, C. (2005). Constructing globalized ethnicity: Migrants from India in Hong Kong. *International Sociology*, *20*(2), 201–224.

Polden, J. (2002). *Regeneration: Journey through mid-life crisis*. London: Continuum.

Polivy, J., Herman, C. P., Mills, J. S. & Wheeler, H. B. (2003). Eating disorders in adolescence. In R. G. Adams & D. M. Berzonsky (Eds.), *Blackwell handbook of adolescence* (pp. 523–549). Malden, MA: Blackwell.

Pool, M. M., Koolstra, C. M. van der Voort, T. H. A. (2003). The impact of background radio and television on high school students' homework performance. *Journal of Communication, 53*, 74–87.

Popenoe, D. & Whitehead, B. D. (2001). *The state of our unions, 2001: The social health of marriage in America*. Report of the National Marriage Project, Rutgers, New Brunswick, NJ. Available: http://marriage.rutgers.edu

Popp, D., Lauren, B., Kerr, M., Stattin, H. & Burk, W. K. (2008). Modeling homophily over time with an actor-partner independence model. *Developmental Psychology*, *44*(4), 1028–1039.

Population Reference Bureau (2009). *World population data sheet*. Washington, DC: Author.

Population Reference Bureau (2000). *The world's youth 2000*. Washington, DC: Population Reference Bureau.

Porfeli, E. J., Hartung, P. J. & Vondracek, F. W. (2008). Children's vocational development: A research rationale. *The Career Development Quarterly*, 57, 25–37.

Portes, A., Fernández-Kelly, P. & Haller, W. (2005). Segmented assimilation on the ground: The new second generation in early adulthood. *Ethnic and Racial Studies*, *28*(6), 1000–1040.

Portes, P. R., Dunham, R. & Castillo, K. D. (2000). Identity formation and status across cultures: Exploring the cultural validity of Eriksonian theory. In A. Comunian & U. P. Gielen (Eds.), *International perspectives on human development* (pp. 449–459). Lengerich, Germany: Pabst Science Publishers.

Posner, R. B. (2006). Early menarche: A review of research on trends in timing, racial differences, etiology and psychosocial consequences. *Sex Roles, 5–6*, 315–322.

Potter, A. S. & Newhouse, P. A. (2004). Effects of acute nicotine administration on behavioral inhibition in adolescents with attention-deficit/hyperactivity disorder. *Psychopharmacology*, *176*(2), 183–194.

Poulou, M. (2005). Educational psychology within teacher education. *Teachers and Teaching: Theory and Practice*, *11*(6), 555–574.

Power, M. & Prasad, S. (2003). Schools for the future: inner city secondary education exemplar. *arq: Architectural Research Quarterly*, *7*(3–4), 262–279.

Power, S. & Clark, A. (2000). The right to know: parents, school reports and parents' evenings. *Research Papers in Education*, *15*(1), 25–48.

Pratt, M. W., Skoe, E. E. & Arnold, M. L. (2004). Care reasoning development and family socialisation patterns in later adolescence: A longitudinal analysis. *International Journal of Behavioural Development, 28*, 139–147.

Prediger, S. (2001). Mathematics learning is also intercultural learning. *Intercultural Education*, *12*(2), 163–171.

Presser, S. & Stinson, L. (1998). Data collection mode and social desirability bias in self-reported religious attendance. *American Sociological Review, 63*, 137–146.

Pressley, M. & Schneider, W. (1997). *Introduction to memory development during childhood and adolescence*. Mahwah, NJ: Erlbaum.

Prevatt, F. & Kelly, F. D. (2003). Dropping out of school: A review of intervention programs. *Journal of School Psychology, 41*, 377–395.

Prinstein, M. J., Boergers, J. & Spirito, A. (2001). Adolescents' and their friends' health-risk behaviour: Factors that alter or add to peer influence. *Journal of Pediatric Psychology, 26*(5), 287–298.

Prinstein, M. J., Boergers, J. & Vernberg, E. M. (2001). Overt and relational aggression in adolescents: Social-psychological adjustment of aggressors and victims. *Journal of Clinical Child & Adolescent Psychology, 30*, 479–491.

Prinstein, M. J. & Dodge, J. A. (Eds.) (2008). *Understanding peer influence in children and adolescence.* New York: Guilford Press.

Prinstein, M. J. & La Greca, A. M. (2004). Childhood peer rejection and aggression as predictors of adolescent girls' externalizing and health risky behaviours: A 6-year longitudinal study. *Journal of Consulting & Clinical Psychology, 72*, 103–112.

Prinstein, M. J. & Wang, S. S. (2005). False consensus and adolescent peer contagion: Examining discrepancies between perceptions and actual reported levels of friends' deviant and health risky behaviours. *Journal of Abnormal Psychology, 33*, 293–306.

Prokopy, L. S. (2009). Determinants and benefits of household level participation in rural drinking water projects in India. *The Journal of Development Studies, 45*(4), 471–495.

Pryke, S. (2001). The Boy Scouts and the 'girl question.' *Sexualities, 4*(2), 191–210.

Psychological Corporation (2000). Technical/product information [On-line]. Available: www.psychcorp.com

Pullen, L., Modrcin-Talbott, M. A., West, W. R. & Muenchen, R. (1999). Spiritual high vs high on spirits: is religiosity related to adolescent alcohol and drug abuse? *Journal of Psychiatric & Mental Health Nursing, 6*(1), 3–8.

Purdie, N., Carroll, A. & Roche, L. (2004). Parenting and adolescent self-regulation. *Journal of Adolescence, 27*, 663–676.

Putnam, R. D. (2000). *Bowling alone: The collapse and revival of American community.* New York: Touchstone Books/Simon & Schuster.

Qin, D. (2009). Gendered processes of adaptation: Understanding parent–child relations in chinese immigrant families. *Sex Roles, 60*(7–8), 467–481.

Qin, D. B. (2009). Being 'good' or being 'popular': Gender and ethnic identity negotiations of Chinese immigrant adolescents. *Journal of Adolescent Research, 24*(1), 37–66.

Qin, D. B., Way, N. & Mukherjee, P. (2008). The other side of the model minority story: The familial and peer challenges faced by Chinese American adolescents. *Youth and Society, 39*(4), 480–506.

Qualter, P. and Munn, P. (2002). The separateness of social and emotional loneliness in childhood. *Journal of Child Psychology and Psychiatry* (formerly *Journal of Child Psychology and Psychiatry and Allied Disciplines*), *43*(2), pp. 233–244.

Quillian, L. (2003). The decline of male employment in low income black neighborhoods, 1950–1990. *Social Science Research, 32*, 220–250.

Rabin, B. A., Boehmer, T. K. & Brownson, R. C. (2007). Cross-national comparison of environmental and policy correlates of obesity in Europe. *The European Journal of Public Health, 17*(1), 53–61.

Raby, R. (2002). A tangle of discourses: Girls negotiating adolescence. *Journal of Youth Studies, 5*(4), 425–448.

Rácz, J., Gyarmathy, V. A., Neaigus, A. & Ujhelyi, E. (2007). Injecting equipment sharing and perception of HIV and hepatitis risk among injecting drug users in Budapest. *AIDS Care, 19*(1), 59–66.

Radmacher, K. & Azmitia, M. (2006). Are there gendered pathways to intimacy in early adolescents' and emerging adults' friendships? *Journal of Adolescent Research, 21*(4), 415–448.

Ragnarsson, A., Onya, H. E., Thorson, A., Ekström, A. M. & Aarø, L. E. (2008). Young males' gendered sexuality in the era of HIV and AIDS in Limpopo Province, South Africa. *Qualitative Health Research, 18*(6), 739–746.

Raine, A. (2002). Annotation: The role of prefrontal deficits, low autonomic arousal, and early health factors in the development of antisocial and aggressive behavior in children. *Journal of Child Psychology and Psychiatry* (formerly *Journal of Child Psychology and Psychiatry and Allied Disciplines*), *43*(4), 417–434.

Rainey, D. & Murova, O. (2004). Factors influencing education achievement. *Applied Economics, 36*(21), 2397–2404.

Ramji, H. (2007). Dynamics of religion and gender amongst young British Muslims. *Sociology, 41*(6), 1171–1189.

Ramp, W. (2003). Religion and the dualism of the social condition in Durkheim and Bataille. *Economy and Society, 32*(1), 119–140.

Rankin, L. & Kenyon, D. Y. (2012). Demarcating role transitions as indicators of adulthood in the 21st century: Who are they? *Journal of Adult Development*, Preprint, 1–6.

Ransford, C., Crouter, A. & McHale, S. (2008). Implications of work pressure and supervisor support for fathers', mothers' and adolescents' relationships and well-being in dual-earner families. *Community, Work & Family, 11*(1), 37–60.

Rantala, K. & Sulkunen, P. (2003). The communitarian preventive paradox: Preventing substance misuse without the substance. *Critical Social Policy, 23*(4), 477–497.

Rasmussen, M. L. (2006). Play school, melancholia, and the politics of recognition. *British Journal of Sociology of Education, 27*(4), 473–487.

Rawlings, D., Barrantes, V. N. & Furnham, A. (2000). Personality and aesthetic preference in Spain and England: Two studies relating sensation seeking and openness to experience to liking for paintings and music. *European Journal of Personality, 14*, 553–576.

Ray, J. (1990). The old-fashioned personality. *Human Relations, 43*(10), 997–1013.

Rayner, J., Kelly, T. P. & Graham, F. (2005). Mental health, personality and cognitive problems in persistent adolescent offenders require long-term solutions: a pilot study.

Journal of Forensic Psychiatry and Psychology, *16*(2), 248–262.

Ream, G. L. & Savin-Williams, R. C. (2003). Religious development in adolescence. In G. R. Adams & M. D. Berzonsky (Eds.), *Blackwell handbook of adolescence* (pp. 51–59). Malden, MA: Blackwell.

Reddy, R. & Gibbons, J. L. (1999). School socioeconomic contexts and self-descriptions in India. *Journal of Youth & Adolescence, 28*, 619–631.

Rees, G. & Lee, J. (2005). *Still running II: Findings from the second national survey of young runaways.* The Children's Society, 7 & 24.

Regan, P. C., Durvasula, R., Howell, L., Ureño, O. & Rea, M. (2004). Gender, ethnicity, and the developmental timing of first sexual and romantic experiences. *Social Behaviour & Personality, 32*, 667–676.

Regnerus, M. D. (2007). *Forbidden fruit: Sex and religion in the lives of American teenagers.* New York: Oxford University Press.

Rego, A. & Cunha, M. (2009). How individualism–collectivism orientations predict happiness in a collectivistic context. *Journal of Happiness Studies*, *10*(1), 19–35.

Reid, K. (2006). An evaluation of the views of secondary staff towards school attendance issues. *Oxford Review of Education*, *32*(3), 303–324.

Reid, S., Kauer, S., Dudgeon, P., Sanci, L., Shrier, L. & Patton, G. (2009). A mobile phone program to track young people's experiences of mood, stress and coping. *Social Psychiatry and Psychiatric Epidemiology*, *44*(6), 501–507.

Reifman, A., Arnett, J. J. & Colwell, M. J. (2007). Emerging adulthood: Theory, assessment, and application. *Journal of Youth Development, 1*, 1–12.

Reijonen, J. H., Pratt, H. D., Patel, D. R. & Greydanus, D. E. (2003). Eating disorders in the adolescent population: An overview. *Journal of Adolescent Research, 18*, 209–222.

Reilly, J. J. (2006). Tackling the obesity epidemic: New approaches. *Archives of Disease in Childhood, 91*, 724–726.

Reinders, H. & Youniss, J. (2006). School-based required community service and civic development in adolescents. *Applied Developmental Science, 10*(1), 2–12.

Reinemann, D. H. S., Stark, K. D. & Swearer, S. M. (2003). Family factors that differentiate sexually abused and nonabused adolescent psychiatric inpatients. *Journal of Interpersonal Violence, 18*(5), 471–489.

Reiss, D., Neiderhiser, J., Hetherington, E. M. & Plomin, R. (2000). *The relationship code: Deciphering genetic and social influences on adolescent development*. Cambridge, MA: Harvard University Press.

Rembeck, G. & Gunnarsson, R. (2004). Improving pre- and post-menarcheal 12 year old girls' attitudes toward menstruation. *Health Care for Women International*, *25*(7), 680–698.

Renk, K., Donelly, R., McKinney, C. & Agliata, A. K. (2006). The development of gender identity: Timetables and influences. In K. S. Yip (Ed.), *Psychology of gender identity: An international perspective* (pp. 49–68). New York: Nova Science Publishers.

Renold, E. (2003). 'If you don't kiss me, you're dumped': Boys, boyfriends and heterosexualised masculinities in the primary school. *Educational Review*, *55*(2), 179–194.

Renold, E. (2002). Presumed innocence: (Hetero)sexual, heterosexist and homophobic harassment among primary school girls and boys. *Childhood*, *9*(4), 415–434.

Repetto, P. B., Zimmerman, M. A. & Caldwell, C. H. (2004). A longitudinal study of the relationship between depressive symptoms and alcohol use in a sample of inner-city black youth. *Journal of Studies on Alcohol, 65*, 169–178.

Resnick, D. (2008). Life in an unjust community: a Hollywood view of high school moral life. *Journal of Moral Education*, *37*(1), 99–113.

Rew, L., Wong, J., Torres, R. and Howell, E. (2007). Older adolescents' perceptions of the social context, impact, and development of their spiritual/religious beliefs and practices. *Issues in Comprehensive Pediatric Nursing*, *30*(1–2), 55–68.

Reyna, V. F. & Farley, F. (2006). Risk and rationality in adolescent decision making: Implications for theory, practice, and public policy. *Psychological Science in the Public Interest, 7*(1), 1–44.

Reynolds, T. (2006). Family and community networks in the (re)making of ethnic identity of caribbean young people in Britain. *Community, Work & Family*, *9*(3), 273–290.

Rhodes, J. R. & DuBois, D. L. (2008). Mentoring relationships and programs for youths. *Current Directions in Psychological Science, 17*(4), 254–258.

Richards, M. H., Crowe, P. A., Larson, R. & Swarr, A. (2002). Developmental patterns and gender differences in the experience of peer companionship in adolescence. *Child Development, 69*, 154–163.

Rickards, T. & Wuest, J. (2006). The process of losing and regaining credibility when coming-out at midlife. *Health Care for Women International*, *27*(6), 530–547.

Rigg, A. & Pryor, J. (2007). Children's perceptions of families: What do they really think?. *Children & Society*, *21*(1), 17–30.

Ringwood, S. (2008). Pro anorexia and social networking sites. *Child and Adolescent Mental Health*, *13*(2), 97–97.

Rissanen, M.-L., Kylmä, J. P. O. & Laukkenan, E. R. (2008). Parental conceptions of self-mutilation among Finnish adolescents. *Journal of Psychiatric & Mental Health Nursing*, *15*(3), 212–218.

Ritvo, R., Ritvo, E., Guthrie, D., Yuwiler, A., Ritvo, M. & Weisbender, L. (2008). A scale to assist the diagnosis of autism and Asperger's disorder in adults (RAADS): A pilot study. *Journal of Autism and Developmental Disorders*, *38*(2), 213–223.

Rivadeneyra, R. & Ward, L. M. (2005). From Ally McBeal to Sábado Gigante: Contributions of television viewing to the gender role attitudes of Latino adolescents. *Journal of Adolescent Research, 20*, 453–475.

Rivlin, E. & Faragher, E. B. (2007). The psychological effects of sex, age at burn, stage of adolescence, intelligence, position and degree of burn in thermally injured adolescents: Part 2. *Developmental Neurorehabilitation*, *10*(2), 173–182.

Roberto, C. A., Steinglass, J., Mayer, L. E. S., Attia, E. & Walsh, B. T. (2008). The clinical significance of amenorrhea as a diagnostic criterion for anorexia nervosa. *International Journal of Eating Disorders, 41*(6), 559–563.

Roberts, B. W., Caspi, A. & Moffitt, T. E. (2001). The kids are alright: Growth and stability in personality development from adolescence to adulthood. *Journal of Personality and Social Psychology, 81*, 670–683.

Roberts, D. F., Foehr, U. G. & Rideout, V. (2005). *Generation M: Media in the lives of 8–18 year-olds*. Washington, DC: The Henry J. Kaiser Family Foundation.

Roberts, J. L. (2005, June 6). World tour: MTV has mastered a nifty trick. *Newsweek*, 34–35.

Roberts, K. (2004). School-to-work transitions: Why the United Kingdom's educational ladders always fail to connect. *International Studies in Sociology of Education*, *14*(3), 203–216.

Roberts, K. A. (2005). Associated characteristics of stalking following termination of romantic relationships. *Applied Psychology in Criminal Justice, 1*(1), 15–35.

Robins, R. W., Hendin, H. M. & Trzesniewski, K. H. (2001). Measuring global self-esteem: Construct validation of a single-item measure and the Rosenberg Self-Esteem Scale. *Personality and Social Psychology Bulletin, 27*(2), 151–161.

Robins, R. W., Trzesniewski, K. H., Tracy, J. L., Gosling, S. D. & Potter, J. (2002). Global self-esteem across the life span. *Psychology & Aging, 17*, 423–434.

Robinson, C. (2005). Buffalo hunting and the feral frontier of Australia's Northern Territory. *Social & Cultural Geography*, *6*(6), 885–901.

Robinson, G. (1997). Families, generations and self: Conflict, loyalty and recognition in an Australian aboriginal society. *Ethos, 25*(3), 303–332.

Robinson, K. (2005). Reinforcing hegemonic masculinities through sexual harassment: issues of identity, power and popularity in secondary schools. *Gender and Education*, *17*(1), 19–37.

Roche, M. & Skinner, D. (2009). How parents search, interpret, and evaluate genetic information obtained from the Internet. *Journal of Genetic Counseling, 18*(2), 119–129.

Roebroeck, M. E., Hempenius, L., Van Baalen, B., Hendriksen, G. J. M., van den Berg-Emons, H. J. G. & Stam, H. J. (2006). Cognitive functioning of adolescents and young adults with meningomyelocele and level of everyday physical activity. *Disability & Rehabilitation*, *28*(20), 1237–1242.

Roeschl-Heils, A., Schneider, W. & van Kraayenoord, C. E. (2003). Reading, metacognition, and motivation: A follow up study of German students in grades 7 and 8. *European Journal of Psychology of Education, 18*, 75–86.

Rogers, M., Wiener, J., Marton, I. & Tannock, R. (2009). Supportive and controlling parental involvement as predictors of children's academic achievement: Relations to children's ADHD symptoms and parenting stress. *School Mental Health, 1*(2), 89–102.

Rogoff, B. (2003). *The cultural nature of human development.* New York: Oxford University Press.

Rogoff, B. (1995). Observing sociocultural activities on three planes: Participatory appropriation, guided participation, and apprenticeship. In J. V. Wertsch, P. del Rio, & A. Alvarez (Eds.), *Sociocultural studies of mind* (pp. 273–294). New York: Cambridge University Press.

Rogoff, B., Baker-Sennett, J., Lacasa, P. & Goldsmith, D. (1995). Development through participation in sociocultural activity. In J. Goodnow, P. Miller, & F. Kessen (Eds.), *Cultural practices as contexts for development* (pp. 45–65). San Francisco: Jossey-Bass.

Rohde, P., Lewinsohn, P. M., Clarke, G. N., Hops, H. & Seeley, J. R. (2005). The adolescent coping with depression course: A cognitive behavioral approach to the treatment of adolescent depression. In E. D. Hibbs & P. S. Jensen (Eds.), *Psychosocial treatments for child and adolescent disorders: Empirically based strategies for clinical practice* (pp. 219–237). Washington, DC: American Psychological Association.

Rohde, P., Noell, J., Ochs, L. & Seeley, J. R. (2001). Depression, suicidal ideation, and STD-related risk in homeless older adolescents. *Journal of Adolescence, 24*, 447–460.

Rohlen, T. P. (1983). *Japan's high schools*. Berkeley: University of California Press.

Roisman, G., Booth-LaForce, C., Cauffman, E. & Spieker, S. (2009). The developmental significance of adolescent romantic relationships: Parent and peer predictors of engagement and quality at age 15. *Journal of Youth and Adolescence, 38/10*, 1294–1303.

Roisman, G. I., Madsen, S. D., Hennighausen, K. H., Sroufe, L. A. & Collins, W. A. (2001). The coherence of dyadic behavior across parent–child and romantic relationships as mediated by internalized representations of experience. *Attachment & Human Development, 3*, 156–172.

Roisman, G. I., Padrón, E., Sroufe, L. A. & Egeland, B. (2002). Earned–secure attachment status in retrospect and prospect. *Child Development, 73*(3), 1204–1219.

Romens, S., Abramson, L. & Alloy, L. (2009). High and low cognitive risk for depression: Stability from late adolescence to early adulthood. *Cognitive Therapy and Research*, *33*(5), 480–498.

Romer, D. & Hennessy, M. (2007). A biosocial-affect model of adolescent sensation seeking: The role of affect evaluation and peer-group influence in adolescent drug use. *Prevention Science, 8*(2), 89–101.

Rommes, E., Overbeek, G., Scholte, R., Engels, R. & de Kamp, R. (2007). 'I'm not interested in computers': Gender-biased occupational choices of adolescents. *Information, Communication & Society, 10*(3), 299–319.

Roos, E., Karvonen, S. & Rahkonen, O. (2004). Lifestyles, social background and eating patterns of 15-year-old boys and girls in Finland. *Journal of Youth Studies*, *7*(3), 331–349.

Rosario, M., Schrimshaw, E. W. & Hunter, J. (2005). Psychological distress following suicidality among gay, lesbian, and bisexual youths: Role of social relationships. *Journal of Youth and Adolescence, 34*(2), 149–161.

Rosario, M., Schrimshaw, E. W. & Hunter, J. (2004). Ethnic/racial differences in the coming-out process of lesbian, gay, and bisexual youths: A comparison of sexual indentity development over time. *Cultural Diversity & Ethnic Minorities, 10*, 215–228.

Rose, A. J., Swenson, L. P. & Waller, E. M. (2004). Overt and relational aggression and perceived popularity: Developmental differences in concurrent and prospective relations. *Developmental Psychology, 40*, 378–387.

Rose, J. P., Endo, Y., Windschitl, P. D. & Suls, J. (2008). Cultural differences in unrealistic optimism and pessimism: The role of egocentrism and direct versus indirect comparison measures. *Personality and Social Psychology Bulletin, 34*(9), 1236–1248.

Rose, R. & Doveston, M. (2008). Pupils talking about their learning mentors: What can we learn? *Educational Studies, 34*(2), 145–155.

Rose, R. J. (2002). How do adolescents select their friends? A behaviour-genetic perspective. In L. Pulkinnen & A. Caspi (Eds.), *Paths to successful development: Personality in the life course* (pp. 106–125). New York: Cambridge University Press.

Rosenberg, M. (1986). Self concept from middle childhood through adolescence. In J. Suls & A. Greenwald (Eds.), *Psychological perspectives on the self* (Vol. 3). Hillsdale, NJ: Erlbaum.

Rosenberg, M. (1965). *Society and the adolescent self-image*. Princeton, NJ: Princeton University Press.

Rosenberger, J. (2003). Discerning the behavior of the suicide bomber: the role of vengeance. *Journal of Religion and Health, 42*(1), 13–20.

Rosenbloom, S. R. & Way, N. (2004). Experiences of discrimination among African American, Asian American, and Latino adolescents in an urban high school. *Youth & Society, 35*, 420–451.

Rosenblum, G. D. & Lewis, M. (1999). The relations between body image, physical attractiveness, and body mass in adolescence. *Child Development, 70*, 50–64.

Rosenthal, D. & Rotheram-Borus, M. J. (2005). Young people and homelessness. *Journal of Adolescence, 28*, 167–169.

Rosenthal, M. (1986). *The character factory: Baden-Powell and the origins of the Boy Scout movement*. New York: Pantheon.

Rotundo, E. A. (1993). *American manhood: Transformations in masculinity from the revolution to the modern era*. New York: Basic Books.

Rowe, R., Maughan, B. & Eley, T. (2006). Links between antisocial behavior and depressed mood: the role of life events and attributional style. *Journal of Abnormal Child Psychology, 34*(3), 283–292.

Rowley, S. J., Kurtz-Costes, B., Mistry, R. & Feagans, L. (2007). Social status as a predictor of race and gender stereotypes in late childhood and early adolescence. *Social Development, 16*(1), 150–168.

Roy, R., Benenson, J. F. & Lilly, F. (2000). Beyond intimacy: Conceptualizing sex differences in same-sex relationships. *Journal of Psychology, 134*, 93–101.

Rozencwajg, P. (2003). Metacognitive factors in scientific problem-solving strategies. *European Journal of Psychology of Education, 18*, 281–294.

Rubie-Davies, C., Hattie, J. & Hamilton, R. (2006). Expecting the best for students: Teacher expectations and academic outcomes. *The British Journal of Educational Psychology, 76*(3), 429–444.

Rubin, G. J., Brewin, C. R., Greenberg, N., Simpson, J. & Wessely, S. (2005). Psychological and behavioural reactions to the bombings in London on 7 July 2005: cross sectional survey of a representative sample of Londoners. *BMJ (British Medical Journal), 31*(7517), 606.

Rubin, K., Fredstrom, B. & Bowker, J. (2008). Future directions in friendship in childhood and early adolescence. *Social Development, 17*(4), 1085–1096.

Rueger, S., Malecki, C. & Demaray, M. (2010). Relationship between multiple sources of perceived social support and psychological and academic adjustment in early adolescence: Comparisons across gender. *Journal of Youth and Adolescence, 39*(1), 47–61.

Ruggiero, M., Greenberger, E. & Steinberg, L. (1982). Occupational deviance among first-time workers. *Youth and Society, 13*, 423–448.

Ruiz, S. A. & Silverstein, M. (2007). Relationships with grandparents and the emotional well-being of late adolescent and young adult grandchildren. *Journal of Social Issues. 63*(4), 793–808.

Ruschena, E., Prior, M., Sanson, A. & Smart, D. (2005). A longitudinal study of adolescent adjustment following family transitions. *Journal of Child Psychology and Psychiatry* (formerly *Journal of Child Psychology and Psychiatry and Allied Disciplines), 46*(4), 353–363.

Russo, N. F. (2008). Understanding emotional responses after abortion. In J. C. Chrisler, C. Golden, & P. D. Rozee (Eds.), *Lectures on the psychology of women* (4th ed., 173 189). New York: McGraw-Hill.

Rutter, M. (1983). School effects on pupil progress: Research findings and policy implications. *Child Development, 54*, 1–29.

Rutter, M., Maughan, B., Mortimore, P. & Ouston, J. (1979). *Fifteen thousand hours: Secondary schools and their effects on children*. Cambridge, MA: Harvard University Press.

Ryan, A. M. (2001). Personality and social development: The peer group as a context for the development of young adolescent motivation and achievement. *Child Development, 72*(4), 1135–1150.

Ryan, J. J. & Lopez, S. J. (2001). Wechsler adult intelligence scale-III. In I. W. Dorfman & M. Hersen (Eds.) *Understanding psychological assessment* (pp. 19–42). Dordrecht, Netherlands: Kluwer.

Rydstrøm, H. (2006). Sexual desires and 'social evils': Young women in rural Vietnam. *Gender, Place and Culture: A Journal of Feminist Geography, 13*(3), 283–301.

Saadawi, N. (1980). *The hidden face of Eve: Women in the Arab world*. London: Zed Press.

Sabat, S. N. (2008). Human rights in Indian culture: A bird's eye view. *The International Journal of Human Rights, 12*(1), 143–156.

Sadler, W. J. & Haskins, E. V. (2005). Metonymy and the metropolis: Television show settings and the image of New York City. *Journal of Communication Inquiry, 29*(3), 195–216.

Sagestrano, L. M., McCormick, S. H., Paikoff, R. L. & Holmbeck, G. N. (1999). Pubertal development and parent–child conflict in low-income, urban, African American adolescents. *Journal of Research on Adolescence, 9*, 85–107.

Saharso, S. (2003). Feminist ethics, autonomy and the politics of Multiculturalism. *Feminist Theory, 4*(2), 199–215.

St. Louis, G. R. & Liem, J. H. (2005). Ego identity, ethnic identity, and the psychosocial well-being of ethnic minority and majority college students. *Identity, 5*, 227–246.

Saldana, L. & Henggeler, S. W. (2006). Multisystemic therapy in the treatment of adolescent conduct disorder. In W. M. Nelson, III, A. J., Finch, Jr. & K. L. Hart (Eds.), *Conduct disorders: A practitioner's guide to comparative treatments.* (pp. 217–258). New York: Springer.

Salkind, N. J. (2003). *Exploring research*. Upper Saddle River, NJ: Prentice Hall.

Salmela-Aro, K., Kiuru, N. & Nurmi, J-E. (2008). The role of educational track in adolescents' school burnout: A longitudinal study. *The British Journal of Educational Psychology, 78*(4), 663–689.

Salmela-Aro, K., Kiuru, N., Pietikäinen, M. & Jokela, J. (2008). Does school matter? The role of school context in adolescents' school-related burnout. *European Psychologist, 13*(1), 12–23.

Saluja, G., Iachan, R. & Scheidt, P. (2004). Prevalence and risk factors for depressive symptoms among young adolescents. *Archives of Pediatrics and Adolescent Medicine, 158*, 760–765.

Sampson, R. J. & Laub, J. H. (1990). Crime and deviance over the life course: The salience of adult social bonds. *American Sociological Review, 55*, 609–627.

Samuels, S. & Casebeer, W. (2005). A social psychological view of morality: Why knowledge of situational influences on behaviour can improve character development practices. *Journal of Moral Education, 34*(1), 73–87.

Sanders, M. R., Montgomery, D. T. & Brechman-Toussaint, M. L. (2000). The mass media and the prevention of child behavior problems: The evaluation of a television series to promote positive outcomes for parents and their children. *Journal of Child Psychology and Psychiatry* (formerly *Journal of Child Psychology and Psychiatry and Allied Disciplines*), *41*(7), 939–948.

Sanghera, G. (2008). The 'politics' of children's rights and child labour in India: A social constructionist perspective. *The International Journal of Human Rights, 12*(2), 215–232.

Santana, V., Almeida-Filho, N., Roberts, R. & Cooper, S. P. (2007). Skin Colour, perception of racism and depression among adolescents in urban Brazil. *Child and Adolescent Mental Health, 12*(3), 125–131.

Saraswathi, T. S. (2006). India. In Arnett, J. J. (Ed.). *International Encyclopedia of adolescence* (two volumes). New York: Routledge.

Saraswathi, T. S. (1999). Adult–child continuity in India: Is adolescence a myth or an emerging reality? In T. S. Saraswathi (Ed.), *Culture, socialization, and human development: Theory, research, and applications in India* (pp. 213–232). Thousand Oaks, CA: Sage.

Sass, R. (1999). The unwritten story of women's role in the birth of occupational health and safety legislation. *International Journal of Health Services, 29*(1), 109–145.

Sato, C. (2007). Learning from weaknesses in teaching about culture: the case study of a Japanese school abroad. *Intercultural Education, 18*(5), 445–453.

Savin-Williams, R. (2006). *The new gay teenager*. Cambridge, MA: Harvard University Press.

Savin-Williams, R. (2001). *Mom, Dad, I'm gay*. Washington, DC: American Psychological Association.

Savin-Williams, R. C. (1998). The disclosure to families of same-sex attractions by lesbian, gay, and bisexual youth. *Journal of Research on Adolescence, 8*, 49–68.

Savin-Williams, R. C. & Ream, G. L. (2007). Prevalence and stability of sexual orientation components during adolescence and young adulthood. *Archives of Sexual Behavior, 36*(3), 385–394.

Sbarra, D. A. & Emery, R. E. (2008). Deeper into divorce: Using actor-partner analyses to explore systemic differences in coparenting conflict following custody dispute resolution. *Journal of Family Psychology, 22*(1), 144–152.

Scarr, S. (1993). Biological and cultural diversity: The legacy of Darwin for development. *Child Development, 64*, 1333–1353.

Schaaf, R. C. & Miller, L. J. (2005). Occupational therapy using a sensory integrative approach for children with developmental disabilities. *Mental Retardation and Developmental Disabilities Research Reviews, 11*(2), 143–148.

Schachter, E. P. (2005a). Context and identity formation: A theoretical analysis and a case study. *Journal of Adolescent Research, 20*, 375–395.

Schachter, E. P. (2005b). Erikson meets the postmodern: Can classic identity theory rise to the challenge? *Identity, 5*, 137–160.

Scharf, M., Shulman, S. & Avigad-Spitz, L. (2005). Sibling relationships in emerging adulthood and in adolescence. *Journal of Adolescent Research, 20*, 64–90.

Scherf, K. S., Sweeney, J. A. & Luna, B. (2006). Brain basis of developmental change in visuospatial working memory. *Journal of Cognitive Neuroscience, 18*(7), 1045–1058.

Schlegel, A. (2008). A cross-cultural approach to adolescence. In D. L. Browning (Ed.), *Adolescent identities: A collection of readings. Relational perspectives book series* (pp. 31–44). New York: Analytic Press/Taylor & Francis Group.

Schlegel, A. (2001). The global spread of adolescent culture. In L. Crockett & R. K. Silbereisen (Eds.), *Negotiating adolescence in a time of social change*. Cambridge: Cambridge University Press.

Schlegel, A. & Barry, H. (1991). *Adolescence: An anthropological inquiry*. New York: Free Press.

Schmidt, J. R. & Thompson, V. A. (2008). At least one problem with some formal reasoning paradigms. *Memory & Cognition, 36*(1), 217–229.

Schneider, B. & Stevenson, D. (1999). *The ambitious generation: America's teenagers, motivated but directionless*. New Haven, CT: Yale University Press.

Schneider, B. & Waite, L. J. (Eds.) (2005). *Being together, working apart: Dual-career families and the work-life balance*. New York: Cambridge University Press.

Schneiders, J., Drukker, M., Van Der Ende, J., Verhulst, F. C., Van Os, J. & Nicolson, N. A. (2003). Neighbourhood socioeconomic disadvantage and behavioural problems from late childhood into early adolescence. *Journal of Epidemiology & Community Health, 57*(9), 699–703.

Schubot, D. B. (2001). Date rape prevalence among female high school students in a rural midwestern state during 1993, 1995, and 1997. *Journal of Interpersonal Violence, 16*(4), 291–296.

Schubotz, D., Rolston, B. & Simpson, A. (2004). Sexual behaviour of young people in Northern Ireland: First sexual experience. *Critical Public Health, 14*(2), 177–190.

Schulenberg, J. (2000, April). *College students get drunk, so what? National panel data on binge drinking trajectories before, during and after college*. Paper presented at the biennial meeting of the Society for Research on Adolescence, Chicago.

Schulenberg, J. E. & Maggs, J. L. (2000). *A developmental perspective on alcohol use and heavy drinking during adolescence and the transition to adulthood*. Washington, DC: National Institute on Alcohol Abuse and Alcoholism.

Schulenberg, J. E. & Zarrett, N. R. (2006). Mental health during young adulthood: Continuity and discontinuity in courses, causes, and functions. In J. J. Arnett & J. L. Tanner (Eds.), *Young adults in America: Coming of age in the 21st century* (pp. 135–172). Washington, DC: American Psychological Association.

Schumer, G. (1999). Mathematics education in Japan. *Journal of Curriculum Studies, 31*(4), 399–427.

Schwartz, S. J. (2005). A new identity for identity research: Recommendations for expanding and refocusing the identity literature. *Journal of Adolescent Research, 20*, 293–308.

Schwartz, S.J., Cote, J. E., and Arnett, J. J. (2005). Identity and agency in emerging adulthood: Two developmental routes in the individualization process. *Youth & Society, 37*, 201–229.

Scott, M. J. & Strading S. G. (2006). *Counseling for post-traumatic stress disorder*. London: Sage.

Scrase, T. J. (2002). Television, the middle classes and the transformation of cultural identities in West Bengal, India. *International Communication Gazette, 64*(4), 323–342.

Sears, H. A. (2004). Adolescents in rural communities seeking help: who reports problems and who sees professionals? *Journal of Child Psychology and Psychiatry* (formerly *Journal of Child Psychology and Psychiatry and Allied Disciplines*), *45*(2), 396–404.

Sears, H. A., Simmering, M. G. & MacNeil, B. A. (2006). Canada. In J. J. Arnett (Ed.), *International encyclopedia of adolescence*. New York: Routledge.

Seaton, E. K., Scottham, K. M. & Sellers, R. M. (2006). The status model of racial identity development in African American adolescents: Evidence of structure, trajectories, and well-being. *Child Development, 77*(5), 1416–1426.

Sedgh, G., Jackson, E. & Ibrahim, B. (2005). Toward the abandonment of female genital cutting: Advancing research, communication and collaboration. *Culture, Health & Sexuality, 7*(5), 425–427.

Segal, U. A. (1998). The Asian Indian-American family. In C. H. Mindel, R. W. Habenstein, & R. Wright, Jr. (Eds.), *Ethnic families in America* (4th ed.; pp. 331–360). Upper Saddle River, NJ: Prentice Hall.

Segall, M. H., Dasen, P. R., Berry, J. W. & Poortinga, Y. H. (1999). *Human behaviour in global perspective: An introduction to cross-cultural psychology*. Boston: Allyn & Bacon.

Seginer, R. (1998). Adolescents' perceptions of relationships with older siblings in the context of other close relationships. *Journal of Research on Adolescence, 8*, 287–308.

Seiffge-Krenke, I. (2003). Testing theories of romantic development from adolescence to young adulthood: Evidence of a developmental sequence. *International Journal of Behavioural Development, 27*, 519–531.

Selfhout, M., Branje, S. & Meeus, W. (2009). Developmental trajectories of perceived friendship intimacy, constructive problem solving, and depression from early to late adolescence. *Journal of Abnormal Child Psychology, 37*(2), 251–264.

Selfhout, M. W. H., Delsing, M. J. M., ter Bogt, T. F. M. & Meeus, W. H. J. (2008). Heavy metal and hip-hop style preferences and externalizing problem behavior: A two-wave longitudinal study. *Youth & Society, 39*(4), 435–452.

Selman, R. (1980). *The growth of interpersonal understanding: Developmental and clinical analyses*. New York: Academic Press.

Selman, R. (1976). Social-cognitive understanding. In T. Lickona (Ed.), *Moral development and behaviour*. New York: Holt, Rinehart & Winston.

Selman, R. & Byrne, D. (1974). A structural developmental analysis of levels of role-taking in middle childhood. *Child Development, 45*, 803–806.

Selvan, M., Ross, M. W., Kapadia, A. S., Mathai, R. & Hira, S. (2001). Study of perceived norms, beliefs and intended sexual behaviour among higher secondary school students in India. *AIDS Care, 13*(6), 779–788.

Sen, K. & Samad, A. Y. (Eds.) (2007). *Islam in the European Union: Transnationalism, youth and the war on terror*. New York: Oxford University Press.

Senior, K. & Chenhall, R. (2008). 'Walkin' about at night': The background to teenage pregnancy in a remote Aboriginal community. *Journal of Youth Studies, 11*(3), 269–281.

Sentse, M., Scholte, R., Salmivalli, C. & Voeten, M. (2007). Person-group dissimilarity in involvement in bullying and its relation with social status. *Journal of Abnormal Child Psychology, 35*(6), 1009–1019.

Sercombe, H. & Paus, T. (2009). The 'teen brain' research: An introduction and implications for practitioners. *Youth & Policy, 103*, 25–38.

Shaftoe, H. S., Turksen, U. T., Lever, J. L. & Williams, J-S. (2007). Dealing with terrorist threats through a crime prevention and community safety approach. *Crime Prevention and Community Safety: An International Journal, 9*(4), 291–307.

Shakin, M., Shakin, D. & Sternglanz, S. H. (1985). Infant clothing: Sex labeling for strangers. *Sex Roles, 12*, 955–964.

Shalatin, S. & Phillip, M. (2003). The role of obesity and leptin in the pubertal process and pubertal growth: A review. *International Journal of Obesity and Related Metabolic Disorders, 27*, 869–874.

Shanahan, L., McHale, S. M., Crouter, A. C. & Osgood, D. W. (2007). Warmth with mothers and fathers from middle childhood to late adolescence: Within- and between-families comparisons. *Developmental Psychology, 43*(3), 551–563.

Shand, A. (2007). Semen anxiety: Materiality, agency and the Internet. *Anthropology & Medicine, 14*(3), 241–250.

Shapka, J. D. & Keating, D. P. (2005). Structure and change in self-concept during adolescence. *Canadian Journal of Behavioural Science, 37*, 83–96.

Sharp, J., Briggs, J., Yacoub, H. & Hamed, N. (2003). Doing gender and development: understanding empowerment and local gender relations. *Transactions of the Institute of British Geographers, 28*(3), 281–295.

Sharpe, A. (2002). English transgender law reform and the spectre of Corbett. *Feminist Legal Studies, 10*(1), 65–89.

Sharpe, D. & Baker, D. (2007). Financial issues associated with having a child with autism. *Journal of Family and Economic Issues, 28*(2), 247–264.

Sharples, M., Graber, R., Harrison, C. & Logan, K. (2009). E-safety and Web 2.0 for children aged 11–16. *Journal of Computer Assisted Learning, 25*(1), 70–84.

Shaw, P., Greenstein, D., Lerch, J., Clasen, L., Lenroot, R., Gogtay, N. Evans, A. (2006). Intellectual ability and cortical development in children and adolescents. *Nature, 440*, 676–679.

Shayer, M. and Ginsburg, D. (2009). Thirty years on – a large anti-Flynn effect? (II): 13-and 14-year-olds. Piagetian tests of formal operations norms 1976–2006/7. *British Journal of Educational Psychology, 79*(3), 409–418.

Sheeder, J., Tocce, K. & Stevens-Simon, C. (2009). Reasons for ineffective contraceptive use antedating adolescent pregnancies Part 1: An indicator of gaps in family planning services. *Maternal and Child Health Journal, 13*(3), 295–305.

Sheehan, G., Chrzanowski, A. & Dewar, J. (2008). Superannuation and divorce in Australia: An evaluation of post-reform practice and settlement outcomes. *International Journal of Law, Policy and the Family, 22*(2), 206–230.

Sheehan, G., Darlington, Y., Noller, P. & Feeney, J. (2004). Children's perceptions of their sibling relationships during parental separation and divorce. *Journal of Divorce & Remarriage, 41*, 69–94.

Shek, D. (2005). Perceived parental control and parent–child relational qualities in Chinese adolescents in Hong Kong. *Sex Roles, 53*(9–10), 635–646.

Shek, D. & Lee, T. (2007). Family life quality and emotional quality of life in chinese adolescents with and without economic disadvantage. *Social Indicators Research, 80*(2), 393–410.

Shelton, J. N., Richeson, J. A. & Salvatore, J. (2005). Expecting to be the target of prejudice: Implications for interethnic interactions. *Personality and Social Psychology Bulletin, 31*(9), 1189–1202.

Shenassa, E. D., Catlin, S. N. & Buka, S. L. (2003). Lethality of firearms relative to other suicide methods: a population based study. *Journal of Epidemiology & Community Health, 57*(2), 120–124.

Sheppard, A. (2007). An approach to understanding school attendance difficulties: Pupils' perceptions of parental behaviour in response to their requests to be absent from school. *Emotional and Behavioural Difficulties, 12*(4), 349–363.

Shernoff, D. J. & Csikszentmihalyi, M. (2003). Pupil engagement in high school classrooms from the perspective of flow theory. *School Psychology Quarterly, 18*, 158–176.

Sherrod, L. R., Flanagan, C. & Youniss, J. (2002). Dimensions of citizenship and opportunities for youth development: The what, why, when, where, and who of citizenship development. *Applied Developmental Science, 6*, 264–272.

Shiotsu, T. & Weir, C. J. (2007). The relative significance of syntactic knowledge and vocabulary breadth in the prediction of reading comprehension test performance. *Language Testing, 24*(1), 99–128.

Shirtcliff, E. A., Dahl, R. E. and Pollak, S. D. (2009). Pubertal Development: Correspondence between hormonal and physical development. *Child Development, 80*(2) 327–337.

Shisslak, C. M. & Crago, M. (2001). Risk and protective factors in the development of eating disorders. In J. K. Thompson & L. Smolak (Eds.), *Body image, eating disorders, and obesity in youth: Assessment, treatment, and prevention* (pp. 103–125). Washington, DC: American Psychological Association.

Shonk, S. M. & Cicchetti, D. (2001). Maltreatment, competency deficits, and risk for academic and behavioral maladjustment. *Developmental Psychology, 37*, 3–17.

Shulman, S. & Scharf, M. (2000). Adolescent romantic behaviours and perceptions: Age-and gender-related differences, and links with family and peer relationships. *Journal of Research on Adolescence, 10*, 99–118.

Shweder, R. (2003). *Why do men barbecue? Recipes for cultural psychology*. Cambridge, MA: Harvard University Press.

Shweder, R. A. (2002). 'What about female genital mutilation?' And why understanding culture matters in the first place. In R. A. Shweder & M. Minow (Eds.), *Engaging cultural differences: The multicultural challenge in liberal democracies* (pp. 216–251). New York: Russell Sage Foundation.

Shweder, R. A., Goodnow, J., Hatano, G., Levine, R. A., Markus, H. & Miller, P. (2006). The cultural psychology of development: One mind, many mentalities. In W. Damon (Ed.), *Handbook of child development* (5th ed, vol 1, 865–937). New York: Wiley.

Sidorowicz, L. S. & Lunney, G. S. (1980). Baby X revisited. *Sex Roles, 6*, 67–73.

Siegel, J. M. (2002). Body image change and adolescent depressive symptoms. *Journal of Adolescent Research, 17*, 27–41.

Sieving, R. E., Perry, C. L. & Williams, C. L. (2000). Do friendships change behaviours, or do behaviours change friendships? Examining paths of influence in young adolescents' alcohol use. *Journal of Adolescent Health, 26*, 27–35.

Sigfusdottir, I-D., Farkas, G. & Silver, E. (2004). The role of depressed mood and anger in the relationship between family conflict and delinquent behavior. *Journal of Youth and Adolescence, 33*(6), 509–522.

Silverberg-Koerner, S., Wallace, S., Jacobs, L., S., Lee, S-A. & Escalante, K. A. (2004). Sensitive mother-to-adolescent disclosures after divorce: Is the experience of wons different from that of daughters? *Journal of Family Psychology, 18*(1), 6–57.

Silvestre, J. (2008). Workplace accidents and early safety policies in Spain, 1900–1932. *Social History of Medicine, 21*(1), 67–67.

Simmons, R. (2008). Raising the age of compulsory education in England: A NEET solution? *british Journal of Educational Studies, 56*(4), 420–439.

Simmons, R. (2004). *Odd girl speaks out: Girls write about bullies, cliques, popularity, and jealousy*. New York: Harvest.

Simmons, R. (2002). *Odd girl out: The hidden culture of aggression in girls*. New York: Harcourt.

Simmons, R. G. & Blyth, D. A. (1987). *Moving into adolescence*. New York: Aldine de Gruyter.

Simons-Morton, B. (2007). Parent involvement in novice teen driving: Rationale, evidence of effects, and potential for enhancing graduated driver licensing effectiveness. *Journal of Safety Research, 38*(2), 192–202.

Simons-Morton, B. G., Hartos, J. L. & Leaf, W. A. (2002). Promoting parental management of teen driving. *Injury Prevention, 8* (Suppl 2), ii24–ii31.

Simons-Morton, B. G., Hartos, J. L., Leaf, W. A. & Preusser, D. F. (2006). Increasing parent limits on novice young drivers: Cognitive mediation of the effect of persuasive messages. *Journal of Adolescent Research, 21*(1), 83–105.

Sin, C. H. (2006). Expectations of support among White British and Asian-Indian older people in Britain: the interdependence of formal and informal spheres. *Health & Social Care in the Community, 14*(3), 215–224.

Singer, E. & Doornenbal, J. (2006). Learning morality in peer conflict: A study of schoolchildren's narratives about being betrayed by a friend. *Childhood, 13*(2), 225–245.

Singh, S. & Darroch, J. E. (2000). Adolescent pregnancy adolescent pregnancy and childbearing: Levels and trends in developed countries. *Family Planning Perspectives, 32*, 14–23.

Singleton, G., Rola-Rubzen, M., Muir, K., Muir, D. & McGregor. M. (2009). Youth empowerment and information and communication technologies: A case study of a remote Australian Aboriginal community. *GeoJournal, 74*(5), 403–413.

Sinnott, J. D. (2003). Postformal thought and adult development: Living in balance. In J. Demick & C. Andreotti (Eds.), *Handbook of adult development* (pp. 221–238). New York: Kluwer.

Sinnott, J. D. (1998). *The development of logic in adulthood: Postformal thoughts and its applications*. New York: Plenum. Strahan, D. B. (1983). The emergence of formal operations in adolescence. *Transcendence, 11*, 7–14.

Sirin, S. R., McCreary, D. R. & Mahalik, J. R. (2004). Differential reactions to men and women's gender role transgressions. *Journal of Men's Studies, 12*, 119–132.

Sirin, S. R. & Rogers-Sirin, L. (2005). Components of school engagement among African American adolescents. *Applied Developmental Science, 9*, 5–13.

Sivanandan, A. (2006). Race, terror and civil society. *Race & Class, 47*(3), 1–8.

Skeggs, B. (2004). *Class, self, culture,* London: Routledge.

Skevik, A. (2004). The new family's vulnerable vanguard: Child maintenance reform in Norway. *Social Policy and Society, 3*(1), 11–19.

Skoe, E. E. & Gooden, A. (1993). Ethic of care and real-life moral dilemma content in male and female early adolescents. *Journal of Early Adolescence, 13*, 154–167.

Slater, M. D. (2007). Reinforcing spirals: The mutual influence of media selectivity and media effects and their impact on individual behavior and social identity. *Communication Theory, 17*(3), 281–303.

Slicker, E., Patton, M. & Fuller, D. (2004). Parenting dimensions and adolescent sexual initiation: Using self-esteem, academic aspiration, and substance use as mediators. *Journal of Youth Studies, 7*(3), 295–314.

Sligh, A. C., Conners, F. A. & Roskos-Ewoldsen, B. (2005). Relation of creativity to fluid and crystallized intelligence. *Journal of Creative Behavior, 39*(2), 123–136.

Slomkowski, C., Rende, R., Conger, K. J. , Simons, R. L. & Conger, R. D. (2001). Sisters, brothers, and delinquency: Evaluating social influence during early and middle adolescence. *Child Development, 72*(1), 271–283.

Slonje, R. & Smith, P. K. (2008). Cyberbullying: Another main type of bullying? *Scandinavian Journal of Psychology, 49*(2), 147–154.

Smart, C. (2004). Changing landscapes of family life: Rethinking divorce. *Social Policy and Society, 3*(4), 401–408.

Smetana, J. G. (2005). Adolescent–parent conflict: Resistance and subversion as developmental process. In L. Nucci (Ed.), *Conflict, contradiction, and contrarian elements in moral development and education* (pp. 69–91). Mahwah, NJ: Erlbaum.

Smetana, J. G., Metzger, A. & Campione-Barr, N. (2004). African American late adolescents' relationships with parents: Developmental transitions and longitudinal patterns. *Child Development, 75*, 932–947.

Smetana, J. G. , Metzger, A., Gettman, D. C. & Campione-Barr, N. (2006). Disclosure and secrecy in adolescent–parent relationships. *Child Development, 77*(1), 201–217.

Smiler, A. (2006). Living the Image: A quantitative approach to delineating masculinities. *Sex Roles, 55*(9–10), 621–632.

Smith, C. & Denton, M. L. (2005). *Soul searching: The religious and spiritual lives of American teenagers*. New York: Oxford University Press.

Smith, D. (2000). Jocks and couch potatoes. *Washington Post,* p. A13.

Smith, D. W. & Brodzinsky, D. M. (2002). Coping with birth-parent loss in adopted children. *Journal of Child Psychology and Psychiatry* (formerly *Journal of Child Psychology and Psychiatry and Allied Disciplines*), *43*(2), 213–223.

Smith, M., Calam, R. & Bolton, C. (2009). Psychological factors linked to self-reported depression symptoms in late adolescence. *Behavioural and Cognitive Psychotherapy, 37*(1), 73–85.

Smokowski, P., David-Ferdon, C. & Stroupe, N. (2009). Acculturation and violence in minority adolescents: A review of the empirical literature. *The Journal of Primary Prevention, 30*(3–4), 215–263.

Sneeding, T. M. & Phillips, K. R. (2002). Cross-national differences in employment and economic sufficiency. *Annals of the American Academy of Political Social Science, 580*, 103–133.

Snyder, J., Reid, J. & Patterson, G. (2003). A social learning model of child and adolescent antisocial behavior. In B. B. Lahey & T. E. Moffitt (Eds.), *Causes of conduct disorder and juvenile delinquency* (pp. 27–48). New York: Guilford.

Soethout, M., Heymans, M. & ten Cate, O. T. J. (2008). Career preference and medical students' biographical characteristics and academic achievement. *Medical Teacher, 30*(1), e15–e22.

Soland, B. (2000). *Becoming modern: Young women and the reconstruction of womanhood in the 1920s*. Princeton: Princeton University Press.

Solberg, M. E., Olweus, D. & Endresen, I. M. (2007). Bullies and victims at school: Are they the same pupils? *British Journal of Educational Psychology, 77*(2), 441–464.

Solomon, A., Ruscio, J., Seeley, J. R. & Lewinsohn, P. M. (2006). A taxometric investigation of unipolar depression in a large community sample. *Psychological Medicine, 36*(7), 973–985.

Solomon, Y. (2002). Intimate talk between parents and their teenage children: Democratic openness or covert control? *Sociology, 36*(4), 965–983.

Somers, C. L. & Surmann, A. T. (2005). Sources and timing of sex education: Relations with American adolescent sexual attitudes and behavior. *Educational Review, 57*(1), 37–54.

Sommers, C. H. (2001). *The war against boys: How misguided feminism is harming our young men*. New York: Simon and Schuster.

Sommers, C. H. (2000). The war against boys. *Atlantic Monthly*, (May), 59–74.

Søraker, J. H. (2008). Global freedom of expression within nontextual frameworks. *The Information Society, 24*(1), 40–46.

Sorell, G. T. & Montgomery, M. J. (2002). The ubiquity of gendered cultural contexts: A rejoinder to Kroger, Archer, Levine, and Côté. *Identity, 2*, 281–285.

Sorell, G. T. & Montgomery, M. J. (2001). Feminist perspectives on Erikson's theory: Their relevance for contemporary identity development research. *Identity, 1*, 97–128.

Sotelo, M. J. (1999). Gender differences in political tolerance among adolescents. *Journal of Gender Studies, 8*(2), 211–217.

Sowell, E. R., Thompson, P. M., Holmes, C. J., Jernigan, T. I. & Toga, A. W. (1999). In vivo evidence for post-adolescence brain maturation in frontal and striatal regions. *Nature Neuroscience, 2*, 859–861.

Sowell, E., Trauner, D., Ganst, A. & Jernigan, T. (2002). Development of cortical and subcortical brain structures in childhood and adolescence: A structural MRI study. *Developmental Medicine and Child Neurology, 44*, 4–16.

Sowerwine, C. (2003). Woman's brain, man's brain: feminism and anthropology in late nineteenth-century France. *Women's History Review, 12*(2), 289–308.

Spear, P. (2000). The adolescent brain and age-related behavioral manifestations. *Neuroscience and Biobehavioral Review, 24*, 417–463.

Spence, J. & Helmreich, R. (1978). *Masculinity and femininity: Their psychological dimensions, correlates, and antecedents*. Austin: University of Texas Press.

Spence, S. H. (2003). Social skills training with children and young people: Theory, evidence and practice. *Child and Adolescent Mental Health, 8*(2), 84–96.

Spencer, N. J. (2006). Social equalization in youth: Evidence from a cross-sectional British survey. *The European Journal of Public Health, 16*(4), 368–375.

Spencer, R., Porche, M. V. & Tolman, D. L. (2003). We've come a long way – maybe: New challenges for gender equity in education. *Teachers College Record, 105*, 1774–1807.

Spencer-Dawe, E. (2005). Lone mothers in employment: Seeking rational solutions to role strain. *The Journal of Social Welfare & Family Law, 27*(3), 251–264.

Spencer-Rodgers, J., Peng, K., Wang, L. & Hou, Y. (2004). Dialectical self-esteem and East–West differences in psychological well-being. *Personality and Social Psychology Bulletin, 30*(11), 1416–1432.

Spengler, E. A. (2002, April 29). Career choice: It's a tough job. *Washington Post*, p. C10.

Spera, C. (2005). A review of the relationship among parenting practices, parenting styles, and adolescent school achievement. *Educational Psychology Review, 17*, 125–146.

Sperber, J. (2008). *Europe 1850–1914: Progress, participation & apprehension. Longman History of Modern Europe*. Harlow: Pearson/Longman.

Spielhofer, T., Benton, T. & Schagen, S. (2004). A study of the effects of school size and single-sex education in English schools. *Research Papers in Education, 19*(2), 133–159.

Spirito, A. & Overholser, J. C. (2003). *Evaluating and treating adolescent suicide attempters: From research to practice*. San Diego, CA: Academic Press.

Spirito, A., Valeri, S. & Boergers, J. (2003). Predictors of continued suicidal behavior in adolescents following a suicide attempt. *Journal of Clinical Child & Adolescent Psychology, 32*, 284–289.

Spreckels, J. (2008). Identity negotiation in small stories among German adolescent girls. *Narrative Inquiry, 18*(2), 393–413.

Sreenivasan, K. K. & Jha, A. P. (2007). Selective attention supports working memory maintenance by modulating perceptual processing of distractors. *Journal of Cognitive Neuroscience, 19*(1), 32–41.

Sroufe, L. A., Carlson, E. & Schulman, S. (1993). Individuals in relationships: Development from infancy through adolescence. In D. C. Funder, R. D. Parke, C. Tomlinson-Keasey, & K. Widaman (Eds.), *Studying lives through time: Personality and development* (pp. 51–60). Norwood, NJ: Ablex.

Sroufe, L. A., Egeland, B., Carlson, E. A. & Collins, W. A. (2005). *The development of the person: The Minnesota study of risk and adaptation from birth to adulthood*. New York: Guilford.

SSCB (Swansea Safeguarding Children Board) (2010). Executive Summary of the Overview Report of the Serious Case Review Concerning Child B. Swansea: SSCB March 2010 at http://www.swansea.gov.uk/media/pdfwithtranslation/q/a/child-b-executive-summary-201003.pdf accessed 21 02.2011.

Staff, J., Mortimer, J. T. & Uggen, C. (2004). Work and leisure in adolescence. In R. M. Lerner & L. Steinberg (Eds.), *Handbook of adolescent psychology* (2nd ed., pp. 429–450). Hoboken, NJ: John Wiley & Sons.

Stake, J. E. & Nickens, S. D. (2005). Adolescent girls' and boys' science peer relationships and perceptions of the possible self as scientist. *Sex Roles, 52*(1–2), 1–11.

Stallard, P., Simpson, N., Anderson, S., Carter, T., Osborn, C. & Bush, S. (2005). An evaluation of the FRIENDS programme: a cognitive behaviour therapy intervention to promote emotional resilience. *Archives of Disease in Childhood, 90*(10), 1016–1019.

Stams, G., Brugman, D., Dekovic, M., van Rosmalen, L., van der Laan, P. & Gibbs, J. (2006). The moral judgment of juvenile delinquents: A meta-analysis. *Journal of Abnormal Child Psychology, 34*(5), 692–708.

Stams, G-J., Juffer, F., Rispens, J. & Hoksbergen, R. A. C. (2000). The development and adjustment of 7-year-old children adopted in infancy. *Journal of Child Psychology and Psychiatry* (formerly *Journal of Child Psychology and Psychiatry and Allied Disciplines*), *41*(8), 1025–1037.

Stanley, S. M., Rhoades, G. K. & Markman, H. J. (2006). Sliding versus deciding: Inertia and the premarital cohabitation effect. *Family Relations, 55*(4), 499–509.

Stanley, S. M., Whitton, S. W. & Markman, H. J. (2004). Maybe I do: Interpersonal commitment and premarital or nonmarital cohabitation. *Journal of Family Issues, 25*, 496–519.

Stanton-Salazar, R. D. & Spina, S. U. (2005). Adolescent peer networks and a context for social and emotional support. *Youth & Society, 36*(4), 379–417.

Star, C. & Hammer, S. (2008). Teaching generic skills: Eroding the higher purpose of universities, or an opportunity for renewal? *Oxford Review of Education, 34*(2), 237–251.

Stearns, E. & Glennie, E. J. (2006). When and why dropouts leave high school. *Youth & Society, 38*(1), 29–57.

Steca, P., Alessandri, G., Vecchio, G. M. & Caprara, G. V. (2007). Being a successful adolescent at school and with peers. The discriminative power of a typological approach. *Emotional and Behavioural Difficulties, 12*(2), 147–162.

Steele, C. M. & Aronson, J. (1995). 'Stereotype threat and the intellectual test performance of African Americans'. *Journal of Personality and Social Psychology, 69*(5): 797–811.

Steele, J. R. (2002). Teens and movies: Something to do, plenty to learn. In J. D. Brown, J. R. Steele, & K. Walsh-Childers (Eds.), *Sexual teens, sexual media: Investigating media's influence on adolescent sexuality* (pp. 227–252). Mahwah, NJ: Erlbaum.

Steele, J. R. & Brown, J. D. (1995). Adolescent room culture: Studying media in the context of everyday life. *Journal of Youth & Adolescence, 24*, 551–576.

Stein, J. H. & Reiser, L. W. (1993). A study of White middle-class adolescent boys' responses to 'semenarche' (the first ejaculation). *Journal of Youth & Adolescence, 23*, 373–383.

Steinberg, L. (2008). A social neuroscience perspective on adolescent risk-taking. *Developmental Review, 28*, 78–106.

Steinberg, L. (2006). *Adolescence* (7th Ed.). New York: McGraw-Hill

Steinberg, L. (2001). *We know some things: Parent–adolescent relations in retrospect and prospect*. Presidential Address: presented at the biennial meeting of the Society for Research on Adolescence, Chicago. *Journal of Research on Adolescence, 11*, 1–19.

Steinberg, L. (1996). *Beyond the classroom: Why school reform has failed and what parents need to do*. New York: Simon & Schuster.

Steinberg, L. & Cauffman, E. (2001). Adolescents as adults in court: A developmental perspective on the transfer of juveniles to criminal court. *SRCD Social Policy Report, 15*(4), 9–13.

Steinberg, L. & Silk, J. S. (2002). Parenting adolescents. In M. H. Bornstein (Ed.), *Handbook of Parenting, Vol. 1: Children and parenting* (2nd ed., 103–133). Mahwah, NJ: Erlbaum.

Steinberg, S., Parmar, P. & Richard, B. (2005). *Contemporary youth culture: An international encyclopedia*. Westport: Greenwood Press.

Steinhausen, H.-C., Boyadjieva, S., Griogoroiu-Serbanescue, M. & Neumärker, K.-J. (2003). The outcome of adolescent eating disorders: Findings from an international collaborative study. *European Child & Adolescent Psychiatry, 12*, i91–i98.

Steinman, K. J. & Zimmerman, M. A. (2004). Religious activity and risk behavior among Africa American adolescents: Concurrent and developmental effects. *American Journal of Community Psychology, 33*, 151–161.

Stephenson, M. (2006). Travel and the 'freedom of movement': Racialised encounters and experiences amongst ethnic minority tourists in the EU. *Mobilities, 1*(2), 285–306.

Steptoe, A. & Feldman, P. (2001). Neighborhood problems as sources of chronic stress: Development of a measure of neighborhood problems, and associations with socioeconomic status and health. *Annals of Behavioral Medicine: A Publication of the Society of Behavioral Medicine, 23*(3), 177–185.

Steptoe, A. & Wardle, J. (2001). Health behavior, risk awareness, and emotional well-being in students from Eastern and Western Europe. *Social Science and Medicine, 53*, 1621–1630.

Stern, D. & Briggs, D. (2001). Does paid employment help or hinder performance in secondary school? Insights from US high school students. *Journal of Education and Work, 14*(3), 355–372.

Stern, P. (2003). Upside-down and backwards: Time discipline in a Canadian Inuit town. *Anthropologica, 45*, 147–161.

Sternberg, R. J. (1988). Triangulating love. In R. J. Sternberg & M. L. Barnes (Eds.), *The psychology of love* (pp. 119–138). New Haven, CT: Yale University Press.

Sternberg, R. J. (1987). Liking versus loving: A comparative evaluation of theories. *Psychological Bulletin, 102*, 331–345.

Sternberg, R. J. (1986). A triangular theory of love. *Psychological Review, 93*, 119–135.

Sternberg, R. J., Conway, B. E., Ketron, J. L. & Berstein, M. (1981). People's conceptions of intelligence. *Journal of Personality and Social Psychology, 41*, 37–55.

Sternberg, R. J. & Nigro, C. (1980). Developmental patterns in the solution of verbal analogies. *Child Development, 51*, 27–38.

Stevenson, H. C. (2004). Boys in the men's clothing: Racial socialisation and neighborhood safety as buffers to hypervulnerability in Africa American adolescent males. In N. Way & J. Y. Chu (Eds.), *Adolescent boys: Exploring diverse cultures of boyhood* (pp. 59–77). New York: New York University Press.

Stevenson, H. W. & Zusho, A. (2002). Adolescence in China and Japan: Adapting to a changing environment. In B. B. Brown, R. Larson, & T. S. Saraswathi (Eds.), *The World's Youth: Adolescence in Eight Regions of the Globe* (pp. 141–170). New York: Cambridge University Press.

Stewart, R. B., Kozak, A. L., Tingley, L. M., Goddard, J. M., Blake, E. M. & Cassel, W. A. (2001). Adult sibling relationship: A validation of a typology. *Personal Relationships, 8, 299–324.*

Stice, E., Shaw, H. & Marti, C. N. (2006). A meta-analytic review of obesity programs for children and adolescents. *Psychological Bulletin, 132,* 667–691.

Stickney, L. & Konrad, A. (2007). Gender-role attitudes and earnings: A multinational study of married women and men. *Sex Roles, 57*(11–12), 801–811.

Stockwell, T., Toumbourou, J. W., Letcher, P., Smart, D., Sanson, A. & Bond, L. (2004). Risk and protection factors for different intensities of adolescent substance use: When does the prevention paradox apply? *Drug & Alcohol Review, 23,* 67–77.

Stoll, B. M., Arnaut, G. L., Fromme, D. K. & Felker-Thayer, J. A. (2005). Adolescents in stepfamilies: A qualitative analysis. *Journal of Divorce & Remarriage, 44*(1–2), 177–189.

Stone, M. R., Barber, B. L. & Eccles, J. S. (2000, April). *Adolescent 'crowd' clusters: An adolescent perspective on persons and patterns*. Paper presented at the biennial meeting of the Society for Research on Adolescence, Chicago.

Stoneman, Z., Brody, G. H., Churchill, S. L. & Winn, L. L. (1999). Family, school, and community effects of residential instability on Head Start children and their relationships with older siblings: Influences of child emotionality and conflict between family caregivers. *Child Development, 70*(5), 1246–1262.

Stonewall (2010). Press release at http://www.stonewall.org.uk/media/current_releases/4867.asp accessed 02.12.10.

Storch, E. A., Bagner, D. M., Geffken, G. R. & Baumeister, A. L. (2004). Association between overt and relational aggression and psychosocial adjustment in undergraduate college students. *Violence & Victims, 19,* 689–700.

Strahan, D. B. (1983). The emergence of formal operations in adolescence. *Transcendence, 11,* 7–14.

Straker, J. (2007). Youth, globalisation, and millennial reflection in a Guinean forest town. *The Journal of Modern African Studies, 45*(2), 299–319.

Strand, S. & Winston, J. (2008). Educational aspirations in inner city schools. *Educational Studies, 34*(4), 249–267.

Strandh, M. & Nordenmark, M. (2006). The interference of paid work with household demands in different social policy contests: Perceived work-household conflict in Sweden, the UK, the Netherlands, Hungary & the Czech Republic. *British Journal of Sociology, 57*(4), 597–617.

Strasburger, V. (2006). Super peer. In J. J. Arnett (Ed.), *Encyclopedia of children, adolescents, and the media*. Thousand Oaks, CA: Sage.

Strasburger, V. (1999). Media violence. *Indian Journal of Pediatrics, 66*(4), 603–612.

Strasburger, V. & Wilson, B. (2002). *Children, adolescents, and the media*. Thousand Oaks, CA: Sage.

Strauch, B. (2003). *The primal teen: What the new discoveries about the teenage brain tell us about our kids*. New York: Anchor.

Striegel-Moore, R. H. & Franko, D. L. (2006). Adolescent eating disorders. In C. A. Essau (Ed.), *Child and* adolescent psychopathology: Theoretical and clinical implications. (pp. 160–183). New York: Routledge/Taylor & Francis.

Striegel-Moore, R. H., Seeley, J. R. & Lewinsohn, P. M. (2003). Psychosocial adjustment in young adulthood of women who experienced an eating disorder during adolescence. *Journal of the American Academy of Child & Adolescent Psychiatry, 42*, 587–593.

Stroggilos, V. & Xanthacou, Y. (2006). Collaborative IEPs for the education of pupils with profound and multiple learning difficulties. *European Journal of Special Needs Education, 21*(3), 339–349.

Stromquist, N. P. (2007). Gender equity education globally. In S. S. Klein, B. Richardson, D. A. Grayson, L. H. Fox, C. Kramarae, et al. (Eds.), *Handbook for achieving gender equity through education* (2nd ed., 33–42). Mahwah, NJ: Lawrence Erlbaum.

Stroobant, E. & Jones, A. (2006). School refuser child identities. *Discourse, 27*(2), 209–223.

Stroud, L. R., Foster, E., Papandonatos, G. D., Handwerger, K., Granger, D. A., Kivlighan, K. T. & Niaura, R. (2009). Stress response and the adolescent transition: Performance versus peer rejection stressors. *Development and Psychopathology, 21*, 47–68.

Strough, J., Leszczynski, J., Neely, T., Flinn, J. & Margrett, J. (2007). From adolescence to later adulthood: Femininity, masculinity, and androgyny in six age groups. *Sex Roles, 57*(5–6), 385–396.

Suárez-Orozco, C. (2004). Formulating identity in a globalized world. In M. Suárez-Orozco, D. Baolian, & M. Hilliard-Qin (Eds.), *Globalisation: Culture and education in the new millennium* (pp.173–202). Berkeley: University of California Press.

Suárez-Orozco, C. & Qin-Hilliard, D. B. (2004). Immigrant boys' experiences in U. S. schools. In N. Way & J. Y. Chu (Eds.), *Adolescent boys: Exploring the diverse cultures of boyhood* (pp. 295–316). New York: New York University Press.

Sue, D. (2005). Asian American masculinity and therapy: The concept of masculinity in Asian American males. In G. E. Good & G. R. Brooks (Eds.). *The new handbook of psychotherapy and counseling with men: A comprehensive guide to settings, problems, and treatment approaches* (pp. 357–368). San Francisco: Jossey-Bass.

Suizzo, M-A. (2000). The social-emotional and cultural contexts of cognitive development: Neo-Piagetian perspectives. *Child Development, 71*(4), 846–849.

Sullivan, H. S. (1953). *The interpersonal theory of psychiatry*. New York: Norton.

Sun, S. S., Schubert, C. M., Liang, R., Roche, A. F., Kulin, H. E, Lee, P. A., Himes, J. H. & Chumlea, W. C. (2005). Is sexual maturity occurring earlier among U. S. children? *Journal of Adolescent Health, 37*(5), 345–355.

Sund, A. M., Larsson, B. & Wichstrøm, L. (2003). Psychosocial correlates of depressive symptoms among 12–14-year-old Norwegian adolescents. *Journal of Child Psychology and Psychiatry* (formerly *Journal of Child Psychology and Psychiatry and Allied Disciplines*), *44*(4), 588–597.

Super, D. (1992). Toward a comprehensive study of career development. In D. H. Montross & C. J. Shinkman (Eds.), *Career development: Theory and practice* (pp. 35–64). Springfield, IL: Charles C. Thomas.

Super, D. E. (1980). A life-span life-space approach to career development. *Journal of Vocational Behavior, 16*, 282–298.

Super, D. E. (1976). *Career education and the meanings of work*. Washington, DC: U. S. Office of Education.

Super, D. E. (1967). *The psychology of careers*. New York: Harper & Row.

Supple, A. J., Aquilino, W. S. & Wright, D. L. (1999). Collecting sensitive self-report data with laptop computers: Impact on the response tendencies of adolescents in a home interview. *Journal of Research on Adolescence, 9*, 467–488.

Susman, E. J., Dorn, L. D. & Schiefelbein, V. L. (2003). Puberty, sexuality, and health. In R. M. Lerner & A. M. Easterbrooks (Eds.), *Handbook of psychology: Developmental psychology*, (Vol. 6, 295–324). New York: Wiley.

Susman, E. J. & Rogol, A. (2004). Puberty and psychological development. In R. Lerner & L. Steinberg (Eds.), *Handbook of adolescent psychology*. New York: Wiley.

Sussman, S., Pokhrel, P., Ashmore, R. D. & Brown, B. B. (2007). Adolescent peer group identification and characteristics: A review of the literature. *Addictive Behaviours, 32*(8), 1602–1627.

Sutherland, P. (2005). A comparison of Piaget's and Bigg's conceptions of cognitive development in adults and their implications for the teaching of adults. In P. Sutherland, and J. Crowther (Eds.), *Lifelong Learning: Concept and Contexts*. London: Routledge.

Sutherland, P. (1999). The application of Piagetian and neo-Piagetian ideas to further and higher education. *International Journal of Lifelong Education, 18*(4), 286–294.

Swanson, D. P., Spencer, M. B. & Petersen, A. (1998). Identity formation in adolescence. In K. Borman & B. Schneider (Eds.), *The adolescent years: Social influences and educational challenges: Ninety-seventh yearbook of the National Society for the Study of Education, Part 1* (pp. 18–41). Chicago: National Society for the Study of Education.

Swardson, A. (1999, September 28). In Europe's economic boom, finding work is a bust. *Washington Post*, pp. 1, 20.

Sweeney, M. M. (2007). Stepfather families and the emotional well-being of adolescents. *Journal of Health & Social Behavior, 48*(1), 33–49.

Sweeting, H., Young, R., West, P. & Der, G. (2006). Peer victimization and depression in early–mid adolescence: A longitudinal study. *The British Journal of Educational Psychology, 76*(3), 577–594.

Swenson, C. C., Henggeler, S. W., Taylor, I. S. & Addison, O. W. (2005). *Multisystemic therapy and neighborhood partnerships: Reducing adolescent violence and substance abuse*. New York: Guilford.

Swinbourne, J. M. & Touyz, S. W. (2007). The co-morbidity of eating disorders and anxiety disorders: A review. *European Eating Disorders Review*, *15*(4), 253–274.

Swinson, J. & Cording, M. (2002). Assertive discipline in a school for pupils with emotional and behavioural difficulties. *British Journal of Special Education*, *29*(2), 72–75.

Sykorova, D. (2002). Family system of help and aid against the background of social transformation. *European Journal of Social Work*, *5*(2), 123–138.

TADS (Treatment for Adolescents with Depression Study) (2004). Fluoxetine, cognitive-behavioral therapy, and their combination for adolescents with depression: Treatment for Adolescents with Depression Study (TADS) randomized controlled trial. *JAMA: Journal of the American Medical Association*, *29*, 807–820.

Taga, K. A., Markey, C. N. & Friedman, H. S. (2006). A longitudinal investigation of associations between boys' pubertal timing and adult behavioral health and well-being. *Journal of Youth and Adolescence*, *35*(3), 401–411.

Taillon, G. (2004). *Remote control wars: The media battle for the hearts and minds of our youths*. Frederick, MD: Publish American Baltimore.

Takahashi, K. & Takeuchi, K. (2007). Japan. In J. J. Arnett, R. Ahmed, B. Nsamenang, T. S. Saraswathi, & R. Silbereisen (Eds.), *International encyclopedia of adolescence*. New York: Routledge.

Tamis-LeMonda, C. S., Way, N., Hughes, D., Yoshikawa, H., Kalman, R. K. & Niwa, E. Y. (2008). Parents' goals for children: The dynamic coexistence of individualism and collectivism in cultures and individuals. *Social Development*, *17*(1), 183–209.

Tamplin, A. & Gooyer, I. M. (2001). Family functioning in adolescents at high and low risk for major depressive disorder. *European Child & Adolescent Psychiatry*, *10*(3), 170–179.

Tang, C. S., Yeung, D. Y. L. & Lee, A. M. (2004). A comparison of premenarcheal expectations and postmenarcheal experiences in Chinese early adolescents. *Journal of Early Adolescence*, *24*, 180–195.

Tang, C. S., Yeung, D. Y. L. & Lee, A. M. (2003). Psychosocial correlates of emotional responses to menarche among Chinese adolescent girls. *Journal of Adolescent Health*, *33*, 193–201.

Taniguchi, S. (2006). Current status of cataloging and classification education in Japan. *Cataloging & Classification Quarterly*, *41*(2), 121–133.

Tanner, J. M. (1991). Growth spurt, adolescent. In R. M. Lerner, A. C. Petersen, & J. Brooks-Gunn (Eds.), *Encyclopedia of adolescence* (Vol. 2, 419–424). New York: Garland.

Tanner, J. M. (1971). Sequence, tempo, and individual variation in the growth and development of boys and girls aged twelve to sixteen. *Daedalus*, *100*, 907–930.

Tanner, J. M. (1970). Physical growth. In P. H. Mussen (Ed.), *Carmichael's manual of child psychology* (Vol. 2, 3rd ed., 77–156). New York: Wiley.

Tanner, J. M. (1962). *Growth at adolescence* (2nd ed.). Springfield, IL: Thomas.

Tanon, F. (1994). *A cultural view on planning: The case of weaving in Ivory Coast*. Tilburg: Tilburg University Press.

Tarter, R. E., Vanyukov, M., Kirisci, L., Reynolds, M. & Clark, D. B. (2006). Predictors of marijuana use in adolescents before and after licit drug use: Examination of the gateway hypothesis. *American Journal of Psychiatry*, *163*(12), 2134–2140.

Tasker, F. & McCann, D. (1999). Affirming patterns of adolescent sexual identity: the challenge. *Journal of Family Therapy*, *21*(1), 30–54.

Tasker, M. (2008). Smaller schools: A conflict of aims and purposes? *FORUM: For Promoting 3–19 Comprehensive Education*, *50*(2), 177–184.

Tawake, S. (2006). Cultural rhetoric in coming-out narratives: Witi Ihimaera's The Uncle's Story. *World Englishes*, *25*(3–4), 373–380.

Taylor, A. (2005). It's for the rest of your life: The pragmatics of youth career decision making. *Youth & Society*, *36*, 471–503.

Taylor, C. S., Lerner, R. M., von Eye, A., Bobek, D. L., Balsano, A. B., Dowling, E. M., et al. (2003). Positive individual and social behavior among gang and nongang Africa American male adolescents. *Journal of Adolescent Research*, *18*, 548–574.

Taylor, D. (2006). From 'It's All in Your Head' to 'Taking Back the Month': Premenstrual syndrome (PMS) research and the contributions of the Society for Menstrual Cycle Research. *Sex Roles*, *54*(5–6), 377–391.

Taylor, J. M., Veloria, C. N. & Verba, M. C. (2007). Latina girls: 'We're like sisters – most times!' In B. J. Leadbeater & N. Way (Eds.), *Urban girls revisited: Building strengths* (pp. 157–174). New York: New York University Press.

Taylor, P. (2003). Age, labour market conditions and male suicide rates in selected countries. *Ageing and Society*, *23*(1), 25–40.

Teitelman, A. M. (2004). Adolescent girls' perspectives of family interactions related to menarche and sexual health. *Qualitative Health Research*, *14*, 1292–1308.

Teitler, J. O. (2002). Trends in youth sexual initiation and fertility in developed countries: 1960–1995. *Annals of the American Academy of Political Science Studies*, *580*, 134–152.

Tervo, R. C., Azuma, S., Fogas, B. & Fiechtner, H. (2002). Children with ADHD and motor dysfunction compared with children with ADHD only. *Developmental Medicine & Child Neurology*, *44*(6), 383–390.

TfL (Transport for London) (2005). *Street Management* LAAU topic 2005–4 September 2005 London Road Safety Unit. At http://www.tfl.gov.uk/assets/downloads/2005–4-Young-Car-Drivers.pdf accessed 21.01.2011.

Thomaes, S., Bushman, B. J., Stegge, H. & Olthof, T. (2008). Trumping shame by blasts of noise: Narcissism, self-esteem, shame, and aggression in young adolescents. *Child Development*, *79*(6), 1792–1801.

Thomas, M. E. (2007). The implications of psychoanalysis for qualitative methodology: The case of interviews and narrative data analysis. *The Professional Geographer*, *59*(4), 537–546.

Thompson, A. E., Morgan, C. & Urquhart, I. (2003). Children with ADHD transferring to secondary schools: Potential difficulties and solutions. *Clinical Child Psychology and Psychiatry*, *8*(1), 91–103.

Thompson, J. K., Shroff, H., Herbozo, S., Cafri, G., Rodriguez, J. & Rodriguez, M. (2007). Relations among multiple peer influences, body dissatisfaction, eating disturbance, and self-esteem: A comparison of average weight, at risk of overweight, and overweight adolescent girls. *Journal of Pediatric Psychology*, *32*(1), 24–29.

Thompson, M. S. & Keith, V. M. (2001). The blacker the berry: Gender, skin tone, self-esteem, and self-efficacy. *Gender & Society*, *15*(3), 336–357.

Thompson, P. M., Giedd, J. N., Woods, R. P., MacDonald. D., Evans, A. C. & Toga, A. W. (2000). Growth patterns in the developing brain detected by using continuum mechanical tensor maps. *Nature*, *404*(6774), 190–193.

Thompson, S., Grant, B. & Dharmalingam, A. (2002). Leisure time in midlife: what are the odds? *Leisure Studies*, *21*(2), 125–143.

Thompson, T. & Massat, C. (2005). Experiences of violence, post-traumatic stress, academic achievement and behavior problems of urban African-American children. *Child and Adolescent Social Work Journal*, *22*(5–6), 367–393.

Thomson, P. & Russell, L. (2007). *Mapping the alternatives to permanent exclusion*. Research Report. York: Joseph Rowntree Foundation.

Thurlow, C. (2001). The usual suspects? A comparative investigation of crowds and social-type labelling among young British teenagers. *Journal of Youth Studies*, *4*(3), 319–334.

Tienda, M. & Wilson, W. J. (Eds.) (2002). *Youth in cities: A cross-national perspective*. New York: Cambridge University Press.

Tierney, T. & Dowd, R. (2000). The use of social skills groups to support girls with emotional difficulties in secondary schools. *Support for Learning*, *15*(2), 82–85.

Tilton-Weaver., L. C. & Galambos, N. L. (2003). Adolescents' characteristics and parents' beliefs as predictors of parents' peer management behaviours. *Journal of Research on Adolescence*, *13*, 269–300.

Timmer, S. G., Borrego, J. Jr. & Urquiza, A. J. (2002). Antecedents of coercive interactions in physically abusive mother-child dyads. *Journal of Interpersonal Violence*, *17*(8), 836–853.

Timmerman, G. (2005). A comparison between girls' and boys' experiences of unwanted sexual behaviour in secondary schools. *Educational Research*, *47*(3), 291–306.

Tims, F. M., Dennis, M. L., Hamilton, N., Buchan, B. J., Diamond, G., Funk, R. & Brantley, L. B. (2002). Characteristics and problems of 600 adolescent cannabis abusers in outpatient treatment. *Addiction*, *97*(1), Supp.1, 46–57.

Tinklin, T. (2003). Gender differences and high attainment. *British Educational Research Journal*, *29*(3), 307–325.

Titus, M. A. (2006). Understanding college degree completion of students with low socioeconomic status: The Influence of the Institutional Financial Context. *Research in Higher Education*, *47*(4), 371–398.

Titzmann, P. F., Silbereisen, R. K. & Schmitt-Rodermund, E. (2007). Friendship homophily among diaspora migrant adolescents in Germany and Israel. *European Psychology*, *12*(3), 181–195.

Tobach, E. (2004). Development of sex and gender: Biochemistry, physiology, and experience. In A. M. Paludi (Ed.) *Praeger guide to the psychology of gender* (pp. 240–270). Westport, CT: Praeger.

Tobin, K. G. & Capie, W. (1981). The development and validation of a group test of logical thinking. *Educational and Psychological Measurement*, *41*, 413–423.

Tolman, D. L., Kim, J. L., Schooler, D. & Sorsoli, C. L. (2007). Rethinking the associations between television viewing and adolescent sexuality development: Bringing gender into focus. *Journal of Adolescent Health*, *40*(1), e9–e16.

Tordjman, S. (2008). Reunifying autism and early-onset schizophrenia in terms of social communication disorders. *Behavioral and Brain Sciences*, *31*(3), 278–279.

Torney-Purta, J. (2004). Adolescents' political socialization in changing contexts: An international study in the spirit of Nevitt Sanford. *Political Psychology*, *25*, 465–478.

Tracey, T. J. G., Robbins, S. B. & Hofsess, C. D. (2005). Stability and change in interests: A longitudinal study of adolescents from grades 8 through 12. *Journal of Vocational Behavior*, *66*, 1–25.

Triandis, H. C. (2001). Individualism-collectivism and personality. *Journal of Personality*, *69*(6), 907–924.

Triplett, R. & Payne, B. (2004). Problem solving as reinforcement in adolescent drug use: Implications for theory and policy. *Journal of Criminal Justice*, *32*(6), 617–630.

Troe, E-J. W. M., Kunst, A. E., Bos, V., Deerenberg, I. M., Joung, I. M. A. and Mackenbach, J. P. (2007). The effect of age at immigration and generational status of the mother on infant mortality in ethnic minority populations in The Netherlands. *The European Journal of Public Health*, *17*(2), 134–134.

Tse, J., Strulovitch, J., Tagalakis, V., Meng, L. & Fombonne, E. (2007). Social skills training for adolescents with Asperger syndrome and high-functioning autism. *Journal of Autism and Developmental Disorders*, *37*(10), 1960–1968.

Tseng, V. (2004). Family interdependence and academic adjustments in college: Youth from immigrant and U.S.-born families. *Child Development*, *75*, 966–983.

Tsouroufli, M. (2002). Gender and teachers' classroom practice in a secondary school in Greece. *Gender and Education*, *14*(2), 135–147.

Tubman, J. G., Gil, A. G. & Wagner, E. F. (2004). Co-occurring substance use and delinquent behaviour during early adolescence: Young relations and implications for intervention strategies. *Criminal Justice & Behavior*, *31*, 463–488.

TUC (2002). *Black and excluded 12 April 2002*. London: Trades Union Council.

Tudge, J. R. H. & Scrimsher, S. (2002). Lev S. Vygotsky on education. In B. J. Zimmerman & D. H. Schunk (Eds.), *Educational psychology*. Mahwah, NJ: Erlbaum.

Turnbull, J. & Beese, J. (2000). Negotiating the boundaries: The experience of the mental health nurse at the interface with the criminal justice system. *Journal of Psychiatric & Mental Health Nursing*, 7(4), 289–296.

Twenge, J. M. & Crocker, J. (2002). Race and self-esteem: Meta-analyses comparing Whites, Blacks, Hispanics, Asians, American Indians and comment on Gray-Little and Hafdahl (2000). *Psychological Bulletin*, *128*, 371–408.

Twisk, D. A. M. & Stacey, C. (2007). Trends in young driver risk and countermeasures in European countries. *Journal of Safety Research*, 38(2), 245–257.

Tyack, D. B. (1990). *The one best system: A history of American urban education*. Cambridge, MA: Harvard University Press.

Tyler, K. A., Hoyt, D. R. & Whitbeck, L. B. (2000). The effects of early sexual abuse on later sexual victimization among female homeless and runaway adolescents. *Journal of Interpersonal Violence*, *15*, 235–250.

Tyler, K. A., Whitbeck, L. B., Hoyt, D. R. & Cauce, A. M. (2004). Risk factors for sexual victimization among male and female homeless and runaway youth. *Journal of Interpersonal Violence*, *19*, 503–520.

Uddin, M. S. (2006). Arranged marriage: a dilemma for young British Asians. *Diversity in Health and Social Care*, 3(3), 211–219.

Uggen, C. & Blackstone, A. (2004). Sexual harassment as a gendered expression of power. *American Sociological Review*, *69*, 64–92.

Uline, C. L. & Johnson, J. F. (2005). Closing the achievement gap: What will it take? Special Issue of *Theory Into Practice*, *44(*1), Winter.

Umans, T., Collin, S-O. & Tagesson, T. (2008). Ethnic and gender diversity, process and performance in groups of business students in Sweden. *Intercultural Education*, 19(3), 243–254.

Underwood, L. E. & Van Wyk, J. J. (1981). Hormones in normal and aberrant growth. In R. H. Williams (Ed.), *Textbook of endocrinology* (6th ed., 11–49). Philadelphia: Saunders.

Underwood, M. K. (2003). *Social aggression among girls*. New York: Guilford Press.

UNESCO (2008). *The global literacy challenge: A profile of youth and adult literacy at the mid-point of the United Nations Literacy Decade 2003 – 2012*. Paris: UNESCO.

Unger, J. B. (2003). Peers, family, media, and adolescent smoking: Ethnic variation in risky factors in a national sample. *Adolescent & Family Health*, *3*, 65–70.

UNICEF (2005). *Gender achievements and prospects in education: The Gap Report*. New York: UNICEF.

United Nations Department of Economic and Social Affairs (UNDESA) (2005). *World youth report, 2005*. New York: Author.

United Nations Development Programme (2009). *Human development report*. New York: Oxford University Press.

United Nations Economic Commission for Europe (2005). *Gender statistics database*. Retrieved September 30, 2005, from http://w3.unece.org/stat/scriptsdb/show-Results.asp

Unterhalter, E. (2008). Cosmopolitanism, global social justice and gender equality in education. *Compare*, *38*(5), 539–553.

Unterrainer, J. M., Kaller, C. P., Halsband, U. & Rahm, B. (2006). Planning abilities and chess: A comparison of chess and non-chess players on the Tower of London task. *The British Journal of Psychology*, *97*(3), 299–311.

Updegraff, K. A., McHale, S. M. & Crouter, A. (2002). Adolescents' sibling relationship and friendship experiences: Developmental patterns and relationship linkages. *Social Development*, *11*, 182–204.

Updegraff, K. A., McHale, S. M. & Crouter, A. C. (2000). Personality and social development adolescents' sex-typed friendship experiences: Does having a sister versus a brother matter? *Child Development*, *71*(6), 1597–1610.

Updegraff, K. A., McHale, S. M., Whiteman, S. D., Thayer, S. M. & Crouter, A. C. (2006). The nature and correlates of Mexican-American adolescents' time with parents and peers. *Child Development*, *77*(5), 1470–1486.

Updegraff, K. A., Thayer, S. M., Whiteman, S. D., Denning, D. J. & McHale, S. M. (2005). Relational aggression in adolescents' sibling relationships: Links to siblings and parent–adolescent relationship quality. *Family Relations*, *54*, 373–385.

Urberg, K. A., Luo, Q., Pilgrim, C. & Degirmencioglu, S. M. (2004). A two-stage model of peer influence in adolescent substance use: Individual and relationship-specific differences in susceptibility to influence. *Addictive Behaviours*, *28*(7), 1243–1256.

Urberg, K. A., Degirmencioglu, S. M. & Tolson, J. M. (1998). Adolescent friendship selection and termination: The role of similarity. *Journal of Social and Personal Relationships*, *15*, 703–710.

Urberg, K. A., Degirmencioglu, S. M., Tolson, J. M. & Halliday-Sher, K. (2000). Adolescent social crowds: Measurement and relationship to friendships. *Journal of Adolescent Research*, *15*, 427–445.

Utter, J., Neumark-Sztainer, D., Wall, M. & Story, M. (2003). Reading magazine articles about dieting and associated weight control behaviors among adolescents. *Journal of Adolescent Health*, *32*, 78–82.

Utz, S. (2009). The (potential) benefits of campaigning via social network sites. *Journal of Computer-Mediated Communication*, *14*(2), 221–243.

Vadocz, E., Siegel, S. & Malina, R. (2002). Age at menarche in competitive figure skaters: variation by competency and discipline. *Journal of Sports Sciences*, *20*(2), 93–100.

Vaizey, E. (2005). Connecting with young voters. *Parliamentary Affairs*, *58*(3), 627–631.

Valencia-Martín, J. L., Galán, I. & Rodríguez-Artalejo, F. (2007). Binge drinking in Madrid, Spain. *Alcoholism: Clinical and Experimental Research*, *31*(10), 1723–1730.

Valentine, G., Skelton, T. & Butler, R. (2003). Coming out and outcomes: Negotiating lesbian and gay identities with, and in, the family. *Environment and Planning D: Society and Space*, *21*(4), 479–499.

Van Aelst, P. & Walgrave, S. (2002). New media, new movements? The role of the internet in shaping the 'anti-globalization' movement. *Information, Communication & Society*, 5(4), 465–493.

Van Beurden, E., Zask, A., Brooks, L. & Dight, R. (2005). Heavy episodic drinking and sensation seeking in adolescents as predictors of harmful driving and celebrating behaviors: Implications for prevention. *Journal of Adolescent Health*, 37, 37–43.

van den Berg, S. M. & Boomsma, D. J. (2007). The familial clustering of age at menarche in extended twin families. *Behavior Genetics*, 37, 661–667.

van den Broek, A. (2002). *Leisure across Europe. Comparing 14 populations, conveying 1 pattern.* Paper to International Association for Time Use Research, Annual Conference, Lisbon, 2002.

van der Klis, M. & Mulder, C. (2008). Beyond the trailing spouse: the commuter partnership as an alternative to family migration. *Journal of Housing and the Built Environment*, 23(1), 1–19.

van der Lippe, T., Jager, A. & Kops, Y. (2006). Combination pressure: The paid work–family balance of men and women in European countries. *Acta Sociologica*, 49(3), 303–319.

Vandereycken, W. & Van Deth, R. (1994). *From fasting saints to anorexic girls: The history of self-starvation.* New York: New York University Press.

van der Slik, F. & Konig, R. (2006). Orthodox, humanitarian, and science-inspired belief in relation to prejudice against Jews, Muslims, and ethnic minorities: The content of one's belief does matter. *International Journal for the Psychology of Religion*, 16(2), 113–126.

van Hoof, A. (1999). The identity status approach: In need of fundamental revision and qualitative change. *Developmental Review*, 19(4), 622–647.

Van Hoof, J. T. C. & Raaijmakers, Q. A. W. (2003). The search for the structure of identity formation. *Identity*, 3, 271–289.

Van Horn, K. R. & Cunegatto M. J. (2000). Interpersonal relationships in Brazilian adolescents. *International Journal of Behavioural Development*, 24, 199–203.

Van Houtte, M. (2000). Why boys achieve less at school than girls: The difference between boys' and girls' academic culture. *Educational Studies*, 30(2), 159–173.

van Langen, A., Bosker, R. & Dekkers, H. (2006). Exploring cross-national differences in gender gaps in education. *Educational Research and Evaluation*, 12(2), 155–177.

Van Leeuwen, K., De Fruyt, F. & Mervielde, I. (2004). A longitudinal study of the utility of the resilient, overcontrolled, and undercontrolled personality types as predictors of children's and adolescents' problem behaviour. *International Journal of Behavioral Development*, 28, 210–220.

van Lier, P., Vitaro, F., Barker, E., Koot, H. & Tremblay, R. (2009). Developmental links between trajectories of physical violence, vandalism, theft, and alcohol-drug use from childhood to adolescence. *Journal of Abnormal Child Psychology*, 37(4), 481–492.

van Poppel, F., Monden, C. & Mandemakers, K. (2008). Marriage timing over the generations. *Human Nature*, 19(1), 7–22.

Van Ryzin, M., Gravely, A. & Roseth, C. (2009). Autonomy, belongingness, and engagement in school as contributors to adolescent psychological well-being. *Journal of Youth and Adolescence*, 38(1), 1–12.

Varga, M. (2008). How political opportunities strengthen the far right: Understanding the rise in far-right militancy in Russia. *Europe-Asia Studies*, 60(4), 561–579.

Vasquez, M. J. T. & de las Fuentes, C. (1999). American-born Asian, African, Latina, and American Indian adolescent girls: Challenges and strengths. In N. B. Johnson, M. C. Roberts, & J. Worell (Eds.). *Beyond appearance: A new look at adolescent girls* (pp. 151–173). Washington, DC: American Psychological Association.

Vaughan, K. (2005). The pathways framework meets consumer culture: Young people, careers, and commitment. *Journal of Youth Studies*, 8, 173–186.

Vazsonyi, A. T. & Snider, J. B. (2008). Mentoring, competencies, and adjustment in adolescents: American part-time employment and European apprenticeships. *International Journal of Behavioral Development*, 32(1), 46–55.

Veenman, S., Kenter, B. & Post, K. (2000). Cooperative learning in Dutch primary classrooms. *Educational Studies*, 26(3), 281–302.

Veenstra, R., Lindenberg, S., Zijlstra, B. J. H., De Winter, A. F., Verhulst, F. C. & Ormel, J. (2007). The dyadic nature of bullying and victimization: Testing a dual-perspective theory. *Child Development*, 78(6), 1843–1854.

Venkatakrishnan, H. & Wiliam, D. (2003). Tracking and mixed-ability grouping in secondary school mathematics classrooms: A case study 1. *British Educational Research Journal*, 29(2), 189–204.

Verkooijen, K. T., de Vries, N. K. & Nielsen, G. A. (2007). Youth crowds and substance abuse: The impact of perceived group norm and multiple group identification. *Psychology of Addictive Behaviours*, 21(1), 55–61.

Verkuyten, M. (2002). Multiculturalism among minority and majority adolescents in the Netherlands. *International Journal of Intercultural Relations*, 26, 91–108.

Verkuyten, M. & Thijs, J. (2004). Psychological disidentification with the academic domain among ethnic minority adolescents in The Netherlands. *The British Journal of Educational Psychology*, 74(1), 109–125.

Verma, S. & Larson, R. (1999). Are adolescents more emotional? A study of the daily emotions of middle class Indian adolescents. *Psychology and Developing Societies*, 11, 179–194.

Verma, S. & Saraswathi, T. S. (2002). Adolescents in India: Street urchins or Silicon Valley millionaires? In B. B. Brown, R. Larson, & T. S. Saraswathi (Eds.) *The world's youth: Adolescence in eight regions of the globe* (pp. 105–140). New York: Cambridge University Press.

Verma, S. & Saraswathi, T. S. (2000, February). *The current state of adolescence in India: An agenda for the next millennium.* Paper prepared for the meeting of the Study Group on Adolescence in the 21st Century, Washington, DC.

Vernberg, E., Ewell, K., Beery, S. & Abwender, D. (1994). Sophistication of adolescents' interpersonal negotiation strategies and friendship formation after relocation: A naturally occurring experiment. *Journal of Research on Adolescence*, *4*, 5–19.

Veugelers, W. & Vedder, P. (2003). Values in teaching. *Teachers and Teaching: Theory and Practice*, *9*(4), 377–389.

Vigil, J. M., Geary, D. C. Byrd-Craven, J. (2005). A life history assessment of early childhood sexual abuse in women. *Developmental Psychology*, *41(3)*, 553–561.

Vijayakumar, L. (2005). Suicide and mental disorders in Asia. *International Review of Psychiatry*, *17*(2), 109–114.

Vijayakumar, L., Kannan, G. K., Kumar, B. G. & Devarajan, P. (2006). Do all children need intervention after exposure to tsunami? *International Review of Psychiatry*, *18*(6), 515–522.

Vincent, M. A. & McCabe, M. P. (2000). Gender differences among adolescents in family and peer influences on body dissatisfaction, weight loss, and binge eating disorders. *Journal of Youth & Adolescence*, *29*, 205–221.

Vitaro, F., Larocque, D., Janosz, M. & Tremblay, R. (2001). Negative social experiences and dropping out of school. *Educational Psychology*, *21*(4), 401–415.

Volk, A., Craif, W., Boyce, W. & King, M. (2006). Adolescent risky correlates of bullying and different types of victimization. *International Journal of Adolescent Medicine and Health*, *18*(4), 575–586.

Volling, B. L., McElwain, N. L. & Miller, A. L. (2002). Emotion Regulation in context: The jealousy complex between young siblings and its relations with child and family characteristics. *Child Development*, *73*(2), 581–600.

Vondracek, F. W. & Porfeli, E. (2003). World of work and careers. In G. R. Adams & M. Berzonsky (Eds.), *The Blackwell handbook of adolescence* (pp.109–128). Oxford, UK: Blackwell Publishers Ltd.

Voracek, M. (2006). Smart and suicidal? The social ecology of intelligence and suicide in Austria. *Death Studies*, *30*(5), 471–485.

Votta, E. & Manion, I. (2004). Suicide, high-risk behaviors, and coping style in homeless adolescent males' adjustment. *Journal of Adolescent Health*, *34*, 237–243.

Voydanoff, P. (2004). The effects of work demands and resources on work-to-family conflict and facilitation. *Journal of Marriage and Family*, *66*(2), 398–412.

Vukman, K. B. (2005). Developmental differences in metacognition and their connections with cognitive development in adulthood. *Journal of Adult Development*, *12*(4), 211–221.

Vulliamy, G. & Webb, R. (2003). Supporting disaffected pupils: perspectives from the pupils, their parents and their teachers. *Educational Research*, *45*(3), 275–286.

Wahlstrom, K. & Ponte, P. (2005). Examining teachers' beliefs through action research: Guidance and counseling/pastoral care reflected in the cross-cultural mirror. *Educational Action Research*, *13*(4), 543–562.

Waizenhofer, R. N., Buchanan, C. M. & Jackson-Newsom, J. (2004). Mothers' and fathers' daily activities: Its sources and its links with adolescent adjustment. *Journal of Family Psychology*, *18*, 348–360.

Walcott, D. D., Pratt, H. D. & Patel, D. R. (2003). Adolescents and eating disorders: Gender, racial, ethnic, sociocultural and socioeconomic issues. *Journal of Adolescent Research*, *18*, 223–243.

Walford, G. (2001). Funding for religious schools in England and the Netherlands. Can the piper call the tune? *Research Papers in Education*, *16*(4), 359–380.

Walker, L. J. (2004). What does moral functioning entail? In T. A. Thorkildsen & H. J. Walberg (Eds.), *Nurturing morality* (pp. 3–17). New York: Kluwer.

Walker, L. J. & Moran, T. J. (1991). Moral reasoning in a communist Chinese society. *Journal of Moral Education*, *20*, 139–155.

Walker, L. J., Pitts, R. C., Hennig, K. H. & Matsuba, M. K. (1999). Reasoning about morality and real-life moral problems. In M. Killen & D. Hart (Eds.), *Morality in everyday life* (pp. 371–407). New York: Cambridge University Press.

Wallace, J. M., Yamaguchi, R., Bachman, J. G., O'Malley, P. M., Schulenberg, J. E. & Johnston, L. D. (2007). Religiosity and adolescent substance use: The role of individual and contextual influences. *Social Problems*, *54*(2), 308–327.

Wallace, L. M., Evers, K. E., Wareing, H., Dunn, O. M., Newby, K., Paiva, A. & Johnson, J. L. (2007). Informing school sex education using the stages of change construct: Sexual behaviour and attitudes towards sexual activity and condom use of children aged 13–16 in England. *Journal of Health Psychology*, *12*(1), 179–183.

Wallerstein, J. S., Lewis, J. M. & Blakeslee, S. (2000). *The unexpected legacy of divorce*. New York: Hyperion.

Ward, L. M., Gorvine, B. & Cytron, A. (2002). Would that really happen? Adolescents' perceptions of sexual relationships according to prime-time television. In J. D. Brown, J. R. Steele, & K. Walsh-Childers (Eds.), *Sexual teens, sexual media: Investigating media's influence on adolescent sexuality* (pp. 95–123). Mahwah, NJ: Erlbaum.

Warren, T., Rowlingson, K. & Whyley, C. (2001). Female finances: Gender wage gaps and gender assets gaps. *Work, Employment & Society*, *15*(3), 465–488.

Warrington, M., Younger, M. & Williams, J. (2000). Student attitudes, image and the gender gap. *British Educational Research Journal*, *26*(3), 393–407.

Waterman, A. S. (2007). Doing well: The relationship of identity status to three conceptions of well-being. *Identity*, *7*(4), 289–307.

Waterman, A. S. (1999). Issues of identity formation revisited: United States and the Netherlands. *Developmental Review*, *19*, 462–479.

Waters, E., Weinfield, N. S. & Hamilton, C. E. (2000). The stability of attachment security from infancy to adolescence and early adulthood: General discussion. *Child Development*, *71*, 703–706.

Watson, I. (2009). Sovereign spaces, caring for country, and the homeless position of Aboriginal peoples. *SAQ: The South Atlantic Quarterly (Highwire)*, *108*(1), 27–51.

Watt, H. (2006). The role of motivation in gendered educational and occupational trajectories related to maths. *Educational Research and Evaluation*, *12*(4), 305–322.

Watt, H. M. G. (2004). Development of adolescents' self-perceptions, values, and task perceptions according to gender and domain in 7th- through 11th-grade Australian students. *Child Development*, *75*(5), 1556–1574.

Way, N. (2004). Intimacy, desire, and distrust in the friendships of adolescent boys. In N. Way & J. Chu (Eds.), *Adolescent boys: Exploring diverse cultures of boyhood* (pp. 167–196). New York: New York University Press.

Way, N. (1998). *Everyday courage: The lives and stories of urban teenagers.* New York: New York University Press.

Way, N. & Chen, L. (2000). Close and general friendships among African American, Latino, and Asian American adolescents. *Journal of Adolescent Research*, *15*, 274–301.

Way, N., Reddy, R. & Rhodes, J. (2007). Pupils' perceptions of school climate during the middle school years: Associations with trajectories of psychological and behavioral adjustment. *American Journal of Community Psychology*, *40*(3–4), 194–213.

Webb, M. (2007). Music analysis down the (You) tube? Exploring the potential of cross-media listening for the music classroom. *British Journal of Music Education*, *24*(2), 147–164.

Webster, L., Hackett, R. K. & Joubert, D. (2009). The association of unresolved attachment status and cognitive processes in maltreated adolescents. *Child Abuse Review*, *18*(1), 6–23.

Wechsler, H. & Nelson, T. F. (2001). Binge drinking and the American college student: What's five drinks? *Psychology of Addictive Behaviors*, *15*, 287–291.

Weerd, P. De, Smith, E. & Greenberg, P. (2006). Effects of selective attention on perceptual filling-in. *Journal of Cognitive Neuroscience*, *18*(3), 335–347.

Weichold, K., Silbereisen, R. K. & Schmitt-Rodermund, E. (2003). Short-term and long-term consequences of early vs. late physical maturation in adolescents. In C. Haywood (Ed.), *Puberty and Psychopathology*. New York: Cambridge University Press.

Weinberg, R. A., Scarr, S. & Waldman, I. D. (1992). The Minnesota transracial adoption study: A follow-up of IQ test performance. *Intelligence*, *44*, 98–104.

Weiner, I. B. (1992). *Psychological disturbance in adolescence.* (2nd ed.) New York: Wiley.

Weinfield, N. S., Sroufe, L. A. & Egeland, B. (2000). Attachment from infancy to early adulthood in a high-risk sample: Continuity, discontinuity, and their correlates. *Child Development*, *71*, 695–702.

Weinreich, H. E. (1974). The structure of moral reasoning. *Journal of Youth and Adolescence*, *3*, 135–143.

Weinstein, N. D. (1998). Accuracy of smokers' risk perceptions. *Annals of Behavioral Medicine*, *20*, 135–140.

Weinstock, H., Berman, S. & Cates, W. (2004). Sexually transmitted diseases among American youth: Incidence and prevalence estimates, 2000. *Perspectives on Sexual and Reproductive Health*, *36*, 6–10.

Weinstock, M., Assor, A. & Broide, G. (2009). Schools as promoters of moral judgment: The essential role of teachers' encouragement of critical thinking. *Social Psychology of Education*, *12*(1), 137–151.

Weiskop, S., Richdale, A. & Matthews, J. (2005). Behavioural treatment to reduce sleep problems in children with autism or fragile X syndrome. *Developmental Medicine & Child Neurology*, *47*(2), 94–104.

Weiss, R. S. (1973). *Loneliness: The experience of emotional and social isolation.* Cambridge, MA: MIT Press.

Weissman, D. (2007). Jewish religious education as peace education: from crisis to opportunity. *British Journal of Religious Education*, *29*(1), 63–76.

Wells, S., Graham, K., Speechley, M. & Koval, J. J. (2005). Drinking patterns, drinking contexts and alcohol-related aggression among late adolescent and young adult drinkers. *Addiction*, *100*(7), 933–944.

Wells, Y. D. & Johnson, T. M. (2001). Impact of parental divorce on willingness of young adults to provide care for parents in the future. *Journal of Family Studies*, *7*, 160–170.

Welti, C. (2002). Adolescents in Latin America: Facing the future with skepticism. In B. B. Brown, R. Larson, & T. S. Saraswathi (Eds.) *The world's youth: Adolescence in eight regions of the globe* (pp. 276–306). New York: Cambridge University Press.

Werner, B. & Bodin, L. (2007). Obesity in Swedish school children is increasing in both prevalence and severity. *Journal of Adolescent Health*, *41*, 536–543.

Werner, E. E. & Smith, R. S. (2001). *Journeys from childhood to midlife: Risk, resilience, and recovery.* Ithaca, NY: Cornell University Press.

Werner, E. E. & Smith, R. S. (1992). *Overcoming the odds: High risk children from birth to adulthood.* Ithaca, NY: Cornell University Press.

Werner, E. E. & Smith, R. S. (1982). *Vulnerable but invincible: A study of resilient children.* New York: McGraw-Hill.

Westenberg, P. M., Drewes, M. J., Goedhart, A. W., Siebelink, B. M. & Treffers, P. D. A. (2004). A developmental analysis of self-reported fears in late childhood through mid-adolescence: Social-evaluative fears on the rise? *Journal of Child Psychology and Psychiatry* (formerly *Journal of Child Psychology and Psychiatry and Allied Disciplines*), *45*(3), 481–495.

Westling, E., Andrews, J. A., Hampson, S. E., & Peterson, M. (2008). Pubertal timing and substance use: The effects of gender, parental monitoring and deviant peers. *Journal of Adolescent Health*, *42*, 555–563.

Wetz, J. (2009). *Urban village schools. Putting relationships at the heart of secondary school organisation and design.* London: Calouste Gulbenkian Foundation.

Wetz, J. (2006). *Holding children in mind over time.* Bristol: Business West.

Weyers, S., Monstrey, S., Hoebeke, P., De Cuypere, G. & Gerris, J. (2012). Laparoscopic hysterectomy as the method of choice for hysterectomy in female-to-male gender dysphoric individuals. *Gynecological Surgery* (January 2012), 1–5.

Whalen, C. K., Jamner, L. D., Henker, B., Delfino, R. J. & Lozano, J. M. (2002). The ADHD spectrum and everyday life: Experience sampling of adolescent moods, activities, smoking, and drinking. *Child Development, 73*(1), 209–227.

Whitbeck, L. B. & Hoyt, D. R. (1999). *Nowhere to grow: Homeless and runaway adolescents and their families*. New York: Aldine de Gruyter.

Whitbeck, L. B. & Hoyt, D. R. (1999a). A risk-amplification model of victimization and depressive symptoms among runaway and homeless adolescents. *American Journal of Community Psychology, 27*, 273–296.

Whitbeck, L. B., Johnson, K. D., Hoyt, D. R. & Cauce, A. M. (2004). Mental disorder and comorbidity among runaway and homeless adolescents. *Journal of Adolescent Health, 35*, 132–140.

Whitbourne, S. K. & Willis, S. L. (Eds.). (2006). *The baby boomers grow up: Contemporary perspectives on midlife*. Mahwah, NJ: Lawrence Erlbaum.

White, J. & Gardner, W. (2009). Think *women*, think *warm*: Stereotype content activation in women with a salient gender identity, using a modified Stroop task. *Sex Roles, 60*(3–4), 247–260.

White, M. J. & White, G. B. (2006). Implicit and explicit occupational gender stereotypes. *Sex Roles, 55*(3–4), 259–266.

Whiting, J. W. M. & Child, I. (1953). *Child training and personality*. New Haven, CT: Yale University Press.

Whiting, S. J., Vatanparast, H., Baxter-Jones, A., Faulkner, R. A., Mirwald, R. & Bailey, D. A. (2004). Factors that affect bone mineral accrual in the adolescent growth spurt. *The Journal of Nutrition, 134*(3), 696S–700.

Whitty, M. (2002). Possible selves: An exploration of the utility of a narrative approach. *Identity, 2*, 211–228.

WHO (World Health Organization) (2010). Fact Sheet 311 at http://www.who.int/mediacentre/factsheets/fs311/en/index.html accessed 28th July 2010.

WHO (World Health Organization) (2008). *Inequalities in young people's health: Health behavior in school-aged children*. Retrieved on February 12, 2009, from http://www.hbsc.org/

Whyte, W. F. (1943). *Street corner society*. Chicago: University of Chicago Press.

Wichstrom, L. (2001). The impact of pubertal timing on adolescents' alcohol use. *Journal of Research on Adolescence, 11*, 131–150.

Wichstrom, L. (1999). The emergence of gender difference in depressed mood during adolescence: The role of intensified gender socialisation. *Developmental Psychology, 35*, 232–245.

Wichstrom, L. & Rossow, I. (2002). Explaining the gender difference in self-reported suicide attempts: A nationally representative study of Norwegian adolescents. *Suicide and Life-Threatening Behavior, 32*, 101–116.

Wikeley, F. & Stables, A. (1999). Changes in school students' approaches to subject option choices: a study

of pupils in the West of England in 1984 and 1996. *Educational Research, 41*(3), 287–299.

Wilansky-Traynor, P. & Lobel, T. (2008). Differential effects of an adult observer's presence on sex-typed play behavior: A comparison between gender-schematic and gender-aschematic preschool children. *Archives of Sexual Behavior, 37*(4), 548–557.

Wilcox, W. B. (2008). Focused on their families: Religion, parenting, and child well-being. In K. K. Kline, (Ed.), *Authoritative communities: The scientific case for nurturing the whole child* (pp. 227–244). The Search Institute series on developmentally attentive community and society. New York: Springer Science + Business Media.

Wild, L. G., Flisher, A. J., Bhana, A. & Lombard, C. (2004). Associations among adolescent risk behaviors and self-esteem in six domains. *Journal of Child Psychology & Psychiatry, 45*, 1454–1467.

Williams, A. F. (1998). Risky driving behavior among adolescents. In R. Jessor (Ed.), *New perspectives on adolescent risk behavior* (pp. 221–237). New York: Cambridge University Press.

Williams, A. F. & Ferguson, S. A. (2002). Rationale for graduated licensing and the risks it should address. *Injury Prevention, 8*(Suppl. 2), ii9–ii16.

Williams, J. E. & Best, D. L. (1990). *Measuring sex stereotypes: A multination study*. Newbury Park, CA: Sage.

Williams, J. M. & Dunlop, L. C. (1999). Pubertal timing and self-reported delinquency among male adolescents. *Journal of Adolescence, 22*, 157–171.

Williams, K., Jamieson, F. & Hollingworth, S. (2008). 'He was a bit of a delicate thing': White middle-class boys, gender, school choice and parental anxiety. *Gender and Education, 20*(4), 399–408.

Williams, S. (2008). Women ninety years on: a quiet revolution. *Women's History Review, 17*(5), 807–815.

Williams, S. T., Conger, K. J. & Blozis, S. A. (2007). The development of interpersonal aggression during adolescence: The importance of parents, siblings, and family economics. *Child Development, 78*(5), 1526–1542.

Willits, F. K. & Crider, D. M. (1989). Church attendance and traditional religious beliefs in adolescence and young adulthood: A panel study. *Review of Religious Research, 31*, 68–81.

Wills, R., Kilpatrick, S. & Hutton, B. (2006). Single-sex classes in co-educational schools. *British Journal of Sociology of Education, 27*(3), 277–291.

Wills, T. A., Resko, J. A., Ainette, M. G. & Mendoza, D. (2004). Role of parent support and peer support in adolescent substance use: A test of mediated effects. *Psychology of Addictive Behaviours, 18*, 122–134.

Wills, W., Backett-Milburn, K., Gregory, S. & Lawton, J. (2005). The influence of the secondary school setting on the food practices of young teenagers from disadvantaged backgrounds in Scotland. *Health Education Research, 20*(4), 458–465.

Wilson, I., Griffin, C. & Wren, B. (2002). The validity of the diagnosis of gender identity disorder (child and adolescent criteria). *Clinical Child Psychology and Psychiatry, 7*(3), 335–351.

Wilson, J. Q. & Herrnstein, R. J. (1985). *Crime and human nature*. New York: Simon and Schuster.

Wilson, W. J. (2006). Social theory and the concept 'underclass.' In D. B. Grusky, & R. Kanbur (Eds.), *Poverty and inequality: Studies in social inequality* (pp. 103–116). University Press.

Windfuhr, K. L., While, D. T., Hunt, I. M., Turnbull, P., Lowe, R., Burns, J. M., Shaw, J., Appleby, L., Kapur, N. N. (2008). Suicide in juveniles and adolescents in the United Kingdom. *Journal of Child Psychiatry and Psychology*, *49*,1165–1175.

Witenberg R. T. (2007). The moral dimension of children's and adolescents' conceptualisation of tolerance to human diversity. *Journal of Moral Education*, *36*(4), 433–451.

Wodarz, N., Bobbe, G., Eichhammer, P., Weijers, H. G., Wiesbeck, G. A. & Johann, M. (2003). The candidate gene approach in alcoholism: are there gender-specific differences? *Archives of Women's Mental Health*, *6*(4), 225–230.

Wolak, J., Mitchell, K. J. & Finkelhor, D. (2007). Does online harassment constitute bullying? An exploration of online harassment by known peers and online-only contracts. *Journal of Adolescent Health*, *41*(Suppl. 6), S51–S58.

Wolbers, M. H. J. (2007). Patterns of labor market entry: A comparative perspective on school-to-work transitions in 11 European countries. *Acta Sociologica*, *50*(3), 189–210.

Wolfe, D. A., Scott, K., Wekerke, C. & Pittman, A. (2001). Child maltreatment: Risk of adjustment problems and dating violence in adolescence. *Journal of the American Association of Child and Adolescent Psychiatry*, *40*, 282–289.

Wolke, D. & Samara, M. M. (2004). Bullied by siblings: association with peer victimisation and behaviour problems in Israeli lower secondary school children. *Journal of Child Psychology and Psychiatry* (formerly *Journal of Child Psychology and Psychiatry and Allied Disciplines*), *45*(5), 1015–1029.

Wolpert, M., Fuggle, P., Cottrell, D., et al. (2006). *Drawing on the evidence: Advice for mental health professionals working with children and adolescents* (2nd ed.) CAMHS Publications.

Wong, M. M., Nigg, J. T., Zucker, R. A., Puttler, L. I., Fitzgerald, H. E., Jester, J. M. Glass, J. M. & Adams, K. (2006). Behavioral control and resiliency in the onset of alcohol and illicit drug use: A prospective study from preschool to adolescence. *Child Development*, *77*(4), 1016–1033.

Wong, M. S. W. & Watkins, D. (2001). Self-esteem and ability grouping: A Hong Kong investigation of the Big Fish Little Pond effect. *Educational Psychology*, *21*(1), 79–87.

Wong, S-S. (2008). Judgments about knowledge importance: The roles of social referents and network structure. *Human Relations*, *61*(11), 1565–1591.

Wong, S. Y. S., Chan, F. W. K., Lee, C. K., Li, M., Yeung, F., Lum, C. C. M., Choy, D. & Woo, J. (2008). Maximum oxygen uptake and body composition of healthy Hong Kong Chinese adult men and women aged 20 - 64 years. *Journal of Sports Sciences*, *26*(3), 295–302.

Woodward, L. J. & Fergusson, D. M. (2001). Life course outcomes of young people with anxiety disorders in adolescence. *Journal of the American Academy of Child and Adolescent Psychiatry*, *40*, 1086–1093.

Woodward, L. J. & Fergusson, D. M. (2000). Childhood Peer Relationship Problems and Later Risks of Educational Underachievement and Unemployment. *Journal of Child Psychology and Psychiatry (formerly Journal of Child Psychology and Psychiatry and Allied Disciplines)*, *41*(2), 191–201.

Woodward, L., Fergusson, D. M. & Belsky, J. (2000). Timing of parental separation and attachment to parents in adolescence: Results of a prospective study from birth to age 16. *Journal of Marriage & the Family*, *62*, 162–174.

Woolfolk, A., Hughes, M. & Walkup, V. (2008). *Psychology in education*. 10th edition, Allyn & Bacon, Harlow, England: Pearson Education.

World Organization of the Scout Movement (2008). Facts and figures. Retrieved on August 7, 2008, from www.scout.org/en/about_scouting/facts_figures

Worsley, H. (2008). Church of England schools as centres for religious abuse or avenues for religious nurture? (The rights of children to encounter faith in the school context.) *International Journal of Children's Spirituality*, *13*(1), 75–83.

Worthington, A. & Higgs, H. (2003). Factors explaining the choice of a finance major: the role of students' characteristics, personality and perceptions of the profession. *Accounting Education*, *12*(1), 1–21.

Worthman, C. M. (1987). Interactions of physical maturation and cultural practice in ontogeny: Kikuyu adolescents. *Cultural Anthropology*, *2*, 29–38.

Wright, L. (1967). The pediatric psychologist : A role model. *American Psychologist*, *22*, 323–325.

Wright, M. J., Gillespie, N. A., Luciano, M., Zhu, G. & Martin, N. G. (2008). Genetics of personality and cognition in adolescents. In J. J. Hudziak (Ed.), *Developmental psychopathology and wellness: Genetic and environmental influences* (pp. 85–107). Arlington, VA: American Psychiatric Publishing.

Wu, C-J. (2006). Look who's talking: Language choices and culture of learning in uk chinese classrooms. *Language and Education*, *20*(1), 62–75.

Wu, L., Schlenger, W. & Galvin, D. (2003). The relationship between employment and substance abuse among pupils aged 12 to 17. *Journal of Adolescent Health*, *32*, 5–15.

Wu, Z. (1999). Premarital cohabitation and the timing of first marriage. *Canadian Review of Sociology and Anthropology*, *36*, 109–127.

Wubbels, T., den Brok, P., Veldman, I. & van Tartwijk, J. (2006). Teacher interpersonal competence for Dutch secondary multicultural classrooms. *Teachers and Teaching: Theory and Practice*, *12*(4), 407–433.

Wulff, H. (2007). *The emotions: A cultural reader*. Oxford:Berg Publishers.

Wulff, H. (1995). Inter-racial friendship: Consuming youth styles, ethnicity and teenage femininity in south London.

In V. Amit-Talai & H. Wulff (Eds.), *Youth cultures: A cross-cultural perspective* (pp. 63–80). New York: Routledge.

Wyatt, J. M. & Carlo, G. (2002). What will my parents think? Relations among adolescents' expected parental reactions, prosocial moral reasoning, and prosocial and antisocial behaviors. *Journal of Adolescent Research, 17*, 646–666.

Wynne, L. C., Tienari, P., Nieminen, P., Sorri, A., Lahti, I., Moring, J., Naarala, M., Läksy, K., Wahlberg, K-E. & Miettunen, J. (2006). Genotype–environment interaction in the schizophrenia spectrum: Genetic liability and global family ratings in the finnish adoption study. *Family Process, 45*(4), 419–434.

Xu, W. H., Xiang, Y-B., Zheng, W., Zhang, X., Ruan, Z. X., Cheng, J. R., Gao, Y-T. & Shu, X-O. (2006). Weight history and risk of endometrial cancer among Chinese women. *International Journal of Epidemiology, 35*, 159–66.

Yamawaki, N. (2007). Rape perception and the function of ambivalent sexism and gender-role traditionality. *Journal of Interpersonal Violence, 22*(4), 406–423.

Yaremko, S. K. & Lawson, K. L. (2007). Gender, internalization of expressive traits and expectations of parenting. *Sex Roles, 57*, 675–687.

Yasui, M., Dorham, C. L. & Dishion, T. J. (2004). Ethnic identity and psychological adjustment: A validity analysis for European American and African American adolescents. *Journal of Adolescent Research, 19*, 807–825.

Yates, M. & Youniss, J. (1996). A developmental perspective on community service in adolescence. *Social Development, 5*, 85–101.

Yates, S. & Payne, M. (2006). Not so NEET? A critique of the use of 'Neet' in setting targets for interventions with young people. *Journal of Youth Studies, 9*(3), 329–344.

Ybarra, M. L. & Mitchell, K. J. (2005). Exposure to internet pornography among children and adolescents: A national survey. *CyberPsychology & Behaviour, 8*(5), 473–486.

Yeh, Y-Y., Yang, C-T. & Chiu, Y-C. (2005). Binding or prioritization: The role of selective attention in visual short-term memory. *Visual Cognition, 12*(5), 759–799.

Yeung, D. Y. L. (2005). Psychosocial and cultural factors influencing expectations of menarche: A study on Chinese premenarcheal teenage girls. *Journal of Adolescent Research, 20*, 118–135.

Yingling, V. (2009). A delay in pubertal onset affects the covariation of body weight, estradiol, and bone size. *Calcified Tissue International, 84*(4), 286–296.

Yip, T. & Fuligni, A. J. (2002). Daily variation in ethnic identity, ethnic behaviors, and psychological well-being among American adolescents of Chinese descent. *Child Development, 73*, 1557–1572.

Yoder, K. A., Hoyt, D. R. & Whitbeck, L. B. (1998). Suicidal behavior in homeless and runaway adolescents. *Journal of Youth & Adolescence, 27*, 753–772.

Yonkers, K. A., Holthausen, G. A., Poschman, K. & Howell, H. B. (2006). Symptom-onset treatment for women with premenstrual dysphoric disorder. *Journal of Clinical Psychopharmacology, 26*(2), 198–202.

Yonkers, K. A., O'Brien, P. M. & Shaughn, E. E. (2008). Premenstrual syndrome. *Lancet, 371*, 1200–1210.

Yost, K. J., Haan, M. N., Levine, R. A. & Gold, E. B. (2005). Comparing SF-36 scores across three groups of women with different health profiles. *Quality of Life Research, 14*(5), 1251–1261.

Yoshimoto, K., Inenaga, Y. & Yamada, H. (2007). Pedagogy and andragogy in higher education – a comparison between Germany, the UK and Japan. *European Journal of Education: Research, Development and Policies, 42*(1), 75–98.

Young, A. M. & D'Arcy, H. (2005). Older boyfriends of adolescent girls: The cause or a sign of the problem? *Journal of Adolescent Health, 36*, 410–419.

Young, D., Bebbington, A., Anderson, A., Ravine, D., Ellaway, C., Kulkarni, A., de Klerk, N., Kaufmann, W. & Leonard, H. (2008). The diagnosis of autism in a female: Could it be Rett syndrome? *European Journal of Pediatrics, 167*(6), 661–669.

Young, R., Sweeting, H. & West, P. (2006). Prevalence of deliberate self harm and attempted suicide within contemporary Goth youth subculture: longitudinal cohort study. *BMJ (British Medical Journal), 332*(7549), 1058–1061.

Youniss, J. (2006). G. Stanley Hall and his times: Too much so, yet not enough. *History of Psychology, 9*(3), 224–235.

Youniss, J., McLellan, J. A. & Yates, M. (1999). Religion, community service, and identity in American youth. *Journal of Adolescence, 22*, 243–253.

Youniss, J. & Smollar, J. (1985). *Adolescent relations with mothers, fathers, and friends*. Chicago: University of Chicago Press.

Youniss, J. & Yates, M. (2000). Adolescents' public discussion and collective identity. In N. Budwig & I. C. Uzgiris (Eds.), *Communication: An arena of development* (pp. 215–233). New York: Greenwood.

Youniss, J. & Yates, M. (1997). *Community service and social responsibility in youth: Theory and policy*. Chicago: University of Chicago Press.

Yu, J. (2008). Perspectives of Chinese British adolescents on sexual behaviour within their socio-cultural contexts in Scotland. *Diversity in Health and Social Care, 5*(3), 177–186.

Yu, L., Winter, S. & Xie, D. (2010). The child Play Behavior and Activity Questionnaire: A parent-report measure of childhood gender-related behavior in China. *Archives of Sexual Behavior, 39*(3), 807–815.

Zagefka, H. & Brown, R. (2005). Comparisons and perceived deprivation in ethnic minority settings. *Personality and Social Psychology Bulletin, 31*(4), 467–482.

Zakaria, F. (2008). *The post-American world*. New York: Norton.

Zalsman, G., Oquendo, M. A., Greenhill, L., Goldberg, P. H., Pamali, M., Martin, A. & Mann, J. J. (2006). Neurobiology of depression in children and adolescents. *Child and Adolescent Psychiatric Clinics of North America, 15*(4), 843–868.

Zedd, Z., Brooks, J. & McGarvey, A. M. (2002). Educating America's youth: What makes a difference? *Child Trends Research Brief*. Washington, DC: Author.

Zeijl, E., te Poel, Y., de Bois-Reymond, M., Ravesloot, J. & Meulman, J. J. (2000). The role of parents and peers in the leisure activities of young adolescents. *Journal of Leisure Research*, *32*, 281–302.

Zettergren, P. (2003). School adjustment in adolescence for previously rejected, average and popular children. *British Journal of Educational Psychology*, *73*, 207–221.

Zhang, J., Jia, S., Jiang, C. & Sun, J. (2006). Characteristics of Chinese suicide attempters: An emergency room study. *Death Studies*, *30*(3), 259–268.

Zhang, W. & Fuligni, A. J. (2006). Authority, autonomy, and family relationships among adolescents in urban and rural China. *Journal of Research on Adolescence*, *16*(4), 527–537.

Zhou, M. (1997). Growing up American: The challenge confronting immigrant children and children of immigrants. *Annual Review of Sociology*, *23*, 63–95.

Zhu, W. X., Lu, L. & Hesketh, T. (2009). China's excess males, sex selective abortion, and one child policy: analysis of data from 2005 national intercensus survey. *BMJ (British Medical Journal)*, *338*(4), b1211-b1211.

Zierold, K. M., Garman, S. & Anderson, H. A. (2005). A comparison of school performance and behaviors among working and nonworking high school pupils. *Family & Community Health*, *28*, 214–224.

Zimmer-Gembeck, M. J. & Collins, W. A. (2003). Autonomy development during adolescence. In G. Adams & M. Berzonsky (Eds.), *Blackwell handbook of adolescence*. Malden, MA: Blackwell.

Zimmer-Gembeck, M. J., Hunter, T. A., Waters, A. M. & Pronk, R. (2009). Depression as a longitudinal outcome and antecedent of preadolescents' peer relationships and peer-relevant cognition. *Development and Psychopathology*, *21*(2), 555–577.

Zimmerman, M. A., Copeland, L. A., Shope, J. T. & Dielman, T. E. (1997). A longitudinal study of self-esteem: Implications for adolescent development. *Journal of Youth and Adolescence*, *26*(2), 117–141.

Zontini, E. (2007). Continuity and change in transnational italian families: the caring practices of second-generation women. *Journal of Ethnic and Migration Studies*, *33*(7), 1103–1119.

Zsolnai, A. (2002). Relationship between children's social competence, learning, motivation and school achievement. *Educational Psychology*, *22*(3). 317–330.

Zuckerman, M. (2007). *Sensation seeking and risky behaviour*. Washington, DC: American Psychological Association.

Zuckerman, M. B. (2003). The times of our lives. In V. N. Gordon & T. L. Minnick (Eds.), *Foundations: A reader for new college students*, New York: Thompson.

Žukauskaite, S., Lašiene, D., Lašas, L., Urbonaite, B. & Hindmarsh, P. (2005). Onset of breast and pubic hair development in 1231 preadolescent Lithuanian schoolgirls. *Archives of Disease in Childhood*, *90*(9), 932–936.

Zukow-Goldring, P. (2002). Sibling caregiving. In M. H. Bornstein (Ed.), *Handbook of parenting*, *Vol. 3: Being and becoming a parent* (pp. 253–286). Mahwah, NJ: Erlbaum.

Zumwalt, M. (2008). Effects of the menstrual cycle on the acquisition of peak bone mass. In J. J. Robert-McComb, R. Norman, & M. Zumwalt (Eds.), *The active female: Health issues throughout the lifespan* (pp. 141–151). Totowa, NJ: Humana Press.

Zunquin, G., Theunynck, D., Sesboue, B., Arhan, P. & Bougle, D. (2009). Evolution of fat oxidation during exercise in obese pubertal boys: Clinical implications. *Journal of Sports Sciences*, *27*(4), 315–318.

Zwane, I. T., Mngadi, P. T. & Nxumalo, M. P. (2004). Adolescents' views on decision-making regarding risky sexual behaviour. *International Nursing Review*, *51*(1), 15–22.

Zwingel, S. (2005). From intergovernmental negotiations to (sub)national change. *International Feminist Journal of Politics*, *7*(3), 400–424.

INDEX